Egypt

EGYPT.

HANDBOOK FOR TRAVELLERS

EDITED BY

K. BAEDEKER.

PART FIRST:

LOWER EGYPT, WITH THE FAYÛM

AND THE

PENINSULA OF SINAI.

WITH 16 MAPS, 30 PLANS, 7 VIEWS, AND 76 VIGNETTES.

SECOND EDITION, REVISED AND AUGMENTED.

LEIPSIC: KARL BAEDEKER, PUBLISHER.
LONDON: DULAU AND CO., 37 SOHO SQUARE, W.
1885.

'Go, little book, God send thee good passage,
And specially let this be thy prayere
Unto them all that thee will read or hear,
Where thou art wrong, after their help to call,
Thee to correct in any part or all.

CHAUCER.

20/-

LOWER EGYPT

AND THE

PENINSULA OF SINAI.

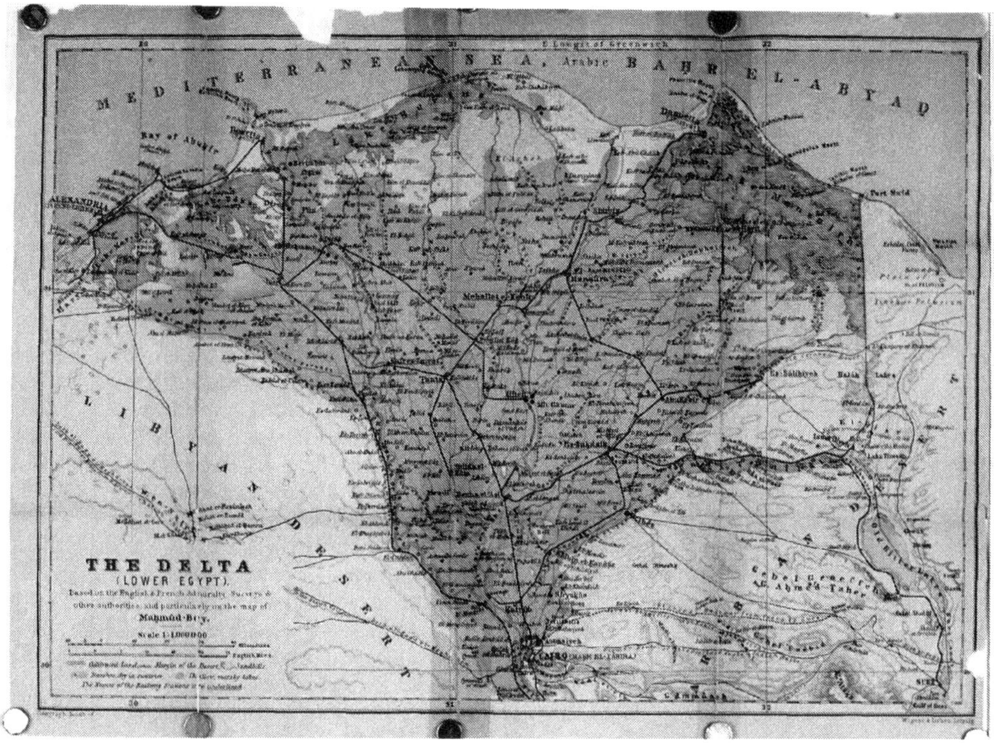
MEDITERRANEAN SEA, Arabic BAHR EL-ABYAD
E. Longit. of Greenwich
ALEXANDRIA
Bay of Abukir
Damietta
Port Said
Mansura
Tanta
Zagazig
CAIRO
Suez
LIBYAN DESERT
THE DELTA
(LOWER EGYPT).
Based on the English & French Admiralty Surveys & other authorities and particularly on the map of
Mahmûd-Bey.
Scale 1:1000000
English Miles

PREFACE.

The present volume is the second of a series of Handbooks for the East now in course of preparation, and designed, like the Editor's European handbooks, for the guidance of travellers.

The materials from which the first edition of the Handbook for Lower Egypt was compiled were partly furnished by *Professor G. Ebers* of Leipsic, while articles on special subjects, as well as many additions and emendations, were contributed by a number of other writers. The Editor is specially indebted to *Professor Ascherson* and *Dr. Klunzinger* of Berlin, *Dr. G. Schweinfurth* and *Franz Bey* of Cairo, *Professor Springer* of Leipsic, and *Professor Socin* of Tübingen. To several English gentlemen who contributed a number of valuable corrections and suggestions, and particularly to the distinguished Egyptologist, *Dr. Samuel Birch*, the Editor also begs to tender his grateful acknowledgements. The corrections and additions for the second edition have been mainly furnished by *Dr. Schweinfurth, Dr. Spitta Bey* (late librarian to the Khedive), and *Emil Brugsch Bey*, all of Cairo.

The Editor has also repeatedly visited Lower Egypt for the purpose of obtaining the most recent practical information, of the kind most likely to be useful to travellers. As, however, a tour in the East is attended with far greater difficulty than in Europe, and sources of information are far less abundant, the Handbook must necessarily contain many imperfections, and the Editor will therefore gratefully avail himself of any communications which his readers may kindly contribute, as many of them have so generously done in the case of his European handbooks. As Oriental life and scenery differ widely in many respects from European, and can hardly be appreciated without some previous study, the Editor has endeavoured to supply the traveller with all the most necessary preliminary information, believing that it will be acceptable to most of his readers, although somewhat beyond the province of an ordinary guide-book.

The Maps and Plans have been an object of the Editor's special care, as he knows by experience how little reliance can be placed on information obtained from the natives, even when the traveller is conversant with their language. The maps of the Handbook are based upon the large maps of

Mahmûd Bey, *Linant*, *Lepsius*, and *Kiepert*, together with the English and French Admiralty charts, and the map of the French expedition, so far as still serviceable; while numerous corrections and additions have been specially made on the spot. The plans of the mosques and the sketch of the Tombs of the Khalîfs have been contributed by *Franz Bey*, the architect. It is therefore hoped that the maps and plans will, on the whole, be found the most serviceable that have yet been published for the use of travellers in Egypt.

Heights above the sea-level and other measurements are given in English feet, from the latest and most trustworthy English and other sources.

The Prices and various items of expenditure mentioned in the Handbook are given in accordance with the Editor's personal experience, but they are liable to very great fluctuation, in accordance with the state of trade, the influx of foreigners, the traveller's own demeanour, and other circumstances. In some cases the traveller's expenditure may be within the rate indicated in the Handbook, but as many unexpected contingencies may arise on so long a journey, an ample pecuniary margin should always be allowed.

Hotels, etc., see p. 17.

Transliteration. The vowel sounds of Arabic words mentioned in the Handbook are represented by *a*, *e*, *i*, *o*, and *u*, as pronounced in Italian (ah, eh, ee, o, and oo). The ê used in the Handbook is a contracted form of *ei*, and is used in preference to it, as it exactly represents the usual pronunciation (*viz.* that of the *a* in fate). The diphthong sound of *ei* is rarely used except in the recitation of the Ḳorân. Arabic words written in accordance with this system will generally be found to correspond with the forms used by German, French, and Italian philologists.

CONTENTS.

CONTENTS.

Maps.

Plans.

Views.

Vignettes.

Asterisks

are used as marks of commendation.

INTRODUCTION.

'I shall now speak at greater length of Egypt, as it contains more wonders than any other land, and is pre-eminent above all the countries in the world for works that one can hardly describe.'

HERODOTUS (B C. 456).

At the close of 1st century Egypt was in a great measure rediscovered by the French savants attached to Bonaparte's Egyptian expedition. Since that period it has attracted the ever-increasing attention of the scientific, its historical and archæological marvels have been gradually unveiled to the world; it is the most ancient, and was yet at one time the most civilised country of antiquity, and it therefore cannot fail to awaken the profoundest interest in all students of the history and development of human culture.

Like other countries of the far East, Egypt possesses for the 'Frank' traveller the twofold attraction of scenery and history. To the first category belong the peculiar charms of its Oriental climate, the singularly clear atmosphere, the wonderful colouring and effects of light and shade, such as are unknown in more northern climates, the exuberant fertility of the cultivated districts contrasted with the solemn, awe-inspiring desert, and the manners, customs, and appearance of a most interesting, though not always pleasing, population. At the same time Egypt is pre-eminent among the countries of the East, and indeed among those of the whole world, as the cradle of history and of human culture. At every step we encounter venerable monuments which have survived the destructive influences of thousands of years and the vandalism of invaders and conquerors, and which are executed on so grand a scale, with so much artistic skill, and with such historical consistency, as at once to excite our highest admiration and command our most profound respect.

Owing to its distance from the homes of most travellers, and to the expense involved in exploring it, Egypt will never be overrun by tourists to the same extent as Switzerland or Italy; but it is now reached without difficulty by one of the numerous Mediterranean steamboat lines, and increased facilities are afforded to travellers by the recent construction of railways (p. 11) within the country itself, while its unrivalled attractions abundantly reward the enterprising traveller and supply him with a subject of life-long interest.

I. Preliminary Information.

(1). Plan of Tour. Season. Companions. Routes.

PLAN. The facilities for travel in Egypt are now such that the intending visitor may make an outline of his tour at home with almost as great ease as for most of the countries of Europe. During the travelling season, moreover, the weather is always fine (comp. p. 67), and never causes disappointment and derangement of plans as in most other countries. If, therefore, the traveller from a more northern region retains his energy in this somewhat enervating climate, and resists the undoubted attractions of the 'dolce far niente', he will have no difficulty in disposing of every day to advantage.

SEASON. From the beginning of November till the middle or end of April there are but few days of bad weather in the interior of Egypt; the prevalent temperature is that of a delicious spring or moderate summer, and the few drops of rain that occasionally fall will hardly be observed by the European traveller. The fertilising inundation of the Nile (p. 57) has by this time subsided, and the whole face of the country smiles with fresh verdure. About the end of April, and sometimes as early as March, begins the period of the Khamsîn (p. 69), a sultry, parching, and enervating wind from the desert, prevailing at longer or shorter intervals for about fifty days (whence the name), though in some seasons it does not make its appearance at all. Winter is therefore the proper season for a tour in Egypt. Those travellers, however, who can endure the fierce glare of an African summer sun will at that season have the advantage of seeing the extent of the overflow of the Nile, and will find that prices are then generally much lower than in winter. (Compare also p. 74.)

COMPANIONS. The traveller can hardly be recommended to start alone for a tour in a country whose customs and language are so entirely different from his own; but, if he has been unable to make up a suitable party at home, he will probably have an opportunity of doing so at Alexandria or Cairo, or possibly at Suez or Port Sa'îd. Travelling as a member of a party is, moreover, much less expensive than travelling alone, many of the items being the same for a single traveller as for several together. Apart, however, from the pecuniary advantage, a party is more likely to succeed in making satisfactory arrangements with the natives with whom they have to deal. (Voyage up the Nile, see vol ii; journey to Mt. Sinai, R. 10.)

ROUTES. A glimpse at Lower Egypt, i.e. Alexandria, Cairo, and the Suez Canal, may be obtained in three weeks (exclusive of the journey out); and the traveller may distribute his time as follows: —

Alexandria	1½ Days.
Railway to Cairo 1, or including Ṭanṭa . . .	1½ -
Cairo and its environs, the Pyramids, etc. . .	10 -
Railway to Suez and stay there	3 -
Visit to the Springs of Moses	1 -
Railway to Ismaʿîlîya	1 -
Steamer on the Suez Canal to Port Saʿîd . . .	1 -
Days of rest	2 -
	21 Days.

These three weeks, however, might be spent very pleasantly at Cairo alone.

A visit to Mt. Sinai requires	18-24 Days.
The Fayûm	4-6 -
Voyage up the Nile and back —	
(a) By steamer, as far as Assuân, and back, 21; thence, from above the first cataract to Abu Simbel near the second cataract, and back 11	32 -
(b) By dahabîyeh to Assuân, and back, about	60 -
(c) By dahabîyeh to Abu Simbel and back . .	90 -

A complete tour through Egypt, including the Nile and the peninsula of Mt. Sinai, will thus occupy 3-5 months in all.

(2). Expenses. Money.

EXPENSES. The cost of a tour in Egypt, and in Oriental countries generally, is considerably greater than that of a visit to any part of Europe, the reasons being that most travellers cannot conform with the simple habits of the natives, that they are ignorant of the language, and that special arrangements have to be made to meet their requirements. The average charge at the hotels for a day's board and lodging is 15-25 fr., without wine (compare p. 17). The cheapest wine costs 3-4 fr. per bottle; English beer 2-2½ fr.; fee ½-1 fr.; the traveller's hotel expenses will therefore amount to at least 20-30 fr. a day, to which must be added the hire of donkeys and carriages and the inevitable 'pourboires'. The total day's expenditure should therefore be estimated at 30 fr. at least. (Steamboat-fares are of course extra; p. 10).

The traveller whose time is very limited, or who is accompanied by ladies, will also require the services of a guide or valet-de-place, or 'dragoman', as they prefer to style themselves (5-8 fr. per day).

MONEY. A small sum of money for the early part of the journey may be taken in English or French gold, or in English banknotes, but large sums should always be in the form of circular notes. These notes, which if kept separate from the 'letter of indication' cannot be cashed by a thief or a dishonest finder, are issued by the principal London banks. Fresh supplies may be forwarded from England by post-office order, in sums not exceeding 500 fr.

The current rate of exchange should always be ascertained from a banker (pp. 206, 232, see also Table, p. 5), and money should be changed as rarely as possible at an ordinary money-changer's, at a hotel, in the bazaars, or through a dragoman. For excursions in the country the traveller should be provided with an ample supply of small change (silver piastres, half-piastres, and copper coin), as the villagers sometimes refuse to change money of any kind, and the traveller may thus be very seriously inconvenienced. They also frequently decline to take a coin if the inscription is worn away by use, and in their examination of gold pieces they attach great importance to the ring of the metal. The traveller should also be on his guard against counterfeit dollars and piastres. A favourite ornament with Oriental women consists of a string of gold coins worn round the head, or as a necklace, and coins with holes in them are accordingly often met with, but they are very apt to be rejected by the natives In changing money, therefore, all these points should be attended to It need hardly be observed that money should always be carefully kept under lock and key, and that it should be shown as little as possible, in order that the cupidity of the people with whom the traveller has to do may not be aroused.

Paper money is unknown in the East. Besides the Egyptian coinage, which moreover has two different rates of exchange†, Turkish, French, English, Italian, Austrian, and Russian gold and silver coins are freely circulated.

The unit of reckoning in the Egyptian currency is the *Piastre*, which contains 40 *Paras*. In ordinary retail traffic accounts are kept in *current-piastres*, which are worth one-half of the government *tariff-piastres*. As, however, these do not, as might be supposed, indicate two different coins, this twofold mode of reckoning is exceedingly puzzling to strangers. It should be particularly observed that at the shops and bazaars the prices are always fixed in current piastres, so that half the number of silver coins only has to be given. The shopkeepers, however, generally convert their prices into francs for the benefit of strangers, and although their demands are then somewhat raised, they are at least more intelligible. On the other hand, in making small purchases, and in dealing with country-people, it is more advantageous to keep to the reckoning in current piastres, as the sellers are very apt to demand as many francs as the amount of the price in piastres.

† There are indeed three rates of exchange · 'Tariff', 'Current', and 'Copper', and the latter is also liable to considerable fluctuation in the interior of the country In Cairo, at present, 1 tariff piastre is worth 8 copper piastres (At Cairo and Alexandria, however, copper money may be declined) The value of copper increases as we penetrate into the interior Thus at the beginning of 1877, 1 Napoleon realised 480 copper piastres at Alexandria 450 at Cairo and beyond it as far as Siût and 420 only higher up the river No advantage, however, can be derived from this difference in value except when very large payments are made in copper, as is the custom with the peasantry. As all the taxes are

Arabian Name	European Name	Value in Egyptian Money: Tariff, Piastres	Tariff, Paras	Current, Piastres	Current, Paras	Value in French Money: Francs	Centimes	Remarks
Gold Coins.								
Ginêh Masri	Egyptian pound	100	—	200	—	26	—	
Nusseh „	half „ „	50	—	100	—	13	—	
Rub'a „	quarter „ „	25	—	50	—	6	50	
Maṣrîyeh	fifth „ „	20	—	40	—	5	20	
Nuṣṣêh Maṣrîyeh	tenth „ „	10	—	20	—	2	60	
Rub'a „	twentieth „ „	5	—	10	—	1	30	
Ginêh Stambûli	Turkish pound	87	30	175	20	[a] 22	75	*a.* In mercantile
Nusseh „	half „ „	43	35	87	30	11	40	transactions fre-
Rub'a „	quarter „ „	21	37	43	35	5	70	quently reckon-
Ginêh Ingilisi or Frengi	English sovereign	97	20	195	—	25	25	ed as 23 fr.
Nuṣṣeh „ „	half „ „	48	30	97	20	12	62	
Bintu	Napoléon d'Or	77	6	154	12	20	—	
Nusseh Bintu	half „ „	38	20	77	6	10	—	
Rub'a „	quarter „ „	19	10	38	20	5	—	
Ginêh Moskûfi	Russian Imperial[b]	79	18	158	36	20	45	*b.* Not often met
Magar	Austrian Ducat	45	37	91	34	12	8	with, and can-
Silver Coins.								not be changed
Riyâl Maṣri	Egyptian Dollar	19	20	39	—	5	8	without a slight
Nuṣṣeh Riyâl Maṣri	half „ „	9	30	19	20	2	50	loss.
Rub'a „ „	quarter „ „	4	35	9	30	1	25	
Tumneh „ „	eighth „ „	2	17	4	35	—	60	
Bârîseh	Parisi[c]	8	30	17	20	2	35	*c.* Egyptian coins
Nuṣṣeh Bârîseh	half „	4	15	8	30	1	16	struck at Paris.
Rub'a „	quarter „	2	7	4	15	—	56	
Kirsh	Silver piastre	1	—	2	—	—	25	
Nuṣṣeh Ḳirsh	half „ „	—	20	1	—	—	12	
Rub'a „	quarter „ „	—	10	—	—	—	6	
Riyâl Shinku	5-franc piece	19	10	38	20	5	—	
Ferank	Franc	4	—	8	—	1	—	
Nusseh Ferank	half „	2	—	4	—	—	50	
Rûbîyeh	Rupee[d] (2*s.*)	8	—	16	—	2	—	*d.* The Anglo-In-
Nuṣṣeh Rûbîyeh	half „	4	10	8	20	1	10	dian coin, much
Rub'a „	quarter „	2	5	4	10	—	55	circulated.
Abu Medfa'[e]	Spanish Douro	19	—	38	—	5	—	*e.* Called 'father
Riyâl Abutêra	Maria Theresa dollar	17	—	34	—	4	50	of the cannon'
Riyâl Moskûfi	Ruble	14	27	29	14	3	80	by the Arabs,
Riyâl „ illa rub'a	three-quarters ruble	11	—	22	—	2	85	who mistake
NuṣṣehR.Moskûfi	half „	7	14	14	27	1	90	the columns for
Rub'a „ „	quarter „	3	27	7	14	—	95	cannons.
Rub'a Fiorini	Quarter Austr. florin	2	14	4	—	—	60	
Shilling		4	35	9	30	1	25	
Nuṣṣeh „		2	17	4	35	—	62	

payable in gold and silver only, the precious metals flow steadily from the country to the gove nment coffers in the towns, where Greek and Jewish money-changer rofit largely by these variations in the exchange. The 'shêkhs-el-beled' or village-chiefs, who always endeavour to depreciate the value of copper, also gain considerably by similar transactions.

(3). Passports. Custom House.

Passports are usually asked for at all the Egyptian ports, and if the traveller is unprovided with one he is liable to detention and great inconvenience. The passport is given up at the custom-house and reclaimed at the traveller's consulate.

Custom House. The custom-house examination at Alexandria is generally carried out with great thoroughness, though with perfect politeness, and no article of luggage is allowed to escape unopened. One of the objects chiefly sought for is cigars, on which 75 per cent of the estimated value is charged. Considerable difficulty is also made about admitting firearms and cartridges. The custom-house is now under European management, and it is on the whole advisable to refrain from an attempt to facilitate matters by bakshîsh (p. 16)

On all goods exported, one per cent of duty is charged on the estimated value, and luggage is accordingly examined again as the traveller quits the country. The exportation of antiquities is strictly prohibited (p. 25). If luggage be forwarded across the frontier, the keys must be sent with it; but, if possible, the traveller should always superintend the custom-house examination in person.

(4). Consulates.

Consuls in the East enjoy the same privilege of exterritoriality as ambassadors in other countries. A distinction is sometimes made between professional ('consules missi') and commercial consuls, the former alone having political functions to discharge; and there are consuls, vice-consuls, and consular agents, possessing various degrees of authority. In all cases of emergency the traveller should apply for advice to the nearest consul of his country, through whom the authorities are most conveniently approached, and who will effectually watch over his interests. It is therefore very desirable that travellers should take the earliest possible opportunity of entering into friendly relations with these most useful officials, and the more so as access to some of the principal objects of interest cannot be obtained without their intervention. The kavasses, or consular officers, also render important services to travellers, for which they expect a fee, although not entitled to demand payment.

On 1st Jan 1876 an important reform in the Egyptian Legal System came into operation for a provisional period of five years. Foreigners had hitherto been entirely withdrawn from the civil and criminal jurisdiction of the Egyptian authorities, their consul alone being competent to take cognisance of cases in which they were concerned. Besides the native authorities there thus existed no fewer than seventeen co-ordinate consular tribunals, each of which administered the law of its own country, and, as it was often uncertain before which tribunal and by what law a case would ultimately be decided, the system caused serious inconvenience both to the landed and commercial interests. The Egyptian government at length made a proposal, which was specially supported by the then minister Nubar Pasha, and was acceded to by the powers represented by consuls, that mixed tribunals should be appointed, consisting of courts of first and second instance, for the trial of all civil cases arising between natives and foreigners, or between foreigners of different nationalities, in accordance with Egyptian law, founded on that of France and Italy. Cases in which the Khedive himself and the Egyptian government are concerned are also tried before this new tribunal, so that the system of appeals, formerly so much abused, is now done away with. The courts of the first instance are at Alexandria and Cairo. The judges consist of natives and foreigners, the latter being elected by the Khedive out of the qualified officials nominated by the Great Powers. The appeal court at Alexandria is constituted in the same manner. Some of the judges of the first instance are also chosen from members of the smaller European states These courts enjoy a constitutional guarantee for the independence of their jurisdiction, and, so far as necessary, they execute their judgments by means of their own officers. The languages used are Arabic, French, and Italian From 1881 to 1884 the jurisdiction of these mixed tribunals was prolonged by the consent of the Powers from year to year, and at the beginning of the latter year it was agreed to continue it for another period of five years. — Besides these new courts, the consular and local tribunals still continue to subsist, their jurisdiction being, however, limited to criminal cases and to civil suits between foreigners of the same nationality, provided the question does not affect land.

At the beginning of 1884 there was called into existence a new system of *Native Courts*, which take precedence of the mixed courts in deciding criminal cases between natives and foreigners. The general procedure is based on the Code Napoléon. Courts of the first instance have been, or are to be erected at Cairo, Alexandria, Tanta, Zakâzîk, Benha, Beni Suêf, Siût, and Kene, while the courts of appeal are at Cairo and Siût. With the native judges are associated ten Belgians, two Dutchmen, and one Englishman. — A scheme is, however, on foot to appoint a commission to extend to the mixed tribunals the criminal jurisdiction in cases where different nationalities are engaged.

(5). Steamboats on the Mediterranean.

Alexandria, the chief seaport of Egypt, is regularly visited by English, French, Austrian, Italian, Russian, Greek, and Egyptian steamers. Whether the traveller returns westwards on leaving Egypt, or intends to proceed to Syria or elsewhere, it is important that he should be familiar with the principal steamboat services.

The time-tables of the *Peninsular & Oriental Steam Navigation Co.* may be obtained in London at 122 Leadenhall St, E.C, or at 25 Cockspur St., S.W. Those who purpose including Syria, Greece, and Constantinople in their Oriental tour should also, before leaving home, write to the '*Administration des Services des Messageries Maritimes, 16 Rue Cannebière, Marseilles*' for a '*Livret des Lignes de la Méditerranée et de la Mer Noire*', and to the '*Verwaltungsrath der Dampfschifffahrtsgesellschaft des Oesterreich-Ungarischen Lloyd, Trieste*' for '*Information for Passengers by the Austrian Lloyd's Steam Navigation Company*' (published in English). With the aid of these time-tables, the traveller will have little difficulty in making out his programme See also '*Baedeker's Palestine and Syria*' (sold at the bookshops of Alexandria and Cairo).

In selecting a route the traveller must of course be guided by circumstances and his own inclination. The shortest sea-voyage is that from Brindisi, three days and a half, from Trieste (viâ Corfu), or from Venice (viâ Ancona and Brindisi), five days; from Naples, four days. The last-named route is perhaps the best for returning, as the temperature of Naples and Rome forms a pleasant intermediary between the warmth of Egypt and the colder climate of N. Europe. The vessels of the principal lines are all nearly on a par with regard to comfort and speed, many of them being large and handsomely fitted up, while others are inferior.

The First Class cabins and berths are always well furnished; those of the Second Class, though less showy, are tolerably comfortable, and are often patronised by gentlemen travelling alone. In autumn and winter the vessels bound for Alexandria, and in spring those returning westwards, are apt to be crowded.

The Food, which is included in the first-class fare and usually in the second also, is always abundant and of good quality. Passengers begin the day by ordering a cup of coffee at 7 or 8 o'clock; at 9 or 10 a déjeuner à la fourchette of three courses is served; lunch or tiffin is a similar repast at 12 or 1; and at 5 or 6 there is a very ample dinner, after which tea is generally provided. Many travellers prefer the cookery on board the French and Austrian steamers as being lighter and better suited to the climate than that of the English vessels. Passengers who are prevented by sickness from partaking of the regular repasts are supplied with lemonade and other refreshments gratis.

The Steward's Fee, which the passenger pays at the end of the voyage, is generally from ½ fr. to 1 fr. per day; but more is expected if unusual trouble has been given.

The Baths provided for the use of passengers in the English and some of the other vessels may be used without extra charge, but the attendant expects a fee at the end of the voyage.

Difference in Solar

(in minutes, + or — signifying that the time of the place at the head of the

	Alexandria	Ancona	Assuân	Athens	Berlin	Brindisi	Cairo	Constantinople	Corfu	London	Marseilles
Alexandria	0	— 65	+ 12	— 25	— 66	— 47	+ 6	— 4	— 40	— 119	— 98
Ancona	+ 65	0	+ 77	+ 41	— ½	+ 18	+ 71	+ 62	+ 26	— 54	— 33
Assuân	— 12	— 77	0	— 36	— 78	— 59	— 6	— 15	— 52	— 131	— 110
Athens	+ 25	— 41	+ 36	0	— 41	— 23	+ 30	+ 21	— 15	— 95	— 73
Berlin	+ 66	+ ½	+ 78	+ 41	0	+ 18	+ 72	+ 62	+ 26	— 54	— 32
Brindisi	+ 47	— 18	+ 59	+ 23	— 18	0	+ 53	+ 44	+ 8	— 72	— 51
Cairo	— 6	— 71	+ 6	— 30	— 72	— 58	0	— 9	— 46	— 125	— 104
Constantin	+ 4	— 62	+ 15	— 21	— 62	— 44	+ 9	0	— 36	— 116	— 94
Corfu	+ 40	— 26	+ 52	+ 15	— 26	— 8	+ 46	+ 36	0	— 80	— 58
London	+ 119	+ 54	+ 131	+ 95	+ 54	+ 72	+ 125	+ 116	+ 80	0	+ 21
Marseilles	+ 98	+ 33	+ 110	+ 73	+ 32	+ 51	+ 104	+ 94	+ 58	— 21	0
Messina	+ 57	— 8	+ 69	+ 33	— 9	+ 10	+ 63	+ 54	+ 17	— 62	— 41
Munich	+ 73	+ 8	+ 85	+ 48	+ 7	+ 26	+ 79	+ 69	+ 33	— 46	— 25
Naples	+ 62	— 3	+ 74	+ 38	— 3	+ 15	+ 68	+ 59	+ 23	— 57	— 36
New York	+ 415	+ 350	+ 427	+ 391	+ 350	+ 368	+ 421	+ 412	+ 376	+ 296	+ 317
Paris	+ 110	+ 45	+ 129	+ 86	+ 44	+ 63	+ 116	+ 107	+ 70	— 9	+ 12
Pesth	+ 43	— 22	+ 55	+ 19	— 23	— 4	+ 49	+ 40	+ 3	— 76	— 55
Rome	+ 70	+ 4	+ 81	+ 45	+ 4	+ 22	+ 75	+ 66	+ 30	— 50	— 28
St. Petersb.	— 2	— 67	+ 10	— 26	— 68	— 49	+ 4	— 5	— 42	— 121	— 100
Trieste	+ 61	— 1	+ 76	+ 40	— 1	+ 17	+ 70	+ 61	+ 25	— 55	— 34
Venice	+ 70	+ 5	+ 82	+ 46	+ 4	+ 23	+ 76	+ 66	+ 30	— 49	— 28
Vienna	+ 54	— 15	+ 66	+ 29	— 12	+ 7	+ 60	+ 50	+ 14	— 66	— 44

Tickets should never be taken at foreign ports through the medium of commissionnaires or other persons who offer their services, but the traveller should, if possible, purchase them at the office in person. The tickets bear the name of the passenger and the name and hour of departure of the vessel. Return or circular tickets (to Syria and Constantinople) and family tickets for three or more persons are generally issued at a reduced rate, but no reduction is made on the charge for food. A child of 2-10 years pays half-fare, but must share the berth of its attendant; but for two children a whole berth is allowed.

Luggage of 150-220 lbs. is allowed to first-class, and of 85-135 lbs. to second-class passengers.

Embarkation. Passengers should be on board an hour before the advertised time of starting. At Marseilles, Trieste, and Brindisi the vessels start from the quays, so that passengers can walk on board; but at Venice and Naples passengers are conveyed to the steamers in small boats, for which the charge at all the Italian ports is 1 franc or lira for each person, including luggage. Good order is kept at these ports by the police. Payment of the boat-fare should not be made until the passenger and his luggage are safe on deck. Before the heavier luggage is lowered into the hold, the passenger should see it properly labelled.

All complaints should be addressed to the captain. On board the foreign steamers a kind of military precision is affected, and questions addressed to the officers or crew are apt to be answered very curtly.

From Trieste to Alexandria *(Austrian Lloyd)* every Friday at midday. On Saturday and Sunday the Dalmatian and Albanian

Time between: —
column is before or behind that of the place on the left side of the page)

	Messina	Munich	Naples	New York	Paris	Pesth	Rome	St. Petersburg	Trieste	Venice	Vienna
Alexandria	— 57	— 73	— 62	— 415	— 110	— 43	— 70	+ 2	— 64	— 70	— 54
Ancona	+ 8	— 8	+ 3	— 350	— 45	+ 22	— 4	+ 67	+ 1	— 5	+ 12
Assuân	— 69	— 85	— 74	— 427	— 122	— 55	— 81	— 10	— 76	— 82	— 66
Athens	— 33	— 48	— 38	— 391	— 86	— 19	— 45	+ 26	— 40	— 46	— 29
Berlin	+ 9	— 7	+ 3	— 350	— 44	+ 23	— 4	+ 68	+ 1	— 4	+ 12
Brindisi	— 10	— 26	— 15	— 368	— 63	+ 4	— 22	+ 49	— 17	— 23	— 7
Cairo	— 63	— 79	— 68	— 421	— 116	— 49	— 75	— 4	— 70	— 76	— 60
Constantin.	— 54	— 69	— 59	— 412	— 107	— 40	— 66	+ 5	— 61	— 66	— 50
Corfu	— 17	— 33	+ 23	— 376	— 70	— 3	— 30	+ 42	— 25	— 30	— 14
London	+ 62	+ 46	+ 57	— 296	+ 9	+ 76	+ 50	+ 121	+ 55	+ 49	+ 66
Marseilles	+ 41	+ 25	+ 36	— 317	— 12	+ 55	+ 28	+ 100	+ 34	+ 28	+ 44
Messina	0	— 16	— 5	— 358	— 53	+ 14	— 12	+ 59	— 7	— 13	+ 3
Munich	+ 16	0	+ 11	— 342	— 37	+ 30	+ 3	+ 75	+ 9	+ 3	+ 19
Naples	+ 5	— 11	0	— 353	— 48	+ 19	— 7	+ 64	— 2	— 8	+ 9
New York	+ 358	+ 342	+ 353	0	+ 305	+ 372	+ 346	+ 417	+ 351	+ 345	+ 361
Paris	+ 53	+ 37	+ 48	— 305	0	+ 67	+ 41	+ 112	+ 46	+ 40	+ 56
Pesth	— 14	— 30	— 19	— 372	— 67	0	— 26	+ 45	— 21	— 27	— 11
Rome	+ 12	— 3	+ 7	— 346	— 41	+ 26	0	+ 71	+ 5	— 1/2	+ 16
St. Petersb.	— 59	— 75	— 64	— 417	— 112	— 45	— 71	0	+ 66	— 72	— 56
Trieste	+ 7	— 9	+ 2	— 351	— 46	+ 21	— 5	+ 66	0	— 6	+ 10
Venice	+ 13	— 3	+ 8	— 345	— 40	+ 27	+ 1/2	+ 72	+ 6	0	+ 16
Vienna	— 3	— 19	— 9	— 361	— 56	+ 11	— 16	+ 56	— 10	— 16	0

coast lies on the left. Arrival at Corfu on Sunday at noon, and halt of 4-5 hours; arrival at Alexandria generally about 4 p.m. on Wednesday. — FROM ALEXANDRIA to Trieste every Tuesday at 4 p.m.; arrival at Trieste on Sunday at 6 p.m. — Fares to Alexandria: 1st class 120 fl., 2nd class 80 fl., in gold. The journey may be broken at any of the intermediate ports.

FROM VENICE AND BRINDISI to Alexandria. The steamers of the *Peninsular and Oriental Company* leave Venice every Thursday afternoon, touch next morning at Ancona, and on Sunday morning at Brindisi, where they receive the English mails for India (arriving from London viâ Paris and Turin in 56 hrs.). They then leave Brindisi at 4 a.m. on Monday for Alexandria, where they generally arrive on Thursday. — FROM ALEXANDRIA to Brindisi the departures take place on Thurs., Frid., Sat., or Sun., 36 hrs. after the arrival of the Indian mail in Suez, notice of which is given at the post-office. — The fare to Alexandria, either from Venice or Brindisi, is 12*l.* for the 1st cabin and 9*l.* for the 2nd cabin, so that passengers embarking at Venice effect a considerable saving.

FROM MARSEILLES AND NAPLES. Vessels of the *Messageries Maritimes* leave Marseilles every Thursday about noon, arrive at Naples on Saturday morning, start again after a halt of some hours, and arrive at Alexandria on Wednesday about 5 p.m. On the voyage from Marseilles to Naples these vessels pass through the Strait of Bonifacio, but on the return-voyage they steer round Capo Corso in order to avoid adverse currents. In quitting the harbour at Naples the passenger enjoys a delightful view in fine weather. On the voyage out the vessel passes through the Strait of Messina at night. — FROM ALEXANDRIA to Naples and Marseilles every Tuesday at 9 a.m. On Friday about noon the vessel sights the Calabrian coast with the Capo Spartivento, and to the W. the pyramidal Ætna, which is covered with snow until summer. It then steers through the Strait of Messina on the E. side, commanding a view of the beautiful promontory of Aspromonte on the right; towards evening it passes close to the island of Stromboli, and next day (Saturday) arrives at Naples about 2 p.m. — Fares from Marseilles to Alexandria 375 and 250 fr., from Naples 275 and 175 fr.

Besides these steamboats may be mentioned those of the Italian SOCIETÀ FLORIO-RUBATTINO, which ply between Genoa, Leghorn, Naples, Messina, and Alexandria once weekly (leaving Alexandria on Saturdays), and those of the French firm FRAISSINET & Co. which ply between Marseilles, Leghorn, and Alexandria twice monthly. The fares are about one-third lower than those above mentioned. The departures are advertised at the hotels of the different ports

The RUSSIAN and EGYPTIAN STEAMERS, the former of which are tolerably comfortable, ply between Alexandria and the eastern ports only (Syrian coast, Constantinople), and are not recommended to ordirary travellers. Fares and departures advertised at the hotels — ENGLISH FREIGHT STEAMERS, with accommodation for a few passengers, ply between Alexandria and Leghorn at irregular intervals, which may be ascertained at the Alexandrian agency, *Messrs R. J. Moss & Co.*

(6). Modes of Travelling in Egypt.

Railways. A network of railways constructed by the Egyptian government now connects most of the important places in the Delta. The engineer of the oldest of these lines, that from Alexandria to Cairo, was Mr. Stephenson, and the others were planned by Faiḍ-Bey. The railways are under the management of a board of administration, the president of which is a native, while most of the members are Englishmen or other Europeans. The carriages resemble those of other countries, but the third class is insufferably dirty. The dust and heat render railway travelling in Egypt exceedingly unpleasant in hot weather.

The traveller should be at the station fully half-an-hour before the hour for starting, as the process of issuing tickets and booking luggage is often very slow, and the ticket-clerks are entitled to close the office 10 minutes before the departure of the train. Gold coins that are in any degree either defaced or of light weight are not accepted at the booking-office. The personal tickets are printed in English and Arabic, the luggage tickets in Arabic only. The hours of departure are seldom altered, and those at present fixed are given in the following pages.

Steamboats on the Suez Canal, see R. 7.

Donkeys (Arab. *ḥomâr*) form the best means of conveyance both in the narrow streets of the towns and on the bridle-paths in the country. They are of a much finer, swifter, and more spirited race than the European, and at the same time patient and persevering. Those in the towns are generally well saddled and bridled in Oriental style. The attendants are either men or boys †, who contrive to keep up with their beasts at whatever pace they are going, and often address long sentences to them in their Arabic patois. As the gait of the donkeys is sometimes very uneasy when they break into a trot, care should be taken not to engage one with this defect for an excursion of any length. As the stirrups are often in bad condition they had better not be used at all. The donkey-boys (Arab. *ḥammâr*) are fond of showing off the pace of their beasts, and often drive them unpleasantly fast. The rider who prefers a slower pace shouts *'ala mahlak* or *'ala mahlakum*; if a quicker pace is wanted, *yalla, yalla*, or *mâshî*, or *sûk el-ḥomâr*, if a halt is to be made, *oṣbur*, or the English word 'stop'. The donkey-boys, especially at Cairo, are generally remarkably active, intelligent, and obliging. Many of the donkeys, particularly in the country, will be observed to have been deprived of part of one or both ears. This has been done, according to the somewhat cruel practice of the country, as a punishment for trespass, an additional

† The boys are preferable to the men, as the latter are generally more exorbitant in their demands and less obliging, and even their donkeys appear to partake of their unpleasant disposition.

fragment being cut off for each repetition of the offence, and the delinquents are known as *harâmîyeh*, or thieves. The horse and donkey-shoes consist of plates of metal with a hole in the middle.

The CAMEL (for riding *hegîn*, in Syria *delûl*; for baggage *gemel*; those with one hump are the only kind found here) is generally used for the Mt. Sinai tour (R. 10) only, but for the sake of experiment may be ridden on one of the shorter excursions from Cairo (*e.g.* to the Petrified Forest or to Helwân). The patient 'ship of the desert' is always surly in appearance, and though he commands our respect never wins our affection. Those only which have been properly trained can be ridden with any comfort, the baggage-camels being as unsuitable for the purpose as the ponderous Flemish cart-horse. If well mounted on a tall and well trained *hegîn*, the traveller will find that camel-riding is quite undeserving of the vituperation so often bestowed upon it by the inexperienced (comp. also R. 10).

(7) Dealings with the Natives. Dragomans.

The traveller, apart from his ignorance of the language, will find it exceedingly difficult to deal with the class of people with whom he chiefly comes in contact. The extravagance of their demands is boundless, and they appear to think that Europeans are absolutely ignorant of the value of money (p. 16). Every attempt at extortion should be firmly resisted, as compliance only makes the applicants for bakhshîsh doubly clamorous. Payment should never be made until the service stipulated for has been rendered, after which an absolutely deaf ear should be turned to the protestations and entreaties which almost invariably follow. Thanks, it need hardly be said, must never be expected from such recipients (comp p. 16). Even when an express bargain has been made, and more than the stipulated sum paid, they are almost sure to pester the traveller in the way indicated. When no bargain has been made, the fees and prices mentioned in the Handbook, all of which are ample, should be paid without remark; and if the attacks which ensue are not silenced by an air of calm indifference the traveller may use the word *rûh* or *imshi* (comp. p. 204) in a quiet but decided and imperative tone. The Egyptians, it must be remembered, occupy a much lower grade in the scale of civilisation than most of the western nations, and cupidity is one of their chief failings, but if the traveller makes due allowance for their shortcomings, and treats the natives with consistent firmness, he will find that they are by no means destitute of fidelity, honesty, and kindliness.

Notwithstanding all the suggestions we have ventured to offer, the traveller will to some extent have to buy his experience. In most cases the overcharges to which he will be exposed will be comparatively trifling, but if extortion is attempted on a larger scale, he had better refer the matter to his consul.

Travellers about to make a tour of any length may avoid all the petty annoyances incident to direct dealings with the natives by placing themselves under the care of a DRAGOMAN (Arab. *turgemân*).

The word *dragoman* is derived from the Chaldæan *targem*, 'to explain', or from *targûm*, 'explanation'. The Arabic *targam* also signifies 'to interpret'. The dragoman was therefore originally merely a guide who explained or interpreted Since the 7th cent B C when Psammetichus I. threw open the country to foreign trade, against which it had previously been jealously closed, this class, which is mentioned by Herodotus as a distinct caste, has existed in Egypt. That author informs us that Psammetichus caused a number of Egyptian children to be educated by Greeks in order that they might learn their language, and it was these children who afterwards became the founders of the dragoman caste The great historian himself employed a dragoman, from whom he frequently derived erroneous information A dragoman, who was employed by the governor Ælius Gallus to accompany him up the Nile, is accused by Strabo of absurdity, conceit, and ignorance The ignorant Arabian, Nubian, or Maltese dragomans of the present day do not attempt to explain or translate the ancient inscriptions An effort was recently made with some success to educate young Arabs for this calling in a school founded for the purpose; but, like most Oriental undertakings, the scheme has not been persevered with.

The dragomans, who speak English, French, and Italian, undertake for a fixed sum per day to defray the whole cost of locomotion, hotel accommodation, fees, and all other expenses, so that the traveller is enabled to obtain, as it were, a bird's eye view of the country without being concerned with the cares of daily life. On the other hand the traveller is frequently imposed upon by the dragoman himself.

The charge made by the dragoman varies very greatly according to circumstances, such as the number and the requirements of the travellers, the length of the journey, and the amount of the demand for the services of such a guide A dragoman is usually employed for the longer tours only, such as the voyage up the Nile, the journey to Mt. Sinai, the excursion to the Fayûm, and a visit to the less frequented towns in the Delta. Visitors to Alexandria, Cairo, Suez, Isma'îlîya, and Port Sa'îd may well dispense with a dragoman, as every necessary service will be rendered them by the commissionnaires of the hotels (5-10 fr. per day). Dragomans of the better class, moreover, usually consider it beneath their dignity to escort their employers through the streets of the towns, and are apt to consign them to the guidance of the local cicerones.

For the above-named longer tours the charges vary so greatly, and the services to be rendered on each are so different, that a separate contract with the dragoman should be drawn up in each case. (Thus, for the Nile voyage he has to procure a dahabîyeh, for the Fayûm horses, for Mt. Sinai camels, for the Delta canal-boats and donkeys, and, for the last three journeys, tents also) Information regarding expenses and other details, as well as the names of some of the best dragomans, will be prefixed to each of the routes in question. The larger the party, the less will be the expense for each member of it, while for a single traveller a dragoman is of course a very costly appendage.

In conclusion, we may add that most of the dragomans are fond of assuming a patronising manner towards their employers, while they generally treat their own countrymen with an air of vast superiority. The sooner this impertinence is checked, the more satisfactory will be the traveller's subsequent relations with his guide; and the hints already given with reference to the traveller's intercourse with the natives may not unfrequently be applied to the dragomans themselves. On the successful termination of the journey travellers are too apt from motives of good nature to write a more favourable testimonial for their dragoman than he really deserves; but this is truly an act of injustice to his subsequent employers, and tends to confirm him in his faults. The testimonial therefore should not omit to mention any serious cause for dissatisfaction. Information with regard to dragomans (name, languages spoken, conduct, and charges) will always be gratefully received by the Editor of the Handbook for the benefit of later editions.

(8). Equipment for the Tour.

Dress. It is less important now than it formerly was to purchase every requirement for the journey before leaving home, as the traveller can easily supplement his outfit at some of the modern shops of Alexandria or Cairo. For all ordinary purposes a couple of light Tweed suits, a few flannel and soft cotton shirts, a supply of thin woollen socks, one pair of light and easy boots, one of shoes, and one of slippers, a moderately warm Ulster or long travelling cloak, a pith-helmet and a soft felt hat, together with the most necessary articles of the toilet, will amply suffice. It is advisable, for the prevention of colds and chills, to wear a woollen fabric next the skin; but light underclothing, with an Oxford shirt, will be found more suitable to the climate than a heavy flannel shirt. Those who intend making a prolonged stay at the principal towns may add a dress-suit and a few white shirts. If a muslin 'puggaree' be used for covering the hat, it should be made to fall over the back of the neck and ears as broadly as possible. This favourite European head-dress, however, invariably attracts hosts of importunate candidates for 'bakshîsh'. Some travellers prefer the *fez* or *tarbûsh*, a red cloth skull-cap with black-silk tassel (1-15 fr.), over which, in native fashion, they tie a silk keffiyeh (manufactured in Egypt, 15-20 fr.), falling down behind in a triangle. This head-dress protects the neck and cheeks admirably against the scorching Egyptian sun, especially when a folded handkerchief or a white skull-cap (*ṭâkîyeh*) is worn under the ṭarbûsh. In prolonged riding tours, a sun-shade is a fatiguing encumbrance. All these articles should be new and strongly made, as it is often difficult and troublesome to get repairs properly executed in Egypt. White shirts, collars, and wristbands, which require frequent and skilful washing, should be as far as possible eschewed, as good laundresses are rare and expensive (2-4 fr. per dozen articles, irrespective of size). Few travellers walk in Egypt, except for very short distances, but sportsmen should add a stout pair of waterproof shooting-boots to their equipment.

For tours on horse or camel-back two small portmanteaus are much more suitable than a box or trunk of larger size.

Miscellaneous. Among the most important extras are a drinking cup of leather or metal, a flask, a strong pocket-knife, note-books, writing-materials, straps and twine, a thermometer, a pocket-compass of medium size, and a supply of magnesium wire for lighting caverns and dark chambers. To these may perhaps be added a 'remontoir', or keyless watch, as a watch-key lost during the journey is not easily replaced.

Health. Fine as the climate of Egypt generally is, the chilly mornings and evenings are often treacherous, and if cold is caught it is apt to result in a tedious intermittent or other fever. There are good chemists at Alexandria and Cairo, from whom small medicine-chests adapted for the climate may be purchased. In serious cases of illness a European doctor, when procurable, should always be consulted, as the traveller's own experience acquired at home is of little avail in the climate of Egypt.

Fits of shivering are the usual prelude to an attack of fever. Quinine is the best remedy, of which 1-3 doses should be taken on the days when the patient is free from fever. Rest and copious perspiration will also afford relief

Diarrhœa, which is apt to turn to dysentery, is a very common complaint in this climate, and is generally the result of eating unripe fruit or of catching cold. The patient should first take a slight aperient, and afterwards tincture of opium or concentrated tincture of camphor. A simple farinaceous diet (such as well-boiled rice), with tea or well matured, unfortified, and unsweetened red wine, will be beneficial, while fruit, meat, and fatty substances should be avoided. In cases both of diarrhœa and fever all remedies are sometimes unavailing except change of climate, especially if the patient is in a marshy or unhealthy locality

Sprains, which often result from exploring ruins and caverns, are most effectually treated with cold compresses, while the injured limb should be tightly bandaged and allowed perfect rest

The sting of a scorpion (seldom dangerous) or bite of a snake is usually treated with ammonia

Sunstroke is very common in Egypt, even in spring when the air is still cool The head and neck should therefore always be carefully shielded in one of the ways above indicated The usual remedies are rest and shade, cold compresses, and warm baths with cold douches applied to the head and neck.

Grey spectacles or veils may be used with advantage when the eyes suffer from the glare of bright weather Zinc eye-wash, or some other innocuous lotion, should be used in such cases

The sticking-plaster, lint, as well as all effervescing powders, and other medicines carried by the traveller should be carefully kept from exposure to moisture

(9). Beggars. Bakshish.

Most Orientals regard the European traveller as a Crœsus, and sometimes too as a madman, — so unintelligible to them are the objects and pleasures of travelling. Poverty, they imagine, is unknown among us, whereas in reality we feel its privations far more keenly than they. That such erroneous notions prevail is to some extent the fault of travellers themselves. In a country where the requirements of the natives are few and simple, and money is scarce, a few piastres seem a fortune to many. Travellers are therefore often tempted to give for the sake of affording temporary pleasure at a trifling cost, forgetting that the seeds of insatiable cupidity are thereby sown, to the infinite annoyance of their successors and the demoralisation of the recipients themselves. As a rule, bakshîsh should never be given except for services rendered, or to the sick and aged

Sir Gardner Wilkinson has justly observed that the cry of '*Bakshîsh, bakshîsh, yâ khawâgeh*' (oh, sir! a gift!), with which Europeans are invariably assailed, is an insulting substitute for the 'good day' of other countries. The Arab reserves his pious benedictions for his own countrymen, but never hesitates to take advantage of that he considers the folly of foreign travellers. The best reply to such applications is '*mâ fîsh, mâ fîsh*' (I have nothing for you), which will generally have the effect of dispersing the assailants. Or a beggar may be silenced with the words '*Allâh ya'tîk*' (may God give thee!).

The word *bakshîsh*, which resounds so perpetually in the traveller's ears during his sojourn in the East, and haunts him long afterwards, simply means 'a gift', and, as everything is to be had in return for gifts, the word has many different applications. Thus with bakshîsh the tardy formalities of the custom-house officer are accelerated, bakshîsh supplies the place of a passport, bakshîsh is the alms bestowed on a beggar, bakshîsh means black mail, and lastly a large proportion of the public officials of the country are said to live by bakshîsh or bribery.

(10). Public Safety. Weapons. Dogs.

Public Safety. The authority of the Khedive is so well established throughout the whole of Egypt that travellers are very rarely exposed to predatory attacks, even on the Sinai journey, and travelling is indeed safer than in some parts of Europe. The protection of an escort is therefore never necessary as it is in certain regions of Palestine and Syria. Travellers, however, who have scientific objects in view, and who require the co-operation of the natives or of the pasha or mudîr of a district, or those who have reason to apprehend any difficulty or danger, may obtain through their consulates a viceregal recommendation (*firmân* or *teskireh*), which will often be found very useful.

Weapons for self-defence are an unnecessary encumbrance. Guns for purposes of sport, see p. 79.

Dogs, being regarded by the Muslims as unclean (p. 79), are never touched by them. Their barking is sometimes a source of alarm, especially in country places, but they fortunately never bite. As they are never domesticated in Oriental countries, it is quite useless to attempt to establish friendly relations with them.

(11). Hotels. Hospitality.

Hotels. The traveller will find good, first-class hotels at Alexandria, Cairo, Isma'îlîya, Port Sa'îd, and Suez, kept by Germans, Frenchmen, or Greeks, with European waiters. The charges are generally high, 15-25 fr. per day being charged during the season for board, lodging, and attendance, whether all the meals are partaken of or not. For a prolonged stay a lower rate should be stipulated for in advance. Wine is generally extra. The waiter expects a fee of 2-3 fr. per week, his native assistant $1^1/_2$ fr., and the porter about 2 fr.; for errands in the neighbourhood there is generally a separate tariff. Orientals attract the attention of waiters by clapping their hands, and sometimes with the exclamation — '*yâ weled*' (ho, boy!). — Tolerable inns have also sprung up of late years at Ṭanṭa, Manṣûra, Zaḳâzîḳ, Damietta, and at Minyeh and Siûṭ in Upper Egypt.

Hospitality. In all other parts of Egypt the traveller who is not provided with tents must apply to the principal natives or officials, or to European merchants for accommodation. The latter are to be met with in every part of the Delta, and will be found most courteous and hospitable. Letters of introduction may be obtained without difficulty at Alexandria and Cairo.

(12). Cafés.

Story-tellers, Musicians, Singers, etc.

European Cafés are to be found at the towns above mentioned, beer being one of the refreshments they afford ($^1/_2$ fr. per glass). The beer either comes from Vienna or Gratz, or is made in Cairo by the Société Genevoise.

Arabian Cafés (*ḳahwa*) abound everywhere, even in the smallest and dirtiest villages. In the country they usually consist of wooden booths, with a few seats made of plaited palm-twigs (*gerîd*), and even in the large towns, like Cairo, they are very small and uninviting. The ḳahwas are frequented by the lower classes exclusively. The front generally consists of woodwork with a few open arches. Outside the door runs a *masṭaba*, or raised seat of stone or brick, two or three feet in height and of about the same width, covered with mats, and there are similar seats on two or three sides of the interior. Coffee is served by the *kahwegi* at 10 paras per cup (*fingân*), and several *nargîlehs* and *shîshehs* or *gôzehs* (water-pipes) are kept in readiness for the use of customers. The *tumbâk* (p. 27) smoked in the latter is sometimes mixed with the intoxicating hashîsh (hemp, Cannabis Indica), the strong and unmistakeable smell of which is often perceptible even in the street. The sale of hashîsh is now nominally prohibited in Egypt.

'The leaves and capsules of hemp, called in Egypt *hasheesh*, were employed in some countries of the East in very ancient times to induce an exhilarating intoxication. Herodotus (iv. 75) informs us that the Scythians had a custom of burning the seeds of this plant in religious ceremonies, and that they became intoxicated with the fumes. Galen also mentions the intoxicating properties of hemp. The practice of chewing the leaves of this plant to induce intoxication prevailed, or existed, in India in very early ages, thence it was introduced into Persia; and about six centuries ago (before the middle of the thirteenth century of our era) this pernicious and degrading custom was adopted in Egypt, but chiefly by persons of the lower orders. . . The preparation of hemp used for smoking produces boisterous mirth. Few inhalations of the smoke, but the last very copious, are usually taken from the gózeh. After the emission of the last draught from the mouth and nostrils, commonly a fit of coughing, and often a spitting of blood, ensues, in consequence of the lungs having been filled with the smoke. Hasheesh is to be obtained not only at some of the coffee-shops. there are shops of a smaller and more private description solely appropriated to the sale of this and other intoxicating preparations: they are called *mahsheshehs*. It is sometimes amusing to observe the ridiculous conduct, and to listen to the conversation, of the persons who frequent these shops. They are all of the lower orders. The term *hashshash*, which signifies a smoker, or an eater, of hemp, is an appellation of obloquy: noisy and riotous people are often called *hashshasheen*, which is the plural of that appellation, and the origin of our word assassin, a name first applied to Arab warriors in Syria, in the time of the Crusades, who made use of intoxicating and soporific drugs to render their enemies insensible'.

'The use of opium and other drugs to induce intoxication is not so common in Egypt as in many other countries of the East: the number of Egyptians addicted to this vice is certainly not nearly so great in proportion to the whole population as is the relative number of persons in our own country who indulge in habitual drunkenness'....

'*Boozeh* or *boozah*, which is an intoxicating liquor made with barley-bread, crumbled, mixed with water, strained, and left to ferment, is commonly drunk by the boatmen of the Nile, and by other persons of the lower orders.' — LANE (1833-35).

Numerous taverns now exist exclusively for the sale of bûzeh, kept chiefly by Nubians. It is usually dispensed immediately from a large boiler with a wooden ladle, which is passed from mouth to mouth, the customers being of both sexes. The liquor is intoxicating in a very slight degree.

Many of the kahwas are frequented, especially on the eves of festivals (p. 236), by story-tellers and musicians. The performances range from those of a very simple character to gorgeous entertainments with dancing, music, and fireworks; and these 'fantasîyas', as they are called by the modern Arabs, afford unbounded delight.

STORY-TELLERS (who in private domestic circles are generally women) still form a characteristic Oriental institution. Wherever they make their appearance, whether in the public streets or the coffee-house, in the densely peopled alleys of the large towns, or in the smallest country villages, or among the tents of the wandering Arabs, they are sure to attract an attentive, easily pleased, and exceedingly grateful crowd. The more sensational the tale, the better, and the oftener is the narrator applauded with protracted cries of 'Aah', or 'Allâh', or 'Allâhu akbar!'.

The story-teller generally occupies a small stool on the maṣṭaba, whence he delivers his address. Most of the members of this class belong to the so-called *sho'ara* (sing. *shâ'ir*), literally 'singers'. They are also known as *'Anâtireh* (sing. *'Antari*) or *Abu-Zêdîyeh*, according as their theme consists of tales and romances from the history of 'Antar, a Beduin hero, or from that of Abu Zêd. Others again are called *Moḥadditîn*, i. e. narrators of history, their province being the recital in prose of passages from the history of Sultan Eẓ-Ẓâhir Bêbars, who reigned over Egypt in 1260-77 (p. 104). The entertainments of the '*alf lêleh u lêleh*' (thousand and one nights) are, however, no longer heard, as popular superstition has branded this collection of tales as 'unlucky'. There are also professional improvisors and travelling singers, whose performances are very popular; but the themes of the whole fraternity are too often of an immoral character.

Musicians by profession, called *âlâtîyeh* (sing. *âlâti*), are indispensable on every festive occasion. The usual instruments are the *reḳḳ* or tambourine with little bells, the *naḳḳâreh*, or semi-spherical tambourine, the *zemr* or hautbois, the *ṭabl beledi* or drum, the *ṭabl shâmi* or kettle-drum, and the *darabûkeh*, a kind of funnel-shaped drum (generally made of earthenware, but sometimes of mother-of-pearl and tortoise-shell, with a fish-skin stretched over the broad end), which last is accompanied by the *zummâra*, a kind of double flute. A better class of instruments, used for chamber music, consists of the *nâi*, a kind of flute, the *kemengeh* or two-stringed violin, the body of which consists of a cocoa-nut shell, the *rebâbeh*, or one-stringed violin with a square wooden body, the *ḳânûn*, a kind of zither with strings of sheep-gut, and lastly the *'ûd*, the lute or mandoline, the oldest of all the instruments.

The Egyptians consider themselves a highly musical people, and the traveller will indeed often be struck by the frequency of their singing. The Egyptian sings when indulging in his kêf (p. 23), whether sitting on his heels or stretched out on his mat, when driving his donkey, when carrying stones and mortar up a scaffolding, when working in the fields, and when rowing. He sings whether alone or in company, regarding his vocal music as a means of lightening his labour and of sweetening his repose. A peculiarity of the Egyptian songs, however, is that they have no tune, though they have a certain rhythm, which is always dependent on the text. They are sung through the nose on seven or eight different notes, on which the performer wanders up and down as he feels inclined.† The character of this so-called music is exceedingly monotonous, and to a European ear displeasing. The songs (*mawwâl* or *shughl*) are all of a lyrical description, most of them are erotic and often grossly obscene, and many are at the same time pointless and meaningless. Some of

† In the large work entitled the 'Book of Songs' an endeavour is made to reduce Arabic music to a system, and the notes are divided into seven different keys, each having the same notes, differently arranged; but the popular songs are sung without the least regard to these artificial rules.

them, however, extol the pleasures of friendship and rational enjoyment, or express derision of an enemy, or contempt for the rustic fellaḥ. Thus a favourite song of the donkey-boys derides a young fellaḥ called 'Alî, the favourite of his village, and is usually sung in mockery of some one of the name

Shuftum 'Ali yâ nâs
Lâbis 'amîs wilbâs
Wâ'if 'ala-l-'abbâs
Yil'ab el-birgâs
Wal 'anṭaret ethaddit
Nus il beled haggit
Kulluh 'ala shân 'Ali
Ya'ni ya'ni
Kulluh 'ala shân 'Ali.

Shuftum 'Ali fîkum
Wallâhṭaf ṭawâ'îkum
Wâhrûḥ beled min dôl
Wâ''ud telâtîn yôm
Kulluh 'ala shân 'Ali
Ya'ni ya'ni
Kulluh 'ala shân 'Ali.

1 Have you seen 'Ali, ye people, in shirt and drawers, standing on the bridge of 'Abbâs and showing off his equestrian tricks? But the bridge is now destroyed, and half the village has flown away. And all this for 'Ali's sake, yes, for 'Ali's sake.

2. Have you seen 'Ali among you? If not, I will run off with your skull-caps (p. 14) and will go into one of the villages and remain there thirty days. All this for 'Ali's sake, yes, for 'Ali's sake.

The pleasures of hashîsh-smoking are thus extolled: —

Gôzeh min el-hind wumrakkeb 'alêha ghâb
Wumdandisheh bil wa' wumgamm'a el aḥbâb
Akhatteh minhâ nefes el-'aḳl minni ghâb
Ba'êt abaldam zei el gamâl guwwa 'lghâb
Tub 'aléya yâ tawwâb
Min shurb el gôzeh wal ghâb.
hâ hâ hâ †
Min shurb el gôzeh wal ghâb.

Oh cocoa-nut †† of India, in which is fixed the stem inlaid with shells, that collects friends around it. I have taken a whiff from it — and my understanding fled I drew so that the tube gurgled like a camel. Oh! forgive me, thou Blotter out of sins! that I smoke out of the cocoa-nut with its stem

Thwarted love is another favourite theme. One of these songs begins — *Hôi, hôi, yâ ḥabîbi! Hôi, hôi, kun ṭabîbi!* (come, come, oh beloved! come and be my physician!) These songs also frequently describe the charms of the beloved object with great minuteness.

Female Singers (*'Awâlim*, sing. *'Almeh* or *'Alimeh*; i. e. 'learned women') of a good class are now very rare, and those who still exist perform only in the harems of wealthy natives, so that the traveller will seldom or never have an opportunity of hearing them. Others of a low class are frequently seen in the streets accompanied by one or two musicians, who are generally blind.

The Female Dancers, or caste of the *Ghawâzi* (sing. *Ghâziyeh*), which is quite distinct from that of the 'Awâlim, were formerly one of the chief curiosities of Egypt, but for some years past they have been prohibited from performing in the streets. Really good dancers are said to be now rare, but on the Nile voyage the traveller will have

---

† These syllables represent the coughing caused by the great quantity of smoke inhaled by the hashîsh smoker at intervals of $^1/_4$-$^1/_2$ hour, after which he gradually becomes intoxicated and insensible.

†† The water-pipe out of which the hashîsh is smoked has generally a cocoa-nut (gôzeh) as a receptacle for the water through which the smoke passes.

an opportunity at Keneh, Lukṣor, and Esneh of seeing very curious and elaborate, though to his taste often ungraceful performances. Most of the dancers congregate at the fair of Ṭanṭa (p. 226), but the most skilful decline to exhibit unless paid with gold. The *Ḥawal*, or men in female attire, who frequently dance at festivities instead of the Ghawâzi, present a most repulsive appearance.

The Snake Charmers (*Rifâ'îyeh*, sing. *Rifâ'i*), who form another distinct caste, exhibit performances of a very marvellous character, as credible European residents in Cairo have testified; but the traveller will rarely come in contact with them. The ordinary exhibition of dancing snakes may, however, occasionally be seen in the Ezbekîyeh. The boys who exhibit small snakes at the hotels must of course not be confounded with the Rifâ'îyeh.

The Jugglers (*Ḥâwî*) of Egypt are similar to those of other countries. The performances of the Buffoons (*Kurûdâti* or *Moḥabbazi*), which are chiefly intended for the amusement of the young, are disgracefully indelicate.

(13). Baths.

The baths of Egypt, with their hot-air chambers, are those commonly known as Turkish, but they are neither so clean nor so well fitted up as some of those in the larger cities of Europe.

The *Ḥarâra* (see Plan), as well as the *Maghṭas* and *Ḥanafîyeh*, have flat ceilings in which are openings covered with stained glass. The maghṭas and the Hanafîyeh each contain marble basins for washing, provided with taps for warm water; the maghṭas contain besides a bath sunk in the pavement. Cold water is brought in ewers. The *ḥarâra*, or general bath-chamber, is less heated than the separate rooms, and is filled with steam. All the chambers are paved with marble slabs and heated by flues under the pavement and behind the walls.

When a cloth is hung up at the entrance to the baths, it indicates that women only are admitted. The baths are always cleanest in the early morning. Fridays are to be avoided, as numerous Muslims bathe early on that day, which is their Sabbath.

The visitor first enters a large vaulted chamber covered with a cupola (*hôsh el-ḥammâm*), having a fountain of cold water in the centre (*faskîyeh*), and the bathing towels hung around on strings, these last being swung into their places or taken down with bamboo rods according to requirement. Having taken off his shoes and given them to the attendant, the visitor is next conducted to one of the raised divans which are still unoccupied, where he proceeds to undress. Valuables may, if desired, be entrusted to the bath owner. Wrapping a cloth round his loins, he leaves his divan, is provided with pattens or wooden shoes (*ḳabḳâb*), and is conducted to the hot room (*ḥarâra*) in the interior of the establishment. Near one of the basins here a linen cloth is spread for the bather, and he is now left to perspire. As soon as the skin is thoroughly moist, he calls for the attendant (comp. Arabic vocabulary, p. 198), who pulls and kneads the joints till they crack, a process to which Europeans are not generally subjected. This is followed by the pleasanter operation of shampooing, which is performed by the *abu kîs* or *abu ṣâbûn*, who is requested to do his duty with the word '*keyyisni*' (rub me), and who then rubs the bather with the *kîs*, a rough piece of felt. The attendant next thoroughly soaps the bather, and concludes the operations by pouring bowls of warm water over his

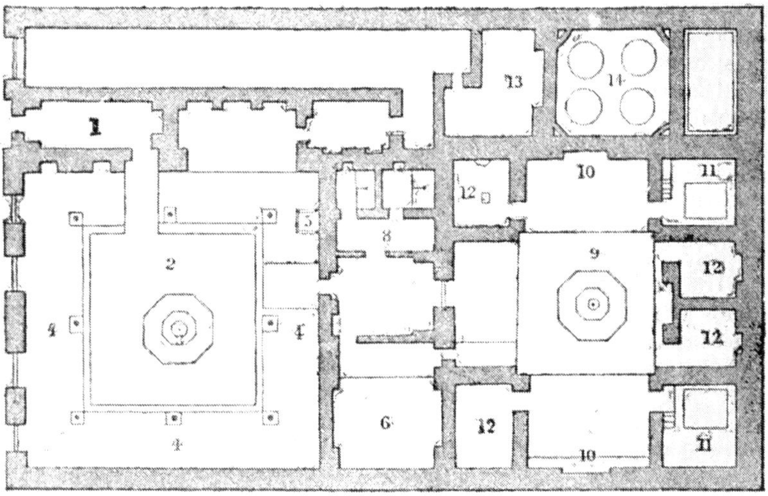

1. Entrance. 2. *Hôsh el-hammâm* (a kind of antechamber, used also by the poorer classes as a dressing-room). 3. *Faskîyeh* (fountain). 4. *Lîwân* (better dressing-rooms, generally consisting of two divisions). 5. Coffee-seller. 6. *Bêt-el-awwel* (warmed dressing-room for cold weather). 8. Latrines. 7. Entrance to the — 9. *Harâra* (or 'sudatorium'). 10. *Lîwân*. 11. *Maghṭas* (cabinets with basins). 12. *Hanafîyeh* (chambers with basins and taps for hot water). 13. Furnaces. 14. Boilers.

head. If the water is too hot the bather may ask for cold (*'hât môyeh bârideh'*), or say 'enough' (*bes*). After this process douches of hot or cold water may be indulged in according to inclination, but the most refreshing plan is to change the temperature gradually from hot to cold, the direction to the attendant being '*môyeh bârideh!*' When desirous of leaving the hot room, the bather says to the attendant '*hât fûṭa*' (bring a towel), whereupon he is provided with one for his loins, another for his shoulders, and a third for his head. The slippers or pattens are then put on, and the antechamber re-entered. When the *kabkâbs* are removed, cold water is sprinkled over the feet, fresh towels are then provided, and the bather at last throws himself down on his divan, wonderfully refreshed, yet glad to enjoy perfect repose for a short time. This interval of tranquil enjoyment is the favourite Oriental '*kêf*' (i. e. luxurious idleness). Every bath contains a coffee and pipe establishment. Coffee and hot *eau sucrée* are the favourite beverages. Before dressing, the bather is generally provided with two or three more relays of fresh towels, and thus the proceedings terminate. The whole of these operations need not occupy much more than an hour, but Orientals often devote a whole morning to the bath. — Many of the baths are charitable foundations, where the natives pay little or nothing. Europeans are generally expected to pay 8 piastres or more (including coffee and nargîleh), and a fee of about 1 p. is given to the 'soap man'. — A Turkish bath is particularly refreshing after a long journey, and is an admirable preventive of colds and rheumatism, but if too often repeated sometimes occasions boils.

'The women who can afford to do so visit the hammâm frequently; but not so often as the men. When the bath is not hired for the females of one family, or for one party of ladies exclusively, women of all conditions are admitted In general all the females of a house, and the young boys, go together. They take with them their own seggâdehs, and the napkins, basins, etc., which they require, and even the necessary quantity of sweet water for washing with soap, and for drinking; and some carry with them fruits, sweetmeats, and other refreshments. A lady of wealth is also often accompanied by her own *bellaneh* or *mash'tah*, who is the washer and tire-woman. Many women of the lower orders wear no covering whatever in the bath, not even a napkin round the waist; others always wear the napkin and the high clogs. There are few pleasures in which the women of Egypt delight so much as in the visit to the bath, where they frequently have entertainments; and often, on these occasions, they are not a little noisy in their mirth. They avail themselves of the opportunity to display their jewels and their finest clothes, and to enter into familiar conversation with those whom they meet there, whether friends or strangers. Sometimes a mother chooses a bride for her son from among the girls or women whom she chances to see in the bath. On many occasions, as, for instance, in the case of preparations for a marriage, the bath is hired for a select party, consisting of the women of two or more families, and none else are admitted; but it is more common for a lady and a few friends to hire a *Khilweh:* this is the name they give to the apartment of the hanafiyeh. There is more confusion among a mixed company of various ranks, but where all are friends, the younger girls indulge in more mirth and frolic. They spend an hour or more under the hands of the belláneh, who rubs and washes them, plaits their hair, applies the depilatory, etc. They then retire to the beyt-owwal or meslakh, and there, having put on part of their dress, or a large loose shirt, partake of various refreshments, which, if they have brought none with them, they may procure by sending an attendant of the bath to the market. Those who smoke take their own pipes with them. On particular occasions of festivity, they are entertained with the songs of two or more 'Al'mehs, hired to accompany them to the bath' — LANE.

(14). Bazaars.

Shops in the East, which are frequently connected with the workshops where the wares are made, are generally congregated together according to handicrafts in a certain quarter of the town, or in a certain street or lane. They are named after the respective trades, such as '*Sûk en-Nahhâsîn*' (market of the copper-smiths), '*Gohargîyeh*' (of the jewellers), *Khurdagîyeh*' (of the ironmongers), *Kassâbîn*' (of the butchers), and sometimes after a neighbouring mosque. These bazaars are generally crowded with customers and idlers, and afford the traveller an excellent opportunity of observing Oriental manners. In all the larger towns and villages there are extensive *Khâns*, or depôts of the goods of the wholesale merchants, who however often sell by retail to strangers.

The shop (*dukkân*) is a recess, quite open to the street, and generally about 6 ft. in width, the floor being on a level with the *mastaba*, or seat in front, on which the owner smokes his pipe, retails his goods, chats with his friends, and performs his devotions. The inscriptions over many of the shops do not announce the name or business of the occupant, but consist of pious phrases, such as 'O Allah! thou who openest the gates of profit!' 'O Allah! thou who helpest us in want!' 'Aid from Allah, and rapid victory!' These and similar ejaculations are invariably repeated by the shopkeeper as he takes down his shutters in the morning. When he leaves the shop he either hangs a net in front of it, or begs a neighbour to keep guard over it. The intending purchaser seats himself on the mastaba, and after the customary salutations proceeds to mention his wishes. Unless the purchaser is prepared to pay whatever is asked, he will find that the conclusion of a satisfactory bargain involves a prodigious waste of time and patience.

As a rule, a much higher price is demanded than will ultimately be accepted, and bargaining is therefore the universal custom. If the purchaser knows the proper price of the goods beforehand, he offers it to the seller, who will probably remark '*kalîl*' (it is little), but will nevertheless sell the goods. The seller sometimes entertains the purchaser with coffee from a neighbouring coffee-shop in order to facilitate the progress of the negotiations. If the shopkeeper persists in asking too high a price, the purchaser withdraws, but is often called back and at last offered the article at a reasonable price. A favourite expression with Oriental shopkeepers is '*khudu balâsh*' (take it for nothing), which is of course no more meant to be taken literally than the well known '*bêtî bêtak*' (my house is thy house) When in the course of the bargaining the purchaser increases his offer in order to make a concession, he generally uses the expression '*min shânak*' (for thy sake).

Nothing raises the traveller so much in the estimation of Orientals as firmness in resisting imposition; but even the most wary and experienced must be prepared to pay somewhat higher prices for everything than the natives themselves The various prices mentioned in the Handbook will give the traveller a fair idea of what may be justly demanded, and will prove a safeguard against any serious extortion.

The dragomans and valets-de-place are always in league with

the shopkeepers, from whom they receive 10-20 per cent on all articles purchased by travellers under their guidance.

Travellers are cautioned against purchasing antiquities, their exportation being moreover strictly prohibited (p. 6). Spurious 'antiquities' (particularly scarabæi) are largely manufactured both in Egypt and Syria, and the name is unhesitatingly applied to everything in the seller's possession, especially in Upper Egypt, if he sees that the traveller is disposed to make purchases of the kind. Remains of mummies are frequently offered for sale in the neighbourhood of all the ancient burial-places.

Both at Alexandria and Cairo there are goods-agents (pp. 206, 235), who will undertake the transmission of all purchases to the traveller's home at moderate cost. Their services are especially recommended if the traveller intends making a tour through the continent of Europe on his return from Egypt, in which case every new article, or object not intended for personal use, is liable to duty at half-a-dozen different frontiers.

(15). Intercourse with Orientals.

Orientals reproach Europeans with doing everything the wrong way, such as writing from left to right, while they do the reverse, and uncovering the head on entering a room, while they remove their shoes, but keep their heads covered.

The following rules should be observed in paying a visit at an Oriental house. The visitor knocks at the door with the iron knocker attached to it, whereupon the question '*mîn*' (who is there?) is usually asked from within. The visitor answers, '*iftaḥ*' (open). In the case of Muslim houses the visitor has to wait outside for a few minutes in order to give the women who happen to be in the court time to retire. He is then conducted into the reception-room, where a low divan or sofa runs round three sides of the room, the place of honour always being exactly opposite the door. According to the greater or less degree of respect which the host desires to show for his guest he rises more or less from his seat, and approaches one or more steps towards him. The first enquiries are concerning the health (see p. 199); the salutation '*Salam aleikum*' is reserved for Muslims. The transaction of business in the East always involves a prodigious waste of time, and as Orientals attach no value whatever to their time, the European will often find his patience sorely tried. If a visitor drops in and interrupts the business, it would be an unpardonable affront to dismiss him on the plea of being engaged. Again, when a visitor is announced at meal-time, it is *de rigueur* to invite him, at least as a matter of form, to partake. At all other hours of the day visitors are supplied with coffee, which a servant, with his left hand on his heart, presents to each according to his rank. Under the coffee-cup (*fingân*) there is generally a *zarf*, or kind of saucer of egg-cup shape. To be passed over when coffee is handed round is deemed by the Beduins an insult of the gravest kind. Having emptied his cup, the visitor must not put it down on the ground, which is contrary to etiquette, but keep it in his hand until it is taken from him by the servant, after which he salutes his host in the usual Oriental fashion by placing his right hand † on his breast and afterwards raising it to his forehead, and pronouncing the word '*dâiman*' (*i. e.* 'ḳahweh dâiman', may you never want coffee). This custom originated with the Beduins, who only regard the persons of their guests as inviolable after they have eaten or drunk with them. When visited by natives, the European should in his turn regale them liberally with coffee. It is also usual to offer tobacco to the visitor, the cigarette being now the ordinary form. The long pipe (*shibuḳ*) with amber mouth-piece, and its bowl resting on a brazen plate on the ground, is more in vogue with the Turks Visits in the East must of course be returned as in Europe. Those who return to a place after an absence receive visits from their acquaintances before they are expected to call on them

Europeans, as a rule, should never enquire after the wives of a Muslim, his relations to the fair sex being sedulously veiled from the public. Even looking at women in the street or in a house is considered indecorous, and may in some cases be attended with danger. Intimate acquaintance with Orientals is also to be avoided, disinterested friendship being still rarer in the East than elsewhere. Beneath the interminable protestations of friendship with which the traveller is overwhelmed, lurks in most cases the demon of cupidity, the sole motive of those who use them being the hope of some gain or bakshish. The best way of dealing with persons who 'do protest too much' is to pay for every service or civility on the spot, and as far as possible to fix the price of every article beforehand, a plan which is usually effectual in limiting their mercenary designs.

On the other hand the most ordinary observer cannot fail to be struck with the fact that the degraded ruffianism so common in the most civilised countries is unknown in Egypt. The people of the country, even the poorest and the entirely uneducated, often possess a native dignity, self-respect, and gracefulness of manner, of which the traveller's own countrymen of a far more favoured class are sometimes utterly destitute. Notwithstanding their individual selfishness, too, the different native communities will be observed to hold together with remarkable faithfulness, and the bond of a common religion, which takes the place of 'party' in other countries, and requires its adherents to address each other as '*yâ akhûya*' (my brother), is far more than a mere name.

---

† The right hand is alone used in greeting and as much as possible in eating, stroking the beard, and the like, the left hand being reserved for less honourable functions

While much caution and firmness are desirable in dealing with the people, it need hardly be added that the traveller should avoid being too exacting or suspicious. He should bear in mind that many of the natives with whom he comes in contact are mere children, whose waywardness should excite compassion rather than anger, and who often display a touching simplicity and kindliness of disposition. He should, moreover, do his utmost to sustain the well established reputation of the '*kilmeh frengîyeh*', the 'word of a Frank', in which Orientals are wont to place implicit confidence.

(16). Tobacco.

Cigar-smokers will find it very difficult to become accustomed to the Oriental tobacco, but they will find tolerable cigar-shops at Alexandria and Cairo, most of which have been established quite recently. As a general rule smokers are recommended to carry with them, both in going to and returning from Egypt, as little tobacco as possible, especially if they travel by the overland route, as a rigorous search is often made and a heavy duty exacted, both at the Egyptian, and at the French, Austrian, and Italian frontiers. Travellers returning to England direct, with their luggage booked through, are allowed half-a-pound of tobacco or cigars free of English duty, or they may bring three pounds on payment of the duty (5*s.* per lb.) and a small fine.

Tobacco *(dukhân)* is kept in good condition by covering it with a moist cloth, with which, however, it must not come in contact. Strong *(hâmi)* or mild *(bârid)* may be asked for according to taste. *Stambûli* is a long and fine cut tobacco, the best qualities of which (40-60 fr. per okka = 2 lbs $11\frac{1}{2}$ oz.) come from Roumelia and Anatolia, and the inferior from the Greek islands. The Syrian tobacco (15-20 fr. per okka), which is cut less regularly, and contains parts of the stalk, is considered less drying to the palate than the Turkish. It is of two kinds, the *kûrâni*, or light-brown, and the *gebeli*, or dark-brown, a mixture of which may be used. The latter, which derives its colour from being dried in the smoke of resinous woods, is known in Europe as '*Latakia*', from the region of N. Syria where it is chiefly grown (Lâdikîyeh), but that name is not applied to it in the East. The native Egyptian tobacco (*dukhân beledi*, or *akhdar*, green tobacco) is of very inferior quality (about 15 piastres tariff
per okka). The natives often gather the leaves from the pl... Reeded
dry them in the sun, rub them to pieces, and smoke th... Bogos,
fresh. *Tumbâk*, or Persian tobacco, is used in a m...tier of Abys-
dition in the long *nargîlehs* or water-pipes only, and ...is of their war-
a particular kind of charcoal. The smoke of the... in the long run to
into the lungs. monarch for their

The stems of these pipes, with their decoratio...t of the Mahom-
alone are of native manufacture. The reservoirs ...eatens to entail
mouth-pieces are imported from Europe, chiefly fro... Egypt proper.

(17). Post and Telegraph Offices.

The Egyptian Postal System is admirably organised in all the principal towns, and now also in many smaller ones. The officials, who are very civil, are often Italians. The addresses of letters destined for Egypt should always be written very distinctly (particularly the initial letters), and they had better be directed to the hotel at which the traveller intends to stay, or to the consulate. Registered letters are not delivered to the person whose address they bear unless he gets a resident to testify to his identity. The forwarding of letters up the Nile or elsewhere in the interior may be entrusted to the landlord of the hotel. The *General Post Office* for the whole of Egypt is at Alexandria. Postage-stamps, bearing a sphinx and a pyramid, are issued at 5, 10 and 20 paras, and at 1, 2, $2^1/_2$ and 5 tariff piastres. There are letter-boxes in the streets and at the hotels of the principal towns. Egypt is now a member of the Postal Union, and the postage for letters within Egypt and to other countries in the union is 1 piastre tariff for every 50 grammes ($1^1/_2$ oz.), and for book-packets 10 paras for the same weight. Post-cards cost 20 paras. Parcels not exceeding $6^1/_2$ lbs. in weight may be sent to the countries of the union for 11 piastres tariff. Post-office orders, see p. 3.

The Egyptian Telegraph System, the various lines of which are about 3750 English miles in length, extends northwards as far as Palestine, and southwards along the Nile to Kharṭûm, a town at the confluence of the Blue and White Nile, whence a line diverges to Kassala, and another by Kordofân to Dâr-Fûr (comp. Map, p. 30). All the larger towns in the Delta have telegraph-offices, and even the Fayûm is included in the system. Telegrams to Alexandria, Cairo, Isma'ilîya, Port Sa'îd, and Suez may be sent in English, French, or Italian, but Arabic must be used for messages to all the smaller stations. Within Egypt the Egyptian telegraph must be used (5 piastres tariff per 10 words), but telegrams to Europe should be sent by the *English* wires, viâ Malta, and certainly not by the Egyptian, viâ Constantinople, a provokingly dilatory route. The following is the tariff of the English telegraph: each word (not exceeding ten letters; if longer, it is reckoned as two words) to Austria, France, or Germany 1*s.* 8*d.*; to London 1*s.* 10*d.*; to other parts of Great Britain 1*s.* 11*d.*; to Italy 1*s.* 5*d.*; to America 2*s.* 2*d.*

(18). Weights and Measures.

1 Dirhem = $3._{93}$ grammes = $60._{65}$ grains troy; 1 roṭl = $445._{46}$ grammes = $1._{0134}$ lbs. avoirdupois (about 1 lb. $^1/_5$ oz.); 1 oḳḳa = $1._{237}$ kilogrammes = $2._{7274}$ lbs. (about 2 lbs. $11^1/_2$ oz.); 1 ḳanṭar = 100 roṭl = $44._{546}$ kilogrammes = $101._{31}$ lbs. (about 101 lbs. 5 oz.). The usual weight of a bale of wool in Egypt is about 282 kilogrammes, or $5^1/_2$ cwt.

1 Rubʿa = $3._{75}$ litres = $6^1/_2$ pints; 1 wêbeh = 30 litres = 6 gals. $2^2/_5$ qts.; 1 ardeb = 7 wêbeh = 210 litres = 46 gals. $1^3/_5$ qt.

1 Pik = $0._{67}$ mètre = $26._{37}$ inches; 1 pik, land measurement, = $29._{527}$ (about $29^1/_2$) inches; 1 ḳassaba = $3._{55}$ mètres = 11 ft. $7._{763}$ (about 11 ft. $7^3/_4$) inches.

1 Feddân = 4200 square mètres = about 5082 sq. yds. = $1^1/_{20}$ acre.

II. Geographical and Political Notice.

By Dr. Schweinfurth of Cairo.

Boundaries and Area (comp. Map, p. 30). The countries subject to the supremacy of the Khedive embrace by far the greater part of N.E. Africa, or nearly the whole of the territory adjacent to the Nile. The natural boundaries of the vassal kingdom founded by Moḥammed ʿAli and bequeathed by him to his successor in 1848 are formed by the Mediterranean Sea on the N., the Libyan Desert on the W., the Red Sea on the E., and Abyssinia, which may be called the Quito of Africa, on the S.E. These boundaries include Egypt Proper, with the five oases of the Libyan desert and part of the peninsula of Sinai, the Nubian Valley of the Nile, with the Nubian desert regions, and lastly the so-called Egyptian Sûdân, which consists of the districts of *Tâka*, *Sennâr*, and *Kordofân*. The Khedive Ismaʿîl, whose dominions were secured to him as a fief hereditary in the male line, extended his boundaries still farther to the S., S.E., and S.W. Thus he purchased *Sauâkin* and *Masauʿa* on the Red Sea, and *Zêlaʿ* and *Berbera* on the Gulf of ʿAden, four important seaports and commercial places, together with the coast districts adjoining them, which formerly belonged directly to the Turkish government; and in the same way he acquired part of the coast of the *Somâli*, extending to the equator, a district replete with still untouched natural treasures. The districts of the *Bogos* and *Galabat* on the frontiers of Abyssinia have been occupied with a view to protect important commercial routes, and together with the Somâli territory of *Harar* have been annexed to the Egyptian empire. *Dâr-Fûr*, once an entirely independent principality in the Mohammedan Sûdân, and the terror of its neighbours, has lately been conquered by the Egyptians, and the empire of the Khedive has thus been increased by four very populous provinces, while Moḥammed ʿAli, who was less fortunate in his designs on that region, succeeded in gaining possession of Kordofân only, the E. part of it. Bogos, Galabat, and the other provinces adjoining the N. frontier of Abyssinia are, however, constantly exposed to the inroads of their warlike neighbours, and it will probably be impossible in the long run to resist the importunate demand of the Abyssinian monarch for their restitution. The rebellion which broke out in most of the Mahommedan provinces of the Egyptian Sûdân in 1883 threatens to entail the entire loss of Ismaʿîl's acquisitions to the S. of Egypt proper.

The boundaries of Egypt in a due S. direction were still more boldly extended by Isma'îl. They now comprise the whole course of the *White Nile* and the greater part of the river region of the *Bahr el-Ghazâl*, where merchants from Khartûm had already for many years possessed settlements and by force of arms had subdued the negro tribes. At the time of Moḥammed 'Ali's death the S. boundary of the Egyptian dominions on the White Nile was formed by the corn-magazines of *El-'Esh* and the wharves near it, situated about 13° N. latitude, while it now extends to the military station of *Fauîra* (on the river connecting the Victoria and the Albert Nyanza), situated about 2° N. latitude, so that the whole length of the empire is now about 2000 English miles. The S. frontier, from Dâr-Fûr to Berbera, a distance of 1560 M., now almost entirely surrounds the kingdom of Abyssinia.

Down to 1883 the whole of the vast territory within these boundaries was, nominally at least, immediately subject to the Khedive, though but sparsely occupied by his comparatively small army, and it contained no tributary peoples mediately subject to him. These enormous tracts, on the other hand, are utterly disproportionate to the population, the desert regions are immeasurably more extensive than the fertile districts, and the barbarous and unprofitable inhabitants far more numerous than the civilised and wealth-producing. The geographer and the political economist therefore would vary widely in their description of the real boundaries of the country. The country which (until the most recent events) owned no other master than the Khedive or his representatives is of immense extent, but the cultivable part of Egypt, which forms the sole source of its wealth, is of very limited area. The extensive dominions of the Khedive which lie to the S. of Egypt proper are still entirely profitless, and hence it was that Isma'îl did his utmost to extend the commerce in this direction, and to improve the means of communication.

Thus while Egypt is nominally as extensive as two-thirds of Russia in Europe, it shrinks to the size of Belgium when the Valley of the Nile, its only productive part, inhabited by a tax-paying population, is alone taken into consideration. The total area of the empire is fully one and a quarter million square miles, including that part of the Libyan Desert which falls within the western boundary drawn from the oasis of Sîwa to the west end of Dâr-Fûr, and which alone measures 525,000 sq. M. in extent. On the other hand Egypt proper, extending towards the desert so far only as it is irrigated by the fertilising Nile, the 'Bilâd Maṣr' (the *Miṣraim* of the Bible), though 550 M. in length, is the narrowest country in the world. The area of this cultivable tract, which has remained unaltered since the remotest antiquity, is about 11,342 sq. M. only (or 21 sq. M. less than Belgium), excluding Wâdi Ḥalfa and the other districts above Assuân In 1882 Amici Bey calculated the entire in-

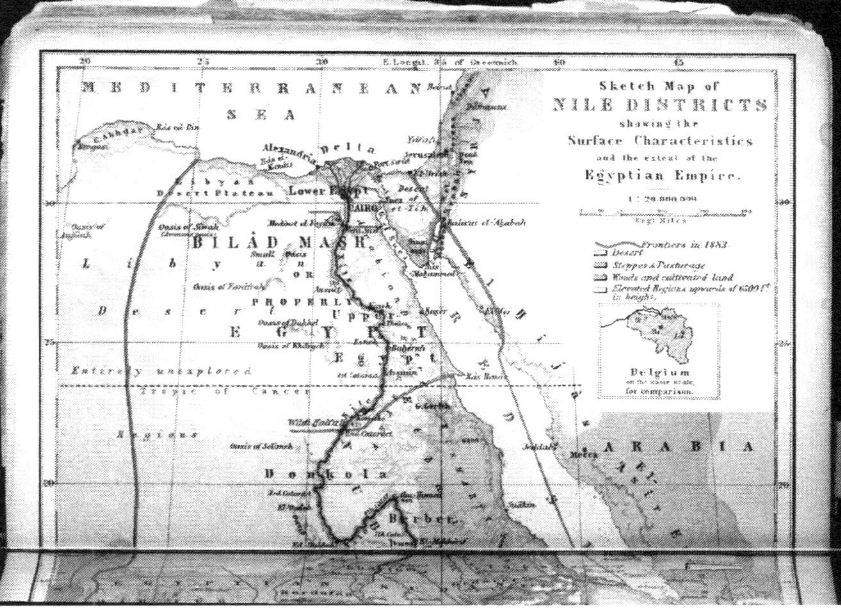

Sketch Map of
NILE DISTRICTS
showing the
Surface Characteristics
and the extent of the
Egyptian Empire.
1 : 20,000,000
Engl. Miles
Frontiers in 1883
Desert
Steppes & Pasturage
Woods and cultivated land
Elevated Regions upwards of 6500 ft. in height.
Belgium
on the same scale,
for comparison.
MEDITERRANEAN
SEA
Alexandria
Delta
Lower Egypt
CAIRO
Libyan Desert Plateau
BILÂD MASR
Libyan Desert
OR
PROPERLY
EGYPT
Upper Egypt
Entirely unexplored
Tropic of Cancer
Regions
Dongola
Berber
ARABIA
Jerusalem
Benghazi
Oasis of Siwah
Oasis of Farafrah
Oasis of Dakhel
Oasis of Khargeh
Oasis of Selimeh
Assiut
Assuan
Ras Benas
Mecca
Suakin

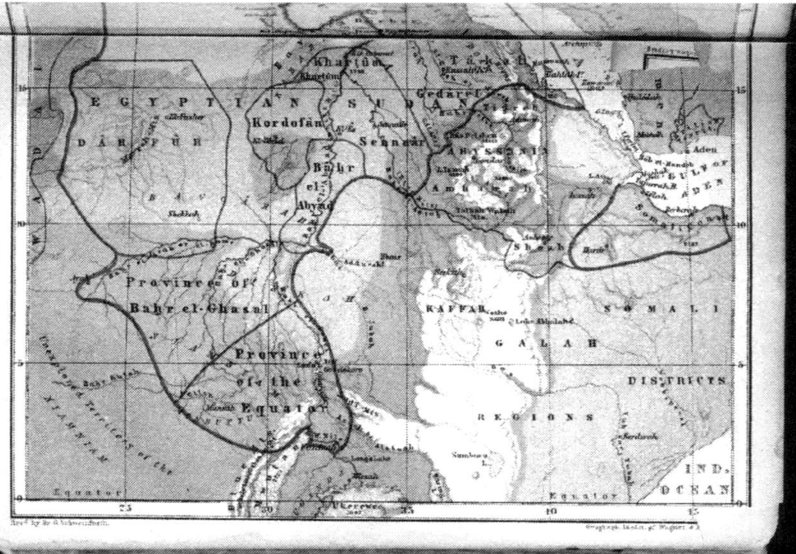
EGYPTIAN SUDAN
DÁR FÜR
Kordofán
Sennaar
Khartúm
Bahr el Abyad
ABYSSINIA
Aden
GULF OF ADEN
Province of Bahr el-Ghasal
Province of the Equator
KAFFA
GALAH
SOMALI
DISTRICTS
REGIONS
IND. OCEAN
Equator
Unexplored Territory of the NIAMNIAM

INSERT FOLD-OUT OR MAP HERE!

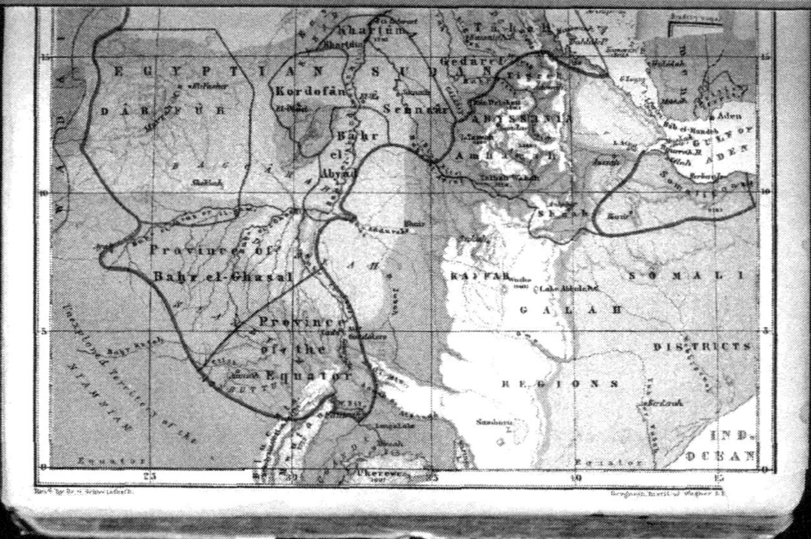
EGYPTIAN SUDAN
DÂR FÛR
Kordofân
Sennâr
Bahr el Abyad
Khartûm
Gedaref
ABYSSINIA
GULF OF ADEN
Aden
Provinces of Bahr el-Ghasal
Province of the Equator
KAFFAR
GALAH
SOMALI
DISTRICTS
REGIONS
IND. OCEAN
Equator
NIAMNIAM

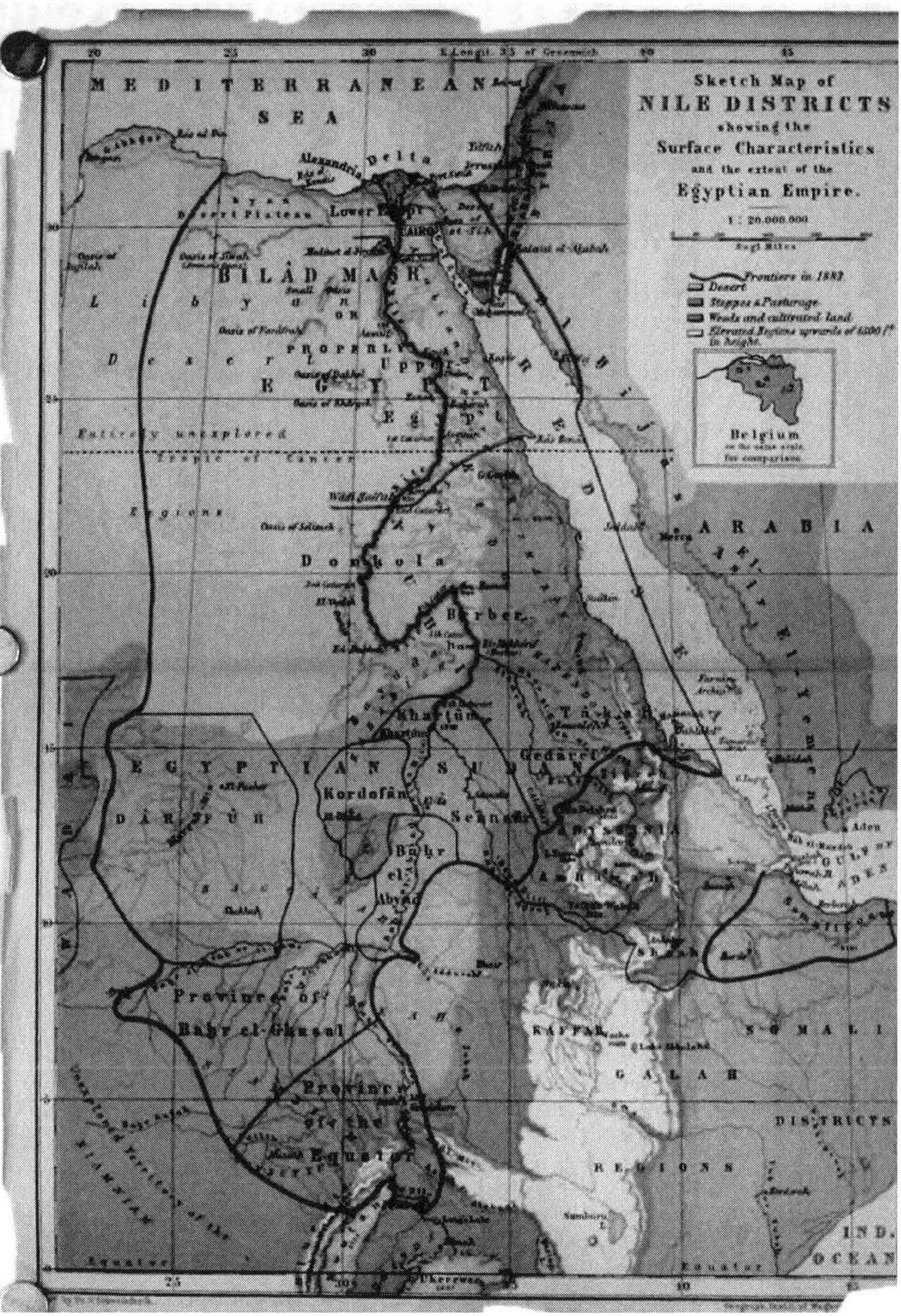

Sketch Map of
NILE DISTRICTS
showing the
Surface Characteristics
and the extent of the
Egyptian Empire.
1 : 20.000.000
Frontiers in 1882
Desert
Steppes & Pasturage
Woods and cultivated land
Belgium
for comparison
MEDITERRANEAN
SEA
Alexandria
Delta
Lower Egypt
Libyan
Desert Plateau
Libyan Desert
EGYPT PROPERLY OR
Upper Egypt
Entirely unexplored Regions
Tropic of Cancer
Dongola
Berber
Khartum
Kordofan
Sennaar
Gedaref
EGYPTIAN SUDAN
DAR FUR
Bahr el Abyad
ABYSSINIA
ARABIA
Aden
GULF OF ADEN
Province of Bahr el-Ghasal
Province of the Equator
SOMALI
GALLA
DISTRICTS
REGIONS
IND. OCEAN
Equator

habited area of Egypt, excluding the deserts, as 12,830 sq.M. and the area actually under cultivation as 9460 sq. M. The alluvial soil of the Nile Valley, in contradistinction to the desert, known among the natives by the Arabic word '*Er-Rîf*', begins at Kharṭûm, at the confluence of the White and the Blue Nile. Following the wide curve described by the Nile through Nubia, the length of the valley as far as the first cataracts is 989 M., but as the space between the river and its rocky banks is very limited, and the irrigation system is imperfectly developed, the cultivable area in this part of the valley is only about 1050 sq. M. The Nubian portion of the alluvial soil of the Nile is thus very insignificant; and when the ancient oracle described Egypt as the country watered by the Nile, and the Egyptians as the people who quenched their thirst with its water, the river below the first cataract must obviously have been meant.

Divisions and Administration. The ancient prehistoric Egyptians were at first subdivided into numerous tribes, who formed a number of distinct small and independent states, with their own laws and their peculiar tutelary gods. These states were afterwards gradually united into the two large principalities of Lower Egypt or the Northern Country (*To Mera*, or *To Meḥ*), and Upper Egypt or the Southern Country (*To Res*, or *To Ḳemâ*). At a later period these two larger states, united under one sceptre, formed the empire of the Pharaohs, or the land of *Ḳemi*. The smaller states then constituted provinces or nomes (Egyptian *ḥesoph*; Greek *nomoi*). The ancient Egyptians divided each nome into four principal parts: — (1) The capital (*Nut*), the religious and administrative centre of the province; (2) The cultivated land (*Un*), subject to the annual inundation; (3) The marshy land which remained in a moist condition after the inundation; (4) The district traversed by canals conducted out of the Nile. The civil and military administration of the nome was presided over either by hereditary governors (*hiḳ*), or by nomarchs (*mer-nat-t'ât-to*) appointed by the king. Under the Ptolemies these governors were called *strategoi (nomu)* or *nomarchoi*, and over a group of these presided an *epistrategos*. The chief authority in religious matters was the high priest of the temple, whose appointment was sometimes hereditary and sometimes elective; and his staff consisted of a prophet, a temple-scribe, a stolistes or custodian of the vestments, and an astrologer.

The number of the nomes varied at different periods. Most of the classical authors (thus Diodorus, liv. 3; Strabo, xxviii. 1, 3) enumerate thirty-six. The Egyptian lists, such as that of Edfu, mention forty-four, half of them being in Upper and half in Lower Egypt (but two of those in Upper Egypt and three in Lower Egypt are counted twice). The Greeks and Romans sometimes divided Egypt into three parts — Upper, Central, and Lower Egypt, or the Thebaïs, Heptanomis, and Delta.

The following is a list of the ancient Egyptian nomes: —

UPPER EGYPT.

	NOMES		CAPITALS		
	Egyptian	Greek	Egyptian	Greek	Arabic
1	TO KENS	OMBITES	ABU (ELEPHANTINE - GEZÎRET-ASSUÂN)	OMBUS (Egypt. NUBI)	KÔM OMBU
2	TES ḤOR	APOLLINOPOLITES	ṬEB (Copt. ATBO)	APOLLINOPOLIS MAGNA	EDFU
3	TEN	LATOPOLITES	NEKHEB (SNI)	EILEITHYIA (LATOPOLIS)	ESNEH
4	UAS	DIOSPOLITES PHATYRITES HERMONTHITES	NI AMON, afterwards ḤER MONT (AN RES AN MUNT)	THEBAI Diospolis magna HERMONTHIS	EL UKṢÛR KARNAK MEDÎNET ABU ERMENT
5	ḤORUI	KOPTITES	QEFTI (Copt. KEBTO)	KOPTUS	ḲUFṬ
6	? EMSUḤ ?	TENTYRITES	TA RER, TAN TA RER (TA NUTRI; Copt. PI TENTORE)	TENTYRIS (TENTYRA)	DENDERA
7	ḤA SEKHEKH	DIOSPOLITES	ḤA, ḤU	DIOSPOLIS PARVA	ḤÛ
8	TENAI(?)	TINITES	TIN (TENI), afterwards AB-ṬU	TIS (TINIS), ABYDUS	KHARÂBEH EL MADFÛNEH
9	KHEM	PANOPOLITES	APU, KHEM (Copt. KHMIN, SHMIN)	CHEMMIS (PANOPOLIS)	AKHMIM
10	ṬUF	ANTÆOPOLITES	NI ENT BAK	ANTÆOPOLIS	ḲAU EL KEBÎR
11	BÂAR	HYPSELITES	SHAS ḤOTEP (Copt. SHÔTP)	HYPSELE (IS)	SAṬB
12	ATEF KHENT	LYKOPOLITES	SIAUT (Copt. SIUT)	LYKOPOLIS	ASYÛṬ
13	ATEF PEḤU		QUS	CHUSAI	ḲÛSÎYEH
14	UAZ		TEBTI		
15	UNNU	HERMOPOLITES	SESUNNU (Copt. SHMUN)	HERMOPOLIS	ASHMUNÊN
16	MEḤ	Northern part of HERMOPOLITES	ḤEBENNU (Copt. TUHO)	THEODOSIOPOLIS	?ṬAḤA EL MEDÎNEH
17	ANUP	KYNOPOLITES	KO, HA SUTEN	KYNOPOLIS	EL ḲÊS
18	UAB	OXYRRHYNCHITES	PA MAZA (Copt. PEMKE)	OXYRRHYNCHUS	BEHNESA

UPPER EGYPT.

	NOMES.		CAPITALS		
	Egyptian	Greek	Egyptian	Greek	Arabic
9	NEḤT KHENT	HERACLEOPOLITES	ḤA KHNEN SU (Copt. Hnês)	HERACLEOPOLIS MAGNA	AHNÂS EL MEDÎNEH
0	PA		ḤA BENNU	HIPPONON	
1	NEḤT PEḤT	. . . .	MERI TUM (Meïtum)		MÊDÛM
		ARSINOITES	SHED	KROKODILOPOLIS	MEDINET EL FAYÛM
2	MATENNU	APHRODITOPOLITES	TEP AḤE	APHRODITOPOLIS	AṬFIḤ

LOWER EGYPT.

1	ANEB ḤAT	MEMPHITES	MEN NOFER (HA KA PTAḤ)	MEMPHIS	
2	AA	LETOPOLITES	SOKHEM	LETOPOLIS	
3	AMENT	NOMOS LIBYA	NI ENT ḤA PI	APIS	
4	SEPI RES	SAÏTES	ZOQA	CANOPUS	
5	SEPI EMḤIT	SAÏTES	SAÏ	SAÏS	ṢÂ EL ḤAGER
6	KA-SIT	XOITES	KHESAUU	XOÏS	
7	AMENT	?	SONTINOFER	METELIS	?
8	. . . ABOT	SETHROÏTES	PI-TUM (Sukot)	(SETHROË)	?
9	AT PI	BUSIRITES	P-USIR-NEB-ṬAṬ	BUSIRIS	
0	KA KEM	ATHRIBITES	HA TA ḤIR AB	ATHRIBIS	TELL ATRÎB
1	KA ḤEBES	CABASITES	KA ḤEBES	CABASUS	
2	KA THEB	SEBENNYTES SUPERIOR	THEB EN NUTER	SEBENNYTUS	SEMENNÛD
3	ḤAQ-AṬ	HELIOPOLITES	ANU	HELIOPOLIS	
4	KHENT ABOT	TANITES	ZOÂN PIRAMSES (ZOAN-RAMSES)	TANIS	ṢÂN
5	THUT	HERMOPOLITES	PI THUT	HERMOPOLIS	
6	KHAR	MENDESIUS	PIBI NEB ṬAṬ	MENDES	? TMEY EL AMDID ?
7	ṢAM ḤUṬ	DIOSPOLITES	PI KHUN EN AMEN	TACHNAMUNIS or DIOSPOLIS	
8	AM KHENT	BUBASTITES	PI BAST	BUBASTIS	TELL BASṬA
9	AM PEḤU	BUTICUS, or PTHENOTES	PI UZO	BUTO	
0	LAPT	PHARBÆTHITES	SHETEN	PHARBÆTHUS	HORBÊT

Lower and Upper Egypt (the latter known as *Sa'îd*) are now each divided into seven PROVINCES or *Mudîrîyeh*. Those of Upper Egypt are. (1) *Kalyûb*, at the head of the Delta; (2) *Sharkîyeh*, *i.e.* 'the eastern', with Zakâzîk as its capital; (3) *Dakahlîyeh*, with Manṣûra as its capital, (4) *Menûf;* (5) *Gharbîyeh*, *i.e.* 'the western', with Ṭanṭa as its capital; (6) *Behêreh*, *i.e.* 'of the lake', with Damanhûr as its capital, (7) *Gîzeh*, opposite to Cairo. The seven Upper Egyptian provinces are those of Beni-Suêf, Minyeh, Siûṭ, Girgeh, Keneh, Esneh, and Wâdi Ḥalfa. The seat of the mudîr or governor of Girgeh has recently been transferred to the not far distant Ṣûhâg. The Fayûm forms a mudîrîyeh by itself. The following capitals and commercial towns are presided over by governors of their own, and are independent of the provincial administration: Cairo, Alexandria, Suez, Port Sa'îd, Damietta, Rosetta, Isma'îlîya, and lastly the small seaport of Ḳoṣêr on the Red Sea.

The administration of the Upper Egyptian provinces, and still more those of the Sûdân, is liable to frequent change, several of them being sometimes united under a governor-general, and at other times again disjoined, or managed by a commission appointed by the minister of the interior. The recently acquired seaports on the Red Sea have governors *(mudîrs)* of their own, and they in their turn are under the supervision of a governor-general *(ḥokmdâr)* resident at Kassala. These last districts are (or were) known as the East Sûdân, while the government of the West Sûdân was centralised at Kharṭûm Before the outbreak of the revolution the West Sûdân consisted of the provinces of Kharṭûm, Sennâr, Bahr el-Abyaḍ, Kordofân, four of Dâr-Fûr, and the provinces of Bahr-el-Ghazal and the Equator. The last two provinces include almost the whole region of the Upper White Nile and are inhabited solely by negro tribes. Kharṭûm was the seat of a governor-general whose jurisdiction extended over the whole of the provinces beyond the limits of Egypt in the narrower sense. Lastly, the Nubian part of the Valley of the Nile is divided into the provinces of Donḳola and Berber, which are administered independently of each other, the capital of the former being El-'Ordeh, that of the latter El-Mekhêrif (or Berber)

The chief official in every province is the *Mudîr*, or governor, who is assisted by a council, or 'dîwân', of other officers. This council consists of a *Wekîl*, or vice-governor; a chief clerk, tax-gatherer, and accountant, who is always a Copt; a *Kâḍi*, or supreme judge, and the chief authority in spiritual matters; sometimes the president of a chamber of commerce and chief authority in civil affairs; a superintendent of police; an architect for the supervision of canals and other public works, and lastly the chief physician of the province. The sub-governors in the smaller towns, who are under the jurisdiction of the Mudîr, are sometimes called *Kâshif*, or *Nâẓir el-Kism.* Subordinate to the nâzir again is the *Shêkh el-Beled*, or chief magistrate or mayor of the village, usually known simply as *shêkh* (plur. *shuûkh*).

In the larger towns there is a magistrate of this kind in each quarter (at Cairo fifty-three), over whom are placed prefects of larger sections *(shêkh et-tumn)*. Over the whole of these presides the Mudîr, and lastly over the latter in some cases a Ḥokmdâr with very extensive powers. Other provinces again are governed by specially appointed inspectors, who occupy the highest rank in their respective jurisdictions.

If the administrative reforms proposed by England actually come into effect, the duties of the provincial governors will be very materially circumscribed. The police administration has been made a separate department, and Egypt has been divided into the three police districts of Cairo, Alexandria, and Upper Egypt, each under an inspector general. The administration of justice is to be committed entirely to the native courts, while a special minister is to have the charge of canal-making and other public works. In order, however, to afford some idea of the importance of the Mudîr in the public life of the provinces, we give here a short account of the functions he has hitherto had to perform.

The Duties of the Mudîr were very multifarious He presided over the administration, the finances, and the police of his province. He was required to watch over the public safety, to superintend public works, to regulate all sanitary matters, to register all transfers of property, contracts of sale, title-deeds, and mortgages, to pronounce judgment in all law-suits which do not fall exclusively within the jurisdiction of the spiritual court (the Mehkemeh), and lastly to collect the taxes The four chief taxes are as follows: (1) *Land-tax (khârâg)*, levied from the *Arâdi el-Mîrîyeh* (see below; the *Ab'âdîyeh* pay ten per cent only, while the *Shiflik* is entirely exempt) It is levied monthly by the ṣarrâf A feddân of the best land in Lower Egypt pays about 25*s*. per annum, but medium and inferior land is taxed at a lower rate A valuation is made annually, and the different estates and farms registered under one of these three classes. (2) *Income-tax*, paid by merchants, bazaar-keepers, and artizans (*werko*, i e. the Turkish *wergi*, *firdeh*, or 'tax'), and varying from 4 to 20 per cent (3) *Market-tax (himl)*, levied according to a certain tariff on all produce brought to the markets, at a rate varying from 2 to 9 per cent This tax is now confined to the four largest towns. (4). *Palm-tax*, levied at the rate of 20 piastres per tree.

Distribution of Land Down to 1879 the Khedive and his family possessed one million and a half feddâns of landed property, or about one-fourth of cultivable Egypt; valued at forty million pounds sterling, and practically forming his private property This land is officially called *Shiflik* (or properly *tshiftlik*, the Turkish for 'estate', or 'farm') Part of these vast estates came into the hands of the reigning monarch by the confiscation of the fiefs (*iktâ'a*) held by the Mamelukes, who were exterminated by Mohammed 'Ali on 11th March, 1811, and by the appropriation of all family foundations (*irsâd*), estates belonging to mosques (*wakf*), and land which in consequence of the depopulation caused by the Mameluke régime had ceased to have any owner The great bulk of the crown estates was, however, amassed during the 15 years' rule of Khedive Isma'îl, who was not over-scrupulous as to the methods he employed in doing so Shortly before his abdication he was forced to resign almost the entire estates of himself and his family to the board of domains appointed by the international financial commission.

Another kind of landed property is called *Ab'ādîyeh*, by which is meant the uncultivated land presented by the Khedive to suitable persons with full right of property on condition of its being reclaimed or cultivated. Estates of this kind pay no taxes for the first three years, after which 10 per cent on the value of the produce is levied (*'ushr*). The rest of the land is officially known as *El-Arādi el-Mîrîyeh*, i.e. government estates. Nearly the whole of the soil of Egypt is thus in the hands of government. The fellāhîn or peasants are merely tenants for life, or so long as they continue to pay their ground-rent (*kharāg*). According to the Korān, an estate on the death of the life-tenant reverts to the *bêt el-māl*, or government treasury, as the common property of all Muslims; but a humane law of 1857 provides that it may be claimed by the next of kin of both sexes on payment of 24 tariff piastres per feddān for registration of the title. The trees planted by the life-tenant, and the buildings and irrigating apparatus erected by him, are his property, and pass to his heirs. The right of occupation, or usufruct, of these lands may also be sold, let, or mortgaged, but the contract must be ratified by government in each case; and where mortgaged lands are not redeemed within fifteen years, they continue in possession of the mortgagee and become his property. A piece of land may at any time be taken possession of by government for public purposes (railways, canals, embankments), in which case the occupant receives another piece of land elsewhere as compensation.

The ground-tax (*kharāg*) is in some cases as high as 20 per cent. Instead of a certain tax being imposed on each village as formerly, the tax payable by each estate is now fixed by the Mudîrîyeh or chief authorities of the province. To facilitate the collection of taxes, all landed estates are formed into groups, generally consisting of properties taxed at the same rate, and known in Lower Egypt as *hōd*, and in Upper Egypt as *kabāleh*.

In certain poor districts where there was a difficulty in collecting the taxes in the reign of Mohammed 'Ali, payment was undertaken by a number of capitalists, who were empowered to recover them from the fellāhîn. This right, however, was not transferable, and it could be resumed by the government at any time. Groups of estates where this system still prevails are called *'uhdeh*.

Since 1822 several attempts have been made at a comprehensive scheme of land valuation, but none has been carried out for more than a few limited districts. In 1879, however, a land valuation office was established at Cairo in connection with the projected reforms in the land-tax.

Population. The population of Egypt has been ascertained to have been greater in ancient than in modern times; for, disregarding the exaggerated calculation of Theocritus, based on a mere assumption, it appears to have numbered at least $7^1/_2$ million souls in the time of Josephus and the Emperor Nero. This number is quite reasonable in itself, as it is estimated that the country could support 8-9 million inhabitants.

According to the enumeration made by Amici Bey in 1882 the present population of Egypt proper is 6,811,448, or about 600 per square mile, and is therefore denser than that of most European states. The thickest population is found in the province of Esneh, the thinnest in the Fayûm and in Behêreh. The sexes occur in almost equal proportions. The number of houses enumerated in the same census is 1,090,000, distributed among 12,876 towns, villages, and hamlets. The population of the provinces beyond the limits of Egypt proper, on the other hand, has never been ascertained by any regular census, and can therefore only be estimated in a conjectural way. The densest population is that of the province of Bahr el-Abyad, where in the case of the Shilluk tribe, numbering about one million souls, the proportion of inhabitants to the square mile is the same as in Egypt proper. The total population of the empire, including Dâr-Fûr and Harar, is now estimated at between 16 and 17 millions.

Origin and Descent of the Egyptians. For thousands of years the banks of the Nile have been occupied by the Egyptians, the oldest nation known to history, and still exhibiting many of their ancient personal characteristics unaltered. Notwithstanding the interminable series of immigrations and other changes affecting the character of the inhabitants, the Egyptian type has always predominated with marvellous uniformity. As Egypt is said to be the 'gift of the Nile', so has the character of its inhabitants been apparently moulded by the influences of that river. No country in the world is so dependent on a river which traverses it as Egypt, and no river presents physical characteristics so exceptional as the Nile; so, too, there exists no race of people which possesses so marked and unchanging an individuality as the Egyptians. It is therefore most probable that this unvarying type is the product of the soil itself, and that the character of the peoples who settled at different periods on the bank of the Nile, whatever it may originally have been, has in due course of time been moulded to the same constant form by the mysterious influences of the river. In all countries, indeed, national characteristics are justly regarded as the natural outcome of soil and climate, and of this connection no country affords so strong an illustration as Egypt, with its sharply defined boundaries of sea and desert, and in its complete isolation from the rest of the world. These considerations tend to throw serious doubts on all the current theories as to the origin of the Egyptians. According to the Bible, Mizraim (Misraîm) was the son of Ham and brother of Canaan and the Ethiopian Cush; and, as his name was applied by the Hebrews to Egypt, it is probable that he migrated with his sons from Asia to the banks of the Nile. The name, moreover, of Ludim, his eldest son, corresponds to the word Rotu, or Lotu, the hieroglyphic name for the Egyptians. Philologists, who have discovered points of resemblance in the roots and inflections of the ancient Egyptian and the Semitic languages, likewise come to the conclusion that the Egyptians originally came from Asia, either by way of Suez, or across the Red Sea from Arabia. The ethnographer †, on the other hand, who observes that many of the

† No inference can legitimately be drawn from the fact that the skulls of the ancient and modern Egyptians, which are very similar in form, have no affinity with those which are usually described as of the negro type, as our craniological collections are very incomplete, and our knowledge of the negro races imperfect The fact is, that several negro races, such as the Nubians and the Shilluk, might be named, whose characteristics undoubtedly belong to the negro type, while their skulls are just as little prognathous as those of the Egyptians.

domestic utensils employed by the ancient Egyptians, as well as many of their customs, are similar to those of the dwellers on the banks of the Zambezi and Niger, but totally different from those seen on the banks of the Indus or Euphrates, will always maintain an opposite view. The considerations already mentioned, however, tend to show that the truth lies between these extremes. Even those who most strongly maintain the Asiatic origin of the Egyptians will probably admit that the immigrants found an aboriginal race already settled on the banks of the Nile, which in its persistent opposition to all foreign influences was doubtless similar to the race usually known as the Egyptian. We start with the cardinal fact, that, although the country has been at various periods overrun by Hyksos, Ethiopians, Assyrians, Persians, Greeks, Romans, Arabs, and Turks, and although the people were tyrannised over, ill-treated, and in most cases compelled to intermarry with these foreigners, the Egyptians have for thousands of years retained the same unvarying physical types, while their character has been but slightly modified by the introduction of Christianity and Mohammedanism. If it now be borne in mind that these foreigners generally invaded the country in the form of an army, that they formed but a small body compared with the bulk of the population, and that they either married native women or sought wives in other countries, it is obvious that they would either continue to exist for a time as a foreign caste, a condition apparently repugnant to nature and necessarily transient, or that they would gradually succumb to the never-failing influences of the soil and be absorbed in the great mass of the aboriginal inhabitants. An excellent illustration of this process is afforded by the Arabian invasion, with the circumstances and results of which we are better acquainted than with the history of the other foreign immigrations; for, disregarding the Beduin tribes, who are entirely distinct from the Egyptian population, we now find that the Arabian element has entirely disappeared, and we meet with genuine Arabs in the towns only, where the merchants, pilgrims, and other members of that people form a class entirely distinct from the natives, and where their existence is only maintained by means of reinforcements from abroad. Another proof of the transforming influences of the Egyptian climate is afforded by the uniform character of the domestic animals. The oxen, in particular (which, however, are gradually being replaced by the buffalo), though they have often been repeatedly exterminated in a single century by murrain, and have been succeeded by foreign races from every quarter of the globe, invariably after a few generations assume the well-known Egyptian type with which the representations on the ancient temples render us so familiar.

The Modern Egyptians. The population of Egypt is composed of the following ten different elements.

(1). The Fellâḥîn (sing. *fellâḥ*), the 'tillers' or 'peasants', form the bulk of the population, and may be regarded as the sinews of the national strength. They are generally slightly above the middle height; their bones, and particularly their skulls, are strong and massive; and their wrists and ankles are powerful and somewhat clumsy. In all these respects the fellâḥîn, as well as their domestic animals, contrast strongly with the inhabitants of the desert, the fellâḥ and the Beduin differing from each other precisely in the same points as their respective camels. Notwithstanding this largeness of frame, however, the fellâḥ never grows fat. The woman and girls are particularly remarkable for their slender build, and they often speak of each other as 'zei el-ḥabl', or slender as a rope. The men generally keep their heads shaved, but the hair of the soldiers and the long tresses of the girls, though always black and often curly, is by no means of the short, woolly negro type.

The chief peculiarity of the Egyptians is the remarkable closeness of their eyelashes on both lids, forming a dense, double, black fringe, which gives so animated an expression to their almond-shaped eyes. The very ancient and still existing custom of blackening the edges of the eyelids with antimony ('koḥl'), which is said to serve a sanitary purpose, contributes to enhance this natural expression. The eyebrows are always straight and smooth, never bushy. The mouth is wide and thick-lipped, and very different from that of the Beduin or inhabitant of the oases. The high cheek-bones, the receding forehead, the lowness of the bridge of the nose, which is always distinctly separated from the forehead, and the flatness of the nose itself, are the chief characteristics of the Egyptian skull; but, as the jaws project less than those of most of the other African coloured races, it has been assumed that the skull is Asiatic, and not African in shape. The Egyptian peasantry have a much darker complexion than their compatriots in the towns, and their colour deepens as we proceed southwards, from the pale brown of the inhabitant of the Delta to the dark bronze hue of the Upper Egyptians. There is also a difference between the tint of the Nubians and that of the Upper Egyptians, even where they live in close contiguity, the former being more of a reddish-brown.

The dwelling of the fellâḥ is of a miserably poor description, consisting generally of four low walls formed of crude bricks of Nile mud, and thatched with a roof of dura straw, rush, rags, or old straw-mats. In the interior are a few mats, a sheep's skin, several baskets made of matting, a copper kettle, and a few earthenware pots and wooden dishes. Instead of using the crude bricks, the fellâḥîn in Upper Egypt often form the walls of their huts of a mixture of mud and straw. The dark, windowless interior is entered by a small opening, in front of which the proprietor usually forms an enclosure of circular shape, with a wall of mud about 5 ft. in height. This is the court-yard of the establishment, and the usual resort of the family and their domestic animals in summer. The walls of the yard generally contain round hollows, used as receptacles for the grain which forms the food of the family. Within the yard are usually placed a square pillar, about 5 ft. in height, with openings in its sides as receptacles for objects of value, and a thick column of the same height, terminating in a platform shaped like a plate, with the edges bent upwards, which is used by the proprietor as a sleeping-place in hot weather. The fact is, that beneath an Egyptian sky, houses are not of the same paramount importance as in more northern regions, all that is wanted being shelter for the night.

The poorer peasant's mode of life is frugal in the extreme. The staple of his food consists of a peculiar kind of bread made of sorghum flour in Upper Egypt, or of maize in the Delta, wheaten bread being eaten by the wealthier only. This poor kind of bread often has a greenish colour, owing to an admixture of bean-flour (Fœnum Græcum). Next in importance in the bill of fare are broad beans (fûl). For supper, however, even the poorest cause a hot repast to be prepared. This usually consists of a highly salted sauce made of onions and butter, or in the poorer houses of onions and linseed or sesame oil. Into this sauce, which in summer acquires a gelatinous consistency by the addition of the universal bâmia (the capsular fruit of the Hibiscus) and various herbs, each member of the family dips pieces of bread held in the fingers. Both in town and country, goats', sheeps', or buffaloes' milk also forms a daily article of food, but always in a sour condition or half converted into cheese, and in very moderate quantities only. In the height of summer the consumption of fruit of the cucumber and pumpkin species, which the land yields in abundance, is enormous. In the month of Ramaḍân alone, when a rigorous fast is observed during the day, and on the three days of the great Beirâm festival (Korbân Beirâm), even the poorest members of the community indulge in meat, and it is customary to distribute that rare luxury to beggars at these seasons.

The dress of the Egyptian peasant calls for little remark, especially as he usually works in the fields divested of everything. The chief articles of his wardrobe at other times are an indigo-dyed cotton shirt *(kamîs)*, a pair of short and wide cotton breeches, a kind of cloak of brown, home-spun goats' wool *(za'bûṭ*, *'abâyeh*, or *'aba)*, or simply a blanket of sheep's wool *(ḥirâm)*, and lastly a close-fitting felt skull-cap *(libdeh)*. He is generally barefooted, but occasionally wears pointed red *(zerbûn)*, or broad yellow shoes *(balgha)*. The shêkhs and wealthier peasants, when they go to market, wear wide, black woollen cloaks and the thick red 'Tunisian' fez *(ṭarbûsh)* with a blue silk tassel, round which they coil a white or red turban *('immeh)*. In their hands they usually carry a long and thick stick *(nabbût)*, made from the central stalk of the palm leaf.

The agricultural population of Egypt does not exceed two million souls, an unnaturally low proportion when we consider the nature of the country. The sole wealth of Egypt is derived from its agriculture, and to the fellâḥîn alone is committed the important task of tilling the soil. They are, indeed, neither fitted nor inclined for other work, a circumstance which proves how completely the stationary character of the ancient Egyptians has predominated over the restless Arabian blood, which has been largely infused into the native population ever since the valley of the Nile was conquered by the armies of El-Islâm. The modern Egyptians, moreover, resemble the ancient in the lot to which they are condemned. In ancient times the fellâḥ, pressed into the service of the priests and the princes, was compelled to yield up to them the fruits of his toil, and his position is nearly the same at the present day, save that the names of his masters are changed, and he has obtained some relief owing to the almost entire abolition of compulsory work.

In early life the Egyptian peasant is remarkably docile, active, and intelligent, but at a later period this freshness and buoyancy is crushed out of him by care and poverty and his never-ceasing task of filling the pitcher of the Danaïdes. He ploughs and reaps, toils and amasses, but he cannot with certainty regard his crops as his own, and the hardly earned piastre is too frequently wrested from him. His character, therefore, becomes like that of a gifted child, who has been harshly used and brought up to domestic slavery, but at length perceives that he has been treated with injustice, and whose amiability and intelligence are then superseded by sullenness and obstinacy. Thus, as in the time of Ammianus Marcellinus, the fellâh will often suffer the most cruel blows in dogged silence rather than pay the taxes demanded of him.

In his own fields the fellâh is an industrious labourer, and his work is more continuous than that of the peasant of more northern countries. He enjoys no period of repose during the winter, and the whole of his spare time is occupied in drawing water for the irrigation of the land. Notwithstanding his hard lot, however, he is an entire stranger to any endeavour to better his condition or to improve his system of farming. As soon as he has accomplished the most necessary tasks he rests and smokes, and trusts that Allâh will do the remainder of his work for him.

The fellâḥ is a believer in the religion of Moḥammed, although he knows but little of the prophet's doctrines and history. Followers of all other religions he believes to be doomed to eternal perdition; but travellers are not on that account disliked by him. We serve rather to confirm his belief in eternal justice, for he is convinced that all the comforts and luxuries we now enjoy will be counterbalanced by torments hereafter. At the same time he admires and overrates our knowledge, which is so superior to his own. Every well-dressed European is in the estimation of the natives a prodigy of wisdom; and, as their ideas of a scholar and a physician are identical, they place implicit reliance on our ability to heal the sick and to save the dying. The traveller who comes in contact with the fellâhîn will often be applied to for medicine, and will often find drugs more effective than money in securing their good will.

(2). COPTS *(kubt, ubt).* While we have regarded the fellâḥîn as genuine Egyptians in consequence of their uninterrupted occupation of the soil, the religion of the Copts affords us an additional guarantee for the purity of their descent. The Copts are undoubtedly the most direct descendants of the ancient Egyptians, there being no ground for the assumption that their ancestors were foreign immigrants who embraced Christianity after the conquest of the country by the Mohammedans, while on the other hand the obstinacy with which they defended their monophysite Christianity for several centuries against the inroads of the creed of Byzantium affords another indication of their Egyptian character. The Coptic population is officially stated as 250,000, but these figures are obviously too low, and the number is more probably about 400,000, *i.e.* about a fifth of the purely indigenous population of the valley of the Nile † They are most numerous in the towns of Northern Egypt, around the ancient Coptos, at Negâda, Lukṣor, Esneh, Dendera, Girgeh, Ṭahṭa, and particularly at Siûṭ and Akhmîm. A large proportion of the population of all these places is Coptic

The Coptic Patriarch is elected from their own number by the monks of the five chief monasteries of Egypt These are the monasteries of St. Anthony and St Paul in the western desert, the two in the valley of the Natron Lakes, and the large convent of Marrag, near Monfalût.

Most of the Copts are dwellers in towns, and are chiefly engaged in the more refined handicrafts (as watchmakers, goldsmiths, jewellers, embroiderers, tailors, weavers, manufacturers of spurious antiquities, etc.), or in trade, or as clerks, accountants, and notaries. Their physique is accordingly materially different from that of the fellâḥîn. They are generally somewhat below the middle height, and of delicate frame, with small hands and feet, their skulls are higher and narrower than those of the peasantry, and with less protruding cheek-bones; and, lastly, their complexion is fairer. These differences are sufficiently accounted for by their mode of life; for, when we compare those Copts who are engaged in rustic pursuits, or the Coptic camel drivers of Upper Egypt, with the fellâḥîn, we find that the two races are not distinguishable from each other. The two distinct types have also been recognized in the skeletons of the ancient mummies.

Few nations in the East embraced the Gospel more zealously than the dwellers on the Nile. Accustomed as they had long been to regard life as a pilgrimage to death, as a school of preparation for

† The total number of Christians in Egypt, including Europeans, Armenians, and Syrians, is about 600,000, or one tenth of the entire population.

another world, and weary of their motley and confused Pantheon of divinities, whose self-seeking priesthood designedly disguised the truth, they eagerly welcomed the simple doctrines of Christianity, which appeared so well adapted to their condition and promised them succour and redemption. Like Eutyches, they revered the divine nature of the Saviour only, in which they held that every human element was absorbed, and when the Council of Chalcedon in 451 sanctioned the doctrine that Christ combined a human with a divine nature, the Egyptians, with their characteristic tenacity adhered to their old views, and formed a sect termed Eutychians, or Monophysites, to which the Copts of the present day still belong.

The name of the Copts is an ethnical one, being simply an Arabic corruption of the Greek name of Egyptians. The theory is now exploded that they derive their name from a certain itinerant preacher named Jacobus, who according to Makrîzî was termed El-Berâdi'i, or 'blanket-bearer', from the old horse-cloth worn by him when he went about preaching. This Jacobus promulgated the monophysite doctrine of Eutyches, which had found its most zealous supporter in Dioscurus, a bishop of Alexandria, who was declared a heretic and banished after the Council of Chalcedon, and his disciples were sometimes called Jacobites. If this name had ever been abbreviated to Cobit or Cobt, it would probably have occurred frequently in the writings of Monophysites, but there we find no trace of it. It is, on the other hand, quite intelligible that the word Copt, though originally synonymous with Egyptian, should gradually have come to denote a particular religious sect, for, at the period when the valley of the Nile was conquered by 'Amr, the native Egyptians, who almost exclusively held the monophysite creed, were chiefly distinguished by their religion from their invaders, who brought a new religious system from the East.

These Egyptian Christians strenuously opposed the resolutions of the Council of Chalcedon, and thousands of them sacrificed their lives or their welfare in the fierce and sanguinary conflicts of the 6th century, the causes of which were imperfectly understood by the great majority of the belligerents. The subtle dogmatic differences which gave rise to these wars aroused such hatred among these professors of the religion of love, that the defeated Monophysites readily welcomed the invading armies of El-Islâm, or perhaps even invited them to their country.

After the conquest of Egypt by 'Amr the Copts were at first treated with lenity, and were even appointed to the highest government offices; but they were soon doomed to suffer persecutions and privations of every description. These persecutions were mainly due to their unbounded arrogance and their perpetual conspiracies against their new masters, and their Mohammedan contemporaries even attributed to them the disastrous conflagrations from which the new capital of the country so frequently suffered (p. 242). Accustomed for many ages to regard themselves as the most civilised of nations, and the Greeks as their inferiors, they perhaps imagined, that, if they succeeded in throwing off the yoke of the barbarous children of the desert, they could prevent the revival of the hated Byzantine supremacy. Their hopes, however, were doomed to bitter disappointment, and their national pride to utter humiliation. Their conquerors succeeded in maintaining their position, and though apparently at first inclined to moderation, were at length driven by the conduct and the previous example of the Copts themselves to persecute and oppress them to the uttermost.

In spite, however, of all these disasters, a numerous community of Copts has always existed in Egypt, a fact which is mainly to be accounted for by the remarkable tenacity and constancy of the Egyptian character. Owing, however, to the continual oppression and contempt to which they have been subjected, the grave disposition of the subjects of the Pharaohs has degenerated into sullen gloom, and their industry into cupidity. The rancour which they have so long cherished has embittered their character, while the persecutions they have suffered have taught them to be at one time cringing, and at another arrogant and overbearing. They are in very few respects superior to their Mohammedan countrymen. They generally possess an hereditary aptitude for mathematical science, and are therefore in great request as book-keepers and accountants, but on the other hand they are entirely destitute of the generous and dignified disposition of the Arabs. They obey their law which forbids polygamy, but constantly abuse that which permits them to indulge in spirituous liquors, drunkards being frequently met with, even among their priests. Their divine worship will strike the traveller as strange, and anything but edifying or elevating.

The traveller may distinguish the Copts from the Arabs by their dark turbans, which are generally blue or black, and their dark-coloured clothes. This costume was originally prescribed by their oppressors, and they still take a pride in it as a mark of their origin, though now permitted to dress as they please. A practised eye will also frequently detect among them the ancient Egyptian cast of features Towards strangers the Copt is externally obliging, and when anxious to secure their favour he not unfrequently appeals to his Christian creed as a bond of union. Many Copts have recently been converted to Protestantism by American missionaries, particularly in Upper Egypt, chiefly through the foundation of good schools and the distribution of cheap Arabic Bibles. Even the orthodox Copts have a great reverence for the sacred volume, and it is not uncommon to meet with members of their sect who know the whole of the gospels by heart. The Roman propaganda, which was begun by Franciscans at the end of the 17th and beginning of the 18th cent , has been less successful among the Copts, and there now exist a few small Roman Catholic communities in Upper Egypt only (at Girgeh, Akhmim, and Negâda). To the Romanists, however, is partly due the preservation of the old Coptic language, into which they caused the gospels to be translated by the most learned scholars of the day (accompanied by a preface asserting the supremacy of the pope) for circulation in Egypt. Notwithstanding the serious defects to which we have alluded, the Coptic community boasts of a number of highly respectable members, and in spite of the frequent heavy contributions levied from the sect by previous governments, it contains several wealthy landowners and merchants, some of whom we shall hereafter have occasion to name.

3. Beduins. *Bedu* (sing. *bedawi*) is the name applied to the nomadic Arabs, and *'Arab* to those who immigrated at a later period and settled in the valley of the Nile. They both differ materially from the dwellers in towns and from the fellâḥîn, who usually call themselves 'Sons of the Arabs' (*Ibn el-'Arab*). The subdivisions of the Beduin tribes are called *Ḳabîleh* (whence the name Kabyles, applied to some of the Algerian Beduins). Though differing greatly in origin and language, the wandering tribes of Egypt all profess Mohammedanism. Again, while some of them have immigrated from Arabia or Syria, partly in very ancient, and partly in modern times, and while others are supposed to be the aboriginal inhabitants of the territories claimed by them (as the Berbers of N. Africa and the Ethiopians or Blemmyes of Nubia), or former dwellers on the Nile expelled from their homes by foreign invaders, they all differ greatly from the stationary Egyptian population; and this contrast is accounted for by the radical difference between the influences of the desert and those of the Nile valley. The Beduins may be divided into two leading groups: (1) Beduins in the narrower sense, *i. e.* Arabic speaking tribes, most of whom have probably immigrated from Arabia or Syria, and who occupy the deserts adjoining Central and Northern Egypt, or who are to be found in different regions of Southern Nubia as a pastoral people; (2) 'Bega', who range over the regions of Upper Egypt and Nubia situated between the Nile and the Red Sea, and extending to the frontiers of the Abyssinian mountains (their territory being known as 'Edbai'). To these last the name of Ethiopians may as accurately be applied as that of Arabs to the first group; and they are believed by Dr. Lepsius to be the descendants of the Blemmyes, who occupied the Nubian part of the valley of the Nile down to the 4th cent. after Christ, when they were expelled by 'Nubian' invaders from the south. The second group consists of three different races, the *Hadendoa*, the *Bisharîn*, and the *Ababdeh*. The last-named, who are widely scattered in the valleys of the desert between the tropics and the latitude of Keneh and Ḳoṣêr, and who lead a poverty-stricken life with their very scanty stock of camels and goats, are those with whom alone we have to deal as inhabitants of Egypt. Though closely resembling the other Bega tribes in appearance, the Ababdeh (sing. Abâdi, the *Gebadei* of Pliny) possess an original language of their own ('to-bedyawîyeh'), which, however, they have long since exchanged for bad Arabic. Besides the girdle round their loins they wear a kind of long white

shirt, and in winter a light-coloured striped woollen mantle, while the Bisharîn and Hadendoa tend their large flocks of sheep and herds of camels in a half-naked condition, girded with a leathern apron and wrapped in a kind of blanket *(melâyeh)*. All these 'Ethiopians' are *Dolichocephali*, with orthognathous skulls, and are remarkable for their fine and almost Caucasian cast of features, their very dark, bronze-coloured complexion, and their luxuriant growth of hair, shading their heads like a cloud, or hanging down in numberless plaits over their necks and shoulders, while in front it is short and curly. Their figures are beautifully symmetrical, and more or less slender in accordance with their means of subsistence, and their limbs are gracefully and delicately formed. In other respects they resemble all the other children of the desert, as in the purity of their complexion, the peculiar thinness of their necks, and the premature wrinkling of the skin of their faces. Compared with their bold and quarrelsome neighbours the Bisharîn, the Ababdeh, who are armed with a dagger worn in a sheath attached to the upper part of the left arm, or with a long, straight sword, but never with a gun, are exceedingly gentle and inoffensive. The Egyptian government has put an end to the old feuds between the Bisharin and the Ababdeh by entrusting to the latter the superintendence of the great commercial route through the Nubian desert (from Korusko to Abu Hammed), and by placing the nine tribes of the Bisharîn under the jurisdiction of the chief shêkh of the Ababdeh, who is personally responsible for the safety of the routes through the desert, and is therefore obliged to reside in the valley of the Nile. (His present headquarters are at the small village of Beḥêreh, at the foot of the hill of Redesîyeh, opposite to Edfu.) The total number of the Ababdeh amounts to about 30,000. The chief shêkh whose dignity is hereditary, appoints over the principal villages a number of sub-chiefs, who are appealed to as judges in family quarrels which the head of the family has been unable to settle.

The dwellings of the Ababdeh consist of low and miserable hovels constructed of stakes covered with ragged straw-mats, and placed in groups of not more than 4-8 together. They also sometimes live in caves, like genuine Troglodytes, although exposed to danger from snakes. Like the other Bega tribes, they are chiefly occupied as shepherds and camel-drivers. The wealthier purchase a little sorghum grain, which they eat either raw, or roasted, or in the form of unleavened cakes, but the poorer seem to have a marvellous power of sustaining life on homœopathically minute quantities of goats' milk and the game which they occasionally capture. The Bisharîn also live exclusively on milk and a little meat, while the Arabian Beduins of the North till the soil to some extent when an opportunity offers. A considerable number of the Ababdeh and Bisharîn who live near the coast and possess no cattle or other property, subsist precariously on the produce of the sea. They are not fishermen, as they possess no boats or other appliances, with the exception of spears and landing-nets, but merely 'Ichthyophagi', who pick up shell-fish, octopoda, or small fish thrown up on the beach. Occasionally they make a prize of turtle's eggs, and sometimes succeed in reaching the sandy islands of the Red Sea where the sea-swallow (sterna) lays its eggs. This poor mode of life of course has an influence on their mental capacity, which is not of a very high order; but they are intelligent in their own affairs, and remarkably skilful trackers, so much so that they are often employed by the government in pursuing criminals. They are nominally Mohammedans, but they do not pray, or keep the fast of Ramaḍân, or make pilgrimages, except on rare occasions. Nor do they, like orthodox Mohammedans, fear 'ginn' and 'ghûls', but they permit polygamy, observe the rite of circumcision, and worship saints.

Besides the Bega, there are numerous Beduins who inhabit the steppes and deserts belonging to the region of the Nile, but beyond the limits of Egypt, and range as far as the confines of the heathen negro-races on the left bank of the Nile, nearly to 9° N. latitude; but with these we have not at present to deal. Among the Arabian Beduins of the North, there are three important tribes in the peninsula of Mount Sinai: the *Terâbiyîn*, who carry on a brisk caravan traffic between Suez and Cairo, and claim territorial rights as far as the banks of the Nile near Basâtîn above Cairo; the *Tîhâya*, who occupy the heart of the peninsula, between Suez and 'Aḳaba; and the *Sawârkeh* or *El-'Arayîsh*, to the north of the latter. In Upper Egypt, besides the Ababdeh, the only Beduins who occupy the eastern bank of the Nile are the *Beni Waṣel* and the *Atûni*, or *Hawâdât*, who, however, have now settled on both banks of the Theban Nile valley and are gradually blending with the fellâḥîn, and the *Ma'azeh* (about 3000 in number), who dwell in groups among the limestone mountains between Suez and Ḳeneh, where there are good pastures at places. Most of the Arabian Beduins, on the other hand, who belong to Egypt, confine themselves to the western bank of the Nile. They occupy the whole of this side of the river from the Fayûm as far as Abydus near Girgeh, and it is mainly with their aid that communication is maintained with the western oases, peopled by a totally different race (p 65), who till the ground and possess no camels, being probably allied to the Berbers of Northern Africa (one of the numerous Libyan tribes mentioned in ancient inscriptions).

The Beduins of the North have inherited with comparative purity the fiery blood of the desert tribes, who achieved such marvellous exploits under the banner of the prophet, but the traveller will rarely come in contact with them unless he undertakes a journey across the desert. The loiterers who assist travellers in the ascent of the pyramids and pester them to buy antiquities, which are generally spurious, call themselves Beduins, but, even if originally of that race, they have entirely lost all its nobler characteristics in consequence of their intercourse with strangers and their debasing occupations. Genuine Beduins are to be found nowhere except in their desert home, where to a great extent they still retain the spirit of independence, the courage, and the restlessness of their ancestors. As in the time of Herodotus, the tent of the Beduin is still his home. Where it is pitched is a matter of indifference to him, if only the pegs which secure it be firmly driven into the earth, if it shelter his wife and child from the burning sunshine and the chilly night air, and if pasturage-ground and a spring be within reach. In consequence of the frequent wars waged between the different tribes, every Beduin is a warrior. Most of them, too, as might be expected, are extremely poor. Thus at Ramleh on the coast, near Alexandria, the traveller will have an opportunity of seeing a whole colony of the poorest class encamped in their tents, where they live in the most frugal possible manner, with a few miserable goats and the fowls which subsist on the rubbish in their neighbourhood. Though professors of El-Islâm, they are considerably less strict in their observances than the fellâhîn of the valley of the Nile, who are themselves sufficiently lax, and above all they sadly neglect the religious duty of cleanliness. They do not observe the practice of praying five times a day, and they are as a rule but slightly acquainted with the Korân Relics of their old star-worship can still be traced among their customs.

The traveller will occasionally observe Beduins in the bazaars of the armourers and leather-merchants, and will be struck with the proud and manly bearing of these bronzed children of the desert, whose sharp, bearded features and steady gaze betoken firmness and resolution. In Egypt the traveller need not fear their predatory propensities, but they have frequently attacked travellers in Turkish Tripolitania and in the eastern part of Arabia Petræa.

(4). Arabian Dwellers in Towns. Those Arabs with whom the traveller usually comes in contact in towns are shopkeepers, officials, servants, coachmen, and donkey-attendants, or perhaps these last only, as most of the best shops are kept by Europeans, while in official and legal matters his intercourse with the natives is carried on through the medium of his consul. The indolence and duplicity of these Arabs, which proceed to some extent from the character of their religion, have often been justly condemned, while their intelligence, patience, and amiability are too often ignored. They are generally of a much more mixed origin than the fellâḥîn, as the various conquerors of Egypt usually made the towns their headquarters. Alexandria, for example, was chiefly favoured by the Greeks and Arabs, and Cairo by the Arabs and Turks. It thus happens that the citizens of the Egyptian towns consist of persons of every complexion from dark brown to white, with the features of the worshippers of Osiris or the sharp profile of the Beduins, and with the slender figure of the fellâḥ or the corpulence of the Turk. Among the lower classes frequent intermarriage with negro women has darkened the complexion and thickened the features of their offspring; while the higher ranks, being descended from white slaves or Turkish mothers, more nearly resemble the European type. As the inhabitants of the towns could not be so much oppressed by their rulers as the peasantry, we find that they exhibit a more independent spirit, greater enterprise, and a more cheerful disposition than the fellâḥîn. At the same time they are not free from the dreamy character peculiar to Orientals, nor from a tinge of the apathy of fatalism; and their indolence contrasts strongly with the industry of their European rivals in political, scientific, artistic, and all business pursuits. A glance at the offices of the ministers, the bazaars of the merchants, the schools of the Arabs, and the building-yards and workshops constructed by natives will enable the traveller to observe with what deliberation and with what numerous intervals of repose they perform their tasks. From such workers it is in vain to expect rapidity, punctuality, or work of a highly finished character, and the caustic remark of Prince Napoleon that the Egyptians are 'capable of making a pair of pantaloons, but never of sewing on the last button', was doubtless founded on experience. The townspeople profess Islamism, but, in their youth particularly, they are becoming more and more lax in their obedience to the Korân. Thus the custom of praying in public, outside the house-doors and shops, is gradually falling into disuse. The European dress, moreover, is gradually superseding the Oriental, though the latter is far more picturesque, and better suited to the climate †. On the whole, however, they are bigoted Mohammedans, and share the contempt with which the fellâḥîn regard all other religions. Their daily intercourse with unbelievers and their dread of the power of the Christian nations tend, however, to keep their fanaticism, which otherwise would be unbounded, in check, and has even induced them to admit strangers to witness the most sacred ceremonies in their mosques.

(5). Berbers. The name *Berberi* (plur. *barâbra*) is believed by many authorities to be identical with 'barbarians', a word which is said to have been adopted by the Greeks from the Egyptians, who used it to denote all 'non-Egyptians', and to be derived from *brr*, *i. e.* 'to be unable to speak', or 'to speak imperfectly'. The 'Berbers' of N. Africa and the town of 'Berber' in S. Nubia also doubtless have the same origin. In Egypt the name is applied in a half contemptuous way to the numerous immigrants from the Nubian

† About the year 1865 a kind of uniform called the 'Stambulina' was prescribed by the government for all the officials of the higher classes (black coat with a row of buttons and low upright collar), but they are allowed to wear ordinary European clothing in their offices. All the officials, however, in the pay of the Egyptian government, including Europeans, and even the members of the mixed court of justice, must wear the red fez (ṭarbûsh).

part of the valley of the Nile, who form the largest foreign element of the community, and who never entirely assimilate with it, as the Nubians make it a rule never to marry Egyptian wives. The Nubians, on the other hand, speak slightingly of the Egyptians as 'Wod-er-Rîf', or sons of the Nile valley (comp. p. 31). The two races entertain a great dislike to each other, and their dispositions are fundamentally different. The Nubians are inferior to the Egyptians in industry and energy, especially in tilling the soil, and also in physical strength; and they are more superstitious and fanatical, as is indicated by the numerous amulets they wear round their necks and arms. They are, however, superior to the Egyptians in cleanliness, honesty, and subordination, and possess a more highly developed sense of honour. The Nubian doorkeepers who are to be found in all the mercantile houses of Alexandria and elsewhere are noted for their honesty. The traveller must not expect to find them very sincerely attached or grateful, any more than the native Egyptians (comp. pp. 12, 25), but as servants they are certainly preferable. The inhabitants of the Nubian part of the valley of the Nile are not all strictly Nubians; for in the southern parts of that region a colony of *Shêgîyeh* and other Arabian tribes has settled in comparatively recent times. The genuine Nubians (a name unknown to themselves, and of ancient origin) occupy the valley of the Nile from Gebel Barkal near the fourth cataract down to the first cataract, and are divided in accordance with the principal idioms of their language into *Mahâs*, *Kenûs*, and *Donkolas*. Their language belongs to the Libyan group of the N. African tongues, and Dr. Brugsch is of opinion that it may afford a clue to the interpretation of the still undeciphered Ethiopian (Meroïtic) inscriptions of the Nubian part of the Nile valley. Dr. Lepsius, on the other hand, who has published an admirable work on the subject, maintains that the 'to-bedyawîyeh' language of the Bega (p. 45) is more likely to be cognate with that of the inscriptions, as he believes that the Blemmyes, the ancestors of the Bega, were the original inhabitants of the region in question, and were expelled by the handsome and intelligent 'Nuba' negroes from the district to the S. of Kordofân. Friedrich Müller places the Nuba tongue in a separate category along with the dialects of a few other tribes in different parts of Africa, and there is certainly much to be said in favour of this distinction of it from the languages of the Hamitic races on the one side and the typical negro races on the other.

Those Berbers who do not learn Arabic grammatically never speak it thoroughly well; but it is generally, though imperfectly, understood in Nubia. The traveller must therefore not expect to learn good Arabic from his Nubian servants. In their native country they till the banks of the Nile, but their land is of very limited extent and poorly cultivated; and as their harvests are scanty they are rarely able to support large families. They accordingly often emigrate at an early age to the richer lowlands, chiefly to the large towns, and particularly to Alexandria, in quest of employment; and they find no difficulty in attaining their object, for they are generally active, intelligent, and honest, while the older immigrants, who are strongly attached to their country, are always zealous in procuring them work and rendering them assistance. When the Berber has succeeded in amassing a moderate fortune, he returns to settle in his native country, of which throughout his whole career he never entirely loses sight, and to which he frequently remits his hardly earned savings for the benefit of his relations. The cold winter nights in Egypt are very trying to the poor Berbers, who often have to sleep in the open air outside the doors, and many of them are attacked by consumption. They are most commonly employed as doorkeepers *(bawwâb)*, as house-servants *(khaddâm)*, as grooms and runners *(sâis)*, for which their swiftness renders them unrivalled, as coachmen *('arbagi)*, and as cooks *(tabbâkh)*. Each of these five classes is admirably organised as a kind of guild, with a shêkh of its own, who levies a tax from each member, and guarantees the character and abilities of members when hired. Thefts are very rarely committed by the Nubians, but in cases of the kind the shêkh compels the whole of his subjects to contribute to repair the loss, and cases have been known in which several hundred pounds have been recovered in this way. The result is that there is a strict mutual system of supervision, and suspected characters are unceremoniously excluded from the fraternity. Nubian women are seldom seen in Egypt.

(6.) Negroes. Like the Berbers, most of the negroes in Egypt are professors of El-Islâm, to the easily intelligible doctrines of which they readily and zealously attach themselves. Most of the older negroes and negresses with whom the traveller meets have originally been brought to Egypt as slaves, and belong to natives, by whom they are treated more like members of the family than like servants. Although every slave who desires to be emancipated may now with the aid of government sever the ties which bind him to his master, most of the negroes prefer to remain on the old footing with the family which supports them and relieves them of the anxiety of providing for themselves. The eunuchs, who also belong almost exclusively to the negro races, but are rapidly becoming rarer, very seldom avail themselves of this opportunity of regaining their liberty, as their emancipation would necessarily terminate the life of ease and luxury in which they delight. The slave-trade is now very rapidly approaching complete extinction in Egypt, not so much owing to the penalties imposed (which the rapacious officials take every opportunity of enforcing), as from changes in the mode of living, and the growing preference of the wealthy for paid servants. Down to 1870 the trade was still carried on in secret with some success, but since then it has been at a standstill. Since 1878 the government has kept a complete register of domestic slaves, and special officials are appointed to watch over their interests.

The negroes, who voluntarily settle in Egypt in considerable numbers, form the dregs of the people and are employed in the most menial offices. Most of the negro races of Central Africa to the N. of the equator are represented at Cairo, particularly in the rank and file of the negro regiments

Ethnographers, linguists, or other scientific men who desire to see specimens of as many different races as possible should obtain an introduction to an Arabian merchant in the Gameliyeh, who will conduct them to merchants from every part of the interior and of the African coast, each attended by his staff of negro servants. The latter, however, especially if long resident in Egypt, cannot give trustworthy information about their country and their origin Some of them have forgotten their mother tongue and even the name of their native country.

Foreigners are prohibited from taking negro servants out of the country, but if through the intervention of their consul they obtain permission they must find security for their subsequent restoration.

(7). Turks. Although the dynasty of the viceroys of Egypt is of Turkish origin (see p. 106), a comparatively small section of the community belongs to that nation, and their numbers appear to be diminishing. The Turks of Egypt are chiefly to be found in the towns, where most of them are government officials, soldiers, and merchants. The Turkish officials are much to blame for the maladministration which so long paralysed the rich productiveness of the valley of the Nile, having always with few exceptions been actuated in their proceedings by motives of reckless cupidity without regard to ulterior consequences. Now, however, that the government of the Khedive has adopted more enlightened principles, it has admitted other nationalities also to its highest civil appointments, some of which are held by able Europeans, and under their auspices a brighter future is probably in store for Egypt. The Turkish merchants are generally a prosperous class, and, although fully alive to their pecuniary interests, they are dignified and courteous in their bearing, and are often remarkable for the handsomeness of their features.

(8). Levantines. A link between the various classes of dwellers in Egypt and the visitors to the banks of the Nile is formed by the members of the various Mediterranean races, known as Levantines, who have been settled here for several generations, and form no inconsiderable element in the population of the larger towns. Most of them profess the Latin form of Christianity, and Arabic has now become their mother tongue, although they still speak their old national dialects. They are apt linguists, learning the European languages with great rapidity, and good men of business, and owing to these qualities they are often employed as shopmen and clerks. Their services have also become indispensable at the consulates as translators of cocuments destined for the native authorities, and as bearers of communications between the respective offices. A large proportion of them are wealthy. Being Christians, the Levantines all live under the protection of the different consuls, and thus unfairly escape payment of taxes, although they derive the whole of their wealth from the country.

(9). Armenians and Jews. This section of the community is about as numerous as the last, and in some respects contrasts favourably with it. The Armenians generally possess excellent abilities, and a singular aptitude for learning both Oriental and European languages, which they often acquire with great grammatical accuracy. Many of them are wealthy goldsmiths and jewellers, and they often hold important government offices.

The Jews are often distinguishable by their red hair from the native Egyptians, as well as by other characteristics. Most of them are from Palestine, but many have recently immigrated from Wallachia. All the money-changers in the streets (*ṣarrâf*), and many of the wealthiest merchants of Egypt, are Jews, and notwithstanding the popular prejudice entertained against them, owing as is alleged to their disregard of cleanliness, they now form, thanks to the impartiality of the present government, one of the most highly respected sections of the community.

(10). Europeans. The number of European residents and visitors in Egypt at the census of 1882 was 82,000, exclusive of the British army of occupation. The Greeks are most numerously represented, then the Italians, French, English (including Maltese), Austrians (including many Dalmatians), and Germans. The numerous Swiss residents in Egypt, who are not represented by a consul of their own, are distributed among the above leading classes (French, Italian, German). Beside these nationalities, there are also a few representatives of Russia, America, Belgium, Scandinavia, and other countries Each of the above leading nationalities shows a preference for one or more particular occupations, in which they sometimes enjoy a complete monopoly. The Greeks of all classes are generally traders. They constitute the aristocracy of Alexandria, and the victual-dealers (*baḳḳâl*) in all the other towns are mostly Greeks. They are the proprietors of the numerous small banks which lend money on good security, both to the peasantry and the government officials, at a rate of interest sometimes amounting to 6 per cent monthly, the maximum permitted by law; and they are the only Europeans who have established themselves permanently as merchants beyond the confines of Egypt proper. The Greeks also have the unenviable notoriety of committing numerous murders, thefts, and other crimes, but it must be borne in mind that they are by far the most numerous section of the European community (35,000 from Greece alone, besides many Turkish subjects), and that some 30,000 of them belong to the lowest class of emigrants from an unhappy and ill-conditioned country. Many of these crimes must, moreover, be regarded as the outcome of the sadly misdirected daring and ability which characterise their nation. The superiority of the Greeks to the

Orientals is nowhere so strikingly manifested as in Egypt, where it affords a modern reflex of their ancient, world-renowned supremacy. Most of them are immigrants from the various Greek islands, and the purity of their type is specially noteworthy.

The Italian residents, 16,000 in number, consist chiefly of traders of a humble class, advocates, and musicians, from the operatic singer down to the Calabrian itinerant. Of French nationality (15,000) are all the artizans of the higher class, who are generally noted for their skill, trustworthiness, and sobriety, and indeed form the most respectable stratum of the European community. Most of the better shops are kept by Frenchmen, and the chief European officials of the government, including several architects and engineers, are French The English settlers number about 5000, exclusive of the troops, of which there were about 7000 at the beginning of 1885. Until recently their specialities were the manufacture of machinery and the construction of railways and harbours; but of late they have also almost monopolised the chief posts in those branches of the administration (post and telegraph office, railways, custom-house) that have been remodelled after the European pattern. A large majority of the residents who enjoy the protection of the British consulate are Maltese, and to them apply even more forcibly most of the remarks already made regarding the Greeks. It has been ascertained that the Maltese settlers in foreign countries are more numerous than those resident in their two small native islands, and of these a considerable proportion belongs to Egypt. At home, under the discipline of British institutions, they form a pattern little nation of their own, but in Egypt, where they are freed from the restraint of these influences, they are very apt to degenerate and to swell unduly the ranks of the criminal class. Many of the Maltese, however, are enterprising tradesmen and industrious artizans, such as shoemakers and joiners. To the Austrian (3000) and German (1000) community belong a number of merchants of the best class, all the directors of the principal banks, many physicians and teachers, innkeepers, musicians, and lastly handicraftsmen of humble pretensions.

With regard to the capability of Europeans of becoming acclimatised in Egypt, there are a number of widely divergent opinions. Much, of course, must depend on the nature of the climate of their own respective countries. It has been asserted that European families settled in Egypt die out in the second or third generation, but of this there is no sufficient proof, as the European community is of very recent origin, and many examples to the contrary might be cited. The climate of Egypt is less enervating than that of most other hot countries, an advantage attributed to the dryness of the air and the saline particles contained in it; while the range of temperature between the different seasons is greater than in Ireland or Portugal.

The Nile (comp. Map, p. 30). The Nile ranks with the Amazon and the Congo as one of the three longest rivers in the world (about 4000 M.), since its headstream is probably to be found in the Shimiju, which rises five degrees to the S. of the Equator. Throughout nearly the whole of its course the river is navigable, with two great interruptions only (at Abû Ḥammed-Barkal and Donḳola-Wâdi Ḥalfa). Though it is greatly surpassed by the Amazon and Congo in volume, neither these nor any other river in the world can vie in historical and ethnographical interest with the 'father of rivers'.

The discovery of the true sources of the Nile and the cause of its annual overflow are two scientific problems which for upwards of 2000 years European scholars laboured to solve, while the Egyptians themselves regarded the river as a deity, and its origin and properties as the most sacred of mysteries, to be revealed to the curious spirit of man only when he should have quitted this earthly scene. As it is the *Egyptian Nile* only with which we have at present to deal, we shall advert but briefly to the subject of the sources of the river, and mention the principal affluents only which affect Egypt.

The Nile is formed by the confluence of the *White* and the *Blue* Nile at the town of Kharṭûm, from which point to its principal mouths at Damietta and Rosetta, a distance of upwards of 1800 miles, it traverses an absolutely barren country, and receives one tributary only, the *Atbara*, on the east side, about 180 miles below Kharṭûm. Throughout the whole of this distance, in the course of which it falls 1240 ft., the river has to contend against numerous absorbing influences, for which it receives no compensation beyond the rare showers attracted in winter by the mountains between its right bank and the Red Sea. Nothwithstanding the immense length of the river, it very rarely presents the picturesque appearance of some of the great European and other rivers, as its banks are generally flat and monotonous, and it contains hardly a single island worthy of mention. The broadest parts of this portion of the Nile are a little below Kharṭûm, a little above its bifurcation near Cairo, and also near Minyeh, at each of which places it attains a width of about 1100 yds., while the White Nile is of greater breadth throughout a long part of its lower course. As the river pursues its tortuous course through thirsty land, for a distance of 15 degrees of latitude, much of its water is consumed by evaporation and infiltration (a process by which it is probable that Libyan oases are supplied with water from the Nubian Nile), and still more so by the extensive system of artificial canals requisite for the irrigation of a whole kingdom. M. Linant estimates this loss at the time of the inundation within Egypt proper, *i.e.* between Gebel Selseleh and Cairo, as one-third of the total volume; he found that 1,093,340,222 cubic mètres of water passed Gebel Selseleh in 24 hrs., while on the same day only 705,588,389 cubic mètres passed Cairo. At the confluence of the White and Blue Nile their average volumes are in the proportion of three to one, but the latter assumes far greater importance when swollen by the Abyssinian rains. The Blue Nile is in fact a species of mountain-torrent, being liable to rise suddenly and sweep away everything it encounters on its rapidly descending course. It is therefore called the *Bahr el-Azrak*, *i. e.* the blue, 'dark', or 'turbid', in contradistinction to the *Bahr el-Abyad*, *i. e.* the white, or rather the 'clear' river, whose water descends from clear lakes and is farther filtered by the vast grassy plains and occasional floating plants through which it passes. The Blue Nile (together with its coadjutor the Atbara) may therefore be regarded as the sole origin of the fertility of Egypt, and also as the cause of the inundation, while on the other hand the regular and steady supply of water afforded by the White Nile performs the very important office of preventing the lower part of the river from drying up altogether in summer. The White Nile is not only much larger than the Blue in average volume, but is, with its tributaries, more than double the length. It does not, however, remain very long undivided. Higher up, in 9° N. latitude, it receives on the east side the waters of the *Sobât*, a stream descending from the mountains to the south of Abyssinia, and resembling the Blue Nile in character, though much smaller. A little farther up, on the opposite side, the White Nile is joined by the *Bahr el-Ghazâl*, or Gazelle River, a very sluggish stream, fed by numerous springs rising in the Nyam-nyam and Kredy regions, between 4° and 5° N. latitude. Higher up the river takes the name of *Bahr el-Gebel*, and is considerably smaller in volume, and beyond 5° N. latitude it ceases to be navigable, as it descends in a series of rapids from the *Albert Nyanza* or *Mwutan Lake*. This sheet of water is connected by another river, the '*Somerset*', which may be regarded as the continuation of the White Nile, with the *Victoria Nyanza* or *Ukerewe Lake;* while the *Shimiju* and other S. feeders of the latter may be called the ultimate sources of the Nile.

The Valley of the Nile from Khartûm to the Delta, although from its great length (15° of latitude) necessarily possessing great varieties of climate, forms one long unbroken tract of country, the fertilising soil of which is brought down by the Blue Nile from the Abyssinian mountains.

The breadth of the Valley of the Nile, including the barren land immediately flanking it, varies from $4^1/_2$ to 10 miles in Nubia, and from 14 to 32 miles in Egypt. The banks, of which the eastern is called the 'Arabian', and the western the 'Libyan', rise at places to upwards of 1000 ft., resembling two large canal embankments, between which the river has forced its passage through the plateau of 'Nubian sandstone' (which extends to the Gebel Selseleh above Edfu), and through the nummulite limestone of Upper and Central

Egypt. The breadth of the cultivable alluvial soil corresponds with the above varying width, but nowhere exceeds 9 miles. The soil deposited by the Nile averages 33-38 ft. deep in Egypt, but near Ḳalyûb at the head of the Delta it increases to about 50 ft., the bottom of it being at places below the level of the sea. The bed of the river is also of considerable depth, and at low water the mud-banks *(gef)* rise above its surface to a height of 25 ft. in Upper Egypt, and 14 ft. at Cairo. These are also the depths of the various irrigation wells.

'Throughout the whole (?) of Egypt the Nile mud rests on a bed of sea-sand. The whole country between the first cataract and the Mediterranean was formerly a narrow estuary, which was probably filled by degrees during the pleiocene period with lagoon deposits, washed down from the crystalline Habesh. At a later period, when Egypt had risen from the sea (and after the isthmus had been formed), the river forced its passage through these deposits of mud, sweeping away many of the loose particles at one place and depositing them again farther down' *(Fraas)* The Nile soil is unlike any other in the world in its composition. According to Regnault it contains 63 per cent of water and sand, 18 per cent of carbonate of lime, 9 per cent of quartz, silica, felspar, hornblende, and epidote, 6 per cent of oxide of iron, and 4 per cent of carbonate of magnesia.

Nothing certain is known regarding the average increase of the alluvial land, all the calculations regarding it having hitherto been based on erroneous or insufficient data. Thus the Nilometer of antiquity furnishes the depth relatively to the level of the sea, but not absolutely. The thickness of earth accumulated around buildings of known age has also been found a fallacious guide, and lastly local measurements lead to no result, as the river often capriciously washes away what it has deposited in previous years. An approximate calculation might possibly be made if the proportion of solid matter annually brought down by the river could be ascertained, but no investigation of this kind has ever been made. It has sometimes been asserted that the desert has begun to encroach upon the cultivated part of the valley, but Sir G. Wilkinson has shown, that, while the sand of the desert may be advancing at places, the cultivable bed of the valley is steadily increasing in thickness and width.

The Inundation, as is obvious from what has already been said, is more or less favourable according to the greater or less amount of rain that falls among the Abyssinian mountains, for that which falls in Central Africa is a more constant quantity, being regulated by the influence of the trade-winds. Like the waterspouts which descend on equatorial Africa, the overflow always recurs at the same season of the year, varying in its advent by a few days only, and in its depth by several yards. At the beginning of June the river slowly begins to swell, and between the 15th and 20th of July the increase becomes very rapid. Towards the end of September the water ceases to rise, remaining at the same height for a fortnight or more, but during the first half of October it rises again and attains its highest level (comp. p. 239). After having begun to subside, it generally rises again for a short time, sometimes regaining and even passing its first culminating point. At length it begins to subside steadily, and after a time the decrease becomes more and more rapid. In January, February, and March the fields from which the water has receded gradually dry up, and in April, May, and the first few days of June the river is at its lowest. The height of the inundation most favourable for agriculture at the present day has been ascertained by long observation to be 23 cubits 2 inches (i.e. about 41 ft. 2 in., the cubit being $21._{386}$ inches), while in the time of Herodotus 16 cubits sufficed, and the god of the Nile in the Vatican is therefore represented as surrounded by sixteen children. A single cubit more is apt to cause terrible devastation in the Delta, and elsewhere to cover many fields destined for the autumn crop (*nabâri*, p. 74), while a deficiency of two cubits causes drought and famine in Upper Egypt. As health depends to a great extent on the regularity of the pulsations of the heart, so the welfare of the whole of this singular country is jeopardised by a too powerful or a too scanty flow of the great artery on which its very existence depends. An excessive overflow, especially if it does not give notice of its approach in due time, is far more disastrous now than formerly, as the extensive cotton-fields in the Delta will not bear flooding, and have to be protected by embankments.

Egypt is now no longer a vast lake during the inundation as it formerly was, nor does the overflow of the fields take place in a direct manner as is commonly supposed. The water is conducted into a vast network of reservoirs and canals, and distributed as required (comp. p. 71), and special engineers are appointed for their supervision. The whole of the cultivable land is divided into huge basins, in which the water introduced by the canals is maintained at a certain height until it has sufficiently saturated the soil and deposited the requisite quantity of mud. After the water in the river has subsided, that in the basins may either be discharged into the river or into the canals, or it may be used for filling other basins lying at a lower level. During these operations many of the villages are connected by means of embankments only, while others can only be reached by boat, and the whole country presents a very peculiar and picturesque appearance.

If the river and the system of canals connected with it are in any way neglected, the consequences are very disastrous, as was notably the case during the latter part of the Byzantine supremacy and under the disgraceful sway of the Mamelukes, when the fertile soil of Egypt yielded less than one-half of its average produce. The mean difference between the highest and the lowest state of the river is about 25 ft. at Cairo, 38 ft. at Thebes, and 49 ft. at Assuân. Even in March and April the traveller will have an opportunity of observing how powerful and rapid the flow of the river still is, although its fall from Assuân (by the first cataract) to Cairo is 299 ft. only, or about seven inches per mile. The rapidity of the stream, however, which averages 3 miles an hour, is not so serious an impediment to the navigation as the frequent changes which take place in the formation of its channel, sometimes occasioning difficulties which the most careful of captains is unable to foresee.

If we now enquire what influence this remarkable river has exercised on the history of civilisation, we can hardly avoid the conclusion that it was the Nile, with its unique character, that stimulated the ancient Egyptians to those great physical and intellectual exertions which rendered them the most famous and the most civilised among the nations of antiquity. The necessity of controlling its course and utilising its water taught them the art of river-engineering and the kindred science of land-surveying, while in the starry heavens they beheld the eternal calendar which regulated the approach and the departure of the inundation, so that the river may perhaps have given the first impulse to the study of astronomy. As the annual overflow of the water obliterated all landmarks, it was necessary annually to measure the land anew, and to keep a register of the area belonging to each proprietor, and above all it became an important duty of the rulers of the people to impress them with a strong sense of the sacredness of property. Every succeeding year, however, there arose new disputes, and these showed the necessity of establishing settled laws and enforcing judicial decisions. The Nile thus led to the foundation of social, legal, and political order, and it is also natural that the mighty and mysterious river on which the welfare of the entire population depended should have awakened their religious sentiment at a very early period. Subsequently, when the engineers and architects, in the service of the state or in the cause of religion, erected those colossal structures with which we are about to become acquainted, it was the Nile which materially facilitated the transport of their materials, and enabled the builders of the pyramids and the other ancient Egyptians to employ the granite of Assuân for the structures of Memphis, and even for those of Tanis, on the coast of the Mediterranean. As the river, moreover, not only afforded a convenient route for the transport of these building materials, but also an admirable commercial highway, we find that the Egyptians had acquired considerable skill at a very early period in constructing vessels with oars, masts, sails, and even cabins and other appliances.

From the earliest historical period down to the present time the course of the Nile, from the cataracts down to its bifurcation to the north of Cairo (the ancient Kerkasoros, *i. e.* the mutilation of Osiris), has undergone very little change. This, however, is not the case with its EMBOUCHURES; for, while ancient writers mention seven (the Pelusiac, the Tanitic, the Mendesian, the Bucolic or Phatnitic, the Sebennytic, the Bolbitinic, and the Canopic), there are now practically two channels only through which the river is discharged into the sea. These are the mouths at Rosetta (Reshîd) and Damietta (Dumyâṭ), situated near the middle of the Delta, while the Pelusiac and Canopic mouths, the most important in ancient times, lay at the extreme east and west ends of the coast respectively The water was afterwards gradually compelled to seek other outlets. The Pelusiac arm found a convenient exit through the Phatnitic near Damietta, while the Canopic was artificially conducted into the Bolbitinic All the principal arms of ancient times at length entirely disappeared, combining to form the modern outlets. These last will in their turn be abandoned, as the river will doubtless again force for itself a more direct passage with a greater fall.

Geological Notice (*by Prof Zittel*). (1) EGYPT PROPER. There is no exaggeration in the often repeated saying that Egypt is 'the gift of the Nile'. But for the bounties dispensed by the river, what is now the most fertile country in N. Africa would be a wilderness of bare rock or sand. With the greatest height attained by the inundation and the extreme length of the irrigation canals corresponds precisely the line which divides the Sahara from the cultivated land. The whole of the alluvial soil deposited by the Nile is an entirely foreign element in the geological structure of N Africa, and its geological character is uniform and easily determined

The origin, composition, and thickness of the alluvium has already been stated The perpendicular, black, and furrowed mud-banks, which often rise to a height of 25-35 ft, are composed of distinct parallel strata of somewhat different colours, with thin layers of sand occasionally intervening In Lower Egypt the mud is rather more thinly spread over the whole Delta, in the form of a blackish or reddish-brown laminated mass, a few isolated spots only remaining uncovered.

Wherever the ground is denuded of its alluvium, apart from which there is no permanent soil in Egypt, it is absolutely sterile; for in this hot and dry country there is no winter, with its protecting mantle of snow, to retard the decomposition of vegetable matter, and to promote its admixture with disintegrated rock, so as to form fertile soil. Owing to the want of vegetation and moisture, without which the progress of disintegration is reduced to a minimum, the surface of the naked rock in Egypt and the neighbouring deserts retains its character almost unaltered The huge masses of debris observed at the foot of the rocks in the valley of the Nile, and particularly at the mouths of the wâdies, and the curious isolated hills with which every traveller through the desert is struck, could not possibly have been formed during the present state of the Egyptian climate They prove that at some pre-historic period the now parched and sterile ground must have been overflowed by copious volumes of water which produced these and various other effects on the appearance of the earth's surface

The geologist will find little to attract his attention in the alluvial soil of Egypt; but on the sea-coast, and in that part of the isthmus which is intersected by the canal there are several points of interest.

On entering the harbour of Alexandria the traveller will observe the massive blocks of stone from the quarries of Meks of which the quays are constructed They consist of recent tertiary, light-coloured, sandy limestone, composed chiefly of innumerable broken fragments of conchylia, a kind of rock which extends far to the W of Alexandria, and probably constitutes the greater part of the lofty Cyrenæan plain. This rock forms the building-stone generally used at Alexandria, and is also employed in the harbour-structures of Port Sa'id

Amidst the desert sand of the isthmus, which even in Lower Egypt forms a substratum underlying the Nile mud, and which in the E part of the desert is nearly covered with a solid gypseous and saline crust, the rock occasionally crops up, or has been uncovered in the course of the excavation of the canal Near the Shalûf station (p. 432) a greenish-grey, gypseous marl overlies the solid limestone, which contains the tertiary marine conchylia, sharks' teeth, and remains of crocodiles and amphibious mammalia. The same formation occurs in other places also, and ridges of the early tertiary nummulite limestone likewise occasionally rise from the plain. At several points on the coast of the Red Sea, particularly near Kosêr, at a height of 600-950 ft above the sea-level, we find rock of the late tertiary or diluvial era containing coral, which shows how much the land must have risen since that period. With these coral-reefs the petroleum wells of Gebel ez-Zêt and the sulphur which occurs on the Râs el-Gimsâh appear to be closely connected.

To the miocene, or middle tertiary period, belong several isolated deposits of sandstone near Cairo, in which are found the beautiful fossil sea-urchins (*Clypeaster Aegyptiacus*) frequently offered for sale near the Pyramids. The place where they occur, on the margin of the desert, about 2 M. to the S. of the Sphinx, has been visited and described by Prof. Fraas.

One of the principal geological curiosities near Cairo is the *Petrified Forest* (comp. p. 339). About 5 M to the E. of the town begins the Khashab ('wood') desert, the surface of which for many miles is sprinkled with whole trunks and fragments of silicified wood. Few travellers go beyond the 'small' petrified wood; the 'great' lies about 20 M. to the E. of Cairo. 'The desert here is so completely covered with trunks, that, except the fine sand itself, no other kind of stone is visible than the flint into which the *Nicoliae* have been converted'. (Fraas) Trunks of 60-90 ft. in length and 3 ft. in thickness have sometimes been found. These have been described by Unger as *Nicolia Aegyptiaca* (of the family of the *Sterculiaceae*), but, according to more recent investigations, it would seem that the forest contained various other trees also (palms and dicotyledonous plants). Whether the trunks have grown and been silicified on the spot, or were brought here by inundations from the south, is still an open question At all events these remarkable deposits date from the late tertiary period

Above Cairo, to the S, the Nile is flanked by ranges of hills, the valley between which is generally 4-9 M. in width On the east side of the Nile begins the Arabian, and on the west side the Libyan desert, both of which are very inhospitable, being ill provided with water, and covered at places only with scanty vegetation From the northernmost spur of the Arabian desert (the Mokattam near Cairo) to a point above Edfu, both banks of the Nile consist of early tertiary nummulite limestone. The strata dip gradually from south to north, so that the farther we ascend the Nile the older are the strata that we meet with. The limestone of the Moḳaṭṭam, with its millions of nummulites, is the material of which the new buildings of the European suburbs of Cairo are constructed, and it was from the venerable quarries of Ṭura and Ma'ṣara that the ancient Egyptians obtained the stone for their pyramids. The blocks for these stupendous structures were conveyed to them by means of a huge stone dyke, of which all trace has now disappeared On the Moḳaṭṭam, near Minyeh, Beni Ḥasan, Siûṭ, Thebes, Esneh, and at other places the limestone is rich in fossils, and in the vicinity of Cairo geologists can easily form a considerable collection of them. The quarrymen on the Mokattam offer visitors fossil crabs (*Xanthopsis Paulino-Wurtembergicus*) and sharks' teeth for a moderate bakhshîsh

To the south of Edfu the nummulite limestone disappears, being replaced by marl and rocks of calcareous and sandy character, which, according to Figari-Bey, contain chalk fossils. After these we come to quartzose sandstone, belonging to the middle chalk formation, and forming considerable cliffs at the Gebel Selseleh, which confine the river within a narrow bed

This last formation, known as 'Nubian sandstone', which covers many thousands of square miles of Nubia and the Sûdân, was the material almost exclusively used for the construction of the ancient temples of Upper Egypt; and near Selseleh, and in the Arabian desert between Keneh and Koṣêr, are still to be seen the extensive quarries which yielded the material for the colossal structures of Thebes.

From Assuân to Selseleh the Nile flows through Nubian sandstone, but near the ancient Syene a transverse barrier of granite and 'syenite' advances from the east, forming the boundary between Egypt and Nubia.

This barrier extends eastwards for about 150 miles, forming a very irregular chain of barren hills 900-1300 ft in height.

The Nile has forced a passage for itself through this hard rock, exposing to view at places the beautiful red felspar crystals which it contains, and forms a wild cataract at Assuân. Near the cataracts are the deserted quarries of the ancient Egyptians, where to this day we still observe a number of unfinished gigantic obelisks, and columns half hewn out of the solid rock

(2) The Arabian Desert Parallel with the coast of the Red Sea, a broad and massive range of mountains, consisting of crystalline rocks (granite, syenite, diorite, porphyry, hornblende slate, gneiss, mica-slate, etc), runs through the Arabian Desert, sending forth numerous ramifications into the interior of the country. At Ḥammâmât, on the caravan-route from Kosêr to Thebes, we pass the quarries whence the dark-coloured stone (aphanite, diorite, and verde antico) used for the ancient sarcophagi and sphinxes was obtained by the Egyptian sculptors. Near the Red Sea, almost opposite the southern extremity of the peninsula of Sinai, rises the Gebel Dukhân, which yielded the beautiful red porphyry (porfido rosso) so highly prized by the Greeks and Romans at a later period, and used by them for vases, columns, sarcophagi, busts, and mosaics. The granite quarries of the Gebel Fatîreh yielded both building stone and copper Most celebrated of all, however, were the emerald mines of the Gebel Zebâra, situated on the Red Sea in the latitude of Selseleh.

This extensive range of mountains of crystalline formation, rising to a height of 6600 ft, of which those of the peninsula of Sinai form a counterpart, terminates towards the east in roof-shaped, stratified formations. At first there occurs a considerable stratum of Nubian sandstone, next to which we find a series of clayey and calcareous strata, identified by Figari-Bey with the Triassic and Jura formations, probably erroneously, as the collection of specimens of the rock at lorence shows that apparently the chalk alone is completely developed These strata are succeeded by extensive masses of limestone, belonging to the nummulite formation, and stretching to the Nile. Among these last formations is found the pale yellow, brownish, and snow-white alabaster, a kind of limestone composed of nodulous masses, which was formerly quarried at the ancient Alabastron near Siût, and still occurs on the Gebel Urakam near Beni-Suêf. In the reign of Mohammed ʿAli this alabaster was largely used in the construction of his alabaster mosque (p. 263), and it was extensively exported in ancient times for the embellishment of buildings and for sculptural purposes Blocks of it are even found among the ruins of the Oasis of Ammon.

These extensive mountains, with their numerous profound ravines and boldly shaped masses of rock, impart a most imposing character to the Arabian Desert. This region is by no means so destitute of vegetation as is usually supposed, for, although without oases, it contains, particularly in the N. part, a number of springs and natural cisterns, which are filled by the rare, but often copious, rains of winter.

(3) The Libyan Desert. This region again presents an entirely different character. It consists of an immense, monotonous, and stony table-land, 650-1000 ft. above the level of the Nile, extending between the Nile and the oases of Khârgeh, Dâkhel, Farâfra, and Bahrîyeh. Throughout this vast area there occur neither mountains, nor valleys, nor even isolated hills of any considerable height; and there is no trace of crystalline or volcanic formations. The surface of the desert rises in gradations, each preceded by a broad girdle of isolated mounds, which have been obviously formed by erosion, the materials having been washed down from the adjoining plateau The whole of this stony and absolutely unwatered plain, the monotony of which is only varied by a few solitary ranges of sand-hills, consists of nummulite limestone. In the direction of the oases it descends in precipitous slopes, furrowed with numerous ravines, and occasionally nearly 1000 ft. in height. The different strata of the earlier nummulite formation, as well as those of the upper chalk, are here exposed to view, and generally contain numerous fossils. The

oases, particularly those of Dâkhel and Khârgeh, are remarkable for their fossil wealth The soil of the deep depressions in which these oases lie, partly below the level of the Nile, consists of the variegated clayey or sandy strata of the upper chalk The ground is so strongly impregnated with alum at places that it was thought worth while about thirty years ago to erect manufactories for its preparation, but the undertaking was afterwards abandoned owing to the difficulties of transport. Numerous thermal springs well up from the upper strata of the chalk, and the soil thus irrigated is luxuriantly clothed with vegetation (see p. 64).

The barrier of Nubian sandstone which abuts on the valley of the Nile at Selseleh extends far into the Libyan desert. It forms the south-western boundary of the oases of Khârgeh and Dâkhel, beyond which it stretches for an unknown distance into the heart of the desert. This formation contains silicified wood and iron and manganese ores in abundance.

About six days' journey to the W. of the oases begins a complete ocean of sand. As far as the eye can reach we discover nothing but a vast expanse of loose yellow sand, which generally forms itself into ranges of sand-hills, many miles in length, and occasionally rising to a height of 300 ft or upwards above the level of the plain.

The oasis of Farâfra lies in a recess eroded in the nummulite limestone, and enclosed by precipitous slopes, except on the S side where there is an opening. To the N and W. of Farâfra extends the eocene limestone plateau as far as the neighbourhood of Sîwa, between which oasis and Bahrîyeh it is remarkable for its numerous basin-shaped and sharply defined depressions These basins, especially those which are filled with salt-lakes, impart a peculiarly attractive character to the scenery. The whole of the desert around the Oasis of Ammon consists of recent tertiary deposits, the fossil wealth of which was once extolled by Herodotus and Eratosthenes

Approximately speaking, the Libyan Desert consists of Nubian sandstone, the upper chalk, the nummulite limestone, and the more recent tertiary formations, arranged in this sequence, and extending in broad successive strips from S.S.E. to N N W.

The Oases *(by Prof. P Ascherson)* In the midst of the Libyan Desert, the most bleak and desolate part of the whole of the African Sahara, at a distance of several days' journey to the W of the Nile, there have existed since hoar antiquity a number of highly favoured spots, which are abundantly irrigated by subterranean supplies of water, and richly covered with vegetation almost vying in luxuriance with that of the valley of the Nile. The Coptic word 'Wâh', according to Brugsch, is of ancient Egyptian origin, and signifies an inhabited station; in its Greek form 'oasis' (properly Οὔασις or Αὔασις), the word is used as the geographical term for irrigated and cultivable spots, or islands of vegetation, in the midst of the stony and sandy ocean of the desert

Four of the five Egyptian oases lie in a somewhat curved line drawn from S.E. to N.W., and converging at the S. end to the valley of the Nile: — (1) *Wâh el-Khârgeh*, i.e. 'the outer oasis' (already so named by Olympiodorus in the 5th cent. A D.), or Oasis-Major of antiquity, situated 3-4 days journey from Thebes or from Girgeh on the Nile. (2) *Wâh ed-Dâkheliyeh*, or more commonly *Dâkhel*, i e the 'inner oasis' (also so named by Olympiodorus), 3 days' journey to the W. of Khârgeh, and about 6 days' journey from the valley of the Nile near Siût. (3) *Farâfra* (i.e. the bubbling springs), about 5 days' journey to the N N W. of Dâkhel, and 8-10 days' journey from the valley of the Nile near Siût. (4) *Sîwa*, anciently the celebrated oasis of Jupiter Ammon, 16 days' journey to the W.S W of Alexandria and about 14 from Cairo. The direct route from Sîwa to Farâfra (traversed by Rohlfs and Zittel in 1874 in $10^1/_2$ days) is little known as yet, as most European travellers make the long circuit towards the E. viâ — (5) *Wâh el-Bahrîyeh*, i e 'the northern oasis', or Oasis Minor of antiquity, situated $5^1/_2$ days' journey to the S.W of Medinet el-Fayûm, about 4 days' journey from Behnesch in the valley of the Nile, 9 days from Sîwa, and 5 days from Farâfra.

The oases always lie at a considerably lower level than the stony plateau of the desert, which rises above them in picturesque rocky precipices, and the oasis of Sîwa is about 78 ft. below the sea-level. The flat surfaces of these depressions do not always form a single cultivated area, but consist, even in the case of the smallest oases like Farâfra, of a number of comparatively small parcels of cultivable soil, separated by belts of sterile ground. One of the large oases, like that of Khârgeh, when surveyed from the neighbouring heights, presents the appearance of a large expanse of desert, flecked with isolated spots of light and dark green, the former being fields of corn and other crops, and the latter palm-groves. These islands of vegetation, the extent of which depends on the copiousness of the springs in their midst and the amount of care used in the distribution of the water, have often since the time of Strabo been not inaptly compared to the spots on a panther's skin, but the simile applies to the oases individually, and not to those of the Libyan desert as a whole, as they are but few in number and very far apart.

As already observed, these Libyan oases owe their fertility to the copiousness of their water supply. Inexhaustible subterranean channels, or an immense reservoir, perhaps common to all the oases, are believed to connect them with the Nubian Nile, or possibly with the Sûdân; and of this supply it is probable that a very limited portion only comes to the surface in the form of springs. Within the last thirty years Hasan-Effendi, a well-digger from the valley of the Nile, and formerly servant to a French engineer, has sunk about sixty new wells in the oasis of Dâkhel, some of which, though close to older wells, do not seem to diminish the copiousness of the latter. With the aid of this additional supply a large area of sterile soil has been brought under cultivation, and it is therefore probable that by means of Artesian wells, such as those sunk by the French in the Algerian oases, the extent of the cultivable soil might still be largely increased. The high temperature of the water, both in the natural springs and in the wells, shows that it comes from a great depth; and it is strongly impregnated with mineral ingredients, as in the case of the bath-springs of Kasr Dâkhel and Bahrîyeh (97° Fahr.), and the beautiful sun-spring ('Ain Hammâm) at Sîwa (85°), the curative properties of which, owing to their remote situation, are seldom utilised. At Bahrîyeh the stratum from which the water more immediately bursts forth seems to lie at no great depth below the surface of the soil. The thermal waters of Dâkhel contain iron, and, like those of Farâfra and Khârgeh, are not unpleasant to drink when cooled; but the water of Sîwa is brackish and nauseous to the taste. The wells are generally very deep (90-320 ft. and upwards), and in ancient times the inhabitants of the oases, as we are informed by Olympiodorus, were celebrated for their skill in sinking them. The invasion of the Arabs, however, was succeeded by several centuries of barbarism, during which the art of boring wells was well nigh forgotten; many wells were filled up, and extensive tracts of cultivated land, still traceable by the old divisions of the fields, were abandoned; but, as above mentioned, the practice is beginning to be revived. The considerable force with which the water comes up from its profound reservoirs enables the inhabitants to construct wells or artificial dams on the highest parts of the oases. The fields are always arranged in terraces of picturesque appearance, over which the fertilising element is conducted downwards in succession, so that the laborious system of sâkiyehs and shâdûfs used in the valley of the Nile is dispensed with. Among the southern oases, on the other hand, we frequently observe extensive water-conduits, carried by artificial embankments to long distances for the purpose of conveying the precious liquid over sterile salt ground to good soil, or necessitated by the requirements cf the curiously involved rights of property. These conduits not unfrequently cross each other at different levels. The springs are generally the property of the communities, rarely that of wealthy individuals; and it is in proportion to their number, and that of the date-palms, that the inhabitants have to pay taxes, while the soil itself is nominally free.

Where the springs are common property, the periodical distribution of the water has from time immemorial formed the subject of statutory regulations. The cultivable land consists of open fields and of gardens, which are carefully enclosed with earthen walls about 6 ft. high, crowned with twisted palm-leaves, for the purpose of keeping out intruders, or are more rarely hedged in with branches of the sunt or other thorny plant

In the oases, as in the valley of the Nile, a regular rotation of winter and summer crops is observed (comp p 72), although, with their uniform supply of water, there is not the same necessity for it The winter crops are wheat and barley; those of summer are rice, dura (*Sorghum vulgare*), and a small proportion of dukhn (*Penicillaria spicata*), while in Dâkhel and Khârgeh indigo is grown in considerable quantities Cotton is also cultivated to a small extent, but the yield is hardly adequate for even the local requirements By far the most important fruit yielded by the gardens is that of the date-palm. The delicious dates are very superior to those of the Nile valley, and they form, particularly at Dâkhel and Sîwa, the only important article of export Olive-trees also occur in all the oases, especially in Farâfra, Bahriyeh, and Sîwa, where they yield a considerable quantity of oil, besides which there are apricots, oranges, lemons, and melons, but very few other fruit trees. The ordinary vegetables grown in the valley of the Nile, such as lettuces, cabbages, and kulkâs, are never met with, nor have the recently introduced sugar-cane and the beautiful lebbek acacia (p 76) yet found their way to the oases. The venerable sunt-trees (p 77) form a very characteristic feature of the southern oases They generally shade the wells, or the sites of old wells now filled up owing to neglect, and they indicate the course of the water-conduits to the still distant traveller.

The most prominent of the indigenous plants of the oases is the 'oshr (*Calotropis procera*), which is also common on the banks of the Nile in Upper Egypt It is a broad-leaved shrub or small tree, attaining a height of 6 ft or more, with a copious milky and very poisonous sap, and round fruit of the size of a large apple containing woolly seeds, and known on the banks of the Dead Sea as the 'apple of Sodom'.

The indigenous animals of the oases are much fewer in number than those of the valley of the Nile The only large mammal that occurs is the gazelle, which is also found in the sterile parts of the Libyan desert. The only beasts of prey are several varieties of jackals (Arab. *dib*) and foxes (Arab. *ta'leb*) Among the latter is the pretty fenek, which is only half the size of the European fox, yellowish-grey in colour, and with ears longer than the breadth of the head Hyenas seem to be unknown, except in Bahriyeh The timid ostrich rarely visits the Libyan oases

The domestic animals kept by the inhabitants of the oases consist of a few horses, numerous donkeys of a small and weakly type, which will not bear comparison with their strong and active congeners of Alexandria and Cairo, and a few oxen, sheep, and goats Buffaloes are also kept in Khârgeh and a few in Bahriyeh. It is surprising how few camels are to be found in the oases, but it is said that the bite of a certain fly endangers their lives in summer Turkeys and fowls are plentiful.

The population of the oases is not of a uniform character. According to Brugsch, the original inhabitants were Libyan (or Berber) tribes, but after the oases were annexed to Egypt many new settlers were introduced from the valley of the Nile and from Nubia The Berber nationality of the inhabitants of the oasis of Ammon, notwithstanding its having been connected with Egypt for several thousand years and its reception of immigrants from the west in the middle ages, is still very marked, while the population of the other oases, like that of the Nile valley, has adopted the Arabic language In Bahrîyeh (where, besides the natives of the place, there is a colony of Sîwanese who still speak the Berber dialéct) and Farâfra the physiognomic type of the Berber race still predominates; in Dâkhel the features of most of the population are not materially different from the fellâh type; while in Sîwa, through which the great caravan route from Alexandria and Cairo viâ Murzuk to the Sûdân leads, and in Khârgeh, which lies on the route to Dâr-Fûr, the admixture of negro blood imparts its unmistakable stamp to the features of the inhabitants There are no Coptic settlers in the oases, but they are sometimes temporarily met with there in the capacity of merchants or government clerks; and Europeans are still more rarely encountered. The population of the oases is comparatively small (Khârgeh, according to Schweinfurth, possessing 6340 souls; according to Rohlfs, Dâkhel 17.000, Farâfra 320, Bahrîyeh about 6000, and Siwa 5600), and the narrow limits of the cultivable soil prevents it from increasing; but a more auspicious era may now be in store for these isolated communities if they follow the example set by the inhabitants of Dâkhel by sinking fresh wells and thus extending their territory. As a rule, even in the most favourably circumstanced oasis of Dâkhel, the physique of the population is poor and stunted, owing partly to their almost exclusive vegetable diet (of which Prof Virchow has found evidence in the condition of the teeth of skulls from the ancient tombs of Dâkhel), and partly to the unhealthiness of the climate, which has been notorious from the remotest antiquity In the early Egyptian period, and also during the domination of the Roman emperors, the oases were generally used as places of banishment, partly because their isolation rendered escape well nigh impossible, and partly perhaps because the climate was expected to aggravate the misery of the exiles The overplus of the water used for agricultural purposes forms a series of marshes, ponds, and lakes on the saline soil, and these last contribute greatly to the picturesqueness of the landscape in Siwa, which is farther enhanced by a number of isolated rocky heights; but the exhalations of these watery tracts in summer are very unhealthy Within the last few centuries this evil has been aggravated by neglect, and the artificial swamps required for the rice cultivation are fraught with additional danger. Some measure for utilising the superfluous water, or at least rendering it harmless, is perhaps more urgently needed for the well-being of the oases than an increase of the water supply Under present circumstances Europeans had better abstain from visiting the oases from the beginning of April till the end of November, but in the winter months they may visit them safely. With regard to the construction of the dwellings in the oases it may be remarked that they all have more or less the character of town-houses, as, even at the present day, the unsafe state of the country requires them to be strongly built in close proximity to each other. Instead of the low hovels of the Nile valley, we therefore find in all the oases houses of several stories in height, somewhat rudely built of mud (and sometimes of stone, as at Bahrîyeh) and palm logs A curious feature of these towns (recurring in the other oases of the Sahara also, as, for example, in the famous commercial town of Ghadames, to the S.W. of Tripoli) is the covered streets running under the upper stories of the houses, and sometimes of such length as to be perfectly dark. As, moreover, like most Oriental streets, they are generally crooked, it is hardly prudent for a stranger to venture into them without a guide. The main street of the town of Siwa winds in this manner up the rocky eminence on which the houses are built, and the place is indeed in this respect one of the most curious in the East

As is usually the case with places lying at a distance from the outer world, the government of these communities is in the hands of the most respectable and wealthy members; and at Farâfra this paternal oligarchy is under the control of no government. Even at Siwa the Mudîr appointed by the Egyptian goverment finds it difficult to assert his authority, and it is only the interminable and sometimes bloody quarrels of the leading parties of the Lifâyeh and the Gharbîn (of whom the latter, as the name indicates, are immigrants from the west) that afford him an opportunity of interposing in his judicial capacity. In the other oases also, down to the middle of the present century, the power of the government officials was always to a great extent paralysed by that of the obstinate shêkhs; but after the repression of the Beduin revolt Sa'îd Pasha succeeded in firmly establishing the viceregal authority in the oases also. Since that period peace has reigned throughout the oases, and as the pressure of taxation is not nearly so heavily felt here as in the valley of the Nile the inhabitants are comparatively wealthy. Of late years, however, they have occasionally suffered from the predatory attacks of nomadic marauders from the Cyrenaica, and even by the Arabs of the Nile valley. A new disturbing element, too, has unfortunately sprung up within the last ten years in Sîwa, Bahrîyeh, and Farâfra, in the establishment and rapid spread of the Senûsi order of Mohammedans, by whom the introduction of all Christian culture is bitterly opposed This religious order was founded about the middle of the present century by Sîdi Snûsi (or Senûsi, as the name is pronounced in Eastern Africa, where the vowels are more distinctly pronounced than by the Moghrebbins of Algeria and Morocco), a tâlib (or scripture scholar) of Tlemsen in Algeria, for the purpose of restoring the observance of Islâm to its original purity, and, above all, of warring against Christianity Although the members of the order are regarded by other Mohammedan sects as Khoms, or heretics, they have rapidly acquired great power in the districts surrounding the eastern Sahara, and, like the Jesuits in Christian countries, have amassed considerable wealth, their principal treasury being at Sarabûb, the chief seat of the order, two days' journey to the W. of Siwa Sarabûb is also the residence of Sîdi-Mahdi, the general of the order and son of its founder, who has succeeded in obtaining certain privileges from the Sultan of Turkey. At Sîwa he has established a richly endowed Zâwiyeh, or school of religion; at Farâfra the Zâwiyeh is all-powerful, having within the ten years of its existence bought up a considerable part of the landed property there, and at Bahrîyeh the order has succeeded in monopolising the schools, so that the rising generation may be expected to succumb to their influence. The hostility of this new sect to all modern culture is obviously a serious obstacle to the progress which the Egyptian government is now anxious to promote.

Climate. The climate of Egypt is to some extent influenced by the great artery on which the country's life depends, but the desert may be regarded as its chief regulator. But for the immense absorbing power of the desert the winter rains of the Mediterranean regions would extend far up the Nile valley; and, but for its proximity, the great expanse of nearly stagnant water at the mouths of the Nile, covering an area of upwards of 2500 sq. M., would render the Delta one of the most unhealthy and uninhabitable regions in the world. The air of the desert is pleasantly cool, and possesses the most refreshing and health-giving qualities; indeed, to borrow Bayard Taylor's expression, it is a true 'elixir of life'. To the delicious purity of the air † of the desert a kind of parallel is afforded by the excellence of the water of the life-giving Nile.

Rain, throughout a great part of Egypt proper, is a very rare phenomenon. At Cairo the fogs of winter are rarely condensed into showers of any duration, and the rain occasionally blown inland from the sea seldom lasts long. Observations carried on at Cairo for five years show a mean annual rainfall of only 1½ inch, while the mean at Alexandria for a period of fourteen years was 8 inches. The unusual frequency of rain during the last few years has been absurdly attributed to the great increase of the area planted with

† It may be noticed here that the air is largely impregnated with saline particles from the limestone rocks of the desert, and it is chiefly to their presence that the beneficial effect of the air on the respiratory organs is supposed to be due

trees, a boon which the country owes to the government of the Khedive Isma'il. The winters of these same years were also unusually wet in Greece and other regions adjoining the Mediterranean where but little rain generally falls, so that the weather of these exceptional seasons was doubtless affected by unknown climatic influences extending far beyond the limits of Egypt. The recent formation of the extensive Bitter Lakes in the Isthmus of Suez has also no influence on the climate except in their own immediate neighbourhood. If the banks of the Red Sea still remain desert in spite of the huge evaporating surface beside them, what change of importance could be expected from the artificial creation of a few square miles of water? The whole of the base of the Delta lies within the region of the winter rains, which from January to April are blown inland by the then prevailing sea-breezes to a distance of 30-50 English miles. In Upper Egypt, on the other hand, rain is almost unknown, and it is not uncommon to meet with adult natives who have never seen a single shower. In that part of the country a thunder-shower, or perhaps the extreme fringe of the tropical rains, falls at rare intervals in April or May to the no small wonder of the natives. These showers are more frequent above the first cataract and they recur regularly a little to the N. of New Donkola or 'Ordeh (19° N. lat.), while to the S. of Shendi there is annually a short wet season, with its concomitants of malaria and fever. The rainfall in the deserts on each side of the Nile is very unequally distributed, but of these regions also it is approximately true that rain is of very partial and sporadic occurrence. Thus there are vast tracts of the Libyan desert which for years together derive their sole moisture from the damp north and north-westerly winds, and when the wind is in any other quarter they are even deprived of their nightly refreshment of dew. On the Arabian side the case is materially different. There, along the coast of the Red Sea, runs a range of mountains 4800-10,000 ft. in height, where occasional, but very violent showers fall between October and December, hollowing out the deep valleys which descend to the Nile. Although these desert rains are of too short duration permanently to affect the character of the country, their fertilising effect on the light and loose soil is far greater than if they had to penetrate a heavier soil covered with thick vegetation.

As the year is divided in the valley of the Nile by the rise and fall of the river into two well-defined seasons, one when the soil is moist and easily cultivated, and the other when nothing will grow without artificial irrigation, so also it may be divided in accordance with the prevalent WINDS into two different periods of eight and of four months. North winds prevail as a rule from the middle of June to the middle of February, and south (S.E. and S.W.) during the rest of the year (while in the Red Sea the prevalent winds at these seasons are almost exactly in the reverse directions). Early in the afternoon of a day during the second of these seasons the wind, as is the case in all tropical regions, sometimes rises to a hurricane, in which case it is called a 'Samûm'. Of this wind there are two or three different varieties: (1) It is called a 'Shôbeh' when it blows chiefly from the east, and (2) a 'Merîsi' when it comes directly from the south. In the latter case it is also sometimes called a 'Khamsîn', but this name more properly applies to the very hot, dry, and dust-laden winds which frequently blow unremittingly for one or two whole days together, and render the climate peculiarly trying in March and April (comp. p. 2).

The name **Khamasîn**, as it is more correctly written, is the plural of *Khamsîn*, signifying 'fifty', and is applied to these winds in consequence of the fact that they prevail only during a period of fifty days before the summer solstice, after which they invariably cease. The Arabs confine this name to the period, and name the winds themselves *shard*. The wind to which the name is applied in winter affords but a feeble idea of the Khamsîn of the hotter season, which forms the only disagreeable feature of the Egyptian climate, and one from which there is no escape. The impalpable sand finds its way into the most carefully closed rooms, boxes, and even watches, and the parching heat is most destructive to the blossoms of fruit-trees.

In accordance with the TEMPERATURE the Egyptian year may also be divided into two seasons, a period of hot weather, lasting eight months (April to November), and a cool season of four months (December to March). Throughout the whole country the heat gradually increases from April till the middle or end of June, and many of the superstitious natives believe that a perceptible freshening of the air takes place on the night of the 'dropping' (17th June; see p. 239). In Alexandria the blowing of the N. N.W. wind sometimes interrupts the regular increase of the heat, so that the maximum may be reached as early as May or June or may be postponed to September or October. The maximum heat in the Delta is about 95° Fahr. in the shade, in Upper Egypt about 109°. At Cairo the thermometer sometimes rises as high as 114° during the prevalence of the Khamsîn. In December, January, and February the temperature is at its lowest, falling in the Delta to 35°, in Alexandria to 40°, and in Upper Egypt to 41°. The quicksilver rarely sinks to the freezing-point, except in the desert and at night. On 16th Feb. 1874, during Rohlfs' expedition in the Libyan desert, the thermometer fell to 23°. About sunrise the traveller will sometimes find a thin coating of ice in his basin, or on neighbouring pools of water, where, owing to the rapid evaporation, the temperature falls several degrees lower than in the surrounding air. As a rule, throughout the whole country, and at every season, the temperature is highest from 1 to 5 p.m., and lowest during the two hours before sunrise. The result of the observations of ten years has been that the mean temperature in the Delta and at Cairo is 58° Fahr. in winter, 78° in spring, 83° in summer, and 66° in autumn. M. Pirona's observations, carried on for fourteen years, fix the mean temperature on the coast near Alexandria at 60° in winter, 66° in spring, 77° in summer, and 74° in autumn. At Alexandria the summer days are much cooler and the winter nights much warmer than at Cairo, but the moisture of the air makes the heat much more oppressive. In the drier air the constant absorption of moisture from the skin keeps the body at a much lower temperature than that of the surrounding air, and thus renders the great heat of the desert much more bearable than one would expect. The strong sea-breezes at Alexandria also make the heat of summer less oppressive than it is at many places on the Mediterranean situated much farther to the N.

As three different thermometers are used in Europe, — those of Fahrenheit, Celsius, and Réaumur (1° F. $= {}^5/_9{}^\circ$ C. $= {}^4/_9{}^\circ$ R.), — the traveller may find the following table convenient for reference.

Fahrenheit	Réaumur	Celsius	Fahrenheit	Réaumur	Celsius	Fahrenheit	Réaumur	Celsius	Fahrenheit	Réaumur	Celsius
+124	+40.89	+51.11	+99	+29.78	+37.22	+74	+18.67	+23.33	+49	+7,56	+9,44
123	40.44	50.56	98	29.33	36.67	73	18.22	22,78	48	7.11	9,89
122	40.00	50.00	97	28.89	36.11	72	17.78	22,22	47	6,67	8,33
121	39.56	49.44	96	28.44	35.56	71	17.33	21.67	46	6.22	7,78
120	39.11	48.89	95	28.00	35.00	70	16.89	21.11	45	5,78	7,22
119	38.67	48.33	94	27.56	34.44	69	16.44	20.56	44	5,33	6,67
118	38.22	47.78	93	27.11	33.89	68	16.00	20.00	43	4,89	6,11
117	37.78	47.22	92	26.67	33.33	67	15.56	19.44	42	4,44	6,56
116	37.33	46.67	91	26.22	32.78	66	15.11	18.89	41	4,00	5,00
115	36.89	46.11	90	25.78	32.22	65	14.67	18.33	40	3.56	4,44
114	36.44	45.56	89	25.33	31.67	64	14.22	17.78	39	3.11	3.89
113	36.00	45.00	88	24.89	31.11	63	13.78	17.22	38	2,67	3.33
112	35.56	44.44	87	24.44	30.56	62	13.33	16.67	37	2,22	2,78
111	35.11	43.89	86	24.00	30.00	61	12.89	16.11	36	1.78	2.22
110	34.67	43.33	85	23.56	29.44	60	12.44	15.56	35	1.33	1,67
109	34.22	42.78	84	23.11	28.89	59	12.00	15.00	34	0,89	1,11
108	33.78	42.22	83	22.67	28.33	58	11.56	14.44	33	0,44	0,56
107	33.33	41.67	82	22.22	27.78	57	11.11	13.89	32	0,00	0,00
106	32.89	41.11	81	21.78	27.22	56	10.67	13.33	31	—0,44	—0,56
105	32.44	40.56	80	21.33	26.67	55	10.22	12.78	30	0,89	1.11
104	32.00	40.00	79	20.89	26.11	54	9.78	12.22	29	1.33	1,67
103	31.56	39.44	78	20.44	25.56	53	9.33	11.67	28	1.78	2,22
102	31.11	38.89	77	20.00	25.00	52	8.89	11.11	27	2,22	2,78
101	30.67	38.33	76	19.56	24.44	51	8.44	10.56	26	2,67	3,33
100	30.22	37.78	75	19.11	23.89	50	8.00	10.00	25	3,11	3,89

Agriculture. I. Capabilities of the Soil. In the time of the Pharaohs the Egyptian agricultural year was divided into three equal parts, the period of the inundation (from the end of June to the end of October), that of the growing of the crops (from the end of October to the end of February), and that of the harvest (from the end of February to the end of June). At the present day there are two principal seasons, corresponding to our summer and winter, besides which there is a short additional season, corresponding with the late summer or early autumn of the European year. The land is extremely fertile, but it is not so incapable of exhaustion as it is sometimes represented to be. Many of the crops, as elsewhere, must occasionally be followed by a fallow period; others thrive only when a certain rotation is observed (such as wheat, followed by clover and beans), and some fields require to be artificially manured. Occasionally two crops are yielded by the same field in the same season (wheat and saffron, wheat and clover, etc.). The recent great extension of the cultivation of the sugar-cane, which requires a great deal of moisture, and of the cotton-plant, which requires extremely little, has necessitated considerable modifications in the modes of irrigation and cultivation hitherto in use. As both of these crops are of a very exhausting character, the land must either be more frequently left fallow, or must be artificially manured. The industry and powers of endurance of the Egyptian peasantry are thus most severely tried, and no imported agricultural labourers could ever hope to compete with them, as has sometimes been thought possible. Although the homogeneous soil of the valley of the Nile breaks up of its own accord after its irrigation, and requires less careful tilling and ploughing than ours, it exacts more uniform attention throughout the whole year, while its irrigation involves a great additional amount of labour to which the European farmer is quite unaccustomed. The increasing use of artificial manures, which were formerly but little known, is another source of great labour. As the country is thickly peopled and supports numerous cattle, there ought to be no lack of natural manure; but, as the dung of the domestic animals is used as fuel throughout Egypt, where wood is very scarce, that of pigeons (p. 79) is almost the only kind available for agricultural purposes. An abundant source of manure is afforded by the ruins of ancient towns, which were once built of unbaked clay, but now consist of mounds of earth, recognisable only as masses of ruins by the fragments of pottery they contain. Out of these mounds, which conceal the rubbish of thousands of years, is dug a kind of earth sometimes containing as much as 12 per cent of saltpetre, soda, ammonia, and other salts. This manure possesses extremely fertilising properties, but if used at the wrong time or place is very injurious to the soil.

II. Irrigation. The whole of the cultivable soil of Egypt is divided into two classes in accordance with its relative height above the surface of the Nile: (1) The '*Rai*', or fields which retain their moisture after the subsidence of the overflow long enough (or nearly long enough) to admit of the ripening of the crop without additional irrigation; (2) The '*Sharâki*', or those which always require artificial irrigation. The irrigation is effected by means of (1) The '*Sâkiyeh*', or large wheels (rarely exceeding 30 ft. in diameter), turned by domestic animals of various kinds, and fitted with scoops of wood or clay, resembling a dredging-machine. (In the

Fayûm a peculiar kind of water-wheel is in use, so contrived as to
be turned by the weight of the water.) According to Figari-Bey,
the number of sâḳiyehs used in Central and Lower Egypt in 1864
was about 50,000, which were turned and superintended by 200,000
oxen and 100,000 persons, and which irrigated 4,500,000 acres of
land. (2) The '*Shâdûf*', an apparatus resembling that of an ordinary
well, set in motion by one person only, and drawing the water in
buckets resembling baskets in appearance; as a substitute for the
sâḳiyeh several shâdûfs are sometimes arranged one above the other.
(3) When it is possible to store the water in reservoirs above the
level of the land to be watered, it is allowed to overflow the fields
whenever required. This is the only method available in the oases,
where fortunately the water rises from the springs with such force
as to admit of its being easily dammed up at a sufficiently high
level. (4) Pumps driven by steam are also used, particularly when
a large supply of water is required, as in the case of the sugar-
plantations on the 'Gefs' of the Nile in Northern Egypt, where they
are seen in great numbers. (5) Lastly the '*Tâbût*', a peculiar, very
light, and easily moved wooden wheel, which raises the water by
means of numerous fans, is used in the Lower Delta only and in
places where the level of the water in the canals remains nearly
the same   In order to distribute the water equally over flat fields,
they are sometimes divided into a number of small squares by means
of embankments of earth, 1 ft. in height, which, owing to the great
plasticity of the Nile mud, are easily opened or closed so as to
regulate the height of the water within them.

Before describing the different Egyptian agricultural seasons,
we must first observe that they are no longer so sharply defined as
they probably were in ancient times. Besides the old crops, there
are now several others of recent introduction, and so extensively
grown as in some measure to revolutionise the modes of cultivation.
These are maize, rice, the sugar-cane, cotton, ramieh, and indigo.
(This last plant was known to Pliny, but it was probably grown in
his time only to a very limited extent.) The agrarian measures of
the Egyptian government are all directed towards the emancipation
of farming from its dependence upon the inundations, in order that
every crop may be cultivated at the season in which it thrives
best. The embankments and various apparatus for the regulation
of the water supply, recently constructed or founded by the government, vie in importance with the greatest ancient works of the kind.

III. AGRICULTURAL SEASONS. (1) The *Winter Crop*, or '*Esh-
Shitâwi*', grown exclusively on the 'Raï' land (p. 71), is sown
immediately after the subsidence of the inundation, which takes
place progressively from S. to N. In Upper Egypt seed-time accordingly begins as early as the middle of October, in Central Egypt
(from Siût to Cairo) at the beginning of November, and in the
Delta about the end of December. The ground is seldom prepared

for sowing by the use of the plough. The seed is scattered over the still soft and moist soil, and is then either pressed into it by means of a wooden roller, beaten into it with pieces of wood, or trodden in by oxen†. Throughout the whole country a period of four months elapses between seed-time and the completion of the harvest. The winter harvest is, therefore, over in Upper Egypt about the middle of February, in Central Egypt about the middle of March, and in the Delta towards the end of April. In Upper and Central Egypt this is the most important harvest of the whole year. The principal crop everywhere is wheat (occupying 50 % of the fields in Upper Egypt and 30 % in the Delta), next to which are barley (in the proportion of 10 % and 14 % in these regions respectively), clover (10 % and 24 % respectively), and broad beans (20 % and 12 % respectively)

(2) The *Summer Crops* (*'Eṣ-Ṣêfi'* or *'El-Kêḍi'*) are much more varied than those of winter, but they are comparatively unimportant in Upper and Central Egypt, as the cultivable land in these regions is very narrow, and belongs chiefly to the 'Rai' category, two-thirds of it being under water during summer. In the Delta, on the other hand, summer is the farmer's most important season The vegetation with which its whole surface is densely clothed in June and July is marvellously rich and beautiful, thousands of magnificent trees clustered in groups afford delightful shelter from the fierce rays of the sun, and the eye ranges over an immense expanse teeming with luxuriant crops. Another charm of the country in summer consists in its abundantly stocked gardens and orchards but of all these attractions the traveller who, like a bird of passage, merely seeks refuge in Egypt from the cold and rains of a northern winter cannot possibly form any adequate idea At this season every dis-

---

† The Agricultural Implements of the Egyptians are exceedingly primitive and defective. The chief of these is the plough (*mihrât*), the form of which is precisely the same as it was 5000 years ago, and the traveller will recognise it on many of the monuments and in the system of hieroglyphics It consists of a pole about 6 ft long, drawn by an ox, buffalo, or other beast of burden, attached to it by means of a yoke, while to the other end is fastened a piece of wood bent inwards at an acute angle, and shod with a three-pronged piece of iron (*lisân*) Connected with the pole is the handle which is held by the fellâh These rude and light ploughs penetrate but slightly into the ground (On the estates of the Khedive, Fowler's steam-plough is now frequently employed.) The harrow is replaced in Egypt by a roller provided with iron spikes (*kumfud*, literally 'hedgehog'). The only tool used by the natives on their fields, or in making embankments of earth, is a kind of hoe or shovel (*migrafeh*) The process of reaping consists of cutting the grain with a sickle, or simply uprooting it by hand The *nôrag*, or 'threshing-sledge', consists of a kind of sledge resting on a roller provided with sharp semicircular pieces of iron, and drawn by oxen or buffaloes. This primitive machine, being driven over the wheat, peas, or lentils to be threshed, crushes the stalks and ears and sets free the grain or seeds The corn is separated from the fragments of straw by the careful removal of the latter, and by tossing it to and fro in a draughty place The grain is afterwards passed through a sieve

trict of Egypt has its favourite crop, in Upper Egypt, between Assuân and Esneh, the penicillaria, and in the Delta rice are chiefly cultivated, while the peculiar looking indigo-plant, a rich profusion of grapes, and a plentiful growth of cucumbers and melons are seen in every part of the country. The summer cultivation, of which the 'Sharâḳi' land alone is capable, is carried on from April to August; but many of the plants grown at this season require a longer period of development, extending throughout the whole of the autumn and even part of the winter. This is particularly the case with the rice crop, which is sown in May, but does not attain maturity till the middle of November, and with the cotton-plant, sown in April, and harvested in November or December. A large quantity of cotton is also yielded by a second harvest from the pruned plant in the month of August, in the second year of its growth. Summer is also the principal season for the tobacco crop.

(3) The *Autumn Season ('En-Nabâri' or 'Ed-Denûri')*, as already observed, is of very subordinate importance, being sometimes occupied, as in the case of rice and cotton, in bringing the summer crops to maturity. It is also the shortest season, extending to little more than seventy days, and yet within this brief space the rich soil of the Delta yields its harvest of maize, which, next to wheat, is the most important of the Egyptian cereals. (The annual yield of these two grains is said to amount to 24 million bushels.) The autumn cultivation lasts from August to October, and sometimes till November. At the beginning of October, throughout the whole Delta from Suez to Alexandria, the traveller will observe an almost unbroken ocean of maize-fields, seldom varied except by the low villages, resembling mounds of earth, with their neighbouring palm groves. The picture of teeming fertility which the country then presents far surpasses that presented by the rich maize-fields of south-eastern Europe. In Central Egypt maize is also an important summer crop. Along with it is sometimes cultivated the less common Sorghum, or Dura, or Indian millet, which is eaten by the poorest fellâhîn only. It is, however, largely consumed by the Beduins on the Arabian side of the Nile, and in the Sûdân and Nubia forms the chief food of the inhabitants. Another plant cultivated in autumn, rarely seen in Egypt, but common in the Sûdân and Nubia, is the tropical Sesame, from which oil is largely prepared.

4. **Farm Produce of Egypt.** The following is an enumeration of all the most important industrial crops cultivated within the boundaries of Egypt. On hearing the names of those with which he is unacquainted, the traveller may identify them with the aid of the Egyptian names given below. The various products are enumerated in the order of their importance.

a. CEREALS. 1. Wheat (*ḳamh*; that from the Delta, *ḳamh bahri*; from Upper Egypt, *ḳamh sa'îdi*). 2. Maize (*dura shâmi*, i. e. Syrian; called in Syria *dura* only). 3. Barley (*sha'îr*). 4. Rice (*ruzz*), cultivated only in the lower part of the Delta of Alexandria and Rahmânîyeh, as far as Mansûra, Zaḳâzîk, Sâlihîyeh, and in the Wâdi Tumîlât, and also in the Fayûm and in the oases of the Libyan desert. 5. Sorghum vulgare (*dura beledi*, i. e. dura of the country; simply called *dura* in the Sûdân; Ital.

sorgho, Engl. *caffercorn*, and the Tyrolese *sirch*). 6 Penicillaria (*dukhn*) 7. Sorghum saccharatum

b. Podded Fruits 1 Broad beans (*fûl*). 2. Lentils (*'adas*) 3 Chick-peas (*hummus*) 4. Lupins (*turmus*). 5 Peas (*bisilla*) 6. Dolichos Lubia (*lûbiya*). 7. Dolichos Lablab (*lablab*), which is very frequently seen festooning walls and pinnacles, but is also grown in fields in separate plants. 8. Vigna Sinensis 9 White beans (*lûbiya frengi*) 10. Phaseolus Mungo 11. Horse beans (*Canavalia gladiata*)

c. Green Crops 1 White Egyptian clover (*bersîm*) 2 Fœnum Græcum (*helbeh*, frequently ground into flour and used in making bread, also generally eaten raw by the natives in winter, not to be confounded with clover) 3 Medicago sativa, or lucerne (*bersîm hegâzi*) 4 Lathyrus sativus, or flat pea (*gulbân*). 5 Sorghum halepense (*gerau*)

d Stimulants. 1 Virginian tobacco, or Nicotiana Tabacum (*dukhân ahmar*). 2 Peasant's tobacco, or Nicotiana rustica (*dukhân akhdar*) 3. Poppies, for the manufacture of opium (*abu-num*, or 'father of sleep') 4. Indian hemp (*hashîsh*; comp p 18).

e. Textile Materials 1 Cotton (*kotn*), introduced from India in 1821, but extensively cultivated since 1863 only 2 Flax (*kettân*) 3 Hemp (*tîl*) 4 Hibiscus cannabinus

f. Dyes. 1. Indigo argentea, a peculiar kind (*nîleh*) 2. Lawsonia inermis (*henna*), used for dyeing the nails, the palms of the hands, and the soles of the feet yellowish red (a very ancient custom, which has recently been prohibited); properly a tree, but, like the tea-plant, cultivated in fields in the form of a dwarfed bush. 3 Saffron (*kartam* or *'osfur*) 4 Madder (*fûa*), cultivated in small quantities 5 Reseda Luteola (*blîya*), used as a yellow dye

g. Oil Plants 1 Castor-oil plant (*khirwa*) 2 Sesame (*sim-sim*). 3. Lettuce (*khass*), very largely cultivated. 4 Rape (*selgam*). 5 Chicory (*hendebeh*) 6 Mustard (*khardal*, or *kabar*) 7 Arachides, or earth-nuts (*fûl sennâri*, or simply *fûl*) 8. Saffron (as an oil-yielding plant) 9 Poppy (as an oil-plant) 10. Garden cress, or Lepidium sativum (*rishâd*)

h Spices 1 Capsicum annuum, the Italian peperone (*filfil ahmar*) 2. Capsicum frutescens, or Cayenne pepper (*shatta*) 3 Aniseed (*yansûn*, or *ânîsûn*). 4 Coriander (*kusbara*) 5 Caraway (*kemmûn*). 6 Nigella (*kemmûn aswad*) 7 Dill (*shamâr*) 8 Mustard

i The Sugar Cane (*kasab es-sukkar*) has of late been largely cultivated in the N. part of Upper Egypt for the purpose of being manufactured into sugar An inferior variety, which is eaten raw, introduced from India in the time of the khalifs, is cultivated in every part of the country

k Vegetables. 1 Bamyas, or Hibiscus esculentus (*bamiya*). 2 Onions (*basal*) 3 Pumpkins (*kar'a*) 4 Cucumbers (*khiyar*) 5 Egyptian cucumbers (frequently trumpet-shaped and ribbed, different varieties called *'abdelâwi*, *'agûr*, etc) 6 Melons (*kâwûn*, the best, *shammâm*) 7. Water-melons (*battîkh*) 8 Melonzanes (*bâdingân*) 9 Tomatoes (*tomâtin*). 10 Corchorus olitorius (*melûkhîyeh*) 11 Colocasia (*kulkâs*). 12 Garlic (*tûm*). 13 Mallows (*khobbêzeh*) 14 Cabbage (*korumb*) 15 Celery (*kerafs*) 16 Radishes, a peculiar kind, with fleshy leaves, which form a favourite article of food (*figl*). 17. Lettuces (*khass*) 18 Sorrel (*hommêd*) 19 Spinach (*es-sibânikh*). 20. Parsley (*bakdûnis*). 21 Purslane (*rigl*) 22 Turnips (*lift*) 23. Carrots (*gezer*, a peculiar kind, with red juice) 24 Beetroot (*bangar*) A variety of other vegetables are cultivated in small quantities in gardens, exclusively for the use of European residents.

5. **Trees and Plantations.** During recent years new avenues and parks have been so extensively planted that Egypt will soon present a far greener and more richly wooded appearance than formerly. In ancient times every square foot of arable land seems to have been exclusively devoted to the cultivation of industrial crops, the natives preferring to import from foreign countries the timber they required for ship-building purposes, and

probably also the small quantity employed in the construction of their temples. The best proof of the scarcity of good timber in Egypt is afforded by the fact that sycamore-wood, one of the worst possible kinds owing to the knottiness and irregularity of its grain, has been laboriously manufactured into coffins and statues. Mohammed 'Ali, a great patron of horticulture, at one time offered prizes for the planting of trees, but his efforts were unattended with success, as the climatic and other difficulties attending the task were then but imperfectly understood in Egypt. His successors were sworn enemies to trees of every kind, and they were content that their palaces should be exposed to the full glare of the sun. The Khedive Isma'il, however, at length revived the plans of his celebrated ancestor, and by the engagement of M. Barillet (1869), superintendent of the gardens of Paris, one of the most skilful landscape-gardeners of the day, introduced an entirely new feature into Egyptian scenery. This enterprising and able man unfortunately died (1874) before all his plans had been carried out, but the eye of every new-comer will rest with pleasure on the parks and gardens for which Egypt is indebted to him. While, for example, the traveller had formerly to ride all the way to the Pyramids over sterile soil, exposed to the scorching rays of the sun, he now drives comfortably thither in a carriage on a well-shaded road. M. Barillet's most important works are the Ezbekîyeh Garden at Cairo, the extensive pleasure-grounds at Gezîreh, and the plantation of trees which shades the roads on the left bank of the Nile, opposite the city. Hundreds of thousands of trees were planted within a few years, and their annually increasing shade has converted many of the dusty and stifling roads in and around Cairo into pleasant promenades. The finest of all these trees, both on account of its umbrageousness and the excellence of its wood, and one which thrives admirably, is the *lebbek* (Albizzia Lebbek), which has long been erroneously called by travellers the acacia of the Nile (the latter being properly the *sunt* tree). Within forty years the lebbek attains a height of 80 ft. and a great thickness, while the branches project to a long distance over the roads, densely covering them with a dense leafy canopy within a remarkably short time. Thus, an avenue planted in 1866 near the German Protestant church already forms a complete arcade over the road. Another very valuable and interesting property of the tree is, that cuttings consisting of branches more than a foot thick, and even portions of the trunk, will strike root and thrive, while in the case of most other trees the cuttings must consist of mere twigs. In the course of a single summer the shady avenues leading to the Pyramids were thus formed. About two hundred different kinds of trees, chiefly of E. Indian origin, are now planted in the parks of the Khedive (about twenty in number), and they are constantly multiplied in nurseries laid out for the purpose. Among the most important of these are the magnificent 'Flamboyer des Indes' (Poinciana pulcherrima) and the rapidly-growing Eucalyptus, tropical fig-trees, and several rare varieties of palms.

The commonest Trees of an Earlier Period which the traveller will encounter in every town in Egypt are the following — The Acacia Nilotica *(sunt)*, the thorn-tree of antiquity, the pods of which, resembling rosaries *(gárrat)*, yield an excellent material for tanning purposes. Next to the palm, this is the tree most frequently seen by the way-side and in the villages. The Acacia Farnesiana *(fatneh)*, with blossoms of delicious perfume. The sycamore *(gimméz)*, anciently considered sacred The zizyphus, or Christ's thorn-tree *(nebk)* Tamarisks *(tarfa;* not to be confounded with tamarinds) The Parkinsonia *(sésebán,* a name also applied to the wild Sesbania shrub). Mulberry-trees *(tût)*, in Lower Egypt only. Carob-trees, or bread of St John *(kharrûb)* The cypress, olive, poplar, plane, myrtle, Aleppo pine, Shinus, Melia, and various fig-trees of Indian origin are of less frequent occurrence.

Among the Fruit Trees the most important is the date-palm *(nakhleh*, the date, *balah;* the rib of the leaf, *gerîd*, the leaf, *lîf;* the points of the leaf, *sa'af*, the crown, *gummâr)* There are no fewer than twenty-seven kinds of date commonly offered for sale The largest attain a length of three inches, and are called *ibrîmi*, or *sukkôti*, as they come from N Nubia. The most delicately flavoured are the small dark brown ones known as *amhât*, which are eaten fresh. The Beduins offer for sale at the hotels a kind of date-preserve packed in what professes to be gazelle-skins, but is usually goats' leather *('agweh)* Palm-wine *(lagbi)*, obtained by boring the heart of the crown of the palm, whereby the tree is killed, is met with in the oases only. Excellent brandy, however, is distilled from the fruit The value of the dates exported annually amounts to about one million francs only, as they realise too high a price in the country itself to remunerate the exporter. The date-palms blossom in March and April, and the fruit ripens in August and September. Fresh dates are rough in appearance, blood-red or pale yellow in colour, and harsh and astringent in taste. Like the medlar, they become more palatable after fermentation has set in.

The vine thrives admirably in Egypt, and grapes *('oenab)* abound from July to September. Wine was extensively made from them in ancient times, and this might still easily be done, were it not that Egypt is already amply supplied with cheap and excellent wines from every part of the Mediterranean The vine blossoms in March and April, like the palm, and the grapes ripen in June and July. Oranges are abundant and cheap (the harvest beginning in September), and so also are mandarins and lemons (the small and juicy fruit of the Citrus limonium), citrons, and cedros are of less frequent occurrence Among other fruit-trees we may also mention the pomegranate *(rummân)*, which is specially cultivated for the benefit of the Turks, who are very partial to them, and which yields a handsome return. Apricots are common, but quite destitute of flavour, and the same remark applies to the peaches *(khôkh);* almonds *(lôz)* are also frequently seen. Throughout the whole of Lower Egypt figs *(tîn)* abound in summer, and the cactus-fig *(tîn-shôk)* is also a favourite fruit Apples, quinces, pears, and plums abound, particularly in the region of Girgeh and in the Fayûm, but these last are perfectly tasteless; these fruits, moreover, are so abundantly brought to the market from the Mediterranean regions that no attempt is made to extend their cultivation in Egypt Within the last ten years the banana *(môz)* has gradually become naturalised in Egypt, but it is still a somewhat expensive fruit (1-1½fr per pound). A delicacy imported from the W Indies for the benefit of strangers is the Anona squamosa *(kishta*, i e 'cream') Pine-apples are very rarely seen Fine tropical fruits of this kind (including also the mango) are only to be found in the gardens of the Khedive, where, however, their capability of acclimatisation has been abundantly proved

The principal Decorative Plants are roses *(ward;* of which the Rosa Damascena moschata and the sempervirens are specially cultivated for the manufacture of otto of roses), oleanders of astonishing height, carnations, and geraniums, all of which have been grown in Egypt from a very early period A bushy tree, which in its half leafless condition attracts the attention of every traveller on landing at Alexandria in winter, is the Poinsettia pulcherrima. The insignificant blossom is surrounded by leaves of the most brilliant red, presenting a very picturesque and striking appearance Natural forests, or even solitary wild trees, are never met with in the valley of the Nile or in the valleys of the northern deserts. On the embankments and on the brink of the rivers we occasionally find wild tamarisks and willows (*safsâf*), but always in the form of mere bushes In the desert-valleys of Upper Egypt, however, grow five different kinds of acacia and several other shrubs of inferior interest. Another tree of considerable importance is the beautiful *dûm* palm, which grows wild in the valleys of S Nubia and even in the oases, but those which occur in N Egypt are always planted Even in Lower Egypt it is not met with beyond 27° N latitude (indeed hardly beyond Keneh), and attempts to acclimatise it at Cairo have never been successful. Lastly we may mention two circumstances which throw some light on the botanical position of Egypt One of these is, that the commonest weeds associated with the industrial crops of Egypt, and which occur nowhere else, are of E Indian origin; and the other, that numerous plants cultivated by the Egyptians are only now to be found in their wild condition in the central regions of Africa

The Animal Kingdom in Egypt. (By *Dr M Th. v Heuglin.*)

I DOMESTIC ANIMALS The *Horse* (*hosân*; horses, *khêl*; mare, *faras*; foal, *muhr*; the rider, *khayyâl*) was probably unknown to the most ancient Egyptians, and was first introduced by the Hyksos (p 88). It is now to be met with throughout the whole of the valley of the Nile, and even in the oases Owing to want of proper care and insufficiency of food, the Egyptian horses are generally of insignificant appearance.

The Egyptian *Donkey* (Arab *homâr*; comp p. 11) is noted for its power of endurance, its spirited temper, and its moderate requirements.

The *Mule* (Arab. *baghl*, or *baghleh*), although admirably adapted for carrying heavy burdens, is less frequently bred in Egypt, but is sometimes imported from Abyssinia, Spain, and other parts of southern Europe, Syria, and Asia Minor.

The *Camel* (Arab *gemel*, fem *nâka*; the camel for riding, *hegîn*), was not unknown to the ancient Egyptians, as it is mentioned in several papyri, but it was probably rarely used, particularly during the early monarchy. During the hottest weather the camel can dispense with water for three days or more, while its scanty provender consists of a few handfuls of maize or beans, of the dry and wiry desert grass, of straw, or of prickly acacia leaves

The *Buffalo* (Arab *gamûs*) seems to have been long domesticated in Egypt Its flesh is not esteemed, but the cows yield milk and butter The buffalo requires little food and attention, but does not thrive except in swampy ground or in the vicinity of flowing water The hide forms strong and valuable leather

The *Ox* (Arab. *tôr*; cow, *bakara*; calf, *'igl*; milk, *leben*; sweet milk, *halîb*, sour milk, *hâmed* or *rôb*) thrives in Egypt on the dry soil of the arable land, and is also reared in the oases Down to the year 1863 Egypt possessed a long-horned race of oxen which is often represented on the monuments, but the breed was entirely swept away by a cattle-plague during that year. The fellâhîn make both butter and cheese from the milk Instead of a churn they use a leathern bag suspended from a rope (*kirbeh*)

The *Goat* (Arab *me'za* or *'anzeh*; he-goat, *tês*; kid, *gidi*) is to be found in every cottage on the banks of the Nile, and in every tent in the desert Its milk is palatable and wholesome. The hide makes durable and waterproof water-bags

Sheep (Arab *kharûf*, *na'geh*, *ghanam*, *ramis*; ram, *kebsh*) are almost as generally kept by the Egyptian peasantry as goats, the most esteemed being the fat-tailed varieties *(ovis pachycera recurvicauda* and *ovis platyura)*. The wool of the Egyptian sheep is harsh and wiry, while many of those in the desert have stiff, straight hair, and are altogether destitute of wool.

The *Pig* (Arab. *khanzîr*), which was regarded by the ancient Egyptians as the emblem of Typhon, and is considered unclean by the Arabs, can hardly be called one of the domestic animals of Egypt, but it is kept by the Greek tavern-keepers.

The *Dog* (Arab *kelb*) throughout the whole of the East is a masterless and half-wild animal. The usual breed resembles the jackal type, its colour being of a light rusty tint. Every canine family has its regular beat, from which intruders are rigorously excluded Most of the Egyptian dogs feed on street refuse

The *Cat* (Arab *kott*, *kotteh*), which was one of the sacred animals of the ancient Egyptians (comp p 136), is now domesticated in almost every Egyptian and Beduin family.

The *Weasel (mustela semipalmata;* Arab. *'ersa*, or *abu 'arûs)*, is occasionally kept, like the cat, for the purpose of keeping in check the mice of numerous kinds with which the country is infested It is chiefly met with in a half-wild condition in Central and Lower Egypt, in the towns, farm-buildings, warehouses, and deserted dwellings

Foremost among the various kinds of poultry kept by the Egyptians is the domestic *Hen* (Arab *farkha;* cock, *dik*), the usual breeds of which are of small size. The artificial hatching establishments in Egypt are of very ancient origin

. The *Turkey* (Arab. *farkha rûmi*) is imported

The domestic *Goose* (Arab. *wuzzeh*) is chiefly met with in Lower and Central Egypt, but nowhere in large numbers The Egyptian *Domestic Pigeon* (Arab *hamâm*) is very common throughout the Nile Valley. The peasants erect large dovecots for these pigeons, which they keep solely for the sake of the manure they yield

II Wild Animals As there are no game-laws in Egypt, any one provided with a license from the police to carry fire-arms is at liberty to shoot anywhere and at any season, provided enclosed gardens be not entered, and growing crops respected Permission to shoot on Lake Menzaleh, however, must be obtained from the farmer of the fishings, an introduction to whom may easily be procured from the traveller's consul at Cairo.

Tolerable guns and other requirements for the *chasse* may be purchased at Cairo (p. 235), but gunpowder is bad and dear Sportsmen who bring their own guns will find it very troublesome to clear them at the custom-house

One of the favourite objects of the chase is the Arabian *Mountain Goat (Ibex beden;* Arab *beden* or *wa'al)*, which still frequents the mountains between the Nile and the Red Sea

Another inhabitant of the mountains is the '*Maned Sheep*' *(Ovis tragelaphus;* Arab *kebsh el-md*, or *kebsh el-gebel)*, which is occasionally met with among the rocky hills near Minyeh and in the neighbourhood of the Fayûm

A denizen of the plains between Cairo and Suez, and of the sand-hills and heights which bound the valley of the Nile and the oases, is the *Dorcas Gazelle (Antilope dorcas*, Arab *ghazâl)*, particularly during the dry and hot season.

On the Libyan side of the Nile, in the region of the Natron Lakes and the Fayûm, and the tract extending thence to the oases, occur also the 'Spear Antelope' *(Antilope leptoceros;* Arab *abu-'l harâb)* and the *Addax Antelope (Antilope addax;* Arab *a'kas*, or *bakar el-wahsh)*, besides which the Arabs mention a kind of '*Cow Antelope*' (perhaps the *Antilope bubalis)*

The *Wild Boar* (Arab *hallûf*) now occurs in a few districts only in the Delta and the Fayûm

In similar localities the sportsman will also meet with the *Marsh Lynx (Felis chaus;* Arab. *tifah)*, the small-footed *Wild Cat (Felis manicu-*

lata, Arab *kott*), the Egyptian *Wolf* (*Canis variegatus*; Arab *dîb*), and the *Ichneumon* (*Herpestes ichneumon*; Arab *nims*), which last, however, prefers gardens and the neighbourhood of farms and villages.

The *Genet* (*Viverra genetta*; Arab *kott zebâd*) is said to be met with occasionally in Egypt. Among the beasts of prey common in the lower part of the Nile Valley we may also mention the various species of *Foxes* and *Jackals* (*Canis vulpes*, *C. mesomelas*, *C. niloticus*, *C. aureus*, *C. famelicus*, and *Megalotis zerda*, Arab. *abu-'l-husên*, *âleb* or *ta'leb*, *abu shôm* or *bashôm* and *abu sûf*) and the *Skunk* (*Rhabdogale mustelina*; Arab *abu 'afen*). The fox and the jackal haunt cliffs, quarries, ruins, and heaps of rubbish. The long-eared *Fennec* (Arab *Fenek*, *Zerdo*), a kind of fox which subsists partly on vegetable food, lives gregariously in extensive burrows which it excavates in the sand of the desert.

Another beast of prey of frequent occurrence is the striped *Hyena* (*Hyaena striata*, Arab *dab'a*), which usually secretes itself among ruins, quarries, or rocks during the day, and scours the country at night in search of dead or disabled domestic animals. The professional Egyptian hyena hunters (Arab *dabba'a*), who are to be met with in many parts of the country, will generally undertake to catch any wild animal of which the traveller desires a specimen, and their services as guides to the sportsman will often be found useful.

An animal of rare occurrence in Egypt, being confined to the side of the Egyptian coast-hills next to the Red Sea, is the *Porcupine* (*Hystrix cristata*; Arab *abu shû'a*, or *hanhan*, or *en-nîs*), which lives in deep hollows excavated by itself.

On the banks of the Nile, and particularly in Upper Egypt, the Egyptian *Hare* (*Lepus aegyptiacus*; Arab. *arnab*) is frequently met with. It usually haunts those tracts which are overgrown with tamarinds.

Among the mountains of Sinai we frequently observe the *Daman*, or *Cony* (*Hyrax syriacus*; Arab *wabr*), which lives in troops on the cliffs and stony slopes, and often lies basking in the sun on overhanging rocks, especially in the forenoon.

Wild fowl abound in Egypt, and frequently come within range of the sportsman's gun. Among these are the *Ganga* or *Sand Grouse* (*Pterocles exustus*, *Pt. guttatus*, and in Upper Egypt the *Pt. coronatus* also; Arab *kata*), and the *Red Partridge* (*Ammoperdix Heyi*; Arab *hagel*), which frequents the hills around the cataracts at Assuân, the E. slopes of the Arabian mountains in the direction of the Red Sea, and Mt. Sinai and its environs, extending as far as the Dead Sea. A kind of *Red-legged Partridge* (Arab *abu zerad*, or *sena*) is also found in the Sinai range. The *Quail* (*Coturnix communis*, Arab *summan*, or *selû*) usually visits the Nile valley during its spring and autumn migrations only.

On the N. coast of Egypt the *Little Bustard* (*Otis tetrax*) is frequently seen in winter, and farther to the W. occurs the '*Collared Bustard*' (*Otis habara*, Arab *habara*).

We may also mention the *Nile Goose* and the *Turtle Dove* (*Turtur senegalensis* and *T. isabellinus*; Arab *kumri*) as natives of Egypt. The Nile Valley and the lagoons of the Delta are also largely visited by BIRDS OF PASSAGE. Many of these proceed still farther to the S., but by far the greater number remain for three or four months among the swamps of Lower Egypt, and in the region of the Natron Lakes and the Birket el-Kurûn in the Fayûm.

Among the numerous water-fowl, including ducks and flamingoes, several species of heron, and perhaps swans also, which breed in the Delta and partly in the Fayûm, are the superb '*Sultan Bird*' (*Porphyrio smaragdonotus*; Arab *dikmeh*) and the beautiful *Golden Snipe* (*Rhynchaea capensis*).

Lastly we must mention the *Crocodile* (Arab. *timsah*), the largest and most famous of Egyptian reptiles, which sometimes attains a length of thirty feet. Although gradually disappearing before the march of modern civilisation, it is still sometimes to be found in the valley of the Nile above Girgeh, and more frequently between the cataracts of Assuân and the Wâdi Halfa, while occasionally, having lost its way during the inundation, it descends to the vicinity of the Delta Crocodiles are sometimes seen fast asleep, often with widely opened jaws, basking in the sun on flat sandbanks or on the ends of low islands, to which they most frequently resort after cool nights In Egypt, however, where it is oftener hunted than in more southern regions, the crocodile is generally too wary to be caught napping, though it sometimes becomes entangled in the nets and falls a prey to the fishermen The Arabs of the Sûdân, who eat the flesh of the reptile and prepare a kind of musk from its glands, frequently angle for it with large hooks baited with meat

It is seldom worth while to fire at crocodiles when swimming, as they usually disappear in the turbid water, even when mortally wounded The sportsman should therefore endeavour to get within range of one of these monster saurians when on shore As they always keep within easy reach of the water, they are occasionally observed on the banks of the river by the traveller navigating the Nile, in which case they should be approached in a small boat as noiselessly as possible. Success is most likely to be achieved in cases where the haunt of the reptile is known, so that the sportsman may lie in ambush at some convenient spot in the vicinity Unless, as rarely happens, the first bullet kills the animal on the spot, it generally contrives to find its way back to the water, and thus effects its escape.

Another saurian of great power, and extremely rapid in its movements, is the *Monitor* (Arab *waran*), which attains a length of 4-5 ft., and derives its name from its supposed habit of giving warning of the approach of a crocodile

III Other Mammalia and Birds. Although not indigenous to Egypt, several varieties of *Apes*, which are imported from the S and W provinces, are seen in the larger towns Among these are the *Cynocephalus hamadryas* and *C. anubis* (both called *ḳird* by the Arabs), the *Inuus ecaudatus* (Arab *nisnas*), the *Cercopithecus ruber*, *C griseo-viridis*, and, more rarely, the *C pyrrhonotus*

The Nile Valley and the neighbouring desert hills are largely infested by *Bats* (Arab *watwat*). The commonest kinds are the *Kalong (Pteropus)*, the *Long-eared Bat (Plecotus, Vespertilio Taphozous, Nyctinomus)*, and the *Spectre Bat (Rhinolaphus, Nycteris, Rhinopoma)*

Besides the beasts of prey already enumerated (p 79), we may also mention the *Mustela Africana*, several kinds of *Hedgehog (Erinaceus;* Arab *ḳonfud)*, and the *Shrew* (Arab *umm sîsi)*

Egypt contains numerous species of the Rodentia The fields, dwelling-houses, and sailing-vessels are often infested with *Mice* and *Rats (Mus, Acomys)*, and in the Sinai Peninsula is found the *Dormouse (Eliomys melanurus)*, all of which are called *fâr* by the Arabs The *Jumping Mouse (Dipus;* Arab. *yerbû'a)* and the *Sand Mouse (Meriones,* Arab *gebeli)* live in the desert, and the '*Fat Rat*' *(Psammomys obesus)* in the sand-hills around Alexandria

Besides the Birds indigenous to Egypt, there are, as already mentioned, a great number which winter there, while others merely pass through the country when on their way to other regions About 360 different species have been ascertained to occur in Egypt, but we shall merely enumerate a few of the most important of those which remain permanently in the country

The commonest *Birds of Prey* are the *Golden Vulture (Gypaetus meridionalis;* Arab *big)*, the *White-headed Vulture (Vultur fulvus,* Arab. *nisr)*, the *Eared Vulture (V auricularis)*, the *Goose Vulture (V cinereus)*, which, however, is a bird of passage only, the *Carrion Vulture (Neophron percnopterus,* Arab. *rakhameh)*, the *Harrier (Milvus aegyptiacus;* Arab *hedâyeh)*, and the *Elanet (Elanus melanopterus)* The white-tailed *Sea Eagle (Haliaetus albicilla;* Arab *'oḳab,* or *shomêta)* breeds in the Delta, the *River Eagle (Pandion haliaetus;* Arab *mansûr* or *ḳetaf)* on the cliffs of the Red Sea, the *Dwarf Eagle (Aquila pennata)* among the palm-groves of Lower Egypt, and the *Lanner Falcon (Falco lanarius variet.;* Arab. *shâhîn)* and *Falco barbarus* on the pyramids and rocky heights Great numbers of '*Screaming Eagles*' pass the winter in Egypt. Of rarer occurrence are the *Imperial Eagle*, the *Hawk Eagle*, the *Migratory Falcon*, the *Stone* and *Red-footed Falcons*, the white-tailed *Buzzard*, the *Hawk*, and the *Sparrow-hawk* (Arab *bâz*). Several species of the European *Harrier* are more common than these last The *Tower Falcon* breeds in every part of Egypt, and probably the *Castrel Hawk (Falco cenchris)* also. The *Gabar (Nisus gabar)* is said to be sometimes met with in Upper Egypt.

The commonest *Owls* are the sub-tropical *Church Owl (Athene noctua var.;* Arab. *umm kûḳ)* and the *Eagle Owl (Bubo ascalaphus;* Arab. *bûm*, or *bufa)*

The family of *Goatsuckers* is represented in Egypt by the peculiar *Caprimulgus aegyptiacus* A small *Swift (Cypselus parvus)*, the chief representative of its family, frequents the regions planted with the dûm palm. The *Swallows (khottâf*, or *ʿasfûr el-yenneh)* most frequently seen are the red-breasted *Hirundo cahirica*, which remains permanently in the country, and a kind of *Rock Swallow (Cotile obsoleta)*

Of the *Fishing Birds* the most common is the *Kingfisher (Ceryle rudis)*, which frequents the banks of every part of the Nile.

The *Bee Eaters* are represented by the *Merops apiaster*, the *M. aegyptiacus*, and the *M viridissimus*, all of which breed in Egypt; but the last only, which is called *shehagh* by the natives, and chiefly occurs in Central and Upper Egypt, remains throughout the year

The most numerous of the *Thin-billed Birds* are the *Hoopoes* (Arab. *hudhud*), and to the *Promeropides* belongs the pretty, lustrous *Honey-sucker (Nectarinia metallica)*, which frequents the frontiers of Upper Egypt

Singing Birds (ʿasfûr) are not numerous in Egypt, with the exception of numerous species of *Larks* and *Stonechats* We may next mention the *Drymoeca*, or *Drymoecus gracilis*, the *Cisticola cursitans*, the *Tree Nightingale (Aedon galactodes)*, the *Acrocephalus stentoreus*, the African *Water-wagtail (Motacilla vidua)*, the *Wedgetail (Argia acaciae)*, and the *Bulbul (Pycnonotus Arsinoe*, found in the Fayûm and N Nubia, while a second species, the *P. xanthopygius* occurs in Arabia Petræa and the valley of the Jordan)

There are no *Flycatchers* peculiar to Egypt Among the *Butcher-birds* we may mention the '*Masked Shrike*' *(Lanius nubicus)*, and among the *Ravens (ghurâb)*, the *Short-tailed Raven (Corvus affinis)* and the *Desert Raven (C umbrinus)*. The lofty mountains of the Sinai Peninsula are the haunt of the *Red-legged Crow (Fregilus graculus)*, and among the tamarisk bushes and on the rocky margins of the valleys of Arabia Petræa occurs the *Starling (Amydrus Tristramii)*

Among the *Finches* peculiar to Africa is the '*Desert Trumpeter*' *(Bucanetes githagineus)* On the upper part of the Nile, beyond the Wâdi Ḥalfa, occur several species of a more tropical character such as the *Fire-finch (Euplectes franciscana)*, the *Steel-finch (Hypochera nitens)*, the '*Lancetail*' *(Uroloncha cantans)* and the *Dwarf Bloodfinch (Lagonosticta minima)*

Woodpeckers are not met with on the Lower Nile The *Wryneck* and grey *Cuckoo* occur as birds of passage, and the *Spurred Cuckoo (Centropus aegyptiacus*, Arab *abu burbur)* as a denizen of the Delta The *Jay (Coccystes glandarius)* is more widely diffused throughout the country.

Among the native *Running Birds* we may mention the *Desert Runner (Cursorius isabellinus)*, the *Stone Curlew (Oedicnemus crepitans;* Arab. *kerwân)* the *Crocodile-Watcher (Pluvianus aegyptiacus;* Arab *ṭêr et-timsâh)*, and the sprightly *Spurred Plover (Hoplopterus spinosus*, Arab. *siksak)* The commonest of the *Herons* are the '*Cow Heron*' *(Ardea Ibis;* Arab. *abu kerdân)* and the white '*Great Heron*' *(Ardea alba* and *Ardea garzetta)*. Near the Wâdi Halfa occurs the *Abdim Stork (Ciconia Abdimii;* Arab. *simbileh)* To the family of the *Ardeidae* belong the rare *Ibis Tantalus* and the *Sacred Ibis (Ibis aethiopica*, Arab *naʿaneh herêz*, or *abu mingal)*.

Besides the European aquatic and other birds already enumerated, which frequent the lagoons, lakes, and marshes (p 81), we may also mention the *Rose-backed Pelican (Pelecanus rufescens)* of N.Nubia; the curious *Scissor-beak (Rhynchops flavirostris;* Arab *abu mokâs)* and the *Fox Goose (Chenalopex aegyptiacus;* Arab *wiz)*, which are found throughout the whole of the Nile Valley, the former especially in summer; and the

Brown Booby (*Sula fiber*; Arab *shomet*), several peculiar species of *Gulls* and *Sea Swallows* (*Larus leucophthalmus*, *Larus gelastes*, *Larus Hemprichii*, *Sterna media*, *Sterna Bergii*, *Sterna albigena*, *Sterna infuscata*, and *Anous stolidus*), and the singular-looking *Dromas* (Arab *hankôr*), on the shores of the Red Sea. The *Flamingo* (*Phœnicopterus antiquorum*; Arab. *bûsha rosh*) haunts the Red Sea and the lagoons of the Delta throughout the whole year, usually congregating in enormous flights, and breeds in the region to the E of Lake Menzâleh

IV. Reptiles. Of this class of animals there are but few species peculiar to Egypt. The *Salamanders* and *Batrachians* (Arab *dufda'a*) are but scantily represented There are about twenty species of *Snakes* (Arab *ta'bân*), including the *Horned Viper* (*Cerastes*; Arab *mohâreneh*) which appears in the ancient inscriptions as a hieroglyphic, the *Echis* (Arab *gharibeh* or *dashshâsha*), the *Cobra da Capello*, *Hooded*, or *Spectacle Snake* (*Naja Haje*; Arab *nâsher*), the *Telescopus* (Arab *abu 'ayûn*), the *Psammophis* (Arab. *abu suftr*), the *Tropidonotus*, the *Periops* (Arab. *arkam*), the *Zamenis* (Arab *gidari*), and the *Eryx* (Arab *dassâs*). The horned viper, the echis, and the hooded snake are highly venomous, and their bite is often fatal, the other snakes are not venomous, but their bite is sometimes dangerous. The Egyptian snake-charmers (Arab *hawi*), all of whom belong to a gipsy tribe (*ghagar*), usually exhibit a number of cobras, the teeth in which the venom is secreted having been extracted (comp p 81)

To the order of the *Saurians* belong the *Crocodile* (*Crocodilus vulgaris*, Arab *timsâh*), of which there are several varieties, and the *Monitor* (*Varanus niloticus*; Arab *waran*), both of which have been already mentioned (pp. 80, 81) Other species occurring in Egypt are the *Ablepharus*, the *Gongylus*, the *Plestiodon*, the *Euprepes*, the *Scincus* (Arab *sakankûr*), the *Ophiops*, the *Eremias* and *Acanthodactylus* (Arab *sehliyeh*), the *Psammosaurus griseus* (Arab *waran*, a name also applied to the monitor), the *Uromastix spinipes* (Arab *dab*), the *Uromastix viridis*, the *Stellio vulgaris* (Arab. *hardûn*), several kinds of *Agama*, the *Chameleon* (Arab *herbâyeh*), and numerous *Ascalabotes* (Arab *abu burs*) To the *Turtle Family* belong the *Nile Turtle* (*Trionyx aegyptiaca*; Arab *tirsa*) and a small *Tortoise* (*Testudo marginata*; Arab *zelhafeh*), while in the Red Sea occur six varieties of *Chelonia* (Arab *bisa* or *sakar*), several of which yield excellent tortoise-shell (Arab *bagha*)

V. Fish of the Nile (by *Dr. C B Klunzinger*) The finny inhabitants of the Nile are in keeping with the palms growing on its banks, being of a tropical and African type They are generally the same as those found in the Senegal and other African rivers, while European species are very rare There are in all about 70-80 varieties The following sketch is merely designed to afford an idea of the commonest species, particularly of those brought to market Many of them are represented and described in the 'Description de l'Egypte' (p 200)

The fish of the Nile are most abundant during the time of the inundation, when a number of varieties, not found at other seasons, are brought down from the higher regions to Lower Egypt At these seasons the canals yield abundant spoil, especially after the subsidence of the water. The flesh is generally soft, watery, and insipid, but the mode of cooking it is perhaps partly in fault The colours are wanting in variety, white with a dark-coloured back predominating

To the *Perch Family* (scaly fish with serrated head-bones) belongs the *Keshr*, and to the *Carp Family* (scaly fish without teeth) belong the *Lebîs*, or *Debs*, and the *Binni*, with a thorn in its dorsal fin. The various kinds of *Siluridae* are very abundant (fish without scales, with barbels, and generally with an adipose fin) Among these are the *Shilbeh* (a fish with a high neck, a short dorsal fin near the head, and without the adipose fin), which is of three kinds, the *shilbeh 'arabi*, the *shilbeh sherîfiyeh*, and the *shilbeh wudni* (the first two with, the last without a spinous ray in its dorsal fin) The *Shâl*, called *kurkâr* in Upper Egypt owing to the sound which they emit, is easily recognised by the bony armour covering its head and its fringed barbels The varieties are the *shâl beledi*, the *shâl senîn* or *sheilân*, and the *shâl ḳamari* or *baṭn sôda*, the last of which has a blackish stomach. The *shâl karafsheh*, or *samr*, has a layer of bone over its neck. The *shal abu riyâl* more nearly resembles the following varieties The *Bayâd* and the *Dokmâk*, provided with very long barbels, and generally of large size, are abundant. Another important member of the Siluridæ is the long and large *Karmût*, with its long dorsal and posterior fins The *karmût hâleh* has an adipose fin, while the *karmût 'arabi* has none To the same family belongs also the famous *Ra'âd*, or electric eel (with one adipose fin on its back, and black spots on its skin)

The following families are peculiar to the tropics The *Characini* (salmon of the Nile) are scaly and provided with an adipose fin Among these are the high-backed and almost rhombic *Kamr el-Bahr*; the oblong *Ray* with its small and somewhat flat teeth; the *Roshâl*, or *Kelb el-Bahr* (river-dog), with strong, conical teeth protruding from its mouth; and the *Nefâsh*, with its small, narrow, and closely-set teeth with double points, and somewhat high shoulders To the family of the *Chromides* (scaly fish with spinous fins and sides of irregular shape) belongs the *Bolti*.

A family occurring in Africa only is that of the *Mormyrides*, or scaly fish with remarkably small mouths, and heads covered with a thick and bare skin Among the members of this family is the well-known *Mormyrus oxyrrhynchus* (*Kanûma*, or *Khashm el-Banât*), with its long snout turned downwards, which was so frequently represented by the ancient Egyptians, then the blunt-mouthed *Banes*, including the *Kashua* and *Kashua kamûra*, or *'Ersat el-Bahr*, the last of which has an almost square muzzle

An interesting, but not common, fish is the *Finny Pike* (*Polypterus*, Arab *abu bishir*), with its numerous dorsal fins and rhomboidal scales covered with enamel, forming one of the few surviving members of the abundant antediluvian Ganoids The *Ball Fish* (*Tetrodon*; Arab. *fakâka*), which is not an edible variety, is frequently offered for sale, either fresh or stuffed (p 236), on account of its curious shape and its singular faculty of puffing itself out like a bladder. It differs from the common ball-fish of the Red Sea in having seven brown or blackish oblique stripes on its sides. The Red Sea contains many fish of a similar kind, but they are not known to exist in the Mediterranean From the latter sea the *Harder* (Mugil), *Bûri*, or *Gharana*, frequently ascend the Nile, where they form the herrings of the Arabs (*fesîkh*) The same remark applies to the '*Finte*' (*sabûgha*), a fish resembling the herring, which occurs in many of the seas, rivers and lakes of Europe. The *Eel* of the Nile (*ta'bân el-bahr*) does not differ from that of European waters

VI Insects *Butterflies* are very rare in Egypt, but *Moths* are much more numerous Among the not very numerous *Beetles* we may mention the *Ateuchus sacer*, the celebrated Scarabaeus (p 125) of the ancient Egyptians This sacred beetle was believed to be of the male sex only, and its act of rolling the clayballs containing its eggs was supposed to be its manner of propagating its species (Plutarch de Iside, l. x. 74). The Egyptians accordingly consecrated the scarabæus to Ptah, the god of origin and creation, who is often represented on the monuments with a scarabæus in place of a human head Among other varieties occur the *Buprestis*, the *Cicindela* or sand-beetle, the *Hister*, the *Dermestes*, and numerous *Water Beetles*.

The various kinds of *Wasps* in Egypt attain a very large size. *Bees* are not often kept by the natives The so-called black honey eaten by the lower classes is sugar-cane treacle The white honey, which is the genuine produce of bees, is imported from Arabia

The commonest of the *Orthoptera* are *Grasshoppers* and *Cockroaches*; and of the *Neuroptera* we may mention the *Ephemera* or day-flies, the beautiful and often reddish-coloured *Dragon-fly*, and the *White Ant* (rare). Among the *Diptera* are the troublesome *House-fly*, and the *Mosquito*. Vermin of all kinds abound, such as *Fleas*, *Bugs*, *Lice*, *Scorpions*, *Tarantulas*, and *Centipedes*

III. Outline of the History of Egypt.

Chronological Table.

Introduction. There is no people in the world whose history is traceable to so remote a period as that of the Egyptians. Other nations may possibly have understood the art of writing as early as they, but no specimens of it have been preserved; whereas the Egyptian records, hewn in stone, burned in clay, or written on leather or on scrolls of papyrus, have survived the ravages of thousands of years. The preservation of these memorials, however, is mainly due to the dryness of the air in the rainless valley of the Nile, and to the property possessed by the hot sand of the desert of hermetically sealing everything committed to its keeping.

The remote dates with which Egyptian chronology deals seem mythical when judged by the standards of Jewish and Christian chronographers, and particularly when compared with the supposed date of the creation of the world; but they are derived from the lists given by Manetho, which have been confirmed by the monuments themselves.

The priest Manetho (Egypt. *Mai en Thot*, i e 'beloved of Thoth') of Sebennytus (the modern Semennûd, p 445), being acquainted with the Greek language, was employed by King Ptolemy II. Philadelphus (B C 284-246) to translate the ancient historical works preserved in the temples This 'Egyptian History' of Manetho enjoyed a high reputation at a later period, but was subsequently lost, with the exception of his lists of kings and their dates, which have been transmitted to us partly by Flavius Josephus, the Jewish historian (1st cent. A D.), and partly by Christian historians.

The monuments and inscriptions in some cases confirm, and in others supplement, the records transcribed by Manetho for the Ptolemies, our information being derived from the series of kings' names inscribed on tablets found at Abydus, Karnak, and Saḳḳâra, from papyrus scrolls, particularly one in the Museum of Turin, and lastly from historical and genealogical notices on the walls of temples and tombs, on statues, implements, and trinkets. A methodical mode of utilising these fragmentary historical records was first taught by the learned Prof. Lepsius (d. 1884).

The lists of the Pharaohs are arranged in the families or dynasties of the Thinites, Memphites, and others. If it be assumed that these different houses reigned in succession, and their reigns be simply added together, the sum which results is very large But, if it be assumed that many of the dynasties mentioned by Manetho reigned contemporaneously in different parts of the country, the reigns of members of the leading dynasties alone have to be added together, and a comparatively moderate sum is the result Adopting the former method of computation M Mariette has fixed the date of Menes, the first King of Egypt, as B C 5004, while Sir Gardner Wilkinson, proceeding on the latter assumption, assigns the date B C. 2700 to the same monarch Lepsius, on the other hand, believes the true date to be B C 3892, as Manetho states that an interval of 3555 years (or 3553, taking into account the difference between the Egyptian and the Julian year) elapsed between the reign of Menes, the first King of Egypt, and that of Nectanebus II (B C 340), the last of the native sovereigns. Our information becomes more definite after the beginning of the New Empire, while from the 26th Dynasty (B C 685) downwards the dates of the different kings are well ascertained.

In accordance with the arrangement of the history of Egypt

given by Lepsius, and now generally accepted, the mythical period was succeeded by that of the *Primaeval Monarchy*, the *Hyksos Domination*, and the *New Empire*, which were followed by the supremacy of the *Persians*, the *Ptolemies*, and the *Romans* in succession. Another system recognizes between the Old and the New Empire a *Middle Monarchy*, which includes the period of the Hyksos. These divisions, in conformity with the lists of Manetho, are again subdivided into *Dynasties*, or different families of kings, named after the districts or *nomes* (p. 32) of which their founders were natives.

Chronological Table.

Primæval Monarchy.

M 5004†. L. 3892 W 2700. I. DYNASTY (*Thinites*, i.e. from Teni, the Greek This, near Abydus in Upper Egypt).

Menes (Egyptian *Mena*), the first earthly king of Egypt, who is said to have founded Memphis (see p 373)

Athothis (Eg. *Teta*, p 373).

Usaphais (Eg. *Hesepti*), who is said to have written anatomical works.

II DYNASTY (*Thinites*)

III DYNASTY (*Memphites*, from Memphis, which soon obtained precedence over the more southern royal city of This).

Tosorthros (Eg. *Tefa*), who studied medicine. In his reign the calendar is said to have been regulated, and the year of 365 days introduced (consisting of twelve months of thirty days, with five supplementary days).

M 4235 L. 3124 W 2450. IV. DYNASTY (*Memphites*; p. 344).

Snefru (pp. 344, 468, 479, 491), the founder of the 4th Dynasty, and the first king of whose reign we possess contemporaneous monuments. Long after his death he continued to be highly extolled, and was even revered as a god.

Khufu (the *Cheops* of the Greeks)
Khâfrâ (the *Chephren* of the Greeks; pp. 159, 345)
Menkaurâ (the *Mycerinus* of the Greeks)
} Builders of the three great Pyramids of Gîzeh (p. 343 *et seq.*).

Khufu and Khafra have been handed down to the detestation of posterity as profligate despisers of the gods, chiefly owing to the account of them given by Herodotus (ii 124, see p. 314 *et seq.*), who, however, was ill informed with regard to the earliest period of Egyptian history The monuments themselves bear testimony to the fact that the family and court of the builders of the Great Pyramids were pious worshippers of the gods, that they were prosperous and wealthy, and that they were industrious and persevering in their undertakings. At that period the fine arts, and particularly that of sculpture, attained a perfection which the Egyptians never again reached. The inscriptions on the monuments also exhibit a high degree of technical skill.

† M is the initial letter of Mariette, L. of Lepsius, and W. of Wilkinson; comp. p 85 — The most important names only in each dynasty are given.

M. 3951 L. 2956. **V. DYNASTY** (*Memphites; pp.* 368, 372, 389, 491).

W. 2240. **VI. DYNASTY** (*Elephantines*, from Elephantine, near Syene, the modern Assuân, situated in Upper Egypt; p. 491).

Teta (p. 376).
Pepi I. (p. 402).
Pepi II. (p. 402).
Nitokris (Eg. *Neitaker*).

VII. DYNASTY (*Memphites*).

VIII. DYNASTY (*Memphites*).

IX. DYNASTY (*Heracleopolites*, from Heracleopolis Parva †, the Karba of Egyptian and Karbanis of Assyrian inscriptions, situated in the N.E. part of the Delta; see pp. 412, 453).

X. DYNASTY (*Heracleopolites*)

XI DYNASTY (*Diospolites*, from Diospolis, *i.e.* Thebes, now Eluksûr-Karnâk-Medînet Abû in Upper Egypt; pp. 160, 453).

On the coast of the Delta, which at this remote period was most probably a very swampy district, densely overgrown with marsh vegetation, and which was first brought under cultivation in the neighbourhood of This, and afterwards around Memphis, the towns of Tanis and Heracleopolis Parva had been founded at a very early epoch by seafaring peoples of Semitic origin They thence penetrated into the interior of the country, where they came into collision with the Egyptians coming from the south, whose culture they adopted At the same time, however, they retained their independence under kings of their own, who during the period of the 6th, 7th, and 8th Dynasties formed the 9th and 10th contemporaneous Dynasties of Heracleopolites, from the year 2691 onwards, and who ruled over the Delta and perhaps the whole of Lower Egypt The 11th Dynasty, which put an end to the sway of the Heracleopolites, is called Diospolite, or Theban, but in the estimation of the Egyptians was not a strictly legitimate line.

Middle Monarchy.

M. 2851. L. 2380 W. 2080 **XII. DYNASTY** (*Diospolites; pp.* 160, 164, 334, 453).

Amenemha I. (Gr. *Ammenemes*).
Usertesen I. (Gr. *Sesonchosis; pp.* 334, 459).
Amenemha II. (Gr. *Ammanemes*).
Usertesen II. (Gr. *Sesostris; p.* 491).
Usertesen III. (Gr. *Lachares*).
Amenemha III. (Gr. *Ameres*, pp. 457, 461, 522).
Amenemha IV. (Gr *Amenemes*).
Sebek-nefru (Gr. *Skemiophris*).

† Heracleopolis, or City of Hercules. The Phœnician god Melkart was called by the Greeks Heracles, as he is said to have performed similar prodigies of strength. Brugsch identifies the Heracleopolitan with the Sethroitic nome (the capital of which was Pithom or Pi-Tum); see p. 412.

Under this Dynasty the sceptres of Upper and Lower Egypt were united. All the kings were powerful and prosperous, and art again flourished. The Sun Temple at Heliopolis (see p. 334) was magnificently restored, and in the Fayûm the practice of building pyramids was revived (see p. 459 *et seq.*) During this period, too, fortifications were erected on the N.E. frontier of the kingdom which appear to have extended across the whole of the present Isthmus of Suez (p. 451).

The Hyksos Period (pp. 298, 373, 453, 479).

In the 12th Dynasty we already hear of Semitic families applying for admission to Upper Egypt †, and in the 13th Dynasty these immigrations became more frequent. The newcomers met with kinsmen in the seaports of the Delta, allied with whom and with Arabian tribes they at length became so powerful as to defeat the armies of the Pharaohs and obtain possession of the whole of Lower Egypt. They made Tanis their capital, and under the name of **Hyksos** ruled over N. Egypt for five centuries, while the exiled royal family was compelled to retire to Upper Egypt. (The name of 'Hyksos', according to Josephus, Manetho, and others, is derived from *hyk*, a king, and *sos*, a shepherd, and thus signifies 'shepherd kings'; some modern authorities, however, derive it from *hyk shasu*, signifying 'Robber Kings'.) The Hyksos soon conformed to the ancient culture of the valley of the Nile. They applied the name of the Egyptian god Set to their own gods (Be'alîm); and the sphinxes preserved at Tanis with the portrait-heads of their kings (p. 298) prove that they took Egyptian artists into their service, and perhaps themselves acquired a knowledge of the Egyptian plastic art (p. 162). At the same time they adopted all the titles of the Pharaohs and the whole of the court ceremonies of the legitimate monarchs of Egypt. ††

XIII. DYNASTY (*Diospolites*).

† In the tomb of the governor Khnum-hotep, at Beni Hasan, *Absha*, a Semitic chief with his family and attendants, is represented approaching with gifts. The occasion was perhaps similar to that on which Abraham and Sarah were induced to visit Egypt (Gen. xii. 10). The record of their sojourn there forms the earliest notice of Egypt to be found in the Bible.

†† From this it appears that when *Joseph* came to Egypt at the end of the Hyksos period he found on the throne a monarch of a race kindred to his own, though conforming in all respects to the ancient customs of the Pharaohs. A famine mentioned in a tomb at El-Kâb is perhaps identical with the one which brought Jacob and his family to Egypt. This tomb belonged to the father of Aahmes, a naval officer, who took part in the expulsion of the Hyksos about four centuries before the Exodus. The inscription runs thus: — 'When a famine prevailed for many years, then I gave the city corn during each famine'.

XIV DYNASTY (*Khoites*, from Khoïs, situated to the N.E. of Saïs).
XV. DYNASTY (*Hyksos*).
XVI. DYNASTY (*Hyksos*).
XVII. DYNASTY (*Diospolites*)

We learn from a papyrus in the British Museum that the Hyksos monarch *Apepi* demanded the cession of an important well from *Rasekenen*, the king of Upper Egypt (17th dyn) This incident gave rise to the outbreak of a war of independence which lasted for eighty years

M. 1703. L. 1591. W 1520. XVIII. DYNASTY (*Diospolites*; pp. 446, 479)

Aahmes I. (*Amosis*, or *Amasis*; p. 302) captured Abaris (Ha-war) after a long siege by land and by water The Hyksos (numbering, according to Manetho, 24,000 men capable of bearing arms) were obliged to retreat and to seek a new territory, and most of them accordingly settled in S. Palestine. The successors of Aahmes penetrated far into Asia, subjugated one nation after another, exacted heavy tribute from the vanquished, and embellished Thebes, their capital, with magnificent edifices.

Amenhotep I. (Gr. *Amenophthis*)

Tutmes (Thothmes) I. (Gr. *Amensis*).

Tutmes II. (Gr. *Misaphris*) and *Ramaka*, his sister and wife.

Tutmes III. (Gr. *Misphragmuthosis*, pp 298, 363, 522) extended his conquests as far as the vicinity of the Tigris.

Tutmes IV. (Gr. *Tuthmosis*).

Amenhotep III. (Gr. *Amenophis*, pp. 385, 405) not only continued to exact tribute from the Oriental nations as far as Mesopotamia, but succeeded in extending his dominions towards the south He was also remarkable for his extraordinary building enterprise.

Amenhotep IV. (Gr. *Horus*) returned to the earlier and ruder religion of worshipping the sun. For his name Amenophis ('peace of Ammon') he therefore substituted *Khuen-aten* ('reflection of the sun's disk)

Ramses I. (*Rhamesses*; pp. 427, 435, 453)

M 1462 L 1443 W 1340. XIX. DYNASTY (*Diospolites*, pp. 162, 427, 453).

Seti I. (pp. 313, 427, 435, 453) undertook several campaigns against the Aramaic tribes, who had formed a league under the hegemony of the powerful *Kheta* (or *Khittim*, the Hittites of the Bible), and penetrated as far as the Orontes. He erected the Memnonium at Abydus, and caused a sepulchre to be hewn for himself in the rock at Thebes. He caused Ramses, his son and successor, to be educated along with other young Egyptian nobles, and it is possible that Moses formed one of the number (Exod. ii. 10). Seti devoted special attention to the Delta and to Tanis, the ancient capital of the Hyksos, where he erected extensive buildings with the aid of the Semites, among whom the Israelites must also be included. During this reign a great canal was completed in Goshen (see p. 411), leading from the Nile to the E. frontier of the kingdom, and probably thence through the Bitter Lakes to the Red Sea, but chiefly destined for the irrigation of the land of Goshen

Ramses II. the *Sesostris* of the Greeks (pp. 313, 374, 410, 413, 427, 453, 481), with a view to vindicate his supremacy over the nations subjugated by his ancestors, undertook campaigns towards the S. to Donkola, towards the N. to Asia Minor, and towards the E. to the Tigris, to commemorate which he erected monuments of victory in various parts of the conquered countries. He exhibited great zeal as a builder, and was a patron of art and science. He erected the Ramesseum at Thebes, and presented it with a library. Pentaur, Amenemapt, and other poets flourished during this reign. Ramses II. was the Pharaoh who oppressed the Israelites (Exod. i. 11).

Merenptah (Gr. *Amenephthes*), the 'Pharaoh of the Exodus' (pp. 316, 453, 481). During his reign (in the year 1325, according to Brandis) the termination of a Sothis period† was celebrated. A conflict which broke out between this monarch and the Israelites settled in Goshen resulted in his discomfiture (Exod. xiv.).

The New Empire.

M 1288 XX. DYNASTY (*Diospolites*; p. 479).

L 1209 **Ramses III.** (the *Rhampsinitus* of Herodotus, ii. 121; see

W 1200. also pp. 334, 408), though successful in his campaign against the Libyans and in other warlike enterprises, could not vie with his ancestors in military glory, but endeavoured to surpass them in the magnificence of his buildings. His monument at Bibân el-Mulûk, near Thebes, is one of the finest now in existence. Most of the rock-tombs in this city of royal mausolea were founded by his successors of the same Dynasty, all of whom also bore the name of Ramses (IV-XIII.).

† The course of Sothis, or the dog-star, afforded the Egyptians a means of ascertaining the true astronomical year. They began their first year with the early rising of this star, at the beginning of the inundation (on 1st Thoth). The Egyptian solar year, being six hours too short, differed from the Sothis year by a quarter of a day. This discrepancy soon became very perceptible. After 40 years the end of the solar year fell by 10 days, and after 400 years by 100 days, short of the end of the true Sothis year, and festivals recurred at seasons to which they did not properly belong. At length, after 365×4 years, the error corrected itself, and the beginning of the new year again coincided with the rise of Sothis. Thus in a period of 1460 fixed, or 1461 variable, years the error in the Egyptian calendar was rectified

M. 1110. L. 1091. W. 1085. XXI. DYNASTY (*Tanites*, from Tanis, in the N.E. part of the Delta; pp. 373, 452).

The throne of the Ramessides was now usurped by ambitious hierarchs of Tanis, headed by *Herhor*, the chief prophet of Ammon; and Thebes was thus deprived of her ancient pre-eminence. This dynasty of priest-kings reigned ingloriously. Being unable to exact obedience from their Asiatic vassals by force, they endeavoured to maintain their suzerainty by a conciliatory policy. (See also the relations of Solomon with Egypt: 1 Kings iii 1; ix. 16; x. 28.)

M. 980. L. 961. W. 990. XXII. DYNASTY (*Bubastites*, from the Bubastis of the Greeks, the Pibeseth of the Bible, the Pibast of the Egyptian monuments, the modern Tell Basṭa in the Delta; pp. 163, 410, 457).

Sheshenk I. (the *Sesonchis* of the Greeks, the *Shishak* of the Bible; p. 454) assisted Jeroboam against Rehoboam, and besieged and captured Jerusalem

Osorkon (Gr. *Osorthon*, the *Zerah* of the Bible, 2 Chron. xiv. 9; xvi. 8; see p. 457) invaded Palestine, but was signally defeated by Asa

M. 810 L. 787 W 818 XXIII. DYNASTY (*Tanites*; p. 453).

Tefnekht, prince of Sais and Memphis, attempted to possess himself of the sovereignty of Lower Egypt, but was defeated by *Piankhi*, King of Ethiopia, who captured Memphis, but afterwards returned to his own country (see p. 299).

XXIV. DYNASTY (*Saïtes*, from Saïs, the modern Ṣâ el-Ḥager; p. 445).

Bek-en-ranf (Gr. *Bocchoris*) vainly endeavoured by a new legislation to arrest the decline of the empire. In 716 Egypt fell into the hands of the **Ethiopians.** — Interregnum.

M. 715. L. 716. W. 714. XXV. DYNASTY (*Ethiopians*). **Shabako** (Gr. *Sabacon*) conquered Upper Egypt, and resided at Thebes, but made no alteration in the religion or the constitution of the country. His sister *Ameneritis* (p. 297) became the wife of King *Ra-men-kheper Piankhi*, and their daughter *Shep-en-apet* married Psammetikh I. (see below).

Shabataka (Gr. *Sebichos*) led an army to the assistance of the Jewish king Hezekiah, but was defeated at Altaku by *Sennacherib*, King of Assyria

Taharka (Gr. *Tearco*, the *Tirhakah* of the Bible, the *Tarku-u* of the Assyrian monuments; pp. 299, 303) formed an alliance with the kings of Phœnicia and Cyprus against Assyria, but was defeated in Egypt by *Esarhaddon*, the son and successor of Sennacherib, and driven back to Ethiopia. The Assyrians then plundered Thebes and divided the country among twenty princes, among whom *Nekho* (the Necoh of the Bible), prince of Sais, became the most prominent. After Esarhaddon's death Taharka endeavoured to shake off the Assyrian yoke, but was defeated and driven out of Egypt by *Assurbanipal (Sardanapalus)*, Esarhaddon's son and successor. The vassal princes assisted Taharka, but were pardoned by Assurbanipal and reinstated in their provinces on a solemn vow of future obedience.

Nut-Amen (Assyr *Urdamani*) captured Memphis and won back the whole of Lower Egypt, but was in his turn defeated by Sardanapalus, who again invaded Egypt.

After the departure of the Assyrians and the decline of their power under the successors of Sardanapalus, the petty Egyptian princes attained complete independence and established the so-called 'Dodekarchy'. An end, however, was put to this by *Psammetikh*, son of Nekho, and prince of Sais and Memphis, with the aid of Ionian and Carian mercenaries. As the nephew (by marriage) of Shabako (p. 91) Psammetikh was the legitimate heir of the Ethiopian dynasty, and he accordingly ascended the throne of Egypt and founded the —

M 665 L 685 W 664 XXVI. DYNASTY (*Saïtes*; pp 163, 427, 446).

664-610 **Psammetikh I.** (Egypt. *Psemtek*, Gr. *Psammetichus*; p. 385), in order to consolidate his empire, assigned dwellings to the Greek mercenaries in the fertile region of Bubastis, and favoured foreigners in many ways. The warrior caste of Egypt, highly offended at this proceeding, emigrated to Ethiopia, and there founded the kingdom of the Sembrides. Profiting by the decline of the power of Assyria, Psammetikh made war against the wealthy Phœnician seaports, but was stoutly opposed by the Philistines.

610-594 **Nekho** (Grk *Nechos*, Egypt. *Nekau*, p 427), the son of Psammetikh, was more concerned for the domestic welfare of the country than for military glory During his reign the S. extremity of Africa was circumnavigated for the first time (Herod. iv. 42). Nekho began to construct a canal from the Nile to the Red Sea, but discontinued the work on being informed by an oracle that it would only benefit 'strangers.' Hearing of the campaign of the Medes and Babylonians against the Assyrians, he also marched against Assyria, and defeated Josiah, King of Judah, the ally of the Assyrians, who opposed him at Megiddo. Meanwhile, however, Nineveh had fallen, and the Assyrian empire been divided by Cyaxares, King of Media, and Nabopolassar, King of Babylon; and Nekho's further progress was arrested by Nebuchadnezzar, King of Babylon and son of Nabopolassar, who defeated him at Karkemish (Circesium). Nekho thus lost his possessions in Syria and Palestine.

594-589. *Psammetikh II.* (*Psammis*, or *Psammuthis*).

589-564. **Uahbrâ** (Gr. *Apries* or *Uaphris*; the *Hophrah* of the Bible), observing that the Babylonians were encroaching on Palestine, fitted out an army and fleet, captured Sidon, defeated the Cyprians and the Tyrians in a naval battle, and marched to the relief of Zedekiah, King of Judah, who was besieged in Jerusalem by Nebuchadnezzar. That city having been again besieged by Nebuchadnezzar and captured, Uaphris accorded an asylum to its exiled inhabitants. He afterwards sustained a defeat from Battus II., King of Cyrene, in consequence of which his army rebelled against him. *Aahmes*, who had been dispatched by him to treat with the insurgents, was then proclaimed king, and he himself was dethroned.

564-526. **Aahmes II.** (Gr. *Amasis*; p. 386) succeeded in securing his supremacy by alliances with Cyrene, with the tyrant Polycrates of Samos, and with the Greeks. He assigned land to foreign colonists, granting them religious toleration, and diverted the stream of commerce from the semi-Phœnician cities of the Delta (Tanis, Mendes, and Bubastis) towards the Greek city of Naucratis (see p 207). During his reign the country enjoyed peace and prosperity, but the balance of power among the great nations of that era underwent a considerable change. Cyrus had meanwhile founded the vast Persian empire, and consolidated it by means of the conquest of the Babylonian and Lydian kingdoms. His son *Cambyses* next marched against Egypt, the only great power which still rivalled Persia. Having advanced to Pelusium with a large army, he there defeated **Psammetikh III.**, son of Amasis, who was now dead (p. 374), captured Memphis, and took the king prisoner. Psammetikh was afterwards executed for attempting to organise an insurrection to shake off the foreign yoke.

The Persian Domination.

XXVII. DYNASTY (*Persians*).

525-521. **Cambyses** (Pers. *Kambuziya II.*, Egypt. *Kembut*; pp. 374, 386, 446) at first behaved with great moderation. He tolerated the Egyptian religion, and to his own name he added the Egyptian agnomen of *Ramesut*, or 'child of the sun'. After, however, he had failed in several rash enterprises, such as his campaigns against the inhabitants of the oasis of Ammon and against the Ethiopians, his temper became soured, and his conduct violent and cruel. He died at Acbatana in Syria, while marching to Persia against *Gaumata*, a usurper who personated *Bardiya* (Gr. *Smerdis*), the deceased brother of Cambyses, who had been assassinated long before this period by order of the king himself.

521-485 **Darius I.** (Pers. *Daryavus*), son of Hystaspes (Vistaspa), became king of the Persian empire on the dethronement of the usurper Gaumata (the personator of Smerdis). His policy consisted in modifying his rule over each part of his territory in accordance with its own special requirements. He endeavoured to promote the prosperity of Egypt in every possible way. He established new commercial routes from Koptos in Upper Egypt to the Red Sea, and from Siûṭ and Abydus to the Sûdân; he resumed the construction of the canal from the Nile to the Red Sea (p. 428); he improved the roads of Egypt; he sent a strong garrison to the oasis of Khârgeh (p. 63), and erected a temple to Ammon there; he coined money for the use of the Egyptians, whose currency had hitherto consisted of stamped rings and weights; and he appointed Amasis, a scion of the 26th Dynasty, his satrap in Egypt. Hearing that the Persians had been defeated by the Greeks (in 492 and 490), the Egyptians

486 revolted against the Persian yoke under the leadership of *Khabbash*, a descendant of the family of Psammetikh. The insurrection, however, was soon quelled by —

485-465. **Xerxes I.** (Pers. *Khshayarsha*), son of Darius; Khabbash disappeared, and Achaimenes, the king's brother, was appointed satrap.

465-425 **Artaxerxes I.** (Pers. *Artakhshathra*), surnamed *Makrocheir*, or *Longimanus*, next ascended the Persian throne. During

463 his reign the Egyptians again revolted. Prince *Inarus of Marea*, aided by the Athenians, defeated Achaimenes, the Persian satrap, but the allied Egyptians and Greeks were in their turn defeated by the Persian general Megabyzus near Prosopitis, an island in the Nile, and Inarus was crucified. *Amyrtaeus*, a scion of a princely Egyptian family, and a partizan of Inarus, then sought an asylum in the marshy coast district, where he succeeded in maintaining his independence.

454 *Herodotus* travels in Egypt

425-405 **Darius II.** (Pers. *Daryavus*), surnamed *Nothos*, or the Bastard. The Egyptians now revolted for the third time. *Pausiris*, son of the Amyrtæus above mentioned, had

405-399 meanwhile been succeeded by a second *Amyrtaeus*, who still maintained the independent position of his predecessor in the Delta. This Amyrtæus headed the new insurrection, which became general in 404; and he was soon recognised as king of the whole of Egypt. He founded the 28th Dynasty,

399-393. which, however, lasted for six years only. *Naifâurut (Ne-*

pherites) of Mendes at length succeeded in completely throwing off the Persian yoke, and became the founder of the 29th Dynasty. His chief endeavour was to secure the friendship of the Greeks, with a view to strengthen himself against the Persians.

405-362. **Artaxerxes II.,** surnamed *Mnemon.*

393-383. The Persian king endeavoured to recover Egypt, but *Akhoris*, the successor of Naifâurut, threw obstacles in his way by supporting his enemies, particularly Euagoras, the tyrant of Salamis in Cyprus, and by improving the defences of his country.

383-382. *Psamut (Psammuthis)* and —

382-378. *Naifâurut (Nepherites) II.*, the successors of Akhoris, reigned for short periods only.

378-362. *Nekht-hor-heb (Nectanebus I.)*, however, the next native monarch, a Sebennytic prince, the founder of the 30th Dynasty, completed the warlike preparations of the Egyptians, and entrusted the chief command of his troops to Chabrias, an Athenian general, who signally defeated Pharnabazus, the Persian general, at Mendes.

362-340 **Artaxerxes III.,** *Ochus*

361-345. *Tachos* or *Teos*, who succeeded Nekht-hor-heb, invaded Persian Phœnicia, supported by a body of Greek allies. During his absence, his nephew *Nekht-nebf (Nectanebus II.)* usurped the Egyptian crown, but was defeated by Artaxerxes III. and driven into Ethiopia. Egypt now surrendered to Artaxerxes, and again became a Persian satrapy (345).

337-330. **Darius III.,** *Codomannus.*

332-323 **Alexander the Great,** after having defeated Darius on the Granicus (334), and at Issus (333), and captured the Philistine town of Gaza, marched to Pelusium, and was received with open arms by the Egyptians, who regarded him as their deliverer from the Persian yoke. He tolerated the native religion, visited the Oasis of Ammon, and founded Alexandria (p. 207), which, under the Ptolemies, became the great centre of Greek culture and of the commerce of the whole world.

In the lists of the Pharaohs we find the 28th, 29th, and 30th Dynasties mentioned as contemporaneous with the 27th or Persian Dynasty.

405-399 **XXVIII. Dynasty** *(Saites)*: *Amyrtaeus (Amen-rut)*

399-378 **XXIX. Dynasty** (*Mendesites*, from Mendes, in the Delta; see p 442): —

399-393 *Nepherites I*
393-383 *Akhoris.*
383-382 *Psammuthis.*
382-378 *Nepherites II.*

378-345 **XXX. Dynasty** (*Sebennytes*, from Sebennytus, the modern Semennûd, in the Delta; p. 445): —

378-364 *Nekht-hor-heb (Nectanebus I).*
364-361 *Tachos (Teos)*
361-345 *Nekht-nebf (Nectanebus II)*

323-30 **Period of the Ptolemies.**

323 **Ptolemy I. Soter** (p. 212), son of Lagus, and one of Alexander's generals, now became Macedonian governor of Egypt. He defeated Antigonus and Perdiccas, who threatened the independence of his province, and in 305, after the assassination of Alexander II. Ægus, the son of Alexander the
305-284 Great, he assumed the title of King of Egypt. In consequence of the foundation of the *Alexandrian Museum* (p. 212) for the reception of learned men, as well as of literary treasures, Alexandria soon superseded Athens as the chief nursery of Greek literature. Two years before his death, which took place in 284, Ptolemy I. abdicated in favour of his son,

286-247 **Ptolemy II. Philadelphus** (pp. 85, 212, 441)

247-222 **Ptolemy III. Euergetes I.** (p. 212, 314), in the course of two campaigns, conquered the empire of the Seleucides and Cilicia in Asia Minor. The power of Egypt abroad was now at its zenith

222-205 **Ptolemy IV. Philopator.** Under this king and his successors, a series of degenerate monarchs, the great empire of the Ptolemies hastened to its destruction. He defeated Antiochus the Great of Syria, who had marched towards the
217 Egyptian frontier, at the Battle of Raphia, but concluded a dishonourable peace with him.

205-182 **Ptolemy V. Epiphanes** (p. 450) ascended the throne, when five years of age, under the guardianship of Agathocles and Œnanthe, the mother of the latter. In consequence of revolts at Alexandria and Lycopolis, and an attack by Antiochus the Great of Syria, his guardians were obliged to resign their office in favour of the *Roman Senate*, by whom Cœlesyria and Palestine were ceded to Antiochus, while Egypt continued to be independent. Ptolemy V., having been prematurely declared of full age in 196, married
192 Cleopatra I., daughter of Antiochus the Great. This alliance not only secured peace abroad, but caused a portion of the revenues of Cœlesyria, Phœnicia, and Judæa again to flow into the treasury of Alexandria. The internal affairs of the country, however, fell into a state of deplorable confusion; one rebellion succeeded another, and anarchy prevailed everywhere.

182 Ptolemy V. was poisoned.

182. **Ptolemy VI. Eupator,** his son, died the same year.

182-146 **Ptolemy VII. Philometor,** the second son of Ptolemy V.

(p. 408), when six years of age, ascended the throne under the protectorate of his mother Cleopatra I.

171. Battle of Pelusium. Philometor is taken prisoner, and Memphis captured, by Antiochus IV. of Syria.

Ptolemy VIII. was now placed on the throne, but was immediately assassinated by **Ptolemy IX. Euergetes II.** (nicknamed *Physcon*, or 'big belly').

170-165. Ptolemy VII. Philometor and Ptolemy IX. Physcon, having become reconciled, reign jointly.

165. The brothers quarrel; Philometor flies to Rome, is reinstated by the Roman senate, and thenceforth reigns alone; while Euergetes, by command of the Roman senate, reigns at Cyrene.

146. Philometor dies.

Ptolemy Physcon besieges Alexandria, and becomes the guardian of the heir-apparent, a minor.

132. He is overthrown by a revolution, and retires to Cyprus.

125. He regains possession of the throne.

117. Physcon dies. *Cleopatra III. Cocce*, his niece and widow,

117-81. and her son **Ptolemy X. Soter II. Philometor II.** *(Lathyrus)* reign jointly.

106. Lathyrus is banished, and his brother **Ptolemy XI. Alexander I.** becomes co-regent in his stead.

89. Alexander is exiled by insurgents.

87. Alexander is slain in a naval battle, and Lathyrus is recalled.

Thebes rebels and is destroyed.

81. Lathyrus dies. Alexander marries *Berenice III.*, with whom he reigns jointly, under the name of **Ptolemy XII. Alexander II.**

81. He assassinates his wife, and is himself slain.

81-52. **Ptolemy XIII. Neos Dionysos** (or *Auletes*, the 'flute-player'), an illegitimate son of Lathyrus, ascends the throne, and is formally recognised by Rome (59).

60. *Diodorus* visits Egypt.

57. Auletes flies from Alexandria to Rome, but is reinstated

54. by Gabinius.

52. Auletes dies, leaving a will by which he appoints his eldest children —

52-48. **Cleopatra VII.** (pp. 428, 213) and **Ptolemy XIV. Dionysos II.** his joint heirs, commands them to marry each other, and nominates the Roman senate their guardian. **Pompey** is appointed to that office.

49. Ptolemy XIV. banishes Cleopatra. Pompey, having been defeated by Cæsar at the Battle of Pharsalia, seeks an asylum in the territory of his wards, but on landing in Egypt is

48. slain at the instigation of Ptolemy.

48. **Cæsar** lands at Alexandria, takes the part of the banished
Cleopatra, and defeats the rebellious Ptolemy.
Ptolemy XIV. is drowned in the Nile.
Cæsar, having meanwhile become dictator of Rome, ap-
47. points **Ptolemy XV.**, the brother of Cleopatra VII., a boy
of eleven, co-regent.
Ptolemy XV. is assassinated at the instigation of Cleopatra,
45. and *Ptolemy XVI. Caesarion*, her son by Cæsar, is appointed
co-regent.

44. Cæsar is murdered.

42. **Antony**, having summoned Cleopatra to Tarsus to answer
for the conduct of her general Allienus, who contrary to her
wishes had aided the army of Brutus and Cassius at Philippi,
is captivated by her beauty and talent. After having spent
31. years of debauchery with the Egyptian queen, he is at
length declared by the Roman senate to be an enemy of his
country. *Octavianus* marches against him, defeats him at
Actium, and captures Alexandria.

30. Antony commits suicide, and Cleopatra is said to have
also caused her own death by the bite of an asp.
Egypt now became a Roman province, and was governed
by prefects down to A.D. 362.

B.C. 30-A.D. 362.

Roman Period.

27. *Caesar Octavianus*, under the title of **Augustus**, becomes
sole ruler of the vast Roman empire (p. 213). The Egyptian
priesthood accord to the Roman emperors the privileges enjoyed by their own ancient monarchs, and in their temple-
inscriptions style them *autocrator* (absolute sovereign).

24. The Ethiopians, under their queen *Candace*, invade Egypt.
Strabo travels in Egypt.

A.D. 14-37. **Tiberius** erects the Sebasteum at Alexandria.

16. Germanicus visits Egypt.

37-41. **Caligula.** A persecution of the Jews takes place, to which
we are indebted for the valuable treatise of Josephus in
answer to Apion, who had written against the Jews.

41-54. **Claudius.** Rights of citizenship guaranteed to the Jews.
Lake Mœris gradually dries up.

54-68. **Nero.** Egypt acquires a new source of wealth as a commercial station between India, Arabia, and Rome.

62. *Annianus*, first bishop of Alexandria

68-69. *Galba. Otho. Vitellius.*

69-79. **Vespasian** (p. 213) visits Alexandria. From this city Titus
starts on his expedition against Palestine, which terminates
with the destruction of Jerusalem in the year 70.
Domitian (p. 443) encourages the worship of Isis and
81-96. Serapis at Rome.

98-117. **Trajan** (p. 428). The canal connecting the Nile with the Red Sea is re-opened (Amnis Trajanus).

116. Rebellion of the Jews at Alexandria.

117-138. **Hadrian** (p. 213) visits Egypt (twice according to some accounts). His letter to Servianus (p. 216).

136. Termination of a Sothis period (comp. 90).

161-180. **Marcus Aurelius.**

1 2. Rebellion of the *Bucolians*, or cowherds of Semitic origin who had long been settled among the marshes of the Delta, quelled by *Avidius Cassius.*

175 Avidius Cassius is proclaimed emperor by the Egyptian legions, but is assassinated in Syria.

176. Marcus Aurelius visits Alexandria (p. 213).

out 179. *Demetrius*, first patriarch of Alexandria.

180-192. **Commodus.**

193-211. **Septimius Severus.** The philosopher Ammonius Saccas founds the Neo-Platonic School.

199 Severus visits Egypt.

204. Edict prohibiting Roman subjects from embracing Christianity. The Delta at this period is thickly studded with Christian communities. Schools of Catechists flourish at Alexandria (Pantænus, Clement, Origen).

211-217 **Caracalla** (p. 213) visits Egypt. Massacre at Alexandria. Caracalla is assassinated by the prefect of his guards —

217-218. **Macrinus**, who is proclaimed emperor by the Egyptians. After his death a series of contests for the possession of the throne take place at Alexandria.

249-251. **Decius** (p. 214).

250 Persecution of the Christians under Decius. Beginning of the anchorite and monastic system, perhaps in imitation of the hermit life led by the devotees of Serapis (p. 384). The history of these Christian ascetics (comp. pp. 385, 480) soon to came be embellished with myths of every kind.

253-260. *Valerianus.* Persecution of the Christians (p. 214).

260-268. **Gallienus** accords religious toleration to the Christians. Plague in Egypt.

260. Rebellion of *Macrianus*, who is recognised as emperor by the Egyptians. He marches into Illyria against Domitian, the general of Gallienus.

265. *Æmilianus (Alexander)* is proclaimed emperor by the army at Alexandria and recognised by the people, but is defeated and put to death by the Roman legions.

268. Egypt invaded by an army of Queen *Zenobia* of Palmyra.

268-270. *Claudius II.*

270-275. **Aurelian.**

270. Renewed invasion of the Palmyrenes. Zenobia recognised as Queen of Egypt.

273. Zenobia dethroned. Insurrection of *Firmus*, a Syrian (p. 214). Invasions of the Blemmyes. Firmus defeated.

276-282 **Probus** obtains the purple at Alexandria (p. 214).

278 His successful campaign against the Blemmyes.

284-305. **Diocletian** (pp. 214, 218).

292. Rebellion in Upper Egypt.

294. Insurrection of the Alexandrians.

295-296. Diocletian takes Alexandria and marches to Upper Egypt.

296. Erection of Pompey's Column (p. 218).

304. Persecution of the Christians.

307-313 *Maximinus*. Beginning of the Arian controversies.

324-337. **Constantine the Great**, first Christian emperor.

325 *Council of Nice.* The doctrine of the presbyter *Arius* of Alexandria (p 214) that Christ was begotten by God before all time, and was godlike, but not very God, is condemned; while the teaching of *Alexander*, bishop of Alexandria, to the effect that Father and Son are *homousioi*, or of the same nature, is sanctioned, chiefly owing to the powerful eloquence of his deacon Athanasius, who accompanied him to the Council.

328. Constantine founds *Constantinople* as a new metropolis of Greek art and science.

337. Death of Constantine.

337-361. **Constantius** favours Arianism. Athanasius is deposed, and *Georgius*, who is made bishop of Alexandria, opposes the followers of Athanasius with the sword.

373. Athanasius dies, after having spent the last years of his life in the midst of his flock.

379-395 **Theodosius I. the Great.** He formally declares Christianity to be the religion of the empire. Persecution of the Arians and heathens (pp. 214, 374).

395. Partition of the Roman empire, Arcadius being emperor of the East, and Honorius of the West.

395-638. **The Byzantines.**

395-408 **Arcadius** permits *Theophilus*, the bigoted patriarch of Alexandria (p. 214), to exterminate with fire and sword the opponents of the doctrine that God must be considered to have a human form.

408-450. **Theodosius II.**

413 Theophilus, patriarch of Alexandria, dies, and is succeeded by *Cyril* (p. 214).

431. The view of the patriarch Cyril, that Christ and the Virgin (as ἡ θεοτόκος) possess a double nature, prevails over that of the patriarch of Constantinople at the third œcumenical Council, held at Ephesus.

444 Death of Cyril.

450-457 **Marcianus** (p. 214).

451 At the fourth œcumenical Council, that of Chalcedon, the doctrine of the archimandrite Eutyches of Constantinople, to the effect that Christ possessed a double nature before his incarnation,

but that this human nature was afterwards absorbed by his divine, is condemned, chiefly through the influence of Pope Leo the Great At the same time the doctrine that Christ possesses two natures, ἀσυγχύτως and ἀτρέπτως, but at the same time ἀδιαιρέτως and ἀχωρίστως, i e. unmixed and unchangeable, but also indistinguishable and inseparable, is formally accepted by the Church. The Egyptians, to this day, adhere to the monophysite doctrine of Eutyches.

474-491. **Zeno.**

482. With a view to put an end to these doctrinal controversies, Zeno issued the so-called Henoticon, in which the question whether Christ possessed a single or a double nature was evaded. The doctrine stated, however, was so vague, that this attempt at reconciliation proved entirely fruitless.

481-518 **Anastasius.**

502. Famine in Egypt.

517. Rebellion of the Alexandrians on the occasion of the election of a patriarch.

527-565. **Justinian** (p. 214). New administration.

536. The emperor appoints a new orthodox patriarch. The Monophysites, who far outnumbered the orthodox party, separate from the dominant church and choose a patriarch of their own. They were afterwards called *Copts* (p 42)

610-641. **Heraclius** (p. 215).

619. The Persians under *Chosroes* invade Egypt (p. 215). Alexandria is taken. Chosroes rules with moderation.

629. The Persians expelled by Heraclius.

Mohammedan Period.

638. *'Amr Ibn el-'Âṣi*, general of Khalîf **'Omar** (pp. 241, 324, 374, 428), conquers Egypt and founds *Fosṭâṭ*.

641. 'Amr enters Alexandria.

643. 'Omar is assassinated.

644-656. **'Othmân.** A number of Arabian tribes settle in the valley of the Nile, and many Copts embrace El-Islâm. Fosṭâṭ becomes the capital of the new government.

656. 'Othmân is put to death.

661-750. **'Omayyades.** The last of this dynasty was —

Merwân II., who, having been defeated by Abu'l-'Abbâs, fled to Egypt, and was put to death there. The Omayyades were then exterminated, with the exception of 'Abd er-Raḥmân, who fled to Spain, and founded an independent Khalifate at Cordova.

750-870. The **'Abbasides** govern Egypt.

813-833. **Mâmûn** (p. 352), the son of Harûn er-Rashîd, visits Egypt, promotes scientific pursuits of all kinds, and supports the school of learned men which had sprung up at Fosṭâṭ.

870-884. **Aḥmed ibn Ṭulûn**, governor of Egypt (p. 242), profiting by the weakness of the 'Abbasides reigning at Baghdâd, declares himself an independent sultan, and founds the dynasty of the **Ṭulunides.** Arabian writers extol Ṭulûn for his fabulous wealth and love of magnificence. Numerous buildings were erected during this reign (pp. 242, 265).

884-896. **Khumarûyeh** (p. 242), son of Ṭulûn.

The 'Book of Lands', a geographical work by Ja'ḳûbi, published about the year 891, informs us that *Fosṭâṭ* occupied about one-third of the area of Alexandria at that period, that *Alexandria* was the most important commercial city in Egypt, that *Ashmunên* in Upper Egypt (see vol ii of the Handbook) was noted for its extensive cloth factories, *Tinîs* for its weaving and gold embroidery, *Alexandria*, *Damyâṭ*, and *Shaṭa* for their brocades and cloth of gold (*dabîki*, *kasab*, *washy*), the *Fayûm* for its canvas (*khêsh*), *Siûṭ* for its carpets, *Akhmîm* for its straw mats and leather-work, and *Taha* for its pottery The chief export at that period, as in ancient times, was corn, which was chiefly sent to the Ḥijâz

904. The Ṭulunides are put to death by the 'Abbaside Khalîf *Muktafi*, who marched with an army to Egypt.

925. The Shî'ite *Fâṭimites*, who had gained possession of the supreme power at Tunis, commanded by 'Obêdallâh, attack Egypt, but are defeated.

935. *Moḥammed el-Ikhshîd*, a Turk, and governor of Egypt, takes possession of the throne.

965-968 *Kâfûr*, a black slave, who had for a time conducted the government for the second son of El-Ikhshîd, usurps the throne, and recognises the suzerainty of the 'Abbasides.

969. *Gôhar* conquers Fosṭâṭ for his master, the Fâṭimite **Mu'izz**, great-grandson of 'Obêdallâh. Mu'izz (p. 242) assumes the title of khalif and transfers his seat of government to Egypt, after having founded the city of Maṣr el-Ḳâhira (Cairo) as a residence for himself near Fosṭâṭ (p. 242). Egypt now becomes the most important part of the territory of the Fâṭimites.

969-1171. **Fâṭimite** sovereigns of Egypt. The earlier of these governed the country admirably. The population increased with wonderful rapidity, and the whole of the commerce of India, as well as that of the interior of Africa, flowed to Egypt.

975. Mu'izz dies.

975-996. **'Azîz,** his son, distinguishes himself by his tolerance and his love of science (p. 287).

996-1020. **Ḥâkim** (pp. 242, 279), son of 'Azîz, a fanatic, declares himself to be an incarnation of 'Ali, and becomes the founder of the sect of the Druses (see Baedeker's Palestine and Syria, p. 100).

1020-1036. **Ẓâhir,** Ḥâkim's son, rules with sagacity.

1036-1094. **Abû Tamîm el-Mustanṣir,** a weak and incapable prince.
1074. The country is ravaged by a pestilence. *Bedr el-Jemâli*,
1077. governor of Damascus, is summoned to Egypt to act as chief vizier.

1094-1101. **Musta'li,** son of Mustanṣir, conquers —

1096. Jerusalem and the towns on the Syrian coast, but is deprived of his conquests by the army of the First Crusade.

1099. King *Baldwin* of Jerusalem attacks Egypt unsuccessfully.

1160-1171. **ʿAḍid Ledinallâh,** the last Fâṭimite.

Contests for the office of vizier take place during this reign between *Shawer* and *Ḍargham*. The former, being exiled, obtains an asylum with *Nûreddîn*, the ruler of Aleppo, who assists him to regain his office with Kurd mercenary troops, commanded by the brave generals *Shirkuh* and *Ṣalâḥeddîn* (Saladin). Shawer, quarrelling with the Kurds, invokes the
1164. aid of *Amalarich I.*, King of Jerusalem (1162-73), who comes to Egypt and expels the Kurds. A second army of
1168. Kurds, which was about to invade Egypt, is driven back in the same way, whereupon Amalarich himself endeavours to obtain possession of Egypt. Shawer next invokes the aid of his enemy Nûreddîn, whose Kurdish troops expel Amalarich. Egypt thus falls into the hands of the Kurds Shirkuh and Ṣalâḥeddîn. Shawer is executed. Shirkuh becomes chief
1169 vizier, and on his death **Ṣalâḥeddîn** rules in the name of the
1171. incapable khalîf. On the death of the latter Ṣalâḥeddîn becomes sole ruler of Egypt, and founds the dynasty of the —

1171-1250. **Eyyubides.**

Ṣalâḥeddîn (pp. 242, 262, 266, 443, 519), being a Sunnite, abolishes the Shîʿite doctrines and forms of worship.

1173-1183 After Nûreddîn's death he gains possession of the whole of that sovereign's Syrian dominions.

1187. By the victory of Ḥittîn he overthrows the Christian kingdom in Palestine.

1193. Death of Ṣalâḥeddîn.

1193-1218. **Melik el-ʿAziz** (p. 353), his brother and successor, preserves intact the dominions bequeathed to him; but the empire is dismembered at his death, and Egypt falls to the share of his son —

1218-1238. **Melik el-Kâmil** (p. 439), in whose reign the country began to play a prominent part in the history of the Crusades.

1219 Damietta (Dumyaṭ) is captured by the army of the Fifth Crusade, but is compelled to surrender in 1221 (p. 443).

While the sons of the last sultan are fighting with each other and with other members of the family for the throne of Egypt, the Mameluke —

1240-1249. **Melik eṣ-Ṣâleḥ** usurps the supreme power, and founds the **Mameluke Dynasty.** † His power being somewhat kept in

† The Mamelukes were slaves (as the word *mamlûk* imports), purchased by the sultans and trained as soldiers, for the purpose of forming their body-guard and the nucleus of their army. They placed Melik eṣ-Ṣâleḥ on the throne, hoping to govern him without difficulty. But when the new sultan found his authority sufficiently well established, he dismissed them from his service, and formed a new body-guard of the

check by his body-guard of Bahrite Mamelukes, he endeavours to extend his supremacy abroad. He attacks his uncle Isma'îl, the ruler of Damascus. The latter allies himself with other Syrian princes and with the Christians of Palestine, but is defeated by Melik eṣ-Ṣâleḥ, whose army has been reinforced by the Turkish mercenaries of the prince of *Kharezmia*. The Egyptians take Jerusalem, Damascus, Tiberias, and Ascalon.

1249. *Louis IX., the Saint*, of France, roused by the loss of Jerusalem, and with a view to prevent the Egyptians from further encroaching on the Holy Land, undertakes a campaign against Egypt, takes Damietta (p. 443), but while marching to Cairo is captured along with his army at Manṣûra, and is only released on payment of a heavy ransom.

1250-1380. Bahrite Mameluke Sultans. The first of these monarchs was *Mu'izz Eibeg*.

1260-1277. **Bêbars**, who had risen from being a slave to the position of leader of the Mamelukes, was one of the ablest of this dynasty. In the course of four campaigns he annihilates the last remnants of the kingdom of Jerusalem, and rules with sagacity, moderation, and justice. He brings to Cairo the last representative of the 'Abbaside khalifs, who had recently been dethroned by the Mongols, recognises his authority, and permits him nominally to occupy the throne.

1277-1290. **Kalaûn** (*Kilâwûn*, p. 275) successfully opposes the Mon-
1289. gols, and conquers Tripoli.

1291. **El-Ashraf Khalîl** (pp. 255, 278, 282), captures 'Akka, the last place in the Holy Land held by the Christians.

1346-1361. **Ḥasan**, the builder of the finest mosque at Cairo (p. 260).

1382-1517. Circassian Mameluke Sultans *(Burgites)*. The founder of this dynasty was —

1382-1399. **Barkûk** (pp. 242, 282), who overthrew the Bahrite Mamelukes. The reigns of these sultans present a series of revolutions and atrocities (see p. 242).

1422-1438. **Bursbey** (*Berisbai*, p. 285) conquers Cyprus.

1468-1496. **Kait Bey** (pp. 268, 286).

1501-1516. **El-Ghûri** (p. 274).

1517. *Ṭûmân Bey* (pp. 243, 272) is dethroned by the **Osman Sultân Selîm I.** of Constantinople (pp. 243, 333). Cairo is taken by storm. Egypt thenceforth becomes a *Turkish Pashalic*. Selîm compels Mutawakkil, the last scion of the family of the 'Abbaside khalîfs, who had resided at Cairo in obscurity since the time of Bêbars, to convey to him his

---

Bahrite Mamelukes (who were so called from the fact that their barracks were situated in the island of Rôḍa in the Nile or *Bahr*). Ere long, however, the new guards succeeded in gaining possession of almost the whole of the supreme power.

nominal supremacy, and thus claims a legal title to the office of *Khalîf*, the spiritual and temporal sovereign of all the professors of El-Islâm. †

The authority of the Osman sultans soon declined, and with it that of their governors. The Egyptian pashas were now obliged, before passing any new measure, to obtain the consent of the 24 Mameluke *Beys* (or princes) who governed the different provinces, and who merely paid tribute to the pasha. The most distinguished of these beys was —

1771. *'Ali Bey*, originally a slave, who raised himself to the dignity of an independent sultan of Egypt by taking advantage of the difficulties of the Turks, who were involved in war with Russia. He conquers Syria and Arabia, but on his return to Egypt is imprisoned by order of his own
1773. son-in-law *Abu Ḍabad*, and dies a few days afterwards. Abu Ḍabad obtains a ratification of his authority from the Turkish sultan. After his death, the beys —

Murâd and *Ibrâhîm* share the supremacy, and render themselves almost independent of Turkey.

The French Occupation.

1798, 1st July. **Napoleon Bonaparte** (pp. 243, 429) arrives at Alexandria, hoping to destroy the English trade in the Mediterranean, and, by occupying Egypt, to neutralise the power of England in India.

2nd July. Storming of Alexandria.

13th July. The Mameluke Bey Murâd defeated.

21st July. Battle of the Pyramids.

1st Aug. Destruction of the French fleet at Abuḳîr by the English fleet commanded by Nelson (p. 447).

25th Sept. Insurrection at Cairo quelled.

1799, Jan., May. Central and Upper Egypt conquered.

25th July. Defeat of the Turks at Abuḳîr.

24th Aug. Napoleon returns from Alexandria to France, leaving General Kléber in Egypt.

1800, 21st Mar. Kléber defeats the Turks at Maṭarîyeh (p. 333).

14th June. Kléber is assassinated at Cairo (p. 243).

1801, Sept. The French are compelled by an English army to capitulate in Cairo and Alexandria, and to evacuate Egypt.

† The Turkish Khalîfs, however, have never been recognised by the Shî'ites, as not being descended from 'Ali. Most of the Sunnites also, especially among the learned Arabs, regard them merely as temporal monarchs. Relying on an ancient tradition, they maintain that none but descendants of the Koreishites, the family to which Moḥammed belonged, can attain the office of Imâm, or spiritual superior. They accordingly regard the great Sherîf of Mecca as their true Imâm.

Mohammed 'Ali and his Successors.

1803 In the year 1803 the French consul *Matthieu de Lesseps* was commissioned by his government to seek for some suitable man to counteract the influence of the English and the Mamelukes in Egypt, and he accordingly recommended for the purpose Mohammed 'Ali, who was born at Kavala in Roumelia in 1769, and who was at that period colonel *(bimbashi)* of an Albanian corps of 1000 men in Egypt.

1805-1848 Mohammed 'Ali, having succeeded in removing most of his enemies, is appointed Pasha of Egypt. In 1807 he frustrates an attempt of the English to take possession of Egypt, and on
1811 1st March, 1811, causes the Mameluke beys, who prevented the progress of the country, to be treacherously assassinated, together with their followers (470 in number). His son, Tusûn Pasha, wages a successful war against the Wahhabites in Arabia, and deprives them of Mecca and Medina. Mohammed improves the agriculture of Egypt by introducing the cotton-plant, and by restoring the canals and embankments, appoints Frenchmen and other Europeans to various public offices, and sends young Egyptians to Paris to be educated. During the Greek war of independence he sends 24,000 men to the aid of the sultan, as a reward for which he is presented with the island of Candia at the close of the war.
1831 In 1831, aiming at complete independence, he makes war against the Porte. His son Ibrâhîm invades Syria, and cap-
1832 tures 'Akka (27th May, 1832), Damascus (8th July), and Haleb (21st Dec.), destroys the Turkish fleet at Kônyeh (Iconium), and threatens Constantinople itself. His victorious career, however, was terminated by the intervention of Russia and France. Syria is secured to Mohammed by the peace of *Kutâhyeh*, but he is obliged to recognise the suzerainty of the Porte. At the instigation of the English, Sultân Mahmûd renews hostilities with Egypt, but is decisively
1839 defeated by Ibrâhîm at *Nisibi* on 24th June, 1839. In consequence of the armed intervention of England and Austria, however, Ibrâhîm is compelled to quit Syria entirely, and Mohammed is obliged to yield to the Porte a second time.
1841 By the so-called firman of investiture in 1841 *Sultân Abdu'l-Medjid* secured the hereditary sovereignty of Egypt to the family of Mohammed 'Ali, the pasha renouncing his provinces of Syria, Candia, and the Hijâz, and binding himself to pay an annual tribute of 60,000 purses (about 306,000*l.*) to the Porte and to reduce his army to 18,000 men. During the last years of his life Mohammed fell into a state of imbecility, and died on 2nd Aug. 1849 in his palace at Shubra.

1848. **Ibrâhîm Pasha**, Moḥammed 'Ali's adopted son, had already taken the reins of government, in consequence of Moḥammed's incapacity, in January 1848, but he died in November of the same year, and before his adoptive father.

1849-1854. **'Abbâs Pasha**, a son of Tusûn Pasha and grandson of Moḥammed 'Ali, has generally been described by Europeans as a brutal, vicious, and rapacious prince. This, however, would seem to be a somewhat distorted view of his character, arising from the fact that he had inherited from his Arab mother a certain amount of ferocity and even cruelty, coupled with the dislike of a true son of the desert for European innovations. He, however, maintained the strictest discipline among his officials, and the public security in Egypt was never greater than during his reign. His death is attributed to assassination.

1854-1863. **Sa'îd Pasha**, his successor, was Moḥammed 'Ali's third son. Thanks to his enlightened government and his taste for European civilisation, Egypt made considerable progress during his reign, although her finances were far from being in a satisfactory condition. He equalised the incidence of taxation, abolished monopolies, improved the canals, completed the railways from Cairo to Alexandria and to Suez, and, above all, zealously supported the scheme of M. Ferdinand de Lesseps for constructing a canal through the Isthmus of Suez, which was opened in 1869 under his successor. During the Crimean war he was obliged to send an auxiliary army and considerable sums of money to the aid of the Porte. He died on 18th Jan. 1863, and was succeeded by his nephew —

1863. **Ismâ'îl Pasha**, the second son of Ibrâhîm Pasha, who was born on 31st Dec. 1830. He had received the greater part of his education in France and had there acquired the strong preference for European institutions which characterised him throughout his reign. Unfortunately, however, he combined with this enlightenment a profound egotism and a tendency to duplicity and cunning, which in the end, in spite of his natural talents, proved his ruin. Most of his innovations, such as the foundation of manufactories and the construction of canals, railways, bridges, and telegraphs, were planned mainly in his own interest, though of course the country shared in the advantage, while even in the establishment of schools, the reorganisation of the system of justice (p. 6), and the like, he acted rather with an eye to produce an impression in Europe than from real concern for the needs of his subjects. As time went on he succeeded in appropriating for his own use about one-fifth of the cul-
1866. tivable land of Egypt. In 1866, in consideration of a large

sum of money, he obtained the sanction of the Porte to a new order of succession based on the law of primogeniture, and
1867. in 1867 he was raised to the rank of *Khedive*, or viceroy, having previously borne the title of *wâli*, or governor of a
1873. province only. In 1873 the Khedive obtained a new firmân confirming and extending his privileges (independence of administration and judiciaries; right of concluding treaties with foreign countries; right of coining money; right of borrowing money; permission to increase his army and navy). The annual tribute payable to the Porte was at the same time raised to 133,635 purses (about 681,538*l.*). With regard to the warlike successes of the Khedive and the extension of his dominions, see pp. 29, 30. — The burden of the public debt had now increased to upwards of 100 million pounds, one loan after another having been negotiated by the finance minister Isma'îl Siddîk, who finally became
1878 so powerful that the Khedive deposed him in 1878 and caused him to be privately put to death. The Powers now brought such a pressure to bear on the Khedive, that he was compelled to resign his private and family estates to the state and to accept a ministry under the presidency of Nubar Pasha, with the portfolio of public works entrusted to M. Blignières and that of finance to Mr. Rivers Wilson. This coalition, however, soon proved unworkable; Nubar Pasha quitted the ministry in consequence of the Khedive's encouragement of a rising among the disbanded officers of the army,
1879. and early in 1879 the whole cabinet was replaced by a native ministry under Sherîf Pasha. The patience of the Great Powers was now at an end; and on the initiative of Germany they demanded from the Porte the deposition of Isma'îl, which accordingly took place on June 26th.

Isma'îl was succeeded by his son **Tewfik** (pronounced *Tevfik*) or **Taufik**, under whom the government was carried on in a more rational spirit, especially after Riaz Pasha became the head of the ministry. The debts were regulated, an international commission of liquidation was appointed, and an extensive scheme of reform was undertaken. In Sept.,
1881. 1881, however, a military revolution broke out in Cairo, which had for its objects the dismissal of the ministry, the grant of a constitution, and above all the emancipation of Egypt from European influences. The Khedive was besieged in his palace and had to yield, he appointed Sherîf president of a new ministry and arranged for an election of Notables, or representatives. As the latter espoused the 'national' cause, Sherîf resigned in Feb., 1882, and Mahmûd Pasha formed a new ministry, the programme of which tallied exactly with the demands of the national party. The new

cabinet, the soul of which was Arabi Bey, the energetic minister of war, at once proceeded, without receiving the consent of the Khedive, to pass several measures intended to diminish the European influence in the political and financial administration of the country. The consuls general were assured that no danger threatened the Europeans, but were also told that any foreign intervention in the internal affairs of Egypt would be resisted by force. The Khedive, to whom both France and England had promised protection, declared that he would offer a determined resistance to the measures of the cabinet. At the end of May the British and French fleets made their appearance before Alexandria. In the middle of June serious disturbances broke out in that town, in the course of which many Europeans were killed, while the others found refuge on board the ships. On July 11th and 12th Alexandria was bombarded by the British fleet, and on Sept. 13th the fortified camp of Arabi at Tell el-Kebîr was stormed by a British force under Sir Garnet Wolseley. Arabi and his associates were captured and sent as exiles to Ceylon. Since these events English influence has been paramount in Egypt. In the autumn of 1883 a wide-spread rebellion broke out among the Nubian tribes of the Sûdân under the leadership of Moḥammed Aḥmed, the so-called 'Mahdi' (p. 153), which threatened to be fatal to the Egyptian supremacy in the Sûdân. An Egyptian army of 10,000 men under an Englishman named Hicks
1883. Pasha was annihilated in Nov., 1883, by the Mahdi's forces, and a second expedition of 3500 regular troops of the Egyptian army, led by Baker Pasha, was also completely defeated
1884. at Tokar in February, 1884. On the 18th of the same month General Gordon, after a perilous ride across the desert, entered Kharṭûm, which he had untertaken to save from the Mahdi; while on Mar. 1st and Mar. 13th the rebel tribes under the Mahdi's lieutenant Osman Digna were defeated at *El-Teb* and *Tamanieb* by the British troops under Graham. The Mahdi himself, however, still maintained his position near Kharṭûm, and towards the close of the year a second British expedition (of 7000 men) was sent out under Wolseley to rescue Gordon.

Wolseley selected the Nile route for this expedition in preference to the shorter but more dangerous desert route from Souâkin to Berber, but the ascent of the river proved a very tedious operation and it was not till the beginning of
1885. 1885 that he was able to concentrate his troops at Korti, between the third and fourth cataracts (a little above Ed-Dabbe on the Map at p. 30). The Nile here makes an enormous bend, and a detachment of 1500 men was now sent on

in advance to cut off this bend and open communication with Kharṭûm from Shendy, while the main body continued its laborious ascent of the Nile. The advanced brigade under General Stewart accomplished its march across the *Bayûda Desert* (see Map, p. 30) with complete success, gaining severely contested victories over large bodies of the Mahdi's followers at *Abû Klea* (Jan. 17th) and at a point near *Metemmeh* (Jan. 19th). Stewart, however, was mortally wounded at the latter engagement. The British reached the Nile at *Gubat*, just above Metemmeh, on the evening of Jan. 19th, and on Jan. 24th a small body of men under Sir Chas. Wilson set out for Kharṭûm in two steamboats which Gordon had sent to meet them. Sir Charles reached Kharṭûm on the 28th, but found that it had already fallen on the 26th, apparently through treachery, and that Gordon was either dead or in the hands of the Mahdi. Upon the news of the fall of Kharṭûm the British government, after consultation with General Wolseley, decided that it was necessary to arrest the progress of the Mahdi, and determined to dispatch reinforcements of 10,000 men to Souâkin, to co-operate with Wolseley from that base. The construction of a railway from Souâkin to Berber was also resolved upon. At the time the Handbook went to press the plan of Wolseley's farther operations was not definitely known; but the loss of Kharṭûm and the approach of the hot season had greatly complicated his task, and the advanced brigade had been recalled to join the main body. Though an absolutely trustworthy account of the fate of General Gordon has not yet been received, there is almost no room to doubt that he perished at the capture of Kharṭûm.

IV. Hieroglyphics.

By Professor G. Ebers of Leipsic.

The ancient Egyptians used three kinds of writing, the *Hieroglyphic*, the *Hieratic*, and the *Demotic*, to which, within the Christian era, was added the *Coptic*. The first and earliest is the pure *Hieroglyphic* writing, which consists of figures of material objects from every sphere of nature and art, together with certain mathematical and arbitrary symbols. Thus  owl,  snail,  axe, □ square,  senti. This is the monumental writing, which is oftener found engraved on stone than written with a pen. For the speedier execution of long records the Egyptians next developed the *Hieratic* writing, in which the owl (, i.e. ) almost ceases to be recognisable, and in which we possess literary works of every kind except dramas. The most ancient hieratic papyrus now extant was written in the third millennium before Christ. The language used in the hieroglyphic and hieratic writings alike was the ancient sacred dialect of the priests. The *Demotic* writing, which was first employed in the 9th century before Christ, diverges so widely from the hieroglyphic that in some of the symbols the original sign from which they were derived is either not traceable, or can only be recognised with difficulty. The sign of the owl, for example, was curtailed to ⊃. This writing was chiefly used in social and commercial intercourse; as, for example, in contracts and letters, whence it was sometimes termed the 'letter character' by the Greeks. The more the spoken language diverged from the sacred dialect, which assumed a fixed form at a very early period, the more urgent became the want of a new mode of writing appropriate to the living language. Thus arose the demotic style, and lastly, in the 3rd century after Christ, the *Coptic*, in which the language spoken at that time by the Christian Egyptians was written, the characters being Greek, with a few supplementary symbols borrowed from the demotic (such as ϣ *sh*, ϥ *f*, ϧ *ch*, ϩ *h*, ϭ *c*, ϫ *j*, and the syllabic ϯ *ti*). Many Coptic writings, chiefly of a religious character, have been handed down to us, the finest of them being the books of the Old and New Testament.

Down to the end of the 18th century scholars had been misled in their endeavours to find a clue to the hieroglyphic writing by a work of the Egyptian grammarian *Horapollon*, translated into Greek, who represented the characters as being purely symbolical, and as having each an independent meaning of its own. At length in 1799 *M. Boussard*, a French officer of artillery, discovered at Rosetta a trilingual inscription (pp. 449 *et seq.*), in hieroglyphic and demotic characters and in Greek. The demotic part of the inscription was examined by *M. Silvestre de Sacy*, a French savant, and *Hr. Ackerblad*, a Swede, in 1802, and, chiefly owing to the exertions of the latter, the signification of a number of the symbols was ascertained. In 1814-18 the hieroglyphic part of the inscription was studied by *Dr. Th. Young*, an English scholar, who, by comparing it with the demotic part, succeeded in dividing it into a number of corresponding groups, and, by directing his attention to the cartouches (p. 117), discovered the signification of several of the hieroglyphic symbols. In 1821 *François Champollion*, usually surnamed *Le Jeune*, who possessed an intimate acquaintance with the Coptic language and literature, directed his attention to the hieroglyphics, and in the course of the following year discovered the hieroglyphic alphabet, which afforded him a clue to the whole of the ancient Egyptian literature. His method, which he has explained in his hieroglyphic grammar, though at first vehemently opposed, soon obtained able adherents, who after his early death in 1832 zealously took up and prosecuted the same line of research.

Among these were the French savants *MM. Ch. Lenormant*, *Nestor l'Hôte*, and *Emmanuel de Rougé*, the last of whom was the first to translate with philological accuracy a hieroglyphic text of any length, and the Italian scholars *MM. Salvolini*, *Ungarelli*, and *Rosellini*. The most distinguished English Egyptologists of the same school are *Messrs. Osburn* and *Hincks*, and *Dr. Birch*, who has compiled the first complete dictionary of the ancient language, and has translated numerous inscriptions. The most celebrated German Egyptologist is *Prof. Richard Lepsius* (d. 1881), the founder of the critical method of prosecuting philological and historical research. Thanks to the discoveries of these savants and others of the same school, the study of the subject has progressed so rapidly that the time is probably not far distant when students will be able to translate a hieroglyphic inscription with as great philological accuracy as the work of a Greek or Latin author.

A glance at a single temple wall, or even at the annexed list of the names of the Egyptian kings, will show the traveller that we have not to deal here with an alphabetical mode of writing, the signs (about 2000 in number) being far too numerous. The ancient Egyptian writings were based on two different, but intimately connected systems. (1) the *Ideographic*, which, by the use of well-known objects as symbols of conceptions, sought to render its meaning intelligible to a certain class of the community; and (2) the *Phonetic*, which represents words by symbols of their sounds. Although we cannot now trace the rise and progress of hieroglyphic writing, as even the earliest specimens manifestly belong to an already perfected system, we may at least safely assert that the ideographic element preceded the phonetic; for, as a child employs gestures earlier than speech, so nations use a symbolical form of writing before they arrive at a method of expressing sounds. The newer and more serviceable phonetic system must ultimately have superseded the ideographic, although occasionally calling in its aid as an auxiliary. In the perfected system, therefore, the symbols for sounds and syllables are to be regarded as the foundation of the writing, while symbols for ideas are interspersed with them, partly to render the meaning more intelligible, and partly for ornamental purposes, or with a view to keep up the mystic character of the hieroglyphics.

The *Phonetic* signs are divided into alphabetical letters, such as  *a*,  *b*,  *q* or *k*,  *f*, etc., and syllabic signs, such as  *ar*,  *hā*,  *sch*,  *ânkh*,  *ancr*, etc. The syllable signs may, in order to fix their sounds with greater precision, have as 'phonetic complements' one, several, or all of those sounds which the name of the syllable representing the sign in question contains. Thus , which stands for ânkh, may also be represented by (1) , (2) , (3)  or (4) . The reading is, however, facilitated by the fact that, in order to ensure the correct pronunciation of each syllabic sign, none but the most definite sounds were added to it. The symbol 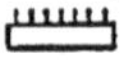 *men*, for example, is never written 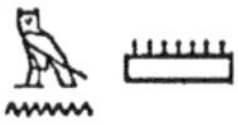, as it might be, but almost invariably 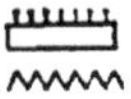 or 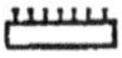. It represents a chess-board with figures. The ideographic signs, or determinatives, are placed as explanatory adjuncts after the phonetically written groups. They are indispensable in elucidating the signification, for the Egyptian language, having been arrested in its development, is poor, and full of homonyms and synonyms. The symbol 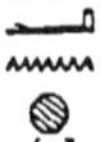 *ânkh*, for example, means 'to live', 'to swear', 'the ear', 'the mirror', and 'the goat'. The reader would easily fall into errors, such as mistaking *ânkh nefer* for 'a beautiful life' instead of 'a beautiful goat', if the determinative, or class, sign did not come to his aid, and show to what category of ideas the object belonged. Thus, after *ânkh*, the goat, the Egyptians either placed a figure of that animal, or a piece of hide with a tail , which served as a common symbol for all quadrupeds. The symbol used to represent a particular word is termed a *special*, while one chosen to denote a class is termed a *general*, determinative. An elephant  placed after the group of , *āb*, 'the elephant', is a special determinative, while a lock of hair  placed after  *senem*, 'the mourning', is a general determinative, a lock of hair being the conventional emblem of grief, as the men were in the habit of cutting off their hair in token of sorrow. A word is frequently followed by several determinatives. Thus  *âsh* is 'the cedar'; but the wood of the tree being scented, the group representing *āsh* was not only followed by the figure of a tree , but also by the symbol , which signifies that a perfumed object is spoken of. The special determinative always precedes the general. Symbols that were not capable of being very clearly engraved on stone were sometimes omitted, and the special determinative given alone. Instead of semsem, 'the horse', often stands alone. In such cases we know the sense of the word, while its pronunciation must be gathered from other and fuller forms of it. The following words, which are written in various ways, may be given as an illustration.

(1)

ahu-u   apet-u   arp-u
Bullocks   Geese   Wine

(2)

Bullocks   Geese   Wine.

In the first of these groups ⸢ahu⸣ *ahu* corresponds to the Coptic ⲉϩⲟⲟⲩ *chou*, and signifies bullocks, as the determinative symbol shows. (The three strokes are the sign of the plural.) In the next place *apet-u* signifies geese, and is determined by the figure of that bird. Lastly *arp* (Coptic ⲏⲡⲛ, *erp*) means wine, and is associated with the general determinative ⊕, *i. e.* the jars in which the juice of the grape used to be kept. In the second form of the sentence the syllabic writing is omitted, and the plural, instead of being denoted by three strokes, is expressed by the repetition of the special determinative. This leaves no doubt as to what is meant, while the first form gives us the actual words.

We now give the most important symbols of sound of the ancient Egyptian writing, and also a few syllabic signs.

Hieroglyphic Alphabet.

1. a
2. a.
3. ā.
4. , b.
5. f
6. h.
7. h.

8. \\ i.
9.
10. k.
11. q or ḳ.
12. l.
13. m.
14. ᷈ᷢ , n.
15. ▯ p.

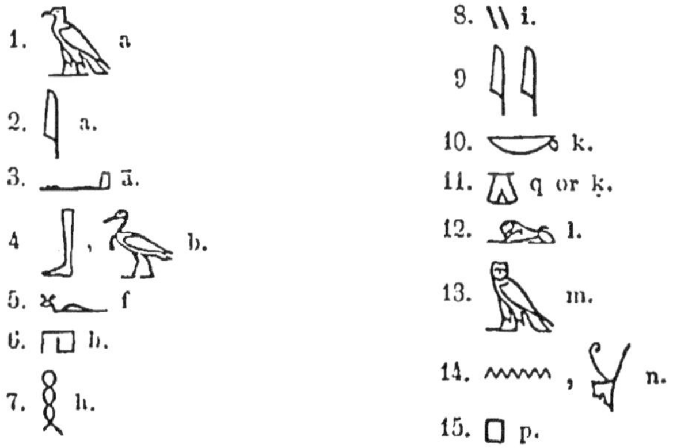

16. q.

17. r.

18. , s.

19. , š (sh).

20. t.

21. , ϑ (th).

22. t.

23. , i (z).

24. , u.

25 , χ (kh).

Important Syllables in Annexed List of Kings.

1. *men.*

2. *nofer.*

3. *râ.*

4. *khâ.*

5. *ka* or *qa.*

6. *user.*

7. *ṭaṭ.*

8. *ân.*

9. *ḥâ.*

10. *kheper.*

11. *neb.*

12. *peḥ.*

13. *aḥ, ab, a.*

14. *Taḥuti, Thoth* (god of science, etc.).

15. *mes.*

16. *Hor* (the god Horus).

17. *ḥeb.*

18. *ser.*

19 *â-a, â*

20. *mer*

21 *su.*

22. *Mаâ* (goddess of truth)

23 *Set* (the god Seth)

24. or *sih*, the son.

25. *sotep* (approved).

26. *Râ* (god of the sun).

27. *Amen* (the god Ammon).

28. *Ptaḥ* (the god Ptah).

29. *ba.*

30.  *ḥotep.*

31.  *me* and *mer.*

32.  *ḥaḳ.*

33.  *an* (On, Heliopolis)

34. *ta.*

35.  *nuter.*

36.  *ase(t)* (Isis)

37.  *khu*

38.  *sa.*

39.  *Net* (goddess Neith)

40.  *uaḥ*

41.  *ab* and *ȧhti.*

42.  *ka.*

43.  *ȧnkh.*

44.  *nekht*

45.  *ruṭ.*

46.  *ba.*

47.  *menkh.*

48.  *fuȧ.*

49.  *sen*

50.  *ṭata*

51.  *khu.*

52.  *seb, ṭua.*

53.  *nub.*

54.  *maȧ*

55.  *sebek.*

56.  *ḥem*

The form of the hieroglyphic signs is not invariable. During the primæval monarchy they were simple and large, while under the new empire they diminished in size but increased in number. The writing of the reigns of Thothmes III. and of Seti I. (18th and 19th dynasties) is remarkably good. In the 20th and following dynasties the hieroglyphics show symptoms of decadence. The writing of the 24-26th dynasties is distinct and elegant, but has not the boldness peculiar to the primæval monarchy. Under the Ptolemies the symbols acquired characteristics peculiar to this period alone, while many new hieroglyphics were added to the old; the individual letters are, as a rule, beautifully executed, but the eye is offended by their somewhat overladen and cramped style. The method of writing, too, is changed. The phonetic element makes large concessions to the ideographic, and acrophony becomes very predominant: *i. e.*, a number of symbols are used to stand for the first letter only of the word they represent. Thus the syllabic symbol *ser* ('the prince') is used for the letter *s* alone; *nehem* ('the lotus-bud') for *n* alone; and so on.

The frames within which the groups of hieroglyphics are enclosed are termed 'cartouches'. Where they occur, the inscription generally records the names of kings, and occasionally, but very rarely, those of gods. Above them usually stands the group *suten sekhet*, i. e. 'king of Upper and Lower Egypt', or *neb taui*, 'sovereign of both lands', or *neb khâ-u*, 'lord of the diadems'.

When the name of a king is to be deciphered, the alphabetical signs must first be noted, and then the syllabic symbols. The following examples will illustrate this.

The builder of the great pyramids is named —

i. e. Khufu; (25) being *kh*; (24) *u*; (5) *f*; and (24) *u*.

The builder of the second pyramid was

Khafra. Here is the 3rd syllabic sign *ra*; , the 4th syllabic sign *kha*; the letter *f*. This would give us *râ-khâ-f*; but it is to be read *khâ-f-râ*, or Khafra, as the syllable ra, wherever it occurs in the name of a king, is always placed first without regard to its proper place in the structure of the word. This was done out of respect for the holy name of Ra, the god of the sun, to which the Egyptians thus piously gave precedence. On the same principle the name of the builder of the Third Pyramid, (3), (1), and (5), or *ra-men-ka*, is to be read Menkara or Menkera. — Several celebrated kings of the 18th Dynasty are termed

. Now is the 14th syllabic sign *tehuti* or *thut*, the 15th syllabic sign *mes*, and the 18th alphabetical letter, which is added as a phonetic complement to *mes*. The name is therefore to be read *Tahut-mes* or *Thut-mes*, the Greek form of which was Tuthmosis (commonly known as Thothmes).

VI. Frequently recurring Names of Egyptian Kings.†

Selection by Prof. Ebers in Leipsic.

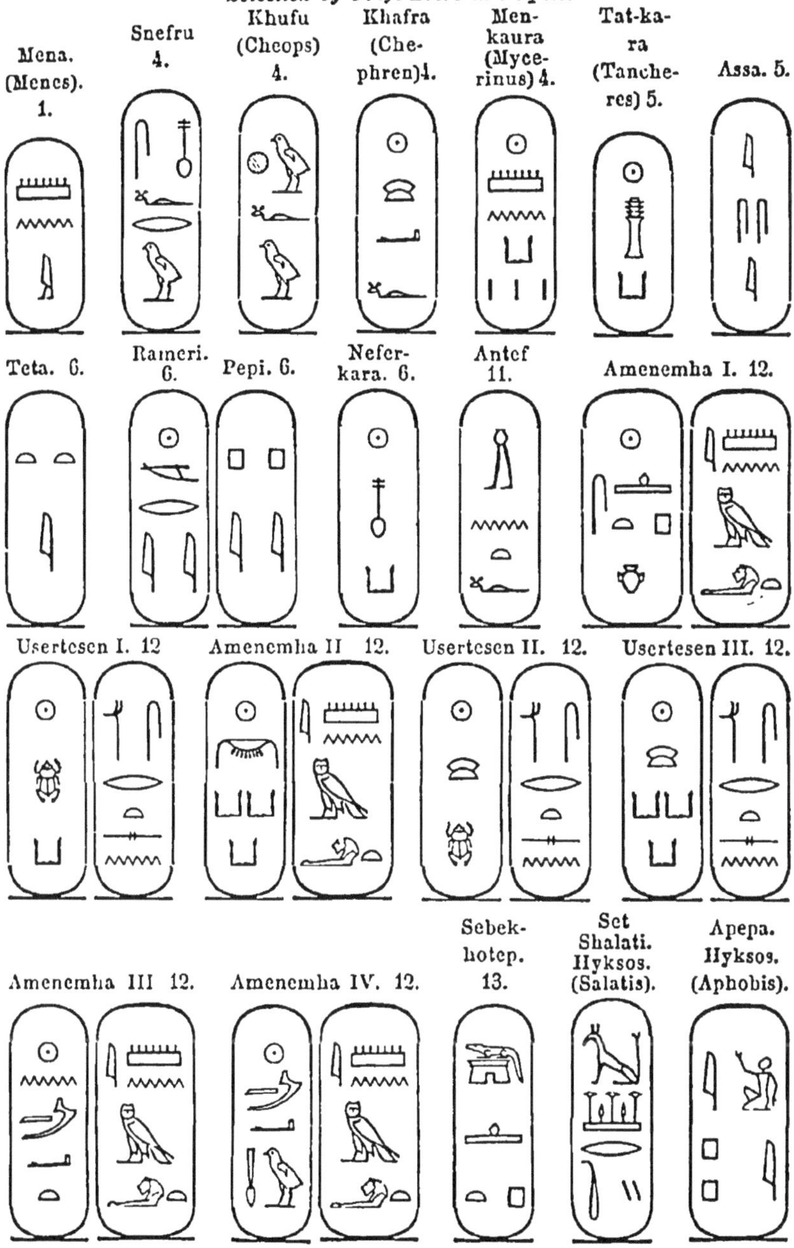

† The numbers placed after the names are those of the different dynasties.

The life-dispensing favourite of (the god) Set. | Rasqenen. | Aahmes (Amosis). 18. | Amenhotep (Amenophis) I. 18. | Tutmes (Tuthmosis) I. 18.

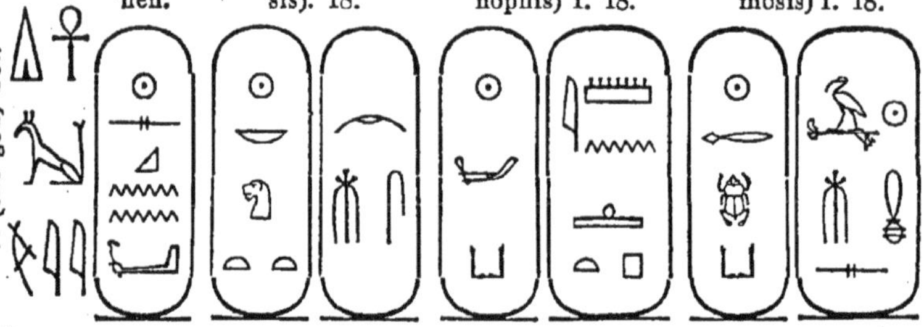

Hatasu. 18. | Tutmes III. 18. | Amenhotep II. 18. | Amenhotep III. 18.

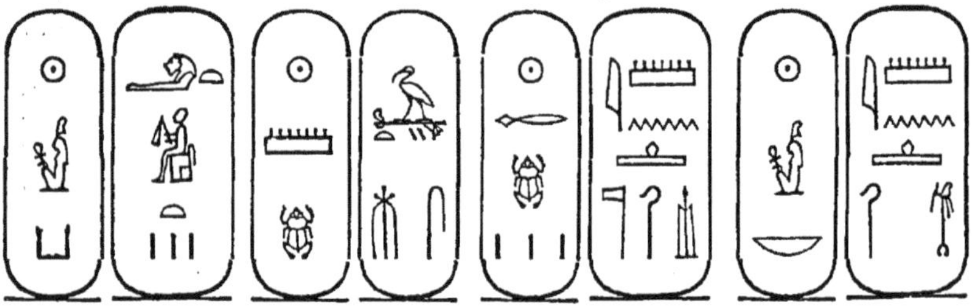

Amenhotep IV. (Khu-en-aten) 18. | Hor-em-heb (Horus) 18. | Ramses I. 19. | Seti I. (favourite of Ptah) 19.

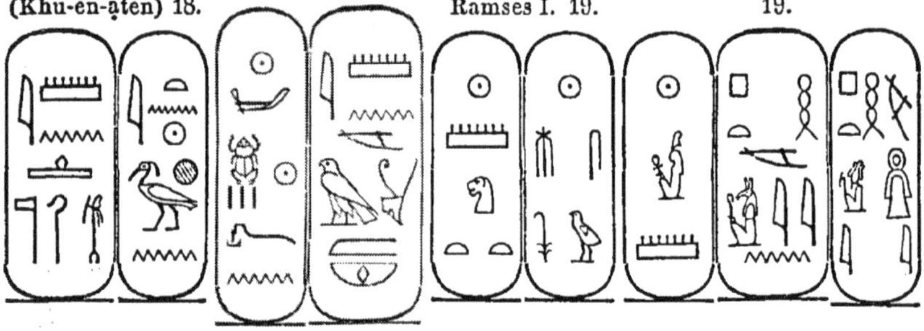

Ramses II., favourite of Ammon, and his father Seti I., the Sesostris of the Greeks.

Sesetsu (Sesostris.)

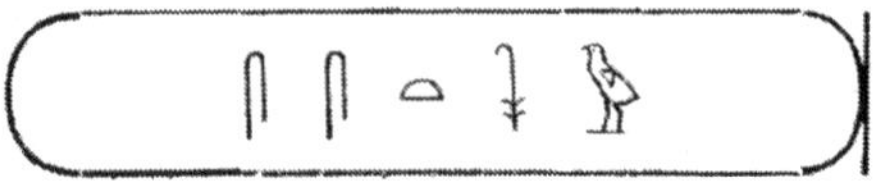

Prince Khaemus.

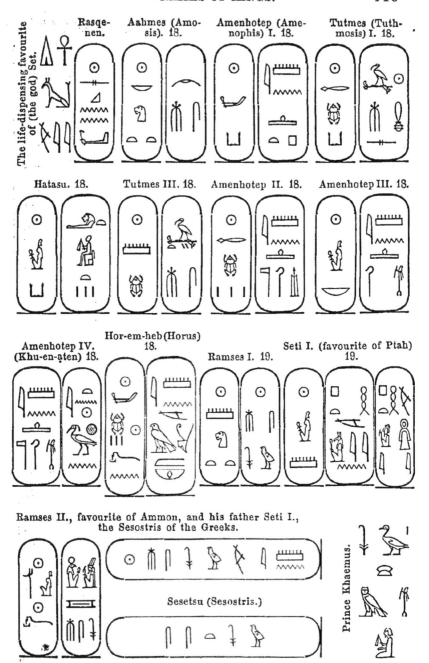

Merenptah I. (Menephthes). 19.

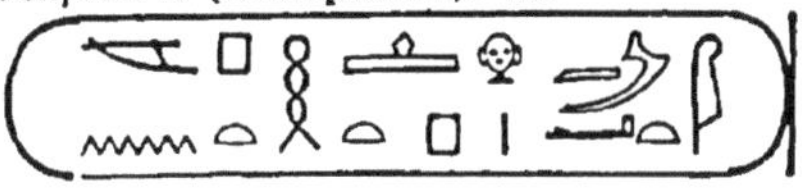

Seti II. (Merenptah). 19.

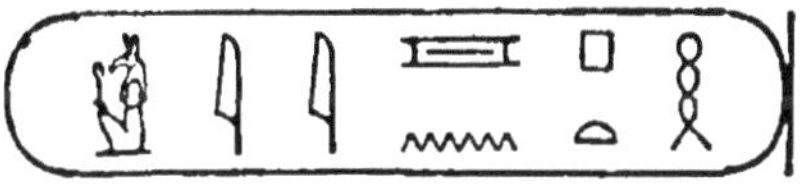

Ramses III. 20.

Ramses IV. 20.

Ramses V. 20.

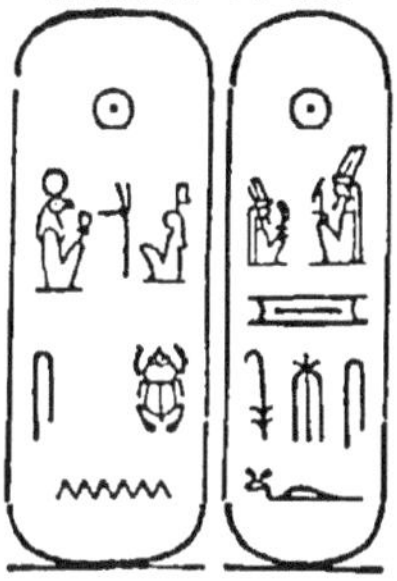

Ramses VI. 20.

Ramses VII. 20.

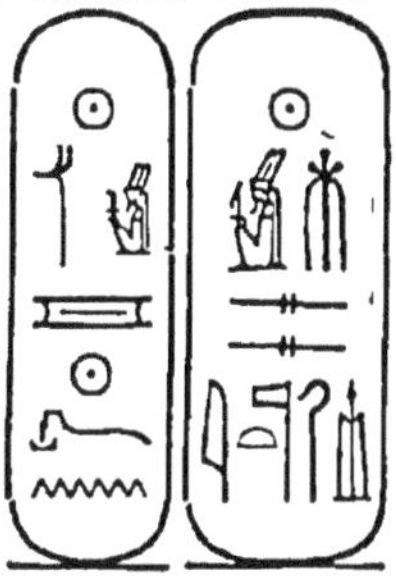

Ramses VIII. 20.

Ramses IX. (Leps. Ramses XI.) 20.

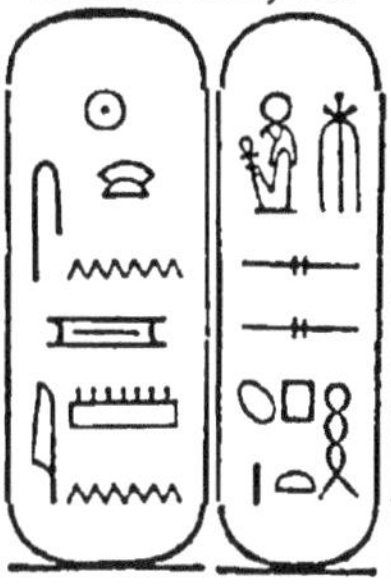

Ramses X. (Leps. Ramses IX.) 20.

Ramses XI. (Leps. Ramses XII.) 20.

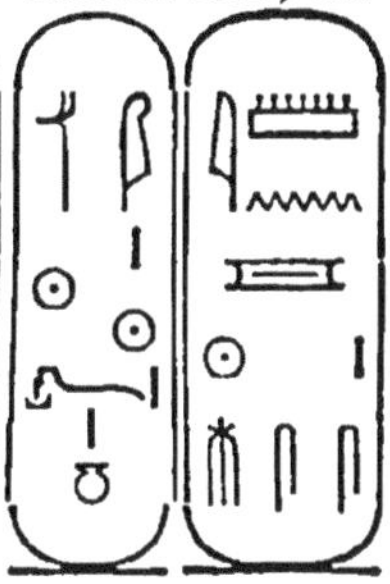

Ramses XII. (Leps. Ramses XIII.) 20

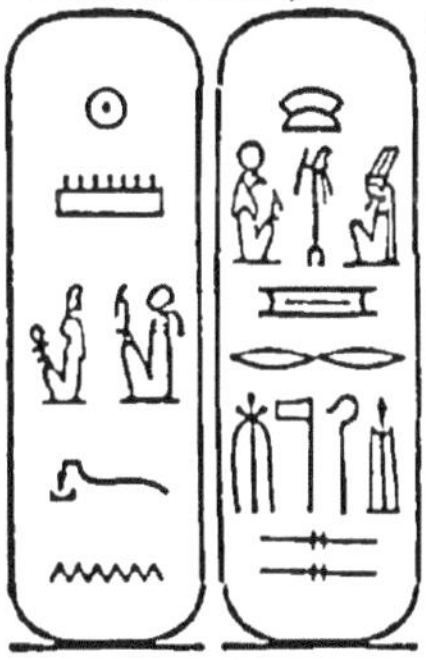

Sheshenk (Sesonchis) I 22.

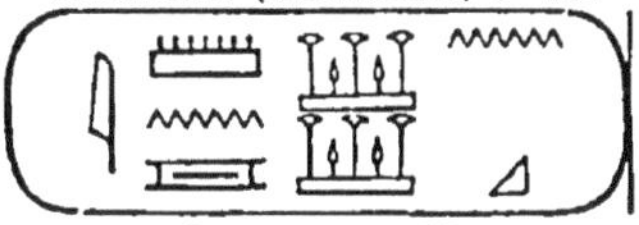

Osorkon I. 22.

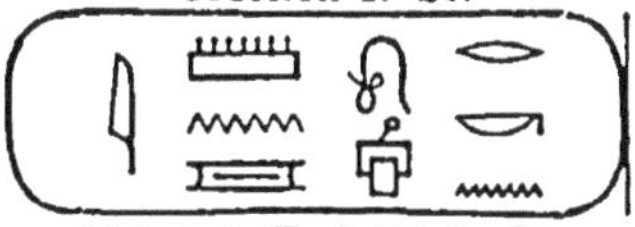

Takelut (Tiglath) I. 22.

Sheshenk IV. 23.

Bokenranf (Bocchoris). 24.

Shabak (Sabaco). 25.

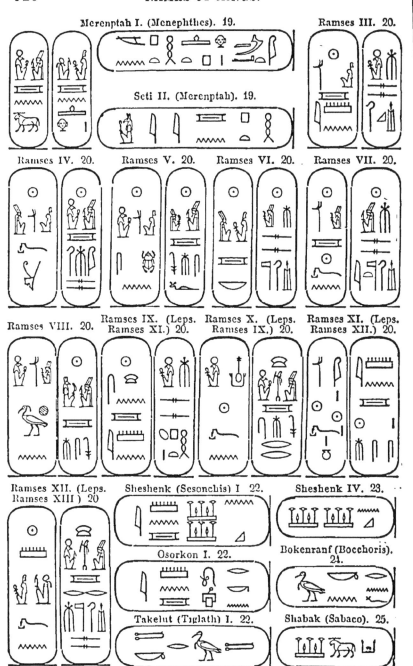

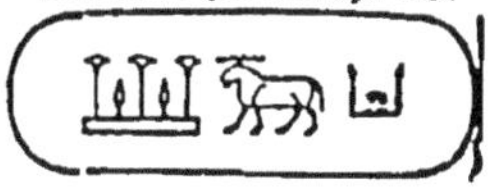

Taharka. 25.

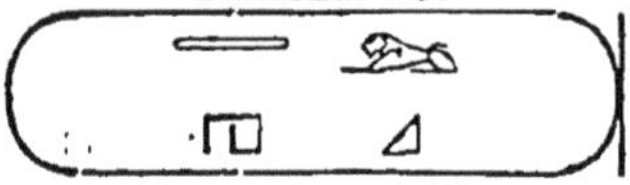

Queen Ameniritis

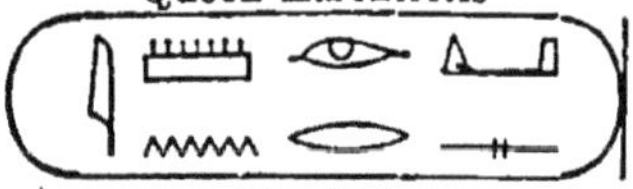

Piankhi.

Psammetikh I. 26 Nekho 26. Psammetikh II. 26.

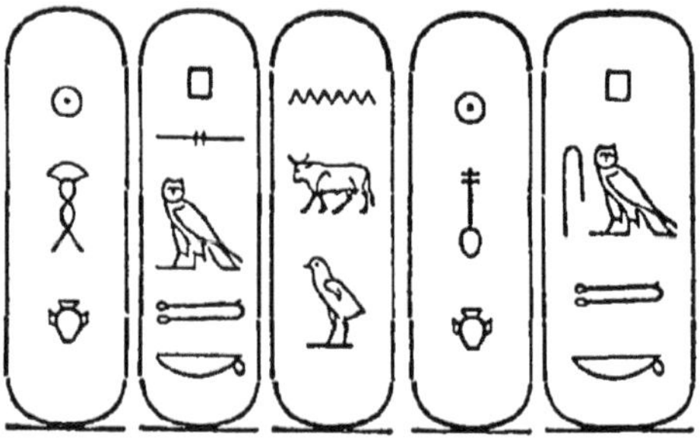

Uahphrahet (Uaphris. Hophrah). 26. Aahmes II. (Amasis). 26. Kambatet (Cambyses) 27. Ntariush (Darius). 27. Darius. 27. Kheshe-rish (Xerxes). 27.

Amenrut (Amyrtæus) 28. Nekht-nebf (Nectánebus). 30. Alexander I. 32. Philip-pus Aridæus. 32. Ptolmis (Ptolemy I. Soter). 33.

Ptolemy II. Philadelphus I. 33

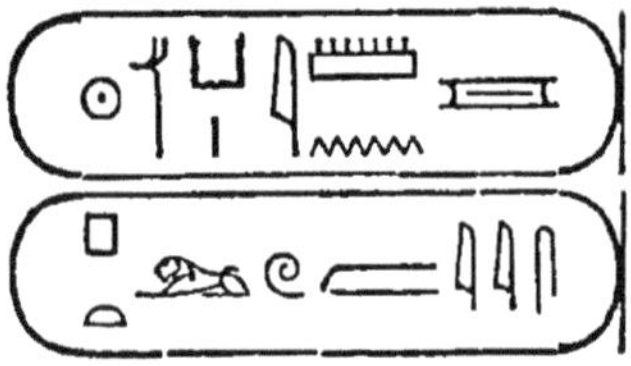

Queen Arsinoë. 33.

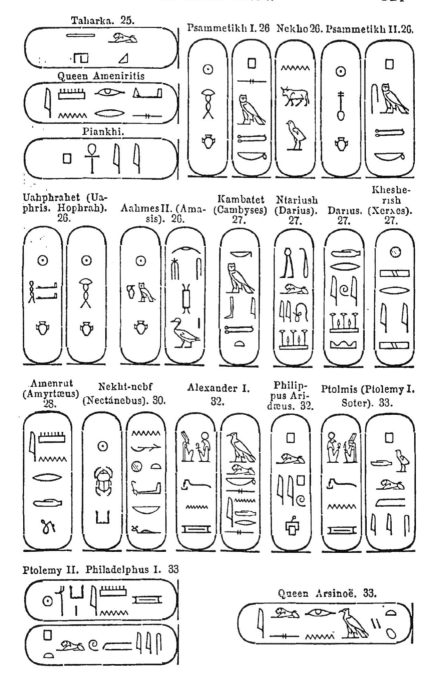

Ptolemy III. Euergetes I. 33.

Queen Berenice II. 33.

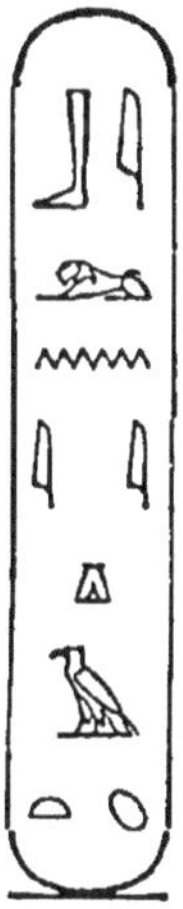

Ptolemy IV. Philopator I. 33.

Ptolemy V. Epiphanes. 33.

Ptolemy IX. Euergetes II. (Physcon). 33.

Seven Ptolemaic princesses of the name of Cleopatra occur.

Ptolemy X. Soter II or Philometor II. usually known as Lathyrus. 33

Cleopatra VI., mistress of Cæsar and Antony. 33.

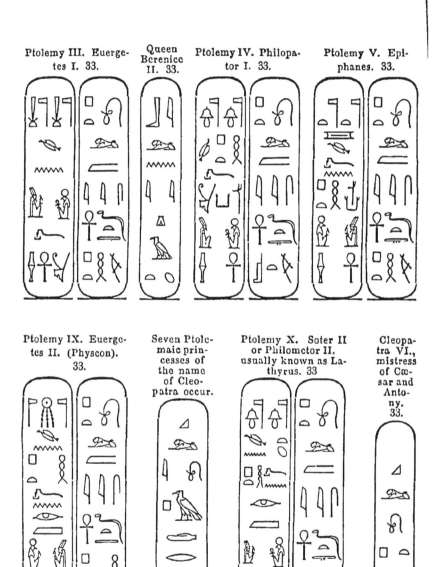

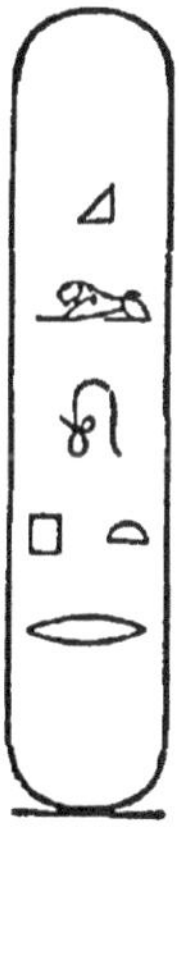

Cleopatra VI., with Cæsarion, her son by Cæsar, and nominal co-regent. 33.

The famous Cleopatra and her son Cæsarion.

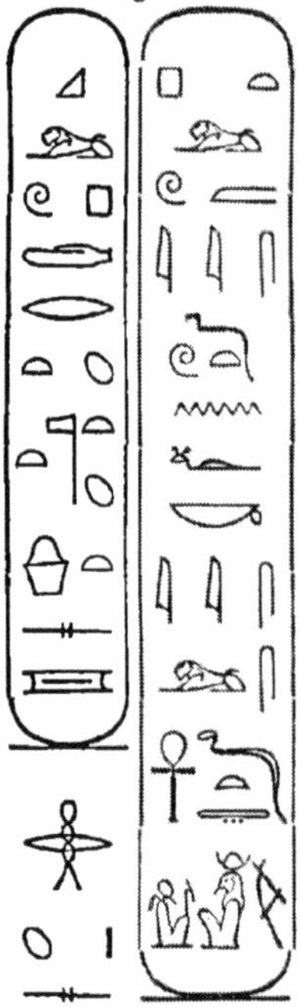

Cleopatra and her son Cæsarion, her co-regent.

Autocrator (absolute monarch) and Kisaros (Cæsar). Epithets of all the emperors. 34.

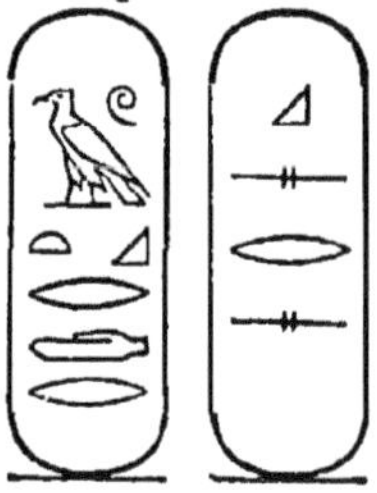

Cæsar Augustus 34.

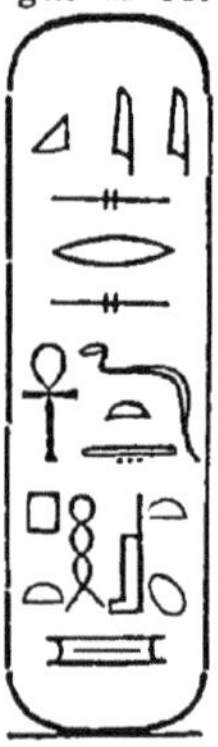

Tiberius. 34.

Caius Caligula. 34.

Claudius. (Tiberius). 34.

Nero. 34.

Vespasian. 34.

Domitian. 34.

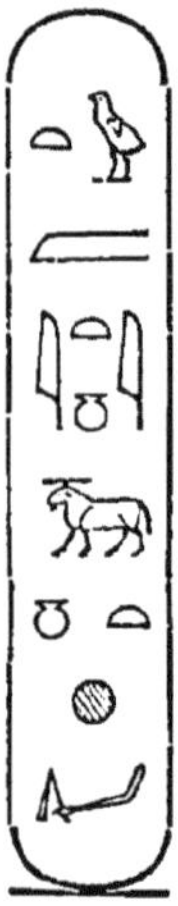

Trajan. 34.

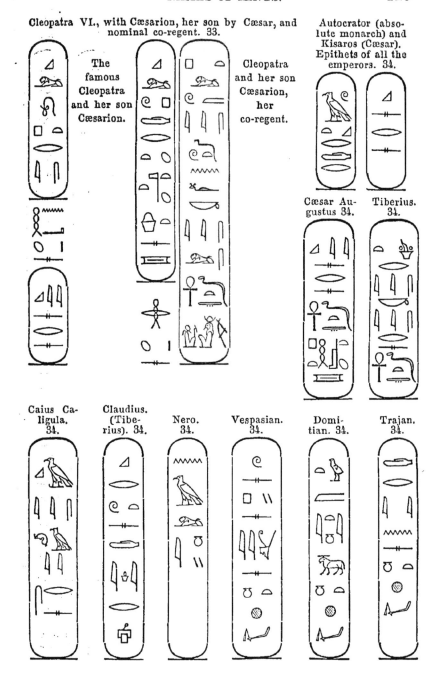

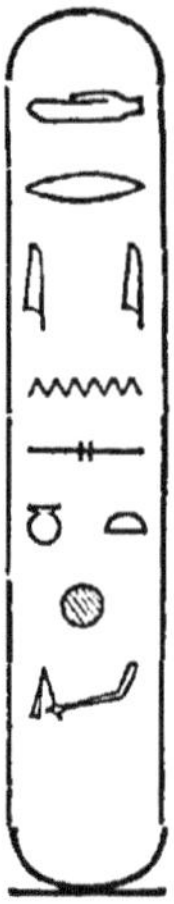

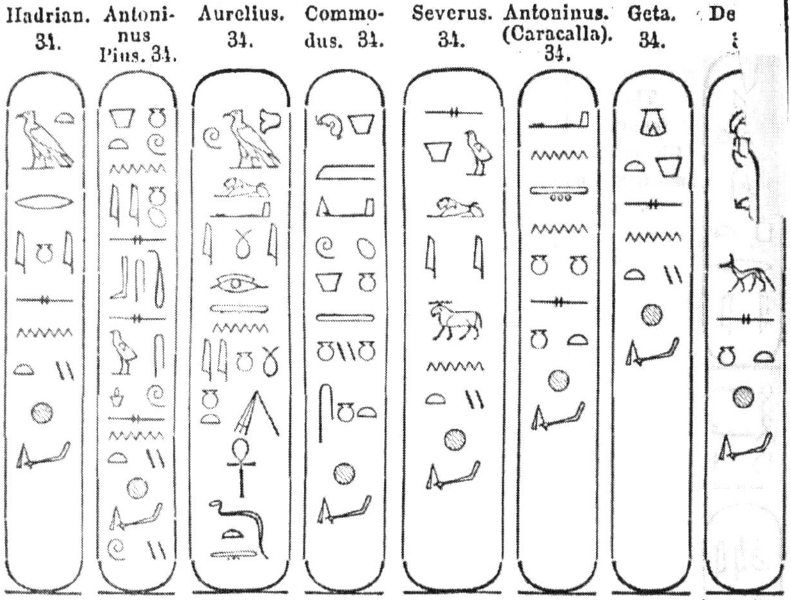
Hadrian. 34.
Antoninus Pius. 34.
Aurelius. 34.
Commodus. 34.
Severus. 34.
Antoninus. (Caracalla). 34.
Geta. 34.
De

VI. Religion of the Ancient Egyptians.

The difficulty of thoroughly comprehending the fundamental ideas which underlay the religion of the ancient Egyptians is increased by two important circumstances. The first of these is, that the hierarchy of Egypt studiously endeavoured to obscure their dogmas by the use of symbolical and mysterious language; and the second is, that each nome possessed its own local divinity and colleges of priests, and invented its own cosmological and metaphysical allegories. This accounts for the differences of doctrine in a number of forms of worship bearing the same name, and for the frequency with which the attributes of one god trench on those of another. The primitive religion, moreover, underwent great changes as the capacity of the hierarchy for more profound speculation increased, until at length the relations of the divinities to each other and to the fundamental ideas represented grew into a complicated system, understood by the limited circle of the initiated alone. This was styled the Esoteric Doctrine †, the leading idea of which was, that matter, though liable to perpetual modifications, was eternal and fundamentally immutable, incapable of increase or decrease, but endowed with intelligence and creative power. In the opinion

† Esoteric (from ἐσωτερικός, inner, hidden) is a term applied to a mysterious doctrine, known to the initiated only, the antithesis of which is the exoteric doctrine (from ἐξωτερικός, external, popular).

those who held this doctrine there could be no original act of creation, and no plurality of gods; but a metaphysical conception so difficult of apprehension could not be propounded to the great body of the people. For the use of such persons it was, therefore, simplified, and clothed with allegorical forms, through the medium in which they might behold it as through a veil, somewhat obscured, but at the same time embellished and shorn of its terrors. This constituted the Exoteric Doctrine, with which was connected the theogony, or theory of the origin and descent of the divinities who represented the various forces and phenomena of nature. These gods, however, though not existent from all eternity, were neither created nor begotten, but were regarded as having been self-created in the wombs of their own mothers, and are therefore spoken of as 'their own fathers', 'their own sons', and the 'husbands of their mothers'. The deities accordingly are seldom spoken of as single individuals, but in triads, as father, mother, and son (comp. p. 130).

The primary source from which all life proceeds, the first cause of all things, was clothed with a personal form, called **Nun.** The principle of light, and the creative power of nature, which implants in matter the germs of existence and light, was **Khepera**, or the scarabæus with the sun's disk, whose emblem was the beetle (*scarabaeus sacer*). As that insect rolls up into a ball the eggs which produce its offspring, and was supposed to have no female, so this deity was believed to have concealed within the globe of the world the germs of organic life. **Ptah** is the greatest of the gods, and is the embodiment of the organising and motive power developed from moisture (Nun). It is he who imparts form to the germs sown by Khepera, and under the name of *Sekhem Nefer* breaks the ball rolled along by the scarabæus, or in other words the egg of the universe, from which emerge his children, the elements and the forms of heaven and earth. **Ra**, a deity who bears seventy-five different forms, at first appears in the Nun under the name of **Tum**, or the evening sun; during his passage through the lower hemisphere, that of night, he is known as *Khnum*, and is born anew on the next morning of the creation, bursting forth in the form of a child (*Harmachis*) from a lotus-flower floating on the Nun. Evening and night precede the morning and day; and *Amenthes*, or the infernal regions, were believed to have existed before the upper regions which formed the scene of human life.

After the breaking of the egg of the world, the universe is resolved into three empires: — (1) The heavenly *Nut*, represented as a woman 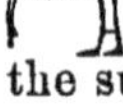, bending over the earth, on whose back float the vessel of the sun, the planets, and the constellations. (2) *Seb*, or the earth, which possesses the power of eternal rejuvenescence, and was regarded by the Egyptians as the symbol of eternity, a deity somewhat resembling the Greek Chronos. (3) The *Infernal Regions*, which are presided over by Ptah, the power productive of new forms, the germinating principle of seeds, and god of light and heat (sometimes represented in the shape of a deformed child), and, after him, by Ra, who appears from the inscription on the royal tombs at Thebes to have been a purely pantheistic conception, the 'frame of the universe' and 'the universe', and whose sphere therefore embraced the lower as well as the upper regions. (See also Ra and Ammon.)

The Sacred Animals and the Mixed Forms, which generally consist of human bodies with the heads of animals, frequently recur as companions of the gods, or are used as emblems of the deities themselves. In each case those animals were selected whose inherent dispositions and habits corresponded to the power or phenomenon of nature personified in the god. Specimens of these animals were kept in and near the temples, and the finest of them were embalmed after death and revered in the form of mummies. Thus, the maternal divinities were appropriately represented by the cow, the patient mother and nurse; the goddess of love, the bride of Ptah, was represented with the head of a fierce lion or a cat; the crocodile was sacred to Sebek, the god who caused the waters of the Nile to rise; and the hawk, which soars towards heaven like the sun, was dedicated to Ra. The symbol of Ptah was the black Apis bull, whose great power of generation seemed analogous to the never ceasing creative energy of the black soil of Egypt.

The Egyptian Gods. The chief of the gods, as we have already mentioned, was **Ptah**, the Greek Hephæstus. He was the ancient god of Memphis, who delivered to Ra the germs of creation, and was assisted in his labours by the seven *Khnumu* or architects. As from him were supposed to emanate the laws and conditions of existence, he is also styled 'lord of truth'. He is represented in the form of a mummy, but with his hands protruding from the bandages, and grasping the symbol of life , that of stability , and the sceptre 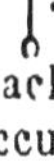. The neck-ornament called 'menat' is generally attached to his back, and on his head he usually wears a smith's cap. He sometimes occurs with a scarabæus instead of a head. In view of his connection with the doctrine of immortality and with the infernal regions, he sometimes appears in the inscriptions as *Ptah-Sokar-Osiris*, who prescribes to the sun that has set, as well as to the mummies of the dead, the conditions under which they may rise again and enter on a new life. The 'primæval Ptah' is also spoken of as the head of the solar gods, and also occasionally as the creator of the egg, from which, according to an older myth, the sun and the moon came forth. Thence, too, is derived his name, which signifies 'the opener'. By his side are often placed the goddess *Sekhet* (Pasht), and his son *Imhotep* (Æsculapius).

His sacred animal was the *Apis* bull, which was the offspring of a white cow impregnated by a moonbeam. In order to represent Apis worthily, a bull had to be sought which possessed a black hide, a white triangle on his forehead, a light spot on his back in the form of an eagle, and under his tongue an excrescence shaped like the sacred scarabæus. After his death the representative of Apis was embalmed and preserved in a sarcophagus of stone (p. 386). He was the symbol of the constantly operative fashioning power of the deity, and is on that account represented as the son of the moon, which, though never changing, appears to re-fashion itself every hour. The era of time named after Apis was a lunar period, containing 309 mean synodic months, which almost exactly corresponded with 25 Egyptian years.

Ptah.

Ra, the great god of Heliopolis (On) in Lower Egypt, as the king of gods and men, ranks next to Ptah, and is, from the exoteric point of view, the sun who illumines the world with the light of his eyes, and the awakener of life. He rises as a child, under the name of *Harmachis* (Har-em-khuti), at midday he is called *Ra*, and at sunset he is represented as *Tum*, an old man subduing the enemies of Ra, who obstruct his entrance to the lower regions which he traverses at night. During his course through the nether world he becomes the ram-headed *Khnum* (p. 129), or the nocturnal link between Tum and Harmachis, or evening and morning. As man in the region of the shades has to undergo many trials, so the ship of the sun, as soon as he has crossed the western horizon, no longer sails along the blue back of the goddess Nut, but along the sinuosities of the serpent Apep, the enemy of the setting sun, who is subdued and held in bondage by the companions of Ra.

In rising Ra is born, and in setting he dies; but his life is daily renewed by an act of self-procreation taking place daily in the bosom of nature, which was termed *Isis*, *Muth*, or *Hathor*. This goddess is frequently called the ruler of the nether regions, and is represented with the head of a cow, or in the form of a cow, which every morning gives birth to the young sun. Twelve human figures, each bearing the orb of the sun or a star on his head, represent the hours of the day and night. The animals specially sacred to Ra were the hawk; the Upper Egyptian light-coloured Mnevis bull, which also belonged at a later period to Ammon Ra, and a specimen of which had even before that time been kept in the temple of the sun at Heliopolis; and, lastly, lions with light skins. The *Phoenix*, or bird from the land of palms, called by the Egyptians *bennu*, which, according to the well known myth, awakes to new life after being burned, and brings its ashes to Heliopolis once every five hundred years, was also associated with the worship of Ra. As Apis is associated with Ptah, so this bird by the side of Ra is a symbol of the soul of Osiris. — Ra is generally represented with the head of a hawk, and coloured red. He holds in his hands the symbols of life and sovereignty, and wears on his head a disk with the Uræus serpent, or basilisk. According to the esoteric and pantheistic construction of the inscriptions on the tombs of the kings, Ra is the great Universe (τὸ πᾶν), and the gods themselves are merely so many impersonations of his various attributes (see Ammon Ra, p. 138).

Harmachis, the great god.

Tum, or *Atum*, a manifestation of Ra, whose name is perhaps akin to *temt*, signifying the universe, was first worshipped in Lower Egypt, particularly at Heliopolis and at the city of Pa-tum, that is, 'the place of Tum', the Pithom of Scripture. His rites were also celebrated in Upper Egypt at an early period. He is one of the oldest of the gods, having existed 'on the waters' in the dark chaos of the embryonic world, prior to the first sunrise, or birth of Harmachis from the lotus flower. According to the later exoteric views he was the setting sun, the harbinger of the coolness of evening. Under his guidance mankind was created by Khnum, and he was the dispenser of the welcome northerly breezes. He was also the approved warrior against the dark powers of the infernal regions which obstruct the progress of the sun's bark, and is represented as a bearded man with a combined Upper and Lower Egyptian crown, or the orb of the sun, on his head, and the emblems of sovereignty and life in his hands. As the creator he sometimes has a scarabæus for a head; as *Nefer-Tum* he has the head of a lion, surmounted by a hawk crowned with lotus flowers, and holds an *ut'a* eye  in his hand. As representing the setting of the sun preparatory to its rising again, he

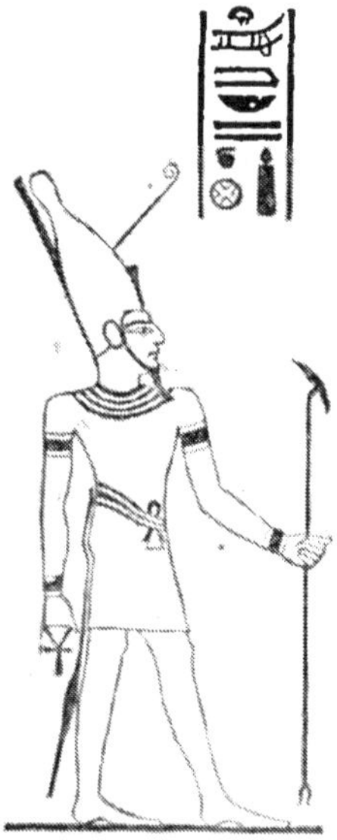
Tum of Heliopolis, lord of the world.

is also regarded as the god of the resurrection, as the hawk on his head indicates.

Khnum (Greek *Chnubis*, *Knuphis*, or *Kneph*), one of the most ancient of the gods, who, while retaining his own attributes, was often blended with Ammon, was chiefly worshipped in the region of the cataracts and in the oases of the Libyan desert. Being regarded as a link between the setting and the rising sun, he receives the sceptre of Ra beyond the western horizon (in which direction also lay the oases), and takes the place of that god during the progress of the sun through the nether world. Khnum ('khnem', the uniting) was also the power which united the days of sterility with those of fecundity, and was therefore specially revered in the island of Elephantine, near the first cataract, where the fertilising Nile first enters Egypt, as the god of the inundation and the dispenser of the gift of water. By his side usually stand the goddesses *Anukeh* and *Sati*. Khnum is one of the cosmic gods, who created the inhabitants of heaven. He and his assistants are associated with Ptah, and he is sometimes represented as moulding the egg of the world on a potter's wheel out of matter furnished by Ptah, and fashioning mankind. He is generally represented with the head of a ram, and coloured green. He occurs as often sitting as standing, wears the *âtef* crown on his head, and wields the sceptre and the symbol of life; while from his hips, proceeding from his girdle, depends a generative organ resembling a tail, which is appended to the most ancient form of his apron.

Khnum.

Ma, the goddess of truth and justice, is the radiant daughter of the god of the sun. She is easily recognised by the ostrich feather on her head, while in her hands she grasps the flower-sceptre and the symbol of life. In the more recent form of the ancient language she is termed *T-mei* (with the article),

Ma, daughter of Ra.

from which name an attempt has been made to derive that of the Greek goddess Themis, like whom Ma is represented as blind, or at least with bandaged eyes.

GODS OF THE OSIRIS AND ISIS ORDER. We owe to Plutarch a detailed account of this myth, which has been uniformly corroborated by the monuments, and which may be briefly told as follows.

The mythological Trinity or Triad.
Osiris. Horus. Isis.

Isis and **Osiris** were the children of Rhea and Chronos, that is, of Nut, the goddess of space, and of Seb, the god of the earth, which, owing to its eternal rejuvenescence and imperishableness, symbolises time. While still in the womb of their mother, that is, in the bosom of space, the children became united, and from their union sprang *Horus*. Typhon and Nephthys, children of the same parents, likewise married each other. Osiris and Isis reigned as a happy royal pair, bestowing on Egypt the blessings of wealth and prosperity. Typhon conspired against Osiris, and at a banquet persuaded him to enter a cunningly wrought chest, which he and his seventy-two accomplices then closed and threw into the Nile. The river carried the chest northwards, and so down to the sea by way of the estuary of Tanis; and the waves at length washed it ashore near the Phœnician Byblus. Meanwhile Isis roamed in distress throughout the country, seeking her lost husband; and she at length succeeded in discovering his coffin, which she carried to a sequestered spot and concealed. She then set out to visit her son Horus, who was being educated at Buto. During her absence Typhon, while engaged in a boar-hunt, found the body of the god, cut it into fourteen pieces, and scattered them in every direction. As soon as Isis learned what had happened, she collected the fragments, and wherever one had been found erected a monument on the spot to its memory; and this accounts for the numerous tombs of Osiris mentioned as existing in Egypt and elsewhere. Osiris, however, was not dead. He had continued his existence and his reign in the lower regions, and after his burial he visited his son Horus, whom he armed and trained for battle. The young god soon began a war against Typhon, and was at length victorious, although he did not succeed in totally destroying his enemy.

Osiris is the principle of light, while Typhon is that of darkness, which Osiris defeats and banishes to the infernal regions. Isis Hathor mourns over his disappearance, follows him towards the West, where she gives birth to Horus, who annihilates darkness and restores his father to his lost position. When *Ra* is termed the soul of Osiris, the meaning is that he renders visible the hidden principle of light (Osiris). When, on the other hand, Osiris is regarded as emblematical of the principle of moisture, the most perfect embodiment of which is the god Hapi, or the Nile, Typhon and his seventy-two companions represent the days of drought. Like the dead body of Osiris, the water flows towards the North, and the languishing Isis, that is, the fruit-bearing earth, mourns over the loss of the fertilising power; but this is for a short period only, for Horus soon vanquishes Typhon in the southern districts, and the rising Nile again begins to impregnate the black soil with abundant fertility. Lastly, when Osiris is regarded as the principle of life, Isis, the earth, is the scene of the operation of that principle, while Typhon represents death, and Horus the resurrection. If we regard Osiris, as the monuments so frequently do, as a pure and perfect being, the principle of the good and the beautiful, in which case he receives the surname of *Un-Nefer*, we recognise in Typhon the discords with which life is so replete, but which seem to be permitted only in order that the purity of the harmonies into which they are resolved through the intervention of Horus may be the more thoroughly appreciated. Osiris, according to the exoteric doctrine, is also the sovereign of the lower regions and the judge of souls, which, if found pure, are permitted to unite with his. The dead, therefore, do not merely go to Osiris, but actually become Osiris. Osiris is always represented with a human head. He either sits as a king on his throne, or appears in the form of a mummy. He always wields the scourge and crook, and sometimes other emblems also. The crown of Upper Egypt which he wears on his head is usually garnished before and behind with the ostrich feathers of truth. Beside him, even in very ancient representations, stands a kind of thyrsus or entwined

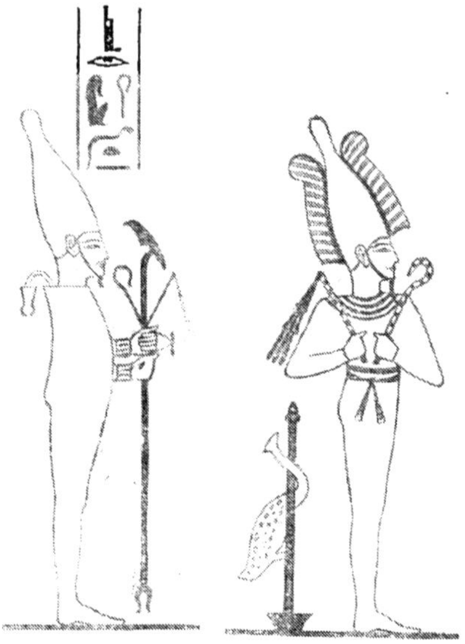

Osiris, prince of eternity.

rod, to which a panther-skin, the garb of his priests, is attached. In consequence of his function of promoting vegetable life, his wanderings, and perhaps also on account of this staff and skin, he was termed Dionysos (or Bacchus) by the Greeks.

Typhon-Seth. The name Typhon is most probably of Greek origin. The Egyptians named him *Seth*, or *Sutekh*, and represented him as a fabulous animal , or with the head of this animal , and subsequently as an ass, an animal which was sacred to him, or with an ass's head. His name is met with in the most remote period, but he appears originally to have been worshipped merely as a god of war and the tutelary deity of foreigners. He is usually styled the brother of Horus, and the two are called the *Reḥeḥui*, or hostile twins, who wounded each other in the battle above described. At a later period, after the god of battles and of foreigners had shown himself permanently unfavourable to the Egyptians, they ceased to render service to him, and erased his name from the monuments on which it occurred, and even from the cartouches of the most highly extolled kings. With regard to his connection with the myth of Osiris and Isis, see p. 130.

Nephthys, the wife of Seth, was called by the Greeks Aphrodite or Nike (Victory), probably on account of her being the wife of the god of war. Her proper sphere was the nether world. In the upper world she occurs as the nurse or instructress of the youthful Horus, and she appears with Isis, mourning and beating her forehead, at the funeral rites of Osiris, whom she had loved, and to whom, being mistaken by him in the dark for Isis, she had borne Anubis. She is also associated with Osiris and Isis, with the youthful Horus and Isis, and even, as one of a tetrad, with Osiris, Isis, and Horus. She is usually represented with the symbol  (i.e. *neb-ḥat*, mistress of the house) on her head, which is adorned with the vulture cap, and grasping in her hands the flower-sceptre and the symbol of life.

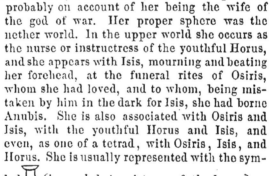

Neb-ḥat (Nephthys).

Anubis was the guide of the dead to the infernal regions and the guardian of Hades, of which he is termed the master. In the form of a jackal, or with the head of a jackal, he presides over funeral rites and guards the kingdom of the West.

Horus, who occurs in many different forms, invariably represents the upper world or region of light, and also regeneration, resurrection, and the ultimate triumph of good over evil, of life over death, of light over darkness, and of truth over falsehood. He is constantly called the 'avenger of his father'; and detailed illustrations of his contest with Typhon, dating chiefly from the period

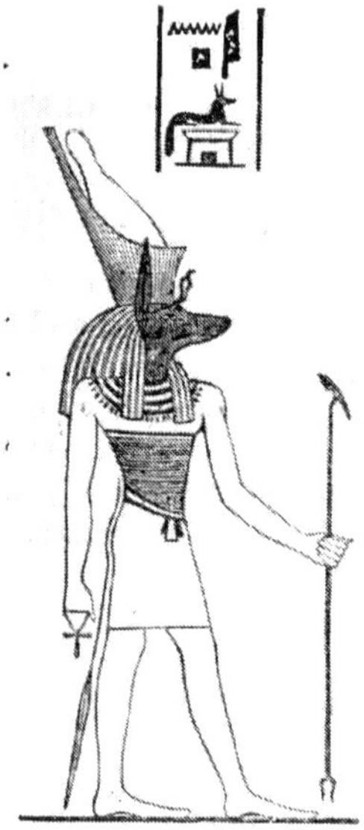

Anubis.

Horus, son of Isis, master of heaven.

Horus, avenger of his father, son of Isis and Osiris.

Horus.

of the Ptolemies, have been handed down to us. In the form of a winged disk of the sun he opposed Typhon and his companions, being aided by the Uræus serpents entwined on the disk. As the god of light (Harmachis, *i.e.* Horus on the horizon) he merges into Ra, as

he personifies the resurrection of the young light from darkness. The 'young Horus' springs in the form of a naked child with the lock of infancy from the lotus flower. Under the name of Hor-hut (Horus, the wing-expander) he overthrows Seth and his associates in behalf of Ra Harmachis, who, as a god of light, is considered equal to Osiris. Ra is equivalent to the Helios of the Greeks, and the young Horus and Hor-hut to Apollo. The hawk, with whose head he is represented, is the animal sacred to him

, and the bird itself with a scourge on its back sometimes stands for him.

Thoth (Egyptian *Taḥuti*, Greek *Hermes*) is primarily revered as the god of the moon, and in this capacity often takes the place of Khunsu (p. 138). As the phases of the moon formed the

basis of the earliest reckoning of time, Thot was regarded as the dispenser of time and the god of measures, numbers, and indeed of everything subject to fixed laws. Lastly he was also regarded as the mediator by whose aid human intelligence manifests itself, as the god of writing, of the sciences, of libraries, and of all the arts which tend to refine life. In the infernal regions he records the result of the weighing of hearts, keeps a register of the trials of the dead, and exhorts their souls to return to the radiant spirit of the universe. He is represented as an ibis on a standard , or with the head of an ibis, and frequently crowned with the disk of the moon and the ostrich-feather of truth. In his hands are a reed and a writing tablet, or, instead of the latter, a palette. He sometimes appears with a crown and sceptre, but very rarely has a human head. The animals sacred to him are the dog-headed ape and the ibis.

Thoth.

Dog-headed ape of Toth.

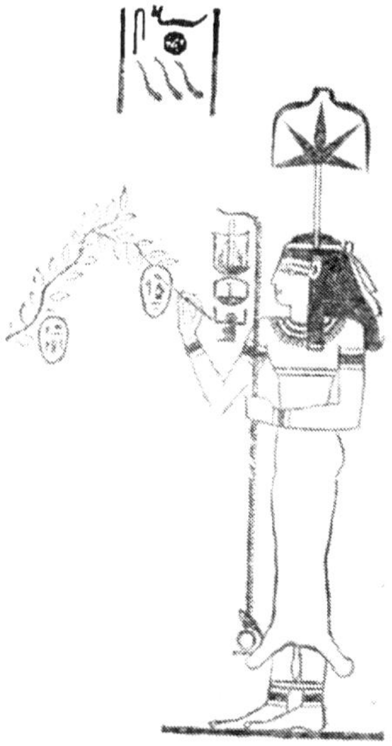

Safekh.

Safekh. A goddess who is associated with Thoth, but whose precise name is unknown, is always designated as *Safekhu*, *i.e.* one who has laid down her horns, as she bears these appendages reversed over her forehead. She is the tutelary deity of libraries, of sacred writings and lists, and therefore of history also. She holds in her left hand a palm-branch with innumerable notches marking the flight of time, and with her right she inscribes on the leaves of the persea tree all names worthy of being perpetuated.

Isis. Muth. Hathor. These three goddesses, although externally regarded as separate, were really different modifications of the same fundamental idea. As a counterpart of the male generative principle, they all represent the female element, the conceiving and gestative principle, or the receptacle in which the regeneration of the self-creating god takes place. *Muth*, whose name signifies mother, is represented as a vulture, or with a vulture's head. She is the great birth-giver, who protects Osiris and Pharaoh with her outspread wings, and she guards the cradle of the Nile, whose mysterious source is defended by a serpent. The functions of *Isis* (p. 130), who endows everything that is capable of life on earth with the good and the beautiful, have already been mentioned. She wears on her head the vulture cap, cow's horns, and the disk of the moon, or the throne , or all four combined. As *Isis Selk*, she is represented with a scorpion hovering over her head, as *Isis Neith*, who is also equivalent to Muth, usually with a weaver's shuttle , while as *Isis Sothis*, or the dog-star, she sails in a boat. She is also represented as suckling the infant Horus in her lap. Her sacred animal is the cow, which belongs also to *Isis Hathor*. The name Hathor signifies 'house of Horus', for within

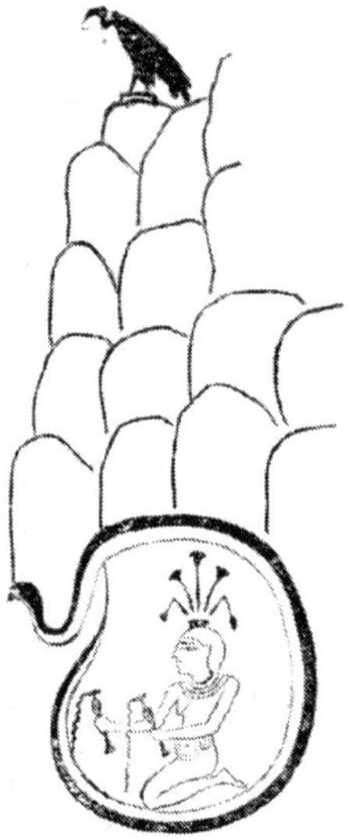

Muth.

Isis and Horus.

Isis Sothis.

the bosom of this goddess the young god gave himself new life. She is the goddess of love, the great mother, who accords her divine protection to all earthly mothers, the dispenser of all the blessings of life, the beautiful goddess who fills heaven and earth with her beneficence, and whose names are innumerable. At a later period she was regarded as the muse of the dance, the song, the jest, and even of the wine-cup. The cord and tambourine in her hand denote the fettering power of love and the joys of the festivals

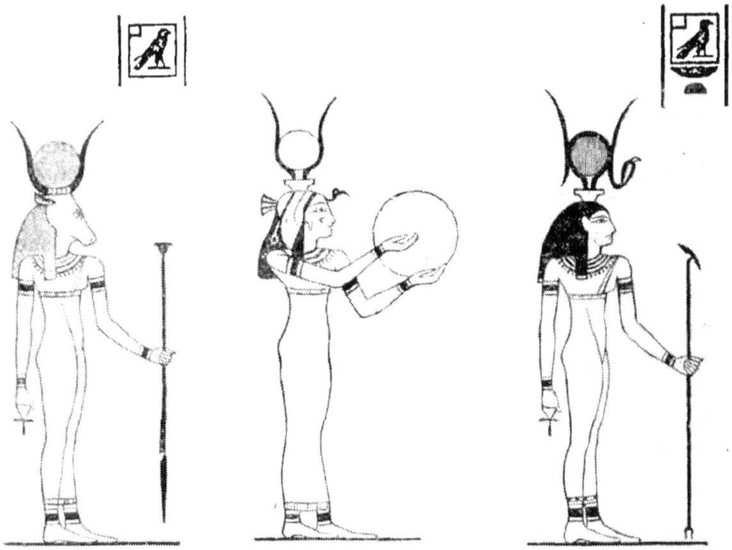

Isis Hathor. Hathor. Hathor.

over which she presided. Her sacred animal was the cow, and she generally appears in the form of a youthful woman with a cow's head, bearing the disk between her horns; and she is even spoken of as the mother of the sun (p. 127). Hathor also plays an important part as mistress of the nether world, where she is usually called *Mer-Sekhet*.

Sekhet. Bast (or *Pasht*). These goddesses likewise coincide more or less with the many-named Hathor; but the lion or cat-headed deity known by these and many other names possesses several characteristics entirely peculiar to herself. She is called the daughter of Ra and the bride of Ptah, and personifies sexual passion. Represented as a Uræus basilisk of the crown of Ra, she is a symbol of the scorching heat of the orb of day; in the nether regions she fights against the serpent Apep, and in the form of a lion-headed woman or a cat, brandishing a knife, she chastises the guilty. But she also possesses kindly characteristics. 'As Sekhet', we are informed by an inscription at Philæ, 'she is terrible, and as Bast she is kind.' The cat, her sacred animal, was long an object of veneration. She wears on her head the disk with the Uræus serpent, and holds in her hands the sceptre and the symbol of life.

Sebek, a god who also appears in union with Ra as Sebek

Ra, is represented with the head of a crocodile, and was chiefly revered in the region of the cataracts at Silsili, Kôm-Ombu, and in the Fayûm (p. 457). At Kôm-Ombu Sebek forms a triad in conjunction with Hathor and Khunsu. His crocodile head is crowned with the disk, the Uræus basilisks, and the double feather. He grasps the sceptre and the symbol of life in his hands, and is coloured green. His sacred animal, the crocodile, was kept in his honour, but a certain Typhonic character was attributed to the reptile, as the sacred lists omit those nomes where it was worshipped.

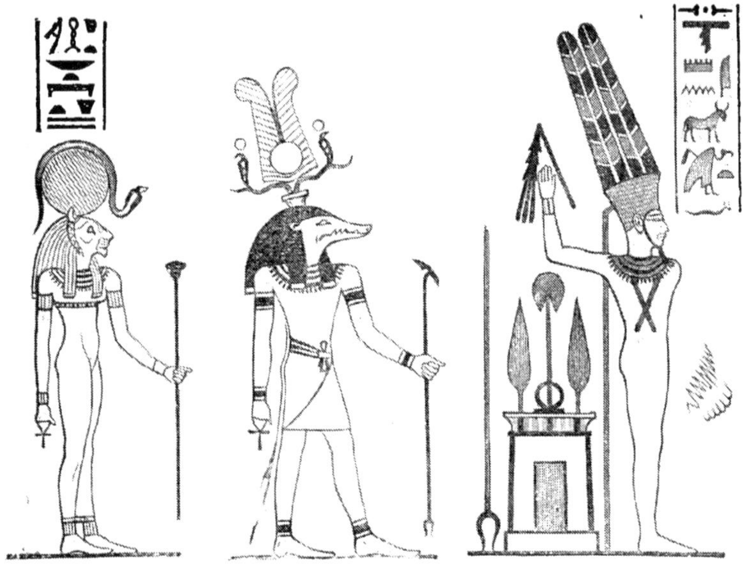

Sekhet Bast. Sebek. Khem Amun.

Ammon-Ra. Ra (p. 127), with whose worship the rites of many other divinities were combined, and whose attributes were frequently merged in those of Osiris, reigned, according to the later inscriptions, as the great monarch of the gods, but Ammon, who was revealed to the exoterics as a son of Ptah, obtained possession of the throne of this world, while Ra continued his sovereignty in Amenthes, or the nether regions. Ammon, whose name signifies 'the hidden one', is a deity of comparatively late origin, having been at first merely the local god of Thebes; but after the valley of the Nile had been delivered from the Hyksos under his auspices, and after Upper Egypt and Thebes had gained the supremacy over Lower Egypt and Memphis, he was raised to the rank of king of all the gods. The attributes of almost the entire Pantheon of Egypt were soon absorbed by this highly revered deity. He reposes as a hidden power in Nun, or the primordial waters, and during the process of his self-procreation he is termed *Khem*. As soon as he has manifested himself, he, as 'the living Osiris', animates and spiritualises all creation, which through him enters upon a higher stage of existence. On the human beings fashioned by Tum he operates mysteriously, disposing them to a love of discipline and order, and to an abhorrence of all that is irregular, evil, and unsightly. Justice, which punishes and rewards, is subject to him, and even the gods 'prostrate themselves before him', acknowledging the majesty of the great Inscrutable. Every other god now came to be regarded as little else than a personification of some attribute of the mysterious Ammon, god of the gods, standing in the same relation to him as models of parts of a figure to the perfect whole. The monu-

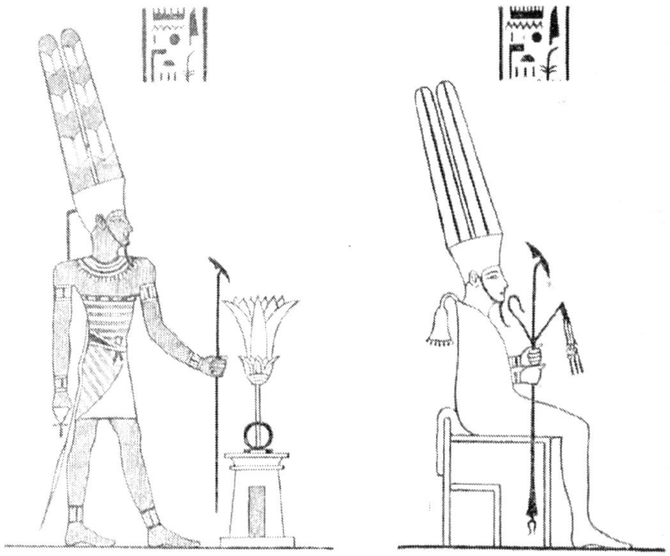

Ammon-Ra, King of the gods.

ments at Thebes represent him enthroned or standing, coloured blue or black, generally adorned with the long feather head-dress termed *shuti*, sometimes with the crown of Upper Egypt alone , or with that of Upper and Lower Egypt, and sometimes with a helmet or diadem on his head. In his hands he wields all kinds of royal insignia, such as the sceptre, the scourge, the crook, and the symbol of life. When represented with a ram's head he is termed Ammon-Khnum, Knuphis, or Kneph (p. 129). Beside him in the great triad of Thebes stand *Muth*, the maternal principle (p. 135), and *Khunsu* or *Khons*, who represents the operation of divine intelligence in the external world, and particularly in its relation to human affairs. He is the 'destroyer of enemies', he aids mankind in the battle of life, and he heals the sick. To his head the moon is attached by the infantine lock. From his wanderings as the god of the moon, and from the vigour with which he destroyed evil spirits, he was identified with Heracles by the Greeks.

Doctrine of Immortality. From the account of the worship of Isis and Osiris it is obvious that the Egyptians believed in the immortality of the soul (whence arose the prevalent worship of ancestors), in a moral responsibility, and in a future state of rewards and punishments. The doctrine with regard to the life of the soul after death was not, however, at all times and in all places the same. According to the Egyptian belief, every human being consisted of three distinct parts, which during the period of life were closely united: (1) the body, a portion of matter; (2) the '*sahu*', or soul, which belonged to the nether world and ultimately returned thither; and (3) the '*khu*', an emanation of the divine intelligence Each of these elements could be separated from the others, but whatever changes it underwent, it was immutable in quantity and quality. As the god of the sun is always the same and yet hourly different, being at first Horus, then Ra, next Tum, and finally Khnum, so it was with the soul and the intelligence which fills and illuminates it, and which, as soon as the gates of the tomb are opened for its reception, speaks and acts for it. Once within the gates of Amenthes, the soul had to undergo many trials. Ferocious beasts had to be conquered, demons to be subdued, and castles to be stormed, and all this was to be done with the aid of texts and hymns written on papyrus and scarabæi, *ut'a* eyes, and other amulets swathed in the bandage of the mummy. At length the soul reached the hall of double justice, where the heart in its vase  was placed in one scale and the goddess of truth in the other. Horus and a cynocephalus conducted the process of weighing, Anubis superintended, Thoth recorded the result, and Osiris with forty-two counsellors pronounced sentence If the heart was found too light, the soul was condemned so suffer the torments of hell, or to continue its existence in the bodies of animals, within a certain period after which it returned to its original body to begin life anew, and had afterwards to undergo another trial by the judges of Hades. If the heart was found sufficiently heavy, Osiris restored it to the soul; the 'sahu' might then return to its mummy; its intelligence, after a period of purification in the regions of the blessed, might unite with the divinity from which it had emanated, and, merged in Horus, Osiris, etc , might traverse the heavens in the boat of the sun, or walk anew among the living in any form it pleased. Finally both the 'sahu' and the intelligence were reunited to the dead body they had quitted, which its mummification had preserved from decay, and which awaited the return of the soul from Amenthes or from its sojourn in the bodies of animals.

Index to the Egyptian Deities.

VII. Doctrines of El-Islâm.

Manners and Customs of the Mohammedans.

(By Prof. Socin, of Tubingen.)

Mohammed†, as a religious teacher, took up a position hostile to the 'age of ignorance and folly', as he called heathenism. The revelation which he believed it was his mission to impart was, as he declared, nothing new. His religion was of the most remote antiquity, all men being supposed by him to be born Muslims, though surrounding circumstances might subsequently cause them to fall away from the true religion. Even in the Jewish and Christian scriptures (the Thorah, Psalms, and Gospels), he maintained, there were passages referring to himself and El-Islâm, but these passages had been suppressed, altered, or misinterpreted. So far as Mohammed was acquainted with Judaism and Christianity, he disapproved of the rigour of their ethics, which were apt to

† Mohammed ('the praised', or 'to be praised') was a scion on the paternal side of the family of Hâshim, a less important branch of the noble family of Kureish, who were settled at Mecca, and were custodians of the Ka'ba. His father 'Abdallah died shortly before his birth (about 570). In his sixth year his mother Amina took him on a journey to Medîna, but died on her way home. The boy was then educated by his grandfather 'Abd el-Muttalib, and, after the death of the latter two years later, by his uncle Abu Tâlib. For several years Mohammed tended sheep. He afterwards undertook commercial journeys, at first in company with his uncle, and then, when about twenty-five years of age, in the service of the widow Khadija, who became his first wife. On one of these journeys he is said to have become acquainted with the Christian monk Bahira at Bosra.

About that period a reaction in the religious life of the Arabs had set in, and when Mohammed was about forty years of age he too was struck with the vanity of idolatry. He suffered from epilepsy, and during his attacks imagined he received revelations from heaven. He can scarcely, therefore, be called an impostor in the ordinary sense. A dream which he had on Mt. Hira, near Mecca, gave him the first impulse, and he soon

degenerate into a body of mere empty forms, while he also rejected their dogmatic teaching as utterly false. Above all he repudiated whatever seemed to him to savour of polytheism, including the doctrine of the Trinity, as 'assigning partners' to the one and only God. Every human being who possesses a capacity for belief he considered bound to accept the new revelation of El-Islâm, and every Muslim is bound to promulgate this faith. Practically, however, this stringency was afterwards relaxed, as the Muslims found themselves obliged to enter into pacific treaties with nations beyond the confines of Arabia. A distinction was also drawn between peoples who were already in possession of a revelation, such as Jews, Christians, and Sabians, and idolaters, the last of whom were to be rigorously persecuted.

The Muslim creed is embodied in the words· 'There is no God but God (Allâh †), and Mohammed is the prophet of God' *(lâ ilâha ill' Allâh, wa Muḥammedu-rrasûl-Allâh)*. This formula, however, contains the most important doctrine only; for the Muslim is bound to believe in three cardinal points: (1) God and the angels, (2) written revelation and the prophets, and (3) the resurrection, judgment, eternal life, and predestination.

(1). God and the Angels. According to comparatively modern inscriptions ('Syrie Centrale', pp. 9, 10) it would appear that the emphatic assertion of the unity of God is by no means peculiar to Mohammedanism. As God is a Spirit, embracing all perfection within Himself, ninety-nine of his different attributes were afterwards gathered from the Ḳorân, each of which is represented by a bead of the Muslim rosary. Great importance is also attached to the fact that the creation of the world was effected by a simple effort of the divine will. (God said 'Let there be', and there was.)

The story of the creation in the Ḳorân is taken from the Bible, with variations from Rabbinical, Persian, and other sources. God first created his throne; beneath the throne there was water; the

---

began with ardent enthusiasm to promulgate monotheism, and to warn his hearers against incurring the pains of hell. It is uncertain whether Moḥammed himself could read and write His new doctrine was called Islâm, or subjection to God At first he made converts in his own family only, and the 'Muslims' were persecuted by the Meccans Many of them, and at length Moḥammed himself (622), accordingly emigrated to Medîna, where the new religion made great progress After the death of Khadîja, Moḥammed took several other wives, partly from political motives

He now endeavoured to stir up the Meccans, and war broke out in consequence. He was victorious at Bedr, but lost the battle of the Uhud. His military campaigns were thenceforth incessant He obtained great influence over the Beduins, and succeeded in uniting them politically In 630 the Muslims at length captured the town of Mecca, and the idols in it were destroyed. Moḥammed's health, however, had been completely undermined by his unremitting exertions for about twenty-four years; he died on 8th June, 632, at Medîna, and was interred there

† Allâh is also the name of God used by the Jews and Christians who speak Arabic.

earth was then formed In order to keep the earth steady, God caused it to be supported by an angel, placed on a huge rock, which in its turn rests on the back and horns of the bull of the world. And thus the earth is kept in its proper position.

Simultaneous with the creation of the firmament was that of the *ginn* (demons), beings occupying a middle rank between men and angels, some of them believing, others unbelieving. These ginn are frequently mentioned in the Korân, and at a later period numerous fables regarding them were invented. To this day the belief in them is very general. When the ginn became arrogant, an angel was ordered to banish them, and he accordingly drove them to the mountains of Kâf by which the earth is surrounded, whence they occasionally make incursions. Adam was then created, on the evening of the sixth day, and the Muslims on that account observe Friday as their Sabbath. After the creation of Adam came the fall of the angel who conquered the ginn. As he refused to bow down before Adam he was exiled, and thenceforward called *Iblîs*, or the devil. After this, Adam himself fell, and became a solitary wanderer, but was afterwards re-united to Eve at Mecca, where the sacred stone in the Ka'ba derives its black colour from Adam's tears. At Jidda, the harbour of Mecca, the tomb of Eve is pointed out to this day. Adam is regarded as the first orthodox Muslim; for God, from the earliest period, provided for a revelation.

Besides the creative activity of God, his maintaining power is specially emphasised, as being constantly employed for the preservation of the world. His instruments for this purpose are the angels. They are the bearers of God's throne, and execute his commands They also act as mediators between God and men, being the constant attendants of the latter. When a Muslim prays (which he does after the supposed fashion of the angels in heaven), it will be observed that he turns his face at the conclusion first over his right and then over his left shoulder. He thereby greets the recording angels who stand on each side of every believer, one on the right to record his good, and one on the left to record his evil deeds The traveller will also observe the two stones placed over every grave in a Muslim burial-ground. By these sit the two angels who examine the deceased, and in order that the creed may not escape his memory it is incessantly chanted by the conductor of the funeral.

While there are legions of good angels, who differ in form, but are purely ethereal in substance, there are also innumerable satellites of Satan, who seduce men to error and teach them sorcery. They endeavour to pry into the secrets of heaven, to prevent which they are pelted with falling stars by the good angels. (This last is a notion of very great antiquity.)

(2) Written Revelation and the Prophets. The necessity for a revelation is based on the dogma of original sinlessness, and

on the natural inclination of every human being towards Islamism. The earliest men were all believers, but they afterwards fell away from the true faith. A revelation therefore became necessary, and it is attained partly by meditation, and partly by direct communication. The prophets are very numerous, amounting in all, it is said, to 124,000; but their ranks are very various. Some of them have been sent to found new forms of religion, others to maintain those already existing. The prophets are free from all gross sins; and they are endowed by God with power to work miracles, which power forms their credentials; nevertheless they are generally derided and disbelieved. The greater prophets are Adam, Noah, Abraham, Jesus, and Moḥammed.

Adam is regarded as a pattern of human perfection, and is therefore called the 'representative of God'. — *Noah's* history is told more than once in the Ḳorân, where it is embellished with various additions, such as that he had a fourth, but disobedient son. The preaching of Noah and the occurrence of the Deluge are circumstantially recorded. The ark is said to have rested on Mt. Jûdi, near Mossul. The giant 'Uj, son of 'Enak, survived the flood. He was of fabulous size, and traditions regarding him are still popularly current.

Abraham (Ibrâhîm) is spoken of by Moḥammed as a personage of the utmost importance, and in the Ḳorân, as well as in the Bible he is styled the 'friend of God' (comp. James ii. 23). Mohammed professed to teach the 'religion of Abraham', and he attached special importance to that patriarch as having been the progenitor of the Arabs through Ishmael. Abraham was therefore represented as having built the Ka'ba, where his footprints are still shown. One of the most striking passages in the Ḳorân is in Sûreh vi. 76, where Abraham is represented as first acquiring a knowledge of the one true God. His father was a heathen, and Nimrod at the time of Abraham's birth had ordered all new-born children to be slain (a legend obviously borrowed from the Slaughter of the Innocents at Bethlehem); Abraham was therefore brought up in a cavern, which he quitted for the first time in his fifteenth year. 'And when night overshadowed him he beheld a star, and said — This is my Lord; but when it set, he said — I love not those who disappear. And when he saw the moon rise, he said again — This is my Lord; but when he saw it set, he exclaimed — Surely my Lord has not guided me hitherto that I might go astray with erring men. Now when he saw the sun rise, he spake again — That is my Lord; he is greater. But when it likewise set, he exclaimed — O people, I will have nothing to do with what ye idolatrously worship; for I turn my face steadfastly towards Him who created heaven and earth out of nothing; and I belong not to those who assign Him partners!'

Besides the slightly altered Bible narratives, we find a story of

Abraham having been cast into a furnace by Nimrod for having destroyed idols, and having escaped unhurt (probably borrowed from the miracle of the three men in the fiery furnace).

The history of *Moses*, as given in the Korân, presents no features of special interest. He is called the 'speaker of God'; he wrote the Thorah, and is very frequently mentioned. — In the story of *Jesus* Mohammed has perpetrated an absurd anachronism, Mary being confounded with Miriam, the sister of Moses. Jesus is called 'Isâ in the Korân; but 'Isâ is properly Esau, a name of reproach among the Jews; and this affords us an indication of the source whence Mohammed derived most of his information. On the other hand, Jesus is styled the 'Word of God', as in the Gospel of St. John. A parallel is also drawn in the Korân between the creation of Adam and the nativity of Christ; like Adam, Jesus is said to have been a prophet from childhood, and to have wrought miracles which surpassed those of all other prophets, including even Mohammed himself. He proclaimed the Gospel, and thus confirmed the Thorah; but in certain particulars the latter was abrogated by him. Another was crucified in his stead, but God caused Jesus also to die for a few hours before taking him up into heaven.

Modern investigation shows with increasing clearness how little originality these stories possess, and how Mohammed merely repeated what he had learned from very mixed sources (first Jewish, and afterwards Christian also), sometimes entirely misunderstanding the information thus acquired. The same is the case with the numerous narratives about other so-called prophets. Even Alexander the Great is raised to the rank of a prophet, and his campaign in India is represented as having been undertaken in the interests of monotheism. Alexander is also associated with the *Khiḍr*, or animating power of nature, which is sometimes identified with Elijah and St. George. The only other matter of interest connected with Mohammed's religious system is the position which he himself occupies in it. Moses and Christ prophesied his advent, but the passages concerning him in the Thorah and Gospels have been suppressed. He is the promised Paraclete, the Comforter (St. John xiv. 16), the last and greatest of the prophets; but he does not profess to be entirely free from minor sins. He confirms previous revelations, but his appearance has superseded them. His whole doctrine is a miracle, and it therefore does not require to be confirmed by special miracles. After his death, however, a number of miracles were attributed to him, and although he was not exactly deified, the position assigned to him is that of the principal mediator between God and man. The apotheosis of human beings is, moreover, an idea foreign to the Semitic mind, and it was the Persians who first elevated 'Ali and the imâms (literally reciters of prayers) who succeeded him to the rank of supernatural beings.

The Korân itself was early believed to be of entirely supernatural origin. The name signifies 'rehearsal', or 'reading', and the book is divided into parts called *Sûrehs*. The first revelation vouchsafed to the Prophet took place in the 'blessed night' in the year 609. With many interruptions, the 'sending down' of the Korân extended over twenty-three years, until the whole book, which had already existed on 'well-preserved tables' in heaven, was in the prophet's possession. During the time of the 'Abbaside khalifs it was a matter of the keenest controversy whether the Korân was created or uncreated. (The Oriental Christians have likewise always manifested a great taste for subtle dogmatic questions, such as the Procession of the Holy Ghost.) The earlier, or Meccan Sûrehs, which on account of their brevity are placed at the end of the book, are characterised by great freshness and vigour of style. They are in rhyme, but only partially poetic in form. In the longer Sûrehs of a later period the style is more studied and the narrative often tedious. The Korân is nevertheless regarded as the greatest masterpiece of Arabic literature. The prayers of the Muslims consist almost exclusively of passages from this work, although they are entirely ignorant of its real meaning. Even by the early commentators much of the Korân was imperfectly understood, for Mohammed, although extremely proud of his 'Arabic Book', was very partial to the use of all kinds of foreign words. The translation of the Korân being prohibited, Persian, Turkish, and Indian children learn it entirely by rote.

The Korân has been translated into English, French, German, Italian, and Latin The best English translations are those of *Sale* (1734; with a 'preliminary discourse' and copious notes; published in a cheap form by Messrs Warne & Co, London) and *Rodwell* (London, 1861).

(3). Future State and Predestination. The doctrine of the resurrection has been grossly corrupted by the Korân and by subsequent tradition; but its main features have doubtless been borrowed from the Christians, as has also the appearance of Antichrist, and the part to be played by Christ at the Last Day. On that day Christ will establish El-Islâm as the religion of the world. With him will re-appear El-Mahdi, the twelfth Imâm (p. 153), and the beast of the earth (p. 142), while the peoples of Gog and Magog will burst the barrier beyond which they were banished by Alexander the Great (p. 144). The end of all things will be ushered in by the trumpet-blasts of the angel Asrâfîl; the first of these blasts will kill every living being; a second will awaken the dead. Then follows the Judgment; the righteous cross to Paradise by a bridge of a hair's breadth, while the wicked fall from the bridge into the abyss of hell. Some Muslims believe in a kind of limbo, like that of the Hebrews and Greeks, while others maintain that the souls of the dead proceed directly to the gates of Paradise. At the Judgment every man is judged according to the books of the recording angels (p. 142). The good have the book placed in their right hands, but it is placed in the left hands of the wicked, bound behind their backs. The scales in which good and evil deeds are weighed play an important part in deciding the soul's fate, a detail which gave rise to the subsequent doctrine of the efficacy of works. This doctrine is carried so far that works of supererogation are believed to be placed to the credit of the believer. The demons and animals, too, must be judged. Hell, as well as heaven, has different regions; and El-Islâm also assumes the existence of a purgatory, from which release is possible Paradise is depicted by Moḥammed, in consonance with his thoroughly sensual character, as a place of entirely material delights.

The course of all events, including the salvation or perdition of every individual, is, according to the strict interpretation of the Korân, absolutely predestined; although several later sects have endeavoured to modify this terrible doctrine. It is these views, however, which give rise to the pride of the Muslims. By virtue of their faith they regard themselves as certainly elect, and as a rule they make no attempt to convert others, as they have no power to alter the irrevocable decrees of God.

In the second place the Ḳorân is considered to contain, not only a standard of ethics, but also the foundation of a complete code of law.

The Morality of El-Islâm was specially adapted by its founder to the character of the Arabs. Of duties to one's neighbour, charity is the most highly praised, and instances of its practice are not unfrequent. Hospitality is much practised by the Beduins, and by the peasantry also in those districts which are not overrun with travellers Frugality is another virtue of the Arabs, though too apt with them to degenerate into avarice and cupidity. The law of debtor and creditor is lenient. Lending money at interest is forbidden by the Ḳorân, but is nevertheless largely practised, the lowest rate in Syria being 12 per cent. The prohibition against eating unclean animals, such as swine, is older than El-Islâm, and, like the prohibition of intoxicating drinks, is based on sanitary considerations. Wine, however, and even brandy, are largely consumed by the upper classes, especially among the Turks.

Although Polygamy is sanctioned, every Muslim being permitted to have four wives at a time, yet among the bulk of the population monogamy is far more frequent, owing to the difficulty of providing for several wives and families at once. The wives, moreover, are very apt to quarrel, to the utter destruction of domestic peace, unless the husband can afford to assign them separate houses. Few men remain unmarried. The treatment of women as mere chattels, which is of very remote Oriental origin, constitutes the greatest defect of the system of El-Islâm, although the position of the female sex among the Oriental Christians and Jews is little better than among the Muslims. It is probably owing to this low estimate of women that the Muslims generally dislike to see them praying or occupying themselves with religion. The practice of wearing veils is not confined to the Muslim women, but is universal in the East. An Oriental lady would, indeed, regard it as an affront to be permitted to mingle in society with the same freedom as European ladies. Even in the Christian churches, the place for women is often separated from the men s seats by a railing. The peasant and Beduin women, on the other hand, are often seen unveiled The ease with which El-Islâm permits divorce is due to Moḥammed's personal proclivities. A single word from the husband suffices to banish the wife from his house, but she retains the marriage-portion which she has received from her husband. The children are brought up in great subjection to their parents, often showing more fear than love for them.

The repetition of Prayers five times daily forms one of the chief occupations of faithful Muslims. The hours of prayer *(adân)* are proclaimed by the *mueddins* (or muezzins) from the minarets of the mosques: (1) *Maghrib*, a little after sunset; (2) *'Ashâ*, nightfall, about 1$^1/_2$ hour after sunset; (3) *Ṣubḥ*, daybreak; (4) *Duhr*, midday; (5) *'Aṣr*, afternoon, about 1$^1/_2$ hour before sunset. These periods of prayer also serve to mark the divisions of the day. The day is also divided into two periods of 12 hours each, beginning from sunset, so that where clocks and watches are used they require to be set daily. Most people however content themselves with the sonorous call of the mueddin: *Allâhu akbar* (three times); *ashhadu an lâ ilâha ill' Allâh; ashhadu anna Muḥammeda rrasûlu'llâh* (twice); *ḥeyya 'ala-ṣṣalâh* (twice); *ḥeyya 'ala'l-falâḥ* (twice), *Allâhu akbar* (twice), *lâ ilâha ill'allâh*, i. e. 'Allâh is great; I testify that there is no God but Allâh, and Moḥammed is the prophet of Allâh; come to prayer; come to worship; Allâh is great; there is no God but Allâh'. This call to prayer sometimes also reverberates thrillingly through the stillness of night, to incite to devotion the faithful who are still awake. — The duty of washing before prayer is a sanitary institution, and tanks are provided for the purpose in the court of every mosque. In the desert, where water is scarce and precious, the faithful are permitted to use sand for this religious ablution.

The person praying must remove his shoes or sandals and turn his face towards Mecca, as the Jews and some of the Christian sects turn towards Jerusalem or towards the East. The worshipper begins by putting his hands to the lobes of his ears, and then holds them a little below his girdle; and he intersperses his recitations from the Ḳorân with certain prostrations performed in a given order. On Fridays the midday recital of prayer takes place three quarters of an hour earlier than usual, and is followed by a sermon, preached from the Mambar (p. 184) by a respectable, but unlearned layman, whose audience sits on the ground in rows before him. Friday is not, however, regarded as a day of rest, business being transacted as on other days. It has, however, of late become customary to close the courts of justice in imitation of the Christian practice of keeping Sunday.

The Muslims frequently recite as a prayer the first Sûreh of the Korân, one of the shortest, which is used as we employ the Lord's prayer. It is called *el-fâtha* ('the commencing'), and is to the following effect: — 'In the name of God, the merciful and gracious. Praise be to God, the Lord of creatures, the merciful and gracious, the Prince of the day of judgment; we serve Thee, and we pray to

Thee for help; lead us in the right way of those to whom thou hast shown mercy, upon whom no wrath resteth, and who go not astray. Amen'.

Another important duty of the believer is to observe the Fast of the month *Ramadân*. From daybreak to sunset throughout the month eating and drinking are absolutely prohibited, and the devout even scrupulously avoid swallowing their saliva. The fast is for the most part rigorously observed, but prolonged repasts during the night afford some compensation. Many shops and offices are entirely closed during this month. As the Arabic year is lunar, and therefore eleven days shorter than ours, the fast of Ramadân runs through all the seasons in the course of thirty-three years, and its observance is most severely felt in summer, when much suffering is caused by thirst.

The Pilgrimage to Mecca †, which every Muslim is bound to

† The conduct of the caravan, with the gifts presented to the town of Mecca, the escort, and other items, costs the Egyptian government 13,000 purses (about 66,300*l.*) annually.

undertake once in his life, is also deserving of mention. Most of the pilgrims now perform the greater part of the distance by water. On approaching Mecca the pilgrims undress, laying aside even their headgear, and put on aprons and a piece of cloth over the left shoulder. They then perform the circuit of the Ka'ba, kiss the black stone, hear the sermon on Mt. 'Arafât near Mecca, pelt Satan with stones in the valley of Mina, and conclude their pilgrimage with a great sacrificial feast. On the day when this takes place at Mecca, sheep are slaughtered and a festival called the Great Beiram (*el-'îd el-kebîr*) observed throughout the whole of the Mohammedan countries. (The 'Lesser Beiram', Arab. *el-'îd eṣ-ṣughayyir*, follows Ramaḍân.) The month of the pilgrimage is called Dhul-ḥiggeh (that 'of the pilgrimage'), and forms the close of the Muslim year. For an account of the feast in connection with the pilgrimage see p. 236. — In order approximately to convert a year of our era into one of the Muslim era, subtract 622, divide the remainder by 33, and add the quotient to the dividend. Conversely, a year of the Mohammedan era is converted into one of the Christian era by dividing it by 33, subtracting the quotient from it, and adding 622 to the remainder. On 21st October, 1884, began the Muslim year 1302. The Gregorian calendar has recently been introduced into Egypt, but is used by government in the finance department only.

Most of the Arabic Literature is connected with the Ḳorân. Commentaries were written at an early period to explain the obscure passages in it, and there gradually sprang up a series of exegetical writings dwelling with elaborate minuteness upon every possible shade of interpretation. Grammar, too, was at first studied solely in connection with the Ḳorân, and a prodigious mass of legal literature was founded exclusively upon the sacred volume. Of late years, however, some attempts have been made to supersede the ancient law, and to introduce a modern European system. The Beduins still have their peculiar customary law.

With regard to theological, legal, and still more to ritualistic questions, El-Islâm has not always been free from dissension. There are in the first place four *Orthodox* sects, the *Ḥanefites*, the *Shâfe'ites*, the *Malekites*, and the *Ḥambalites*, who are named after their respective founders. In addition to these must be mentioned the schools of *Free Thinkers*, who sprang up at an early period, partly owing to the influence of Greek philosophy. The orthodox party, however, triumphed, not only over these heretics, but also in its struggle against the voluptuousness and luxury of the most glorious period of the khalifs.

Ascetism and fanaticism were also largely developed among professors of El-Islâm, and another phase of religious thought was pure Mysticism, which arose chiefly in Persia. The mystics (*ṣûfi*) interpret many texts of the Ḳorân allegorically, and their system therefore frequently degenerated into Pantheism. It was by mystics who still remained within the pale of El-Islâm (such as the famous Ibn el-'Arabi, born in 1164) that the *Orders of Dervishes* were founded.

DERVISHES (*darwîsh*, plur. *darâwîsh*). The love of mysticism which characterises Mohammedans is due partly to the nature of El-Islâm itself, and partly to external circumstances. That earthly life is worthless, that it is a delusion, and at best a period of probation, are sentiments of frequent recurrence in the Korân. This pessimist view of life has been confirmed by Mohammed's conception of the Supreme Being, on whose awe-inspiring attributes he has chiefly dwelt, thus filling his adherents with a profound dread of their Creator. The result of this doctrine was to induce devout persons to retire altogether from the wicked world, the scene of vanity and disappointment, and to devote themselves to the practice of ascetic exercises, with a view to ensure their happiness in a future state. The fundamental aim of this asceticism was to strive after a knowledge of God by cultivating a kind of half-conscious and ecstatic exaltation of mind. A mystic love of God was deemed the great passport which enabled the worshipper to fall into this ecstatic trance, and to lose himself so completely in contemplation as to destroy his own individuality (*fanâ*) and blend it with that of the Deity (*ittihâd*). As in Europe the monastic system and the mendicant orders sprang from the example of penitents and hermits who had renounced the world, so in the Mohammedan world asceticism was rapidly developed into an organised system of mendicancy, although in the Korân Mohammed had expressed his strong disapproval of the Christian monastic system. At an early period many noble thinkers (such as the Persians Sa'di and Hâfiz) and talented poets enrolled themselves in the ranks of the ascetics, but the dervishes who represent the sect at the present day have entirely lost the spirit of their prototypes, and have retained nothing but the mere physical capacity for throwing themselves into a mechanical state of ecstasy and rendering themselves proof against external sensations.

The following are the principal orders of dervishes (*tarîkat ed-darâwîsh*) in Egypt: —

(1) The *Rifâ'iyeh* (sing. *rifâ'i*), an order founded by Seyyid Ahmed Rifâ'a el-Kebîr, possess a monastery near the mosque of Sultân Hasan (see p. 260), and are recognisable by their black flags and black or dark blue turbans. The best-known sects of this order are the *Aulâd 'Ilwân*, or *'Ilwâniyeh Dervishes*, and the *Sa'diyeh Dervishes*. The former are noted for their extraordinary performances at festivals, such as thrusting iron nails into their eyes and arms, breaking large stones against their chests, as they lie on their backs on the ground, and swallowing burning charcoal and fragments of glass. The Sa'diyeh, who usually carry green flags, are snake-charmers (p. 21), and on the Friday on which the birthday of the prophet is celebrated used to allow their shêkh to ride over them on horseback (the *dôseh*, p. 237).

(2) The *Kâdiriyeh* (sing. *kâdiri*), an order founded by the celebrated Seyyid 'Abd el-Kâdir el-Gilâni, have white banners and white turbans. Most of them spend their time in fishing, and in their processions they

carry nets of different colours, fishing-rods, and other insignia of their chief pursuit.

(3) The *Aḥmedîyeh* (sing. *aḥmedi*), the order of Seyyid Ahmed el-Bedawi, are recognised by their red banners and red turbans. This order is very numerous and is much respected. It is divided into many sects, but of these the two most important only need be mentioned. One of these is the *Shinnâwîyeh*, who play an important part in the ceremonies at the tomb of Seyyid Ahmed at Tanṭa (p. 225). The other sect is that of the *Aulâd Nûḥ*, who are generally young men, wearing high pointed caps with a plume of strips of coloured cloth, and a number of small balls strung across their breasts, and carrying wooden swords and a kind of whip made of a thick plait of rope.

There are also many other orders which it is unnecessary to enumerate. The ceremony of the admission of members to all these orders is a very simple matter. The candidate *(el-murîd)* performs the customary ablution sits down on the ground beside the superior *(el-murshid*, or spiritua, leader), gives him his hand, and repeats after him a set form of words, in which he expresses penitence for his sins and his determination to reform, and calls Allâh to witness that he will never quit the order. The ceremony terminates with three recitals of the confession of faith by the murîd, the joint repetition of the *fatḥa* (p. 148), and a kissing of hands.

The religious exercises of all the dervishes consist chiefly in the performance of *Zikrs* (i. e. pious devotions, or invocations of Allâh; see below, and p. 239). Almost all the dervishes in Egypt are small tradesmen, artizans, or peasants. Most of them are married men, and they take part in the ceremonies peculiar to their order at stated seasons only.

Dancing Dervishes.

Some of them, however, make it their business to attend festivals and funerals for the purpose of exhibiting their zikrs. These last are called *fuḳara* (sing. *faḳîr*), i. e. 'poor men'. Others again support themselves by drawing water *(ḥemali;* see p. 248). Those who lead a vagrant life and subsist on alms are comparatively few in number. The dervishes of this class usually wear a kind of gown *(dilḳ)* composed of shreds of rags of various colours sewn together, or a shaggy coat of skins, and carry a stick with strips of cloth of various colours attached to the upper end. A considerable number of them are insane, in which case they are highly revered by the people, and are regarded as specially favoured by God, who has taken their spirits to heaven, while he has left their earthly tabernacle behind.

The *Zikrs* (see p. 239) to which the traveller will most conveniently obtain access are those of the *Dancing* and the *Howling Dervishes*. The dancing dervishes are called *Mevlewis* after the founder of their order, the *Môla Jelal ed-dîn er-Rûmi* of Balkh in Persia (who flourished about A D. 1208), mevlewi being the Turkish form for môlawi, or adherent of the Môla or learned master. They perform their zikr within a circular space about 20 ft in diameter and enclosed by a railing. With slow, measured tread the shêkh comes forward, followed by a dervish, and takes his seat on a carpet opposite the entrance. The other dervishes next enter the circle one after another, in the order of their ages, wearing long gowns and conical hats. They walk solemnly up to their superior, make him a profound obeisance, kiss the hem of his robe, and take up their position to his left. From the galleries is presently heard a rude and weird kind of music, consisting of a single prolonged tone of a stringed instrument accompanied by a flute and a human voice rising and falling in cadences. Time is beaten by a tambourine, with varying rapidity and vigour. The singer recites a hymn expressing the most ardent love of God. As soon as the singing ceases, the dervishes rise, and walk in procession three times round the circle, headed by the shêkh. Each of them, including the shêkh himself, makes a low bow in passing the spot from which the shêkh has just risen. They then resume their seats, and the shêkh, with closed eyes, and in a deep, sepulchral voice, begins to murmur a prayer, in which the word Allâh alone is audible. When the prayer is over the dervishes divest themselves of their gowns, under which they wear a long, loose, light-coloured skirt or kilt, reaching down to their ankles, and a more closely fitting vest. They then present themselves before the shêkh, each in his turn make him a profound obeisance, and begin to move slowly round in a circle. They turn on the left foot, propelling themselves by touching the waxed floor from time to time with the right. Most of them make about forty gyrations per minute, but some of them accomplish sixty and even more. The whole of the zikr is performed by the dervishes noiselessly, with closed eyes, and outstretched arms, the palm of one hand being turned upwards and the other downwards, and their heads either thrown back or leaning on one side. During the dance soft strains of music are heard, while the beat of the tambourine gradually accelerates, and the skirts of the performers fly out in a wide circle. The tones of the flute become shriller and shriller, until on a signal given by the shêkh the music ceases, the dancers stop, cross their arms over their chests, and resume their seats. The dance is performed three times by all except the superior. The latter, however, walks several times noiselessly through the midst of the dancers, who, although their eyes are closed, touch neither him nor one another. The whole zikr occupies about an hour.

The howling or shouting dervishes perform their zikr in a kneeling or crouching posture, with their heads and chests bent downwards. In this attitude they sometimes remain for hours, incessantly shouting the Muslim confession of faith — 'lâ ilâha', etc, until they at length attain the ecstatic condition, and finish by repeating the word *hû*, i. e. 'he' (God) alone. On the occasion of great festivals some of them fall into a kind of epileptic convulsion, and foam at the mouth; but no notice is taken of them, and they are left to recover without assistance. It need hardly be added that the European traveller will find these performances unpleasing and painful.

The Worship of Saints and Martyrs was inculcated in connection with El-Islâm at an early period. The faithful undertook pilgrimages to the graves of the departed in the belief that death did not interrupt the possibility of communication with them. Thus the tomb of Moḥammed at Medîna, and that of his grandson Ḥusên at Kerbela, became particularly famous, and every little town soon boasted of the tomb of its particular saint. In many of the villages of Syria the traveller will observe small dome-covered buildings, with grated windows, and surmounted by the crescent. These are the so-called *Weli's*, mausolea of saints, or tombs of shêkhs. In the interior there is usually a block of stone, hewn in the shape of a sarcophagus and covered with a green or red cloth, on which texts from the Ķorân are embroidered in gold or silver. The walls are generally embellished with paintings representing the sacred cities of El-Islâm, and executed in an amusingly primitive style. Suspended from the ceiling by cords and threads are little boats, ostrich eggs, and numerous paper bags filled with sacred earth from Mecca. In one corner are a thick wax candle and a heap of bones of all kinds. The tomb is usually surrounded by a burial-ground, where certain persons have the privilege of being interred. Schools are also frequently connected with these weli's. Shreds of cloth are often seen suspended from the railings of these tombs, or on certain trees which are considered sacred, having been placed there by devout persons. This curious custom is of ancient origin.

About the end of the 18th century a reaction against the abuses of El-Islâm sprang up in Central Arabia. The WAHHABITES, or Wahhabees, named after their founder 'Abd el-Wahhâb, endeavoured to restore the religion to its original purity; they destroyed all tombs of saints, including even those of Mohammed and Ḥûsên, as objects of superstitious revemence, and sought to restore the primitive simplicity of the prophet's code of morals; and they even forbade the smoking of tobacco as being intoxicating. They soon became a great political power, and had not Mohammed 'Ali deemed it his interest to suppress them, their influence would have been far more widely extended than it now is. — As to the Senûsi order, see p. 67.

We have hitherto spoken of the doctrines of the *Sunnites* (from *sunna*, 'tradition'), who form one great sect of El-Islâm. At an early period the SHI'ITES (from *shî'a*, 'sect') seceded from the Sunnites. They assigned to 'Ali, the son-in-law of Mohammed, a rank equal or even superior to that of the prophet himself; they regarded him as an incarnation of the Deity, and believed in the divine mission of the imâms descended from him. El-Mahdi, the last of these, is believed by them not to have died, but to be awaiting in concealment the coming of the last day. The Persians are all Shî'ites. Towards the West also Shî'itism was widely disseminated at an early period, particularly in Egypt under the régime of the Fâṭimite sovereigns. The Shî'ites are extremely fanatical, refusing even to eat in the society of persons of a different creed. The other sects, which are chiefly confined to Syria (the *Metâwileh*, the *Isma'îliyeh*, the *Nosairîyeh*, the *Druses*, etc.), are noticed in Baedeker's Syria and Palestine.

Remarks on Mohammedan Customs.

The birth of a child is celebrated on the seventh day of its life by a domestic festival, attended by the ḳâḍi or some learned theologian, who dissolves in his mouth a piece of sugar-candy presented to him by the host and drops a little of his sweetened saliva into the infant's mouth, as it to give it a sweet foretaste of the world's gifts and also for the purpose of 'giving it a name out of his mouth'. Muslims, it is well known, are usually named by their pronomens only. If a more precise designation is desired, the name of the father is placed after the pronomen, with or without the word *ibn* ('son of') placed between the names. Nicknames, such as 'the one-eyed', etc., are also not uncommon.

When the child is forty days old the mother takes it to the bath, and causes forty bowls of water (thirty-nine in the case of a girl) to be poured over its head. This bath forms the purification of both mother and child.

The rite of circumcision is performed on boys up to the age of six or seven, or even later, the ceremony being attended with great pomp. The child is previously conducted through the streets in holiday attire, the procession being frequently united with some bridal party, in order to diminish the expense of the proceedings. The boy generally wears a turban of red cashmere, girls' clothes of the richest possible description, and conspicuous female ornaments, which are designed to attract attention, and thus avert the evil eye from his person. A handsomely caparisoned horse is borrowed to carry him; he half covers his face with an embroidered handkerchief; and the barber who performs the operation and a noisy troop of musicians head the procession. The first personage in the procession is usually the barber's boy, carrying the '*heml*', or barber's sign, a kind of cupboard made of wood, in the form of a half-cylinder, with four short legs. The flat front of the heml is adorned with pieces of looking-glass and embossed brass, while the back is covered with a curtain. Two or more boys are often thus paraded together, being usually driven in a carriage and attended by music.

Girls are generally married in their 12th or 13th, and sometimes as early as their 10th year. A man in search of a bride employs the services of a relative, or of a professional female match-maker, and he never has an opportunity of seeing his bride until the wedding-day, except when the parties belong to the lowest classes. When everything is arranged, the affianced bridegroom has to pay a bridal-portion *(mahr)* amounting to about 25*l.*, more being paid when the bride is a spinster than if she is a widow. Generally speaking, about two-thirds of the sum, the amount of which always forms a subject of lively discussion, is paid down, while one-third is settled upon the wife, being payable on the death of the husband, or on his divorcing her against her will.

The marriage-contract is now complete. Before the wedding the bride is conducted in gala attire and with great ceremony to the bath. This procession is called '*Zeffet et Hammâm*'. It is headed by several musicians with hautbois and drums; these are followed by several married friends and relations of the bride in pairs, and after these come a number of young girls. The bride is entirely concealed by the clothing she wears, being usually enveloped from head to foot in a cashmere shawl, and wearing on her head a small cap, or crown, of pasteboard. The procession moves very slowly, and another body of musicians brings up the rear. The hideous shrieks of joy which women of the lower classes utter on the occurrence of any sensational event are called *zaghârît*. The bride is afterwards conducted with the same formalities to the house of her husband.

The ceremonies observed at funerals are not less remarkable than those which attend weddings. If the death occurs in the morning, the funeral takes place the same day; but if in the evening, it is postponed till next day. The body is washed and mourned over by the family and the professional mourning women (*neddâbehs;* a custom prohibited by Mohammed, but one dating from the remotest antiquity); the *fikih*, or schoolmaster, reads several Sûrehs of the Korân by its side; after this, it is wrapped in its winding sheet, placed on the bier, covered with a red or green cloth, and then carried forth in solemn procession. The foremost persons in the cortége are usually six or more poor, and generally blind, men, who walk in twos or threes at a slow pace, chanting the creed— 'There is no God but God; Mohammed is the ambassador of God; God be gracious to him and preserve him!' These are followed by several male relatives of the deceased, and sometimes by a number of dervishes with the flags of their order, and then by three or more schoolboys, one of whom carries a copy of the Korân, or of parts of it, on a stand made of palm-branches, covered with a cloth. The boys usually chant in a loud and shrill voice several passages from the '*Hashrîyeh*', a poem describing the last judgment. The bier, with the head of the deceased foremost, comes next, being borne by three or four of his friends, who are relieved from time to time by others. After the bier come the relations and friends in their everyday attire, and the female relatives, with dishevelled hair, sobbing aloud, and frequently accompanied by professional mourning women, whose business it is to extol the merits of the deceased. If the deceased was the husband or father of the family, one of the cries is — 'O thou camel of my house', the camel being the emblem of the bread-winner of the household.

The body is first carried into that mosque for whose patron saints the relatives entertain the greatest veneration, and prayers are there offered on its behalf. After the bier has been placed in front of the tomb of the saint, and prayers and chants have again been recited, the procession is formed anew and moves towards the cemetery, where the body is let down a perpendicular shaft to a spacious vault excavated on one side of it, and there placed in such a position that its face is turned towards Mecca. The entrance to the lateral vault is then walled up, and during this long process the mourners recite the words. — '*Allâhu mughfir el-muslimîn wa l-muslimât, el-mûminîn wa'l-mûminât*' (God pardons the Muslim men and the Muslim women, the faithful men and the faithful women). A Khaṭîb, Imâm, or other person then addresses a few stereotyped words to the deceased, informing him how he is to answer the two examining angels who are to question him during the ensuing night (p. 145). A fâtḥa having again been whispered, and the perpendicular shaft filled up, while the mourners incessantly repeat the words — '*bismillâh er-raḥîmir raḥmâni*' (in the name of God, the merciful), the bystanders shake hands, and the male mourners disperse. The women, however, who have stood a little on one side during the ceremony, now come forward and inspect the tomb.

Another custom peculiar to the Muslims is that the separation of the sexes is as strict after death as during life. In family vaults one side is set apart for the men, the other for the women exclusively. Between these vaults is the entrance to the tomb, which is usually covered with a single large slab. The vaults are high enough to admit of the deceased sitting upright in them when he is being examined by the angels Munkar and Nekîr on the first night after his interment (see p. 155); for, according to the belief of the Mohammedans, the soul of the departed remains with his body for a night after his burial. For particulars regarding the tombs, see p. 185.

The Religious and Popular Festivals of the Egyptians may all be seen to the best advantage at Cairo. For farther particulars, see p. 236. Fair at Ṭanṭa, see p. 226.

VIII. Historical Notice of Egyptian Art.

In the ancient Egyptian poem which extols the achievements of Ramses the temples in the valley of the Nile are called 'everlasting stones'; and the works of Egyptian art do indeed seem to lay claim to perpetuity. Some of the monuments have existed for forty or even fifty centuries, so that, compared with them, the works of all other nations appear recent and modern; and a still greater marvel is that the skill displayed in the execution of these monuments must have been the growth of many antecedent ages, all memorials of which are now buried in the obscurity of the remotest antiquity.

The Egyptian people belonged to the so-called Chamite race, and, like the Semites and, the Indo-Germanians, had their original home in Asia (comp. pp. 37, 38). Whether they brought any of their arts to the Valley of the Nile, or whether their taste for art and their imagination were awakened for the first time by the Father of Rivers, must of course remain for ever unknown. Some of the very earliest of the products of Egyptian art are indeed more akin to those of Asia than the later, but Egyptian art as a whole presents so peculiar and unique a character that its origin was most probably local. The question might indeed be settled if we were in a position to compare early Egyptian art with that of the Oriental nations of the same period; but of the latter we can now find no trace. The only sources from which we can form any opinion regarding the original condition and the earliest development of Egyptian art are the technical execution of the oldest known monuments and the forms and style of decoration employed in them. Thus the ceiling-painting in the pyramidal tombs reveals its indebtedness to the textile handicraft; for it is in the art of weaving alone that the margins and seams there represented have any use or significance. Again, the walls of the most ancient tomb-chambers contain horizontal and vertical bands and convex mouldings, the design of which has obviously been borrowed from a system of building in wood. The sloping ridges of the pyramids point to an original style of building with crude brick, as walls of that material required to be tapering in form to ensure their durability. We thus gather that the Egyptians of a very remote period were weavers and potters, familiar with the arts of building in wood and in brick. If we go a little farther, and venture to draw inferences from the subjects and forms of their earliest works of art, we find that the Egyptians of the remotest traceable period must have been a cheerful and contented people, free from that taste for the mystic and the symbolical which afterwards characterised all their exertions in the sphere of art, and endowed with a love of life and nature which they zealously manifested in the earliest products of their imagination.

An attempt to gather a history of Egyptian art from the information we possess regarding the various dynasties of the Egyptian monarchs has led to the following results, which, however, may be much simplified or modified by future discoveries. The first period of the steady development of Egyptian art closes with the sixth dynasty, and the monuments of Memphis are the most important, though not the only structures of the early dynasties. Some of these (such as the pyramid of Cochome, p. 382) are supposed to date as far back as the time of the fourth king; and there is reason to believe that they were originally built of sun-dried bricks encrusted with stone, instead of, as subsequently, in solid stone. This would also account for the mode of construction observed in the stone pyramids, which consist of repeated incrustations of tapering courses of ma-

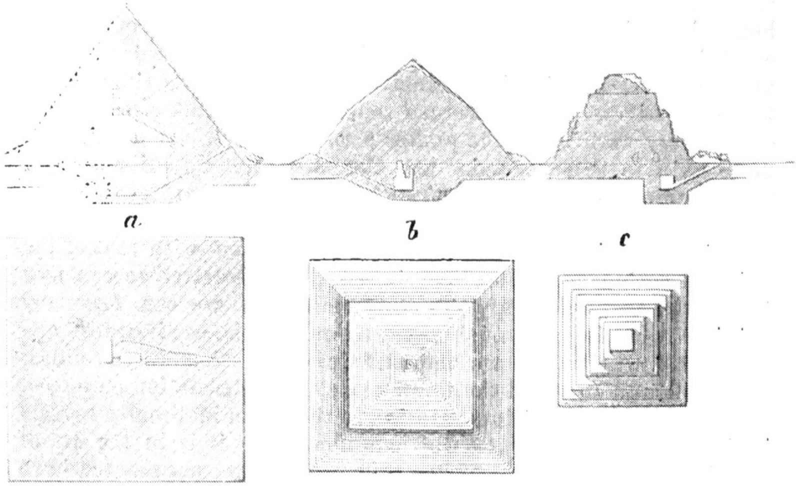

a. Pyramid of Cheops (usual form of pyramids). *b*. Pyramid of Dahshûr, with bent sides. *c*. Step-pyramid of Saḳḳâra.

sonry. According to the well-known hypothesis of Dr. Lepsius, the famous German Egyptologist, these different layers or crusts, like the concentric rings in the trunk of a tree, perhaps corresponded to the number of years during which the deceased monarch reigned. Besides the pyramids of the usual regular form (Fig. I. *a*), there are others with sides forming an obtuse angle, and others again with sides in steps. Of the pyramid with bent sides there is an example at Dahshûr (Fig. I. *b*), and of the pyramid in steps one at Saḳḳâra (Fig. I. *c*). The terrace, or step, form seems, however, to have been uniformly used in all the pyramids up to the apex (which was probably tapered), and in most of them the angles formed by the steps were afterwards filled up with stone. There can now be no reasonable doubt that the pyramids were intended to form the inaccessible tombs of great monarchs, near which their courtiers and magnates erected mortuary chapels for themselves (Maṣṭaba) in the form of blunted pyramids, in order, as it were, to pay homage to the memory of their illustrious masters. The pictorial decorations of these temples, as well as the plastic works of the same period, serve most impressively to complete the artistic effect of the pyramids. While their marvellously perfect execution alone indicates a high state of artistic development, our admiration is specially aroused by the striking fidelity to nature and expressiveness of the sculptures. The unfavourable criticisms on Egyptian sculpture formerly current may indeed now be regarded as entirely refuted. Even in European museums an opportunity is afforded to the traveller of becoming acquainted with the noble style by which the early Egyptian art alone is characterised. What visitor to the Louvre, for example, can fail to remember the striking impression produced by the statue of the 'Writer?' The expressive eyes are formed of dark quartz containing a transparent pupil of rock crystal fixed with a small knob of metal, while the attitude is remarkable for its lifelike fidelity and strong individuality. This statue dates from the fifth or sixth dynasty. and the museum at Bûlâḳ contains other plastic works of the same period in which an almost overdrawn realism is still more apparent. The limestone statue of Ra-Nefer, a priest of Ptah-Sokar at Memphis, and the wooden figure of the 'village shêkh' (p. 305), which the Paris Exhibition of 1867 has brought into so favourable notice, are the best-known specimens of a style of art of which the very existence was unsuspected a few decades ago, and the discovery of which has tended greatly to modify the old supposition that the Egyptian sculptors executed their works in mere mechanical accordance with a prescribed canon. The chief merit of the earliest Egyptian sculpture is the faithfulness of the portraiture, which is such that the identity of the person represented by two different statues may often be determined by the similarity of the features, even when executed at different periods of the person's life. In this way have been identified eight statues of Khafra, the third king of the fourth dynasty, although all differing in measurement, material, and the age represented (comp. pp. 305, 307). Observation of nature in the case of these earliest works has evidently been carried into the minutest details. The race of men represented is uniformly of the same character, somewhat resembling that of the modern fellâhîn, the figures are of a powerful, thickset type, and their muscles are faithfully represented, occasionally to exaggeration. These early sculptors, however, were incapable of producing works of a more complex character, where excellence of general effect required to be superadded to accuracy of detail, and in this respect they were far surpassed by their successors. Even the reliefs in the tomb-chambers of Memphis are executed in a singularly fresh and unsophisticated style, and the spectator will hardly regret the absence of the mystic symbolism of the later period.

After the sixth dynasty there occurs a sudden falling away from this vigorous style of art, occasioned perhaps by political dissensions, by internal wars, and possibly by a change of religious convictions. It was not until the rise of the Eleventh Dynasty that the state of the country became more settled, and that art began to revive. The new style, however, differed materially from the old. As the ancient capitals of Memphis and This now began to yield precedence to Thebes, the new centre of the kingdom, and as the system of writing, the laws, and the constitution, had all undergone material alteration, so, too, it may rather be said that the cultivation of art began anew than that the style then practised was a development of that of the fourth and sixth dynasties. Of this second efflorescence of art no great monuments have been handed down to us, the most important works being the obelisks of Heliopolis and the Fayûm and several colossi dug up at Tanis and Abydus. The rock tombs of Beni Hasan are also interesting relics of the period of the Twelfth Dynasty. In these we find a reversion to the rock-building style, which, according to Lepsius, is nearly identical with that of the grotto architecture, and owed its origin to the prevalence of ancestor-worship, and to the popular desire, arising from the Egyptian doctrine of immortality, for the preservation of the bodies of the dead. The rock-tomb was safe from the overflow of the Nile, while its equable temperature arrested the decay of the corpse, and a chapel connected with it afforded the relations an opportunity of paying homage and presenting offerings to the deceased. The division of the tomb into a series of chambers, leading at length to the actual sepulchre, soon led to their being architecturally decorated. Where there were several chambers, one behind the other, it was natural that openings should be made in the walls for the sake of admitting light. The next step was to convert the remaining portions of wall into pillars for the support of the roof, and to plane off their corners, part of the pillar being, however, left square at the top so as to blend the octagonal column with the roof. In the next place the octagonal pillar was sometimes converted into one of sixteen sides, so as to resemble a column, and in some cases the flat surfaces were grooved or fluted, a sharp angle being thus formed between each of them. Polygonal columns of this character, which occur in the first tomb of Beni Hasan, have been called Proto-Doric or Egypto-Doric by Champollion and Falkener, from their resemblance to the Doric columns of the Greeks (Fig. 11). The points of resemblance are the marked fluting, the tapering, and the absence of bases; but the Proto-Doric differs from the Greek Doric in being destitute of the 'echinus', a member resembling an overhanging wreath of leaves, and forming the capital of the Doric column. In some cases there is the still greater difference that the Proto-Doric columns are unfluted, the surfaces being left smooth for the reception of coloured inscriptions In such cases the column loses its structural significance, being degraded to a mere surface for inscriptions, and presents a marked contrast to the Doric, where each member and each line fulfils a definite requirement of the building.

The architects of the tombs of Beni Ḥasan, however, were not unacquainted with a light and elegant mode of building above ground, which cannot have originated in the grotto architecture

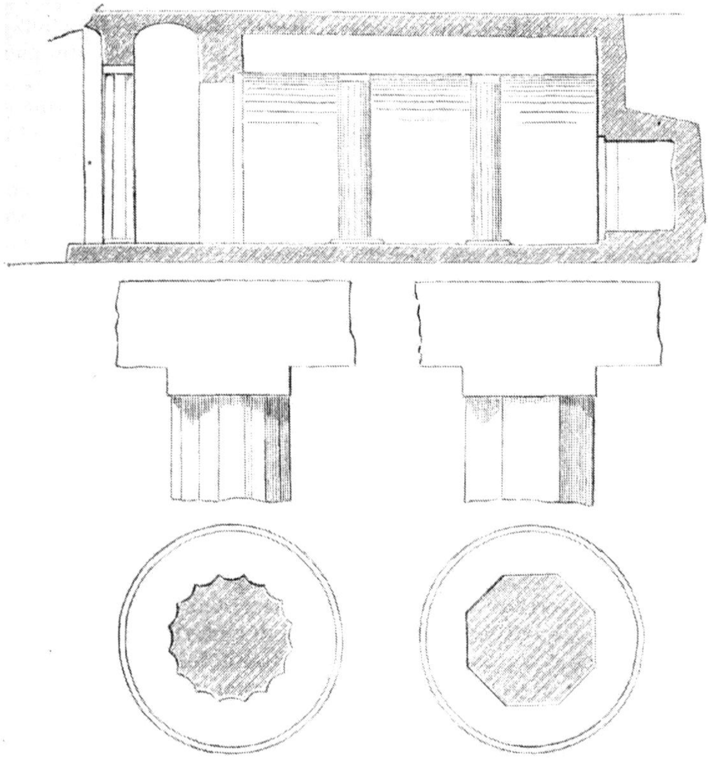

II. Section of the N. Tomb and Columns of Beni Ḥasan.

This is proved by their use of the lotus-column (Fig. III), the prototype of which is a group of four lotus-stalks bound together and secured at the top by rings or ligatures, the capital being formed by the blossoms. These columns, which contrast strongly with the massive Proto-Doric, suggest a light style of garden architecture in wood.

While the architecture of the eleventh and twelfth dynasties bears some slight resemblance to the earlier style, the sculpture of the same period presents an almost total deviation from the ancient traditions. The primitive, lifelike realism to which we have already alluded is displaced by the rigorous sway of the Canon, by which all proportions are determined by fixed rules, and all forms are necessarily stereotyped. There seems, however, to have been no retrogression in point of technical skill; for, as in the time of Khafra, the hardest materials still became compliant, and the difficulties of the minutest detail were still successfully overcome by the sculptors of the Pharaohs.

Another considerable break now took place in the progress of Egyptian art. This dreary interval began with the invasion of the Hyksos or Shepherds, and lasted throughout the whole of their domination. To them is attributed the destruction of the older monuments, and they themselves have left no architectural remains behind them. They were not, however, entirely insensible to the charms of art, and after the first terrors of the invasion were over, they did not prevent the Egyptian artists from prosecuting their calling. As the Normans in Sicily adopted the culture of the conquered Arabs, so the Hyksos turned to account the knowledge of art and the technical skill possessed by the Egyptians. The sculptures excavated at Tanis, the capital of the Hyksos (four sphinxes and particularly a group of river-gods in granite), are of Egyptian workmanship, and there is nothing to betray their origin in the Hyksos period except the type of the features, the bushy beards, and the thick tufts of hair.

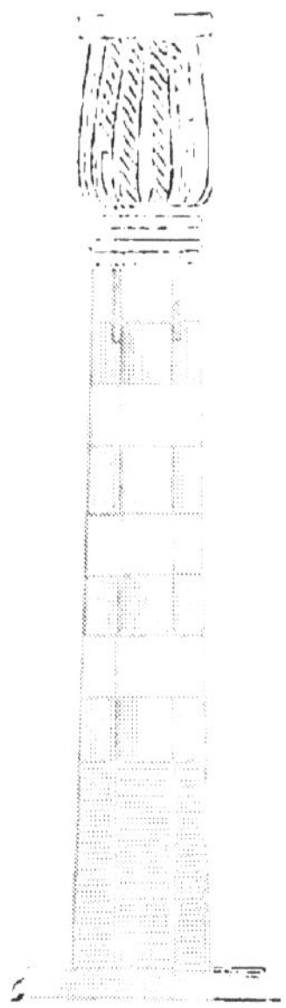

III. Lotus Column.

With the expulsion of the Hyksos begins a new period, in the history of art as well as in that of politics. The warlike and victorious monarchs of the Eighteenth and Nineteenth Dynasties, in particular, have perpetuated their memory by astonishingly numerous monuments. The compulsory labour of captive enemies afforded the architects an opportunity of carrying out their most gigantic designs, while the achievements of their sovereigns, such as the campaigns of Thothmes, Amenophis, and Ramses, supplied the sculptors with an inexhaustible theme for the decoration of the façades of their temples. To this period of the new empire belong most of the Theban monuments. The taste for the great and the colossal, and for symmetry of proportion had attained its culminating point, but the stagnation of the lifesprings of art, the dependence of the drawing and colouring on formal rules, and the over-loading of the ornamentation with symbolical signs (such as the Uræus and the Hathor masks) become unpleasingly apparent. It can hardly, however, be said that the decline of Egyptian art had yet begun; for this period lasted so long as to give rise to a general belief that the Egyptians had never possessed any other style, and entirely to obliterate the recollection of the more ancient and materially different period of development. At the same time a careful inspection of the monuments of this period will convince the observer that no farther development could be expected afterwards to take place on the basis of a system so lifeless and entirely mechanical. Shortly before the conquest of the country by the Persians, however, a slight improvement in artistic taste appears to have taken place. While the monuments of the Twenty-second and following Dynasties are unattractive, being mere reproductions of earlier works, the sculptures of the Twenty-sixth Dynasty (such as the alabaster statue of Queen Ameniritis of the XXV. Dynasty) exhibit a considerable degree of elegance and refinement. But this revival was of brief duration. After the establishment of the Ptolemæan dynasty the native art became entirely extinct, though for a time a semblance of life was artificially maintained. Political interests required the restoration of the temples, and numerous artists were employed for the purpose; the traditional style continued to be practised, and every branch of art was liberally patronised The style of this period, however, had well-nigh degenerated into mere mannerism, and therefore does not possess the historical interest attaching to the earlier stages of Egyptian art.

The art of the Ptolemæan era, moreover, in spite of all its richness and apparent vigour, not only shows manifest symptoms of decline, but was threatened with the loss of its originality and independence owing to foreign influences. As soon as Hellas came into contact with Egypt, the innate charms of Hellenic art, which even remote India was unable to resist, began to affect the hitherto strongly conservative and self-satisfied Egyptians.

Having thus given a slight chronological outline of the progress of Egyptian art, we must now endeavour to supplement it by a description of the chief characteristics of each period. Our attention will be chiefly directed to the monuments of the new empire, owing to their great number and extent.

The *Column* in Egypt, as elsewhere, constitutes the most important of all architectural members. Its absence indicates a very elementary stage of the art of building, when artistic development has yet to begin. The column imparts to the edifice an appearance of organic life, it lightens and breaks the outline of its different masses, and affords strength and support. When compared with the Greek columnar orders, the Egyptian column is of a very imperfect character. Its decoration and its form do not immediately and exclusively express its proper office, as is the case with the Greek column, and the Doric in particular. Its dependence on its natural prototype, the wreath-crowned canopy-support, still continues apparent, and its proportions, though not altogether independent of rule, still appear too arbitrary. Lastly, the height and thickness of the columns do not stand in an appropriate ratio to the weight they have to bear. It must, nevertheless, be admitted that the eye is delighted with the brilliance of their colouring and the perfection of their execution.

Egypt possesses a considerable number of different orders of columns. Some of these occur in the old empire only, while others are found for the first time in monuments of the new empire, without, however, belonging to a higher grade of art. In the tombs of Beni-Hasan (XII. Dynasty) we have become acquainted with the polygonal or Proto-Doric column, and also with that with the bud-capital. The latter was perhaps suggested by a form of pillar which occurs in the tombs of the VI. Dynasty near Antinoë (the modern El-Bersheh). The surfaces of the pillars are hollowed out, and in the hollows rise lotus stalks, crowned with a bunch of buds or closed blossoms (Fig. IV). Akin to the lotus columns of Beni

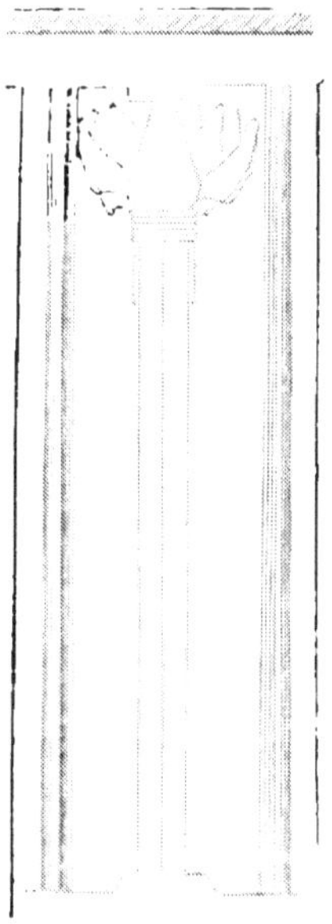

IV.

V. Papyrus Columns.

Hasan is an order of column of the new empire, which was adorned partly with sculpture and partly with painting, and which afterwards gradually adopted the conventional form. This column tapers at its base, where it is encircled with a slight wreath of reed leaves. It also tapers again upwards, and in some cases presents a shaft painted with horizontal bands and hieroglyphics, and in others a shaft grooved so as to imitate the stalks of a plant (the papyrus) which are bound together at the top with a ligature. The capitals, somewhat simple in form, and tapering upwards, are sometimes decorated on the lower part with a wreath of upright reed leaves, and sometimes, like the shafts, are treated as surfaces for painting, in which case their origin in the vegetable kingdom is indicated by a few painted buds only (Fig. V. *a*, *b*).

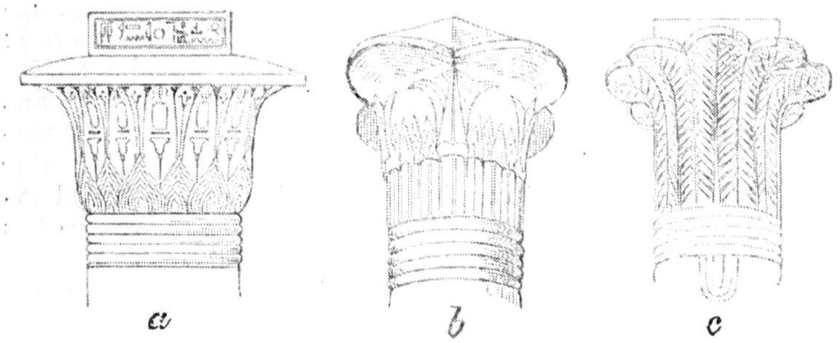

VI. Calyx Capitals.

While the columns hitherto described performed the structural function in temples and tombs of supporting massive stone roofs, the order of columns with *Calyx Capitals* was chiefly used for the decorative purpose of enclosing the processional approach in the anterior halls of the temples, and was required to support but little weight. The shafts of these columns rest on round bases resembling discs, they taper downwards, and are treated as surfaces for painting. The flowers and leaves on the capitals sometimes seem to be attached superficially only (Fig. VI. *a*), while in other cases the leaves appear to form a wreath, growing out of a columnar stem, and leaning slightly outwards so as to assume the calyx form. Of this style the papyrus (Fig. VI. *b*) and the palm (Fig. VI. *c*) formed the natural prototypes, and even at a late period several other very pleasing types were added. Another kind of column, which seems to have been much in vogue during the latest period of independent Egyptian art, is of inferior importance and artistic merit. It has a shaft terminating at the top in masks attached to four sides, usually representing the goddess Hathor with the cow's ears, and above these are placed miniature temple façades, forming a kind of abacus. Both in this case and in that of the Osiris pillars (Fig. VII), where the figure of the god,

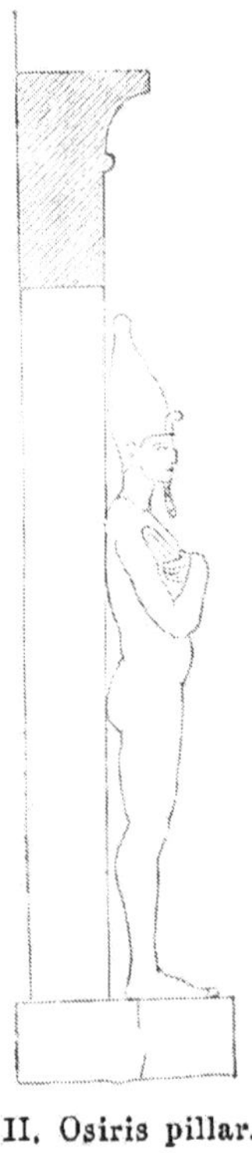

II. Osiris pillar.

with the crook in his left hand and the scourge in his right, stands quite detached from the pillar, and bears no part of the weight, the structural function has been treated as a matter of very subordinate importance.

Immediately connected with the columns are the beams above them. The inner apartments of the temples were ceiled with stone beams exclusively, extending from the abacus (or crowning slab) of one column to that of another; and the rectangular spaces thus formed were filled with slabs of stone, adorned sometimes with astronomical designs. The chief characteristics of the outer parts of the beams are, that the architrave rests immediately on the abacus, and that there is a furrow hollowed out above it, forming a deep shadow. The architrave is generally inscribed with hieroglyphics, so that its structural office is rendered less apparent; but the concave moulding above it presents the appearance of a proper crowning cornice (Fig. VIII, *b*), thus serving to counterbalance the

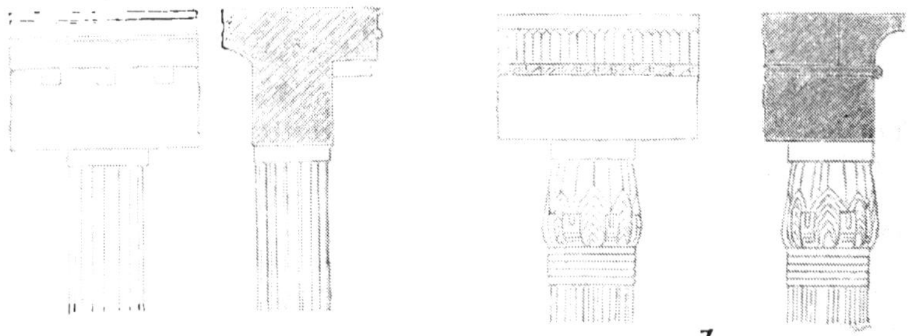

a *b*

VIII*a*. Entablature from the Tombs of Beni Hasan. VIII*b*. Entablature with hollowed cornice.

effect of the inwardly sloping walls, and giving the building an appropriate finish. The hollowed cornice is usually embellished with upright leaves or staves; and, when it crowns a portal, a winged sun-disc generally hovers over the centre. The architectural idea embodied in the entablature of the tombs of Beni Hasan is materially different. Above the architrave lies a straight projecting slab, which presents the appearance of being borne by a series of beams (Fig. VIII, *a*). The resemblance here to cognate Oriental modes of building is very apparent, while the entablature above described is peculiar to Egyptian art. The crowning of the walls with the concave cornice, and its frame-like embellishment of roll-moulding, constitute the chief articulation of the edifice; but this would have afforded insufficient relief had it not been supplemented with colouring, whereby the cold surface of the walls was covered with a pattern resembling that of a gorgeous carpet.

In order that the traveller may thoroughly understand and appreciate Egyptian architecture, he should make himself acquainted, not merely with the different modes of building and their details, but with the peculiarities of the national religious rites. The costly stone edifices of the ancient Egyptians were used exclusively for religious purposes. It is an error to suppose that the temples contained the royal residences within their precincts; the nature of the climate alone would have rendered them uninhabitable. The kings' palaces, as we learn from the representations of them in tombs, were edifices of a very light and airy description, adorned with balconies, colonnades, and bowers, and surrounded by gardens and ponds. They were built of brick and wood, and, as the sole object of the architects was to provide a convenient and pleasant dwelling, they were richly decorated with colouring.

With regard to the architecture of the temples, it is important to keep in view the fact, that they were neither destined for the reception of a congregation like Christian churches, nor, like the Greek temples, erected as mere receptacles for the image of the god. The Egyptian worshippers approached the temple precincts in solemn procession, and the profane remained outside, while the initiated and the ordained penetrated to different parts of the interior in accordance with the degree of their knowledge of the divine mysteries, the high priest alone being privileged to enter the innermost sanctuary.

The multitude would first arrive in their festively decorated boats by the great highway of the Nile, and they would then traverse the avenue leading to the temple, which was flanked by sphinxes on each side. The sphinxes consist of a lion's body with the head of a man (Androsphinx), or that of a ram (Kriosphinx), and according to an inscription at Edfu they were intended to symbolise the conflict of Horus with Typhon-Seth. The sphinx avenue led to the precincts of the temple proper, the Temenos of the Greeks, which were completely enclosed by a wall, built of bricks of the Nile clay, or, as at Edfu, of solid stone. The sacred lakes, generally two in number, and the sacred grove were usually the only accessories of the temple which lay without the precincts. At the end of the avenue the eye is confronted by two huge towers with the entrance between them, called the Pylons, which are in the form of truncated pyramids, with walls divided into sections by round staves, and affording admirable surfaces for plastic or pictorial decoration. The pylons and the portal between them are both crowned with the usual hollowed cornice Under ordinary circumstances these pylons present a very imposing appearance, but their grandeur must have been much enhanced when they were festively decorated (as in Fig. IX) on solemn occasions, and when gaily hung with flags to welcome the arrival of the worshippers. Within the pylons, in the larger temples, lay a large open court *(Peristyle)*, flanked on two or three sides with colonnades, and beyond it a large hall borne by columns *(Hypostyle)*, of which those in the centre, differing in size and form of capital, marked out the route to be followed by the procession. In many of the temples a smaller columnar hall, and chambers of smaller size and decreasing height, all lying in the line of the processional route (and together called

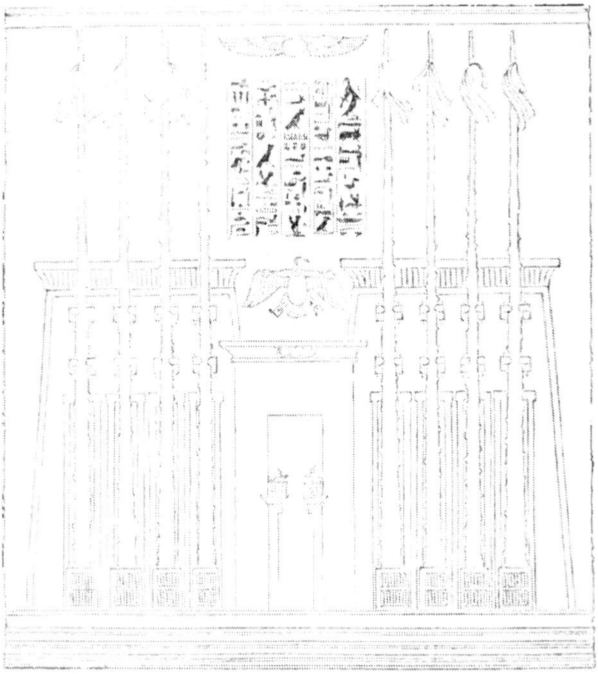

IX. Decorated Portal and Pylons.

the *Prosecus*) separated the hypostyle from the small, dark, and secluded sanctuary, called the *Adytum* or *Secus*, sometimes consisting of a single huge hollowed block of stone, where behind rich curtains lay the symbol of a god and a sacred animal. The sanctuary was surrounded by a number of chambers of various sizes, and staircases led to the roof and to other apartments which either served as dwellings for the custodians and receptacles for the temple furniture, or for the celebration of sacred rites.

Having thus glanced at the internal arrangements of the temple, we may now retrace our steps and rejoin the devout procession. The lower classes of the people (the 'Pasu'), forming the great bulk of the procession, were not permitted to advance beyond the sacred grove and the courtyard, where on certain days they offered sacrifices. The 'Patu', or lowest grade of the instructed, the 'Rekhiu', or esoterics, who were initiated into the sacred mysteries, and the 'Ammiu', or enlightened, advanced into the great hall, and from the portal of the Prosekos, or hall 'of the manifestation of majesty', they were permitted to behold from afar the sacred emblem of divinity. These worshippers were now passed by the king and the officiating priests, who ascended in solemn procession to the roof, while the high priest entered the small and sombre chamber of the god. The annexed ground-plan of the S. temple at Karnak will render the foregoing description more intelligible (Fig. X), and analogous arrangements might easily be pointed out in the temples of other nations, such as those of Semitic race. The erection of obelisks or colossi (or both) in front of the pylons is also susceptible of easy explanation. The obelisks, the form of which was well adapted to break the monotonous outline of the walls, record in

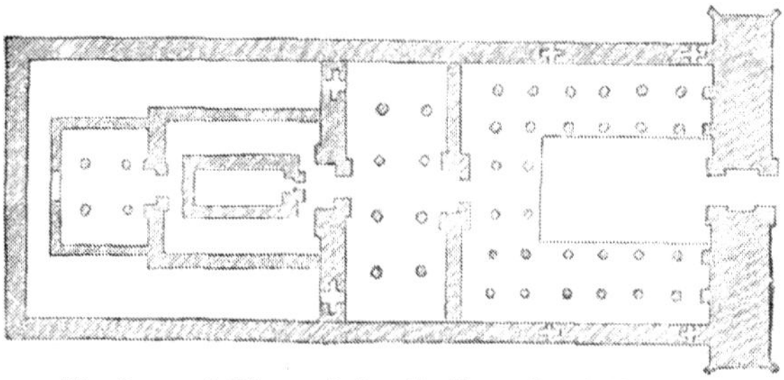

X. Ground Plan of the S. Temple at Karnak.

hieroglyphic inscriptions the victorious power bestowed on the Pharaohs by the god, while the royal statues remind beholders of the duty of monarchs to show their gratitude by erecting temples to the gods. The winged disk of the sun with the heads of the Uræus serpent over every entrance has also a noteworthy signification. It symbolises the victory of Horus over Typhon, and the triumph of good over evil; and an inscription at Edfu informs us that, after the victory of Horus, Thoth (reason) commanded this symbol to be placed over all entrances. On the other hand the way in which architecture is constantly made subservient to painting, for the purpose of obtaining surfaces for symbols and inscriptions, is unpleasing. Every column, every pillar, every roof-beam, and every wall is embellished with raised or engraved figures and characters, all of which are painted. The scenes which portray the victories of the Pharaohs, and their intercourse with the gods, are always accompanied by explanatory inscriptions, and even the simplest ornaments used under the new empire have some symbolical signification.

The form of temple above described sometimes required to be varied in consequence of the nature of the site. In Lower Nubia the sandstone rocks approach so near the Nile that the temples had to be partially or wholly excavated in their sides. At Girgeh, for example (Fig. XI), the pylons and the colonnaded courtyard were built in the open air in front of the temple, while the hypostyle and the sanctuary were excavated in the rock. The larger temple of Abu Simbel, on the other hand, including the pylons and the colossi, is entirely excavated in the rock. During the Ptolemæan era other deviations from the traditional types came into vogue. Differences in

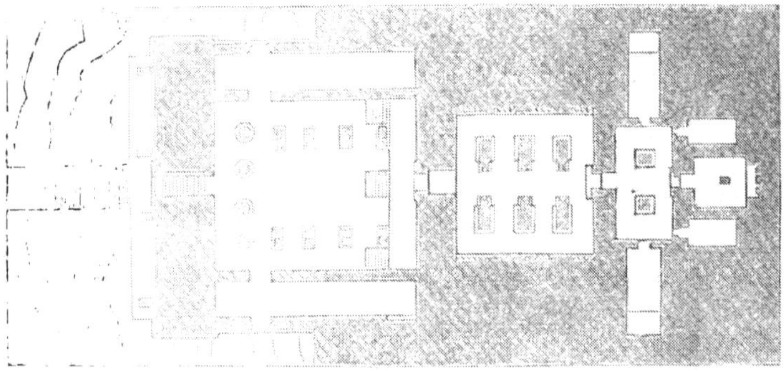

XI. Ground Plan of the Grotto of Girgeh.

the forms of the capitals, in the ornamentation, and other details, as well as a more arbitrary disposition of the temple arrangements themselves, now clearly betray the invasion of Greek influences.

Several of these late buildings, entirely enclosed by columns, with intervening walls rising to half the height of the columns, or even higher, so strongly resemble the Greek peripteral temples externally, that some internal similarity is involuntarily expected. The probable object of some of these edifices, namely to serve as enclos ures for sacred animals, proves them to be of purely Egyptian origin; but, owing to the abnormal disposition of the different members, it is difficult to conceive them to be products of purely native art. Besides the temples in the island of Philæ, the imposing edifices of Edfu (Apollinopolis Magna), Kôm Ombu (Ombos), Esneh (Latopolis), Tentyris (Dendera), and Erment (Hermonthis), afford ample opportunities for the study of the Ptolemæan style of architecture, the impression produced by which is apt to procure for Egyptian art a less favourable general verdict than it strictly deserves.

While the edifices dedicated to the service of the gods belong exclusively to the period of the new empire, there still exist Mortuary Temples the origin of which may be traced back to the remotest periods of the ancient empire. The oldest of these temples are called *Mastabas* (comp. p. 379), and contained a chapel for the celebration of sepulchral rites, as well as a tomb. The kings, however, were not satisfied with a monument in which their tombs and mortuary chapels were united, but adjacent to their pyramids erected temples in which sacrifices were to be offered for the welfare of their souls. The handsome pillar-structure of granite and alabaster near the great Sphinx appears to have been a temple of this kind in connection with the pyramid of Chefren. Under the new empire also the kings constructed their actual burial-places at a distance from the monuments dedicated to their memory. The deep rock vaults in the ravines of the royal tombs were the resting-places of their remains, while the great 'Memnonia' (which are placed exclusively on the W. bank of the Nile at Thebes) were the temples where rites were celebrated in their memory. The most interesting feature of the mortuary temples is their pictorial decoration. The subjects of those in the memnonia are of course the power and prosperity, the victories and achievements, of the monarchs, while the private chapels contained scenes from the domestic life of the deceased. The memnonia sometimes covered a very extensive area, like that of Ramses II., which contained a library and a school. Most of them have pylons and large colonnaded halls, but it cannot now be ascertained whether they were uniform in their arrangements.

By far the greater number of Egyptian sculptures are in immediate connection with architectural works. Colossal statues mount guard over pylons and pillars, and every available surface is adorned with reliefs. If these plastic works are to be fairly judged, they must be regarded as component parts of the building they adorned. Speaking of the colossal statues, Dr. Lepsius justly remarks · — 'The features of these statues, which even received divine honours, and were enthroned in, or in front of, temples in a commanding position, either as structural supports, or detached from the pillars behind them, wear the same character of monumental repose as the statues of the gods themselves, and yet without the possibility of their human individuality being confounded with the universally typical features of the divine images'. — This is chiefly the case with the colossal sitting statues, whose position (with their legs bent at a right angle, their arms firmly pressed against their sides, and their heads looking in a perfectly straight direction) may well be called stiff, but not properly conventional. Many peculiarities of Egyptian art, especially during the earlier period, are apt to be attributed to the imperative requirements of sacerdotal authority, but they are perhaps rather to be accounted for by the imperfection of artistic development. The sculptors exhibit great skill in detail, but they seem incapable of making their skill subserve the general effect of their works. They have obviously striven to represent each member of the body with the utmost fidelity, but they were incapable of combining them harmoniously. Thus, we generally see reliefs with the faces in profile, the chest nearly facing us, and the legs again in profile, a peculiarity which recurs in the works of other Oriental nations, and even in those of the Greeks of the early period. This defect was at length overcome by the Greeks, but of the Egyptian artists it continued permanently characteristic, just as their heroes invariably retain the primitive distinction of being delineated in much larger proportions than other persons. Hampered by these immutable rules as to proportion (which were modified twice only in the course of several thousand years), Egyp-

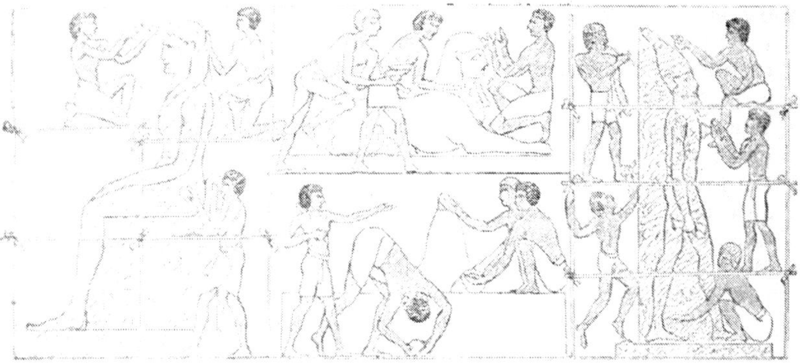

tian art appears to have been seriously checked in its growth, and to have entered, after a brief period of efflorescence, on a long era of what may be termed Byzantinism, — and yet in many respects the Egyptian sculptures merit our highest admiration. The artistic effects capable of being produced in any given material, such as granite, were always calculated with the nicest discrimination; nothing capable of achievement is left undone, and beyond this nothing is attempted. The sculptors are notable for their knowledge of anatomy, for their accuracy in the delineation of muscle, for their skill in portraiture, and for their fidelity in representing animal life. Of all the Egyptian works the figures of the gods are perhaps the least happy. To us they seem to exhibit a want of taste and intelligence; but this is perhaps to be accounted for by the fact that they were intended to be worshipped only, and not admired. That the practice of art was very highly developed in Egypt is proved not merely by the great extent to which the division of labour was carried, but by the fact that the artists understood the process of copying figures by dividing them into squares and calculating their proportions so as to be able to reduce or enlarge them at pleasure. As all authorities, however, concur in pronouncing the Egyptian artists perfect in point of technical skill, it would be superfluous to say more on this branch of the subject.

Besides the painting of the Egyptian plastic works, another peculiarity is the incision of the reliefs, which recede from the surface instead of being raised above it. These 'cœlanoglyphs', or 'reliefs en creux', which somewhat resemble pieces of embroidery, produce nearly the same effect as paintings. Their object is the same, and the style of composition, design, and artistic execution are nearly identical. No attention whatever was paid to tastefulness in grouping or uniformity of arrangement, the separate scenes being merely placed beside or over each other; but, individually, these are remarkable for distinctness and excellence of execution, and they afford us a far more vivid picture of the life of the ancient Egyptians, their customs, their wars, and their religious rites, than any written chronicle could have afforded. In artistic finish, on the other hand, these scenes are defective, and the colouring has no independent value, being merely used to make the figures stand out more distinctly, and imitating nature in the crudest possible manner.

In the province of artistic conception we find Egyptian imagination fettered by traditional bonds which it made no effort to break; but in the practice of the handicrafts Egypt was perfect. The goldsmiths and workers in metal in particular had attained the most complete mastery of their craft; they thoroughly understood all its ancillary arts, such as enamelling and Damascene work, and they were thus able to produce works of a degree of finish such as a highly civilised nation alone could execute and appreciate.

The traveller should note the signification of some of the SYMBOLS and SIGNS most commonly used in the ornamentation of the columns and other parts of the Egyptian temples. Thus,  is the crook or shepherd's staff, the emblem of the leader or monarch;  a scourge, the symbol of kingly power. When both are in the hand of the same figure they perhaps import the power of restraining and of urging onwards. Then  a seal, the symbol of life;  Nilometer, the symbol of steadfastness;  the red crown of Lower Egypt;  the white crown of Upper Egypt;  the united crown of Upper and Lower Egypt; 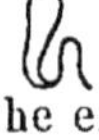 and  the Uræus serpent. On diadems and suns was placed the emblem 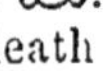. The Uræus serpent, possessing the power of life and death, was the emblem of kingly power. The sceptre, 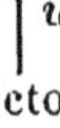 *user*, denoted authority of various kinds, power, wealth, and victorious strength. The sceptre 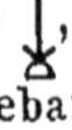, which is read *ûs*, *t'am*, or *ouab*, indicates the name of the Theban nomos; , a basket, signifies a master; , a decorated basket, a festival, or solemn assembly, at which offerings were made in such receptacles;  *mâa*, an ostrich-feather, truth and justice; , *ran*, the frame surrounding the names of kings, signifies the name;  *kheper*, the scarabæus or beetle, the principle of genesis and regeneration. The precise meaning of the symbol  is unknown, but it is read *sam*, and signifies union. It is frequently observed at the foot of statues, entwined with aquatic plants, where it is symbolical of the union of Upper and Lower Egypt, and perhaps of the union of this world with the next. The lock  on the temple of a figure marks it as a child, generally the offspring of the gods or of the kings.

IX. Buildings of the Mohammedans.

Mosques. Dwelling Houses.

By Franz-Bey, Architect at Cairo.

The Mohammedan style of architecture in the valley of the Nile was not, as might perhaps be expected, the immediate successor of the Egyptian, but was separated from it by that of the early Christian epoch, a period of six or seven centuries. This new style was not of native growth, but was imported from abroad, being of Arabian origin, considerably modified by the forms of art which the victorious Arabs found in vogue among the Byzantines, and by those of Persian art of the era of the Sassanides. Different as the Arabian buildings at Baghdâd and Cairo may appear from those at Tunis and in Spain, they all possess certain features in common. The fundamental idea of all Mohammedan architecture originated in the nomadic life of the Arabs. The tent was the prototype, alike of the house and of the temple. The walls in particular, with their carpet-like decoration, and their extensive, unrelieved surfaces, remind one of this origin. This style of architecture is that of the fickle children of the desert, whose edifices, even after they had become a settled and stationary nation, continue to convey an idea of unsubstantiality, and who never attained to a clear perception of the proportion to be observed between the support and the burden to be borne. This defect is less apparent in cases where the Arabian builders were brought under the influence of more civilised nations, where they employed columns, entablatures, and other fragments of ruined edifices which they found available, or where, as sometimes happened, they were aided by Byzantine or other foreign architects, than in purely Arabian edifices like the Alhambra in Spain; but in every case the national characteristic is more or less distinctly traceable.

The buildings most immediately connected with the national traditions are the RELIGIOUS EDIFICES, the leading feature of which consists of the *Court*, such as that seen at Mecca, which dates from a period even earlier than that of Mohammed himself. The walls of the court, indeed, lost their primitive simplicity after their designers had been brought into contact with the colonnaded courts of Egypt and the Syrian regions, and the *Columnar Court* was thus developed; but the Arabian builders avoided using or imitating Egyptian columns. They preferred the columns or remains of columns of the Alexandrian and Roman period, as the massive proportions of those of the Egyptian style were less appropriate to a light and open structure than the columns of the richly decorated Corinthian order.

They borrowed their cornicings, which they employed but sparingly, and their mosaic ornamentation, such as arabesques, from the Byzantine models which they found in Syria and in the oldest Byzantine-Christian edifices of Egypt, and their pointed arches and domes chiefly from the region of the Euphrates. At the same time they contrived to impart to their works a certain individuality of character, partly by the elegance of their forms and the preference given to superficial over architectural decoration, and still more so by the peculiar character of their ornamentation, resembling the patterns of textile fabrics, and obviously imitated from wall-tapestry. Similar patterns appear also in their latticed windows, their carved doors, and their diapered balconies

The *Exterior* of these buildings is generally plain, consisting of a lofty, rectangular enclosing wall of quadrangular plan, but not entirely without relief in the form of projections and indentations. In the mosques there are usually minarets and domes projecting beyond this general outline, and this is still more commonly the case with the public fountains (sebîl) and the mosque schools (medreseh) above them. The portal, on the other hand, and certain perpendicular sections of the building of various widths, generally recede a little, the latter a few inches only, being again brought forward immediately below the cornicing to the level of the façade by means of a 'stalactite' corbelling. In these last also the windows are often inserted with little regard to symmetry. In the corners of the projections thus formed, as well as in the other angles of the building, we frequently find columns of marble inserted, or columns hewn out of the material of the building, and detached to the extent of three-fourths of their thickness. The whole plan of the stone façades, which is not devoid of a certain degree of grandeur, reminds us of those of the ancient Egyptian temples, although the Muslims were generally scrupulously careful to avoid every resemblance to the pagan buildings. The portal is generally the richest part of the edifice. The windows are simpler, and less importance is given to the principal cornice than the height and other dimensions of the building would seem to demand.

The *Portals* consist of rectangular niches, of such depth as to allow room on the left and right outside the door for the mastabas, or stone-benches used by the doorkeeper (bawwâb). This door-niche in the mosques rises nearly to the full height of the façade, and terminates at the top either in a sphere, or in a polygonal half-dome, partly ribbed, and partly embellished with pendentives or 'stalactites'. The two perpendicular mural pillars of the niche approach each other towards the top, either in curved or in straight lines converging at an acute angle. In neither case, however, do they actually meet, the niche terminating above in a hemispherical dome, which springs from the converging lines. The form of the entrance varies considerably. In some cases it terminates above in an architrave, in others in a round or pointed arch, while fantastically waved or broken-arch forms are also not uncommon. The commonest style in the mosques is the architrave form with segmental relieving arches. A favourite practice was to pave the threshold with an ancient block of red or black granite, even if covered with hieroglyphics, and in many cases these venerable inscriptions are still traceable. In the mosques, on the resting-place in front of the door, is a low railing which marks the boundary to which the visitor may penetrate without removing his shoes or sandals. †

The *Windows* are more commonly rectangular than arched, and are sometimes grouped in twos and threes, in which case they are often tastefully adorned with round, oval, or star-shaped rosettes in plaster, perforated, and filled with coloured glass. This arrangement has many points of resemblance to the Byzantine and Romanesque styles. The window in the façades are frequently surrounded with scrolls in low relief, and with flat bands or roll-mouldings. On the inside they are usually adorned with friezes in plaster with arabesques.

Special importance was attached to the principal doors of monumental buildings, which as a rule were massively mounted with iron or bronze, or were constructed of pieces of wood of different colours, ingeniously fitted together. The portals of some of the mosques are embellished with bronze decorations, beautifully embossed and chased. The doors in the interior of the buildings are often richly inlaid with ebony and ivory.

The *Dome*, a very salient feature in Mohammedan buildings, especially in the mosques and mausolea, varies much in form; the base of the structure projects beyond the square ground-plan of the edifice, and the summit rises above the enclosing wall. The dome, which tapers upwards in an elliptical form and is adorned with knobs and crescents, is blended with the quadrangular interior of the mausoleum by means of pendentives; while, externally, the union of the cube with the sphere is somewhat masked by the polygonal base of the dome. In some cases the transition is effected by means of gradations resembling steps, each of which is

† In the more frequented mosques the custodians provide slippers for the use of Frank visitors. Fee 1 silver piastre.

crowned with a half-pyramidal excrescence of the height of the stnep These excrescences might be regarded as external prolongations o. the pendentives of the interior, but do not correspond with them if position. The architects, however, doubtless intended to suggest some such connection between the internal and external ornamentation. The domes are constructed partly of stone and partly of brick, the pendents being of stone, or of plaster and lath-work, and they are sometimes of considerable length. The finest are probably those of the Khalifs' Tombs The greatly elongated domes of the Mameluke tombs have a second dome structure in their interior. The latter, lying much lower, supports walls placed in a radiating form, which bear the upper dome. One of these dilapidated tombs (p. 327) affords a good opportunity of examining this mode of construction. Near it there is also a dome with a lantern, a form quite foreign to the customary style of Arabian dome building.

It is a mistake to suppose that the joints are not cut in a straight direction, but were formed in curved or broken lines which required each stone to be an exact counterpart of its neighbour. This arrangement is occasionally seen in the case of straight or flat segment-shaped plinths, but even there this kind of construction is often merely simulated by means of inlaid marble of different colou /.

The *Minarets* (from the Arabic *menârch*, 'a signal' or 'signal-post') are generally square at the base, tapering upwards, story by story, until the form at length changes to that of an octagon or cylinder. On these towers the architects have expended their utmost skill, and the spectator will not fail to be stuck by their graceful proportions. The highest story is sometimes formed of pilasters, or columns, which bear a roof, either consisting of one or more dome-shaped protuberances with the symbol of El-Islâm, or of a simple conical point. They are generally built of substantial masonry, and contain *Winding Staircases* of stone leading to the galleries of the different stories and to the balconies between them. From these last the mueddins summon the faithful to prayer (p. 147). The galleries are borne by projecting cornices, and the balconies by brackets of similar construction. The wooden rods and hooks at the top of the minarets are used for hanging up the lamps during the fasting month of Ramaḍân. The mosques were also formerly provided with external platforms (called *mabkharas*), on which incense used to be burned on high festivals, so as to diffuse sweet perfumes throughout the whole neighbourhood. The mosque of El-Ḥâkim is now the only one which still possesses platforms of this kind.

The *Public Fountains (sebîls)*, with the *Mosque Schools (medrcschs)* on the first floor, are frequently included within the rectangular precincts of the mosques, but they sometimes project from them in a circular form. The exterior of these buildings, and also of the open colonnades used for scholastic purposes, is frequently adorned with detached columns, which is not the case with the religious edifices.

The *Interiors* of the mosques, on the other hand, are freely embellished with columns, the court being usually bordered by a colonnade, which is doubled or trebled on the side next the prayer-niche (*ḳibla*).

Cairo presents no example of a distinct Arabian order of column, and hardly a single Arabian capital, those actually executed by Arabs (such as those adjoining the prayer-recess of the mosques) being imperfectly developed, and copied from Byzantine and Ptolemæan models. The form of capital which seems peculiar to Cairo is very simple and is also used as a base. Proceeding from the four corners of the abacus in curved lines are four surfaces which unite below with the ligature of the round or octagonal column. The numerous columns which adorn the mosques and private houses originally belonged, almost without exception, to Roman or Ptolemæan structures, and sometimes to Christian churches. The Mohammedans did not, however, employ columns belonging to the ancient Egyptian temples unless they had already been remodelled and used in Greek or Roman structures. Thus the Roman pedestals with remains of hieroglyphics occasionally seen in the mosques must originally have belonged to Egyptian temples. The architects of the mosques collected the columns they required for their purpose with little regard to their dimensions. If they were too short, a pedestal, or a reversed capital was placed beneath them, regardless of the order to which it belonged. Ionic and Corinthian columns are mingled promiscuously, and a certain degree of uniformity in the architecture is only observed when the abacus is reached. On this last lies a second abacus of sycamore wood secured by a wooden bar, from which lamps are frequently suspended.

The arches of the *Arcades* are almost invariably pointed, being at first round, while their sides go off at a tangent near the top; or they gradually assume the keel-shape, being slightly curved inwards below in the shape of a horseshoe. There are also other forms which approach still more nearly to the Gothic pointed arch; and there seems little doubt that this form, so early and so generally employed at Cairo, was exported thence to Sicily, and became the type which afterwards extended to Northern Europe. Beyond this resemblance in the form of the arch, however, and in some of the details of the windows, the pointed style possesses nothing in common with the Arabian. The Gothic gateway of marble between the mosques of Kalaûn and Barḳuḳîyeh (p. 278) in the Derb el-Naḥḥâsîn must, therefore, be regarded as a work executed under European influence. The popular account of it is that it was brought from some island.

The arcades of the mosques and other spacious halls are covered with a flat *Ceiling* of open-work, of almost uniform height. The junction of the walls and ceiling is generally masked by a pendent cornice, or a cornice with a frieze for inscriptions. The beams used in the construction of the ceilings are generally square at both ends to a length of 3-5 ft., beyond which they are rounded below, and frequently carved. The interstices between the beams are sometimes divided into 'coffers'; and proper coffered ceilings also occur, as in the mosque Ṣalâḥeddîn Yûsuf in the citadel (p. 264). In the corners of the apartments, as well as under the principal architraves, pendents are generally placed to conceal the angles. The earliest ceilings appear to have consisted of palm-trunks, and then covered with boards of sycamore wood, which were often richly carved. The space immediately in front of the ḳibla (prayer niche) usually terminated in a dome borne by columns. Spherical and groined vaulting was used for smaller chambers only; but the arcades of the Barḳûḳ mosque (p. 282), with their depressed spherical brick vaulting, form an exception to this rule. In secular buildings the use of vaulting is much more frequent, as in the case of the city-gate Bâb en-Nasr (p. 280) and other arched passages. The entire ground-floors of palaces are also sometimes vaulted, and bridges and aqueducts were usually executed in barrel vaulting, or with pointed arches

The *Decorations* generally consist of panelling or flat paintings, destitute of structural meaning, while pilasters, cornices, and other architectural embellishments are rare. This species of ornamentation was doubtless originally suggested by the carpets, fringes, and mats, used by the Arabs for covering their walls. The stalactite corbellings, on the other hand, which mask the union of the vertical with the horizontal parts of the building, and take the place of the vaulting used in western architecture, are of a more structural character; but even these perform no real architectural function, and form a mere fantastic decoration of the angles of the domes.

The panel and frieze decorations are either foliage, geometrical figures, or written characters. The *Foliage* is usually shaped in rectangular relief, with a few incisions to divide the broader surfaces. The moulding is generally more or less in conformity with the spirit of the classical style, but in the conventional arabesques the leaves and other parts of plants of a southern climate are recognisable. The *Geometrical Figures* consist either of a kaleidoscopic arrangement of constantly recurring fantastic forms, or of a series of intertwined and broken lines. Lastly, the Arabic *Written Characters* with which the friezes are often decorated, and more particularly the Cufic and Sullus characters, are peculiarly well adapted for ornamental purposes, as they resemble decorative foliage, although destitute of its strictly symmetrical and continuous character. When the writing is employed for lengthy inscriptions in low relief, the ground on which it is placed is generally covered with slightly raised arabesques.

Panels or friezes bearing inscriptions of this character produce a very rich and pleasing appearance. When viewed from a moderate distance, especially if enhanced by colouring, the broad characters stand out with great effect. The ground then resembles a network of lace, the delicate lines of the arabesques being indistinguishable except on close inspection. Sultan Hasan's mosque (p. 260) contains a remarkably handsome frieze of this description. The large and bold characters on the mosques or private houses which strike the eye of the traveller are almost invariably texts from the Korân, while historical notices in a small running character are often inscribed on marble slabs over the entrances and the lattice-work of the sebils, where they are sometimes carved in wood. Similar inscriptions also occasionally occur in the halls of the interior.

The observer can scarcely fail to be struck with the apparently capricious way in which this ornamentation is distributed, the artist having sometimes lavished the whole richness of his arabesques upon certain spots to the neglect of others. When this peculiarity is more closely examined, it will be found that the parts thus favoured are — (1) the Portals, which are embellished with a framework of rich friezes, with rosettes to mark certain points, with artistic sculpturing on the architrave, and with pendents in the ceiling of the niche; (2) the Minarets, which it was customary to place over or adjacent to the portals, but seldom from structural motives; (3) the external surfaces of the Dome, which are sometimes covered with arabesques, and sometimes with roll-mouldings or wreaths; (4) the Kibla, with its handsome border, its capitals and columns, which are often rich and beautiful, its fine mosaics, its miniature pseudo-arcades; (5) the Pendents in the interior of mausoleums; (6) the Ceilings; (7) the Mambar (pulpit), which is partly in stone and partly in wood. The lattice-work, windows, doors couches or sofas *(dikkeh)*, lanterns, and lamps are also much ornamented. These last are sometimes made of very curious enamelled glass, but few are now to be found in the mosques.

Colour does not perhaps play quite so conspicuous a part in the Egypto-Arabian monuments as in the Spanish; but the Egyptian artists, like those of the Alhambra, were also much addicted to the use of bright colours, especially red, blue, yellow, gold, and white. The ground of the decorative inscriptions is frequently deep blue, while the letters are usually gilded. On the whole, however, painting was never so highly developed here as in Spain, where the artists showed a certain appreciation of perspective by painting the lower parts of their walls with dark colours and gradually shading them upwards with lighter and more brilliant tints. In their colouring, as well as in their ornamental reliefs, it is obvious that the Egyptian artists aimed at producing effect by contrasts. The pavement consists of the richest marble mosaic, for the most part in dark colours, the walls are generally painted, and the cornice and ceiling richly coloured and gilded. In the more important private houses we sometimes find the walls covered with majolica. The traveller will also be struck with the beautiful effects of colour produced by the *Inlaid Work* in the ḳiblas of certain mosques (the tombs of Ḳalaûn, Ṭulûn, and Ḳait Bey), where marble, porphyry, mother-of-pearl, and Venetian enamel have been combined. In the case of *Cabinet Work* the colours used for inlaying are dark brown, black (ebony), white (ivory), and bronze. Externally the dark yellowish stone of which the buildings were constructed produced a naturally pleasing effect, which the architects occasionally endeavoured to enhance by colouring every alternate course red or black; while important parts were adorned with marble mosaic, majolicas, panelling, and gilding. Owing to the mildness of the climate of Egypt much of the original colouring has been preserved, but it must not be confounded with the rude and staring painting of stone façades and marble ornaments executed on the occasion of the opening of the Suez Canal in 1869.

The secular edifices, like the sacred, and particularly the *Dwelling Houses*, have also their characteristic peculiarities. The ordinary town-houses are constructed of stone on the ground-floor, and generally have an overhanging upper story. The projecting parts sometimes rest on pillars, but more commonly on beautifully carved brackets of peculiar form, and are provided with a kind of bow-window, which serves the double purpose of ventilating the house and of affording a view of the street to the women concealed behind the lattice-work. The small perforated and generally octagonal balconies, with round holes at the bottom, are used for cooling the drinking-water in porous vessels (*ḳullehs*), whence they derive their name of *Mushrebîyehs* (from *sharâb*, a draught). These balconies are rectangular in shape, but their sides are sometimes arched, and the lattice-work round them, composed of turned pieces of wood, often forms an ingenious and elaborate pattern. The roofs of these mushrebîyehs usually project in a tent-like form, and instead of cornices they have pendent friezes cut out of boards. The union of these projections with the surface of the wall below is generally masked by means of richly carved and elegantly waved mouldings with tasteful rosettes. Above the mushrebîyehs, which rarely extend to the height of the apartment within, there are usually introduced upper windows, with stucco frames, filled with stained glass. — The *Cornices* of the houses project but slightly, curving a little outwards when pendentives are not employed; and they are almost always crowned with pinnacles, which are often most elaborately executed. We may also mention the curious form of cornice seen in the Mameluke Tombs, where the projecting ends of the roof-beams are serrated.

While bestowing their full meed of praise on the wonderfully rich ornamentation and other details of Arabian architecture, one cannot help feeling that the style fails to give entire æsthetic satisfaction Want of symmetry in plan, poverty of articulation, insufficiency of plastic decoration, and an incongruous mingling of stone and wood, are the imperfections which strike most northern critics. The architects, in fact, bestowed the whole of their attention on the decoration of surfaces; and down to the present day the Arabian artists have always displayed far greater ability in tracing elegant outlines, and designing the most complicated ornaments and geometrical figures on plane surfaces, than in the treatment and proportioning of masses. Although we occasionally see difficulties of construction well overcome, as in the case of the interior of the Bâb en-Nasr, these instances seem rather to be successful experiments than the result of scientific workmanship. The real excellence of the Arabian architects lay in their skill in masking abrupt angles by the use of 'stalactites' or brackets.

If we enquire into the causes of these defects in the development of art we shall find that the climate is one of the principal. Its remarkable mildness and the rareness of rain have enabled architects to dispense with much that appears essential to the inhabitant of more northern latitudes; and hence the imperfect development and frequent absence of cornices. The extraordinary durability of wood in Egypt, again, has led to its being used in the construction of walls, and in connection with stone, in a manner which would never occur to northern architects. Another circumstance unfavourable to the development of native art has doubtless been the ease with which the architects obtained abundance of pillars and capitals in ancient buildings ready to their hand. There were also political obstacles to the progress of art, such as frequent intestine struggles and dissensions, and the sway of despotic rulers and their servile officers; and, lastly, the characteristic Egyptian tenacity and veneration for tradition and religious precept have not been without their influence. The original design of the mosque, for example, was borrowed from Mecca, and no deviation could be made from its plan; and this accounts for the invariable recurrence of the same forms in the mosques of Egypt. In a few instances architects ventured to introduce innovations, but they never failed to revert sooner or later to the established style. The external architecture of private houses, however, being unfettered by religious considerations, might have progressed more favourably but for the powerful influence of superstition and fear An external display of wealth, according to the popular notion, drew upon its possessor the 'evil eye' of the covetous, the consequence of which was misfortune or death, while, on the other hand, it afforded the government a pretext for extorting heavy taxes from the occupant. It therefore became customary with the Egyptians to restrict any appearance of luxury to the interior of their harems, where it is exhibited in the sumptuous furniture and hangings, and in the jewellery of the women. These indications of wealth are never seen except by the proprietor's nearest relations and the female friends of his wives, and are effectually concealed from the view of the government and of the general public.

With regard to *Sculpture* and *Painting* it will strike the traveller that the modern Egyptian chisel and brush have been reserved exclusively for the decoration of wall surfaces. Representations of animals occur rarely, while those of the human figure were prohibited by the Korân (comp. p. 218). The latter, however, are occasionally met with. One of the Tulunides, for example, caused a festal hall to be adorned with painted wooden statues of himself, his wives, and his favourite dancers; and at Cairo there was even a famous manufactory of figures of men and animals at that period. In the 11th cent., as we are informed, there were two celebrated painters at Cairo who vied with each other in the execution of relief pictures. One of them painted a dancer, who seemed to be disappearing into the wall, while his rival painted another who seemed to be coming out from it. El-Kitami's picture of Joseph in the pit was also a far-famed work. On the whole, however, these branches of art were but little developed, the Egyptians resembling the Israelites in this respect. The Arabs were more successful, however, in the prosecution of artistic handicrafts, and excelled in the embellishment of all kinds of implements in metal-work, enamel, inlaying, engraving, etc. Their decorative ingenuity, developed by these arts quite as much as by the wall decorations, and applied to textile fabrics also, has attained so wide a celebrity, that the word 'Arabesque' is now nearly synonymous with 'ornament'. The word 'Grotesque' was once similarly applied to the western style of decoration borrowed by Raphael and Giovanni da Udine from the 'Grottoes' of the Baths of Titus at Rome, and employed by them with singular success in the loggie of the Vatican, but this word has long since lost its original meaning.

The **Mosques** are divided, in accordance with their religious importance, into two kinds: (1) those in which the sermon *(khutbeh)* is preached on Fridays, called *Gâmí*; (2) those in which prayer only is offered daily except on Fridays, named *Mesgid*†, or *Zâwiya*. The name *mesgid*, which has been imported from Constantinople, is less frequently used than Zâwiya, which denotes a small mosque, consisting of one chamber only.

† It is from this word *mesgid* (which means a place for prostration), that we derive the word mosque, through the Spanish *mezquita* and the French *mosquée*.

The Muslims also repeat their prayers at the grated windows of the mausolea of their saints (*shêkh*, or *weli*; see p. 152), behind which is visible a catafalque, covered with bright coloured carpets, but by no means invariably containing the remains of the holy man. These weli's, or tombs of shêkhs, occur in every part of the country, being frequently built into the houses, and are easily recognised by their cubic form and their domes. They are rarely more than 4-6 yds. square, and are generally whitewashed. The interior is often empty and infested with scorpions and vermin.

Every Gâmi has a court of considerable size, generally uncovered, called the *Fasha*, or *Sahn el-Gâmi'*, in the centre of which is the *Hanefîyeh*, or fountain for religious ablution. On the E. side the court is adjoined by the *Lîwân*, covered with carpets or mats (*Hasîreh*), where the sacred vessels are kept. Between the Lîwân and the court there often runs a mushrebîyeh railing which separates the holy place of the Gâmi' from the court.

In the Lîwân we observe: (1) the *Kibla* or *Mihrâb*, the prayer-niche turned towards Mecca; (2) the *Mambar*, or pulpit, to the right of the Kibla, from which the *Khatîb* or *Imâm* addresses the faithful; (3) the *Kursi* (pl. *Kerâsi*), or reading-desk, on which the Korân (which is kept at other times in a cabinet of its own) lies open during divine service; (4) the *Dikkeh*, a podium borne by columns, and surrounded by a low railing, from which the *Moballigh* (assistants of the Khatîb) repeat the words of the Korân, which is read at the Kibla, for the benefit of the people at a distance; (5) the various lamps and lanterns (*Kindîl* and *Fânûs*). By the side of the Sahn el-Gâmi' is another small court with a basin of water and other conveniences, which the faithful almost invariably visit before entering the sacred precincts. Adjoining the Lîwân is usually placed the mausoleum of the founder of the mosque, called *Maksûra*, and farther distant, by the principal entrance, is the *Sebîl* (fountain) with the *Medreseh* (school). Under the Sebîl is a cistern, which is filled during the inundation of the Nile. These fountains are often richly adorned with marble and bronze railings. They are protected by a very projecting roof, and above them is the more or less handsome school hall. The railings whence the water is distributed are usually approached by several steps. The interior of the Sebîl consists of a single large chamber, the pavement of which is about 3 ft. below the level of the surrounding soil, and in it the water drawn from the cistern is placed in vessels for distribution at the railings. Adjacent to the Sebîls are sometimes placed troughs for watering animals. The water stored in these cisterns is generally in great request in June, when the Nile water becomes unwholesome, assuming a green colour caused by the presence of myriads of microscopically small plants. The *Medreseh* usually consists of a single hall, with a store-room for its simple furniture.

Considered with respect to their ground-plans, the mosques are classed in two leading groups: (1) those of *rectangular plan*, with *hypaethral* columns or pilasters round the open court (see plan of the mosques of ʿAmr, p. 324, and Barḳûḳ, p. 282); and (2) those which have a *rectangular* or *cruciform* court surrounded by closed rooms, like the mosque of Sultan Ḥasan and most of the tomb mosques, or those where the tomb is of large size compared with the Ṣaḥn el-Gâmiʿ.

The Tombs of the Muslims (comp. also p. 155) are generally situated on high ground, uninfluenced by the moisture of the river, and sometimes in the desert. The chambers are destitute of decoration. Within is a catafalque of stone resting on a more or less decorated pedestal, and bearing two upright columns (*Shâhid*) of marble or other stone, one of which, placed immediately over the head of the deceased, bears his name and age, with texts from the Korân. At the top of the shâhid is represented the turban of the deceased, the form of which indicates his rank. Over the catafalques of persons of distinction are erected dome-shaped canopies, resting on four columns or pilasters, or their tombs have the closed form of those of the shêkhs already mentioned. On festivals the catafalques and hollow parts of the pedestals are covered with palm-branches, flowers, and basilicum. On these occasions the friends, and especially the female relatives, of the deceased often spend whole days by the tomb, engaged in prayer and almsgiving. For these mourners it was necessary to provide accommodation, and the result is that a complete mausoleum, with its rooms for the family, sebîl, school, stables, custodian's residence, etc., is often nearly as extensive as the mosques themselves, while some of them are so large as almost to present the appearance of a small deserted town. To buildings of this kind the name of *Ḥôsh* is applied. One of the most imposing of these is the tomb-mosque of Sultan Barḳûḳ.

The **Dwelling-Houses**, which rarely have more than two stories, are built in very various styles, but the following rules are generally observed in their construction: — (1) The principal rooms, particularly those of the *Harem* (p. 187), look into the court or garden, if there be one. (2) The windows looking to the street are small, placed very high, and strongly barred, while those of the upper floors are closed with mushrebîyeh (p. 181), which, however, are gradually being superseded by glass-windows with shutters. (3) The entrance-door (Pl. I, 1), behind which is the seat (*Masṭaba*, Pl. I, 2) of the doorkeeper, is generally low and narrow, and the passage (Pl. I, 3) leading from the street to the court is built in the form of an angle, to prevent people from seeing into the court. (4) The court (*Ḥôsh*, Pl. I, 4) is planted with trees and unpaved, and contains a well of water that has filtered through from the Nile. This water, however, is generally more or less brackish, and is used only for washing purposes and for the cattle. (5) By the entrance to the court, and on the same level, is the *Mandara*

(Pl. I, 7), or reception-room of the proprietor, with at least one *Khazneh*, or cabinet (Pl. I, 15), and other conveniences. The Mandara of the best class is of symmetrical construction, and the door is in the middle of one of the sides. The central part of this hall, called the *Durkâ'a*, which is paved with marble mosaic and contains a fountain *(Faskîyeh)*, is one step lower than the sides on the right and left. The ground-plan is generally the same as that of the Kâ'a (Pl. I, 14). Opposite the entrance of the durkâ'a there is generally a *Suffeh*, or kind of stand in stone or marble, on which are placed the household utensils for washing, drinking, etc. The more elevated sides of the Mandara, called the *Lîwân*, are covered with carpets and mats, thus forming a kind of couch, and are never stepped upon except with shoeless feet. Visitors leave their shoes in the Durkâ'a. Along the walls are often placed cupboards, richly decorated with inlaid work and majolica. The ceilings are generally tastefully ornamented. Adjoining the court there is usually another hall, situated a little above its level, adorned

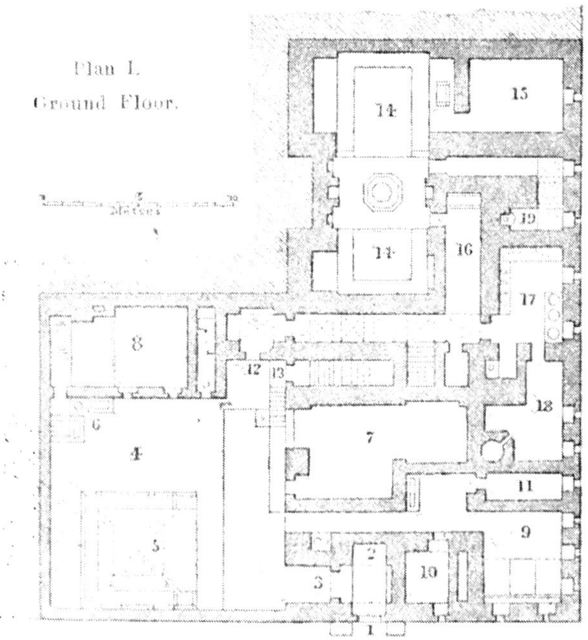

1. Entrance of the House. 2. Seat (Mastaba) for the doorkeeper. 3. Corridor. 4. Court. 5. A kind of bower (Muk'ad) in which visitors are received in summer. 6. Fountain. 7. Guest-chamber. 8. Servants' rooms 9. Donkey-stable. 10. Saddle-room. 11. Room for fodder. 12. Door leading to the women's apartments (Bâb el-Harim). 13. Staircase leading to the proprietor's apartments. 14. Principal saloon (el-Kâ'a). 15. Khazneh. 16. Small court. 17. Kitchen. 18. Bake-house. 19. Privy.

with a column, and open towards the north. This is called the *Takhta Bôsh*, and is used in temperate weather for the same purposes as the Mandara. Lastly the *Muḳ'ad* (Pl. I, 5), where the proprietor receives visits in summer, is usually raised, like the Takhta Bôsh, half the height of the ground-floor above the level of the court, and is adorned with several columns, while below it are small chambers used as store-rooms and for various other purposes, and frequently the well with its drawing apparatus.

The principal part of the *Harem* (women's apartments), which in smaller houses is accessible from the court only by the *Bâb el-Ḥarim* (Pl. I, 12; II, 3), is the *Ḳâ'a* (Pl. I. 14). The ceiling of the Durḳâ'a is higher than that of the Lîwân, and has a dome in the centre with mushrebîyeh openings. The walls of the Lîwân are

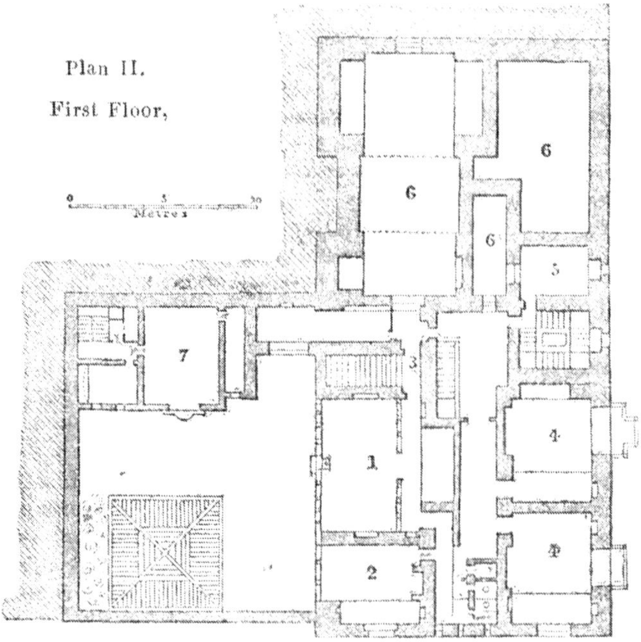

1. Open hall (Takhta Bôsh). 2. Cabinet. 3. Door of the Harem. 4. Rooms of the Harem with mushrebîyehs. 5. Magazine. 6. Open courts. 7. Guest-chambers.

frequently lined with rows of shelves, with valuable porcelain, crystal, or plate. In the larger houses a separate staircase for the women-servants ascends from the ground-floor to the upper stories. On its way it passes the intervening floor forming their dwelling, which is built over the less important rooms of the ground-floor

Another door usually leads direct from the apartments of the proprietor into the harem (Pl. I, 3). At the back of the building are kitchens and stables, and frequently a mill also. — In the country, and even at Cairo, the entrance-door is sometimes painted with very rude figures of camels, lions, steamboats, etc., which are intended to indicate that the owner has performed the pilgrimage to Mecca (p. 148).

X. The Arabic Language.

Arabic belongs to the Semitic group of languages, and has no relationship with the tongues of Europe. A knowledge of Hebrew, however, will materially facilitate the learning of Arabic. The golden era of Arabic literature is coeval with the introduction of El-Islâm, and the Koran in the dialect of the Kureish (the family of Mohammed) is still regarded as an unrivalled model of style and language. As El-Islâm spread from its narrow home over the vast territories that gradually acknowledged the Crescent, Arabic lost many of its older and fuller forms and was greatly simplified for daily use. In this way arose the vulgar dialects of Arabic, of which that spoken in Egypt is one. In writing, however, an attempt was made to retain the older forms, and the written language of the present day, known as Middle Arabic, occupies a position midway between the original classical tongue and the popular dialects. Egypt was conquered by the Arabs in the 19th year of the Hegira (640 A.D.) and the Coptic language was replaced by Arabic. The dialect of the latter developed in the valley of the Nile differs considerably in the pronunciation of the consonants, vocalisation, and accent from the ordinary Arabic dialects of Syria and elsewhere. Thus the letter ج is pronounced hard in Egypt and soft in Syria (see p. 190). The variations, however, are not so great as to prevent the Syrians and Egyptians being mutually intelligible.

A sharply defined and exact pronunciation of the consonants is characteristic of Arabic and is absolutely essential to any satisfactory use of the language. The learner should endeavour at once to master the pronunciation of the more difficult Arabic consonants, such as ح, ط, ع, ص, and ض, so as, for example, to be able to make a distinct difference between *bêt* (house) and *bêḍ* (eggs). Many of the sounds have no representatives in English. Owing to the increasing intercourse between the native Egyptians and Europe, the former have of late adopted many words from other languages, chiefly from Italian and French. Many Arabic words have, moreover, long since been replaced by Turkish equivalents. The Egyptian dialect also contains many Coptic or ancient Egyptian words. Very few Europeans learn to pronounce Arabic accurately, even after a residence of many years in the country.

The language of the peasantry and the inhabitants of the desert is purer and more akin to the classical language than that of the dwellers in towns. The Muslims generally speak more correctly than the Christians, being accustomed to a refined diction and pronunciation from their daily repetition of passages of the Korân. The chief difference between the language of the Korân and the modern colloquial dialect is that a number of terminal inflexions are dropped in the latter.

Alphabet. The Arabic alphabet was developed from that of the Nabataeans, who in turn adopted their written characters from the Palmyrenes. In spite of its external attractions, it is one of the most imperfect in existence In written or printed Arabic the short vowels are usually omitted and have to be supplied by the reader, a feat which demands considerable skill and experience In the Korân, however, the vowels are all indicated by appropriate signs. It is greatly to be wished that the Arabs would adopt a simpler alphabet, with a regular use of the vowel-signs, and that they would agree to write the ordinary spoken language. The present condition of affairs not only seriously increases a stranger's difficulties in learning the language, but is a serious obstacle to the education of the Arabs themselves.

We give below the sounds corresponding to the different letters, so far as it is possible to represent or describe them to the English reader. It should also be observed that in the following pages we use the vowel sounds of *a*, *e*, *i*, *o*, *u* as they are used in Italian (ah, eh, ee, o, oo). The *ê* used in the Handbook is a contracted form of *ei*, and is used in preference to it, as it exactly represents the ordinary pronunciation (viz. that of *a* in fate) The original diphthong sound of *ei* is only used in the reading of the Korân and in a few isolated districts. Where a sound resembling the French *u* occurs it is represented by *ü* (as in *tutün*). This system of transliteration will be found most convenient, as the words will then generally resemble the forms used in German, French, and Italian, instead of being distorted to suit the English pronunciation. Thus *emîr*, which is pronounced 'aymeer'; *shêkh* (or sheikh), pronounced 'shake' (with a guttural k); *tulûl*, pronounced 'toolool'; *Abusîr*, pronounced 'Abooseer'; etc.

Vowels The short vowel symbols, *Fathah*, *Kesrah*, and *Dummeh* (*ă*, *ĕ*, *ŭ*), which are generally omitted, become long when connected with *Alef*, *Wau*, and *Ye* (*â*, *ê*, *î*, *ô*, *û*, *au*).

The numerous gutturals of Arabic render the language unpleasing to the ear. The consonants Nos. 15, 16, and 21, which are sometimes called 'emphatic', are very peculiar, and modify the vowels connected with them: thus after them *a* and *u* approach the sound of *o*, and *i* that of *e*. The sounds of the French *u* and *eu* (German *ü* and *ö*) are rare in colloquial Arabic.

Consonants.

1.	Elif, Alef	ا		accompanies an initial vowel, and is not pronounced except as a hiatus in the middle of a word.
2.	Bâ	ب	b	as in English.
3.	Tâ	ت	t	
4.	Thâ	ث	th	as *th* in 'thing', but generally pronounced *t* or *s*.
5.	Gîm	ج	g j̣	in Syria and Arabia like the French *j* (sometimes also like the English *j*), but pronounced *g* (hard) in Egypt.
6.	Ḥâ	ح	ḥ	a peculiar guttural *h*, pronounced with emphasis at the back of the palate.
7.	Khâ	خ	kh	like *ch* in the Scotch word 'loch', or the harsh Swiss German *ch*.
8.	Dâl	د	d	as in English.
9.	Dhâl	ذ	dh	as *th* in 'the', but generally pronounced *d* or *z*.
10.	Rê	ر	r	like the French or German *r*.
11.	Zê, Zên	ز	z	as in English.
12.	Sîn	س	s	
13.	Shîn	ش	sh	
14.	Ṣâd	ص	ṣ	emphasised *s*.
15.	Ḍâd	ض	ḍ	both emphasised by pressing the tongue firmly against the palate.
16.	Ṭâ	ط	ṭ	
17.	Ẓâ	ظ	ẓ	an emphatic *z*, now pronounced like No. 11 or No. 15.
18.	ʿÊn	ع	ʿ	a strong and very peculiar guttural.
19.	Ghên	غ	gh	a guttural resembling a strong French or German *r*.
20.	Fê	ف	f	as in English.
21.	Ḳâf	ق	ḳ	emphasised guttural *k*, replaced by the natives of Lower Egypt, and particularly by the Cairenes, by a kind of hiatus or repression of the voice.
22.	Kâf	ك	k	
23.	Lâm	ل	l	as in English.
24.	Mîm	م	m	
25.	Nûn	ن	n	
26.	Hê	ه	h	
27.	Wau	و	w	
28.	Ye	ى	y	

Accentuation. If a word terminates with a long syllable ending in a consonant (indicated by a circumflex accent over the vowel), or with a syllable ending in a double consonant, the accent is placed on the last syllable (as in *maghnâtîs*, *bâdingân*, *al'mâz*, *ketébt*, *taghtámm*, each of which has the stress on the last syllable). If the last syllable has any other form, *i. e.* if it terminates in a vowel only, or in a consonant preceded by a short vowel, the accent in the case of a *dissyllable* is on the first syllable (as in *gézmeh*, *búrnus*, *fúrsha*, *rédi*), and in the case of a *trisyllable* or *polysyllable* on the third syllable from the end (as *mármala*, *mâhbara*, *mâdeneh*), except when the penultimate is a long syllable (as in *sibânikh*), in which case the accent is on that syllable.

Address. The inhabitants of towns use the 2nd person plural in addressing a person, or a periphrasis, such as *genâbak* (your honour), *hadretak* (your presence), or to a patriarch *ghubtatkum*, to a pasha *sa'âdetak*. *Yâ sîdi* (O sir) is also frequently used, and to Europeans, *ya khawâgeh*.

Possessives These are expressed by means of affixes Thus, *binti*, my daughter; *bintak* (*ik* when the person addressed is feminine), thy daughter; *bintu*, his daughter; *bintha*, or *bintahâ*, her daughter, *bintnâ* or *bintinâ*, our daughter, *bintkum* or *bintukum*, your (pl 1) daughter, *bintuhum*, their daughter The idea of possession is colloquially expressed by the use of the word *betâ'* ('property'), as *el-'abd betâ'i*, my slave ('the slave my property').

Article The definite article *el* or *al* is assimilated before dentals, sibilants, and the letters *n* and *r* thus, *esh-shems*, the sun, etc.

Demonstratives In Egypt the word 'this' is rendered by *de*, fem *di*; as *er-râgil de*, this man; *el-bint di*, this girl The Beduins use the old Arabic and Syrian *hâda* 'These', *dôl* 'That', *dikha*, *dukha*, *dukhauwa*, *dikhaiya;* plural *dukhamma*

Relative · *elli*, omitted after substantives used in a general sense.

Interrogatives Who, *mîn;* what, *êh*, *êsh*.

Declension The substantive is not declinable. The genitive of a substantive is formed by simply placing it immediately after the substantive to be qualified, the latter being deprived of its article. thus, *ibn el-bâsha*, the son of the pasha The feminine terminations *a*, *e*, *i* are in such cases changed into *at*, *et*, *it:* thus *mara*, wife; *marat el-ḳâḍi*, the wife of the judge

Dual. The dual termination is *ên*, fem *etên:* thus *seneh*, year; *senetên*, two years, *rigl*, foot, *riglên*, two feet

Plural In the masculine the termination is *în* (as *fellâhîn*, peasants), in the feminine *ât* (as *ḥâra*, town, quarter, etc, pl *ḥârât*) The plural is, however, usually formed by a radical change of the vowel sounds of the singular, the change being effected in thirty or forty different ways, so that it becomes necessary for the learner to note carefully the plural form of every substantive thus, *'ain*, spring, pl *'uyûn*; *tâgir*, merchant, pl *tuggâr; gebel*, mountain, pl *gibâl; ḳabîleh*, tribe of Beduins, pl. *ḳabâil*.

Verbs. Many of the verbs consist of slightly differing cognate roots, connected somewhat in the same manner as the English verbs *lay* and *lie* Each verb consists of a perfect and present imperfect tense, an imperative, a participle, and an infinitive.

The above remarks are made merely in order to afford a slight idea of the structure of the language, the difficulties of which are such that few persons will venture to encounter them, unless they make a prolonged stay in the country. We should, however, recommend the traveller to commit to memory the following words and phrases of everyday occurrence, a knowledge of which will often prove useful.

Arabic Vocabulary.

one	— *wâhed*,	fem. *wahdeh*;	the first	— *el-âwwel*,	fem. *el-auwaleh* or *el-ûla*.	
two	— *etnên*,	- *etnên*;	the second	— *tâni*,	fem.	*tâniyeh*
three	- *telâteh*,	- *telât*;	the third	— *tâlet*,	-	*tâlteh*
four	— *arba'a*,	- *arbá*,'	the fourth	— *râbé*,	-	*râb'eh*
five	- - *khamseh*	- *khams*;	the fifth	— *khâmis*,	-	*khâmseh*
six	— *setteh*,	- *sitt*,	the sixth	— *sâdis*,	-	*sâdseh*
seven	- *sab'a*,	- *seb'a*,	the seventh	— *sâbé*,	-	*sâb'eh*
eight	- - *temânyeh*	- *temân*,	the eighth	— *tâmen*,	-	*tâmneh*
nine	— *tes'a*,	- *tis'a*;	the ninth	— *tâse'*,	-	*tâs'eh*
ten	— *'ashara*,	- *'asher*,	the tenth	— *'âshir*,	-	*'âshra*

11	— *hadâsher*	100	— *mîyeh*; before nouns, *mît*.
12	— *etnâsher*	200	— *mîtên*
13	— *telatâsher*	300	— *tultemîyeh*
14	— *arba'tâsher*	400	— *rub'amîyeh*
15	— *khamstâsher*	500	— *khumsemîyeh*
16	— *settâsher*	600	— *suttemîyeh*
17	— *sab'atâsher*	700	— *sub'amîyeh*
18	— *temantâsher*	800	— *tumnemîyeh*
19	— *tes'atâsher*	900	— *tus'amîyeh*
20	— *'eshrîn*	1000	— *alf*
30	— *telâtîn*	2000	— *alfên*
40	— *arba'în*	3000	— *telat alâf*
50	— *khamsîn*	4000	— *arba't alâf*
60	— *settîn*	5000	— *khamast ălâf*
70	— *sab'în*	100,000	— *mît alf*
80	— *temânîn* 90 — *tes'în*	1,000,000	— *milyûn*

once	— *marra wahdeh marra* or *nôba*	a half	— *nuss*
		a third	— *tult*
twice	— *marratên*	a fourth	— *rub'a*
thrice	— *telât marrât*	three fourths	— *nuss u rub'a*
four times	*arba marrât*	a fifth	— *khums*
five times	— *khams (khamas) marrât*	a sixth	— *suds*
six times	— *sitt (setteh) marrât*	a seventh	— *sub'eh*
seven times	— *seb'a marrât*	an eighth	— *tumn*
eight times	— *temân marrât*	a ninth	— *tus'eh*
nine times	*tes'a marrât*	a tenth	— *'ushr*
ten times	— *'ashara marrât*		

The substantives following numerals above ten are used in the singular; thus 4 piastres, *arba' kurûsh*; 100 piastres, *mît kirsh*.

I, *ana*, thou, *inteh*, fem. *enti*; he, *hûweh*; she, *hîyeh*; we, *ehna*; ye or you, *entu*, or *entum*; they, *hum*, or *huma*.

Yes, *eywa*, to be sure, *na'am*; no, *lâ*, no, I will not, *lâ*, *mush 'âuz*, or *'âuz*; it is not necessary, *mush lâzim*; not, *mâ*; there is nothing, *mâ fîsh*, I will, *ana biddi*; wilt thou, *biddak*; we will, *biddina*, will you, *biddukum*.

I go, *ana râiḥ;* I shall go, *âna arûḥ;* we shall go, *nerûḥ;* go, *rûḥ;* will you not go, *mâ terûḥ*, go ye, *rûḥu.*

See, *shûf;* I have seen, *shuft.*

I speak, *betkallim;* I do not speak Arabic, *ana mâ betkallim-shi bil-'arabi;* what is your name, *ismak ê.*

I drink, *bashrab;* I have drunk, *ana shiribt;* drink, *ishrab.*

I eat, *ana bâkul*, or *ana wâkil;* I have eaten, *ana kalt;* eat, *kul;* we will eat, *biddina nâkul.*

He sleeps, *binâm*, he is now asleep, *huweh nâim;* get up, *ḳûmu;* I am resting, *besterîḥ* or *bastaraiyah.*

I have ridden, *rikibt;* I mount, *barkab*, I will mount, *arkab;* I start, *ana besâfir*, or *musâfir.*

I am coming, *ana gâi;* come, *ta'âleh, ta'âla*, or *ta'âl.*

To-day, *en-nahâr-deh;* to-morrow, *bukra*, the day after to-morrow, *ba'deh bukra;* yesterday, *embâreḥ*, the day before yesterday, *auwel embâreḥ.*

Much or very, *ketîr;* a little, *shuwaiyeh (shwaiyeh);* good, *ṭayyib*, not good, *mush ṭayyib*, very good, *ṭayyib ketîr;* slow, slower · *shwaiyeh shwaiyeh, 'ala mahlak;* go on, *yallah, yallah.*

How much, *kâm*, for how much, *bikâm;* enough, *bess;* how many hours, *kam sâ'a.*

For what purpose, *min-shân-êh* or *'ala-shân-êh*, no matter, *mâ 'alêsh.* This last is a favourite expression with the Arabs, who use it to express indifference and also as an apologetic interjection.

Everything, *kull*, together, *sawa, sawa;* every, *kull wâḥed;* one after the other, *wâḥed, wâḥed*

Here, *heneh* (Syrian *hôn*), come here, *ta'âla heneh;* come from here, *ta'âleh min heneh;* there, *henâk* (Syrian *hônîk*); above, *fôḳ;* below, *taḥt;* over, *'ala;* deep, *ghamîk, ghawît;* far, *ba'îd*, near, *ḳuraiyîb;* inside, *guwwa;* outside, *barra;* where, *fên* (pronounced by the Beduins *wên*); yet, *lissa;* not yet, *mâ lissa* (with a verb); when, *emta;* after, *ba'd;* later, afterwards, *ba'dên*, never, *abadan;* always, *dâiman tamallî*, perhaps, *belki, yumkin*, or *yimkin.*

Old, *kebîr, 'atîḳ kadîm*, deceitful, *khâin;* intoxicated, *sakrân;* blind, *a'ma;* stupid, awkward, *ghashîm;* lazy, *keslân;* strange, *gharîb;* healthy, *salîm, ṣâgh salîm, ṭayyib, biṣ-ṣaḥḥa*, or *mabsûṭ* (also 'contented'); hungry, *gi'ân;* small, *ṣughayyar;* short, *ḳuṣayyar;* long, *ṭawîl;* untruthful, *kaddâb*, tired, *ta'bân*, satisfied, *shab'ân;* weak, *ḍa'îf;* dead, *meyyit*, mad, *magnûn* (Syrian *mejnûn*); trust-worthy, *amîn.*

Bitter, *murr;* sour, *ḥâmeḍ;* sweet, *ḥelu*

Broad, *'arîḍ;* narrow, *ḍayyiḳ;* large, *'azîm, kebîr;* hot (weather), *ḥarr*, (of food, etc.) *sukhn;* high, *'âli;* empty, *khâli, fâḍi;* new, *gedîd;* low, *wâṭi;* bad, *baṭṭâl;* dirty, *wusekh;* dear, *ghâli.*

White, *abyaḍ;* black, dark, *iswid;* red, *aḥmar;* yellow, *aṣfar*, blue, *azraḳ;* green, *akhḍar.*

Hour, *sâ'a;* what o'clock is it, *es-sâ'a kâm*, it is 3 o'clock, *es-*

sâʿa telâteh; it is half past 4, *es-sâʿa arbaʿ unuṣṣ;* it is a quarter to 5, *es-sâʿa khamseh illa rubʿa.*

Forenoon, *ḍaḥâ;* noon, *ḍuhr;* afternoon ($2^1/_2$ hours before sunset), *ʿaṣr;* night, *lêl;* midnight, *nuṣṣ-el-lêl.*

Sunday, *yôm el-ḥad*, *nehâr el-ḥad;* Monday, *yôm el-etnên;* Tuesday, *yôm et-telât;* Wednesday, *yôm el-arbaʿ;* Thursday, *yôm el-khamîs;* Friday, *yôm el-gumʿa;* Saturday, or Sabbath, *yôm es-sebt.* *Yôm* or *yûm* (day) is generally omitted. Week, *gumʿa;* month, *shahr*, pl. *ushhur.*

Instead of the Arabic names of the months used in Syria, the Egyptians employ the Coptic (ancient Egyptian) names of the solar months, which, however, are always about nine days behind the European months. Each Coptic month has thirty days, and in order to complete the year five or six intercalary days are added at the end (in the beginning of September). The European names, however, are gradually coming into general use.

English	January	February	March	April	May	June
Syrian	*kânûn el-tâni*	*shobâṭ*	*adâr*	*nîsân*	*eyâr*	*ḥazîrân*
European	*yenaîr*	*febraîr*	*mâres*	*abrîl*	*mayeh*	*yûnia*
Coptic	*ṭûba*	*amshîr*	*baramhât*	*barmûdeh*	*bashens*	*baûna*
English	July	August	September	October	November	December
Syrian	*tamûz*	*âb*	*êlûl*	*tishrîn el-awwel*	*tishrîn el-tâni*	*kânûn el-awwel*
European	*yûlia (lûliyeh)*	*aghostôs*	*sebtember*	*oktôber*	*november*	*dezember*
Coptic	*ebîb*	*misra*	*tût*	*bâba*	*hâtûr*	*kiâḥk*
The intercalary days (which come after Misra) are called *ayyâm en-nesi.*						

The Muslim months form a lunar year only (comp. p. 149). Their names are: *Moḥarrem, Ṣafar, Rabîʿ el-Awwel, Rabîʿ et-Tâni, Gemâd el-Awwel, Gemad et-Tâni, Regeb, Shaʿbân, Ramaḍân* (month of fasting), *Shawwâl, Dhil-Ḳiʿde, Dhil-Ḥiggeh* (month of the pilgrimage).

Winter, *shita;* summer, *ṣêf;* spring, *rabîʿ;* autumn, *kharîf;* rain, *maṭar;* snow, *telg;* air, *hawa.*

Heaven, *sema;* moon, *ḳamar;* new moon, *hilâl;* full moon, *bedr;* sun, *shems;* sunrise, *ṭulûʿ esh-shems;* sunset, *maghreb;* star, *nigm*, pl. *nugûm;* constellation, *kaukab.*

East, *sherḳ;* west, *gharb;* south, *ḳibla;* southern, *ḳibli, ḳubli;* north, *shemâl.*

Father, *ab*, or, before genitives and affixes, *abû;* mother, *umm;*

son, *ibn*, or *weled*, pl. *ûlâd;* daughter, *bint*, pl. *benât;* grandmother, *gidda*, or *sitt;* brother, *akh*, before genitives and affixes *akhû*, pl. *ikhwân;* sister, *ukht*, pl. *ukhwât;* parents, *ab u umm*, or *wâlidên;* woman, *mara*, *ḥurmeh*, women, *ḥarîm*, *niswân;* boy, *weled;* youth, fellow, *gada'*, pl *gid'ân;* man, *râgel*, pl. *rigâle;* person, *insân*, pl. *nâs*, or *beni âdam* (sons of Adam); friend, *ḥabîb*, *ṣâḥeb*, pl. *aṣḥâb;* neighbour, *gâr*, pl. *gîrân;* bride, *'arûs;* bridegroom, *'arîs;* wedding, *'urs.*

Cord for fastening the kuffîyeh, *'oḳâl;* cloak, *'abâyeh;* fez, *ṭarbûsh;* felt cap, *libdeh;* girdle, *ḥezâm;* leathern girdle, *kamar;* trousers (wide), *shirwâl;* trousers (of women), *shintyân;* European trousers, *banṭalûn;* long white blouse, *galabîyeh;* jacket, waistcoat, *salṭa*, *'anteri;* dressing-gown, *ḳufṭân;* coat (European), *sitra*, skull-cap, *ṭaḳîyeh;* silk, *ḥarîr;* boot, *gezma;* slipper, *babûg;* shoe, *markûb*, *ṣarma;* wooden shoe, *ḳabḳâb;* stocking, *shurâb;* turban, *'emma.*

Eye, *'ên*, dual *'ênên;* beard, *daḳn*, *leḥyeh;* foot, *rigl*, dual *riglên;* hair, *sha'r;* hand, *yedd*, *îd*, dual *îdên*, my hands, *îdeyyeh;* right hand, *yemîn;* left hand, *shemâl;* palm of the hand, *keff;* fist, *ḳabḍa;* head, *râs;* mouth, *fumm;* moustache, *sheneb.*

Diarrhœa, *ishâl*, fever, *sukhûna*, *ḥomma;* China, *kîna;* quinine, *melḥ el-kîna;* opium, *afiyûn;* pain, *wag'a.*

Abraham, *Ibrâhîm;* Gabriel, *Gabriân*, *Gebraîl*, *Gubrân*, George, *Girgis;* Jesus, *Seyyidna 'Isa* (the Mohammedan name), *Yesû' el-Mesîḥ* (used by the Christians); John, *Hanna;* Joseph, *Yûsuf*, *Yûsef;* Mary, *Maryam*, Moses, *Mûsa;* Solomon, *Selîmân*, *Islêmân.*

American, *Amerikâni*, *Malekâni;* Arabian, *'arabi;* Arabs (nomads), *'Arab;* Austria, *Bilâd Nemsa;* Austrian, *Nemsâwi;* Beduin, *Bedawi*, pl. *Bedwân*, *'Arab*, *'Orbân;* Cairo, *Maṣr*, *Medînet Maṣr;* Constantinople, *Istambûl;* Egypt, *Bilâd Maṣr;* Egyptians (non-nomadic Arabs), *Ûlâd 'Arab;* England, *Bilâd el-Ingilîz;* English, *Ingilîzi;* France, *Feransa;* Frank (*i. e.* European), *Ferangi*, *Afranki*, pl. *Afrank;* French, *Feransâwi;* Germany, *Alemânia;* German, *Alemâni;* Greece, *Rûm;* Greek, *Rûmi;* Italy, *Bilâd Itâlia;* Russia, *Bilâd el-Moskof;* Russian, *Moskûwi*, *Moskûfi*, Switzerland, *Switzera;* Syria, *Esh-Shâm;* Turkish, *Turki.*

Saint (Mohammedan), *wali*, *weli;* St. George (Christian), *Girgis el-ḳaddîs*, *mâr Girgis;* prophet, *nebi*, or (applied to Moḥammed) *rasûl.*

Army, *'askar;* baker, *khabbâz*, *farrân;* barber, *ḥallâḳ*, *mozeyyin;* Beduin chief, *shêkh el-'Arab;* bookseller, *kutbi;* butcher, *gezzâr;* caller to prayer, *mueddin* (p. 147); consul, *ḳonsul;* consul's servant (gensdarme), *ḳawwâs;* cook, *ṭabbâkh;* custom-house officer, *gumruktshi;* doctor, *ḥakîm*, plur. *ḥukama;* dragoman, *turgemân* (p. 13); gatekeeper, *bawwâb;* goldsmith, *ṣâigh;* judge, *ḳâḍi;* money-changer, *ṣarrâf;* pilgrim (to Mecca), *ḥagg* (Syrian *ḥâjji*), plur. *ḥegâg;* police, *ẓabṭîyeh;* porter, *ḥammâl*, *sheyyâl;* robber, *ḥarâmi*, plur. *ḥarâ-*

mîyeh; scholar, *'âlem*, plur. *'ulama;* schoolmaster, *fikîh;* servant, *khaddâm;* soldier, *'askari;* tailor, *kheyyâṭ;* teacher, *mo'allim;* village-chief, *shêkh el-beled;* washer, *ghassâl;* watchman, *ghafîr*, plur. *ghufara.*

Apricot, *mishmish;* banana, *môz;* beans (garden), *fûl*, (lupins) *lûbiyeh;* citrons or lemons, *lîmûn;* cotton, *koṭn;* dates, *balâḥ;* date-palm, *nakhleh*, figs, *tîn;* flower (blossom), *zahr*, plur. *azhâr;* garlic, *tûm;* grapes, *'ŭnab*, *'enab*, melons (water), *baṭṭîkh*, (yellow) *kâwûn*, *shamâm*, olives, *zêtûn;* onions, *baṣal;* oranges, *bortukân;* peach, *khôkh* (Syrian *dorrâk*); pistachios, *fustuk;* plums, *berkûk* (Syrian *khûkh*); pomegranate, *rummân;* St. John's tree (carob), *kharrûb;* tree (shrub), *shagara*, plur. *ashgâr.*

Brandy, *'araki;* bread, *'êsh* (Syrian *khubz*); bread, loaf of, *raghîf*, plur. *aghrifeh;* cigarette-paper, *warakat sigâra;* coffee, *kahwa*, egg, *bêd*, (boiled) *bêḍ maslûk*, (baked) *bêḍ makli;* honey, *'asal*, milk, *leben*, (fresh) *leben ḥalîb*, (sour) *leben ḥâmeḍ;* oil, *zêt;* pepper, *filfil;* poison, *simm;* rice, *ruz;* salt, *melḥ;* sugar, *sukkar;* water, *moyêh;* wine, *nebîd.*

Book, *kitâb*, plur. *kutub*, letter, *gewâb*, *maktûb.*

Carpet, *siggâda*, *busâṭ;* chair (stool), *kursi*, plur. *kerâsi;* gate, *bâb*, *bawwâba;* hospital, *isbitâlia;* house, *bêt*, plur. *biyût;* minaret, *mâdana*, monastery, *dêr*, (of dervishes) *tekîyeh;* mosque, *gâmi'* (or more rarely *mesgid*); prayer-niche, *maḥrâb;* pulpit, *mambar*, *mimbar*, room, *ôḍa*, sofa, *dîwân;* straw-mat, *ḥaṣîra;* table, *sufra;* tent, *khêma*, plur. *khiyam*, (Beduins') *'eshsha*, *bêt;* tent-peg, *watad*, plur. *autâd;* tent-pole, *'amûd*, tomb, *kabr*, plur. *kubûr;* window, *shibbâk*, plur. *shebakîk*, or *ṭâka.*

Bridle, *ligâm;* candle, *sham'a;* dagger, *khangar;* glass (for drinking), *kubâyeh;* gun, *bundukîyeh*, gunpowder, *bârûd;* knife, *sikkîneh*, lantern, *fânûs;* luggage, *'afsh;* pistol, *tabanga*, *ferd;* rope, *ḥabl*, saddle, *serg*, saddle-bag, *khurg;* stick, *'asâyeh;* stirrup, *rikâb*, plur. *rikâbât;* sword, *sêf.*

Bath (warm), *ḥammâm;* cistern, *bîr sahrîg;* fountain (public), *sebîl*, pond, *birkeh*, plur. *birak;* spring, *'ain*, *'ên.*

Charcoal, coal, *faḥm;* fire, *nâr;* iron, *ḥadîd;* lead, *ruṣâṣ;* light, *nûr;* stone, *ḥagar;* timber, *khashab;* wood for burning, *ḥaṭab.*

Anchorage, *mersa;* harbour, *mîna;* island, *gezîreh;* land, mainland, *barr;* Nile, *baḥr en-Nîl*, *baḥr;* Nile-barge, *dahabîyeh;* promontory, *râs;* river, *nahr;* sea, *baḥr;* ship, *merkeb*, *markab*, plur. *marâkib;* steamboat, *wabûr*, swamp, *baṭîḥa*, *ghadîr.*

Bridge, *kanṭara;* castle, fortress, *kal'a;* cavern, *maghâra;* desert, *ḥala*, *gebel;* district, native country, *bilâd;* earth, *arḍ;* embankment, *gisr*, hill, *tell*, plur. *tulûl;* market, *sûk*, plur. *aswâk;* market-town, *bandar;* meadow, *merg*†; mountain, *gebel*, plur. *gibâl;*

† The words *merg* and *ghaba* (forest) are almost unknown in Egypt, where neither meadows nor woods exist.

palace, *ḳaṣr*, *serâyeh*; plain, *sahl*, (low ground) *waṭa*; road, *ṭarîḳ*, *darb*, *sikkeh*, (main road, high road) *ṭarîḳ sulṭâni*, (by-road) *ḥâra*, *darb*, *sikkeh*; ruin, *kharaba*, *birbeh*; school, (reading) *kuttâb*, (more advanced) *medreseh*, plur. *madâris*; street, (main) *shâriʿ*, (lane) *zuḳâḳ*; thicket, *ghêt*; town (large), *medîneh*, plur. *medâin*; valley, *wâdi*; wood, *ghâba*; village, *beled*, *kafr*.

Ass, *homâr*, plur. *ḥamîr*; bee, *naḥla*; bird, *têr*, plur. *ṭiyûr*, (small) *ʿaṣfûr*, plur. *ʿaṣâfîr*; boar (wild), *hallûf*; bug, *baḳḳa*, camel, *gemel*, plur. *gimâl*, fem. *nâḳa*; camel for riding, *hegîn*; fowl, *farkha*, plur. *ferâkh* (used in Upper Egypt for 'young pigeons'); cock, *dîk*; dog, *kelb*, plur. *kilâb*; dove, *ḥamâme*; duck, *baṭṭ*; eagle, *nisr*; fish, *semaka*, plur. *semak*; fleas, *berâghît*; fly, *dubbâna*; foal, *muhr*; gazelle, *ghazâl*; hedgehog, *ḳumfud*; hen, *farrûga* (Syrian *jejeh*); horse, *ḥoṣân*, plur. *khêl*; leech, *ʿalaḳa*, plur. *ʿalaḳ*; lizard, *seḥlîyeh*; louse, *ḳamle*; mare, *faras*; pig, *khanzîr*; pony, *kedîsh*; scorpion, *ʿaḳraba*, plur. *ʿaḳârib*; sheep, *kharûf*, fem. *naʿga*; snake, *taʿban*, *ḥayyeh*; stallion, *faḥl*, *ḥoṣân*; tortoise, *ziḥlifeh*; turtle, *tirsa*; vulture, *rakham*.

On Arrival. For how much will you take me ashore? (to the ship?) *Teṭallaʿni fil-bair bikâm? Tenezzilni fil-merkeb bikâm?*

For five francs, *Bikhamas ferankât*, *bikhamseh ferank*.

Too much; I will give you one. *Ketîr*, *aʿdîk wâḥed*, *bess*.

You shall take me alone; or I will give you nothing. *Tâkhudni* (or *tewaddîni*) *waḥdi*, *willa mâ baʿdîkshi ḥâgeh*.

There are three of us. *Eḥna telâteh*.

Four piastres each. *Kullu wâḥed bi arbaʿ ḳurûsh*.

Put this box (these boxes) into the boat. *Nezzil eṣ-ṣandûḳ-deh (eṣ-ṣanadîk-dôl) fil felûke*.

At the Custom-House (*Gumruk*). Open this box. *Iftaḥ eṣ-ṣandûḳ*.

I have nothing in it. *Mâ fîsh ḥâgeh*, *mâ fihâsh ḥâgeh*.

Give me your passport. *Hât et-tezkereh (bassâbôrto)*.

Here is my passport. *Âho el-bassâbôrto betâʿi*.

I have no passport. *Mâ ʿandîsh tezkereh*.

I am under the protection of the English (American) consul. *Ana fi ḥemâyet* (or *âna taḥte*) *ḳonṣul el-Ingilîzi (el-Amerikâni)*.

At a Café (p. 17). Boy, bring me a cup of coffee. *Hât fingân ḳahwa, ya weled* (*kahwa bisukkar*, with sugar; *mingher sukkar*, or *sâde*, without sugar).

Bring me a chair. *Hât kursi*. Bring me water. *Hât li môyeh*.

Bring me a water-pipe. *Hât shîsheh (nargîleh)*.

Bring me a live coal. *Hât wilʿa (baṣṣat nâr, baṣṣa)*.

Change the pipe (i.e. bring a newly filled bowl). *Gheyyar en-nefes.*

At the Bath (p. 21). *Fil Ḥammâm.* Bring the wooden shoes. *Hât el-kabkâb.* — Take me in. *Waddîni gûwwa.* — Leave me for a little. *Khallîni shwaiyeh.* — I do not perspire yet. *Mânîsh 'arkân lissa.* — Rub me well. *Keyyisni ṭayyib (melîḥ).* — It is not necessary to rub me. *Mûsh lâzim tekeyyisni.* — Wash me with soap. *Ghassilni biṣâbûn* — Enough; it is sufficient. *Bess; yikeffi; bikeffi.* — Bring me cold water. *Hât môyeh bârideh.* — Bring some more. *Hât kamân.* — We will go out. *Niṭla' barra.* — Bring me a sheet (sheets). *Hât fûṭa (fuwaṭ).* — Bring me water, coffee, a nargîleh. *Hât môyeh, ḳahwa, nargîleh.* — Where are my clothes? *Fên hudûmi; hudûmi fên?* — Bring my boots. *Hât el-gezmeh.* — Here is your fee. *Khud bakshîshak, âdi el-bakshîsh betâ'ak.*

Washing. Take the clothes to be washed. *Waddi el-hudûm lil-ghasîl.* (The articles should be counted in the presence of the washerman.) — How much does the washing cost? *Kâm (ḳâddi ê) temen el-ghasîl?*

On the Journey. When will you start? *Emta tesâferu?* — We will start to-morrow at sunrise. *Nesâfer bukra, ma'ash shems;* an hour before sunrise, *sâ'a ḳabl esh-shems;* two hours after sunrise, *sâ'etên ba'd esh-shems.* — Do not come too late. *Mâ tit'akh-kharshe.* — Is everything ready? *Kull shê ḥâder?* — Pack; load (the camel). *Sheyyilu; sheddu.* — Hold the stirrup. *Imsik er-rikâb.* — Wait a little. *Istanna (istenna) shwaiyeh.*

What is the name of this village, mountain, valley, tree, spring? *E* (or *êsh*) *ism el-beled de;* or *el-beled-de ismo ê (el-gebel, wâdi, shegara, 'ên)?*

We will rest, breakfast. *Nestereyyaḥ (nisterîḥ), niftar.* — Is there good water there (on the way)? *Fî môyeh ṭayyiba (fiddarb)?* — Where is the spring? *Fên el-'ên?* — Keep at a little distance. *Khallîk ba'îd 'anni.* — Bring the dinner. *Hât el-akl, eṭṭabîkh, el-ghada.* — Take away the dinner. *Shîl el-akl.*

Stop. *Ukaf, 'andak.* — Go on. *Yalla.* — Where are you going to? *Enta râiḥ fên?* — Where do you come from? *Gâi min ên?*

Shall we go straight on? *Nerûḥ dughri?* — Straight on. *Dughri, dughri* — Turn to the left. *Ḥawwud 'ala shmâlak.*

Do not be afraid of me. *Mâ tkhafsh minni.* — What am I to do? *Weana mâ li?* — I will have nothing to do with it; it does not concern me. *Ana mâ li.* — What are we to do? *Esh el-'amal; na'mel ê?*

O sir, a gift. *Bakshîsh, yâ khawâgehi* — There is nothing for you; be off. *Mâfîsh; rûḥ!*

Open the door. *Iftaḥ el-bâb.* — Shut the door. *Ikfil el-bâb.* — Sweep out the room, and sprinkle it. *Iknus (iknis) el-ôḍeh u rushshaha.*

We will eat. *'Auzîn nâkul.* — Cook me a fowl. *Iṭbukhli farkha.* — Clean this glass well. *Naḍḍef ṭayyib el-kubaiyeh-di.* — Give me some water to drink. *Iskîni, idîni moiyeh.*

At a Shop (see p. 24). What do you want? What are you seeking? *'Auz ê? 'Aiz ê?* — What may it cost? *Bikâm deh? Deh bikâm?* — What does this cost (what is it worth)? *Byiswa kâm?* — That is dear, very dear. *Deh ghâli, ghâli ketîr.* — Cheap, sir. *Rakhiṣ, yâ sîdi.* — No, it won't do. *Lâ, mâ yiṣaḥḥish.* — Yield a little. *Zîd shwaiyeh.* — Give the money. *Hât el-flûs.* — Change me a piece of gold. *Iṣrif li-gineh.* — For how much will you take the gold piece? *Tâkhod el-gineh bikâm?*

Salutations and Phrases Health (peace) be with you. *Es-salâm 'alêkum.* Answer And with you be peace and God's mercy and blessing. *U 'alêkum es-salâm waraḥmet Allâh wa barakâtu.* These greetings are used by Muslims to each other. A Muslim greets a Christian with — Thy day be happy. *Nehârak sa'îd.* Answer: Thy day be happy, blessed *Nehârak sa'îda wemubârak (umbârak).*

Good morning. *Ṣabâḥkum bil-khêr,* or *ṣabâh el-khêr.* Answer: God grant you a good morning. *Allâh iṣabbeḥkum bil-khêr.*

Good evening. *Misâkum bil-khêr,* or *mesîkum bil-khêr.* Answer: God vouchsafe you a good evening. *Allâh yimessîkum bil-khêr;* or *messâkum Allâh bil-khêr.* — May thy night be happy. *Lêltak sa'îdeh.* Answer: *Lêltak sa'îdeh we mubâraka.*

On visiting or meeting a person, the first question after the usual salutations is: How is your health? *Ezeiyak,* or *kêf ḥâlak (kêf kêfak)?* Thanks are first expressed for the enquiry: God bless thee; God preserve thee. *Allâh yibârek fîk, Allâh yiḥfazak.* Then follows the answer: Well, thank God. *El-ḥamdu lillâh, ṭayyib.* — The Beduins and peasants sometimes ask the same question a dozen times.

After a person has drunk, it is usual for his friends to raise their hands to their heads and say: May it agree with you, sir. *Hanî'an, yâ sîdi.* Answer: God grant it may agree with thee. *Allâh yehannîk.*

On handing anything to a person: Take it. *Khud* (Syrian *dûnak*). Answer: God increase your goods. *Kattar Allâh khêrak,* or *kettar khêrak.* Reply: And thy goods also. *Ukhêrak.* (This form of expressing thanks, however, will not often be heard by the

ordinary traveller, as the natives are too apt to regard gifts presented to them by Europeans as their right.)

On leaving Good bye. *'Al Allâh.* Or: To God's protection. *Fî amân Illâh.* Or: Now let us go on. *Jalla bina.* — Generally speaking, the person leaving says nothing, unless when about to start on a long journey, in which case he says: Peace be with you. *Ma'as-salâma.*

On the route: Welcome. *Ahlan wasahlan,* or *marḥaba.* Answer: Twice welcome. *Marḥabtên.*

I beg you (to enter, to eat, to take something). *Tafaḍḍal (tefaḍḍal, itfaḍḍal),* fem *tafaḍḍâli (itfaḍḍâli);* plur. *tafaḍḍâlu (itfaḍḍâlu, tefaḍḍâlu).* — Will you not join us (in eating)? *Bismillah* (literally 'in God's name). Answer: May it agree with you, *Bilhâna*

Take care; beware. *Ûka (û'a);* fem. *ûḳi (û'i).*

I am under your protection; save me. *Fa'rḍak (fi'arḍak).* — My house is thy house. *Bêtî bêtak* (p. 24) — Be so good. *Emel ma'ruf.*

What God pleases ('happens', understood). *Mâshallah* (an exclamation of surprise). — As God pleases. *Inshallah.* — By God. *Wallâh,* or *wallâhi.* — By thy head. *Waḥyât râsak.* — By the life of the prophet. *Waḥyât en-nebi.* — God forbid. *Istaghfir Allâh!*

XI. Works on Egypt.

The traveller who desires more than a mere superficial acquaintance with the land of the Pharaohs, the history of which is the most ancient and in some respects the most interesting in the world, should of course before leaving home read some of the standard works on the subject, and also select a number of others for reference or entertainment during the journey. This is all the more necessary if the traveller is entirely ignorant of the ancient and modern languages of the country, in which case he will find it difficult, if not impossible, to institute independent enquiries as to its manners, literature, and art. From the appended list, which might easily be extended, the traveller may make a selection in accordance with his individual taste. Those indicated by asterisks are among the most indispensable.

Before enumerating the works which most English travellers will read, we may mention a few of the leading foreign authorities on Egypt. Foremost among these are Lepsius's 'Denkmäler aus Ægypten und Æthiopien', Champollion's 'Monuments de l'Égypte et de la Nubie', Rosellini's 'Monumenti dell' Egitto e della Nubia', and the 'Description de l Égypte' published by the members of the French expedition. Schnaase, Kugler, Lübke, Erbkam, and Reber have written valuable works on the history of Egyptian art; Forskal,

Schenk, Unger, Schweinfurth, Ascherson, and Boissier, on botany; and Brehm, Hartmann, Fraas, Pruner, and Klunzinger on natural history and medicine.

With regard to the Greek and Roman writers on Egypt, see p. 344. The Arabian historians are mere chroniclers, who narrate a series of facts and traditions, and are entirely deficient in method and the faculty of criticism. The following are the most important writers on the general history of Egypt: — *El-Mas'ûdi* (d. 956), of Fosṭâṭ; *Ibn el-Athîr* (d. 1232), of Mossul in Syria; *Ibn Khaldûn* (d. 1406), one of the most learned of Arabian authors, a philosophical historian, and chiefly famous for the preface to his history, which was printed at Bûlâḳ, in four volumes, in 1868; *Abulfidâ* (d. 1331), prince of Hama in Syria. The following are authors of important works on limited epochs of Egyptian history and of valuable descriptive works: — *El-Maḳrîzi* (d. 1442, at Cairo), the author of a geographical, physical, historical, and political description of Egypt, and of Cairo in particular, printed at Bûlâḳ in 1854; *Abul-Maḥâsin* (d. 1469), the author of a detailed history of Egypt from the Arabian conquest nearly down to the time of his death; *Es-Siyûṭi* (d. 1506), of Siûṭ in Upper Egypt; *El-Manûfi* (d. 1624); *Abu Shâma* (d. 1224), who wrote the history of Nûreddîn and Ṣalâḥeddîn; *Bahâeddîn* (d. 1234), who for many years was a follower of Saladin; *'Abdellaṭîf* (d. 1232), a physician at Baghdâd, the author of a very important and interesting description of Egypt.

Historical, Descriptive, and Scientific Works.

Birch, Dr. S., Egypt, down to B C. 300, London, 1875
**Birch, Dr S.*, Sir Gardner Wilkinson's Ancient Egyptians; London, 1877.
**Brugsch*, Histoire d'Égypte, 2nd ed ; Leipzig, 1874
**Brugsch*, L'Exode et les Monuments Égyptiens, Leipzig, 1875
Bunsen, Egypt's Place in Universal History; London, 1867
Ebers, Egypt, Descriptive, Historical, and Picturesque, translated from the German by Clara Bell and furnished with notes by Dr Sam Birch; 800 illustrations; London, 1882
**Lane*, Modern Egyptians, new ed, London, 1871
Leon, E. de, The Khedive's Egypt, London, 1877
**Lepsius*, Letters from Egypt, Æthiopia, etc, London, 1852
Mariette, Aperçu de l'Histoire Ancienne d'Egypte. Paris, 1867
Mariette, Monuments of Upper Egypt, London, 1877
Maspero, Histoire Ancienne des Peuples de l'Orient, Paris, 1875
**M'Coan*, Egypt as it is, London, 1877
Merval, Du Barry de, Architecture Égyptienne; Paris, 1873.
Osburn, Monumental History of Egypt, London, 1854
Palmer, Egyptian Chronicles, London, 1861
Paton, Egyptian Revolution, from the Period of the Mamelukes to the death of Mohammed 'Ali, London, 1870.
Perring, The Pyramids of Gizeh; London, 1839.
Perrot & Chipiez, History of Art in Ancient Egypt, translated from the French by W. Armstrong, London, 1883
Poole, Egypt, in Sampson Low's series of manuals of Foreign Countries.
Records of the Past, Translations of Egyptian inscriptions by *Dr. Birch* and others.
Rikart, Carl von, Menes and Cheops identified in History; London, 1869.

Sharpe, History of Egypt; new ed., London, 1876 (most useful for the Ptolemæan, Roman, and Byzantine periods).
Sharpe, Hieroglyphics, London, 1861.
Shelly, Handbook of the Birds of Egypt; London, 1872.
Vyse, The Pyramids of Gizeh; London, 1840.
Vyse, Egypt, Political, Financial, and Strategical.
Wallace, Egypt and the Egyptian Question; London, 1883.
Wilkinson, *Sir Gardner*, The Ancient Egyptians (new edition by *Dr. Birch*, see above)
Zincke, Egypt of the Pharaohs and the Khedive; London, 1873.

WORKS OF A MORE POPULAR CHARACTER, AND WORKS OF FICTION.

About, Le Fellah, Paris, 1869.
Arabian Nights, by Lane, London, 1841. The learned editor is of opinion that these popular tales were written in 1474-1525, being based mainly on earlier traditions, that they were probably compiled by an Egyptian, and that they afford an admirable picture of Arabian, and particularly of Egyptian, life at that period.
Bovet, Egypt, Palestine, and Phoenicia, translated from the French by Canon Lyttleton, London, 1883
Cooke, Leaves from my Sketchbook; Second Series; London, 1876
Curtis, Nile Notes of a Howadji, or The American in Egypt.
Ebers, Series of novels on Egyptian subjects, all of which have been translated into English.
Eden, The Nile without a Dragoman, London, 1871.
Fleming, A Nile Novel; London, 1877
**Gordon*, *Lady Duff*, Letters from Egypt; London, 1866, 1875.
**Kingsley*, Hypatia; London, 1863.
Leland, Egyptian Sketchbook; London, 1873.
Moore, The Epicurean; London, 1864
Poole, Englishwoman in Egypt; London, 1844-48.
Poole, Cities of Egypt; London, 1883
Smith, *A. C.*, The Nile and its Banks; London, 1868.
Werner, *Carl*, Nile Sketches; London, 1871-72
Whately, *M. L.*, Ragged Life in Egypt, new ed., London, 1869.
Whately, *M. L.*, Among the Huts in Egypt; 3rd ed., London, 1873.
Whately, *M. L.*, Scenes from Life in Cairo; London, 1882.
Wilson, *Erasmus*, *F. R. S.*, Cleopatra's Needle, with Brief Notes on Egypt and Egyptian Obelisks; London, 1877.

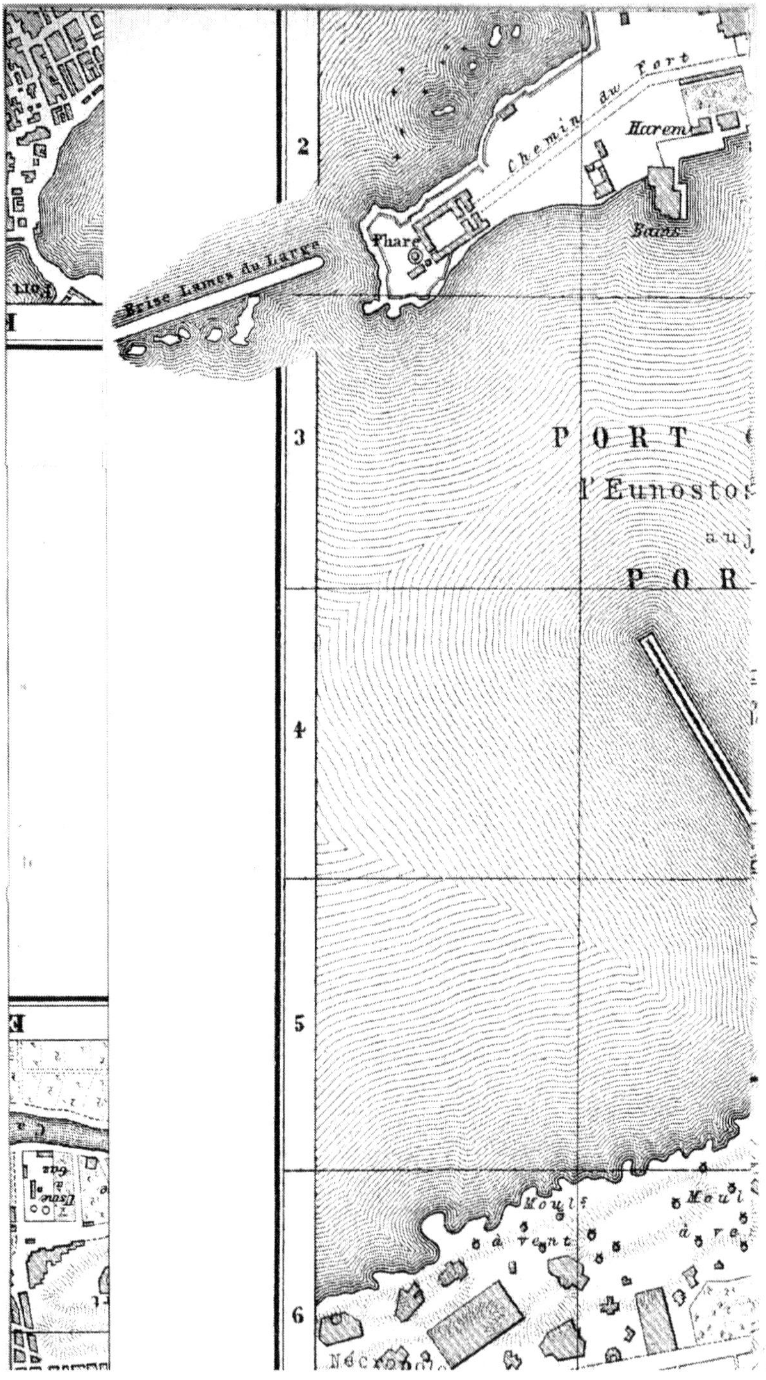

Chemin du Fort
Harem
Bains
Phare
Brise Lames du Large
PORT
l'Eunostos
auj
POR
Moul
à vent
Moul
à ve
Nécropole
Usine à Gaz
2
3
4
5
6

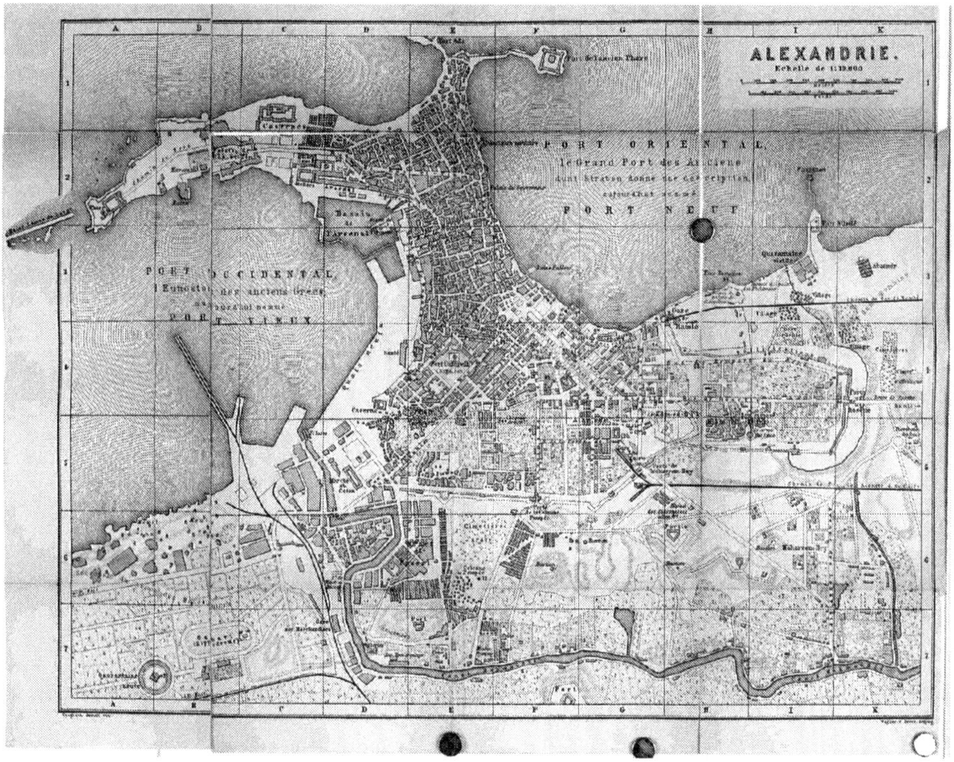
ALEXANDRIE.
PORT ORIENTAL,
PORT NEUF
PORT OCCIDENTAL,
PORT VIEUX

1. Alexandria.

Arrival. The perfectly flat N.E. coast of Egypt, and even Alexandria itself, are not visible to the steamboat passenger until very shortly before the vessel enters the harbour. We first observe the lighthouse rising conspicuously above the flat and colourless line of the coast, and then a row of windmills, light-coloured buildings, and the smoke of the steamboats in the harbour. On a hill to the left rises the château of the Khedive at Ramleh (p. 222), and on the coast, to the right, at the beginning of the entrance to the harbour, we perceive the so-called *Bâb el-ʿArab* (Beduin Gate), the extremity of a line of fortifications extending between the sea and Lake Mareotis (p. 223). It was this western harbour only, the Eunostos, or harbour of those 'returning home in safety' of the Greeks, that European vessels were formerly permitted to enter, while they were rigorously excluded from the 'Great Harbour' on the E. side, which was described by Strabo (p. 208), and is now erroneously called the 'New Harbour'. The latter, which Mohammed ʿAli attempted again to utilise, but found too much choked up with sand, is now chiefly used by fishing-boats, but larger vessels sometimes enter it when compelled by stress of weather.

Before passing Bâb el-ʿArab the steamer takes a pilot on board and is steered by him through a narrow, shallow, and rocky channel *(Bôghaz)* into the harbour. As the passage can only be effected by daylight, vessels arriving in the evening must ride at anchor outside until next morning. On the coast, to the right, we observe the grotesque half-ruined *Château of Meks* (p. 221), with its numerous domes and slender towers. It was erected by the viceroy Saʿîd Pasha (p. 107), who used to

---

Plan of Alexandria.

1. Arsenal . . . D, 2

Railway Stations.

2. For Rosetta, Cairo, and Suez . . . G, 5
3. For Ramleh. . H, 3
4. Bains de Turin. F, 5

4a. Banque Impériale Ottomane . . F, 4

Steamboat Offices.

5. Egyptian Mail Steamers . . . E, 3
6. Fraissinet & Co. G, 4
7. Austrian Lloyd . G, 4
8. Messageries Maritimes . . . . F, 4
9. Peninsular and Oriental Co. . F, 4
10. Rubattino & Co. F, G, 4
11. Russian Steamers F, 4

Consulates.

12. American . . . G, 4
13. Belgian. . . . F, 4
14. Danish . . . . F, 3
15. German . . . G, 4
16. British . . . G, 4
17. French . . . . G, 4

17a. Greek . . . G, 4

18. Italian . . . . G, 4
19. Dutch . . . . F, 4
20. Austrian . . . G, 4
21. Russian . . . G, 4
22. Swedish . . . G, 4
23. German Club . F, 4
24. Custom House D, E, 3

Churches.

25. English. . . . F, 4
26. Armenian. . . F, 5
27. Coptic . . . . G, 4
28. Greek Cath. . . F, 4
29. Greek Orthodox F, 4
30. St. Catherine (Rom. Cath.). . F, 4
31. Lazarist . . . F, 4
32. Maronite . . . F, 3
33. Presbyterian. . F, 3
34. Protestant. . . F, 3
35. Equestrian Statue of Mohammed ʿAli F, 4
36. Palais Zizinia . F, 3
37. Pompey's Column E, 6
38. Porte de la Colonne Pompée, or du Nil F, 5
39. Porte de Moharrem Bey. . . . . G, 5
40. — de Rosette . K, 4
41. Egypt. Post Office F, 3
42. Quarantine . A, B, 7
43. Râs et-Tîn, Palace B, 1, 2
44. Roman Tower . H, 3
45. Telegraph Office, Egyptian . . F, 4
46. — British . F, G, 4

Theatres.

47. Rossini . . . . F, 3
48. Zizinia. . . . G, 4
49. Politeama . . F, 4
50. Tribunal . . . F, 4

Hotels.

a. H. Khédivial . . G, 4

b. — Abbat. . . . F, 4

S. Synagogues . . G, 4

reside here, surrounded by his army, for a considerable part of the year. The older palace, to the left, on the prominent *Râs et-Tîn* (cape of figs, p. 219), and the Arsenal are comparatively uninteresting, especially as the busy harbour itself now engrosses the whole attention. The steamer is soon surrounded by numerous small boats, the occupants of which proffer their services with animated gesticulations. As soon as the brief sanitary inspection is over, the boatmen swarm wildly on deck like a piratical crew, eager to secure a fare, and reminding the traveller of a scene from Meyerbeer's Africaine. In the midst of this bustle and confusion the following Arabic words may be found useful: — *ta'âl*, come; *shûf*, look here, *mush 'âuzak*, I don't want you, *mush lâzim*, it is not necessary. *imshi* or *rûh*, begone. A supply of half-franc pieces and sous should be kept in readiness for the occasion.

Having sufficiently surveyed the novel and picturesque scene, the traveller engages a boatman to convey him and his luggage ashore, or, especially if ladies are of the party (see below), he gets one of the hotel agents to manage everything for him. Before leaving the vessel he should keep a watchful eye on his luggage, and see that the whole of it is placed in the boat which he himself is going to use. As soon as the boat is clear of the steamer the Arab hoists his sail, for he never rows unless absolutely obliged, and steers for the custom-house. Any importunity as to the fare may be simply answered with — '*tayyib, yalla, yalla*' (all right, make haste).

On reaching the landing-stage of the *Custom-House* (Pl. 24), the traveller is first conducted to the passport-office (to the left, in the passage), and gives up his passport, which is afterwards restored to him at the consulate at Alexandria, or he may have it sent after him to Cairo.

Meanwhile the luggage has been landed, and the traveller, if alone, and with ordinary luggage, pays the boatman 2½-3 fr., or for 2 persons 4-5 fr., and for each additional person 1 fr. more. The porter who carries the luggage into the custom-house and afterwards to a cab expects 25c. for each package. All these rates of payment are amply remunerative, but 'bakshîsh' (p. 16) is invariably asked for, and the word will resound in the traveller's ears throughout the whole of his journeyings in the East, and even long afterwards.

The custom-house examination is generally pretty rigorous, the articles chiefly sought for being tobacco, weapons, and diamonds. No fee need be given to the officials.

As already observed, it is preferable, especially when ladies are of the party, to secure the services of one of the hotel agents, who relieves the traveller of all trouble, pays boatmen and porters, and assists in clearing luggage at the custom-house. In addition to his outlay, he receives a fee of 2½fr. from a single traveller, or more in proportion for a party. The principal hotels now send their own boats to meet the steamers. The traveller who wishes to ensure a comfortable disembarkation may write beforehand to the hotel at which he means to put up, and desire a commissionnaire, a boat, and a carriage to meet him. The usual charge in this case for a party of three persons is: — boat from the steamer to the custom-house 5 fr., luggage-boat 2 fr., porter and fee to custom-house officers 2fr. 75c., carriage to the hotel 4½fr., carriage of luggage 2fr., or 16fr. 25c. in all.

At the egress of the custom-house a noisy and importunate crowd of carriage-drivers and donkey-boys lies in wait for new-comers. Neither walking nor riding is recommended to the traveller on his first arrival, and he had better drive straight to his hotel. Carriage to the hotels (¾ M.) 2½fr., or for 3-4 persons 3-4fr.; donkey ½fr., porter for each large package ½fr.

Hotels. (It may again be remarked here that all the hotels in the East charge a fixed sum per day for board and lodging, exclusive of liquors, whether the traveller takes his meals in the house or not.) *HÔTEL KHEDIVIAL (Pl. a, G, 4), near the Cairo station, in the finest part of the town, with good cuisine; *HÔTEL ABBAT (Pl. b; F, 4), in the Place de l'Eglise, well situated. — Second class. HÔTEL CANAL DE SUEZ, behind the **Palais Zizinia**, close to the Place Méhémet-Ali, with good cuisine; HÔTEL DES VOYAGEURS, in the street which leads from the statue in the Place Méhémet-Ali to the sea; HÔTEL DES ETRANGERS, Rue Mosquée Attarine (Pl. F, 4).

Café (comp p 17), in the European style: *Paradiso*, Rue de la Poste Française, on the coast. 'Café noir, in the European style, or 'café fort' in the Arabian, 2 piastres current (25 c.) per cup. — **Beer.** *Brasserie Française*, next door to the Hôtel des Voyageurs; *Brasserie Sphinx*, *Maury*, *Rupnik*, in a side-street near the Palais Zizinia; *Stern*, Place de l'Eglise (Pl F, 4); also at the *Café Paradiso* (see above)

Baths. *European:* at the *Hôtel Abbat* (see above); *Bains de Turin* (Pl. 4; F, 5), Rue de la Colonne Pompée *Arabian* (comp p 21)· the best are in the Rue Râs-et-Tîn, opposite the Zabtiyeh (police-office) *Sea Baths* in the Port Neuf

Clubs. The *Deutsche Verein* (Pl. 23), Rue de la Mosquée d'Atarine, has a good reading-room, to which admission is obtainable through a member. The *Club Mohammed 'Ali* resembles the Club Khédivial at Cairo (p. 234).

Cabs (in the European style) There is a tariff, but the Arab drivers invariably ignore it. The fare for a short drive in the town, without luggage, is on ordinary days 50 c.; to the steamboats, see above, to the railway station, see p. 223 Per hour, during the day, 2 fr., but more on holidays, when the demand is greater After the first hour each additional half-hour only should be charged for Drives beyond the fortifications according to bargain The usual charge for a whole day, in which case also a bargain should be made, is 20-25 fr

Donkeys (comp p 11). Per ride of 1/4 hr 50 c; per hour 1 1/2 fr.; longer excursions according to bargain, whole day 5-6 fr.

Commissionnaires (p 13), who are useful when time is limited, abound. They charge 5-7 fr. per day, but the fee should be fixed beforehand Most of them offer to escort the traveller to Cairo and even up the Nile; but such proposals should be disregarded, as the best dragomans are always to be found at Cairo in winter For the mere journey to Cairo, and for the ascent of the Nile by steamer, no dragoman is necessary. On arriving at the Cairo station (p 231) travellers are met by the commissionnaires of the principal hotels, so that the services of any other attendant are unnecessary

Post Office (Pl 41; F, 3), open from 7 a m to 7.30 p m, except for an hour after noon Letter-boxes at the hotels and in several of the streets. France and Austria have post-offices of their own, but these will soon be closed, as Egypt has now joined the Postal Union

Telegraph Office (Pl 45; F, 4) The rate for telegrams within Egypt is 5 piastres tariff per ten words — *English Telegraph Office* (Pl 46; F, G, 4) The English wires may not be used for inland telegrams.

Consulates (comp. p 6) BRITISH (Pl 16; G, 4), Boul de Ramlé· consul-general, *Sir Evelyn Baring;* vice-consul, *Mr Cookson* — AMERICAN (Pl 12, G, 4), St Mark's Buildings, Place Méhémet-Ali consul-general, *Mr Pomeroy;* consul, *Baron de Menasci.* — FRENCH (Pl 17; G, 4), Place Méhémet-Ali· consul-general, *M Barrère;* consul, *M. Monge* — GERMAN (Pl 15, G, 4), Rue de la Porte Rosette *Hr. v Derenthall;* vice-consul, *Dr. Michadelles.* — AUSTRIAN (Pl. 20; G, 4), Rue de la Mosquée d'Atarine: *Hr v Hoffenfels*, consul-general; *Hr. Gsiller*, consul. — ITALIAN (Pl 18; G, 4), Boul. Ismail *Sign. G. de Martino;* vice-consul, *Sign. Machiavelli* — BELGIAN (Pl 13; F, 4), Okella Dimitri, Rue de la Porte Rosette *Baron de Vinck*, consul-general; *M. Franquet*, consul — DUTCH (Pl 19, F, 4), Rue de la Citerne-du-Four 31 *Hr Van der Does de Willebois* — RUSSIAN (Pl. 21; G, 4), Rue de l'Obélisque 97: *M. de Hitrovo;* vice-consul, *M. Svilarich.* — SPANISH, *Señ de Ortega Morejon.* — SWEDISH (Pl 22; G, 4), Boulevard de Ramlé· *M. Heidenstamm*, consul-general; *Mr. Barker*, vice-consul. — DANISH (Pl 14; F, 3), Okella Dumreicher, *M de Dumreicher.* — GREEK (Pl. 17a; G, 4); *M. Byzantios*, consul-general; *M Buffides*, consul

Steamboat Offices (fares, etc., see p 10) *Peninsular & Oriental Co.*

(Pl. 9; F, 4), *Messageries Maritimes* (Pl. 8; F, 4); *Austrian Lloyd* (Pl. 7; G, 4); *Florio-Rubattino & Co.*, Italian (Pl. 10; G, 4); *Fraissinet & Co.*, French (Pl. 6; G, 4), *Russian Steamers* (Pl. 11; G, 4); *Egyptian Postal Steamers* (Pl. 5; E, 3), all in or near the Place Méhémet-Ali.

Railway Stations. The station for *Cairo* (p. 223), *Suez* (p. 414), and *Rosetta* (p. 449) is outside the Porte Moharrem Bey, ½ M. from the Place Méhémet-Ali (Pl. 2; G, 5). The station for *Ramleh* (Pl. 3; H, 3) is at the Port Neuf.

Booksellers. The *Stationers & Booksellers Co.* (formerly *Robertson*), St. Mark's Buildings, Place Méhémet-Ali, chiefly for English books; *Librairie de la Bourse* or *Exchange Stationery Co.*, adjoining the Exchange (large stock of photographs). — Several NEWSPAPERS (in French, English, and Italian) are published at Alexandria.

Bankers. *Banque Impériale Ottomane* (Pl. 4a), which has branches throughout the whole of the Turkish dominions; *Bank of Egypt*, Rue Méhémet-Tewfik; *Anglo-Egyptian Banking Co.*, Rue Chérif Pacha; *Franco-Egyptienne*, Boulevard de Ramlé; *Bank of Alexandria*, Rue Chérif Pacha; *Crédit Lyonnais*, Rue Chérif Pacha.

Physicians. *Dr. Mackie*, *Dr. Waller*, and *Finney Bey*, English; *Dr. Varenhorst Bey*, *Dr. Kulp*, *Dr. Schiess*, *Dr. Walther* (skin and ear diseases), German; *Dr. Neruzzos Bey*, *Dr. Kartullis*, Greek; *Dr. Zancarol*. Dentist, *Dr. Love*. All the addresses may be obtained at the apothecary Huber's (see below).

Chemist. *Otto Huber*, Rue Chérif Pacha.

Hospitals. The *Deaconnesses' Institute*, Avenue de Moharrem Bey, is an admirable establishment, which may be commended to the liberality of travellers. *European Hospital*, Boulevard Ismail Pacha; *Egyptian Hospital & Foundling Asylum*, near the Ramleh station; *Greek Hospital*.

Shops for all kinds of European articles are to be found in the Place Méhémet-Ali. *Cordier*, St Mark's Buildings, near the English Church; *Chalons*, near Cordier; *A la Ville de Paris*, below the Deutsche Verein (p. 205); *Camoin*. Ready-made clothing: *Meyer & Co.*, *Stein*, *Goldenberg*, all in the Place Méhémet-Ali. The Arabian bazaar presents no attraction.

Churches. *English* (Pl 25), Place Méhémet-Ali, *Rev. E. J. Davis;* service on Sundays at 11 and 3 o'clock. — *Presbyterian* (Pl. 33), *Rev. Mr. Kean;* service at 11. — *Protestant Church* (Pl 34), a handsome new building in the Rue de l'Eglise Anglaise; German and French service on alternate Sundays at 10. — *Roman Catholic:* St Catherine (Pl. 30) and Lazarist Church (Pl 31). — *Greek Orthodox* (Pl 29). — *Greek Catholic* (Pl. 28). — *Armenian* (Pl 26). — *Maronite* (Pl 32). — *Coptic* (Pl. 27). — Several *Synagogues*, the largest of which is near the Ramleh Station, and the handsomest in the Rue de l'Okelle Neuve, 46.

At Alexandria there are eight different Freemasons' Lodges, which, however, possess two buildings only, called the *Loge des Pyramides* or *English Lodge* (Boul. Ismail) and the *Scotch Lodge* (Okella Neuve, Place Méhémet-Ali).

Theatres. The large *Zizinia Theatre* (Pl 48; G, 4), in the Rue de la Porte Rosette, opposite the German Consulate, is frequently closed, even in winter. — Italian operas are given in the *Politeama* (Pl 49), a wooden building, elegantly fitted up, opposite the Italian Consulate (also used as a circus). — Italian plays, and occasionally operas, are performed in the small *Rossini Theatre* (Pl. 47; F, 3), Rue d'Anastasi.

DISPOSITION OF TIME. Unless the traveller desires to visit all the points of historical interest at Alexandria, he may easily, by taking a carriage, inspect the town with its few relics of antiquity in half-a-day; or a whole day will be required if the drive be extended to the new quays at Meks (p. 221) and along the Mahmûdîyeh Canal. Those who have never seen an Oriental town will be interested in observing the street scenes and the picturesque faces and costumes; but to travellers returning home Alexandria presents an almost European appearance, and is unattractive. Starting from the Place Méhémet-Ali (p. 218), we may first ride or drive to *Pompey's Column* (p. 218). We then return to the Place Méhémet-Ali and traverse the long *Rue Râs-et-Tin* to the palace of that name, after which we may drive to the new *Quays* at *Meks* (p. 221) If time permits, a drive may also be taken (best in the afternoon) along the *Mahmûdiyeh Canal* to the *Palace Number Three* (Nimreh Telâteh) and the public gardens of *Ginênet en-Nuzha* (p 220), both situated on the canal.

History. Alexandria was founded in B.C. 332 by Alexander the Great, forming a magnificent and lasting memorial of his Egyptian campaign. With the foundation of the city are associated a number of legends to the effect that the coast, opposite the island of Pharos, was specially pointed out by divine omens to the Macedonian monarch as a suitable site for the foundation of a new seaport. † In the time of Alexander there were several harbours on the N. coast of Egypt. The most important were those of Naucratis, at the W. (Canopic) mouth of the Nile, chiefly used by Greek vessels after the 26th Dynasty (p. 92), and Tanis and Pelusium on the N.E. side of the Delta, at the two embouchures bearing the same names, to which Egyptian and Phœnician vessels only seem to have been admitted. Alexander, who had overthrown the barriers which had hitherto separated the nations dwelling on the E. shores of the Mediterranean, conceived the plan of founding a new and splendid seaport town in Egypt, both to facilitate the flow of Egypt's wealth towards Greece and the Archipelago, and to connect the venerable kingdom of the Pharaohs with that widely extended Greek empire which it was his great ambition to found. The site chosen by the king was not, however, an entirely new one. On the coast opposite the island of Pharos (p. 208), as we learn from the monuments, had long stood the Egyptian village of Rhakotis, where, as Strabo records, a guard was posted to ensure the safety of the frontier. It seems strange at first sight that the new seaport should have been founded at the W. extremity of the coast of the Delta instead of on the old harbour of Pelusium at the E. end, which lay close to the Red Sea and to the caravan route between Egypt and Syria, and might easily have been extended so as to suit Alexander's requirements. The fact is, however, that the far-seeing founder really made a most judicious choice; for it has been recently ascertained that a current in the Mediterranean, beginning at the Strait of Gibraltar, washes the whole of the N. African coast, and, when it meets the waters of the Nile, it carries the vast deposits of the river towards the E., and

† A venerable old man is said to have appeared to the king in a dream and to have repeated to him the following lines from Homer (Od. iv 54, 55):

'One of the islands lies in the far-foaming waves of the sea,
Opposite Egypt's river, and its name is *Pharos*'.

The following incident was also regarded as a favourable omen. As Dinocrates, the king's architect, was marking out the plan of the town and the sites of the principal buildings, the white earth used for the purpose ran short, and he supplied its place with the flour belonging to his workmen The flour soon attracted numerous birds, by which it was speedily devoured, whereupon Aristander pronounced this incident to be a prognostication of the future wealth and commercial prosperity of the city.

has thus filled the old harbour of Pelusium with mud. The action of this current also endangers the new harbour (Port Sa'îd, p. 436), and on its way towards the N. it has already choked up the famous ancient ports of Ascalon, Sidon, and Tyre. Even Herodotus remarked that the Nile mud rendered the water shallow off the coast of the Delta; and it was doubtless a knowledge of these circumstances which led to the selection of a site for the city of Alexander on the W. side of the mouths of the Nile.

Topography of Ancient Alexandria. The site selected for the new city, which the able architect Dinocrates laid out in the form of a Macedonian cloak (chlamys), was in every respect a favourable one. On the N side it was washed by the Mediterranean, and on the S. side by Lake Mareotis, which was abundantly fed by numerous canals connected with the Nile. The products of Egypt could be brought down by the river to the city, and thence at once shipped to any part of the Mediterranean. The island of Pharos lay opposite to the mainland. 'Now Pharos', says Strabo (B C 66-24; Bk xvii c. 1, § 6), who describes Alexandria in the 17th Book of his Geography, 'is a long-shaped island, almost connected with the mainland, where it forms a harbour with two entrances. For the two promontories thrown out by the shore form a bay, and between these lies the island by which the bay is closed. ... The E. end of the island of Pharos is nearest to the mainland and to the promontory called *Lochias*, and makes the entrance to the harbour narrow. This strait is further narrowed by rocks, partly covered by the water, and partly above the water, which cause the waves of the sea to break into surf as they enter. The extremity of the island itself is also a rock washed by the sea, bearing a tower beautifully constructed of white stone with many stories, and named after the island. This tower was erected by Sostratus of Cnidus' — The tower mentioned by Strabo was the famous lighthouse built in the reign of Ptolemy Philadelphus, which was regarded by the ancients as one of the wonders of the world, and gave its name of 'Pharos' to all lighthouses afterwards erected. It bore the inscription: 'Sostratos, the Cnidian, son of Dexiphanes, to the gods who protect mariners'. It is said by an Arabian historian to have stood at the E. end of the peninsula now called *Burg ez-Zefer*; and he describes its ruins as consisting of a square substructure 110 ells in height, an octagonal second story of 60 ells, and a round superstructure of 63 ells, or 233 ells in all, while its original height is said to have been 400 ells (590 ft.).

'The W. entrance to the harbour', continues Strabo (ib., § 6), 'is also somewhat difficult of access, but does not demand so great caution as the other. It forms a second harbour, called *Eunostus*† (or 'harbour of the happy return'), which lies outside of the artificial and enclosed harbour. The other, which has its entrance by the already mentioned tower of Pharos, is the *Great Harbour* (comp. p. 203). The others are separated from it by an embankment called the *Heptastadium*, and lie contiguous to each other in the recess of the bay. The embankment forms a bridge which extends from the mainland to the western part of the island, and has two passages, bridged over, and leading into the harbour of Eunostus. This structure, besides forming a bridge to the island, served also as an aqueduct when the island was inhabited. But, as it took the side of the kings in the war against Alexandria, the island was laid waste by the divine Cæsar.'

The Heptastadium, a vast embankment of seven stadia in length (1300 yds.), as its name imports, was constructed by Ptolemy Soter, or his son Philadelphus, and having since that period been artificially enlarged by debris from the ancient city, thrown into the sea, as well as by natural deposits, it has now attained a width of more than 1600 yds. The

† This is the 'Old Port' which is almost exclusively used at the present day, and where a number of handsome new buildings are being erected (comp. p. 203).

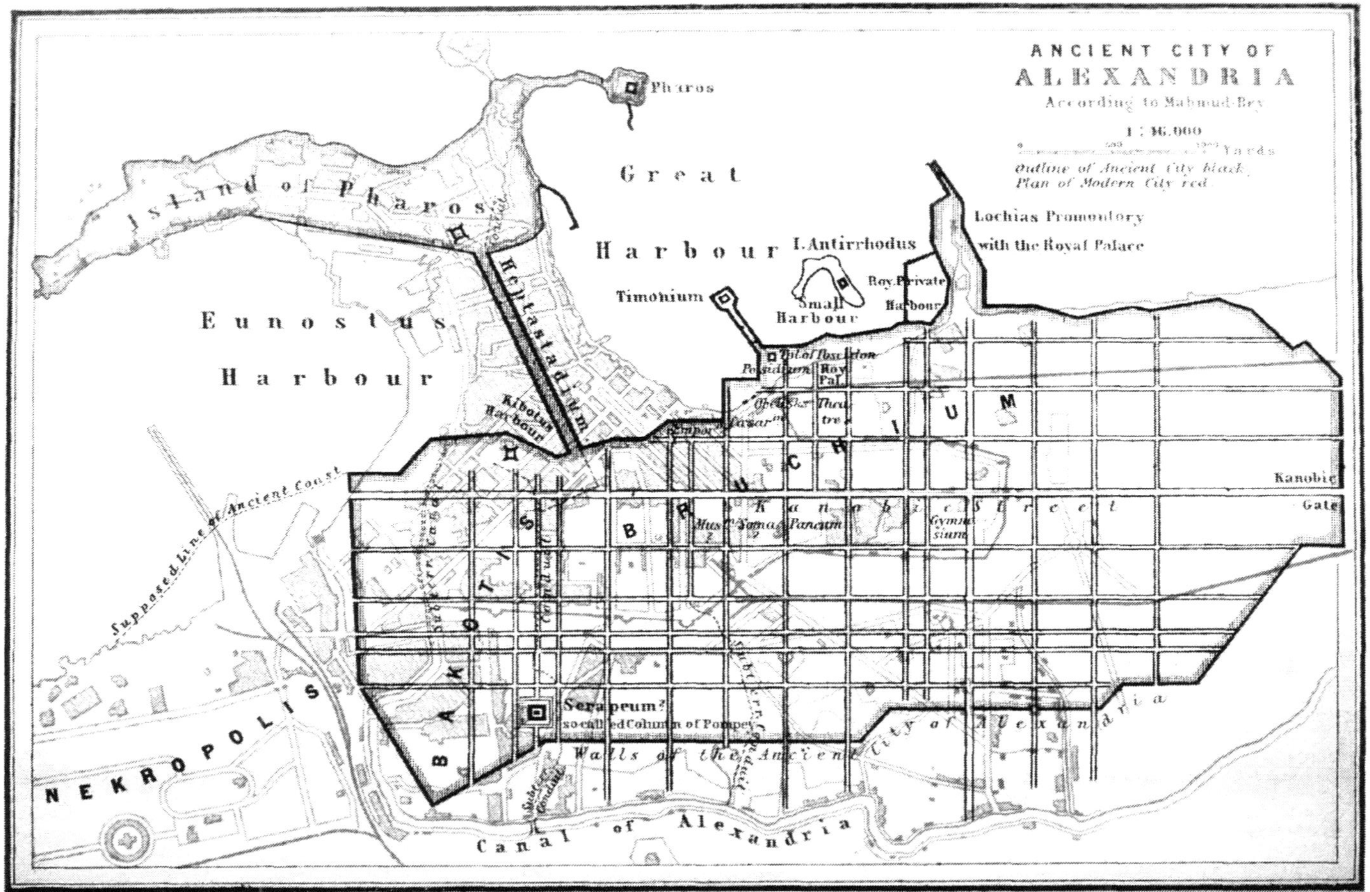

Geograph. Instit. of Wagner & Debes, Leipzig

embankment now forms the site of a great part of the modern city, and on its W. side is situated the Custom House, where the traveller first sets foot on Egyptian soil

'To the right of the entrance to the Great Harbour', Strabo then goes on to say (ib , § 9), 'lies the island with the tower of Pharos, and on the side are the rocks and the promontory of Lochias†, on which stands a royal castle. To the left of persons entering are the inner royal buildings connected with Lochias, which comprise painted saloons and groves Below these lies an artificial harbour, appropriated to the kings, and closed, and opposite to it is the small island of Antirrhodus, with a royal castle and another small harbour The island was so named from being, as it were, a rival of Rhodes Above it lies the theatre Beyond this is the Poseidium, a curved promontory which runs out from the Emporium (or market-place), and to which Antony added an embankment projecting still more towards the middle of the harbour. At the end of this embankment he erected a royal residence which he called Timonium. This was his last work, when after his defeat at Actium, deserted by his friends, he crossed to Alexandria and determined for a time to lead the life of a Timon (or misanthrope) ... Next follows the Cæsarium (or Temple of Cæsar), with the market-place and warehouses Such are the surroundings of the Great Harbour. (§ 10) Immediately beyond the Heptastadium is the harbour of Eunostus, and above it the artificial harbour, sometimes called Cibotus (literally, the box), which also has docks. From this harbour runs a navigable canal to Lake Mareotis'.

Among the Principal Quarters of the ancient city we may first mention the Necropolis, or city of the dead, at the extreme W. end, 'where there are many gardens, tombs, and establishments for embalming bodies' (Strabo, xvii. 10), and Rhakotis, 'the quarter of Alexandria situated above the ships' magazines' (Strabo, xvii 6), the most ancient part of the city, and chiefly inhabited by Egyptians The Bruchium quarter, which was walled in, and contained the palaces and public buildings, lay on the mainland between Lochias and the Heptastadium, while the Jews' quarter was situated to the E of Lochias, between the sea and the main street, the E end of which was closed by the Canopic gate Outside the gate lay the hippodrome, and farther to the E was the suburb of Nicopolis, 30 stadia from Alexandria, which possessed an amphitheatre and a race-course, and where the quinquennial games were celebrated (Strabo, xvii. c 1, § 10).

With regard to the Streets of ancient Alexandria, Strabo (ib. § 8) has the following passage. 'The whole town, indeed, is intersected with streets practicable for waggons and riders, but the two broadest of them are more than a hundred feet in width and cross each other at a right angle' — This statement has been confirmed and supplemented by the excavations of Mahmûd-Bey, who has discovered traces of a rectangular network of streets, seven of them running lengthwise, from W.S.W. to E.N.E., and twelve breadthwise, from N N W to S S E He has also identified the two main streets mentioned by Strabo, the more important of which probably coincided with the modern Rue de la Porte Rosette, beginning at the Gate of Rosetta, the ancient Canopic gate, intersecting the town, and at its W end deviating from the straight line This street is still the most important in the town, and it is probably indebted for its long existence to the conduit constructed under it at an early period, which still supplies the cisterns with Nile water. Of the buildings which once flanked this street a few relics only now exist, but the excavations have brought to light distinct traces of the old pavement, which consisted of blocks of granite, and have established the fact that the street was about 45 ft. in width, or double that of the other streets. On each side of the causeway ran foot-pavements with arcades, of which, however, the traces are but scanty — The important cross-street mentioned by Strabo has been discovered by Mahmûd-Bey on the E side of the town.

† Now much reduced in extent, owing to the dilapidation of the breakwaters and the damage done by earthquakes.

Here, between two causeways, each 20 ft. in width, he found a deep band of soil. on which probably grew a row of trees; and this street was also provided with a water-conduit The side-streets, which were 23 ft. in width only, were generally about 300 yds. apart

Of the PRINCIPAL BUILDINGS of ancient Alexandria the relics are now so scanty that it is impossible to determine the character of the edifices to which they belonged (With regard to the so-called Cleopatra's Needle and Pompey's Pillar, see pp. 218, 222) The locality least free from doubt is the site of the **Paneum**, which according to Strabo (ib., § 10) was 'an artificial circular mound, resembling a rocky hill, to which a winding way ascends From its summit one can survey the whole of the surrounding town in every direction'. This spot is doubtless identical with the modern Kôm ed-Dik, the highest ground in the town, 112 ft in height, where the reservoir of the waterworks (p 216) is now situated.

The **Gymnasium**, according to Prof Kiepert, who has minutely examined the plans of Mahmûd-Bey, and not the Sema and Museum, occupied the site of the old German consulate and its garden. 'The most beautiful building, however,' says Strabo (ib , § 8), 'is the Gymnasium, with its colonnades, which are more than a stadium in length. In the middle lie the courts of justice and groves'

The theatre, the Sema or Soma, and the Museum were situated in the quarter of the *Royal Palaces* (p 209), which belonged to the Bruchium (p. 209), and occupied 'a fourth or even a third part of the whole extent of the city' (ib , § 8). This quarter must have lain to the N of the great street leading to the Canopic Gate, and to the S. of Lochias, and must have adjoined the harbour and 'all that lay beyond it'. The Alexandrian **Theatre** lay opposite the island of Antirrhodus (p. 209), in accordance with the custom that obtained at Greek seaports of placing theatres where they could command a view of the sea. Speaking of the **Sema**, Strabo (ib., § 8) describes it as 'another part of the royal buildings, an enclosed space, within which are the tombs of the kings and that of Alexander. For Ptolemy Lagi had taken away the body of the latter from Perdiccas, who had brought it from Babylon. ... Now Ptolemy brought the body of Alexander to Alexandria and buried it where it now lies, though not in the same coffin. The present coffin is of hyalus (glass or alabaster), but the former was of gold, which was carried off by Ptolemy . . . surnamed Parisactus, son of Cocces' (probably Ptolemy XI, Alexander I). — A sarcophagus carried off by the French, and afterwards captured by the English and deposited in the British Museum, was once supposed to be that of Alexander, but, when the hieroglyphics upon it were deciphered, they were found to have no reference to him.

The **Museum**, like the Sema, belonged to the quarter of the royal palaces, and probably stood on the spot where some huge ruins, since described by Brugsch, were discovered in 1853 when a Greek school was being built These ruins lay on the S. side of the Place Méhémet-Ali and to the W. of Cleopatra's Needle, a site which would correspond with the quarter of the palaces. The library undoubtedly was connected with the Museum, and it is noteworthy that among these ruins a hollowed stone was found bearing the inscription, 'Dioskorides, 3 vols.', though it can hardly have been used as a receptacle for scrolls. From these walls, now buried beneath the earth, once flowed a copious stream of knowledge, the benefits of which continue to be traceable even at the present day. According to Strabo (ib , § 8), the Museum contained 'a hall for walking, another for sitting, and a large building with the dining-room of the scholars residing at the Museum The society also possesses revenues in common, and the Museum is presided over by a priest, formerly appointed by the kings but now by the emperor'. This 'hall for walking' was an extensive court shaded with trees and provided with fountains and benches, while the hall for sitting was used for purposes of business and study. The latter was a covered colonnade, closed on one side, where the scholars assembled, and where their pupils, thirsting for knowledge, listened to the precepts of their masters Like all the Egyptian dining-halls, that of the Museum probably had a flat roof, a polished pavement, and a balustrade of short columns around it. The members of the Museum were arranged at their repasts according to the schools to which they belonged (Aristotelians, Platonists, Stoics) Each department elected a president, and the body of presidents formed a council, whose deliberations were presided over by the 'neutral' priest appointed by government With the vast and artistically embellished buildings of the Museum various other important establishments were connected, chief among which was doubtless the library, with copying and binding rooms, where the manuscripts were reproduced, adapted for use, and fitted with rollers and cases Besides the revenues enjoyed by the Museum in its corporate capacity, a yearly salary was paid to each member from the time of Philadelphus downwards Parthey estimates the members in the time of the first Ptolemies at one hundred at least, but it was probably much smaller at a later period The Alexandrian School was chiefly celebrated for its distinguished professors of the exact sciences, including geography, astronomy, mathematics, mechanics, natural history, medicine, and anatomy. Among its most celebrated scholars were Eratosthenes and Strabo, the geographers, Hipparchus and Ptolemæus, the astronomers, Archimedes, the mechanician, Euclid, the founder of geometry; and Herophilus and Erasistratus, the anatomists The branch of learning most successfully cultivated by the members of the Museum, however, was grammar, or philology, as it would now be called 'The task of transmitting to posterity in a pure form the whole of the knowledge and intellectual creations of an earlier period may perhaps be regarded as the noblest aim of philology, and this task was most ably performed by the philologists of Alexandria It is to their critical labours that we owe the preservation of the Greek literature, which has exercised so great an influence on the culture of the West and on modern history generally'. In these words Parthey sums up the result of the labours of the Alexandrian scholars, whose individual merits we cannot here discuss.

The chief **Library** at Alexandria, the nucleus of which consisted of the library left by Aristotle, belonged to the Museum, having been founded by Ptolemy Lagi with the assistance of Demetrius Phalereus It was arranged in the reign of Philadelphus, and rendered accessible by being placed in the Museum Zenodotus, Callimachus, and Eratosthenes were the first librarians Callimachus provided the scrolls with titles. As to the number of volumes in the library our chief source of information is a scholium on Plautus, with Ritschl's commentary In the time of Ptolemy Philadelphus the number was about 400,000, which, by deducting duplicates, was reduced to 90,000 In Cæsar's time, when the library was burned, the number had probably risen to about 900,000 The Pergamenian collection of books, which Antony presented to Cleopatra, contained 200,000 scrolls. These treasures, collected in one place and easily accessible, enabled the members of the Museum to pursue the studies most congenial to them. A second library was placed in the apartments of the Serapeum.

The site of the **Serapeum**, or great temple of Serapis, which Strabo mentions very briefly, may be approximately determined by the fact that it must have stood near Pompey's Pillar. The god to whom it was dedicated was introduced by the Ptolemies, in order that both Greeks and Egyptians might have a deity recognised by both, who might be worshipped in common Ptolemy Soter is said to have caused the image of the god to be sent from Sinope on the Pontus, the inhabitants of which were most unwilling to part with it At length, after three years, the colossus is said himself to have entered the vessel and by a miracle to have arrived at Alexandria in three days To the Greeks he was introduced as Pluto, while the Egyptian priests called him Osiris-Apis. They both regarded him as the god of the infernal regions, and as the Greeks associated him with Pluto, the Egyptians connected him with Ptah The introduction of the new god was the more easily accomplished as it was favoured by the priesthood of both nations, their well-intentioned object being to attract worshippers of different races to the same shrine, and, at one spot at least, to blend the religious sentiments of the Greeks and Africans. After his arrival in Egypt Serapis was of course transformed into an entirely new divinity, and his rites were remodelled so as to suit the Greek, and more particularly the Egyptian, forms of worship. The place where the Apis bull was chiefly worshipped down to a very late period is ascertained to have been Memphis (p. 372). The *Temple of Serapis*, when completed, is said to have been surpassed in grandeur by no other building in the world except the Roman Capitol. It lay to the W of Alexandria, in the suburb of Rhakotis, and not far from the Necropolis, on an eminence ascended on one side by a carriage-road and and on the other by a flight of steps, widening towards the top and leading to a platform with a vaulted roof borne by four columns Beyond this were colonnades containing chambers set apart for the worship of the god, and a number of lofty saloons which at the time of Philadelphus contained a library of 42,000 vols This collection was afterwards much enlarged, and is said to have comprised 300,000 vols at a later period. There were also numerous subterranean chambers, used for various purposes, and a number of dependencies, as at the Serapeum of Memphis (p. 383). The interior of the colonnades was enriched with extraordinary magnificence. The walls were richly painted, and the ceilings and capitals of the columns gilded Within the sanctuary stood the statue of the god, which probably consisted of a wooden figure overlaid with various precious metals. An opening ingeniously introduced in the sanctuary admitted rays of light falling on the mouth of the idol, 'as it kissing him'. Most of the extant images of Serapis are of dark stone. That of Alexandria, which is sometimes said to have consisted of emerald, was probably coloured dark blue. On its head was the calathos, and at its feet lay Cerberus, with the heads of a wolf, a lion, and a dog, around which was entwined a serpent.

After Alexander's death, when his empire was divided among his generals, Ptolemy, the son of Lagus (p. 96), came into possession of Egypt, and Alexandria became his capital. The population of the city increased greatly, and it attracted a large number of Jewish settlers, to whom Ptolemy assigned a suburb on the coast, towards the E. During his wise and upright reign Alexandria became a great resort of artists and scholars, including Demetrius Phalereus, the orator (p. 211), Apelles and Antiphilus, the painters, Euclid, the mathematician, and Erasistratus and Herophilus, the physicians, in whose society the king spent much of his time. A history of Alexander the Great written by Ptolemy himself has unfortunately been lost Under his successor, Ptolemy II. Philadelphus (p. 96), the Museum (p. 210) attained its highest prosperity. Among its distinguished members were Sosibius and Zoilus, the grammarians; Strato, the natural philosopher; Timochares and Aristarchus, the astronomers; Apollodorus, the physician; Hegesias, the philosopher; Zenodotus, Theocritus, Callimachus, and Philetas, the poets; and the versatile Timon. It was about this period that the Old Testament was translated from Hebrew into Greek, the new version being called the Septuagint from the tradition that seventy translators were engaged in the work. Under Ptolemy III. Euergetes (p. 96), Aristophanes of Byzantium, the grammarian and critic, became the director of the Museum, while the mathematical school was superintended by Eratosthenes of Cyrene, the founder of the science of mathematical geography. At this period Alexandria was also the residence of the orator Lycon of Troas, of the poets Apollonius, the Rhodian, and Lycophron, and of the great astronomer Conon. Notwithstanding the continual dissensions among the Ptolemies with regard to the succession to the throne (p. 96), which seriously disturbed the peace of the city, the fame of Alexandria, as the greatest centre of commerce in the world and the chief seat of Greek learning, steadily increased, and in B.C. 48, when the Romans interfered in the quarrels of Cleopatra VII. and her husband and brother Ptolemy XIV., had reached its zenith. After the murder of Pompey at Pelusium, Cæsar entered Alexandria in triumph (p. 98), but was attacked by the citizens and the army of Ptolemy XIV., and had considerable difficulty in maintaining himself in the Bruchium p. 209). During the siege of the city occurred the irreparable (calamity ofthe burning of the Great Library of the Museum, but it was afterwards to some extent replaced by the Pergamenian collection, presented to Cleopatra by Antony. Cæsar was afterwards conquered by the charms of the Egyptian queen, but Antony fell more fatally into her toils, and spent years of revelry with her at Alexandria (comp. p. 98). Augustus treated Alexandria with clemency, and enlarged it by the addition of the suburb of Nicopolis on the E. side of the city.

Under the successors of Augustus, Alexandria was almost uninterruptedly the scene of sanguinary civil dissensions, caused chiefly by the Jews, who in the reign of Tiberius constituted one-third of the whole population In A.D. 69 Vespasian was proclaimed emperor by the Alexandrians, his election having been to a great extent due to the influence of the philosophers Dion, Euphrates, Apollonius of Tyana, and others then resident at the Museum. Under the following emperors also the sciences continued to flourish at Alexandria. In the reign of Hadrian, Valerius Pollio and his son Diodorus, and Apollonius Dyscolus, the grammarians, Ptolemy Chennus, the mythographer, Appian, the historian, and Claudius Ptolemy, the astronomer, lived at Alexandria; and the emperor himself. who visited the city twice, held public disputations with the professors at the Museum. In A.D. 176 Marcus Aurelius came to Alexandria for the purpose of quelling an insurrection, but treated the citizens with great leniency, and attended the lectures of the grammarians Athenæus, Harpocration, Hephæstion, Julius Pollux, and others. Lucian also lived at Alexandria at this period, in the capacity of secretary to the prefect of Egypt. In the reign of Marcus Aurelius the Temple of Serapis was burned down, but the library escaped without injury, and the temple was soon rebuilt. In 199 Severus visited Alexandria, and established a senate and a new municipal constitution. The visit of Caracalla, whom the citizens had previously derided, was fraught with disaster. Having attracted the whole of the male population capable of bearing arms to one spot, he caused them to be massacred in cold blood. He closed the theatres and the public schools, and to prevent future rebellions he caused a wall fortified with towers to be erected between the Bruchium and the rest of the city.

The first great persecution of the Christians, which took place in the reign of Decius (250), was a terrible blow to the Alexandrians. The city had for a considerable time been the seat of a bishop, and had since 190 possessed a theological school, presided over by Pantænus and at the beginning of the 3rd cent. by Clement of Alexandria, who endeavoured to combine Christianity with the Neo-Platonism which sprang up about this period at Alexandria and was taught by Ammonius Saccas, Herennius, Plotinus, Porphyrius, Jamblichus, and others. A second persecution took place in 257, during the reign of Valerian; and shortly afterwards, in the reign of Gallienus, the plague carried off a large portion of the population. The incessant revolts which broke out in Alexandria and other parts of Egypt led repeatedly to the elevation of usurpers and rival emperors to the throne. Thus, Firmus was proclaimed emperor at Alexandria as a rival of Aurelian, and Probus owed the purple mainly to the Egyptian legions. The Alexandrians afterwards revolted against Diocletian and declared themselves in favour of Achilleus; but Diocletian besieged the city, took it by storm, and chastised the inhabitants with great severity.

Christianity, however, still continued to gain ground, and Alexandria was even regarded as the chief seat of Christian erudition and of the orthodox faith. The dogmatic dissensions between Arius, who filled the office of presbyter, and Athanasius, who afterwards became a bishop, at length broke out, and were fraught with disastrous consequences. Alexandria was also soon obliged to yield to Constantinople its proud position as the centre of Greek thought and science. The sanguinary quarrels between the Athanasian party and the Arians under their unworthy bishop Georgius further contributed to the rapid decline of the city. On the accession of Julian to the purple the pagans of Alexandria again instituted a persecution of the Christians, and Georgius became one of their victims. In the reign of Theodosius, however, paganism received its deathblow, and Theophilus, the patriarch of Alexandria, displayed the utmost zeal in destroying the heathen temples and monuments. The famous statue of Serapis was broken in pieces and burned in the amphitheatre amidst shouts of derision from a Christian crowd. The material prosperity of the city also fell off so greatly, that the municipality was no longer able to defray the cost of cleansing the Nile and keeping the canals open. After the death of Theophilus (in 413) the revenues of Alexandria were still farther diminished by the proceedings of the new patriarch Cyril, who led the armed mob against the synagogues and expelled the Jews from the city; and in 415 the learned and beautiful heathen Hypatia, daughter of the mathematician Theon, was cruelly murdered by an infuriated crowd.

The reigns of Marcian, Leo I., and Justinian were also signalised by new revolts, chiefly occasioned by religious dissensions. Under Justinian all the still existing heathen schools were finally closed, and the few scholars of any eminence who had remained till then were obliged to leave the place. A new insurrection which broke out in the reign of Phocas was attended with greater success than previous revolts, for Heraclius, whom the Alexandrians now proclaimed emperor, contrived in 610 to maintain his possession of the purple. The sway of the Eastern emperors in Egypt, however, soon came to an end. In 619 Alexandria was captured by Chosroes, King of Persia, but the Christians were left unmolested. Ten years later Heraclius succeeded in recovering possession of Egypt, but the troops of the Khalîf ʿOmar soon afterwards invaded the country and took Alexandria after a prolonged siege In December, 641, Amr Ibn el-ʿAṣi, ʿOmar's general, entered the city; but by order of his master, he treated the inhabitants with moderation. The decline of Alexandria now became still more marked, and about this period ʿAmr founded Fosṭâṭ (p. 241), as a new capital and seat of government, free from Christian influences. The new town, which gradually developed itself into the modern Cairo, soon became an important and prosperous place at the expense of the famous ancient Greek city. During the middle ages Alexandria sank into insignificance. Its commerce received a deathblow by the discovery of the sea-route to India round the Cape of Good Hope, and the discovery of America entailed new losses. After the conquest of Egypt by the Turks (in 1517) the city languished under the infamous régime of the Mamelukes, the harbours became choked with sand, the population, which had once numbered half a million souls, dwindled down to 5000, and the environs were converted into a sterile and marshy wilderness. With regard to the history of the French invasion, see p. 105.

The decay of the once powerful seaport was at length effectually arrested by the vigorous hand of Moḥammed ʿAli, who improved the harbours and constructed several canals. The chief benefit he conferred on Alexandria was the construction of the *Mahmûdîyeh Canal*, which was so named after the reigning Sultan Mahmûd. By means of this channel fresh water was conducted to the town from the Rosetta branch of the Nile, the adjoining fields were irrigated anew, and Alexandria was again connected with the Nile and the rest of Egypt, the products of which had long found their only outlets through the Rosetta and Damietta mouths of the river. The enterprising pasha began the work in 1819, employing no fewer than 250,000 labourers, and completed it at a cost of $7^1/_2$ million francs. He also improved the whole canal-system of the Delta, the works being chiefly superintended by the aged and eminent Linant de Belleville-Pasha, general director of public works, and other French engineers. The subsequent viceroys have also made great efforts to improve the prospects of the town; and the Egyptian cotton-trade, which received a strong impulse from the American war, and found its chief outlet through Alexandria, has proved a source of great profit to the citizens. Several regular steamboat services and two telegraphic cables now connect Alexandria with Europe, while it communicates with the rest of Egypt by river, railway, and telegraph. The town suffered severely during Arabi's rising in 1882, and a great part of the European quarter was laid in ashes by the fanatical natives. Owing to the continued state of political uncertainty and the delay of the Egyptian government to pay an indemnity, little has been done to repair the mischief, and the spirit of enterprise seems for the time being completely lamed.

Gas and Water. The city was provided with gas in 1865, and is also now well supplied with water. The old cisterns, the number of which is said still to exceed a thousand, and the situation of which enables us to determine the direction of the ancient streets, have been superseded by the modern waterworks, completed in 1860, which are supplied by the Moharrem-Bey Canal, a branch of the Mahmûdîyeh Canal. The reservoir, into which the water is pumped by steam, after having been filtered, is situated on the top of the Kôm ed-Dik hill, the site of the Paneum of antiquity (p. 210), and is capable of containing 10,000 cubic mètres of water (about 360,000 cubic feet). The water-rate per cubic mètre (36 cubic feet) is now 1 fr. only, while for the same quantity the old water-carriers used to receive 2 fr. 25 c.

Harbours (comp. pp. 203, 208). The maritime traffic of Alexandria is of considerable importance, although it is said to have decreased since the opening of the Suez Canal. The port is entered annually by about 2000 vessels. In 1883, which was commercially a somewhat dull year, the value of the imports was 7,500,000*l.*, of the exports 12,150,000*l.*, the former paying 135,000*l* and the latter 520,000*l.* of duty. The most important export is cotton, of which 2½-2¾ million cwt are annually despatched. Next in order are cotton-seed, grain, leguminous seeds, sugar, and onions; and lastly we may mention the not unimportant items of elephants' tusks, ostrich feathers, and mother-of-pearl. England possesses the lion's share of the trade and shipping, next in order coming France, Germany, and Austria.

Alexandria now contains a population of upwards of 200,000 souls, including at least 50,000 Europeans. In its palmy days it is said to have numbered more than half-a-million inhabitants, consisting of Egyptians, Greeks, Jews, Phœnicians, and Italians, all of whom were animated in common with the spirit of enterprise which attracted them to the recently founded city. The Greek element predominated at that period, next in importance to which was the Egyptian, while a numerous, but exclusive, Jewish community was settled here as early as the 4th cent. B.C. According to tradition the Gospel was first preached to the Alexandrians by St. Mark, and it is an historical fact that the Christian community was already numerous in the time of Hadrian (2nd cent.). In a letter to Servianus the emperor himself gives a very unfavourable, but hardly accurate account of the Christians.

'Egypt, my dear Servianus', writes Hadrian, 'which you extolled to me, I have found to be inhabited by a very frivolous and vacillating people, who are easily swayed by every passing rumour. Those who worship Serapis are the Christians, and men who call themselves bishops of Christ are nevertheless devoted to Serapis. There is not a single president of a Jewish synagogue, not a single Samaritan, not a single Christian presbyter that is not at the same time an astrologer, an interpreter of signs, and a quack. The patriarch himself, whenever he comes to Egypt, is compelled by one party to worship Serapis, and by another to worship Christ. They are a refractory, good-for-nothing, and slanderous set of people — The city (Alexandria) possesses treasures and resources in abundance No one's hands here are idle At one place glass is manufactured, at another paper, and at another linen All these busy people seem to carry on some kind of handicraft Men with gouty feet, blind persons, and even those with gouty hands, all find some occupation. They all really recognise one god only (probably Mammon), the same who is worshipped by Christians, Jews, and all nations. It is a pity that the people are of so bad a disposition, as the importance of the city, even in point of size, makes it well worthy of being the capital of the whole of Egypt. I made every possible concession to the city, restored its ancient privileges, and added so many new ones that the citizens came and thanked me in person, and yet as soon as I had left the place they calumniated my son Verus'

As at that period, so at the present day, the population of Alexandria consists of members of every nation dwelling on the banks of the Mediterranean. The language most generally understood is Italian, which the Arabs, as well as other nations, learn readily.

Sights. Unless the traveller proposes to make archæological researches and to study the ancient topography of Alexandria, he will easily become acquainted with its principal points of interest in a single day (comp. p. 206). Cairo affords a far better insight into Oriental life than its half-European seaport, while its delightful winter climate, notwithstanding the proximity of the two cities, is far superior to that of Alexandria. In summer the reverse is the case, as the heat at Alexandria is then tempered with cool sea-breezes, but even as early as April, especially when the S. or S E. wind prevails, the atmosphere there also is often hot and dusty. The European should avoid any undue exertion, which may easily be followed by very prejudicial effects.

The new-comer will nevertheless find it interesting to walk through the town, and particularly to observe the busy streets with their Oriental and European throng; and he will encounter, chiefly beyond the precincts of the Frank quarter, a number of isolated relics of antiquity, in the shape of stumps of columns, blocks of stone, and heaps of broken pottery. It is not an easy matter to give the traveller distinct directions as to his route through the city, as only the principal streets have well-recognised names. Most of the new names given them by government are unfamiliar to Europeans and Arabs alike, and have practically superseded the older names in a few cases only. Some of the streets again are differently named by Europeans ot different nationalities. If the traveller loses his way he will soon meet with a donkey-boy who will take him back to his hotel (comp. p. 205). On the W. side of the city, and on the neck of land between the two harbours, the ancient Heptastadium, to the N. of the Place Méhémet-Ali, the inhabitants are chiefly of Arabian extraction (p. 206), while the quarter which was once the island of Pharos, farther to the N., is occupied by the Turks. The streets here are somewhat broader than in the other quarters, and the houses are sometimes handsomely built and provided with gardens. Pompey's Column is easily found and forms a convenient landmark.

The great centre of European life is the **Place Méhémet Ali** (formerly *Place des Consuls*), which is embellished with plantations of trees and two fountains. It was the principal scene of destruction in 1882. In the centre rises the *Equestrian Statue of Moḥammed 'Ali* (Pl. 35), the founder of the reigning dynasty of Egypt, designed by *Jaquemard*, and cast in Paris. The statue is 16 ft. in height, and stands on a pedestal of Tuscan marble 20 ft. in height. As the Mohammedan religion forbids the pictorial or plastic representation of the human form, the erection of this monument was long opposed by the 'Ulama, or chief professors of 'divine and legal learning'. On the N.E. side stands the *English Church* (Pl. 25), adjoined by *St. Mark's Building* and the *International Tribunal* (Pl. 50), the only buildings which escaped the fury of the natives in 1882. The wooden booths and sheds which were erected after this period of devastation have now been removed, and their place has been taken by temporary shops and warehouses of a more substantial character.

From the S.E. corner of the square we reach the triangular *Place de l'Eglise*, or *Square Ibrâhîm*, the former name being derived from the Roman Catholic church of *St. Catharine* (Pl. 30) situated here. The Rue de la Colonne Pompée leads hence to the S. to the *Porte de la Colonne Pompée*, or *Porte du Nil*. Outside this gate we pass a large Arabian cemetery, lying on the right, and soon reach an eminence covered with rubbish and fragments of ruins, on which rises **Pompey's Column** (Pl. 37; E, 6). The monument is composed of red granite from Assuân, which has withstood centuries of exposure to the elements; and it is now the only important relic of antiquity in the city. The pedestal, composed of several blocks which once belonged to other buildings, was formerly covered by the earth and is much damaged. The height of the column, together with the disintegrated, or perhaps never quite completed, Corinthian capital, and the pedestal, is 104 ft.; the shaft is 67 ft. high, and is about 9 ft. in diameter below, and not quite 8 ft. at the top. The proportions produce an exceedingly harmonious effect.

This handsome monument does not derive its name from Pompey the Great, who was murdered on the Egyptian coast (p. 97) after the Battle of Pharsalia, but from the Roman prefect Pompeius, who, according to the inscription, erected it in honour of the unconquered Diocletian, the defender of the city of Alexandria'.† There is no ground for supposing that this column once bore the brazen horse which the citizens are said to have erected as a token of gratitude to Diocletian. After that emperor had besieged Alexandria for eight months, and had destroyed the waterworks, he at length took the city, and slew the usurper Achilleus. According to the popular story, he then commanded his soldiery to massacre the seditious populace until their blood should

---

† Τὸν (ὁσ)ιώτατον αὐτοκράτορα, τὸν πολιοῦχον Ἀλεξανδρείας Διοκλητιανὸν τὸν ἀνίκητον Πο(μπήι)ος ἔπαρχος Αἰγύπτου (τὸν εὐεργέτην).

reach his horse's knees. His hôrse soon afterwards stumbled over a dead-body and wetted its knee in human blood, whereupon the emperor was pleased to regard this as a sign that the unhappy citizens had been sufficiently chastised. Out of gratitude, particularly to the horse, they are said to have erected the brazen horse which was known as that of Diocletian. That the horse did not, however, occupy the summit of the column is proved by an ancient illustrated plan of Alexandria, in which Pompey's Pillar is represented with the figure of a man on the top The inscription, moreover, indicates that the column was erected by Pompeius II, whose prefecture did not begin till A D 302, whereas the defeat and death of Achilleus took place about 296 The column has, therefore, no connection with the story of the brazen horse, but was probably erected chiefly in commemoration of a gift of corn presented by Diocletian to the citizens during a period of scarcity

Near the extensive cemetery at the foot of the column are several fragments of columns which probably belonged to the *Serapeum* (p. 211). If we are to believe the accounts of Maḳrîzi and 'Abdellaṭîf, this temple was encircled by a colonnade of 400 columns, and once contained the library which was burned by 'Omar.

Following the road a little farther, and diverging to the right near a manufactory, we skirt the S. slope of a low plateau and soon reach the **Catacombs** (Pl. D, 7), about 1/2 M. from Alexandria.

From this point to the vicinity of the Serapeum (see above) the sloping, rocky ground was honeycombed by a great number of subterranean passages and tomb-chambers, but as there is now a quarry here, all traces of the ancient constructions will soon be obliterated. Several ornamented sarcophagi are still seen lying about The workmen offer coins, chiefly of the time of Constantine, for sale, and it is from that period that the construction of the catacombs probably dates One only of the tomb-chambers, which was discovered in 1858, is tolerably preserved, and it is now exposed to view owing to the fall of the stories above it We enter by a wooden gate, generally open, and descend by an ancient flight of steps on the W. side to a group of three chambers On the left (N side) we observe an apse with traces of paintings and Greek inscriptions (Christ between Peter and Andrew in the middle, on each side a love-feast). The vault opposite the entrance, with remains of tasteful decoration in stucco, contains three recesses, the paintings in which represent (W. side) the Maries at the Sepulchre, (N side) Christ, like the Egyptian god Horus, treading on serpents, with a quotation from Ps xci 13; and (E. side) the Ascension On each side of the central recess is a large Greek cross with the inscription at the four corners IC XC NIKA (Jesus Christ conquers) These very rude frescoes probably date from about the 6th cent, being doubtless a second restoration of the original, as we still find three layers of plaster, one above the other, and each bearing traces of painting. The third vault, a long chamber on the E side, contains sixteen recesses, which were once closed by means of upright slabs of stone. A flight of steps descending hence to the S, the outlet of which is now built up, led to a lower series of tombs

We now return to the Porte de la Colonne Pompée (Pl. 38), and follow the Rue de la Colonne back to the (1/4 hr.) Place Méhémet-Ali (p. 218), from the N.W. corner of which diverges the *Rue Râs et-Tîn*, the longest street in Alexandria. This street describes a wide curve through the Arabian quarter situated on the ancient Heptastadium (p. 217), traverses the Turkish quarter on what was formerly the island of Pharos (p. 217), some of the houses in which present a very handsome appearance, and leads to the *Viceroyal Palace* on the **Râs et-Tîn** (Pl. 43), or 'promontory of figs.' This walk affords a good view of the street-traffic of the city, but the palace itself, which was built by Moḥammed 'Ali and restored by Isma'îl Pasha, is uninteresting, especially as the Dîwân, or Council Chambers, were destroyed by a fire in 1870. The balcony, however, commands a fine view of the extensive harbour. (Admission by ticket procured at the Consulate; but the hotel commissionnaires sometimes obtain access by payment of a bakshîsh.) The Harem, a separate building, facing the sea, is built on the model of the seraglio at Constantinople. A visit to the neighbouring *Lighthouse* is very interesting, especially in the early morning, but admission is granted only to those provided with an order from the governor, which may be obtained through the English or American consulate. The *Arsenal* (Pl. 1) is not worth visiting.

A drive (3 M.; road very dusty; carriage in the afternoon 10 fr., or after 5 p.m. 5-7 fr., fee 1 fr.) should also be taken to the *Gmênet en-Nuzha*, or public garden (usually called the *Jardin Pastré*). Turning to the right outside the Porte de Rosette (Pl. 40), leaving the European cemeteries to the left, and avoiding the road which leads in a straight direction to Ramleh, we pass the waterworks on the left, cross a small mound of ancient rubbish, and reach the *Maḥmûdîyeh Canal* (p. 215). We then turn to the left, drive for a short time along the canal, and soon reach the entrance to the gardens, where a band plays on Fridays and Sundays from 4 to 6 p.m. Europeans will be interested by the profusion of exotic plants which thrive here in the open air. A little higher up is a fine garden belonging to M. Antoniadis, a rich Greek merchant, who has liberally thrown it open to the public. On the days on which the band plays this part of the canal is the resort of the fashionable world of Alexandria.

Retracing our steps, and following the bank of the canal, which lies on the left, we observe on the right a long succession of villas and gardens, including the viceroyal château *Nimreh Telâteh* ('Number Three'), with its handsome entrance, and the château and garden of *Moḥarrem-Bey*. We may now re-enter the city by the Porte Moharrem-Bey, or by the Porte de la Colonne Pompée.

Adjoining the W. side of the city is the site of the original Macedonian *Necropolis*, a reminiscence of which is preserved in the Arabic name *Gabari* (see below). No traces of the cemetery now remain, the ground being occupied by a dirty suburb intersected by very bad roads. About 4½ M. farther W. are the *Quarries of Meks* (see below), which are hardly worthy of a visit (carriage there and back in 2-3 hrs., 10-12 fr.).

Starting from the Place Méhémet-Ali, we follow the new *Rue Ibrâhîm* (Pl. E, F, 4, 5), which has been constructed straight through an old Arabian quarter, and at the end of it cross the Maḥmûdîyeh Canal. We then turn to the left, crossing the rails which lead to the extensive new quay, and immediately afterwards proceed to the right by the *Route du Meks* (Pl. A, B, 6), which skirts the coast. A little to the left of the road is the new *Hippodrome*, the race-course of Alexandria, sometimes known as the *Gabari* (see above). To the W. of it is an old palace with a mosque, recently converted into a *Quarantine* (Pl. 42) or lazzaretto. In the friable limestone of the coast-hills are a number of tomb-chambers, the ceilings of which are borne by pillars of the rock left for the purpose; but most of them have been destroyed by the inroads of the sea, and are now covered up. These chambers, which contain nothing interesting, have been styled the *Baths of Cleopatra*. Farther on, to the left of the road, is the château of Sa'îd Pasha (p. 203), and to the right, close to the sea, is the *Bâb el-'Arab* (p. 203).

At **Meks** were established the works of Messrs Greenfield & Co., an English firm which contracted for the construction of the imposing new **Harbour Works** of Alexandria. These consist, in the first place, of an outer breakwater, beginning near the W. end of the island of Pharos (Râs et-Tîn, p. 219), and extending to the S.W. towards Meks, forming an obtuse angle, and nearly 2 M. in length. This huge barrier, completed in Dec. 1873, is formed of a foundation of 26,000 solid masses of masonry, each 20 tons in weight, faced on the side next the sea with natural blocks, each 15-25 cwt. in weight. The horizontal surface is 19ft in width, and, at low tide, 10 ft. above the level of the water. The admirably sheltered harbour thus formed is nearly 1800 acres in area, and 20-60 ft. in depth. A second pier, or Molo, nearly 1000 yds. in length, and connected by lines of rails with the old railway-station, protects the inner harbour, which is about 475 acres in area and on an average 27 ft. deep. From the beginning of this pier (near Gabari, at the S.W. extremity of the town) a series of new quays extends along the whole E. side of the old harbour to the Arsenal, whereby about 75 acres of very valuable land have been reclaimed. The whole length of the berthage thus obtained for large vessels, including the inside of the Molo, extends to nearly 2 M. No fewer than 30,000 artificial blocks, weighing 20 tons each, and 2 million tons of natural blocks of stone, manufactured and quarried respectively at Meks, were used in the construction of the harbour-works.

To the E. of Meks, and to the S. of the road, lies the extensive *Lake Mareotis* (p. 223).

Ramleh ($6^1/_2$ M., see below) is connected with Alexandria by two railways; the direct line, on which a train runs hourly to Ramleh in 20 min. (fares 4 pias. 20, 3 pias. 20 paras, 2 pias. tariff); and the Rosetta railway (station outside the Porte Moharrem-Bey), which runs two trains daily to Ramleh in 27 min. (same fares). There is also a new carriage-road (carriage about 10 fr.), which will be preferred by those who wish to inspect the fragments of statues and half-excavated ruins of buildings lying scattered about the fields.

A few paces from the station of the direct or English line to Ramleh, and close to the sea, rises the so-called *Roman Tower* (Pl. 44), which, however, seems to be of Arabian origin. It was adjoined, down to March 1880, by the famous obelisk called **Cleopatra's Needle**, which vied with Pompey's Column in general interest as a monument of antiquity. One of the last acts of the Khedive Isma'il was to present this obelisk to the city of New York. Both the native and foreign residents of Alexandria looked on with indignation while this interesting relic was raised by American machinery from the place it had occupied for 2000 years and removed to the specially constructed vessel that was to convey it to New York. Indeed it was only the public sympathy with the young Khedive Tewfik, who looked upon the presentation as a legacy of his father's government that prevented a popular outbreak over this piece of vandalism The obelisk now forms one of the prominent features of the Central Park in New York, where, however, it is feared that it will rapidly become defaced by the severity of the climate — A companion obelisk, that lay for centuries prone in the sand by the side of Cleopatra's Needle, now adorns the Thames Embankment at London

The direct local railway traverses the rubbish heaps of the ancient *Nicopolis*. Projecting into the sea, to the left, is the small *Fort Silseleh*. We here obtain a retrospective glimpse of the sickle-shaped S.E. side of the town.

Nicopolis, situated beyond the Hippodrome (of which no trace is now left), about 30 stadia to the E of the city, is said to have been 'no smaller than a town', and received its name, 'town of victory', from Octavian (Augustus) in memory of the victory he gained here over Antony and his adherents. A small *Temple*, recently discovered close to the sea, and to the N W of the ruins of the *Kasr el-Kayâsereh* (castle of Cæsar), the ruined walls of which have been pulled down to afford material for the new palace of the Khedive (see below), was perhaps also erected by Octavian on the same occasion

To the right, skirting the Maḥmûdîyeh Canal, runs the Rosetta railway (p. 447). Near the station of (4 M.) *Sîdi Gaber*, on a slight eminence to the left, and not far from the site of the old Roman castle above mentioned, is a new viceroyal palace, called *Muṣṭafa Pasha*. The *Catacombs* situated to the N.E. of this point are almost entirely destroyed. The train now passes a series of villas and gardens full of luxuriant vegetation, the most attractive of which lie beyond the fourth of the five stations.

$6^1/_2$ M. **Ramleh** (*i.e.* 'sand') is a modern place, consisting chiefly of numerous country-houses (*Pensions Beauséjour* and *Miramare*, both good), some of which are occupied by Alexandrian families throughout the whole year. It possesses waterworks of its own, which greatly facilitate horticulture. On the way to the sea the traveller will observe a few relics of the Greek and Roman periods.

From Alexandria to Ramleh by the *Rosetta Railway*, and thence viâ Abuḳir to Rosetta, see p. 447.

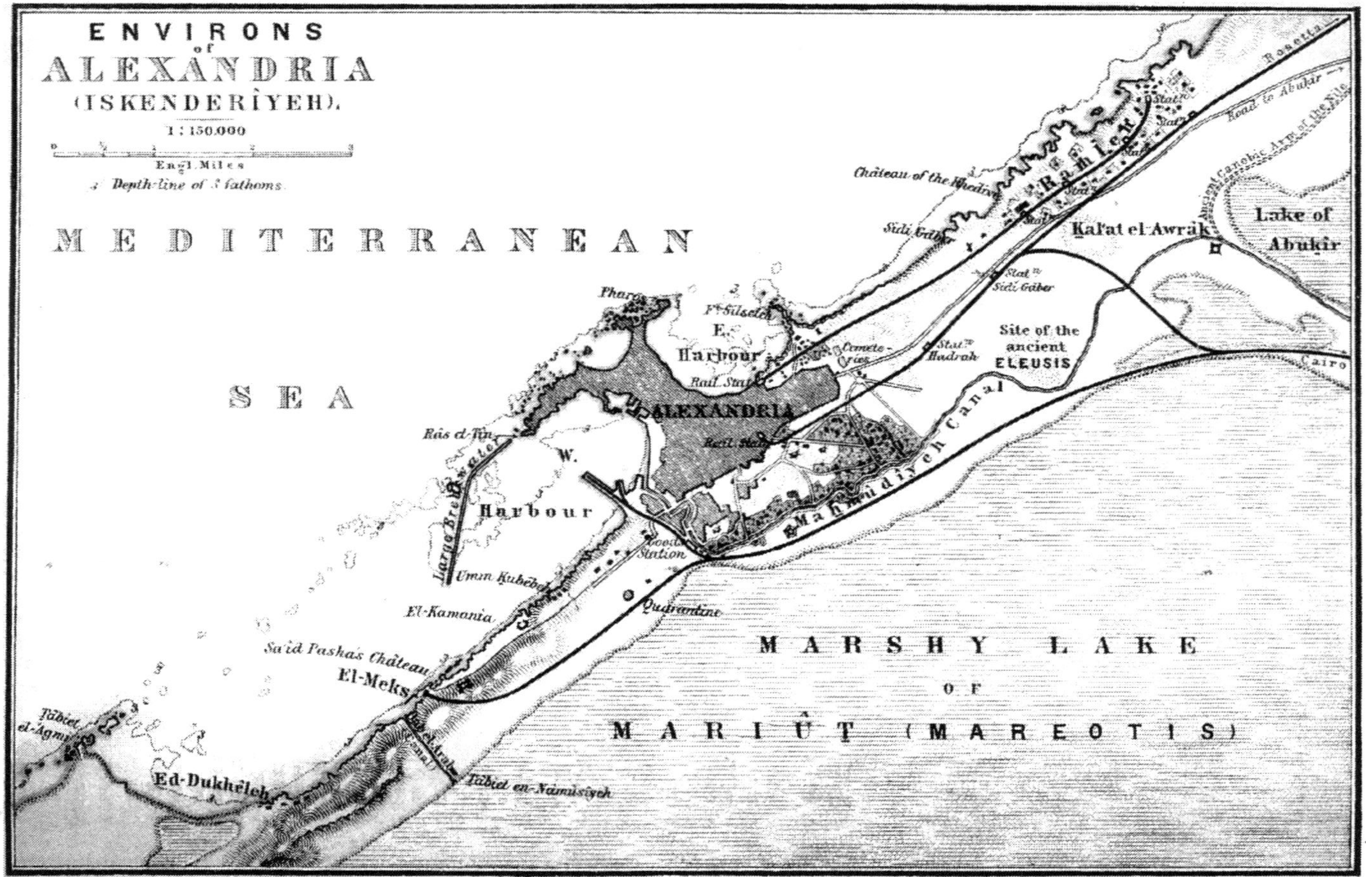

Drawn by H. Kiepert.
Geograph. Instit. of Wagner & Debes, Leipzig.

2. From Alexandria to Cairo.

128 M. RAILWAY. Express train in $4^1/_3$ hrs, fares $30^1/_2$ fr (117 piastres), $20^1/_4$ fr. (78 piastres); return-tickets, available till the first train on the second day after, 175 piastres 20 paras or 117 piastres tariff. Ordinary trains in $5^1/_2$-6 hrs, fares 97, 65, 39 piastres Each first-class passenger has 35 kilogrammes of luggage free, second 26, third 17 (or about 77, 57, and 37 lbs. respectively) The first and second class carriages resemble those in France and Italy; the third are often excessively dirty Five trains daily each way, starting at the same hours. express at 6 p m, ordinary at 8 (from Cairo 8 30) a m, 10 a m, 2.45 p m, and 10 30 p m — From stat. Benha viâ Zakâzîk direct to Suez at 1 p m, reaching Zakâzîk at 2 p m. and Suez at 6 30 p.m (fares from Alexandria to Suez 169 and 113 piastres tariff) At Kafr ez-Zaiyât (p. 225) there is a European restaurant The only refreshments obtainable at the other stations are boiled eggs (bêd), Arabian bread (ʿêsh), water (môyeh), and oranges (bortukân) and sugar-cane (kaṣab) in their seasons ($^1/_2$-2 copper piastres).

The railway-station (Pl 2, G, 5) is not far from the hotels, but the traveller had better drive to it, starting from his hotel at least half-an-hour before the advertised time of departure New-comers and travellers burdened with much luggage should engage the commissionnaire of the hotel or a valet-de-place (2s) to assist in booking their luggage, an operation carried on by the employés with those alternations of apathetic indolence and violent hurry which are so characteristic of Orientals. The Alexandria and Cairo line, the first railway constructed in the East, was made under Saʿîd Pasha in 1855 and was to have been continued by another line from Cairo across the desert to Suez, but the latter project has been abandoned. The names of the stations are not called out. The Arabian villages (comp p 39) seen from the line present a very curious appearance, and the interior of their half-open mud-hovels is frequently visible ' The dust is very annoying in hot weather, forcing its way into the carriages even when the windows are closed

The train first traverses gardens towards the N.E., and beyond *Sidi Gâber* diverges to the right from the line to Rosetta (p 447). To the left is the ruin of the *Kaṣr el-Kayâsereh* (p. 222), situated on the coast, with the château of *Ramleh* (p. 222) in the distance. It then crosses the *Mahmûdîyeh Canal* (p. 448) and skirts its S. bank nearly as far as stat. Damanhûr (see below). To the left lies the *Lake of Abukîr (Beḥeret Maʿadîyeh)*; to the right is *Lake Marcotis (Beḥêret Maryût)*, the water of which washes the railway embankment at places during the period of the inundation, while in summer it is a considerable distance from it.

The **Lake Mareotis**, or *Marcia*, as it was also called in ancient times, bounds Alexandria on the S. side In Strabo's time it was filled from the Nile by means of numerous canals, both from the S and E, which brought great traffic to this inland harbour, while the sea-harbour was more important for the export trade The lake, which lies 8 ft. below the sea-level, was once surrounded by a luxuriantly fertile tract of country, irrigated from the Nile as early as the time of Herodotus. The banks once yielded excellent white wine, which has been extolled by Horace and Virgil, and is mentioned by Athenæus as having been particularly wholesome Egypt now produces very little wine, but reminiscences of its culture in the region of Lake Mareotis are still preserved in the name Karm (*i e* 'vineyard', pl kurûm), which the Arabs apply to some ancient ruins here, and in numerous wine-presses hewn in the rocks which still exist Mahmûd-Bey and Professor Kiepert divide this coast region into four parallel zones: (1) The chain of sand-hills on the coast, where many old ruins are still observable; (2) The depression of the Wâdi Maryût, a western prolongation of the lake, the water of which covers the eastern and lower half of that valley, while the western half consists of marshy ground with several islands, bearing ruins of ancient buildings; (3) The chain of hills to the S. of the lake, about 5 M. in width, and consisting of fertile land, with the ruins of about forty ancient villages; (4) The Mareotic plain, stretching to the margin of the desert, and also containing many ruins.

During the Arabian and Turkish régime the waters of the lake gradually subsided, but in 1801, during the siege of Alexandria, the English cut through the neck of land between the lake and the sea near the so-called Maison Carrée, a little to the W. of Abukîr, thus laying an extensive and fertile region under water and destroying about 150 villages. The present Es-Sett marks the spot where the fatal cutting was made and afterwards closed. Moḥammed 'Ali did all in his power to repair the damage and to improve the environs of Alexandria, but about 100,000 acres of cultivable land are said still to be covered by the sea-water. The water is now evaporated for the sake of its salt, the right to manufacture which is farmed out by government for 4000 purses (nearly 20,000 *l.*) per annum.

We observe at intervals the sails of the barges on the Maḥmûdîyeh Canal, and long strings of laden camels traversing the embankments. 17 M. *Kafr ed-Dawâr* was the point at which Arabi erected his strongest fortifications in 1882, after the English had occupied Alexandria and Ramleh. We now perceive the first cotton-fields on the right. — 28 M. *Abu Ḥomṣ*, a group of mud-hovels.

$38^1/_2$ M. **Damanhûr** (first station at which the express stops, reached in $1^1/_4$ hr.), the capital of the province of *Beḥêreh*, with 25,000 inhab., was the ancient Egyptian *Tema-en-Hor* (city of Horus), and the Roman *Hermopolis Parva*. The town lies on an eminence, and contains some tolerably substantial buildings. Among them are several manufactories for the separation of the cotton from the seeds, and above them tower several minarets. The Arabian cemetery lies close to the railway. In July, 1798, Bonaparte, on his expedition to Cairo, selected the route viâ Damanhûr, which at the time was so excessively parched and burned up that his officers and men suffered terribly, while he himself narrowly escaped being taken prisoner. On 21st July, however, he succeeded in defeating the troops of the Mamelukes at the 'Battle of the Pyramids', and on the 25th he entered Cairo. In Nov., 1802, the Mamelukes here inflicted a signal defeat on the Turks. A large market is held at Damanhûr on Sundays, and a smaller one on Fridays. (From Damanhûr to *Fum el-Baḥr* and *Rosetta*, see p. 448.)

55 M. *Tell el-Bârûd*, a village with a large mound of ruins.

From Tell el-Bârûd to Bûlâḳ ed-Dakrûr (p. 231) a direct railway connecting our line with the Upper Egyptian Railway, was opened in 1875. The traveller bound for Cairo, however, will not care to take this route except in case of necessity. The train leaves Alexandria at 10.30 p.m., reaches (55 M.) Tell el-Bârûd at 1.20 a.m. (halt of 40 min.), and arrives at (130 M.) Bûlâḳ ed-Dakrûr at 7.5 a.m.; it starts again at 8.30 a.m. and arrives at ($358^1/_2$ M.) Siûṭ at 6.45 p.m. — In the reverse direction the train leaves Siûṭ at 8.30 a.m. and arrives at Bûlâḳ at 7.5 p.m.; it starts again at 8.30 p.m., reaches Tell el-Bârûd at 2 a.m., and Alexandria at 5.20 a.m. — Fares: to Bûlâḳ 97 piast. 20 par., 65 piast.; to Siûṭ 269 piast. 10 par., 179 pias. 20 paras.

As far as Bûlâḳ the train follows the W. bank of the Rosetta branch of the Nile, skirting the boundary between the Libyan desert and the cultivated Delta of the Nile. The stations between Tell el-Bârûd and Bûlâḳ are *Kôm Ḥamâdeh*, *Eṭ-Ṭaryeh*, *Kafr Dâwud*, *El-Wardân*, and *El-Menâshi*. The station at Bûlâḳ is nearly $1^1/_2$ M. from the Muski. Carriages not always to be had.

The cultivated land becomes richer, and we pass villages, groups of trees, and even tamarisks. The train reaches the broad Rosetta arm of the Nile, crosses it by a long iron bridge (fine view to the left), and enters the station of (65 M.) **Kafr ez-Zaiyât** (second station at which the express stops, 2 hrs. after leaving Alexandria; halt of 20 min.; restaurant). The town, which carries on a busy trade in grain, cotton, and the other products of the Delta (p. 73), lies on the right bank of the river. Excursion to the ruined site of *Saïs*, the modern *Ṣâ el-Ḥager*, see R. 8, d.

The Delta in Winter. 'The fields are still wet at places, and straight canals are seen in every direction All the cereals grown in ancient times still flourish here, and the slender palm still rears its fruit-laden crown beside the less frequent sycamore, with its slender umbrageous foliage. The cotton-plants are successfully cultivated where the soil is well irrigated, and form extensive plantations of underwood, bearing a profusion of yellow, red, and white blossoms, which somewhat resemble wild roses. Vineyards are rare, but they sometimes occur in the northern part of the Delta, the plants being trained on the trelliswork which we often see represented in the paintings of the ancient Egyptian tombs. The water-wheels (sâḳiyeh) are turned by buffaloes and donkeys, and sometimes by camels or by steam, and the water-pail (shâdûf), though less common than in Upper Egypt, is occasionally plied by slightly clad men and boys. The canals are flanked with embankments to protect the fields from inundation, and the paths on these banks are enlivened with strings of camels, donkeys with their riders, and men, women, and children on foot. From a distance the villages look like round, grey hillocks, full of openings, and around them rise dovecots and palm-trees. On closer examination we distinguish the mud-huts, huddled together on rising ground where they are safe from the inundation. Many of these hamlets are adorned with very handsome groups of palms, while the minarets which overtop the larger villages and towns seem to point as devoutly to heaven as our Gothic church-spires'. (*Ebers*, 'Goshen', etc)

76 M. **Ṭanṭa** ($3^3/_4$ hrs. from Alexandria, $1^1/_2$ hr. from Cairo).

Opposite the station is an *Inn* kept by a Greek, which looks not uninviting. The Greek *Restaurant* on the Canal, near the Bazaar, is patronised by European merchants from Cairo and Alexandria during the fair of Ṭanta

Consular Agents. British, *Mr. Joyce*; German, *Hr. Dahhân*; French, *M. Athanasi*.

Ṭanṭa, the handsome capital of the province of *Gharbîyeh*, which lies between the Rosetta and Damietta arms of the Nile, with a population estimated at 60,000 souls, possesses large public buildings and an extensive palace of the Khedive. The bazaars present a very busy scene at the time of the fairs (see below).

The *Mosque of the Seyyid el-Bedawi*, having been recently restored, presents a handsome appearance. The large court contains the basin for ablutions (pp. 147, 184).

Seyyid Ahmed el-Bedawi is probably the most popular saint in Egypt, and the most frequently invoked. He is said to have been born in the 12th cent. at Fez, or according to others at Tunis, and to have settled at Ṭanṭa after a pilgrimage to Mecca. He is credited with the possession of great personal strength, and is therefore invoked in times of danger or exertion, and by women also who desire the blessing of children.

Travellers may generally visit the mosque without an attendant, but must not omit to deposit their shoes at the door. During the fair, however, which attracts among other visitors a number of fanatical Mohammedans from countries rarely visited by Europeans, it is advisable to procure the escort of the shêkh of the mosque, to whom an introduction may be obtained through the consular agent (fee 1-2 fr.).

The catafalque of the saint is covered with red velvet richly adorned with embroidery, and is enclosed by a handsome bronze railing. The dome is still unfinished. One large and two small schools are connected with the mosque. The sebîl, or tank, with the small medreseh (school) above it, situated in the space adjoining the mosque, is an interesting old building.

The most important of the three annual FAIRS OF TANTA is that of the 'môlid' (nativity) of the saint in August. The other two fairs are in January and April. Each fair lasts from one Friday to the following, presenting an interesting and picturesque scene, but too often marred by the licentiousness so prevalent among Orientals. In August upwards of half-a-million persons congregate here from all the Eastern countries bordering on the Mediterranean, and from the Mohammedan part of Africa. The Egyptian peasantry, who purchase cattle, implements, clothing, and trinkets at the fair, are always largely represented, and a number of European merchants are also to be met with. The number of visitors to the April fair is said to average 200,000, and to the January fair 50,000. Upwards of a million head of cattle are sold annually at these fairs. Beggars and pilgrims farther contribute to swell these vast crowds, and the merchants themselves usually combine a pious visit to the shrine of the saint with their commercial business; for the Prophet permits even the Mecca pilgrims to engage in trade, although he has imposed on them many unpleasant restrictions. In August and April we also encounter here the greater number of the Ghawâzi and 'Awâlim (comp. p. 20), of the singing and dancing and unveiled women, and of the jugglers and showmen of every kind who dwell on the banks of the Nile. The fair of Ṭanṭa may indeed almost be regarded as a modern reflex of the pilgrimage to Bubastis (p. 411) described by Herodotus. Women uttering the peculiar crowing sound which they use to express great emotion still approach the sacred shrine in boats as in the time of Herodotus, and license is everywhere prevalent. — Long processions of camels laden with chests and bales are seen converging towards the town, accompanied by crowds of men and large herds of cattle. The banks of the canal are thronged with persons washing themselves and drawing water. The streets teem with the most animated traffic, and are filled with long rows of boats, in many of which the occupants are seen plying their handicrafts. Dervishes with dishevelled hair and ragged clothes, cripples, and idiots, who are treated with great respect, are clamorous for bakshîsh; and pilgrims returning from Mecca are saluted with flags and symbols at the gate of the mosque. On the first Friday of each fair the vast concourse of visitors, headed by the chief authorities of the town, move in procession towards the mosque of the sainted Seyyid. In the large space set apart for shows, adjoining the horse-market, the jesters usually attract a numerous audience. When they pronounce the name of Allâh the whole of the assemblage seated around bow their heads with one accord. The gestures of terror and astonishment made by the children and negroes at the performances of the jugglers are very amusing. Among the most popular exhibitions are those of the obscene Karagyûz, and the dances performed by men in female dress (comp. p. 21).

From Ṭanṭa to *Mahallet Rûh*, *Manṣûra*, and *Damietta*, see pp. 445, 439.

A short branch-line runs from Ṭanṭa to the S. to *Shibîn el-Kôm*, a small town on this side of the Rosetta branch of the Nile, in the *Menûfiyeh*, one of the most fertile regions in the Delta.

Beyond Ṭanṭa the train traverses a fertile tract, and beyond (87 M.) *Birket es-Sab'a* crosses a small arm of the Nile. A number of cotton-cleaning mills afford an indication of the wealth of the country. A little farther on, near Benha, on the Damietta arm of the Nile, is a large viceroyal palace, where 'Abbâs Pasha (p. 107), Sa'îd Pasha's predecessor, was murdered in 1854. The train crosses the Damietta branch of the Nile by an iron bridge, and, immediately beyond it, reaches —

101 M. **Benha** (reached from Alexandria in 3½ hrs., from Cairo in ¾ hr.; railway to Zaḳâzîḳ, Isma'îlîya, and Suez, see p. 407), or *Benha l-'Asal*, i.e. 'Benha of the honey', so called from a jar of honey which Makaukas, the Copt (p. 374), is said to have sent from this place to the Prophet. The red oranges and the 'Yûsuf Efendi' mandarins of Benha are much esteemed at Cairo, and excellent grapes are also produced here.

To the N.E. of Benha, not far from the town, and intersected by the railway, are the ruins of the ancient **Athribis**, the 'heart-city' of antiquity, situated in the 10th Nomos of Lower Egypt, and named *Kôm el-Atrib* by the natives of the village of *Atrib* or *Etrib*. The site of the ancient town is still traceable, but the remains hardly repay a visit, and no inscriptions are now left. The heaps of rubbish begin near the Rosetta branch of the river and end by a small canal. A lion bearing the name of Ramses II., found here and carried to Europe, and the fact that the town and the deities belonging to it are mentioned in a few hieroglyphic inscriptions, indicate that it was founded in the time of the Pharaohs. A Roman-Egyptian necropolis was at a later period founded at the end of the long street on the remains of ancient buildings. Brugsch, who visited the place in 1854, describes it thus — 'The dead lay in their coffins in tomb-chambers which were situated immediately below the surface of the mound of rubbish and were constructed of black Nile-bricks dried in the sun. The chambers were vaulted and lay adjacent to each other. I sought in vain for inscriptions and paintings, but one of the chambers was coloured red. The coffins consist of square boxes of cedar-wood, the sides being about an inch in thickness. The mummies were admirably preserved and elaborately encased in their cerements. Neither they nor the coffins bore any trace of hieroglyphics, but on the lid of one of the latter I found the word ΠΑΤΡΑΣ and a date. Many statues and busts of the Græco-Roman period have also been found here, which indicate that the town of Athribis was a place of considerable importance at this late epoch of Egyptian history.'

Near (109 M.) *Ṭûkh* the mountains enclosing the Nile higher up become visible in the distance, those on the E. (Arabian) side appearing lower than those on the W. (Libyan) side. About 5 min. later the outlines of the pyramids begin to loom in the distance towards the S.W., and near (120½ M.) **Ḳalyûb** these stupendous structures become distinctly visible. About 3 M. to the W. of this point is the *Barrage du Nil* (p. 408), to which a disused branch-line diverges. Railway to Zaḳâzîḳ, Isma'îlîya, and Suez, see R. 5. The Libyan chain becomes more distinctly visible, and we also observe the Moḳaṭṭam range with the citadel, and the mosque of Moḥammed 'Ali with its slender minarets. The scenery now becomes more pleasing. The fields are enlivened with numerous trees, and gardens and villas come in sight. To the left lie the site of the ruins of Heliopolis (the obelisk of which is not seen from the railway), and the garden of Maṭarîyeh with its sycamores, and the large château of ʿAbbâsîyeh, while on the right we perceive the beautiful avenue leading to Shubra (p. 330). The environs of the city become more and more prominent, and about 50 min. after leaving Benha the train enters the station of (128 M.) **Cairo.**

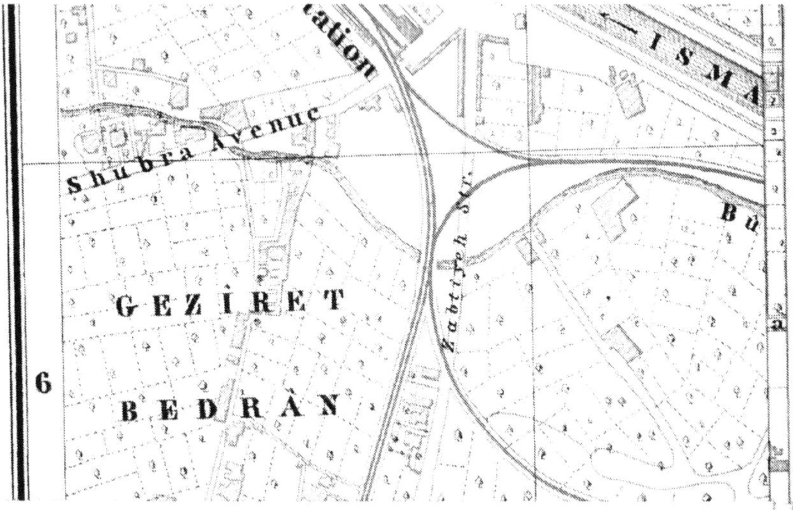

Shubra Avenue
GEZÎRET
BEDRÂN
Zabtiyeh Str.
6

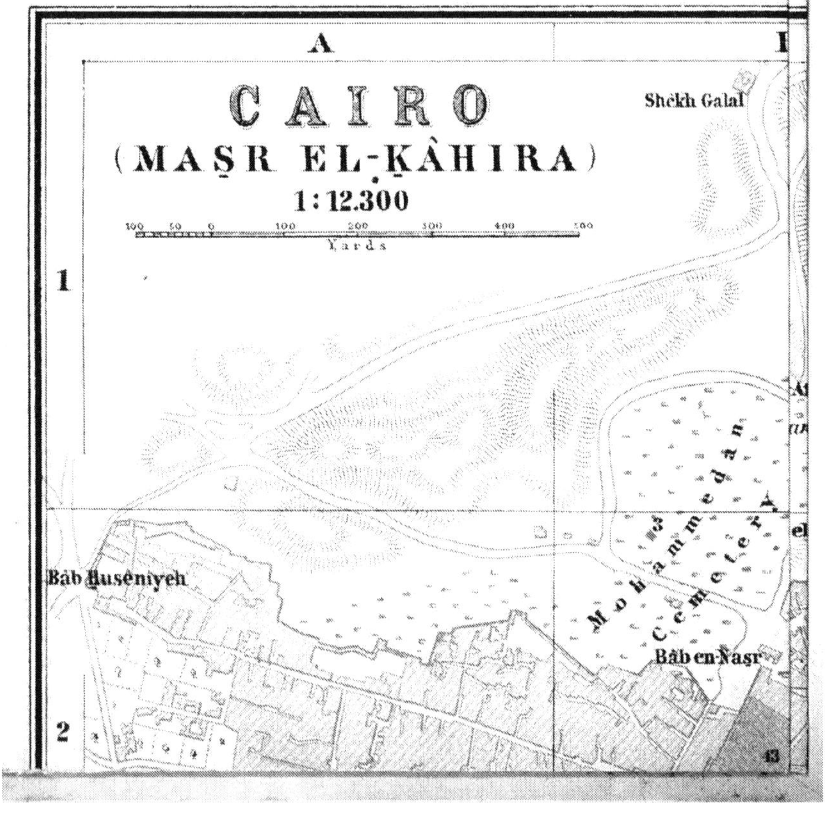

A
CAIRO
(MAṢR EL-ḲÂHIRA)
1:12.300
Yards
1
2
Shêkh Galal
Mohammedan Cemetery
Bâb Ḥuseniyeh
Bâb en-Naṣr

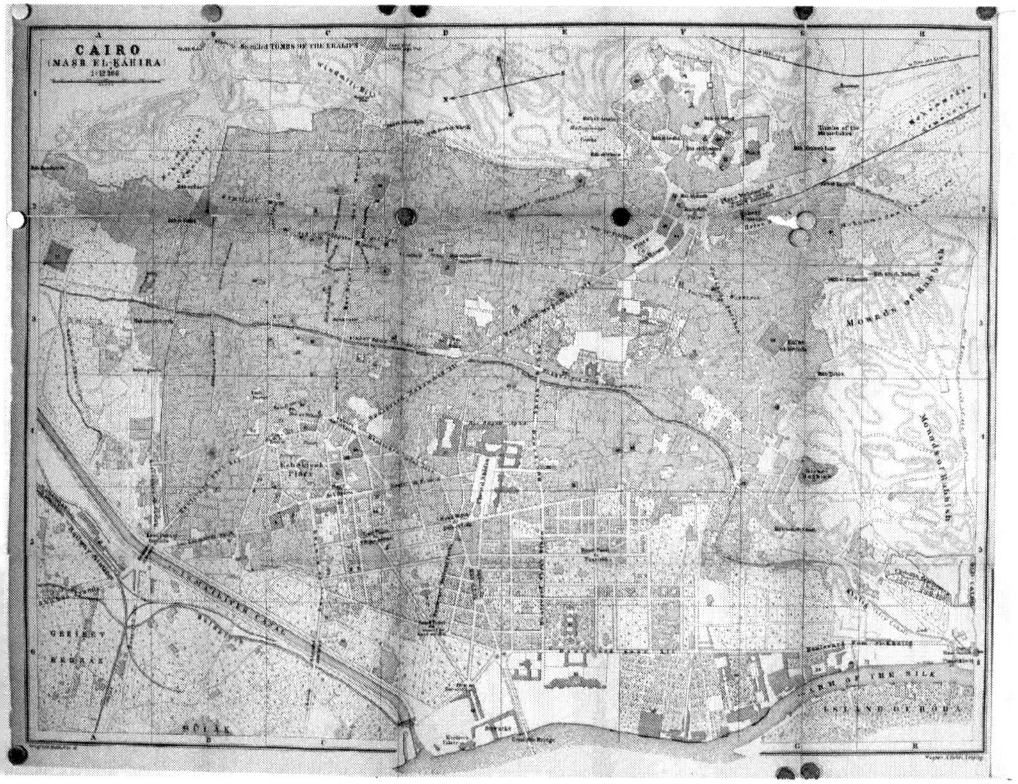
CAIRO
(MASR EL-KAHIRA)
TOMBS OF THE KHALIFS
Windmill Hill
Tombs of the Mamelukes
Mounds of Rubbish
Ezbekiyeh Place
ISMAILIYEH CANAL
GHEZIREH
BULAK
ARM OF THE NILE
ISLAND OF RODA

Explanation of Numbers in Plan of Cairo.

1. American Mission . . . C,5
2. Bêt el-Kâḍi. C,2
3. Burckhardt's Grave. . . B,2

Churches.

4. Armenian C,3
5. Armenian-Catholic . . C,3
6. Coptic-Catholic C,3,E,4
7. Coptic-Jacobite B,4,5
8. English. C,5
9. French C,3
10. German C,5
11. Greek Catholic. . . . C,3
12. Maronite C,3
13. Roman Catholic (Latin) C,3
14. Sisters of Sacred Heart B,4
15. Syrian C,3
16. Citadel F,G,1,2
17. Club Khédivial C,4

Consulates.

18. British C,4
19. French C,5
20. German C,5
21. Austrian C,4
22. Deaconesses' Institute . C,6
23. Dervish Monastery in the Habbanîyeh E,3
24. Exchange. C,4
25. Fum el-Khalîg H,6
26. Geographical Institution C,4
27. Joseph's Well F,1
28. Kaṣr el-ʿAin, Hospital . G,6
29. Ḳaṣr en-Nîl, Barrack . . D,6
30. Library, viceroyal . . . E,3,4
31. Ministry of Public Works E,6
32. Medreseh Gamelîyeh . . C,2

Mosques.

33. Gâmiʿ ʿAbbâs Pasha . B,3
34. — Abul Seba. D,5
35. — El-Akhḍar. E,4
36. — El-Akbar (Tekîyet el-Maulawîyeh) F,3
37. — El-Ashraf C,2
38. — El-Azhar C,2
39. — Barkûkîyeh C,2
40. — El-Benât. D,3
41. — ʿAbderraḥmân . . . F,2
42. — El-Ghûri C,D,2
43. — Ḥâkim B,2
44. — Sulṭân Ḥasan . . . F,2
45. — Ḥasan Pasha . . . F,3
46. — Ḥasenên C,2
47. — Ibrâhîm Agha . . . E,2
48. — Kait Bey G,5
49. — Ḳaṣr el-ʿAin G,6
50. — Ḳessûn E,3
51. — El-Kirkia C,5
52. — Maḥmûdi F,2
53. — Moḥammed ʿAli . . F,2
54. — Moḥammed Bey C,2
55. Gâmiʿ Moḥ. Bey Mabdûl E,4
56. — Moḥ. en-Nâṣir . . . C,2
57. — El-Muaiyad D,2,3
58. — Nûreddîn G,2
59. — Rifâʿîyeh F,2
60. — Salâheddîn Yûsuf . F,1
61. — Shêkh Ramaḍân . . E,4
62. — Shêkh Ṣâleḥ. . . . E,4
63. — Shekhûn. F,3
64. — Sîdi Bedreddîn . . G,2
65. — Sîdi el-Ismaʿîli . . F,4
66. — Seiyideh Safîya . . E,4
67. — Sulêmân Pasha . . F,1
68. — Ibn Tulûn E,3
69. — El-Werdâni E,3
70. — Yûsuf Gamali . . . C,2
71. — Ez-Ẓâhir. A,2,3
72. — es-Seiyideh Zênab . F,G,4
73. Muristân Kalaûn C,2
74. Okella Sulfikar Pasha . C,2
75. Opera House C,4

Palaces.

76. ʿAbidîn (viceroyal) . . D,E,4,5
77. ʿAli-Pasha D,4
78. Chérif-Pasha D,5
79. Helmîyeh. E,F,3
80. Ibrâhîm-Pasha F,5
81. Ismaʿilîyeh E,6
82. Kaṣr ʿAli F,G,6,7
83. — Ed-Dubara E,6
84. Kiâmil-Pasha. C,5
85. Manṣûr-Pasha D,3
86. Police Office C,4
87. Post Office (Egyptian) . C,4
88. Place of Execution . . . D,2
89. Railway Station A,5
90. Rosetti Garden C,4
91. Sebîl of ʿAbderraḥmân Kikhya C,2
92. — of Moḥammed ʿAli . D,2
93. — of the Khedive's grandmother B,5
94. — of ʿAbbâs Pasha . . . F,3
95. Shêkh Mufti (ul-Islâm) . C,3
96. — Es-Sadad E,3
97. Telegraph Office, British C,4
97a. — — Egyptian C,5
98. Theatre, French C,4
99. Tribunal, International . C,4
100. Waterworks, head of old H,6

S. Synagogues C,3

Hotels.

a. New Hotel C,5
b. Shepheard's Hotel. . . . C,5
c. Hôtel du Nil C,3
d. — Royal B,4,5
e. — d'Angleterre C,4
f. — d'Orient C,4
g. Pension Fink D,5

Gates, Streets, etc.

Gates.

Bâb ʿArab el-Isar G,1,2
— El-Attabey E,1
— El-Azab F,2
— Derb el-Mârûk D,1
— Faghalla. B,3
— El-Futûḥ B,2
— El-Gebel F,1
— El-Gedîd F,1
— El-Ghorâyib. C,D,1
— Ḥasanîyeh. A,2
— El-Kabasseh. G,3
— El-Ḳarâfeh G,2
— Kaṣr en-Nîl D,6
— En-Naṣr B,2
— Esh-Shaʿrîyeh B,3
— Seiyideh Nefîseh H,3
— Seiyideh Zênab G,5
— Ṭulûn. G,3
— El-Wezîr E,2
— El-Wusṭâni F,1
— Ez-Zuwêleh (Mutawelli) . D,2

Bazaars.

Booksellers. C,2
Gamelîyeh C,2
Khân el-Khalîli C,2
Sûḳ el-ʿAṭṭârîn C,2
— El-Faḥḥâmi D,2
— El-Gôhargîyeh. C,2
— El-Ḥamzâwi. C,2
— En-Naḥḥâsîn C,2
— Eṣ-Ṣâigh C,2
— Es-Selâf. B,3
— Es-Sellâḥa. E,F,2
— Es-Sûdân C,2
Sukkarîyeh D,2

'Places.'

ʿÂbidîn D,4,5
Atab el-Kadra C,4
Bâb el-Khalk D,3
Bâb el-Lûk D,5
Place de la Bourse. C,4
Ezbekîyeh C,4,5
Fish Market B,4
Karamêdan F,G,2
Sulṭân Ḥasan F,2
Méhémet Ali (Menshîyeh Gedîdeh) F,G,2
Place de l'Opéra C,4,5
Rumêleh F,2
Rond Point du Bâb el-Louq D,5
— — de Faghalla B,5
— — de l'Hippodrôme . . . C,5
— — du Caracol de Kaṣr en-Nîl. D,6
— — du Mouski C,3
— — de Nasrieh E,5

Streets.

Abbasieh, Route de l' . . . A,B,2,5
Boulaq, Route de C,5,6
Boulevard ʿAbdul ʿAzîz . . C,D,4
— Clot Bey. B,4,5
— Fumm el-Khalîg. G,H,6
— Kaṣr ʿAli E,F,5
— Moḥammed ʿAli C,D,E,3,4
— Shêkh Rîḥân. E,3,6
— Soliman Pasha D,5,6
Derb el-Aḥmar. D,E,2
— El-Gamâmîz. E,F,4
— El-Yahûdi. C,3
Gamelîyeh C,2
Gâmiʿ el-Benât, Sikket . . C,D,3
Ghûrîyeh. C,D,2
Habbanîyeh E,3,4
Ḥawala, Route de D,4
Ḳanṭarat ed-Dikkeh, Sikket B,5
Margûsheh, Sikket B,2,3
Muski C,2,3
Neuve, Rue C,2,3
Rageb Agha, Rue D,E,4
Rugbîyeh. F,G,3
Ṣalîbeh. F,2,3
Shubra Avenue A,5,6
Sérafs, Rue des C,3
Siûfîyeh F,3
Sukkarîyeh. D,2
Tribunal, Rue du C,4

3. Cairo.

Railway Stations (comp. p 11) The station for Alexandria (R. 2), Zaḳâzîḳ, Isma'îlîya, and Suez (R. 5), and for the whole of the Delta, lies beyond the Isma'îlîyeh Canal (Pl. A, 5), 1/2 M. from the end of the Muski The station for Bedrashên (Saḳḳâra), the Fayûm, and the Nile railway as far as Siûṭ (p 371), and also for the branch-line of the Alexandria and Cairo railway (p. 224), diverging at Tell el-Barûd (opened in 1875), is at Bûlâḳ ed-Dakrûr, 1½ M. from the Muski. The station for the line to Ṭura and Ḥelwân (p. 403) is in the Place Méhémet-Ali, below the Citadel (Pl F, G, 2)

The hotel commissionnaires with their omnibuses or carriages await the arrival of each train and take charge of luggage. As it not unfrequently happens that all the hotels are full, it is a wise precaution to telegraph for rooms from Alexandria Carriage with two horses from the station to one of the hotels 2½-3 fr, donkey ½ fr, luggage-donkey ½ fr. (but an attempt to extort more is always made; comp p 12)

Hotels (see remark on p 204). *New Hotel (Pl a; C, 5), in the Ezbekîyeh, a large building with handsome rooms (landlord, *Sign Pantellini*); *Shepheard's Hotel (Pl b; C, 5), also in the Ezbekîyeh (proprietor *Hr. Zech*, manager *Hr Gross*), patronised by English and American travellers. Each of these hotels has a terrace and garden, and the charge at each is 12-16*s*. per day. *Hôtel du Nil (Pl. c; C, 3), in a narrow street off the Muski (p 253), the main artery of traffic; a good house, though uninviting externally, with a pleasant garden (proprietor *Hr Friedmann*), 15-16 fr per day. *Hôtel Royal (Pl d, B, 4, 5), in the Ezbekîyeh, moderate charges; Hôtel d'Orient (Pl. f, C, 4), *Hôtel d'Angleterre (Pl. e; C, 4), both in the Ezbekîyeh, with good cooking, and moderate charges. All these hotels have baths and reading-rooms

Pensions. At the following houses board and lodging may be obtained for 250-500 fr. a month according to the size and position of the rooms, wine included: *Madame Fink* (Pl g, D, 5), in a healthy situation in the Quartier Isma'îlîya (good table); *Hôtel Couteret*, opposite Shepheard's Hotel; *Hôtel d'Angleterre* (see above), *Hôtel de Byzanze* (rooms only), in the Ezkebîyeh

Private Apartments for the winter may also now be procured without much difficulty A slight knowledge of the language, however, is indispensable, as the servants seldom speak foreign languages The cost of living in this way is lower than at a hotel, but it is seldom possible to secure private lodgings for a shorter period than six months A sunny aspect should be chosen, and a detailed written contract drawn up A bargain as to food may be made with some neighbouring restaurant Wine, see p. 235 Information as to rooms may be obtained at the cigar-shop of *Livadas* in the Ezbekîyeh, but it is advisable to submit the contract before signing to an impartial resident.

Restaurants. **Santi*, in the garden of the Ezbekîyeh, déjeuner 3, dinner 3½ fr; *Hôtel d'Angleterre*, *Kovats*, both in the Ezbekîyeh.

Confectioners: *Berti* (an Italian) in the Ezbekîyeh and the Muski; *Schneider*, *Mathieu*, both in the Ezbekîyeh

Cafés in the European style abound (beer ½ fr. per glass) Most of them have a separate room in which roulette is played, and the traveller need hardly be cautioned against joining in the game **De la Bourse* in the Ezbekîyeh; also in the *Ezbekîyeh Garden*, by the music tents (p. 258). Beer is sold by *Bohr*, near the post-office, *Muller*, *Café du Square*, near Shepheard's Hotel; *Mayr*, in the Ezbekîyeh, *Kovats*, near the Café Egyptien (see below). — *Bodega*, with various English beverages, next door to the Café Royal. — The following are *Cafés Chantants*, where Bohemian musicians and singers perform in the evening *Café Egyptien*, opposite Shepheard's Hotel; *Eldorado*, in the Ezbekîyeh.

The *Arabian Cafés* (p 17), of which there are upwards of a thousand at Cairo, each consisting of a single booth with a few cane-bottomed seats, are hardly worth visiting. Small cup of coffee with sugar 30, without sugar 20, 'Stambûli' coffee 40 paras copper. — Outside the European cafés are usually congregated a number of *Shoeblacks* ('Bôyeh' i. e. 'colour' in Turkish), a lively but sometimes too importunate fraternity, who jabber a few words in several of the European languages. Shoe-cleaning 10 paras in silver. The negroes always seem specially anxious to have their boots well polished.

Money Changers, Arabic *Sarrâf* (comp. p. 4), who endeavour to attract customers by rattling their money, are to be found in every street. Although it is very desirable always to be well provided with small change, the traveller is cautioned against dealing with these people until he is thoroughly conversant with all the coins. He should also be on his guard against spurious piastres. The usual exchange for a Napoleon is 154 piastres current, and for a franc 7 piastres and 10 paras.

Bankers (comp. p. 3). *S. Müller*, in the Rosetti Garden; *Bank of Egypt*, Rondpoint du Mouski; *Crédit Lyonnais*, at the Egyptian Post Office; *Banque Ottomane; Banque Anglo-Égyptienne; Suares*. The chief Alexandrian firms (p. 206) also have branch-offices at Cairo. English circular notes and French banknotes always realise the best exchange.

Consulates (comp. p. 6). The consuls general have their chief offices at Alexandria, but most of them reside at Cairo in winter. *American*, Mr. Comanos; secretary, Mr. Walmass. — *British* (Pl. 18), in the Ezbekîyeh; Mr. Borg. — *Austrian* (Pl. 21), in the Ezbekîyeh; consul, Hr. Neumann. — *Belgian*, in the Ezbekîyeh; M. Franquet. — *Danish*, in the Rosetti Garden; Hr. Schulz. — *Dutch*, near the Muski, in the narrow street leading to the Hôtel du Nil; consul, Hr. Fabricius. — *French* (Pl. 19), in the Ezbekîyeh; consul, M. Lequeux; secretary, M. Eymar. — *German* (Pl. 20), in the Quartier Isma'ilîya; consul, Hr. Martens; secretary, Hr. Wilhelm. — *Greek*, in the Place de l'Opéra; consul, M. Rhalli. — *Italian*, in the Place de l'Opéra; consul, Sign. Venanzi. — *Persian*, in the Ezbekîyeh; consul-general, Hadji Mohammed Khân; secretary, Mirza 'Ali Effendi. — *Russian;* vice-consul, M. Grégoire d'Elie. — *Portuguese;* M. Caprara. — *Swedish;* Hr. Borg.

Carriages, generally good, and with two horses, abound at Cairo. The principal stand is to the right of the entrance to the Muski, and there are others in the Ezbekîyeh, near the Hôtel d'Orient, and in the Place 'Abidîn, near the offices of the minister of finance. The new tariff of 1882 is never strictly adhered to. For a short drive the usual fare is 1-$1\frac{1}{2}$ fr.; for $\frac{1}{2}$-1 hr. 2-3 fr.; for a whole day 20 fr., or for the better carriages 25 fr. — The following are the fares for the principal drives and excursions in a carriage and pair: —

Destination	francs	fee	Destination	francs	fee
Rail. Station	$1\frac{3}{4}$	—	Fumm el-Khalîg	3-4	—
— with luggage	$2\frac{1}{2}$	—	Kasr en-Nîl (starting-point of Nile Steamers)	2	—
Rail. Station at Bûlâk ed-Dakrûr	$3\frac{1}{2}$	$\frac{1}{2}$	Kasr el-'Ain	3	—
Citadel	$2\frac{1}{2}$	$\frac{1}{2}$	Old Cairo (Masr el-'Atîka, Island of Rôda)	5	$\frac{1}{2}$
Bûlâk (Museum)	4-5	—	Atar en-Nebi	6	$\frac{1}{2}$
Shubra Garden	6-8	$\frac{1}{2}$	Pyramids of Gîzeh, 2 persons	15-20	$1\frac{1}{2}$-2
Shubra Avenue, as far as Kasr en-Nuzha	5	$\frac{1}{2}$	Pyramids of Gîzeh, 4 persons	20-25	2-$2\frac{1}{2}$
'Abbâsîyeh	5	$\frac{1}{2}$			
Kubbeh	6-8	$\frac{3}{4}$			
Matarîyeh (Heliopolis, Virgin's Tree)	9-10	1			

These fares include the return-journey, except in the case of the railway stations and the Kasr en-Nîl.

When, however, a drive of any length is contemplated, the traveller had better enquire of the landlord or manager of his hotel as to the proper fare. On Sundays and holidays the fares rise considerably, and it is then often difficult to get a good vehicle. The *sáïs*, or boy who runs before the carriage to clear the way in the crowded streets, is a very useful attendant (p 247). His services are included in the carriage-fare, but he expects a small additional fee (2 piastres).

Omnibuses ply from the Place de la Bourse (Pl. C, 4) to the railway stations and to the ministries, the Khân el-Khalîli, and the Shubra-Allée. Fares, 1st class 1 piastre tariff, 2nd class 20 paras 'Correspondences' at half fares.

Donkeys (comp p 11) afford the best and most rapid mode of locomotion in the narrow and crowded streets of Cairo, and they are to be met with, day and night, in every part of the town The attendants often thrust them unceremoniously on the traveller's notice by placing them directly in his path These animals are to be found in great numbers at all the most frequented points, and if one is wanted in the middle of the night the word 'ḥammâr' (p 11) shouted out immediately attracts a large assortment of them. The donkey-boys of Cairo have all the *savoir vivre* of denizens of a large city, and they often possess a considerable fund of humour, which they show most readily when well paid They delight in excursions into the country (to Saḳḳâra, for instance), which afford them a 'fantasîya', or special treat, and the European will be astonished at the smallness of their requirements and those of their beasts. The donkeys are particularly serviceable in the narrow streets of the Arabian quarter, which afford shade and coolness, but are not accessible to carriages. For a short ride in the town the usual charge is 1-2 piastres tariff (25-50 c); for 1 hr, 1 fr; for a forenoon in the town, $2^1/_2$ fr., for excursions 4-6 fr per day (ladies' saddle 1 fr. extra), and a bakshîsh of $^1/_2$-$^3/_4$ fr. to the boy, unless he has been uncivil. When a donkey is hired to carry baggage, its attendant should be required to follow the same route as the travellers themselves, and always to remain in sight Persons making a prolonged stay, as soon as they have found a good donkey with proper gear and a satisfactory attendant, had better secure its future services by the payment of an extra bakshîsh Care should be taken to choose a donkey with sound fore-legs

Commissionnaires (comp p. 13). The traveller who is pressed for time, and wishes to see as much as possible, cannot well dispense with a cicerone The best guides (5-8 fr per day) are to be had at the hotels They often try to induce their employers to engage them for distant tours, such as that to Mt Sinai, or the voyage up the Nile, but for such expeditions they are totally unfitted. As a rule, purchases should never be made in their presence. If, however, the traveller knows a few words of Arabic, and is not in a hurry, he will soon find his way through every part of the city and the environs with the aid of his donkey-boy alone.

Dragomans (comp. pp 13, 205). Information as to trustworthy dragomans may be obtained at the traveller's consulate, at the hotels, at *Kauffmann's*, the bookseller, or at *Zigada's*, in the Muski The following may be recommended *Michael Shaija*, a Syrian Christian; *Muḥammed Sâlim; Shall.*

Post Office (Pl. 87; C, 4), on the E side of the Ezbekîyeh, open daily from 7 a m to 6 p m, and also for a short time after the arrival of the last mail train, or for a longer time when the British, Indian, and other important mails come in. Letter-boxes at most of the hotels, at Berti's (the confectioner), at the railway-stations, and in various other places.

Telegraph Offices. *Egyptian* (Pl 97a, C, 5), in the Quartier Isma'îliya; *British* (Pl 97; C, 5), next door to the New Hotel The Egyptian telegraph only can be used for messages within Egypt. Telegrams for Upper Egypt must be in Arabic. Comp p. 28

Theatres. *Italian Opera* (Pl. 75; C, 4). The winter season depends, however, entirely on the subsidy of the Khedive, which is not always granted. — *Summer Theatre* in the Ezbekîyeh Garden, see p. 258.

Physicians. *Dr. Grant-Bey*, English, *Dr Hess; Dr. Wildt; Dr. Becker; Dr. Comanos*, a Greek. who has studied in Germany — Oculists *Dr. Tachau. Dr. Brugsch* — Dentists *Mr. Broadway* and *Mr Waller*, both English. — The addresses may be obtained at the hotels.

Chemists. *Sommer* (a German), in the Ezbekîyeh and the Muski (English and homœopathic prescriptions made up); *Ducrot* (a Frenchman), also in the Ezbekîyeh; *Nardi*, in the Muski, *Swiss Pharmacy* of Dr Hess, in the Ezbekîyeh, *Pharmacie Centrale (Perrot)*, Boulevard Clot-Bey.

Churches. *English Church* (Pl 8; C, 5), Route de Boulaq, in the Isma'ilîya quarter. — *American Service* in the American Mission (Pl. 1; C, 5), near Shepheard's Hotel — *Protestant Church* (Pl. 10), in the Isma'ilîya quarter; German service in the morning, French in the afternoon. — *Roman Catholic Church* (Pl 13; C, 3), in a street off the Muski, opposite the street in which the Hôtel du Nil is situated *Convento Grande di Terra Santa*, with 18 chaplains of different nationalities. *Jesuit Church*, in the Rosetti Garden *Franciscan Church*, near the Boul Clot Bey *Church of the Mission of Central Africa*, under Mgr Sogaro — *Orthodox Greek Church* (Pl. 11; C, 3), in the Hamzâwi (p 253) — *Coptic Catholic Church* (Pl. 6; C 3, E 4), at the back of the Roman Catholic Church, *Coptic Jacobite Church* (Pl 7; B, 4, 5), in a side street between the Boulevard Clot Bey and the Ezbekîyeh These two sects have, in all, 32 churches at Cairo — The *Jews* here are of two sects, the Talmudists and the Karaites, the former being by far the more numerous. They possess 13 synagogues, most of which are situated in the Jewish quarter (Derb el-Yahûdi) The religious affairs of both sects are presided over by a chief rabbi

Schools. The new *School of the American Mission* (Pl 1), conducted by *Messrs Lansing* and *Watson*, whose sphere of operations is chiefly among the Copts, adjoins the English Consulate in the Ezbekîyeh. — The *Anglican Mission School* is presided over by Miss Whateley. — The *German School*, managed by the *Rev Hr Graeber*, is largely patronised by all nationalities and sects — Besides these, there is a *European Girls' School (Mme Castel* and *Fraul. Im Hof)*, an *École Gratuite*, an *École des Soeurs du Sacré Cœur*, a *Pensionnat des Soeurs du Bon Pasteur*, a *Collège de la Ste Famille* (school of the Jesuits), and an *École de Frères*. — Permission to visit the Egyptian schools may be obtained at the office of the general inspector, in the Derb el-Gamâmîz (p. 269).

Hospitals. The large *Kasr el-'Ain* (Pl 28; G, 6), a hospital with a school of medicine, lies on the Nile, on the route to Old Cairo (p. 373). — The *European Hospital* (physician, *Dr Martini*), in the 'Abbâsîyeh, is admirably fitted up, and under the supervision of the consuls The patients are attended by sisters of mercy The charges are 6-12 fr per day, according to the accommodation, and poor patients are also admitted at lower rates — The large German *Deaconnesses' Institute* (Pl. 22; C, 6), in the new Isma'ilîya quarter, opened in 1884, is intended mainly for sick strangers in Cairo — The new *Austrian Hospital* is also in the 'Abbâsîyeh.

Teachers of Arabic. *Ibrâhîm Effendi Zên-eddîn* (address ascertained from the porter of the Hôtel du Nil); *Serkis*. a Syrian.

Clubs. The *Geographical Society* (Pl. 26; C, 1), founded by *Dr. Schweinfurth* the celebrated African traveller, possesses an extensive library and a reading-room, which are open to visitors at certain hours — The *Club Khédivial* (Pl 17, C, 5), in the Ezbekîyeh, is fitted up in the English style, and is patronised by some of the higher government officials among other members Strangers are not admitted without difficulty.

Exchange, with reading-room and café, in the New Hotel

Baths (comp p 21) *European Baths* at the hotels, and in the Rosetti Garden (*Bagni Tosi*, kept by a native of Trieste). The best of the numerous *Arabian Baths* are those near the Bâb esh-Sha'rîyeh (Pl. B, 3), one at Bûlâk, and the *Mandolfo Baths* in the 'Abbâsîyeh (also with a European bath)

Booksellers. *Kauffmann*, in the Muski, an old-established firm. *Penasson*, *Barbier*, both in the Ezbekîyeh Photographs (see below) are also sold at *Kauffmann's* — Writing and drawing materials are sold by *Kauffmann*, *Penasson* and *Zollikofer*, the last in the Muski. Visiting cards may be ordered at *Zollikofer's* and at *Boehm-Anderer's*, in the Ezbekîyeh.

Photographs. *Schoefft*, 'Abbâsîyeh Street (Place Faghalla), with a good background for groups, also a fine collection of *groups of natives, and a few desert scenes some of which are very striking (various prices;

a collection of 25, of small size, is sold for 25 fr.). *Stromeyer & Heymann*, in the Kantaret ed Dikke (Pl. B, 5), with a charming garden and well-equipped studio. *Laroche & Co.*, in the Ezbekîyeh Garden. Among the numerous photographs of Egyptian landscapes and temples the best are those by **Sebah* of Constantinople, which may be purchased at his depôt, adjoining the French consulate in the Ezbekîyeh, or at Kauffmann's. *Hr. E. Brugsch*, the keeper of the Bûlâk Museum (p. 295), has caused a number of the objects in the museum to be photographed. This collection, which costs 25 fr. (small size 15 fr.), may be purchased at the museum, or at Kauffmann's, but is not sold by the photographers.

European Wares. All the ordinary wants of the traveller may now be supplied at Cairo. Clothing and many other articles, chiefly for the use of travellers, are sold by *Paschal & Co.*, *P. Cicolani*, *Mayer & Co.*, *Stein*, *Camoin*, the *Magasin au Soleil*, and the *Cordonnerie Française*, all in the Ezbekîyeh, and at the *Bazar Universel*, opposite the post-office (p. 232). Ladies' requirements are sold by *Cécile*, *Camille*, and others in the Ezbekîyeh. Good watchmakers and goldsmiths are *Bongerber*, beyond the rondeau of the Muski, and *Buchsbaum*, in the Muski. Optical instruments and rifles may also be obtained at the last-named, ammunition at *Cassegrain's* und *Bajocchi's*, both in the Ezbekîyeh.

Goods Agents. Those who make purchases in Egypt to any considerable extent are recommended to send them home through the medium of a goods-agent, in order to avoid custom-house examinations, porterage, and various other items of expense and annoyance. The post-office forwards parcels not exceeding 7 lbs. in weight. For larger packages the following agents may be employed: *Cesare Luzzatto*, in the same street as the Hôtel du Nil; *Dombre & Levi*, in the Muski; *Dagregorio*, in the Ezbekîyeh. The charges are comparatively moderate.

Hairdressers abound in and around the Ezbekîyeh. Their charges are usually exorbitant, 1½-2½ fr. being charged for hair-cutting, and 1 fr. for shaving. Most of the *Arabian Barbers* have their shops open to the street. Their principal occupation consists in shaving the heads of their customers in Oriental fashion, an art in which they are very expert. When the operation is over, they hold a looking-glass before the customer, saying — '*na'îman*', (may it be pleasant to you), to which the usual reply is — '*Allâh yin'im 'alêk*' (God make it pleasant to thee).

Wine, Preserves, etc., are sold by *Niccolo Zigada*, *Monferrato*, and *Dracatos*, all near Shepheard's Hotel; by *N. A. Ablitt*, in the Muski; and by *Class & Co. (Fleurent Bodega)* and *Walker & Co.*, in the Ezbekîyeh.

Tobacco (comp. p. 27). Syrian tobacco (Korâni and Gebeli) is sold at a shop in the Gâmi' el-Benât street (p. 272), near the Muski, but had better be purchased in small quantities only. Turkish tobacco (Stambûli) and cigarettes are sold by *Nestor Gianaclis*, in the Muski, by *Voltera Frères*, in the same building as the post-office, and by *Cortessi*, in the Ezbekîyeh, next door to the Café de la Bourse. The last also keeps a stock of good cigars, generally of Dutch or German manufacture. Good cigars cost 10 fr. per hundred and good tobacco 40 fr. per okka (p. 28).

Arabian Bazaars, see pp. 23, 251. Near the end of the Muski is a shop kept by a Nubian, who sells various *Egyptian* and *Nubian* articles, suitable for presents. Thus an ostrich-egg costs 3 fr. and upwards, a specimen of the fakâka, or ball-fish (p. 84) 3-5 fr., a Nubian lance 1 fr., bow with six arrows 12-15 fr., small fiddle 12 fr., square fiddle 20 fr., leopard skin 15-30 fr. (the skins, however, are insufficiently tanned, and almost entirely stripped of their hair). Unless the proprietor of this shop happens to be in want of money, it is difficult to obtain anything from him at a reasonable price, and he sometimes closes his shop entirely. — Sticks and whips of *Hippopotamus Skin* are sold by a Pole (who speaks a little Italian) near the Roman Catholic church.

Arabian Woodwork is sold by **Parvis*, an Italian, on the left side of a court near the entrance to the Muski. Strangers should not fail to visit his interesting workshop, which they may do without making any purchase. Similar objects may be obtained at a more moderate rate from *Venisio*, opposite Shepheard's Hotel, and *Bertini*, adjoining the Hôtel du Nil, but their workmanship is scarcely so artistic as that of Parvis.

The dates of the **Religious Festivals of the Mohammedans**, of which Cairo is the principal scene, cannot easily be given according to the European computation of time, owing to the variable character of the Arabian lunar year. Calendars reducing the Mohammedan and Coptic reckoning of time to the European system may, however, be obtained at any bookseller's.

The first month of the Arabian year is the *Moharrem*, the first ten days of which (*ʿashr*), and particularly the 10th (*yôm ʿashûra*), are considered holy. On these days alms are distributed, and amulets purchased. Mothers, even of the upper classes, carry their children on their shoulders, or cause them to be carried, through the streets, and sew into the children's caps the copper-coins presented to them by passers-by. On the 10th Moharrem, the highly revered *ʿAshûra* day, on which Adam and Eve are said first to have met after their expulsion from Paradise, on which Noah is said to have left the ark, and on which Ḥusên, the grandson of the prophet, fell as a martyr to his religion at the battle of Kerbela, the Gâmiʿ Ḥasanên (p. 292) is visited by a vast concourse of religious devotees, whose riotous proceedings had better not be inspected except from a carriage, especially if ladies are of the party. Troops of Persians in long white robes parade the streets, cutting themselves with swords in the forehead until the blood streams down and stains their snowy garments. Two boys, representing Ḥasan and Ḥusên, are also led through the streets on horseback, with blood-stained clothes. Strangers may also obtain admission to the Persian mosque, in which the orgies are continued, by special introduction. Towards evening a great zikr of whirling dervishes takes place here (p. 239).

At the end of *Safar*, the second month, or at the beginning of *Rabîʿ el-awwel*, the third, the MECCA CARAVAN (p. 148) returns home, its approach being announced by outriders. Some of the faithful who go to meet the procession proceed as far as three days' journey, but most of them await its arrival at the *Birket el-Ḥagg* (p. 335), or pilgrims' lake. Detached groups of pilgrims occasionally return before the rest of the cavalcade, and their arrival is always signalised by the blowing of trumpets and beating of drums. A pyramidal wooden erection, called the *Maḥmal* hung with beautifully embroidered stuffs, and carried by a camel, accompanies the procession as a symbol of royalty. The interior of the Maḥmal is empty, and to the outside of it are attached two copies of the Korân. The procession usually enters the city by the *Bâb en-Naṣr* (p. 280). In 1½-2 hrs. it reaches the Rumêleh (p. 262), the large open space in front of the citadel, from which last twelve cannon-shots are fired as a salute. The cortége then sweeps round the Rumêleh, and finally enters the citadel by the Bâb el-Wezîr (Pl. E, 2). The departure of the pilgrims (p. 238) is attended with similar ceremonies.

The great festival of the Môlid en-Nebi, the birthday of the prophet, is celebrated at the beginning of *Rabî' el-awwel*, the third month The preparations for it begin on the second day of the month, and the most important ceremonies take place on the evening of the eleventh The city, and particularly the scene of the festival, is then illuminated by means of lamps hung on wooden stands made for the purpose Processions of dervishes (p 150) parade the streets with flags by day, and with lamps hoisted on poles by night. On this evening the sellers of sweetmeats frequently exclaim — 'A grain of salt for the eye of him who will not bless the prophet!' The *Dôseh*, or ceremony of riding over the dervishes, also took place on the eleventh of this month Some fifty dervishes or more lay close together on the ground, and allowed the shêkh of the Sa'dîyeh dervishes on horseback to ride over them Accidents rarely happened, although the horse trod on every one of the prostrate figures. During this ceremony the spectators shouted incessantly, 'Allâh-lá-lá-lá-láh-láh!' This barbarous custom was forbidden by the Khedive Tewfik, and the ceremonies are confined to the procession of the shêkh and the reading of the Korân in the Khedive's tent. At night a great zikr is performed by the dervishes (p 239). On this festival, as on all the other 'môlids', the jugglers, buffoons, and other ministers of amusement, ply their calling with great success (comp p 150)

In the fourth month, that of *Rabî' el-Akhir (et-tâni)*, occurs the peculiarly solemn festival of the birthday or *Môlid of Husên*, the prophet's grandson, the principal scene of which is the mosque of Hasanên, where the head of Husên is said to be interred This festival lasts fifteen days and fourteen nights, the most important day being always a Tuesday (*yôm et-telât*). On this occasion the *'Ilwânîyeh Dervishes* (p 150) sometimes go through their hideous performance of chewing and swallowing burning charcoal and broken glass, and their wild dances On the chief days of this festival, and on their eves, great crowds congregate in and around the mosque, and especially by the tomb of Sultân es-Sâleh in the bazaar of the Nahhâsîn (p. 256) On these occasions the Korân is read aloud to the people, the streets adjoining the mosque are illuminated, the shops are kept open, and story-tellers jugglers, and others of the same class attract numerous patrons.

In the middle of *Regeb*, the seventh month, is the *Môlid of Seiyideh Zênab* ('Our Lady Zênab'), the grand-daughter of the prophet The festival, which lasts fourteen days, the most important being a Tuesday, is celebrated at the mosque of the Seiyideh Zênab (p 268), where she is said to be buried

On the 27th of this month is the *Lêlet el-Mi'râg*, or night of the ascension of the prophet the celebration of which takes place outside the Bâb el-'Adawi, in the N suburb of Cairo

On the first, or sometimes on the second, Wednesday of *Sha'bân*, the eighth month, the *Môlid of Imâm Shâfe'i* is commemorated, the centre of attraction being the burial-place of El-Karâfeh (p. 327) This festival is numerously attended, as most of the Cairenes belong to the sect of Imâm Shâfe'i (p 149) The ceremonies are the same as those at the other môlids

The month of *Ramadân* (p 148), the ninth, is the month of fasting, which begins as soon as a Muslim declares that he has seen the new moon. The fast is strictly observed during the day but the faithful indemnify themselves by eating, drinking, and smoking throughout the greater part of the night At dusk the streets begin to be thronged, the story-tellers at the cafés attract large audiences, and many devotees assemble at the mosques. The eve of the 27th of the month is considered peculiarly holy. It is called the *Lêlet el-Kadr*, or 'night of value', owing to the tradition that the Korân was sent down to Mohammed on this night. During this sacred night the angels descend to mortals with blessings, and the portals of heaven stand open, affording certain admission to the prayers of the devout On this night the traveller should visit the Hasanên mosque, or, especially if accompanied by ladies, that of Mohammed 'Ali (p. 263) in the citadel, in order to see the great zikrs of the whirling and howling dervishes, of whom some thirty or forty take part in the performances. The scene is of an exciting, but somewhat painful character, particularly if any of the performers become '*melbûs*', a condition resembling that of epileptic convulsion (p. 152)

The month Ramadân is succeeded by that of *Shawwâl*, on the first three days of which is celebrated the first and minor festival of rejoicing, called by the Arabs *El-'Id es-Sughayyir* (the lesser feast), but better known by its Turkish name of *Beirâm* The object of the festival is to give expression to the general rejoicing at the termination of the fast; and, as at our Christmas, parents give presents to their children, and masters to their servants at this festive season. Friends embrace each other on meeting, and visits of ceremony are exchanged. During this festival the Khedive also receives his principal officials, ambassadors, and other dignitaries

At this season the traveller may also pay a visit to the cemetery by the Bâb en-Nasr or to one of the others where numerous Cairenes assemble to place palm branches or basilicum (*rihân*) on the graves of their deceased relatives, and to distribute dates, bread, and other gifts among the poor.

A few days after the Beirâm, the pieces of the *Kisweh*, or covering manufactured at Constantinople, at the cost of the Sultan, for the Ka'ba (the most sacred sanctuary in the interior of the temple at Mecca), whither it is annually carried by the pilgrims, are conveyed in procession to the citadel, where they are sewn together and lined. The ceremonies which take place on this occasion are repeated on a grander scale towards the end of the month of *Shawwâl* (generally the 23rd), when there is a gay procession of the escort which accompanies the pilgrimage caravan to Mecca, and which takes charge of the Mahmal (p. 236). On this occasion every true believer in the prophet, if he possibly can, spends the whole day in the streets. The women don their smartest attire. Many of the harem windows are opened, and the veiled inmates gaze into the streets The chief scene of the ceremonies is the Rumêleh (Pl F, 2), at the foot of the citadel, where a sumptuous tent of red velvet and gold is pitched for the reception of the dignitaries. The procession is headed with soldiers, who are followed by camels adorned with gaily coloured trappings, and bearing on their humps bunches of palm-branches with oranges attached. Each section of the cavalcade is preceded by an Arabian band of music, the largest section being that which accompanies the *Takht Rawân*, or litter of the Emîr el-Hagg, and the next in order that of the *Delil el-Hagg*, or leader of the pilgrims, with his attendants. Next follow various detachments of pilgrims and dervishes with banners, and lastly the Mahmal (see above) A picturesque appearance is presented by the camp of the assembled pilgrims (Haggi) at the Birket el-Hagg (p. 335), whence the caravan finally starts for Mecca

On the 10th of *Dhul-higgeh*, the twelfth month, begins the great festival of *El-'Id el-Kebir*, which resembles the lesser feast (el-'id es-sughayyir) already mentioned. On this day, if on no other throughout the year, every faithful Muslim eats a piece of meat in memory of the sacrifice of Abraham, and the poor are presented with meat for this purpose by the rich

The Muslims also celebrate the Christian *Easter Week*, although in a different manner, and of course for different reasons from the Christians. On Palm Sunday (*had el-khus*) the women bind palm twigs round their heads and fingers On the following day (*Monday*) it is customary to eat *fakûs* (cucumbers) with cummin On the *Tuesday* the diet of the faithful consists of a kind of cheese-broth with onions, and the day is therefore called *yôm el-mish wa'l-basal* ('cheese-soup-and-onion-day') *Wednesday* is called *arba' Eyûb*, or 'Job's Wednesday'. On this day the *ghubera* herb is said to have addressed to Job the words — 'Wash thyself with my juice, and thou shalt recover' He did so, and recovered, and to this day the whole of the Egyptian Muslims wash themselves with *gharghara Eyûb* in memory of the miracle *Maundy Thursday* is the Pea-Thursday of the Muslims (*khamîs el-bisilla*). *Good Friday* is called *gum'a el-mafrûka*, or 'day of the butter-cakes'. *Saturday* is the *sebt en-nûr* or 'sabbath of light' (so named from the sacred fire which on this day bursts forth from the Holy Sepulchre at Jerusalem) On this day it is customary for the Muslims to use a kind of eye-powder for the purpose of strengthening their eyes, to get themselves bled, and to eat coloured Easter eggs On *Easter Sunday* (*'îd en-nusâra*) the Mohammedans usually visit their Christian friends, and these visits are returned during the feast of Beirâm

With the RISING OF THE NILE there are also connected several interesting festivals, closely resembling those of the ancient period of the Pharaohs, which even the Christian epoch was unable entirely to obliterate. As, however, they take place in summer, few travellers will have an opportunity of witnessing them As these festivals have reference to a regularly recurring phenomenon of nature, their dates are necessarily fixed in accordance with the Coptic solar reckoning of time, instead of the variable Arabian lunar year. — The night of the 11th of the Coptic month Ba'ûna (17th June) is called *Lêlet en-Nuḳta*, i e. the 'night of the drop', as it is believed that a drop from heaven (or a tear of Isis, according to the ancient Egyptian myth) falls into the Nile on this night and causes its rise The astrologers profess to calculate precisely the hour of the fall of the sacred drop The Caireues spend this night on the banks of the Nile, either in the open air, or in the houses of friends near the river, and practise all kinds of superstitious customs One of these consists in the placing of a piece of dough by each member of a family on the roof of the house; if the dough rises, happiness is in store for the person who placed it there, while its failure to rise is regarded as a bad omen On 21st June the river begins slowly to rise (comp. p. 57). On the 27th of the Coptic month Ba'ûna (3rd July) the *Munâdi en-Nîl*, or Nile-crier, is frequently heard in the morning, announcing to the citizens the number of inches that the river has risen. The munâdi is accompanied by a boy, with whom he enters on a long religious dialogue by way of preface to his statements, which, however, are generally inaccurate The next important event is the *Cutting of the Dam* (*yôm gebr el-bahr*, or *yôm wefa el-bahr*), which takes place between the 1st and the 14th of the Coptic month of Misra (i e. between 6th and 19th August), when the principal ceremonies are performed on and near the island of Rôda (p 318). The Nile-crier, attended by boys carrying flags, announces the *Wefa en-Nîl* (the plenitude. or superfluity of the Nile), or period when the water has reached its normal height of sixteen ells (p 58) The cutting through of the dam takes place amid general rejoicings and noisy festivities. It appears from inscriptions on columns found on the Nile near the Gebel Selseleh, that similar festivals connected with the rise of the river were celebrated as early as the 14th cent before Christ

Dervishes (comp p 150). The 'Dancing Dervishes' perform their 'zikr' in the Tekîyet el-Maulawîyeh (p 265) every Friday from 2 to 3 p m ; visitors walk in and take their seats outside the space enclosed by boards, no permission being necessary (bakshîsh of 1-2 piastres on leaving) A visit may be paid in the same way to the performances of the 'Howling Dervishes', whose zikr takes place in the Gâmi' Kasr el-'Ain (p 317), also on Fridays from 2 to 3 p m Both these curious scenes may be witnessed on the same day if the traveller goes early to one of them, leaves after 25 min., and then visits the other, thus seeing quite enough of each.

SIGHTS AND DISPOSITION OF TIME.

The duration of the traveller's stay at Cairo depends of course on his own inclination and the objects he has in view. He may wish to devote his attention chiefly to the mosques, or to the street-scenes; he may endeavour to find his way through the intricacies of the city alone, or with the assistance of a donkey-boy, or he may prefer to hire a carriage and a commissionnaire. By carefully preparing a plan beforehand, and starting early every morning, the traveller may succeed in visiting all the chief objects of interest in six days, but it need hardly be said that a satisfactory insight into Oriental life can not be obtained without a stay of several weeks.

Principal attractions when time is limited: — *(a) In the Town.* Street-scenes (p. 244); Ezbekîyeh Garden (p. 258); Citadel (p. 262), either about sunset, or before 11 a.m.; Tombs of the Khalîfs (p. 282) and Mamelukes (p. 327); the mosques of Sulṭân Ḥasan (p. 260), 'Amr (p. 324) at Old Cairo, Ibn Ṭulûn (p. 265), Ḳalaûn (p. 275), Barḳûḳîyeh (p. 278), and El-Azhar (p. 287), the last being shown only by permission obtained through the traveller's consulate; Bâb en-Nasr (p. 280); Museum at Bûlâḳ (p. 295). — *(b) In the Environs* (by carriage). Pyramids of Gîzeh (p. 340); Heliopolis (p. 333); Shubra Avenue (p. 330); Tombs of Apis and the Maṣṭaba of Saḳḳâra (p. 371).

The above outline will serve as a guide to those who are pressed for time; a more leisurely visit may be arranged as follows: —

First Day. *Forenoon* (by carriage, or on donkey-back): *Citadel (p. 262), with *View of Cairo, and visit to the Gâmi' Moḥammed 'Ali; Gâmi' Sulṭân Hasan (p. 260); Gâmi' ibn Tulûn (p. 265); Bâb ez-Zuwêleh (p. 272); Gâmi' el-Muaiyad (p. 272); street and mosque of El-Ghûri (p. 274). — *Afternoon:* drive on the 'Abbâsîyeh road to Kubbeh, Maṭarîyeh, the Virgin's Tree, and Heliopolis (p. 332).

Second Day. *Forenoon* (on donkey-back): Bazaars (to which a whole day may also be devoted on foot); Muristân Ḳalaûn (p. 275); tomb-mosque of the sultan Mohammed en-Nâṣir ibn Ḳalaûn (p. 277); Gâmi' Barḳuḳîyeh (p. 278); Gâmi' el-Ḥâkim (p. 279); Bâb en-Naṣr (p. 280); Tombs of the Khalîfs (p. 282). — *Afternoon* (by carriage). Nile Bridge (p. 328; closed from 1 to 3 p.m.); garden and palace of Gezîreh (p. 329; admission by tickets procured at the traveller's consulate).

Third Day. *Forenoon:* Museum of Bûlâḳ (p. 295). — *Afternoon* (on donkey-back, starting early in winter): Moses' Spring and the smaller Petrified Forest (p. 337), returning by the Moḳaṭṭam (view of Cairo by sunset), and past the Citadel (p. 336).

Fourth Day. *Forenoon:* Mosques of El-Azhar (p. 287) and Ḥasanên (p. 292), most conveniently visited in succession, as both are shown by special permission only, and with the escort of a ḳawwâs. The same remark applies to the Gâmi' Seiyideh Zênab (p. 268), a visit to which, however, had perhaps better be omitted, as its situation is somewhat remote. The mosque of El-Azhar should not be visited on a Friday, as there is no teaching on that day, and the traveller would thus miss one of the chief attractions. — *Afternoon* (by carriage): Old Cairo (p. 317) and the island of Rôda (p. 318); Babylon with the early Christian churches (p. 320); the Gâmi' 'Amr (p. 324); also, if time permit, the Imâm Shâfe'i, Hôsh el-Basha (p. 327), and the Tombs of the Mamelukes, after which we return by the quarter of the Ṭulunides (p. 265).

Fifth Day (by carriage): Pyramids of Gîzeh (p. 340; which may be seen in the course of a forenoon, if necessary); visit Shubra, if time remains, in the afternoon, with Cicolani's Gardens in the Shubra Avenue.

Sixth Day (by railway and on donkey-back): Memphis and Saḳḳâra (p. 371).

Seventh Day (by railway). Baths of Ḥelwân (p. 403), and (on donkey-back) quarries of Ṭura and Maʿṣara (p. 405).

Eighth Day (by railway): Barrage du Nil (p. 406).

The above itinerary will on the whole be found the most convenient, although some riders will perhaps consider several of the days somewhat too fatiguing.

The following places deserve repeated visits: — the Museum at Bûlâḳ; the Citadel, or the windmill-hill at the E. end of the Rue Neuve (prolongation of the Muski), for the sake of the view of the Tombs of the Khalifs and the hills of Moḳaṭṭam; the Tombs of the Khalifs; the Ezbekîyeh Garden; the Shubra Avenue, on a Friday; the Bazaars (and street-traffic), on a Thursday.

Special permission is necessary for the following places: —

(a) From the Waḳf Office (p. 259), through the consulate, for all the mosques, including the Tombs of the Khalîfs and the Mamelukes (pp. 282, 327). Fridays and festivals are unsuitable days for a visit to the mosques. The ḳawwâs of the consulate who escorts the visitors usually receives a fee of 5 fr.

(b) From the minister of war, through the consulate, for the Gâmiʿ Ṣalaḥeddîn Yûsuf (p. 264), the Gâmiʿ Sulêmân Pasha (p. 264), and the fortifications at the Barrage du Nil (p. 406).

(c) From the master of the ceremonies, through the consulate, for the gardens and château of Gezîreh (p. 328).

(d) An introduction from the consulate is also requisite in order to procure admission to the house of the Shêkh es-Sadad, the representative of the descendants of Mohammed.

History of Cairo. When Egypt was conquered by Cambyses (B C 525) the Babylonians are said to have founded New Babylon on the site now occupied by Old Cairo, and during the Roman period that city became the headquarters of one of the three legions stationed in Egypt. Remains of the Roman *castrum* are still preserved here In A D. 638 New Babylon was captured by *ʿAmr ibn el-ʿAsi*, the general of Khalîf ʿOmar; and when he started on his victorious progress towards Alexandria, he commanded the tent (fosṭâṭ) he had occupied during the siege to be taken down. As it was discovered, however, that a pigeon had built her nest upon it, ʿAmr ordered the tent to be left standing until the young birds should take wing After the capture of Alexandria, ʿAmr requested the Khalif to allow him to take up his residence there, but ʿOmar refused to accord permission, as Alexandria appeared to him to be rife with elements of discord, and, moreover, too far distant from the centre of the conquered country to be suitable for its capital. ʿAmr accordingly returned to his tent, around which his adherents encamped. A new city thus gradually sprang up, and the name of Fostât continued to be applied to it in memory of its origin. ʿAmr afterwards erected a mosque (p 324), and he is also said to have begun the construction of the canal *(Khalig)*, which, leaving the Nile opposite the island of Rôda, intersects the town, and is supposed to have been intended to connect the Nile with the Red Sea The city was considerably extended in the reign of the splendour-loving *Ahmed ibn Ṭulûn*, the founder of the dynasty of the Tulunides, who erected the new quarter of *El-Khatîya*, to the S W. of the present citadel Among the buildings ascribed to him is the mosque (p 265) which still bears his name. The town of Fostât was favoured by his successors also, and particularly by his son *Khamarûyeh*, who erected a palace here; and at length, under the Fâtimite Khalîfs (p 102), the modern city of Cairo was built adjacent to the old The new city was founded by *Jôhar*, the general of the Fâtimite Khalîf *Mu'izz*, to the N. of El-Khatîya, as a residence for the khalîf, and as barracks for the soldiers commanded by him. At the hour when the foundation of the walls was laid, the planet Mars, which the Arabs call Kâhir, or 'the victorious', crossed the meridian of the new city; and Mu'izz accordingly named the place *Maṣr el-Kâhira*, or *Kâhira*. Masr, the name of Egypt or of its capital, seems also already to have been applied to Fostât, which, to distinguish it from Maṣr el-Kâhira, was now called *Maṣr el-'Atîka* (the present Old Cairo) The new town extended rapidly. Bricks were easily made of the Nile mud, the Mokattam hills afforded excellent stone, while the gigantic ruins of the ancient Memphis on the opposite bank of the river were also used as a quarry, as the foundations of the houses still show In 973 the new city of Cairo was constituted the capital of Egypt, and for many centuries after that period the destinies of the country were determined here. In 1166 the citadel which still commands the city was erected by Ṣalâheddîn (Saladin) on the slope of the Mokattam hills, and the same sultan caused the whole town, together with the citadel itself, to be enclosed by a wall, 29,000 ells in length Under his luxurious and extravagant successors Cairo was greatly extended and magnificently embellished According to the Arabian historians, the most enterprising of these sultans was Mohammed en-Nâṣir (d 1341), who constructed numerous handsome edifices both within and without the citadel, as well as canals and roads, thus converting the ruins and sand-hills in the environs into beautiful suburbs, with palaces and pleasure-grounds At that period, however, Cairo was fearfully devastated by the plague, as it had been on two former occasions (in 1067 and 1295), and was also several times subsequently, and, according to Makrîzi, no fewer than 900,000(?) persons died in Old and New Cairo between November, 1348, and January, 1349. The town suffered severely in other ways also, and indeed its whole history, so far as recorded, like that of the sultans and the Mamelukes themselves, seems to have presented an almost continuous succession of revolutions, rapine, and bloodshed As most of the Mameluke sultans who resided in the citadel died a violent death, so the reign of almost every new potentate began with bitter and sanguinary contests among the emirs for the office of vizier, while but few reigns were undisturbed by insurrections in the capital During the third régime of Mohammed en-Nasîr, who had been twice deposed, and as often recovered his throne, a persecution of the Christians took place at Cairo The Christians, of whom great numbers resided in Cairo and throughout the whole of Egypt, were accused by the people of incendiarism. Their churches were accordingly closed or demolished, while they themselves were so ill-treated and oppressed, especially in the reign of Sultân Ṣâleh (1351-54), that many of them are said to have embraced Islamism In 1366 and 1367, in the reign of Sultân *Sha'ban*, sanguinary conflicts took place in the streets of Cairo between hostile parties of Mamelukes and in 1377 Sha'bân himself was tortured and strangled in the citadel Even greater disorders attended the dethronement of Sultân *Barkûk* (1389), when the wildest anarchy prevailed at Cairo, the convicts escaped from their prisons, and in concert with the populace plundered the houses of the emirs and the public magazines The following year a rebellion again broke out among the Mamelukes, who stormed the citadel, in consequence of which Barkûk regained possession of the throne, and celebrated his triumphal entry into Cairo Scarcely, however, had he closed his eyes and been succeeded by *Farag*, when the Mamelukes again revolted, and renewed conflicts took place for possession of the citadel, during which the city was partly plundered. Similar scenes were repeated on almost every change of government. The turbulence of the Mamelukes, who were always treated with too much consideration by the sultans, now became more and more unbearable, they robbed the people in the markets, assaulted citizens in the public streets, and grossly insulted respectable women. Hitherto the outrages committed by these troops had been chiefly connected with some political object, but from the middle of the 15th century downwards they were generally perpetrated with a view to plunder Thus in 1458, when fires repeatedly broke out at Cairo and Bûlâk, it was generally believed that the Mamelukes had caused them in order to obtain opportunities for robbery. In the course of the following year they forcibly entered the mosque of 'Amr at Old Cairo on a Friday, and robbed the numerous women who were then attending divine service In the sultanate of Khoshkâdem (1461-67) the Mamelukes plundered the bazaars of Old Cairo, and in the reign of Mohammed (1496-98), son of Kait-Bey, they roved through the streets at night, maltreated the police, and plundered various quarters of the city. In 1496, when rival emîrs were almost daily fighting in the streets of Cairo, the Mamelukes of course utilised the opportunity for plunder.

On 26th Jan. 1517, the Osman Sultân *Selîm I.*, after having gained a victory in the neighbourhood of Cairo, entered the city Tûmân Bey, the last Mameluke sultan, again gained possession of the ill-guarded town on 28th Jan, but was obliged to evacuate it on the following day, and was taken prisoner and executed (p. 272). Before Selîm returned to Constantinople, he caused the finest marble columns which adorned the palace in the citadel to be removed to his own capital. Thenceforward Cairo became a mere provincial capital, and its history is almost an entire blank down to the period of the French expedition On 22nd July, 1798, after the Battle of the Pyramids, Cairo was occupied by *Bonaparte*, who established his headquarters here for several months, and who quelled with sanguinary severity an insurrection which broke out among the populace on 23rd-25th September At the beginning of the year 1799 Bonaparte started from Cairo on his Syrian expedition, and on his return to France, Kléber was left as commander-in-chief of the French troops at Cairo, where he was assassinated on 14th June, 1800. In 1801 the French garrison under Belliard, being hard pressed by the grand vizier, was compelled to capitulate. On 3rd August, 1805, *Mohammed 'Ali*, as the recognised pasha of Egypt, took possession of the citadel, which for the last time witnessed a bloody scene on 1st March, 1811, when the Mameluke Beys were massacred by Mohammed's order Since then nothing has interrupted the peaceful development of the city.

Cairo, *Kahira*, or *Masr el-Kahira* ('Masr the victorious', Masr being the ancient Semitic name for Egypt; p. 30), or symply *Masr* or *Misr*, is situated in 30° 6′ N. latitude, and 31° 26′ E. longitude, on the right bank of the Nile, about 9 M. to the S. of the so-called 'cow's belly', the point where the stream divides into the Rosetta and Damietta arms, and has not inaptly been styled 'the diamond stud on the handle of the fan of the Delta'. On the E. side of the city, which covers an area of about 11 square miles, rise the barren, reddish cliffs of the Mokattam Hills (p. 335), about 650 ft. in height, which form the commencement of the eastern desert. The city has extended so much towards the west of late years that it now reaches the bank of the river and has entirely absorbed Bûlâk (p. 293), which was formerly its harbour.

Cairo is the largest city in Africa, as well as in the Arabian regions, and is the second city in the Turkish empire. It is the residence of the Khedive, and of the ministers and principal authorities, and is presided over by a governor of its own. Owing to the secluded habits of the Mohammedan families, and in consequence of the fact that a large section of the lower classes of the community have no fixed abode, it is a very difficult matter to ascertain the number of the inhabitants with even approximate precision. Judging from the average annual number of births in Egypt and at Cairo, the population of the city may be estimated at 400,000 souls, although at the census of 1882 it was returned as 368,108 only. The number of resident Europeans is about 21,000, including 7000 Italians, 4200 Greeks, 4000 French, 1600 English, 1600 Austrians, and 1200 Germans. Natives of all the principal Oriental states are also to be found at Cairo. The mass of the population consists of Egypto-Arabian townspeople (p. 48), Fellâḥ settlers (p. 39), Copts (p. 42), Turks (p. 52), and Jews (p. 53), the last of whom number 7000 souls. Besides the natives and the European residents, the traveller will frequently encounter negroes of various races, Northern Africans, Beduins, Syrians, Persians, Indians, and other Oriental settlers.

The *Hospitals* mentioned at p. 234 are fitted up in the European style, and so likewise is the *Military School* (*Ecoles Militaires;* in the ʿAbbâsîyeh), with its four departments (staff, artillery, cavalry, and infantry), connected with which there is a *Veterinary School.* Cairo also possesses a *Girls' School*, maintained by government (founded through the exertions of Dr. Dor, a Swiss), and a *Chemical-Pharmaceutical Laboratory*, presided over by M. Gastinel, and possessing an excellent pharmaceutical collection. The medicines required for all the hospitals in the country are prepared at the laboratory, and the yield of the 12 saltpetre manufactories of Egypt (about 1000 tons per annum) is tested here.

The *Police Force* (*Zabṭîyeh*, Pl. 86), an admirably organised institution, consists of about 300 officials, including a number of Europeans (chiefly Italians), who are very obliging to strangers, and who preside so effectually over the public safety that the traveller may explore the remotest and dirtiest purlieus of the city without apprehension of danger. If, however, he should have any cause for complaint, he should lay the matter before his consulate (p. 6).

The ***Street Scenes** presented by the city of the Khalîfs afford an inexhaustible fund of amusement and delight, admirably illustrating the whole world of Oriental fiction, and producing an indelible impression on the uninitiated denizen of the West. 'What makes Cairo so romantic and novel is the contrasts of barbarous and civilised scenes and incidents it presents, which forcibly strike and interest even the most utterly *blasé* European, and which recur in every department and phase of life in this Arabian capital of the desert, and indeed throughout all Egypt. Cairo may be compared to a mosaic of the most fantastic and bizarre description, in which all nations, customs, and epochs are represented, — a living museum of all imaginable and unimaginable phases of existence, of refinement and degeneracy, of civilisation and barbarism, of knowledge and ignorance, of paganism, Christianity, and Mohammedanism. In the Boulevards of Paris and on London Bridge I saw but the shadow, and at Alexandria the prelude only, of the Babel of Cairo, to which the Roman or the Venetian carnival is tame and commonplace. These marvellous scenes cannot fail to strike every one, and particularly the uninitiated new-comer, most forcibly. In order to enjoy them thoroughly, one cannot help wishing for eyes behind, as well as before, and for the steady power of forcing one's way possessed by the camel of burden'. *(B. Goltz.)* There is, however, no great difficulty in forcing one's way through the crowd in the Muski, although the chaotic, carnival-like scene which it presents can hardly be depicted in too bright colours.

Most of the streets in the old part of the town are still unpaved and inaccessible to carriages, and they are too often excessively dirty. The Khedive, however, is annually increasing the number of carriage-ways by the demolition of old streets and the erection of buildings in the modern style. The lanes separating the rows of houses in the Arabian quarter are so narrow that there is hardly room for two riders to pass, and the projecting balconies of the harems with their gratings often nearly meet. The new quarter on the W. side of the city possesses broad, shadeless streets, handsome avenues, and the beautiful Ezbekîyeh Garden (p. 258); but Oriental life seems to find this atmosphere uncongenial, and it must therefore be sought for in the old quarters, and particularly in the Muski, the chief business thoroughfare. The busy traffic in this street often presents an 'interminable, ravelled, and twisted string of men, women, and animals, of walkers, riders, and carriages of every description. Add to this the cracking of the drivers' whips, the jingling of money at the table of the changers established at every corner of the street, the rattling of the brazen vessels of the water-carriers, the moaning of the camels, braying of donkeys, and barking of dogs, and you have a perfect pandemonium'. Europeans, and even ladies, may ride with perfect safety through the midst of all this confusion, and they will often have opportunities of observing most picturesque and amusing scenes. The denseness of the crowd sometimes seems to preclude the possibility of farther progress, but the ḥammâr, or donkey-boy, is pretty sure to elbow a passage without much difficulty.

'Having carefully learned the expressions *ana 'âwiz humâr* (I want a donkey) and *bikam kirsh deh* (how many piastres), I yielded to the temptation of plunging recklessly into the thick of Arabian life, its conversation, and its equestrianism I therefore pronounced the mystic words with the satisfaction of a child which utters articulate expressions for the first time, and when I was instantly so perfectly understood by a score of donkey-boys that they all offered me their donkeys at once (though perhaps they would have done so had I not spoken at all), I felt like a magician who has succeeded in discovering an effectual formula of conjuration. After this display of my abilities, I vaulted into the saddle with as much ease and assurance as if Cairo had been my home. The donkey-boy next probably asked me — 'where to'? Whereupon, feeling that my stock of Arabic phrases and cabalistic formulæ was nearly exhausted, I replied in a very abbreviated style — *kullo, kullo*, that is, 'everything' (meaning that I wanted to see everything). The donkey-boy then nodded his *tayyib ana aref* ('all right, I understand'), and I now felt perfect confidence in my powers of speech . . My donkey now set off at a gallop and plunged into the midst of a labyrinth of lanes full of riders and walkers, but where I was going to, or how far, or why, I was unable to tell That, however, was precisely the joke of the thing' *(Goltz.)*

Lovers of the picturesque will find such rides very enjoyable. When they have sufficiently explored the narrower streets, they may direct their attendant to return to the Muski ('lil Muski, yâ ḥammâr'), whence the hotels are easily reached.

It is not, however, until the traveller has learned to distinguish the various individuals who throng the streets, and knows their different pursuits, that he can thoroughly appreciate his walks or rides. We may therefore give a brief description of some of the leading characteristics of the different members of the community. The traveller will probably first be struck with the differences of colour in the *Turbans.* From a very early period it has been customary for the Arabs to distinguish their different sects, families, and dynasties by the colour of their turbans. Green turbans form the badge of the 'Sherîfs', or descendants of the prophet, and they are also frequently worn by the Mecca pilgrims, green being also the colour of the banner of the prophet. The 'Ulama, or clergy and scholars, usually wear a very wide and broad, evenly folded turban of light colour. The orthodox length of a believer's turban is seven times that of his head, being equivalent to the whole length of his body, in order that the turban may afterwards be used as the wearer's winding sheet, and that this circumstance may familiarise him with the thought of death. The dress and turbans of the Copts, Jews, and other non-Muslim citizens, are generally of a dark colour, those of the Copts being blue, and those of the Jews yellow, in accordance with a decree issued in the 14th century (p. 242). Blue is also the colour indicative of mourning. The *Women* of the poorer and rustic classes wear nothing but a blue gown and a veil. Their ornaments consist of silver or copper bracelets, earrings, and ankle-rings, while their chins, arms, and chests are often tatooed with blue marks. In Upper Egypt nose-rings are also frequently seen. The women of the upper classes are never so handsomely dressed in the streets as at home. Their figures, in early life, are generally upright and graceful They colour their eyelashes and eyelids dark, and their finger and toe-nails with henna, which gives them a brownish yellow tint. When equipped for riding or walking, most ladies wear a light-coloured silk cloak, with very wide sleeves *(tôb* or *sebleh)*, over their home attire. They also don the *burḳo'*, or veil, which consists of a long strip of muslin, covering the whole of the face except the eyes, and reaching nearly to the feet. Lastly they put on the *ḥabara*, a kind of mantle, which in the case of married women consists of two breadths of glossy black silk. Thus disguised, they look unnaturally broad and unwieldy, and not unlike bats. The wealthier ladies, who drive in their carriages attended by eunuchs, usually veil their faces up to their eyes with thin gauze in accordance with the fashion of Constantinople. With regard to circumcision, weddings, and funerals, the ceremonies attending which are similar in all the Egyptian towns, see p. 153. Among other customs we may also mention the peculiar mode in which a woman carries her child, either astride her shoulder, or resting on her hip.

Amid this busy throng of men and animals resound the various cries of street-vendors and other persons who transact their business in the open air, and the warning shouts of outrunners (*sâis*), coachmen, donkey-attendants, and camel-drivers. The words most commonly heard are — *'riglak'*, *'shemâlak'*, *'yemînak'*, *'guarda'*, *'û'â, û'â'*. As a rule, however, the Cairenes pay no attention to these warnings unless addressed to them individually. Thus, *'riglak yâ khawâgeh'* ('your foot, sir', *i.e.* 'take care of your foot'; *khawâgeh* is the usual title given to Europeans by the Arabs, and is said to have originally meant 'merchant' only); *'shemâlak yâ shêkh'* ('your left side, O chief'); *'yemînak yâ bint'* ('your right side, girl'); *'ḍahrik yâ sitt'* ('your back, lady'); *'yâ 'arûseh'* (bride); *'yâ sherîf'* (descendant of the prophet); *'yâ efendi'* (Turkish official). — BEGGARS are very numerous at Cairo, most of them being blind. They endeavour to excite compassion by invoking the aid of Allah: *'yâ Moḥannin, yâ Rabb'* ('O awakener of pity, O Master'); *'ṭâlib min allâh ḥakk lukmet 'êsh'* ('I seek from my Lord the price of a morsel of bread'); *'âna ḍêf Allâh wa'n-nebi'* ('I am the guest of God and of the Prophet'). The usual answer of the passer-by is, *'Allâh yiḥannin 'alêk'* ('God will have mercy on you'), or *'Allâh ya'ṭîk'* ('God give thee'; comp. p. 16).

One of the most popular characters to be met with in the streets of Cairo is the Saḳḳa, or Water-Carrier, with his goatskin of water, carried either by himself or by a donkey, who still plies his trade, although the new waterworks (p. 381) could easily supply every house in the city, as well as the public sebîls (p. 177), with water, and though on many of the houses there are brass tubes through which passers-by may take a draught from the main pipes. His usual cry is — '*yâ 'auwaḍ Allâh*' ('may God recompense me'). The labour he undergoes during eight months in the year, when he brings his heavy load all the way from the Nile, is very severe and miserably underpaid; but during the four months when the river is rising he obtains his supply from the canal by which Cairo is intersected. The springs, being generally brackish, are not suitable for drinking. Many of the saḳḳas sell water to the people in the streets. These are known as '*saḳḳa sharbeh*', and they carry their supply of water either in a skin or in a large earthen-ware vessel on their backs. They offer a draught to passers-by in a brazen saucer or in a ḳulleh (porous bottle), for which they receive a small copper coin, and sometimes no payment at all. On the occasion of festivals, and particularly on the môlids (birthdays) of saints, persons who desire to do a pious work frequently hire one

of the saḳḳas to dispense water gratuitously. The saḳḳa then shouts in a singing tone, '*sebîl Allâh yâ'aṭshân yâ môyeh*', thus inviting all thirsty persons to drink gratuitously; while he occasionally turns to his employer, who generally stands near him, with the words, 'God forgive thy sins, O dispenser of the drink-offering', or 'God have mercy on thy parents', to which the persons who have partaken of the water reply, '*amîn*' (amen), or 'God have mercy on them and on us'. After numerous blessings of a similar kind have been interchanged, the saḳḳa hands the last cup of water to his employer, with the words, 'The remainder for the liberal man, and Paradise for the confessor of the Unity! God bless thee, thou dispenser of the drink-offering!'

The *Hemali*, who belong to one of the orders of dervishes (p. 151), are also engaged in selling water, which they flavour with orange-blossom *(zahr)*, while others add a little brandy *('erḳ-sûs)* or grape-juice *(zebîb)*. There are also numerous itinerant vendors of different kinds of sweetmeats, which to Europeans look very uninviting. Thus, *saḥlab* is a thin jelly made of wheat-starch and sugar, the sellers of which shout, '*ḥalâweh, yâ sukkar bimismâr yâ ḥalâweh!*' (confection, O sugar, for a nail, O confection!). These vendors, who resemble the rag and bone collectors of European towns, often barter their wares for nails or pieces of old iron, as their call indicates. Lastly, there are itinerant cooks, with portable kitchens, who sell small meat puddings, fish, and other comestibles, and whose customers eat their dinners sitting cross-legged by the side of the street. This custom is noticed by the old German geographer Sebastian Münster (d. 1552), who says that 'the city of Cairo is said to be five times as large as Paris. There are few people, who, as with us, buy food to prepare at home; but when they are hungry they buy from the cooks, of whom the city contains nearly thirty thousand'.

The way in which fruit and vegetables are cried is particularly curious. The commonest expressions are perhaps the following: '*Allâh yehawwinheh yâ lêmûn*' ('God will make them light, O lemons'; i. e., he will make light, or empty the baskets containing the lemons); '*'asal yâ burtuḳân, 'asal*' ('honey, O oranges, honey'; i. e., sweet as honey); '*meded yâ Embâbeh meded! tirmis Embâbeh yaghlib el-lôz!*' '*yâ maḥlâ bunei el-baḥr*' ('help! O Embâbeh, help! the lupins of Embâbeh are better than almonds; Oh, how sweet is the little son of the river!'). The best lupins are grown at Embâbeh, and they are called 'children of the river' from the fact that they require to be soaked in Nile water for a considerable time before they are boiled. Other cries are '*ya muselli'l-ghalbân yâ libb*' ('O comforter of those in distress, kernels', i. e., of the melon); or, more commonly, '*el-moḥammaṣ*' ('roasted kernels'); '*yâ fustuḳ*

gedîd' (new pistachios); '*el-ward kân shôk min 'arak en-nebi fettah'* ('the rose was a thorn; it blossomed from the sweat of the prophet'). This legend resembles that of the thorns at Subiaco among the Sabine Hills, which were converted into rose bushes by the blood of St. Francis. '*Rawâyeh el-genneh yâ temer henna'* ('odours of Paradise, O flowers of henna'). With regard to the henna plant, see p 75.

When the work of the day is over, the solemn and sonorous cry of the mueddin, summoning the faithful to prayer (see p. 147), reverberates from the tops of the minarets; but much of the busy street-traffic goes on till nearly midnight, and during the month of Ramadân it even continues throughout the whole night, while the barking of hungry dogs and the braying of donkeys frequently form an additional interruption to repose. At a very early hour in the morning the same scenes recommence, and on leaving his hotel the traveller is tempted to believe that Cairo is celebrating a never-ending Carnival.

While perambulating the streets of the city the traveller will frequently have occasion to observe the *Schools (kuttâb)*, which are open on the side next the street, and one of which is attached to almost every public fountain He will find it very amusing to watch the efforts of the *fikîh*, or schoolmaster, in teaching his pupils with the aid of admonitions and blows, while the boys themselves recite verses of the Korân with a swaying motion of their bodies, bending over their metal writing-tablets, and yet finding time for the same tricks as European schoolboys. Unless the visitor has an order of admission from the minister of public instruction, it is not advisable to watch the fikîh too closely, as he is easily disconcerted and is then apt to be uncivil.

These schools all have a purely religious character, and are exclusively creations of El-Islâm The mere reading and recitation of verses from the Korân being in itself considered a meritorious act, the great object of these schools is to teach the pupils to recite the Korân by heart Each boy is provided with a copy of the sacred book, if he can afford to buy one, an ink and pen case (*dawâyeh*), and a tablet of metal or of wood painted white. After learning the alphabet, the pronunciation and the values of numbers, he is then taught the ninety-nine 'beautiful names of Allâh' contained in the Korân, a knowledge of which is necessary to enable him to repeat the ninety-nine prayers of the Mohammedan rosary (sebha). The boy is then made to write out the *Fâtha*, or first chapter (sûreh) of the Korân, which he reads often enough to impress it perfectly on his memory, swaying his body to and fro the while, whereby, as he imagines, his memory is rendered more pliant. After learning the first chapter, he next proceeds to learn the last, the last but one, and the others in the same inverted order, until he reaches the second, the reason being that the chapters gradually diminish in length from the second to the last Although the language is often difficult and obscure, no explanations are given, so that the boy who knows the whole book by heart usually understands but little of it As soon as the boy has learned the whole of the Korân in this way, the completion of his studies is commemorated by the celebration of the *Khatmeh*, a family festival, to which the schoolmaster is invited.

These schools are maintained by the private enterprise of the schoolmasters themselves, who exact payment of 1-2 piastres per week from each pupil. There are in all about 280 schools of this kind at Cairo, presided over by 290 teachers, and attended by 8600 pupils, at Old Cairo there are 26 schools with 30 masters and 909 boys, and at Bûlâk 41 schools with 42 masters and 1320 boys — The 11 higher government schools are attended by 1480 pupils, while the foreign settlers support 57 schools with 247 teachers and 4340 pupils.

In walking through the bazaars (see below) and other streets, the traveller will be interested in observing how industriously and skilfully most of the artizans work with their very primitive tools. The *Carpenters (naggâr)*, for example, seem to ply their craft with very tolerable success, without bench, vice, rule, or drill In order to steady the piece of wood on which they are working they make use of the weight of their bodies, and sometimes of their teeth and their toes. For a rule they substitute a piece of string or a palm-twig, and for boring holes they use an iron spike imbedded in a circular piece of wood, which they turn by means of an instrument resembling a fiddle-bow (p. 257). Their principal tool consists of a small axe, which serves many different purposes. A number of other primitive tools are described at pp. 256, 257. — After the closing of the shops in the evening it is customary for the porters or watchmen to place their beds *(serîr)* of palm-twigs outside the entrances, where they spend the night, thus presenting a very curious and characteristic phase of Egyptian out-of-door life.

The **Bazaars**† of Cairo (comp. p. 23), though inferior to those of Damascus and Constantinople, present to the European traveller so many novel features, and so many interesting traits of Oriental character, that he should endeavour to pay them repeated visits, in order to become acquainted with their peculiarities.

Most of the bazaars consist of narrow, and often dirty, lanes, generally covered over with an awning to shade them from the sun, and flanked with rooms of various sizes, open towards the street, and about 3 ft above the level of the ground (comp. p. 24). These lanes usually enclose a massive building of considerable size *(khân)*, consisting of two stories, and containing an inner court, around which are grouped a number of magazines for goods. Some of the older of these buildings, particularly those in the Gamelîyeh (p. 257) and the Khân el-Khalîli (p 255), are architecturally interesting, and possess handsome mushrebîyehs. A considerable number of these khâns form separate quarters of the city *(ḥâra)*, which were formerly closed by massive, iron-mounted gates, still in some cases preserved; and they were carefully guarded at night by watchmen appointed for the purpose. No one was permitted to

† *Bazâr* is properly speaking a Persian word, the Arabic equivalent for which is *sûk*. The magazines of the wholesale merchants, with their large courts, are called *wakkaleh*, which the Franks have corrupted to *Occaleh*, *Occal*, or *Okella* (pp. 257, 279).

pass through the gates without undergoing an examination by the custodian, and this custom still prevails at Damascus and in the towns of Upper Egypt, such as Siûṭ. In former times, during the prevalence of the Mameluke conflicts, which were always attended with the pillaging and assassination of many peaceful citizens, the gates of the khâns frequently remained closed for several days together, for the purpose of affording protection against the outrages of these lawless mercenaries.

The principal market-days are Monday and Thursday, when the traffic in the narrow streets is so great that it becomes difficult or impossible to traverse them; but it is on these occasions that the most characteristic scenes of Oriental life are witnessed. Pedlers are seen forcing their way through the crowd, shouting at the top of their voices, sometimes carrying a small table with them, and frequently selling their wares by auction. So, too, we observe coffee-sellers, water-bearers, nargileh-hawkers, and others, elbowing their way, lauding their commodities, and escaping accidents almost by a miracle. One of the noisiest frequenters of the bazaars is the *dallâl*, or auctioneer, who carries on his head or shoulders the goods he is instructed to sell, and runs up and down the lanes shouting '*ḥarâg, ḥarâg*', and adding the amount of the last bid he has received. However great the confusion may be, his practised ear instantly detects each new bid issuing from one of the dukkâns, and he immediately announces the new offer — '*bi'ishrîn ḳirsh*', '*bi'ishrîn u nuṣ*', and so on. The seller of the goods always accompanies the dallâl to give his consent to the conclusion of the transaction.

It is hardly possible to give the traveller any idea of the prices of the various commodities, as they depend on the demand, which is greater in winter than in summer, and also on the character of the seller and the demeanour of the purchaser. We may also mention that many so-called Oriental articles, particularly silks and woollen stuffs, are now manufactured of inferior materials by European firms, and exported to Egypt. Some articles again, such as rugs and hangings, please the eye amid their native surroundings, but are rarely suitable for European rooms; while others are more advantageously purchased in most European capitals than from the Oriental merchants themselves, with whom bargaining is difficult and troublesome. So-called antiquities are largely sold at the hotels at exorbitant prices, far exceeding their true value, and many of them are even specially manufactured for the purpose. Caution in making a purchase is far more requisite in the East than in Europe, as Orientals regard skill in cheating simply as a desirable accomplishment. Those who purpose making large purchases had better defer doing so until they have gained a little experience of the national peculiarities, and they should in no case rely on the recommendations or advice of commissionnaires and persons of a similar class (comp. p. 233). Natives of the country may often be consulted with advantage as to prices, but the traveller must be prepared to pay more than persons familiar with the language and customs.

The following description of the city is so arranged that even a new-comer will have little difficulty in finding his way without any other guide If, however, time be limited, the traveller is recommended to get a commissionnaire or local dragoman (p. 233), to show him the bazaars in the following order.

The **Muski**, with its E. continuation the *Rue Neuve*, is the chief thoroughfare of Cairo, nearly 1 M. in length, and runs in a nearly straight direction from W. to E., from the Ezbekîyeh *place* to the tombs of the khalifs. This street, the beginning of which has frequently been sketched by European artists, has now to a great extent lost its Oriental characteristics, but it still presents many picturesque and attractive features (comp. p. 244). Among the shops, many of which present quite a European exterior, are numerous tobacco and cigar stores, emporiums of clothing, and stalls of fez-makers, with the peculiarly shaped iron they use in their trade. (The price of a fez or ṭarbûsh varies from 2 fr. to 15 fr. according to the material with which it is lined.)

On entering the Muski we observe on the right, above us, an Arabian school (p. 250) We ascend the street to a small *place* called the *Rond-Point* (Pl. C, 3). Immediately before this *place* is reached, we diverge to the right, and follow the first lane to the left (running parallel with the Muski), passing a red and yellow mosque on the right, and disregarding the attraction of the European glass wares sold here. Pursuing a straight direction (*i.e.*, as straight as the crooked lanes admit of), we pass the end of a narrow lane on the right, through which we perceive the entrance to an uninteresting Greek church, and the covered entrance to a bazaar lately burned down, on the left. Turning to the right, we next enter the **Sûḳ el-Ḥamzâwi** (Pl. C, 2, 3), or bazaar of the Christian merchants (Syrians and Copts), who vie with their Mohammedan fellow-tradesmen in the exorbitance of their demands, and whose chief wares are European calico, porcelain, and drugs (which last are sold at all the bazaars). Near the end of this street, a little before its junction with the broader street *El-Ghûrîyeh* (see below), we observe on the right the **Sûḳ el-ʿAṭṭârîn**, or spice-market, which is easily distinguished by its aromatic odours. The perfumes of Arabia, genuine and adulterated, wax-candles, and drugs are the chief commodities here. Attar of roses is sold by weight at high prices. The small bottles into which it is put have very narrow necks, through which one drop at a time only can pass. Customers should of course see that the bottles are accurately weighed beforehand.

Beyond the ʿAṭṭârîn Bazaar (still keeping the El-Ghûrîyeh carriage way on our left) we next enter its continuation, the **Sûḳ el-**

Fahhâmi (literally, coal-market; Pl. D, 2), the bazaar for wares from Tunis and Algiers. We first observe drug-stalls, and then magazines of light-coloured woollen and other stuffs, which, however, are imported from Nîmes and other places in Southern France, being now seldom or never manufactured at Tunis.

Pursuing the same direction, parallel with the El-Ghûrîyeh street, and passing a number of shoemakers' stalls (bawâbîshi), we come to a broader covered passage (exactly opposite which is a modern okella, presenting no attraction), which we follow to the right for a few paces, and then take the first lane to the left. At the end of this lane lies a more open spot where undressed wool is exposed for sale Lower down, a little to the left, we reach the **Sukkarîyeh**, or bazaar for sugar, dried fruits (nukl), and similar wares. Adjoining it is the *Gâmi el-Muaiyad* (p 272), now undergoing restoration, while facing us, at the end of the street, rises the handsome *Bâb ez-Zuwêleh* (see p. 272), or *Mutawelli*. Opposite the outside of the gate is a house with a large grated window, and in the corner is a column built into the wall, at which executions by strangulation formerly took place In a straight direction we next enter the **Shoemakers' Bazaar**, formerly a school, an interesting building, the first story of which overhangs the lower and is borne by large brackets. The large gateway (on the right) is still preserved; part of the interior has been altered, while the rest of it is in a dilapidated condition. — The same street then passes the stalls of the tent and flag-makers, and leads to the *Boulevard Mohammed 'Ali* (p. 260), at the W. end of which are the mosques of Sultân Hasan (p. 260) and Rifâ'îyeh (p 260), the latter being still unfinished. On the left, before this last is reached, is the entrance to the once celebrated **Sûk es-Sellâha** (Pl. E, 2), or bazaar of the armourers, now reduced to three or four miserable stalls, where European weapons are sold. Keeping to the left, we traverse several crooked lanes and reach the Sebîl Mohammed 'Ali (see below) in the Ghûrîyeh street. This last digression, however, is uninteresting.

We return from the Shoemakers' Bazaar to the Bâb ez-Zuwêleh, before reaching which we pass the unattractive **Saddlers' Bazaar** (*Sûk es-Surûgîyeh*), and a police-office at the corner to the right. We now follow a broader street, the first part of which is called the Sukkarîyeh (see above). Beyond the Sebîl Mohammed 'Ali this street is named **El-Ghûriyeh** from the mosque erected by Sultân El-Ghûri (p 274), the small minaret of which, with its domes, rises nearly in the middle of the street.

We follow this street in a straight direction nearly as far as the post of the (lower) sentry on the left, a little before reaching whom we turn to the right into the **Sûk es-Sûdân**, or bazaar for wares from the Sûdân, consisting of chests, gum, dûm-palm nuts, ill-tanned tiger skins, etc. (see p. 236). Farther on, in a straight direction, are the stalls of the **Booksellers** and **Bookbinders**.

Most of the booksellers are also scholars, but they are not so fanatical as their brethren of Damascus, who sometimes decline to sell their books to Christians. Seated on their mastabas are frequently to be found various other members of the learned, or would-be learned, world, who spend whole days here in interminable colloquies Some of the booksellers sell those works only which they have themselves published, while others keep an assortment of books from the printing-offices of Bûlâk and others (p 294) As the prices vary greatly in accordance with the demand and other circumstances, and there is no such thing as a fixed publishing price, purchasers should always endeavour to ascertain beforehand the true value of any work they wish to buy As in the case of many other wares, the line between new and second-hand books is not so strictly drawn in the East as in Europe The booksellers generally keep catalogues, several feet in length, to refresh their memories regarding the state of their stock The Korân, which is shown very reluctantly to non-Muslims, is generally kept under lock and key, or at least separate from the other books. The books are not arranged side by side as in European shops, but piled up in a very inconvenient fashion. Many of them are sold in loose sheets, in which case the purchaser should see that the work is complete, as gaps are of frequent occurrence The bindings usually consist of leather and pasteboard Valuable books are often kept in cases of red sheepskin, out of which they are drawn by means of a loop. — The workmanship of the bookbinders, who like other Oriental artizans work in the open street, is generally cheap and durable. Red is their favourite colour

At the point where the street expands a little, before reaching the handsome W. entrance of the El-Azhar mosque (p. 287), we observe several houses with picturesque mushrebîyehs (p. 181). The next lane to the left leads us across the Rue Neuve, the prolongation of the Muski (passing a large new school at the corner to the right), towards the large new minaret of the Hasanên Mosque (p. 292). Opposite to it, on the left, is a gateway through which we enter the **Khân el-Khalîli** (Pl. C, 2), which once formed the centre of the commercial traffic of Cairo. This building, which is said to have been founded so early as the end of the 13th cent. on the site of ruined tombs of the Khalîfs by El-Ashraf Ṣalâḥeddin Khalîl (1290-93), one of the Baḥrite Mameluke sultans, forms a distinct quarter of the city, and is intersected by a main street and numerous cross-lanes, formed by long rows of stalls of tradesmen and artizans, all covered over. This is the headquarters of the silk and carpet merchants and the vendors of trinkets.

The usual price of a light *keffiyeh* (shawl for the head) is 12-14 fr, and of one of heavier quality, with red and yellow stripes and interwoven with gold thread, 20-25 fr The fringes are generally loosened and adjusted after the completion of the purchase Many of the so-called Damascene silks, and particularly the lighter keffîyehs in pleasing colours, are manufactured at Lyons and Crefeld The table-covers of red, blue, or black cloth, embroidered with coloured silk (35-100 fr.), are well worthy of notice. The letters with which they are adorned rarely have any meaning.

The Khân Khalîli contains two large Carpet Bazaars, one (the smaller) immediately to the right of the entrance (see above), and the other at the W. end, to the left, a little before we reach the broader and better lighted Sûḳ en-Naḥḥâsîn (p. 256). The latter of these two bazaars, established in the court of a building in the early Arabian style, is a favourite subject with European artists.

The prices of the carpets, like those of other Oriental goods, are liable to great fluctuation Those of Baghdâd and Brussa (in Asia Minor) are the most sought after, but imitations, manufactured at Brussels, are said to be not uncommon. They are chiefly remarkable for the harmonious arrangement of their colours. As soon as a purchaser appears, the dealers spread their wares over the whole court for his inspection. If the traveller is pressed for time he had better not attempt to make a purchase, as several hours must not unfrequently be spent in negociation before a satisfactory bargain is concluded.

Leaving this court, we cross the Sûḳ en-Naḥḥâsîn (see below) in a somewhat oblique direction, and pass through a very insignificant gate into the **Sûḳ eṣ-Ṣâigh** (pl. *Ṣiyâgh*), or bazaar of the gold and silversmiths, which consists of several crooked lanes, barely a yard in width, through which the traveller will sometimes find it difficult to thread his way. The occupants of these crowded alleys keep their wares in glass cases or under glass shades. Their stalls present a very poor appearance, but their filagree-work is sometimes very good. Spurious gold and silver wares are not unfrequently sold as genuine. The bellows of the silversmith are generally of amusingly primitive construction, consisting of a conical bag of goatskin, open at one end, where it is provided with wooden handles, and terminating at the other end in a tube, usually an old gun-barrel, which runs under a small mound of clay to the fire.

The finest ninety-carat silver, which is never sold except in its native condition, is frequently purchased with a view to the manufacture of plate and trinkets in the house of the purchaser himself and under his immediate supervision, in order that all possibility of fraud may be obviated. The finest quality manufactured at the shops is the eighty-carat silver, the workmanship bestowed on which is usually worth a quarter to a half the value of the raw material; the next quality is the seventy-five carat; and, lastly, there are inferior qualities containing fifty per cent or less of pure silver. The silver manufactured at the shops ought to bear a government stamp, indicating the number of carats it contains As soon as a standard of price is agreed on, the article is paid for in accordance with its weight in dirhem (drachms), and with its assay as stated by the seller. The quality of the metal is then attested by a government official, who is always in attendance, and the article is taken to the customs-office, where a duty is exacted from the purchaser. The whole transaction is therefore of a somewhat complicated character, and the formal attestation by the official affords no guarantee whatever of the true quality of the metal. The only satisfactory plan is to purchase the raw material, and, like the natives of the country, get it manufactured under one's personal supervision

In the Jewish quarter, to the W of the Sûk eṣ-Ṣâigh, are the booths of the *Jewellers (Góhargiyeh)*, where, however, there is nothing to see, as they show their wares to intending purchasers only.

From this labyrinth of lanes we return to the **Sûḳ en-Naḥḥâsîn**, or market of the copper-smiths, immediately to the left of which are the imposing façades of several contiguous mosques, the first two of which contain the tombs of Sultân Ḳalaûn and his son Moḥammed en-Nâsir (p. 277). This bazaar presents little attraction, but one of the Arabian copper ink-bottles (*dawayeh;* 4-10 fr., according to the style of the engraving with which they are adorned) may be purchased as a souvenir. Several pipe-makers *(shibukshi)* are also established here.

The chief occupation of the pipe-makers is the boring of pipe-stems. Their primitive apparatus consists of an instrument resembling a bow with which they turn a wooden cylinder terminating in an iron spike. The string of the bow is pressed against the wood, and the bow is moved to and fro, somewhat like that of a violin, so as to turn the borer Notwithstanding the simplicity of this tool, and although they merely steady the stem with their hands, they execute their work with surprising rapidity and accuracy — The same kind of implement is used by the turners. The wood on which they are working is secured on two nails in two parallel upright pieces of wood and turned with the bow with the right hand, while the work is done with a chisel held in the left.

Leaving the bazaars for a short time, we may now turn to the right, and follow the broad, newly constructed street to the **Bêt el-Ḳâḍi** (Pl. 2), or 'House of the Judge'. The appointment of ḳâḍi is made by the government at Constantinople, and is usually bestowed on favourites, as it is said to be a very lucrative post. In the large court on the right is an open verandah, resting on columns with early Arabian capitals (*takhta bôsh*; p. 186). Part of the building still dates from the time of Saladin (1193). Within the building, the entrance to which consists of an open verandah, the ḳâḍi holds his court on Thursdays. This court was formerly the supreme tribunal of the country, but its jurisdiction is now limited to cases in which the law laid down by the Ḳorân is to be administered, and particularly to actions between married persons The large extent to which the court is patronised shows that polygamy is not particularly conducive to domestic harmony.

Crossing the court, and passing through the gate opposite, we next follow the windings of the narrow lane to the left as far as a sentry posted by the *Gâmiʿ Yûsuf Gamali*.

[To the right of this mosque begins the street called **Gameliyeh,** leading to the Bâb en-Naṣr (p. 280). It consists of a number of large warehouses (okellas; p. 251), and is the headquarters of the Red Sea trade.

The staple commodities here are gums, coffee, mother-of-pearl, tortoiseshell, skins, ostrich-feathers, wax, incense, attar of roses, and various essences, the ports from which they are brought being Jedda, Ḥodêda, ʿAden, Zêlaʿ, Berbera, Masauaʿ, Souâkin, and Koṣêr

As we shall have to traverse the Gameliyeh on our way to the Tombs of the Khalifs, we need not now visit it.]

Where the street divides, beyond the above-mentioned sentry, we keep to the left until we regain the Sûḳ en-Naḥḥâsîn, near a fountain (Sebîl ʿAbder-Raḥmân Kikhya; p. 279). We then follow the bazaar-street to the right to the Bâb el-Futûḥ (p. 280), and proceed thence to the left to the Rue Neuve (Muski, p. 253).

The above-named bazaars are the most important at Cairo, the others being unattractive We may, however, add the names of some of the other trades, as given by Mr. Lane: — *Tâgir*, cloth and stuff merchants; *khurdagi*, dealers in iron goods and small wares; *khaiyâṭ*, tailors; *ṣabbâgh*, dyers; *reffa*, stocking-makers;

ḥabbâk, embroiderers and silk-lace makers; *'akkâd*, manufacturers of silk braid; *'aṭṭâr*, druggists and perfumers; *dakhâkhni*, tobacconists; *fâkihâni*, fruiterers; *zeiyât*, oil-merchants, who also sell butter, cheese, honey, etc.; *khuḍari*, vegetable dealers; *gezzâr*, butchers; *farrân*, bakers; *ḳahwegi*, coffee-dealers; *shammâ'a*, wax and candle-dealers; *simsâr*, brokers; *samkari*, tinsmiths; *ḥaddâd*, smiths; *sâ'âtı*, watchmakers; *faṭâṭrı*, cake-sellers; *sammâk*, fish-dealers; *kharrât*, turners.

The Ezbekîyeh and the New Isma'îliya Quarter.

The central point of the *Isma'îliya Quarter* (p. 258), which is intersected by broad and shadeless streets bearing French names, is the —

Place Ezbekiyeh (Pl. C, 4, 5), or simply the *Ezbekîyeh*, which is named after the heroic Emîr Ezbek, the general of Sulṭân Ḳait Bey (p. 268), who brought the general and son-in-law of Bajesid I. as a captive to Cairo. A mosque was erected here in honour of his victory; and, though the building no longer exists, its name still attaches to the site. This was once the focus of the Oriental traffic of Cairo, but the native industries have gradually to a great extent been absorbed by Europeans. The principal hotels, several of the consulates, numerous cafés, palatial dwelling-houses, handsome shops, and the theatres are situated in this magnificent *place*, in the centre of which are *Pleasure Grounds*, with the luxuriant vegetation peculiar to the marvellous climate of Egypt. The gardens afford a delightful promenade, especially in the afternoon, and also present a very attractive appearance by gaslight. They were laid out in 1870 by M. Barillet (p. 76), formerly chief gardener to the city of Paris. They are octagonal in shape, and cover an area of $20^1/_2$ acres; the walks are altogether $1^1/_2$ M. in length. The gardens contain a variety of rare and beautiful trees and shrubs, and the open spaces are planted with the *Lippia nodiflora*, to supply the place of grass, which does not thrive in this dry climate. The grounds are open to the public in the forenoon, but in the afternoon a charge of 10 paras silver (no change given) is made for admission. An Egyptian band, which generally performs European music, plays here daily from 5 to about 8 p.m. Among the other attractions of the place are several cafés, a theatre, where Italian comedies are performed in summer (p. 233), a French restaurant, where a good supper is procurable, and a photographer's studio. An artificial hill with a belvedere commands a fine view, and below it is a pretty grotto. The garden was at first visited almost exclusively by Europeans, but it is gradually becoming the fashion for Arabs to send their veiled wives and their children to promenade here, while the Europeans of the better classes now treat it with unreasonable neglect. The trees, shrubs, and flowers thrive admirably, the greatest show of blossom being in May and June. Invalids who spend the winter in Cairo for the sake of their health will find these beautiful grounds a very pleasant resort, though they should be careful to leave them before sundown, after which the air here is very damp

Similar gardens, but of smaller extent, have been laid out by M Barillet at Gezîreh (p. 328), in the island of Rôda (p 318), at Shubra (p. 331), at Kubbeh (p. 332), and at Gîzeh (p 341) The present superintendent of gardens is M Delchevallerie. — Private gardens of M. Ciccolani, see p. 331

. The **New Town of Isma'îliya** was begun about the year 1865, when the Khedive presented sites here gratuitously to any one who would undertake to erect on each a house worth at least 30,000 fr. within eighteen months. Most of the houses are architecturally uninteresting, but there is a fair sprinkling of handsome buildings.

At the end of the Muski, on the left, is the small *place* named *Atab el-Kadra* (Pl. C, 3) It was formerly adorned with an equestrian statue of Ibrâhîm Pasha, but this was removed during the revolution of 1882 and is now in the magazine of the Bûlâk Museum. On the W. side of the *place* is the *International Tribunal* (Pl. 99, C 4; p. 7), beyond which is the *Théâtre Français* (Pl. 98). On the S. side of the Ezbekîyeh is the *Opera House* (Pl. 75), and to the right of it (W.) the ponderous *New Hotel* (Pl. a). Opposite, on the W. side of the Ezbekîyeh, is a large house belonging to Sign. Matatia, the banker, built in the Louis XV. style, and let out in *quartiers* To the W. of the New Hotel are the *German Church* (Pl. 10) and the *English Church* (Pl. 8), which still lacks its spire. Still farther to the W. is the residence of M. Delort, the banker, in the early Arabian style, the interior of which, partly fitted up with relics from old Arabian houses, is worthy of a visit. The ministerial offices and several palaces of the Khedive, including the *Palais 'Abidîn* (Pl. 76), built in the form of a horse-shoe, are also situated in this new quarter of the city. Opposite the Palais 'Abidîn is the *Dîwân el-Wakf*, or government office for mosques and other ecclesiastical property. The consulates are also all in this neighbourhood (comp. p. 232). Near the French consulate (Pl. 19; C, 5) is the house of Count St. Maurice, in the Arabian style, now occupied by the French consul-general. The palaces of the Egyptian grandees are generally enclosed by high walls, so that only the roofs are visible to passers-by. Some of them will be briefly mentioned when we have occasion to pass them (pp. 317, 341).

It need hardly be added that the traveller in search of Oriental scenes will not care to devote much time to this modern and almost entirely European quarter, but will hasten to make acquaintance with the Arabian parts of the city.

Southern Quarters. Boulevard Moḥammed 'Ali. Gâmi' Sulṭân Ḥasan. Citadel. Gâmi' Moḥammed 'Ali. Gâmi' Salâḥeddîn Yûsuf and Sulêmân Pasha. Joseph's Well. Gâmi' ibn Ṭulûn, Ḳait Bey, and Seidiyeh Zênab. Viceroyal Library at Derb el-Gamâmîz. Monastery of Dervishes in the Ḥabbanîyeh. Bâb ez-Zuwêleh. Gâmi' el-Muaiyad. Gâmi' el-Ghûri.

Starting from the Place Atab el-Kadra, between the Muski and the Ezbekîyeh (see above), the *Boulevard Moḥammed 'Ali*, 1860 yds. in length, leads straight to the foot of the citadel. At the end of this long street is the *Place Sulṭân Ḥasan* (Pl. F, 2), with two large mosques. That on the left is the **Gâmi' Rifâ'îyeh** (Pl. 59), named after an order of dervishes (p. 150), and erected entirely at the expense of the mother of the ex-Khedive Isma'îl, but still unfinished. On the right, adjoining the Place Rumêleh, rises the—

****Gâmi' Sulṭân Ḥasan** (Pl. 44), the 'superb mosque', and the finest existing monument of Arabian architecture. It was begun in the year 757 of the Hegira (A.D. 1356), and completed in three years by Melik en-Nâṣir Abu'l-Ma'âli Ḥasan ibn Ḳalaûn, but is now in a neglected and dilapidated condition.

Sulṭân Ḥasan, the sixth son of Sulṭân Nâṣir (p. 277), was still a minor when he ascended the throne in A.D. 1346. At the end of the vigorous reign of Nâṣir (d. 1341), which lasted 43 years, the Mamelukes and emîrs revolted, and the state of anarchy which now ensued was farther aggravated by the prevalence of the plague or 'black death' (1348-49), which exterminated whole families, whose property was immediately seized by the government. Makrîzi (p. 242), with the usual exaggeration of Orientals, records that no fewer than 15-20,000 persons died at Cairo in a single day. After having been dethroned in 1351, Ḥasan regained possession of his sceptre three years later, but in 1361 he was again dethroned and assassinated.

The lofty walls with their shallow niches, pierced with six or seven windows one above the other, the huge gateway (see below), and the S. minaret which is still preserved, present a majestic appearance, especially now that the incongruous additions of later date have been removed. The building is in the form of an irregular pentagon, on the E. side of which the minarets and the mausoleum (see below) form symmetrical projections. The windows in the side are disposed somewhat irregularly, and the wall terminates in a broad cornice. The angles of the edifice are embellished with columns built into the wall, with a wreath of pendentives or 'stalactites' at the top, forming to some extent a new order of capital.

According to the legend, Sulṭân Ḥasan, after the completion of the work, ordered the architect's hands to be cut off, in order that he might not erect a second building of equal splendour. (Similar myths in various parts of Europe record that architects have been blinded from the same motive.) The mosque of Ḥasan has always been the chief rallying point of the ringleaders of insurrections and all kinds of public demonstrations.

One of the *Minarets*, as Maḳrîzi informs us, was overthrown by an earthquake, killing three hundred persons. The southernmost is the highest minaret in existence, measuring 280 ft. (that of *El-Ghûri* 213 ft., *Kalaûn* 193 ft., *Muaiyad* 167 ft., *El-Azhar* 167 ft., *Kait Bey* and *Barkûk* 164 ft., *Tulûn* 132 ft., *ʿAmr* 105 ft.).

The ***Gateway* on the N. side, in the Boulevard Moḥammed ʿAli, situated 10 ft. above the street, is unrivalled in its imposing dimensions. It forms a niche, 66 ft. high, with regular arabesques in sculptured stone, and the principal cornice is in the 'stalactite' form. An insignificant flight of steps ascends to the entrance.

From the *Entrance* (Pl. 1) we first enter a *Vestibule* (Pl. 2), with an interesting cupola and stone arabesques, where a black spot, said to be a blood-stain, is shown on the floor. We then turn to the left, then to the right, and afterwards to the left again, and thus reach the *Inner Court* (Pl. 3; before entering which we must put on straw-shoes; fee 1 piastre on leaving), 38 yds. in length, and 35 yds. in width, presenting a very interesting and picturesque appearance. In the centre is the *Mêḍa* (Pl. 4), or foun-

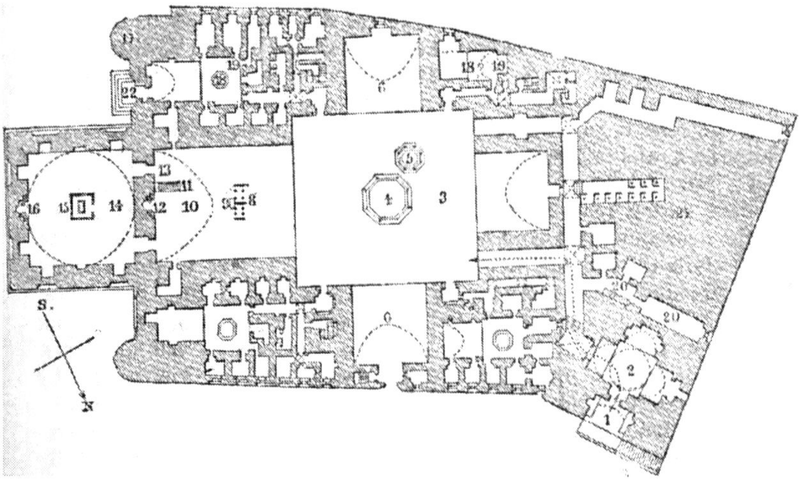

1. Chief Entrance (from the Boul. Moḥammed ʿAli). 2. Vestibule. 3. Hôsh el-Gâmiʿ. 4. Mêḍa, or Fountain for the ablutions of the Egyptians. 5. Ḥanefîyeh, or Fountain for the ablutions of the Turks. 6. Open chambers for prayer. 8. Dikkeh. 9. Kursi. 10. Sanctuary. 11. Mambar. 12. Kibla. 13. Entrance to the Mausoleum. 14. Maksûra. 15. Tomb of Sulṭân Ḥasan. 16. Kibla. 17. Minaret. 18. Fountain. 19. Schools. 20. Chambers for carpets. 21. Offices. 22. Sultan's Entrance.

tain where Egyptian worshippers perform their ablutions, to the right of which is the *Ḥanefîyeh* (Pl. 5), or fountain for the Turks, who formerly kept entirely aloof from their fellow-worshippers. Notwithstanding their dilapidated condition, both these fountains are very characteristic examples of Arabian architecture. Over the entrance to the principal dome is inscribed the date 764 of the Hegira (A.D. 1363).

The interior of the mosque is cruciform, and the four arms of the cross are roofed with lofty, pointed vaulting. In the S.E. arm is the *Lîwân el-Gâmi'* (Pl. 10), or Sanctuary, with a stone Mambar (Pl. 11), from which the sultan sometimes addressed the people. The frieze is embellished with a finely executed Cufic inscription. Numerous lamps hang from the ceiling. To the right of the mambar is the entrance (Pl. 13) to the *Maḳṣûra* (Pl. 14), an interesting and majestic structure, which has been recently restored; it is covered with a dome, 180 ft. in height, and contains the Tomb of Sulṭân Ḥasan. The pendentives in the corners, which are still partly preserved, betray the influence of the classical style. Around the walls runs a frieze with texts from the Ḳorân in large letters intertwined.

On leaving this mosque, we proceed to the E. (right) to the circular **Place Rumêleh**, from which the Mecca pilgrimage starts (p. 238), and to the **Place Méhémet Ali** (*Menshîyeh Gedîdeh*, or New Place), formerly called the *Ḳaramêdan*, on the S. side of the Rumêleh. From the E. side of the Rumêleh a broad carriage-road, passing two mosques (on the left. the *Gâmi' Maḥmûdi*, Pl. 52, and beyond it the *Gâmi' 'Abderrahmân*, Pl. 41, with a decaying minaret), and affording a view of the Tombs of the Khalîfs to the left, ascends in windings to the Citadel. A shorter and steeper route, which may be ascended on donkey-back, diverges to the right near the beginning of the carriage-road, passing through the *Bâb el-Azab*, flanked with its huge towers. It was in this narrow and crooked lane, enclosed by lofty walls, and formerly the chief approach to the citadel, that the massacre of the Mamelukes took place on 1st March, 1811, by order of Moḥammed 'Ali (p. 106). Amîn Bey, the only one who survived, effected his escape by making his horse leap into the moat, through a gap in the wall.

The **Citadel** (*El-Ḳal'a;* Pl F, G, 1, 2), which should be visited repeatedly for the sake of the view, was erected in 1166 by Ṣalâḥeddîn (p. 242), with stones taken from the small pyramids at Gîzeh, the site having been selected, according to Arabian historians, owing to the fact that meat could be kept fresh here twice as long as in any other part of Cairo. Although the fortress commands the city, its site is unfavourable in respect that it is itself completely commanded by the heights of the Moḳaṭṭam, rising above it immediately to the S.; thus in 1805 Mohammed 'Ali was enabled, by means of a battery planted on the Gebel Giyûshi (p 335), to compel Khurshîd Pasha to surrender the Citadel.

We enter the inner court of the Citadel by the *Bâb el-Gedîd* ('New Gate), and traversing a walled passage, we observe on a terrace before us the —

***Gâmi' Moḥammed 'Ali** (Pl. 53), the 'Alabaster Mosque', whose lofty and graceful minarets are so conspicuous from a distance as to form one of the landmarks of Cairo. The building was begun by Moḥammed 'Ali, the founder of the present Egyptian dynasty, on the site of a palace which was blown up in 1824; and in 1857 it was partly completed in its present form by Sa'îd Pasha (p. 107). In plan it resembles the Turkish mosques built on the model of the Hagia Sofia at Constantinople. The execution of the design displays but little artistic taste, and the treatment of the material is somewhat unsatisfactory. The alabaster used for the incrustation of the masonry consists partly of blocks, and partly of slabs, and was obtained from the quarries near Beni Suêf, which were known in ancient times, but had long been disused and forgotten. The beautiful yellow tint of the stone soon fades when exposed to the sun. The alabaster incrustation of the S. façade, is, however, new and fresh.

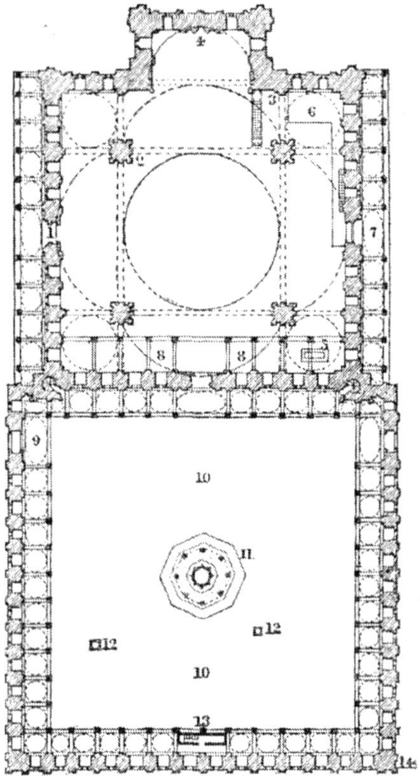

1. Entrance. 2. Kursi. 3. Mambar. 4. Kibla. 5. Grated space for the Sultan. 6. Tomb of Mohammed 'Ali. 7. Sultan's Entrance. 8. Great Gallery. 9. Entrance to the — 10. Ṣaḥn el-Gâmi'. 11. Ḥanefiyeh. 12. Small Fountain. 13. Ascent to the clock-tower. 14. Point of view.

The Entrance (Pl. 1; where we put on straw or cloth shoes; fee 1 p.t.) is on the N. side. The interior, consisting of a large quadrangle, with domes resting on 4 huge pillars, presents an imposing appearance; and the ceiling is effectively painted. The Kursi, Mambar, and Kibla possess no particular attraction. At the S.E. angle is the *Tomb of Moḥammed 'Ali* (d. 1849), enclosed by a handsome railing (Pl. 6), opposite to which is a space set apart for the Sultan, also enclosed by a railing (Pl. 5).

To the S. of the last is the *Sahn el-Gâmiʿ* (Pl. 10), or *Anterior Court*, enclosed by vaulted galleries, in the upper parts of which plain limestone has been used instead of alabaster. In the centre is the Hanefîyeh (p. 184), designed in the debased Turkish style. On the W. side is the approach to a tower, terminating in pavilions in the Chinese style, and containing a clock which was presented to Mohammed ʿAli by Louis Philippe of France.

A magnificent *View is obtained from the parapet at the S.W. end of the mosque, which is reached by walking round the building. (The palace of the Khedive, fitted up in the European style, is uninteresting.) From this point we survey the yellowish grey city, with its countless minarets, domes, and gardens. At our feet stands the mosque of Sultân Hasan. To the N. and W. are the windmill-hills † and the green plain traversed by the Nile. To the W. in the distance are the Pyramids, towering above the desert. On the flat roofs of the houses we observe innumerable air-pipes, called malkaf, known also by the Persian name of bâdgir, by means of which the cool north-wind is introduced into the houses.

The other mosques in the citadel cannot be visited without special permission (p 241) Many of the chambers have been diverted from their original uses, so that they are not easily inspected, and are moreover in a very ruinous condition.

The **Gamiʿ Salaheddin Yûsuf** (Pl. 60), situated to the S.E. of the Mosque of Mohammed ʿAli, was erected in A.D 1171-93, in a style betraying the influence of Western architecture, and in many points resembling that of a basilica Here, too, the pointed arch predominates. The openings under the arcades are of the elongated Moorish form. The dome was once supported by nine magnificent columns of granite, but it has now fallen in, the only remains of it being the deeply sculptured pendentives. As in the case of most of the other mosques, the columns have been taken from ancient monuments The Kibla is handsomely embellished with miniature arcades, in the interior of which are rich arabesques. The coffered ceiling of carved wood is painted white and gilded, with a blue ground. The windows are still partly filled with tracery in plaster The whole edifice up to the roof is of solid masonry The minarets, each consisting of a cube with a cylinder above it, are covered at the top with slabs of green porcelain, and are encircled with a band of 'Sullus' characters in white on a brown ground.

Immediately to the S E of the Mosque of Saladin is the so-called **Well of Joseph** (Pl. 27), a square shaft sunk in the limestone rock to a depth of 280 ft , containing somewhat brackish water, which is brought to the surface by means of two sâkiyehs, one above the other, worked by oxen halfway down the opening Since the introduction of the steam-pumps (p 281), however, the well has lost its former importance. When the citadel was constructed here in the 12th cent , the builders discovered an ancient shaft filled with sand, which *Salaheddin Yûsuf* caused to be re-opened and named after himself Yûsuf's, or Joseph's, Well. This circumstance gave rise to the tradition, which was chiefly current among the Jews that this was the well into which the Joseph of scripture was put by his brethren, and the story is still faithfully repeated by the dragomans.

The **Gamiʿ Sulemân Pasha** (Pl 67) was erected in the year 391 of the

† Windmills were first erected in Egypt by the French, before which period all the grain in the country was ground in the houses in hand-mills (tâha) The latter are still chiefly used and the windmills have comparatively little to do.

Hegira by Sulêmân, the Mameluke, afterwards Sultân Selim. The architecture is a mixture of Arabian and Turkish, but the plan is rather Byzantine in character The mosque is small, but carefully executed. It contains Cufic inscriptions, marble mosaics, and a mambar in marble.

Route from the Citadel to the *Mokattam* and to the *Petrified Forest*, see p. 336.

On the W. side of the Place Méhémet Ali (p. 262) is the railway-station for Ḥelwân (p. 403). From this point a street called the *Salibeh* runs to the W., traversing the oldest, and now partly ruined, quarter of Cairo, which was erected by the Tulunides (p. 102), and is almost exclusively inhabited by the lower classes. About 440 yds. from the Place this street is intersected by another, running from N. to S., the N. (right) part of which is called the *Siûfîyeh*, and the S. (left) part the *Rugbîyeh*. At the beginning of the Siufîyeh, on the right, is a new Arabian Girls' School, and beyond it, on the same side, is the *Tekîyet el-Maulawîyeh* (Pl. 36; F. 3), where the dervishes perform their dances (p. 239), with a dome adorned with carefully sculptured arabesques. (This street terminates in the Boulevard Mohammed 'Ali) At the corner opposite the mosque is the recently completed *Sebîl of the Mother of 'Abbâs Pasha* (Pl. 94), in marble, rich and effective in general appearance, but lacking finish in its details. The large school above it is hardly worth visiting.

We now proceed in a straight direction to the *Place Seiyideh Zênab*, where we show our order of admission at the office of the Waḳf. Visitors on foot or on donkey-back follow an attendant with the key, who leads the way up the direct and somewhat steep path to the mosque. Those who are driving return to the Sebîl of the Mother of Abbâs Pasha and enter the Rugbîyeh street, follow it for about 300 yds., and turn down a street to the right, in which, after about 130 yds. more, we observe on the right the —

*Gâmi' ibn Tulûn (Pl. 68). This mosque, the oldest in Cairo, was erected by Abu'l-'Abbâs Aḥmed ibn Tulûn, the independent governor of Egypt under the suzerainty of Khalîf Mu'tamid (A.D. 870-92), in the year 265 of the Hegira (A.D. 879), on the once fortified hill of *Kal'at el-Kebsh* (see p. 268).

Aḥmed ibn Tulûn, the founder of the dynasty of the Tulunides (p. 102), was so successful in war that he extended the boundaries of Egypt beyond Syria and as far as Mesopotamia, but was proclaimed a rebel from the mambar of every mosque by the 'Abbaside khalif El-Mu'tamid of Baghdâd (see above), and fell a victim to disease in Syria in A D 884 According to one legend the mosque occupies the spot where Abraham sacrificed the goat *(kebsh)* instead of his son, whence the appellation Kal'at el-Kebsh (i e , 'castle of the goat') Another legend points to this as the spot where Noah's ark ran aground on the 10th Moharrem (p. 236), although the Muslims generally believe that this event took place on Mt. Jûdi near Mosul in Syria (see p. 143). According to a third tradition the name is derived from the winding staircase which ascends the still existing minaret (see below) in the form of a twisted ram's horn.

The construction of the edifice, which, as Makrizi informs us

(p. 201), was designed by a Christian in imitation of the Kaʿba at Mecca, occupied two years. Contrary to the practice followed in the case of earlier mosques, the whole of the building was constructed of entirely new materials. The walls consist of brick, coated with stucco.

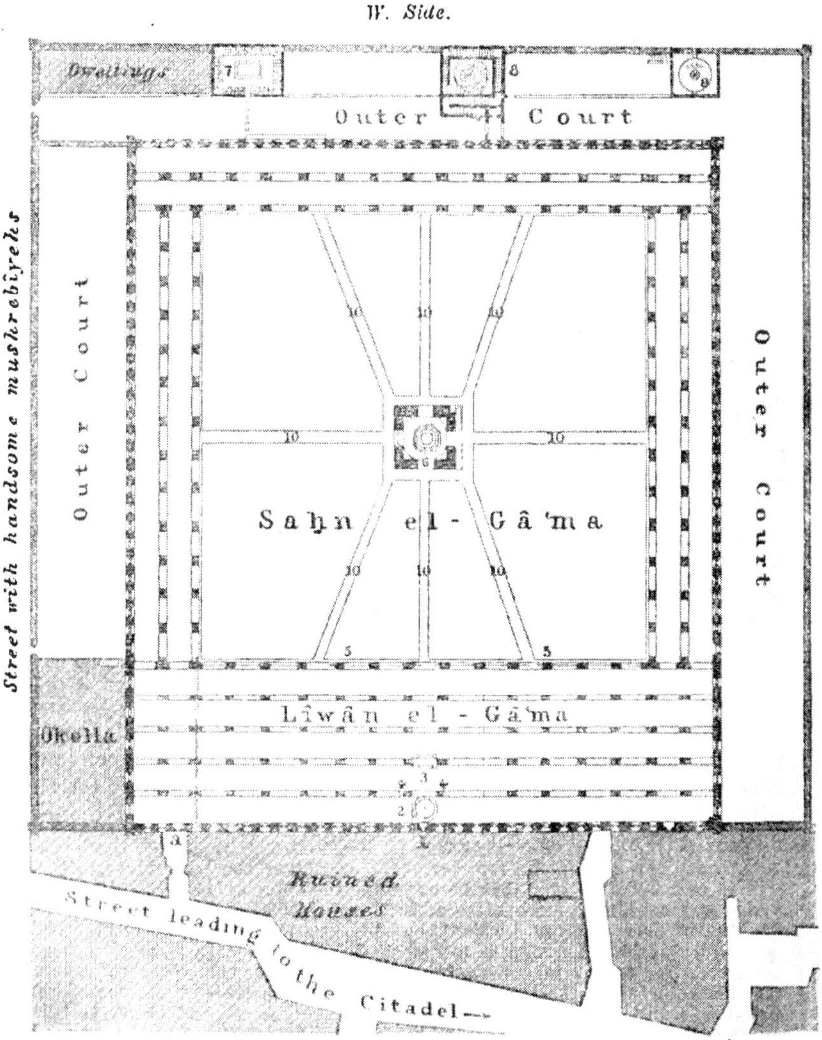

a. Entrance. 1. Kibla. 2. Mambar. 3. Dikkeh. 4. Kursi. 5. Railing and pillars (all of which fell in 1875), separating the Lîwân el-Gâmiʿ (sanctuary) from the court of the mosque. 6. Hanefîyeh. 7. Latrines. 8. Minaret. 9. Sâkiyeh. 10. Paved paths.

The Entrance (Pl. a) to the mosque is on the E. side, and we reach the interior by traversing the S. part of the Lîwân. The mosque originally had two entrances from each of the three outer courts (see Plan). The Ṣahn el-Gâmiʿ, which we first enter, is a spacious quadrangle, 99 yds. square. The dome-covered structure (Pl. 6) in the centre was destined to be the tomb of the founder; but, as he died in Syria (see p. 265), it was fitted up as a Ḥanefîyeh, or basin for ablution before prayer, and still serves that purpose.

On the N., W., and S. sides of the court of the mosque run arcades, which were at one time converted into cells for the reception of paupers and cripples. The character of the building, which must once have presented a very imposing and harmonious appearance, has thus been seriously injured. The Arabian historians relate that Aḥmed was so charmed with the edifice when completed that he presented the architect with 10,000 dinârs, and he is said to have defrayed the whole of the cost of its construction out of one of the treasures found by him (p. 102).

The pointed arches of the arcades are slightly depressed, and have a tendency towards the horseshoe form, a shape which is completely developed in the lower stories of the minaret (see below) Between the openings of the arcades are introduced pointed arches or niches, partly for purposes of support, and partly by way of ornament. The central pillars, which fell in 1814, once bore marble tablets with Cufic inscriptions, recording the date of the building of the mosque, but these have since been destroyed.

The Lîwân, or Sanctuary, on the E. side, through which we have entered the building, contains five series of arcades, and in each of the other sides of the court there are two series. With a view to exclude all sound of the outside world, the external wall of this chamber of prayer was separated from the street by a row of shops, and the three other sides were isolated by the introduction of outer courts beyond them, enclosed by lofty walls (see Plan).

All the angles in the interior are filled with columns built into the walls, extending two-thirds of the way up, without bases, and with imperfectly defined capitals in plaster. At certain places in the pillars and the masonry longitudinal beams of wood have been introduced for the purpose of strengthening the building, but they are visible only where the external incrustation has fallen off. The perforated attics, the gratings of stucco, the ornamentation, and the Cufic inscriptions in stucco are all executed in strict conformity with the Byzantine-Arabian style. In the *Ḳibla* (Pl. 1), however, we observe two marble columns with capitals of more pronounced Byzantine form. The upper part of the niche is adorned with gilded mosaic, and the lower part with inlaid marble, while above is a dome with stalactites. The *Mambar* (Pl. 2), a masterpiece of wood-carving, was probably restored when the mosque was repaired by El-Melik el-Manṣûr in the year 696 of the Hegira.

The roof, with its open timber-work and octagonal recesses, constructed of the trunks of date-palms and overlaid with sycamore wood, formerly rested on 158 rectangular pillars of brick, coated with stucco. The friezes, bearing Cufic inscriptions, are also of sycamore wood.

The outer court on the W. side contains a Ṣâkiyeh (P. 9) and the singular Minaret (Pl. 8), with its external winding staircase, the design of which is said to have been suggested to Ṭulûn by a strip of paper wound round his finger, and which is the only one of the kind except that of the Mabkhara of the Gâmiʿ Ḥâkim (p. 279). The minaret commands a good survey of the oldest buildings of Cairo, but, owing to its ruinous condition, the ascent is now prohibited. (Fee to the attendant who shows the Lîwân 1-2 piastres).

Outside the entrance to the mosque we turn to the right, and then to the right again. Passing the S. side of the mosque, where we observe several handsome mushrebiyehs on the left side of the street, and turning a little to the left, we traverse several lanes and alleys, built on what was formerly the hill of Ḳalʿat el-Kebsh (p. 265), and reach the small, but once handsome —

Gâmiʿ Ḳait Bey (Pl. 48), which, like most of the buildings of its period, long lay in a neglected condition, and was only lately saved from complete ruin. This mosque was erected in the 15th cent., and in plan resembles the Tomb of Ḳait Bey (p. 286).

Ḳaid or *Ḳait Bey* (1468-96) was one of the last independent Mameluke sultans of Egypt. Both as a general and a diplomatist he successfully maintained his position against the Porte (Sultans Mohammed and Bajazid), and even inflicted serious losses on the Turks, but the refractory Mamelukes obstructed his undertakings, and in 1496 compelled him to abdicate in favour of his son Mohammed, a boy of fourteen

The door, with its bronze covering, is about 45 ft. in height. The mosque is about 26 yds. in length and 22 yds. in width. The attics have almost entirely fallen in, but a graceful minaret still exists. Opposite the Ḳibla is a gallery, serving as a dikkeh, which is accessible from the staircase to the minaret. The principal arches, which approach the horseshoe shape, though distinctly pointed, are tastefully decorated. The mambar is richly embellished with wood-carving. The mosaics on the pavement and the walls are also worthy of notice. Bakshîsh, $^1/_2$ piastre for each person.

In a small *place* on the Khalîg, or canal traversing the city, about 550 yds. to the N.W. of the mosque of Ḳait Bey, lies the **Gâmiʿ es-Seiyideh Zênab** (Pl. 72; F, G, 4), which was begun at the close of last century, but not completed until after the French invasion (in the year of the Hegira 1216), and which has been recently enlarged. The mosque, richly embellished with ancient columns, contains the tomb of Zênab, daughter of Imâm ʿAli, and granddaughter of the Prophet (her môlid, see p. 237), consisting of a sarcophagus, enclosed by a bronze railing, with a lofty dome above it (shown by special permission only). — Outside the mosque, to the right of the entrance, is the sarcophagus of another Mohammedan saint.

A long series of tortuous streets, called *Derb el-Gamâmîz* ('sycamore street'), running not far from the canal, leads hence towards the N. to the Boulevard Méhémet Ali. After fully half-a-mile we come to a small open space by the canal, shaded by some fine acacias. The gate on the right leads to the viceroyal *Library (*Kutubkhâneh*, Pl. 30), founded by the Khedive Isma'îl on 24th March, 1870, in the left wing of the office of the minister of public worship. The collection consists of a number of books formerly preserved in various other institutions, and of others purchased or presented by the Khedive, and is dedicated to the use of the public. One of the finest presentations to the collection is the valuable library of Muṣṭafa Pasha, which occupies a separate room. The whole library consists of about 25,000 vols., chiefly Arabic and Turkish works, and there is a small European department, principally containing scientific works in French, which is to be gradually extended. The library is open to the public from 3 to 6 and from 7 to 10 o'clock by Arabian time, *i.e.* about three hours in the forenoon and three hours in the afternoon, and the officials are instructed to afford visitors all the information in their power. Books must be consulted in the reading-room, the use of which is accorded to persons provided with a permission from the ministry of public instruction or with a certificate from their consul, bearing their names, and available for a year. The library is closed on Fridays; and during the month of Ramaḍân it is open in the afternoon only. The chief credit of arranging and increasing this fine collection of books belongs to two Germans, Dr. Stern and Dr. Spitta-Bey (d. 1883), but the present director is an Arab shêkh, named Murad Effendi.

The liberality with which the treasures of Muslim literature are thus thrown open to the European public is deserving of all praise. A special feature of the library, possessed by no other Oriental collection available to Franks, consists of the *Maṣâhif*, or copies of the Korân, collected from various mosques of Cairo, and now preserved from destruction. They are remarkable for their large size, superb execution, and great age, and constitute the finest existing specimens of Arabian art.

The oldest specimen of the Korân is one in the *Cufic*, or early Arabian, character, 12 inches in length, and 8¾ inches in width. It contains one-half of the Korân only, and is in a very damaged condition, having, moreover, once been injured by fire The titles of the sûrehs are bordered with gold, and the carefully written text illuminated with coloured letters. According to the testimony of a shêkh who saw the 'noble book' in its perfect condition this Korân was written by *Ga'far es-Ṣâdik*, son of Moḥammed el-Bakir, son of 'Ali Zên el-'Abidîn, son of Ḥusên, son of 'Ali, son of Abu Ṭâlib and son-in-law of the Prophet. This Ga'far was a great chemist and scholar, whose pupil Ṭartûsi, according to Ibn Khallikân (1,147, ed. of Bûlâk), once stated that he had written about 500 different pamphlets. He lived in the years 80-148 of the Hegira, and this Korân would thus be about 1150 years old There is considerable doubt as to the accuracy of this story, but the MS. is certainly of very early date

The other fine large copies of the Korân, about twenty in all, are of later origin, most of them having been executed by order of the sultans of the Bahrite Mamelukes (1260-1382) and of the Circassian Mamelukes (1382-1516), while a few of them date from the still later period of the Osman sultans.

One of the most interesting of these is the copy of *'Abd er-Razzâk*, written by *'Abd er-Rahmân ibn Abulfath* in the year 590 of the Hegira, and dedicated to the mosque of Husên, 11¼ by 8¾ inches. This Korân is more remarkable for age than beauty. To the superscription of each sûreh are added both the number of verses and that of the words and letters it contains, besides traditional utterances of the Prophet connected with the chapter in question, — a most laborious piece of work, resembling what has been done by Jewish scholars in preparing copies of the Old Testament. Another copy, dating from 635 of the Hegira, 12¾ by 10½ inches, which once belonged to the mosque of Husên, has its titles in gold, but it is in a damaged condition.

Next in interest is a Korân of Sultân *Mohammed en-Nâsir ibn Sêfeddîn Kalaûn* (1293-1341), 21 by 14 inches, written by *Ahmed Yûsuf*, a Turk, in 730 of the Hegira. It is written entirely in gilded characters, and there is also a second copy of a similar description. Several other Korâns date from the reign of Sultân *Sha'ban* (1363-77), grandson of the last named, to whose mosque they were dedicated. The first of these, dating from 769, 27½ by 19½ inches, has not its titles written in the usual Cufic character, and the headings 'in the name of God the all-merciful' are in gold. Of the same date and similar size is the Korân of *Khondabaraka*, mother of Sultân Sha'bân. The first two pages are written in gilded and coloured characters, blue being the prevailing colour, and are illuminated with stars and arabesques, the next two are in gold, embellished with faint arabesques, and the whole work is written in a bold and excellent style. Another copy of Sultân Sha'bân, dating from 770, of the same width, but a little longer, contains some beautiful workmanship on the early pages. The text is wider than that of the last, and the book is bound in two volumes. Another and still larger copy, dating from the same year, measures 32¾ by 21 inches. All these last were destined for the school in the *Khutt et-Tabbâneh* (street of the straw-sellers), founded by *Khondabaraka*, the sultan's mother. Lastly we may mention another copy written in 778, by order of the same prince, by *'Ali ibn Mohammed el-Mokattib*, and gilded by *Ibrahim el-Amedi*, from which we gather that these Korâns were sometimes the work of several different hands. This copy measures 28 by 20¼ inches, and above each sûreh is recorded the number of words and letters it contains. All these masâhif are written on thick and strong paper, and vie with each other in magnificence. The designs exhibit no great variety, but they are executed with the most elaborate care and neatness. The text of these Korâns is provided with red letters written above certain passages to indicate where the tone of the reader's voice is to be raised, lowered, or prolonged.

The collection contains three Korâns of the reign of Sultân *Barkûk* (1382-99), the oldest of which, executed in 769, measures 41 by 32 inches. It was written by order of Muhammed ibn Muhammed, surnamed Ibn el-Butût, by *'Abderrahmân es-Sâïgh*, with one pen in sixty days, and revised by Muhammed ibn Ahmed ibn 'Ali, surnamed Elkufti. A second copy, of the same sultan's reign, and of similar size, has its first and last pages restored in the same style as those of other copies, but the modern workmanship is inferior to the ancient. A smaller Korân, of the year 801, measuring 23 by 19½ inches, is written entirely in gilded characters.

To Sultân *Farag* (1399-1412), the son of Barkûk, once belonged a copy of the Korân dating from 814, and brought to the library from the mosque of Muaiyad. It measures 37 by 29¼ inches, and was also written by 'Abderrahmân es-Sâïgh, the same skilful penman who had been previously employed by Barkûk, and the author of a pamphlet, entitled *'Sanâ'at el-Kitâbeh'* (the art of writing), and now preserved in this library. From the year 810 dates a fine copy, 38½ by 27 inches, written by *Mûsa ibn Ismâ'îl el-Kinani*, surnamed *Gagini*, for Sultân *Shêkh el-Mahmûdi Muaiyad* (1412-21).

A copy which once belonged to *Kait-Bey* (1468-96), dating from the year 909, or a century later than the last, and unfortunately in a very injured condition, is the largest Korân in the collection, measuring 44¾ by 35 inches. To the period of the Osman sultans belongs the small muṣḥaf of *Ṣafiya*, mother of Sultân Mohammed Khân, who caused fifty-two copies to be written by *Mohammed ibn Ahmed el-Khalîl el-Tebrîzî*. It dates from 988, and measures 14 by $9^1/_3$ inches. In it, as in one of the other copies, a black line alternates with a gilded one, and the first few pages are very beautifully executed. A copy of *Husên-Bey Khemashûrgi*, $21^1/_2$ by $16^3/_4$ inches, is written in a smaller character.

The library also boasts of many other valuable Korâns, chiefly written in the Persian character. One of these, $17^1/_2$ by 12 inches, presented by an Indian hokmdâr to the Khedive, has a Persian commentary written in red between the lines of the text, and is beautifully illuminated at the beginning and at the end. Another copy, presented by a prince of Bukhâra, contains four commentaries two in Arabic by Bêdâwi and Gelalên, and two in Persian. Another gift of the same donor was the prayer-book '*Dalâil el-Khairât*', written on a golden ground, and furnished with a Persian translation. There is also a Korân about 9 inches only in length, illuminated with gilded flowers, and dating from the year 1109 of the Hegira. It was written by Mohammed Ruh Allâh, and contains the thirty different parts of the Korân on thirty pages. Each line begins with an *alif*, the first letter of the Arabic alphabet — a most laborious performance. Another Korân, once the property of the Sultân *Elga Elyusfi*, measuring $20^1/_4$ by 16 inches, is written in two different handwritings, the larger being named Thuluthi, and the smaller Neshi. The highest efforts of Arabian calligraphy and illumination are also displayed in several Moghrebin MSS., and in a number of single leaves bearing texts from the Korân or sayings of the prophet.

The ancient Muslims bestowed the utmost care on these precious copies of the Korân, and their descendants still entertain profound veneration for the sacred volume sent from heaven. The library possesses many other ancient and valuable MSS., but they are all entirely eclipsed by these Maṣâhif. They possess, however, great interest for the Arabic scholar, to whom they are willingly exhibited, and form the first collection of the kind in the world. The library is especially rich in numerous commentaries on the Korân and books containing traditions of the prophet, as well as works on the law of the four Muslim sects, particularly the Hanefites and Shâfe'ites. The library likewise contains a number of historical, grammatical, and astrological works, some of which are very ancient, not a few being in the handwriting of their authors. Among the poetical MSS. the most important is that of Mutanebbi, dating from 553 of the Hegira, with a commentary by Ibn Ginni, who also wrote a commentary on the Hamâsa. A MS., entitled 'Poems of the Arabs', dates from the same year, and among the MSS. of the Hamâsa is a Moghrebin or Algerian work, written 'from the recitation of the best-informed persons', and dating from 597. There is also an old MS. of the commentary of Merzûki upon the collection of poems made by him. The fine MS. of Firdusi, embellished with many coloured illustrations, was presented by the Shah of Persia. The above enumeration will convey some idea of the valuable contents of the library, of which at present there is only an Arabic index, though a French catalogue is now in course of preparation. The printed books are less numerous than the MSS., and they are chiefly from the Bûlâk press. Some of the surplus copies derived from that source have been sold by the library.

After visiting the library the traveller may inspect the neighbouring *Dervish Monastery* in the *Habbanîyeh* (Pl. 11; permission must be procured from the minister of public worship). The monastery was erected in 1174 of the Hegira by Muṣṭafa Agha, vizier of Sulṭân Selîm. The round sebîl is the most interesting object in the establishment. The building possesses a large court, raised considerably above the street, and containing a few trees. Around the court are the cells of the dervishes, and adjoining it is a small mosque. With regard to the dervishes, see p. 150.

Continuing to follow the same street, we cross the new *Boulevard Shêkh Rîḥân*, and beyond it the Boulevard Moḥammed ʿAli (see p. 260). Beyond the latter we pass an open space, on the right side of which is the *Palace of Manṣûr Pasha* (Pl. 85; unattractive), and enter the street named after the *Gâmiʿ el-Benât* (Pl. 40; 'mosque of the girls'), which rises on the right. On the left, a little beyond the mosque, and on the farther bank of the canal, is the entrance to the house of *Shêkh Mufti*, or *Shêkh ul-Islâm* (Pl. 95), the interesting interior of which is shown by special permission only (p. 241). The street then runs on towards the N., in a straight direction, and terminates in the Muski, near the Hôtel du Nil (p. 231).

If we leave the Palace of Manṣûr Pasha (see above) on the left, and follow a lane leading to the S.E. (right) corner of the *place* called after the old gate *Bâb el-Khalk*, we reach after about 500 paces more the (left) old town-gate **Bâb ez-Zuwêleh** (Pl. D, 2), built of solid blocks of stone, and resembling the Bâb el-Futûḥ (p. 280) in plan. The S. side consists of two huge towers; by that to the right are a number of stone and wooden balls, probably dating from the Mameluke period. Ṭûmân Bey, the last of the Circassian sultans of Egypt, was hanged outside this gate by Sulṭân Selîm II., on 19th Rabîʿ el-Awwel, 923 of the Hegira (15th April, 1517; p. 243). This gate is also called *Bâb el-Mutawelli*, from the old tradition that the most highly revered saint Ḳuṭb † el-Mutawelli has his abode behind the western gate, where he sometimes makes his presence known by a gleam of light. A beggar who spends the day here endeavours, by loudly invoking the saint, to excite the compassion of passers-by. From the inner (E.) gate hang bunches of hair, teeth, shreds of clothing, and other votive offerings placed here by sick persons who hope thereby to be cured of their diseases.

Passing through the gate, we enter the street called *Sukkarîyeh* (p. 254), where on the left we observe the handsome portal of the **Gâmiʿ el-Muaiyad** (Pl. 57), a mosque which is connected with the gate of the city. The interior is undergoing restoration, and is, therefore, not easily accessible. This mosque was erected by Sulṭân Shêkh el-Maḥmûdi Muaiyad (1412-21), of the dynasty of the Circassian Mamelukes, who had once been the leader of the

† *Kutb* properly means pole or axis This greatest of the Mohammedan saints is so named because the other weli's, who are divided into three classes (*naḳib*, pl. *nuḳaba; negib*, pl *nugaba; bedil*, pl. *abdâl*), are considered, as it were, to revolve round him. According to the generally received belief of the Muslims the favourite abode of this saint is on the roof of the Kaʿba, but the Egyptians regard the Bâb ez-Zuwêleh as at least his next most favoured dwelling-place, and therefore sometimes call it the gate of El-Mutawelli, *i e.* 'of the reigning ḳuṭb'. The tomb of Seyyid Ahmed el-Bedawi (p. 225) is another resort of the ḳuṭb, who of course can instantaneously transport himself from Mecca to Cairo or elsewhere at pleasure.

rebellion against Sulṭân Farag (p. 284), and who had been defeated by the sultan and imprisoned for a time at this spot. The edifice is also known as the *Gâmiʿ el-Aḥmar*, or the red mosque, from the colour of its exterior.

Sultân Shêkh el-Mahmûdi Muaiyad, after having defeated and executed Sulṭân Farag, his predecessor, who was the son of Barkûk, the founder of the Circassian Mameluke dynasty of the Burgites (from the Arabic *burg*, or castle, and so called from their service in fortresses), ascended the throne in Nov. 1412. His reign was chiefly occupied with victorious campaigns against his unruly Syrian vassals, in which he was greatly aided by the military talents of his son *Ibrâhîm*. He was a man of weak constitution, and the early death of Ibrâhîm is said to have accelerated his end; while some authors state, on the other hand, that he caused Ibrâhîm to be poisoned from jealousy on account of his greater popularity Muaiyad died on 13th Jan. 1421 Although, according to Egyptian historians, he died very wealthy, his coffers did not contain money enough after his death to defray the expenses of his funeral, all his property having been carried off by his emirs, while no one cared for the dead body Though successful in his foreign policy, he had neglected to secure the good will of his people His emirs were never sure of their lives, many of them having been imprisoned or executed on mere suspicion. As most of the public offices were sold to the highest bidder, his subjects were oppressed and maltreated by his judges and officials, who sought to indemnify themselves by practising all kinds of extortion. Notwithstanding all the misfortunes he brought upon Egypt by his maladministration and cupidity, Muaiyad had no lack of panegyrists, who remembered only that he was a pious Muslim, that he associated much with scholars, that he was distinguished as a theologian, an orator, and a poet, and that he had founded a mosque, a hospital, and a *medreseh*, or theological school. On several occasions, after having perjured himself with a view to compass the destruction of his opponents, he spent several days in a dervish monastery, attended the zikrs, and loaded the monastery with presents Like the dervishes, he usually wore nothing but a woollen robe, and to prove his humility he commanded the preachers to descend one of the steps of their pulpits when they had occasion to mention his name Towards religionists of other creeds he was intolerant in the highest degree He exacted heavy contributions from Christians and Jews, and he re-enacted and rigorously enforced the sumptuary laws of ʿOmar (A D 634-44), Mutawakkil (849-50), the Fâtimite Khalîf Ḥâkim (996-1020; see p. 279), and Sultân Moḥammed en-Nâsir (1293-1341; p 277) Not only were the colours to be worn by the Christians and Jews prescribed (the costume of the former being dark blue, with black turbans, and a wooden cross weighing 5lbs. hung round their necks, that of the latter, yellow, with black turbans, and a black ball hung from their necks); but the fashion of their dress and length of their turbans, and even the costume of their women, were so regulated as entirely to distinguish them from the followers of the prophet.

The handsome bronze gate at the entrance originally belonged to the mosque of Sulṭân Ḥasan (p. 260). The plan of the mosque resembles that of the mosque of ʿAmr (p. 324); but this edifice is richer in its details, although without any strongly defined characteristics. Here, too, columns of many different kinds have been employed. On the right, by the Maḳṣûra, is the mausoleum of the sultan, and on the left that of his family. The sanctuary is separated by a railing from the inner court (Ṣaḥn el-Gâmiʿ), which is shaded with acacias and sycamores. The ruins on the S. side are those of a public bath which was formerly connected with the mosque, but its plan is scarcely now traceable. The mosque has three minarets, two of which rise above the outbuildings of the *Bâb ez-Zuwêleh* (see above), the city-gate connected with the sacred edifice.

[Outside the gate, towards the S.E., to the left of the sentry, is the *Derb el-Aḥmar*, or 'red way', recently called Rue de la Citadelle, leading to the Citadel (p. 262). About 450 yds. from the Bâb Mutawelli, by a bend of the road towards the right, rises the *Gâmi' el-Werdâni* (or *Mardâni;* Pl. 69), with its graceful minaret. The court, now closed, and used as a magazine, is adorned with slender columns and pointed arches.]

Following the Sukkarîyeh street to the left (N.) for about 100 yds. more, we observe on the right the modern *Sebîl of Moḥammed 'Ali*, in marble (Pl. 92), a fountain of pleasing appearance, though imperfect in its details. To the left, about 270 yds. farther on, where the street now takes the name of *El-Ghûrîyeh* (p. 254), we observe, slightly projecting into the road, the ***Gâmi' el-Ghûri** (Pl. 42), and opposite to it the **Sebîl* and *Medreseh* erected by the same founder. The two façades, dating from the second half of the 10th cent. of the Hegira, and presenting a very harmonious effect, are most interesting. The walls of the interior are adorned with inlaid figures. A shirt of the Prophet brought by Sulṭân el-Ghûri from Mecca, was formerly shown at this mosque, but it is now said to be preserved in the Citadel, where it is shown once annually to the higher government officials only, who have the privilege of kissing the precious relic. The Sebîl and Medreseh have been skilfully restored by the architect of the Waḳf, a German named *Franz-Bey*, and are to be extended and adapted to contain the viceroyal library (p. 269).

Kansuweh el-Ghûri (1501-16), once a slave of Sultân Kait Bey, was chosen sultan on 20th April, 1501, after the downfall of Ṭûmân Bey, who had reigned for one hundred days only. Although upwards of sixty years of age when he ascended the throne, he still possessed considerable vigour and energy. He kept the unruly emîrs in check, and neutralised the influence of the older Mamelukes by the purchase of new slaves. Although himself of servile origin, he was as great a lover of splendour as if he had belonged to a princely family. His stables contained the finest horses in Egypt, his rings the most precious jewels, his dinner-service was of the purest gold, and his palace and citadel were the resort of poets, minstrels, and musicians. He improved the roads and canals of Egypt, founded schools and mosques, and constructed fortifications; but, in order to accomplish all this, he imposed burdensome taxes on his people. On one occasion he levied a subsidy on all landed property in Egypt and Syria amounting to the value of ten months' produce, and he taxed the estates of religious institutions still more heavily than those of private individuals. A similar tax was imposed on mills, ships, beasts of burden, and irrigation machinery, and all government pensions were withheld for ten months, while large sums were arbitrarily extorted from the merchants. At the same time he levied heavy dues on imports and exports, debased the coinage, and taxed the inspectors of markets, who indemnified themselves by exactions from the dealers. Already seriously injured by the discovery of the Cape route to India by the Portuguese, the trade of Egypt was terribly depressed by these tyrannical proceedings. Having at length been made aware by the Venetians of the dangers which threatened his country, Kansuweh el-Ghûri endeavoured to protect its commerce by equipping a fleet for service against the Portuguese in India, and with it in 1508 he gained a naval victory over Lorenzo, son of the viceroy Francisco d'Almeida, near Shawl in Beluchistan, but the following year his fleet was compelled to retreat to Arabia in a shattered condition Meanwhile Ḥusên had conquered Ḥijâz and Yemen, and added them to the Egyptian dominions, on which occasion El-Ghûri caused the whole of the S. side of the Ḥarâm at Mecca to be rebuilt (in 906 of the Hegira), as recorded there by an inscription under the Bâb Ibrâhim; but these districts soon threw off his yoke and placed themselves under the suzerainty of the Osmans, and, before his newly equipped fleet reached India, the sultan himself died On 24th Aug. 1516, while fighting against the army of the Osman sultan Selim I. in the plain of Dâbik (to the N. of Aleppo), he is said to have fallen down in a fit of apoplexy, and to have been slain by his own followers, either from motives of cupidity, or to prevent his being captured by the enemy His head was afterwards cut off and carried as a trophy to the victor.

Farther on, we leave the *Gâmiʿ el-Ashraf* (Pl. 37; uninteresting) to the left, and, about 220 yds. from the Gâmiʿ el-Ghûri, reach the Rue Neuve (Muski, p. 253).

N.E. Quarters. Mûristân Ḳalaûn.   Tomb of Sultân Moḥammed en-Nâṣir ibn Ḳalaûn. Gâmiʿ Barkukîyeh.   Gâmiʿ Ḥâkım.   Bâb en-Naṣr. Bâb el-Futûḥ. Tombs of the Khalîfs.

Starting from the Ezbekîyeh and ascending the Muski as far as the El-Ghûrîyeh street, on the right (p. 254), and the Bazaar of the Coppersmiths (en-Naḥḥâsîn; Pl. C, 2; p. 256), on the left, we follow the latter, passing the entrance to the Khân el-Khalîli on the right (p. 255), and after a few hundred paces observe on the left three mosques, adjoining each other, with staring red and white striped façades (p. 180). The first of these is the —

Mûristân Ḳalaûn (Pl. 73), once a vast hospital ('mûristân', from the Persian word bîmaristân), the greater part of which is now in a ruinous condition, and used as a workshop by coppersmiths and tinkers. The tomb of the founder, however, which also serves the purpose of a mosque, is tolerably preserved. The foundation-stone was laid by Sulṭân el-Manṣûr Ḳalaûn (1279-90) in the year 683 of the Hegira, and the whole edifice is said to have been completed within thirteen months.

Passing over a son of Bêbars, who was a minor, Ḳalaûn ascended the throne of Egypt in Nov. 1279 He gained a victory over a rebellious governor of Damascus, he defeated the Mongolians, who were threatening Syria, at Homs; he chastised the princes of Armenia and Georgia for allying themselves with the Mongolians, who had invited Pope Nicholas IV., Edward I. of England, and Philip le Bel of France to attack Syria, offering them the necessary horses, beasts of burden, and provisions; he entered into treaties with Emperor Rudolph, the Genoese, Alphonso III of Castile, Jacopo of Sicily, the prince of Yemen, and the prince of Ceylon, he took the town of Lâdikîyeh (Laodicea) from the prince of Tripoli, and then Tripoli itself, which after the death of Bohemund had fallen into the hands of Bertram of Gibelet; and he made preparations to wrest from the Christians their fortress of ʿAkka (Acre), the only one still held by them in Syria Before, however, he could proceed to carry out this last enterprise, he died on 10th Nov. 1290 Ḳalaûn is immoderately praised by the Egyptian historians. He was, indeed, less bloodthirsty than Bêbars, and less tyrannical towards his subjects, but in the prosecution of his schemes

18ᵃ

of aggrandisement he committed flagrant breaches of justice and honour, deeming no treaty sacred, if its violation promised him any advantage.

The Mûristân, the finest monument of Kalaûn's reign, was so extensive, that it contained a separate ward for every known disease (see Plan), besides rooms for women; and connected with it were abundant stores of provisions and medicines. It also contained a large lecture-room, in which the chief physician delivered medical lectures. Not only the poor, but even persons of means, were received gratuitously as patients, and the con-

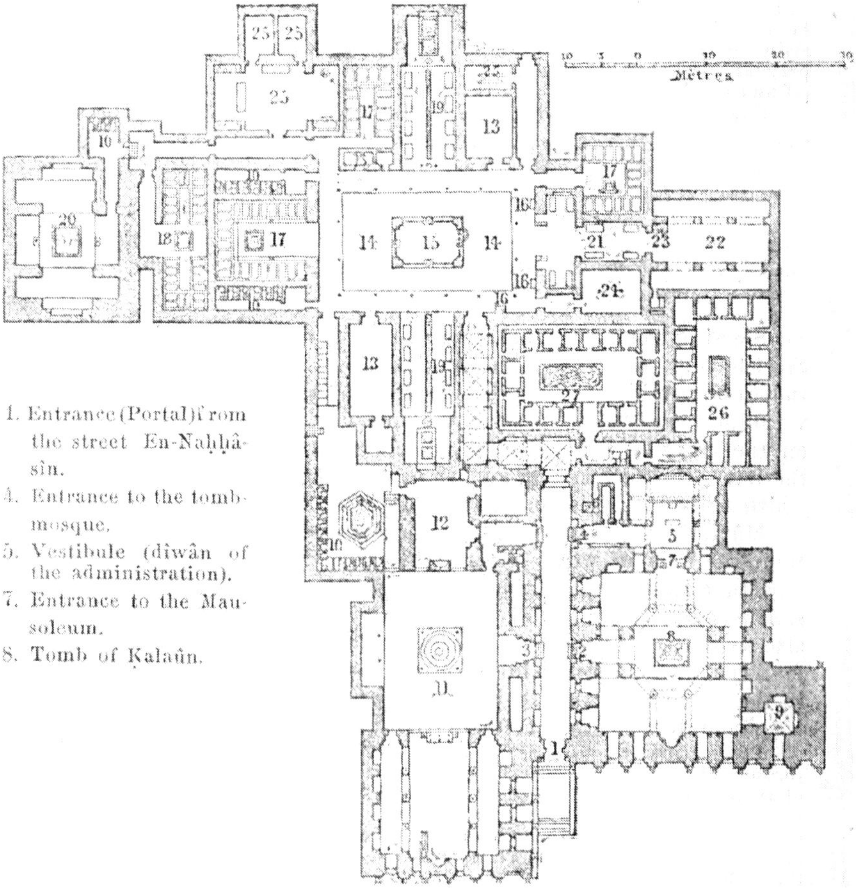

1. Entrance (Portal) from the street En-Naḥḥâsîn.
4. Entrance to the tomb-mosque.
5. Vestibule (dîwân of the administration).
7. Entrance to the Mausoleum.
8. Tomb of Kalaûn.

The other numbers in the Plan are intended to convey an idea of the *former* arrangements of the hospital, but some of the rooms are in a dilapidated condition, while others are now used for various other purposes. No. 2. Closed entrance to the Mausoleum; 3. Entrance to No. 11. formerly part of the mosque; 9. Minaret; 10. Basin; 12. Room for prayer; 13. Magazines; 14. Surgical room; 15. Rooms of the physicians; 16-19. Rooms for patients; 20. Attendants' room; 21. Court; 22. Shêkh; 23. Magazine; 24. Dead-house; 25. Kitchen; 26, 27. Cells for the insane.

sumption of food was so large that the hospital employed several officials for the sole purpose of buying provisions and keeping accounts. Besides these officials there were a number of others, whose duty it was to collect the various revenues set apart for the support of the institution In the tomb-mosque the Korân and the religious traditions connected with it were publicly taught, the teachers and the pupils both being supported by government A large adjacent apartment contained the library, which was well stocked with exegetical treatises on the Korân, books of traditions, grammars, and medical, theological, legal, and literary works, and was kept in good order by a librarian and five assistants. The school-building contained four lecture-rooms for the teachers of the four schools of Mohammedanism (p. 149); and there was also a school for children, where sixty orphans were maintained and educated gratuitously.

In the tomb-chamber are still preserved articles of dress which once belonged to Kalaûn, and are populary supposed to possess miraculous virtues. Thus, the shawl (*'immeh*) of his turban is supposed to cure headaches, and one of his heavy kaftâns, wrapped round the body of the patient for 24 hours, is said to be an infallible remedy for ague This superstitious belief in the healing powers of the sultan's clothing is probably due to the fact that he devoted much attention to medicine

The Portal (Pl. 1; Nos. 1-8 are the only parts of the building now preserved; the other numbers on the plan show the *former* arrangements), the most interesting part of the whole edifice, is constructed of black and white marble, and is of imposing height. The doors still show traces of their former covering of bronze. The ceiling of the entrance, with its open beams, is also very effective.

The corridors, most of which are vaulted in the Gothic style, appear to some extent to have lost their original regularity in consequence of their restoration by Seyyid el-Mabrûki and Ahmed Pasha Ṭâher during the present century.

The second door (Pl. 4) on the right leads to the Vestibule (Pl. 5) of the *Tomb of Ḳalaûn*, now used as an office by the administrators of the Waḳf. The tomb itself contains a fine granite column, and the lower parts of the walls are covered with mosaics in marble. The ḳibla (prayer-recess), with its mosaics, its beautiful dwarf-arcades, and its shell-shaped ornamentation, is also worthy of notice. The disposition of the pairs of windows resembles that which occurs in Christian churches of the Romanesque period. The stucco tracery with which the windows are filled should also be inspected.

Adjacent to the Mûristân is the *****Tomb of Sulṭân Moḥammed en-Nâṣir ibn Ḳalaûn** (1293-1341; Pl. 56), dating from 698 of the Hegira.

In 1293 *Mohammed en-Nâsir ibn Kalaûn*, son of the Kalaûn above mentioned, when only nine years of age, succeeded his elder brother Khalîl, who is better known as El-Ashraf (p 255) At the beginning of his reign sanguinary feuds broke out between Ketboga, his vicegerent, and Shujâi, his vizier In Dec. 1294, Ketboga, having got rid of his antagonist, usurped the sceptre, but two years later was dethroned by the discontented emîrs, and was succeeded by Lajîn, son-in-law of Bêbars, and once a slave of Kalaûn, who is said to have been a German by birth, and to have been brought to Egypt when ten years old Lajîn having been assassinated in Jan 1299, Nâsir, who had meanwhile resided at Kerak, a Syrian fortress to the E of the Dead Sea, was recalled Although he had gained several victories over the Mongolians, who were threatening Syria and even Egypt itself, he was still treated by his emîrs as a youth under age, and the real rulers of the country were Sallar, his chancellor, and Bêbars II Jashengir, the prefect of his palace, who had originally been a Circassian slave. In 1309 Nâṣir returned to Kerak, for the avowed purpose of undertaking a pilgrimage to Mecca, but on his arrival there he announced his intention to throw off the trammels of tutelage, and for a time to establish his residence at Kerak. The consequence was that he was declared at Cairo to have forfeited his throne, and Bêbars II was proclaimed sultan in his stead (April, 1309). The Syrian emîrs, however, remained faithful to Nâṣir, and with their aid he succeeded in re-establishing his authority in Egypt, although the nominal 'Abbaside Khalif residing at Cairo had pronounced him an outlaw and declared war against him. The three chief traits in Nâṣir's character, distrust, vindictiveness, and cupidity, now became very prominent, and there was no promise or oath which he deemed inviolable. He treated his emîrs with the utmost capriciousness, presenting them with rich gifts, or ordering them to be executed, as the humour seized him, and this feature of his character has been aptly described by an Arabian historian, who declares 'that he fattened his emîrs, and killed them when thoroughly fattened, in order that all they had swallowed might return to him.' Isma'îl Abul Fidâ (p. 201), however, one of his emîrs, retained his master's favour till the time of his death, and even had the title of sultan conferred upon him. Towards the mass of the population, on the other hand, Nâṣir was always liberal and condescending, he abolished oppressive taxes, punished hoarders of grain, and distributed corn in times of famine. He was tolerant towards the Christians also, and was anxious to abrogate the regulations about dress (p. 273) which certain fanatics had induced him to make in his earlier years, but was unable to carry out his wish. He even appointed Christian officials, particularly in the custom-house and finance departments. His chief object was to surround himself with officers who could procure him money, to defray the enormous expenses of his court, to gratify his taste for horses (of which no fewer than 3000 are said to have been reared in his stables annually), and his love of building. He connected Alexandria anew with the Nile by means of a navigable canal, and constructed other canals also, such as that from Khânkâh to Siryâkûs, and embankments. In spite of his tyranny, he therefore enjoyed a considerable share of popularity, to which his stringent enforcement of the religious laws and his indulgence towards the clergy, so long as they did not interfere in politics, farther contributed. On 6th Jan. 1341 Nâṣir died the death of a pious and penitent Muslim. As soon as the emîrs perceived that his end was near, they seized upon the whole of his property, so that after his death not even a suitable pall to cover the corpse could be found. His miserable funeral took place by night, attended by a few emîrs only, and lighted by a single lantern. Thus, according to his Arabian biographers, terminated the reign of the powerful sultan whose dominions had extended from the frontier of Abyssinia to Asia Minor, and from the Euphrates to Tunis, but who, though wealthy and the father of twelve sons, died like a stranger and a childless man, and was buried like a pauper.

The late-Romanesque portal, in marble, with its round arch, is strikingly different from all other Arabian portals of the kind. It was originally erected at Acre in Syria, after the destruction of which it was transferred to Cairo in A.D. 1291 by the Egyptian Mameluke Sultân El-Ashraf (p. 255) as a trophy of victory. The only object of interest in the interior is the well-defined and beautifully moulded Arabian stucco-work, remains of which are preserved.

The third large building is the **Barkûkiyeh Mosque** (Pl. 39), erected at the close of the 14th cent. and containing the tomb of the daughter of Barḳûḳ. It possesses a marble portal and a bronze door, but the interior is uninteresting.

Barḳûḳ (1382-99), a Circassian slave, succeeded in raising himself to the throne by setting aside Ḥâggi, a boy of six years, and great-grandson of Moḥammed en-Nâṣir. He was proclaimed sultan in Nov. 1382, being the first of the Circassian Mameluke sovereigns (p. 104) His accession to the throne, which had been the result of treachery and intrigues of every kind, so exasperated the emîrs that they conspired against him and dethroned him in June, 1389 In Jan 1390, however, after having defeated his enemies, Barkûk celebrated his triumphal entry into Cairo. During his reign the Mongolians under Timur and the Osmans under Bajesid encroached on the frontiers of his empire, but Barkûk was not sufficiently energetic to resist their advances He died in 1399

These three mosques, with their three lofty minarets, present an imposing, though not quite regular, façade. Opposite to them is a modern sebîl. Continuing to follow the Naḥḥâsîn Bazaar (p. 256), which is generally enlivened by busy traffic, towards the left, we come to another fountain with a School (Pl. 91), erected by a certain *ʿAbder-Raḥmân Kikhya*, the founder of several religious edifices (p. 291). An arm of the Nile is said once to have flowed between the Tomb of Kalaûn and this fountain.

Passing to the right of the fountain, we reach the beginning of the *Gamelîyeh* street, the seat of the wholesale trade of Cairo (p. 257), the warehouses of which occupy the okellas (p. 257), or inner courts, of this part of the town The finest of these courts, which present no great attraction, is the *Okella Sulfiḳar Pasha* (Pl. 74), opposite the corner where our street bends to the N. The entrance, with a kind of star-vaulting, and the court, with its colonnades and mushrebîyehs, should be noticed. To the left, at the corner of the lane by which we have come, is the *Medreseh Gamelîyeh* (Pl. 32), with a late-Romanesque gateway, the original form of which is scarcely now traceable owing to the restoration and bedaubing it has undergone. At the back of this school is a tomb-mosque. Following the lane towards the N. for about 500 paces more, we reach a transverse lane on the left, which leads to the entrance of the —

· **Gâmiʿ el-Ḥâkim** (Pl. 43), erected at the beginning of the 5th cent. of the Hegira, on the plan of the Gâmiʿ ibn Tulûn, by Khalîf El-Ḥâkim, of the Fâtimite dynasty (p 102), the founder of the sect of the Druses. A Cufic inscription over the E. gate gives the date 393 of the Hegira (A.D. 1003).

El-Ḥâkim (996-1020), the third Fâtimite Khalif, succeeded his father ʿAzîz when scarcely eleven years old His bigoted attachment to the Shiʿite views (p. 153), and his intolerance towards the Sunnites, Christians, and Jews, rendered him unpopular with most of his subjects of the upper ranks. With the lower classes, on the other hand, consisting partly of Shiʿites and partly of Sunnites, he ingratiated himself by his liberality, his religious and unassuming mode of life, his zeal for the discipline of his soldiers, his rigorous administration of justice, and his persecution of the Jews and Christians. But while he wore the plainest kind of clothing and prayed daily among the people, he frequently caused his viziers and officials to be executed from mere caprice Down to the year 1017 he was a benefactor to the poor, but a sanguinary tyrant towards the rich, the great, and those who differed from him in creed. Till then he had been a devout Shî'ite and exacted obedience from his subjects as their lawful Imâm, but had repudiated any homage approaching to deification. He now, however, devoted himself entirely to the Ultra-Shî'ites, who elevated him to the rank of a god He was persuaded of his divinity by Mohammed ibn Isma'îl ed-Darazi, a cunning Persian sectary, who called on his people to recognise him as a deity. Thenceforward El-Ḥâkim discontinued his attendance at the mosques, ceased to organise pilgrimages, and exacted from his subjects the veneration due to a god Islâm became a matter of indifference to him, and he permitted the Christians and Jews who had embraced the religion of the prophet to return to their former faith, although by Mohammedan law such conduct was punishable with death. All the suppressed churches and synagogues were re-established, and their property restored to them, and the sumptuary laws were repealed. At length, on the night of 12th Feb. 1021, El-Ḥâkim disappeared, having probably been assassinated while taking one of his nightly walks on the Mokaṭṭam hills The Druses (the sect founded by Ed-Darazi, above mentioned), however, believe, that El-Ḥâkim voluntarily withdrew from the world in consequence of its sinfulness, and that he will one day re-appear and be worshipped by all nations as the last incarnation of the Deity.

Until quite recently the greater part of the old mosque lay in ruins, but the heaps of rubbish have now been removed or levelled, so as to clear the great court for the reception of the building materials of the Waḳf. The central part of the sanctuary was restored, as far as its advanced stage of dilapidation allowed, in order to contain a museum of Arabian art, which will shortly be opened. The court of the old mosque is to be occupied by a school of art.

The whole building occupies an area about 400 ft. long and 350 ft wide. The great court was adjoined on the side next the sanctuary by five aisles or arcades, on the W. by two, and on the N. and S. by three. These were supported by brick pillars, 10 ft. high and $4^{1}/_{2}$ ft. thick, incrusted with stucco. The pillars are rounded at the corners and bear pointed arches approaching the horseshoe form. The ceiling and the wooden bolts were formed of the stems of the date-palm. The Cufic inscriptions and arabesques are of little artistic value, and the entire structure was much less carefully and artistically built than its model, the Gâmi' Tûlûn. — On the N. side of the mosque are two massive Mabkhara (p. 177), with bases executed in the style of the Egyptian pylons. That at the N.E. corner is connected with the old town-walls, the bastions of which bear inscriptions dating from the French occupation of 1799.

Returning to the lane by which we have come, we follow it to the N., passing on the left an okella with an interesting gateway enriched with stalactite decoration, and a façade adorned with Arabian wood-carving. We now reach the —

Bâb en-Naṣr, or 'Gate of the Help of God', the plan of which was probably derived from the Roman castle of Babylon (p. 320). The ancient city-wall to the W. connects this gate with the similar **Bâb el-Futûh,** or 'Gate of Victory'. These two gates, together with the fortified mosque of Sulṭân Ḥâkim situated between them (see above), formed a strong position for the troops of Napoleon, whose cannons have only recently been removed from the terraces of the gates. The casemates and towers still bear French names cut in the bastion walls. On payment of a small bakshîsh, the visitor may ascend the Bâb en-Naṣr and the city-wall, and walk along the top of the latter to the Bâb el-Futûḥ. These gates, the most important of the sixty which once existed in the walls of Cairo, were erected by the vizier Berd Gamali in the 11th century. The Bâb en-Naṣr in particular is built of well-hewn stone, and has vaulted winding staircases in the interior, groined vaulting in the gateway, girders with a kind of hatched moulding, and cornices with a corbeled frieze. Over the entrance are a slab with a Cufic inscription, and decorative shields. The principal entrance of the Bâb el-Futûḥ is flanked with semicircular towers, and that of the Bâb en-Naṣr with square towers. The spaces between the inner and outer gates are vaulted.

We leave the Bâb en-Naṣr and turn to the right, crossing a Mohammedan burial-ground, on the left side of which, on a small

Bâb en-Naṣr. *Bâb el-Futûḥ.*
(From the side next the town.)

eminence not far from the road, is interred *J. L. Burckhardt* (d. 1817), the distinguished Oriental traveller, whose works are still of high authority.

Before leaving the city-wall to the right, we observe on the left two towers with iron basins, being the reservoirs of the **Waterworks** supplying the palace of the Khedive in the ʿAbbâsîyeh and the Citadel. In front of these, but less visible, are the five large filters for purifying the town supply.

The water is pumped into these filters by engines of 150-horse power, situated in the Ismaʿîlîya quarter, on the canal of that name. A smaller pump adjoining the filters is used for providing the Citadel with water. The first temporary pumping machinery, erected in 1865-66, at Kaṣr el-ʿAin, was employed in filling the basins in the desert, and also in supplying a small part of the city. The distribution of water is now effected by a double system of pipes, through one set of which the filtered water is forced to a height of about 80 ft., while the other brings unfiltered water from the neighbourhood of Bûlâḳ for the purpose of watering the streets and the gardens, conducting it to a height of about 30 ft. only. The engines in the Ismaʿîlîya quarter are capable of supplying the town with 30,000 cubic mètres, or about 111,000 cubic feet, of water per day. The government pays 40 centimes for each cubic mètre of filtered water consumed, and 25 centimes for the same quantity of unfiltered water. The lowest rate payable by small families for filtered water is 8 fr. per month. The whole length of the pipes for filtered water, the largest of which are 2 ft. in diameter, amounts to 19 miles, and that of the pipes for unfiltered water to about 6 miles. The cost of the works amounted to 5 million francs.

The very dusty road next leads to the unimportant tomb of *Shêkh Galal*, a little beyond which we reach the so-called —

**Tombs of the Khalifs,

which extend along the E. side of the city, and which, beyond the Citadel, are known as Tombs of the Mamelukes (p. 327)†.

All these tombs, most of which are of vast extent, were once richly endowed, each being provided with a numerous staff of shêkhs and attendants, who with their families resided within their precincts. At the beginning of the present century the revenues of these establishments were confiscated, so that the tombs are now falling to ruin. The descendants of the mosque attendants and other Arabs have since taken up their quarters among the ruins, and the old necropolis has thus been converted into a kind of suburb of Cairo, the inhabitants of which often pester strangers with their importunities.

A visit to the tombs is exceedingly interesting, particularly towards sunset, owing to the very curious and novel picture they present. They may be reached by carriage, but the traveller will be more independent on donkey-back. The necessary order of admission from the Wakf ministry may be obtained through the consulate (see p. 241).

Points of View. (1) From the road, approaching from the Bâb en-Nasr, a little beyond the tomb of the shêkh; (2) From the S.W. corner (see Plan), at the foot of the Citadel; (3) From the **Windmill Hill opposite the end of the Rue Neuve, the E. prolongation of the Muski. This last point is specially recommended as it also affords an admirable survey of the town, the Nile, and the Pyramids, and is very easily reached. Half-an-hour of leisure before sunset can hardly be better spent than on this hill (p. 287), but the beggars are often troublesome.

The N.E. group of these mausoleums (on the left when approached from Bâb en-Nasr) consists of the *Tomb of Sultân Abu Sa'îd Kanṣuweh el-Ghûri* (p. 274), a cube surmounted by an elongated dome, and two tomb-mosques, one of *Sultân el-Ashraf*, with a handsome minaret, the other of *Emîr Yûsuf*, son of Bursbey (see p. 285). These two mosques, which present no attraction, are now used for military purposes, and are not shown without special permission from the minister of war. As visitors are prevented by the sentry from approaching them, we leave them to the left, and proceed in a straight direction to the —

***Tomb-Mosque of Sulṭân Barḳûḳ** (p. 279), with its two superb domes and its two minarets. Under the N. dome are the tombs of the male, and under the S. dome those of the female members of the family. The present Entrance (Pl. 1) at the S.W. corner is in a ruinous condition. The old Principal Entrance (Pl. 18) at the

† The name 'Tombs of the Khalifs' is historically a misnomer. Both the Baḥrite (1258-1382) and the Circassian Mameluke sultans (1382-1517) were nominally dependent on Khalifs of the house of the 'Abbâsides resident in Egypt (p. 101), but treated them as mere puppets; and it was these real monarchs of Egypt, and not the Khalifs, who built these large and superb mausoleums.

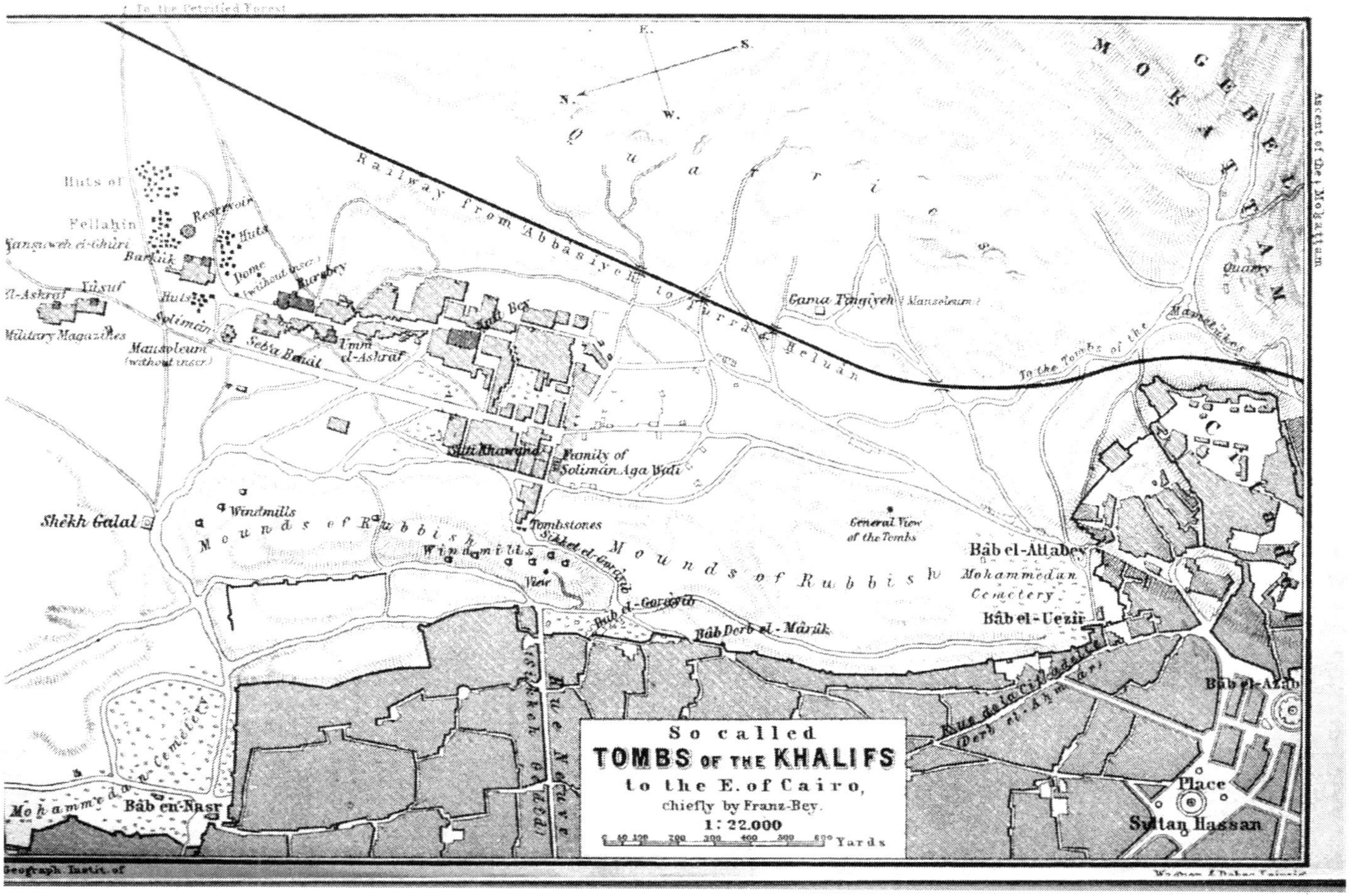
So called
TOMBS OF THE KHALIFS
to the E. of Cairo,
chiefly by Franz-Bey.
1: 22.000
Yards
Mokattam
Gebel
Quarries
Quarry
Railway from Abbasiyeh to Turra & Heluan
To the Tombs of the Mamelukes
Gama Tangiyeh (Mausoleum)
Huts of Fellahin
Reservoir
Huts
Dome (without inscr.)
Barsbey
Barkûk
Yûsuf
El-Ashraf
Military Magazines
Solimân
Mausoleum (without inscr.)
Seba Banât
Umm el-Ashraf
Sitti Khawand
Family of Solimân Aga Wali
Windmills
Shêkh Galal
Mounds of Rubbish
Tombstones
View
Bâb el-Goraiyib
Bâb Derb el-Mârûk
General View of the Tombs
Bâb el-Attabey
Mohammedan Cemetery
Bâb el-Uezir
Bâb el-Azab
Place
Sultan Hassan
Rue Neuve
Bâb en-Nasr
Mohammedan Cemetery
Ascent of the Mokattam
To the Petrified Forest
N.
S.
E.
W.

The accompanying plan of Barḳûḳ's Tomb-Mosque will convey an idea of its original extent and arrangements; but a considerable part of it is now in ruins.

1. Present Entrance. 2. Vestibules. a, b, c, d. Large Quadrangle (Hôsh, or Ṣaḥn el-Gâmiʿ). c, d, e, f. Sanctuary (or Lîwân el-Gâmiʿ). 3. Small Court with Fountain. 4. Large Basin (Ḥanefîyeh). 5. Kibla. 6. Mambar. 7. Kursî. 8. Dikkeh. 9, 10, 11. Colonnades (almost all in ruins). 12. Tomb of Sulṭân Barḳûḳ. 13. Tombs of members of the Harem. 14. Vestibule. 15. Apartments once occupied by the shêkh and officials of the mosque. 16. Rooms for guests and students. 17. Sebîl with School. 18. Principal Entrance. 19. Hall in which the Sulṭân granted audiences.

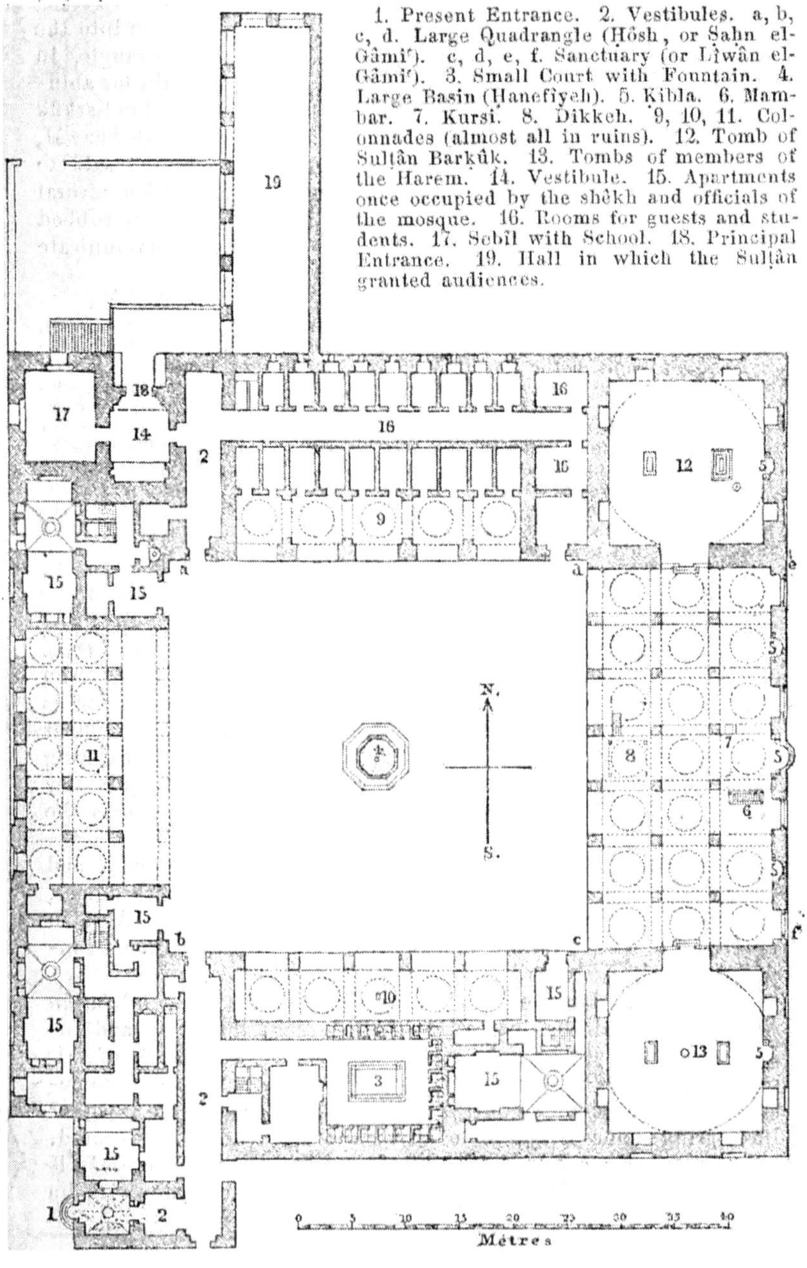

N.W. angle, now closed, has an architrave of alabaster; the threshold is of granite, and the ceiling consists of a dome with pendentives.

The Vestibule (Pl. 2) of the S. façade, through which we reach the interior, has a fine star-shaped dome. We pass thence into the Hôsh, or Ṣaḥn el-Gâmiʿ (Pl. a, b, c, d), the large Quadrangle, in the centre of which is the Ḥanefîyeh (Pl. 4), or fountain for ablution. Beneath the larger (N.E.) dome is the Tomb of Sulṭân Barḳûḳ (Pl. 12), who reigned from 19th Ramaḍân, 784, to 15th Shawâl, 801 (comp. p. 279). Adjoining the tomb is a column, said to represent the height of the deceased, and inscribed with several biographical data. A black stone here (ironstone), when rubbed on granite under water, is believed by the Muslims to communicate sanatory properties to the discoloured water.

The adjacent tomb is that of *Sulṭân Farag*, son of Barḳûḳ.

Farag (1399-1412) had scarcely ascended the throne (20th June, 1399), as a boy of thirteen years of age, before the Osmans began to threaten the Syrian dominions of the Egyptian empire; and Timur (Tamerlane), in his war against the Osmans, shortly afterwards defeated the Syrian emirs, who had opposed him, near Aleppo. Farag himself thereupon headed a campaign against Timur, and proceeded victoriously as far as Damascus; but owing to dissensions among his emîrs he was obliged to return to Cairo and leave Syria to its fate. After the defeat of the Turks under Bajesid by the Mongols under Timur at the battle of Angora, Farag was compelled to enter into negociations with Timur, and he is even said to have sent him Egyptian coins bearing the Mongolian conqueror's name in token of his subjection. The death of Timur, however (18th Dec. 1403), saved Egypt from the risk of being conquered by the Mongols. The latter years of Farag's reign were constantly disturbed by the rebellions of his emîrs, particularly Shêkh el-Maḥmûdi Muaiyad (see p. 273). He was at length compelled by the insurgents to capitulate at Damascus, whither he had proceeded with his army, and was executed (May, 1412).

The third tomb contains the remains of a brother of Farag, who reigned seventy days only. The S. Mausoleum (Pl. 13) contains the tombs of the female members of the family. The *Mambar (Pl. 6), in hard limestone, one of the most beautiful existing specimens of Arabian sculpture, was presented by Kait Bey (p. 268). The *Minarets, with their three galleries (besides the balconies below them), are borne by pendent cornices.

The symmetrical plan of the edifice, its massive masonry, and the symmetrical disposition of the rows of pilasters with domes, constitute this mosque one of the most perfect examples of Arabian architecture in existence; and, notwithstanding its ruinous condition, it still presents a most imposing appearance.

To the W. (right) of this tomb-mosque is the *Tomb of Sulṭân Sulêmân*, containing interesting sculpture in the dome and inscriptions in fayence, now partly destroyed. To the E. of this tomb (and to the S. of Barḳûḳ's mosque) is another handsome dome-covered tomb, the founder of which is unknown; and there are other interesting dome-structures of various forms, carefully executed, but of uncertain origin. Adjoining the mausoleum of Sulêmân is the tomb of the *Sebʿa Benât* (seven maidens). The dome, with its

Tombs of the Khalifs.

South East side, seen from a distance of 200 yds. in approaching the tombs from the Citadel.)

pendentives, is of a very elongated form, and differs considerably from those of the neighbouring mausolea, being more similar to those of the so-called Mameluke tombs (p. 327).

Opposite the last-named tomb, to the E. (left), is the **Tomb-Mosque of Bursbey** *(Berisbai)*, completed in 1431.

Bursbey (1422-38), who had for a time been the vicegerent of a young son of Ṭatar, ascended the throne on 1st April, 1422. After having defeated some of his rebellious vassals, he determined to attack Cyprus, one of the chief hotbeds of piracy. In the course of the third of his expeditions he succeeded in capturing Janus, King of Cyprus, whom he carried in triumph to Cairo. On paying a ransom of 200,000 denarii, and promising to pay the sultan an annual tribute, he was sent back to Cyprus as a vassal of Egypt. Bursbey was, however, less successful in his battles with the Turcoman Kara Yelek, who had allied himself with Timur, the prince of the Mongols. A contemplated expedition against Egypt, which was to have been commanded by Shah Rokh, a son of Timur, had to be abandoned in consequence of the breaking out of a pestilence throughout the East. In order to prevent Kara Yelek from joining Shah Rokh, Bursbey attacked him in N. Syria in 1436, but was compelled by his refractory emîrs to conclude a dishonourable peace, notwithstanding which he shortly afterwards entered Cairo with all the pomp of a conqueror. Shah Rokh then demanded the cession to himself of the privilege of sending to Mecca the materials for the covering of the Kab'a, a right which had belonged to the sultans of Egypt since the decline of the khalifate of Baghdâd, but Bursbey was successful in resisting this claim. He also defeated the Sherîf of Mecca, and thus became the protector of the holy city, while the possession of Jedda, the seaport of Mecca (p. 423), afforded him great commercial advantages. This was owing to the fact that Jedda had recently become a favourite resort of the Indian spice-merchants who had previously traded with 'Aden, but had there been subjected to gross extortion by the princes of Yemen. Bursbey availed himself so thoroughly of these advantages that he incurred the hostility of Venice, Catalonia, and Arragon, but he succeeded in monopolising the trade in some of the most important articles, so that the interests of private dealers were seriously prejudiced. He died a natural death in 1438.

Various data regarding the building of the mosque and the legacies bequeathed for its preservation were engraved on a long marble frieze on the okella which adjoins the edifice on the right, and a considerable part of it is still to be seen in the *place*. The Lîwân contains good mosaics. Some of the handsome perforated stucco windows are still preserved, but the bronze gratings have been removed, and the openings built up. Several severe conflicts between the French troops and the Mamelukes are said to have taken place around this mosque.

The admirably executed gateway with its pendentives, and the wall enclosing the three monuments, were erected by Moḥammed, an intendant of the Ḥôsh, about the year 1142 of the Hegira.

Adjoining the mosque is the *Ma'bed er-Rifâ'i*, a mausoleum with a remarkably depressed dome, next to which is the *Tomb of the Mother of Bursbey*, a poorly executed work. The form of the openings in the latter is worthy of notice, as the arches with straight sides, placed below an acute angle, though not uncommon, seldom occur quite alone. The oldest arches of the kind are to be found in the 'Amr and Azhar mosques.

In the same street, a few paces farther to the S., we observe on the right the long *Okella Ḳait Bey*, with its carefully executed gateway and characteristic ornamentation. The façade is built of massive stone, and is tolerably regular, but the mushrebîyehs are of inferior workmanship and probably of later date. The gate is mounted with large iron nails. The ground-floor is vaulted, while the upper floor has an open ceiling. The edifice was completed in the year 877 of the Hegira.

A little farther to the S., projecting in an angle, is a public fountain, now in ruins, also erected by Ḳait Bey. The shallow niches, the upper parts of which are shell-shaped, are in the form of fantastic arches.

Beyond this sebîl is an open space, on the right side of which is the *Tomb-Mosque of Ḳait Bey (p. 268), the finest edifice among the Tombs of the Khalîfs, with a lofty dome and beautiful minarets.

The Ṣaḥn el-Gâmiʿ was once closed by a mushrebîyeh lantern, which fell in 1872. The rest of the edifice has an open ceiling, as in the case of the manḍaras (p. 185). The *Dikkeh*, in the form of a balcony, resembles that in the mosque of Ḳait Bey adjacent to the mosque of Ṭulûn. The details are very elaborately executed. Within the mausoleum are shown two stones, one of red, and the other of black granite, which are said to have been brought from Mecca by Ḳait Bey, and to bear impressions of the feet of the prophet. One of them is covered with a wooden canopy, and the other with a bronze dome. The mosque also contains a finely carved kursi for the Korân. The whole edifice is erected of solid and regular masonry. The *Minaret* is remarkable for the elegance of its form. The *Dome*, richly adorned with bands of sculpturing, is constructed of limestone.

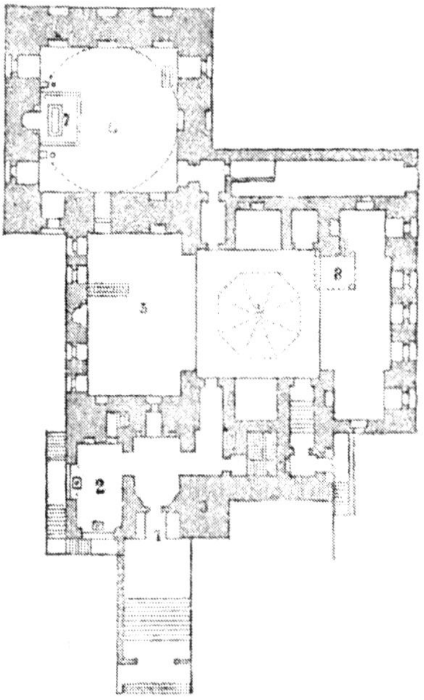

1. Principal Entrance. 2. Sebîl with Medreseh. 3. Lower part of the Minaret. 4. Ṣaḥn el-Gâmiʿ. 5. Lîwân with Kibla and Mambar. 6. Mausoleum. 7. Tomb of Ḳait Bey. 8. Dikkeh.

With a visit to this mosque the traveller may conclude his inspection of the great necropolis. Those who are not fatigued may now walk towards the Citadel (p. 262), examining the different ḥôshes, domes, and smaller monuments on the right and left, and may then visit the Tombs of the Mamelukes (p. 327) beyond the Citadel. The embankment of the new railway which runs between the Tombs of the Khalîfs and the quarries of the Moḳaṭṭam, affords a good survey of the scene. The traveller who quits the Tombs about sunset should not omit to ascend the *Windmill Hill* from the side next the town (comp. Plan, p. 282), for the sake of the view. A fine effect, especially by evening light, is produced by the domes and the peculiar colouring of the valley and the opposite heights of the Moḳaṭṭam. This mound of rubbish should indeed be frequently visited (comp. p. 282). To the W. are the city, the plain of the Nile, and the Pyramids. The red building to the N.E. is the 'Abbâsîyeh (p. 332), to the left of which is a mosque (Gâmi' el-'Adil). In front of the latter is the N.E. group of the Tombs of the Khalîfs (p. 282), a little to the right of which are the two minarets of Sulṭân Barḳûḳ (p. 282). Beyond these rises the Gebel el-Aḥmar (p. 337), adjoining which are the Moḳaṭṭam hills, with the other Tombs of the Khalîfs at their base.

Mosques of El-Azhar and Ḥasanên.

The **Gâmi' el-Azhar** (Pl. 38; C, 2) presents few features of architectural interest, and is so shut in by houses that very little of the exterior is visible. The plan of the principal part was originally the same as that of the 'Amr Mosque (p. 324), but the numerous additions made at various periods have somewhat modified its form, and since the conversion of the mosque into a university the aisles have been separated from the court by walls and railings. The first great alterations took place in the year 1004 of the Hegira, in the reign of Moḥammed ibn Murâd, the next were made by Shêkh Isma'îl Bey in 1131 of the Hegira, and the last by Sa'îd Pasha about 1848, all exhibiting the decline of Arabian architecture.

The *Minarets* (Pl. 12), some of which are brightly painted, were erected at different periods, one of them having been built by 'Abder Raḥmân Kikhya (p. 279).

The mosque has six gates the *Bâb el-Muzeyinîn* (Pl. a), or Gate of the Barbers (see below), on the W. side, forming the principal entrance, and possessing an interesting portal; the *Bâb Goharîyeh* (Pl. b), on the N. side; the *Bâb esh-Shurba* (Pl. c), or Soup Gate, on the E.; the *Bâb es-Ṣa'îdîyeh*, or Gate of the Upper Egyptians; the *Bâb esh-Shawwâm* (Pl. e), or Syrian Gate; and the *Bâb el-Maghârbeh* (Pl. f), or Gate of the W. Africans, the three last being on the S. side.

The mosque was converted into a **University** (now the most important in Mohammedan territory) by Khalîf 'Azîz Billâh (A.D. 975-96), at the suggestion of his vizier Abu'l Farag Ya'ḳûb, in the year 378 of the Hegira, and the establishment is attended by students from almost all the countries professing El-Islâm.

On the side of the court looking towards Mecca is a spacious colonnade (see below), which forms the principal hall for prayer and tuition On the other three sides are smaller colonnades, divided by wooden partitions or railings into a number of *Riwâks*, or separate chambers (literally, colonnades). Each of these is set apart for the use of the natives of a particular country, or of a particular province of Egypt. The most important of these riwâks are as follows:

Riwâk et-Turk (the word *Turk* being applied to all Mohammedans from the N provinces of the Turkish empire), attended by	64 students
Riwâk el-Maghârbeh (W Africans)	88 „
Riwâk esh-Shawwâm (Syrians)	94 „
Riwâk el-Baghdâdiyeh (natives of Baghdâd)	1 „
Riwâk el-Hunûd (Indians)	7 „
Riwâk el-Akrâd (Kurds)	12 „
Riwâk ed-Dakarna, or *Dârfûriyeh* (natives of Dârfûr)	56 „
Riwâk es-Sennâriyeh (natives of Sennâr)	37 „
Riwâk el-Barâbra (Nubian Berbers)	36 „
Riwâk el-Gabart (E Africans from the Somâli coast, from Zêla, Berbera, and Tajurra)	98 „
Riwâk el-Haramên (natives of the holy cities of Mecca and Medina)	8 „
Riwâk el-Yemen (natives of Yemen)	26 „
Riwâk esh-Sharâkweh (natives of the Egyptian province of Sherkîyeh)	380 „
Riwâk el-Fashniyeh (natives of Fashneh in Upper Egypt)	703 „
Riwâk el-Fayûmeh, or *Fayâyimeh* (natives of the Fayûm)	181 „
Riwâk el-Baharweh (natives of Lower Egypt)	454 „
Riwâk eṣ-Ṣa'idiyeh (natives of Upper Egypt)	1462 „

The university is attended by about 7700 students in all, who are taught by 231 shêkhs or professors.

The different sects are distributed as follows.

Shâfe'ites	3723,	with 106 shêkhs
Malekites	2855,	with 75 shêkhs.
Hanefites	1090,	with 49 shêkhs.
Hambalites	23,	with 1 shêkh.

The students *(Mugâwirîn)* usually remain three, and sometimes from four to six years in the mosque They pay no fees, but each riwâk is supported by an annual subsidy from the endowments of the mosque, although these were much diminished by Mohammed 'Ali, who appropriated the revenues of most of the religious foundations in Egypt to government purposes. The shêkhs, or professors, receive no salary, either from the mosque or from government, but support themselves by teaching in private houses, by copying books, or by filling some religious office to which a salary is attached, and they occasionally receive donations from the wealthier students. When teaching, the shêkh sits cross-legged on a straw-mat and reads from a book placed on a desk *(rahleh)* before him, explaining each sentence as he proceeds; or he directs one of the more advanced students to read aloud, adding his own explanations from time to time The students sit in a circle around the teacher, listening, or attentively taking notes. As soon as a student knows by heart the whole of the book which is being studied by the class, the shêkh makes an entry in his copy of the work, called the *Igâzeh*, whereby authority to lecture on the book is conferred on the student himself. The president of the university, who is usually the most distinguished of the shêkhs, is called *Shêkh el-Azhar*, and receives a salary of about 20 purses, i. e. 10,000 piastres.

Most of the students, particularly those whose native tongue is not Arabic, begin their university education by learning the Arabic grammar (*'ilm en-nahu*). The next branch of study is religious science (*'ilm el-kelâm*), the introduction to which consists of a series of preparatory lectures on the attributes of God and the prophet (*'ilm et-tauhîd*, i e the doctrine of the unity of God) The chief attributes of God are said to be the following twelve existence, source of all being, eternity, independence, unity, omnipotence, will (in accordance with which he rules the universe, man being powerless to save himself from sin or to be pious without the assistance and grace of God), omniscience (or knowledge of everything that happens between the lowest foundations of the earth and the loftiest heights of the firmament), life, vision (which enables him to see everything everywhere, without the aid of light, and without eyes), hearing (without ears, in the same way as he knows without a brain, and overthrows without hands), and speech (in a language that has had no beginning, a language without letters or sounds, which is inherent in his nature, and does not resemble human speech)

After having completed his course of religious instruction, the student proceeds to study law (*'ilm el-fikh*)

'Jurisprudence', says Ibn Khaldûn, one of the greatest of Arabian thinkers, 'is a knowledge of the precepts of God in relation to the actions of men, some of which it is our duty to perform, while others are forbidden, or recommended, or permitted, and this knowledge is derived from the book of God, i e the Korân, from the Sunna (i e tradition), and from the inferences drawn by the lawgiver (Mohammed) from sufficient materials afforded by the Korân' The study of law is therefore based upon the exegesis of the Korân (*tafsîr*) and of tradition (*hadîth*).

The science of law is divided into two branches· —

(1) The doctrine of the *Chief Religious Commandments* of El-Islâm, viz (a) *Et-Tauhîd*, or the recognition of God's unity and of Mohammed as his prophet, (b) The *Salât* and *Tahâra*, or the duty of repeating the canonical prayers in connection with the ablutions, (c) The *Sadaka* and *Zakât*, or giving of alms and payment of a religious tax, (d) The *Siyâm*, or fasting during the month of Ramadân, (e) The *Hagg*, or duty of performing a pilgrimage to Mecca

(2) The doctrine of *Secular Law*, civil and criminal, either as expressly laid down by the Korân, or as deducible from it The legal literature again is divided into two classes, one embracing systematic expositions of the law of the Korân, and the other consisting of the decisions (*fetwa*) and opinions of celebrated jurists in special and difficult cases

Besides these leading branches of instruction, logic (*'ilm el-mantik*) rhetoric (*'ilm el-ma'âni wal bayân*), the art of poetry (*'ilm el-'arûd*), the proper mode of reciting the Korân (*'ilm el-kirâ'a*), and the correct pronunciation of the letters (*'ilm et-tejwîd*) are also taught.

The above list of the subjects taught at the most important of Mohammedan schools will serve to convey an idea of the intellectual condition of Orientals at the present day. The most conspicuous defect of their culture consists in the entire absence of independent thought, in consequence of which they are the mere recipients of the knowledge of the past. Their minds are thus exclusively occupied with the lowest grade of intellectual work, their principal task consisting in the systematic arrangement or encyclopædic compilation of the knowledge handed down to them. Some of the shêkhs of the Azhar are men of marvellous erudition, but they are destitute of creative power, or of the ability to utilise their old materials for the construction of any new edifice, and they adhere faithfully to the notion of their forefathers that the greatest triumph of mental labour is to learn by heart any work of acknowledged literary value. Doubt and criticism, which so often serve to open up fresh sources of knowledge, are unknown to them, with natural history they are entirely unacquainted; and even geometry, algebra, and astronomy, so assiduously cultivated by the ancient Arabs, have now fallen into oblivion. So well satisfied are they, moreover, with their own wisdom, that they utterly despise the scientific pursuits of the Western world.

We enter the mosque by the Gate of the Barbers (Pl. a), from the Street of the Booksellers (p. 254). On each side of the Entrance

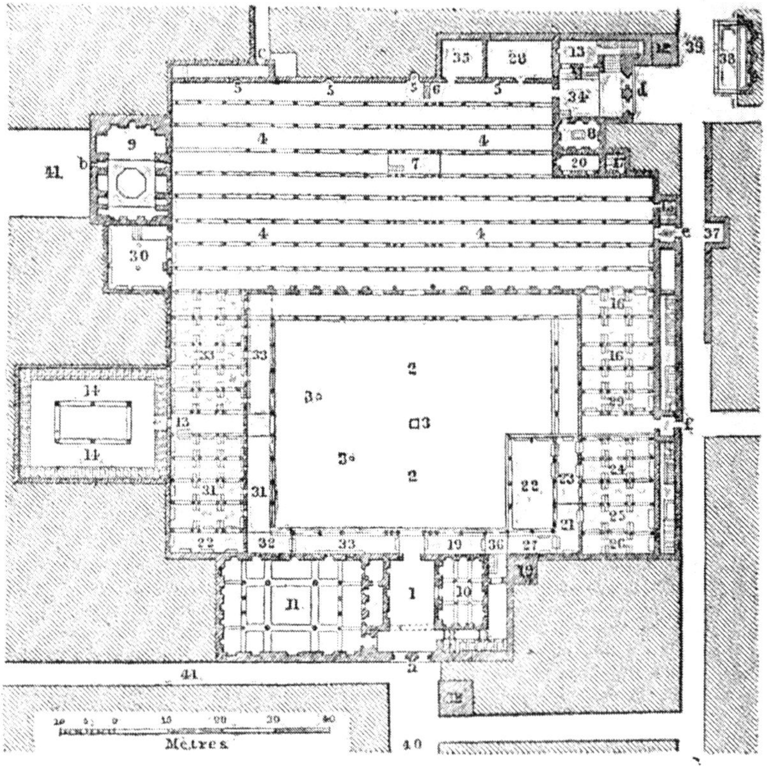

a, b, c, d, e, f. Gates (see p. 287). 1. Entrance Court (barbers'). 2. Hôsh el-Gâmi', or Great Court. 3. Cisterns. 4. Lîwân el-Gâmi', or Sanctuary, now the principal hall for instruction. 5. Kibla. 6. Mambar. 7. Dikkeh. 8. Tomb of 'Abder-Rahmân Kikhya. 9. Mesgid (mosque) Gôharîyeh. 10. Mesgid Tabarset. 11. Mesgid Ebthahawîyeh (in ruins). 12. Minarets. 13. Fountain. 14. Latrine. 15-34. Riwâks (or rooms for study). 15. Riwâk et-Turk (Turks from N. provinces of the empire); 16. Riwâk el-Maghârbeh (W. Africans); 17. Staircase to the Riwâk esh-Shawwâm (Syrians); 18. Staircase to the Riwâk el-Baghdâdîyeh (natives of Baghdâd); 19. Riwâk el-Akrâd (Kurds); 20. Riwâk ed-Dakarna or Dârfûrîyeh (natives of Dârfûr); 21-27. Riwâk es-Sennârîyeh (natives of Sennâr), Riwâk el-Barâbra (Nubian Berbers), Riwâk el-Gabart (E. Africans from the Somâli coast, Zêla', Berbera, and Tajurra); 28. Riwâk el-Haramên (natives of Mecca and Medîna); 29. Riwâk el-Yemen (natives of Yemen); 30. Riwâk esh-Sharâkweh (natives of the province of Sherkîyeh); 31. Riwâk el-Fashnîyeh (natives of Fashneh); 32. Riwâk el-Fayûmeh, or Fayâyimeh (natives of the Fayûm); 33. Riwâk el-Bakârweh (natives of Lower Egypt); 34. Riwâk eṣ-Ṣa'îdîyeh (natives of Ṣa'îd, or Upper Egypt). 35. Receptacle for carpets. 36. Steps to the Terrace. 37. Gate of the Okella Kait Bey. 38. Public Fountain. 39. Road to the Tombs of the Khalîfs. 40. Booksellers' Street (p. 254). 41. Street to the Rue Neuve (Muski).

(Pl. 1), which was restored by Edhem Pasha at the beginning of the present century, we frequently observe barbers engaged in shaving the heads of the students with admirable skill, but we of course avoid stopping to watch the process for fear of giving offence. This being one of the fountain-heads of Mohammedan fanaticism, the traveller should, of course, throughout his visit, be careful not to indulge openly in any gestures of amusement or contempt. Beyond the entrance, which forms a kind of fore-court, we reach the Ḥôsh el-Gâmi' (Pl. 2), or Great Court, where the students are seen sitting on their mats in groups and conning their tasks. This court does not contain the usual fountain for ablution, but there are three small Cisterns (Pl. 3) for the purpose. The arcades enclosing the court have arches approaching the keel shape, but the sides are straighter than usual. The openings and niches over the arcades are less systematically arranged than in the case of the Ṭulûn Mosque (p. 265), from which they seem to have been copied.

On the E. side, in the direction of Mecca, is the Lîwân el-Gâmi' (Pl. 4), or Sanctuary, now the principal hall of instruction, covering an area of about 3600 sq. yds., with a low ceiling resting on 380 columns of granite and marble, all of ancient origin, and arbitrarily arranged. The hall is entirely destitute of architectural enrichment, and presents a heavy and sombre appearance. Here again, as in the court, we observe various groups of students in the usual crouching attitude, and others devoutly praying in front of the ḳiblas (Pl. 5), of which there is one for each of the four recognised sects of the Shâfe'ites, the Malekites, the Ḥanefites, and the Ḥambalites (comp. p. 149). The domes over these ḳiblas and their walls are adorned not unpleasingly in stucco. On the S. side is the Tomb of 'Abd er-Raḥmân Kikhya (Pl. 8), by whom the S.E. part of the mosque was restored (d. about 1750). To the W. (right) of this tomb is the Riwâḳ (see above) of the students from Upper Egypt (Pl. 34), and to the left of the latter, on the E. side, is that of the natives of Mecca and Medîna (Pl. 28). The N. side is bounded by the *Mesgid Gôharîyeh* (Pl. 9), a smaller mosque, and the oldest part of the whole structure.

After having inspected the great hall, the visitor is conducted into a number of smaller apartments (riwâḳs), some of which are indicated in the plan of the edifice, but they contain nothing noteworthy. There is also a separate riwâḳ, called the *Zâwiyet el-'Omyân*, for blind students, for whose maintenance a portion of the funds is set apart. These blind youths, who have a shêkh of their own, were frequently guilty of riotous conduct in former years, and used to parade the streets armed with bludgeons, whenever they conceived their rights infringed, the disputes being generally concerning the quality of their food. To this day they are said to be the most fanatical of their sect, and to entertain the most bitter hatred and contempt for the kâfir, or unbelieving Christian.

On the right and left of the W. Entrance (Pl. a) are two old mosques. The *Medreseh of Emîr Ṭaibar* (Pl. 10), on the S. side, built in 1309, contains a ḳibla richly adorned with mosaic. The mosque on the N. side (Pl. 11) is now in ruins, as indeed are several other parts of the mosque of El-Azhar ('the flourishing').

Returning to the Rue Neuve, we observe to the N., opposite us, the handsome minaret of the —

***Gâmiʿ el-Ḥasanên** (Pl 46; C, 2), the mosque of Hasan and Ḥusên, the sons of ʿAli, the son-in-law of the prophet (p. 153; the termination *ên* indicating the dual), which has recently been restored. The interior is constructed with considerable symmetry and care. The wooden ceiling, from which hang a number of lamps, is painted. A marble column is said to contain the head of Ḥusên, who was slain at Kerbela by Shemîr Ibn el-Gaushan by order of Yezîd. The head is said to have been brought to Cairo in a green silk bag. This tomb-mosque is chiefly frequented by men on Thursdays, and by women on Saturdays. †

† The visitors to the tombs, burial-mosques, and welis, which are to be found near almost every village, generally have a twofold object in view, one being to do honour to the memory of the deceased and to invoke the blessing of heaven upon them, and the other to obtain through their mediation the fulfilment of some special wish. On arriving at the tomb, the visitor must turn towards the face of the deceased and pronounce the greeting of peace He then walks round the *maḳsûra*, or monument, from left to right, repeating the fâtha at the door, or at each of the four sides, in a very low voice. A sûreh of the Korân is sometimes also repeated, and even the khatmeh, or recitation of the whole volume, is not unfrequently performed In conclusion the praises of God and the prophet are usually recited, coupled with a prayer that the merit of the whole performance may be placed to the credit of the weli's soul Before the concluding prayer, the worshipper sometimes introduces a prayer for his own temporal and spiritual welfare When wealthy persons visit the tomb of a saint, they distribute bread among the poor, and pay one sakka or more to dispense water gratuitously. Some of the tombs are chiefly visited on certain days of the week; and there are certain days of the year (especially about the middle of the month of Shaʿbân) on which festivals are celebrated in honour of the patron saints of the different towns and villages The most important of these are that of Seyyid Ahmed el-Bedawi at Ṭanta in Lower Egypt, and that of ʿAbd er-Raḥîm at Keneh in Upper Egypt. A week or a fortnight before the day of the festival, booths for the sale of coffee and sweatmeats begin to spring up around the shrine, and crowds of devotees flock to the tomb from all directions, some of them to perform the zikr, and others to take part in various fantasîyas Dancing women, singers, musicians, jugglers, snake-charmers, buffoons, as well as swings and merry-go-rounds, present their various attractions to young and old. On the feast-day itself, when the crowd is greatest, a solemn procession takes place. The *maḥmal*, a kind of wooden frame which usually lies on the roof of the tomb is covered with the gold and silver-embroidered winding-sheet of the saint and placed on the back of a camel, gorgeously decorated with ribbons, carpets, and bells The procession is headed by outriders galopping to and fro on camels, by fife-players and drummers, and by the arm-bearing population of the village, whose chief delight consists in firing off their guns Immediately before the camel with the *maḥmal* walk a number of venerable old men reciting passages from the Korân, and on each side of it are flag-bearers. Behind it come a band of music, female

The battle of Kerbela, at which Husên fell, took place on 10th Moharrem of the year 61 of the Hegira (10th Oct 680) Historians record that Husên's head was sent to Damascus, while his body was interred in the Meshhed Husên on the N.E frontier of Persia, to which Persian pilgrims still resort in great numbers

Neither *Hasan* nor *Husên* was remarkable for moral worth or political greatness. The veneration paid to these young 'saints' seems to have sprung solely from the persecutions to which the whole family of 'Ali was subjected, coupled with the fact that they were the grandsons of the prophet. Their misfortunes doubtless at first excited pity, a feeling which led to their being honoured with a kind of deification, particularly in Persia, where divine honours had at a still earlier period been paid to the sovereigns of the country as being descended from the gods. It is still the custom in Persia, during the month of Moharrem, to represent the events which led to Husên's death in nine successive theatrical performances, somewhat resembling the Passion plays of Europe

Opposite the egress of the mosque is the entrance to the Khân Khalîli (p. 255). At the E. end of the Rue Neuve is the Windmill Hill mentioned at pp. 282 and 287, adjoining which is the road to the Tombs of the Khalîfs (pp. 282-287).

Bûlâk and the Museum of Egyptian Antiquities.

Owing to the expansion of Cairo towards the W., in the direction of the Nile, **Bûlâk** (or *Boulaq*), situated beyond the Isma'ilîyeh Canal, and formerly an island, has become the river-harbour of the city of the khalifs. Its narrow streets present a very busy scene, affording a more characteristic picture of Oriental life than the capital, as the inhabitants of distant provinces are proportionally more numerous here. Natives of Dâr-Fûr, Wadai, Donkola, Kordofân, and Khartûm, and members of the various negro tribes are seen mingling in picturesque confusion; and popular festivals and amusements are very frequently provided for their entertainment in the evening. Goods are conveyed hither from Upper Egypt, from Nubia, from the interior of Africa, and from the fertile Delta; and the Nile barges are then laden with other cargoes for the return-journey. The principal quay is nearly opposite the palace of Gezîreh, adjacent to a large timber-yard; and it is most frequented between October and December, when the rapids of the river are most easily navigated. The merchants of Cairo congregate here every morning to make purchases, frequently as early as 7 o'clock. When there is a scarcity of goods, they sometimes go out to the vessels in boats; but when there is no scarcity, the goods are sold by auction in Bûlâk. Caravans bringing merchandise also arrive here not unfrequently, the most important being from Tunis viâ Kufra and Sîwa, and from Wadai and Dâr-Fûr. On one part of the route from Dâr-Fûr, it is said that the caravans obtain no fresh water for twelve days.

dancers, men on camels thumping on huge drums, and lastly a promiscuous crowd of holiday makers The procession often marches about the town for an hour or more, and thence out into the desert. Towards evening the mahmal is brought back to its usual place, and the festival then terminates.

The chief wares brought to Bûlâḳ are gum, ostrich-feathers, ivory, and senna-leaves The best quality of gum, called 'ṣamgh kordofâni', comes from Kordofân, while the inferior 'talh' is from Sennâr. The ostrich-feathers come from Kordofân, where the birds are reared, and also from Wadai and Dâr-Fûr The feathers are carefully tied up in bundles, and well peppered to protect them against moths. They are sold by weight, a rotl (pound) of good and pure white feathers realising as much as 30*l.* A single white feather of good quality is worth 10-20 frs. The black and grey feathers are much less expensive. After reaching Europe they require to be washed before being used. Of late years it has become usual to pick out the finest feathers, and to offer them for sale to travellers at high prices, even as far up as Assuân.

At Bûlâḳ, and at the moorings of *Embâbeh*, farther to the N., the traveller will find the dahabîyehs, or boats fitted up for the voyage to Upper Egypt. At the N. end of the town is situated the *Arsenal*, founded in 1835, with a manufactory of weapons attached to it. Machinery for Egyptian manufactories arriving from Europe is put together at Bûlâḳ before being sent to its final destination, and all repairs of machinery are also executed here. Bûlâḳ also boasts of a large *Iron Foundry*, an *Ecole des Arts et Métiers*, a *Paper Manufactory*, a *House of Correction for Women*, a *Lunatic Asylum*, and the *Government Printing Office*, none of which establishments will interest ordinary travellers.

The **Viceregal Printing Office** (*el-maṭba'a*; director, *'Ali-Bey Gaudat*) was founded by Mohammed 'Ali, chiefly for the purpose of printing and disseminating translations of European scientific works of all kinds, and particularly school-books The introduction of printing had at first to contend against serious prejudices, as many of the Muslims feared that the name of God would be defiled by contact with impure substances used in the process. To this day, indeed, the Korân is preferred in a written form; but, thanks to the perseverance of the government, the prejudice against other printed books has now almost entirely disappeared, and there are few of the many modern institutions recently introduced into Egypt which have thriven so well as this printing-office. Within the last fifty years there have been printed here, according to the government statistics, 418,375 copies of 226 works (393 vols.) of various kinds, without reckoning works printed at the cost of private individuals.

The number of private printing-offices is also increasing from year to year, the most important being that of Muṣtafa Wahabi, where works published by a scientific society (gem'iyet el-ma'ârif) are printed. Lithography is also beginning to come into use, but the execution is often defective.

Of the works printed in Egypt 1000-4000 copies are usually struck off, and the fact that the whole of them are generally sold within a few years affords a proof that the taste for literature in the East is again on the increase. Some works, such as Bokhâri's collection of traditions, have an immense sale Energetic attempts are still being made to render European works accessible to Orientals in the form of translations, chiefly from the French Thus, among the legal works, may be mentioned a translation of the Code Napoléon, among the geographical the works of Malte Brun, and among the historical the Life of Charles XII by Voltaire, and a few years ago the libretto of Offenbach's Belle Hélène was even thought worthy of being printed in Arabic at the government printing-office of Bûlâḳ — At the same time the national literature has not been neglected, and a number of valuable early Arabian works have recently been brought into notice by the agency of the printing-press, such as the historical works of *Ibn el-Athîr* (comp p. 201), those of *Maḳrizi* (p. 201), those of *El-Maḳḳari*, the writer of Spanish history (17th cent.), and the 'Book of the Songs' by *Abulfarag el-Isbahâni* (d. 966).

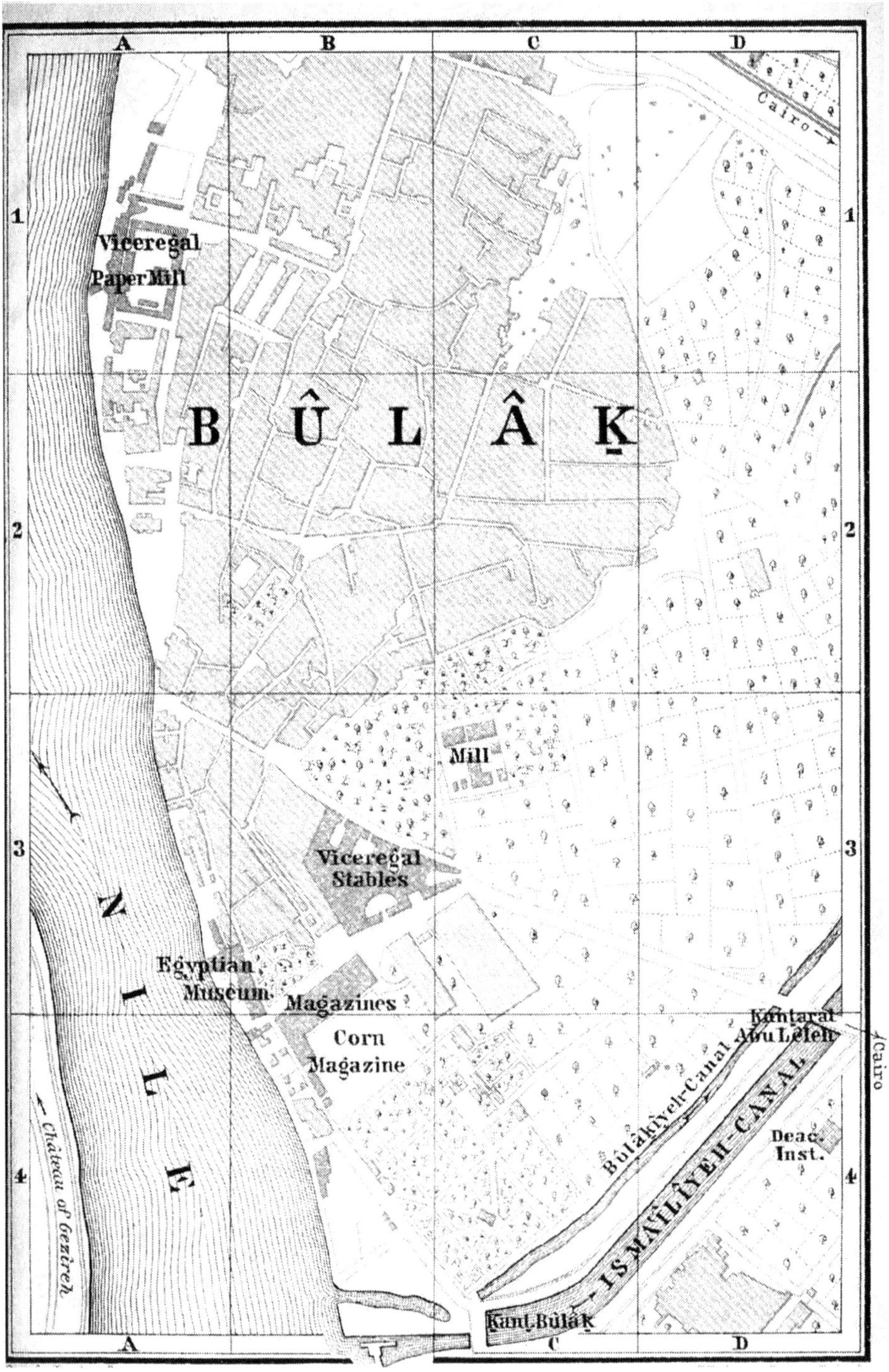
A
B
C
D
1
2
3
4
Cairo
Viceregal
Paper Mill
B Û L Â Ḳ
Mill
Viceregal
Stables
Egyptian
Museum
Magazines
Corn
Magazine
N I L E
Château of Gezireh
Kantarat
Abu Leleh
Cairo
Bûlâkîyeh-Canal
ISMAÎLÎYEH-CANAL
Deac.
Inst.
Kant. Bûlâk

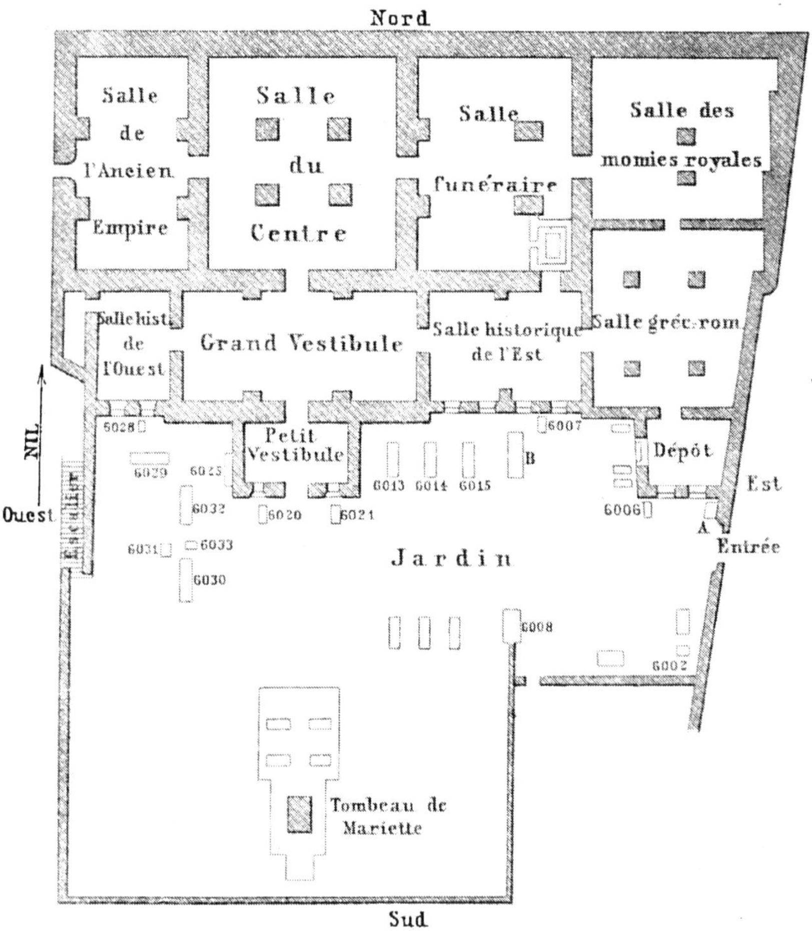

Nord
Salle de l'Ancien Empire
Salle du Centre
Salle funéraire
Salle des momies royales
Salle hist. de l'Ouest
Grand Vestibule
Salle historique de l'Est
Salle gréc.-rom.
Petit Vestibule
Dépôt
NIL
Ouest
Est
Entrée
Jardin
6028
6029
6025
6032
6031
6033
6030
6020
6021
6013
6014
6015
B
6007
6006
A
6008
6002
Tombeau de Mariette
Sud

A peculiarity of many of the books recently printed at Bûlâk is that smaller works illustrative of the text are printed on the margins of the pages. The paper used for the purpose is made in Egyptian manufactories, chiefly from maize-straw, which accounts for its yellowish tint.

The great attraction at Bûlâḳ is the —

****Museum of Egyptian Antiquities** (the traveller bound for which has only to direct his donkey-boy 'lil Antikât'), a magnificent collection, and entirely unrivalled of its kind. A great advantage possessed by it over all the European museums is that the places where all its monuments and relics have been found are known, and indicated by labels, a circumstance of the greatest importance in assisting historical and geographical research. The collection was founded by *M. Mariette-Pasha*, who died in 1881 and has been succeeded as director by *Prof. Maspero*, another Frenchman. The keeper of the museum is *Herr Brugsch-Bey*, who is assisted by *M. Bouriant.*

The arrangement of the museum has recently been entirely altered, and most of the treasures formerly stored in the magazines have now found a place in the building itself Several of the rooms have been enlarged and an addition has been built to receive the objects found at Dêr el-Bahri, near Thebes, in 1881. Prof. Maspero has also caused a room to be fitted up for monuments of the Greek, Roman, and Coptic periods.

The Museum is open daily, except on Fridays, from 8 to 12 and from 2 to 5; in winter from 8 to 12 and 1 to 4 o'clock (no fee). Strangers, who wish to make special studies, will receive every facility from the director and keepers.

Court. To the right of the gateway is a colossal figure of King Usertesen I. (Pl. A), in rose-coloured granite, brought from Abydos in 1884. Farther on, placed against the external wall of the Museum, are four dark-grey granite figures, in a sitting posture, of the lion-headed goddess Sekhet (No. 6006), all brought from the temple of the goddess Muth at Karnak. To the right, between the windows, 6007. Double statue representing the god Ammon and an Ethiopian queen.

This group, which is of rough workmanship, was found in 1882 at Naga (Meroe) by Herr Berghoff, who some months later was captured and beheaded by the Mahdi.

On the left side of the court are two large fragments of a granite Naos, or shrine, with elaborate decorations and the name of King Nectanebus II. In the corner to the left, 6002. Large eagle in marble, from the island of Thasos. To the left of the entrance to the garden is a large *Sphinx* (No. 6008) in rose-coloured granite, from Tanis in Lower Egypt; the cartouches of Ramses II. are a later addition. To the right is a cast of the same figure (Pl. B)

We now enter the **Garden.** To the right · 6013, 6014. Sarcophagi in grey granite from Saḳḳâra, belonging to two brothers named Takhos, who were high officials in the time of the first Ptolemies.

Adjacent, 6015. Granite sarcophagus of Ankh-hapi, also from Saḳḳâra (Greek period). Opposite are three marble sarcophagi of the Græco-Roman epoch, from Alexandria.

Opposite the entrance of the Museum, in the middle of the garden, is the *Tomb of Mariette*, who is interred in a marble sarcophagus made in the ancient style. The four small limestone sphinxes in front of it are from the sacred avenue leading to the Serapeum at Saḳḳâra (p. 384). — Nearer the river, 6030, 6032. Two sphinxes in rose-coloured granite from Karnak, with inscriptions and the name of Thothmes III Between these: 6031. Colossal figure of Ramses II. (from Tanis), and 6033. Sacrificial tablet of Thothmes III. (from Karnak). To the right (E.): 6025. 'Stele' or sepulchral tablet, in limestone, with an inscription referring to Ptah-hotep (5th dynasty; from Saḳḳâra). To the N., by the wall of the Museum, are several sepulchral slabs and the sitting figure (in grey granite; No. 6028) of the Princess Nefert, daughter of Usertesen I. (12th dynasty). In front, 6029. Sarcophagus in brownish granite, found at Damanhûr, with an inscription containing the name of Psammetikh II. (26th dynasty).

The building of the Museum is painted blue, green, and red in the manner of the Egyptian temples, and above the door is the winged disk of the sun (see p. 133). To the right and left of the door are two seated granite figures from Tanis (6020, 6021), both 'usurped' by Ramses II., *i.e.* provided with his cartouches, but really of earlier origin (13th or 14th dynasty?).

Petit Vestibule. Maspero's new *Catalogue*, several of Mariette's works, and photographs of objects in the Museum are sold here. The best collections of the latter are the *Monuments Choisis du Musée de Boulaq* (25 fr., small size 15 fr.) and *La Trouvaille de Deïr el Bahari* (1st vol. 40 fr., 2nd vol. 15 fr.). Sticks and umbrellas must be given up here.

The walls are covered with tombstones and basreliefs, most of them from Abydos and Saḳḳâra. Among the most interesting are: No. 21. Stele of Hormin (20th dynasty), with a burial scene; 3. Stele of Unnefer, who died at the age of 51 years, 1 month, and 27 days (from Luḳṣor); 19. Tombstone of Pa-nefer-haf, who died aged 57 years, 10 months, and 4 days. — To the left, 82. Base of a column in alabaster, with the cartouche of Ramses III., found at Tell el-Yehûdîyeh (Shibîn el-Ḳanâṭir). In front is the capital of a porphyry column, with an inscription of a later date. Sarcophagi in basalt and close-grained limestone, dating from the time of the Ptolemies

Grand Vestibule. The walls are completely covered with 'steles' or sepulchral slabs, chiefly from Abydos. No. 165. Monument of Phra-em-heb. In the uppermost row are two figures standing before Osiris; in the second row, the mummy of Phra-em-heb is represented in an upright position before the tomb, while his sister embraces his knees; in the third field is a sacrificial scene (20th dynasty; from Saḳḳâra). — 166. The gods Usurhapi, Ammon-Ra, Muth, and Khunsu receiving the sacrifice of a king, whose cartouche has been left empty (from Saḳḳâra). — 167. Tombstone of Entef, with well-preserved colouring (11th dynasty; from Thebes). — 292. The scribe Anawa, major-domo of Memphis, in the act of worshipping Tum and Harmachis (19th dyn.; from Saḳḳâra). The inscription is a hymn to the sun. — 330. Stele of Piankhi, son of Herhor, high-priest of Ammon and viceroy of Ethiopia (21st dyn.; Abydos). — 378. Tombstone. In the uppermost field are represented Phra-unem-emamf, the chief scribe of Ammon, and his wife Niuhai, priestess of Ammon, kneeling before the jackal Anubis; in the second row the deceased are seen arriving before Osiris and Isis; the third field represents a sacrifice for the dead (20th dyn.; Saḳḳâra). — 420. Roma, keeper of the royal diadems and of the perfumes of the royal treasury, with his wife Sukha, his daughter Tapu, and his grandson Nihiaï, all in adoration before Osiris, Isis, and Horus. In the second field Roma and Sukha receive sacrificial gifts from their son Apii and other members of the family; the third contains a hymn to Osiris (19th dyn.; Abydos). — Nos. 199, 229, 255, and 327 are the best examples of steles of the 6th dynasty.

To the left, in the middle. 446. Statue of Sebek-em-saf, a king of the 13th dynasty, in rose-coloured granite (from Abydos). No. 445, used as a base for the last, is the shaft of a column in red granite, inscribed with the 5th year of the reign of Merenptah (19th dyn.). Adjacent, to the left: 442. Tai and his wife Naï, sitting figures in limestone; at the back the same figures are represented in the act of receiving sacrificial gifts from Tinro, priestess of Ammon (19th dyn.; Saḳḳara). — In the middle of the room, to the right: *468. *Alabaster Statue of Queen Ameneritis*, on a base of grey granite. The cartouches are those of her father Kashta and her brother Shabako (25th dyn., Karnak). — *465. Lion, admirably pourtrayed in bronze, with the cartouches of King Apries of the 26th dynasty, probably designed to adorn a staircase. — 469. Group of Ammon and Muth, dedicated by Seti I. (19th dyn.; Thebes).

At the sides of the door leading to the Salle du Centre are two large limestone steles, inscribed with the name of Ramses IV and with hymns to various deities. In front, 285, 286. Two limestone figures, in a crouching posture, of Khai, keeper of the treasures in the mortuary chapel of Ramses II. No. 285 holds a small shrine with an image of Osiris, and No. 286 another with an image of Ra. — By the four pilasters are finely-executed sarcophagi in basalt and limestone. 409. Limestone coffin of a woman named Ankh; 160. Coffin in green basalt of a woman named Betaita, both of the Ptolemaic period. Opposite, 284, 287. Coffin and lid of Hor-em-heb, dating from the Saite period (p. 91), and covered inside and out with funereal representations and inscriptions.

We now turn to the left and enter the —

Salle historique de l'Ouest. This room contains historical steles of various epochs and also the monuments of the period of the Hyksos (p. 88), which is represented in Europe by a solitary head in the Villa Ludovisi at Rome. — In the centre of the room: **107. *Hyksos Sphinx* in black granite, from Tanis, the restored parts recognisable by their darker hue.

The head shows the coarse and foreign-looking features of the race which oppressed Egypt for so long a period. An inscription on the right shoulder, almost effaced, mentions Apepi (Apophis), one of the last Hyksos kings. Merenptah, the Pharaoh of the Exodus, and Ramses II. subsequently caused their names to be inscribed on the base, and Psusennes, of the 21st dynasty, engraved his on the breast of the statue.

106. Head of a sphinx, resembling No. 107, with the name of Merenptah, added at a later date. — 108. Sacrificial tablet of black granite, with the name of the Hyksos king Apepi. — 100. Torso of a Hyksos statue in grey granite, found at Mît Farês in the Fayûm, and thus proving that the Hyksos dominion extended at least as far as this district.

123. Double statue of grey granite, found at Tanis and dating from the Hyksos period.

Two foreign-looking figures are standing before the sacrificial tables, which are lavishly adorned with aquatic plants (*Baskhuiu*), fishes, and birds. The features of the figures resemble those of the sphinxes; their matted beards, their plaited hair, and the bracelets on their arms distinguish them strongly from the figures on other Egyptian monuments. The name of Psusennes, engraved both on the front and on the back of the monument, was added at a later date.

**89. *Stele of the Diadoch*, in black granite, found in 1870 among the ruinous foundations of the mosque of Shêkhûn in Cairo.

In the arch above the proper inscription is a representation of Ptolemy I. Lagi (p. 96), before his accession to the throne. He is still styled a 'satrap' here, but the empty cartouches adjoining his figure seem to indicate that he is free to ascend the throne. On the left he is consecrating to Horus, the avenger of his father, a piece of planted land (), and on the right he is presenting gifts to Isis-Buto, the tutelary goddess of the cities of Peh and Tep. The inscription extols the satrap Ptolemy as a hero, who brought back from Asia to the Nile the treasures removed from the temples of Egypt, and who fixed his residence in the '*Fortress of Alexander I., which was formerly called Rhakotis*' (*i.e.* Alexandria). His victories over Syria and the western regions of Egypt, and his beneficence to the gods of Egypt are also praised, and there follows a eulogium of his liberality in renewing a grant to the goddesses (*i.e.* to the priests) of the cities of Peh and Tep, the so-called quarters of Buto, whose worship had been abolished by the 'Arch-enemy Xerxes'.

*127. Celebrated monument of the time of *Thothmes III*, in black granite (19th dyn.; Karnak).

The upper part of the inscription was erased by Khu-en-aten, who overthrew the worship of Ammon in Thebes, or by some other early monarch, but was afterwards restored, perhaps by Ramses II. The traces of this double change are distinctly visible on the upper half of the stele. Below is an inscription in 25 lines celebrating the victories of Thothmes III. in a highly poetic manner. This monument was often copied by subsequent dynasties to celebrate the exploits of Seti I. and Ramses III.

101. Portrait-head in dark granite of *Taharka* (the Tirhakah of the Bible), the Ethiopian conqueror (25th dyn.); negro cast of features, nose mutilated.

The following steles are also of historical interest: 98. *Stele of Piankhi*, in grey granite, covered with inscriptions (23rd dyn.; Gebel-Barkal).

In the 6th cent. before Christ the power of the Ethiopian monarchs extended to Thebes, while several native princes still maintained themselves in N. Egypt One of these named Tefnekht (p 91) organises a rising against the usurper Piankhi, but is finally conquered and forced to yield to the Ethiopian, who, after pacifying the country, returns to his capital Napata.

99. Stele of Hor-sa-tef, in grey granite, from the end of the Persian period (Gebel-Barkal).

The king gives an account of the wars carried on by him against the tribes dwelling between Abyssinia, Dârfûr, and the Red Sea, particularly of the expedition to the Gebel-Barkal in the 6th year of his reign

114. The so-called Coronation Stele, on which the name of the king has been effaced. — 122. Stele of Amen-meri-nut, recounting a campaign undertaken by him at the instigation of a dream. — 112. Tablet known as the Stele of Excommunication. These three steles were all found at Gebel-Barkal.

In the corner of the room · 97. Door-post of grey basalt, with the name and titles of Tau, brother of Queen Ra-meri-ankh-ens, wife of Pepi I. (6th dyn.; Abydos). — 127. Limestone stele, with inscriptions on each face and the cartouches of Usertesen III. and Amenemha III. (12th dyn.; Abydos).

The rose-coloured granite door, leading from the Grand Vestibule to the Salle du Centre, was found at Abydos, amid the ruins of an ancient temple of Osiris. The central portion bears the cartouche of Seti I., while at the sides are full-length figures of the same monarch.

Salle du Centre. Along the walls are arranged twelve cabinets, containing statuettes of the Egyptian deities in bronze, stone, and porcelain, and objects connected with the burial ceremonies of the Egyptians. To the left, *Case B*. Osiris and Apis. 2490. Apis-bull with the sacred triangle on its forehead; 2497-2502. Apis steles, in limestone, from the Serapeum at Saḳḳâra; 2494. Serapis (human body with the head of a bull); 2434. Relief of the transportation of a dead Apis, with figures of Isis and Nephthys to the right and left of the reliquary.

Case C. 2416. Statuette of Osiris in limestone, with fragments of the kneeling figures of a brother and sister, each presenting a sacrificial tablet, 2415. Hawk with the crown of Upper and Lower Egypt; 2386. Upper part of a sceptre, consisting of a lotus blossom and a hawk; 2381. Upright mummy of Osiris in basalt; 2383. Stele with relief of an Osiris mummy; on the arch at the top is the sun (a red disk with a scarabæus), while to the right and left are two dog-faced baboons in an attitude of adoration. 2359. Harpocrates emerging from the calyx of a lotus; 2325. Statue of the child Horus, with its finger at its lips, formerly gilded; 2391, 2364. Two bronze chairs, with feet and arms in the form of lions, while the back of the second consists of a hawk with outspread wings.

Cabinet D. 2209 Bronze naos, with a cat; 2276. Wooden obelisk with a mummy of Osiris; 2299. Jackal; 2315. Statuette of Anubis with the jackal's head, and the linen case in which it was found, 2260. Beak and neck of an ibis; 2129. Statuette of a priest, holding a shrine of Osiris, 2134, 2223. Ibises in bronze.

Cabinet E. Figures of Isis. 2167. Isis with wings attached to her arms; 2170. Isis and Horus, in stone, gilded; 2141, 2142. Same subject, in bronze; 2154 Osiris mummy on a pedestal adorned with basreliefs of gods (in bronze); 2185. Tombstone representing Isis sheltering the god Harmachis with her wings and receiving sacrificial offerings.

Cabinet F Statuettes of the goddesses Isis, Nephthys, and Thueris 2028. Sitting figure of Nephthys in yellowish marble; 2038. Sitting figure of Isis, with her hands resting on her knees, the face and neck gilded; 2105. Bronze ægis with a head of Hathor, furnished with cow-horns, 2033. Same subject; 2063. Porcelain statuette of Thuëris; 2061. Tombstone, with the singer Anarimes offering sacrifices to a hawk.

Cabinet G. 2009, 2013. Bronze figures of the Theban Ammon, with the double feather on his head; 1967. Bronze ægis with the head of a lion, bearing a solar disk and a uræus serpent; 1957. Bronze figure of Imhotep (the Æsculapius of the Greeks), with a papyrus roll on his knees, 1925. Ptah as a mummy, in bronze. — 1933. Figure of the 'Primæval Ptah' (see p. 126) in green porcelain; the deity is represented in the shape of a distorted child, standing upon two crocodiles and strangling two snakes. Behind is Ma, the goddess of justice, with outspread wings. — 1883, 1863. Bronze figures of the goddess Sekhet, with the lion's head, one sitting and the other standing; 1857. Bronze cat; 1882. Bronze figure of Sekhet, with the solar disk and a uræus serpent on her head.

Cabinet I. *1813, *1750. Bronze statuettes of the god Nefer-Tum, one inlaid with gold and enamel; 1831. Sceptre ending in a lotus, surmounted by a bronze statuette of Serapis; 1829. Bronze statuette of the goddess Neith; 1826. Bronze group of Horus and Thoth pouring water over a figure kneeling between them; 1775. Horus with the head of a hawk, leaning against an obelisk; 1770. Uræus serpent with a human head, wearing the crowns of Upper and Lower Egypt; 1764. Sceptre with a lotus and head of a hawk. 1734. Pectoral plate in the form of a shrine; in the middle is a shield bearing the head of Hathor supported by two uræus snakes; at the sides are Ptah and Sekhet. — 1710. The god Shu, in porcelain.

Cabinet J. chiefly contains statuettes of Osiris. 1558. Wooden

Stele, with wonderfully preserved gilding and colouring; the scene represents a priest of Mentu in adoration before Harmachis and Tum. 1530. Stele of Besmut; 1510, 1511. Two small coffins of baked clay, containing statuettes of Osiris; *1547. Wooden statuette of Osiris; 1562. Perforated slab of porcelain, representing a scarabæus in blue, green, and black enamel; 1493. Wooden head-rest, such as is still used in the Sûdân and Japan.

Cabinet K. 1445. Side of a sarcophagus of Besmut, dating from the period of the Saïte kings. The inscriptions are taken from the Ritual of the Dead. — 1483. Naos of elegant workmanship for a person named Nekht, a sitting figure of whom, in serpentine, occupies the interior (13th dyn ; Abydos). — In the front part of the cabinet is a necklace, consisting of small statuettes of Osiris in green enamel and the emblems  and .

Cabinet L. 1393. Papyrus written for the mummy of Amenmes and containing a treatise on the lower world. 1307. Osiris statuette of the scribe Neferhotep, in alabaster. 1306. Alabaster statuette of Awi, the royal scribe for the sacrificial offerings. Several wooden hawks, partly from coffins and shrines, partly from wooden statuettes of Osiris. This cabinet also contains numerous 'cartonages' (p. 312) of the Græco-Roman era, many of them with elaborate designs and wonderfully fresh colouring.

Cabinet M. also contains cartonages and masks. 1200, 1201. 'Canopi' or Canopic jars of terracotta, adorned with boldly and elegantly executed designs, and inscribed with the name 'Baâu'. These jars contained the embalmed viscera of the mummy and were generally interred with it. They invariably occur in groups of four, either all with covers in the shape of human heads, or with the heads of a man, an ape, a hawk, and a jackal. — 1243, 1244. Two similar vases. Mummies of animals: 1271, 1274. Crocodiles, 1275 Jackal, 1272. Ibis. Also shrines and statuettes of Osiris in wood and other materials.

Cabinet N. 1123-1126. Canopi of painted limestone; 1156. Small stone naos of the 13th dynasty 1171 et seq. Conical tiles of baked clay, of a kind found only at Thebes; they were perhaps votive offerings.

Between the pillars and the N. and S. walls are four glass-cases.

Case A. (by the S. wall, to the left) contains a selection of figures from the Egyptian Pantheon in bronze, porcelain, and lapis lazuli. 2625. (in the middle of the case) kneeling bronze figure with the head of a hawk and the arms raised in adoration. 2512. Group in bronze: Osiris seated between Nefer-Tum and Horus, and in front a kneeling worshipper. 2626. Sitting figure of Osiris, with Isis and Nephthys behind him; 2665. Anubis: 2664. Figure worshipping Isis, whose headgear consists of a fish; 2700. Horus; 2697. Osiris as a mummy, in bronze inlaid with gold; 2595. Isis with the head of a cow; 2597. Ammon; 2581. Apis-bull, with Isis on the right and Nephthys on the left; 2583. Mummy of Osiris between Isis and Nephthys; 2576. Apis-bull, with a Carian inscription on the base; 2709. Serapis, with a papyrus plant on his head. — Among the *Porcelain Figures* the following are the most noteworthy: 2558. Isis, Horus, and Nephthys; 2675. Thuëris; 2552. Figure of the god Set (almost unique); 2548. Ptah as a child; 2566. Thoth, Isis, Nephthys, and Khnum; 2559. Bes strangling a lion; 2687. Ptah Sokar as a mummy, with a sceptre in his hand; 2640. Hathor-Isis with a child at her breast, while behind is an Isis sheltering her with her wings; 2635. Harpocrates; 2542. Cynocephalus or dog-faced ape, the emblem of the god Thoth. — *Lapis lazuli Figures:* 2643. Ma, the goddess of truth, with a golden feather on her head; 2638. Isis and Horus, with golden horns and the solar disk; 2565. Horus holding a serpent (finely executed); *2646. Small figure of Horus in iridescent glass.

Cabinet II. (N. wall) contains the **Jewels of Queen Aah-hotep*, mother of Aahmes (18th dyn.), found with the mummy of the Queen at Drah abu'l Negga (Thebes). In front: 3448. Bracelet for the upper arm, adorned with turquoises; in front is a vulture with wings of lapis lazuli, cornelian, and paste in a gold setting (not enamelled). 3476. Dagger with a handle formed of four female heads in gold and a blade damascened with the same metal; 3475. Axe with a handle of cedar wood encased in gold and inlaid with the name and titles of Aahmes in precious stones; 3477. Pliable chain of gold, 36 inches long, to which is attached a scarabæus with wings inlaid with lapis-lazuli; 3508. Diadem with the cartouche of Aahmes and two sphinxes; 3510. Gold bracelet inlaid with lapis lazuli, representing King Aahmes kneeling between Seb and his acolytes; 3509. Bracelet formed of pearls strung upon gold wire. 3582. Golden boat, resting upon a wooden frame with four wheels of bronze and containing twelve rowers, a steersman, and a figure holding a baton of command. The end of the boat, which is in the form of a lotus, bears the cartouche of King Kames (end of the 17th dyn.). — On the N. side of the cabinet: 3564. Necklace *(usekh)* of gold, the links of which are in the form of coils of rope, cruciform flowers, antelopes chased by lions, jackals, vultures, and winged uræus serpents; the clasps represent the heads of hawks. — 3565. Breastplate of gold inlaid with precious stones. In the middle is a boat with a naos or ark, containing King Aahmes, on whose head Ammon and Ra are pouring the water of life; at the back is an engraved representation of the same scene. — 3580. Golden diadem with the head of Medusa, dating from the Greek period. — On the W. side of the cabinet: 3595. Gold chain with three flies in gold foil; 3605. Wooden staff, with a crook at the end, overlaid with gold; 3607. Fan of gilded wood, with the holes left by the ostrich feathers with which it was originally furnished. — On the S. side of the cabinet: Bracelets and anklets of massive gold; 3628. Mirror of Queen Aah-hotep, made of wood, bronze, and gold. Adjacent are numerous rings and bracelets of the Græco-Roman period. — Opposite —

Case P. Historical relics. 3834. Roll of mummy linen with the cartouche of King Pepi (6th dyn.), found at Saḳḳâra; 3956. Large alabaster vase, the capacity of which is indicated as '21 hin'; 3870. Circular vase with enamelled inscription mentioning Amenhotep III. and his wife Tii (18th dyn.); 3894. Scarabæus, admirably executed in green serpentine, with the cartouche of Ramses II.; 3901, 3902. Alabaster vase, with the name of King Mer-en-Ra on the bowl and that of his brother and successor, Pepi II. Ra-nefer-ka, on the lid. 3874. Bronze cube found at Tanis along with 15 others of the same kind; the inscriptions, with several names and cartouches that belong, perhaps, to the 13th dynasty, are inlaid in silver. 3868. Piece of enamel with the cartouches of Ramses III., found at Tell el-Yehûdîyeh (Shibîn el-Ḳanâṭir). — 3960. Fragment of a statue of Taharka (25th dyn.). On the base are 14 fettered Asiatics and 14 negroes, emblematical of the tribes conquered by Taharka. — 3893. Vase in blue enamel, with the cartouche of Thothmes III. (18th dyn.); 3910. Statuette of Ramses IV. as Osiris, in blue enamel; 3908. Fragment of a statue of Seti I.; 3914. Large scarabæus in blue enamel, with the cartouche of Ramses IV. (20th dyn.); 3925. Small heart-shaped amulet, inscribed with a chapter from the Ritual of the Dead and dedicated to Seti I.; 3928. Small sphinx in green felspar, with the cartouches of Apries (26th dyn.); 3897. Bronze ægis with the head of a king. — The case also contains a number of scarabæi inscribed with the names of kings and gods.

Case O, between the pillars and the S. wall of the room, contains statuettes of Osiris, canopi, and objects connected with the dead. 1606, 1607, 1648, 1649. Alabaster canopi of the period of the 26th dyn., very finely executed. — 1621. Small votive sarcophagus, in limestone, made in the time of the 22nd dynasty and dedicated to Ra. It contained the bier of black granite, now placed in front of it, on which lies the mummy of the deceased, guarded by the soul in the form of a hawk with a human head. — 1622. Wooden stele, the lower part of which is adorned with an Egyptian landscape, a representation of extremely rare occurrence; 1594. Bronze statuette of Osiris; 1678. Papyrus with extracts from the Ritual of the Dead, prepared for a Theban named Mapui.

Adjoining the four pillars in the centre of the hall are eight cabinets. Of these *Cabinets R.* and *Q.* contain models for sculptures, while the other six contain articles of daily life. Several of the slabs in Case Q. have reliefs on both sides. The most striking is No. 3393. Fragment of a ram, exceedingly delicate both in design and execution.

Cabinet Y. 3240. Hippopotamus in blue enamel, the body adorned with representations of plants, birds, and butterflies (11th dyn.; Thebes). — *3622. *Statuette of Osiris*, in white enamel, inlaid with blue, yellow, and violet. The inscription mentions the name of Ptahmes (20th dyn.). This unique work is the most beautiful statuette of Osiris that has been found. — 3277. Wooden case for perfume. The handle consists of a nude female figure in the act of swimming and holding in her outstretched arms a duck, the body of which is hollowed out to receive the perfume, while the wings form the cover. — 3289. 3305, 3306, 3314. Enamel works from Tell el-Yehûdîyeh. No. 3306. represents a garland of lotus flowers and buds. — 3278. Head of a king of the 26th dynasty, in blue porcelain. 3304. Small wooden reel or bobbin of thread, terminating at each end in a human head, 3315. Fine bronze figure of the goddess Bast.

Cabinet U. contains glass phials and vases. *3159. Head of a girl, carved in wood, found near the pyramids of Gîzeh; 3179. Green enamelled brick with the cartouches of Ramses III. (almost unique); 3181. Tortoise in wood, with holes containing wooden hair-pins (11th dyn.; Thebes). — 3182. Board for a game resembling draughts; the drawer contains seven of the pieces used in the game, inlaid with ivory. 3183. is another board of the same kind. — 3195. Reed-basket (11th dyn.), almost identical with the parti-coloured baskets still made by the natives of Assuân.

Cabinet V. contains vases and other vessels for eye-powder (3063, 3066, 3068, 3069). 3080. Vase of green jasper in the shape of a heart, with a scarabæus engraved on the one side and the 30th chapter of the Ritual of the Dead on the other; 3092. Inkstand in green porcelain for red and black ink; *3098. Bust of Isis in blue enamel, with the cartouches of Ramses III.; 3059. Blue colouring material, retaining the shape of the little bag that contained it (Tell el-Yehûdîyeh); 3090. Small piece of stone, for grinding the colours used in writing; 3093. Split rings of cornelian, ivory, and glass, found in mummy-cases (use unknown); 3107. Sceptre in bronze of the Saite period, with a crocodile bearing a boat, which in turn supports a naos.

Cabinet X. 2929. Palette used by scribes, with six different colours and the cartouche of Thothmes III. (18th dyn.). *2949, 2950, 2960, 2961, 2968. Five silver vases of elaborate workmanship, found at Tell Tmai (Mendes); the details consist of the flowers, buds, and leaves of the lotus. 2965. Lion's head, in red jasper, 2966. Silver boat with ten rowers and a steersman, found with the trinkets of Queen Aah-hotep; 2984. Statue in green enamelled clay, standing on a base covered with inscriptions, which mention the name of Nefer-abra (26th dyn.); 2986. Dies, resembling those still in use; 2991. Small bronze sphinx of the Persian era.

Cabinets S and *T.* contain vases of terracotta and bronze, for holding perfume, water, meal, etc.

In the centre of the room: **3961. *Statue of King Khefren* or *Khafra*, the builder of the second pyramid, found in the well of the granite temple near the Great Sphinx (p. 365).

The king is represented in life-size, sitting on a throne, the arms of which terminate in lions' heads. At the sides of the seat are papyrus and lotus plants intertwined around the symbol of union , which indicates the junction of Upper with Lower Egypt, and is perhaps emblematical of the transition from this life to the next. On the pedestal, to the right and left of the feet of the statue, is inscribed in distinct hieroglyphic characters: 'The prince and victorious Horus, Khafra, the good god and lord of the diadem'. In his right hand the monarch holds a roll of papyrus. On the top of the back of the throne is a hawk, protecting the king's head with its outspread wings. The torso is of a more thickset type than is the case with the statues of the modern empire, having been modelled in accordance with the rules prescribed by the hieratic canon at that early period, and the whole figure breathes a spirit of strength and repose. The muscles of the breast and legs are reproduced with wonderful accuracy. The statue is made of an extremely hard diorite, the difficulty of working which has been overcome by the artist in a marvellous manner.

**3962. (railed in) *Wooden Statue* from Saḳḳâra known as the *Shêkh el-beled* (village-chief), a name given to it by the Arabs on account of its resemblance to a well-fed specimen of that modern functionary.

The figure, which dates from the early part of the old empire, affords a proof that the Egyptian sculptors were quite capable of executing really artistic work whenever they could shake off the fetters of their rigid canon. The individuality and realism of this figure will afford a pleasant surprise to those who have found it difficult to admire the stiff conventional forms of Egyptian art. The feet, which had been broken off, are restored, but the rest of the figure is in its original condition. The upper part of the body and the legs are bare, while from the hips hangs a kind of apron folded in front. In the hand is the long rod of office. The round head with its short hair, and the portrait-like, good-natured face are remarkably life-like. The eyes, which have a somewhat rigid expression, were put in, as in the case of other similar statues, after the work was completed. They consist of pieces of opaque white quartz with pupils formed of rock-crystal, in the centre of which is placed a polished metal knob for the double purpose of securing them and giving them light and sparkle; and they are framed with thin plates of bronze, the edges of which form the eyelids. The figure was originally covered with a thin coating of plaster of Paris and painted. — The female torso in the Salle de l'Ancien Empire (No. 1044) was found in the grave of the Shêkh el-Beled and probably represents his wife.

**5243. *Statue of Hathor*, the goddess of the infernal regions, bending her head, adorned with the disk and double feather, protectingly over the deceased Psametik. Nos. 5245 (Osiris), 5246 (Isis), and 5244 (sacrificial slab) were found in the same tomb.

This group, executed in green basalt, and found at Sakkâra, is one of the best works of the 26th dynasty. The heads are remarkably attractive, but the treatment of the other parts of the body is much inferior to that of the ancient empire. The technical execution, however, shows the utmost care and skil.

By the N. wall, behind the statue of Khefren, are numerous Canopi (see p. 301). — 1841. Small stele in black basalt, representing 'Horus on the crocodiles'; the inscription contains magical formulæ and formed a talisman against evil. — 1846. (behind the last), Papyrus found at Thebes, containing moral precepts couched in the form of a dialogue. Above, 1847. Ritual of the Dead with coloured representations, prepared for a person named Senhotep (20th dyn.; Thebes). *1848. Geographical papyrus, describing, after a somewhat mythical and allegorical fashion, the Fayûm and Lake Mœris (Thebes; Greek period). — Along the walls and between the cabinets are wooden coffins of various periods, most of them found in Thebes.

The door on the W. side of the Salle du Centre leads to the **Salle de l'Ancien Empire**, which contains the largest existing collection of monuments of the primæval empire, *i. e.* of the time of the builders of the pyramids In the middle of the N. side: *1050. Double group in limestone, found in 1870 in a maṣṭaba near Mêdûm, the colouring still remarkably fresh. It represents Prince Rahotep and his wife Nefert, a princess of the blood, both in the costume of the period (4th or 5th dyn.). The eyes, made of coloured quartz, impart a very lifelike air to the figures. — To the left of the last, 1052. Statue of Ti, in limestone, found in the Serdâb of his tomb at Saḳḳâra (p. 388); to the right, 1049. Statue of Nefer-kha-ra (5th dyn.). — By the E. Wall: *1037-1039. Three wooden panels with reliefs.

These panels, taken from the walls of a tomb, represent the figure of 'Hosi', the deceased, while the hieroglyphics above give his name and his titles The work is executed by a master hand and is not unworthy of comparison with the Shêkh el-Beled (4th dyn.; Saḳḳâra).

N. side, in the cabinet in the corner to the right: 1051. Fragment of the inner lining of a tomb, found in a grave at Mêdûm.

The six geese represented here are drawn and coloured with great accuracy, while the treatment shows considerable cleverness and humour. The material is a kind of hardened clay coated with plaster of Paris.

Below, Models of boats used in transporting mummies (11th dyn.; Saḳḳâra). — The cabinet in the left corner of the same side contains small and lifelike figures, differing entirely from the ordinary stiff attitudes of Egyptian statues· 1002. Man in a crouching position cleaning a vase: *1006. Scribe in a kneeling posture, with his arms crossed (inlaid eyes); 1001. Man with a sack on his shoulder and his sandals in his hand; 1012, 1013. Two women grinding corn, 1014. Dwarf named Khnumhotep, 'keeper of the linen for embalming'. These figures all belong to the 4th, 5th, and 6th dynasties. — 1007. Small sacrificial chest, probably used by the priests. It contains a sacrificial slab, vases, knives, etc. (6th dyn.). — On the walls are several tombstones in the form of doors, chiefly from Saḳḳâra. — In front of the window: 1053. Large limestone sarcophagus from Thebes, of which a drawing was made by Lepsius in 1842, but which was afterwards again lost under heaps of rubbish and not rediscovered till 1882. It belongs to the 11th dynasty and was made for a person named Tagi. The interior is adorned with numerous inscriptions and scenes relating to the dead, most of them in good preservation.

In the middle of the S. Wall. *975. *Statue of Ra-nefer*, a priest, wearing a wig (in limestone). The muscles of the arms and breast are executed with great realism, and the statue ranks among the most perfect specimens of Egyptian art (5th dyn.; Saḳḳâra). — To the right, 974. Basaltic statue of King Khefren at a more advanced age than in No. 3961 (p. 305); the statue, which was found with the latter in the granite temple near the Sphinx, has been freely restored. — *964. A large and very perfectly executed sarcophagus in rose-coloured granite, of great antiquity, which once contained the remains of a priest of Apis named Khufu-ankh.

The sides recall the domestic rather than the sepulchral style of architecture, but in Egypt these styles were similar in many respects. The ancient Egyptians used to call their earthly dwellings 'inns' or 'lodgings', while they styled their tombs 'everlasting houses'. The ends of the beams, resembling triglyphs, should be noticed

965. Similar but plainer sarcophagus, prepared for Prince Hirbaif. 970. Similar sarcophagus with the angles rounded, bearing the name of Prince Kamskhem. These three sarcophagi were all found near the Pyramids of Gîzeh and date from the time of the 4th dynasty.

Adjacent, by the W. Wall: 886. Stele of limestone, with an inscription of 50 lines, in which the deceased Uni records his exploits under the three Pharaohs, Teta, Pepi I., and Mer-en-ra, including his work on the pyramids constructed by the last two kings (both in Saḳḳâra, opened in 1880-81; comp. p. 402). — 882. Celebrated tombstone of the 25th dynasty, probably a copy of an original of the 4th dynasty.

The inscription is a record by King Cheops of various works and restorations carried out by him. It contains a representation of the great sphinx of Gîzeh, with an intimation 'that the dwelling of the sphinx Harmachis lies to the S of the temple of Isis and to the N. of the temple of Osiris'.

Also on the S. side of the room are various fragments from tombs at Saḳḳâra, with scenes of great life and humour. 887. Boatmen, engaged in the transportation of fruit and other provisions, fall into a quarrel and attack each other with the oars. 889. In the upper row are represented the various stages in the making of bread; below are slaves pouring wine into jars. 890. Shepherds conducting their flocks across the inundated fields, and scaring off the crocodiles, which lurk amid the reeds, by loud cries and gestures. 908. Fruit-seller teasing an ape, which has seized him by the leg.

W. Wall. 958. The two upper rows represent field workers, the third the making of wine and bread In the lowest row are goldsmiths weighing gold and sculptors at work with their polishing stones. — 959. Shepherds pasturing their flocks; below, shepherds and fishermen preparing for a meal. — To the right and left of the door, 881, 1046. Steles from the grave of Sabu at Saḳḳâra (p. 401).

The first of these represents the deceased sitting at a table covered with slaughtered cattle, eggs, flowers, fruit, and other offerings, which are being brought in by servants; on the other slab we see Sabu seated in a kind of litter, while a number of men and women are bringing their gifts to the tomb. Below are represented the cutting up of slaughtered oxen, the deceased navigating the Nile, and his cattle being driven before him to be counted. All these scenes are intended to imply that in the next world the just continue the same life as they lived in this, but in a state of greater felicity.

In front of the steles, 986, 988. Two sacrificial tables in alabaster.

Two lions support each of the tables in a slightly tilted position, so that the libations ran down into a vase placed between the tails of the lions (4th dyn.).

The door on the E. side of the Salle du Centre leads to the **Salle Funéraire,** which contains wooden sarcophagi from Thebes, chiefly belonging to the priests of Mentu, and also others found in 1884 in the necropolis of Akhmîm (Panopolis). To the right and left are two large octagonal glass-cases containing scarabæi, amulets of glass, enamelled clay, and cornelian, and objects used in the adornment of the dead.

Cases AN, AO, and *AP.* contain scarabæi, the finest of which are No. 4572, in felspar; No. 4567, in gold; and No. 4566, in light-coloured serpentine, of very delicate workmanship.

Case AQ. contains figures of deities in bronze. 4585. Isis, with winged arms raised in an attitude of protection; the indented portions were formerly filled with enamel. 4587. Two wooden tablets with figures of the god Bess.

Case AR. Scarabæi, the emblem of the heart, found in the bodies of mummies whence the heart had been removed, and other smaller scarabæi, made of cornelian and granite. 4555. Heart with a man's head in amethyst, perhaps dating from the 11th dynasty; 4562. Amulets in the form of outstretched fingers, probably interred with the mummy to avert the evil eye (26th dyn.). — *Case AS.* contains objects in bronze, used as ornaments for the heads of small statues, including Ammon and Osiris feathers, Isis horns, false beards, and the like. — *Case AT.* Pectorals, or ecclesiastical breast-ornaments, in the form of shrines, some of them inlaid with glass. 4333. Scarabæus in blue enamel, with expanded wings; 4328. Scarabæus made of coloured glass beads; 4327. Scarabæus in perforated work.

Case AU. Small sceptres in wood and bronze. 4274. Pectoral plate, representing Isis on a lotus between two winged serpents; 4303. Kukupha, or sceptre of wood; 4271. Ægis, head of Isis with the solar disk and horns; 4278. Small ægis of quartz.

W. Side. *Cabinet AE.* Wooden chests in the shape of a naos, wooden statuettes of Osiris, chains of cornelian, glass, and other beads. 4402. Fragment of a frieze found in Tell el-Yehûdîyeh, with a fantastic bird, probably meant for a phœnix. Above are two round disks of enamel (No. 4401), with ornamentation resembling stars, found at the same place. 4427. Wooden naos with well-preserved colouring. 4420. Small stele of wood, formerly gilded

The fact that the figure of Osiris alone is intact proves that the mutilation of the stele took place at a very early period, when the thieves did not dare to remove the gold on the figure of the god.

S. Wall. *Case AD.* 4436. Osiris in the first stage of his resurrection (comp. p. 130), a figure of diorite with a double feather of gold on the head (26th dyn.); 4441. Case for a sceptre or standard, in the shape of a boat terminating at each end in a lotus; 4450. Figure of the royal scribe Ani, in black granite, holding a sistrum with the head of Hathor (18th dyn.). — *4454. Small figure of the ancient empire (5th dyn.), in limestone, described by the inscription as the 'steward of the grain for tribute, Nefer'. This is one of the finest specimens of Egyptian sculpture. — 4457. Vase of grey granite, encircled by a serpent and bearing the names of King Piankhi (23rd dyn.) and a queen (the latter illegible); 4449. Uræus serpent in bronze, perhaps used as a sceptre, 4475. Weight of grey granite in the form of a calf's head, with the cartouches of Seti I (19th dyn.) and a stamp indicating the weight (300 Utes), 4479 Door-hinge, in bronze, with the cartouche of Queen Shep-en-apet, daughter of Queen Ameneritis and wife of Psammetikh I. (26th dyn.).

Cabinet AC. Chairs, baskets, wooden instruments of husbandmen and masons, fruits, seeds, and other objects used in common life. 4493. Chair with lion's claws as feet, 4495. Similar chair without the lion's feet, both found in Thebes (11th dyn.), 4497. Wooden hatchet, 4650. Wooden ruler. In the middle of the cabinet is a large basket (No. 4618), filled with the fruit of the dûm-palm (p. 78). In front are saucers of red earth containing grain, olives, and eggs.

E. Wall. *3599. *Tomb Chamber* of the 11th dynasty, found at Thebes and brought to Bûlâḳ in 1883.

The tomb was prepared for a Theban grandee named Herhotep, whose stone sarcophagus, covered with inscriptions, occupies almost the whole available space in the interior. The drawings and hieroglyphics, the latter consisting of citations from the Ritual of the Dead, resemble those of the primæval empire On the wall opposite the door is a list of the sacrificial offerings

N. Side. Octagonal glass-case. *Section AG.* Figures of men and animals in glass paste of different colours. Ram, in green and black; Eagle, black with a white beak; Cow, red and blue; Bird with a human head, representing the soul, in red and green. All the objects in this section were found with mummies from the Fayûm (Labyrinth).

Section AH. 4096. The goddess Ma, with the face coloured light-blue, the body reddish brown, and a necklace of variegated mosaic; 4091. Four female heads, of a light-blue colour; 4090. Two jackals, in obsidian; 4099. Two plates of gold, engraved with amulets.

Section AI. So-called *ut'a* eyes , in various materials. These amulets are emblematical of the eyes of Ra which illumine the world (p. 128), the right eye being called the sun, and the left the moon; the former also symbolising the king, and the latter the queen. The dead, when rising from their graves, are represented as *ut'a* eyes. — Small head-rests, symbolical of the eternal resting-place of pure souls. — Small columns in green felspar or earthenware, emblematical of the renewed spring or rejuvenescence of the deceased.

Section AJ. Paste imitations of precious stones, works in glass, and mosaics. Among the last are an ape, a human head, and small star-shaped flowers; if split into thin sheets, each layer of the mosaic shows the same pattern. Small tortoise, executed with great care and truth to nature.

Section AK Hares, crocodiles, hedgehogs, cows, and other animals in enamelled clay, cornelian, agate, and lapis lazuli. 4163. Elephant (rare); 4173. Ape leaning on its elbow, a work showing a good deal of humour.

Section AL Cornelian rings and serpents. In the middle, Collection of small ornaments for a necklace, several of which, in the shape of cartouches, bear the name of Ramses II.

Section AM. Amulets and emblems: Tat, the symbol of constancy; the heart; the symbol of life (?).

Section AF. Amulets. rising of the sun; emblem of the the goddess Neith; , emblems of impartiality; symbol of the clothing of the dead in the other world; etc.

W. Wall. *Cabinet Z.* 4480. Wooden figure of the ancient kingdom. 4846. Small round naos in terracotta, found at Abydos; over the door is a frieze of uræus snakes, while round the exterior runs a series of scenes representing Osiris receiving sacrifices and worship from a family of Abydos. 4919. Large two-handled terracotta vase, with the inscription 'Year 33, wine prepared for transportation'. 4876. Small models of votive offerings in terracotta, bearing the name of the scribe Nib. The case also contains a collection of terracotta moulds for the preparation of amulets and figures in glazed earthenware. At the top of the case are alabaster vases, of the most varied shapes.

N. Wall. *Cabinet AA.* Palettes for scribes and painters, combs.

needles, phials for salves and cosmetics, nails, and other finely-executed objects in wood. 4737. Double comb, in wood; 4728. Three polishing stones; 4747. Six fish-hooks; 4764. Small lizard in lead, a metal seldom used by the ancient Egyptians. 4791. Model of an Egyptian house, showing that the present natives of Ḳurna and Draḥ abu'l Negga have in no way improved or altered the domestic architecture of their forefathers. 4830. Iron key, probably of the Græco-Roman period.

Cabinet AB. Weapons, darts, chisels, knives, pincers, axes, and arrow-heads. Many of the chisels and axes (*e. g.* 4657, 4463) bear the cartouches of Thothmes III. and Queen Hatasu (18th dyn.). 4705. Bronze chisel with the head of a hawk; 4714-4716. Bows and arrows, some of the latter tipped with flint or bone (see also No. 4720). The two alabaster statues (Nos. 4648, 4685) belong to the 4th or 5th dynasty and are destitute of inscriptions. 4676. Double group in limestone, found at Saḳḳâra (5th or 6th dyn.). — 4673, 4674. Two boards for games: the first is divided into 30 squares, four of which bear special names; the other has three squares, with holes for the insertion of the wooden pins used in the game. Both date from the period of the 17th dynasty and were found at Thebes. — 4713. Sabre of hard wood, with the name of King Rasekenen on the one side and that of the 'royal son' on the other.

Cabinet AV (without glass) contains basreliefs of the period of the 18th dynasty. The titles, as well as the style of execution and design, which recall the monuments of Tell el-Amarna, seem to indicate that the persons here represented lived at the close of the reign of Amenophis III. or the beginning of that of Amenophis IV.

Cabinet AX contains a selection of Canopi (see p. 301). — 5005,5008. Two unfinished statues in grey serpentine, found at Mîtrahîneh (Memphis), the one of a man kneeling and holding a naos, the other a standing figure divided by a still distinguishable red line into two halves. — 5021. Granite statue without an inscription, found at Karnak and probably belonging to the 18th dynasty. The figure is in a kneeling posture and holds in front of it a kind of altar in the form of a column, with the head of Hathor and a lotus.

We now leave the Salle Funéraire and pass into the **Salle des Momies Royales,** which contains the valuable collection of monuments found at Dêr el-Baḥri (Thebes) on July 5th, 1881.

The first suspicions of the existence of the royal tombs at Dêr el-Bahri date from 1871, but the Arabs of the neighbourhood carefully concealed their knowledge of them and long baffled the curiosity of travellers. Statuettes of Osiris, rolls of papyrus, and other objects offered for sale at Luksor gradually put investigators on the right scent, and finally in 1881 the source of these antiquities was discovered, yielding a treasure that surpassed the most sanguine expectations.

We begin with the S. Wall. 5205. Double coffin of Masaherta, high-priest of Ammon, son of King Pinetem II. and father of Queen Hest-em-sekhet (21st dyn.). Adjacent, 5206. Double coffin of

Ta-u-hert, priestess of Ammon (21st dyn.). 5207. Double coffin of Pinetem III., son of Hest-em-sekhet, and of Men-kheper-ra, two high-priests of Ammon (21st dyn.). — On the other side of the passage: 5208. Outer case of the mummy of Queen Hest-em-sekhet. 5209. Double coffin of Princess Nesi-Khunsu. 5210. Exterior mummy-case of Queen Ramaka and her daughter Mutemhat. 5211. Double coffin of Tet-Ptah-auf-ankh, priest of Ammon (22nd dyn.). 5212. Double coffin (blackened with bitumen at a later period) of Nesi-ta-neb-asher, priestess of Ammon (22nd dyn.). 5213. Coffin of Thothmes III. (18th dyn.), much injured and robbed of its rich gilding. 5215. Coffin of Queen Hent-ta-ui (21st dyn.). — By the pillars: 5247. Large mummy-case or 'cartonage', in the shape of Osiris, of Queen Ahmes-nefer-ateri, wife of Amosis I. 5222. Mummy-case of Queen Aah-hotep, wife of Amenophis I. and mother of Amosis I. (similar to the last; see p. 302).

Both these cases are of huge size and are formed of innumerable layers of linen cloth, tightly pressed and glued together and covered with a thin coating of stucco. The solid mass of linen thus prepared is at least as hard as wood, and is adorned with painted and incised ornaments and inscriptions Each of the mummies wears a wig, surmounted by a crown and double feather.

Between the pillars and the N. Wall stands *Cabinet AY*, the upper shelf of which contains a bronze pedestal with four vases for libations, inscribed with the name of Queen Hest-em-sekhet. Adjacent is a wooden chest for containing statuettes of Osiris, bearing the cartouches of Pinetem II. Below are two shelves with Osiris statuettes, in blue glazed clay, dedicated to the memory of Pinetem II., Masaherta, Pinetem III., Tet-Ptah-auf-ankh, Hest-em-sekhet, Hent-ta-ui, Nesi-Khunsu, Ramaka, Nesi-ta-neb-asher, and Ta-u-hert. — Lower down are several votive gifts found with the mummy of Hest-em-sekhet. 5261. Ivory casket with inscriptions and the cartouches of Ramses IX. — 6262 (lowest shelf but one), False mummy of a child, fabricated at a very remote period by thieves, to take the place of the real one; the mummy-case bears the name of Princess Setamu, daughter of Amosis I. (18th dyn.). Adjacent are two small oars found with the mummy of Thothmes III. At the botton of the cabinet are several finely-executed canopi'.

Cabinet BD, between the pillars and the S. wall. On the uppermost shelf are two wigs belonging to Queen Hest-em-sekhet, and between them a small wooden box with the cartouches of Pinetem II. Second shelf: Osiris statuettes. Third shelf: Fruits of the dûm palm, raisins, and dates; small vases in blue glazed earth bearing the name of Princess Nesi-Khunsu; similar vases of glass paste, green, blue, or black and white. 5248. Casket in wood and ivory with the cartouches of Queen Hatasu (18th dyn.). 5249. Fragment of the coffin of Ramses I. Fourth shelf: 5250. Mummy of Sokar-em-saf, found in 1881 in the pyramid built by this king at Saḳḳâra (6th dyn.).

Cabinets AZ and *BC*, placed at the foot of the pillars, opposite each other, contain wigs, boxes made of the papyrus reed, vases for libations, and leaves and flowers found with royal mummies, which have been prepared and described by Dr. Schweinfurth.

In the centre of the room is a large *Funereal Bed*, intended for the reception of the mummy.

The feet of the bed, which was found in Thebes and belongs to the 11th dynasty, are formed of two lions The mummy, which is of later date, is that of a priestess of Ammon, daughter of Prince Takelot (23rd dyn.).

5221. Exact reproduction, on a reduced scale (one-third) of the tent or canopy of the mummy of Hest-em-sekhet, painted by MM. Brugsch and Bouriant.

The original, which is made of dyed leather, has been so damaged, that it cannot be exhibited until it has undergone a long and costly process of restoration

N. Wall, within the recess with panelled sides 5227. Coffin of Raskenen III. (end of the 17th dyn.), 5228. Wooden coffin of Amosis I. (18th dyn.), painted yellow, with ornamention and inscriptions in blue; 5229 Inner case and mummy of Queen Ahmes-nefer-ateri; 5230. Coffin and mummy of Amenophis I. (18th dyn.), the head wearing a mask. In the corner: *5202. Richly gilded lid of the coffin of Aah-hotep, mother of Amosis I. (17th dyn.; p. 312).

E. Wall. 5231. Coffin and mummy of Thothmes II. (18th dyn.); 5232. Coffin and mummy of Seti I., father of Ramses the Great (19th dyn.). 5233. Coffin and mummy of Ramses II., surnamed the Great (19th dyn.).

The two inscriptions on the coffin record that in the 16th year of King Siamu the mummy was removed from the tomb of Seti I, and that in the 10th year of the high-priest Pinetem it was again removed and transferred to the tomb of Amenophis I

Adjacent, *5234. Coffin of Netem-Mut, mother of King Herhor (20th dyn.), finely executed but in a very dilapidated condition; the ornamentation and inscriptions are inlaid with coloured glass.

S. Wall. 5235. Inner case with the mummy of Queen Hest-em-sekhet; 3236. Inner case and mummies of Queen Ramaka and her daughter Mutemhat, who died at the same time. 5237. Coffin and mummy of Nebsenui, a priestly scribe, this mummy is in wonderful preservation, even the eye-lashes are visible. 5238. Coffin and mummy of Pinetem II., with teeth ground to a point.

The two *Stands* contain eight other mummies, also found in 1881.

Salle Gréco-Romaine. This room contains mummies and tombstones of the Græco-Roman period, Greek and Coptic inscriptions, and numerous smaller relics, arranged in eight cabinets. To the right of the entrance, *5400. The famous *Decree of Canopus* (pp. 447, 455), found at Tanis (and usually called the *Tablet of Tanis*, to distinguish it from another copy in the Louvre).

This tablet confirmed the correctness of the method of deciphering discovered by the celebrated Champollion, and employed by Egyptologists since the finding of the Rosetta Stone (p. 450) On the limestone pillar are inscribed three different versions of the same decree, above it appears in hieroglyphics, or the *Ancient Egyptian* written language, below in *Greek*, and on the margins in the popular dialect written in the *Demotic* character The decree was pronounced by an assembly of the priests in the temple of Canopus on 7th March (17th Tybi), B C 238, in the reign of Ptolemy III. Euergetes I., it praises the king for having brought back the images of the gods from Asia, gained many victories, preserved peace in the land, and saved it from imminent famine by his forethought in importing corn, and it concludes with a resolution that the assembly shall call itself 'the priesthood of the Euergetes of the gods', found a new sacerdotal caste to be named after Euergetes, institute new festivals in honour of the king and queen, and introduce an improvement in the popular calendar It is also resolved to pay permanent honour in all the temples throughout the country to the Princess Berenice, who died young and unmarried, and to celebrate certain festivals yearly to her memory. In all temples of the first and second rank costly and beautiful statues were to be erected to the 'princess of virgins', to which various services were to be rendered and offerings presented Her praises were to be sung by specially trained choirs, and chiefly by virgins, and the bread provided for the priestesses was to be stamped 'bread of Berenice'. The inscriptions lastly declare that the decree is to be inscribed on slabs of bronze or of stone in the *holy* (hieroglyphic), the *Egyptian* (demotic), and the Greek languages, and to be exhibited conspicuously in every temple of the first and second rank

To the left of the door, 5401. Another copy of the same decree found at Tell el-Hizn (Lower Egypt) in 1881. The representations above the inscriptions show the royal family in adoration before the gods of Egypt. — 5457. Coptic inscription found at Dêr el-Baḥri in a grave used as a chapel. The text consists of a tirade against heretics and the usual prayer for the emperor and his family. — 5466. Fragment of a marble stele with the names of certain citizens of Memphis, who had erected a monument to a high functionary in the temple of Ptah. 5455. Coffin in baked clay, of the Byzantine epoch, found at Syene (Assuân). Rectangular coffin of lead, of the Græco-Roman period, found at Alexandria. 5426. Stele of the 26th dynasty, representing King Apries offering a sacrifice to Ptah-Sokar-Osiris; on the upper margin, to the right, is a Carian inscription which has not yet been deciphered. — 5492. Stele of the Persian period, representing a god standing on a lion and bearing on his head the disk of the sun and the crescent of the moon; at the sides are lunar crescents surmounted by ears.

5566. White marble statue of a Roman lady, found at Tell Mokhdam. This figure stands on No. 5565, a quadrangular base of red granite, with a Greek inscription dedicated to Antinous by a governor of Thebes — Opposite, 5563. Block of close-grained sandstone, with a frieze containing the cartouches of Psammetichus I. and Shabako. Below is a long Greek inscription with the names of the emperors Valens, Valentinian, and Gratian.

5613, 5614. Two mummies found at Saḳḳâra, dating from the latest period and adorned with reliefs of Christian and Egyptian emblems (3rd or 4th cent. of the present era). — 5574. Lid of the mummy-case of a sacred ram, found in 1871 at Tmaï el-Amdîd, the ancient Mendes. The ornamentation includes representations of the twelve hours of the day and night. — 5515. Porphyry bust of a Roman emperor, unnamed; 5532. Colossal figure in rose-coloured granite, probably representing one of the Ptolemies; 5550. Bust of the Nile, a beautifully executed work of the Roman period; 5569. Siren playing the lyre, a figure of great rarity found in the Serapeum at Saḳḳâra (feet modern). — 5609. Rectangular coffin with a pointed cover, a good work of the Greek period; the triangular ends were adorned with stucco basreliefs ot sirens, painted and gilded, like the one found in the Serapeum. — 5610, 5575. Wooden coffins with inscriptions and representations in black, both of the Græco-Roman period.

Cabinet BE. In the middle, Isis, in white marble. The vases, candelabra, and lamps surrounding this figure date from the Christian epoch, and were found chiefly in the Fayûm and Coptos. *5624. Vase in blue glazed earth, of the Ptolemaic period.

Cabinet BF. Objects like those in Cab. BE, and also carvings in ivory, either enclosed in wooden frames or intended for the adornment of wooden caskets. 5713. Two wooden panels with Greek inscriptions engraved upon a coating of wax. 5709. The triangular ends of No. 5609 (see above) The four heads of Medusa, numbered 5711, also belong to No. 5609, they are made of painted and gilded stucco and are fastened in round wooden saucers. The rest of the collection consists of terracotta lamps and figures.

Cabinet BG. Below, 5767. The god Bess, in painted terracotta; 5765. Grotesque figure of a woman; 5789, 5769, 5808, 5823. Terracotta plaques with reliefs from Grecian history. — 5846. Bacchic procession (lower half mutilated); 5769. Basrelief in perforated work, of earlier date than the foregoing. Nos. 5874 and 5886. are similar pieces of less careful workmanship. — 5777. Two bronze plates, containing military commissions of the time of Domitian, both found at Coptos. *5807. Bronze lamp; the handle ends in a flower from which a lion emerges. *5812. Black terracotta saucer, with busts of the Alexandrian Isis and Serapis in the middle.

Cabinet BH. 5872. Terracotta relief of a goddess sitting on a swan and holding a bow in her left hand; 5830, 5831. Two Assyrian cylinders found in the Isthmus of Suez; 5883. Bronze mirror of the Greek period, finely chased; 5871. Anubis in the garb of a Roman soldier and wielding a club; 5876. Handles of a vase decorated with horses' heads, probably of the early Greek period.

Cabinet BI. 5949. Faun lying on a wineskin, a good Greek work; 4948. Fragment of a similar figure. 5909. Hilt of a Roman sword, in the shape of an eagle's head; the blade is of a later date. 5956. Statuette of Venus in gold, repoussé work; 5920. Gold ring with a piece of lapis lazuli, on one side of which are three deities, on the other a gnostic inscription.

Cabinet BJ. On the top shelf are figures of animals in terracotta. On the second shelf, 6118. Small round altar on a square base; to the right, fragment of a vase. *Bust with an angel's head, the arms pressed against the breast and holding a butterfly. — The two lower shelves contain modern reproductions of stone and bronze figures, small steles, and scarabæi, most of them manufactured in Keneh and Thebes. The terracotta figures in the lowest shelf but one, resembling those of Tanagra, were found at Alexandria, in tombs of the Ptolemaic period.

The cabinet adjoining the N.W. pillar contains trinkets of silver and gold, a beautifully executed little stele in felspar, a 'Horus on the crocodiles', and two tambourines found in Akhmîm. In the lower part of the cabinet are two slabs of serpentine (No. 6106), found at Coptos in 1883, which contain fragments of a long inscription recording a series of works carried out by Roman soldiers under Augustus. The rest of the inscription has not been discovered.

Opposite is a cabinet containing terracotta figures, a figure of Anubis in blue glazed earth, and ivory plaques for caskets with reliefs. Below is a collection of weights in stone and bronze. This cabinet also contains a pair of scales.

The **Salle Historique de l'Est** contains several hundred steles or tombstones, chiefly found at Abydos, Sakkâra, and Thebes, but a few also at Tell el-Amarna. — In the middle of the room (No. 872) is the celebrated *Tablet of Sakkâra*.

This tablet was found in 1861 in a half-ruined mortuary chapel at Sakkâra. On one side is inscribed a hymn to Osiris and on the other a list of 58 kings, in two rows, beginning with Meribah (1st dyn.) and ending with Ramses II. The list is unfortunately very imperfect.

870, 871. Two blocks of close-grained sandstone, intended for votive offerings; on the upper margin of the lateral faces is an inscription mentioning the name of Ameni Antef Amenemha, an unknown king of the 13th or 14th dynasty (Karnak). — 497. Stele of the period of Khu-en-aten (18th dyn.). 488. Serpent in black granite, with the cartouches of King Amenhotep III., who erected it as a guardian of the temple at Athribis (the modern Benha). — *492, 493. Two basreliefs found in old Memphis and showing some of the most delicate workmanship of the Saite period. The one represents the scribe Psamtik-nefer-sa-mer superintending the transportation of gold ornaments intended for his tomb; the other shows him receiving votive offerings.

E. Wall. In the corner to the right, 600. Granite statue of Thothmes III. (18th dyn.). *610. Fine head in black granite with mild and regular features, held by Mariette to be the Pharaoh of the Exodus (Merenptah), but according to Maspero the Pharaoh Horemheb; *617. Head of hard limestone found in the temple of Karnak; other fragments found almost exactly in the same spot make it probable that this is the head of the wife or daughter of King Horemheb. — To the left, 642. Bust of Amenophis II. (18th dyn.); *640. Head of a king (18-20th dyn.).

N. Wall. In the centre, 721. Large granite statue of the Roman period, found at Tanis. In a niche to the right, *3963. Figure

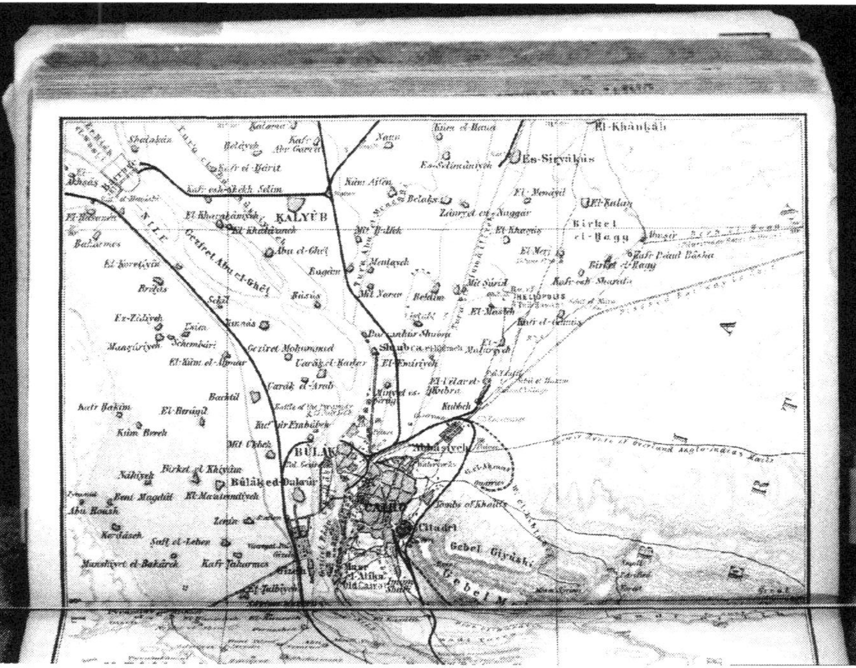

El-Khânkâh
Es-Siryâkûs
KALYÛB
NILE
Gezîret Abu el-Ghêt
Birket el-Ḥagg
HELIOPOLIS
Shubra
BÛLÂK
Bûlâk ed-Dakrûr
CAIRO
Citadel
Abbâsîyeh
Gebel Giyûshi
Tombs of Khalifs
Kubbeh
El-Matarîyeh
Kafr Ḥakim
Kûm Bereh
El-Berâgîl
Birket el-Khiyâm
Nâhiyeh
Beni Magdûl
El-Ma'tamdîyeh
Abu Rowâsh
Kerdâseh
Saft el-Leben
Kafr Ṭahurmes
Manshiyet el-Bakârî
Zenîn
El-Ḳoreiyîn
Ez-Zâwiyeh
Manyûriyeh
Schembâri
Mit Okbeh
Mit Nama
Beltîm
Kalama
Belâkṣ
Zâwiyet en-Naggâr
El-Menâyil
El-Kulah
Kafr Dâud Bâsha
Gezîret Mohammed
Warâk el-Hadar
Warâk el-Arab
Bachtîl

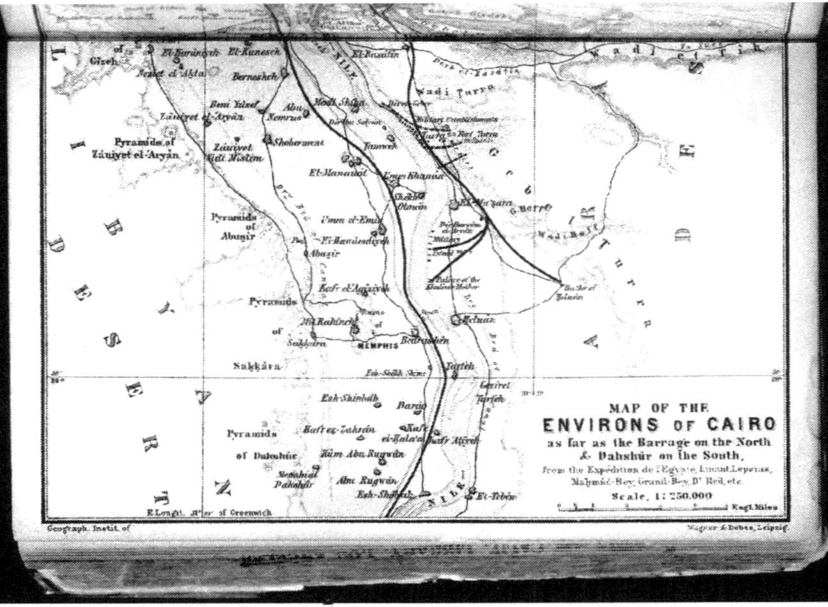
MAP OF THE
ENVIRONS OF CAIRO
as far as the Barrage on the North
& Dahshûr on the South,
from the Expédition de l'Égypte, Linant, Lepsius,
Mahmûd-Bey, Grand-Bey, Dr Reil, etc.
Scale, 1:250,000
Engl. Miles
LIBYAN DESERT
ARABIAN DESERT
Pyramids of Sakkâra
Pyramids of Dahshûr
Pyramids of Abusîr
Pyramids of Zâuiyet el-'Aryân
MEMPHIS
NILE
Geograph. Instit. of
Wagner & Debes, Leipzig

INSERT
FOLD-OUT
OR MAP
HERE!

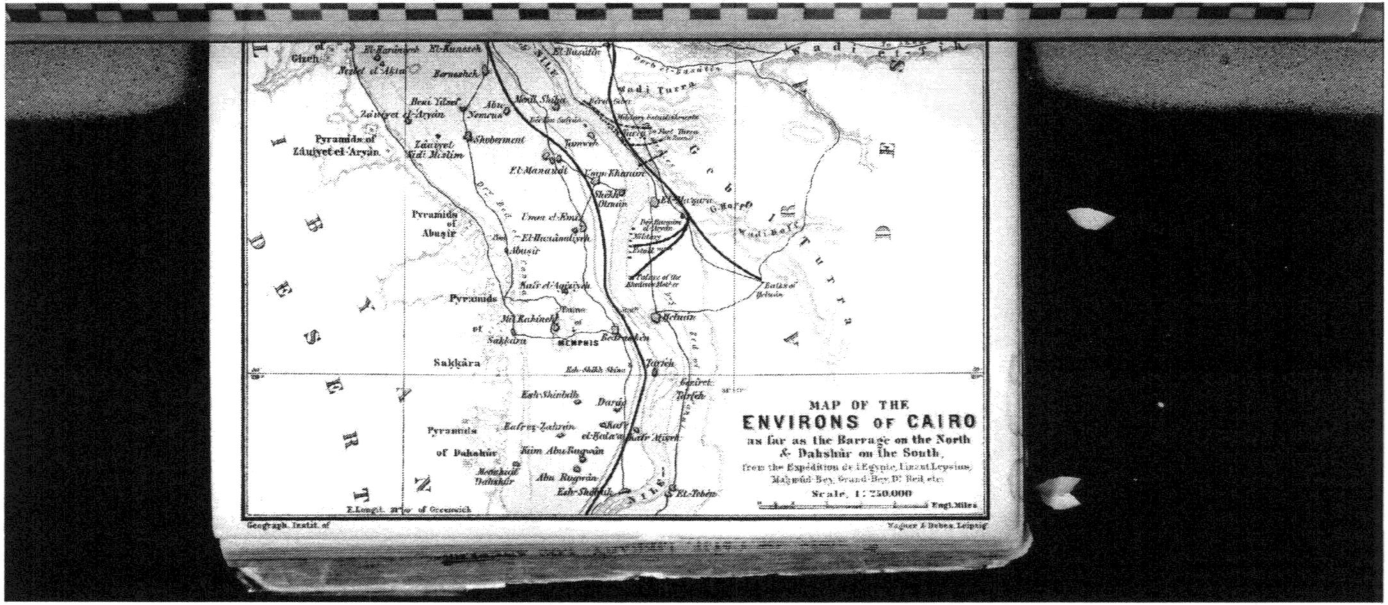
MAP OF THE
ENVIRONS OF CAIRO
as far as the Barrage on the North
& Dahshûr on the South,
Scale, 1 : 250.000
Engl. Miles
Geograph. Instit. of
Wagner & Debes, Leipzig
Pyramids of
Zâuiyet-el-'Aryân
Pyramids
of
Abuṣîr
Pyramids
Saḳḳâra
Pyramids
of Dahshûr
MEMPHIS
L
I
B
Y
A
N
D
E
S
E
R
T

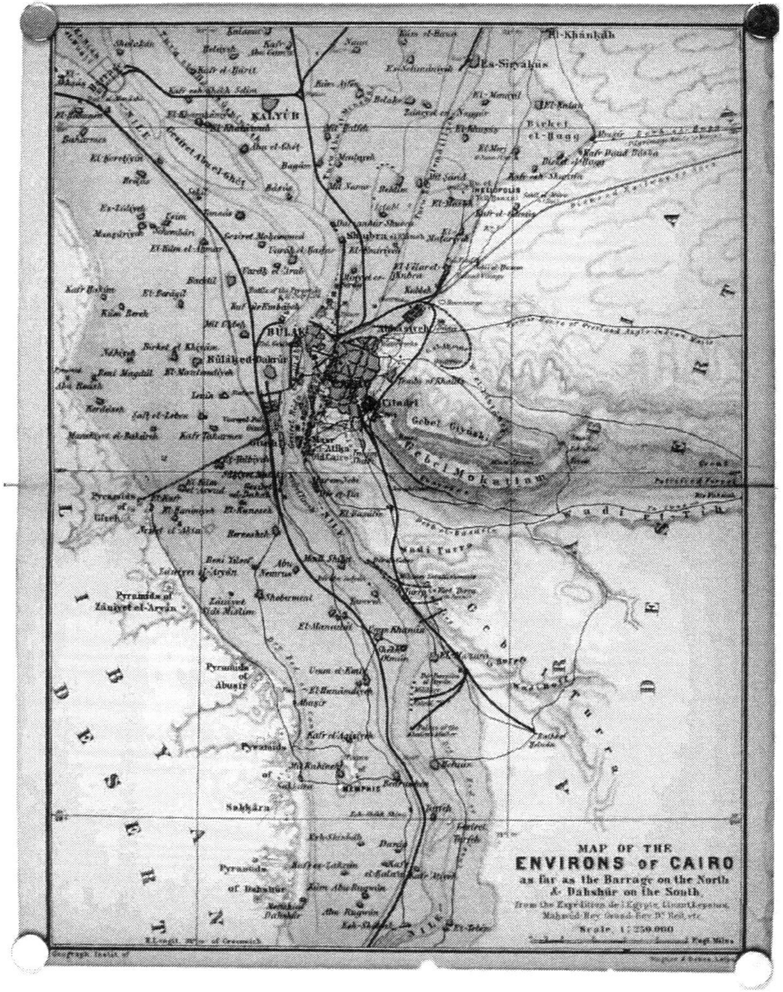
MAP OF THE
ENVIRONS of CAIRO
as far as the Barrage on the North
& Dahshûr on the South
Scale 1:250.000
L I B Y A N   D E S E R T
Pyramids of Gîzeh
Pyramids of Zâwiyet el-Aryân
Pyramids of Abusîr
Sakkâra
Pyramids of Dahshûr
Memphis
Kalyûb
Bulâk
Citadel
Gebel Giyûshi
Gebel Mokattam
El-Khânkah
Es-Siryâkus
Heliopolis

of Thueris in green serpentine, in the form of a hippopotamus (Thebes); this goddess was the guardian of departed souls and her forbidding appearance was supposed to drive away evil spirits. The figure is well preserved and its technical execution is admirable.

S. Wall. In the centre, 561. Limestone statue of Amenhotep III., with inlaid eyes. To the left, by the adjacent window, is a dûm-palm found in a tomb at Thebes in 1884, with a head of Hathor and a hieroglyphical inscription. In front, Naos covered with inscriptions and representations relating to Thot, including a dog-faced ape (p. 134). — Large stele, covered on both sides with inscriptions and bearing the cartouches of King Usertesen (12th dyn.).

The Museum of Bûlâk also possesses a large collection of Papyri, including a number of valuable scrolls found at Dêr el-Bahri. Unfortunately there is at present little space for their exhibition, so that most of them, as well as numerous other monuments, have for the present at least to be kept in the store-rooms.

4. Environs of Cairo.

Old Cairo, Gezîreh, Shubra, Heliopolis, and the Pyramids of Gîzeh are most conveniently visited by carriage, and the Mokattam hills, Moses' Well, the Petrified Forest, and Gebel el-Ahmar on donkey-back. The first-named excursions may also of course be made on the back of a donkey, but this mode of travelling is more fatiguing.

Old Cairo (*Maṣr el-ʿAtîka*).

Fumm el-Khalîg. Old Water Conduit. Christian Cemeteries. Island of Rôḍa. Castle of Babylon. Coptic Church of St. Mary. Gâmiʿ ʿAmr. Tombs of the Mamelukes. Hôsh el-Bâsha.

Traversing the new town of Ismaʿîlîya (p. 259) towards the S.W., we proceed by the *Boulevard ʿAbdul ʿAzîz*, the *Rond-Point Bâb el-Lûk*, and the *Square* of that name (beautifully planted with flowers of the Turkish national colours), to an open space, from which a road to the S. leads to the Nile Bridge (p. 328). Here we turn to the left and follow the *Boulevard Kaṣr ʿAli*. On the left, at the corner, we observe the *Palace of Ḥusên Pasha* (brother of the Khedive), surrounded by lofty walls. Opposite, to the right, are the new *Palais Ismaʿîlîyeh* (Pl. 81; E, 6) and the large palace *Kaṣr ed-Dubara* (Pl. 83), both belonging to the Khedive. To the left, surrounded with pleasure-grounds, is the *Ministry of Public Works* (formerly the Military School; Pl. 31); the kiosque to the right contains the *Institut Egyptien*, that to the left the *Viceregal Laboratory* (p. 244). Farther on, to the right, is the *Palais Ibrâhîm Pasha* (Pl. 80; F, 5), with a large garden; then the spacious *Kaṣr ʿAli* (Pl. 82; F, 6), the palace of the Khedive's grandmother. We next reach the *Kaṣr el-ʿAin* (Pl. 28; G, 6), or large hospital (p. 234), with the *Mosque Kaṣr el-ʿAin* (Pl. 49), where the howling dervishes perform their zikr (p. 239). About 2½ M. from the W. end of the Muski we observe on the right and left large straw magazines *(tibn)*, and opposite to us the —

Fumm el-Khalîg, or influx of the city canal into an arm of the Nile, which, however, is dry from May until the period of the overflow. The festivities connected with the cutting of the Nile embankment take place here in August. The straw-market is bounded on the S. by the *Old Aqueduct of the Citadel*, which has been disused since the completion of the steam-pump in 1872.

The *Head* of this conduit, separated by a street from the arm of the Nile just named, is constructed of solid masonry in a hexagonal form, and consists of three stories, about 150 ft in diameter. The ground-floor contains stables and magazines, and on the first and second is accommodation for about 130 soldiers On the terrace, where there are six water-wheels (sâkiyehs), each worked by two oxen, is a large hexagonal basin from which the water flowed into the aqueduct On the platform there are also stables for the oxen and chambers for the attendants. The aqueduct, constructed of massive blocks of stone, and resting on pointed arches, ascends in four different levels to the citadel, the total height being 278 ft, and the total length 4000 yds. ($2^1/_4$ M) When the Nile was at its lowest, the water had to be raised to a height of 80 ft. to the first basin. A branch of this conduit supplied the Jewish quarter with water in the neighbourhood of Imâm Shafe'i (p. 327) The aqueduct dates from the time of Saladin (12th cent, p 262) The entrance is in the N. wall, at the back of the head of the aqueduct, where a Berber is posted as a custodian (fee $^1/_4$ fr for each person) *Views from the openings of the platform, very fine Easy ascent by an inclined plane.

Towards the left, a few hundred yards from the gate of the head of the aqueduct are situated the *Christian Cemeteries*, surrounded by lofty walls The first is the English Cemetery, the second the Roman Catholic, beyond which are those of the Greeks, Armenians, and Copts, which present no attraction.

Leaving the head of the aqueduct, we follow the direction of the arm of the Nile, which, however, is not always visible, as the houses and walls of the *Manyal* quarter interpose between the road and the water, and reach ($1^1/_4$ M.) the mansion which formerly belonged to *Sulêmân Pasha el-Fransâwi* (Colonel Selves), with two fine Arabian portals (visitors not admitted). The second narrow and short road to the right beyond the château leads to the ferry crossing to the **Island of Rôḍa.** We descend the slope, enter the ferry-boat ($^1/_4$ fr. for one person, there and back; for a party more in proportion; payment made on returning), ascend the opposite path, and turn to the right. A young gardener is usually in waiting at the landing-place to conduct travellers through the intricate lanes to the garden. At the S. extremity of the island is the *Nilometer (Mikyâs)*, situated on land belonging to the heirs of *Hasan Pasha*. The garden, laid out in the Arabian style, is miserably neglected. The paths are paved with a kind of mosaic of round pebbles, obtained partly from the desert, and partly from the island of Rhodes, and the most important of them are bordered with low walls, supporting wooden verandahs and arbours, over which climb immense vines. The gardens contain orange and lemon trees, dates, palms, and bananas, and also the henna plant, which is not met with in the public gardens of Cairo.

The **Nilometer** (*Miḳyâs*), a square well, 16 ft. in diameter, connected by a channel with the Nile, has in the centre an octagonal column, on which are inscribed the ancient Arabian measures and Cufic inscriptions. The four straight sides are constructed of massive masonry, and contain niches adorned with columns with Byzantine capitals. Marble slabs built into the walls bear Cufic inscriptions. The *drâ'*, or old Arabian ell, is 54 centimètres, or about 21¹/₃ inches, and is divided into 24 kirat. The column of the Nilometer, which has been frequently repaired, is 17 ells in height, the first of which is built into the foundations. The upper part is secured by means of a beam attached to the opposite walls. The zero point of the Nilometer (according to Mahmûd-Bey) is 28 ft. above the average level of the Mediterranean, so that the top of the column is nearly 59 ft. above sea-level. The water of the Nile, when at its lowest, covers 7 ells of the Nilometer, and when it reaches a height of 15 ells and 16 kirat, the shêkh of the Nile measurement proclaims the *Wefa* (p. 239), *i.e.* the height of the water necessary for irrigating every part of the Nile valley. The announcement of the wefa is the signal for cutting the embankment. The shêkh, however, has his private meter, the zero of which is nearly 7 inches lower than that of the old Nilometer †.

The mean difference between the low and high level of the Nile at Cairo is 24¹/₂ feet. When, according to the shêkh's mode of reckoning, the height of 23 ells is attained, the island of Rôḍa is overflowed.

The Mikyâs or Nilometer was constructed in the year 97 of the Hegira (A D 716) by order of the Omayyad Khalif Sulèmân (715-17) Mâmûn, the 'Abbaside Khalif (A D 809-33), added the Cufic inscriptions on the N. and W. walls and repaired the whole structure in 814 According to the Cufic inscriptions on the S and E sides, another restoration took place in the year 233 of the Hegira Khalif Mutawakkil (847-61) also repaired the Mikyâs in 247 of the Hegira (A D 859), and transferred the office of measuring the water from the Copts, who had hitherto held

† The rate of taxation was determined in ancient times in accordance with the height of the inundation. All the authorities from Herodotus down to Leo Africanus agree in stating that the Nile must rise 16 cubits, or Egyptian ells, in order that the land may produce good crops The famous statue of Father Nile in the Vatican is accordingly surrounded by sixteen figures of genii, representing these 16 ells. To this day the height of the overflow influences taxation, and the land which is artificially irrigated pays less than that reached by the river itself The object of the government always is to induce a belief that the inundation is favourable, and the sworn shêkh of the Nilometer is therefore subject to the influence of the police at Cairo 'The same political motives, from which in ancient times the custody of the Nilometers was entrusted to the priests alone, still prevent the Egyptian public from obtaining access to the Mikyâs in the island of Rôda The real height of the water is always concealed, and false statements made, as it is the object of the fiscal authorities to levy, if possible, the full rate of taxation every year, whatever the height of the Nile may have been. This traditional dishonesty in the use of the Nilometer was first discovered by the French engineers during the occupation of Egypt by Napoleon'. (C. Ritter.)

it, to the Muslim family of Abû Radah. In 485 of the Hegira (A.D. 1092) the Fâtimite Khalîf Mustanṣir Billâh (1036-94) caused the Nilometer to be covered with a dome, resting on columns, but that structure was destroyed during the siege of this part of the island by the French under Napoleon. A roof in Turkish taste, resting on wooden columns, now covers the well.

Adjoining the Nilometer is a large *Kiosque* in the Turkish style, which may be inspected when not occupied by any harem. The architecture is uninteresting, but the handsome dimensions of the rooms, which are intended for a summer residence, and the bath are worthy of notice. The S. verandah of the kiosque affords an uninterrupted *View of the Nile, with Gîzeh to the right, the pyramids in the background, and Old Cairo on the left (fee 1 fr.).

Near the N. end of the island stands the wonder-working tree of the saint *Mandûra*, a huge nebk tree, the branches of which are hung with innumerable rags According to a popular superstition the patient must thus offer to the saint the cloth which enveloped the affected limb, then encircle the tree seven times, pluck off two leaves, and tie them on the affected part with another cloth

Leaving the island and returning to the opposite bank, we regain the **Old Cairo** road, and after $^1/_4$ M. more we reach the end of the bazaar of this small town. We then turn to the left, and in a few minutes reach a street running from N. to S. Turning to the N. (left), we observe on the right a distinct quarter of the town, built on the ruins of *Fostât* (p. 241) within the precincts of an ancient *Roman Castle*, formerly called **Babylon.** The plan of the fortress is still traceable by means of the numerous characteristic remains of the Roman outer wall. On the S. side, between two projecting towers, is a gateway with a gabled roof, now almost entirely ruined. The castle is said once to have been occupied by one of the three Roman legions stationed in Egypt (p. 241), and to have been connected by a bridge with Rôḍa and with Gîzeh, where another Roman station is said to have been situated. Proceeding in a straight direction for about 100 yds., and then about 35 paces to the right of a low doorway situated in a hollow on the W. side and concealed by a small wall, we reach the middle of the Coptic quarter, where, enclosed by a dense mass of houses, is situated the much frequented —

***Abû Sergeh,** or *Coptic Church of St. Mary.* (A Coptic boy may be engaged as a guide to the church; fee 1 piastre.) According to a wide-spread belief this church was built before the Mohammedan conquest, and a legendary document preserved by the Coptic priests places the date of its erection in the year 329 of the Hegira, *i.e.* 940 A.D. A glance at the poor materials of the building, however, with its wooden ceiling and heterogeneous columns, will at once show the absurdity of this idea. The crypt. however, is undoubtedly much older than the church and may very well date from a pre-Mohammedan epoch. Abû Sergeh is probably equivalent to St. Sergius. According to tradition, the Virgin and Child after their flight to Egypt spent a month in the crypt of this church. One of the Coptic priests (who expects a fee of 1 piastre tariff from each visitor) shows some interesting Byzantine carving and mosaics in ivory, now blackened and discoloured with age. Many valuable art relics have been removed from the church since 1860. A number of old pictures of saints which still remain, some of them on a gold ground and with well preserved colours, possess no artistic value. Above a door to the right of the high-altar, engraved in wood, is the Coptic inscription, 'Greetings to the Temple of the Father!' Below it is a modern Arabic inscription with the date 1195. — This church may be regarded as the original model of all the older Egyptian-Byzantine churches in which the Coptic Christians now worship †.

The basilica consists of a nave and aisles. The tribuna, the two side chapels, the sanctuary, and the parts corresponding to the senatorium and matroneum of northern basilicas are raised a few steps above the level of the nave and aisles, and are almost all as high as the nave, while the aisles are provided with galleries. The nave and tribuna have open roofs, that of the latter being supported by elliptical beams, and both being probably of later date than the church itself. The left side-chapel is surmounted by an Arabian dome, while the aisles have flat ceilings. The lofty side-walls of the nave consist of two rows of columns, one above the other, the columns of the lower row being separated by keel-shaped arches, while the upper series, supporting the gallery, consists of groups of two columns and one pillar alternately, connected by an architrave. The columns of Carrara marble originally belonged to ancient edifices, and, like those in the earlier mosques, have been placed here without the least regard to their suitability in point of diameter, form of capital, or other architectural features. Two of the three original entrances are now built up, while the third, in accordance with the custom of the country, has walls projecting into it in order to prevent passers-by from seeing into the fore-court. The sacristy,

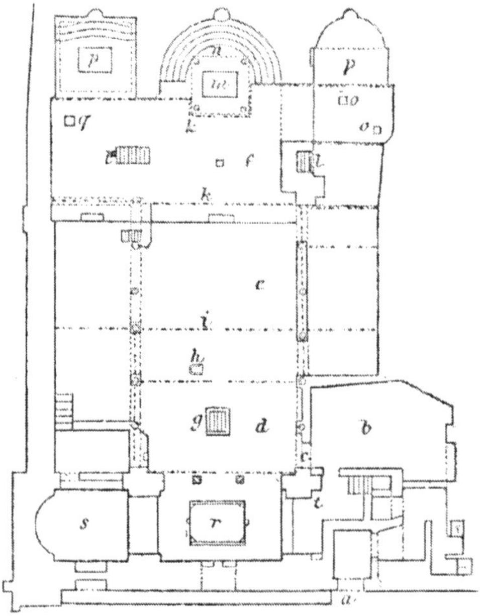

a. Entrance from the street. b. Anterior Court. c. Entrance to the Church. d. Vestibule. e. Women's section. f. Men's section. g. Well. h. Seat for the chief priest. i. Wooden screen. k. Wooden screen adorned with carving. l. Steps to the crypt. m. Altar. n. Presbyterium. o. Reading-desks. p. Side-chapels. q. r. Wells. s. Sacristy. t. Magazines.

† **Coptic Worship.** On entering the church, the members of the con-

now a dark and dirty chamber without a door, contains relics of Coptic paintings on the right wall

The nave is divided by wooden screens into three sections. The first forms a fore-court, or vestibule, the second is set apart for the

---

gregation first pay their homage to a number of pictures of saints hanging on the walls (the veneration of saints and of the Virgin being a prominent feature of the Coptic system), and then kneel before the altar and kiss the hand of the priest They then take their stand (for there are no seats) in the part of the church allotted to them, leaning on crutches which they bring for the purpose, as the service often lasts for three hours. The service begins with the reading or chanting of prayers and passages from the Gospels, partly in the Coptic language, and partly in Arabic, in which the priest is assisted by a schoolmaster and a choir of boys. During this performance the worshippers, with very few exceptions, engage freely in conversation, and the noise is said to be sometimes so great that the priest has to come out of the hêkel, or sanctuary, and enjoin silence After a time the burning of incense begins The priest, swinging his censer, leaves the hêkel and joins the congregation, each member of which he blesses, placing his hand on their heads. He concludes this ceremony in the women's section of the church, and the ordinary service now terminates

The *Celebration of the Eucharist* is very frequent in the Coptic churches, immediately following the ordinary service The celebrant priest wears a white and gaily embroidered gown reaching to his feet, and bearing the Coptic cross on the breast and sleeves After washing his hands, he directs a boy to bring him several small round loaves with the Coptic cross impressed on them He chooses the best of them, places it on a plate, and pronounces over it the blessing of the triune God. He then carries it into the hêkel, places it on the altar, covers it with white cloths, and makes the circuit of the altar several times, reciting prayers, and accompanied by the choristers carrying lighted candles. He next brings the plate with the bread out of the hêkel and holds it up before the people, whereupon the whole congregation kneels Returning to the hêkel, he breaks the bread into small pieces, puts it into a chalice, pours wine over it, and eats it with a spoon, distributing a few pieces to the assistant clergy and the choristers Lest any fragment of the consecrated elements should be profaned, he finally washes all the utensils and his own hands, and drinks the water in which he has washed them. Meanwhile a number of small round loaves prepared in an adjoining apartment, are distributed among the congregation, each member receiving and eating one or more. The laity partake more rarely of the wine, and only after having previously confessed In this case the communicants approach the door of the hêkel, where the priest administers to them with a spoon a piece of the bread dipped in wine

A curious ceremony takes place in the Coptic churches on Palm Sunday (*'id esh-sha'ânîn*) After the usual service and the communion which follows it, several basins of water are placed in the space before the hêkel The priest in his white surplice takes his stand in front of them, turning his face towards the hêkel, while another priest in his ordinary dress reads the Gospel in Arabic, after which the former consecrates the water by pronouncing a prayer over it The moment this ceremony is concluded, the surrounding congregation rushes up to the basins in order to dip palm-wreaths into them; and the crowd is often so unruly that the priest is obliged to restore order with the aid of his stick These wreaths are then worn by the Copts under their tarbûshes during the whole of the following year as amulets against the evil eye, the sting of scorpions, and every other misfortune that can befall body or soul

On 18th-19th January, the anniversary of the Baptism of Christ (*'îd el-ghitâs*), men and boys plunge into the large font or bath which is to be found in most Coptic churches, the water having been first blessed by

women, and the third for the men. Within the vestibule (first section of the nave), as in most of the ancient Christian churches, is a trough in the pavement for washing the feet and other ablutions. Beyond the three sections of the nave, and raised by a few steps, is the choir where the priests officiate; and, lastly, we observe the *Hêkel*, or sanctuary, containing the altar, and enclosed by a wall, doors, and curtains. Inside the apse rise several steps of masonry, in amphitheatrical fashion, towards the place which in European churches is occupied by the episcopal throne, and in Oriental by sacred images. The wall separating the sanctuary from the choir is panelled and richly adorned with carvings in wood and ivory. The oldest of these, probably coeval with the church, represent the Nativity, the Eucharist, and the patron saint of the church, and are surrounded with ornamentation in wood, consisting of rectilineal patterns, the basis of which is generally the Coptic cross (✣). Another favourite device, which is often seen at Jerusalem, and with which the Copts frequently tattoo their arms, consists of the same cross, with four smaller crosses in the angles. A narrow flight of twelve steps descends to the *Crypt*, a small vaulted chapel, consisting of nave and aisles. At the end of the nave is an altar in the form of an early Christian tomb-niche, which tradition indicates as the spot where the Virgin and Child reposed; in the centre of the aisles are apses. The right aisle contains the font, into which, according to the Coptic ritual, the child to be baptised is dipped three times.

The Coptic quarter of Old Cairo contains several other basilicas, used by Coptic, Greek, and Jewish congregations, but interesting only to those who are making a special study of this kind of architecture. Among them we may mention the second *Seiyideh Maryam*, or Greek Church of St Mary, on an elevated site in the castle of Babylon, and sometimes called *El-Mo'allaka*, or 'the hanging', containing ivory carving and stained glass windows. The church of *Mâri Mena* contains a handsome candelabrum. That of *Abû Sefên* has a pulpit in coloured marble, inlaid with mother-of-pearl, and a jug and basin with old Arabian enamel work. The *Synagogue (Esh-Shamyân*, or *Kenîset Eliyâhu)* was formerly a church of St. Michael. The Jews say that Elijah once appeared here, and the synagogue boasts of possessing a scroll of the Thorah written by the hand of Ezra. The scrolls shown however, are all quite modern. Benjamin of Tudela mentions a synagogue at Old Cairo where Moses is said to have prayed for

---

the priest. Or, partly by way of amusement, they perform the same ceremony in the Nile, into which they first pour some consecrated water. On these occasions the river in Coptic districts swarms with boats. On the eve of this festival, as well as on Holy Thursday and on the festival of the Apostles, the priest washes the feet of the whole of his congregation.

It is impossible to resist the impression that the Coptic worship has degenerated into a series of mere empty outward ceremonies, and indeed the more enlightened members of the sect admit this to be the case. Another external form to which they attach great weight is the observance of fasts, and a Copt who is negligent in this respect will rarely be met with. On these occasions all kinds of animal food, not excepting fat, eggs, butter, and cheese, are prohibited, and the usual fare consists of bread, onions, fûl (beans), prepared with walnut or mustard-oil, and dukka (a kind of salad).

the cessation of the plague of the thunder and hail (Exod. ix. 29), and which 'is therefore called the house of prayer of Moses'. — The church of *St. Barbara* is embellished with many carvings in wood and ivory, and with paintings of more than average merit.

Starting from the door of the castle, we pursue our way towards the N., across the rubbish heaps of the ancient Fosṭâṭ (p. 241), skirt the town-wall of Old Cairo, and after 650 yds. reach the —

*Gâmi' 'Amr, sometimes styled the 'crown of the mosques'. The W. side with the entrances, of which that near the S.W. corner (Pl. A) alone is used, the two others having been built up, is partly concealed by peasants' huts and potteries (manufactories of ḳullehs, p 326), the occupants of which pester visitors for baḳshîsh. The entrance is easily recognized by the newly built porch.

So far from being the oldest structure of the kind in Cairo, as is generally asserted, this mosque is in its present form really one of the youngest. The last of its numerous reconstructions dates from the beginning of the 9th cent. of the Hegira (1400 A. D.), when a rich Cairene merchant, named Ibrâhim el-Maḥallî, undertook to restore the building, partly at his own expense and partly with the proceeds of collections made in all parts of Egypt. In this undertaking he pulled down and made use of the materials of the then standing mosque, which had been hastily erected in 1302 after the destruction of a still earlier building by an earthquake. The heterogeneous nature of the columns is accounted for by the fact that they were brought from other buildings in Cairo ruined by the same earthquake and were adapted to their new functions by rude Procrustean methods of lengthening or shortening The N. and S. walls, running parallel with the aisles, are not straight. The N. and S. colonnades are in ruins. The plan of the edifice is in exact accordance with the typical form of the rectangular mosque with a hypæthral arrangement of columns round an open court.

We traverse the great court towards the W., passing the Fountain (Pl. 7), near which rise a palm and a thorn-tree, and enter the E. colonnade of the Sanctuary (Pl. a, b, c, d), which rests on six rows of columns. In front of the Mambar (Pl. 2) is a Column (Pl. 3) bearing the names of Allah, Moḥammed, and Sultan Suleimân in Arabic characters; and by a freak of nature the outline of the prophet's 'kurbatsh' is traced on it by a vein of lighter colour than the rest of the marble, which is of a grey colour. This column is believed by the Muslims to have been transported miraculously from Mecca to Cairo †. In the N.E. corner is the Tomb of Shêkh 'Abdallah, son of 'Amr. The columns, all composed of marble of various kinds, are 366 in number. The masonry consists

† The legend is told by Moritz Busch as follows. — 'When 'Amr was building this mosque, he asked his master, Khalîf 'Omar, for a column from Mecca. The Khalîf thereupon addressed himself to one of the columns there, and commanded it to migrate to the Nile, but the column

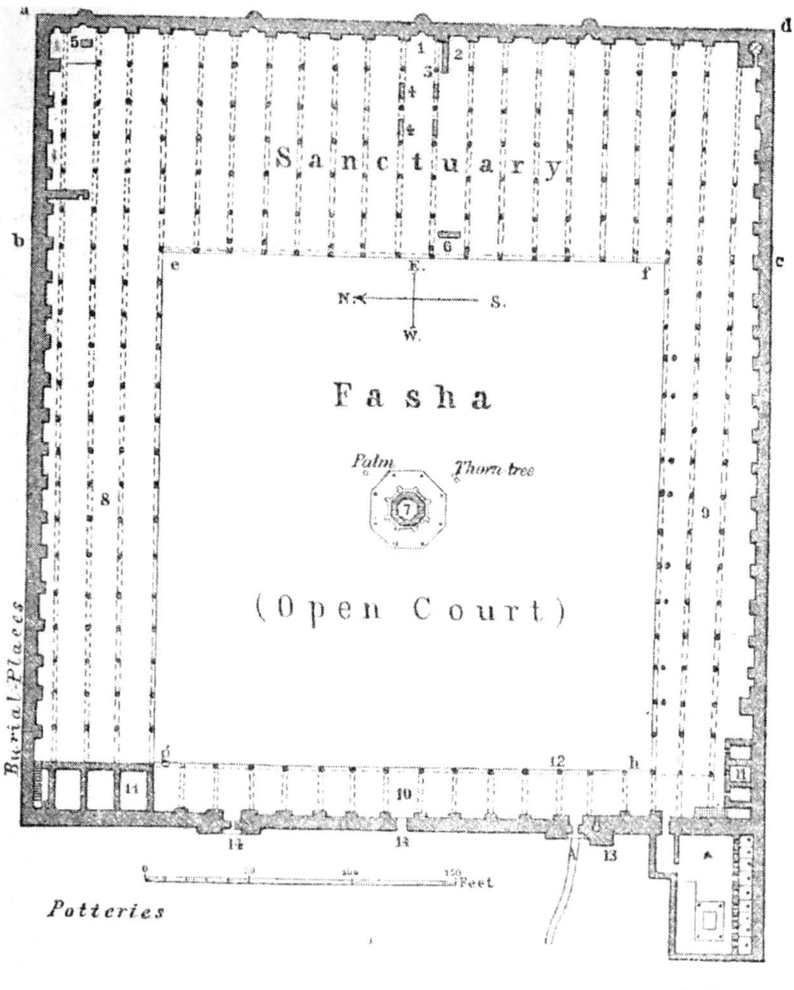

A. Entrance. a,b,c,d. Sanctuary. e,f,g,h. Fasha (large open court). 1. Kibla. 2. Mambar. 3. Column bearing the name of Mohammed. 4. Kursi (destroyed). 5. Tomb of Shêkh ʿAbdallah (son of ʿAmr). 6. Dikkeh. 7. Ḥanefiyeh. 8. Quadruple aisle (in ruins). 9. Triple hall (almost entirely ruined). 10. Hall without aisles. 11. Chambers of later construction. 12. Double column for the faithful. 13. Minarets. 14. Entrances now closed. 15. Potteries and fellâḥ dwellings.

---

would not stir. He repeated his command more urgently, but still the column remained immovable. A third time he repeated his command, angrily striking the column with his 'kurbatsh', but still without effect. At length he shouted, 'I command thee in the name of God, O column, arise, and betake thyself to Cairo!' Thereupon the column went, bearing the mark of the whip, which is still visible'.

of burnt bricks, and evidently belongs to different periods, the oldest part being near the entrance, in the S. façade of the court. The arches are of very various forms, some of them being almost circular, while others, particularly those in the apertures of the wall, form a nearly acute angle with straight sides. Horseshoe arches also occur, and others are constructed in arbitrary and fantastic shapes. The capitals display a great variety of Roman and Byzantine forms, and some of them, not quite completed, in the ruined N. colonnade, were perhaps Arabian imitations of Ptolemaic models. The baths and other buildings once connected with the mosque are no longer traceable.

The colonnades on the W. side (that of the entrance) are now supported by one row of columns only. Of the double columns that once stood here one *Pair of Columns* (Pl. 12) alone remains. They are placed very close together, and it is said that none but honest men could squeeze themselves between them; but the Khedive has abolished this test of character by walling up the interstice.— In 1808 this mosque, which has long been almost disused, witnessed a very remarkable scene. At the usual period of the rise of the Nile, the water began to fall. Dismayed by this strange phenomenon, the whole of the Mohammedan priesthood, the Christian clergy of every sect, and the Jewish rabbis, with one accord, assembled in the mosque of 'Amr to pray for the rise of the water, and so effectual were their prayers that the river ere long rose to its wonted fertilising height. (Fee to the attendant $^1/_2$-1 fr.)

The traveller who does not intend ascending the Nile will find it not uninteresting, on quitting the mosque, to visit one of the above-mentioned *Kulleh Manufactories*, and to inspect its primitive apparatus (bakshîsh, a few copper piastres)

The porous water-jars (Arabic *Kulleh*) used throughout the whole of Egypt are chiefly manufactured at Keneh in Upper Egypt of light grey clay of very equal consistency. The remarkably uniform and delicate porosity of the vessels is produced by mixing the clay with ashes, which, the first time the vessel is used, are partly washed away by the water. The rapid evaporation caused by the porosity of the kulleh cools the liquid within to a temperature of 12-14° lower than that of the surrounding air. — These vessels, including the *balâzeh*, or large jars with handles, chiefly manufactured at *Balâz* in Upper Egypt, are brought down from Upper Egypts in rafts, consisting of thousands of them tied together by the handles and with their mouths covered

Continuing to follow the road across the rubbish-hills of Fosṭâṭ, which we have just left, we observe on our right a Muslim burial-ground, and at a short distance in front of us the old aqueduct. A little to the right, on an eminence, rises an old ruined mosque (*Gâmi' Abû Su'ûd)*, beyond it is the Citadel with the mosque of Mohammed 'Ali, and farther distant are the hills of the Moḳaṭṭam (p. 335) This view is very striking towards sunset.

The road, which becomes bad beyond this point, leads round the ruined mosque and ascends heaps of debris. On the top of the hill it divides. The road to the left leads back to the town, from the houses of which the Mosque of Sulṭân Ḥasan (p. 260) stands

Tombs of the Mamelukes.
(Names unknown.)

Tombs of the Khalifs.
(East Side.)

out conspicuously. The road, first in a straight direction, afterwards inclining to the right, leads to the necropolis known as Imâm Shafe'i (see below), with the burial-mosque of the viceroyal family, which, however, presents no great attraction. Riders may easily make this short digression (see below).

Between this point and the base of the Moḳaṭṭam towards the E., and extending for some distance up the steep slopes of the hills, lies an extensive burial-ground, with several conspicuous, but very dilapidated mausolea, known as the —

Tombs of the Mamelukes, which approach close to the city. Like the so-called Tombs of the Khalîfs (p. 282) their history is obscure, the names of the builders being unknown, and no inscriptions having been preserved. The ruins of these monuments, however, still bear traces of great artistic merit, and several of the minarets in particular are exceedingly beautiful.

In a somewhat detached position, a little way in the direction of the hills, we observe the ruined dome and lantern mentioned at p. 177. Close to the town, in the midst of a group of other tombs, rises the ruins of a mausoleum which once had a double dome. Inside the building are walls arranged in the form of a fan for the support of the outer dome, which has fallen in.

The whole of this region is still used as a Muslim burial-ground, and in some cases the ancient mausolea have been converted into family burial-places.

The gate by which we re-enter the town is the *Bâb el-Ḳarâfeh* (Pl. G, 2). If we quit the main street by the second side-street to the left, we pass through the street El-'Abr eṭ-Ṭawîl, and in about 10 min. reach the S.W. and oldest part of Cairo, containing the venerable *Gâmi' ibn Ṭulûn* (p. 265), which may now be visited if time permits.

The road to the viceroyal burial-mosque in the necropolis of Imâm Shafe'i passes the old mosque of Abû Su'ûd mentioned above, descends the hill at the bifurcation of the road, and leads to a group of dome-buildings nearly 1 M. distant, among which the imposing outline of the tomb of *Imâm Shafe'i*, of a bluish-grey colour, is most conspicuous. Near it is the **Ḥôsh el-Bâsha,** or burial-mosque of the family of the Khedive.

To the left of the entrance is a sebîl. On each side of the large arcade leading to the mosque are apartments for the accommodation of the women who come to pray at the tombs. At the end of this covered passage, on the left, is a small open space, in which, opposite to us, is a small door leading to the entrance of the mosque. (Nearer us is another door on the left, leading to the mausoleum of a wife of ex-Khedive Isma'îl.) As usual in all the mosques, the visitor on entering must put on slippers or linen socks over his boots. (Bakshîsh for one person 2, and to the guide 3 piastres tariff.) The monuments are in white marble, and were executed by

Greek and Armenian sculptors. The inscriptions and ornamentation are richly gilded and painted. The Korân is regularly read here.

Returning to the sebîl already mentioned, we may next visit the neighbouring so-called *Hôsh el-Memâlîk*, erected in the 18th cent., probably the tomb of the Mameluke chief 'Ali Bey and his family, but erroneously pointed out as that of the famous

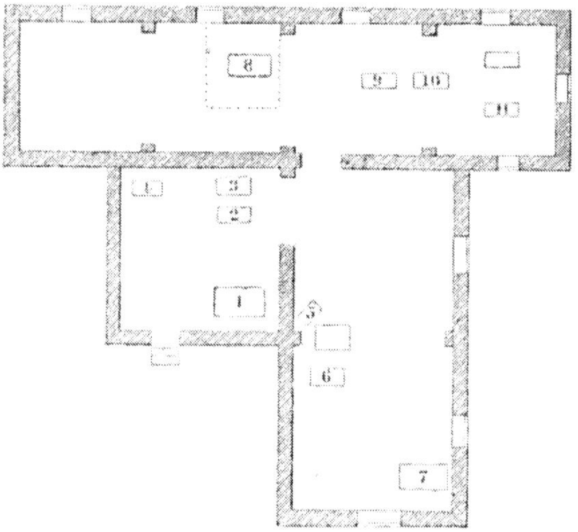

1. Mother of 'Abbâs Pasha.
2. 'Abbâs Pasha (p. 107).
3. El-Hâmi, son of 'Abbâs.
4. Ahmed Pasha Yeken.
5. Mohammed 'Ali Defterdâr.
6. Ibrâhîm Pasha.
8. Tusûn Pasha, father of 'Abbâs, and his family.

. Tomb of Tusûn Imai Bey, whose remains were burned in the Sûdân.

10. Tusûn 'Ali Sefer.

Besides these the mosque contains many other tombs of no importance, chiefly those of the harem.

Mameluke general Murâd Bey (*Hôsh Murâd Bey*), who is interred in the Suhag mosque at Girgeh in Upper Egypt. The principal monuments stand on a hollow pedestal, and the domes rest on marble columns.

Château and Park of Gezireh.

Ticket of admission from the consulate necessary (p. 241). Distance about 3 M. (a drive of $^1/_2$ hr.). It should be borne in mind that the Nile bridge is closed from 1 to about 3 o'clock, the time appointed for the passage of vessels through it. A visit to Gezîreh may also be combined with an excursion to the Pyramids (on the way back from the latter).

The road to the château of Gezîreh crosses the handsome *Iron Bridge* adjoining the *Kasr en-Nîl* (Pl. 17), the extensive barracks of Cairo, which also contain apartments for the use of the Khedive. The bridge, about 420 yds. in length, was built by a French iron company. The buttresses, which were constructed with the aid of air-tight 'caissons', are of solid stone, and are 55 yds. apart. The bottom of the foundations is about 45 ft. below the level of the river when at its lowest. At a very early hour in the morning an interesting and picturesque crowd of peasantry may be seen congregated here for the purpose of paying duty on the wares they are bringing to market.

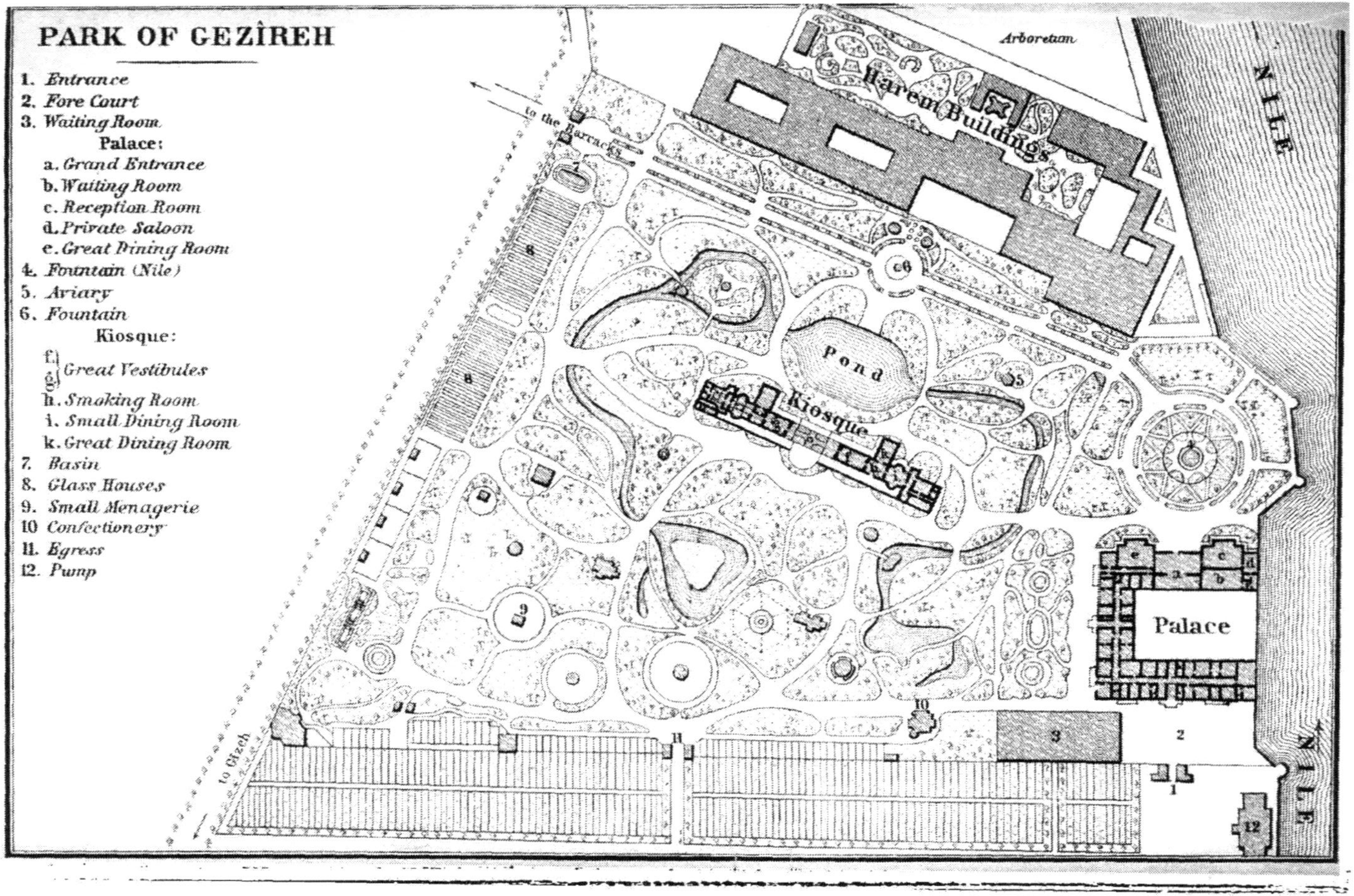
PARK OF GEZÎREH
1. Entrance
2. Fore Court
3. Waiting Room
Palace:
a. Grand Entrance
b. Waiting Room
c. Reception Room
d. Private Saloon
e. Great Dining Room
4. Fountain (Nile)
5. Aviary
6. Fountain
Kiosque:
f. g. Great Vestibules
h. Smoking Room
i. Small Dining Room
k. Great Dining Room
7. Basin
8. Glass Houses
9. Small Menagerie
10 Confectionery
11. Egress
12. Pump
Arboretum
Harem Buildings
NILE
to the Barracks
Pond
Kiosque
Palace
to Gizeh
NILE

Beyond the bridge we turn to the right, and soon observe, close to the Nile, the northernmost part of the great park, the laying out of which is still unfinished. The grounds, which were designed by M. Barillet (p. 76), are intended to extend from Gizeh to Embâbeh, and will be about $5^1/_2$ M. long and 3 M. broad.

The W. Arm of the Nile, which separates Gezîreh from the mainland, is at present closed at the upper end, so that when the river is low the channel is filled with water to a point a little above Embâbeh only. It is intended, however, to use this arm as a kind of waste-pipe, to be opened when the water is so high as to endanger the E. bank near Kasr en-Nil and the new town of Ismaʿîlîya. The bed of this arm of the river has been widened, deepened, and protected by embankments (a work which was begun in 1866) and nearly one-third of the volume of the Nile can be conducted through this channel. The embankments were constructed with the aid of a small transportable railway. The island of Gezîreh was often flooded in former times, rendering horticulture impossible, but the whole surface has been raised about 5 ft., so as to elevate it above the level of the highest inundations.

From the Entrance (Pl. 1) we cross the Fore Court (Pl. 2) to the left, and apply to the custodian (Pl. 3; generally a Frenchman; no fee), who shows the palace and grounds. The **Palace,** which is externally a simple edifice, was erected, after many interruptions and alterations, by Franz-Bey, a German architect, in 1863-68. All the distinguished guests who were invited to attend the ceremony of opening the Suez Canal were entertained here. The palace became state property in 1880 and is now seldom occupied.

The masonry was executed by native workmen the woodwork by J. Maunstein of Vienna, and the marble-work by Bonani of Carrara The decorations of the walls in the principal apartments were designed by C. v. Diebitsch, and the silk-hangings were manufactured by Detrogat of Lyons from designs by Franz Most of the ironwork is from the Lauchhammer foundry near Dresden The furniture in the N wing is chiefly Parisian, and the rest was partly manufactured by Parvis (p. 236), and partly by a Berlin firm

On the N. side is the superb Entrance (Pl a), with bamboo furniture from Paris. Adjoining it on the E. are the Waiting Room (Pl. b) and the large Audience Chamber (Pl. c). Beyond these are a Drawing Room (Pl. d) and the Cabinet of the Khedive. The visitor should notice the magnificent onyx mantel-pieces with mirrors, each of which cost 3000*l*., and the handsome metal cupboard in the cabinet. To the W. (right) of the entrance are a large (Pl. e) and a small dining-room, the latter of which contains Arabian cabinets by Parvis (p. 236).

The other two wings (W. and S.), surrounded by the gardens, contain suites of apartments for visitors, each consisting of a bedroom, dressing-room, and sitting-room. The upper floor contains similar apartments, one suite of which was lined with blue satin when occupied by the Empress Eugénie, and another was fitted up for the reception of the Princess of Wales

We next visit the *Grotto*, a little to the N.W. of the palace, and easily recognised by the rock of which it is constructed. The materials were chiefly brought from the wave-worn coast of Alexandria, and partly from the Petrified Forest (p. 337). The pebbles were imported from the island of Rhodes in the Mediterranean, and the coral and shells from the Red Sea.

Pl. 4, a fountain by Bonani, representing the infant Nile. To the N. of it is the Harem Building, part of which was erected by Moḥammed 'Ali (not shown). Pl. 5, a pleasant resting-place, a 'volière' enclosed with interesting plants. Pl. 6, a fountain. In the centre of the garden is the long **Kiosque*, probably the finest modern Arabian structure of the kind. The ornamentation, in cast iron, is in the Alhambra style. The plan of the building is slightly irregular, as several apartments of an older kiosque have been incorporated with it. The handsome hall and the fountain were executed at the Lauchhammer foundry near Dresden; they weighed 400 tons, and the cost of transport alone amounted to upwards of 2000*l.*; the hall itself, exclusive of the expense of its erection and decoration, cost 8000*l.* On the E. side of the kiosque are the reception chambers, and on the W. side the private apartments of the Khedive, consisting of an ante-chamber (Pl. f, g), a small (Pl. i) and a large dining-room (Pl. k), a smoking-room (Pl. h), chambers for reading, resting, and bathing, and a store-room for plate.

The marble work here is also by Bonani, the principal decorations by Diebitsch, and the others by Ercoleni, Furcy, Girard, and Parvis Roman table in mosaic, presented to Moḥammed 'Ali by the pope. Several handsome tables in Florentine mosaic Furniture in cast metal by Barbedienne of Paris. The bronze candelabra in the palace and in the kiosque were for the most part brought from other palaces, so that there is some incongruity in their styles. Furniture French and English

Pl. 8, green-houses, with a Victoria Regia at the N. end. Pl. 9, a small menagerie with animals from Central Africa (none deserving special mention). Pl. 10, confectionery establishment. Pl. 11, usual exit. Pl. 12, pumps for watering the grounds and the avenues leading to Gîzeh. Adjacent, an ice-manufactory.

The Shubra Avenue.

About $2^1/_2$ M. to the N. of Cairo lies the village of *Shubra*, on the Nile, where a spacious garden and kiosque of Moḥammed 'Ali, now neglected, are situated (permission to visit them obtained through the consulate). The broad ***Shubra Avenue** leading thither is composed of beautiful sycamores and lebbek trees (erroneously called Nile acacias; p. 76). This avenue forms the Rotten Row, or Avenue de Boulogne, of Cairo. The fashionables of the town, both Mohammedan and Christian, drive or ride here daily, but principally on Friday and Sunday evenings. The scene resembles the 'corso' of European cities, but is rendered far more picturesque by its Oriental elements. The carriages of the slightly veiled ladies from the harems of the wealthy, and those of the ministers, the consuls, and the merchants, follow each other in gay procession, while the ubiquitous donkey forms a conspicuous feature in the busy throng.

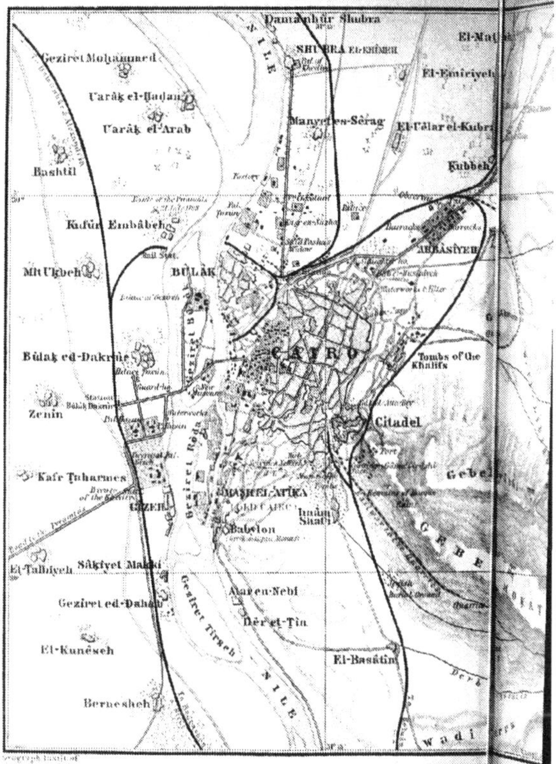

Damanhûr Shubra
SHUBRA
Gezîret Mohammed
Uarâk el-Hadar
Uarâk el-Arab
Manyet es-Sêrag
El-Matarîyeh
El-Emîrîyeh
El-Ualar el-Kubra
Kubbeh
Bashtîl
Kufûr Embâbeh
ABBÂSIYEH
Mît Ukbeh
BÛLÂK
Bûlâk ed-Dakrûr
CAIRO
Tombs of the Khalifs
Zenîn
Citadel
Kafr Tuharmes
Gebel
GÎZEH
Babylon
Et-Talbîyeh
Sâkîyet Makki
Gezîret ed-Dahab
Atar en-Nebi
Dêr et-Tîn
El-Kunêseh
El-Basâtîn
Bernesheh
NILE
Wadi

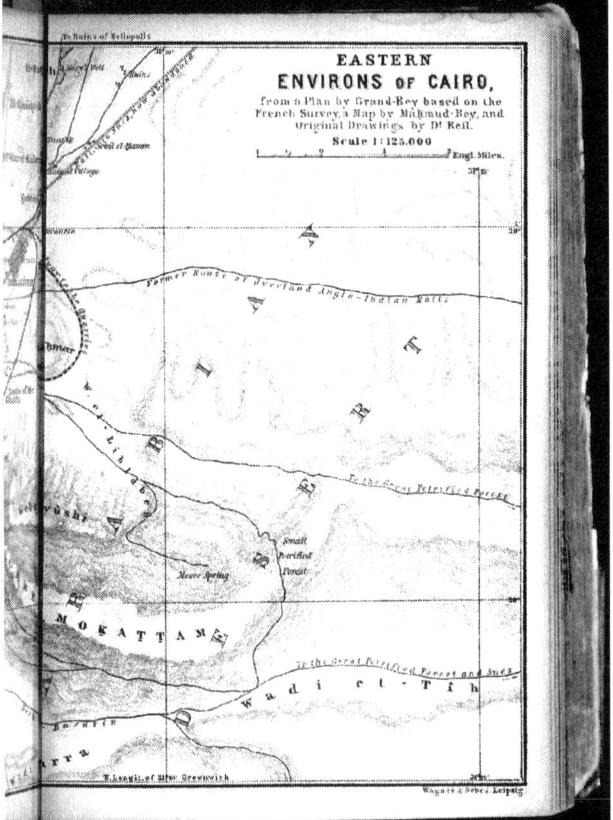
EASTERN
ENVIRONS OF CAIRO,
from a Plan by Grand-Bey based on the French Survey, a Map by Mahmud-Bey, and Original Drawings by Dr Reil.
Scale 1:125.000
Engl. Miles.
To Ruins of Heliopolis
Former Route of Overland Anglo-Indian Mails
To the Great Petrified Forest
Small Petrified Forest
Moses Spring
MOKATTAM
To the Great Petrified Forest and Suez
Wadi et-Tih
Wagner & Debes, Leipzig

INSERT
FOLD-OUT
OR MAP
HERE!

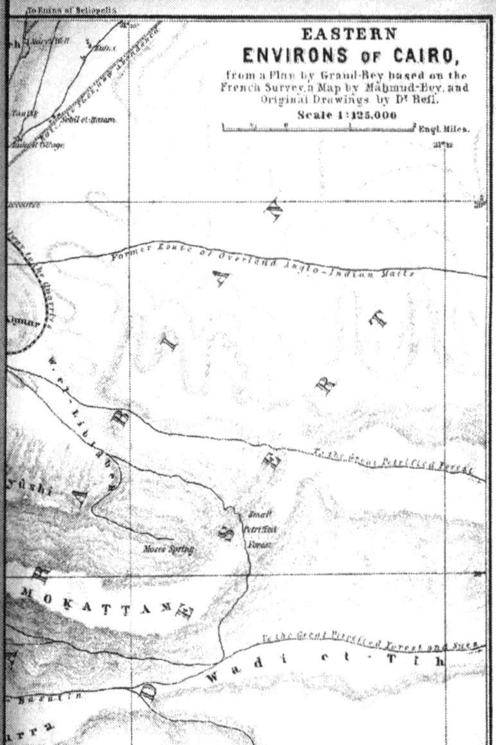

EASTERN
ENVIRONS OF CAIRO,
from a Plan by Grand-Bey based on the French Survey, a Map by Mâhmud-Bey, and Original Drawings by Dr Reil.
Scale 1:125,000
Engl. Miles.
To Ruins of Heliopolis
Former Route of Overland Anglo-Indian Mails
To the Great Petrified Forest
Small Petrified Forest
Moses Spring
MOKATTAM
To the Great Petrified Forest and Suez
Wadi et-Tih
E. Longit. of Grw. Greenwich
Wagner & Debes, Leipzig

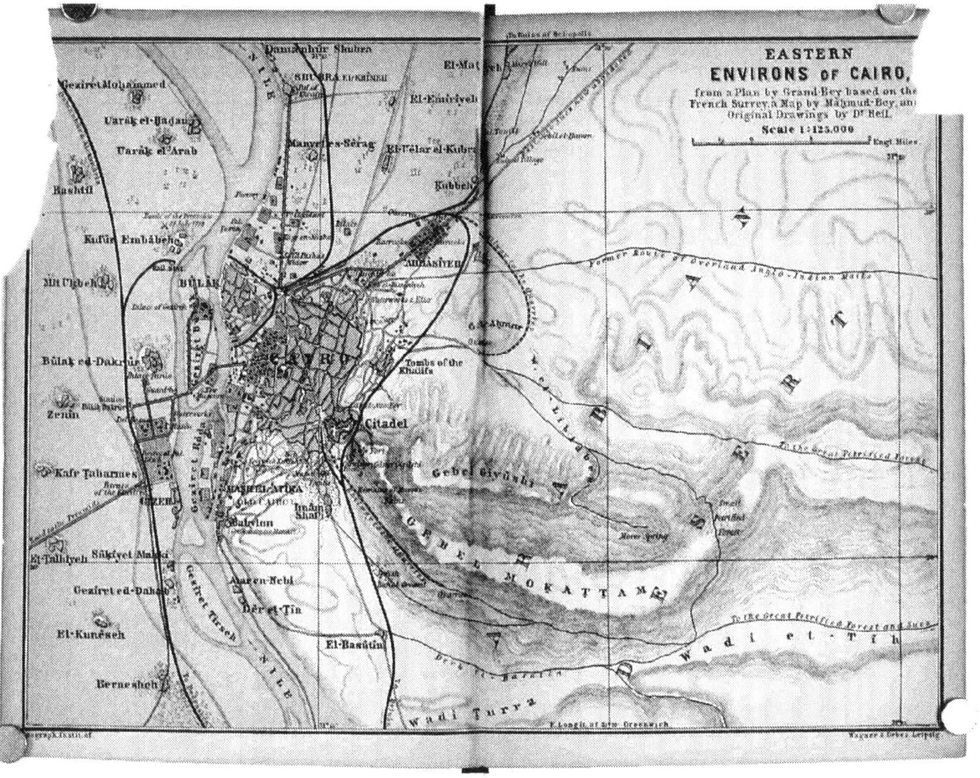

EASTERN
ENVIRONS OF CAIRO,
Scale 1:125,000
CAIRO
Citadel
Tombs of the Khalifs
Gebel Giyûshi
GEBEL MOKATTAM
Wadi et-Tîh
Wadi Turra
Damanhûr Shubra
El-Emîriyeh
Manyet es-Serag
Kubbeh
Kufûr Embâbeh
Mît Uḳbeh
Bûlâḳ ed-Dakrûr
Kafr Ṭaharmes
GÎZEH
El-Ṭâlbîyeh
Sâḳiyet Mekki
Geziret ed-Dahab
El-Kuneseh
Berneshel
Âṯâr en-Nebi
Dêr et-Tîn
El-Basâtîn
NILE

The handsome equipage of the Khedive is also seldom absent on Fridays and Sundays. Beyond the railway-station (Pl. A, 5), where the avenue begins, are a number of cafés and orange and refreshment stalls. Near the beginning of the drive are several villas, one of which, to the right, a little back from the road, is the beautiful *Villa Ciccolani*, a visit to which (on the way back) is recommended. The tower commands a good survey of the environs (fee 1 fr.). On the left is the viceroyal palace *Kaṣr en-Nuzha*, for the reception of distinguished foreign visitors (not shown).

At the end of the avenue, and beyond the first houses of **Shubra**, we turn a little to the right and soon reach the entrance to the garden, where tickets of admission are presented. We first proceed to the kiosque (fee 1 fr), after which a gardener shows the grounds and presents visitors with a bouquet (fee 1 fr.).

The new garden château, which was erected by Halîm Pasha, son of Moḥammed 'Ali, on the site of an older building, presents no architectural interest, but is worthy of inspection as an example of rich and effective garden architecture. The fine large basin, bordered with balustrades and galleries, was left unaltered. The corners and sides of the square reservoir are embellished with small kiosques. The fountains consist of water-spouting lions, and in the centre of the basin rises a kind of balcony, borne by twenty-four water-spouting crocodiles, which remind one of the proximity of the Nile. The pavement, basin, and columns are of Italian marble, while the upper part of the structure is in wood and stucco only. As already observed, the whole place is in a neglected condition. Several of the windows afford a fine view of the Nile. The rooms, which are handsomely fitted up, contain a number of pictures, including an indifferent portrait of Mohammed 'Ali.

The *Garden, which covers an area of nearly nine acres, was somewhat incongruously re-modelled a few years ago by M. Barillet (p. 76) in the old French style, which is ill adapted for the Oriental vegetation, but it also contains some beautiful rose and geranium beds. Among the tropical plants, which have their Latin names attached, we remark the beautiful Indian lemon-shrub and a huge lebbek tree (p. 76). An artificial hill in the garden commands a good survey of the grounds. A large building to the N. has been built for the Khedive's stud.

Heliopolis.

Another pleasant drive may be taken to Matarîyeh, a village 5 M. to the N.E of Cairo, where the Tree of the Virgin and the Obelisk of Heliopolis are situated The drive to the Kubbeh palace takes $^3/_4$ hr, thence to Matarîyeh $^1/_2$ hr, and to the obelisk $^1/_4$ hr. more A donkey takes longer

We follow the *Boulevard Clot Bey*, leading from the Ezbekîyeh to the station and to Shubra (p 330), turn to the right at the

Rond Point de Fagalla (where we observe the Sebîl of the mother of ex-Khedive Isma'îl on the left; Pl. 93), leave the new guard-house on the left, and then follow the *Route de l'Abbasieh*, which soon inclines a little to the left. A few years ago this road was flanked with large heaps of rubbish, but these have now given way to villas and gardens, which extend to the Bâb Ḥasanîyeh. The road is also pleasantly shaded by the lebbek trees (p. 76) planted here some time ago. Immediately after crossing the Khalîg (city-canal), the 'Abbâsîyeh road skirts the old mosque of *Eẓ-Ẓâhir* (Pl. 71), a large square pile of buildings, which was called by the French *Fort Sulkowsky*, was afterwards a government bakehouse, and is now a guard-house. A few paces beyond this building we reach the (right) *Bâb Ḥasanîyeh*, through which the route to 'Abbâsîyeh lay before the completion of the new road (and which, being shorter, may still be followed by riders or walkers). Beyond this gate the carriage-road runs towards the N.E., skirting the desert. At the beginning of it, on the left, is the slaughter-house. A road to the right leads to the pumps of the water company.

A few hundred paces farther on, the road divides again. The branch to the right, the old Suez road, leads to an uninteresting viceroyal château at the base of the *Gebel el-Aḥmar* (p. 337), the ascent of which is recommended.

We follow the road to the left, leading direct to **'Abbâsîyeh.** On the right we pass a modern public fountain, and on the left an old burial-mosque and the 'European Hospital'. 'Abbâsîyeh is a group of houses and cottages, founded by 'Abbâs Pasha in 1849, in order to afford suitable accommodation for the Beduin shêkhs whose friendship he was desirous of cultivating, and who objected to enter the city itself. A large palace which formerly stood here has been replaced by barracks in the most modern style, besides which there are numerous older barracks and a military school with a gymnastic-ground. The English troops are at present encamped here. Near the last barrack on the left is a palace of the ex-Khedive's mother, and a little farther on, also to the left, rises the meteorological and astronomical Observatory. At the end of the houses of 'Abbâsîyeh begin the new gardens which have been reclaimed from the desert. The road crosses two railways, passes the village of *Kubbeh* (left), intersects beautiful orchards and vineyards, and leads under handsome acacias and past numerous sâkiyehs to the *Palace of Khedive Tewfîk*. The vineyards, which were planted by Ibrâhîm Pasha, the grandfather of the Khedive, and contain various kinds of vines from Fontainebleau, are celebrated. This property formerly belonged to the late Muṣṭafa Fazyl-Pasha, the uncle of the Khedive. The present palace, however, has been entirely erected by Tewfîk himself. In the desert, to the right of the road, about $^1/_2$ M. distant, is situated the *Race Course*, where races formerly took place annually in January.

A little before reaching Khedive Tewfîk's palace, the road turns to the right and skirts the garden belonging to the palace. It then enters an olive plantation and leads in a straight direction to Matarîyeh. This plain has been the scene of two important battles. In 1517 the Battle of Heliopolis made Selîm and the Turks masters of Egypt (p. 105); and on 20th March, 1800, General Kléber with 10,000 French troops succeeded in defeating 60,000 Orientals, and in consequence of this victory regained possession of Cairo, although for a short time only.

Near the village of **Matariyeh** are the Tree and Well of the Virgin and the Obelisk of Heliopolis. The *Virgin's Tree* (in a garden to the right of the road) is a sycamore with a decayed and riven trunk, covered with names and inscriptions, but the branches are still tolerably flourishing. According to the legend, the Virgin and Child once rested under the shade of this tree during the Flight to Egypt; and there is another tradition to the effect that the persecuted Mary concealed herself with the Child in a hollow of the trunk, and that a spider so completely covered the opening with its web as to screen her effectually from observation The present tree, the predecessor of which died in 1665, was not planted till after 1672. At the time of the inauguration of the Suez Canal the tree was presented by the Khedive to the Empress Eugénie. The garden is watered by means of a double sâkiyeh, which is supplied from a shallow reservoir fed by springs. This water is good for drinking, while that of all the others, which percolates through the ground from the Nile, is usually brackish. This reservoir has been called the 'Water of An' from a very early period, and figures in the Coptic legends connected with the Virgin. It is an interesting fact that the celebrated balsam shrub, the balm of which is said to have been presented to Solomon by the Queen of Sheba, once throve in this neighbourhood. The plant, however, does not now occur nearer than Yemen, where its juice is an article of commerce. It is said to have been replanted here by Cleopatra, but apparently without success. In 1820-30 the first experiments with the cotton-plant (p. 75), which now plays so important a part in the commerce of Egypt, were made in this neighbourhood. Quails abound here in the month of April (p. 80).

About $^1/_2$ M. beyond the garden are situated the ruins of the famous ancient **Heliopolis**, or city of the sun, of which the obelisk and the outer walls are now the only vestiges. The town was called by the Egyptians the dwelling or seat of Ra (Helios), or of Tum (the evening sun, p. 125), or house of Phœnix (Bennu) or *An*. The latter, the popular name of the place, is frequently mentioned in the Bible under the Hebrew form of *On*. Thus, in Genesis, we are informed that Pharaoh gave Joseph the daughter of Potiphera (i.e. 'dedicated to Ra'), a priest of Heliopolis, named

Asenath, in marriage. *On* lay in the land of Goshen, and we learn from the monuments that even after the Exodus it was still inhabited by a considerable number of Semites. The Arabs named it *'Ain Shems*, which means 'well of the sun'.

From a very early period the Sun Temple of Ra (Tum-Harmachis, p 127), the most famous and ancient shrine in Egypt, with the exception of that of Ptah of Memphis, was the scene of magnificent rites in honour of the cycle of deities connected with the worship of the sun. The chief of these were Tum and Ra-Harmachis, with his companion Thoth, Sehu and Tefnut, children of Tum, Osiris in the character of the soul of Ra (called 'the ancient of Heliopolis'), Horus, and Isis, the last named deity being specially worshipped here under the highly revered name of Isis-Hathor, or Venus Urania, who was sometimes known as Isis of An The Mnevis bull was also revered here, being the animal sacred to Ra, while the Apis bull of Memphis, which abode for a time at Heliopolis before its introduction into its sanctuary in the town of the pyramids, was associated with Ptah The lions which were kept here perhaps had reference to Sehu and Tefnut, the brother and sister, who were represented as lions. or perhaps, owing to the glossiness of their skins and their natural fire, to the shining and glowing orb of day. With regard to the *Phœnix*, the bird of Ra, which was worshipped here, and which brings its ashes to Heliopolis, see p. 127. Cats and a white sow were also regarded as sacred here

The foundation of the temple is of very remote origin. In the 'great hall' here the wounds of Horus, received in his combat with Seth Typhon (p 130), are said to have been healed. Amenemha I., the first king of the 12th Dynasty, restored the shrine of Tum and laid the foundation of the Sun Temple, in front of which his son Usertesen erected the obelisk which still stands here

The immense wealth of this shrine is mentioned by various papyri, and particularly the Harris papyrus in London, which gives a list of the gifts presented to it by Ramses III alone The staff of priests, officials, custodians, and menials connected with the temple is said to have numbered no less than 12 913 As each Pharaoh was regarded as a human embodiment of Ra, it was natural that he should present special offerings to the chief scene of the worship of that god, and should proudly add to his titles that of 'lord of Heliopolis'. The most celebrated of the ancient schools, with the teachers of which Herodotus once conversed, was also established at Heliopolis, while in Strabo's time (born B C 60) the famous seat of learning had ceased to exist, although the houses of the priestly scholars were still standing The guides showed the great geographer the dwelling in which Plato and Eudoxus were said to have resided for thirteen(?) years; 'for', he says, speaking of the professors at this university, 'these persons, so admirably imbued with knowledge of heavenly things, could only be persuaded by patience and politeness to communicate some of their doctrines; but most of them were concealed by these barbarians.' Obelisks, the emblems of the sun's rays, were of course frequently dedicated to the god of the sun and his temple; and we are accordingly informed that Heliopolis was 'full of obelisks'

The ·Obelisk which still stands here is of red granite of Syene (Assuân), and is 66 ft. high. Excepting a small obelisk found by Lepsius in the Necropolis of Memphis, this is the oldest yet discovered, having been erected by Usertesen, with the pronomen Ra-kheper-ka, the second king of the 12th Dynasty. The companion obelisk (for these monuments were always erected in pairs) stood, as Mohammedan writers inform us, down to the 12th century. Each of the four sides bears an inscription in the bold and simple characters of the old empire; but those on two of the sides have been rendered illegible by the bees which have made their cells in the deeply cut hieroglyphics. The pyramidium at the top was covered with metal at a comparatively late period. The ground on which it stands has been so considerably raised by deposits of mud, that a great part of the obelisk is now buried. The inscriptions, which are the same on each of the four sides, record that Usertesen I. (Ra-kheper-ka), King of Upper and Lower Egypt, lord of the diadems and son of the sun, whom the (divine) spirits of An (Heliopolis) love, etc., founded the obelisk on the first day of the festival of Set, celebrated at the close of a period of thirty years. Cambyses is said to have destroyed Heliopolis, but it is ascertained that the city still contained many objects of interest down to a late Mohammedan period.

The excursion may be extended to the village of *El-Merg* (with some ruins of the 18th Dynasty) and the once prosperous, but now ruinous *Khânkâh*, on the outskirts of the desert ($2^1/_2$ hrs from Matarîyeh), but the sole attraction consists in the duck and snipe shooting around the ponds near Khânkâh. An interesting visit may, however, be made without much trouble to an ostrich farm kept by some Frenchmen, about $^1/_2$ hr. to the right

The **Birket el-Ḥagg**, or Lake of the Pilgrims, $4^1/_2$ M to the E. of Matarîyeh, presents no attraction except during the latter half of the lunar month of Shawwâl, when the great caravan which accompanies the new kisweh, or cover for the Ka'ba, to Mecca, assembles here to celebrate the so-called Mahmal Festival (p 236) A similar scene may, however, be more conveniently viewed at 'Abbâsîyeh, where, in the open spaces on each side of the road before its bifurcation, numerous tents are pitched and festivities take place at the time of the departure and arrival of the sacred carpet

The Mokaṭṭam Hills.

The ***Mokaṭṭam Hills** are well worthy of a visit (on donkey-back), especially about sunset, or in the morning between 8 and 9 o'clock; or the ascent may be made by way of termination to the excursion to the Petrified Forest (p. 337). Those who consider the expedition too fatiguing may content themselves with the ascent of the Windmill Hill (p. 287) at the end of the Muski, or with a visit to the Citadel (p. 262).

One route to the Mokaṭṭam (or *Gebel Giyûshi,* as the range of hills to the E. of Cairo is sometimes called after the conspicuous old mosque situated on their summit) starts from the Tombs of the Khalifs, and the other from the Citadel. The former is recommended for going, and the latter for returning. The whole excursion takes 3 hours.

Passing the Tombs of the Khalîfs, and crossing the railway embankment, we ride in the direction of a dark projecting rock, which we afterwards leave to the right. The road, which is fairly good, then ascends along the S.E. side of the large quarry lying on the right, and bears towards the right. In $^3/_4$ hr. we reach a large plateau, on the W. margin of which rises the dilapidated *Mosque of Giyûshi.*

The **View from this point, especially with its sunset colouring, is magnificent. The thousand minarets of the city and the picturesque buildings of the Citadel are then tinted with a delicate rosy hue. The grandest of all the burial-grounds of the desert forms a noble foreground, the venerable Nile dotted with its lateen sails flows below us in its quiet majesty, and to the W., on the borders of the immeasurable desert, tower the huge and wondrous old Pyramids, gilded and reddened by the setting sun. At our feet are the Citadel with the mosque of Moḥammed 'Ali, the old aqueduct on the left, and the domes of Imâm Shâfe'i (p. 327). On a rocky eminence are situated the picturesque ruins of several burial-mosques, which, being of the same colour as the rock, are apt to escape the notice of travellers on the Nile or its banks.

The Mokattam and the adjacent hills which flank the valley of the Nile, belong to the great range of the nummulite mountains which extend from N W. Africa, across Egypt and India, to China. This nummulite formation is one of the Eocene, or oldest deposits of the tertiary period, and immediately follows the chalk It is remarkably rich in fossils, the chief mass of which consists of millions of nummulites (a kind of snail-shell), or large rhizopodes of the polythalamica group The larger kinds are about one inch in diameter, and the smaller about 1/8 inch. On removing the outer coating of limestone, we find the well-defined chambers within. They are also frequently seen, cut into two halves, in the stones of the Pyramids, which are to a great extent constructed of nummulite limestone. The Greeks also noticed these curious fossils, and Herodotus mentions the smallest kinds as being petrified lentils, of the sort eaten by the ancient Egyptians (comp. 318).

The numerous quarries in the slopes of the Mokattam and the higher side-valleys of the range also yield a profusion of sea-urchins (clypeaster, cidaris, echinolampas, etc), various kinds of oysters, cerithium, ovula, strombus, nerina, turritella, nautilus, bivalves, 'sharks' teeth, and bones of the halicore Beautiful crystals of isinglass-stone and of strontian also occur, the shells of the nummulites having frequently been crystallised into the latter mineral

At the N. end of the plateau is an old Turkish fort, whence a bridge descends to the Citadel, but travellers are not permitted to use this route. On the E. and higher part of the Moḳaṭṭam, to the right, adjoining the summit, is a flagstaff erected in 1874 by the English party of scientific men who observed the transit of Venus from this point. The S. (right) end of these hills is skirted by the road to the smaller Petrified Forest, which may be reached from this point in about 3/4 hour.

On the way back our route bears a little to the right, and away from the lofty perpendicular sides of the above-mentioned quarry. The route back to the town viâ the Citadel turns to the left after 1/4 hr., near some ancient tomb-caverns, crosses a new bridge, and enters the Citadel by the *Bâb el-Gebel*, passing a number of dirty canteens. Turning immediately to the left, we pass the Well of Joseph (p. 264) on the left, and reach the broad road leading to the city.

The **Gebel el-Aḥmar**, or *Red Mountain*, which rises to the N.E. of Gebel Giyûshi (p 335; most conveniently visited from ʿAbbâsîyeh on donkey-back; p. 332), and connected with it by means of a substratum of limestone, consists of a very hard meiocene conglomerate of sand, pebbles, and fragments of fossil wood, cemented together by means of silicic acid, and coloured red or yellowish brown with oxide of iron. According to Fraas, the two colossal statues at Thebes are composed of rock from the 'Red Mountain'. For many centuries the quarries here have yielded excellent and durable millstones, and the neighbouring huge heaps of debris afford abundant material for the construction of the macadamised roads of Cairo and Alexandria. Similar meiocene formations, which owe their origin to an eruption of hot springs impregnated with silicic acid, occur to the S.E. of the Gebel el-Aḥmar, in the direction of the Petrified Forest, and even in a side-valley of the Gebel Giyûshi. A railway now encircles the whole of the hill, being used for carrying away the conglomerate and the subjacent limestone yielded by its quarries. Messrs. Fraas and Unger have found a few examples of freshwater conchylia among the fossils of the Gebel el-Aḥmar.

The Red Mountain undoubtedly owes its origin to an eruption of silicic springs, which forced their way through the tertiary limestone rock; and to similar agency is probably to be ascribed the mud-volcano near *Abû Zaʿbel*, beyond Khânkâh, 4-5 hrs to the N of this point A little to the E of Abû Zaʿbel, on the borders of the very smooth slope of the sandy desert, protrudes a black basaltic tufa rock, which has not reached the well-known crystallised form of basalt, but is in an amorphous condition, exactly resembling the black blocks lying on the E side of the Great Pyramid of Gîzeh. As there are traces of very ancient quarries near Abû Zaʿbel, these blocks may possibly have been brought thence.

Moses' Spring and the Petrified Forest.

Since the time of the French expedition the 'Petrified Forest near Cairo', as part of the *Gebel Khashab* is now called, has become one of the sights of Egypt which almost every traveller makes a point of visiting. To the natives the Petrified Forest is known as the 'Great' and the 'Little Gebel Khashab' The scientific traveller will find a visit to the former extremely interesting, but most travellers will be satisfied with an excursion to the latter, the outskirts of which may be reached in 1½ hour. The expedition may be made in half-a-day on donkey-back Carriages require extra horses, and even then sometimes stick in the sand.

A few drops of bitter and brackish water which trickle from a cleft in a narrow and rocky side-valley of the Mokattam are quite erroneously called *ʿAin Mûsa*, or *Moses' Spring*, but a visit to this spot (scarcely ½ hr. from the mouth of the valley) is interesting, and may easily be combined with the excursion to the Petrified Forest

The services of a guide may be dispensed with, as every donkey-boy is well acquainted with the route to the Little Petrified Forest, but a visit to the 'Great', near the Bîr el-Fahmeh, can hardly be accomplished without the aid of a well-informed dragoman

Leaving the Bâb en-Naṣr (Pl. B, 2; p. 280), we turn to the right to the Tombs of the Khalîfs, pass close to the burial-mosque of Sulṭân Barḳûḳ (p. 282), and, between the Moḳaṭṭam and the limestone substrata of the 'Red Mountain' (see above), cross a raised ledge of rock, forming a kind of threshold to the first desert valley towards the E., into which the E. spurs of the Moḳaṭṭam descend. Near a shallow quarry, in the middle of the valley, the well-defined desert track turns towards the S. After a ride of 1/4 hr., during which an isolated hill of red and black sandstone resembling the 'Red Mountain' is visible in the desert on our left, we cross a deep, dry water-course. The path divides here. That to the right leads to Moses' Spring and the Little Petrified Forest (see below), while that to the left is the route to the Great Petrified Forest and the Bîr el-Faḥmeh (p. 340).

Following the path to the right, we observe a yellowish hill at the foot of the spurs of the Moḳaṭṭam, and reach it in 1/4 hr. more. This hill stands at the mouth of the narrow, winding valley, 1 1/4 M. in length, through which the path to Moses' Spring ascends over large blocks of stone and rubble. The ravine terminates in a lofty amphitheatre of rock, which affords welcome shade. Near it stands a fig-tree, which the quarrymen have enclosed with a wall to protect it from the wind. In the higher angle of the valley to the right is the cleft in the rock from which issues the **'Spring of Moses'**, arbitrarily so named. The chief attraction of the gorge consists in the numerous desert plants and the fossils it contains.

In order to reach the smaller Petrified Forest, we return to the mouth of the gorge at the foot of the hill above mentioned, turn to the right, and proceed towards the S., skirting the slopes of the Moḳaṭṭam, which are here more precipitous. We then cross a black projecting rock, which has a glazed appearance, and pass through a square gap in the rock, beyond which we observe opposite to us gently sloping hills, consisting of limestone, marl, and beds of fossil oysters. The route ascends, a little to the right, between these hills, and soon reaches the plateau of the **Gebel Khashab**, where the scattered fragments of fossil wood indicate the beginning of the *Little Petrified Forest*. The farther S. we proceed across this plateau, the more numerous do the fossil trunks become; but they are inferior in length and thickness to those on the Bîr el-Faḥmeh (p. 340). Almost all these trunks and fragments have been ascertained by Unger to belong to the same tree, which he has named the Nicolia Ægyptiaca. On examining the grain microscopically, he found that it did not belong to the palm family, but was more akin to the cotton-plant. The trunks show traces of ramification, but do not now possess either roots or boughs. Whether the trees once grew here, or were floated hither by water, became embedded in the sand, and afterwards converted into stone, is still a matter of controversy. Fraas (see below) is of opinion that the formation resembles that of brown coal of the meiocene period, but that the trunks, instead of becoming carbonised, were converted into flint owing to the abundant presence of silica in the sandstone and to the peculiarity of the climate, which appears to have been much the same at that remote period as at the present day.

'Numerous huge trunks of a kind of balsam-tree lie in every direction among the sand or in the strata of meiocene sandstone The structure of the wood is as follows There are no annual rings The wood consists of prosenchymal and parenchymal cells, variously distributed, the latter having both thick and thin divisions Dotted vessels, filled with cells, are scattered throughout the tissue, either singly or in groups, and short in their articulation. These vessels are divided into chambers, all the walls being alike, but the outer walls are sometimes without these divisions; the radiating marks are prolonged by means of a series of 1-4 parenchymal cells A comparison of the fossil wood with living varieties shows that the vessels of the Sterculia and Astrapæa woods are grouped in the same way, and Unger therefore considers it probable that the wood of the Nicolia belonged to the Byttneriaceæ or to the Sterculiaceæ Thousands of these Nicolia trunks are exposed to view in the desert of Khashab. Where the sandstone became disintegrated and in course of time was converted into the sand of the desert, there the silicised trunks were gradually disengaged from their sandstone bed, and they now cover the surface of the Little Khashab for a distance of 10-15 miles, and that of the 'Great' for a far greater distance . . Travellers who are not familiar with the appearance of a vein of coal will be greatly struck by the appearance of this formation, regarding which all kinds of fanciful theories have been set up The geologist, however, will simply regard it as akin to the coal-measures of the meiocene period, with this difference, that, while the waters of Europe favoured the preservation of the carbon and the fibre of the wood, the silicious sandstone of the Mokattam converted the tissue of the wood into silicic acid The climatic changes, moreover, which have taken place in the region of the Nile since the meiocene period are doubtless much the same as those which must have affected the interior of Germany, where the brown coal is chiefly formed of the remains of balsam-poplars and cypresses.' *(Fraas)*

Crossing the plateau of the Petrified Forest for about 20 min. more towards the S., we suddenly reach the S. slopes of the Moḳaṭṭam, through a gap in which, at a spot now concealed by sand, a path descends past table-shaped ledges of calcareous marl, formed by erosion, into the *Wâdi et-Tîh* (more correctly *Wâdi Dughla*), or 'valley of wanderings'. On the S. horizon rise the hills of Tura (p. 405), recognisable by the old fortress on their right spur and by two heights exactly opposite to us, of which that to the left somewhat resembles a coffin in shape, while that to the right is of semicircular form. Crossing the bottom of the valley in this direction (S.), we perceive in the Ṭura hills the entrance to a desert gorge, bounded by lofty and precipitous slopes. This valley extends for many miles in various windings, communicates with the ravines of the desert which begin in the Gebel Khôf near Ḥelwân, and is abundantly stocked with the plants peculiar to the desert.

We may return from the Little Petrified Forest through the 'Valley of Wanderings', skirting the S. and W. slopes of the Moḳaṭṭam, passing the Tombs of the Mamelukes, and entering the city by the Place Moḥammed 'Ali at the foot of the Citadel. Another interesting return-route is across the Moḳaṭṭam hills to the Giyûshi eminence (p. 335). Thence to the city, see p. 336.

A visit to the Great Petrified Forest near Bîr el-Faḥmeh (4 hrs. to the E. of Cairo, and $2^1/_2$ hrs. beyond the Little Petrified Forest) takes a whole day, and is fatiguing, especially as the traveller has the sun in his face both in going and returning; but it is interesting to geologists. The route is not easily found (p. 338); the Wâdi et-Tîh (p. 339) forms the best starting-point (comp. Maps, pp. 316, 328).

We leave Cairo by the *Bâb el-Karâfeh* (Pl. G, 2), pass the Tombs of the Mamelukes, and, leaving the village of Basâtîn on the right, ascend to the left by the Jewish Cemetery. After reaching the top of the hill in the Wâdi et-Tîh (whence we observe the entrance of the rocky ravine mentioned at p. 339 to the right), we follow the valley towards the E. for $1^1/_4$-$1^1/_2$ hr. more. Above the gradual slopes of the desert, about $1^1/_4$ M. to the left, we then perceive several reddish hills and another of yellowish colour in front. Riding towards the latter, we reach on its E. slopes the debris of the **Bir el-Faḥmeh** ('coal well') and remains of some walls, dating from the period (1840) when Moḥammed 'Ali caused a search for coal to be made here. The shaft is said to be 600 ft. in depth, the bottom being 200 ft. below the level of the Nile. No coal, however, was found. The hills of the desert to the N., N.W., and W. of the Bîr el-Faḥmeh are thickly strewn with trunks and fragments of fossil timber. Some of the trunks which are exposed to view measure 65-100 ft. in length, and are upwards of 3 ft. thick at the lower end. They are generally brown and black, with a polished appearance, and frequently contain chalcedony.

A sand-hill $^1/_2$ hr. to the N. of Bîr el-Faḥmeh, to the base of which the Forest extends, affords a good survey of the district. To the N.W. are the Moḳaṭṭam, the 'Red Mountain' (p. 337), 'Abbâsîyeh, and the plain of the Nile. We may now return in this direction, keeping to the N. of the Moḳaṭṭam hills (comp. Map, p. 328), following a level desert valley. The way cannot be mistaken, but is not easy to find in the reverse direction without an experienced guide, as the point for which we are bound, not being conspicuous, is likely to be missed, and there are no good landmarks on the route beyond the Spring of Moses, opposite to which it enters the valley between the Moḳaṭṭam and the Gebel el-Aḥmar.

The Pyramids of Gizeh.

Now that there is a good road from Cairo to the Pyramids of Gîzeh, the excursion is generally made by carriage (20-25 fr.; a drive of $1^1/_2$ hr; donkey, 2 hrs.) Travellers formerly crossed the Nile at Old Cairo and rode thence to Gîzeh. The inspection of the Pyramids takes 2 hrs. at least (p. 343), the whole excursion thus occupying 5 hrs., so that the traveller can return to Cairo in time for dinner. Those who intend spending a whole day at Gîzeh should take provisions with them. Candles will also be required (and magnesium wire is recommended), if the traveller visits the interior of the Great Pyramid (see p. 356) or of any of the other tombs.

A visit to Saḳḳâra (p. 371) combined with the excursion to Gîzeh takes under ordinary circumstances two days, and, unless the traveller is content to pass the night in a cavern, requires a tent and a dragoman, so that the whole expedition is somewhat troublesome and costly. Those

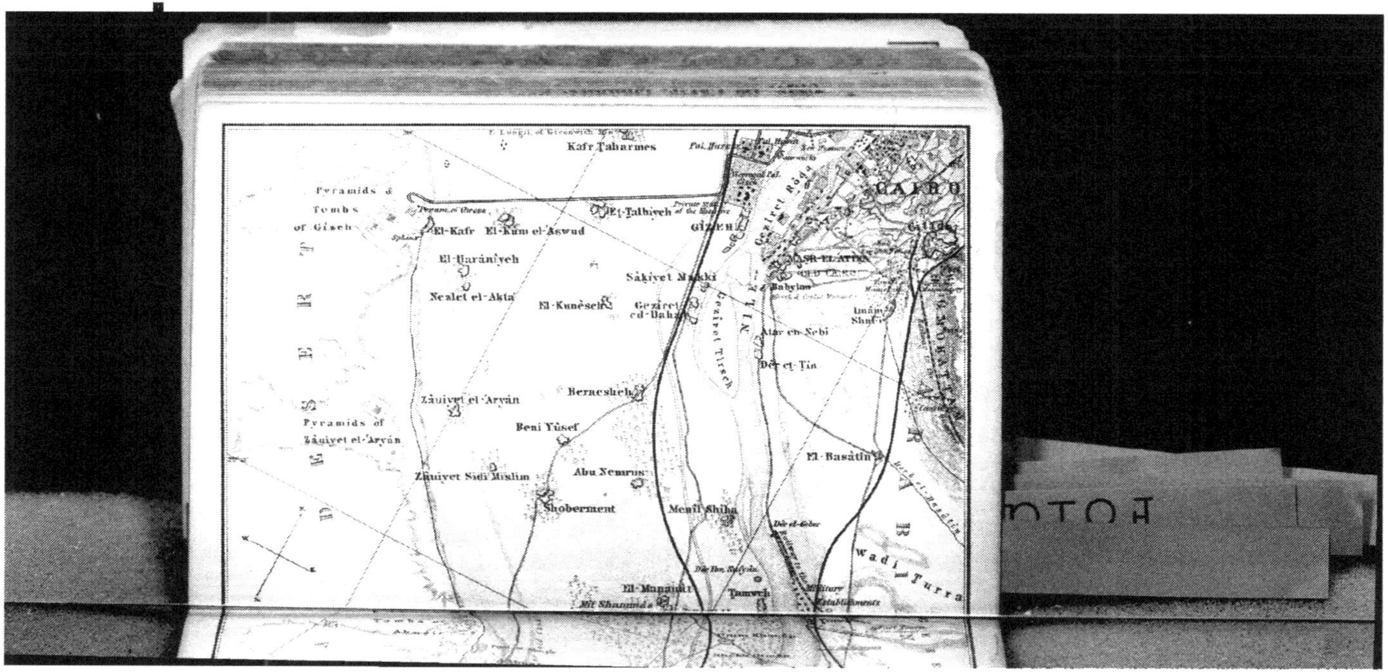

Kafr Taharmes
Pyramids &
Tombs
of Gizeh
El-Kafr
El-Kum el-Aswad
Et-Talbiyeh
GIZEH
Gezíret Róda
CAIRO
Citadel
El-Haraniyeh
Nezlet el-Akta
El-Kunêseh
Sakiyet Mekki
Gezíret ed-Dahab
Babylon
OLD CAIRO
Imâm Shafi'i
Atar en-Nebi
Gezíret Tírseh
Dêr et-Tin
Bernesheh
Zâuiyet el-'Aryân
Pyramids of
Zâuiyet el-'Aryân
Beni Yûsef
Zâuiyet Sidi Muslim
Abu Nemrus
Shoberment
Menil Shiha
El-Basâtin
Wadi Turra
El-Manauat
Tamweh
Mit Shammâs

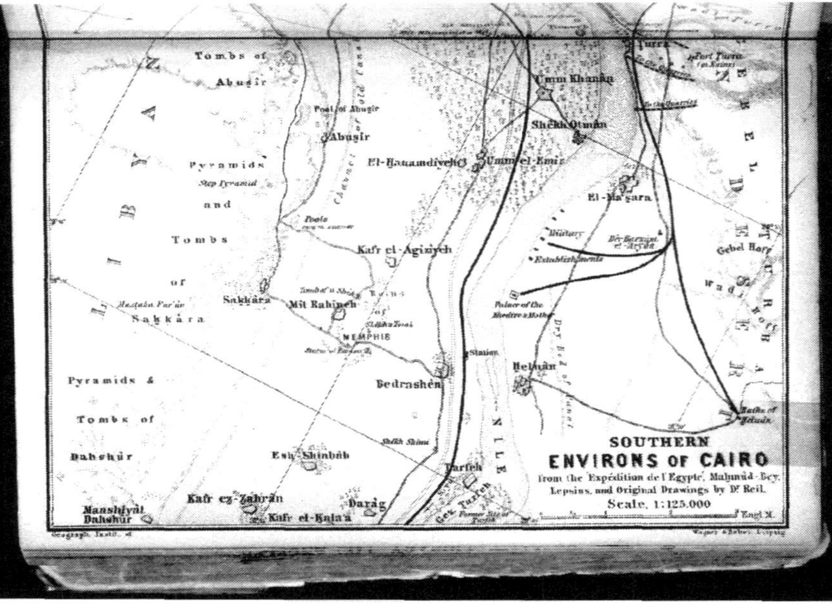
SOUTHERN
ENVIRONS OF CAIRO
from the 'Expédition de l'Egypte', Mahmûd-Bey, Lepsius, and Original Drawings by Dr. Reil.
Scale, 1:125.000
Tombs of Abuṣir
Abuṣir
Pyramids
Step Pyramid
and
Tombs
of
Sakkâra
Sakkâra
Mit Rahineh
MEMPHIS
Kafr el-Ağiziyeh
El-Ḥawamdiyeh
Umm el-Emir
Umm Khanân
Shêkh Otmân
Ṭurra
El-Ma'ṣara
Helwân
Bedrashên
Station
Tarfeh
Dârâg
Esh-Shinbâb
Kafr ez-Zahrân
Kafr el-Ḳala'a
Manshîyat Dahshûr
Pyramids &
Tombs of
Dahshûr
Gebel Hoff
NILE
Dry Bed of Canal
Palace of the Khedive's Mother
Baths of Helwân
Engl. M.

INSERT
FOLD-OUT
OR MAP
HERE!

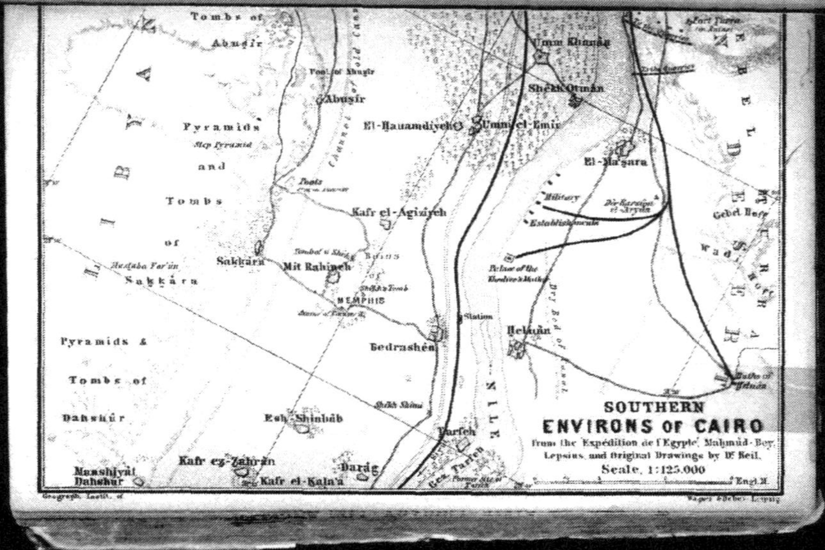

SOUTHERN
ENVIRONS OF CAIRO
from the 'Expédition de l'Égypte', Maḥmûd-Bey, Lepsius, and Original Drawings by Dr. Reil.
Scale, 1:125.000
Engl. M.
Tombs of Abuṣîr
Abuṣîr
Pyramids
Step Pyramid
and
Tombs
of
Sakkâra
Sakkâra
Mastaba Far'ûn
Pyramids &
Tombs of
Dahshûr
Mashîyât Dahshûr
Kafr ez-Zahrân
Kafr el-Kala'a
Esh-Shinbâb
Darâg
Mit Rahîneh
MEMPHIS
Bedrashên
Kafr el-Agîzîyeh
El-Ḥauamdîyeh
Umm el-Emir
Sheikh Otmân
Umm Khunân
El-Ma'sara
Military Establishments
Palace of the Khedive's Mother
Station
Helwân
Dry Bed of Canal
NILE
Tarfeh
Gebel Betr
Wâdi Hôf
Baths of Helwân
Channel of old Canal
Ruins

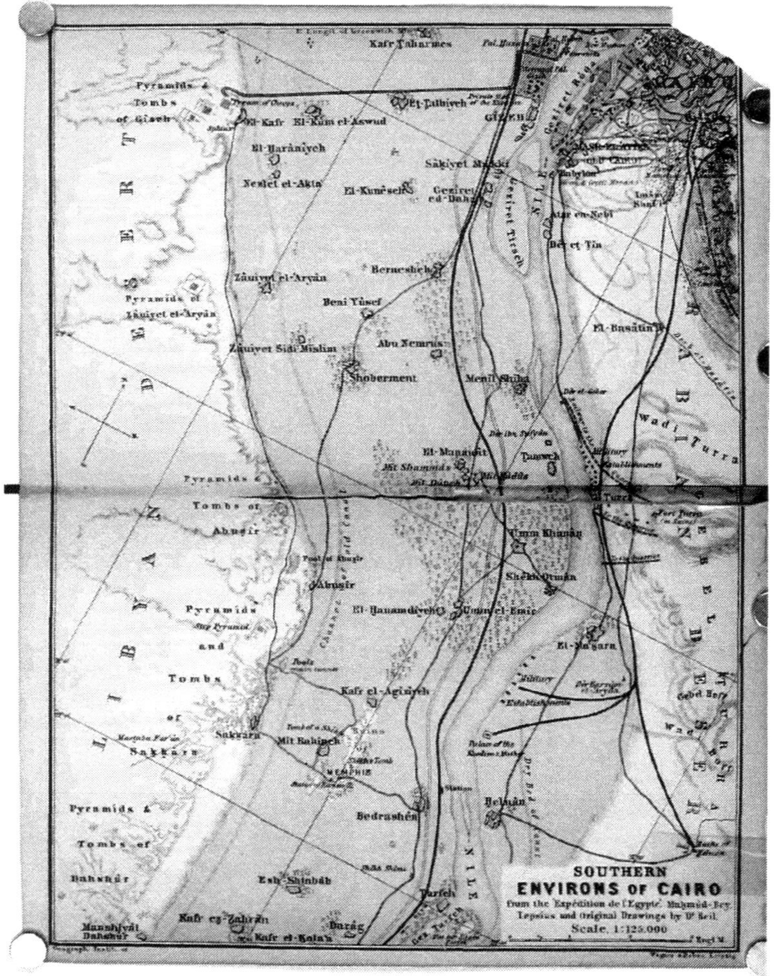

SOUTHERN
ENVIRONS OF CAIRO
from the Expédition de l'Egypte, Mahmûd-Bey, Lepsius and Original Drawings by Dr. Reil.
Scale 1:125,000
Kafr Tahurmes
Pyramids & Tombs of Gîzeh
El-Kafr
El-Kûm el-Aswud
El-Talbiyeh
Gîzeh
El-Harâniyeh
Nezlet el-Akta
El-Kuneseh
Sâkiyet Mekki
Geziret ed-Dahab
Geziret Tîrseh
Atar en-Nebi
Dêr eṭ-Tîn
Zâuiyet el-'Aryân
Bernesheh
Pyramids of Zâuiyet el-'Aryân
Beni Yûsef
El-Basâtîn
Abu Nemrus
Zâuiyet Sidi Muslim
Shoberment
Menîl Shîha
El-Manawât
Tamweh
Mit Shammâs
Pyramids & Tombs of Abusîr
Abusîr
Tura
Wadi Turra
Umm Khanân
Shêkh 'Otmân
Pyramids and Tombs of Sakkâra
El-Hawamdîyeh
El-Ma'sara
Kafr el-Agûzîyeh
Sakkâra
Mit Rahîneh
Memphis
Bedrashên
Helwân
Pyramids & Tombs of Dahshûr
Esh-Shinbâb
Tarfeh
Kafr ez-Zahrân
Barag
Kafr el-'Olâ'a
Menshîyat Dahshûr
L I B Y A N D E S E R T
A R A B I A N
NILE

who do not care to ride the whole way send donkeys to Gîzeh on the day before they start, drive thither early in the morning and dismiss the carriage there (the fare being hardly less than for the journey there and back), and ride in the afternoon or evening along the outskirts of the desert to Sakkâra, where the night is spent. On the following morning the route leads by the site of the ancient Memphis and through palm groves to the railway-station of Bedrashên. Railway thence to Bûlâk ed-Dakrûr, the station for Cairo, together with fares and the time occupied by the journey, see p. 371.

A visit to Ḥelwân (p. 403) may also be combined with the last-mentioned excursion if the traveller crosses the river with his donkey near Bedrashên, and passes the night in the hotel at Ḥelwân. Cairo may then be regained on the third day on donkey-back, or by the railway (p. 403).

Travellers who do not fear a little extra exertion and who are satisfied with a rapid inspection of the pyramids may visit Gîzeh and Sakkâra in one day by observing the following directions. Leaving Cairo at 8 a.m., we drive to Bedrashên and ride thence to Sakkâra (p. 371); quitting the latter at 2 p.m., we next ride along the edge of the desert to the pyramids, which we reach about $1^1/_2$ hr. before dusk. The drive back from the pyramids, where a carriage should be ordered to meet us, is most agreeable when a moonlight night has been chosen for the excursion.

One of the fine and calm days of which there is no lack at Cairo should be selected for the excursion, the driving sand in windy weather being very unpleasant.

Near *Kasr en-Nîl* we cross the Nile by the great iron bridge (p. 328). On the opposite bank we leave *Gezîreh* (p. 328), to which an avenue leads, on the right. The greenhouses and gardeners' dwellings belonging to the Khedive also lie on the right. To the left of the road leading across the island we observe the lofty chimney of a water-pump, and the private gas-manufactory of the Khedive. A second and smaller bridge then crosses the other branch of the Nile, which was long choked with mud, but which has lately been re-opened, so that the name of Gezîreh (*i. e.* island) is now justifiable (comp. p. 329). Immediately beyond the bridge rises a Ḳaraḳol (Turk. 'guard-house'), the road passing which leads to the railway station of Bûlâḳ ed-Dakrûr (p. 371) and to a palace of Tusûn Pasha. The road to Gîzeh, which is well kept and is shaded by beautiful lebbek trees, diverges to the left by the second bridge. Near the entrance to the viceroyal gardens of Gîzeh, which are bounded on the S. by an extensive palace, are waterworks for the raising and distribution of the water, immediately beyond which the road turns to the right. On the left rises the high wall enclosing the property of the Khedive, and on the right are palaces of the princes Husên and Hasan Pasha (none of which are shown to visitors). After crossing the Upper Egyptian railway, the road leads between the railway (on the left) and the canal (on the right) towards the S. to the private station of the Khedive, and thence to the right, direct towards the Pyramids. Or we may follow the better road along the Nile, keeping the wall of the palace to our right. The now decayed village of **Gîzeh** (which was a railway-station until recently, but has ceased to be so since the opening of the Bûlâḳ ed-Dakrûr station), which we leave to the left, is said by Leo Africanus to have once contained magnificent palaces, which the Mameluke princes afterwards used as a summer-residence, and it was a place of some commercial importance in the middle ages. A line of fortification between this point and the Nile, which once protected the entrance to the town on the left bank of the river, has entirely disappeared. On this part of the road two bridges are crossed; on the left lie the huts of two fellâḥîn villages, *Eṭ-Ṭalbîyeh* and *El-Kôm el-Aswad*. The fields on each side are intersected by canals and cuttings, containing more or less water according to the season. Small white herons, erroneously supposed to be the ibis, and vultures with light and dark plumage are frequently observed here. The huge angular forms of the Pyramids now loom through the morning mist, and soon stand out in clear outlines, with all the injuries they have sustained during the lapse of thousands of years.

A few hundred yards before the road begins to ascend, it is protected against the encroachments of the sand by a wall 5 ft. in height. On the left are a Sâḳiyeh (water-wheel) and stables, and on the right a building once destined to be a hotel, the establishment of which the Beduins, apprehensive of infringement of their rights, succeeded in preventing. Carriages have usually to stop here on account of the sand, and the occupants have to complete the excursion on foot; the best walking is on the top of the wall. The road, 26 ft. in width, and now flanked with walls $6^1/_2$ ft. in height, winds up the slope to the left, and reaches the plateau 130 yds. from the N.W. corner of the Pyramid of Cheops. Near the N.E. angle of the Pyramid is the *Viceroyal Kiosque* (Pl. a), where the custodian will generally give visitors the use of some of the rooms on the ground-floor on payment of a fee.

The 'Beduins of Gîzeh', who surround the carriage and importune travellers long before the Pyramids are reached, and who strew the last part of the road with sand in order that they may have a pretext for assisting carriages up the hill, are very pertinacious in their attentions and exorbitant in their demands. No attention should be paid to their demonstrations at first, but one of them may be afterwards engaged for the ascent of the Great Pyramid and a visit to the other antiquities. With the aid of the annexed plan the traveller might indeed easily dispense with their services, but as they seem to regard the privilege of escorting travellers as a kind of birthright, he had better engage one of them for the sake of avoiding farther importunities.

The Pyramids of Gîzeh occupy a plateau gradually ascending from E. to W., the E. and N. margins of which are very precipitous at places, and extending about 1600 yds. from E. to W., and 1300 yds. from N. to S. The three great Pyramids are so situated on this plateau that a line drawn from the N.E. to the S.W. angle of the largest pyramid is exactly in a line with the diagonal of the second pyramid, while the diagonal of the third pyramid is parallel with that line. These Pyramids are thus built exactly facing the four points of the compass, although the magnet seems to show an inclination of 8° 30′ towards the W. Smaller (and uninteresting) pyramids rise to the E. of the Great Pyramid and immediately to the S. of the third. To the S.E. of the Great, and to the E. of the second and third pyramids, are situated the Sphinx, the adjacent temple of granite, a deep rock-tomb (Campbell's Tomb), and an isolated stone building. Numerous tombs (maṣṭabas), almost all in ruins, surround the Great Pyramid and extend over the plateau to the E. and W., or are hewn in the form of grottoes in the external rocky slope towards the E. and in a ledge of rock to the S.E. of the second pyramid.

Chief Attractions. Those who are pressed for time should devote their attention to the ***Great Pyramid* (p. 354, explore the interior, and ascend to the summit), the ***Sphinx* (p. 362), the **Granite Temple* (p. 365), **Campbell's Tomb* (p. 367), and the *Tomb of Numbers* (p. 366). The inspection of these chief objects of interest, which we describe first, occupies about 2 hrs.; but those whose time permits, and who desire to form an accurate idea of the topography of the whole area, should make the **Circuit* described at p. 367, which will occupy 1½-2 hrs. more. Most of the tombs (p. 368) are so badly preserved that they are not worth visiting, unless the traveller is unable to undertake the excursion to Saḳḳâra.

The Pyramids †.

'Everything fears time, but time fears the Pyramids'.
'Abdellatîf (Arabian physician, born at Baghdâd in 1161).

The Pyramids within the precincts of the Necropolis of the ancient capital city of Memphis are the oldest and most wonderful monuments of human industry yet discovered. They stand on the margin of the plateau of the Libyan desert, along a line about 25 M. in length, and may be divided into the five groups of Abû Roâsh (p. 370), Gîzeh (p. 340), Zâwyet el-'Aryân and Abusîr (p. 370), Saḳḳâra (p. 382), and Dahshûr (p. 402). Beyond the boundaries of Egypt, to the S., there also occur the Ethiopian pyramids in the island of Meroeh near Begerawîyeh, at Nûri, and on the Gebel Barkal; but these Ethiopian structures, as Lepsius has shown, are comparatively recent imitations of the Egyptian, those at Nûri and on the Gebel Barkal dating from the 7th cent. B.C. at the earliest, and those of Begerawîyeh from the 1st century.

History of the Erection of the Pyramids. Manetho has ascribed the erection of the First Pyramid, which was surnamed that 'of Cochome' (comp. p. 382), to the fourth king of the 1st Thinite Dynasty (p. 86), but the statement is very improbable. The first

† The name, according to some authorities, is derived from the Egyptian Pi-Rama ('the mountain'), and according to others from πυρός, wheat, and μέτρον, a measure.

Egyptian monuments which bear the names of their founders date from the time of *Snefru*, who formed a link between the 3rd and 4th Dynasties. That monarch was the immediate predecessor of *Khufu* (or *Cheops*, B. C. 3091-67), *Khâfrâ* (or *Chephren*, 3067-43), and *Menkaurâ* (or *Mycerinus*, 3043-20), the builders of the Great Pyramids (comp. pp. 86, 344-347). It continued customary to build pyramids down to the 12th Dynasty (B. C. 2300); but at a later period, especially after the residence of the Pharaohs had been removed from Memphis to Thebes, the kings, as well as their subjects, seem to have preferred rock-tombs to mausolea above ground. The *Greeks* were much struck by these monuments when they first came to Egypt, and even erected similar ones themselves (as at Cenchreæ), akin to the Mastabas (p. 379). The Pyramids are therefore invariably described by Greek travellers†, as well as by their successors, and they afterwards became famous as one of the greatest wonders of the world.

Herodotus, though ill informed as to the history of the founders of the Pyramids, describes the structures themselves admirably, like everything else he saw in person Cheops (Khufu), according to his statement, was addicted to every kind of vice; he closed the temples, prohibited the offering of sacrifices, and oppressed the whole nation by exacting compulsory labour. Some of his subjects were employed by him in quarrying blocks of stone among the Arabian mountains, and in transporting them to the Nile, others had to ferry these stones across the river, while others again conveyed them to the base of the Libyan mountains††. 'Now there were about 100,000 men employed annually for three months in each of these tasks. They took ten years to make the road for the transport of the stones, which, in my opinion, must have been almost as laborious a task as the building of the Pyramid itself; for the length of the road amounts to five stadia (1017 yds.), its breadth is ten fathoms (60 ft), and its height, at the highest places, is eight fathoms (48 ft), and it is constructed entirely of polished stone with figures engraved on it†††. Ten years were thus consumed in making this road and the subterranean chambers on the hill occupied by the Pyramids, which the king caused to be excavated as his burial-place, having made it an island by conducting a canal thither from the Nile. (As to this erroneous statement, see p. 358.)

---

† According to Pliny, the Pyramids have been described by Herodotus, Euhemerus, Duris Samius, Aristagoras, Dionysius, Artemidorus, Alexander Polyhistor, Butorides, Antisthenes, Demetrius, Demoteles, and Apion, to whom we might add Strabo, Diodorus, Pomponius Mela, and others They are mentioned by Aristotle

†† Herodotus is accurate in his statement as to the origin of the stone most of that used in the construction of the Pyramids having been quarried on the E bank of the Nile (p 405)

††† This route is still traceable, and was even restored at a later period for the removal of stones from the Pyramids to the Nile. It terminated on the E. side of the Pyramid of Cheops (see Plan).

Now the construction of the Pyramid occupied twenty years †. Each of the sides, which face the different points of the compass, for there are four sides, measures eight plethra (820 ft.), and the height is the same. It is covered with polished stones, well jointed, none of which is less than thirty feet long.'

'This pyramid was first built in the form of a flight of steps. After the workmen had completed the pyramid in this form, they raised the other stones (used for the incrustation) by means of machines, made of short beams, from the ground to the first tier of steps; and after the stone was placed there it was raised to the second tier by another machine, for there were as many machines as there were tiers of steps; or perhaps the same machine, if it was easily moved, was raised from one tier to the other, as it was required for lifting the stones. The highest part of the pyramid was thus finished first, the parts adjoining it were taken next, and the lowest part, next to the earth, was completed last ††. It was recorded on the pyramid, in Egyptian writing, how many radishes, onions, and roots of garlic had been distributed among the workmen, and if I rightly remember what the interpreter (p. 13) who read the writing told me †††, the money they cost amounted to sixteen hundred talents of silver (upwards of 350,000*l.*). If this was really the case, how much more must then have been spent on the iron with which they worked, and on the food and clothing of the workmen, seeing that they worked for the time already mentioned, and I believe that no shorter time could have been occupied with quarrying and transporting the stones, and with the work and the excavations under the surface of the earth.'

'Cheops is said to have reigned fifty years in Egypt, and to have been succeeded in the kingdom by his brother Chephren, who acted exactly in the same manner as his brother, and who also erected a pyramid, which, however, is not of so great dimensions (for we measured this one also). This pyramid does not contain subterranean chambers, nor is a channel conducted to it from the Nile (comp. p. 358). Chephren constructed the foundations of coloured Ethiopian stone (granite of Assuân), but the pyramid was forty feet lower than the other, near which he erected it; for both stand

† It is not quite clear whether Herodotus means that the 100,000 men were occupied 20 or 30 years in building the Pyramid of Cheops, as he does not say whether it was the building above the subterranean chambers, or the whole of the structure that took twenty years.

†† This account of the mode in which the pyramid was constructed has been entirely confirmed by modern investigations (comp. p. 350).

††† If inscriptions, now destroyed, really once existed on the outside of the pyramid, they doubtless contained much more important information than that which the interpreter professed to read. It is, moreover, unlikely that the interpreters, who attended travellers like the dragomans of the present day, were able to read hieroglyphics. They probably repeated mere popular traditions regarding the pyramids and other monuments, with embellishments and exaggerations of their own.

on the same hill, at a height of about a hundred feet. Chephren is said to have reigned fifty-six years.'

'This makes altogether a hundred and six years, during which the Egyptians suffered all kinds of oppression, and the temples constantly remained closed. Owing to their hatred of these two kings, the people would not even mention their names, and they even call the pyramids after a shepherd named Philitis, who at that period pastured his flocks in the neighbourhood†'.

'After this king (Chephren), Mycerinus, the son of Cheops, is said to have reigned over Egypt. He is said to have had no pleasure in the conduct of his father, but to have re-opened the temples and to have allowed the people, reduced to extreme distress, to return to their occupations and the worship of the gods. He is also said to have pronounced the most just judgments of all the kings.'

'He, too, left behind him a pyramid, but a much smaller one than that built by his father. Each of its sides measures 280 feet only, and half of it consists of Ethiopian stone. Some of the Greeks state that this was the pyramid of Rhodopis, a courtezan, but they are wrong; nay, when they maintain this, they do not seem to me even to know who this Rhodopis was, for she flourished in the time of King Amasis, and not in the reign of this king (comp. p. 348).'

The account given by *Diodorus Siculus* (i. 63, 64) is as follows: — 'The eighth king was Chembes, the Memphite, who reigned fifty years. He built the largest of the three pyramids, which were reckoned among the seven wonders of the world. They are to be found in the direction of Libya, 120 stadia distant from Memphis, and 45 from the Nile. The sight of these great masses and their artistic construction excites surprise and admiration. The base of the largest, the plan of which is quadrilateral, is seven plethra (700 ft.) on each side; and the height is more than six plethra. The sides gradually contract towards the top, where each is still six cubits broad. The whole building is of hard stone, difficult to hew, and it is of everlasting duration. For no less than a thousand (some writers even say three thousand) years are said to have elapsed from the building of the pyramids down to the present time, and yet these stones, in their original jointing, and the whole structure are preserved uninjured by time. The stones are said to have been brought all the way from Arabia, and the building to have been erected by means of embankments, as no lifting machines had yet been invented. And the most wonderful thing is, that, around the place where this enormous work is built, nothing is to be found but sandy soil, and there is no trace either of the embankment or of the hewing of the stones; so that one might believe that the whole mass had not been gradually erected by human hands, but had been placed by some god in this

† Obviously a reminiscence of the Hyksos (p. 88), to whom, even at a later period, every national misfortune was popularly attributed.

sandy plain in a finished condition. The Egyptians attempt partly to explain this by the miraculous story that the embankments consisted of salt and saltpetre, and that they were melted by an inundation; that they thus disappeared, while the solid building remained. But this was not really the case, it was more probably the same number of human hands employed in throwing up the embankments which removed them and cleared the ground. It is said that 360,000 men were compulsorily employed in the work, and that the whole was scarcely completed within a period of twenty years†.'

'On the death of this king, his brother Chephren succeeded to the throne. He reigned fifty-six years. According to others the successor was not a brother of the last king, but a son of his, named Chabryis. In this, however, all the accounts agree, that, imitating his predecessor, he erected the second pyramid, which is indeed as artistically built as the first, but is not nearly so large, each side of the area being a stadium only (193 yds.) . . The kings had built these pyramids as tombs. and yet neither of them is buried in them. For they were so hated on account of the excessively laborious work imposed by them and their many cruelties and oppressions, that the people threatened to drag their bodies from their tombs with derision and to tear them to pieces Both, therefore, commanded their relatives, before their deaths, to bury them quietly in some unknown place.'

'These kings were succeeded by Mycerinus (whom some call Mencherinus), a son of the builder of the first pyramid. He resolved to erect a third pyramid, but died before the work was finished. Each side of the area he made 300 feet long. He caused the sides to be constructed, up to the fifteenth tier, of black stone, resembling the Theban. For the completion of the remaining part he employed the kind of stone which had been used for the other pyramids. Although this work is inferior to the others in point of size, it is superior in its much more artistic construction and its valuable stone. The name of Mycerinus, the builder of the pyramid, is inscribed on its N. side.'

'This king is said to have abhorred the cruelty of his predecessors, and to have endeavoured to be courteous to every one and to become the benefactor of his subjects. He is said to have sought in every possible way to gain the affection of his subjects, and among other things to have presented large sums at the public courts of law to honest people who were thought to have lost their causes undeservedly. There are three other pyramids, the sides of which are 200 feet long In their whole construction they resemble the others, but not in size. The three kings already named are

† These 360,000 workmen (a number perhaps based on the 360 days of which the old Egyptian year consisted), like the 100,000 men of Herodotus, who were relieved every three months, are doubtless a mere myth.

said to have erected them for their wives. These works are unquestionably the most remarkable in all Egypt, whether in respect of the size of the buildings and their cost, or the skill of the artists. And it is thought that the architects deserve even more admiration than the kings who defrayed the cost; for the former contributed to the completion of the work by mental power and praiseworthy exertion, but the latter only by the wealth they had inherited and the labour of others. Neither the natives, however, nor the historians at all agree in their accounts of the pyramids. For some maintain that they were built by these three kings, and others that they were built by different persons'.

Strabo's account is remarkably graphic and concise: — 'If you go forty stadia from the city (of Memphis), you come to a hill on which stand many pyramids, the burial-places of kings. Three are particularly remarkable, and two of these are even reckoned among the seven wonders. They are square in form and a stadium in height, and this height is only slightly greater than the length of each side. One pyramid, too, is a little larger than the other. A moderate distance up one of its sides, this pyramid has a stone which can be taken out. When it is removed, an oblique passage within leads to the tomb. These pyramids are near each other in the same open space; and a little higher up the hill is the third, much smaller than these two, but erected in a much more costly style. For, from its foundation nearly up to the middle, it consists of a black stone, of which mortars are also made, and which is brought from a long distance, namely from the mountains of Ethiopia. Owing to its hardness and the difficulty of working it, the building is rendered expensive'.

Strabo then speaks of the fossils resembling lentils, mentioned at p. 336, but does not share the view current at that period that they were the petrified remains of the workmen's food. With regard to Rhodopis, who is mentioned at p. 346, he tells the following tradition, resembling the tale of the modern Cinderella. While Rhodopis was bathing, an eagle carried off one of her shoes, carried it to Memphis, and dropped it into the lap of the king, who was then sitting on the judgment seat. The king, admiring the neatness of the shoe, and surprised at the strangeness of the occurrence, sent out messengers to search for the owner of the shoe. She was found at Naukratis and brought to the king, who made her his wife, and on her death erected the third pyramid to her memory.

Pliny speaks somewhat slightingly of the Pyramids: — 'We must also in passing mention the Pyramids in this same Egypt, an idle and foolish display by the kings of their wealth; and indeed, as most persons maintain, they had no other object in erecting them than to deprive their successors, and rivals plotting against them, of money, or perhaps for the purpose of keeping the people engaged. The vanity of these people in this matter was very great'.

His description of the Pyramids is borrowed without remark from other authors. Thus he does not hesitate to repeat that embankments for the raising of the stones were made of saltpetre, which was afterwards washed away, or of bricks, which on the completion of the pyramid were distributed among private persons. He also mentions Rhodopis.

Mas'ûdi, one of the *Arabian Historians*, says that the Pyramids were built three hundred years before the flood by Sûrîd, in consequence of the interpretation of a dream which predicted the deluge. Having assured himself that the world would be repeopled after the flood, he caused the Pyramids to be erected, the prophecy to be inscribed on their stones, and his treasures, the bodies of his ancestors, and records of the whole store of knowledge possessed by his priests to be deposited in their chambers and recesses, in order that they might be preserved for the benefit of those who should come after the flood. According to a Coptic legend, he caused the following inscription to be engraved on one of the Pyramids: — 'I, King Sûrîd, have built these Pyramids and completed them in 61 years. Let him who comes after me, and imagines he is a king to compare with me, attempt to destroy them in 600 (years). It is easier to destroy than to erect. I have covered them with silk; let him dare to attempt to cover them with mats!' A tradition recorded by the same author resembles the German myth of the nymph of the Lorelei: — 'On the western Pyramid is enthroned a beautiful naked woman with dazzling teeth, who allures desert wayfarers from the south and west, embraces them in her arms, and deprives them of reason'.

'Fair Rhodope, as story tells,
The bright unearthly nymph, who dwells
'Mid sunless gold and jewels hid,
The lady of the Pyramid'. (MOORE.)

According to other myths the spirit of the Pyramid bears the form of a boy, or that of a man, who hovers around it burning incense.

The Pyramids have been frequently visited and described by Christian travellers to Palestine on their way through Egypt. The spurious itinerary of Antony of Piacenza of the 6th cent. states that he visited the twelve granaries of Joseph (the Pyramids), and the same notion was entertained by pilgrims as late as the 14th, 15th, and 16th centuries. It is worthy of remark that many of the mediæval travellers, even as late as the 17th cent., concur with the most accurate of the Arabian authors in stating that they saw inscriptions on the Pyramids. Thus the knight of Nygenhusen, a pilgrim who assumed the name of William of Boldensele (14th cent.), informs us that he saw inscriptions on the Pyramids in different languages, and he gives six verses of one of them in Latin. 'Abdellaṭîf, speaking of the inscriptions on the Pyramids, which no one could decipher in his time, says that — 'they are so numerous, that, if one attempted to copy on paper those only which appear on the surface of these two Pyramids (those of Cheops and Chephren) they would fill more than 10,000 pages'. A similar account is given by Mas'ûdi, Makrîzi, Ibn Haukal, Edrîsi, and other Arabs; and yet on the incrustation of Chefren's Pyramid which is preserved at the top there is now no trace of a single letter. We must therefore conclude that the slabs which have been removed once bore inscriptions, which were perhaps purposely destroyed.

Construction of the Pyramids. In consequence of the investigations of Lepsius and Erbkam, the mode in which the Pyramids were erected and the meaning of the account given by Herodotus are now well ascertained. The following questions have been asked by Lepsius: — (1) How does it happen that the Pyramids are of such different sizes? (2) After Cheops and Chephren had erected their gigantic mausolea, how could their successors be satisfied with monuments so much smaller, and of so different proportions? (3) How is the fact to be accounted for, that an unfinished pyramid is never met with? (4) How could Cheops, when he ascended the throne and chose an area of 82,000 sq. yards for his monument, know that his reign would be so unusually long as to enable him to complete it? (5) If one of the builders of the great pyramids had died in the second or third year of his reign, how could their sons or successors, however willing to carry out the plan, have succeeded in completing so gigantic a task, and in erecting monuments for themselves at the same time? And how comes it that many other kings did not, like Cheops, boldly anticipate a reign of thirty years and begin a work of the same kind, the design for which might so easily have been drawn, and might so readily have been carried out by his subjects? — To all these questions the researches of Lepsius and Erbkam afford but one entirely satisfactory answer. 'Each king', says Lepsius in his letters from Egypt, 'began to build his pyramid when he ascended the throne. He began it on a small scale, in order that, if a short reign should be in store for him, his tomb might be a complete one. As years rolled on, however, he continued enlarging it by the addition of outer coatings of stone, until he felt that his career was drawing to a close. If he died before the work was completed, the last coating was then finished, and the size of the monument was accordingly proportioned to the length of the builder's reign; so that, had the progress of these structures always been uniform, it would have almost been possible to ascertain the length of each king's reign from the incrustations of his pyramid, in the same way as the age of a tree is determined by the number of the concentric rings in its trunk'. — The first step taken by the king's architect was doubtless to level the surface of the rock on which the pyramid was to be erected, leaving, however, any elevation in the centre of the area untouched, to form a nucleus for the structure, and to save labour and material. The subterranean chambers were first excavated in the rock, and then extended into the superincumbent masonry. A small building, in the form of a truncated pyramid, with very steep walls, was first erected. If the king died at this stage of the construction, a pyramidal summit was placed on the structure, and its surface was then prolonged down to the ground by filling up the angles formed by the nearly upright sides. If, however, the king survived this first period in the pyramid's history, a new series of stones was placed around it, and the same process was repeated until each successive incrustation became in itself a work of prodigious difficulty. The filling up of the angles could then probably be safely entrusted to the piety of the monarch's successor. The annexed plan will serve to illustrate this explanation.

The rock which in some cases served as the nucleus of the structure is marked *a*; the first part of the pyramid is *b*; on this was placed the pyramidal summit *c*; the angles *d* were then filled up, and a pyramid on the smallest scale was now completed. If time permitted, the builder next proceeded to place the two blocks *e* next to the blocks *d*, and above these the blocks *f*. To complete the pyramid on the next largest scale, it was then necessary to crown it with the summit *g*, and to fill up the angles *h* and *i*. If, for some reason or other, the angles were not filled up, the result was a so-called 'step-pyramid' (p. 382).

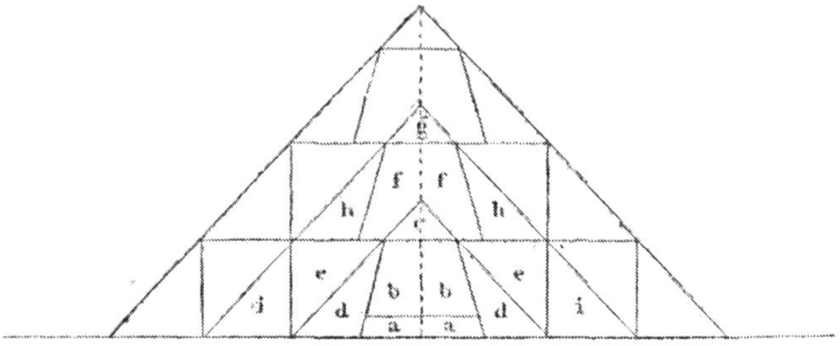

A confirmation of the accuracy of this theory is afforded by the ascertained fact, 'that the more nearly the interior of the pyramid is approached, the more careful does the construction become, while the outer crusts are more and more roughly and hastily executed, in proportion as the probable time for their deliberate completion gradually diminished'. The smallest pyramids always consist of the simple structure already described. The outer sides of the complementary triangular stones were entirely polished, except when, as in the case of the third pyramid, the whole surface was to be, as it were, veneered with slabs of granite.

Object of the Pyramids. In accordance with the ancient Egyptian doctrine of the immortality of the soul (p. 139), it was necessary that the earthly tabernacle of the soul should be preserved.

In order to remove the bodies of the dead from the influence of the inundation of the Nile, they were buried in the dry rocky soil of the desert. Wealthy persons caused tomb-chambers (p. 379) to be excavated for themselves, while the kings, who wished to maintain their royal pre-eminence even in death, were specially anxious to ensure the durability and permanence of their tombs. The burial-place of a king was worthy, in their opinion, of being distinguished by its situation and its magnitude; they desired that it should surpass all others in magnificence, and that the tomb-chamber should be least capable of violation. It was probably, therefore, at first customary to cover the rock-tomb of a king with blocks of stone, or to raise a mound over it, if sand and earth were procurable in the vicinity. The violent winds from the desert, however, rendered it necessary to consolidate these mounds by covering them with stones. The sepulchral mounds thus acquired a definite form; they became square structures, tapering upwards, and gradually assumed the pyramidal shape, ensuring the utmost strength and durability.

Opening of the Pyramids. The Pyramids are said first to have been opened by the Persians (B.C. 525-333), and it is certain that they were examined by the Romans. The Arabs endeavoured to penetrate into the interior of these stupendous structures, chiefly in hope of finding treasures; and the greater the difficulties they encountered, the more precious and worthy of concealment did they imagine the contents to be. According to 'Abdellaṭîf, it was Khalîf Mâmûn (A.D. 813-33), son of Harûn er-Rashîd (p. 101), who caused the *Great Pyramid* to be opened; but it is probable that that prince merely continued the investigations of his predecessors, as Dionysius, the Jacobite patriarch of Antioch, who accompanied him, found that an entrance had already been effected. Mâmûn's workmen are said to have made a new entrance (p. 357) adjacent to the old, with the aid of fire, vinegar, and projectiles. With regard to the success of the undertaking there exist various more or less highly embellished accounts by the Arabian historians; but one thing appears certain, that the hopes of the explorers were disappointed, and that nothing was found in the already plundered chambers and corridors. According to some accounts, the gold found here was exactly enough to defray the cost of the undertaking, having possibly been introduced into the interior by the Khalîf himself, in order to obviate the reproach of having spent so much money for nothing. Many of the Arabs relate, that, after the workmen had penetrated to a considerable depth, they found a vessel containing a considerable sum of gold coin, amounting, strangely enough, to the exact sum which had been spent on the investigation. Along with the treasure was found a marble slab, bearing an old inscription to the effect that the money beside it sufficed to pay for the work of the inquisitive king; but that, if he attempted to penetrate farther, he would expend a large sum and find nothing. The vessel containing the treasure is said to have consisted of an emerald, and to have been taken by Mâmûn to Baghdâd. Other fabulous stories are told of golden statues set with jewels, amulets, talismans, and mummies, which were found here in a golden cabinet, in a box in the form of a human figure, and in a stone sarcophagus. Maḳrîzi speaks of the sarcophagus which still lies in the royal tomb-chamber as in his time, and another author says that its cover bore the words — 'Abû Amad built the Pyramid in 1000 days'

We possess no definite information concerning the opening of the second Pyramid, but 'Abdellaṭîf, who was himself present, gives us an account of the attempted destruction of the *Third Pyramid.* As early as the reign of Saladin (A.D 1169-93), the vizier Ḳara-ḳûsh used the Small Pyramids as a quarry for the material of which he constructed various imposing edifices in Cairo, including the Citadel. El-Melik el-'Azîz 'Othmân (1193-99), Saladin's successor, was persuaded by his courtiers to demolish the so-called 'Red Pyramid', or that of Menkaura. The sultan accordingly organised a party of workmen for the purpose, under the supervision of some of his nobles, caused a camp to be pitched at the base of the Pyramid, and ordered them to begin the work of destruction. After eight months of incessant labour, however, the senseless undertaking, which had cost enormous sums and prodigious exertions, had to be abandoned. 'Nothing was effected by the undertaking', says 'Abdel-laṭîf, 'but the shameful mutilation of the Pyramid, and the demonstration of the weakness and incapacity of the explorers. This occurred about the year 593 of the Hegira (A. D. 1196). When the stones that have been removed are regarded at the present day, one would think that the structure had been entirely destroyed, but when one then looks at the Pyramid itself, one sees that it has suffered no material damage, and that a part of its incrustation has been stripped off on one side only'. — The Pyramids were also used as quarries at a later period, and even during the régime of Mo-ḥammed 'Ali, who moreover is said to have been advised by a prophet to destroy them. With the aid of gunpowder he might perhaps have succeeded in effecting what the workmen of the Khalif had failed to do, had not his European friends represented to him that the blasting operations would probably damage the city of Cairo.

The first modern traveller who carefully and successfully examined the Pyramids was Nicholas Shaw in 1721; but he still entertained the notion that the Sphinx had a subterranean connection with the Great Pyramid He was followed by Norden in 1737, Pococke in 1743, who gives a plan and dimensions; Fourmont in 1755; Karsten Niebuhr in 1761; Davison in 1763, a most meritorious explorer, who discovered many new facts concerning the interior of the Great Pyramid, Bruce in 1768; Volney in 1783, Browne in 1792-98; Denon, Coutelle, Jumard, and other savants of the French expedition under Bonaparte in 1799-1801. Jumard in particular has the merit of having taken very accurate measurements but he exhibited more ingenuity than good sense in attributing to the proportions of the building a hidden significance which they cannot be proved to possess. Hamilton, in 1801, was a dispassionate and critical observer. In 1817, Caviglia, a bold, but illiterate and fanciful seaman, was fortunate in eliciting new facts regarding the interior of the Great Pyramid, and excavated the Sphinx. In 1817, Belzoni (p. 359), an intelligent investigator and discoverer, thoroughly explored the interior of the Second Pyramid. The next eminent explorer was Sir Gardner Wilkinson in 1831. In 1837 and 1838 Col Howard Vyse and Mr. Perring made very thorough investigations and took careful measurements which will always be considered authoritative. In 1842-45 Prof. Lepsius, the distinguished German Egyptologist, who was president of the Prussian expedition, made several very important discoveries, and furnished us with much valuable information. He found no fewer than thirty pyramids which had been quite unknown to previous travellers. To M. Mariette is chiefly due the merit of having explored the burial places of Sakkâra (pp. 378, 388), which yielded him a rich spoil.

Ascent of the Great Pyramid.

Exterior. The traveller selects two of the importunate Beduins by whom he is assailed, and proceeds to the N.E. corner of the Pyramid, where the ascent begins (Payment, see below. The selection of the guides should properly be made by the shêkh; but this is seldom done, and even when it is, the traveller is still pestered by the others for bakshîsh.) These strong and active attendants assist the traveller to mount by pushing, pulling, and supporting him, and will scarcely allow him a moment's rest until the top is reached. As, however, the unwonted exertion is fatiguing, the traveller should insist on resting several times on the way up, if so disposed. Ladies should have a suitable dress for the purpose, and a stool may be brought to facilitate their ascent by halving the height of the steps. The ascent may be made in 10-15 min., but, in hot weather especially, the traveller is recommended to take nearly double that time. As the blocks are generally upwards of 3 ft. in height, the traveller will find the assistance of the guides very acceptable, though not indispensable. Persons inclined to giddiness may find the descent a little trying, but the help of the Beduins removes all danger. Both in going and returning the traveller is importuned for bakshîsh, but he should decline giving anything until the descent has been safely accomplished. At the summit of the Pyramid the patience is again sorely tried by the onslaught of vendors of *spurious* antiquities and dishonest money-changers, all parley with whom should be avoided. Those who make a prolonged stay on the top had better be provided with sunshades and perhaps also with grey or blue spectacles.

Interior. A visit to the interior of the Great Pyramid is interesting, but, though the guides represent it as easy and desirable, it will be found fatiguing and far from pleasant. The explorer has to crawl and clamber through low and narrow passages, which, at places, especially near the entrance, are not above $3^1/_2$ ft. high and 4 ft. wide. The stones on the floor are often extremely slippery, and the close air smells strongly of bats†. Travellers who are in the slightest degree predisposed to apoplectic or fainting fits should not attempt to penetrate into these stifling recesses.

For the ascent a single traveller usually takes two guides, but three suffice for two travellers. For a visit to the interior each traveller is accompanied by one guide. The customary fee for the whole expedition is $2^1/_2$ fr. for each traveller, whether he has been attended by one, two, or three guides. The Beduins are never contented with this sum, but the remuneration is ample. The traveller, however, if not dissatisfied, may give an additional gratuity of 1-2 silver piastres to each of his guides. On no account should any payment be made to any of them un-

† The temperature of the interior is 79° Fahr., *i.e.*, as is usually the case in subterranean chambers, the same as the mean temperature of the outer air in the neighbourhood.

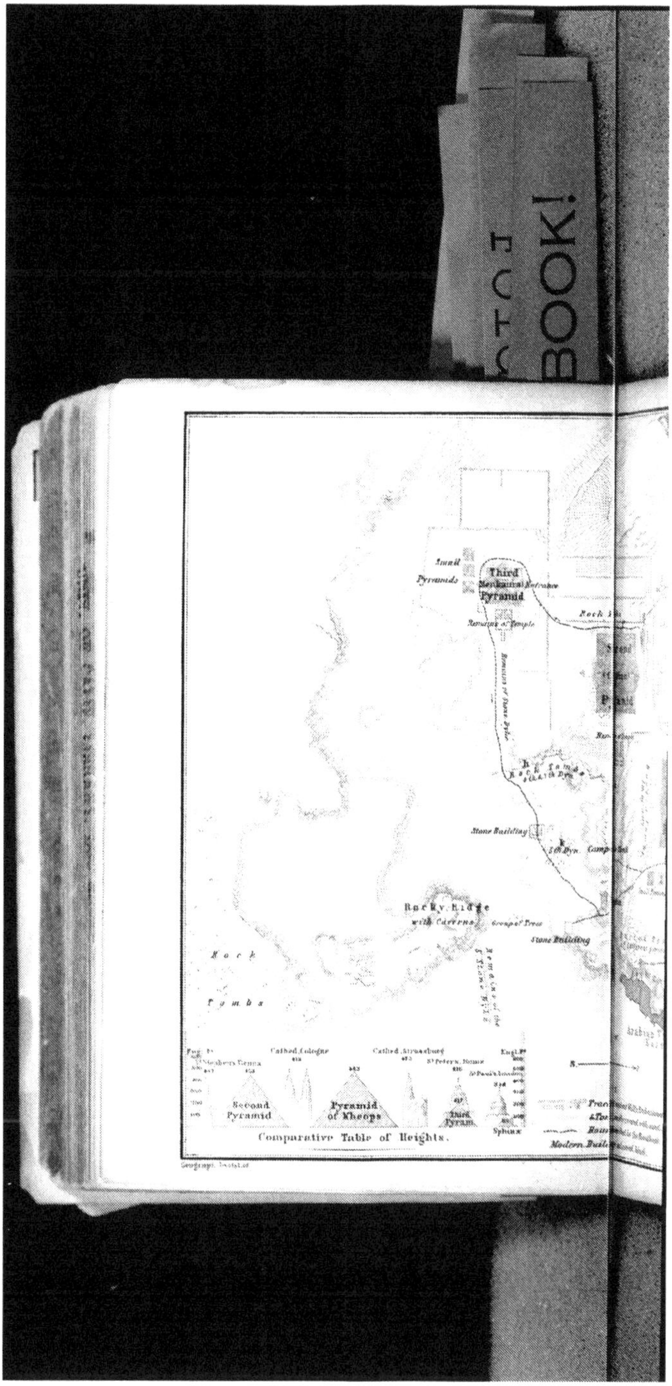
BOOK!
Small
Pyramids
Third
Pyramid
Entrance
Remains of Temple
Stone Building
Rocky Ridge
with Cairns
Group of Trees
Stone Building
Rock
Tombs
Cathed. Cologne
Cathed. Strassburg
Second
Pyramid
Pyramid
of Kheops
Third
Pyram.
Sphinx
Comparative Table of Heights.
Modern Buil

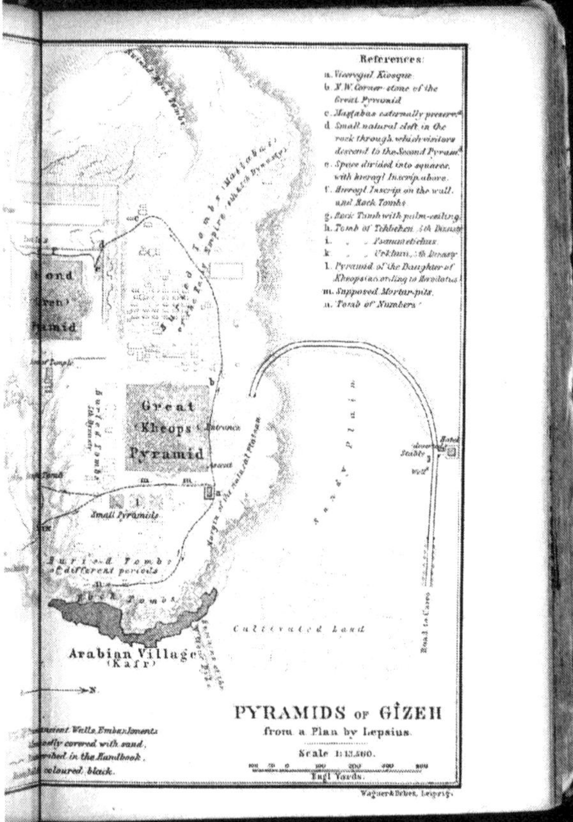
References:
a. Viceregal Kiosque
b. N.W. Corner-stone of the Great Pyramid
c. Mastabas externally preserved
d. Small natural cleft in the rock through which visitors descend to the Second Pyramid
e. Space divided into squares, with hierogl. Inscrip. above.
f. Hierogl. Inscrip. on the wall, and Rock Tombs
g. Rock Tomb with palm-ceiling
h. Tomb of Tekheken 4th Dynasty
i. „ „ Psammetichus
k. „ „ Urkhuu, 5th Dynasty
l. Pyramid of the Daughter of Kheops according to Herodotus
m. Supposed Mortar-pits.
n. 'Tomb of Numbers'
Great (Kheops) Pyramid
Entrance
Small Pyramids
Buried Tombs of different periods
Rock Tombs
Arabian Village (Kafr)
Cultivated Land
Sandy Plain
Road to Cairo
PYRAMIDS OF GÎZEH
from a Plan by Lepsius.
Scale 1:13,860.
Engl. Yards.
Wagner & Debes, Leipzig.

INSERT FOLD-OUT OR MAP HERE!

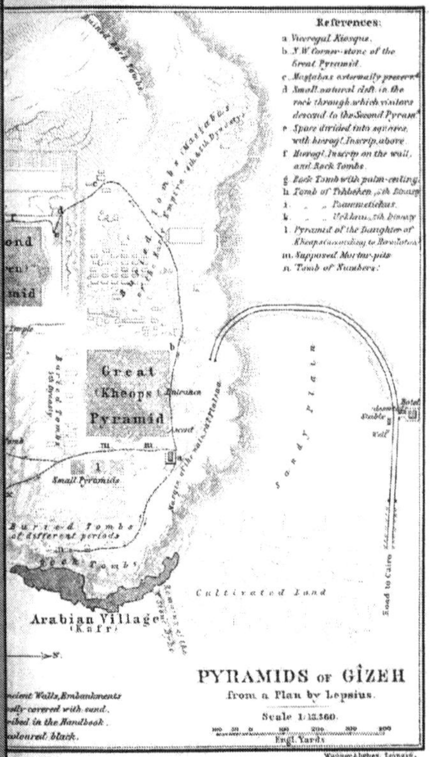

Wagner & Debes, Leipzig.

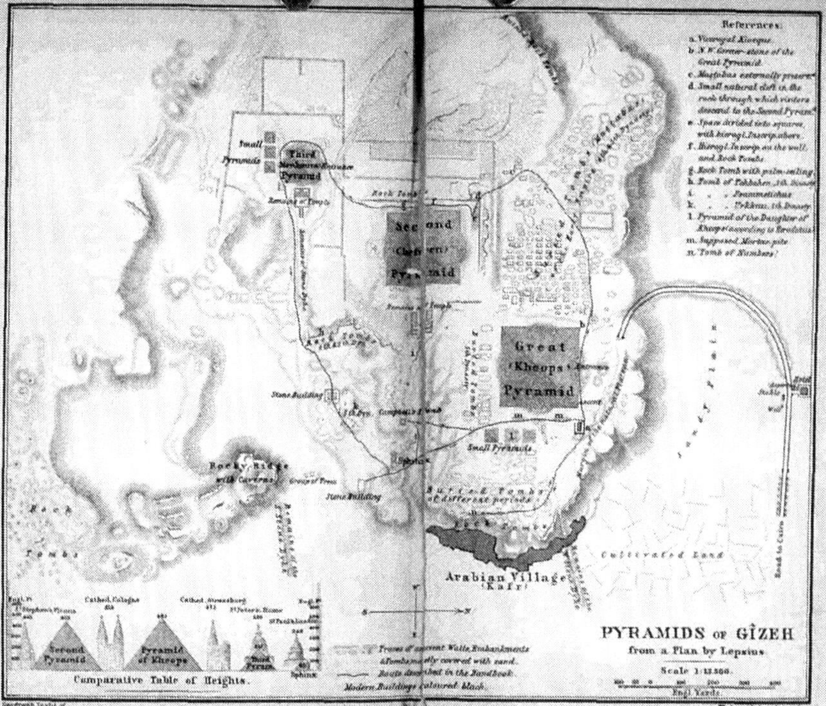
References:
b. N.W. Corner-stone of the Great Pyramid.
d. Small natural cleft in the rock through which visitors descend to the Second Pyramid.
e. Space divided into squares, with hierogl. Inscrip. above.
f. Hierogl. Inscrip. on the wall, and Rock Tombs.
g. Rock Tomb with palm-ceiling.
l. Pyramid of the Daughter of Kheops according to Herodotus.
m. Supposed Mortar-pits
n. Tomb of Numbers?
Third Pyramid
Small Pyramids
Second (Chefren) Pyramid
Great (Kheops) Pyramid
Small Pyramids
Sphinx
Stone Building
Rocky Ridge with Caverns
Rock Tombs
Cultivated Land
Arabian Village (Kafr)
Road to Cairo
Second Pyramid
Pyramid of Kheops
Comparative Table of Heights.
Sphinx
Traces of ancient Walls, Embankments & Tombs, mostly covered with sand.
Routes described in the Handbook.
Modern Buildings coloured black.
PYRAMIDS OF GÎZEH
from a Plan by Lepsius
Engl. Yards.

til the termination of the expedition. One guide of course suffices for a visit to the other objects of interest, the fee for which is 1-2 fr. according to the time occupied.

The **Great Pyramid** is called by the Egyptians 'Khufu Khut'

or the 'glorious throne of Khufu'.

The length of each side (Pl. *AA*) is now 750 ft., but was formerly (Pl. *BB*) about 768 ft.; the present perpendicular height (Pl. *EC*) is 451 ft., while originally (Pl. *EE*), including the nucleus of rock (Pl. *FF*) at the bottom, and the apex (Pl. *CE*), which has now disappeared, it is said to have been 482 ft. The height of each sloping side (*AC*) is now 568 ft., and was formerly (Pl. *BE*) 610 ft. The angle at which the sides rise is 51° 50′. The cubic content of the masonry, deducting the foundation of rock in the interior, as well as the hollow chambers, was formerly no less than 3,277,000 cubic yards, and it still amounts to 3,057,000 cubic yards, which are equivalent to a weight of about

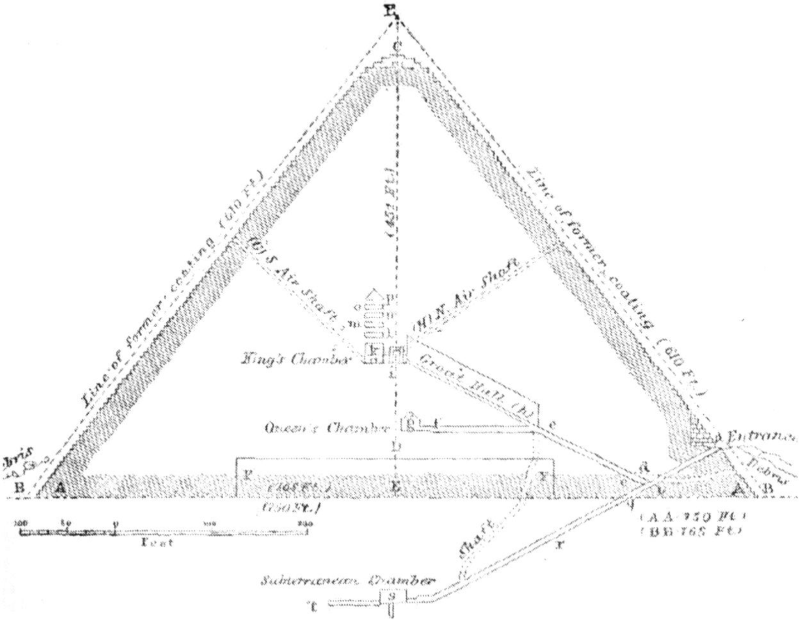

6,848,000 tons. In round numbers, the stupendous structure still covers an area of nearly thirteen acres. With regard to the comparative dimensions of other buildings, see the accompanying Map. The material of which the pyramid is constructed consists of stone from the Mokattam and from Tura, containing numerous fossils, chiefly nummulites (p. 336), as already noticed by Strabo (p. 348). With regard to the history and exploration of the pyramid, see pp. 344, 352. Interior, see below.

Escorted by two Beduins, one holding each hand, and, if desired, by a third (no extra payment) who pushes behind, the traveller begins the ascent of the large granite blocks. '*Iskut wallâ mâfîsh bakshîsh*' (be quiet, or you shall have no fee) is a sentence which may often be employed with advantage. We may again remind the traveller that it is advisable to rest once or oftener on the way up, in order to avoid the discomfort of arriving breathless and heated at the summit. The space at the top at present measures about 12 sq. yds. in area, so that there is abundant room for a large party of visitors.

The **View is remarkably interesting and striking. There is perhaps no other prospect in the world in which life and death, fertility and desolation, are seen in so close juxtaposition and in such marked contrast. To the W. (S.W. and N.W.) extend yellowish brown and glaring tracts of sand, interspersed with barren cliffs. The huge and colourless monuments erected here by the hand of man remind the spectator, like the desert itself, of death and eternity. On a bare plateau of rock stand the other pyramids and the Sphinx, rearing its head from the sand, like some monster suffocated by the dust. To the S., in the distance, rise the pyramids of Abuṣîr, Saḳḳâra, and Dahshûr, and to the N. those of Abû Roâsh. The scene is deathlike, the colouring yellow and brown. Towards the E., on the other hand, glitters the river, on each bank of which stretches a tract of rich arable land, luxuriantly clothed with blue-green vegetation, and varying in breadth. The fields are intersected in every direction by canals, on the banks of which rise stately palms, waving their flexible fan-like leaves, and interlacing their shadows over the fellâḥ villages perched like ant-hills on embankments and mounds. In the direction of Cairo runs the long straight carriage-road. Immediately before us rises the Citadel with the striking minarets of the mosque of Moḥammed ʿAli, while the Moḳaṭṭam hills, which form the chief mass of colour in the landscape, gleam in the morning with a pale golden tint, and in the evening with a violet hue.

The descent of the Great Pyramid is more rapidly accomplished than the ascent, but is hardly less fatiguing, and the traveller will find the help of the Arabs not unacceptable.

Interior (comp. Plan, p. 355). Some of the chambers in the interior of the Great Pyramid are at present closed; but, to prevent confusion, we shall not mention these until we have described those which are still shown. An interval of rest between the ascent and the expedition into the interior is again recommended.

The *Entrance* (Pl. *a*) is on the thirteenth tier of stones, on the N. side of the structure†, and at a perpendicular height of 48 ft. from the ground. The long passage *a r*, which is now only 3 ft. 4 in. in height and 3 ft. 11 in. in width, descends in a straight direction at an angle of 26° 41′, and is altogether 106½ yds. in length. We follow this passage as far as the point *d* only, 20 yds. from the entrance. A huge triangular trap-door of granite (Pl. *b*), let into

† All the pyramids are entered from their N. sides. The stone sarcophagi containing the bodies lay from N. to S.

Granite Temple, Sphinx & Great Pyramid (of Cheops).
(Seen from the South East.)

The Sphinx.
(Seen from the North East.)

the ceiling, and kept in its place by iron cramps, here arrests the farther progress of the explorer. The hardness of the material of which this barrier consists compelled the Arabian treasure-hunters (p. 352) to avoid it, and to force a new passage (Pl. *d*) through the softer limestone. This is the roughest and most awkward spot on the whole route. Beyond the rugged blocks at this point we enter a passage (Pl. *ce*), ascending at about the same angle, and 41 yds. in length, beyond which lies the Great Hall (Pl *h*). Before entering the latter, we diverge at the point *e*, by the horizontal passage *ef*, to the so-called *Chamber of the Queens* (Pl *g*) This passage is at first 3 ft. 9 in. only in height, but at a distance of 6½ yds. from the chamber the flooring sinks a little, so that the height increases to 5 ft. 8 inches. The N. and S. sides of the chamber are each 17 ft. in length, and the E. and W. sides 18 ft. 10 inches. The height is 20 ft. 4 in., including the pointed roof, which consists of enormous blocks of rock placed obliquely and leaning against each other, and projecting beyond the sides of the walls to a distance of 5½ ft. into the surrounding masonry. We now return to *e* and enter the *Great Hall* (Pl. *h*), the handsomest of the comparatively small chambers in the interior of this colossal mass of masonry. The jointing and polish of the fine-grained Mokaṭṭam limestone form an unsurpassable marvel of skilful masonry. As the visitor can now breathe and look about him with more freedom, he may verify the accuracy of ʿAbdellaṭîf's remark, that neither a needle nor even a hair can be inserted into the joints of the stones. The Great Hall is 28 ft. high and 155 ft. long. The lower part is 3 ft. 4 in in width; and the upper part, beyond the last of the panels of stone, each of which is 1 ft. 8 in. thick and 2 ft. high, is 7 ft in width. The seven courses of stone composing the roof, which seem to have been arranged in imitation of the arch-principle, project slightly one above the other, serving to strengthen and support the horizontal slabs which form the ceiling. The parallel incisions in the pavement and on the walls were perhaps used to facilitate the introduction of the sarcophagus, and they now serve to prevent the visitor from slipping. At the end of the Great Hall is a small horizontal passage, 22 ft. long and 3 ft. 8 in. high, expanding about the middle into an Antechamber (Pl. *i*), which was once closed by four trap-doors of granite. The remains of these slabs, in their pendent position, should be noticed. We next enter the *King's Chamber* (pl. *k*), the most interesting of all. The N. and S. sides are each 17 ft. in length, the E. and W. sides 34½ ft., and the height is 19 ft.; the floor of the chamber is 139½ ft. above the plateau on which the Pyramid stands. The chamber is entirely lined with granite, and is roofed with nine enormous slabs of granite, each 18½ ft. in length, the ends of which rest on the lateral walls. It now contains nothing but an empty and mutilated sarcophagus of granite, bearing no trace of an inscription, the lid of which had disappeared before the time of the French expedition. Length 7½ ft., width 3 ft. 3 in., height 3 ft. 4 inches The very massive sides ring with a clear tone when struck. Curiously enough, the King's Chamber does not lie exactly in a line with the diagonal of the Pyramid, but is 16 ft. 4 in. to the S. of it. Owing to the prodigious weight of the superincumbent masses, it would have been extremely hazardous simply to roof the chamber with long horizontal slabs, but the cautious architects of Cheops foresaw the danger and relieved the ceiling of the weight by introducing five hollow chambers above it. The first four *(l, m, n, o)* have flat ceilings, while the last *(p)* is roofed with blocks leaning obliquely against each other. These chambers are accessible from the Great Hall (p. 357), but not without great difficulty.

The first chamber *(l)* is named 'Davidson's chamber', after its discoverer (1763). The four others, discovered by Col Vyse and Mr Perring, were named by them Wellington's *(m)*, Nelson's *(n)*, Lady Arbuthnot's *(o)*, and Col Campbell's *(p)* chambers The discovery of the last of these was particularly important, as the name of Khufu (p 330) was found in it Lady Arbuthnot's Chamber contains the name of Khnum ('builder') Khufu These inscriptions are in red paint, and were doubtless placed on the stones as distinguishing marks by the quarrymen, as some of them are now upside down

About 3 ft above the floor of the King's Chamber are the ends of the *Air Shafts (w, x)* by which the chamber is ventilated, and which were re-opened by Col. Vyse. They are about 6 in. in height and 8 in. in width only, expanding by a few inches at the outer extremities. The N. shaft is 234 ft., and the S. shaft 174 ft. long. We now retrace our steps, and, on emerging from these awe-inspiring recesses, hail the light and air with no little satisfaction.

Chambers not now accessible. The only other chambers in the interior of the Great Pyramid as yet discovered are the following. The first passage *a, b, r*, leading downwards in a straight line, 293 ft. in length, terminates in a horizontal corridor, 27 ft in length, 3 ft. in height, and 2 ft. in width, which leads to the subterranean chamber *s*, hewn in the rock. The E. and W sides of this chamber are each 46 ft. in length, the N. and S. sides 27 ft., and the height 10½ ft. It does not lie in a line with the diagonal of the Pyramid, and its floor is 101½ ft below the level on which the Pyramid is built The subterranean horizontal passage *t* leads nowhere The statement of Herodotus (p. 344) that the subterranean chamber planned by Cheops for the reception of his body lay on a kind of island, surrounded by a canal which was conducted hither from the Nile, is erroneous, as the chamber lies above the highest level of the overflow of the river, and it has, moreover, been ascertained that no channel from the river leads in this direction. From the lower end of the Great Hall a shaft, discovered by Davidson in 1763, descends to the lower passage, and is erroneously known as the 'Well'. The enterprising Caviglia found that it terminated in the passage leading to the subterranean chamber *(r)*, and in 1831 Sir G. Wilkinson rightly explained that it must have been made to enable the workmen to quit the Pyramid after the upper passages had been obstructed by blocks of stone. It must at all events have been constructed at a later period than the masonry itself, as it has been obviously bored through it.

The **Second Pyramid** (which cannot be ascended, but should be entered by scientific visitors), called by the Egyptians 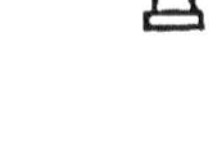 *ur*, the 'great' or 'considerable', was erected by Khafra, who was called Chephren by the Greeks, and whose portrait-statue is preserved in the museum at Bûlâḳ (p. 305), but his name has not been discovered on any part of the structure. Owing to the greater height of the rocky plateau on which it stands, it appears higher than its larger neighbour. As the rocky site rises towards the W. and N., a considerable part of it required to be removed in order that a level surface might be obtained. The levelled space surrounding the base of the Pyramid was paved with blocks of limestone (see p. 369). To the E. are remains of the temple erected for the worshippers of the deceased Pharaoh, a structure of the kind which probably adjoined all large pyramids (p. 368). The incrustation of the Pyramid, which must have been preserved down to the middle of the 17th cent., seems to have been laid on in a rough condition and to have been polished afterwards, beginning from the top. The lower courses were left in the rough, a circumstance which led the French savants to suppose that the Pyramid was once surrounded by a pedestal. The merit of having opened this Pyramid belongs almost exclusively to *Belzoni*, a most enterprising and successful explorer †. An inscription over the entrance records that the opening took place on March 2nd, 1818.

The *Interior* is entered by two passages on the N. side. The mouth of one of these is in the level surface in front of the Pyramid, and was concealed by the pavement, that of the other is on the N. side of the Pyramid itself, now 38 ft., but formerly 49 ft. above the level of the ground. This upper passage, which was lined with granite at the beginning, descends at an angle of 25° 55′ to a depth of 105 ft., leading first to a horizontal corridor, and thence to 'Belzoni's Chamber', which once contained the tomb of the deceased, situated 3 ft. 10 in. to the E. of the diagonal of the

† The traveller will meet with the name of *Giambattista Belzoni* so frequently, and in connection with discoveries of such importance, that a brief notice of his remarkable career may not be unacceptable. He was the son of a poor barber, and was born at Padua in 1778. He was brought up as a monk at Rome, where he was distinguished both for mental and physical endowments, and devoted much of his time to drawing. When Rome was occupied by the French, he quitted that city and went to England, and while in London eked out his livelihood by acting as a model for figures of Hercules and Apollo. At the same time he devoted considerable time to study, and especially to the science of water-engineering. Accompanied by his high-spirited wife, he next went to Egypt, where he arrived in 1815 and was at first obliged to support himself by dancing in public. He at length attracted the attention of Mohammed 'Ali who accorded him relief. His first undertaking of importance was the opening of the Pyramid of Chephren. He next discovered the tomb of Seti I. at Thebes (No. 17), the finest of all the royal tombs; he opened the rock-temples of Abû Simbel, and re-discovered the emerald mines of Zabara and the ruins of the ancient Berenike on the Red Sea. He died in 1823 while on a journey into the interior of Africa. A giant in stature, he inspired the Arabs with such admiration that he could prevail upon them to undertake the most unusual tasks. At the same time he was an intelligent explorer, and a very able and accurate draughtsman. His works, partly published by himself, and partly by his widow, are still valuable.

Pyramid. This chamber is hewn in the rock, and roofed with painted slabs of limestone leaning against each other at the same angle as that formed by the sides of the Pyramid. It is $22^1/_2$ ft. in height, $46^1/_2$ ft. in length from E. to W., and $16^1/_3$ ft in width from N. to S. Belzoni here found a granite sarcophagus let into the ground and filled with rubbish, 3 ft in height, 6 ft 7 in. in length, and $3^1/_2$ ft. in width, and destitute of inscription. The lid was broken. The *lower* passage, entered from the pavement on the N. side of the Pyramid, descends at first at an angle of 21° 10', reaches a trap-door, runs in a horizontal direction for 59 ft., and then ascends, terminating, after a distance of 97 ft. in all, in the horizontal corridor leading to Belzoni's Chamber. On the E. side of the middle of the horizontal portion of this lower passage was introduced a small chamber; and, connected with it on the W. side by means of a descending passage, 22 ft. in length, was another chamber hewn in the rock, 8 ft 5 in. in height, 34 ft. 3 in. in length, and 10 ft. 4 in. in width. The perpendicular height of this Pyramid is now 450 ft. (formerly 458 ft.), each side of the base measures $694^1/_2$ ft (originally $711^3/_4$ ft.), and the height of each sloping side is $560^3/_4$ ft (originally $575^3/_4$ ft.), while the sides rise at an angle of 52° 20'. The solid content of the masonry is now 2,156,960 cubic yds., equivalent to 4,883 000 tons in weight (originally 2,426,710 cub. yds., equivalent to 5,309,000 tons).

The **Third Pyramid**, named by the Egyptians  *her*, or 'the upper', was erected by Menkaura, the Mykerinos of Herodotus. The rock on which it stands has a shelving surface, and the necessary horizontal site was formed by building up a pedestal of enormous blocks, instead of by removing a portion of the rock. The stones of which the Pyramid is constructed are remarkably large and well hewn. The lower part of it is covered with slabs of polished granite, and the upper part with rough stones. The incrustation and the material which once filled the angles of the exterior are now so damaged that the tiers of the internal nucleus are almost everywhere visible. On the E. side are relics of a temple (comp. p 358). With regard to the construction of the Third Pyramid and the attempts which have been made to destroy it, see pp. 346, 347, 353.

The *Interior* of the Third Pyramid is in many respects particularly interesting, and the access to it was formerly easier than that to the Pyramid of Cheops, but the indolent Beduins have unfortunately allowed it to become choked with sand. The entrance is on the N. side, 13 ft. above the ground. A passage *ac* descends at an angle of 26° 2' to a distance of $104^1/_2$ ft., being lined with granite where it passes through the masonry from *a* to *b*, and then penetrating the solid rock from *b* to *c*. From *c* a slightly descending passage *cd* leads to a white-washed antechamber *f*, 7 ft. in height, 12 ft. in length, and 10 ft. in width, and, beyond this chamber, passes three trap-doors *g*, which were intended to arrest the progress of intruders. The passage *hd* then becomes nearly horizontal (gradient 4°) for a distance of $41^1/_2$ ft., and finally descends to the chamber *e*, which is $44^1/_2$ ft long, $12^1/_2$ ft broad, and owing to the unevenness of the rock from which the pavement has been removed, varies from 13 ft to 13 ft. 5 in. in height. The remains of a sarcophagus let into the ground were found here, but not that of Menkaura, which was carefully ensconced in a still lower tomb-chamber.

The pavement of the chamber *e* covers the mouth of a shaft 29 ft. in length, which was closed by a trap-door, and is flanked with a projecting block of granite on each side, 11 ft. wide and 2 ft. 4 in. high, designed to prevent the removal of the sarcophagus. Beyond the trap-door the passage descends 2 ft. 5 in. more, and a horizontal shaft, 10 ft. in length, finally leads thence to the *Tomb Chamber* (Pl. *i*), which is by far the most interesting of all those yet discovered within the pyramids. It is paved with blocks of granite, 2½ ft. in thickness, and its ceiling is arched in the English Gothic form. The arch has been formed by placing the stones against each other at an angle so as to resemble a roof, and then hollowing them out on the inside. The sarcophagus of Menkaura was found here by Col. Vyse in a good state of preservation. It was externally 2 ft. 7 in. high, 8 ft. long, and 3 ft. wide. The lid was gone, but its remains were found in the chamber *e*, and beside them the upper part of the wooden coffin, which, as the inscription on it recorded, once contained the body of Menkaura. The finely executed sarcophagus was composed of brown basalt, showing a blue tint where broken. The vessel in which it was being conveyed to England was unfortunately lost off Carthagena in the S. of Spain, but drawings of the precious relic

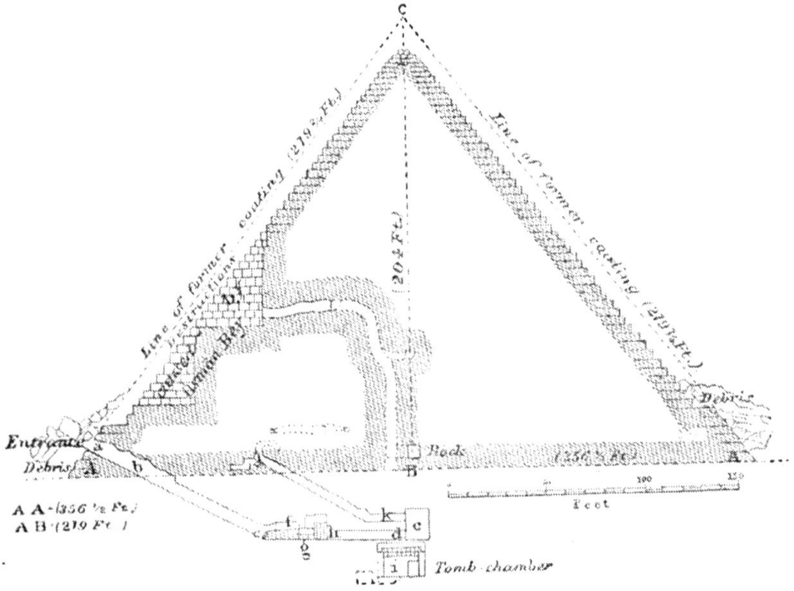

BB. Present perpendicular height of the Third Pyramid, 204 ft. — *BC.* Former perpendicular height, 219 ft. — *AA.* Side of base, 356½ ft. — *ABA.* Sloping sides, each 262¾ ft. — *ACA.* Original sloping sides, each 279¾ ft. — Angles at *AA*, 51°.

have been preserved. The inscription on the wooden lid, now preserved in the British Museum, runs as follows: — 'Osiric King Men-kau-ra

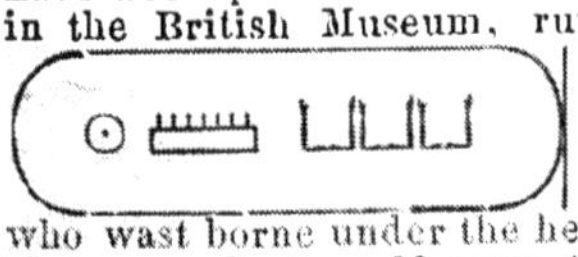

ever-living, who art descended from heaven, who wast borne under the heart of Nut, and heir of the sun. Thy mother Nut spreads herself over thee in her name, which is the mystery of heaven. She has granted thee to be like a god, annihilating thy enemies, King Menkaura, ever-living!' — Herodotus is, therefore, doubtless right in stating that Mykerinos (Menkaura) was the builder of the Third Pyramid, though Manetho mentions Queen Nitokris of the 6th Dynasty (p. 87) as one of the builders.

The three *Small Pyramids* situated to the S. of the Third Pyramid are uninteresting. The tomb-chamber of the one in the centre also contains the name of Menkaura, painted on the ceiling.

About 600 paces to the E. of the plateau of the Second Pyramid, from amidst the sand of the desert, rises the —

****Sphinx** †, which, next to the Pyramids themselves, is the most famous monument in this vast burial-ground. It is hewn out of the natural rock, and where this material has failed it has been moulded into the shape of a recumbent lion with the head of a man. The body was left in a rough form, but the head was originally most carefully executed. The entire height of the monument, from the crown of the head to the pavement on which the fore-legs of the lion rest, is said to be 66 ft. (see below), but the head, neck, and a small part of the back are generally alone visible, the rest being concealed by the constantly shifting sand. The ear, according to Mariette, is $4^1/_2$ ft., the nose 5 ft 7 in., and the mouth 7 ft. 7 in in length; and the extreme breadth of the face is 13 ft. 8 inches. If the traveller stands on the upper part of the ear, he cannot stretch his hand as far as the crown of the head, and the space between these points must have been greater when the head-decoration, which, as well as the greater part of the beard, is now broken off, was still intact. There is a hollow in the head, into which one of the Arabs may be desired to climb. The face was deplorably mutilated at a comparatively recent period by a fanatic, iconoclastic shêkh, and afterwards by the barbarous Mamelukes, who used it as a target. It would appear from 'Abdellaṭîf's (p. 343) account that it was in perfect preservation in his time: — 'This face is very pleasing, and is of a graceful and beautiful type; one might almost say that it smiles winningly'. He also describes the proportions of the head very minutely. An older writer, however, states that the nose was mutilated in his time, and, as it is now entirely destroyed, the face somewhat resembles the negro type, though the mouth still has a smiling appearance. The stone formerly had a reddish tint which has now entirely disappeared. The Arabs have given the Sphinx the name of 'abû l hôl', *i.e.* 'father of terror', or formerly 'belhit', probably derived from the Coptic ⲃⲉⲗ-ϩⲓⲧ (bel-hit), signifying a person who carries his heart or his intelligence in his eyes, or 'the watchful'. This last expression has frequently been used, by authors who were ignorant of its antiquity, as an appropriate epithet for the Sphinx. The Arabs believed that the figure possessed the supernatural power of preventing the encroachment of the sand. The complete excavation of the Sphinx was first undertaken by Caviglia (p. 354), at the cost (450*l.*) of an English society. He discovered the flight of steps

† The Egyptian Sphinx (p 167), being of the masculine gender, is represented with the head of a ram or of a man, and never with that of a woman.

which ascended to the stupendous monument, and also found between the paws of the lion a carefully laid pavement, at the end of which next to the breast of the Sphinx rose a kind of open temple, dvided by two partitions, through which ran a passage, containing a small figure of a recumbent lion, facing the Sphinx, in the middle. In the background rose a pillar, and at the sides were two others, forming a kind of wall. The one next the breast of the Sphinx was particularly interesting from the fact that it bore the date of the reign of Thothmes III. of the 18th Dynasty. Several of these relics are now preserved in the British Museum. The Sphinx was also entirely excavated by M. Mariette.

History of the Sphinx. It was pointed out by Lepsius in 1843 that the Sphinx must have been founded earlier than the 18th Dynasty, notwithstanding the above mentioned inscription on one of the tablets. The date there given is the first year of the reign of Thothmes III., which contains the account of the dream of that monarch while practising at a target and hunting near the Sphinx. From the inscription at the end the Sphinx appears to have been a representation of Khafra or Chephren, whose cartouche

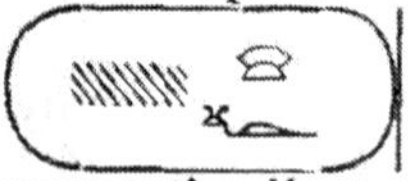

occurs at the left end of the last but one of the consecutive lines of the inscription, the ⊙ alone having been obliterated. In his dream Thothmes is asked by the Sphinx to clear away the encroachments of sand. As the Sphinx lies nearly in a line with the Pyramid of that king, it was not unnaturally thought that he was the founder of both monuments. This conjecture seemed to be confirmed by the discovery of the statue of Chephren in the rock-temple adjoining the Sphinx (p. 365). The monument has even been supposed to be entitled to claim still higher antiquity; for M. Mariette, while examining a ruined building at the foot of the southernmost of the three pyramids which rise to the E. of the Great Pyramid, found a stone built into a wall, bearing an inscription which seemed to imply that the Sphinx already existed in the time of Khufu, the builder of the first pyramid. The inscription on the right side of the stone runs literally thus: — 'The living Horus, the King of Upper and Lower Egypt, Khufu, the life-dispensing, found (in making excavations) the Temple of Isis, the patroness (ḥant) of the Pyramid in the place (*i.e* in the immediate vicinity) of the Temple of the Sphinx'.

The Sphinx is written  *ḥu*, which signifies 'to guard' or 'watch', or 'the watchman', an expression precisely equivalent to the 'bel-hit' (p. 362) of a later period. The above inscription, however, is of later date than the time of Cheops. The large tablet of Thothmes III., found between the paws of the Guardian of the Necropolis, has been already mentioned. This celebrated Pharaoh (p. 89) restored the Sphinx, and seems specially to have revered it, as is indicated by numerous small monuments which bear the figure of the Sphinx coupled with his name or his portrait. In the inscription already referred to, the Sphinx is said to speak to Thothmes 'as a father to his son', and to address him in the words — 'I am thy father Harmachis'. Though more or less buried in sand at various periods, the Sphinx was highly admired and revered down to so late a period as that of the Roman emperors, as numerous inscriptions upon it, now concealed by the sand, testify. Curiously enough, the Sphinx is mentioned neither by Herodotus nor any later Greek traveller.

Signification of the Sphinx. The Greeks and Romans call the Sphinx Harmachis, or Armachis, which is equivalent to the ancient Egyptian Har-em-khu, *i e.* Horus on the horizon, or the sun in the act of rising. Harmachis is the new-born light which conquers darkness, the soul which overcomes death, or fertility which expels barrenness. Being the powerful antagonist of Typhon, he was victorious over evil in different shapes He achieved some of his most brilliant exploits in the form o' the winged disk of the sun, and conquered his enemies in that of a lion with a human head, *i e* in the form of a sphinx. The scene of this victory was the Leontopolitan Nome, the name of which is derived from the myth In a papyrus preserved at Berlin the solar god is said sometimes to take the form of a lion, and other shapes also. Harmachis, in the burial-places, promises resurrection to the dead Turned directly towards the E , his face first reflects the brilliance of the rising sun, and he illumines the world after the darkness of night. Harmachis, dwelling on the outskirts of the desert, overcomes sterility and prevents the sand from overwhelming the fields This last attribute was still ascribed by the Arabs at a late period to the Sphinx-Harmachis, who is called by Greek inscriptions Agathodæmon, or the 'good spirit'. The morning was considered sacred to Harmachis, and it is in the E. that he first shows himself to the world. The East belonged to him; and as Thothmes III carried his sway farther to the E. than any of his predecessors, it was not unnatural that he should have showed special veneration for the Sphinx-Harmachis, and chosen him for his tutelary god. Every Pharaoh was, as we are aware, regarded as an earthly incarnation of Ra, and also, as many monuments testify, of Ra Harmachis. The kings, therefore, afterwards chose the Sphinx to symbolise the divine nature of their mission as monarchs, and it was a favourite practice to crown the lion's body with a head bearing their own features. The sphinx representing a king is called *neb*, or 'lord'. The Assyrians provided their sphinxes with wings as symbols of speed and of the power of rising above earthly things.

About $^3/_4$ hr. in a due S. direction from the Sphinx, on the outskirts of the desert, is a spot known to the Beduins where numerous fossils occur in the meiocene sand-formation. Among the commonest are the curious sea-urchins (Clypeaster), which the Beduins frequently offer for sale. — In the desert, about 4 hrs. farther distant, petrified wood is said to occur (comp. p. 339).

A few paces to the S.E. of the Sphinx is situated the *__Granite Temple__, a large building constructed of granite and alabaster, discovered by M. Mariette in 1853. The different chambers are now kept free of sand, so that they can be examined in every part. The object of the building has not yet been ascertained, but there can be no doubt that it was in some way connected with the Sphinx. The inscription of Khufu mentioned at p. 364 speaks of a Temple of the Sphinx. The statues of Chephren (pp. 305, 307) found here seem to indicate that he was the founder of this structure; and, if so, this would be the only temple handed down to us from the primæval monarchy. At the same time the building so closely resembles a maṣṭaba (p. 379), that, particularly as it stands in the Necropolis of Memphis, it was perhaps rather one of those monuments which were dedicated to the rites of the dead; and it seems not improbable that Chephren, who built the Second Pyramid as his tomb, erected this edifice as a place of assembly for the worshippers, of his *manes*. The building is a fine example of the simple and majestic architecture of that remote period, when the art of working the hardest kinds of stone had already attained perfection. The chisel which in the hand of the stone-mason shaped these blocks of granite with such exquisite skill, could doubtless, when wielded by the sculptor, easily create a statue of Chephren.

Descending by a recently constructed Passage (Pl. *aa*) in steps, protected by walls against the encroachment of the sand, we pass through a door (*b*) into a Passage (*bb*) descending towards the E., 6 ft. 8 in. in width and 79 ft. in length. On the right, halfway down this passage, is the entrance to a Chamber (*c*) constructed entirely of blocks of alabaster; opposite to it, on the left, is the Entrance (*d*) to a flight of steps, which turns at a right angle and ascends to a small chamber, where an opening on the S. side leads to the granite roof of the temple. This passage and chamber are also constructed of alabaster. At the E. end of the corridor we enter a Hall (Pl. *e*), 79 ft. in length (N. to S.) and 23 ft. in width, embellished with six monolithic pillars of granite varying from 3 ft. 4 in. to 4 ft. 7 in. in thickness. The pillars are connected by enormous blocks of similar dimensions which are still *in situ*. Adjoining this hall on the W. is another similar Hall (Pl. *f*), 57$^1/_2$ ft. long and 29 ft. wide, the ceiling of which was borne by ten columns of granite in two rows. At the S.W. corner of Hall *e* is a Door *g*, leading into the Corridor *gg*, which is adjoined on the left by the Chamber *i*. At *hh*, farther on, and also at the end of *gg*, are niches in two stories, one above the other, probably destined for the reception of mummies. Returning to Hall *e*, we proceed to Passage *k*, in the middle of the E. side, which leads between walls 13 ft. in thickness to Chamber *l*, the last on the E. side of the building, and destitute of columns. At the point *m* in this apartment, M. Mariette found a deep well containing water, but now filled with sand, in which he discovered no fewer than nine statues of Chephren. The best of these are now in the Museum of Bûlâḳ (pp. 305, 307). Several dog-headed apes

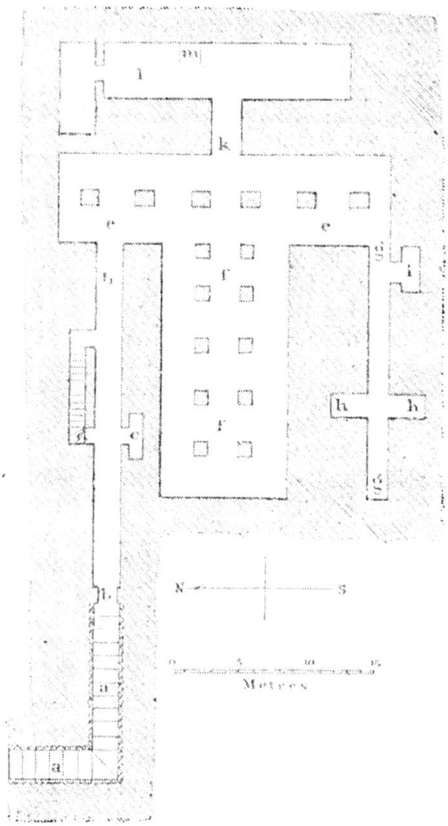

(p. 134), executed in stone, were also found in the sand here. At the N. and S. ends of this apartment are two side-chambers, one of which (Pl. *n*) only is now accessible, the other having been built up.

Between the Granite Temple and the Sphinx recent excavations have laid bare a series of walls, which consist of Nile mud and gravel and obviously date from the Roman period.

Among the tombs surrounding the different pyramids, where the relatives, priests, and state officials of the kings were interred, one of the most interesting is the —

Tomb of Numbers (Pl. *n*), so called from the enumeration it contains (as usual in other tombs also) of the cattle possessed by the deceased. This tomb, which lies on the E. slope of the plateau of the Pyramids (p. 342), belonged to a certain *Khafra-ankh* and his wife *Herneka*. The representations and hieroglyphics it contains are either partly or entirely obliterated. Khafra-ankh was a 'semer' or companion, and a 'suten rekh', or blood-relation of the king, to whom his wife, a priestess of Neith, was also related. He is extolled as the illustrious priest of the Pyramid of Khafra, surnamed 'the great'. On the E. wall of the principal chamber we see writers engaged in recording the number of cattle of each kind possessed by the deceased. The representatives of the different flocks placed beside the numbers are admirably executed, and faithful to nature even in their attitudes. The sign 𓏤 is equivalent to 1, 𓎆 to 10, and 𓍢 to 100, these symbols being repeated so as to represent the hundreds, tens, and units of which the various flocks consisted. Thus 𓍢𓍢𓍢𓍢𓎆𓎆𓏤𓏤𓏤 / 𓍢𓍢𓍢𓍢𓎆𓏤𓏤 coupled with the figure of a bull, indicates that Khafra-ankh possessed 835 bulls, and in a similar manner we are informed that he had 220 cattle without horns, 760 asses, 2235 goats of the antelope kind, and 974 goats. Besides these animals we also distinguish the more or less obliterated representations of a voyage on the river, the measurement of corn, the felling of trees, etc., and on the S. wall we find a portrait of the deceased and his wife, both in a sitting posture, with tables covered with offerings before them.

***Campbell's Tomb**, which may be visited on the way back from the Sphinx to the Great Pyramid, is larger than most of the others mentioned below. It is of comparatively late origin, dating, as the inscriptions record, from the 7th cent. and the 26th Dynasty. The upper part has been entirely destroyed, and the deep and wide shaft, at the bottom of which is a tomb-chamber vaulted with an arch having a span of 11 ft., is now uncovered. The tomb was discovered in the course of excavations made by Col. Vyse in 1837, and named by him after Col. Campbell, the British consul-general of Egypt at that period. The shaft is $30^1/_2$ ft. wide from E. to W., 26 ft. from N. to S., and $53^3/_4$ ft. in depth. The sarcophagi found here were in niches, and not in the vaulted chamber. One of these, now in the British Museum, is composed of red granite, and prismatic in form, and bears numerous inscriptions. The arched lid bears the portrait of a bearded mummy at its upper end, and a profusion of funereal scenes and inscriptions in the style of the 26th Dynasty. Two sarcophagi in basalt and another in whitish quartzose stone were also found here. From all of these the bodies had been removed. The vaulted chapel had also been forcibly entered on the W. side, but the passage is now closed.

***Circuit of the Pyramid Plateau of Gizeh** (comp. p. 343). After having inspected the Great Pyramid externally and internally (p. 354), we turn (following the dotted line on the Map, p. 354) to the left (W.) of the entrance, descend the mound of debris, and proceed to the N.W. angle of the Pyramid, where its foundation-stone (Pl. *b*) has been exposed to view. Towards the W. and S.W. lie numerous tombs (maṣṭabas, p. 379), but they present no attraction, being almost all in very bad preservation and more than half buried in the sand.

We may, however, notice two of these maṣṭabas, situated not far from the above mentioned foundation-stone, but now covered with sand. In one of these, built by a certain Senet' em-ab, were found several carefully executed scenes, including a representation of the deceased in a litter, borne by thirteen servants, and followed by two large dogs. The other tomb belonged to another Senet' em-ab (*i.e.* 'good' or 'perfect name'), surnamed 'Meha', who seems to have been one of the most distinguished dignitaries of his time, and was married to Khent-kau-s, a king's daughter. He was a priest of high rank, treasurer, and superintendent of the corn-magazines, which last office, recalling the history of Joseph, was instituted at a very early period He was at the same time a minister of war, or literally 'president of the double house of war'.

Opposite the N W angle of the Second Pyramid, and also now filled with sand, are the tombs of three other Egyptian magnates of the 5th Dynasty, containing a genealogical record of a family which enjoyed the distinction of being 'suten rekh' (p 367), or related to the king, for four generations As the kings themselves are also mentioned here, these tombs have materially facilitated the compilation of an accurate list of the members of the 5th Dynasty The ancestor of this family Shepseskaf-ankh, lived in the reign of the Pharaoh Shepseskaf. His eldest son Aimeri served under Nefer-ar-ka-ra, and Ptah-bau-nefer, the son of Aimeri, was a priest of Ra-en-user, and is also styled a prophet of Khufu, *i e* of the *manes* of the builder of the First Pyramid Two jambs from this maṣṭaba, and the architrave belonging to them, are now in the museum at Berlin. The eldest son of Ptah-bau-nefer was called Ptah-nefer-sam To the same family belonged Ata, who also served under Ra-en-user, apparently in the capacity of a director of music, as he styles himself 'president of song, who delights the heart of his lord by his beautiful song in the inner chambers (khennu) of the lofty gate'. The Egyptian word 'peraa' which occurs in this inscription is the root of the word Pharaoh used in the Bible

The largest and best preserved of these tombs lie to the N.W. of the Second Pyramid (see dotted line in Plan, p. 354), near the point *e*. A handsome gateway and a well-preserved hieroglyphic inscription are still to be seen here. To the N. of this point are also several rows of tombs now filled up.

We now skirt the W. side of the vast necropolis, and reach the N.W. angle of the rocky enclosure of the court of the *Second Pyramid*. A natural cleft in the rock here facilitates our descent from the top of the rock, which is 16 ft. in height. At the foot of it we reach the plateau which was hewn in the rock in order to prepare a level surface for this pyramid (p. 359). Part of the surface on the N side is divided by means of deep incisions and transverse furrows into six rows of squares, the object of which is unknown. On the rock above is inscribed the name of Ramses II. in hieroglyphics. On the E. side of the Second Pyramid are remains of the temple once connected with it (p. 359). We follow the W. side of the Pyramid. On the rock to the right is a hieroglyphic inscription (Pl. f; the name of an architect, and uninteresting), near which are several rock-tombs. One of these tombs (Pl. *g*), nearly opposite the S.W. angle of the Pyramid, has a "Ceiling hewn in the rock in imitation of palm-stems. (Visitors should beware of falling into the tomb-shaft.)

In passing the W. side of the Pyramid the visitor has an opportunity of observing, that, although several triangular blocks of granite are strewn around, which perhaps once formed the lower portion of the external incrustation of the Pyramid, the upper quarter of the Pyramid is covered with a hard kind of conglomerate composed of limestone, broken bricks, and plaster.

Our route now leads towards the S.W. to the *Third Pyramid* (p. 360), once entirely covered with huge blocks of granite, the lower courses of which are still in tolerable preservation. We walk round the Pyramid on the W and S. sides, near the latter of which stand three smaller pyramids (p. 362), then leave the temple (p. 360) belonging to the Third Pyramid on the left, and descend by a good path towards the E.

We observe here on the left another series of rock-tombs dating from the 4th and 5th Dynasties. Among these is that of **Tebehen** (Pl *h*), containing a long list of offerings with representations of persons dancing with raised arms and feet before the altar In a small hollow a little farther to the N is a tomb embellished with four columns (Pl. *i*), the well-preserved inscriptions of which contain the name of Psametik Another tomb belonged to a priest, a relative of the Khafra 'who had to honour the Pyramid Uer ('the great') of King Khafra'.

In the valley before us, to the right, rises a projecting ridge of rock containing tombs of no interest. Adjoining this rock, on the left, are two sycamores and a date-palm, rising above an Arabian burial-place. Still farther to the E we observe the remains of the stone dam leading from the plain of the Nile to the Third Pyramid (p. 344). To the left of the trees rises a kind of truncated *Tower*, constructed partly of the natural rock and partly of masonry, and supposed to have been a tomb. Passing through it, we come to other tombs on the left, also covered with sand. One of these was that of *Urkhuu* (Pl. *k*), who seems to have been a kind of minister of public instruction in the reign of Neter-ar-ka-ra, as he bore the titles of — 'the royal and learned writer of the lofty gate, the learned president of the art of writing, who brings light into the writings of the double house of the tomb'. We next reach the *Sphinx* (p. 362), 150 paces to the S.E. of which is the entrance to the *Granite Temple* (p. 365). On the S. horizon, at a distance of $6^1/_4$ M., rise the pyramids of Abuṣîr (p. 370) and the step-pyramid of Saḳḳâra (p. 382).

In order to complete our circuit of the plateau of the Pyramids, we proceed from the Sphinx towards the W. to 'Campbell's Tomb' (p. 367), ascend thence to the Great Pyramid, and pass three uninteresting small pyramids on the right. (That in the centre, according to Herodotus, was the tomb of a daughter of Cheops; that to the S, according to an inscription preserved in the Museum of Bûlâḳ, belonged to Hentsen, another daughter of the same king.) We skirt the E. side of the Great Pyramid to the left, where there are two long 'mortar-pits' (Pl. *m*), and soon regain the Kiosque of the Khedive (p. 342), from which we started. The so-called Tomb of Numbers (p. 366) is on the E. side of the plateau, a little above the mud-huts of the Beduins.

The Pyramids of Abû Roâsh, the northernmost group in the Necropolis of Memphis, present little attraction, and are not worth visiting. Standing in front of the viceroyal kiosque on the plateau of the Great Pyramid of Gîzeh, we perceive towards the N. an abrupt ridge of rock descending to a branch of the Nile, and to the right, at its base, two villages shaded by palm trees. The nearer of these is *Kerdâsa*, the inhabitants of which are occupied in cutting flints for the primitive guns still used in Egypt The large quantities of splinters seen here suggest to us that the so-called 'flint tools' (p 485) found in other parts of Egypt may possibly be merely the refuse from similar workshops. Immediately beyond Kerdâsa is **Abu Roash**, which may be reached in 1¾-2 hrs. by a route skirting the desert On the margin of the plateau close to Abû Roâsh on the N.W side, rise the shapeless remains of a *Pyramid of Nile Mud*, which is constructed round a nucleus of massive stone. On a ridge of rock descending precipitously to the margin of the desert, and reached by a path ascending a hollow, near the white tomb of a shêkh, and ¼ hr. before the Mud Pyramid is reached, are situated the remains of two pyramids One of these now consists of four or five courses of stone only, and (according to Col. Vyse) contains a chamber reached from the N side by a passage inclined at an angle of 22°, and 53 yds in length. Each side measures 124 yds. The other pyramid, to the W. of the last, is now a mere heap of ruins. A stone dyke, about 600 yds. in length, leads from the N to the hill on which these two pyramids stand. Numerous fragments of granite strewn about here indicate that this material has been used either for the construction of the tomb-chambers or for the external incrustation of the pyramid No inscriptions were found here Distinct traces of a necropolis now entirely destroyed are observable near these two pyramids, and also on the plateau ascending to the W from the Mud Pyramid. The pyramids of Abû Roâsh seem to belong to one of the first dynasties, but nothing certain is known about them.

From Gîzeh to Abusîr and Sakkâra (p. 371) is a ride of about 2¼ hrs, skirting the margin of the desert To the left lie patches of cultivated land and a number of ponds, containing more or less water in accordance with the height of the last inundation, bordered with vegetation, and frequented by numerous birds; beyond which flows the Bahr Yûsuf arm of the Nile (p 456) After 1 hr we observe the remains of two pyramids on the right. The first of these (N), near the village of *Zâweyet el-'Aryân*, must once have been an important monument, as the sides are still nearly 100 yds in length The second (S.), near the hovels of *Riga*, is now a mere heap of debris In one hour more, passing the village of *Shoberment*, we reach the **Pyramids of Abusîr** (comp. Map, p 378), the ancient *Busiris* (2 hrs. to the S S E. of the Pyramids of Gîzeh, and ¾ hr to the N N E. of Sakkâra), situated on a rocky eminence covered with sand. The masonry of these monuments, having originally been constructed with no great care, is now much damaged, and their bases are covered with sand, so that a visit to them is uninteresting. They were erected by kings of the 5th Dynasty. The entrances are on the N sides, and, as in all the other pyramids, there is a passage, at first slanting and afterwards horizontal, leading to the chamber in the centre. The northernmost of the three largest pyramids (once fourteen in number), lying close together, belonged to a certain *Sahura*, and was styled that of the 'glorious emerging' (*i e* of the deceased into another world). At a very early period divine honours were accorded to this Pharaoh, and sacrifices were offered to his *manes* so late as the time of the Ptolemies. The pyramid was enclosed by a wall, to which a still traceable path ascended from a building (probably a temple) situated in the plain. Its perpendicular height was 163½ ft. (now 118 ft.), its sides were 258½ ft.

(now 217¼ ft.) in length, and they were inclined at an angle of 51° 42′ 35″. With regard to the central one of these pyramids, that to the S of the last, the inscriptions state that 'the dwelling of *Ra-en-user* stands fast'. Ti (p 388) and other priests, whose mastabas were found at Sakkâra, presided over the rites connected with this pyramid According to very ancient inscriptions, a peculiar kind of monument (an obelisk standing on a truncated pyramid), dedicated to the sun, and bearing the name of Rashepuab, is said once to have stood near the pyramid of Ra-en-user. The name of the largest pyramid (sides 108, formerly 120½ yds , perpendicular height 165, formerly 229 ft), situated a little to the S W , is unknown. Perring (p 351) found that all the chambers had been entered and plundered. The other pyramids are mere heaps of ruins, and one of them (to the S.W. of the largest) seems never to have been completed

Continuing our route to Sakkâra, we leave to the left a pond and the village of *Abuṣîr*, situated beyond a group of palms to the S E , and soon reach the sandy eminences of the Necropolis of Memphis, at the beginning of which the tomb of Ti is situated.

The Site of Ancient Memphis and the Necropolis of Sakkâra.

A visit to Memphis and Sakkâra may easily be accomplished in one day by the aid of the railway, but 1½-2 days may profitably be devoted to the excursion There are, indeed, but few of the tombs in the Necropolis of Sakkâra which are accessible to the ordinary visitor, but the interiors of these are so interesting, that many travellers will find them worthy of careful and repeated inspection A tent is not absolutely necessary for the expedition The traveller may pass the night at Mariette's house (p 377), or on its covered terrace, or, if necessary, in one of the numerous caverns in the neighbouring rocks. A blanket is a sufficient covering in spring. Provisions should not be forgotten, and liquors may, if necessary, be procured at Bedrashên at the shop of a Greek 'bakkâl' (on the right, beyond the bridge)

Railway (*Ligne de la Haute-Egypte*) The station of *Bûlâk ed-Dakrûr* is situated on the left bank of the Nile, 3 M from Cairo, a drive of ½ hr (5 fr) The train, starting daily at 8.30 a m , runs thence to Bedrashên (see below) in ½ hr (fares 10 pias 20 paras, 7 pias ; fare for donkey and attendant, 2½ fr ; see below) The inspection of the site of Memphis, and the ride to Mariette's House, occupy 2 hrs , for luncheon and a visit to the tombs 4 hrs should be allowed, and for returning to the station of Bedrashên 2 hrs more The train from Upper Egypt generlaly reaches Bedrashên about 6. 30 p m , so that the traveller should leave Sakkâra a little after 4 o'clock The hotel at Cairo will thus be regained about 8 p.m. It is desirable to arrive in good time both at Bûlâk and Bedrashên, as the train, though generally late, occasionally starts before its time.

Those who wish to spend a night at Sakkâra may return from Bedrashên to Cairo either on the second evening (as above), or at 10 45 a m. by the special train from the Fayûm (see p 456), or the traveller may start at 3 p m. from Bûlâk ed-Dakrûr for Bedrashên by the Fayûm train, ride in the evening to Sakkâra, and thus have the whole of the next dav at his disposal. It should, however, be remarked that the trains to and from the Fayûm start from Bûlâk ed-Dakrûr at the time when the Nile bridge at Gezîreh is open for the passage of vessels (during 2 hrs). Crossing the river in a small boat is not recommended, owing to the great confusion which prevails — Donkeys with good saddles may now be obtained in Bedrashên, so that it is no longer necessary to bring them from Cairo.

On leaving the station we observe the Pyramids of Gîzeh (p. 343) on the right, in such a position, that the Pyramid of Cheops conceals the other two. The view to the left is at first hidden by the lofty walls of the large estate at Gîzeh (p. 341), which formerly belonged to the Khedive but is now state property. At the S. end of the wall is the old private station of the Khedive Ismaʿîl, now disused. On the left, beyond the Nile, we now perceive Old Cairo with its windmill hills, above which rises the long ridge of the Moḳaṭṭam, separated from the heights of the Wâdi et-Tih (p. 339) to the S. by the broad depression of the Gebel Ṭura (p. 403). On the banks of the Nile are the large military establishments of Ṭura. To the right rise the hills of the Libyan desert with the Pyramids of Abuṣîr (p. 370). We next observe the step-pyramid, which, however, soon disappears behind a grove of palms. On the right and left of the line are tracts of arable land.

The (14 M.) station of Bedrashên lies to the left of the line, and near it is a very ancient and most interesting Jewish burial-ground. We ride across the railway, turn to the right, and cross a bridge to the mud-huts of *Bedrashên*, scantily shaded by palm-trees. Beyond the bridge (a Greek 'baḳḳâl' on the right; p. 371) we turn to the S. (left), leaving the village on the right, and ride on the embankment to the W. towards a conspicuous palm-grove. Immediately beyond the last houses of Bedrashên we observe to the right, at a distance of 1/2 M., a lofty heap of rubbish, belonging to a government manufactory of saltpetre. On each side of the embankment lie green fields in spring and summer, and large expanses of water in autumn and the first half of winter. The embankment ends near the first trees of the palm-groves, 20 min. from the station.

There are two different routes hence to Saḳḳâra, used at different seasons. One of these (the 'summer-route') leads due W., past the colossal figure of Ramses II., and, leaving the village of *Mitrahîneh* on the right, to the village of Saḳḳâra, but it is not practicable at the season of inundation. The other route ('winter-road') diverges from the embankment to the right, traverses the whole length of the palm-grove, leaves the village of Mitrahîneh a long way to the left, and reaches another embankment farther on.

The insignificant sandy expanse before us, shaded by palms, and strewn with blocks of granite, broken pottery, and fragments of brick, is the ancient **Site of Memphis**, which is now interesting in an historical point of view only. We observe from the characteristics of the ruins, that the ancient Egyptians built their edifices, with the exception of palaces and temples, of large sun-dried bricks of Nile-mud. Were it not for the vast Necropolis to the W. of the ancient city, no one would imagine that one of the most famous and populous capitals of antiquity had once stood here. It is not now possible to form any precise idea of the situation of the city; and as its stones were carried off in former centuries to build edifices on the right bank of the Nile (see p. 374), the relics found here have been very scanty. The narrow streets, which are still said to have been half-a-day's journey in length down to the

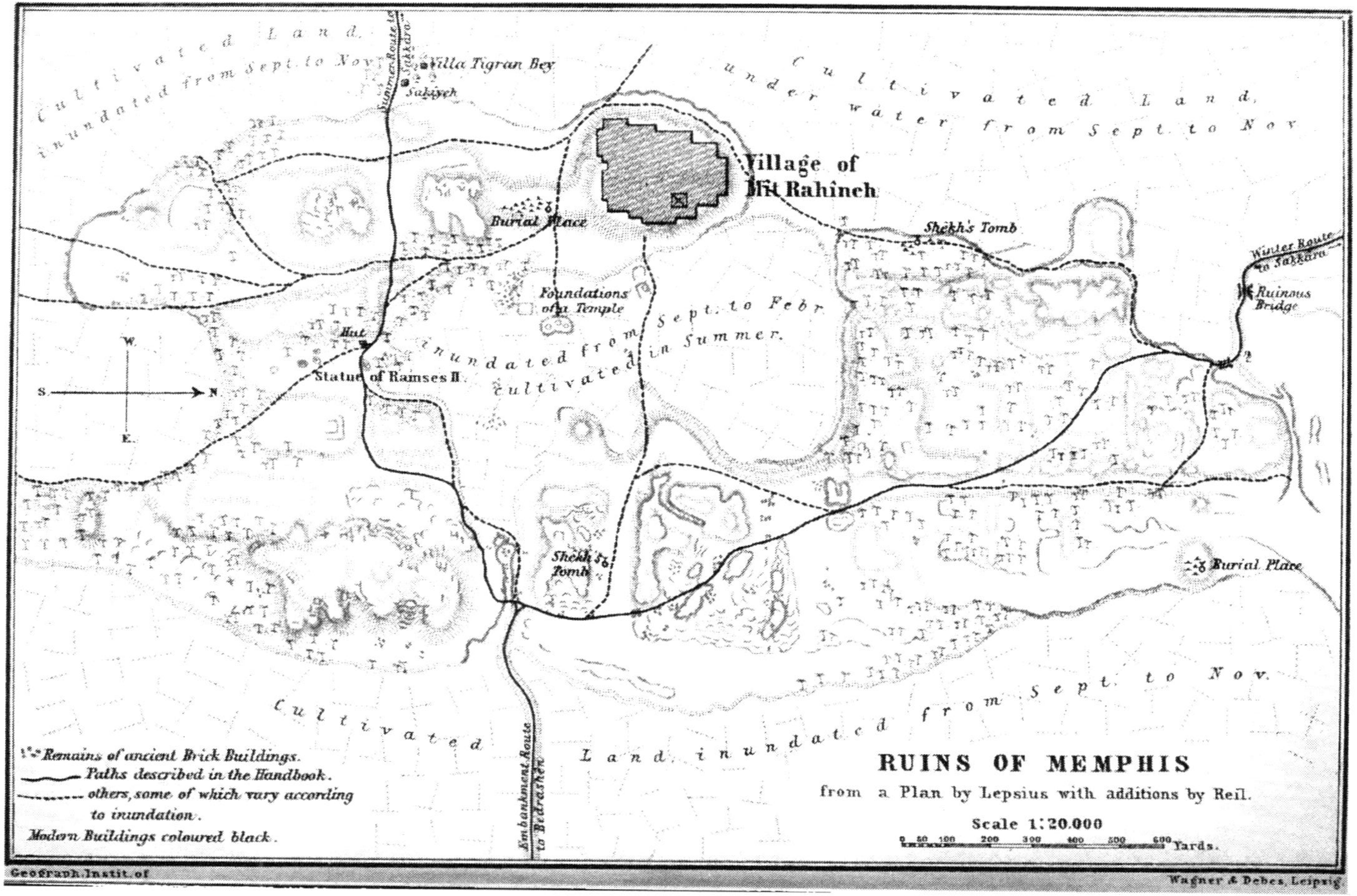
Cultivated Land, inundated from Sept. to Nov.
Summer Route to Sakkara
Villa Tigran Bey
Sakiyeh
Cultivated Land, under water from Sept. to Nov.
Village of Mit Rahineh
Burial Place
Shekh's Tomb
Winter Route to Sakkara
Ruinous Bridge
Foundations of a Temple
inundated from Sept. to Febr. cultivated in Summer.
Hut
Statue of Ramses II
W.
S.
N.
E.
Shekh's Tomb
Burial Place
Cultivated Land, inundated from Sept. to Nov.
Embankment Route to Bedrashen
Remains of ancient Brick Buildings.
Paths described in the Handbook.
others, some of which vary according to inundation.
Modern Buildings coloured black.
RUINS OF MEMPHIS
from a Plan by Lepsius with additions by Reil.
Scale 1:20.000
0 50 100 200 300 400 500 600 Yards.
Geograph. Instit. of
Wagner & Debes, Leipzig

12th cent., extended between the Nile and the Bahr Yûsuf, to the N. as far as Gîzeh, and to the S. about as far as the latitude of the Pyramids of Dahshûr. The most important quarters of the city and many of its public buildings appear to have stood in the fields of the villages of Bedrashên, Mîtrahîneh, and Kasrîyeh.

Menes (p. 86), 'the enduring', 'the eternal', who is placed by the Egyptians at the head of all their dynasties (having been immediately preceded by the dynasty of the gods), and is described as a man of This (near Abydos in Central Egypt, the district which Diodorus calls the oldest part of Egypt), is said to have been the founder of the Empire, and the builder of *Memphis*. Herodotus states that he was told by the Egyptian priests, that Menes had constructed an embankment across the Nile about 100 stadia above Memphis, and thus compelled the river, which had formerly flowed past the Libyan chain, to quit its old channel, and to run between the two ranges of hills. When the land thus reclaimed had become sufficiently firm, he built upon it the city of Memphis, situated in the narrow part of Egypt. To the N. and the W. of the city, as they informed him, Menes caused a lake to be excavated for its defence, and to be filled from the river, which protected the town on the E. side; while within the city he erected the great and memorable *Temple of Ptah*. The whole history of the city is associated with this vast sanctuary, which included within its precincts the temples of other gods, was surrounded by a wall, and must have commanded the city like a huge castle.

Memphis, like all the Egyptian towns, was known by several different names. In the first place, like the nome around it, it was called the 'city of the white wall', after the castle, which was well known even in the Greek period. Another name, derived from the deity most highly revered by the citizens, was *Ha Ptah* ('house of Ptah'), which the Greeks translated *Hephaistopolis*. Lastly it was known by the popular name of *Men-nefer*, *i. e.* 'good place', or 'haven of the good'. The *r* at the end of Men-nefer was then dropped, and thus arose the Coptic form *Menfi* or *Memfi*, which the Greeks and Romans changed to *Memphis*, and the Arabs to *Menf*. The quarter where the licentious rites of the Egyptian and Phœnician goddess of love were celebrated, and where strangers were afterwards allowed to settle, was called *Ta-ankh*, *i. e.* 'the world of life'.

Menes was succeeded by his son Atahuti, or Athothis, who made Memphis his capital, and is said to have built the royal palace. During his reign and that of his successors of the primæval monarchy, Memphis attained its greatest prosperity. Each of the Pharaohs extended and embellished the temple. Memphis suffered severely from the invasion and during the domination of the Hyksos (2194-1683). The Pharaohs of the new empire who expelled the intruders (p. 89) resided at Thebes, the city of Ammon, but by no means forgot their ancient capital, the city of Ptah and Apis. During the 21st Dynasty the seat of government was transferred to Saïs (p. 445), the proximity of which restored to Memphis a share of its ancient glory, though but for a short period. The city was besieged and captured several times by the Assyrians, and also by the Ethiopian Piankhi who offered great sacrifices to Ptah in the 'City of the White Wall'. Cambyses, the first monarch of the Persian dynasty, took the city by storm after his victory at Pelusium (B.C. 525) over Psammetikh III. (the last king of the 26th Dyn.); and two centuries later it was entirely eclipsed by the foundation of Alexandria (B.C. 332), although it still retained some importance during the Roman period (B.C 30). In consequence of the edict of Theodosius (A.D 379-395; comp. p. 100) the temples and statues were destroyed, and under the later Byzantine monarchs the heretical Monophysites (p. 101) seem to have been very numerous here. Makaukas, the leader of the Copts, was established at Memphis while negociating with 'Amr Ibn el-'Asi, the general of 'Omar. The Mohammedan conquerors transferred their residence to the right bank of the Nile (comp. p. 241), opposite the northernmost part of Memphis, using the well-hewn blocks, which had once composed the venerable palaces and temples of the ancient city of Menes, for the construction of their palaces, castles, and mosques. Memphis, however, was so vast, that it was long before its plunderers succeeded in entirely destroying it. Down to a late period its ruins excited the admiration of all visitors. Thus 'Abdellaṭîf (at the end of the 12th cent), after a lively account of numerous attacks sustained by the enormous city, assures us that even in his time, the ruins contained a profusion of wonders which bewildered the mind and baffled description. 'The more profoundly we contemplate the ruins (he says), the greater does the admiration become with which they inspire us; and every new survey we take becomes a source of fresh delight' On beholding the ruins he cannot help regarding as pardonable the popular belief, that the ancient Egyptians were giants of prodigious longevity, who had the power of moving masses of rock with a magician's wand. — After the time of 'Abdellaṭîf the rapidly dwindling ruins of Memphis are rarely mentioned. Stone after stone was transferred as from a quarry to the opposite bank of the Nile, and we are told that the site was systematically explored by treasure-seekers, who took many centuries to exhaust its precious relics.

The * **Colossal Statue of Ramses II.** lies in a hollow, having unfortunately fallen with its face to the ground. The head is turned towards the S.W. This huge statue was discovered by Messrs. Caviglia and Sloane (p. 354) in 1820, and presented to the British Museum, but owing to the difficulty of transport it has never been removed. It consists of remarkably hard and fine-grained limestone, and before it was injured was about 42 ft. in height. The workmanship is admirable. The features, which resemble the Semitic type, are exactly similar to those of this great monarch (the Sesostris of the Greeks) as portrayed on numerous other monuments, particularly at Thebes. He wears the royal head-dress (pshent) with the Uræus snake, which is crowned with a cylinder sloping slightly outwards, and resembling the modius in the head of Serapis. An artificial beard is attached to the chin. On his breast the king wears a shield terminating in a groove at the top (perhaps a kind of pouch, such as were worn by the Jewish priests and those of Serapis), in the centre of which is inscribed his pronomen Ra-user-ma setep en Ra, *i.e.* 'god of the sun, mighty in the truth, approved by the sun', while the god Ptah (p. 126), and the lion-headed Sekhet (Bast) stand by as bearers; the girdle, in which a dagger is worn, bears both the pronomen and the surname of Ramses, the favourite of Ammon, which is also inscribed on the front of the scroll or staff which he holds in his left hand. On the back of the support of the left leg, which is in the attitude of stepping forward, are two vertical rows of hieroglyphics, the lower parts of which are broken off — 1st Line: 'the princess and great . . .'; 2nd Line: 'the king's (daughter), the great . . .' These fragments of inscriptions show that the figure of a daughter of the king was placed at his feet. The figure of a son is still distinctly recognisable, the arm being raised in an attitude of prayer, and the hand touching the knee of the statue. — There can be no doubt that this statue, the face of which, when erect, was turned towards the N., is one of those erected by Ramses II. in front of the temple of Ptah (p. 373) at Memphis. In the time of Strabo it perhaps stood alone in the anterior court, which was used for bull-fights. 'A colossal statue of a single stone', he observes, 'stands in the entrance court before the temple of Ptah. Bull-fights were exhibited here, for which express purpose some persons keep bulls, as horse-trainers rear horses'. According to Herodotus two of these statues were 30 cubits in height, which, as the Greek cubit was only about 1½ ft. in length, nearly corresponds to the 42 ft. which the statue actually measures. Both Herodotus and Diodorus state that Sesostris (Ramses II.), on his return from a great and victorious campaign, was invited at Pelusium on the Egyptian frontier, with his wife and children, to a banquet at the house of his brother. The latter, desiring to assassinate Ramses, caused his tent to be surrounded with dry reeds after the banquet, and to be set on fire. The intoxicated servants rendered inefficient aid, and the king's wife and children were in the utmost danger. The king, thereupon, raised his hands in prayer, dashed into the flames, and rescued them. Out of gratitude he then erected this statue, at the foot of which the figures of a prince and princess were placed. Accessory figures of a similar kind, however, are frequently found with other statues to which no such story attaches.

Close to the statue, on the left, in front of a fellâḥ-hut, are remains of a statue, including a colossal foot, which, however, being of sandstone, probably did not belong to the statue of Ramses, which is composed of limestone. In a number of hollows, to the right of the colossal statue. we observe remains of foundations, the most important of which are 5 min to the N.W., beyond the projecting angle of the palm-grove, and due E. from the village of Mîtrahîneh. M. Mariette supposed these to be the foundation of a temple of Ptah (Vulcan). During the inundation the whole of the low ground is under water, and then resembles a lake surrounded by palm-groves.

In 1851-54 Hekekyan Bey, an Armenian, was employed by the London Geological Society to make excavations here; and having sunk shafts at 96 different places, he found bones of domestic animals, fragments of pottery and bricks, and various implements (*e g* a copper knife), at different depths Near the colossal statue, beneath strata of Nile-mud, which had not been covered with sand from the desert, was discovered a fragment of red terracotta, at a depth of 39 ft It therefore appears, that since the erection of the statue of Ramses, about the middle of the 14th cent B C, the deposit of Nile-mud around it has attained a thickness of nearly 10 ft without reckoning a layer of sand 8 in in thickness. The alluvial deposits at this spot must thus have increased at the rate of 3³/₁in in each century from the middle of the 14th cent. B.C down to the present time If the thickness of the deposit above the terracotta fragment increased at the same rate, it would follow that the earthenware vessels were manufactured on the banks of the Nile 11,646 years before Christ It need hardly be said, however, that this mode of computation is very untrustworthy And yet 'who would venture to deny that this fragment of pottery, buried at a depth of 39 ft, may be at least 4000 years older than the monument of the great Ramses'? *(Peschel.)*

From Mîtrahîneh (Memphis) *to Saḳḳâra.* (1) Spring Route. We ride towards the W. from the statue of Ramses, leaving the village of Mîtrahîneh at a little distance to the right (see Maps, pp. 372, 378). On quitting the palm-grove we obtain an interesting view; immediately to the right, shaded by palm-trees and lebbeks, is a small villa belonging to Tigran Bey, a nephew of Nubar Pasha. About 1 M to the W. is another long palm-grove surrounding Saḳḳâra and bordering the desert; beyond this, on the yellow sand of the desert, rise eleven pyramids. The first of these, to the left, is the outer mud-pyramid, beyond which are the blunted pyramid, the first mud-pyramid, and the great pyramid, all belonging to the group of Dahshûr (p. 402). Not far from these we next perceive the Masṭaba Far'ûn, with the pyramid of Pepi II; then, exactly above the houses of Saḳḳâra, two pyramids, the lesser of which is that of Pepi I.; and, lastly, to the right, the pyramid of Unas. the great step-pyramid, and two smaller ones (to the right, that of Teta). These last eight pyramids belong to the group of Saḳḳâra. — Having nearly reached (3/4 hr from the statue of Ramses) Saḳḳâra, we leave the village, which is uninteresting, to the left, turn towards the N., and skirt the palm-groves. (At the end of these, on the left, is a beautiful, shady sycamore, close to a spring of good water, and the tomb of a shêkh.) We now reach the margin of the desert, the route still leading towards the N., and ascend to the plateau of the Necropolis (p. 378).

(2) Winter Route. During the period of the inundation, after having visited the statue of Ramses, we return to the (5 min.) end

of the embankment (see p. 372), which leads back to Bedrashên, and then turn to the N. and traverse the whole of the plantation, until we reach another embankment which winds across the plain towards the W., and is interrupted by two bridges. Distance from the statue of Ramses to the 1st bridge 20 min.; thence to the second bridge $1/4$ hr.; from this bridge to the margin of the desert 20 min.; and to Mariette's house 20 min. more. (The return-route to the station of Bedrashên will take nearly $1^1/_2$ hr., without stoppage.)

The two routes unite on the outskirts of the desert. and ascend to the plateau over the ruins of an ancient village which was perhaps inhabited by the embalmers of the dead. On the right are grottoes hewn in the rocks. Near the first of these is a deep shaft, now covered up, where human mummies, and those of several cats, were found In the third grotto, on the right, is the figure of a cow hewn in the rock, representing the goddess Hathor (p. 135).

The traveller may inspect the step-pyramid (p. 382) of Saḳḳâra on the way to Mariette's House, at which he is recommended to rest before visiting the rest of the Necropolis. This pyramid is reached by either of the paths indicated on the map (p. 378) in 20 minutes. One of these leads to the N., round the small pyramid nearest to the step-pyramid, and then turns to the W. through a sandy depression; the other path leads more to the left (N.W.), passing several tombs and shafts, straight in the direction of the *Step-Pyramid* (described at p. 382, and most conveniently visited in going or returning). Having crossed the E. enclosing wall, and passed round the N.E. corner, we obtain, near the closed entrance on the N. side, a striking view towards the N. In the foreground lies the green valley of the Nile, bordered by palm-trees, and framed on both sides with the yellowish-grey desert; and we also observe the alabaster mosque of Moḥammed 'Ali at Cairo. On the left tower the three pyramids of Gîzeh, 9 M. distant, and the three nearer pyramids of Abusîr. The path pursues a W. direction for a short distance, then turns to the right beyond the next heap of rubbish (N W.), crosses the hollow, and joins the above-mentioned path leading to Mariette's House. Strangers are quite at liberty to enter and use the broad covered terrace in front of the house, but for any very protracted occupation of it the permission of the museum authorities should be obtained. No charge is made for admission to the terrace, but it is usual to give a fee of 1 fr. or more, according to the number of the party, to the Beduins who take charge of the house, and who are much better conducted than their rapacious brethren of Gîzeh. A guide to the tombs must be taken at Mariette's House, as visitors are not admitted to them unattended. (Baḳshîsh for the tombs of Apis and Ti, 2 fr.)

The Chief Attractions of the Necropolis of Saḳḳâra are the *Step-Pyramid (p 382), the *Tombs of the Apis Bulls (p. 385), and the **Tomb of Ti (p. 388). Nearly 150 tombs dating from the ancient empire have been discovered, but most of them were in a ruined condition. Many of them, however, yielded interesting spoil to the scientific explorer, and copies were made from their monuments and decorations, but most of them have again been covered up to preserve them from the influence of the air and the rapacity of relic-hunters, so that the visitor is now hardly aware of their existence The scientific traveller, however, may obtain special permission from the museum authorities to unearth the interesting tomb of Ptahhotep (p 401), or any of the others.

The rocky margin of the plateau of the desert, between the village of Abusîr (p 370) and the road ascending from Sakkâra, contains numerous *Tomb-Chambers* (comp. p 382), none of which now merit a visit, except perhaps that of Bekenrauf, of the period of Psammetikh I. The Mastaba Far'ûn, see p. 402; the Pyramids of Dahshûr, p. 402

The *Grottoes of the Ibis Mummies and of the Cats*, containing a number of mummies piled up together, are now closed, being considered dangerous. The whole of the soil of the Necropolis is indeed so honeycombed with tombs that great caution should be used in traversing it. Some of the open shafts are no less than 50 ft in depth.

> 'The traveller is lost in the immense expanse of desert, which he sees full of Pyramids before him, is struck with terror at the unusual scene of vastness, and shrinks from attempting any discovery amidst the moving sands of Saccara' *Bruce.*

The **Necropolis of Sakkâra** (from Sokar, p. 126) extends over an undulating tract of the desert, which, according to M. Mariette's computation, is about 7700 yds. in length, and 550-1600 yds. in width. It contains sepulchral monuments of every kind, from the pyramid to the rock-hewn cavern, dating both from the ancient and the later empire. Many of the recent excavations are now covered with loose heaps of light-coloured sand. The whole of the Necropolis has been repeatedly explored both by the Byzantines and the Khalîfs, as well as by modern explorers. Many generations have been enriched by its treasures, and yet an immense profusion of relics was still left to be discovered by the indefatigable M. Mariette. It is nevertheless probable that this mine of antiquities, which has so marvellously preserved everything committed to its keeping, is still far from being exhausted.

Ancient writers have recorded many interesting facts regarding the Necropolis of Memphis, and have mentioned various parts of it by name. The Pyramids, eleven in number, have indeed been identified, and the Serapeum has been excavated, but all trace of many other features have been irrevocably lost. Who, for example, can possibly tell where now to look for the sacred lake across which the mummy of Apis was conveyed by boat; or the beautiful pastures near it, which were once compared with Homer's asphodel meadows; or the temple of the gloomy Hecate, and the gates of Cocytus and of Truth; or the site of the statue of Justice without a head; or the multitude of sacred and profane buildings mentioned by the later Greek papyri as having belonged to this burial-ground? On the other hand, the numerous tombs within its pre-

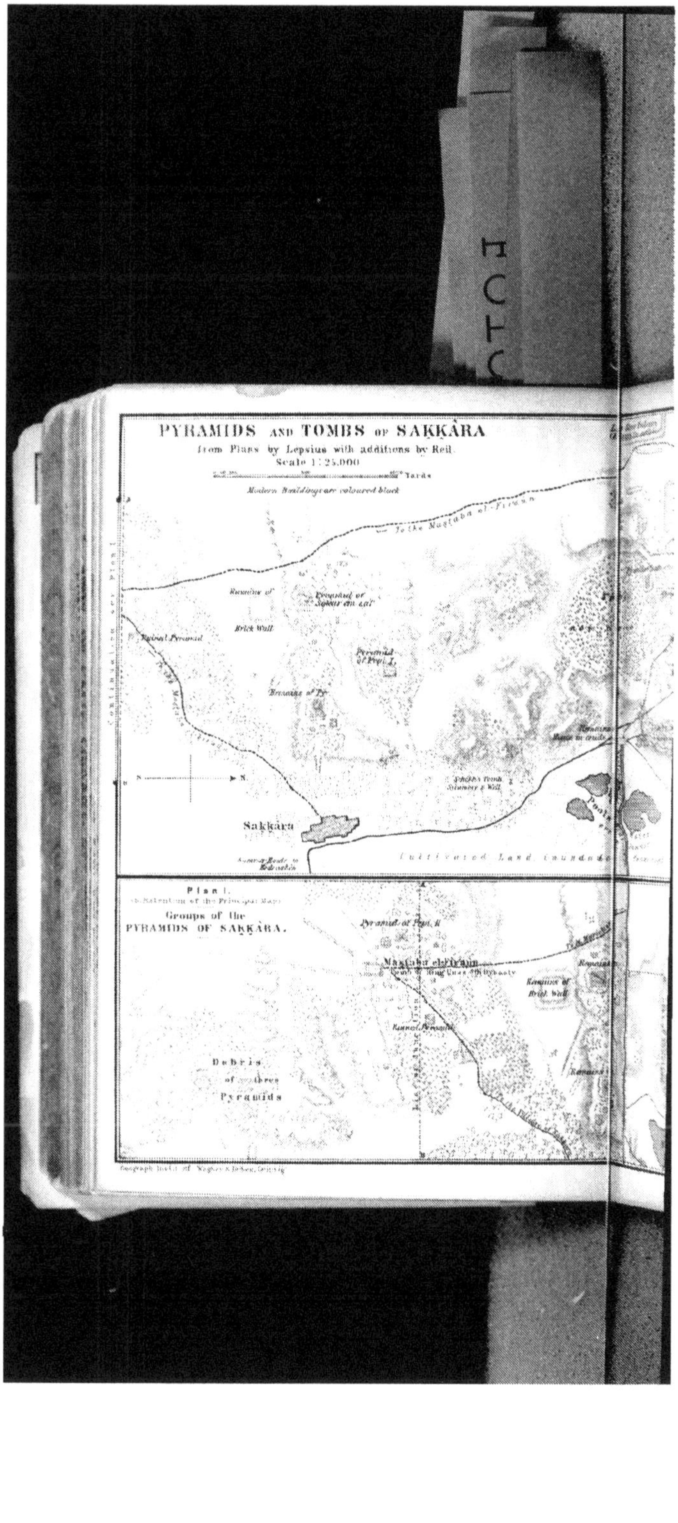
PYRAMIDS AND TOMBS OF SAKKÂRA
from Plans by Lepsius with additions by Reil.
Scale 1:25,000
Yards
Modern Buildings are coloured black
Pyramid of Pepi I.
Brick Wall
Sakkâra
Cultivated Land
Plan I.
Groups of the
PYRAMIDS OF SAKKÂRA.
Pyramid of Pepi II
Mastaba el-Fir'aun
Remains of Brick Wall
Debris of three Pyramids

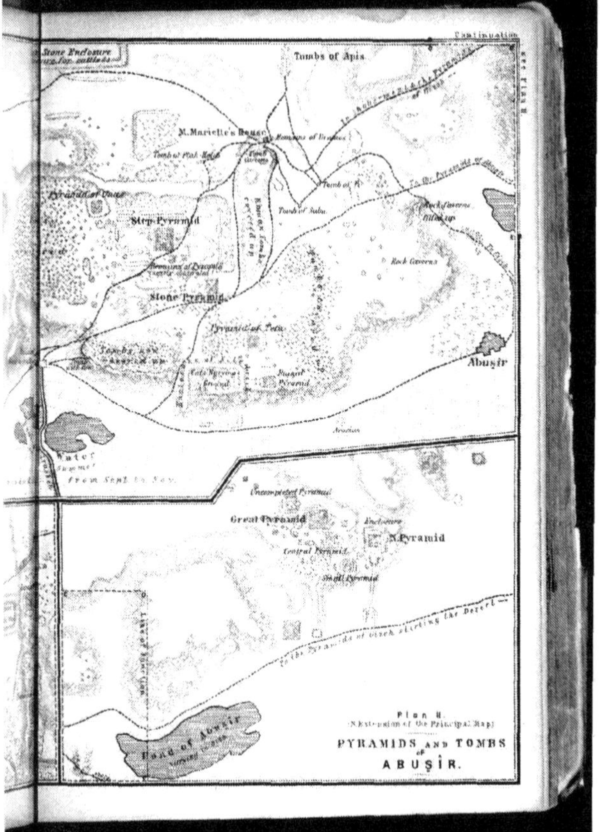
Tombs of Apis
M. Mariette's House
Step Pyramid
Stone Pyramid
Pyramid of Teta
Rock Caverns
Abuṣir
Uncompleted Pyramid
Great Pyramid
Enclosure
N. Pyramid
Central Pyramid
Small Pyramid
Plan II.
(Extension of the Principal Map)
PYRAMIDS AND TOMBS of ABUṢÎR.

INSERT
FOLD-OUT
OR MAP
HERE!

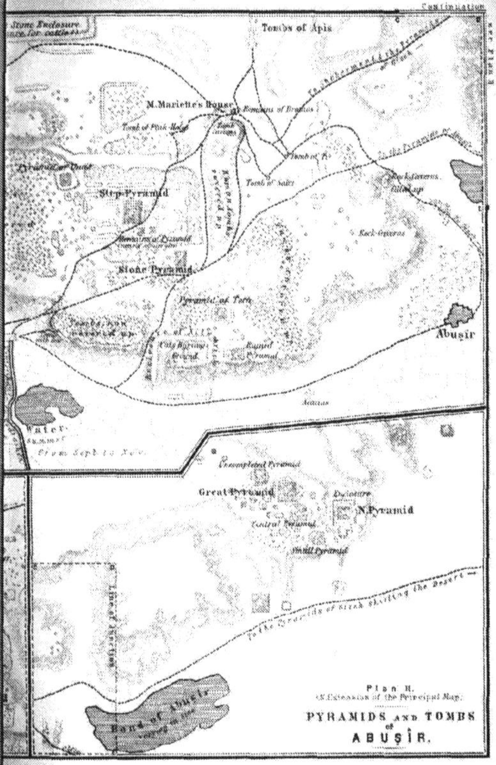
Tombs of Apis
M. Mariette's House
Remains of Bramas
Tomb of Ptah-Hotep
Step-Pyramid
Tomb of Sabi
Rock-Caverns
Stone Pyramid
Pyramid of Teti
Abusîr
Tombs, now covered up
City Burying Ground
Ruined Pyramid
Acacias
Water from Sept. to Nov.
Unfinished Pyramid
Great Pyramid
N. Pyramid
Central Pyramid
Small Pyramid
Line of Junction
Plan II.
PYRAMIDS AND TOMBS of ABUŞÎR.

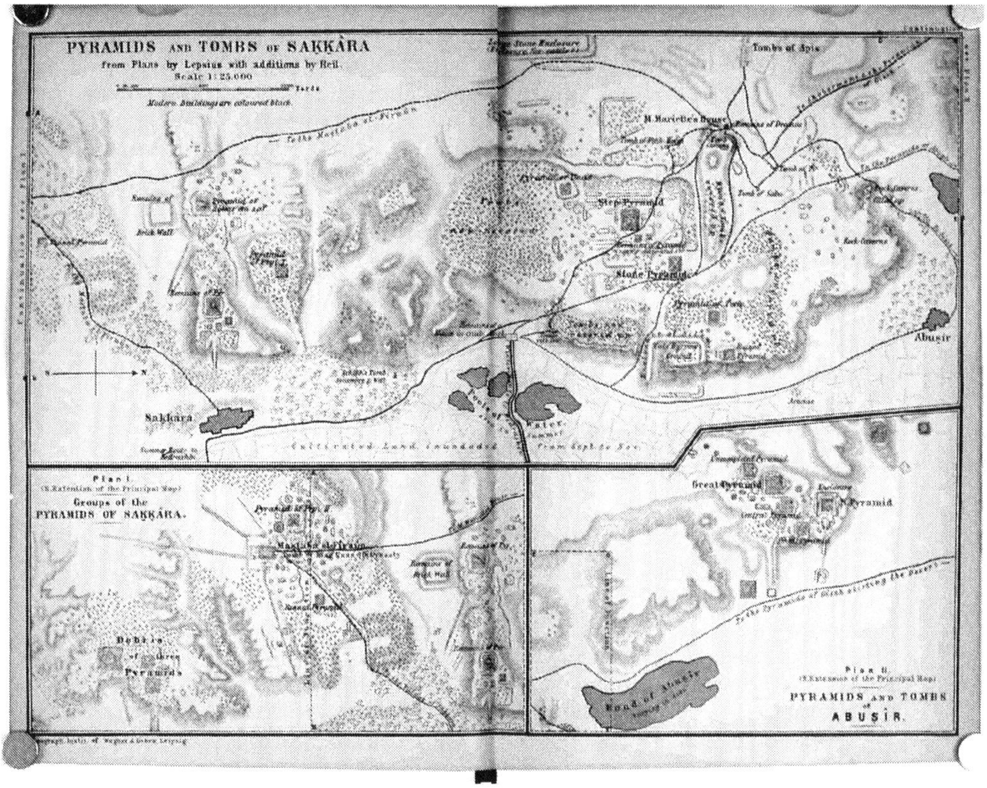

PYRAMIDS AND TOMBS OF SAKKÂRA
from Plans by Lepsius with additions by Reil.
Scale 1:25.000
Modern Buildings are coloured black.
To the Mastaba el-Farun
Brick Wall
Sakkara
Cultivated Land inundated from Sept. to Nov.
Water
Tombs of Apis
M. Mariette's House
Step Pyramid
Stone Pyramid
Abusir
Plan I.
(S. Extension of the Principal Map)
Groups of the
PYRAMIDS OF SAKKÂRA.
Mastaba el-Farun
Debris of three Pyramids
Great Pyramid
N. Pyramid
Plan II.
(N. Extension of the Principal Map)
PYRAMIDS AND TOMBS of ABUSIR.

cincts afford sufficient information with regard to the different periods at which its silent denizens were admitted.

The Tombs are of two kinds, viz. *Maṣṭabas* (literally 'benches') and *Rock-Chambers*. The **Maṣṭaba** is a mausoleum of solid masonry constructed on the surface of the earth. Its form is usually rectangular, and the walls slope inwards, so that the whole structure forms a kind of low truncated pyramid. Many of them are built of limestone-blocks of moderate size, and others of Nile-bricks. While the pyramids are always entered from the N., the door of the Maṣṭaba is usually on the E. side. On the stone door-posts generally rests the drum, a cylindrical block of stone, probably in imitation of the round section of a palm trunk, such as still usually covers the doorways of huts built of Nile-mud or sun-dried bricks. The drum usually bears the name of the deceased, but rarely his titles, which are often very lengthy. Grand-children and other near relations of the Pharaohs, however, are distinguished by the  added to their names, being a title of honour which might be translated — 'blood relation of the king'. The door-posts occasionally bear a full-length representation of the deceased; and, where there is no drum, the architrave of the door sometimes bears an inscription. The arrangements of the interior vary. At the back of the principal chamber there is usually a monument with numerous inscriptions, giving the whole of the titles of the deceased, the names of his nearest relations, and a number of prayers, generally addressed to Anubis, the guide of souls in the infernal regions and the tutelary god of the realms of the dead. In front of these monuments, and in presence of the family, it was usual for the priests appointed for the purpose to perform the rites due to the *manes* of the deceased (p. 139). Osiris is rarely mentioned by the inscriptions, and death is hardly ever alluded to. Near the principal chamber there is generally a niche closed with masonry, to which M. Mariette gave the name of *serdâb* ('hollow space'), and which in many of the maṣṭabas either contains, or formerly contained, a statue of the deceased. Most of the serdâbs are entirely closed, but some of them have small openings in the wall, through which it was probably customary to introduce incense. The well, or perpendicular shaft into which the body of the deceased was sunk, is usually on the W. side of the Maṣṭaba, for it was in the direction of the setting sun that his soul would cross the threshold of the next world. The sarcophagus is usually an oblong stone box with a flat lid, containing a wooden coffin tapering towards the feet, with a human face represented on it at the head. Within this coffin was placed the body, either wrapped in a cloth, or without any covering. There is here no trace of the careful mummifying process of a later age.

The ornamentation of the interior of the maṣṭabas is very rich.

The first chamber usually contains well-executed basreliefs, mostly coloured, of members of the family of the deceased, and short inscriptions in the simple hieroglyphics of that period, with their scanty determinative symbols, recording the dignities of the deceased, and mentioning the estates from which his faithful servants have brought offerings to the *manes* of their master. Other chambers contain carefully arranged lists of the appropriate offerings to be presented to the deceased at different seasons, and on the various festivals, such as meat and poultry, vegetables and fruit, drinks and essences; and adjoining these are represented the altars laden with these gifts. We seldom find any allusion to death, or the life in the next world, but there are generally faithful representations of the favourite pursuits of the deceased (bird-catching, fishing, etc.), of his most valuable possessions (herds of cattle, ships, etc.; but curiously enough, neither camels, sheep, nor horses, which last seem to have been introduced by the Hyksos), and the tasks performed by his servants (agricultural operations, vintage, carpentering, glass-blowing, gold-washing, papyrus-gathering, writing, etc.). These coloured basreliefs form a most interesting link in the history of ancient art, and are not without æsthetic attraction also. They constitute, as it were, a picture-book in stone, illustrative of the manners and customs which prevailed during the earliest known stage of human civilisation.

'If we enquire into the motives of these primordial inhabitants of the Nile Valley in decorating the walls of their tombs with these curious scenes, it would appear that they intended to hand down to posterity a record of the earliest achievements of mankind in the province of art and civilisation. Having hardly emerged from the simplicity of the primæval condition, they seem to have been proud of displaying the results of their peaceful conquests over the animate and inanimate world around them, and to have been desirous of informing posterity of these triumphs. At that remote epoch, to behold was to admire. The chief occupation of the period was apparently to embellish the tombs in the best possible manner, and it is these decorations which constitute the pictorial history of primitive Egypt'. — *Brugsch*

These tombs probably originated somewhat in the following manner. Every Egyptian of moderate means, and particularly the great and wealthy, began during his lifetime to plan the construction of a tomb worthy of his position in society. The longer he lived and the wealthier he became, the handsomer and the more spacious was the structure. When the architect had lined the interior with smoothly hewn stones from the quarries of Ṭura, the task of the draughtsman and the decorator began. In accordance with certain rules regarding the objects to be represented and their grouping, which seem to have been followed in all the tombs of a similar kind, or perhaps according to well-defined patterns, the draughtsman first proceeded to divide the walls into sections of different sizes, and sometimes into regular squares, with red chalk, and then to fill them up with sketches of the representations and the hieroglyphics with which the tomb was to be adorned. The stone-mason then converted these sketches with his chisel into relief figures, some of which were flat, while others were raised about $2^1/_2$ lines or more. Lastly the painter coloured these designs, the most conspicuous tints being black, reddish brown, pale brown, yellow, light and dark blue, and green. Parts of the design that were intended to be white were not painted, but left in the natural colour of the stone. All the colours, so far as they have been chemically analysed, are earthy substances, and are beautifully preserved, except in cases where they have been too long exposed to the sun and wind. The women are always painted of a pale yellow colour, and the men of a reddish brown tint. The metals also have their conventional colours, iron being blue, and bronze yellow or red, while wood is painted brown, or, when in logs, greenish grey. In painting animals the artists endeavoured to imitate their natural colours, and we accordingly find that the cows and calves are black, brown, and dappled. — On the death of the proprietor of the tomb, his remains were deposited at the bottom of the mummy-shaft, and the task of decorating the tomb was at an end, so that the most perfect sculptures are to be seen in juxtaposition with the mere designs in red chalk. If other members of the family died, their mummies were likewise deposited in the common shaft, but no allusion to their history was recorded on the walls of the principal chamber. An exception, however, was made in the case of the widow of the deceased, whose statue was placed on the W. side of the tomb-chamber beside that of her husband, as has been done in the tomb of Ti. It is also worthy of remark that the name of the proprietor of the tomb is always engraved in hieroglyphics on the so-called drum of the doorway and on that of a 'stele' fashioned in imitation of a door on the W. side of the tomb (as in the case of the tomb of Ti, p. 388). In a number of the tombs it has been observed that a single figure has been obliterated, while the whole of the rest of the decorations are well preserved and intact. The figures thus defaced are supposed to have been those of dishonest servants, whose misconduct induced the family to erase their portraits. At stated intervals, on holidays, and probably also on the anniversary of the death of the occupant of the tomb, the family was wont to assemble in the decorated tomb-chamber and the anterior court, bringing offerings of food which they consumed in honour of the deceased, while homage was done to the statue by burning incense around it.

The *Rock Tombs*, placed in long rows, and most of them excavated on the E. and S. slopes of the plateau, are in a far simpler style than the maṣṭabas, both in point of construction and of internal decoration; but they sometimes contain similar decorations, particularly in Upper Egypt.

With regard to the *Construction of the Pyramids*, see p. 350. The peculiarities of the 'Step Pyramid' are mentioned below.

The **Step-Pyramid** of Saḳḳâra (Arab. *El-Haram el-Medarraga*, i.e. 'provided with steps'), a very conspicuous feature in the landscape, and the 'Cognisance of Saḳḳâra', may be inspected by the traveller externally either in going or returning. Egyptologists differ as to the period of its construction. Some authorities, relying on a passage of Manetho, in which it is stated that 'he (Uenephes) built the pyramid at Cochome', attribute the monument to a king of the 1st Dynasty. Cochome was the Greek form of the hieroglyphic name Ka-kam ('the black bull'), which occurs on the 'steles' and sarcophagi of the Apis tombs as a place in the vicinity of the Necropolis. If this view be correct, we have before us the most ancient structure in the world. Other authorities, however, reject this view, and assign the monument to the period of the 5th Dynasty, but for equally slender reasons. The pyramid consists of six stages, the lowest of which is about $37^3/_4$ ft. in height, the next 36 ft., the third $34^1/_2$ ft., the fourth $32^3/_4$ ft., the fifth 31 ft., and the sixth $29^1/_3$ ft., while each stage is about $6^1/_2$ ft. in width. The peculiarity of the pyramid is not its graduated form, as every other pyramid when deprived of its external incrustation would present the same appearance (comp. p. 350), but consists in the facts that it does not stand like all the others exactly facing the principal points of the compass, that the area it covers is oblong instead of square (N. and S. sides 354 ft., E. and W. sides 398 ft.) and in particular that it contains a very numerous and complicated series of passages and chambers in the interior. The unique form of these chambers, which were explored by General Minutoli in 1821, led M. Mariette to conjecture that they once contained the Apis tombs of the primæval monarchy. Two of the chambers are said to have been decorated with convex pieces of green fayence, inlaid in a peculiar way in stucco, so as to form a kind of mosaic. A richly gilded skull and gilded soles of feet, together with other interesting relics found here and numerous treasures collected by Minutoli, were unfortunately lost at the mouth of the Elbe. The door of the step-pyramid with its architrave of white limestone covered with hieroglyphics, and the door-posts formed of somewhat rough blocks of limestone and green glazed bricks, were removed by Lepsius in 1845 to the museum at Berlin. — This pyramid must have been used for different purposes from the great pyramids of Gîzeh, but the scanty inscriptions found here afford no information on the subject. At one point on the S. side, where the outer masonry has been destroyed, the jointing of the stones may be inspected. The material used is an inferior clayey kind of limestone quarried in the neighbourhood. The pyramid may be ascended without danger, but on no account without the help of the Beduins, as the surface is crumbling and treacherous. (On one occasion, during the period of the inundation, M. Mariette met with a troop of wild boars on the third step.) The view from the sum-

Step Pyramid of Sakkâra.
(South East Side.)

Interior of the Apis Tombs.
(Principal Passage.)

mit is very inferior to that from the Pyramid of Cheops (p. 356), as the perpendicular height is 197 ft. only.

About 250 paces to the S.W. of the Step-Pyramid is the **Pyramid of King Unas,** which was opened in 1881 and has been made accessible to the public (cards of admission obtained from Messrs. Thos. Cook & Son, in Cairo, next door to Shepheard's Hotel). The entrance, now provided with an iron gate, was found closed by gigantic blocks of sandstone, occupying the entire width of the corridor, and by three doors of granite, and it required the expenditure of a vast amount of labour to remove these obstacles. The interior contains two large chambers and a smaller one, the former with a lofty pointed roof, the latter with a low and flat roof. The two large chambers contain numerous funereal inscriptions, most of them well preserved. The granite sarcophagus of the king, who was a member of the 5th Dynasty, stands in the second chamber, close to the wall. The three walls enclosing it are of oriental alabaster and are adorned with brightly coloured paintings. The stone beams of the ceilings do not rest on the side-walls, but are separated from them by a considerable interval, thus relieving them of an immense pressure (comp. p. 358).

The best *coup d'oeil* of the inner construction of the pyramids is obtained at the *Pyramid of Pepi I.*, about 3/4 hr. to the W. of the village of Saḳḳâra, which has been opened from the top (comp. p. 402).

The Serapeum. Standing on the terrace of Mariette's House, we observe, immediately to the N., a sandy hollow, from which rise several heaps of stone and hillocks of sand. These mounds mark the site of the statues of the Græco-Egyptian period, standing on the walls which flanked the approach (Dromos) from the Egyptian to the Greek Serapeum (see below). The statues (including a marble Cerberus in the form of a lion with its tail terminating in a snake's head) are in a very mutilated condition, and have been purposely covered with sand. On the W. side was situated the *Egyptian Serapeum*, or *Mausoleum of Apis*, the sacred bull, which had spent its life in its temple (Apieum) at Memphis (p. 373), and after its death was buried in the vaults of Saḳḳâra. Owing to an erroneous translation, the Greeks regarded Serapis as a distinct Egyptian deity.

The *Dead Apis*, or Osiris-Apis (Asar-Hapi, or *Serapis*), is termed the 'reviving Ptah' (p 126), and probably symbolised the perpetual regenerating power of the god So, too, Apis was associated with the moon, which seems to undergo hourly change, while remaining unaltered. Hapi, the genius of death, bears the head of the cynocephalus, which was also a symbol of the moon. The *Nile*, the great regenerator of the parched soil, bore the same name (Hapi), and its rise was associated with the light of the moon, which by one of its rays impregnated the cow which bore Apis. As the embodiment of the soul of Osiris in the infernal regions, Apis was the principle which revives everything dead. The great festival of the rise of the Nile, which at many places measured as many ells as there were days in each phase of the moon, was also called the 'Festival of the Birth of Apis', and the period of 25 years, which was named after Apis, was a lunar epoch, consisting of 309 average synodic months, equivalent to about 25 Egyptian years When Apis survived his allotted period of 25 years, it is said that he used to be drowned in the Nile, but this cannot have been the invariable practice, as the Apis inscriptions mention that one of these sacred bulls lived 26 years

The whole of the area was excavated and explored by Mariette, who in 1850 found a number of sphinxes from Sakkâra in private gardens, and was thus led to conjecture that they belonged to the *Serapis Temple* mentioned by Strabo and in several Greek papyri. The passage in Strabo runs thus: — 'There is also a temple of Serapis there in a very sandy place, so that mounds of dust are heaped up by the wind, by which the sphinxes are either buried up to their heads or half concealed, whence one may understand the danger incurred by a person going to the temple and overtaken by a gust of wind'. — In the course of his excavations M. Mariette first came upon the *Sphinx Avenue*, which led from the Apis tombs to a Serapeum of the Greek period. It terminated on the E. side, where the chief entrance was situated, in a semicircle formed by eleven statues of Greek philosophers and poets, which now grace the Louvre. The narrow approach (Dromos) was flanked by a double wall, on which stood the figures of animals mentioned above.

The **Greek Serapeum**, which was in the best preservation, was a small example of the simple form of a Greek temple 'in antis', and consisted of a cella and a pronaos, approached by a flight of steps, with two Corinthian columns between the 'antæ' or pilasters of the façade. Adjoining this Greek temple stood an Egyptian chapel with walls sloping inwards and a concave cornice, which was once adorned with the fine statue of the Apis bull now preserved in the Louvre In the sand under the pavement in front of these buildings were found an immense number of small bronze images of gods, of which no fewer than 531 were collected in one day The desert and the sterile sand with which it is covered were regarded by the Egyptians as 'typhonic', or under the influence of Typhon, the god of evil, and these images were accordingly placed in it with a view to purge and consecrate it

The upper part of an Egyptian Serapeum, which seems to have been built in the usual form of the Egyptian temples (with pylons, anterior court, etc.), was also discovered here, but was partly destroyed or overthrown in the course of the excavations. These scanty remains, together with those of the Greek Serapeum, are now completely covered with sand, to a depth, it is said, of 60 ft. or more.

Within the extensive chambers of the Serapeum there was also established a colony of hermits, who lived in the strictest seclusion in cells attached to the various chapels of the temple, as appears from recently deciphered Greek papyri in the British Museum and the Louvre, which were brought from Memphis. Connected with the worship of Serapis, the deity revered above all others in the Alexandrian period, there was a regularly organised monastic system. The monks (κάτοχοι, ἐγκάτοχοι, or οἱ ἐν κατοχῇ ὄντες, i e 'recluses') on entering the order gave up all their worldly possessions, and subsisted entirely on food brought to them by their relations. They were not permitted to leave their cells, and a kind of air-hole formed their sole channel of communication with the outer world. They called each other brethren, and spoke of a common father. Some of their dreams and visions, in which battles with demons play an important part, have been recorded. Buried alive in these dismal recesses, they hoped to purify themselves by the prolonged service of Serapis. We also learn from the papyri that similar monastic institutions were connected with other temples of Serapis and with those of Isis, which were often associated with the Serapis temples. There is no doubt that these κάτοχοι in the service of Serapis were the prototypes of the Christian monks and ascetics of a later period. The first Christian hermits (ἐγκεκλεισμένοι) are also said to have received their food through the air-holes of their cells, and to have chiefly aimed at attaining to a condition of ἀπάθεια, or *gradus impatibilitatis* (*i. e.* insensibility to external impressions). — The Christian monastic and ascetic orders are said to have been founded by SS. Paul and Anthony of Thebes, but there is no sufficient historical foundation for the statement (pp. 99, 480).

In the subterranean part of the Egyptian Serapeum, hewn in the rock, where the Apis bulls were interred, there were found no fewer than 3000 monuments, and it was ascertained that the bulls were interred in different ways at different periods of Egyptian history. No Apis sarcophagus dating from the primæval monarchy was discovered, and it would seem that the first placed here dates from the reign of Amenophis III. (18th Dynasty). On the surface above, a chapel was erected in honour of each bull, while his remains were deposited in one of the square chambers hewn in the rock, to which a sloping passage descended from the chapel. No trace of these chapels now remains. Every Apis was interred in this way down to the thirtieth year of the reign of Ramses II. (19th Dynasty), after which the vaults began to take a different form. A subterranean gallery, about 110 yds. in length, was now hewn in the rock, and flanked with rudely excavated chambers, forty in number, which were walled up after having received the remains of the sacred bull. This was done down to the twentieth year of the reign of Psammetikh I., the first king of the 26th Dynasty, when four of the Apis vaults fell in, and another site was chosen for a new series of tombs. In the thirty-third year of that king's reign a new gallery, flanked as before with vaults, was accordingly excavated for the purpose. These vaults, which are much more carefully constructed than the two series of earlier date, are still accessible, while the others have long since been filled up.

Leaving Mariette's house, and turning to the left, we observe on our right (N.) the above mentioned hollow with its heaps of sand and stones, which conceal the badly preserved statues of the Greek period. The trodden path leads hence, to the N.W., in 2 min. to the entrance (Pl. *a*) of the * **Apis Tombs** (*Egyptian Serapeum*), situated between sharply hewn rocks. The ceiling having threatened to fall in at places, Khedive Isma'îl caused the vaults to be thoroughly repaired at considerable expense, and closed with a gate in 1869, so that they can now be visited with perfect safety.

The sixty-four Apis vaults now accessible, which were begun

in the reign of Psammetikh I. and extended at intervals down to the time of the last of the Ptolemies, form a series of vaults on both sides of a lofty horizontal corridor hewn in the solid rock. These chambers average 26 ft. in height, and their pavement and vaulted ceilings are constructed of excellent Mokattam stone. The passages into which they open have an aggregate length of 380 yds., and are about 10 ft. in width and 17½ ft. in height. Twenty-four of the chambers still contain the huge sarcophagi in which the Apis mummies were deposited. These monster coffins average 13 ft. in length, 7 ft. in width, and 11 ft. in height, and no less than 65 tons in weight. The covers, five of which are composed of separate pieces of stone cemented together, have in several instances been pushed on one side, and on the top of some of them the Arabs, for some unexplained reason, have built rude masses of masonry. All the sarcophagi, when discovered by Mariette, had been emptied of their contents, with the exception of two, which still contained a number of trinkets.

Twenty-four of the sarcophagi are of granite, but three of them only bear inscriptions, briefly recording the name of the king by whom they were erected. One of these sarcophagi bears the name of *Amasis* (the last king but one of the 26th Dynasty), another that of *Cambyses*, and a third that of *Khabbash* (p. 94), a king of the house of the Saïtes, who gained possession of the throne during the reign of Darius and occupied it until the second year of Xerxes. The cartouches on a fourth sarcophagus, dating from one of the later Ptolemies, are empty. The most instructive relics found here were the '*Apis Steles*', or small stone votive tablets presented by pilgrims to the shrine of the bull last interred, and which, it is said, could only be received within seventy days of the sacred animal's death. These tablets during the earliest period were attached to the basement of the small temple of Apis erected above the vault, and afterwards to the wall which shut off the vault from the main passage. As time rolled on, they were set up at a still greater distance from the tomb, although, curiously enough, specially favoured persons were permitted to place *Statuettes*, bearing inscriptions similar to those on the steles, near the sarcophagus. These tablets have yielded most valuable information as to the ancient Egyptian mode of reckoning time, and particularly regarding the later periods of Egyptian history, as they record the days, months, and years of the king's reign on which the Apis revered by the donor was born, enthroned, and interred respectively. We have thus been enabled to determine with precision the duration of the reigns of many of the Pharaohs and the order in which they succeeded each other. Most of these relics are now preserved in the Louvre. If the ceremonies which accompanied the obsequies of the Apis bulls were as magnificent as the sarcophagi were costly, Diodorus probably does not exaggerate when he informs us that the chief priest of an Apis bull which died of old age shortly after the accession of Ptolemy Lagi expended on its burial not only the whole of a large sum then in the coffers of the temple, but a farther sum of fifty talents of silver (about 11,700*l.*) advanced by the king. Diodorus also assures us that in his time the keeper of Apis (whose office was doubtless a very honourable one) spent no less than a hundred talents on the obsequies of a bull.

Passing through the gateway, we enter a Chamber (Pl. *b*) of considerable dimensions, with niches of various sizes in the bare limestone walls, where votive tablets of the kind mentioned above were once placed. Visitors light their candles here. The guide now proceeds towards the right. After a few paces we observe at our feet a huge block of black granite (Pl. *c*), which once formed the lid of a sarcophagus. Beyond it we turn to the left, and after ten paces reach an enormous granite sarcophagus (Pl. *d*), which so nearly fills the passage that there is only just room to pass it on its right side. The lid and the sarcophagus belong to each other, having doubtless been executed for the reception of one of the sacred bulls, but were probably stopped here on their way to the vault for which they were destined, in consequence of the crisis in Egypt's history which caused the overthrow of the worship of Apis. Beyond this sarcophagus we continue to proceed towards the W. between bare walls of rock, and then turn to the left (S.) into another passage destitute of ornament. This leads us to the Principal Passage (Pl. A, B), running parallel with the first, from E. to W., and penetrating the solid rock. This passage is flanked with the side-chambers, about 26 ft. in height, which contain the colossal sarcophagi of the Apis bulls (see above), each consisting of a single block of black or red polished granite or of limestone. One of the finest (Pl. *e*), composed of black granite, and bearing the best executed hieroglyphic inscriptions on its polished exterior, may be entered by means of a ladder. After having traversed the whole of the W. part of the main gallery and returned to the point at which we entered it, we next visit the E. part of the gallery, where we observe several more sarcophagi We then reach a side-passage (Pl. *f*) diverging to the right. from which another passage leads to the right, in a direction parallel with the main corridor, but now built up, as it was in a dangerous condition. A little beyond this point we reach the E. end of the main gallery (Pl. B). Retracing our steps for a short distance, we turn to the right, pass over another sarcophagus which blocks the way by means of steps, and thus regain the door by which we entered the vaults. The temperature in these subterranean chambers, to which the outer air has little or no access, is always about 79°, that being the mean temperature of Cairo.

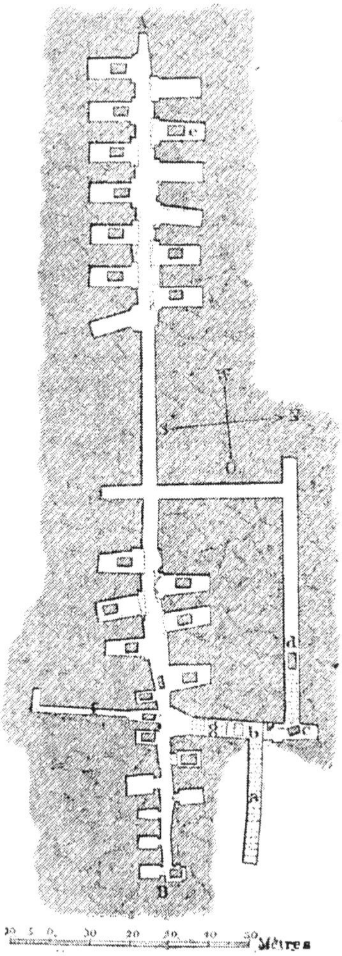

Before taking our leave of this extraordinary place, we may quote the interesting words of its discoverer: —

'I confess', says Mariette, 'that when I penetrated for the first time, on 12th Nov. 1851, into the Apis vaults, I was so profoundly struck with astonishment that the feeling is still fresh in my mind, although five years have elapsed since then. Owing to some chance which it is difficult to account for, a chamber which had been walled up in the thirtieth year of the reign of Ramses II. had escaped the notice of the plunderers of the vaults, and I was so fortunate as to find it untouched. Although 3700 years had elapsed since it was closed, everything in the chamber seemed to be precisely in its original condition. The finger-marks of the Egyptian who had inserted the last stone in the wall built to conceal the doorway were still recognisable on the lime. There were also the marks of naked feet imprinted on the sand which lay in one corner of the tomb-chamber. Everything was in its original condition in this tomb, where the embalmed remains of the bull had lain undisturbed for thirty-seven centuries. Many travellers would think it terrible to live here alone in the desert for a number of years; but such discoveries as that of the chamber of Ramses II. produce impressions compared with which everything else sinks into insignificance, and which one constantly desires to renew'.

The **Maṣṭaba of Ti (260 paces to the N.E. of Mariette's house; see Map, p. 378) is the most interesting and best preserved monument of this kind (comp. p. 379) in the extensive Necropolis of the ancient capital of the primæval monarchy. It lies in an old street of tombs, now covered up; and the surface of the soil has been so raised with deposits of the sand of the desert that the tomb rather resembles a subterranean rock-structure than a building on the surface of the earth. Very little of the exterior is therefore now visible, but the interior, which has been completely excavated, is executed with the utmost care, and the sculptures on the walls exhibit a skill which is truly marvellous when it is remembered that the mausoleum was erected in the 5th Dynasty, in the time of the builders of the pyramids of Abuṣîr, that is, about 4500 years ago. Both the paintings and the hieroglyphics which cover the walls are executed in remarkably delicate and flat bas-relief, the outlines being sharp and distinct, while the projecting parts are at the same time subdued and harmonious. The hieratic canon (p. 161) has already imparted to the human figures a somewhat conventional type, notwithstanding their spirited action, but there is a refreshing fidelity to nature in the attempts of the artists to represent animals. The painting of the figures is preserved at places. Each of the larger scenes is presided over by the commanding figure of Ti himself, the proprietor of the tomb, who is easily distinguishable by his loftier stature. He wears a wig with the usual locks, and his features were doubtless copied from life, as is proved by their resemblance to those of his statue now preserved at Bûlâḳ (p. 306). In some cases his chin is prolonged by a small false beard. Around his loins he wears a kind of apron, carefully folded, and pointed in front, and from his neck hangs a broad necklace. With one hand he leans on a long staff, and in the other he holds his baton of office. Ti (hieroglyphic ), as the inscriptions in the tomb-chamber inform us (p. 396), was a dignitary of the highest rank in the service of Ra-nefer-ar-ka, Ra-en-user, and Kaka, monarchs of the 5th Dynasty. He was a 'semer' (companion, adjutant, or chamberlain) of the king, 'enthroned in the heart of his lord', a 'master of the secrets' (privy counsellor), 'loving his sovereign', a 'president of the gate of the palace', a 'secret counsellor of the king in all his royal assemblies', a 'secret counsellor for the execution of the commands of the king', and a 'president of all the royal works and the royal department of writing'. He also held a high sacerdotal office at the pyramids of Abuṣîr (p. 370), and he is elsewhere called one of the chiefs of the prophets, a president of the sacrifices and purifications, and a guardian of the mystery of the divine speech. His wife Nefer-hotep-s, who is frequently represented by his side, was a member of the royal family, but he himself was a man of humble parentage, who had risen to distinction by his merit. His sons Ti and Tamut (Tamuz) enjoyed the title of princes in consequence of the high rank of their mother. Like other Egyptian ladies of distinction, the wife of Ti is termed the 'beloved of her husband', the 'mistress of the house', and the 'palm of amiability towards her husband'.

Three Entrances (Pl. *A*), the side-walls of which are built of blocks of stone inclining slightly inwards, lead to the first small anterior Court (Pl. *B*), which contains the remains of two pillars. On the E. wall (Pl. *a*) are represented the offering of gifts; on the S. wall, to the left of the entrance (Pl. *b*), a poultry-yard and the fattening of geese (see below); and to the right of the entrance (Pl. *c*), the catching of fish in traps. These three scenes are small and damaged by exposure. On the front-walls of the entrance, on each side of it, is a figure of Ti (see above), above which are mutilated hieroglyphics mentioning several of his titles. We next enter the Great Court (Pl. *C*), an extensive quadrangle, which was once covered with a roof borne by twelve square pillars. The roof has disappeared, but some of the pillars are still standing. This hall is said to have been the scene of the rites performed in honour of the deceased and the sacrifice of victims. In the centre of the court was sunk the mummy shaft (Pl. *d*), not perpendicularly, as usual, but in an oblique direction, communicating with the tomb-chamber below, where a sarcophagus without inscription was found.

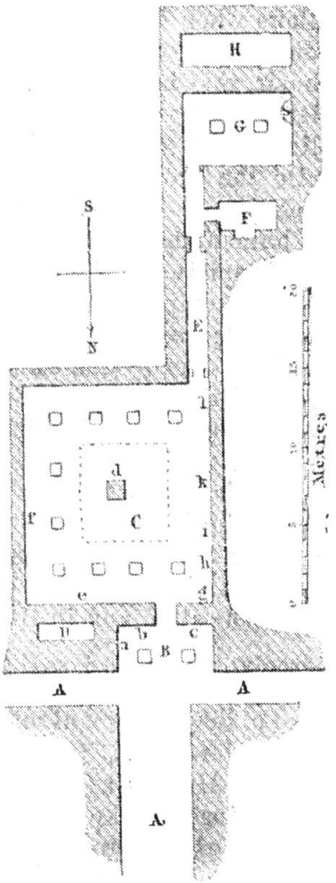

On the N. side (Pl. *e*), which is much injured by exposure, are represented the offering of gifts, the sacrifice of cattle, and the conveyance of

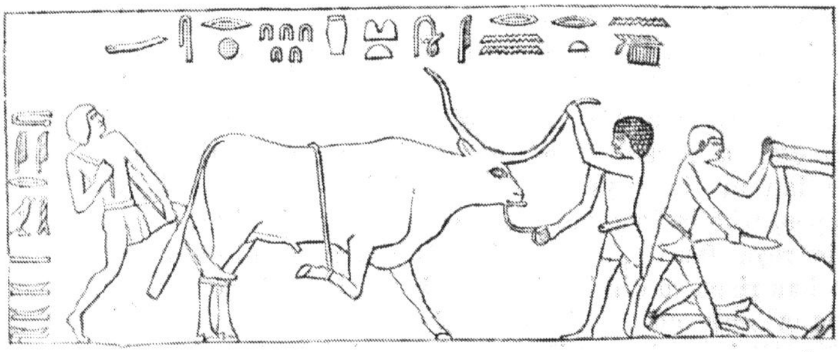

slave in a boat. A particularly successful figure is that of a long-horned bull, whose hind-legs a man is binding togeth r with visible effort, while another is dragging it down to the ground. Beside it lies another victim already slain. The inscription above this scene informs us that the young bull sacrificed here would, 'according to the judgment of the man skilled in slaughtering', yield 50 *men*, or pots (probably of fat). †

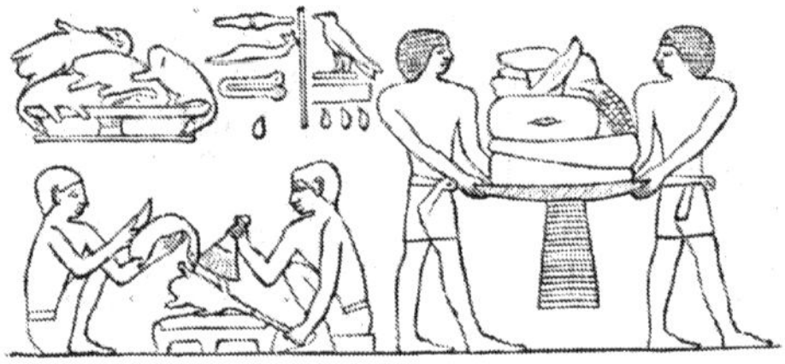
'Slaughtered Victims'. 'Meat for Cooking'.

Behind the wall here is another chamber ('Serdâb'; Pl. *D*), not now accessible, in which nothing was found.

On the E. side (Pl. *f*), which is also much damaged by exposure to the air, are represented the offering of gifts, a number of servants, and other scenes. There are no figures on the S. side. Those on the W. side are well preserved, except towards the top.

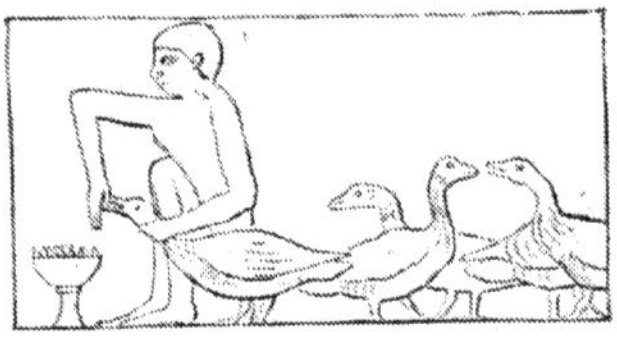

Close to the entrance, on the right (Pl. *g*), is the very interesting scene of the feeding of the geese (showing that the ancient Egyptians were acquainted with the modern modes of fattening poultry), and also that of the 'feeding of the cranes'; above which is represented the 'putting in of the fattening cakes to boil'. We next observe (Pl. *h*) a complete poultry-yard, with geese, pigeons, and cranes, which are being fed with corn, and then the figure of Ti (Pl. *i*). Farther on is a slab of stone (Pl. *k*), 9 ft. long and $1^1/_2$ ft. broad, bearing on the lower part a representation of four Nile barges (the fourth to the right being without rowers), which 'descend the Nile with much corn'; above these are antelopes, a pleasing

† We annex woodcuts of some of the best of these scenes, which will serve to impress them on the traveller's memory. They are from photographs taken from impressions obtained by Dr. Reil (d. 1880), and are therefore almost facsimiles. With the exception of the large tableau of Ti engaged in hunting (p. 399), they are reduced to one-twelfth of the original size.

group of doves, cranes, a mountain-goat, two more antelopes, and to the left, in the corner, four more mountain-goats. Adjoining these figures on the left is another figure of Ti (Pl. *l*).

Adjoining the right corner of the S. side of this court (see above) is a corridor, formerly closed by a door, and also divided by another doorway in the middle. It is now entered by a wooden door, the key of which is brought by the guide.

On each side of this Corridor (Pl. *E*) are several series of bearers of offerings (comp. p. 380), one above the other. On the right is a niche $9^1/_4$ ft. high and 6 ft. wide, containing a 'stele' dedicated to the wife of Ti. On the left, on the inner part of the pillar of the doorway, is Ti with his titles; then (between the first and second doors) the transport of the statue of Ti and persons offering incense. Hieroglyphics in different places inform us that 'this is the statue of thorn-acacia wood of the deceased Ti', and 'this is the statue of ebony, which they are drawing'; 'the drawing of the statue is a good drawing'. — 'The servants pour out water' is the inscription at the place where a servant is wetting the runners of the sledge which bears the statue. — On the right (between the niche and the second door) are several more rows of gift-bearers. On the door-posts (left) two male figures and (right) Ti with his titles. Over the door (N. side) musicians and dancers, and (S. side) Ti in a boat (damaged). We then come to a door on the right, leading into an oblong, covered, and therefore somewhat dark chamber (Pl. *F*), the scenes adorning which afford us an insight into the domestic economy of the deceased. Among them are represented a complete pottery and a bake-house, and numerous vessels of various forms, destined for different uses. On the upper part of the left door-post of this chamber a piece of the sycamore wood to which the door was attached is still in its place.

Above, on each side of the door of this chamber (on the E. side of the corridor), are several barges, some of which are light boats with a number of rowers with broad, shovel-shaped oars, while others of heavier build have lateen sails and are also steered with oars. In the bow of the vessel stands a man with a long pole, used for sounding, in the same way as is done at the present day. These boats are conveying retainers of the deceased to Sakkâra to pay homage to his remains; for we read beside one of the sailing-boats: — 'Arrival from the N. country, from the villages of the family estate, in order that they may behold the chamberlain who is perfect in consequence of his distinction in occupying the first place in the heart of his sovereign, and the master of the mystery of the kingdom of the dead, Ti'. The captain of the vessel, of which we annex a woodcut, wishing to land on the W. bank, is represented as giving the command — 'Direction, starboard, starboard!'

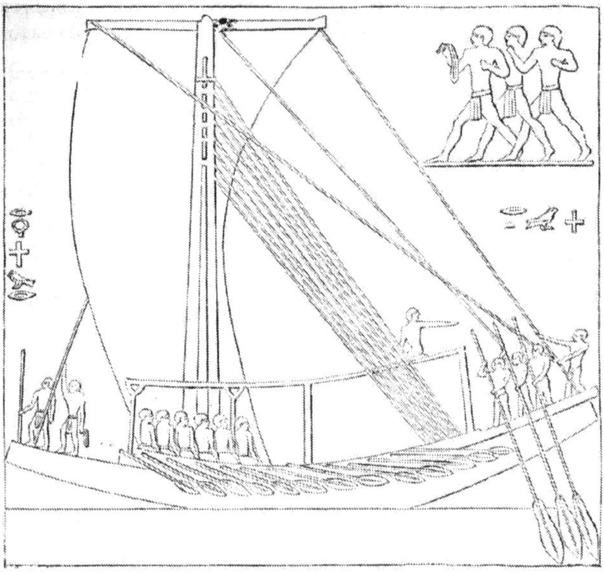

Leaving the corridor, we pass through the door opening to the S. (with a figure of Ti on each side), and enter the Tomb Chamber (Pl. *G*) itself, 22¾ ft. broad, 23¾ ft. long, and 12½ ft. in height, and embellished with special care. The ceiling, in imitation of palm-stems, rests on two massive square pillars, coated with stucco and coloured to imitate red granite, and has two openings on the E. side through which light was introduced.

E. Side of the Tomb Chamber of Ti.

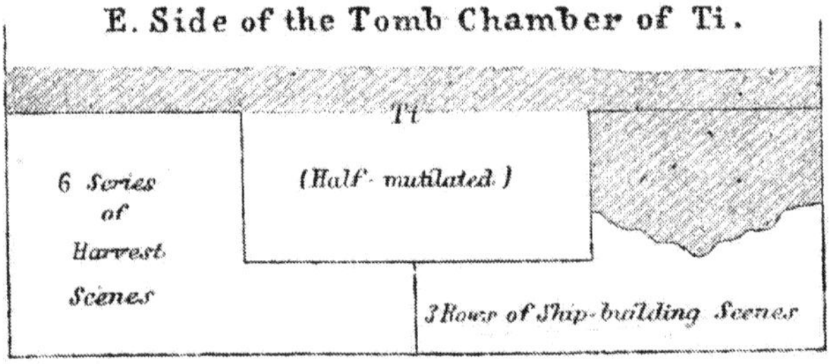

On the E. side (to the left of the entrance) are six series of harvest scenes, representing the reaping, storing, and transport of the corn, the treading of it out by oxen or asses, the separation of the straw from the grain by means of three-pronged forks, the sifting of the grain, and the filling of the sacks, which last operation is done by women. The dress of the female workers is represented as fitting tightly, leaving the form of their figures well-defined. All seem intent on their occupations, the scenes are full of life and spirit, and the imaginative artists have even credited the dumb creation with intelligence. The reaper says to the ears — 'Ye are seasonable',

or 'ye are now large'; and at another place he is made to say — 'this is reaping; when a man does this work he becomes gentle, and so I am'. The driver of a herd of donkeys addresses them with — 'people love those who go on quickly, but strike the lazy'; 'if thou

couldst but see thy own conduct!' Gleaners of the remains *(sep)* left by the reapers are also represented.

In the centre of this wall is a half-mutilated representation of

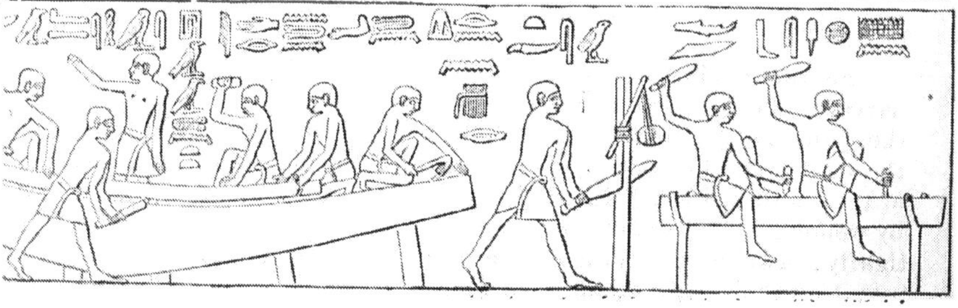

Ti. To the right of it are two perfectly preserved and several damaged ship-building scenes, representing the various operations, from the hewing of the stems to the caulking of the vessel resting on the stocks. The primitive saws, axes, hammers, borers, and other tools used by the workmen are particularly interesting.

S. Side of the Tomb Chamber of Ti.

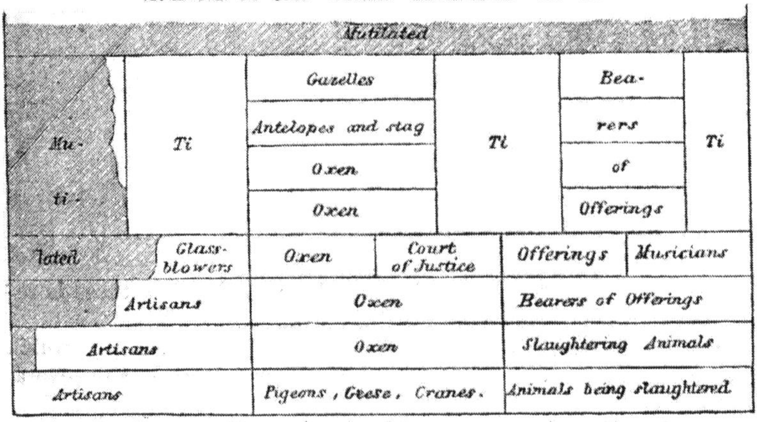

The S. side is richly covered with representations, but the upper parts are damaged. We here find lists of the whole of the domestic animals belonging to the deceased, including oxen, gazelles, and

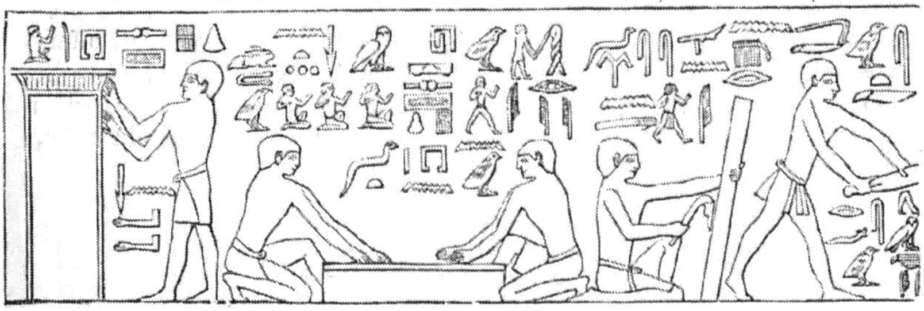

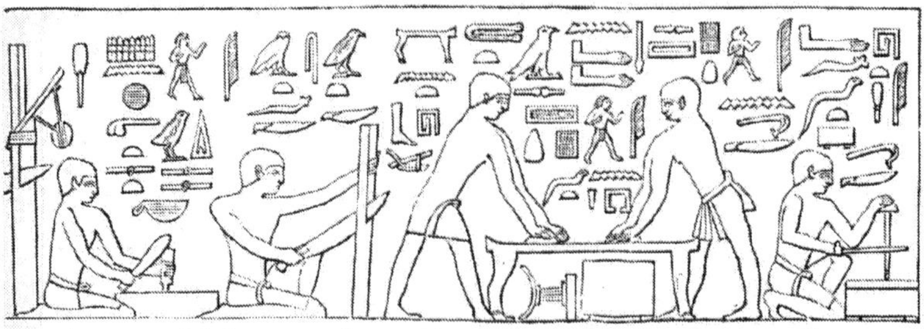

antelopes, which were domesticated at that period, and a stag, which is separately noted by the writers. Then figures of Ti and bearers of offerings. On the lower half of the wall are four rows of workmen of different trades, including carpenters, masons, sculptors, glass-blowers, chair-makers, leather-workers, and water-bearers. To the right of these, at the bottom, are geese, ducks, pigeons, and cranes; above which are oxen, and then a scene in a court of justice, consisting of a number of judges writing, before whom several criminals are being dragged. To the right of the last

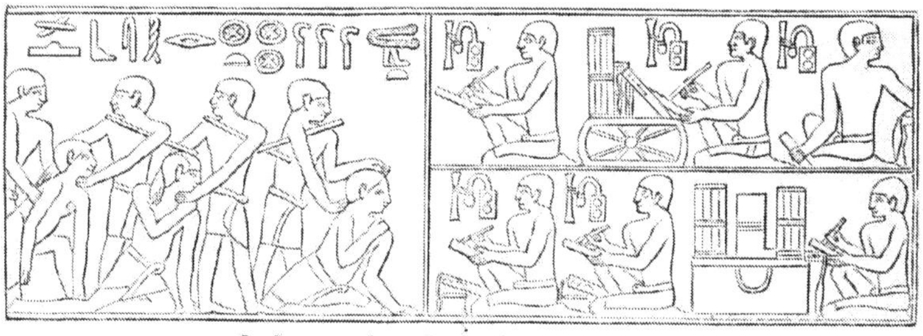

scene are several figures bearing offerings, and below these is represented the slaughtering of various animals.

Behind this wall is concealed another Serdâb (Pl. H), in which a statue of Ti, now preserved in the museum at Bûlâk, and several broken statues were found.

On the W. side are two large 'steles', extracts of the contents of which have already been given (p. 389). These inscriptions also contain an invocation of Anubis, the jackal-headed guardian of the infernal regions, who is to take the deceased under his protection. In front of the left stele is a slab for the reception of offerings (p. 380), of the kind which occurs in every tomb. In the centre of the wall are slaughterers and the presentation of gifts (damaged). In front of these stood statues [of Ti and his wife, which are now in the museum of Bûlâk.

N. Side of the Tomb Chamber of Ti.

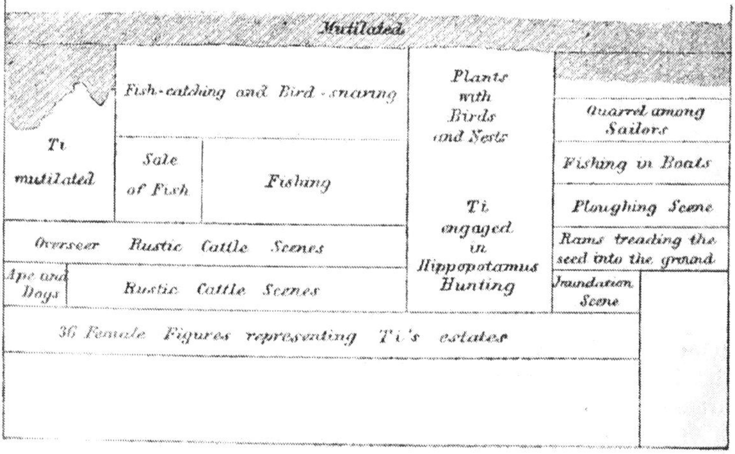

The **North Side of the chamber is adorned with the most elaborate and best preserved scenes. The lowest of these consists of a long procession of 36 female figures (of a pale yellowish colour, see p. 381), bearing on their heads large baskets filled with various kinds of agricultural produce, bottles, jars, and loaves, carrying poultry in their hands (and in one case a porcupine in a cage), and leading cattle by ropes. The inscription above them records that this is an — 'Offering of sacrificial drink and food from the villages of the family estate of the chamberlain Ti situated in Lower and Upper Egypt'. Adjoining each figure is the name of the place which it represents. Each name is accompanied by that of Ti, the proprietor, and the order is in accordance with the most valued products, the industries, and the situation of the place represented. Thus we observe a Water-drawing Ti (probably so call-

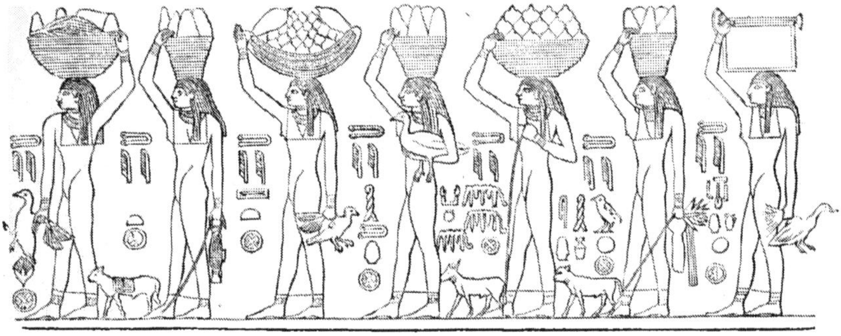

ed from its irrigation system), a Field Ti, a Palm Ti, a Ship Ti, an Island Ti, a Sycamore Ti, a Bread Ti, and a Cake Ti.

Above these are rustic cattle scenes. A cow is represented calving, and another is being milked, while an overseer, apparently

tired with doing nothing leans on his staff and orders the servants to — 'milk while you hold fast the young calf by the knees'. To the right of these are a number of frisky young calves, tethered to blocks of wood, and browsing or skipping about. Near the left angle we observe a dwarf leading an ape, resembling the long-tailed monkeys of the Sûdân, and a man with a deformed shoulder with a couple of prick-eared greyhounds, of the kind known in N. Africa as 'slughi' (p. 401).

Higher up (comp. Plan, p. 396) we observe scenes representing the snaring of birds and the catching of fish in nets and baskets; and we here read the last of the hieroglyphic inscriptions — 'Let

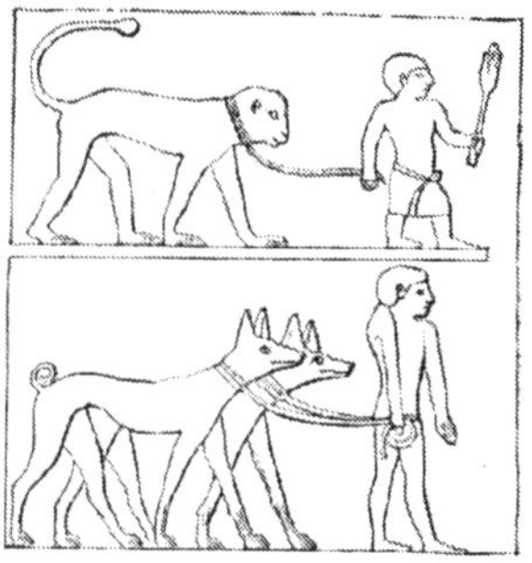

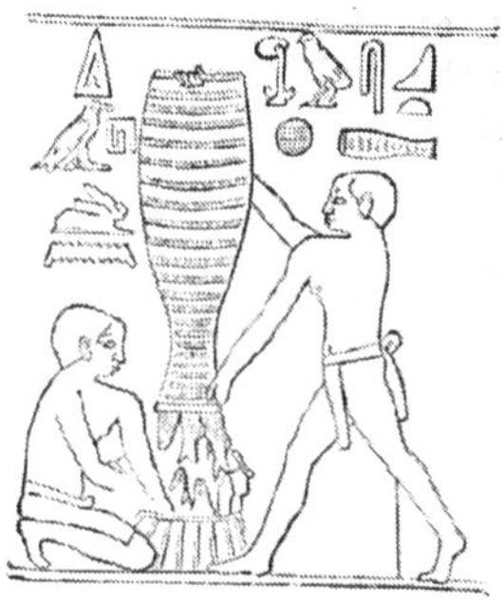

what is in it fall down', and 'the emptying of the receptacle formed of rushes'.

To the right, towards the door, is a large and striking tableau, representing **Ti engaged in hippopotamus hunting. He stands in a light papyrus boat, leaning on a staff, and is more than double the size of his attendants. The hunting of crocodiles and hippopotami on the Nile formed a favourite pastime of the wealthy Egyptians, and we find scenes of this kind recurring frequently, especially in the burial chapels of the earliest period of the Egyptian monarchy. The bearing of Ti is calm and dignified, while the captain of the vessel, 'the chief over the people of the bird-pond Atet', seems to be attending to the directions of his master with a view to communicate them to the crew. In the foremost vessel three of the men are engaged in securing two aquatic monsters floundering in the water, one of which has been caught with a kind of snare and is threatened with the spears of the hunters. An allusion to this kind of hunting is said to be contained in the following passage in the Book of Job (xli. 1,2): — 'Canst thou draw out leviathan with an hook? or his tongue with a cord which thou lettest down? Canst thou put an hook into his nose? or bore his jaw through with a thorn?' — The other hippopotamus which the men are endeavouring to secure has a small crocodile in its mouth. At the stern of Ti's vessel is a smaller boat containing a boy, who is about to strike on the head a silurus which he has caught. The other fish represented in the water are so faithfully drawn that the species to which they belong are easily determined. The three boats are surrounded by papyrus plants, among the tops of which various birds are sitting on their nests or fluttering about. A pair of kingfishers with their young, in a nest faithfully copied from nature, are defending themselves against the threatened attack of some kind of weasel.

This scene is nearly double the size of he others, and the above copy is about 1/19th of the original size.

Below these hunting scenes is the procession of women bearing offerings, already described. Above these, to the right, are cattle being driven through the water during the inundation.

Above the inundation and over the door are a number of rams. According to Herodotus the Egyptians sowed their seed on the wet mud, and caused it to be trodden in by swine, and this task is here

being performed by the rams, stimulated partly by blows and partly by food held before them. The explanatory hieroglyphic inscription is to the effect that — 'it is well for him who loves work!'

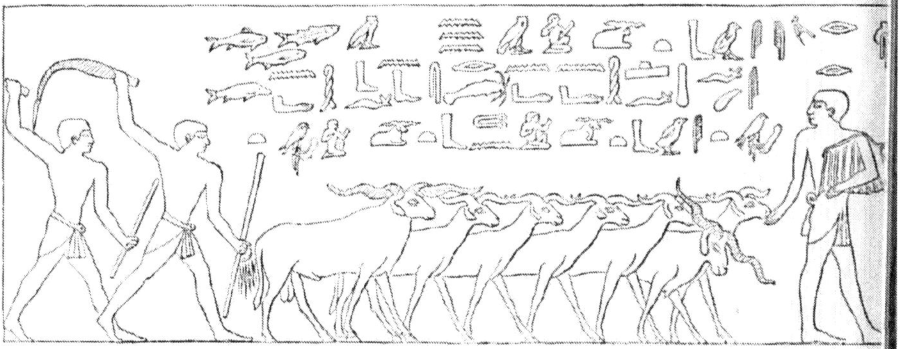

Above the rams is a ploughing scene, adjoining which is a man hoeing the ground, while another is scattering the seed.

In the fishing scene (above) the overseer, leaning on his staff, says to his servants, 'Ye are like apes', to which they good-humouredly reply, 'Thy command is executed; it is done excellently'. At the top (not easily distinguished) is a quarrel among sailors, who appear to be interchanging violent blows and remonstrances — 'Thou art of a pugnacious hand, but I am so gentle'.

Among the maṣṭabas which are now shown only by special permission from the Director of Museum, and from which the sand requires to be removed, the most interesting, and after that of Ti the best preserved, is the —

Maṣṭaba of Ptahhotep, which lies a little to the W. of the path from the step-pyramid to Mariette's House.

Ptahhotep, like Ti, lived in the 5th Dynasty, and was a priest of the Pyramids of Aser, Ra-en-user, and the 'divine dwelling of Men-kau-Hor'. He also bore a number of other titles The best portrait of him is on the E. wall. His costume is similar to that of Ti (p. 398). His young son, with the lock denoting infancy, is holding his staff with his right hand and a hoopoe in his left The visitor should observe the harvest of the papyrus plant, and the games which were probably connected with the vintage festival The grapes are being plucked, trodden, and pressed. A hunting scene lower down is full of humour and life, and some of the animals will interest zoologists. Most of the hounds are 'slughi' (p. 398). The attack and slaughter of the gazelle is a very spirited scene. Ptahhotep also indulges in lion-hunting A lion is represented seizing in its jaws the muzzle of a cow tied up as a bait, and fastening its claws into the animal's neck, while the calf stands behind its mother, and the kneeling hunter with his two hounds points out to them the lion on which he is about to let them loose The fishing and fowling scenes are particularly well executed Another successful representation on the same wall is the procession of the retainers of Ptahhotep bearing offerings from the different villages on his estates Like the modern processions of pilgrims at Cairo, this cortége is headed by pugilists and prize-fighters. Captive lions and other smaller wild animals are being carried in cages, and the master of the dogs is leading his greyhounds and another kind of hound resembling a hyena. Next follow mountain-goats, antelopes, and oxen. A cow is calving with the aid of a veterinary surgeon, and a number of calves on the ground are struggling violently to disengage themselves from the cords with which they are bound. After these come flocks of poultry. If the inscriptions are to be believed, Ptahhotep possessed 121,000 geese of one kind and 11,210 of another, 1225 swans, 120,000 small geese, 121,022 pigeons, and 111,200 goslings. Among the domestic poultry are included cranes, which their keeper brings before his master, counted, and in good order. Ptahhotep, sitting on a throne, wearing a panther-skin, and anointing himself with oil, surveys the rich produce of his estates, watches the slaughter of his cattle, approves of the order kept by his clerks, and listens to the music of harps and flutes The list is exceedingly instructive owing to the distinctness of the determinative symbols which accompany the carefully written words. This maṣṭaba also contains a false door, bearing a representation of the entrance to a tomb as a symbol, on the W. wall.

The **Maṣṭaba of Sabu,** to the E. of that of Ti, contains similar representations, and an enumeration of the various kinds of cattle possessed by the deceased. Of one kind of cattle he possessed 405, of another 1237, and of a third 1300; of calves 1220 of one kind, and 1138 of another Besides these he had 1308 antelopes, 1135 gazelles, 1244 goats of a species resembling the antelope, and 1010 herons. The poultry (geese, ducks, and pigeons) is reckoned by thousands ( = 1000).

After having visited the Necropolis, the traveller may, if time permit, proceed to the '*Maṣṭaba Farʿûn*', which belongs to the

S. group of Saḳḳâra, a ride of $1^1/_4$ hr. to the S. of Mariette's House. We pass the step-pyramid and the pyramid of Unas on the left. Exactly in a line with the step-pyramid, parallel with its W. side, and about a thousand paces to the W. of it, we observe a space of ground enclosed by broad and massive, but now very dilapidated, walls on the E., N., and W. sides, while the S. side is bounded by the natural hills of the desert. The object of this enclosure is a mystery to Egyptologists. M. Mariette, however, conjectured, with much probability, that the place was used as a pen for the numerous cattle slaughtered here as victims. Repeated excavations have been made within the precincts of the enclosure, but without result. Each side is 440 yds. in length.

Proceeding hence towards the Maṣṭaba Far'ûn, we observe the tomb rising before us at no great distance, so that the route to it cannot be mistaken. To the left are the dilapidated *Pyramids of Pepi I.* and *Sokar-em-saf.* On the N.W. side of the maṣṭaba is the still more dilapidated *Pyramid of Pepi II.*, now used by the Arabs as a quarry. All these pyramids are constructed exactly in the same manner as that of King Unas (p. 383), but they are in such a ruined and dangerous condition that the director of the museum has had them all closed again, previously taking an accurate copy of the inscriptions they contain. — The **Maṣṭaba Far'ûn**, which may be ascended, is oblong in form, like all the other tombs of the kind, with walls sloping inwards. The entrance is on the N. side. It was first explored by M. Mariette, who believed that it was the tomb of King Unas (p. 383).

We may either retrace our steps hence to Mariette's House, or traverse a depression to the N. of the maṣṭaba, opening towards the E., and leading direct to the village of Saḳḳâra.

If several days have been allowed for the excursion to Saḳḳâra, the traveller may next proceed to visit **Dahshur**, situated $^3/_4$ hr. to the S. of the Maṣṭaba Far'ûn. This place is perhaps identical with the *Acanthus* of Diodorus, where a leaky cask is once said to have stood, into which water from the Nile was daily poured by 360 priests. On the margin of the desert there still grow numerous sunt trees, as in ancient times. On the desert plateau of Dahshûr rise two large and two smaller pyramids of limestone, and two of brick, together with remains of others, all of which are at a considerable distance from each other. The northernmost brick pyramid, which was once covered with slabs of stone, is curious. It is sometimes pointed out, but without any authority, as the fabulous pyramid which Herodotus mentions as having been erected by King Asychis, who is said to have compelled his labourers to make bricks of mud laboriously obtained from the bottom of a lake by means of poles. The entrance on the N. side was once approached by a vestibule. The present height of the pyramid is about 90 ft. only.

On the S. side of another ruined pyramid, situated to the S.W. of the last, are traces of two embankments (p. 344), descending towards the E. from the larger *Stone Pyramid* on the W. The last is still 326 ft. in height and 234 yds. in width, being nearly as large as the Great Pyramid of Gîzeh, and in its solitude presents a very imposing appearance, even to an accustomed eye.

To the E. and S. are remains of several other pyramids. Still farther to the S. rises a pyramid of peculiar form, sometimes called the *Blunted*

Pyramid (comp p. 159), the lower slopes rising at an angle of 54° 41', while the sides of the apex form an angle of 42° 59' The whole pyramid was probably originally intended to have the same slope as the apex (as the sides of the neighbouring pyramid rise at an angle of 43° 36'), but the lower part was never completed. This pyramid is 206½ yds. square and 321 ft. in height The interior was explored so early as the year 1660 by Mr. Melton, an English traveller. In 1860 M. Le Brun found a small chamber in the interior. No clue to the name of the builder has been discovered. On the extreme S side of the plateau rises a brick pyramid, 99 ft in height, marking the S extremity of the vast Necropolis of Memphis, which extends down to Abû Roâsh (p 370), towards the N., a distance of 23 M. — From Dahshûr to the Pyramid of Mêdûm, and to the Fayûm, see R 9.

Quarries of Ṭura and Baths of Ḥelwân.

Railway to (14 M.) Helwân in ¾-1 hr (fares 11 piastres 10, 7 piastres 20, 4 piastres 20 paras). The trains, of which there are four daily, start from the new station in the Place Mehémet Ali. Another train starts from the Central Station, passes the 'Abbâsîyeh and the Cartridge Factory, joins the first-mentioned line at Basâtîn, and reaches Ḥelwân in 1⅓ hr.

The railway to Ḥelwân, which was constructed mainly for the purpose of connecting the great military establishments at Ṭura with the Citadel, runs from the Place Méhémet Ali, in a S. direction. It skirts the base of the Moḳaṭṭam, on the slopes of which are the interesting ruins of a mosque, and traverses the burial-ground of the Mamelukes (p. 327). To the right lies the oldest part of Cairo, with the Mosque of Ṭulûn (p. 265). On the same side we next observe the Necropolis of Imâm Shafe'i (p. 327), beyond which is the valley of the Nile, with the various groups of pyramids rising above it (p. 404).

Before reaching (4 M.) *Basâtîn*, a village situated in one of the angles of a triangular piece of arable land which extends a considerable way into the desert, we perceive the Jewish burial-ground on the left, and, farther on, the broad Wâdi et-Tîh (p. 339), which separates the Moḳaṭṭam range from the Gebel Ṭura. Traversing a tract of desert sand, the line approaches the Nile, on which lies the village of *Ṭura*. A little to the right are the large military establishments and gunpowder mills. On the hill stand the ruins of an old fort.

9½ M. *Ma'ṣara*, a village on the Nile, is noted for the slabs of stone obtained in the neighbourhood, known as 'palattes', and used for paving purposes in almost every house of the better class in Egypt. From either Ṭura or Ma'ṣara we may visit the *Quarries of Ṭura* (p. 405), which yielded material for the construction of the ancient temples, and are still worked. Their entrances in the rocks are visible from the railway. The ride thither occupies ½ hr., from Ḥelwân 1½ hr. It is advisable to bring good donkeys from Cairo, as the choice at Ḥelwân is very limited.

Beyond stat. Ma'ṣara the line skirts the slopes of the *Gebel Ṭura*, and after ascending a considerable incline reaches the plateau on which the Baths of Ḥelwân are situated.

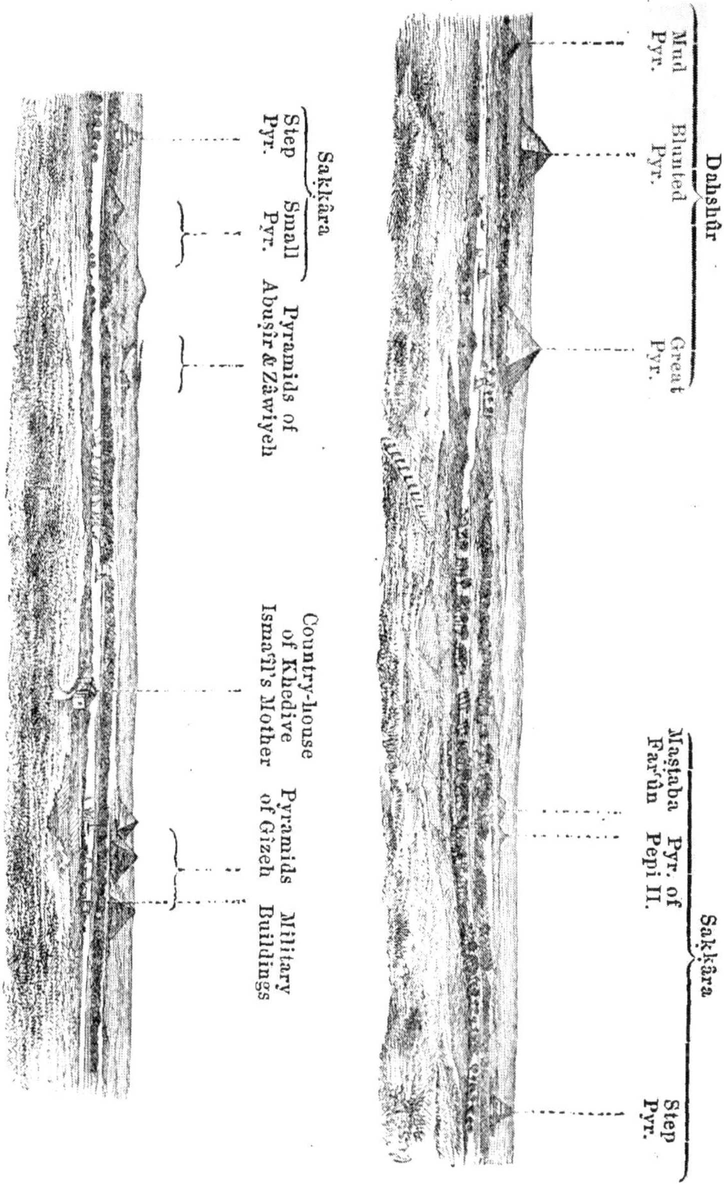

Sketch of the Pyramids as seen from Ḥelwân.

14 M. **Ḥelwân,** French *Hélouan-les-Bains*. — **Hotels.** *Grand Hôtel, belonging to the Egyptian government, with a court planted with trees, a veranda, and airy rooms; 'pens.' 15 fr. Hôtel Ollivier, unpretending, 'pens.' 10 fr. — *Private Lodgings*, at various prices, are easily obtained.

Ḥelwân, an artificial oasis in the desert, 3 M. from the Nile, belongs to the Egyptian government, and is placed under the superintendence of *M. Grand-Bey*, who is represented at the place itself by *M. Onsy*. The medical inspector is *Dr. Engel*, a German. In spite of the disadvantages of its situation, which necessitate the bringing from a distance of drinking water, provisions, and even garden mould, Helwân has hitherto had a very prosperous existence, especially since it came into the hands of the government in 1880. It still, however, presents a dull and new appearance, and the vegetation around is still very scanty. Visitors who have come to Egypt for their health are strongly recommended not to remain in Cairo, but either to go on at once to Upper Egypt or to pass the winter in Ḥelwân, where, besides the baths, they enjoy the advantages of perfect quiet and a remarkably pure and dustless atmosphere (comp. p. 67).

The sulphur springs, which were also probably used in ancient times, resemble those of Aix in Savoy in their ingredients. In 1871 they were utilised for sanatory purposes by Dr. Reil, by order of Khedive Isma'îl. The principal springs are covered in. The bath-house for Europeans contains fourteen cabinets, for warm and tepid baths, shower-baths, and inhalation. There is also a basin containing water strongly impregnated with sulphur, 5-6½ ft. deep, and 1200 sq. yds. in area. The interior of the Khedive's bath-house may also be inspected.

Near the sulphur springs, especially those situated farther to the W., which are still uncovered, a quantity of flint splinters have been found, the largest of which are now in the museum at Bûlâḳ (comp. p. 370). The banks of the Nile afford good wild-fowl shooting, but the desert game is shy and not easily reached.

The subterranean quarries of **Ma'ṣara** and **Ṭura**, which are still worked, yielded the stone used in the construction of the Pyramids. A visit should be paid to these vast caverns, if time permit. The ride thither from Ḥelwân takes 1½ hr; candles and matches should not be forgotten. The stone is transported to the bank of the Nile by means of tramways, carts, camels, and mules.

These immense quarries are hardly less imposing than the Pyramids themselves, for which they afforded material. The Arabs make very poor miners, as they dread the darkness of shafts and pits. They quarry the stone on the outside of the rocky slopes only, while the quarrymen of the Pharaohs penetrated into the interior of the mountain and excavated large chambers, tunnelling their way until they came to serviceable stone, and leaving the inferior untouched. The roofs of the rock-halls, which are of different sizes, are supported by pillars of rock left standing for the purpose. A few remains of hieroglyphics and coloured basreliefs are still preserved in the quarries, but they are of no historical value. During the construction of the railway in 1875 a number of sarcophagi of soft limestone, without inscriptions, were found in a sand-hill in the neighbourhood, belonging probably to a burial-place of the quarrymen of the Pharaohs.

These quarries were also worked during the Ptolemaic and Roman periods, and Strabo, who was generally well-informed, states that the quarries which yielded the stone used in building the pyramids lay on the Arabian bank of the Nile. He says that they were excavated in a very rocky mountain, called '*the Trojan*', and that near them and the Nile lay the village of *Troja*, 'an ancient residence of captive Trojans who had followed Menelaus to Egypt and remained there'. Diodorus gives the same account of the foundation of the Egyptian Troja, but adds that Ctesias has a different version of it Both authors were probably misled by the statement of Herodotus, that Menelaus was hospitably received in Egypt when returning home with Helen from the siege of Troy. There is, however, little doubt that the village called Troja by these authors is the modern Ṭura, which had no connection whatever with the city of Priam. Inscriptions dating from the ancient empire and others of the later monarchy, found in the quarries themselves, inform us that the ancient name of the place was Ta-ro-fu, or more recently Ta-roue, or region of the wide rock-gateway, whence the stone of the pyramids was obtained. This name was corrupted by the Greeks to 'Troja', and as prisoners of state and of war, including many Asiatics, were chiefly employed in the quarries, it was not unnatural to suppose that the colony of quarrymen at the foot of the hill was a settlement of captive Trojans Several slabs of rock bearing figures and hieroglyphics have been found in one of the great rocky halls of Ṭura. One of these represents King Amenophis III (18th Dynasty) sacrificing to the gods Ammon, Horus, and Hersheft, and on the other we find him worshipping Ammon accompanied by Anubis, Sekhet, and Hathor. The inscription under the first slab (with which that on the second is nearly identical) runs thus from the second line onwards· — 'His Majesty ordered new halls (*het-u*) to be opened, for the purpose of quarrying the light-coloured and excellent stone of An for the construction of his buildings founded for perpetuity, after His Majesty had found that the halls of Rufui (Troja) had been tending to great decay since the time of those who had existed at the beginning (i e. former generations). These were newly established by His Majesty'. — Another inscription, of the time of Nectanebus II., runs thus. — 'This excellent quarry of Rufu was opened in order to construct the temple of Thoth, the twice great, the double Aperu, the commander of the divine speech, etc . . . May (its) continuance be everlasting!'

The Barrage du Nil.

RAILWAY. As a train runs from the *Bûlâk ed-Dakrûr* station (p. 224) to (12 M.) *El-Menâshi* (p. 225), the station for the Barrage, in the evening only, and returns on the following morning, travellers cannot visit the Barrage by this line in one day. They will therefore find it more convenient to take a train on the Cairo and Alexandria line as far as (9 M.) *Kalyûb* (p. 227); fare 6 pias. tariff 30, 4 pias. 20, or 2 pias. 30 paras; donkeys and attendants, see p. 233; departure of the trains, see p. 223. Donkeys may be hired at Kalyûb; but, as the saddles are bad, the short ride to the Barrage ($1^1/_4$ hr.) is often uncomfortable. *George Politi* keeps a tolerable restaurant in the bazaar of the village near the Barrage.

Permission to inspect the works connected with the Barrage

must be obtained from the minister of war through the traveller's consulate.

The barrier, which consists of a huge bridge with lock-gates, built across the the Nile at the S. extremity of the Delta, about 12 M. below Cairo, dates from the time of the energetic Moḥammed 'Ali and was constructed from the plans of a French engineer named *Mongel-Bey*.

Fortifications of considerable strength were constructed here by Sa'îd Pasha for the purpose of arresting the progress of any invading army, and storing munitions of war. The place was therefore called *Kal'at Sa'îdîyeh* (Sa'îd's Castle), but is now known as '*Kanâṭir*' (bridges).

The object of the Barrage was to keep the water of the Nile at the same level in all seasons, so that the necessity for irrigation machinery throughout the district below it would have been entirely superseded, while those fields to the S. of it which are on a level with the reservoir would also have benefited. The Barrage was also intended to remove the difficulties of navigation below this point during the three months when the Nile is at its lowest. During that period the water is too shallow for large vessels, and even small vessels are often impeded by shoals and shifting sandbanks; and it was therefore proposed that the whole of the communication by water should then be kept up by means of large canals.

The first trial of the Barrage was unsuccessful; when the gates were closed to retain the water, part of the work gave way and it was hastily concluded that the whole undertaking was a costly failure. For the next twenty years the Barrage was nothing but an impediment to the navigation, as vessels often take several hours to effect the passage of the locks, which is sometimes even attended with danger, and have to pay heavy dues. At the beginning of 1883, however, it was carefully tested by two English engineers, who came to the conclusion that the Barrage might not be so wholly unfitted for its intended purpose as had been generally taken for granted. As the Nile fell, they accordingly lowered the gates inch by inch, and found that no untoward results ensued. On the contrary the water at the Barrage only fell 10 inches while it fell 57 inches at Assuân, and the fellâḥîn were enabled to irrigate their fields without recourse to the expensive steam-pumping apparatus on which they had previously been dependent. It would, however, be rash to make a prophecy from the successful experiment of a single year, and the engineers who conducted it are of the opinion that an expenditure of 200 000*l*. would be necessary to make the Barrage quite secure. As yet, also, no barrier has been constructed for the Damietta branch of the Nile; and for the complete success of the scheme this, of course, would be essential. Comp. the map of the environs of Cairo, p. 316.

5. From Cairo to Suez.

No special preparations need be made for this journey, and a dragoman is superfluous At Suez, Isma'îlîya, and Port Sa'îd there are good hotels in the European style, where local guides may be engaged for the environs These towns present little attraction beyond their situation; but the harbours, the Red Sea, and the Suez Canal will interest most travellers. The excursion may conveniently be made on the way home, as most of the steamers which ply between Alexandria and the European ports touch at Port Sa'îd, besides which it has direct communication with Naples, Marseilles, and Trieste through the Australian and Chinese mail steamers

The journey takes four days 1st Day By train at 11 30 a m. from Cairo to Suez, which is reached at 6 30 p m — 2nd Day. Excursion in the morning to Moses' Spring, and in the afternoon to the harbour of Suez. — 3rd Day. By train at 9 15 a m from Suez to Isma'îlîya, arriving at 11 30 a m (or by steamer if there happens to be an opportunity; see p. 424); excursion in the afternoon to El-Gisr — 4th Day By canal steamer (p. 424) at 7 30 a m to Port Sa'îd, arriving at 2 p m

From Cairo to Suez (149 M) by railway in 7 hrs ; fares 111 piastres tariff 30, 74 pias 20, 44 pias. 30 paras From Cairo to Isma'îlîya only ($97^1/_2$ M), in $4^1/_2$ hrs , fare 73 pias 20, 49 pias , 29 pias. 20 paras. There is only one through-train daily, starting at 11 30 a m , and arriving at Zakâzîk at 1 30 p m , where a stoppage of half-an hour takes place (dinner 3-5 fr.; also quarters for the night) The through-train leaves Suez at 9.15 a m , reaches Isma'îlîya at 11 33 a m , Zakâzîk at 1 46 p m (halt of $^1/_2$ hr), and Cairo at 4 15 p m (A train leaves Zakâzîk for Alexandria viâ Benha at 2 20 p m , reaching Alexandria at 8 45 p.m) — There was formerly a direct railway from Cairo to Suez, traversing the desert, but the line had to be abandoned, partly on account of the want of water, and partly owing to the difficulty in keeping it clear of sand (comp. Map of Lower Egypt).

From Cairo to (9 M.) stat. *Kalyûb*, see p. 227. The slender minarets of the mosque of Mohammed 'Ali (p. 263) and the Mokattam hills (p. 335) remain in sight for a considerable time, and as we approach Kalyûb the Pyramids of Gîzeh become conspicuous to the W. of the line. Beyond Kalyûb a line of rails diverges to the Barrage (p. 406) to the left, and the main line to Alexandria (R. 2) diverges on the same side, farther on. Our train turns towards the N.E., and traverses a fertile and well-watered district, shaded by numerous trees. The next stations are ($13^1/_2$ M.) *Nawa* and ($19^1/_2$ M.) *Shibîn el-Kanâtir*.

About $1^1/_2$ M to the S E. of Shibîn el-Kanâtir is the ruined site of **Tell el-Yehudîyeh** (Hill of the Jews) On this spot Onia, the high priest of the Jews, son of Onia III., aided by Ptolemy Philometor, erected a temple for his countrymen who had been expelled from Palestine by the Syrian party and had met with a hospitable reception in Egypt. To the objection that no true temple could exist anywhere but in Jerusalem he answered in the words of Isaiah (xix 18, *et seq*) — 'In that day shall five cities in the land of Egypt speak the language of Canaan, and swear to the Lord of hosts; one shall be called the city of destruction (or, according to others, 'city of deliverance'). In that day shall there be an altar to the Lord in the midst of the land of Egypt, and a pillar at the border thereof to the Lord'. Some critics have supposed that these and the following verses were interpolated for the purpose of justifying the erection of a temple on the bank of the Nile At all events Onia effected his purpose and erected the sacred edifice. The temple is said to have occupied the site of a ruined sanctuary of Pasht (Sekhet), and recent excavations made here have led to the discovery that a town stood on the spot as early as the time of Ramses II , and attained to great prosperity in the reign of Ramses III., the wealthy Rhampsinitus of Herodotus. The pronomen and surname of the latter monarch (Ramses hak Aan) are of frequent recurrence, and he was probably the founder of the ancient sanctuary, of which but few traces now remain. Every vestige of that edifice, as well as of the Jewish temple, which was built after the model of the Temple of Solomon, and tended materially to widen the breach between the Syrian and Egyptian Jews, had long been lost, when, in 1871, Brugsch found under the rubbish here some massive substructions of Oriental alabaster, and a number of interesting mosaic tiles with which the walls had once been overlaid, and on which were not only rosettes and decorative figures, but representations of battles and sacrificial and other scenes The well-known Oriental type of head, so characteristically drawn by the Egyptian artists, was found to recur very frequently. Cartouches of Ramses III. in fayence and his easily recognised portrait in alabaster were also found at different places. The most valuable are now in the museum of Bûlâk. A walk to this spot is pleasant, and the hills command a picturesque view, especially by evening light, but of the ruins themselves there is very little now to be seen.

Next stations (29 M.) *Inshâṣ*, and (36 M.) *Belbês*, which is supposed to be the ancient *Pharbaethus*. The town was formerly a place of some importance from its situation at the junction of most of the routes leading from Cairo to the East. The railway now approaches the **Fresh-Water Canal**, which was probably constructed by the early Pharaohs, and certainly existed in the 14th cent. B.C., but afterwards fell to decay and was not again utilised until the construction of the modern canal.

Near Zaḳâzîḳ were the sources of those streams which intersected the land of Goshen, rendering it famous for its productiveness, they then fell into the Bitter Lakes, which were connected with the Red Sea by means of an artificial canal. 'Now another canal', says Strabo, 'falls into the Red Sea and the Arabian Gulf near the town of Arsinoe, which some call Kleopatris. It also flows through the so-called Bitter Lakes, which were formerly bitter. But when the canal was constructed they changed their character through the blending of the waters, so that they are now well stocked with fish and frequented by water-fowl' The channel of the old canal, which was re-discovered by the French expedition of 1798, is still traceable at places, and its direction has frequently been followed by the engineers of M de Lesseps. From the not inconsiderable remains of the old canal near Belbês, it appears to have been about 50 yds. (100 ells, according to Strabo) in width, and 16-17½ ft. in depth The somewhat steep banks are still strengthened at places with solid masonry. According to Herodotus the canal was four days' journey, and according to Pliny 62 Roman miles, in length It certainly had a branch, towards the N.E , to Lake Timsâh ('crocodile lake') or it may have flowed entirely in that direction, and been continued thence to the Bitter Lakes The name of Lake Timsâh (p 434), moreover, indicates that it must once have been connected with the Nile. In ancient times the canal was primarily constructed for purposes of navigation, and it is now used by numerous small barges which convey the produce of the Egyptian soil to Ismaʿîlîya for exportation, and bring back cargoes of coal and imported wares in exchange; but the canal is now chiefly important as a channel for conducting fresh water to the towns on its banks, particularly Ismaʿîlîya and Suez, and as a means of irrigating and fertilising the country through which it passes (comp p. 430) Near Cairo the canal diverges from the Nile to the N of the viceroyal palace Kasr en-Nil The volume of water passing through it is regulated by locks, three between Nefisheh and Suez, and another of larger size at Suez itself. The surface of the canal is 54 ft., and the bottom 26 ft. in width, and it averages 7 ft. in depth — The construction of a new and larger fresh-water canal between Cairo and Ismaʿîlîya was begun in 1876

$41\frac{1}{2}$ M. Stat. *Burdên.*

$47\frac{1}{2}$ M. **Zaḳâziḳ** (halt of about half-an-hour; good refreshment-room, with a civil Italian landlord, and tolerable quarters for the night), a thriving, semi-European town, lies on a branch of the fresh-water canal (see above) and on the *Mu'izz Canal* (the ancient Tanite arm of the Nile, p. 438). It is the capital of the E. province of *Sherḳîyeh* and seat of a mudîr, and is said to contain about 40,000 inhabitants.

The situation of Zaḳâziḳ, in the midst of a fertile tract watered by several canals, and connected with the richest districts of the Delta, is extremely favourable, and it is a rapidly improving place. The soil here has been very carefully cultivated since the time of Moḥammed 'Ali (1826), and Zaḳâziḳ forms the chief centre of the Egyptian cotton and grain trade. No less than 50,000 tons of cotton are said to be sold here annually. During the American war the production of cotton in this district was carried to such an extent as to threaten all other branches of agriculture with extinction, but a just equilibrium has fortunately been again restored. Many European merchants have offices here, and the large cotton-factories give the place an almost European appearance. Zaḳâziḳ is also important as a railway junction. — In the vicinity, near *Tell Basṭa*, lay the ancient *Bubastis*, or *Bubastus* (Egyptian *Pi-bast;* the *Pibeseth* of Ezekiel xxx. 17), the capital of the Bubastite nome (p. 91).

The ruins of the ancient Bubastis consist of large and dark mounds of debris, visible from the railway, and situated $\frac{3}{4}$ M. from the station; but the place is uninteresting except to those who endeavour to identify these shapeless remains with the description given by Herodotus (ii. 137, 156) of the town and temple of the Egyptian Artemis (Sekhet, Bast, or Pasht). The site was re-discovered by *Malus.* Wherever an ancient Egyptian town has stood, there are always to be found mounds of earth, rubbish, and potsherds, which the Arabs call 'Kôm'. These mounds here are of unusual height, recalling the account of the place given by Herodotus. He informs us that Sabaco, an Ethiopian monarch, who reigned for 50 years, never caused criminals to be executed, but sent them back to their native places for the purpose of heaping up rubbish to raise the height of the sites (which had already been done in the reign of Ramses II). The town of Bubastis in particular, which contained the beautiful temple of Bubastis, seems to have been specially favoured in this respect, so that, if the story is true, the inhabitants must often have been getting into trouble. It is these mounds which are visible from the railway, but the 'notable temple', of which Herodotus says that 'there are many larger and more costly, but none equal to it for beauty of form', has entirely disappeared. It was situated on an island, which was connected with the mainland by one approach opposite the entrance to the temple, and formed by two moats conducted from the Nile. Each moat was 100 ft in width, and bordered with trees. 'As the temple stands in the centre of the town', says Herodotus, 'it may be seen from every direction, and, as it remained unaltered when the site of the town was raised, the spectator overlooks it wherever he may happen to be. A wall with raised stone-work surrounds it, and another encloses both the temple, containing the image of the goddess, and a grove of trees of considerable height. The temple is a stadium in length, and the same in width. From its entrance runs a paved road, three stadia in length and 400 ft in width, towards the E., across the market-place, and straight to the temple of Hermes. On each side of it rise gigantic trees.' — The temple of Sekhet. the goddess revered here, was the most important of the pilgrimage shrines in Lower Egypt; and the same joyous and licentious festivals which were celebrated in honour of Hathor at Dendera also took place here in presence of Bubastis, another form of Isis Hathor, with similar magnificence and riotousness. 'The young men of Aven (or On, p 333) and of Pibeseth shall fall by the sword', says Ezekiel (xxx. 17), when speaking of their idolatrous practices. Bubastis was the Aphrodite of foreigners, the golden Cypris, and also the Artemis of the Greeks; under the name of Bast she was the Ashera, and under that of Sekhet the Ashtaroth, of the Phœnicians (p. 136) The Upper Egyptians celebrated their joyous festivals at Dendera during the first half of the month corresponding to our October, and the Lower Egyptians probably held theirs at the same season, and also about the period of our Christmas, on the 16th Khoiak (Kiahk, or commonly Kiâk), the 'very auspicious' day dedicated to the goddess Bubastis is represented with the head of a lion or a cat (p. 137). The cat was sacred to her, and, according to Herodotus, cats are said to have received honourable burial at Bubastis.

'When the Egyptians travel to Bubastis', says Herodotus, 'they do so in this manner. Men and women sail together, and in each boat there are many persons of both sexes Some of the women make a noise with rattles, and some of the men blow pipes during the whole journey, while the other men and women sing and clap their hands. If they pass a town on the way, they lay to, and some of the women land and shout and mock at the women of the place, while others dance and make a disturbance. They do this at every town that lies on the Nile; and when they arrive at Bubastis they begin the festival with great sacrifices, and on this occasion more wine is consumed than during the whole of the rest of the year. All the people of both sexes, except the children, make a pilgrimage thither, about 700,000 persons in all, as the Egyptians assert.' — These ancient festivals are recalled to some extent by the modern merry-makings at the fair of Ṭanṭa (p 226)

On leaving Zaḳâzîḳ the train runs round the town, into the market of which we look down on the right. Immediately afterwards the Manṣûra line diverges to the left (p. 438). The fertile tract which we now traverse is part of the *Goshen* of the Bible. During the Turkish régime it fell into a miserable condition, and at the beginning of the century afforded a very scanty subsistence to barely 4000 Arabs; but the cultivation was so rapidly improved by means of the fresh-water canal that it now supports upwards of 12,000 prosperous farmers and peasants. The viceroy Sa'îd Pasha ceded this tract to the company of M. de Lesseps, but it was purchased by his successor Isma'îl Pasha for 10 million francs, erected into a separate province, and garrisoned with cavalry.

The **Goshen** of the Bible (Egyptian *Gosem*) is frequently mentioned by Moses. Thus, in the Book of Genesis (xlv 10), Pharaoh says to Joseph: — 'And thou shalt dwell in the land of Goshen, and thou shalt be near unto me, thou, and thy children, and thy children's children, and thy flocks, and thy herds, and all that thou hast'. Gen. xlvi 28, 29. — 'And he sent Judah before him unto Joseph, to direct his face unto Goshen; and they came into the land of Goshen And Joseph made ready his chariot, and went up to meet Israel, his father. to Goshen, and presented himself unto him'. Gen. xlvii 5, 6. — 'And Pharaoh spake unto Joseph, saying, Thy father and thy brethren are come unto thee. The land of Egypt is before thee; in the best of the land make thy father and thy brethren to dwell; in the land of Goshen let them dwell'. Gen. xlvii. 27: — 'And Israel dwelt in the land of Egypt, in the country of Goshen; and they had possessions therein, and grew. and multiplied exceedingly'. In a later passage the sacred record mentions the cities in Goshen in which the Israelites were compelled to work at the tasks imposed on them by Pharaoh (Exodus i. 11): — 'Therefore they did set over them taskmasters to afflict them with their burdens. And they built for Pharaoh treasure cities, Pithom and Raamses'. Lastly, the first camping-places of the retreating Israelites are enumerated in Numbers xxxiii. 5 *et seq.* — (1) Ramses, (2) Succoth, (3) Etham, and (4) Pi-hahiroth, 'which is before Baal-zephon: and they pitched before Migdol'. Leaving Pi-hahiroth, they then 'passed through the midst of the sea into the wilderness'.

We thus find that the Bible mentions a considerable number of places belonging to Goshen, and as the sites of several of these have been identified with the aid of the Egyptian monuments, we are enabled approximately to determine the boundaries of the district, within which also lay Tell el-Yehûdîyeh (p. 408), Belbês (p. 409), and Bubastis (p. 410). That Goshen lay to the E. of the Delta there can be no doubt, as it was situated between the residence of the Pharaohs and Palestine, and the Scriptures make no mention of the Nile having been crossed. This province was afterwards called the Nomos Arabia, or Arabian nome, and the ancient Egyptian Gosem is spoken of as one of the E. districts of the empire. The name still survives in that of the town called *Kûs* by the Copts, and *Fakûs* by the Arabs (the ancient *Phacusa*; comp. p. 451).

The southernmost point of the triangle formed by the land of Goshen was probably Heliopolis (Matarîyeh), whence the district seems to have extended in a narrow strip as far as Belbês. The S. boundary ran thence, in the latitude of the present Fresh-Water Canal, as far as Lake Timsâh. On the W. the district was probably bounded by the Tanitic arm of the Nile, on the N. by Lake Menzaleh, and on the E. by a branch of the same, as well as by the Balah and Timsâh lakes, which in ancient times were connected by a line of fortifications, and formed a kind of moat behind the bastions erected for the purpose of warding off the attacks of the warlike tribes of W. Arabia. To the S. of the district of Goshen extended a desert tract intersected by ranges of hills, ramifying from the hills which bound the Arabian bank of the Nile. These hills generally run from W. to E., and attain their greatest height in the 'Atâka Mts., which command the N.W. shore of the Gulf of Suez. It is probable that the Jews, who settled in Goshen as shepherds, and afterwards appear as inhabitants of the towns in that region, were compelled to assist in the cultivation of the soil, which seems to have attained a high state of perfection at that period. Several records written on papyrus by Egyptian officials about that epoch are still preserved. They describe the charms of the country in the most vivid colours, stating that life there was 'sweet', and that the soil yielded all kinds of crops in abundance. In a papyrus preserved at Leyden the writer, Keniamen, writes the following report to his superior Hui, an important official under the Pharaoh of the oppression (Ramses II.): — 'Therefore I heard the message of the eye (an official title) of my master, saying: Give corn to the Egyptian soldiers, and to the Hebrews who polish stones for the construction of the great store-houses (bekhennu) in the city of Ramses', etc. — The Israelites were doubtless also employed in the construction of the new canals which converted the sterile land into a smiling agricultural tract, affording abundant subsistence both to man and beast, so that it is not surprising that the emigrants fondly remembered the 'flesh-pots of Egypt'. *Pithom*, where the Israelites made bricks, probably lay, as mentioned below, near *Abû Sulêmân*, which is situated to the S. of the railway between Zakâzîk and Tell el-Kebîr, and near which there is a small lake. Farther on, near the ruin-covered hill of *Rigâbeh*, are several muddy ponds, which contain a considerable volume of water during the inundation, and are probably identical with the 'Barkabuta' (בְּרֵכוֹת), or ponds of Pithom, mentioned in a papyrus of Anastasi VI.†

† According to Brugsch, who relies on the geographical and topo-

Another scene of the forced Israelitish labour was *Ramses*, which has been identified by Lepsius with the ruins of Tell el-Maskhûta (see below), while Brugsch and others suppose it to have been Tanis-Zoân, the modern Sân (see remark, p. 452) The environs of these towns were richly cultivated, while another part of Goshen was, as at the present day, of a sterile character, and probably suitable for pasturage at certain seasons only. In this E province of the empire the Egyptian element of the population preponderated in the towns only. On the coast were settled Phœnician colonists, and the desert tracts bounding and extending into the cultivated land were occupied by Beduins, living in tents, as at the present day; while the marshes in the region around Lake Menzaleh were peopled by cowherds, as to whose Semitic origin the monuments afford conclusive evidence The higher culture of the Egyptians would doubtless in many cases influence and attract these strangers, but the constant influx of immigrants from the vast neighbouring Semitic countries of Asia would on the other hand seriously impede the progress of civilisation in this part of the empire. Down to the present day the character of the population of the N and E parts of the land of Goshen has remained nearly the same as in ancient times The European merchants represent the ancient Phœnicians, the Beduins who haunt the sterile regions are the wandering Semites of antiquity, and the peculiar inhabitants of the Menzaleh region (p. 452) are similar to the primitive pastoral population

Beyond (59 M.) stat. *Abû Hammâd*, on the left, begins the Arabian desert, which is here an undulating sandy plain with scanty desert vegetation. It is intersected in an easterly direction by the fertile *Wâdi Tûmîlât* and the fresh-water canal, which present a striking contrast to their surroundings. On the right, beyond the canal, stretches a beautiful green tract of country, beyond which rise the hills of the desert.

66 M. Stat. *Tell el-Kebîr*, an insignificant place, which lately attained celebrity as the scene of Arabi's defeat by the British troops in 1882. It lays claim to the honour of occupying the site of the *Pithom* of the Bible; but that city must have lain more to the S.W., on the site of the present *Tell Abû Sulêmân* (see above). On leaving Tell el-Kebîr the train passes a cemetery laid out by the English, with a tasteful monument to the British soldiers who fell in the struggle with Arabi. A little farther on a tower and a palace come in sight.

80 M. Stat. **Mahsameh** possesses the remains of a monument which probably belonged to one of the cities of Ramses where the

---

graphical information afforded by the monuments *Pithom* was situated in the Sethroitic Nome, between the Pelusiac and Tanitic arms of the Nile. This district, according to the inscriptions, also bore the Semitic name of *Sukkôt* ('tents'), which it doubtless derived from the nomadic life led by its Semitic shepherd inhabitants, who from a very early period had been permitted by the Pharaohs to pasture their flocks there. Classic authors state that Heracleopolis Parva (see pp 87, 453) was the capital of this nome, while the monuments mention Pi-tom as its capital. The identification of the site of Pithom is farther facilitated by the fact that the ancient itineraries place it on the route from Pelusium to Tanis (p. 452), exactly halfway between these places The surrounding country was covered with lakes and marshes, and was intersected by canals in every direction. At the present day the district is half desert and half swamp, and it is traversed by the canal between Port Sa'îd and El-Kantara.

Israelites made bricks for Pharaoh. We next pass the small station of *Ramses*, which is chiefly used for the traffic connected with the construction of the new fresh-water canal (p. 409).

Near the fresh-water canal is situated the ruin-covered **Tell el-Maskhûta**, the debris of which is not worth visiting. It possesses, however, a large and interesting block of granite, on the front of which is a representation of Ramses II., enthroned between the gods Ra and Tum. The figures were once elaborately executed, but have suffered much from exposure to the air, particularly the heads On the back of the monument the name of Ramses is inscribed six times. Lepsius is probably right in identifying this spot with the *Ramses* of the Bible, and his opinion is corroborated by the existence of huge bricks of Nile mud in the enclosing wall of the buried city, which still contain an admixture of chopped straw, recalling the sacred narrative (Exodus, i. 13, 14): — 'And the Egyptians made the children of Israel to serve with rigour: And they made their lives bitter with hard bondage, in mortar, and in brick, and in all manner of service in the field'. — 'And (Exodus, v. 6, 7) Pharaoh commanded the same day the taskmasters of the people, and their officers, saying, Ye shall no more give the people straw to make brick, as heretofore; let them go and gather straw for themselves'.

Beyond this point the train runs through an entirely desert track, passes the small junction of *Nefîsheh*, and reaches —

$97^1/_2$ M. Stat. **Isma'iliya** (p. 434), where the blue *Lake Timsâh* (p. 434) presents a beautiful and striking contrast to the desert just traversed, especially if some large sea-going steamer happens to be passing, with its masts overtopping the low houses of the town. Isma'îlîya is a terminal station. To the right of the station lies the Arabian quarter of the town.

The Suez train returns by the same line of rails to stat. Nefîsheh (good refreshment-room, embellished with antlers, stuffed birds, and other curiosities), and then turns to the S. (left). On the right we observe a large nursery for trees, the property of ex-Khedive Isma'îl's mother. The train traverses the desert, frequently skirting the fresh-water canal, which it crosses immediately beyond Nefîsheh. This canal runs between the railway and the great Suez Canal, and is navigated by a few small craft only. The Suez Canal, connecting the Mediterranean and the Red Sea, and traversed by large sea-going steamers, and the extensive Bitter Lakes lie on our left (comp. p. 433). Towards the S.W. rises the *Gebel Geneffeh*, or *Gebel Ahmed Daher*, with its productive quarries, which yielded material for the construction of the canal. Beyond ($102^1/_2$ M.) stat. *Serapeum* (p. 433) we obtain a fine view of the bluish green Bitter Lakes (p. 433) on the left. Farther on, the heights of the *Gebel 'Uwêbid* rise on the right. The next station is ($113^1/_2$ M.) *Fâyid*. Near ($125^1/_2$ M.) stat. *Geneffeh* we reach the S. end of the Bitter Lakes. On the left again stretches a vast sandy plain. On the right, above the lower hills, tower the dark masses of the *'Atâka Mts.* (p. 415), the outlines of which stand out very prominently by evening light.

Near ($136^1/_2$ M.) stat. *Shalûf* (p. 432) the canal is visible for a short time. Then (149 M.) *Suez* (see below).

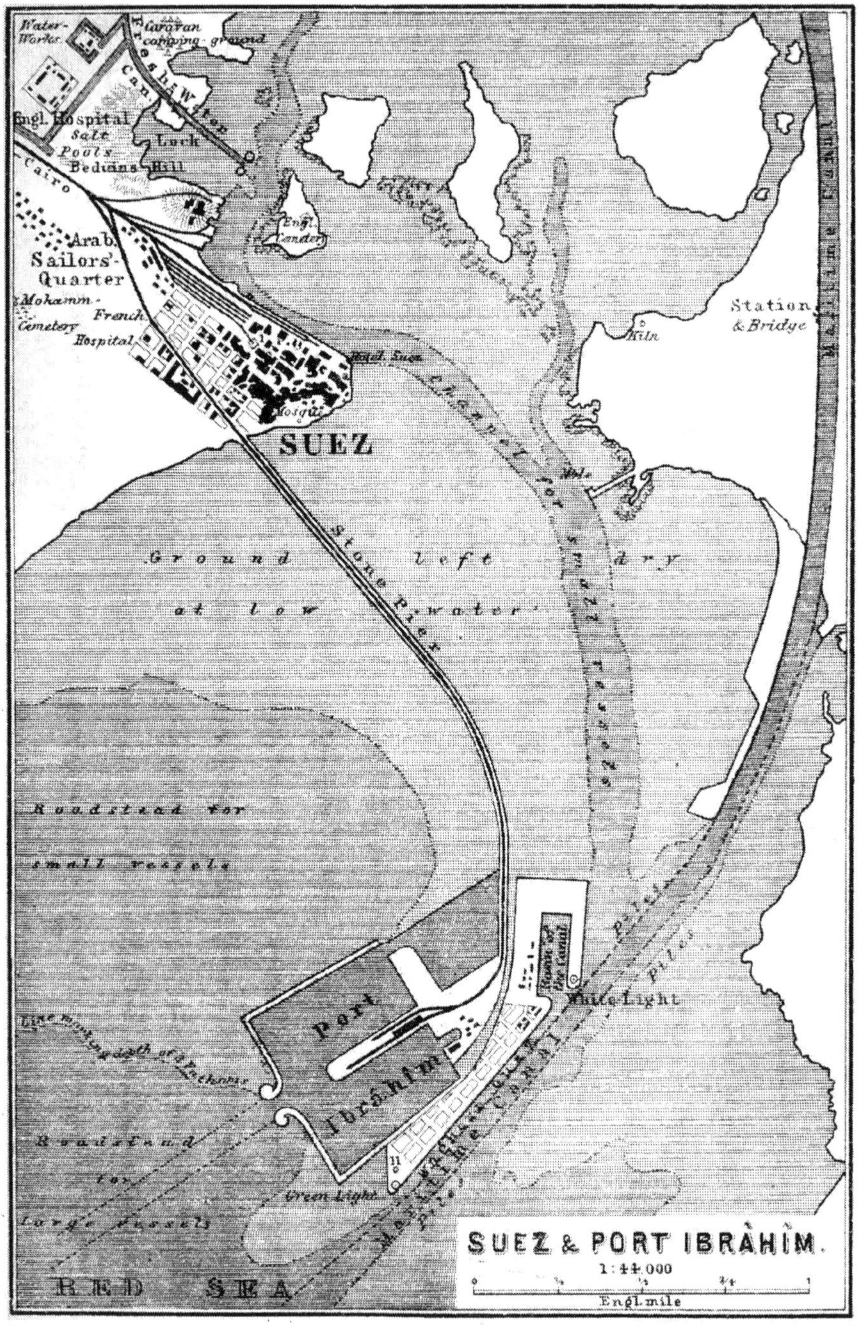

Water-Works
Caravan camping ground
Fresh Water Canal
Engl. Hospital
Salt Pools
Beduins Hill
Lock
Cairo
Arab Sailors' Quarter
Mohamm. Cemetery
French Hospital
Hotel Suez
Mosque
SUEZ
Station & Bridge
Kiln
Mole
Channel for small vessels
Ground left dry at low water
Stone Pier
Roadstead for small vessels
Port Ibrâhîm
Basin of the Canal
White Light
Piles
Maritime Canal
Roadstead for large vessels
Green Light
RED SEA
SUEZ & PORT IBRÂHÎM.
1:44,000
0 1/4 1/2 3/4 1
Engl. mile

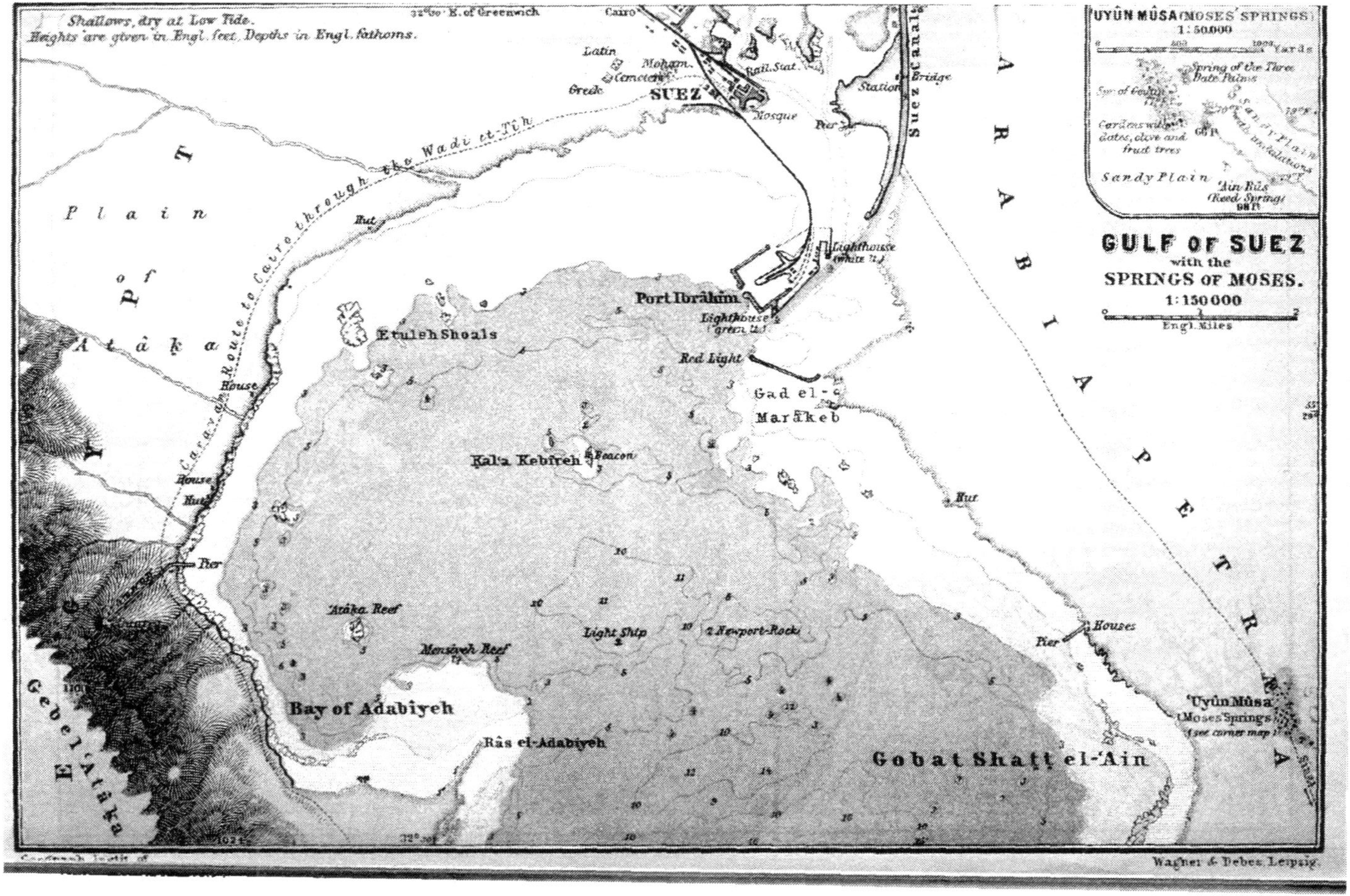
GULF OF SUEZ
with the
SPRINGS OF MOSES.
1:150 000
Engl. Miles
UYÛN MÛSA (MOSES' SPRINGS)
1:50 000
Yards
Spring of the Three Date Palms
Gardens with dates, olive and fruit trees
Sandy Plain
'Ain Rûs (Reed Spring)
Shallows, dry at Low Tide.
Heights are given in Engl. feet, Depths in Engl. fathoms.
32°30' E. of Greenwich
Cairo
Latin
Moham. Cemetery
Greek
SUEZ
Rail. Stat.
Mosque
Pier
Station
Bridge
Suez Canal
ARABIA PETRAEA
Plain of Atâka
Caravan Route to Cairo through the Wadi et-Tih
Hut
House
Lighthouse (white lt.)
Port Ibrâhîm
Lighthouse (green lt.)
Red Light
Gad el-Marâkeb
Etuleh Shoals
Kal'a Kebîreh
Beacon
Light Ship
2 Newport-Rocks
'Atâka Reef
Mensiyeh Reef
Bay of Adabiyeh
Râs el-Adabiyeh
Gobat Shatt el-'Ain
Houses
'Uyûn Mûsa (Moses' Springs) (see corner map)
Gebel 'Atâka
Wagner & Debes, Leipzig.

6. Suez, ʿAin Mûsa, and the Red Sea.

On arriving at the busy station, the traveller is beset by a number of cicerones who speak broken English, French, and other languages.

Hotels. Hôtel Suez (Pl a), situated on the coast, at a considerable distance from the station, a first-class house, fitted up in the English style, and kept by a German; board and lodging 16s. per day (less if a prolonged stay is made) There are two scales of charges. (1st) breakfast 4, tiffin 4, dinner 6s.; (2nd) 2, 2, and 4s. respectively. Bottle of ale or porter 1s. 6d. The servants are Indians, — quiet, attentive people, with delicate features and of slender build. English Church service on Sundays. The shady court of the hotel affords a pleasant lounge. Newspapers for the use of visitors. — Hôtel d'Orient, in the Rue de Colmar, the principal street, 1/4 M from the station; pension, with wine, 10 fr. per day; unpretending, but tolerable — Most of the restaurants and cafés are very disreputable-looking Ladies should not walk in the streets of Suez after dark.

Post and Telegraph Offices (Egyptian) at the station. Telegrams to foreign countries should be despatched by the wires of the Eastern Telegraph Company (English).

Consuls. British, *Mr. West;* French, *M Cravery;* Austrian, *Hr. Margutti;* Russian, *Señ Costa* (p 420), Spanish, *Sen Nacadi.*

Disposition of Time. If the weather is calm, the harbour and entrance to the canal may be visited by small boat. Calm weather is also very desirable for the excursion by land to the Springs of Moses (p 419), as the driving sand is excessively disagreeable in a high wind. The beautiful clearness of the green water, with its curious shells and seaweed, and the almost invariable beauty of the sunsets render a boating excursion here unusually attractive. The situation of the sandbanks and of the navigable channel is of course best inspected at low tide.

A charge of 6-8s. is usually made for a rowing-boat for half-a-day. The boatmen are apt to be extortionate in their demands, as travellers on their way to or from India, and making a short stay only, are often too lavish in their payments In fine weather a day may be pleasantly spent as follows Row early in the morning down the gulf to the mouth of the canal, ascend the canal for a short distance, and land at the usual starting-point for the Springs of Moses. Donkey (which is brought in the boat from Suez) 5-6 fr. for the day We now traverse the desert, which extends down to the sea-shore, to the (2 hrs) Springs, where luncheon (brought from Suez) may be taken An hour or more may be spent here in resting or looking for shells on the shore, after which we regain the boat in 2 hrs. more. We next row (again taking the donkey with us) to the quays, land there, and dismiss the boat Remounting the donkey, we ascend to the docks, inspect them at our leisure, and then return to the hotel The whole excursion may be accomplished without much fatigue in about 8 hrs If the wind is favourable, the traveller may sail as far as the so-called caravan landing-place (comp. Map, p 414), whence the Springs are reached in half-an-hour; but the charge for the boat is then higher, and if the wind is favourable in one direction, it is adverse in the other, so that nothing is to be gained by this arrangement, unless donkeys are altogether dispensed with. In stormy weather the pier and docks only can be visited with comfort.

The ʿAtâka Mountains (p. 418) may be ascended on the S W side, but not without great difficulty, as the rocks are bare and precipitous, and competent guides are not procurable. The view, according to Fraas, is most beautiful and interesting, as the whole of the isthmus and the canal lie at the spectator's feet like a vast map

Natural History of the Red Sea (by *Dr. C B. Klunzinger*) Among the numerous natural products of the Red Sea, which is of a tropical character, with a fauna almost entirely different from that of the Mediterranean, we need only mention those of commercial value and those frequently offered for sale to travellers as curiosities. The prices demanded are usually exorbitant, but may be reduced by bargaining

The *Mother-of-Pearl Shells (sadaf)* of the Red Sea form an important article of commerce, but, owing to the undue extent to which the fishery has recently been carried, the yield has greatly fallen off. The Beduins of the coast, who train slaves as divers, carry on the fishery during the summer. The price of the shells averages 12-15 piastres tariff per okka ($2^1/_2$ lbs), varying according to the size. The largest of the shells are rarely more than two pounds in weight, and the finest are apt to be perforated by worms, in which case they are valueless. The principal mart on the Red Sea for mother-of-pearl and pearls is Jedda (p. 423), the seaport of Mecca. Pearls may sometimes be purchased direct from the Beduins or their slaves, but they ask more than the pearls are worth in Europe, 4-5 fr being often demanded for one of small size The small discoloured pearls, though valueless, are also frequently offered for sale. The Arabs grind them down, and prepare an eye-salve from the powder.

Another common bivalve is the *busr (Tridacna gigas)*, a huge kind of clam-shell The indigestible flesh, called '*surumbâk*', is dried and sold in the markets as an article of food This shell also yields pearls, but they are dull and worthless

Among the univalves the most important is the *Bûk*, a kind of whelk, which the *hâwi*, or conjurer at fairs, uses as a horn. Large and unstained specimens are rare, costing 2-4 fr. each. Other large varieties of the same species are of less value A very common shell-fish is the large *gemel* or *abû sub'âa (Pteroceras lambis)*, which has six long finger-like projections; its flesh is also dried and sold as *surumbâk* (see above). The divers frequently bring up specimens of the large *malha (Cassis cornuta)*, which is of a stone-grey colour externally, and covered with a thick yellow substance at the mouth, in which cameos may be cut The *wad'a*, or cowry, or 'porcelain shell' as it is sometimes called *(Cypraea)*, and the *morsâ'a*, or cone-shell *(Conus)*, are very abundant and rarely worth more than a few paras each. A small white cowry is used in the 'troll-madam' game. A small black-and-yellow striped cowry *(Columbella mendicaria)*, known as the *silêm*, is sometimes exported to the Sûdân, where it is used instead of small coin The glossy mosm'a *(Nerita polita)*, which is often found on the sea-shore, is sometimes used for the same purpose One of the prettiest shells of the Red Sea is the abundant small pink *wardân* or *silesêfu (Monodonta Pharaonis)* with its black and white knobs Among other shells frequently offered for sale are the *Murex*, with its long spines, the *gibrîn (Oliva)*, the long conical *mirwad*, or screw shell *(Terebra)*, the large and thin *Dolium*, and the small *Haliotis*, or ear-shell. The *nehêd*, or top shell *(Trochus)*, and the *sâr'a (Turbo)* are sometimes polished with muriatic acid so as to resemble mother-of-pearl, and are used for ornamental purposes. Black coral, or *yusr*, which realises a high price, is used for the manufacture of rosaries, pipe mouthpieces, and ornaments The purple *dem el akhwân*, or organ coral, is sometimes used as a dye, and the blocks of the porous coral *(Porites)* for building purposes Other kinds of coral, or stony zoophytes, known as *sha'ab*, bleached perfectly white, are frequently seen in the shops They sometimes resemble roses, trees, leaves, and bulbous growths The traveller should, if possible, make a point of seeing the **SUBAQUEOUS CORAL FORMATIONS, which resemble a scene from fairyland A boat is taken in calm weather as far as the slope of the coral reef of Sha'ab which skirts the shore The coral in the immediate vicinity of Suez is not so fine as some of the formations a little farther off Those who are interested in marine zoology should walk along the cliffs at low tide, when they will find thousands of curious shell-fish and zoophytes in the pools, under the stones, and on the beach. They may also amuse themselves by gathering edible mussels, limpets, and sea-urchins and watch the eccentric movements of the crabs. A visit to the FISH-MARKET is also recommended, where the curious and brightly coloured members of the finny tribe are seen to far better advantage than in a museum. The singular looking ball-fish (p. 84) is often stuffed and offered for sale. A large crab, known as the *bint umm er-rubbân*, which is caught on the shore by moonlight without difficulty, is esteemed a delicacy. The tortoise-shell yielded by the loggerhead turtle, and the thick skin of the *gild*, or dugong (*Halicore cetacea*), form considerable articles of commerce. According to some authorities the Jewish ark of the covenant was covered with dugong leather.

History of Suez. Little is known regarding the ancient history of Suez. A town mentioned for the first time by Lucian under the name of *Klysma*, or *Kleisma*, seems to have occupied this site at a very early period. It was a fortified place, and the special task of the garrison was to protect and maintain the old isthmus-canal completed by Darius (p. 427). Ptolemæus calls the place *Clysma Praesidium*, but places it much farther to the S. During the supremacy of the Arabians, who re-opened the old canal for a short time (p. 428), the town was named *Kolzum* or *Kolzim*. After the 8th cent. it seems to have sunk into insignificance, but it is mentioned by Abdulfidâ as the starting-point for Ṭûr (p. 515). — The chief historical interest attaching to the place lies in the fact that it is usually supposed to be close to the point where the Israelites crossed the Red Sea (comp. pp. 419, 483).

Suez, a town with 11,170 inhab., lies at the head of the gulf of that name, one of the N. extremities of the Red Sea, and to the S.W. of the mouth of the Suez Canal. On the W. it is commanded by the picturesque blue heights of the 'Atâḳa Mts., and on the E. by hills belonging to the Asiatic coast range. Before the construction of the great work of M. de Lesseps, Suez was a miserable Arabian village, with 1500 inhab. at most.

'The place', says Dr. Schweinfurth in 1864, 'still consists of confused groups of miserable mud hovels, and ruinous, half-European buildings of lath and plaster. On the quay rises the one-storied block of the English hotel, in front of which are the iron railway shed, a few warehouses, and the consulates of the western powers. Such is the poverty-stricken appearance of the town, where moreover a deathlike stillness prevails, notwithstanding the fact that three different quarters of the globe join hands over its walls. Not a tree, not a spring, not even the meagre saltwort, or a trace of vegetation of any kind, is to be seen on the extensive and flat coast or anywhere in the environs of the town. The blue of the sky and the sea, where half-a-dozen steamers and a few sailing vessels are lying at anchor, affords the only relief to the eye of the spectator.'

To this day the town presents a very dreary appearance, and its trade has again greatly fallen off, the stimulus given to it by the opening of the canal and the large docks having apparently been transient. Neither the Arabian quarter with its seven insignificant mosques, nor the streets of the European quarter, which contain several buildings and warehouses of considerable size, present any attraction. The Arabian bazaar is unimportant, but at the entrance to it are stalls of beautiful shells and coral from the Red Sea, for which exorbitant prices are asked (comp. p. 416). Near the Suez Hotel are several stalls where Chinese articles are sold.

On a mound of debris to the N. of the town, not far from the station and the magazines of the 'Peninsular and Oriental Steam Navigation Company', is a kiosque of the Khedive, commanding a fine view of the mountains of the peninsula of Sinai, the sea, the harbour, and the town. The hill is called by the Arabs *Kôm el-'Olzum*, and was probably the site of the ancient *Ḳolzum* (see above).

A little farther to the N. is the mouth of the *Fresh Water Canal* (p. 409)†, the flow of which into the conduits, as well as its discharge into the sea, is regulated by means of a large lock. The level of the canal is here $6^1/_2$ ft. above that of the Red Sea. The large buildings to the N. of it are the *English Naval Hospital* and the engine-house of the '*Compagnie des Eaux.*' To the E. of the canal is the large camping-ground for the caravans coming from Arabia, which sometimes number as many as a thousand camels and present a most interesting sight. On the way from the kiosque of the Khedive to the canal are a number of salt pools, sometimes tinged red by innumerable microscopically small crabs, which, in the morning especially, diffuse an odour resembling that of violets. The small neighbouring eminence is called the Beduins' Hill. Opposite, to the E., beyond the railway, is the Arabian sailors' quarter, consisting of dirty mud-hovels.

A massive **Pier*, about $1^3/_4$ M. in length, resting on a substructure of artificial stone, 48 ft. in width, extends into the sea to the S. of the town, leading to the **Harbour.* (Boat thither, see p. 415.) The foundation of the pier and of the whole of the quays rests upon a sandbank stretching out from the land in the shape of a hook, and heightened by the addition of large quantities of earth dredged from the S. end of the canal. The deposits of earth thus made also enabled the canal company to embank an area of about 50 acres, on which the arsenal, magazines, workshops, and buildings connected with the docks were erected. The pier affords a pleasant and interesting promenade (donkey 1-2 fr., according to the time), commanding beautiful views of the bay and the mountains enclosing it. At low tide the outline of the sandbank is distinctly traceable.

'The 'Atâka Mts. to the W. of the town looked as if composed of a liquid mixture of molten garnets and amethysts They were reflected in the water at their base, the ebb of which gradually disclosed more and more of the ramparts and buildings around the harbour and the entrance to the canal. The lofty pier, carrying the railway from the anchorage of the large vessels to the town, overtopped all the other buildings, the sandbanks, and the deep pools left isolated by the retiring tide Men riding on donkeys and camels were passing along the pier, and the lower the sun sank, the sharper did their outlines become against the glowing horizon, until at length they looked like black shadows on a transparent golden yellow and violet wall of glass. At length the darkness closed in, and the roads were shrouded in night'.

At the end of the pier we first reach a small dock of the Canal Company on the left, with a lighthouse (white light), beyond which

† Before the construction of the canal the inhabitants of Suez derived a supply of bad water from the Springs of Moses, which was brought to the town by camels and donkeys, and they were afterwards supplied with Nile water by railway, at a cost of $1^1/_2$ centimes per quart. 'What a notable day (29th Dec., 1863) was it then in the town's history when the fresh-water canal was opened, and the life-giving element flowed from the desert into the town in exhaustless abundance! It seemed like a repetition of one of the miracles of Moses.' *H. Stephan.*

is the *Waghorn Quay*, bearing a Statue of *Lieutenant Waghorn*, an enterprising Englishman, who after having spent the best years of his life in establishing regular communication between England and India *viâ* Egypt, died in London in poverty in 1850. M. de Lesseps has placed a French inscription to his memory on the W. side of the monument.

The large basin farther S., which has been named *Port Ibrâhîm*, and is capable of containing 50 vessels of the largest size, is divided by massive bulwarks into two parts, one for vessels of war, and the other for the mail steamers and trading vessels.

The mouth of the dock is protected by gates. The masonry is everywhere admirably constructed, particularly that of the massive breakwater outside the docks. The dry dock is 123 yds. long, 25 yds. wide, and 29 ft. in depth.

On the E. side of these docks are stakes and buoys indicating the entrance to the Suez Canal (p. 431), which is at a considerable distance from the N. extremity of the gulf. (Small boat, see p. 415.)

The **Springs of Moses**, Arabic *'Ain* (pl. *'Ayûn*) *Mûsa*, lie on the E. side of the gulf, about $7\frac{1}{2}$ M. to the S.S.E. of Suez, or $4\frac{1}{2}$ M. from the new docks. (Boats and donkeys, see p. 415.) The whole of the route thither by land traverses the sand of the desert, skirting the sea, which lies to the right. Towards the W. tower the imposing 'Atâḳa Mts. (p. 415), which present a most picturesque appearance on the return route. To the left rise the yellowish ranges of the *Gebel er-Râḥa*, belonging to the long chain of the *Gebel et-Tîh*, and facing the S.E. We are now traversing Asiatic soil, while at the same time the eye ranges over part of the African continent.

'At this point, as at the Hellespont, two different quarters of the globe adjoin each other; but, instead of Europe, we here have the greater continent of Africa lying to the W. of Asia. The meeting of these two neighbours here, however, is of a very different character. While Europe and Asia salute each other across the Bosphorus and Hellespont, adorned with verdant robes and crowned with laurel, as if about to vie with each other in a peaceful contest of song, Asia and Africa seem to scowl at each other across the Red Sea like wrestlers who have divested themselves of their garments and are on the point of entering the lists to fight a fierce battle for the sovereignty of the world. On the African side the 'Ataka Mts. present a bold and menacing appearance, while the dreary desert of Asia, situated among the Gebel er-Râha, bids defiance to its loftier adversary'. *(Schubert.)*

Those who make the excursion by water need hardly be reminded of the profound historical interest attaching to this part of the Red Sea.

'This is the scene of Pharaoh's attempted passage, and these waves were once ploughed by the ships of King Hiram and King Solomon, which every three years brought gold from Ophir, and ivory, ebony, and incense, to the harbours of Elath and Ezion-Geber. Here, too, once plied the light Moorish vessels mentioned in the Old Testament, and similar to the craft now used by the Indo-Arabians. From this point the Phœnician mariners employed by King Necho began their famous circumnavigation of Africa about the year B.C 600, and at a later period enterprising Greek sailors set forth to solve the great geographical problem of the ancient Hellenic world regarding the true character and situation of India The Red Sea was also navigated by the merchantmen of the Ptolemies and the Romans, who by this route imported precious stuffs from India and spices from Arabia — the robes and pearls which decked Cleopatra, and the frankincense which perfumed the halls of the Palatine The waves of this sea, moreover, wash the shores of places deemed sacred by two different religions, viz. Mt. Sinai, and Jedda, the seaport of Mecca' (*Stephan*)

With regard to the Exodus of the Israelites and their passage of the Red Sea, see p 481. If the Red Sea is really meant, and not the Sirbonic Lake, as supposed by Brugsch, the scene of the passage was most probably near the modern Suez.

'Ain Mûsa is an oasis, the property of *M. Costa* (p. 415), about five furlongs in circumference, and watered by several springs. The traveller will easily find a pleasant resting-place for luncheon. The vegetation here is very luxuriant. Lofty date-palms and wild palm saplings, tamarisks, and acacias thrive in abundance; and vegetables are successfully cultivated by the Arabs who live in the mud hovels near the springs, and who expect a bakshîsh from visitors. Their gardens are enclosed by opuntia hedges and palings, at the entrances to which the traveller is beset by barking dogs. The springs, situated in the midst of these gardens, consist of several turbid pools of brackish water. The largest of them, enclosed by an old wall, is said to have been the spring called forth from the rock by the rod of Moses, or the bitter waters which the prophet sweetened by casting a certain tree into them. The scene of these miracles, however, must have been a considerable distance to the S. of this point; but this oasis may have been the spot where Moses and the Israelites sang their beautiful song of praise, recorded in Exodus, xv.

'I will sing unto the Lord, for he hath triumphed gloriously: the horse and his rider hath he thrown into the sea. The Lord is my strength and song, and he is become my salvation he is my God, and I will prepare him an habitation; my father's God, and I will exalt him. The Lord is a man of war. the Lord is his name Pharaoh's chariots and his host hath he cast into the sea· his chosen captains also are drowned in the Red sea. The depths have covered them: they sank into the bottom as a stone Thy right hand, O Lord, is become glorious in power· thy right hand, O Lord, hath dashed in pieces the enemy. And in the greatness of thine excellency thou hast overthrown them that rose up against thee thou sentest forth thy wrath, which consumed them as stubble And with the blast of thy nostrils the waters were gathered together, the floods stood upright as an heap, and the depths were congealed in the heart of the sea. The enemy said, I will pursue, I will overtake, I will divide the spoil, my lust shall be satisfied upon them; I will draw my sword, my hand shall destroy them. Thou didst blow with thy wind, the sea covered them: they sank as lead in the mighty waters'

The oasis is also interesting in a geological point of view, particularly on account of the formation of a number of springs, which lie in funnel-shaped cavities at the top of isolated mounds, 4-6 ft. in height. These springs have been described by Fraas, the geologist, whose account will be best appreciated by the traveller if he visits the mound marked by a solitary palm, about 10 min. to the S.E. of the gardens (view).

'The temperature and character of these springs vary. They range from 70° to 84° Fahr.; and while some of them are quite drinkable and but slightly brackish, others are very bitter and nauseous to the taste. The springs rise in the midst of gardens, where the natural hillocks have been levelled, in funnel-shaped basins, within which the water wells up from numerous small holes; and every new hole the visitor makes with his stick becomes the source of a new spring The natural condition of the springs, however, is more satisfactorily observed in the desert, outside of the opuntia enclosure. About a thousand paces to the E. of the oasis stands a solitary palm, at the foot of a hillock rising about 16 ft. above the level of the plain On the top of this hillock is a pool, 4 ft. in diameter and 1½ ft in depth. The water, 70° in temperature, is very salt and bitter, and the bottom of the pool is covered with inky-black mud. The discharge of the spring forms a stream 3-4 inches in width, which, however, is soon swallowed up by the desert sand at the foot of the hill. Numerous water-beetles, which clung to the hand when touched, the Melania fasciolata Oliv. which seemed to luxuriate in the tepid water, and, as I was much pleased to see, myriads of transparent water-fleas (Cypris delecta Mull.) disported themselves in the basin In the hollow of my hand I caught dozens of them, which swam about for a time with their fringed feelers, and at length got ashore. I next observed in the mud the innumerable transparent scales of dead insects, and I at length discovered that the rock enclosing the hill was entirely composed of Cypris skins It was now obvious that the Cyprides had built the hill. Millions of these little insects had in the course of ages cemented with their calcareous integuments the sand through which the springs rise, thus at length forming a kind of wall around it, and when the surface was in this way raised beyond the height to which the pressure of the water forced the springs, some of them were entirely shut off and compelled to seek some other outlet . . The pressure of the water evidently comes from the Râhah Mts, although they are 10-14 miles distant . . . Had it not been for this organic life, and particularly that of the Cyprides, which gradually walled in the channels of the springs with their remains, so that the surface of the water is at some places 40-50 ft above the level of the desert, and 100 ft above the level of the sea, these waters would simply have been lost among the sands of the desert.' (*O. Fraas*)

Conchologists (p. 416) will find a number of interesting shells on the beach at low tide, but the best places are farther S.

Unless the traveller is bound for Mt Sinai, he will probably not extend his journey farther in this direction. To some of our readers, however, the following brief description of the Red Sea and its shores will not be unacceptable.

The Red Sea and its Coasts (by *Dr. C B Klunzinger*; comp. Map, p 30). The Red Sea, Arab. *El-Bahr el-Ahmar*, or *Bahr el-Hejâz*, the ancient *Sinus Arabicus*, is an arm of the sea extending from the Indian Ocean towards the N W, between Arabia and Africa, to a distance of 1400 miles. It is entered at the S. extremity by the *Bâb el-Mandeb*, a strait 18 M. only in width At the broadest part (in 16° N lat) it is 221 miles in width Towards the N. end it gradually contracts, and at length divides into two arms, the Gulf of 'Akaba (*Sinus Ælanites*), and the Gulf of Suez (*Sinus Heroopolites;* Arab *Bahr Suês*, or *Bahr Kolzum*, so called after the ancient Klysma) The sea averages 400-600, and is at places 1000 fathoms in depth, but the shores are flanked with a network of subterranean coral reefs and islands, which often extend a long way from the coast These reefs render the navigation of this sea very dangerous, particularly at the narrower parts of it, the most dreaded point being the so-called *Bahr Far'ûn* (p. 488), near Ṭûr. The course of the large steamers is in the middle of the sea, which is free from these reefs, but the smaller Arabian vessels always steer close to the shore, with the configuration of which their captains are well acquainted, in order that they may run into one of its numerous creeks *(sherm)* on the slightest threatening of bad weather. The Arabs adopt the cautious policy of never sailing at night or in stormy weather, unless compelled; and when they are obliged to cross the sea, they always wait for settled weather In spite of the miserable construction of their vessels, shipwrecks are accordingly of rare occurrence

No rivers fall into the Red Sea, but a number of intermittent rain-torrents descend from its banks. The water is of a beautiful blue colour, changing to pale green where there are shoals or reefs near the surface. No satisfactory reason for the modern name of the sea has yet been given. The difference between high and low tide is 3½-7 feet The prevalent wind in the N. part of the sea, particularly in summer, is the N. wind, and in the S. part the S E. wind in winter, and the N.W. in summer. The sea is therefore unsuitable for large sailing vessels, which, when bound for India, always sail round the Cape of Good Hope.

The coasts of the Red Sea consist of barren rock or sand, and are almost entirely uninhabited. A little way inland the mountains rise to a height of 4000-7600 feet So far back as the time of Solomon the navigation of the Red Sea was of considerable importance, and several of the seaports, such as Berenike and Myos Hormos, were celebrated. Since the opening of the Suez Canal the sea has been regularly traversed by the Indian steamers, which run direct from Suez to Aden. The traffic between the different places on the coast is carried on by means of the Arabian coasting vessels (*katêra*, barge, *sambûk*, vessel of medium size with a short cutwater; *baghleh*, the same, without cutwater; *dau*, or *dow*, a vessel of considerable size with a prodigious development of stern; *rangeh*, the same, with a long cutwater). Regular communication between some of the more important places is also kept up by Egyptian steamers, which ply fortnightly between Suez, Jedda, Souâkin, and Masau'a. Steamers of the Austrian Lloyd and others also ply between Suez and Jedda at the time of the Meccan pilgrimage

African Coast On this side of the Red Sea there is not a single place of consequence between Suez and Koṣêr. At *Gimsâh*, opposite Ṭûr, sulphur-mines were formerly worked, and it was then a place of some importance; but the mines have been abandoned, and the whole district is now inhabited by a few nomadic Beduins only.

Koṣer (1200 inhab.) is the harbour of Upper Egypt, from which it is 4½ days' journey in a straight line. It was formerly one of the chief outlets for the products of Egypt, particularly grain, and was also the starting-point of numerous pilgrims, but since the opening of the Suez railway it has lost nearly all its importance. It was a place of no importance down to the first decade of the present century, when, under the auspices of Mohammed 'Ali, it increased to a town of 7000 inhabitants It is now a neglected place, as all the pilgrims, except the poorest, now prefer the route by Suez Even its grain trade, its only other resource, has greatly declined, as steamers now convey corn to the Hejaz at a cheaper rate than it can be obtained from Koṣêr The steamers rarely touch here, and the traffic is carried on by native craft only, which ply almost exclusively to Jedda, Yenba', and Wejj.

Koṣêr is the residence of a governor, and possesses a quarantine establishment, a government corn magazine for the supply of the Hejâz (Dakhîreh), and a telegraph office communicating with the valley of the Nile The town is a well-built place, crowned with a citadel, which was erected by Sultan Selîm in the 16th century and still contains a few cannon dating from the French period and a mortar with the inscription, 'L'an III de la Rép française'. In the distant background rise picturesque mountains, culminating in *Gebel Abû Ṭiyûr* and *Abû Suba'a*, 4200 ft. in height. The harbour is sheltered from the prevailing N. wind only. Drinking water has to be brought to the town in skins from the mountains, one day's journey distant.

About 5 M. to the N. is *Old Koṣêr*, with the remains of the ancient *Leukos Limen*, a famous harbour in the time of the Ptolemies, but now blocked up with coral, and accessible to small boats only.

Between Koṣêr and *Râs Benâs*, where *Berenike* was situated, dwell the nomadic 'Ababdeh' (p. 45), and between the latter and Souâkin the 'Bisharîn' (p. 45), both being tribes of a Nubian type.

Souakin (10,000 inhab.), situated in a sterile region with a saline soil, possesses a good harbour. It belonged to the Turks down to 1865, when it was ceded to Egypt, and since that period it has rapidly improved. The principal part of the town lies on a small island, and there are also a number of substantial stone houses belonging to it on the mainland. Behind it extends the busy village of *Gef*, which is inhabited by the native Bisharîn. About 1¼ M. farther inland are the springs which supply the town with water and irrigate the gardens. The chief exports, being products of the district, are cattle, hides, butter, india-rubber, tamarinds, and mother-of-pearl, while ivory, ostrich-feathers, and other commodities from the Sûdân are brought to Souâkin viâ Kassala and Berber, and exported hence. Souâkin was formerly an important depôt of the slave-trade. This seaport is a convenient starting-point for the exploration of the Sûdân, and formed the basis of the English expedition despatched in March, 1885, to co-operate with the Nile army of Lord Wolseley in attacking the Mahdi at Kharṭûm.

Masau'a or *Massowah* (5000 inhab.), the seaport of Abyssinia, belonged to the Turks as early as 1557, and has recently been ceded to Egypt. Like Souâkin, it lies on an island, opposite to which, on the mainland, are the pleasant villages of *Arkiko* and *Mokullu*, with their country-houses and gardens. Masau'a carries on a brisk trade in commodities similar to those of Souâkin. The population consists of Ethiopians, Arabs, and a few Europeans. The climate is very hot, but not unhealthy.

Arabian Side. The seaports of the province of Yemen, on the E. side of the Red Sea, are *Mokhâ*, *Hodêda*, and *Lohâya*. Mokhâ has fallen entirely to decay, and Hodêda alone is visited once monthly by the steamers of the Austrian Lloyd. These places have long since been superseded by the English seaport of *'Aden*.

The most important seaport on the Red Sea, a great focus of Oriental trade, and one of the wealthiest towns in the Turkish empire, is **Jedda**, situated 46 M. to the W. of Mecca, of which it is the port. Pilgrimages from every Mohammedan country converge here, and the merchants transact business with the devotees on their arrival and departure. The inhabitants trade with the interior of Arabia, with Egypt, E. Africa as far as Mozambique, Mesopotamia, Persia, India, and the Malay Islands. Jedda is the chief market for pearls, mother-of-pearl, and black coral, and for the coffee, balsam, senna leaves, aromatic herbs, and horses and donkeys which Arabia produces. It is also a great depôt of Oriental carpets, muslins, woollen and silk stuffs, spices, cocoa-nuts, essential oils, and other products which are exported to the western Mohammedan countries. The imports are corn, rice, butter, oil, and not unfrequently slaves. The covered bazaars and khâns are therefore very interesting, and the markets are well supplied with fruit, which does not grow in the utterly sterile environs, but is imported from El-Yemen by water and still more extensively from *Ṭâif* by land. The harbour lies at a considerable distance from the town, which can only be approached by small craft. Water for drinking is collected in cisterns. The houses are lofty and substantially built, and the town possesses handsome government buildings and a castle. Outside the walls the Muslims point out a stone structure, 120 yds long and 6 yds wide, as 'Eve's Tomb'. Over the 'holy navel' is placed a chapel, containing a hole in the interior through which the visitor can look down on the stone covering that part of the sacred remains. This spot is only one-third of the way from the feet to the head (39 yds.), so that the upper part of Eve's frame must have been disproportionately large. At the time of the Wahhabite wars the town was taken by the Egyptians, but has again belonged to the Turks since 1840. In 1858 a terrible massacre of the Christians took place here, on which occasion the French and English consuls were murdered, and the town was bombarded by the English in consequence

Farther to the N lies **Yenba'**, the seaport of Medîna, which lies about 92 M. to the E. of it *Yenba' el-Bahr*, situated on the coast, with about 2000 inhab only, lies in a sterile region, while the larger town of *Yenba' en-Nakhl*, with about 5000 inhab, situated nearly a day's journey inland, is surrounded with palms and other vegetation. The chief exports are sheep, hides, honey, and dates. Steamers touch here at the season of the pilgrimage only. As Yenba' en-Nakhl is only nominally under the Turkish supremacy, Europeans cannot safely visit it except under the protection of one of the principal inhabitants of the place. Medîna, like Mecca, is forbidden ground to Christians

There are no harbours of note between this point and Suez, but **El-Wejj**, opposite Koṣêr, is an important quarantine station. Since the cholera was brought to Egypt by the Meccan pilgrims in 1865, the quarantine establishment here has been annually fitted up for a month and a half or two months, at the time of the return of the pilgrims after the Great Beirâm. Both the caravans travelling by land, and vessels of every nation from Arabian ports, must undergo quarantine here for five days, or for a longer period if the outbreak of an epidemic is apprehended. While the quarantine lasts, Wejj presents a very busy appearance. The great Mecca caravan, which travels viâ 'Akaba, passes this way both in going and coming The town itself has 600-800 inhab only, a castle built by Sultan Selîm, with a garrison of a few soldiers, a spring of fresh water, and, as the latter is insufficient during the quarantine season, a steam engine for the distillation of sea-water. — The N. part of the Arabian coast, as far as El-Wejj, is under the supremacy of Egypt.

7. From Suez to Port Sa'îd. The Suez Canal.

Between Suez and Isma'îlîya there is no regular steamboat service on the Canal, but large steamers traverse it daily on their route to India and China, and in one of these a passage may generally be obtained by applying to the agent of the company, to whom an introduction may be obtained through the traveller's consul The usual charge for the trip is 10 fr, besides which food must be paid for in accordance with the steward's tariff The vessels of the Messageries Maritimes (p 10), however, issue cabin tickets for the whole trip from Suez to Port Sa'îd for 100 fr., including food and wine.

The S. part of the Canal, from Suez to Isma'îlîya, including the Bitter Lakes and the entrance to Lake Timsâh, is the more interesting. The steamers generally make a very short stay at Suez, where a small boat must be hired by the passenger who desires to land, but they halt at Port Sa'îd for at least 5-8 hrs. to coal, and lay to at the quay, so that passengers can walk ashore. The passage from Suez to Port Sa'îd occupies 16 hrs. (see below), but it now and then happens that vessels run aground, in which case part of the cargo has to be discharged, and a detention of several days takes place

The deck of the large steamers affords a good survey of the surrounding country, but from the small steamboats which ply regularly between Isma'îlîya and Port Sa'îd the passenger cannot see beyond the embankments of the Canal

Railway from Suez to Isma'îlîya, see p 414; a train starts daily at 9 15 a.m, arriving at 11.33 a m (fares 44 pias. 10, 29 pias. 20, 17 pias. 30 paras). From Isma'îlîya to Port Sa'îd a small Egyptian steamer runs every evening, starting about 5 o'clock, after the arrival of the train from Cairo and Alexandria, and arriving at Port Sa'îd about midnight (fare 21½ fr) A small screw-steamer belonging to the Canal Company also runs every alternate day from Isma'îlîya to Port Sa'îd (fare 19½ fr.; the additional 5 fr. charged by the other steamers are paid by them to the Canal Company as a tax). None of these steamers accommodate more than

20-25 passengers. A place on deck should be secured, if possible. The passage from Isma'îlîya to Kanṭara (p. 435), where a halt of $1/2$-$3/4$ hr. is made for refreshments, occupies $2^1/_2$ hrs., and thence to Port Sa'îd $3^1/_4$ hrs., or about $6^1/_2$ hrs. in all. As already mentioned, the large steamers take 16 hrs. to perform the passage between Suez and Port Sa'îd, Isma'îlîya being about half way. They are not allowed to steam at greater speed, as their wash would injure the embankments

The Canal is 160 kilomètres (100 M.) in length, and the E. bank is furnished with posts at intervals of 5 kilomètres. Near the stations, which generally consist of a few wooden huts only, are passing places for the large steamers, named 'Gare du Nord' and 'Gare du Sud' respectively. The Canal is about 26 ft in depth, thus admitting vessels drawing 24-25 ft. of water. The surface varies in breadth from 65 to 120 yds., while the width of the bottom is about 24 yds only. The dues amount to 10 fr. per ton, 10 fr. for each passenger, and 10-20 fr. for pilotage according to the tonnage of the vessel. The use of the Canal is open to vessels of all nationalities.

The **Isthmus of Suez**, a narrow neck of land which connects Africa with Asia, is at its narrowest part $70^1/_2$ M. in width. On the S. side it is washed by the N. part of the *Gulf of Suez* (Arab. *Baḥr Ḳolzum*, Greek *Heroopolite Bay*), the western of the two arms of the Red Sea which separate Africa and Asia. The Isthmus is a low-lying tract of land, the S. part of which may be regarded as a kind of continuation of the gulf. About halfway across it rises an eminence about 50 ft. in height, called El-Gisr (the 'threshold', p. 434), and dividing it into two nearly equal parts. Within the S. half, and adjoining this barrier, lies Lake Timsâḥ, or the Crocodile Lake (p. 434), a little to the W. of which begins the Wâdi Ṭûmîlât (p. 413), a transverse valley, traversed by the Fresh Water Canal, and now partly cultivated. Farther S. we come to a belt of sand-hills in the region known as the Serapeum (p. 433), about 10 M. in width, and beyond them to the Bitter Lakes (p. 433), consisting of a large and a smaller basin. Before the construction of the Canal the deepest part of these lakes, the bottom of which was covered with an incrustation of salt, was 24 ft. below the average level of the Red Sea. In 1856, before the water of the Mediterranean was introduced into the lakes, they covered an area of $14^1/_2$ sq. miles. Between them and the Red Sea extends a desert tract, $12^1/_2$ M. in width, and $2^1/_2$ ft. only above the level of that sea. To the N. of the barrier of El-Gisr lies Lake Ballaḥ, or the Date Lake (p. 435), a little beyond which is Lake Menzaleh (p. 435), originally a shallow sheet of water, extending a long way to the W., as far as the Damietta arm of the Nile, and separated from the Mediterranean by a narrow strip of land only, in which there are now four openings. By the second opening from the E. the harbour of Port Sa'îd has been constructed. The numerous ruins which have been discovered below the surface of this lake indicate that its site was once cultivated land, sprinkled with a number of towns (p. 435).

At a very remote period the Red Sea and the Mediterranean were probably connected, or at all events the former extended as far as Lake Timsâḥ, as fossil conchylia, particularly varieties of the Spondylus, now occurring in the Red Sea, but not in the Mediterranean, have been found there. The isthmus, however, is undoubtedly of very ancient formation, having been as broad at the time of the journey of Herodotus (B. C. 454) as it is now. With regard to the formation of the isthmus we may quote the following passage from M. J. Schleiden: —

'If we suppose a strait substituted for the isthmus, it is not difficult to foresee what would happen. The waves of the Red Sea entering it at one end would soon choke it with sand, while the same result would be caused on the Mediterranean side by the prevalent N. and N.W. winds, the Etesian winds of antiquity. About halfway between the seas these different agents would come into collision, and throw up a bar of sand, the situation of which would naturally be a little to the N. of the central point, as the action of the waves on the S side would be more regular than that of the wind on the N., and thus be generally able to penetrate farther. This bar would gradually be raised by the action of the waves, and that at an accelerating rate in proportion as its growth would present an obstacle to the motion of the water, until its level came to be above the level of low tide The surface would then become dry by exposure to the air, and the loose sand, blown about by the winds, would form sand-hills of the kind found on every sea-shore In this way the connection between the seas would at length be cut off, and the barrier of El-Gisr formed'

The Isthmus of Suez has, from a very early period, formed an important highway between Asia and Africa. A considerable part of its area was occupied with lakes and swamps, while the higher points were fortified to prevent the passage of invaders. Near Pelusium, the 'Key of Egypt', at the E. extremity of the curve formed by the coast of the Delta, to the S.E. of Port Sa'îd, were situated the passes by which the empire of the Pharaohs was entered. The high road from Asia skirted the coast of the Mediterranean, passing Rhinocolura (the modern El-'Arîsh, p. 478), traversed the neck of land separating the Sirbonic Lake from the Mediterranean, and led by Casium (see below), with the temple of Jupiter Casius (the modern Râs el-Kasrûn†), and by the town of Gerrha††, to Pelusium (p. 435), whence several roads di-

† The agnomen of Casius is derived by Brugsch from the Semitic Egyptian word *Hazi* or *Hazion*, signifying the asylum, or land of the asylum, a name which applies admirably to a shrine situated on the extreme E. margin of the Egyptian frontier. He also identifies the *Baal-zephon* of the Bible, which lay 'beside Pi-hahiroth' (Exod xiv 9), with this hill and the shrine of Zeus Casius. The word Ba'al Zephon occurs in a papyrus in the British Museum in the form *Baali Zepûna*, and is the Semitic equivalent ('lord of the north') of the Egyptian Ammon. Pi-hahiroth again literally means the 'entrance to the reed and papyrus swamps', by which was doubtless meant the Sirbonic Lake, so that Pi-hahiroth itself probably lay at the W end of the lake, at the entrance to the neck of land when approached from Egypt (p. 484).

†† *Gerrha* (plur of the Greek *gerrhon*, a wall, or fortified place) is identified by Brugsch with *Anbu* (a word also signifying fortified place), which is mentioned as early as the 19th Dynasty. This place was called *Shur* ('wall') by the Hebrews (Gen. xvi 7, xxv. 18; Exod. xv. 22; 1 Sam. xv. 7, xxvii 8). The town lay a little to the S.W. of Pi-hahiroth, which is mentioned above.

verged to the interior of the Delta. Three other roads, one from Mt. Casius† leading to the E., the second from Gerrha, and the third from Pelusium, converged in the middle of the isthmus (probably near the barrier of El-Gisr), joining the route leading thence past the Serapeum and the W. bank of the Bitter Lakes to the ancient Arsinoe, at the N. end of the Gulf of Suez. The Mediterranean was thus connected with the Red Sea by an overland route at a very early period. After the powerful monarchs of Thebes had expelled the Hyksos and subjugated a great part of the W. side of the continent of Asia, the coast districts of S. Arabia, and many islands and maritime towns of the Mediterranean, Seti I. and Ramses II. (p. 90), the great and warlike princes of the 19th Dynasty, became desirous of establishing communication by water between the Nile and the Red Sea in order that their navies and merchantmen might thus pass between the latter and the Mediterranean. This project was probably carried out as early as the reign of Seti I., as a representation of his time on the outer N. wall of the great banquet hall of Karnak (see vol. ii. of the Handbook), elucidated by inscriptions, informs us that, on his victorious return from Asia, Seti had to traverse a canal (*ta tenat*, or 'the cutting') swarming with crocodiles (so that it must have communicated with the Nile), and defended by bastions, the names of which distinctly indicate that it must have been situated on the frontier of the empire. The construction of the canal is, moreover, attributed by many ancient authors, including Herodotus, Aristotle, Strabo, and Pliny, to Sesostris (Seti I. and Ramses II.). The canal may possibly have led from Lake Timsâḥ to Pelusium, and thus have connected the two seas directly. Blocks bearing the names of Ramses I., Seti I., and Ramses II., found near Ḳanṭara (p. 435), seem to favour this conjecture. At a much later period, after Seti's canal had probably been obliterated owing to neglect, Pharaoh Nekho (p. 92) undertook to construct a canal between the Nile and the Red Sea. The new canal quitted the Nile at Bubastis (p. 410), and entered the Arabian Gulf near the ancient Patumos. No fewer than 120,000 Egyptians perished while engaged in the work, and the king afterwards abandoned the work, as he was informed by the oracle that the barbarians alone would profit by the work. By the 'barbarians' were chiefly meant the Phœnicians, whose fleets at that time commanded both the Mediterranean and the Red Sea. The canal was probably completed, after the conquest of Egypt by the Persians, by Darius, the son of Hystaspes, the great organiser of the Persian empire, and not by Ptolemy Philadelphus, as stated by some authors. Numerous traces

† Brugsch mentions that another route traversed the desert of Shur (to the S. of the Sirbonic Lake) to the Gulf of Suez, but was little frequented, being described by Pliny as '*asperum montibus et inops aquarum*' (mountainous and destitute of water).

of the work, and fragments of monuments with inscriptions both in the Persian and Egyptian character, have been found (p. 432). Under the Ptolemies the canal system was extended. While one arm led from Phakusa on the Nile to the lakes towards the S. of Pelusium, that is, direct to the Mediterranean through the connected lakes of Balah and Menzaleh, another branch was now constructed from Lake Balah to the Bitter Lakes, into which the fresh-water canal watering the scriptural land of Goshen also fell (p. 409). It was thus feasible in the time of the Ptolemies to travel by water from the Nile to the S. part and also to the N. part of a canal, which, like the modern Suez Canal, connected the Red Sea and the Mediterranean in a nearly direct line. When Antony returned to Egypt after the battle of Actium in B. C. 31, Cleopatra made an unsuccessful attempt to convey her ships across the Isthmus of Suez in order to escape with her treasures from Octavian. As, however, it is very improbable that she would have attempted to transport vessels of considerable size for so long a distance by land, there can be little doubt that the canal still existed in her time, although in a dilapidated and unserviceable condition.

The canal is said to have been restored during the Roman period. Another canal, beginning near Cairo, and terminating in the Gulf of Suez, the precise course of which, probably following the earlier channel, is nowhere described, is said to have been called the *Amnis Trajanus*, and was probably constructed during the reign of that emperor (A.D. 98-117). A canal of Hadrian is also mentioned. It is certain, however, that the chief mercantile route between the Red Sea and Italy did not follow the Nile and the canal thence to the Gulf of Suez. The Indian vessels of the Romans touched at Berenike, a little to the N. of the tropic of Cancer, and still more frequently at Leukos Limen, the modern Ḳoṣêr, or at Myos Hormos in the latitude of Siûṭ (Lykopolis) on the Red Sea. From these two last-named seaports, which were much frequented, especially in the month of September, goods were conveyed by the great caravan-route to Koptos on the Nile (near the modern Ḳeneh), and were then transferred to boats which carried them down the Nile to Alexandria, where they were shipped for their ultimate destination. After the Arabs had conquered Egypt, they must have been desirous of connecting the Lower Egyptian part of the Nile as directly as possible with the Red Sea. ʿAmr ibn el-ʿAṣi (p. 101) accordingly restored the ancient canal (of which the Khalîg at Cairo is said to be a portion), and used it for the transport of grain from Fosṭâṭ (p. 241) to Ḳolzum (Suez), whence it was exported by the Red Sea to Arabia. The bed of the ancient canal is said to have been pointed out to ʿAmr by a Copt, to whom a remission of the poll-tax was granted as a reward. The canal is said to have been filled up by the morbidly suspicious Khalîf Al-Manṣûr ibn Moḥammed (754-775), in order to cut off the supplies of the army of the rebel Moḥammed ibn Abû Ṭâlib at Medîna, but the truth of this statement is questionable. It is at all events certain that the canal became unserviceable after the 8th century. At a later period the Venetians frequently thought of constructing a canal through the Isthmus with a view to recover the trade which they had lost owing to the discovery of the route round the Cape of Good Hope, and several travellers advocated the scheme; but no one seriously attempted to carry it out. Leibnitz, too, in his proposal regarding an expedition to Egypt, made in 1671 to Louis XIV., the greatest monarch of his age, strongly recommends the construction of such a canal.

'The lord of Egypt', he says, 'is not only in a position to do great injury to the welfare of the world, as the Turks undoubtedly have done by the stoppage of trade; but he might, on the other hand, confer a great benefit on the human race by uniting the Red Sea with the Nile or with the Mediterranean by means of a canal, in the same way as France has merited the gratitude of Europe by the construction of a canal along the foot of the Pyrenees. The statement that the level of the Red Sea is higher than that of the Mediterranean (as Darius was assured) is a mere myth; and even if such were the case, the opening of such a canal would not expose Egypt to the danger of inundation'.

Sulṭân Musṭafa III., the admirer of Frederick the Great, 'Ali Bey, the enterprising Mameluke prince, and Buonaparte all revived the scheme, and the latter on his expedition to Egypt in 1798 (p. 105) even caused the preliminary works to be undertaken, but the actual execution of the project seemed almost as distant as ever. Lepère, his chief road engineer, and a man of great ability, surveyed the ground under the most unfavourable circumstances, and not without personal danger, but owing to a serious miscalculation he threw great doubt on the feasibility of the undertaking. While in reality the level of the two seas is nearly the same, Lepère estimated that of the Red Sea to be nearly 33 ft. higher than that of the Mediterranean. Laplace among others protested against the accuracy of this calculation, as being in defiance of all the laws of hydrostatics, but the supposed obstacle was sufficiently formidable to prevent any farther steps from being taken, although the scheme still had many supporters, until M. de Lesseps directed his attention to the matter. It was reserved for this shrewd and energetic Frenchman to carry out the task which had seemed impracticable to a series of wealthy and powerful princes. In 1831 he was sent from Tunis to Egypt as a young consular *élève.* At Alexandria, where he had to perform quarantine for a considerable time, he was supplied with books by M. Mimaut, the French consul. Among them was Lepère's Mémoire regarding the scheme of connecting the two seas, which led him to consider its great importance, although Lepère himself doubted its feasibility. In 1838 he made the acquaintance of Lieut. Waghorn, an Englishman (p. 419), whose zealous advocacy of the construction of a route between Europe and India viâ Egypt stimulated his zeal for a similar project. In 1841 and 1847 Linant Bey, the viceroy's engineer of waterworks, and Messrs. Stephenson, Negrelli, and Bourdaloue, demonstrated the inaccuracy of Lepère's observations, and proved that the level of the two seas was nearly the same, so that the construction of a canal between them was possible. In 1854 M. de Lesseps, having matured his plan, laid it before Sa'îd Pasha, who was then viceroy, and who determined to carry it out. Difficulties were thrown in the way of the enterprise by the English government during Lord Palmerston's ministry, but on 5th Jan. 1856 permission to begin the work was formally granted by the viceroy. A considerable time, however, elapsed before the necessary capital was raised, and it was not till 25th April 1858, that the work was actually begun. The viceroy undertook to pay many of the current expenses, and provided 25,000 workmen, who were to be paid and fed by the company at an inexpensive rate, and were to be relieved every three months. In order to provide these workmen with water, 4000 water-casks suitable for being carried by camels had to be constructed, and 1600 of these animals were daily employed in bringing them supplies, at a cost of 8000 fr. per day. On 29th Dec. 1863 the fresh-water canal (p. 409) was completed, so that the company was thenceforth relieved of the enormous expense of supplying the work-people with water. The hands now employed, among whom were a number of Europeans, were less numerous, and much of the work was done by machinery, of 22,000 horse-power in all.

On 18th March, 1869, the water of the Mediterranean was at length allowed to flow into the nearly dry, salt-encrusted basins of the Bitter Lakes, the N. parts of which lay 26-40 ft. below the level of the Mediterranean, while the S. parts required extensive dredging operations.

'The first encounter of the waters of the two seas was by no means of an amicable character; they met boisterously, and then recoiled from the attack; but soon, as if commanded by a 'quos ego' of Neptune, they peacefully mingled, and the ocean once more gained possession of the land which it had covered at a very remote period, but only on condition of rendering service to the traffic of the world'. *(Stephan.)*

The cost of constructing the canal amounted to about 19 million pounds sterling, of which 12,800,000 was paid by the shareholders, while the rest of the sum was almost entirely contributed by the Khedive. [In 1875, however, the British Government acquired the Khedive's shares for a sum of 4,000,000*l.*] The capital was raised in the following manner: —

Original capital, in 400,000 shares of 20*l.* each .	8,000,000*l.*
Loan of 1867-68, repayable in 50 years by means of a sinking fund	4,000,000*l.*
Loan of 1871, repayable in 30 years	800,000*l.*
Total:	12,800,000*l.*

Besides the Canal the company also possesses considerable tracts of land.

The opening of the Suez Canal was inaugurated on 16th Nov. 1869, and the magnificent festivities which took place on the occasion are said to have cost the Khedive no less than 4,200,000*l*.

The great mercantile importance of the Canal is apparent from the following data. The distance from London to Bombay viâ the Cape of Good Hope is 12,548 English miles, and viâ the Suez Canal 7028 M. only. The saving thus effected is 44 per cent of the distance. From Hamburg to Bombay by the Cape 12,903 M., by the Canal 7383, saving 43%. From Trieste to Bombay by the Cape 13,229 M., by the Canal 4816 M.; saving 63%. From London to Hongkong by the Cape 15,229 M., by the Canal 11,112 M.; saving 28%. From Odessa to Hongkong by the Cape 16,629 M., by the Canal 8735 M.; saving 47%. From Marseilles to Bombay by the Cape 12,144 M., by the Canal 5022 M.; saving 59%. From Constantinople to Zanzibar by the Cape 10,271 M., by the Canal 4365 M.; saving 57%. From Rotterdam to the Sunda Strait by the Cape 13,252 M., by the Canal 9779 M.; saving 26%.

The traffic on the Canal is rapidly increasing, as appears from the following statistics, and many vessels (not exceeding 425 ft in length) pass through it at regular intervals.

In 1870	486	vessels of an aggregate burden of	493.911 tons.
1871	765	-	761,467 -
1872	1082	-	1,439,169 -
1873	1172	-	2,085,032 -
1874	1264	-	2,424,000 -
1875	1494	-	2,009,984 -
1880	2026	-	4,350,000 -
1881	2727	-	5,795,000 -
1882	3198	-	7,322,125 -
1883	3307	-	8 051,300 -

In 1883 the British vessels which passed through the Canal were 2537 in number, French 272, Dutch 124, German 122, Austrian and Hungarian 67, Italian 63, Spanish 31, Russian 18; and there were also a number of vessels of other nationalities. The number of passengers on board these vessels was about 115,000.

The net receipts are also steadily increasing: —

Receipts in 1871	340,000*l*	sterling
- - 1872	418,000*l*	-
- - 1873	916,000*l*	-
- - 1874	808,000*l*.	-
- - 1880	1,600,000*l*	-
- - 1881	2,043,000*l*.	-
- - 1882	2 109,000*l*.	-
- - 1883	2 625,000*l*.	-

The fact that the increase in the receipts of the last few years has not kept pace with that of the tonnage of the vessels is explained by the reduction of the tariff.

Passage of the Suez Canal. The entrance to the Canal from the Gulf of Suez is not at the N. extremity of the gulf, but much farther to the S., and is approached by a navigable channel in the sea which is indicated by certain landmarks (p. 419). The vessel first passes the lighthouse (red light) at the end of the pier running out from the Asiatic shore, and then a second (green light) near the docks at the end of the great railway pier. It then follows the deep navigable channel, which at the end of the Canal is 300 yds. in width, but gradually contracts. A number of shoals, which are dry at low tide, lie on the E., and others on the W. side of the ship s course. We pass a handsome pier on the left, from the S. side of which the navigable channel to Suez, bordered by shallows, branches off to the N.W., and then, nearly in the latitude of Suez, we enter the mouth of the canal. On that part of the W. bank of which the Canal has made an island by separating it from the mainland, rise the workshops and coal magazines of the company and the quarantine establishment. At low tide the shallows in the N. part of the gulf are visible, and a series of islands is always to be seen at the extremity of the gulf, which, but for the Canal, might be crossed on foot at low tide. On the westernmost island, situated opposite the railway station and the hotel, is an old burial-ground, and on a larger island farther to the E. are the company's furnaces and workshops.

At the 150th kilomètre (the 83rd on the fresh-water canal) the desert rises in a slight eminence, on which lie a number of huge granite blocks, the remains of two monuments erected here by Darius, during the Persian period, and still bearing traces of hieroglyphics and of the Persian cuneiform characters.

'They were doubtless intended to arrest the eye of the passenger travelling through the canal, and were therefore of imposing dimensions, and placed on a massive pedestal The bed of the ancient canal is, moreover, traceable in the neighbourhood It does not seem to me probable that Darius should have limited himself to the three monuments of which there are still remains, particularly as the distance between the second and third (at Shalûf and Serapeum respectively) is much greater than that between the first and second One other monument at least may therefore be supposed to have stood between the second and third . . . . These three monuments have been destroyed by violence, perhaps during the successful rising of the Egyptians in the reign of Artaxerxes, or after they had finally shaken off the Persian yoke. Fire, which is very injurious to granite, seems to have been used in destroying them'. — *(Lepsius)*

Near *Shalûf et-Terrâbeh* (a station on the left, near the 139th kilomètre, with a village in the midst of vegetation, founded by the company), no less than 40,000 cubic yds. of limestone, coloured red and brown with iron, had to be removed in the course of the excavation of the Canal, and interesting geological formations have been brought to light (comp. p. 60).

'The lower stratum of the bank contains a layer of sharks' teeth (*Carcharodon megalodon Ag*) . . The limestone rock of which the bank consists, and which is rapidly decomposed by exposure to the air, is mingled with salt and gypsum, and betrays its pure oceanic origin; for not only does its lowest stratum contain numerous teeth and vertebræ of the Carcharodon, but the rock itself contains bivalve shells and remains of Bryozoa, which fall out as the rock disintegrates. Above the limestone lies a layer of loose sand A thin stratum of the rock, which is full of remains of boring conchylia and crocodiles' teeth, also contains bones and teeth of large quadrupeds, Cetacea, and sharks'. — *(O. Fraas.)*

Near Shalûf is the second of the monuments erected by Darius (see above), which was discovered by MM. Rozière and Devilliers, two of the savants attached to the French expedition, and was excavated by M. de Lesseps in 1866. The red blocks, which belong to two different monuments, bear Persian cuneiform and hieroglyphic inscriptions. In the latter the name of Darius occurs. The representations still preserved exhibit a curious combination of Persian and Egyptian characteristics. The winged disk of the sun of the Egyptians resembles the 'Feruer' of the Persian monuments. The Persian tiara is adorned with the heads of two kings, opposite to each other. The figures are in the Egyptian style, and between the outstretched hands of each is an Egyptian 'cartouche', or frame for the name of a king. One of the blocks bears hieroglyphics in front (half obliterated) and cuneiform characters at the back.

The Canal now enters what is called the *Small Basin* of the Isthmus, which consists entirely of shell formations, and thence leads into the *Large Basin* of the **Bitter Lakes**† (p. 425). At each end of the large basin rises an iron lighthouse, 65 ft. in height. The water is of a bluish green colour. The banks are flat and sandy, but a little to the left rises the not unpicturesque range of the *Gebel Geneffeh* (p. 414). A little farther on (near the 89th kilomètre) is the cutting which conducts the Canal through the rocky barrier of the **Serapeum**. The railway station (p. 414) is near the fresh-water canal. A flight of steps ascends to the top of the left bank of the Canal. The village, which was founded in 1860, contains several pleasant little gardens.

The ruins from which the station derives its name were formerly supposed to have belonged to a Serapeum, which, according to the itinerary of Antonine, once stood in this neighbourhood; but they can hardly have belonged to a temple of Serapis or to any other sanctuary, and Lepsius is doubtless right in pronouncing them to be the remains of a third monument erected on the bank of the ancient canal by Darius (p. 432). He found here a fragment of the wing of a disk in the Persian style, a stone with cuneiform characters, and a third bearing hieroglyphics, all of which confirmed his opinion. The blocks of limestone lying on the ground belonged to the pedestals of the monuments. The ruins of the real Serapeum have been probably discovered in the remains of a stone building, about 74 paces long (from E. to W.), and 53 paces broad (from N. to S), situated about 1/4 M. to the S of the 14th kilomètre stone on the fresh-water canal. Excavations made there have brought to light a few Egypto-Roman antiquities, which probably once belonged to a village connected with the Serapeum In accordance with the rule regarding the temples of Serapis, the village must have lain entirely beyond the precincts of the sanctuary

At the 85th kilomètre is situated *Tuṣûn*, which is easily recognised by the whitewashed dome of the tomb of a certain *Shêkh Ennedek*, a wealthy chief, who, after having made a pilgrimage to Mecca, is said to have presented his cattle and his gardens to the poor, and to have spent the rest of his life on the Gebel Maryam near Lake Timsâḥ in pious meditation. Excavations in the neighbourhood of Ṭusûn have led to the discovery of many interesting fossil remains of large animals belonging to the meiocene tertiary

† Brugsch identifies the Bitter Lakes with the *Marah* of the Bible (Exod. xv. 23). 'And when they came to Marah they could not drink of the waters of Marah, for they were bitter'.

formation, and pieces of fossil wood have also been found here (p. 338). — Before entering *Lake Timsâḥ* we pass the foot of the *Gebel Maryam*, which an Arabian legend points out as the place where Miriam, when smitten with leprosy for her disapproval of the marriage of Moses with an Ethiopian woman, spent seven days, beyond the precincts of the camp of the Israelites (Numbers, xii.).

At the 80th kilomètre stone the Canal enters **Lake Timsâḥ**, or the *Crocodile Lake* (p. 409), on the N. bank of which lies the town of *Isma'îlîya*. The lake, which is now about 6 sq. M. in area, and of a beautiful pale blue colour, was, before the construction of the Canal, a mere pond of brackish water, and full of reeds. On 18th Nov. 1862 the water of the Mediterranean was let into this basin, which is traversed by two artificial channels for the passage of large vessels.

Isma'îliya. Railway Station, see p 414; steamer to Port Sa'îd, see p. 424 — In the Place Champollion, between the station and the harbour, is the *'Hôtel Paris*, a good though very unpretending inn. On the lake is the small *'Hôtel des Bains de Mer*, pension 12 fr , bath 1 fr.

Post and *Telegraph Offices* and *Chemist's Shop* not far from the railway station

While the Canal was being constructed this town was the central point of the works, and the residence of numerous officials and traders, so that its traffic soon became very considerable, and it has even been extolled by modern poets as a 'wonder of the desert'. Its suddenly acquired prosperity declined almost as suddenly when the canal works were completed, but the town has lately regained a little of its former animation. The houses and gardens and the viceroyal château, which had fallen into a dilapidated condition, have recently been restored. The climate is pleasant and the air dry, notwithstanding the proximity of the water. The ground, which has been reclaimed from the desert by means of irrigation, has been planted with tasteful gardens. On the N.E. side of the town are the château of the Khedive and the waterworks; on the W. side is the Arabian quarter.

The best way of spending a few leisure hours here is to visit the hill of *El-Gisr* (see below; 1-2 hrs.; donkey 1 fr.). The route to it passes the Pierre Gardens and the engine-house of the waterworks.

Canal Journey to Port Sa'îd. The steamer (p. 424) at first follows the navigable channel indicated by stakes. To the S. rises the *Gebel Abû Balaḥ* range. In 1/4 hr. we reach the entrance to the Canal, which now intersects the plateau of **El-Gisr** ('the threshold') in a straight direction. The hills of El-Gisr cross the course of the Canal a little to the N. of Lake Timsâḥ, and presented a serious obstacle to its construction. The average height of the 'threshold' is 52 ft. above the sea-level, and it is now about 82 ft. above the bottom of the Canal. In order to form a cutting through it, no less than 18,767,000 cubic yds. of earth had to be removed, and 20,000 fellâḥîn were employed in the work before machinery could be

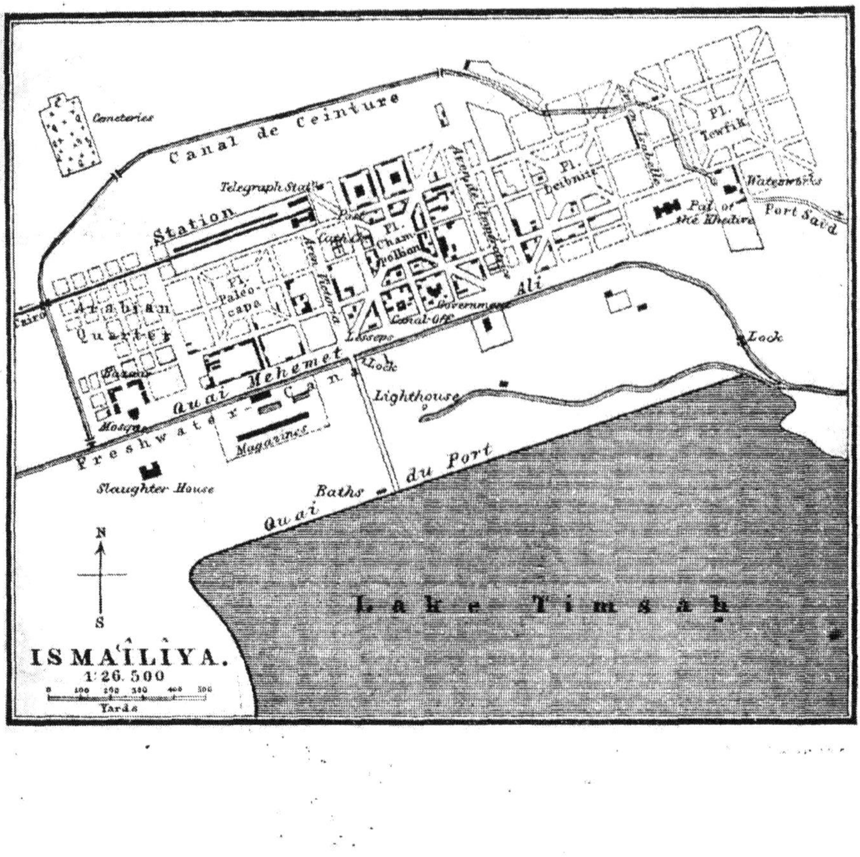
Cemeteries
Canal de Ceinture
Telegraph Stat.
Station
Post
Pl. Champollion
Pl. Paléocapa
Arabian Quarter
Cairo
Bazaar
Mosque
Quai Mehemet Ali
Freshwater Canal
Lock
Magazines
Lighthouse
Slaughter House
Baths
Quai du Port
Government
Canal Off.
Lesseps
Pl. Tewfik
Waterworks
Pal. of the Khedive
Port Said
Lock
Lake Timsah
N
S
ISMAÏLIYA.
1:26.500
0 100 200 300 400 500
Yards

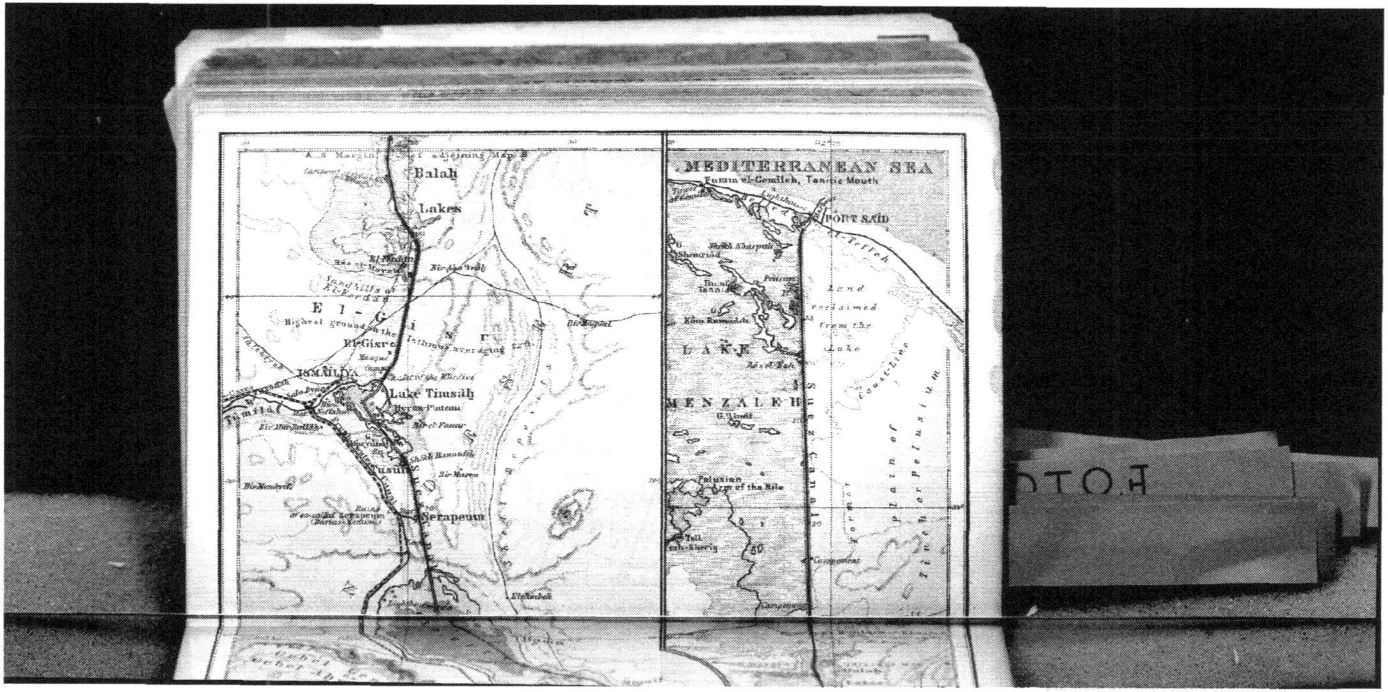
MEDITERRANEAN SEA
Fumm el-Gemileh, Tanitic Mouth
PORT SAID
Balah
Lakes
Land
reclaimed
from the
Lake
LAKE
MENZALEH
Pelusiac Arm of the Nile
Plain of Pelusium
Suez Canal
El-Gisr
ISMAILIYA
Lake Timsah
Tusum
Serapeum

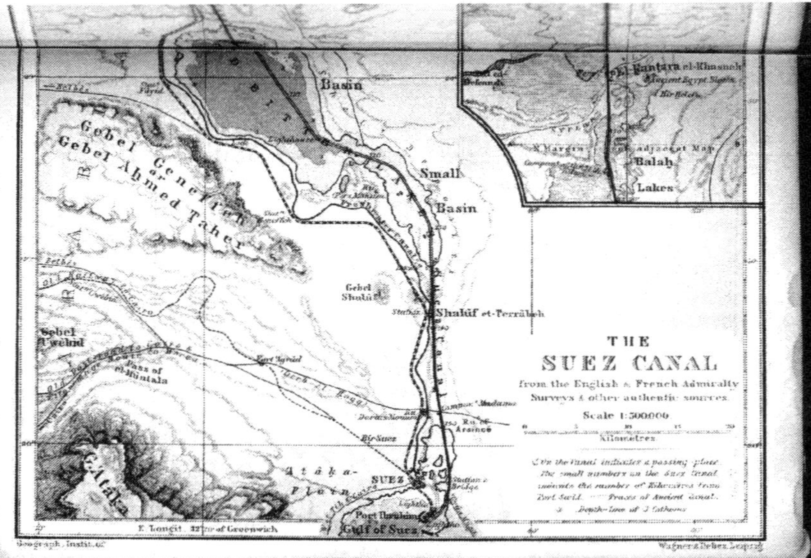
THE
SUEZ CANAL
from the English & French Admiralty
Surveys & other authentic sources.
Scale 1:500000
Kilometres
Basin
Small
Basin
Gebel Geneffeh
or
Gebel Ahmed Taher
Gebel
Shalûf
Shalûf et-Terrâbeh
Gebel
Uwêbid
Pass of
el-Muntala
SUEZ
Port Ibrahim
Gulf of Suez
Balah
Lakes
E. Longit. 32° of Greenwich
Geograph. Instit. of
Wagner & Debes, Leipzig

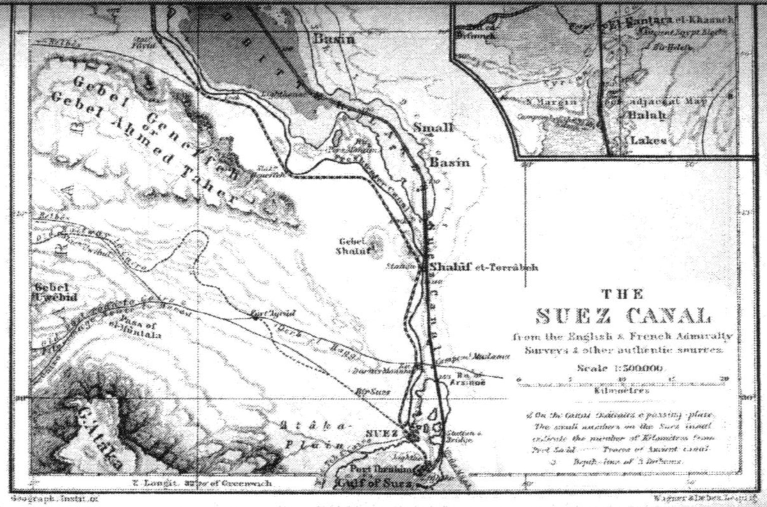
THE
SUEZ CANAL
from the English & French Admiralty
Surveys & other authentic sources.
Scale 1:500000.
Kilomètres
Gebel Geneffeh
or
Gebel Ahmed Taher
Gebel Shalûf
Shalûf et-Terrâbeh
Small
Basin
Gebel Uwêbid
Pass of el-Muntala
SUEZ
Port Ibrahîm
Gulf of Suez
G. Atâka
Atâka Plain
Lakes
Balah
E. Longit. 32° of Greenwich
Geograph. Instit. of
Wagner & Debes, Leipzig

THE
SUEZ CANAL
from the English & French Admiralty Surveys & other authentic sources
Scale 1:500000
Kilometres
MEDITERRANEAN SEA
PORT SAÏD
LAKE
MENZALEH
Balah
Lakes
Lake Timsâh
ISMAÏLIYA
El-Gisr
Serapeum
Great
Basin
Small
Basin
Shalûf et-Terrâbeh
Gebel Geneffeh
Gebel Ahmed Taher
SUEZ
Gulf of Suez
Port Ibrahim

FOLDOUT BLANK

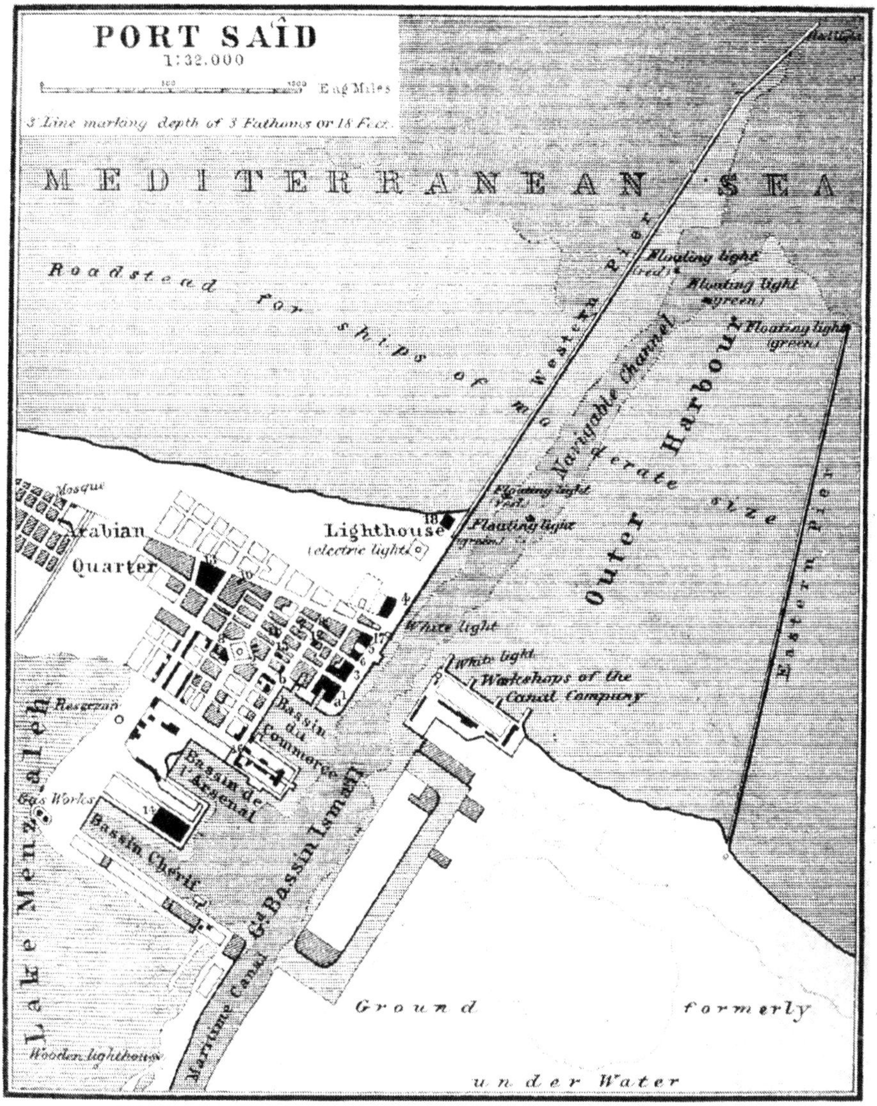

Hôtels:
a. *Hôtel des Pays-Bas.*
b. *Hôtel de France.*
1. *Passport, Custom-house & Egyptian Telegraph Office.*
2. *Austrian Lloyd.*
3. *Messageries Maritimes.*
4. *Peninsular & Oriental Co.*
5. *Russian Steamboat Office.*

Consulates:
6. *German & Russian.*
7. *Austrian.*
8. *British.*
9. *American.*
10. *French.*
11. *Italian.*
12. *Swedish & Norwegian.*
13. *Egyptian Government Offices.*
14. *English Depôt.*
15. *Egyptian Post Office.*
16. *French Post Office.*
17. *Eastern Telegraph.*
18. *Slaughter House.*

brought into operation. At the top of the hill is the deserted village of *El-Gisr*, with a chapel to the Virgin of the Desert, a small Swiss house, and a mosque. A flight of steps ascends to this point from the Canal. In clear weather the view hence embraces a great part of the Isthmus, the frowning 'Atâḳa Mts. rising above Suez, the majestic mountains of the peninsula of Sinai, the course of the Canal, and the green expanse of the Bitter Lakes.

The Canal is flanked with high banks of yellow sand. At the next passing-place we obtain a glimpse of the desert. Near *El-Ferdân* (at the 63rd kilomètre stone) the Canal passes through a cutting, and then traverses *Lake Balah*, from which it is separated by a low embankment. We next reach **El-Ḳantara** ('the bridge'), or properly *Ḳanṭarat el-Khazneh* ('bridge of the treasure'), situated on a rising ground between the Menzaleh and Balâḥ lakes, and forming a kind of natural bridge between Africa and Asia. The caravans starting from the town of Ṣâliḥîyeh, situated on the old Pelusiac arm of the Nile, and the point where the chief commercial routes of the N.E. part of the Delta unite, pass this way, and the projected Egypto-Syrian railway will take the same direction. The old bridge was removed by the Canal Company, and replaced by a ferry. The station here contains several restaurants (*Hôtel de la Poste*, déjeûner 4 fr., very fair; opposite to it are '*Refreshment Rooms*' and a '*Buffet des Voyageurs*'; halt of $1/2$-$3/4$ hr.). The hill to the left commands a tolerable survey of the environs.

About $1^1/_2$ M. from Kantara lie a number of large blocks of the same sandstone conglomerate as that of which the colossal figures of the Memnon consist. They appear to have been used as altars in some monumental edifice, which, as the inscriptions inform us, was erected by Seti I. in honour of his father Ramses I., and completed by Ramses II, the son of Seti. To what ancient town these ruins belonged has not been ascertained. A moderate day's journey distant are situated the extensive ruins of **Pelusium**, the celebrated eastern seaport and key to Egypt, which now contains no objects of interest The ruin-strewn *Tell el-Herr*, and the more extensive *Geziret el-Farama*, which is also covered with debris, were once occupied by the ancient fortress.

Immediately beyond Ḳanṭara begins **Lake Menzaleh,** through which the Canal is constructed in a perfectly straight line to Port Sa'îd (45 kilomètres).

'The brackish waters of this lake extend over an area of about 1000 sq M., covering what was once one of the most fertile districts in Egypt, and was intersected by the three most important arms of the Nile in ancient times, the Pelusiac, the Tanitic, and the Mendesian. Among the numerous towns and villages situated here were the important cities of Avaris, the name of which, afterwards changed to Pelusium, is connected with several important and stirring historical events; Tanis (p. 452), situated on the Tanitic arm and on a canal connecting that arm with the Mendesian, a place where trade and science once prospered; and Tennis (p. 452), of the ruins of which there are still traces on an island in Lake Menzaleh. Not only has this vast tract been lost to cultivation, but the environs of the lake also are in a miserable condition from long neglect ... I have rarely seen a more desolate region than this, which was once so smiling. In the midst of the interminable expanse of sand, swamp, and water, the only relief to the eye was afforded by immense flocks of pelicans and silver herons and a few herds of buffaloes. The right of fishing here is farmed out by government at a rent of 1,500,000 frs. per annum, but what a paltry sum is this compared with the value of the lost land!' *(Stephan).*

The operation of draining the lake has been begun, particularly of the part adjoining the Canal. Curious mirages are sometimes observed here.

Râs el-'Êsh is the last (15th) station. We soon come in sight of the numerous masts of Port Sa'îd, which we reach in $^3/_4$ hr. more. To the N.W. are the white stones of the cemetery, the tombs in which are constructed in the form of vaults of masonry above ground, as the soil is saturated with salt water at a depth of 2 ft. below the surface.

Port Sa'îd.

Hotels. *Hôtel des Pays-Bas (*Netherlands Hotel*, Pl. a), 'pens.' 15 fr.; Hôtel de France et du Louvre (Pl. b), 'pens.' 12 fr. — The *Eldorado* and the *Grand Casino* are two much-frequented music halls, which may be visited by ladies; theatrical performances are given at the former in winter. *Café Paradis*, Quai François-Joseph

Egyptian Post Office, Pl. 15; *French*, Pl 16; *Egyptian Telegraph Office*, Pl. 1; *Eastern Telegraph Co.*, Pl. 17

Consuls. American, *Mr Broadbent;* Austrian, *Hr. v. Reglia;* British, *Mr Burrel*, French, *M Dobignie;* German, *Hr. Bronn;* Greek, *M. Polymeris;* Holland, *Count van der Duyn*, Italian, *Dr. Vitto;* Sweden & Norway, *Mr. Wills;* Belgium, *M. Holbecke;* Denmark, *Mr. O'Connor;* Spain, *Sen. de la Corte;* Russia, *Hr. Bronn*

Banks. Agencies of the *Anglo-Egyptian Banking Co*, the *Crédit Lyonnais*, and the *Banque Ottomane.*

Steamboats, see p 7 Voyage to Jaffa or to Alexandria 15 hrs. — On arriving at Port Sa'îd by sea, as in the case of Alexandria (p. 203), the traveller sees nothing of the low, sandy coast until the steamer reaches the yellowish-green water near it, which is rendered turbid by the mud of the Nile. The lighthouse and the masts of vessels at anchor in the roads first come into view, after which we observe the massive piers (see below) which protect the entrance to the port. The custom-house examination takes place immediately on landing Passports, though asked for, are not indispensable If the vessel does not lay to at the quay, $^1/_2$ fr. is charged for taking each passenger ashore. Travellers wishing to secure a passage in one the steamers bound for Syria during the travelling season (February to April) had better do so by telegraph. — Regular communication with Isma'iliya is maintained by the small screw-steamers of the Suez Canal Co. and of the Egyptian Post Office.

Lake Menzaleh (see p 435) affords excellent *Wild Fowl Shooting* in March and April. Flamingoes are observed among many other species. The charges for the necessary boats vary greatly according to the demand. If possible, the sportsman should return to Port Sa'îd every evening, as the nights are often cold and rainy; but, if provided with a tent, a cook, and other necessary appliances, he may camp out on several of the different islands in succession.

The town of *Port Sa'îd*, which owes its origin to the Suez Canal, lies at the E. extremity of an island which belongs to the narrow strip of land separating Lake Menzaleh from the Mediterranean. It is the seat of the general manager of the Suez Canal. It was expected that the prosperity of the place would increase rapidly, but its progress has hitherto been very gradual. The broad, regular streets consist chiefly of light and temporary brick buildings. The population (17,058, including 6000 Europeans) is similar in character to that of Suez, but the French element preponderates here still more. The construction of the harbour was attended with immense difficulty. It occupies an area of 570 acres, and has been excavated to a depth of 26 ft. by means of laborious dredging. It is protected by two massive piers; the eastern running out into the sea towards the N. for a distance of an English mile; and the western, running towards the N.E. for $1^1/_2$ M., being still unfinished. Where they start from the land these piers are 1440 yds. apart, but their extremities approach within 770 yds. of each other. The navigable entrance, marked by buoys which are lighted at night, is only 100-160 yds. in width. (Those who have leisure may hire a boat for a cruise in the harbour or for the purpose of visiting one of the large steamers lying at anchor.) The most serious risk to which the harbour is exposed is that of being choked up with the Nile mud which is deposited on the Pelusiac coast by a current in the Mediterranean, constantly flowing from the west (comp. p. 207). The western pier is intended to ward off these accumulations of sand and mud, and also to shelter the harbour from the N.W. winds which prevail during two-thirds of the year; and it is therefore of great length and solidity. Both piers were constructed by the Frères Dussaud of blocks of artificial stone, manufactured of seven parts of sand from the desert and one part of hydraulic lime imported from Ardèche in France. The concrete was mixed by machinery and poured into large wooden moulds, in which it remained for several weeks. The moulds were then removed, and the blocks exposed to the air to harden them more thoroughly. Each block weighed 20 tons, and measured about $13^1/_3$ cubic yards in solid content. Thirty of them were manufactured daily, and 25,000 in all were required.

'Above the wooden moulds, which covered an extensive piece of ground, was constructed a tramway, bearing a steam-crane, which could be moved to any required spot, for the purpose of hoisting the blocks and conveying them to their destination. After having been hoisted by the crane, the blocks were transported to a boat, where they were placed on an inclined plane in twos or threes, and secured by means of wedges. They were then conveyed to the place where they were to be sunk, the wedges were removed, and the huge masses then slid down the incline, splitting the wood and emitting sparks of fire on their way, and plunged into the water with a tremendous splash, while the boat staggered from the effects of the shock and was lashed by the waves thus artificially caused. These huge '*pierres perdues*', as they are technically called, were thus gradually heaped up until they reached the surface, and the last layers, rising a little above the level of the water, were finally deposited by means of a crane on board of a steamboat'

On the strip of land separating Lake Menzaleh from the Mediterranean rises the **Lighthouse*, constructed of concrete, 164 ft. in height, and one of the largest in the world. Its electric lights are visible to a distance of 24 M. To the E. of it are quays and workshops. The streets extend along the W. side of the *Inner Harbour*, which consists of three sheltered basins in which vessels discharge and load. The first of these, beginning on the N. side, is the basin of the commercial harbour, the second is that of the quays, and the third the 'Bassin Chérif'. The last is flanked with handsome buildings, which were erected by Prince Henry of the Netherlands as a depôt for facilitating the Dutch goods and passenger traffic between Europe and the colonies of Holland; on his death, however, which happened in 1882, they were purchased by the English government, and they are now used a military depôt and barracks.

8. Towns of the Central and Northern Delta.

A tour in the inland and northern districts of the Delta, including a visit to the towns of Manṣûra, Damietta, and Rosetta, and the exploration of some of the ruins of towns near the embouchures of the Nile, is attended with considerable difficulty and discomfort, with which the attractions are by no means commensurate. A week at least is required for the excursion, unless the traveller confine himself to places lying close to the railway.

Those who are unacquainted with the language, and propose to penetrate into the interior of the country, should be provided with a dragoman or a servant (p. 13), a tent, and a cook, as there are no tolerable hotels except at Ṭanṭa, Damietta, and Rosetta. Introductions should be obtained through the consulate at Cairo to the consular agents at Manṣûra, Rosetta, and Damietta, and to the shêkh of the fisheries at Tanis.

As wet weather and cold nights are not uncommon in the Delta in winter, the traveller should be well provided with warm clothing and rugs. A moderate supply of provisions and wine will also be found useful.

Disposition of Time. The railway traffic in the Delta has much increased of late, so that the following tours can now be accomplished with much less loss of time than formerly. The hours of starting and the fares are so often changed, that it is useless to give them here.

1st Day. From Cairo to Manṣûra. — 2nd Day. At Manṣûra; excursion to Behbît el-Hager; and start from Ṭalkha, opposite Manṣûra, for Damietta. — 3rd Day. Forenoon at Damietta; in the afternoon, by train (1.45 p.m.) to Ṭanṭa. — 4th Day. From Ṭanṭa to Rosetta. — 5th Day: From Rosetta to Alexandria. — A visit to Tanis takes two days more, and to Sais also two days.

The tour may also be made in the reverse direction, and some travellers will find it convenient to proceed from Tanis direct to Port Sa'îd.

The journey itself presents little attraction. The chief characteristics of the monotonous scenery are extensive and often remarkably fertile fields, canals, and dirty villages surrounded by palm-trees.

a. From Cairo to Manṣûra.

92 M. Railway in 6 hrs., fare 69 or 46 piastres tariff.

From Cairo to ($47\frac{1}{2}$ M.) *Zakâzîk*, see R. 5; halt of $\frac{1}{2}$ hr. (*Refreshment Room). The Manṣûra train crosses the Pelusiac arm of the Nile and proceeds to the N.N.E., following the E. bank of the *Mu'izz Canal*, the ancient Tanitic branch of the Nile, and traversing a fertile district. Stations (56 M.) *Mehîyeh* and (62 M.) *Abû Kebîr*.

From Abû Kebîr a branch-line runs to the E. viâ *Tell Fâḳus*, anciently Phacusa (p. 451), to ($20\frac{1}{2}$ M.) *Es-Salihîyeh*, situated on the old Pelusian arm of the Nile (p. 59) and on the caravan road to Syria. — Route viâ Tell Fâkus to *Tanis*, see p. 451.

Beyond Abû Kebîr the line turns to the N.W., crosses the

Mu'izz Canal and a number of other smaller canals, and next reaches (66 M.) *El-Bûha* and ($71^1/_2$ M.) *Abû Shekûk* (route thence to Tanis, see p. 451). — 79 M. *Sinbelâwîn.* — 92 M. *Manṣûra.*

A shorter route from Cairo to Manṣûra is to take the train (leaving Cairo at 10.30 a.m. and 6 p.m.) to *Ṭanṭa* and *Ṭalkha* (p. 442), and then to cross the Nile to Manṣûra.

Manṣûra (*Hôtel de France; Hôtel Papathanasi; Hôtel du Nil; Filiciano's Restaurant;* consular agents for Great Britain, Germany, etc.), a town with 16,000 inhab., surrounded by cotton-fields, lies on the right bank of the ancient Bucolic or Phatnitic arm of the Nile, now the Damietta branch, from which diverges the *Ashmûn* or *Ṣughayyar* ('the little') canal. Next to Ṭanṭa, Manṣûra is the most important provincial town in the Delta; it is the residence of the Mudîr of the province of *Daḳahlîyeh*, and is the chief depôt of the bread-stuffs, cotton, indigo, tobacco, hemp, and flax which this part of the Delta produces. There are several large manufactories here, and many European inhabitants, chiefly Greeks. Most of the houses are badly built and in a dilapidated condition.

History. Manṣûra (i. e. 'the victorious'), a comparatively modern place, was founded by Sultan Melik el-Kâmil in 1220, after the capture of Damietta by the Christians (p. 443), and doubtless as an advantageous substitute for that place in a strategic point of view, as it lies securely ensconced in the angle formed by the Damietta arm of the Nile and the Ashmûn Canal. The new fortress, according to the chronicles of Jordanus, was called New Damietta, to which the epithet of Manṣûra, or 'the victorious', was afterwards added. Melik el-Kâmil constructed the place with great care, and threw a bridge, strengthened with iron, across the Nile, which served both for the purpose of communicating with the opposite bank and as a barrier to prevent the Christians from forcing their way farther up the Nile. The first serious attack made on Manṣûra was by the Crusaders under Louis IX. of France in 1250. After encountering great difficulties they succeeded in crossing the Ashmûn Canal, and on the first day of battle, after a severe struggle, they were eventually victorious. In the neighbourhood of Manṣûra, however, they were repeatedly defeated by the young Sulṭân el-Mo'azzam Ṭuranshah. Their fleet was destroyed, and 'famine-fever' broke out. Negociations of peace proved fruitless, and when the ill-fated Crusaders attempted to escape they were intercepted by the vigilant Turks, who thinned their ranks terribly and captured the king with his brother Charles of Anjou and a number of the knights attending them. Louis thus expresses himself regarding this misfortune in a letter which is still extant. — 'The Saracens with their whole army and in immense numbers fell upon the Christian army during our retreat, and thus it happened that by divine permission, and as our sins merited, we fell into the hands of the enemy. We ourselves, our brothers the counts Alphonso of Poitiers and Charles of Anjou, and all who were retreating with us by land, fell into captivity, though not without many losses by death and much shedding of Christian blood, and not one escaped'. During his captivity at Manṣûra Louis IX. was treated with consideration, even after the young Mo'azzam Ṭuranshah had been assassinated before his eyes, and the crown of Egypt had passed from the house of Saladin to the so-called Bahrite Mamelukes (p. 104). On 6th May, 1250, Louis and his barons were released on payment of a heavy ransom, and on surrendering the town of Damietta.

Leaving the Mudîrîyeh and following the curve described by the street, we pass a small mosque on the left and the German consulate on the right, and after a few hundred paces reach a lane on the left, containing the *Gâmiʿ es-Sign* (here pronounced Sagna), or 'mosque of the prison', which is pointed out as the prison of Louis IX., although Abulfîda has stated that the king was confined in the house of Ibn Fakhreddîn, the scribe of the town, situated on the Nile. (A small room on the bank of the Nile is shown as Fakhreddîn's house, but without the slightest authority.) The mosque contains columns brought from older edifices, with Byzantine capitals of Corinthian tendency, bearing Saracenic arches. The Mambar (pulpit) and ceiling are still embellished with remains of fine wood-carving, which was originally painted. Another, and probably correct tradition points out an old house of Saladin's time, next door to the *El-Muwâfiḳ Mosque*, as the true prison of Louis IX.

The town contains no other sights. The palace of the Khedive is a large and unpleasing building.

Excursion to Behbît el-Hager. The excursion by boat takes 2 hrs. up the river, and $1^1/_2$ hr. in the reverse direction, so that, including a stay of 2 hrs., it occupies 6-7 hrs. in all. The charge for a good boat is 6-8 fr.; bad walkers should take donkeys with them. In ascending the stream, the boat passes the town on the left, lying close to the bank of the river. On the right is the village of *Gôger*, also known from an early period as *Tell el-Yehûdîyeh* ('hill of the Jews'), inhabited by Arabs. Many of the Jews of Manṣûra still cause their dead to be interred here. The next places are *Mît Nâbit* on the right, and *Kafr Wîsh* on the left. The Shêkh el-Beled (mayor of the village) of the latter place possesses a pleasant garden, which is often visited by the inhabitants of Manṣûra, particularly on feast-days, for the purpose of 'smelling the air'. Nearly opposite this village we land (on the right) at an old bulwark of blocks of limestone and bricks, near the *Ḳanṭarat el-Wîsh*, a bridge across a canal which joins the river here. — From the river to the ruins is a pleasant walk of 40 minutes. The luxuriant trees on the route have quite a European appearance, as they include lime-trees, silver poplars, and willows, besides the ṣunṭ-tree, the lebbek, the tamarisk, and the bernûf shrub. We traverse well-cultivated fields, and soon reach the distinct traces of a wall enclosing a heap of ruins, known to the Arabs as '*Ḥager el-Gâmûs*' (buffaloes' stone), which form the remains of the once magnificent **Isis Temple of**  **Ḥebt or Ḥebit,** or *Pa Ḥebit*, i. e. the town of the panegyrics or festive assembly. The words Pa Ḥebit were corrupted by the Arabs to Behbît. The Copts knew the place by its sacred name of *Naisi* (ⲛⲁⲏⲥⲓ), and the Romans called it *Iseum* or *Isidis Oppidum*. It lay in the Sebennytic nome, the capital of which was Sebennytus, situated on the same site as the modern Semennûd (p. 445), once the home of Manetho, and about $6^1/_2$ M. distant from Pa Ḥebit. Some idea of the immense changes which have taken place in the vegetation of this region since the era of hieroglyphics may be formed from the fact that, while the papyrus plant was sedulously and successfully cultivated on both banks of the Nile in the neighbourhood of Sebennytus, not a single specimen of this useful plant is now to be met with, either here or in any other part of the Delta. On the N.W. side of the ruins of the temple lies the village of Behbît, and adjoining it still exists the sacred lake of the temple. The ruins of the venerable sanctuary of Isis form an imposing and most picturesque mass of blocks, fragments of columns and architraves, ceiling slabs, and other remains, altogether about 400 paces in circumference. We are reminded of the animal sacred to Isis by the reliefs of cows and of figures with cows' heads on several of the blocks of stone. The name of Ptolemy II. Philadelphus I. (B.C. 284-246), the founder of the temple, occurs in several places. The structure must have been a very costly one, as it consisted entirely of beautiful granite, chiefly grey, and partly red in colour, brought from a great distance. The sculptures (*hautreliefs* and *reliefs en creux)* are most elaborately executed. Several of the female heads and busts, and some of the cows' heads also, are remarkably fine. In some of the inscriptions the hieroglyphics are unusually large, in others they are of small and elegant form, and in all they are executed in the somewhat flourishing style peculiar to the age of the Ptolemies. The chief deities revered here were Isis, with Osiris and Horus, besides whom occur Seb and Nut, Hathor and Khunsu, the triad of Sehu, Tefnut, and Anhur, Sebek, Hapi (the Nile), and Anubis in the form of Horus, as the avenger of his father. We may also remark here that Anubis, the martyr, was a native of Naisi, or the Iseum, on the site of which we now stand. On the W. side of the ruins is an interesting large slab of grey granite, veined with red, on which is represented the king offering a gift of land to Osiris and Isis, 'the great divine mistress of Ḥebit'. Higher up there is another block of grey granite, with a representation of Isis enthroned, and of the king offering to 'his mother' two small bags of the green mineral called mafkat and *mesṭem*, or eye-paint. The inscriptions consist of the usual formulæ regarding offerings. None of them are perfect, but many must still be concealed among the ruins. The pylons have disappeared, and with them the historical inscriptions also. One of the sculptures represents a procession of the gods of the nome, but unfortunately their names are not given. In one case Isis calls the king 'her brother'. Adjoining a figure of the goddess is the inscription: — 'Isis, mistress of Ḥebit, who lays everything before her royal brother'. On a grey block of granite, lying in an oblique position, is represented the sacred bark of Isis, resembling those seen elsewhere in bronze only. The cabin is like a house of two stories, in the upper of which sits the goddess, with cow's horns and a disk, on a lotus flower, and attended on her right and left by female genii with long wings. Each of the genii bears in her hand the pen of the goddess of truth. The ruins of the temple are now so confused that it is impossible to form even an approximate idea of its original form. A number of blocks resembling mill-stones show that the shafts of the columns were round. The capitals were embellished with the Hathor mask. On the N. side lies an unusually large capital, in granite, and upwards of 7 ft. in circumference. Numerous remains of pillars and architraves also still exist. The steps which led to the roof of the temple, and probably resembled those at Dendera and Edfu, were also of granite. A huge block is still to be seen here with four steps attached to it.

The ruins of *Mendes*, 11 M. to the E. of Manṣûra, whence they may be visited in one day, have recently been excavated, and it is not unlikely that they may afford a rich spoil to the learned explorer.

b. From Manṣûra to Damietta.

40 M Railway from *Talkha* (on the left bank of the arm of the Nile, opposite to Manṣûra, ferry in 5 min, 1/2 fr) The trains leave Ṭalkha at 2 55 and 11 p m and reach Damietta at 4 35 p.m and 1 20 a m. (fares 29 pias 20, 19 pias. 20 paras). — From Tanta (whence the train comes to Ṭalkha) to Damietta, 71 1/2 M, in 3 1/3-4 1/3 hrs. (fares 54 or 36 pias)

The train follows the left bank of the Damietta arm of the Nile. The land is carefully cultivated in the neighbourhood of Manṣûra, and we observe a number of steam engines which are used for the irrigation of the soil. The train stops at (14 M.) *Shirbîn*, an insignificant little town built of crude bricks. The next stations are *Râs el-Khalîg* and *Kafr el-Baṭṭîkh*. The latter lies in a monotonous, sandy plain, extending as far as Lake Burlus, and covered in summer with crops of water-melons. An important melon market is held here in July. The railway-station of Damietta lies on the left bank of the arm of the Nile (ferry in 5 min.; 1 fr.).

40 M. **Damietta**, Arabic *Dumyâṭ*, situated between the Damietta branch of the Nile and Lake Menzaleh, about 4 M. from the sea, possesses a harbour, annually frequented by about 500 vessels of an aggregate burden of 40,000 tons.

Bertrand's Inn, small, French landlord European *Café* kept by *Costi*, a Greek, who also lets a few rooms. Post-office and Arabic telegraph-office. A Roman Catholic and a Greek church

Seen from the railway station, situated near the harbour, Damietta, which now has a population of 43,630 souls, presents an imposing appearance, with its lofty houses flanking the river. The interior of the town, however, by no means fulfils the traveller's expectations. On every side lie ruinous old buildings and walls; many of the houses seem to be uninhabited; and new edifices are sought for in vain. There are few European residents here, the insignificant trade of the place being chiefly in the hands of native merchants (Arabs and Levantines). Small vessels only can enter the Damietta arm of the Nile, as the bar at its mouth is constantly altered in form by the wind and waves, so that vessels are liable to a long detention in the open roads. Under the most favourable circumstances the navigable channel varies from 6 to 16 ft. in depth. The industries to which the town was indebted for its former prosperity (see below) still exist to some extent, and the traveller will find it interesting to visit one of the streets inhabited by the silk and cotton weavers.

History. Little or nothing is known of the early history of Damietta. It is mentioned by Stephanus of Byzantium as *Tamiathis*, a name which has been preserved in the Coptic *Tamiati*. The town must, however, have been a place of some importance during the Roman period, if we may judge from the numerous and occasionally very handsome columns in the mosques, many of which were found on the spot, though others were brought by the Arabs by sea from Alexandria or Pelusium. Domitian seems either to have visited Damietta, or to have been one of its patrons, as a stone bearing his name, doubtless found in the ancient town, now stands in front of the kâḍi's house. At a later period there were probably a good many Christian residents, as a remarkably fine Christian church, which was destroyed by the Crusaders, once stood in ancient Damietta. During the Arabian era Damietta attained a great reputation on account of the resistance it offered to the Crusaders, but the town of that period stood farther to the N. than its modern successor (see below). It was besieged for the first time, but without success, about 1196 by Amalarich and the troops of Manuel, the Greek emperor. Saladin devoted special attention to the fortification of the place. In 1218 Damietta was besieged by King John of Jerusalem with a German, Dutch, English, and French army, under the generalship of the Count of Saarbruck, aided by the knights of three ecclesiastical orders. The Christian army, which was afterwards reinforced by a number of Italian troops, is said to have consisted of 70,000 cavalry and 40,000 infantry, and although this account is probably much exaggerated, it was doubtless very numerous. With the aid of an ingenious double boat, constructed and fortified in accordance with a design by Oliverius, an engineer of Cologne, the Frisians, Germans, and others of the besiegers succeeded after a fight of twenty-five hours in capturing the tower to which the chain stretched across the river was attached. The success of the Christians was however considerably marred by the interference of the ambitious, though energetic Pelagius Galvani, the papal legate, and by the vigilance of the Egyptian prince Melik el-Kâmil. In 1219 many pilgrims, including Leopold of Austria, quitted the camp of the besiegers, believing that they had done their duty. At length, after various vicissitudes, the Christians captured the place. They obtained valuable spoil, sold the surviving townspeople as slaves, and converted the mosques into churches, but in 1221 they were compelled by a treaty to evacuate the town. In 1249, when Louis IX. landed near Damietta, it was abandoned by its inhabitants, who had set all the warehouses on fire. Without striking a blow, the Crusaders marched into the deserted streets of the fortress, but in the course of the following year they were obliged to restore it to the Saracens as part of the ransom of Louis IX., who had been taken prisoner at Manṣûra (p. 439). During the same year, by a resolution of the Emirs, the town was destroyed, and re-erected on the E. bank of the river, farther to the S., on the site which it now occupies. The new town soon became an important manufacturing and commercial place. Its staple products were leather-wares, cloth, and essence of jasmine, for which it was famous, and its harbour was visited by ships of many different nations. After Moḥammed 'Ali's victory over the Turks at Damietta in 1803, he constructed the Mahmûdîyeh Canal with a view to restore Alexandria's ancient importance. Damietta thus lost most of its trade, and its decline was farther accelerated by the foundation of the ports on the Suez Canal.

The town contains no attractions. The principal mosque is a huge, shapeless edifice, the only redeeming features of which are the lofty minarets and the spacious dome. All the houses of more stories than one are provided with handsomely carved wooden jutties and lattice-work, which differ materially in style from the mushrebîyehs of Cairo. The principal street, which is upwards of 1 M. long, forms the busy and well-stocked bazaar of the place.

An interesting excursion may be made to the mosque of *El-Gebâneh*, situated near a cemetery, to the N. of the town (see below). The building appears to date from the period of the old town of Damietta, and has Cufic inscriptions in front. The interior contains numerous columns dating from the Roman period, the bases of which are about 3 ft. below the level of the pavement of the nave. Two of the columns bear curious inscriptions. Some of the shafts are of beautiful verde antico, and others of porphyry. The capitals, including several in the Corinthian style, are partly of Roman and partly of Byzantine workmanship. Two columns standing on the same base are believed, like those in the Mosque of ʿAmr at Cairo, to possess miraculous powers. (Fever-patients, for example, are said to be cured by licking one of them.) The minaret is embellished with early Arabian ornamentation.

About ¾ M. farther from the town is a hollow containing a cemetery and a number of brick houses. The soil here and on the slopes of the adjoining hills is of a dark red colour, whence the place derives its name of *Baḥr ed-Dem*, or 'sea of blood'. According to tradition, 30,000 martyrs of El-Islâm were once massacred here. The neighbouring hills, particularly those on the right, are called *Tell* (plur. *tulûl*) *el-ʿAẓm*, or 'hills of bones', being said to contain multitudes of human skeletons. Reminiscences of the siege of Damietta by the Crusaders in 1219, and of the victory gained here by Moḥammed ʿAli over the Turks in 1803, are curiously mingled in the minds of the natives, and have given rise to various unfounded legends. It is not improbable that part of ancient Damietta once stood on the Tell el-ʿAẓm.

Sportsmen and fishermen will find much to repay them in a visit to Damietta and *Lake Menzaleh* (p 435), ¾ M distant The town is built on both banks of the arm of the Nile, the deposits of which have formed a terrace-like embankment, sloping down to the deeply indented salt lakes at the mouth of the river. In the environs are extensive fields of rice, the harvest of which takes place in Sept and Oct. The fields are intersected in every direction by cuttings and canals, which are crossed by numerous bridges for the use of the cattle Cows are extensively reared here, and the milk and butter of Damietta are the best in Egypt. A walk in the environs will be found interesting The fields are pleasantly shaded at intervals with plantations of sycamores, Cordia, and other trees. The ditches are filled with beautiful white and blue water-lilies (Nymphæa Lotus, N cærulea, and N. stellata) and other aquatic plants. The larger canals are bordered with lofty reeds, the haunt of the ichneumon, which often surprises the traveller by its tameness. Notwithstanding its girdle of inundated plains, canals, and lakes, Damietta enjoys a remarkably healthy climate at all seasons. The atmosphere is never so damp here as at Alexandria, which lies in more immediate proximity to the sea, and even in the height of summer it is often refreshingly cool.

A trip by boat down to the *Mouth of the Nile (Bôghaz)* takes 3-3½ hrs., or, if the wind is favourable, 1½ hr. only (fare 5 fr.). Numerous dolphins will be observed in the river near its mouth.

From Damietta to Rosetta (p 449), viâ *Lake Burlus (Burollos)*, a route which is not recommended, takes 2-3 days at least, and sometimes much longer.

c. From Damietta to Ṭanṭa.

71½ M Railway in 3¼-4¼ hrs (two trains daily, starting at 7 a m. and 1.45 p m.); fares 54 or 36 piastres. To Mahallet-Rûh (junction of the line to Desûk) in 3-3¾ hrs.; fares 47 pias 10, 31 pias 20 paras.

From Damietta to (40 M.) *Ṭalkha (Manṣûra)*, see p. 442. Beyond Ṭalkha the train runs at a little distance to the W. of the Damietta arm, and next reaches (51½ M.) **Semmenûd**, an uninteresting little town, consisting of a densely packed mass of low mud-hovels (no inn). The ruins of the ancient *Sebennytus*, the site of which is now occupied by Semmenûd, are also insignificant. The old Egyptian name of Sebennytus was *Teb-en-nuter*, which the cuneiform inscriptions render *Zabnuti* (Coptic *Sjemnouti* and *Sebennetu*). It was the capital of the nome of Sebennytes Superior, in which Manetho (p. 85) is said to have been born, and where, according to the myth, Horus gained one of his victories over Seth. The figure stamped on the coins of the province represents Horus as a warrior.

Crossing several canals, the train runs towards the S., and stops at (56 M.) **Maḥallet el-Kebir**, a populous town, with numerous European houses, cotton-cleaning mills, and considerable trade. The next stations are (64 M.) **Maḥallet Rûḥ**, the junction for Zifteh and Desûḳ (see below), and (71½ M.) **Ṭanṭa** (see p. 225).

From Mahallet Rûh to Zifteh (20 M), by a branch-line in 1½ hr.; fares 15 or 10 piastres. Stations *Bedrashiyeh*, *Sonṭa*, and **Zifteh**, which lies on the left bank of the Damietta arm.

From Mahallet Rûh to Desûk (33 M.), by an afternoon train (2 30 p.m) in 2½ hrs.; fares 24 pias. 30, 16 pias 20 paras (from Ṭanṭa 31 pias. 20 paras, or 21 piastres). Those travellers only will take this route who intend proceeding from Desûk to Rosetta

The train runs towards the N W, crossing numerous canals Stations *Koṭûr*; *Neshart*, a village on the right bank of the *Bahr Kalin*, which the train crosses; *Shabbâs*, and **Desuḳ**, the ancient *Naukratis*, on the right bank of the Rosetta arm, which is here of considerable width. No accommodation is procurable here, and it is not easy to hire a boat for the whole journey to Rosetta. A small boat may, however, be hired as far as *Fûa*, where a larger craft for the rest of the route is more easily obtained.

d. Saïs.

From the *Kafr ez-Zaiyât* station (p. 225) an excursion may be made to Ṣâ el-Hager, the site of the ancient Sais, the cradle of several royal families (24th, 26th, and 28th Dynasties), but there is no great inducement to visit the place, and even the scientific traveller is not likely to be rewarded unless prepared to make costly excavations At all events a visit to this spot had better be paid in the course of a tour in the Delta, and not on the traveller's first journey to Cairo. A donkey may be hired at Kafr ez-Zaiyât for 15 piastres per day. For a party it is pleasanter and cheaper to make the excursion by boat (easily procured; fare for two days about 25 fr). The journey by land takes 5 hrs., by water 3-8 hrs, according to the wind.

The plain watered by the Rosetta arm of the Nile is extremely fertile. A little to the N. of Kafr ez-Zaiyât the river describes a long curve; and somewhat farther to the N., on the W. bank, a little inland, but visible from the water, rise the ruins known as *Ed-Dahariyeh*, a series of heaps of debris which mark the site of a town of considerable size. On the W. bank, farther on, is the pleasant village of *Nakhleh*. The village of *Sâ el-Hager* (on the E. bank), at which we disembark, lies to the S. of the ruins.

The ancient **Saïs** is mentioned in history at a very remote period, and as early as the 18th Dynasty it was regarded as a cradle of sacerdotal wisdom. The goddess Neith, whom the Greeks identified with their Athene, was the tutelary deity of the place. She was one of the maternal divinities, a manifestation of Isis (p. 135), and was named the 'great cow' which gave birth to the sun. She was worshipped both by the Egyptians and the Libyans. On the Roman coins of the Saite Nome is seen a figure of Minerva with an owl in her right hand and a lance in her left. It was this identification of Neith with Athene that probably led Pausanias to suppose that Pallas-Athene originally came from Libya, to which Saïs was frequently considered to belong. According to an ancient tradition, Athens is said to have been founded by Cecrops of Saïs, and a fanciful corroboration of the myth is sought for in the fact that the letters of A-neth-a and Athena are identical. Most of the Greek scholars who repaired to Egypt for purposes of study went either to Heliopolis or to Saïs. According to Plato, Solon associated here with the learned men of Egypt, Herodotus obtained much information here, and the fame of the Saïte knowledge of mysteries was maintained down to a late period. The 26th Dynasty originated in the city of Neith, and its kings were specially devoted to that goddess, to whom they erected monuments of great splendour. Cambyses also visited Saïs after his conquest of Egypt, and showed himself favourable to the temple of the goddess and her rites. It is not known when the town was destroyed. It was probably an episcopal see at a very early period.

There is now no trace of the famous buildings erected here by Amasis and others (p. 93), or of the chapel formed of a single block of granite brought from Elephantine to Saïs, which must have weighed at least 250 tons. The site of the temple of Neith, which was connected with the royal palace and with a mausoleum for the Pharaohs of the 26th Dynasty, cannot now be identified with any certainty. The columns with palm-capitals, the tomb of Osiris, the obelisks, statues, and androsphinxes, mentioned by Herodotus, have all entirely disappeared. The sacred lake, however, on which, according to Herodotus, mystery-plays were acted at night in honour of Osiris, is probably identical with a sheet of water to the N. of a huge wall enclosing an open space, on the E. side of which the wall is upwards of 500 yds. long and nearly 65ft. in thickness. The outline of the lake was probably once elliptical, but is now of very irregular form. On its S.E. side rise vast heaps of rubbish, marking the site of the royal palace and the temples connected with it. It is, however, impossible to trace the outline of a single building, either here or among the ruins between the village of Ṣâ el-Ḥager and the enclosing wall of the Acropolis, lying to the N. of the cluster of humble fellâḥîn dwellings which have inherited the proud name of Saïs in the form Ṣâ. Mariette's excavations at this spot brought a few antiquities to light, but led to no discovery of importance.

e. Rosetta.

44 M. From Alexandria to Rosetta by railway in $2^1/_2$ hrs; fares 33 pias., 22 pias., 13 pias. 10 paras (two trains daily). The station is outside the Porte Moharrem-Bey, whence the Cairo trains also now start (see p. 206). — From Damanhûr (p. 224) to Rosetta is a journey of one day only, but the start should be made at an early hour. As far as Fumm el-Maḥmûdîyeh a donkey takes $2^1/_2$-3 hrs. (charge about 4 fr.); thence to Rosetta by boat in 5-7 hrs., according to the wind (20-30 fr., or, including stay, which must be specially bargained for, and return, about double that sum).

From Alexandria to Rosetta there is a recently opened railway, skirting the coast, from which short branch-lines are to be constructed to the various coast fortresses. The famous towns which lay on this coast in ancient times have entirely disappeared. As far as *Sîdi Gaber* (p. 223), the second stopping-place, the train runs parallel with the railway to Cairo, which then diverges to the right, while our line follows a N.E. direction. The next station of any importance is ($6^1/_2$ M.) *Ramleh* (p. 222; the station lies $^1/_2$ M. to the E. of the town). Stations *El-Moḥammadîyeh* and *'Azabet es-Siyûf*, the latter of which is a considerable village. Near ($9^1/_2$ M.) *El-Mandara* the train enters upon the neck of land which separates the Lake of Abuḳîr *(Beḥêret Ma'adîyeh)* from the Mediterranean, and reaches (12 M.) **Abuḳîr** (6 M. to the N.E. of Ramleh), an insignificant village, famous for the naval battle of 1st Aug. 1798, in which the English fleet under Nelson signally defeated the French, destroying thirteen of their seventeen vessels. The precise site of the ruins of *Heracleopolis* and *Canopus* is unknown. The latter, which lay 120 stadia from Alexandria, was probably situated a little to the E. of Abuḳîr. Between that village and an opening in the neck of land which separates *Lake Edku* from the sea are some heaps of ruins which perhaps belonged to the ancient **Canopus.**

The city of *Canopus*, which, according to the decree of Tanis (p. 313) passed here, was known by the sacred name of *Pakot*, and by the popular name, still existing in the Coptic language, of *Kah en-Nub*, or 'golden soil', was a very famous place in ancient times. The resemblance of the name Kahennub to Canobus, the helmsman of Menelaus, gave rise to the Greek tradition that that pilot was interred here. Strabo describes the pleasure-loving town as follows. — 'Canobus is a city which lies 120 stadia from Alexandria, if one goes by land, and is named after the helmsman of Menelaus who died there. It contains the highly revered temple of Serapis, which, moreover, works such miracles that even the most respectable men believe in them, and either sleep in it themselves, or get others to sleep there for them. Some persons also record the cures, and others the effects of the oracle dreams experienced there. A particularly remarkable thing is the great number of parties of pleasure descending the canal from Alexandria; for day and night the canal swarms with men and women, who perform music on the flute and licentious dances in the boats with unbridled merriment, or who, at Canobus itself, frequent taverns situated on the canal and suited for such amusements and revelry' — The jars known as 'canopi' (p. 301) derive their name from this place.

On the shore of the semicircular bay of Abuḳîr are several small forts, and on the promontory rises a lighthouse. The train continues to traverse the narrow neck of land between the Lake of Abuḳîr and *Lake Edku* beyond it, on the right, and the Mediterranean on the left. Stations (20 M.) *El-Ma'adîyeh*, near the former Canopic mouth of the Nile (p. 59), and (28 M.) *Edku*, a village situated on a sand-hill to the right. The train finally traverses a dreary expanse of sand, and reaches *Rosetta* (p. 449).

From Damanhûr to Rosetta. We ride past several wells and along the bank of a small canal, traverse some fields, leave the ruins of *Kôm ez-Zargûn* to the right, and in $1^1/_4$ hr. reach the *Maḥmûdîyeh Canal* (p. 223), which lies between lofty banks, and is traversed by barges and small steamers plying between Alexandria and Rosetta. After a ride of about 10 min. more, we observe, on the opposite bank of the canal, a long, desolate-looking, one-storied house, which was used for the accommodation of the workmen employed in cleaning the canal in the reign of Sa'îd Pasha. The canal, which connects Alexandria with Cairo and the Delta, and at the same time supplies the former city with water from the Nile (see p. 215), was constructed by Mohammed 'Ali in 1819 at a cost of $7^1/_2$ million francs. In the execution of the work he employed the forced labour of 250,000 fellâḥîn, of whom no fewer than 20,000 are said to have perished from disease and over-exertion. We follow the bank of the canal, and about $1^1/_2$ M. from Fumm el-Maḥmûdîyeh reach two rows of remarkably fine trees, under the shade of which we continue our route. Near *Fumm el-Maḥmûdîyeh*, where the canal receives its supply of water from the Rosetta arm of the Nile, its banks are lined with solid brick masonry, and at this point we observe a number of barges awaiting the opening of the lock-gates which separate the canal from the river. The engines by means of which an impetus is given to the water so as to cause it to flow towards Alexandria are four in number, each being of 100-horse power. The large and handsome engine-rooms may be visited by the traveller. Adjacent is a workshop for repairs.

The banks of the Rosetta arm are monotonous, but are enlivened by a considerable number of towns. The first place on the right bank is *Sindyûn*, with a handsome minaret. Opposite to it is *Dêrût*. The angular pieces of wood at the top of the minarets are used for bearing lamps on festive occasions. Numerous pumps are observed on the banks. The next places on the left are *Minyet-es-Sa'îd* and *Fezâr*, and on the right *Shemshîr*; then, on the left *Adfîneh*, with a palace erected by Sa'îd Pasha, and on the right *Metûbis*. Farther towards the N., *Dîbeh* lies a little to the left, and on the right are *Kum*, *Minyet el-Murshid*, and the important-looking little town of *Berimbâl*. On the same bank are *Yeggârîn* and the village of *Kasha*, and opposite, to the left, is the town of *Mahallet el-Emîr*, crowned with two minarets. On the right we next observe *Faras*, and on the left *Shemâsmeh* and *El-Khimmâd*; then, on the right, *El-Basreh*, and on the left *El-Gedîyeh*. The citadel of Rosetta (Reshîd), usually known as the *Kal'a* ('castle') next comes in sight. Near it, also on the left, we observe a fine grove of palm-trees rising close to the town, and the hill of Abu Mandûr (see below).

Rosetta, Arabic *Reshîd* (a Coptic name, *Ti Rashit* signifying 'city of joy'), the ancient *Bolbitine*, with 19,392 inhab., almost exclusively natives, lies at the mouth of the Bolbitinic arm of the Nile, which was also called the *Taly* (Τάλυ). As the Rosetta Stone (see below) was found near Fort St. Julien, 4 M. to the N., it is supposed that the ancient town lay in that neighbourhood. — There is no inn at Rosetta, but, if necessary, the traveller may apply for accommodation to the hospitable Franciscan monks.

History. Little is known regarding the early history of the town. It was founded on the site of the ancient *Bolbitine*, and early in the middle ages attained considerable mercantile importance It continued to flourish down to the beginning of the present century, but its prosperity declined rapidly in consequence of the construction of the Mahmûdiyeh Canal and the improvement of the harbour of Alexandria The rice trade of Rosetta is of considerable importance, and shipbuilding is carried on with some success

The town possesses numerous gardens, which yield excellent fruit. The hill of *Abû Mandûr*, to the S. of the town, which commands a fine view, is supposed by some topographers to have been the site of the ancient Bolbitine. The interesting streets contain many small, but substantial houses in a peculiar, half-European style, with projecting stories and windows towards the outside. Numerous columns from edifices of the heathen and Christian periods, many of them of granite and some of marble, are seen lying in various open spaces, particularly one of considerable size near the river, and a number of others are built into the houses. The very spacious *Mosque of Sakhlûn* is embellished with many ancient columns, but is otherwise uninteresting. The fortifications to the N. of the town are not shown except by permission the commandant. In 1799 M. Bouchard, a French captain of engineers, discovered in *Fort St. Julien* the celebrated *Rosetta Stone*, which afforded European scholars a key to the language and writing of the ancient Egyptians, which had been lost for nearly 14 centuries.

The **Rosetta Stone**, now preserved in the British Museum, is a *stele* of black basalt, the corners of which are unfortunately damaged, bearing three different inscriptions on its face. The subject is the same in each case, but the first is in the sacred hieroglyphic language and character of the ancient Egyptians, the second in the demotic, or popular, language and writing, and the third in the Greek language and character. The 54 lines of the Greek text, which is written in 'uncial' letters, are well preserved, but of the 14 hieroglyphic lines all on the right side and twelve on the left are seriously damaged. The subject of the inscription is a decree of the priests in honour of Ptolemy V. Epiphanes (B. C. 204-181), issued on 27th March, 195, when the king was still a boy of fourteen. The high-sounding titles of the king, the date, and the place (Memphis) where the resolution was passed are first set forth in eight lines. Next follow in twenty-eight lines the motives which induced the hierarchy to issue the decree, — viz. the numerous benefits conferred by the king on his country, the gifts presented by him to the clergy and the temples, the reduction and remission of taxes, the indemnity granted to criminals, his leniency towards the rebels who had 'returned to peace', his vigorous resistance to enemies approaching by land and by sea and to the town of Lycopolis, his prudent conduct on the occasion of an inundation which took place in the eighth year of his reign, and his liberal contributions towards the support of the sacred animals and the repair and adornment of the temples. The remainder of the inscription gives the resolution itself, to the effect that a statue, a chapel of gold, and an image of the king should be placed in every temple, decorated on feast-days, and revered; and farther, that the decree, inscribed on a slab of hard stone in hieroglyphic, demotic, and Greek writing should be placed in every temple of the first and second rank. — The last paragraph of the Greek inscription informs us that we shall find the two translations, one in the sacred, the other in the popular language of the Egyptians, adjacent to it. The first step towards deciphering these last was to endeavour to discover the alphabet of each kind of character. The *demotic* part was first scrutinised, and M. S. de Sacy and Hr. Ackerblad, a Swedish scholar, first succeeded in determining the groups which contained the word Ptolemy. In the *hieroglyphic* part (p. 110) some of the groups were framed, and, as had been ascertained from the Roman obelisks and other sources before the finding of the Rosetta Stone, it was inferred that these were names of kings. Dr. Th. Young, an Englishman, and M. F. Champollion, the French Egyptologist, then succeeded, independently of each other, the former in 1819, the latter in 1822, in discovering the missing alphabet by means of a comparison of the names of the different kings. Champollion afterwards prosecuted his researches with such marvellous success, that he justly merits the highest rank among the decipherers of hieroglyphics. Taking the framed group which recurred most frequently on the Rosetta Stone to be Ptolemaios, as the Greek inscription indicated, he compared it with other framed symbols on an obelisk found at Philæ contemporaneously with the Rosetta inscription. The symbols on the obelisk, which occurred in connection with the name of Ptolemy, he conjectured to signify Cleopatra, as the number of letters also indicated. He then proceeded to compare the two groups: —

(1)  he took to be Ptolemy,

(2) 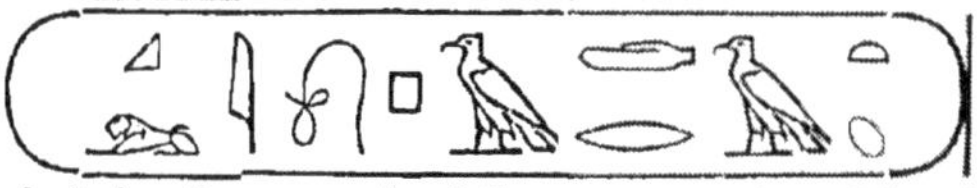 Cleopatra.

The first symbol in the second of these groups is a triangle, which he supposed to represent *k*, and which does not occur in the first group (Ptolemy). The second symbol in the second group, a lion, he took to be *l*, and he was confirmed in this view by the fact that the same symbol occupied the fourth place in the first group. The third symbol in the second group, a reed, according to his hypothesis, would be *e*, and this again was confirmed by the two reeds in Ptolemaios, representing the Greek diphthong αι. The fourth symbol in the second group, a cord with a loop, was also, according to his expectation, found to occupy the third place in the first. So, too, the square, representing *p* in the second group was found to correspond with the first letter of the first group. The sixth letter of the second group, a bird, did not occur in the first group, but was repeated in its proper place in the second. The seventh sign in the second group, a hand, would be *t*, but the same letter was represented in the word Ptolemy by a semicircle. This discrepancy might have misled the decipherer, had he not rightly conjectured that two different symbols might possibly exist for the same letter, and that the semicircle at the end of Cleopatra represented the Coptic feminine article *t*, which, as he afterwards found, is placed at the end of many female names. The eighth letter in the second frame he took to be *r*, and this letter did not occur in the first frame. By this process the nine letters of Cleopatra's name, or ten including the article, were ascertained, while the different letters in the case of Ptolemy were afterwards verified by comparing them with the names of other kings, and particularly with that of Alexander the Great 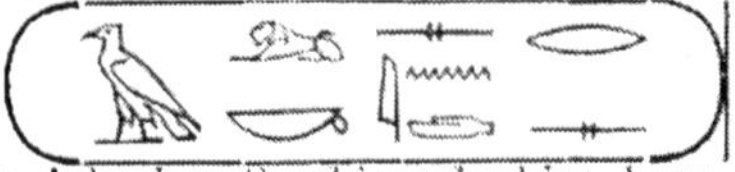. The other steps in the task of deciphering the hieroglyphics have already been noticed at p. 111.

f. Ṣân (*Tanis*).

A visit to the ruins of Tanis is not only somewhat tedious and troublesome, but will not repay the ordinary traveller, as they are now covered by sand. The finest relics discovered there have, moreover, been carried off to grace the museum of Bûlâḳ. Most travellers will require a dragoman, a tent, and rugs for the journey.

Down to the middle of January, that is before the Nile is too low, the traveller may proceed by the Mu'izz Canal from the *Abû Sheḳûḳ* station (p. 439) to Ṣân. Enquiries as to the state of the water should previously be made at Zaḳâzîḳ. The train from Zaḳâzîḳ arrives at 4.27 p.m. at Abû Sheḳûḳ, where the party embarks in a boat previously ordered by the dragoman. Ṣân may be reached the same day (7-8 hrs., but more in the reverse direction), and the night should be spent in the boat. The boats are large, but dirty. The charge for the voyage to Ṣân is about 45 fr., and for the journey there and back about 80 fr., including stoppages, which must be specially stipulated for. If the water in the canal is too low for navigation, the traveller should proceed to the *Abû Kebîr* station only (p. 438), and there take the branch-line to (9 M.) *Tell Faḳûs*, a village on the left bank of the Nile, which is reached at 3.30 p.m. On the opposite bank of the canal, about 1 M. from the ruins of the ancient Phacusa, and near the modern *Mît el-'Azz*, is a cotton factory belonging to an Egyptian bey. *Mr. Robertson*, the manager, an English engineer, accords a kind reception to travellers.

The ruins of Tell Faḳûs, the site of the ancient *Phacusa* (Φακοῦσσα; Φακόεσσα), which was once the capital of the Arabian nome, and of Goshen, and is called Phakos, or, without the article, Kos, by the Copts, are interesting to Egyptologists only. The district of Goshen (p. 411) and the ancient city bear the same name. The scanty remains bear a few inscriptions, some of which date from the period of Ramses II.

Donkeys and a guide should be ordered at Mît el-'Azz in the evening, and the journey continued on the following morning.

The route from Abû Kebîr traverses fertile fields, chiefly planted with cotton, and frequently intersected by ditches and cuttings, through which the traveller must ride or wade. This tract was formerly the pasture-land of the ancient *Amu* (see below), and was overgrown with reeds and marsh-plants. The distance to be traversed depends on the state of the water, and the route varies at different seasons. The villages resemble those on the Upper Nile, except that there are no large dovecots here. About noon we reach the margin of the desert, on the parched and cracked surface of which there are occasional pools of salt water. Towards sunset we regain the cultivated land, and, after a good deal of waiting and shouting, are ferried across the Mu'izz Canal. We then either pitch our tent among the ruins of the ancient Tanis, or ask hospitality of Aḥmed, the wealthy farmer of the fishings. His son Muṣṭafa will be found obliging. Insect-powder should not be forgotten.

From Port Sa'îd (p. 436) to Tanis, across *Lake Menzaleh* (p. 435), is a voyage of 15-35 hrs., according to the wind. No fixed fare. On the island of *Tenîs* are the ruins of the ancient *Tennis*, most of which appear to date from the time of the Crusades. The ruins on several other islands indicate that a great part of the lake was once cultivated land, sprinkled with towns (p. 435). We at length quit the lake and enter the Mu'izz Canal (p. 438), the ancient Tanitic arm of the Nile, and in 1-2 hrs. more we disembark opposite to Sân.

From Tanis to Damietta or Manṣûra by boat in about 18 hrs., viâ *Maṭariyeh*, a miserable fishing village. From Tanis to Sinbelâwîn (p. 439) we may also proceed by land (one day's journey), and continue our journey thence by train, but it will be found difficult to obtain horses or donkeys at Ṣân.

Ṣân is a fishing village (p. 435), where an amusing fish-auction takes place every Tuesday and Friday at the house of Aḥmed. The faces and figures of the inhabitants are peculiar. They are doubtless the descendants of the wild and rebellious Bashmurites and Biamites who gave so much trouble to the troops of the khalîfs Merwân II. (744-50) and Mamûn (813-33), and also of the Semitic shepherds who inhabited the Menzaleh region at a very remote period. They were called Amu, or, with the article, Pi-Amu, by the Egyptians, and the name was afterwards corrupted to Biamites. They were also known as Pi-Shemer, which was corrupted to Bashmurites. In the Christian period they belonged to the orthodox church, and styled themselves Melekites, or 'royalists', a name which they still apply to themselves in the form 'Malakiyîn', although they have long since embraced El-Islâm. The hope of bakshîsh makes them civil to travellers.

Ancient Tanis. The name Tanis is the Greek, and the modern name of Ṣân the Arabic, form of the ancient *Zān* or *Zoān* (Psalm lxxviii. 12). The scriptural name is the same as that given to the place by the Egyptian monuments. A statue found here, and now preserved at Bûlâḳ, for example, bears an inscription to the effect that the dignitary it represents was 'a governor in his town, a magnate in his province, and a prefect of the towns of the field of T'ān' (*i. e.* Zān or Zoān). The Semitic inhabitants also called the town T'ar, *i. e.* Zar, and the Egyptians named it T'a or Za (or Zor, plur. Zoru, signifying 'a fortified place'), while the sacred name was Khont-ab, or Mesent, the place of Horus and of Phœnix, and the Edfu of the north†. Tanis was the capital of the fourteenth

† Brugsch identifies Tanis with the *Ramses* of the Bible (comp. p. 413), and supposes it to have been the town where Moses wrought his

nome of Lower Egypt, and lay on the arm of the Nile named after it, the modern Mu'izz Canal, with which many ancient legends are associated. Thus it was by this arm of the river that the body of Typhon (Seth), when slain by Osiris, floated down to the sea On this account the Tanitic arm of the Nile is said to have been an object of hatred to the Egyptians, but it is more probable that their dislike was caused by the fact that Seth, under the name of Ba'al, was worshipped on its banks by the natives of the district Among the other gods specially revered here were Ammon of Thebes, with Khunsu and Muth, Tum neb-On, or lord of Heliopolis, and Horus along with Isis and Sokar Osiris The favourite deities, however, were Tum and Khunsu, the god of the moon, who in one of his aspects was identified by the Greeks with their Heracles The Egyptian priests who performed the rites of the 'gods of Ramses' in this town, are also called by the monuments Khar-tot, or 'warriors', a name which is identical with the Hebrew name Khartummîm given in the Bible to the Egyptian magicians who attempted to imitate the miracles wrought by Moses (Exodus viii, ix)

We learn from the Bible (Numbers xiii 22) that Tanis was founded seven years later than Hebron, which, however, is mentioned as having been a very ancient place as early as the time of Abraham. This notice of the place was perhaps copied into the sacred writ of the Israelites from some earlier Phœnician work At all events it is probable that it was founded so far back as the primæval monarchy by Phœnician mariners, and that it then lay much nearer to the sea than at the present day. The mud of the Nile has formed the broad piece of land which separates the site of Tanis from Lake Menzaleh In the Sethroitic nome, adjacent to Tanis, lay Heracleopolis (pp. 87, 412), the cradle of the kings of the 9th and 10th Heracleopolite Dynasties, monarchs of foreign origin, who reigned in Lower Egypt until expelled by the 11th and 12th Dynasties Monuments were erected at Tanis by Amenemha and Usertesen (p. 87), but a statue of the 13th Dynasty found here may have been brought from elsewhere at a later period. When the *Hyksos* overran Egypt, they found at Tanis a population of a race kindred to their own While Abaris (Hauâr), on the E frontier of the empire, formed the basis of their military operations, they constituted Tanis their capital. Here they employed Egyptian artists, who executed sculptures for them in the conventional style, faithfully pourtraying the features of their conquerors (p 298) After the expulsion of the Hyksos, Tanis was neglected by the Egyptian kings, but it was again specially favoured by the great monarchs of the 19th Dynasty Seti I, Ramses II, and Merenptah, the Pharaoh of the Exodus, frequently held their courts here, and even condescended to participate in the rites of Seth peculiar to the place. At the same time they embellished the city so liberally, and promoted its prosperity so effectually, that it is described by several papyri as being a particularly beautiful and pleasant place, and the name is therefore written ϫⲁⲛⲏ, *i e* 'the beautiful, the agreeable', by later writers In the time of Isaiah and Ezekiel (8th and 6th cent respectively) Zoan must still have been a very important place 'Surely the princes of Zoan are fools, the counsel of the wise counsellers of Pharaoh is become brutish' (Isaiah xix 11) Before this period the city had surrendered to the armies of the Assyrians, as we also learn from the cuneiform inscriptions, which mention Tanis in the time of Sardanapalus as Sanu, and its prince Pu-tu-bis-ti (Petubastes) Under the 26th Dynasty. which favoured foreigners, Zoan again prospered, but in the reign of Amasis, who patronised Sais and the Greek Naucratis in preference to

miracles before Pharaoh (Ramses II), and from which the Israelites started on their wanderings The now bleak and sterile plain around Zoan is called by the monuments *Sokhot Zoan*, or plain of Zoan It was not till the time of Ramses II, when a new town with temples and shrines was erected adjacent to the ancient fortress of Zor or Zoru (see above), that the place was called Pi-Ramses ('city of Ramses')

Tanis, Mendes, and Bubastis, the half-Semitic cities of the Delta, it began to decline perceptibly, although slowly. Flavius Josephus calls the place a πολίχνη, or small town only, but Strabo and Stephanus of Byzantium call it 'the great'. In the course of the frequent invasions in Egypt from the E., Tanis was usually the first place which suffered after Pelusium, so that its ancient monuments were thus gradually destroyed, and the edicts of Theodosius contributed not a little to the same result. The work of destruction was finally completed in consequence of Turkish misrule, and 'the great Tanis' has thus dwindled down to the fishing village of Sân, the sole attraction of which consists in the scanty ruins in the neighbourhood.

Ruins of Tanis. The wall, built of bricks of Nile mud, enclosing the temple of Ramses II., the sanctuary of which perhaps existed as early as the primæval monarchy, was 250 paces long and about 150 wide. The temple stood in the centre of the town, and the latter lay on the slopes of hills which had been thrown up on both sides of the temple, partly for the protection of the temple itself, and partly to raise the houses above the level of the inundation (p. 410). Ascending a slight eminence close to the village, we first reach a large and much mutilated colossal figure in granite. We next come to a hollow made in the course of Mariette's excavations, with solid substructions of huge blocks of limestone, in the side of which there is a small chapel. Farther to the E. another and larger fragment of ruin was lately excavated, but, like most of the remains mentioned below, it has again been covered up with sand. Among the broken figures in black basalt lying here is a female torso, a singular peculiarity of which is that the left breast is much larger than the right. A damaged colossal figure, prostrate on the ground, is worthy of notice, as it shows that even granite monuments were painted. The flesh parts of these Tanitic coloured statues were painted bright pink, or almost red, the eyebrows reddish brown, and the 'kalantika', or headdress resembling a wig, yellow of various shades. Most of the statues and blocks bear the name of Ramses II. The finest of those of the early monarchy (such as the colossal statue of Usertesen at Berlin) are now deposited in different museums. The name of Merenptah is also observed on a number of ruins, and so also is the cartouche of Sheshenk, or Sesonchis III., of the 22nd Dynasty, of Bubastis, but only on those architectural fragments and statues which owe their origin to Ramses II. A little farther to the E. was probably situated the hypostyle, or colonnaded hall of the temple, as is evidenced by the broken columns lying on the ground, including several huge shafts of granite, crowned with finely executed palm capitals. At the bottom of the opening made by the last excavations, lie shattered obelisks, colossal statues, capitals of columns, shafts, and bases, in grand confusion. All these fragments are of granite, grauwacke, or other hard stone. On a blackish figure in a sitting posture is inscribed the name of Ramses II., who is here called 'lord of the diadems', 'protector of Egypt', and 'destroyer of foreign nations.' The shaft of a huge column also bears the still traceable name of one of his successors. About 20 paces farther on, a large broken obelisk lies prostrate on the ground. Ten other obelisks near it, in a still more shattered condition, testify to the ancient glory of the city. The loftiest of them measured 46 and 49 ft. in height, and nearly 5 ft. in thickness. Some of them consisted of very dark, and others of light-coloured syenite. Even the great temple of imperial Thebes contained fewer obelisks than this vast sanctuary. All these edifices owed their origin to Ramses II. The museum at Bûlâḳ contains the finest of the Hyksos sphinxes (p. 298) found here, while four others, more or less mutilated, still remain here. Besides these there is a sphinx in the Egyptian style, dating from the 19th Dynasty. The visitor should also notice an interesting little chapel, resembling a sarcophagus, and composed of a single block of a granulous kind of alabaster. The cavity is not much wider than the thickness of the sides At the back is represented the triad of Ammon, Tum, and Mut. Another colossal statue here, composed of rose-coloured or almost purple granite, and a lion-headed statue of Sekhet were also erected by Ramses II. Adjacent is a second statue of Ramses II, executed in a flinty kind of sandstone, and coloured. Farther on, towards the S., we next observe a large granite 'stele' with finely executed inscriptions, still easily legible, although damaged, mentioning a mode of reckoning dates which has been met with nowhere else. They are in honour of a distinguished official of the time of Ramses II., and bear the date of 400 years after the Pharaoh Asetpehti, a Hyksos monarch. A considerable way beyond this monument is another excavated hollow containing fragments of a temple, including several remarkably fine columns with curious palm capitals. These capitals, which, like the columns themselves, are of rose-coloured granite, are narrower at their bases than the shafts on which they rest. All the columns, now overthrown, are remarkable for slenderness of form, and the bases on which they stood were no less than 3ft. in height, being higher than any others yet discovered in Egypt. Towards the S.E. are several round blocks, probably dating, according to the two inscriptions, from the period of the Ptolemies. Leaving the hollow containing the palm columns, we ascend without difficulty to the tomb of a shêkh which commands the best survey of the ruins of Tanis. Around the grey plateau of the town rise a series of hills, nearly forming a circle, and once covered with dwelling-houses. The ruins of the temple form a mass of cubical blocks and black and red fragments of obelisks, while the heaps of rubbish are mingled with innumerable chips of broken pottery. The empty houses resemble caverns, and show that the Tanites were contented with dwellings of very moderate size. The limestone 'stele' discovered here by Dr. Lepsius in 1866, known as the *Tablet of Tanis*, or *Decree of Canopus*, is now preserved in the museum at Bûlâḳ (p. 313).

9. The Fayûm.

A Tour through the Fayûm, including a visit to the Labyrinth, the site of Lake Mœris, the Birket el-Kurûn with its abundant wildfowl, and the ruins in its neighbourhood, takes 6-8 days, and requires a tent, a dragoman, and a supply of provisions. A dragoman charges 30-40 fr. a day for each person, according to the requirements of his employers, and for that sum he is bound to provide them with a tent, provisions (wine excepted), and donkeys, or other means of conveyance, and to pay railway fares and all other expenses. A written contract (comp. p. 471), specifying the places to be visited, the points where some stay is to be made (on which occasions a reduced charge per day should be stipulated for), and other particulars, should be drawn up before starting. Those who intend to visit Medînet el-Fayûm and its immediate environs only, and who do not object to rough quarters for one or two nights, may dispense with a dragoman and a tent, but should be provided with a moderate supply of food. An introduction to the mudîr will be of great service in enabling the traveller to procure the necessary horses or donkeys, which the inhabitants are often unwilling to hire (comp. p. 458).

Since the completion of the railway this excursion has usually been undertaken from Cairo, but it may also be combined with a visit to Sakkârah. It was formerly usual to visit the Fayûm in connection with a journey up the Nile, but this plan entails needless expense, as the boat and its crew have to be paid for while lying idle for several days. If, however, the traveller prefers this plan, he disembarks at Wasta and sends on his dhahabîyeh to Beni Suêf, which he afterwards reaches by railway.

Railway from Cairo to Medînet el-Fayûm (*Ligne de la Haute-Egypte*), 75 M., in about 4 hrs. The trains are often late. — A train starts daily at 8.30 a.m. from the Bûlâk ed-Dakrûr station, reaching Wasta (p. 458) at 10.38 a.m. (halt of 20 min.; change carriages) and Medînet el-Fayûm at 12.15 p.m. A second train starts from Bûlâk ed-Dakrûr at 3 p.m., reaching Wasta at 5.29, where the train leaving Assiût at 8.30 a.m. arrives at 4.25 p.m. From Wasta the Fayûm train proceeds at 5.45 p.m., reaching Medîneh at 7 p.m. — From Medînet el-Fayûm the line goes on to Senhûr, but for a visit to the Birket el-Kurûn horses must be brought from Medîneh (comp. p. 463). — A train leaves Medînet-el-Fayûm daily at 9 a.m., reaching Wasta at 10.15 a.m. and Bûlâk ed-Dakrûr at 1.15 a.m.

Situation and History of the Fayûm. In the great plateau of the *Libyan Desert*, which rises 300-400 ft. above the sea-level, is situated the province of the Fayûm (from the ancient Egyptian 'Phiom', *i.e.* marsh or lake district), the first of the oases, which is usually considered to belong to the valley of the Nile, and is justly celebrated for its extraordinary fertility (see below). This tract is in the form of an oval basin, 840 sq. M. in area, and supports a population of 200,000 souls; it is enclosed by the Libyan hills, which are here of moderate height, and lies about three-fifths of a degree to the S. of Cairo. It enjoys a remarkably fine climate, and has but rarely been visited by the plague. This 'land of roses' is still one of the most beautiful parts of Egypt, and more than any other part of the Nile valley deserves the well known epithet of 'the gift of the Nile', bestowed on Egypt by Herodotus, as it is entirely indebted for its fertility to the waters of the Nile with which it is artificially irrigated. The *Bahr Yûsuf*, a channel 207 M. in length, which is more probably a natural branch of the river, artificially adapted, than a canal, diverges from the Nile to the N. of Assiût, and flows through a narrow opening in the Libyan chain into the Fayûm, where it divides into numerous ramifications, abundantly watering the whole district. One of its branches runs towards the N., skirting the E. slopes of the Libyan hills. At the point where the Bahr Yusûf enters the Fayûm, the district forms a plateau of moderate height, descending towards the W. in three gradations towards the Birket el-Kurûn, a long, narrow lake, extending from S.W. to N.E. On the easternmost and highest part of the oasis the Labyrinth and Lake Mœris (pp. 462, 463) were once situated; the central part yields the

THE NILE
from
Cairo to Feshn.including the Fayûm
and the
Pyramids.

1:1.000.000.

0   10   20   30
Kilomètres
0   5   10   15   20
English Miles

Names of Railway Stations are underlined.

Tannas
Kufur Embâbeh
Abu Roâsh
Pyram.
Bûlâk
el-Dakru
Shubrah
HELIOPOLIS
Abbâsiyeh
CAIRO
Gizeh
G. el-Mokattam
el-Arabah
Pyram. of
Gizeh
Zâuivet el-Aryân
Pyr. Shodermein
El-Basâtin
Turrah
El-Masarah
Pyram.
Abusîr
Bedreshên
Sakkârah
Pyr.
MEMPHIS
Sulphur
Baths
Heluân
Pyram.
Esh-Shôbak
Dahshûr
Barnasht
Kafr-Hamûd
El-Teben
Megdûneh
Sherâfeh
kebir
Beshih
Belideh
Gemâzeh
zaghir
Tahmeh
Kasr el-Ayât
Menshireh
Kafr-Lish
l'Aknâz
Pyr.of Lisht
el-Moharrakah
Matânieh
Eshker
Gezîreh
Menivet
el-Kaid
Gergiah
Gibihat
el-Kuttûri
Saidiyeh
Riklah
Dimeh
Medinet Nimrûd
Gezîret el-Karn
Birket el Kurûn
Tânâyeh
er-Rodhah
Kubwât
Sennoris
Banbâr
Masurah
Tirseh
Gebelich
Sirsino
Abuksah
Senhûr
Nakalîleh
el-Mehdis
Beshuai
Fidimin
Moshah
Abu Gonshelt
Senrû
Kelabin
el-Ulam
Atfieh
Kasr Gebali
Bihamu
Seleh
Agamieh
Nawûmis
Nezleh
Medinet el-Fayûm
Demu
Pyr. Medûm
ARSINOE
el-Atf
Tubhûr
Abgig
 Siuleh
Pyr.of Hauâra
en-Nasir
Desiyeho
Saul
Kasr el-Benât
Zâwieh
Kasr Kurûn
Sawâfueh
Mairûb
Illahûn
Abusir
Menûn
Korman
Kerimât
Kefr Magran
Atamneh
Biahmû
Abusir
Mdr Antonios
Mdr Manast
Mardûleh
Abu Kandil
Mawaro Shidmâ
Rabiât
Zerlteh
Bûsh
Behabshe
Medinet Ma'di
Tutûn
Sedement
Benawiyeh
Medinet Garak
Talût
Kalamseh
Al-Jnâs el-Medineh
(HERAKLEOPOLIS)
Benisuéf
Beni Korrâh
Beraweh
Nanah
Tizment
Tensah
G. Gubêh
Bayad
Rayân
Kimbish
el-Matanieh
G.Gharab
Deshâsheh
Dushtut
el-Tahah
el-Balankah
Tahaleljisheh
Rayal
W.Senhûr
Nezleh
el-Kubrah
Nezleh
Tâbele
Sedo
Menkatin
W.Sanaur
el-Mesurah
el-Fûkah
Saft Rashin
Gemhur
Feshn
G.et-Têr

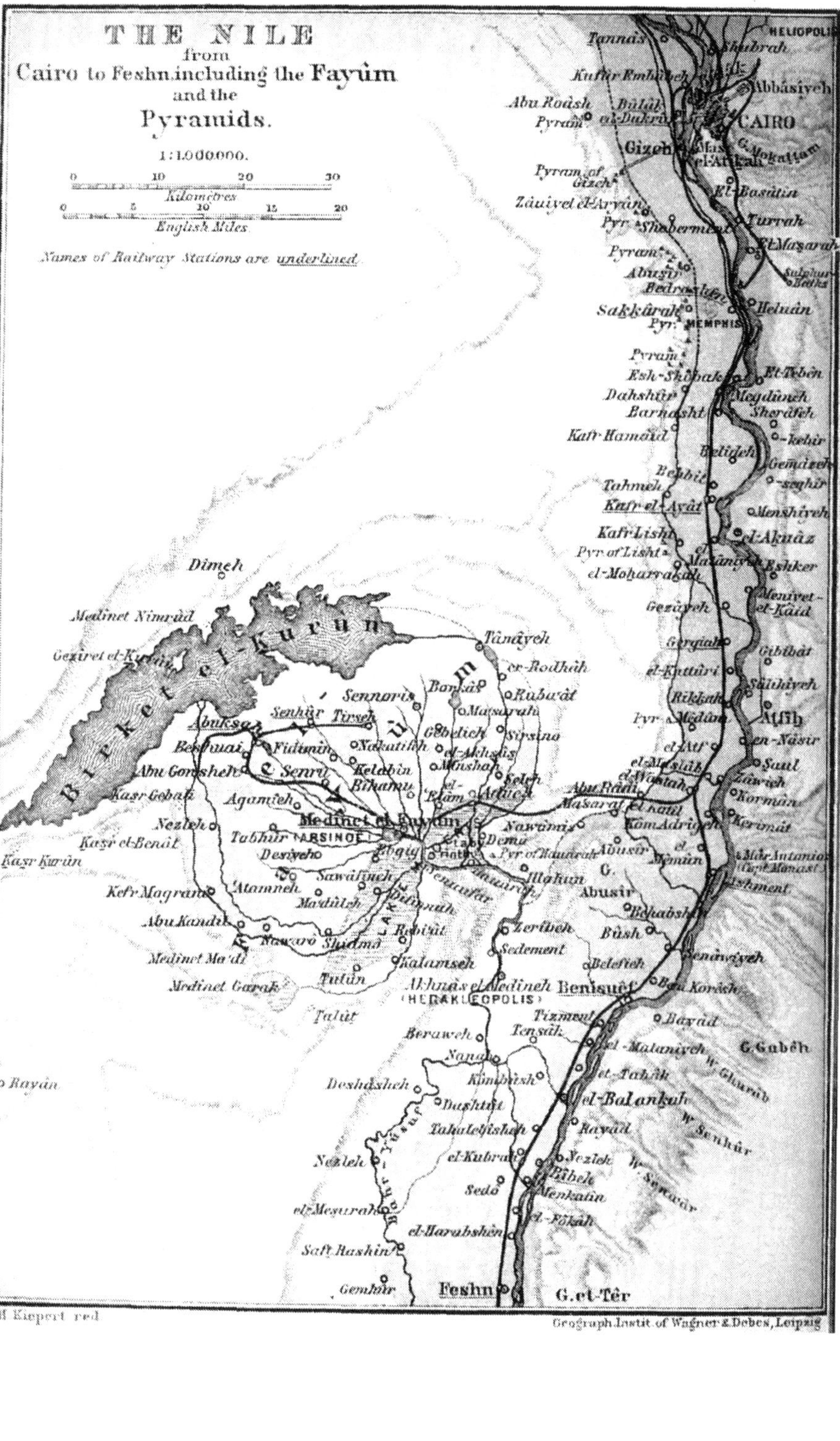

H.Kiepert red.

Geograph.Instit.of Wagner & Debes, Leipzig

luxuriant crops for which the province is famous; while the westernmost part chiefly consists of sterile desert land. To the W. and N. of the Birket el-Kurûn rise precipitous limestone hills, beyond which lies the immense sandy desert of Sahâra. The Fayûm must have been reclaimed from the desert at a very early period, probably during the early empire, in the reign of Amenemha III, as monuments of his period indicate that he was perhaps the first of the Pharaohs who sought to regulate the whole course of the Nile On the Upper Nile Prof Lepsius has found Nilometers constructed by that monarch, and in the Fayûm, on the site of the Labyrinth, a number of blocks of stone inscribed with his name. The Greeks called him *Ameris*, or *Moeris*, and believed that the lake known to them as 'Lake Mœris', which they regarded as a marvel of engineering skill, was named after him. The word *meri*, however, is the Egyptian for lake or overflow, so that the great basin of the Fayûm was simply 'the lake', and it was from his exertions in connection with the irrigation works that Amenemha obtained the name of Mœris. We learn from several inscriptions, and from a papyrus roll treating of the Fayûm, that the province was known in the time of the Pharaohs as *Ta shet*, or the lake-land, and that Lake Mœris was called *hun-t*, signifying the discharge or posterior lake On its bank rose the celebrated Labyrinth, which was probably renewed by the Bubastite monarchs of the 22nd Dynasty About the same period the town of Crocodilopolis, situated on Lake Mœris, and afterwards called Arsinoe after the wife of Ptolemy Philadelphus, was so extended and embellished by Osorkon I that it is called the 'city of Osorkon I' in the inscription on the celebrated stele of Piankhi The whole province was at first called the lake-land, then the district of Crocodilopolis, and lastly the Arsinoite Nome. The deity most highly revered here was the crocodile-headed Sebek, the reptile sacred to whom was carefully tended in Lake Mœris. At the same time the voracious and dangerous monster, notwithstanding the reverence paid to it on account of its connection with the inundation, was also regarded as Typhonic, and the Crocodilopolitan nome was therefore passed over in the lists of nomes — At the period preceding that of the Psamtikides of the 26th Dynasty the Labyrinth appears to have been used as a hall for great imperial assemblies At the period of the Ptolemies and the Romans the products of the Fayûm were much extolled. 'The Arsinoite Nome', says Strabo, 'is the most remarkable of all, both on account of its scenery and its fertility and cultivation For it alone is planted with large, full-grown, and richly productive olive-trees, and the oil is good when carefully prepared; those who are neglectful may indeed obtain oil in abundance, but it has a bad smell. In the rest of Egypt the olive-tree is never seen, except in the gardens of Alexandria, where under favourable circumstances they yield olives, but no oil Vines, corn, podded plants, and many other products also thrive in this district in no small abundance'. — Strabo's description is still applicable at the present day. The oranges and mandarins, peaches, olives, figs, cactus fruit, pomegranates, and grapes grown here are much esteemed, and the beautiful, rich-coloured red roses of the gardens of the Fayûm, which were once so lavishly strewn at the banquets of Cleopatra, still thrive here. At the station of Medinet el-Fayûm small phials of attar of roses, of inferior quality, are frequently offered for sale Isma'îl Pasha devoted special attention to this favoured part of his dominions The fields, which are watered by means of wheels of peculiar construction, yield rice, sugar, cotton, flax, and hemp, besides the usual cereals The beginning of November is probably the season at which the traveller will obtain the most distinct idea of the fertile character of the district. — The *Inhabitants* are fellâhin, or tillers of the soil, and Beduins To the latter race belong the poor fishermen who inhabit the banks of the Birket el-Kurûn Many of the peasants also call themselves 'Arabs', and the wealthier of them are generally well mounted

The Railway Journey is preferable to the voyage up the Nile in point of speed, and the passenger obtains a good view of the left bank of the river, and sometimes of the opposite bank also. The Nile with its lateen sails is frequently visible to the left, while on the right we obtain glimpses of the Pyramids, rich corn-fields, canals, water wheels, palm-groves, and villages with tall dovecots in rapid succession. The journey has already been described as far as (14 M.) *Bedrashên* (see p. 372). We next observe on the right the pyramids of Dahshûr and the so-called false pyramid of Mêdûm (see p. 467). *Abû Ragwân*, *Kafr ed-Dabai*, *Kafr el-ʿAyâṭ*, *Kafr Amar*, and *Gizeh* are unimportant stations.

51 M. **el-Wasta** (post and telegraph office) lies in the midst of a large palm-grove, a few hundred yards to the left of the line, in the direction of the Nile. Travellers coming from Cairo change carriages here; stay of 20 min. in the forenoon, 17 min. in the afternoon.

The branch-line to the Fayûm runs towards the W., across cultivated land, to the village of *Abu Râdi*, beyond which it traverses a desert tract for 35 min., and then crosses the low and bleak Libyan chain of hills, reaching its highest point at a level of 190 ft. above the sea. We then descend, cross the *Bahr el-Wardân*, which flows towards the Bahr Yûsuf from the N., and then the water-course of *el-Bats* (p. 460), and near the station of (19 M.) *el-Adweh* (69 ft.), on the right, we again perceive cultivated land. On the left is a cemetery with the dilapidated tombs of several shêkhs. Numerous palm-branches are placed by the tombstones as tokens of affection. On the right stretches an ancient dyke, which once may have belonged to the embankment of Lake Mœris (p. 462). We pass the station of *el-Maslûb*, traverse rich arable land, and soon reach ($23^1/_2$ M.) —

Medinet el-Fayûm, the 'town of the lake-district', situated to the S. of the site of *Crocodilopolis-Arsinoe*, the ancient capital of the province (*Hôtel du Fayoûm*, 10*s.* daily; with a letter of introduction from Cairo quarters may also be obtained at the American mission-station or at the house of the Italian curé). It contains about 40,000 inhab., and is a not unpleasing specimen of an Egyptian town. Between the station and the town we observe a peculiar, undershot sâkiyeh, or water-wheel driven by the water itself. The very long covered bazaar contains nothing of special interest. The traveller, even if unprovided with an introduction, should pay a visit to the mudîr, who will protect him from extortion in case of any difficulty with the owners of horses and others (comp. p. 34). A broad arm of the Bahr Yûsuf (p. 456) flows through the middle of the town. The mosque of *Kait Bey*, on the N. side of the town, now somewhat dilapidated, is the only interesting building of the kind. It contains numerous antique columns, brought from the ancient Arsinoe, some of which have shafts of polished marble with Arabic inscriptions, and Corinthian and other capitals. Below the mosque, on the bank of the Bahr Yûsuf, are some remains of ancient masonry. No ancient inscriptions have been discovered here, but the walls of some of the houses contain fragments which must have belonged to ancient temples. At the W. end of the town the Baḥr Yûsuf radiates into numerous branches, which water the country in every direction. The dilapidated mosque of *Ṣofi* situated here forms a picturesque foreground.

To the N. of the town are the extensive ruins of **Crocodilopolis-Arsinoë,** which has been entirely destroyed. The site is now called *Kôm Fâris.* Many antiquities, both of the Roman and the Christian period, have been found here, including numerous small terracotta lamps and many thousand fragments of papyri, intermixed with pieces of parchment. Most of the papyri are Greek (among them fragments of Homer, Euripides, Thucydides, also of a Christian catechetical book), many are Arabic from the 2nd cent. of the Hegira down to 943 A.D.; and others are in Coptic, Pehlevi, Sassanide-Persian, and Meroitic-Ethiopian characters. Several fragments in hieratic and hieroglyphic characters, the oldest from the time of Ramses III. (about 1300 B.C.), have also been discovered. As the writings are for the most part tax-papers, it has been supposed that they belonged to a tax office of the town of Crocodilopolis, where old papyri also were used. A large number of the papyri found here were acquired by Consul Travers for the Berlin Museum, and even a larger number by Theod. Graf and Archduke Rainer for the Austrian Museum of Art and Industry at Vienna. The very extensive cemetery of the town, with its picturesque tombstones, covers part of the site of the ancient city; the highest of the mounds of rubbish command a survey of the whole of the Fayûm At the N. end of the ruins, about 1¼ M. from Medîneh, M. Schweinfurth discovered the remains of a large temple with a pylon, in front of which is a sitting figure of Amenemha I., the founder of the 12th Dyn., and inside several slabs with the name of Ramses the Great. A head with Hyksos features, now in the museum of Gizeh, has also been found here. According to Mr. Flinders Petrie, the temple proper, which was 490 ft. wide and had a double colonnade, belongs to the 26th Dynasty.

The village of **Bihamu,** about 4 M. to the N of Medîneh, was doubtless once situated on the bank of Lake Mœris It still contains some shapeless ruins of ancient origin, destitute of inscription, but supposed to be the remains of the pyramids which according to Herodotus once stood in the lake They are now called *Kursi Far'ûn,* or chair of Pharaoh, and resemble dilapidated altars rising above other fragments of solid masonry. If they were once pyramids, the greater part of them must have been removed, as the walls are now but slightly inclined inwards Distinct traces of the water in which they once stood are to be seen on their bases, and they are still surrounded by remains of walls, the purpose of which is unknown

In the fields near **Ebgig,** or *Begig,* 2½ M. to the S W. of Medîneh, lies a fine obelisk, broken into two parts, which must have once been at least 46 ft. in height (route to it rough and dirty) Like other obelisks, it is, horizontally, of oblong rectangular shape, and its summit is rounded. The inscriptions, which are damaged at many places, inform us that the monument was erected by Usertesen I., who also founded the obelisk of Heliopolis (p 333), and belonged to the same family (12th Dyn.) as Amenemha III, the founder of the Labyrinth — A visit to Bîhamu and Ebgîg is chiefly interesting to archæologists, and perhaps to botanists also

Excursions. A whole day is required for a visit to the *Pyramid of Hawârah* and the *Labyrinth* (horse 10, donkey 5 fr.). The route leads at first for $^3/_4$ hr. along the bank of the Bahr Yûsuf. The first village of any importance is *Uhâfeh*. Our path traverses well cultivated land with numerous water-wheels. The corn and cotton fields are shaded by numerous sycamores, lebbeks, palms, and other trees. About $^1/_2$ hr. from Uhâfeh, and beyond two smaller villages, we reach a bridge of ancient brick masonry. Traversing the slightly undulating tract a little farther, we reach the *Bahr Belâ Mâ* ('river without water'), also called *el-Bats*, a deep channel, extending in a wide curve, and terminating near the N.E. end of the Birket el-Kurûn (p. 465). In winter the water, which trickles down from its lofty banks, forms a few scanty pools. At the bottom of the channel grow reeds and tamarisks. The S. bank rises at places nearly perpendicularly to a height of 26 ft., so that the sequence of the strata of the soil is distinctly observable. We now ascend the plateau (the highest in the province, 88 ft. above the sea level) on which lies **Hawâret el-Kasab** or *Hawâret el-Makta*, a considerable village, with a mosque (reached in $1^3/_4$ hr. from Medînet el-Fayûm). The traveller may apply to the Shêkh-el-Beled (prefect of the village) for a guide to the pyramid of Hawâra. If the water is high, and the canals have to be avoided, we have to make a circuit of nearly 2 hrs. to the Labyrinth, but by riding through the water, where necessary, it may be reached in $^3/_4$ hour.

The longer route is preferable, as it passes several relics of antiquity. A little beyond the village rises the bridge of *Kanâtir el-Agami*, the ten buttresses of which rest on a foundation of massive stone. We continue to ride along an ancient embankment, and thus reach the *Katasanta* structure, which consists of a terrace of six carefully jointed steps of large and well-hewn blocks, but bears no inscription whatever. We cross the *Bahr el-Wardân*, which now intersects the ruins near the Pyramid of Hawârah, and which is sometimes called by the Arabs *Bahr el-Melekh* or *Bahr esh-Sherki*, i.e. river of the East. On the E. side lies the mass of buildings, which, according to Lepsius, was probably the *Labyrinth* (see below). In order to obtain a survey of these interesting ruins the traveller is recommended to ascend at once the **Pyramid of Hawâra.** This consists of unburnt bricks of Nile mud mixed with straw (comp. p. 370), and, when its sides were perfect, covered an area of upwards of 116 sq. yards. It has been ascertained that the nucleus of the structure is a natural mass of rock, 39 ft. in height. The dilapidated summit is easily reached in a few minutes by a flight of well-worn steps. The entrance to the pyramid, on the S. side, was discovered in 1889 by Mr. Flinders Petrie. The tomb chamber is 22 ft. long, 8 ft. wide, and 6 ft. high; it was covered with three large slabs of stone and contained two sarcophagi, one of them of polished sandstone without inscription, and fragments of an alabaster vase with the name of Amenemha III. The chamber was filled with water to a depth of 3 ft.

Towards the S. we observe a congeries of chambers and passages of unburnt bricks, bounded by the Baḥr esh-Sherḳi, and pronounced by Lepsius to be the right side of the **Labyrinth**, and the only part of it which is to some extent preserved. On the other side of the Pyramid there was doubtless a similar collection of rooms which has now disappeared; and several other structures beyond them, of which traces still remain, must have once existed there. The whole Labyrinth must have been in the shape of a horseshoe. Between the wing of the Labyrinth which still exists, and that which has disappeared, lies an extensive space strewn with broken pottery, in the middle of which are large fragments of a magnificent ancient temple. The base of the shaft of a small papyrus column, and a capital of the same order, both in the red stone of Assuân, with sculptured stalks and foliage, are worthy of notice. Some blocks disinterred here bearing the name of Amenemha III. have again been covered with sand. Several large blocks of limestone are also observed in the middle of this large court of the Labyrinth. The inscriptions are almost entirely destroyed, but faint traces of painting, and the symbols  (âa) and  (u), are still recognisable. From the traces still existing, the whole structure would appear to have occupied an area of 8800 sq. yds., and the large inner court an area of about 60 acres.

The Ancient Labyrinth. According to Brugsch, the Greek name Labyrinthos, which has been differently interpreted, is derived from 'erpa', or 'elpa-rohunt', i. e. the 'Temple of the mouth of the Lake'. The inscriptions found here by Lepsius prove that it was founded by Amenemha III. of the 12th Dynasty. Herodotus declares that the Labyrinth, which was afterwards reckoned as 'one of the wonders of the world', was so vast as to surpass all the buildings of the Greeks taken together and even the Pyramids themselves. For the best description we are indebted to Strabo, who visited the Labyrinth in person. He says: 'There is also the Labyrinth here, a work as important as the Pyramids, adjoining which is the tomb of the king who built the Labyrinth. After advancing about 30-40 stadia beyond the first entrance of the canal, there is a table-shaped surface, on which rise a small town and a vast palace, consisting of as many royal dwellings as there were formerly nomes. There is also an equal number of halls, bordered with columns and adjoining each other, all being in the same row, and forming one building, like a long wall having the halls in front of it. The entrances to the halls are opposite the wall. In front of the entrances are long and numerous passages which have winding paths running through them, so that the ingress and egress to each hall is not practicable to a stranger without a guide. It is a marvellous fact that each of the ceilings of the chambers consists of a single stone, and also that the passages are covered in the same way with single slabs of extraordinary size, neither wood nor other building material having been employed. On ascending the roof, the height of which is inconsiderable, as there is only one story, we observe a stone surface consisting of large slabs Descending again, and looking into the halls, we may observe the whole series borne by twenty-seven monolithic columns. The walls also are constructed of stones of similar size. At the end of this structure, which is more than a stadium in length, is the tomb, consisting of a square pyramid, each side of which is four plethra (400 ft.) in length, and of equal height The deceased, who is buried here, is called Ismandes It is also asserted that so many palaces were built, because it was the custom for all the nomes, represented by their magnates, with their priests and victims, to assemble here to offer sacrifice and gifts to the gods, and to deliberate on the most important concerns. Each nome then took possession of the hall destined for it. Sailing about a hundred stadia beyond this point, we next reach the town of Arsinoe', etc. This description of Strabo is confirmed by the contents of two papyri, one of which is in the museum of Gîzeh, the other in private possession (Mr. Hood) The deities of 66 districts are enumerated here, 24 of whom belong to Upper Egypt, 20 to Lower Egypt, and 22 to the Fayûm.

It is very doubtful whether we should consider these buildings of Nile bricks as remains of the ancient Labyrinth, or rather as tombs. Certainly nothing is left that recalls in any way the splendour of the old 'wonder of the world'. Except some blocks of limestone, nothing remains of the extensive structures once erected here, save the pyramid 'at the end of the labyrinth'.

To the N. of the pyramid Mr. Flinders Petrie discovered some mummy coffins with carefully painted heads (now in London). Of still greater value are the portraits found at *el-Rubayât*, 13 M to the N.E. of Medînet el-Fayûm, which were purchased and brought to Europe by M. Theodore Graf

Lake Mœris. The object of Lake Mœris, which has long since been dried up, was to receive the superfluous water in the case of too high an inundation, and to distribute its contents over the fields when the overflow was insufficient Strabo describes Lake Mœris in the following terms 'Owing to its size and depth it is capable of receiving the superabundance of water during the inundation, without overflowing the habitations and crops, but later, when the water subsides, and after the lake has given up its excess through one of its two mouths, both it and the canal retain water enough for purposes of irrigation This is accomplished by natural means, but at both ends of the canal there are also lock-gates, by means of which the engineers can regulate the influx and efflux of the water' The lock-gate, which in ancient times admitted the water conducted from the Nile by the canal into the lake, was probably situated near the modern *el-Lahûn* (see below), the name of which is supposed to be derived from the old Egyptian '*Ro-hun*' or '*Lohun*', *i.e.* 'the mouth of the lake', and the site of which was probably once occupied by the town of Ptolemais

There is a difference of opinion as to the *Situation and Form of the Ancient Lake.* Linant-Bey, arguing from the considerable difference of level between the two lakes, maintains that the Birket el-Kurûn (Lake of the Horns, p. 465) could never have formed part of Lake Mœris, as was formerly supposed, and he assigns to the latter a much smaller area than was attributed to it under the earlier theory. Placing it farther to the S E, nearer to the Labyrinth and el-Lahûn, he makes its boundary-line run towards the S S.W of Medînet el-Fayûm to the *Birket el-Gharak*, and intersect the desert of *Shêkh Ahmed*, where the ancient height of the water, which far exceeds the level attained in modern times, has left its traces, it then leads to *Kalamsha*, turns to the N. to *Dêr*, and then to the E. and S E. to *Dimishkîneh*, follows the embankment of *Pillawâneh*, and passes *Hawâret el-Kebîr* and the bridge of *el-Lâhûn* (see below). Hence the boundary leads by *Dimmo* towards the N.E to *Seleh*, and thence to the W. to *Bihamu* (p 459); then again to the S, and thus returns to Medînet el-Fayûm —A somewhat fatiguing journey of 2-3 days will enable the traveller to complete this circuit of the bed of the lake, which is now dried up. Recently, however, Mr F.Cope Whitehouse, relying upon the great circumference assigned by Herodotus (II, 149) to the lake, of 3600 stadia (reduced by Linant to 360) or about 335 M. (Pliny says 230 M), and upon measurements made by himself on the spot, ascribes a considerably larger area to the lake than Linant, and maintains that it extended on the S W. to the *Wâdi Rayân* It is not improbable that in ancient times nearly the whole of the Fayûm could be laid under water, so that even the Birket el-Kurûn belonged to Lake Mœris, but that the entire system was meant for the watering of the Fayûm alone and not of the Nile valley or the Delta. Considering that the bed of the lake must annually have been raised by the deposit of Nile mud, it follows, that as soon as the raising of the embankments and the removal of the mud were discontinued, the lake must have become unserviceable, especially after the lock-gates at el-Lahûn fell to decay, each opening of which, as Diodorus informs us, cost 50 talents (i e. about 11,250*l* ?) The discharge of the superfluous water probably ran through the Bahr Belâ Mâ, which has already been mentioned (p. 460), or through the Wâdi Nezleh (p. 464), both of which fall into the Birket el-Kurûn The ancient conjecture, that the latter discharged part of its water into the Ṣahâra (or, as Herodotus says, the 'Libyan Syrte'), was not an unnatural one.

A visit to the **Pyramid of el-Lahûn** or **Illahûn** is only interesting to those who are desirous of convincing themselves of the truth of Linant's hypothesis, and to make the circuit of the boundaries of the old bed of the lake (see above). The pyramid, which is built of Nile bricks, may be reached from Hawâret el-Kaṣab in 4-5, or from the Labyrinth in 3-4 hours. It has been recently been opened by Fraser. The discovery of an alabaster altar with the name of Usertesen II. renders it probable that the pyramid was built by that monarch A smaller pyramid lies to the N.E. The remains of the ancient embankments, which were tolerably well preserved in the time of the Khalifs, are not without attraction Those who are interested in hydraulic engineering should also inspect the entrance of the Bahr Yûsuf into the Fayûm

About 1/2 M. to the E. of the pyramid of el-Lahûn, Mr. Flinders Petrie discovered a temple in 1889, and close beside it the ruins of the town *Ha-Usertesen-hotep*, now called *Kahun*. The latter was founded by Usertesen II (12th Dyn) for the labourers on his pyramid. Among the articles found here were pottery, flint and copper implements of the 12th Dyn., numerous papyri of the same period, a statuette of Si-Sebek (13th Dyn), a wooden stamp of Apepi, and a large wooden door of Osorkon I

Gurob, 1 1/2 M. to the W S W of Illahûn and close to the edge of the desert, owed its origin to Tutmes III, who built a temple there Many of the inhabitants were foreigners Mr Petrie discovered here fragments of pottery of the time of Tutankhamon and Ramses II., resembling the most ancient potsherds found at Mycenæ. The coffin of Amentursha, discovered here, is now at Oxford. The pottery bears Egyptian stamps, but also letters of the Cyprian, Phœnician, and other alphabets.

Birket el-Kurûn and *Kaṣr Kurûn* (tent, horses, provisions, etc., comp. p. 456). The RAILWAY from Medînet el-Fayûm viâ *Senrú* and *Abu Gonsheh* to (15 M.) *Abuksa* (see below) and thence to *Senhûr* and (7 1/2 M.) *Tirseh* is used almost exclusively for the conveyance of sugar-cane to the manufactories of the Khedive. Travellers going by railway (one train daily from Medîneh to Abuksa, starting about noon, and performing the journey in about 1 hr.) must take horses with them for the continuation of their journey. The following routes are all practicable, but the third is to be preferred: —

(1) We proceed by land viâ *Nezleh* (where boats must be ordered or the passage of the lake) to *Kaṣr Kurûn;* then by water to

Dîmeh, and again by water to the S. bank of the lake, situated in the latitude of *Ṣenhûr*, which lies about 4 M. inland. The horses should be sent on from Ḳasr Ḳurûn to the lake (unless the somewhat refractory guides refuse to obey), in order that we may ride to Ṣenhûr, and thence to Medînet el-Fayûm. Four or five days are required for the excursion; the points of interest are mentioned in the third route. The road from Nezleh (see below) to Ḳaṣr Ḳurûn (4 hrs.) leads through the desert, past the remains of a small temple, called by the Arabs *Kaṣr el-Benât*, or 'Maidens' Castle'.

(2) If the traveller renounces Dîmeh and Ḳaṣr Ḳurûn, and is satisfied with the sport to be obtained in the Baḥr el-Wâdi, he may easily make the excursion in $2^1/_2$-3 days. On the first day the route skirts the railway (see above) to (2 hrs.) *Ṣenrû;* it then leads through a plantation of opuntia, the growth of which is so gigantic that it almost resembles a forest, and across a sandy tract overgrown with tamarisks to (2 hrs.) **Abuksa**, situated on a hill, and commanding a fine survey of the lake and the Libyan mountains. At the N. base of the hill near the railway station (see above) is a sugar manufactory, superintended by a Frenchman, who accords a kind reception to travellers. We now proceed to the S.W. across meadows, and through a somewhat marshy district, to ($2^1/_2$ hrs.) *Absheh*, situated close to *Nezleh*. (The traveller is recommended to spend the night in a tent rather than among the Beduins.) Next day we follow the valley of the *Bahr el-Wâdi* (or *Baḥr Nezleh*), which is bounded by large mud-hills, to the lake ($2^1/_2$ hrs.), where we spend the middle of the day. (The numerous dead fish on the bank of the lake render its proximity unpleasant; boats are to be had from the Beduins.) In the evening we return to Absheh, and on the third day to Medînet el-Fayûm.

(3) Four days at least are required for the somewhat longer route viâ Ṣenhûr and the lake to Ḳaṣr Ḳurûn, if the traveller wishes to visit Dîmeh, and shoot on the lake. The route first skirts the railway and the villa of Maḥmûd Bey, and then passes the tomb of a shêkh, where a draught of good water is offered to the traveller by a dervish. A number of dry ditches must be crossed, and also several canals, where the traveller on horseback will hardly escape from wetting his feet when the water is high; if he rides on a donkey, he should get the Arabs to carry him and his saddle across. The fields which we pass are remarkably well cultivated, and the eye rests with pleasure on trees of various kinds, including fine olives in the gardens, with hedges of cactus. The vegetation is most luxuriant in the neighbourhood of *Fidmîn*, a village picturesquely situated on a slope, but inhabited by a thievish population. The *Baḥr et-Tâḥûneh* ('mill river'), one of the broader canals, must be crossed here. Beyond this point the country is, at places, green and well irrigated, and at others dry and sterile. One part of the route, which is flanked by luxuriant gardens of olives, pomegranates, and

figs, is very muddy. After a ride of fully three hours we reach the locks and the bridge *Ḳanâṭir Ḥasan.* The large body of water of the canal, which is conducted from the Baḥr Yûsuf, here falls into a channel, which, with many ramifications, conveys it to the fields of Ṣenhûr.

The large village of **Ṣenhûr** (rail. station, see p. 463) lies on the border of the second plateau of the province. Those who visit Hawâra (p. 460) reach the first plateau, while the second is crossed on the way to Ṣenhûr; the third lies at our feet when looking down on the Birket el-Ḳurûn from the great *Kôm,* i.e. the ruin-strewn hill to the N. of the village. The handsome house of the Shêkh el-Beled offers good accommodation, and even quarters for the night. The traveller should make a bargain here for a boat with the shêkh of the fishermen. About 30 fr. for the day, and a bakshîsh for the rowers (of whom 6-8 are necessary for speed), are demanded.

Ṣenhûr stands on the site of an ancient, and not unimportant, town, of which large heaps of ruins still remain. Roman walls are traceable in many places. A large building has recently been excavated by the peasants for the sake of obtaining the hard bricks of which it is built, but part of it has already been removed. No remains of columns or inscriptions have been met with.

From Ṣenhûr to the Birket el-Kurûn takes about 1½ hr. The route leads through sugar-plantations. We reach the lake near the peninsula known as *el-Gezîreh,* on which stands a heap of ruins. A short distance to the W. are the scanty remains of *el-Hammam.* The traveller, after having ridden to the lake, should not forget to order his horses, which return to Senhûr, to await him for the return-journey at the spot where he has quitted them, or to order them to meet him in good time on the bank of the lake by Nezleh (see p. 464)

The **Birket el-Ḳurûn** ('lake of the horns') owes its name to its shape, which resembles that of slightly bent cows' horns. It measures 34 M. in length, and, at its broadest part, is about 6½ M. wide. It is situated on the same level as the Mediterranean, and its depth averages 13 ft. The greenish water is slightly brackish (scarcely fit for drinking), and abounds in fish, some of which are very palatable. The right of fishing is let by government, and the whole of the fishermen dwelling on the banks of the lake are in the service of the lessee, who receives one-half of the catch. The boats *(merkeb)* are very simply constructed, being without deck or mast; the traveller must take up his quarters on the flooring in the stern; none of the boats have sails, for, as the fish always go in the same direction as the wind, the fishermen have to row against the wind in order to catch them. Numerous pelicans, wild duck, and other water-fowl, frequent the lake. The banks are extremely sterile; on the N. side are barren hills of considerable height. In the middle of the lake rises a mass of rock, resembling a table, and serving as a landmark. Near the S. bank, from E. to W., lie the villages of *Kafr Tamîyeh, Tirseh, Ṣenhûr, Abuksa, Beshuai,* and *Abû Gonsheh*; the ruins of *Dîmeh* are situated on the N.

bank, but there are no other villages of importance. A the S.W. end of the lake is the promontory of *Khashm Khalîl*, overgrown with tamarisks and reeds, the creeks of which afford good landing-places. Ascending thence across the desert, we reach the temple in about $1^1/_4$ hours. The fishermen object to pass the night on the bank in the neighbourhood of Ḳaṣr Ḳurûn, being afraid of the Beduins and the '*Afrît*' (evil spirits).

Ḳaṣr Ḳurûn is a tolerably well preserved temple, probably of the Roman, or, at the earliest, of the Ptolemaic period. Before reaching it we observe numerous traces of an ancient town, which has now disappeared. The ground is strewn with blocks of hewn stone, burnt bricks, broken pottery, and fragments of glass. A circular foundation wall indicates the site of an ancient cistern, while other walls seem to have belonged to vineyards. The walls of the temple consist of carefully hewn blocks of hard limestone. This temple, like almost all the shrines in the oases, was dedicated to the ram-headed Ammon-Khnum, as is proved by the only two figures of this deity which still exist. They stand opposite to each other at the highest part of the posterior wall of the upper story of the open roof.

The temple is 20 yds in width across the façade, and 29 yds. in length. The entrance, facing the E, is approached by a lofty and carefully constructed platform, 14 yds. in length, forming a fore-court, on the S side of which rises a massive structure resembling a tower. Adjoining the façade of the temple, to the W. of the entrance door, rises a massive, semicircular projection, resembling the half of a huge column. On the lower floor are the apartments of the temple which were dedicated to worship, divided into a triple prosekos, and leading to the Sekos or sanctuary. In the first three rooms the ground slopes down towards the sanctuary, which, built in the form of a cella, adjoins the third room of the prosekos, and (as in the case of other temples) was divided into three small rooms at the back. The sanctuary is flanked by two narrow passages, each of which is adjoined by three rooms. The rooms of the prosekos also have adjacent chambers from which we may enter the cellars, or ascend by two flights of steps to the upper floor with its different apartments, and thence to the roof, whence we obtain an extensive view of the remains of the ancient city, of the lake, and the desert. Each gate of this curious building is surmounted by a winged disc of the sun; and over the doors leading into the second and third rooms of the prosekos and into the sanctuary, instead of the ordinary concave cornice, there is a series of Uraeus snakes, which, with their outstretched heads and bending necks, together form a kind of cornice. The names of several travellers are engraved on the stone of the first room, including those of Paul Lucas, R Pococke, Jomard, Roux, d'Anville, Coutelle, Bellier, Burton, Belzoni, Hyde, and Paul Martin. Kasr Kurûn has also been visited by Lepsius There are no ancient inscriptions remaining

To the E. of the large temple are situated two smaller Roman temples, in tolerable preservation, the larger of which, situated 300 paces from the smaller, is not without interest. Its walls (18 ft. by 19 ft.) consist of good burnt bricks, and its substructures of solid stone; the cella terminates in a niche resembling an apse, on each of the side-walls are two half-columns, which, as the fragments lying on the ground show, belong to the Ionic order There are also some less important ruins covering an extensive area, but nothing has been found among them dating from an earlier period than the Roman. The construction of the walls, the architectural forms, and many coins found here, are Roman;

and none of those small relics of the period of the Pharaohs, which are usually found so abundantly among the ruins of Egypt, have been discovered here. This was perhaps the site of the ancient *Dionysias*, a town which probably sprang up on the ruins of a Roman military station, situated on the extreme western side of Egypt On the outskirts of the ruins are walls which perhaps belonged to gardens; there must also have been once an aqueduct for the purpose of supplying the inhabitants and their gardens with water.

From Kaṣr Ḳurûn to Dîmeh is one day's journey. **Dîmeh** is situated opposite to the point at which we approach the lake from Ṣenhûr. The scanty ruins on the S. bank of the lake (*El-Ḥammâma*, etc.), are not worthy of a visit; but the ruins of Dîmeh, although no inscriptions have been found there, present some attraction. A street, 400 yds. in length, formerly embellished with figures of lions, leads to a platform on which an important temple once stood. The numerous blocks scattered about here, resembling mill-stones, and apparently artificially rounded, are discovered on closer inspection to be of natural formation. The paved court was surrounded by a brick wall, and the temple itself contained several apartments; a peristyle, with columns now in ruins, led to the entrance. Notwithstanding the imperfect state of the ruins, they suffice to prove, that a town of very considerable importance, perhaps the ancient *Bacchis*, once stood here.

Excursion to Médûm.

The Pyramid and Mastabas of Mêdûm, the oldest monuments in the world, deserve a visit, which if the traveller approaches by the river, may be accomplished from the village of *Rikka* in about 6 hrs. (railway travellers may perform it in about the same time from the el-Wasta station; comp. p. 458). Crossing the railway, we proceed on donkey-back in about 1¼ hr. to the pyramid, which rises close to the cultivated country on the soil of the desert, 1½ M. to the N. of the village of *Mêdûm*. This appears to be the oldest of the local names handed down to us, as it is met with on the mastabas of the early period of Snefru.

The **Pyramid of Médum** is so different from all the other structures of the kind that it is called by the Arabs '*El-Haram el-Kaddâb*', or '*the false pyramid*'. From a large heap of rubbish which covers its base, the smooth and steep upper part of the structure rises in three different stages at an angle of 74° 10', and is still preserved to a height of 122 ft. The first section is 69 ft, and the second 20½ ft, while the third, now almost entirely destroyed, was once 32 ft in height The outer walls consist of admirably jointed and polished blocks of Mokattam stone The holes in one of the surfaces were made by Lepsius and Erbkam when they examined the pyramid, the construction of which afforded them an admirable clue to the principle upon which the others were built (comp. p. 350). The Pyramid of Mêdûm was never completed; the heap of debris at its base consists of the material which once filled the angles of the different sections, so as to give the pyramid a smooth surface The pyramid was pillaged as early as in the time of the 20th Dynasty. It was opened in 1881 by Maspero, who found a long corridor and a chamber without sarcophagus Perhaps in this pyramid *Snefru*, the first king of the 4th Dyn., was buried, as in the neighbouring tombs persons related to him are interred.

The **Maṣṭabas of Mêdum**, which were opened by Mariette, lie to the N. of the pyramid. These were the tombs of the relations of Snefru (4th Dyn), and in many respects resemble the mausolea of Saḳḳârah which bear the same name. The façades of the most important of them are partly uncovered. The street of tombs, which is now accessible, presents the appearance of a hill-side covered with masonry, incrusted with stucco, and provided with ante-chambers. The mouth of each tomb is towards the E.; the leaning external walls are generally of Nile bricks, richly embellished with the linear patterns which afterwards formed the favourite decorations of the sides of the sarcophagi (which were imitations of the tomb-façades). The vestibule is in most cases comparatively large, but the inner corridors are narrow, slope downwards, and are covered with representations in a remarkably simple and antiquated style. The archaic character of the scenes and of the hieroglyphics proves the great antiquity of these monuments. The influence of the hieratic canon is already traceable here, but it does not appear to have hampered the efforts of the artists as much as it did at a later age. The admirably preserved colours are also less conventional than those seen in later monuments.

The first open tomb which we reach from the S., was that of Prince (Erpa Ha) *Nefermât*, who lived in the reign of King 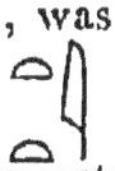 Teta. (There were 3 kings of this name, in the 1st, 3rd, and 6th Dynasty.) On the left wall of the corridor leading to the tomb-chamber, we see the deceased in a sitting posture, and on the right wall he is represented standing, with his wife behind him. Adjacent are men and women presenting offerings, as in the mastabas of Ti and Ptahhotep. The flesh-tint of the men is red, and that of the women pale yellow, and this circumstance, especially in a monument of this early period, is important as tending to prove the Asiatic origin of the Egyptian nobles. The features of the persons represented are of the Caucasian, and not of the Ethiopian type. Among the villages belonging to Nefermât, which offered gifts, there appears on the left the name of the district of 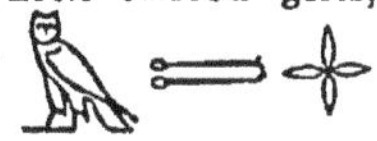  i.e. '*Metun* of the cattle'. Metun is the oldest form of the name Mêdûm. From the neck of the ox, which represents the victim, flows a black stream of blood. On the right side we find among others a district named that 'of the white sow', which proves that pigs were reared in Egypt as early as the time of Snefru. The pig in this group is very true to nature 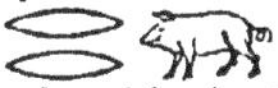 In the name of the district *Hat en Sek*, or 'place of the ploughing', the most ancient form of the plough is used as a determinative symbol. The advanced condition of industrial pursuits, showing that the Egyptians already practised the art in which, according to Pliny, they afterwards excelled, is proved by the character of the dress worn by the women represented on the right side of the first passage, consisting of black and white cotton stuff, with pleasing patterns on the borders. He tells us that they were not in the habit of painting the materials for their dress, but of dipping them in certain fluids. They were coloured with boiling dyes, and came out impressed with a pattern. Although the boilers contained one colour only, it is said to have imparted several different tints to the stuffs dyed in them. — In order to impart a durable colour to the larger figures represented here, an entirely unique process was employed. The outlines were engraved on the stone, while the surfaces enclosed by them were divided into deeply incised squares, which were filled with stucco of different colours, the flesh-tint of the men being red, that of the women yellow, and the colour of the robes being white, etc.

A little farther to the N. is the tomb of *Atet*, the wife of Nefermât. On the architrave over the doorway we see the husband of the deceased engaged in snaring birds, while a servant presents the spoil to the mistress of the house, whose complexion is of a brilliant yellow. On the outside wall, to the left, we observe the cattle of the deceased browsing on reeds. On the right stands Nefermât, who, as the inscription informs us, 'caused this monument to be erected to his gods in indestructible characters'. Among the domestic animals are several cattle of very bright colours. We also notice a gazelle held by the horns by a butcher, who is cutting off its head Offerings of wine were also made at this early period In the passage leading to the Serdâb is a group of labourers busily at work The hunting-scenes are curious, and, notwithstanding their simplicity, remarkably true to nature Among them is a greyhound seizing a gazelle by the leg, and another carrying a long-eared hare.

A few paces to the N E is another mastaba built of well-hewn blocks of limestone. The hieroglyphics and low reliefs, resembling those in the tomb of Ti at Sakkârah, are admirably executed The deceased interred here was named *Khent*, and his wife *Mara* Traversing the vestibule and a narrow passage, we reach a tomb-chapel with a sacrificial table; in the passage, on the right, is a handsome male figure with a lasso, and on the left are stone-masons, engaged in making sarcophagi On the left, in the innermost niche of this tomb, we perceive the deceased, and on the right, his wife We next come to a ruined mastaba, and to another tomb, half excavated, which was constructed for *Rahotep*, a son of Snefru, one of the highest civil and military dignitaries of the kingdom, and his wife *Nefert*, a relation of the royal family. The statues of this married couple, who died young, or at least are so represented, which are now among the principal treasures of the museum of Gîzeh, were found here Farther to the W are several other tombs, now covered up.

On the right bank of the Nile, opposite Rikka, upwards of 3 M. inland, is situated the small town of **Atfih**, where a heap of earth and broken pottery represents the scanty remains of the ancient *Aphroditopolis*, the territory of which, according to Strabo, adjoined that of Acanthus (Dahshûr), while its capital lay on the Arabian bank of the Nile. The city of Aphrodite must have been the same as that of the Egyptian Hathor, to whom also was sacred the white cow, which, as Strabo informs us, was worshipped here. The monuments, however, show us, that in the nome of Aphroditopolis, Horus, the son of Isis, was more highly revered than any of the other gods, among whom Hathor must be included. At an early period the Coptic name of the place was Tpeh, from which Atbo, and the Arabian name *Atfih* are derived

About A.D 310 the city of Aphroditopolis gained some celebrity from St. Anthony, the anchorite, who took up his quarters among the mountains to the E. of the town. So many devotees of every class made pilgrimages to him, that a regular high-road, practicable for camels, had to be constructed, which led the pilgrims through the desert to the cell of the hermit, situated near a group of palms and a spring The saint, however, escaped from his visitors, by retiring farther into the heart of the mountains (see below)

Near the village of *Zâwiyeh* (W. bank) a small canal runs out of the Nile into the Bahr Yûsuf (p. 456); a deep cutting also seems to have connected the river with the Bahr Yûsuf in the latitude of Ahnas el-Medîneh and Beni Suêf. These four channels enclosed an island which has been identified with the *Heracleopolitan Nome*, unanimously described by Greek authorities as an island. Strabo, who visited it on his way to the Fayûm, after leaving the Nome of Aphroditopolis, describes it as a large island, and informs us, that the inhabitants of *Heracleopolis* worshipped the ichneumon, the greatest enemy of the crocodile, which was held sacred in the nome of Arsinoe, for, as he tells us, it crawls down the throat of the sleeping monster and devours its entrails. The large hills of rubbish near *Ahnas el-Medîneh* have been satisfactorily identified with the ruins of Heracleopolis, they lie about 11 M inland from Beni Suêf, and are called by the Arabs *Umm el-Kîmân* ('mother of the heaps of rubbish'). An excursion to them, however, is not recommended, unless the traveller is visiting Beni Suêf from the Fayûm.

On the W. bank of the Nile the mountains recede a considerable distance, while on the E. bank their steep and lofty spurs frequently extend down to the bank in not unpicturesque forms. None of the Nile villages between this point and Beni Suêf are worthy of mention. About 2 M inland (on the W. bank) is the village of *Bûsh*, chiefly inhabited by Copts, with two churches of some interest, and numerous potteries.

Beni Suêf, 72 M. from Cairo, with 5-6000 inhab., the first place where the steamboat stops, and a railway station, is a pleasantly situated town, with beautiful shady avenues, and a palace in bad preservation. It is the capital of a province of the same name, which is said to contain 169 villages with about 100,000 inhabitants, and is the residence of a Mudir. Post and telegraph office, and a small bazaar. The market days present a busy scene, but the dirty streets are almost deserted at other times. The linen manufacture, for which this town was famous in the middle ages, has fallen off.

A road, which was much frequented before the completion of the railway, leads from Beni Suêf into the Fayûm.

Another road, traversing the *Wadi Bayâd*, which opens near the village of that name, on the E. bank of the Nile, opposite Beni Suêf, leads through the desert to the monasteries of *St Anthony* and *St Paul* (pp 99, 385), situated a few miles from the Red Sea. The fraternity of the monastery of St Anthony now occupies the highest rank among the Monophysitic religious corporations

From Beni Suêf railway to Cairo in 4½ hrs.

10. The Peninsula of Sinai.

The journey to Mount Sinai is perhaps the most interesting of Oriental expeditions, particularly to the student of the Bible †, as he will traverse nearly the same route as that of the Israelites described in the Bible (p 481). The peninsula of Mt. Sinai owes its imperishable fame to the vicissitudes undergone by these wanderers under the leadership of their great lawgiver; but the scenery is also so varied that it will amply repay the traveller for all the privations of his journey, which, after all, are not more serious than those of a tour through the interior of Palestine. The usual duration of the Mt Sinai expedition is 17-20 days (comp, however, p. 475)

The best SEASON for the journey is between the middle of February and the end of April, and between the beginning of October and the middle of November. During the months of November, December, and January, the nights are generally very cold, while in summer the glare of the sun, reflected from the granite rocks of the Sinai mountains, is very oppressive Even at the end of May the weather is hot, and the Khamsîn (p. 69) prevalent (setting in sometimes as early as April), but at this advanced season the traveller will have the advantage of seeing the manna (p. 500), or fruit of the tarfa shrub, in its ripe condition.

The PREPARATIONS for the journey require special care. The starting-point is Suez, but all the preliminaries must be arranged at Cairo, where alone are to be found the necessary dragomans and the Shêkhs of the Ṭawara Beduins (p. 478), who act as guides and let camels during the travelling season The first thing is to engage a good dragoman (p. 13), who provides camels, tents, bedding, blankets, and provisions. All these should be examined at Cairo, and the tents pitched by way of experiment. The more carefully this inspection is made, and any defects

† Although it is not the object of the handbook to enter upon the province of Biblical criticism. the views of the principal explorers are briefly given in connection with the different places. As the great charm of a journey through the Peninsula consists in its associations with the Biblical account of the Exodus of the Israelites, and the promulgation of the law (p 481), the traveller should of course be provided with a copy of the whole Sacred Volume, or at least with the books of Exodus and Numbers.

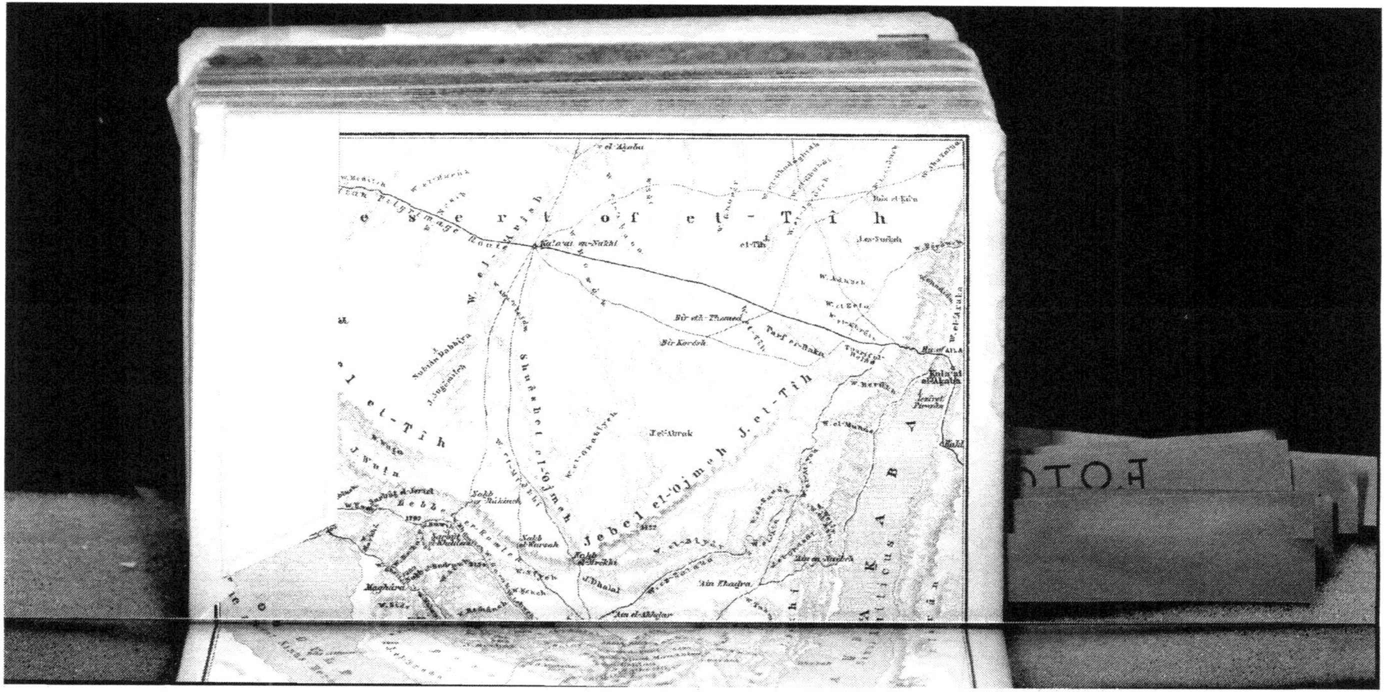
Pilgrimage Route
Jebel el-'Ojmeh
J. et-Tîh
Bir eth-Themed
Ras el-'Aḳaba

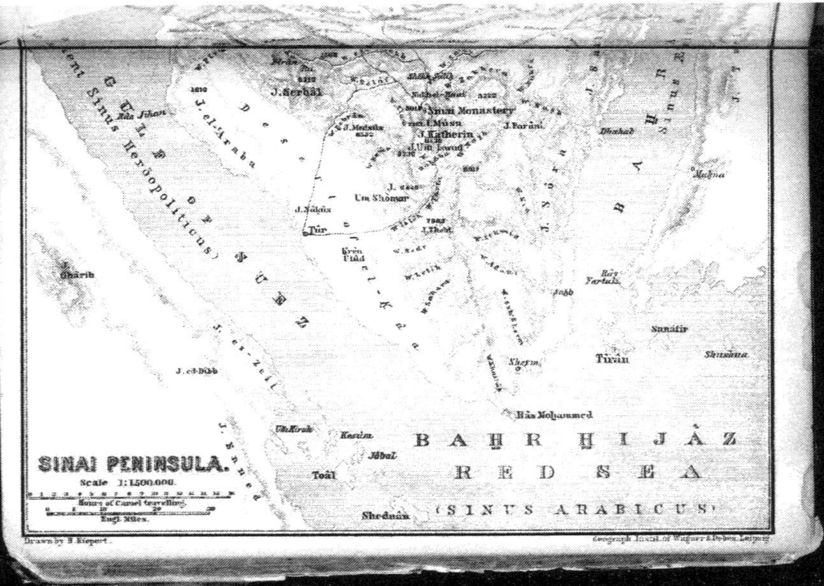
SINAI PENINSULA.
Scale 1:1,500,000.
Hours of Camel travelling.
Engl. Miles.
GULF OF SUEZ
Sinus Heroopoliticus
BAHR HIJÂZ
RED SEA
(SINUS ARABICUS)
J. Serbâl
J. el-Araba
Sinai Monastery
J. Katherin
J. Ferâni
Um Shômar
Tûr
Tîrân
Sanâfir
Râs Mohammed
Shedwân
Toâl
Drawn by H. Kiepert.

INSERT

FOLD-OUT

OR MAP

HERE!

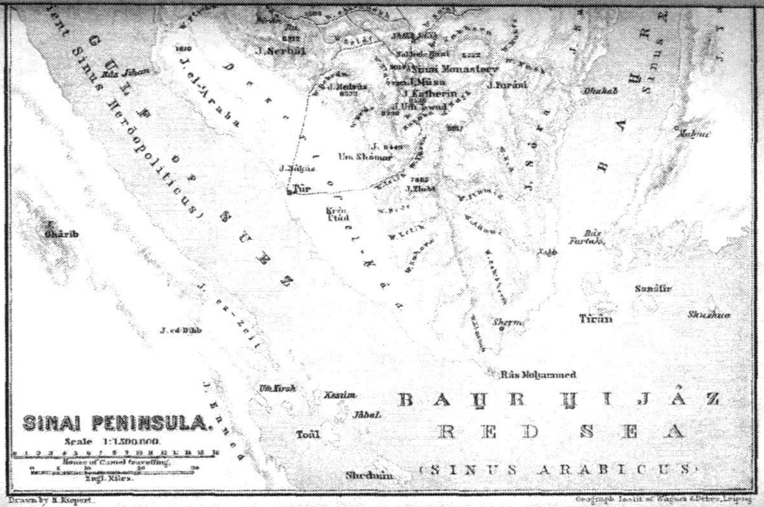

SINAI PENINSULA.
Scale 1:1,500,000.
Hours of Camel travelling.
Engl. Miles.
GULF OF SUEZ
Sinus Heroopoliticus)
J. Serbâl
Sinai Monastery
J. Mûsa
J. Katherin
J. Um Shômar
Tûr
Tirân
Sanâfir
Râs Moḥammed
BAḤR ḤIJÂZ
RED SEA
(SINUS ARABICUS)
Drawn by H. Kiepert.
Geograph. Instit. of Wagner & Debes, Leipzig.

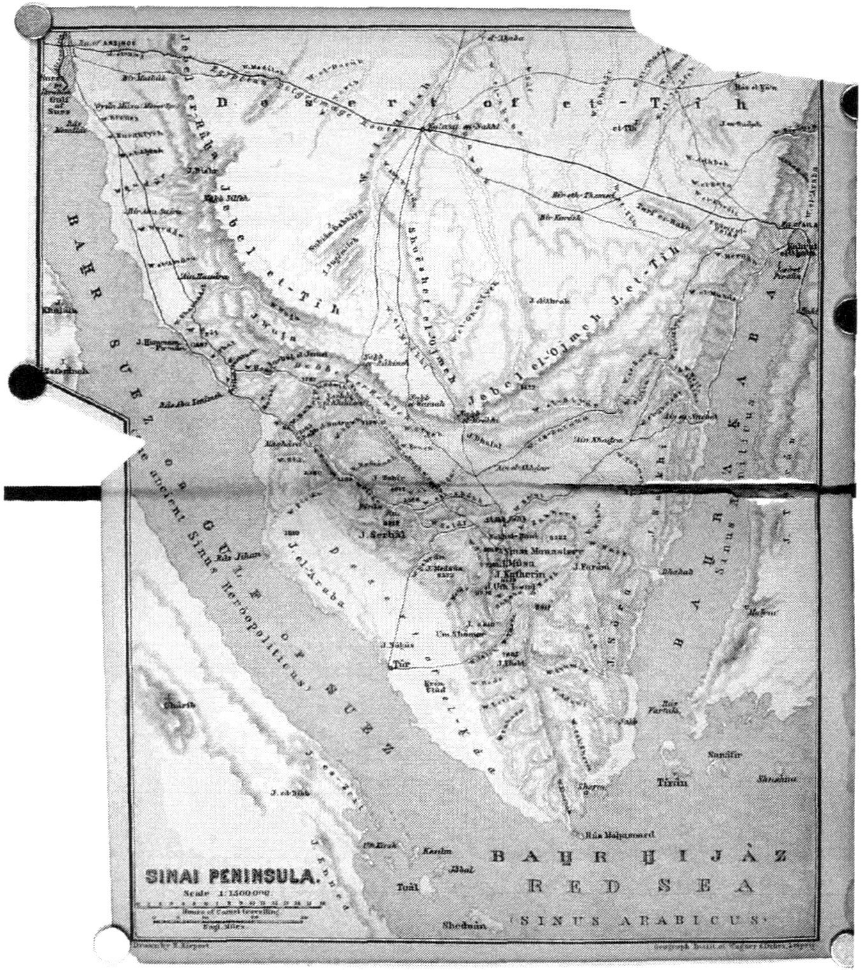
SINAI PENINSULA.
Desert of et-Tih
Jebel et-Tih
Jebel el-'Ojmeh
J. el-'Araba
J. Serbâl
J. Katherîn
J. Mûsa
Tûr
Gulf of Suez
BAHR SUEZ or GULF OF SUEZ
the ancient Sinus Heroöpoliticus
BAHR HIJÂZ
RED SEA
(SINUS ARABICUS)
Tirân
Sanâfir
Shedwân
Râs Muhammed

remedied, the less likelihood will there be of subsequent annoyance. The traveller is particularly cautioned against trusting to the promises of Orientals

The cost of the journey for a party of 3-4 persons, including camels, tents, accommodation in the monastery of Mt. Sinai (and at the Hotel at Suez if necessary), provisions (exclusive of spirits), the dragoman's fee, and all gratuities payable to attendants, will amount to 40-50 fr a day for each person, according to the requirements of the party, and the demand for camels The expense is proportionally less for a large party, but in this case, delays and differences of opinion are more likely to occur.

The following CONTRACT will probably meet the requirements of most travellers.

Contract. Mr. X. and his travelling companions on the one hand, and the Dragoman Y. on the other, have mutually entered into the following contract. —

(1) The Dragoman Y. binds himself to conduct Mr. X. and his party safely through Arabia Petraea to the Monastery of Sinai, and back, by the following route .. (naming the principal points), at a charge of ... shillings per day For the three days, during which the camels are travelling from Cairo to Suez the Dragoman shall receive one-third only of the stipulated daily charge The Dragoman Y undertakes to await at Suez the arrival of the travellers, in perfect order for starting, on the ... day of the month of . The day of starting from Suez shall be deemed the first complete travelling day. For each day after the first twenty days, reckoned from the starting of the camels, and also for days of rest, the right to appoint which is reserved to Mr X., the daily charge shall be reduced to . for each person

(It is advisable to lay down the whole route very precisely, mentioning also the valleys which have to be traversed, but the stages must of course depend on the situation of the springs We may again mention here that the Orientals, and the Beduins in particular, attach no value whatever to their time, so that little or no compensation need be made for delays.)

(2) The whole travelling expenses of the party, for the journey by land and by water, camels, boats, etc., for food, for tents, or for accommodation at hotels (to be chosen by Mr X) in case of any stay at Suez; for lights, service, guides, bakshish to all persons whatsoever, and particularly the fees for escorting the party paid to the Beduins whose territory is traversed, shall be defrayed exclusively by the Dragoman Y., who shall also bear all outlay for the stay in the Monastery, including the usual contributions to the monks Each traveller shall be entitled, without extra charge, to ½-1 bottle of wine per day, but Mr X shall provide any spirituous liquors required by the party (Or the party may prefer to purchase their own wine, as well as spirits, in which case the Dragoman Y. shall be required to carry it free of expense A few bottles of good claret or Burgundy, and of Cognac, should also be taken by each traveller to mix with the water, which is often unpalatable, or to be used in case of illness)

(3) The Dragoman Y. shall provide a good cook, and a sufficient number of servants, and shall take care that they are always polite and obliging to Mr X. and his party, and that they are quiet at night so as not to prevent the travellers from sleeping, and he shall also maintain order among the camel drivers, as well as the other attendants. The Dragoman Y. also undertakes to be himself at all times obliging to Mr. X. and his party (p 13), and to comply with all their wishes so far as possible.

(It is customary for the attendants to ask a bakshîsh for every trifling service, but no attention should be paid to their demands. Another bad habit of theirs, to be carefully provided against, is that of tying up their beasts too close to the tents, and of chattering beside them half the night.)

(4) The Dragoman Y. shall provide ... tents for 2-3 persons each (to

which may be added, if required, a tent to be used by the whole party during the day), and for each traveller a complete bed with clean mattresses, blankets, sheets, and pillows; each person shall have two clean towels every five days, and clean sheets once a week. A sufficient supply of water for washing shall be supplied every morning, and as much drinking water per day as the traveller desires

(The Beduins of Sinai carry the water in small, long-shaped casks. The traveller will find it convenient to have one of these appropriated to his private use Kullehs are best for keeping the water cool, but are easily broken)

(5) The traveller's breakfast shall consist daily of eggs, with tea, coffee, or chocolate; lunch shall consist of cold meat (roast-meat, fowls, etc), and fruit, dinner, at the end of the day, shall consist of . . . courses. The travellers shall be provided with oranges and dates whenever they desire

(The traveller may adjust the bill of fare according to his taste. As the air of the desert is bracing, a liberal diet should be prescribed; preserved meats may also be stipulated for Nothing is to be had on the route except at the monastery, where rice, lentils, bread, dates, and excellent date-brandy may be purchased. The dinner hour should always be fixed for the evening, after the day's journey is over

It need hardly be said that wine and spirits are apt to make the traveller drowsy in hot weather Cold tea quenches the thirst better than anything else The bread which the dragoman proposes to take should be tasted beforehand The Arabian bread, consisting of thin, round cakes, is only palatable when fresh, so that a supply of European bread should be stipulated for — An abundant supply of ordinary tobacco (p. 27) should be taken to give the attendants and Beduins, but the traveller should beware of being too liberal with it at first, lest this attention should be demanded as a right)

(6) The Dragoman Y. shall provide a sufficient number of good and serviceable camels, the riding camels (see below) for Mr. X. and party may be tried by them before starting, and in case they do not suit, may be exchanged for others The same stipulation applies to the saddles (the condition of which should be carefully examined).

(7) In case of the illness or death of any of the camels, Mr. X. and party shall to no extent be responsible.

(8) Neither the Dragoman Y. nor the Arabs, who escort the travellers, shall, without the special permission of Mr. X., allow anyone whomsoever to join the party.

(9) The Dragoman Y. binds himself to conduct Mr. X. and party to any point within Arabia Petræa which they may desire to visit, to allow them to break their journey, whenever, and for as long a time as they may wish, and to provide each member of the party, when making excursions off the main route, with guides and luncheon. The Dragoman Y. shall not, however, be bound to provide more than *one* dinner, and *one* lodging for the night

(10) The Dragoman Y. forfeits all claim to payment for any day when he is the cause of a stoppage for more than half a day; but no such forfeiture shall take place, if Mr. X himself, or unfavourable weather, should be the cause of the delay. Any accidents happening to the camels, or difficulties caused through the fault of the Arabs, shall be reckoned among the delays for which the Dragoman Y. is answerable.

(This last stipulation is quite fair, as the Arabs in Arabia Petræa can always procure fresh camels within a few hours.)

(11) The day for starting from Suez shall be the . . .th day of . . .; for any postponement caused by the Dragoman Y , contrary to the wishes of Mr X. and party, he shall be liable to a fine of . . *l.stg* per day

The CAMELS (p. 12) used for riding are of an entirely different race from the camels of burden, and are called '*Hegîn*', or in Syria '*Delûl*' (i.e. docile). The Delûls, properly speaking, are selected animals of noble breed and very superior to the ordinary camels of the caravans. The saddle, which is placed upon the hump of the animal, consists of a kind of wooden frame, from which two high round crutches project in front and behind. Upon the frame is placed a leather cushion (which is rendered more comfortable by the addition of rugs), and in front of the foremost crutch there is a second cushion. The traveller sits with one leg round the foremost crutch, somewhat in the way in which ladies ride, and rests the heel of one foot against the instep of the other. The camel is urged on by the rider's heel, or a switch. The camels generally march in a long string, one behind the other, with deliberate but long steps, always snatching at herbs by the way-side when they have an opportunity. Their trotting and galloping paces are unpleasant. A camel can also carry two or more persons in a litter, and may also be made to carry the traveller's luggage. Mounting is not easy at first. When the animal kneels down, the rider grasps the two crutches, and places one knee on the cushion; he then swings the other leg into the saddle over the hindmost crutch. The camels have a trick of getting up while the rider is in the act of mounting, but the drivers prevent this by putting their feet on one of the animal's bent fore-legs. The first movements are always somewhat violent, and the novice must hold fast by the crutches; as the camel always gets up with its hindlegs first, the rider should at first lean back, and afterwards forward. The walking motion is very pleasant, and those who are accustomed to it prefer a camel to a horse for a long journey. The rider can read comfortably if he wishes, and need not hold the reins in his hand.

Arabian Saddle-bags (*Khurg*) should be purchased for the journey, as they are very convenient for carrying the requirements of the toilet, books, tobacco, and other articles.

With regard to Dress, see pp. 14, 15. Overcoats, cloaks, or bournouses ('abâyeh', see p. 40), and slippers, should not be forgotten. The traveller should also be provided with Strong Shoes, if he intends to make mountain ascents, as the rocks of the Serbâl and Jebel Mûsa are very sharp and angular.

Lastly a few hints with regard to Health (p. 15; chemists, p. 234) may be acceptable to the traveller, although the climate of the peninsula is extremely healthy, especially if the traveller walk an hour or two in the mornings and evenings. A pair of blue or grey spectacles, with perhaps a second pair in reserve, will be found to protect the eyes against the inflammation which is apt to be caused by the glare of the sun. A supply of zinc or other eyewash will often be useful. Castor oil (two tablespoonfuls) is a good remedy for diarrhœa, even when serious. Seidlitz powders are a specific for indigestion. Pills of quinine should be taken in cases of fever (which frequently attacks the Beduins), and glycerine is useful for softening the skin when cracked by the heat. A supply of lint, sticking-plaster, and linen bandages, may also sometimes be useful. — A cup of tea or coffee will be found refreshing at luncheon; fuel for heating water (camel-dung, and dry plants) can always be obtained by the Beduins. Good cocoa is also considered wholesome and nutritious, and is easily prepared. A supply of Liebig's extract of meat should not be omitted.

At Cairo (or at Suez) the traveller should procure through his consul a letter of introduction from the Monastery of the Sinaites at Cairo to those of the Monastery of St. Catharine, where he will then receive every attention. Those who intend to visit 'Akaba, should, if possible, be provided with an introduction to the commandant of the fortress there, especially if they propose to proceed thence to Petra. — Enquiries should also be made at Cairo whether a journey to Petra is considered safe.

The following are the principal routes (distances see below). —

(a) Land Route. This route leads by Wâdi Maghâra (p. 491), Wâdi Mokatteb (p. 493), Wâdi Firân (p. 494), and Nakb el-Hâwi (p. 501), to the Monastery of Sinai, and returns by Wâdi esh-Shêkh (p. 520), Sarbût el-Khâdem (p. 522), and Wâdi el-Homr (p. 523) near the sea, and to the road leading to Suez. In this way the traveller does not retrace his steps, except on a portion of the route.

(The journey from Mt. Sinai to ʿAkaba, and from Petra to the Holy Land, is very rarely undertaken, and should not be attempted without careful enquiry regarding the safety of the route.)

(b) Sea Voyage. A boat conveys the traveller down the Red Sea to Ṭûr (p 515), whence he rides to Sinai in 2½ days. When the N. wind, which almost always prevails on the Red Sea, is strong enough, the voyage takes about 20 hrs.; but it may take much longer if the breeze subsides. As the vessel skirts the coast, and as violent storms in the Red Sea are very rare, except during the prevalence of the Khamsîn in April and May, the voyage in a boat of sufficient size (about 20 tons' burden) is unattended with danger, though far from pleasant in a bad vessel The return-journey should on no account be made by water, for, owing to the prevalence of the N. wind, constant tacking is necessary, so that the voyage takes 8-10 days or more. The trip may be made in a vessel of 20 tons' burden, with a crew of four men, for 100-150 fr

The master of the vessel should be required to provide himself with the necessary ship's documents The traveller's consul will perhaps give him a letter of introduction to Shêkh Ḥennen, a respectable and obliging Arab who lives at Ṭûr. Even without an introduction the traveller should apply to this shêkh, who will assist him in getting camels. The shêkh speaks Arabic only, but his son speaks a little French and Italian. Travellers who can speak modern Greek or Arabic should go direct to the Greek Convent, show the monks his letter of introduction to the convent on Mt. Sinai, and hire from them the camels necessary for the completion of his journey

The most favourable time for starting is towards evening; we embark from the quay near the Suez hotel After traversing the narrow arm of the sea at the upper end of which Suez is situated, we reach the end of the Suez canal, and the roadstead shortly afterwards. On the right rise the ʿAtâka mountains (p 415), with the promontory of the same name, and to the left are the palms of ʿAin Mûsa (p 419), beyond which is the low chain of the hills of Tîh. Beyond Cape ʿAtâka opens the broad *Wâdi Mûsa*, and the hills recede On the left lies the desert extending between the Tîh hills and the sea; to the right, in the foreground, is the lighthouse of *Râs Zaʿferâneh*, opposite to which, on the left, is the *Jebel Hammâm Farʿûn* (see p. 488), abutting on the sea. For some distance hills on the left now rise close to the coast (see p. 489). The bay expands. To the right, in the foreground, rises the huge and picturesque *Jebel Ghârib* (about 5900 ft. in height), at the foot of which is a second lighthouse. On the left are the conical peaks of the *Jebel el-ʿAraba*, the base of which we now skirt. Beyond the Jebel Ghârib, which becomes more and more prominent, rises the table-land of *Jebel ez-Zêt*, which yields petroleum. The chain of Jebel el-ʿAraba is prolonged by the sandy *Jebel Nâkûs* (p. 516), and the *Jebel Hammâm Mûsa* (p. 516). We at length come in sight of the palm-groves and buildings of Ṭûr, beyond which lies the sterile desert of *El-Kâʿa* (p. 517); above the latter tower the imposing mountains of Serbâl on the left, and of Umm Shômar on the right, between which appear the mountains of Sinai. *Ṭûr*, see p. 515.

Ṭûr is now the quarantine station for the Mecca pilgrims and is consequently called at by the steamers, which may be used for the journey to this point and back. This considerably decreases the trouble and expense of the expedition, but it is necessary to find out beforehand the season and duration of the quarantine, which of course varies with the lunar year of the Arabs and with the state of health of the pilgrims In 1880 81 it lasted from November to January.

The advantages of the sea-voyage consist in the saving of time and money effected by avoiding the fatiguing and monotonous journey between Suez and Wâdi Shebêkeh, while we make the acquaintance of Ṭûr and the picturesque route through the Wâdi es-Slêh (p. 517), and have an opportunity of ascending the Umm Shomar (p. 515) without making any digression On the other hand we miss the route by Ṣarbût el-Khâdem (p 522); but this is of no consequence provided we return the whole way by land, for the sake of seeing the majestic Serbâl (p. 497), the oasis of Fîrân (p. 495), the Wâdi Mokatteb (p 493) with its inscriptions, and the mines of Wâdi Maghâra (p 491), all of which are points of much interest

Camels are always to be had at Ṭûr, but as good saddles are rare, the traveller's dragoman should take an ample supply of rugs from Cairo; moreover it is not so easy to make a satisfactory bargain at Ṭûr as at Cairo, though Shêkh Ḥennen (see above) will render every assistance in his power If the party is numerous, or if the traveller wishes to provide against the possibility of delay, camels should be sent on from Suez to Ṭûr, a journey of three days for unladen animals, the cost of which is not very great.

To the above directions may, lastly, be added a few hints for which we are indebted to a traveller who is well acquainted with the Arabic language, and is accustomed to associate with the Beduins. — Take the railway from Cairo to Suez Dispense with tents and beds; but take at least a couple of warm rugs to fold over the saddle, and to be used at night A hammock will also be found very serviceable, and the camp may be pitched where the trees are large enough to give it support. Before leaving Cairo the traveller should lay in a stock of preserved meats and wine, and buy a lamp and a few cooking utensils Pack these in palm-leaf baskets, which are well adapted for the camels. If necessary the stock of provisions may be reinforced at Ṭûr by fresh bread, a few fowls, lobsters, and fish, and some date paste. At Suez procure introductions to the monks of the Greek convent at Ṭûr and to Shêkh Ḥennen. Proceed from Suez to Ṭûr by boat or by steamer (during the quarantine period). Sleep at Ṭûr in Ḥennen's house or in the Greek convent. Hire a camel through Ḥennen with a Beduin attendant on foot. Start very early and traverse the desert to Wâdi es-Slêh (see p 517), reaching the Sinai Monastery next evening Thence travel slowly to Wâdi Baʿbaʿ Lastly, return to Suez by forced marches, taking about two days and a night. The whole journey may thus be accomplished in eight days. without reckoning the stay at the monastery, and perhaps at Fîrân; and as a sheltered resting-place may always be found among the mountains, the protection of a tent will never be missed, excepting perhaps on the last day of the expedition

Distances and Disposition of Time. There are of course several land-routes to the Monastery of Sinai, but we need only describe the most interesting of them, and those which are generally taken by travellers As a standard of distance we adopt the time usually occupied by the camels in performing the journey. Their average rate of travelling is about $2^1/_2$ M. per hour

When a journey in the East is to last for several days, it will be found impossible to induce the boatmen on the Nile, or the 'Children of the Desert', to start early in the morning, as they invariably seem to think that a late hour in the afternoon is the most suitable time, so that a very short distance only is performed on the first day So on the tour to Sinai the party seldom gets farther than ʿAin Mûsa (see below) on the first day, but on the second and following days more satisfactory progress is made. Patience is therefore indispensable at starting. The journey is usually made without any prolonged halt, except at the mines of Wâdi Maghâra in the Wâdi Mokatteb, in which we spend 3-4 hrs., riding at a slower pace; at the Jebel Serbâl, if it is to be ascended, for one day; and at Ṣarbûṭ el-Khâdem, for $^1/_2$-1 day Mount Sinai, being the great object of the journey, requires a stay of 2-3 days.

Routes to Mount Sinai.

Route I. By Land viâ Suez, Wâdi Maghâra, and Wâdi Fîrân.

1st Day. From Suez to ʿAin Mûsa (p. 419), $2^1/_2$ hrs.

A longer journey cannot well be accomplished on the first day, but the camels and attendants may be sent on thither, while the traveller may follow alone in the evening or early on the following morning, by boat, and there mount his camel for the first time.

2nd Day. From 'Ain Mûsa to the beginning of the Wâdi Werdân (p. 485), 8 hrs.

From 'Ain Mûsa to the beginning of the great plain 3 hrs.; thence to the beginning of the Wâdi Werdân 5 hrs.

3rd Day. From the beginning of the Wâdi Werdân to Wâdi Gharandel (p. 487), 7$^3/_4$ hrs.

From Wâdi Werdân to Wâdi 'Amâra (p 486), 3$^3/_4$ hrs
From Wâdi 'Amâra to Wâdi Hawâra (p 486), 2 hrs.
From Wâdi Hawâra to Wâdi Gharandel, 2 hrs

4th Day. From Wâdi Gharandel to Râs Abû Zenîmeh (p. 489), 8$^3/_4$ hrs.

From Wâdi Gharandel to Wâdi el-Ḥomr (where Route ii. diverges see p 524), 5$^1/_2$ hrs
Thence to Râs Abû Zenîmeh (p 489), 3$^1/_4$ hrs.
The 4th day may be divided into two days, if the Jebel Ḥammâm Far'ûn (p 488) is to be visited The best camping place is at the mouth of the Wâdi Kuwêseh

5th Day. From Râs Abû Zenîmeh to the mines in the Wâdi Maghâra (p. 491), 8$^1/_4$ hrs.

From Râs Abû Zenîmeh to Ḥanak el-Lakam (p. 490), 3$^3/_4$ hrs.
Thence to the mines in the Wâdi Maghâra (p. 491), 4$^1/_2$ hrs.

6th Day. From Wâdi Maghâra to the hill of El-Meḥarret in the Wâdi Fîrân (p. 495), 9 hrs.

From the mines to the Wâdi Fîrân, 3$^1/_4$ hrs
Through the Wâdi Fîrân to El-Meharret, 5$^3/_4$ hrs.
The 6th day's journey should be divided into two parts by those who are specially interested in the mines of Wâdi Maghâra and the inscriptions in the Wâdi Mokatteb On the 7th day we then arrive in good time at the foot of Mt Serbâl, or at the Oasis of Fîrân (p. 495).

7th Day. From the hill of El-Meḥarret to the end of the Wâdi Selâf (p. 501), 7$^3/_4$ hrs

From El-Meharret to the beginning of the Wâdi Selâf, 2 hrs.
Thence to the end of the valley, 5$^3/_4$ hrs
The traveller who desires to ascend Mt. Serbâl (p 497), should devote this day to the excursion, giving notice to the Beduins of this intention on the previous day They will then provide guides, and pitch the tents near the best starting-point for the ascent, which should be begun at an early hour

8th Day. Over the Naḳb el-Ḥâwi (p. 501) to the Monastery of Sinai, 4$^1/_2$ hrs.

If the easier route from the oasis of Fîrân through the Wâdi esh-Shêkh (see below) to the monastery (12$^3/_4$ hrs) is preferred, the party should encamp on the 7th day by the defile of El-Watîyeh (9 hrs, p 521)

Two or three days at least should be spent at the Monastery of Sinai (p 503).

Route 11. From the Monastery of Mount Sinai viâ Ṣarbûṭ el-Khâdem to Suez.

1st Day. From the Monastery of Sinai to the Wâdi eṭ-Ṭarr (p. 521), in the Wâdi esh-Shêkh, 7$^3/_4$ hrs.

From the Monastery of Sinai to El-Watîyeh, 3$^3/_4$ hrs.
Thence to the Wadi et-Tarr, 4 hrs.
This is a moderate day's journey only, as the traveller seldom

succeeds in getting off early from Sinai, especially if the halt is made at the monastery itself The monks will, if requested, aid the traveller in overcoming difficulties raised by the Beduins

2nd Day. From Wâdi eṭ-Ṭarr, viâ Wâdi Ṣolêf, Wâdi Berâḥ, and Wâdi Lebweh, to the lower end of the Wâdi Barak (p. 521), $8^3/_4$ hrs.

From Wâdi et-Ṭarr to the top of the Nakb Wâdi Barak, $6^1/_2$ hrs Thence to the lower end of Wâdi Barak, $2^1/_4$ hrs.

3rd Day. From the lower end of the Wâdi Barak to the beginning of the Wâdi el-Ḥomr (p. 524), $9^1/_4$ hrs.

From the Wâdi Barak to the Wâdi Merattameh in the Wâdi Sûwik (p. 522), $4^1/_4$ hrs Thence to the Wâdi el-Ḥomr, 5 hrs

4th Day. Through the Wâdi el-Ḥomr to the Wâdi Gharandel (p. 487), $9^1/_4$ hrs.

Through the Wâdi el-Homr to its union with the Wâdi Shebêkeh, $3^3/_4$ hrs. Thence to the Wâdi Gharandel (see Route i), $5^1/_2$ hrs.

5th-7th Days. From the Wâdi Gharandel to Suez, see Route i.

Those who desire to visit the monuments of Sarbût el-Khadem (p. 522) should go on the 3rd day as far as the Wâdi Merattameh (see above), and devote the afternoon to the antiquities. They would then proceed on the 4th day as far as the junction of the Wâdi el-Ḥomr and the Wâdi Shebêkeh ($8^3/_4$ hrs). Beyond that point, see R. i.

Route III. From Suez by Sea to Ṭûr, and by Land to Sinai.

1st Day. Sea-voyage from Suez to Ṭûr (p. 474), 15-30 hrs.

2nd Day. Preparations for the journey in Ṭûr (p. 515).

3rd Day. Visit the Jebel Nâḳûs (p. 516). Under favourable circumstances this may be managed on the second day.

From Ṭûr to the Monastery of Sinai, $2^1/_2$ days The pass used by the monks is much shorter than the route described below, but is extremely rugged

4th Day. By the plain of El-Ḳâ'a (p 518) to the Wâdi Ḥebrân (p. 518), 9 hrs.

5th Day. Through the Wâdi Ḥebrân by the Naḳb el-'Ejjâwi to the Wâdi Selâf (p. 501), 10 hrs.

6th Day. Over the Naḳb el-Ḥâwi (p. 501), and through the Wâdi er-Râḥa (p. 502), to the Monastery of Sinai, $5^1/_2$ hrs.

Formation of the Peninsula. At the N. end of the Red Sea two long, narrow bays extend into the mainland, the Gulf of Suez on the W., and the Bay of 'Aḳaba on the East The peninsula thus formed, which belongs to Arabia, is called the Peninsula of Sinai, or Arabia Petræa, after Petra, its capital. It consists entirely of sterile ranges of mountains, furrowed by Wâdis, or valleys with watercourses, which are scantily filled after rain only. The geological formations of the peninsula are extremely interesting. The S. promontory of the peninsula is called Râs, or Cape Moḥammed. This large, triangular region is 9400 sq. M. in area, *i.e* about the same size as Sicily. It is appropriately called the *Peninsula of Sinai*, because 'Mount Sinai constitutes the nucleus of its formation, and presents physical features entirely distinct from those of the surrounding regions. Isolated by the sea and desert from the rest of the earth and its history, it has yet, from a very remote period, formed the highly revered vestibule of all the temples of the civilized world'. (C. Ritter.) The Mount Sinai group, with its masses of granite, forms the S.W. half of the peninsula, while the long limestone range of Jebel et-Tîh, beginning at the Isthmus of Suez, first turns to the S.E., and then sends forth a number of ramifications to the E. and N.E. The Sinai group forms a watershed from which wâdis descend to the E. and W., *i. e.* to the gulfs of Suez and ʿAḳaba respectively; while the 'River of Egypt', which is mentioned as the boundary of Palestine in the Bible, and is now the Wâdi el-ʿArîsh, descends from the Jebel et-Tîh towards the N. to the Mediterranean. Those parts of the *Tîh Mountains* across which our route lies rise to a moderate height, and are formed of limestone, chalk, and, to a smaller extent, of sandstone.

The Mount Sinai Group. 'This huge range, composed of primæval gneiss and granite, or, in more precise geological terminology, of colourless quartz, flesh-coloured felspar, green hornblende, and black slate, rising in majestic and precipitous masses and furrowed by vertical clefts, extends from Serbâl to the Om Shômar, and from the Om Shômar to the Râs Mohammed Since the time of their formation these crystalline masses have undergone no geological change, but have reared their summits above the ocean from the beginning of time, unaffected by the transitions of the Silurian or Devonian, the Triassic or chalk periods. At the base only do these venerable mountains show any trace of alteration. Thus the Red Sea has on one side thrown a girdle of coral around Mount Sinai, and so in recent times produced a coast district; while towards the N the sea, during the chalk period, has formed the limestone plateau of the desert of Tîh (4000 ft above the sea-level), which stretches across the whole of Sinai to Mount Lebanon The crystalline masses of the Sinai chain, which extend from N to S. for a distance of about 40 M , exhibit no great variety. The whole range forms a central nucleus traversed by diorites and porphyries' (O Fraas)

Inhabitants Amid the sterile mountains and valleys of the peninsula, some 4-5000 Beduins manage to obtain a livelihood. They generally have remarkably slight figures, and regular, sharply marked features. The boys, who follow the camels and wait upon travellers, are particularly graceful and engaging; the men are employed in conveying millstones, charcoal, and other wares to Egypt, they supply travellers (who are chiefly pilgrims of the Greek faith) with camels, hunt the mountain goat, celebrate festivals, and, in the W. part of the peninsula at least, rarely indulge in the sanguinary feuds which the different tribes formerly waged with one another Those occupying the E. and the N E. of Arabia Petræa are of a wilder and more warlike character; the boys and girls, and occasionally the men, drive the goats and the speckled sheep, which call to mind the artifice resorted to by Jacob, to the meagre pastures in summer, while the women remain in the tents to look after their children and household work In the best watered parts of the peninsula, the Beduins have built themselves huts, and cultivate plantations of dates, the most productive of which are in the Wâdi Firân (p 495), and in the neighbourhood of Ṭûr on the Red Sea In all other districts the inhabitants live in tents The Ṭâwara are good-natured, honest, and generally of noble bearing, they are quite free from the sordid cupidity of the lower classes in Egypt, and the name of 'Fellâḥ' is used by them as a term of reproach They do not practise polygamy, and their families are generally small The young Beduins have opportunities of seeing the girls of their tribe unveiled, while tending their herds on the mountains, and of forming attachments to them. Marriages from inclination are therefore frequent here, but custom requires that the bridegroom should purchase his bride from her father, the usual price being several camels, and a certain sum of money, but the bargain is seldom concluded without protracted negotiations conducted by a third party. The girl is not permitted to know anything of these negotiations between the father, the suitor, and the match-maker (khâṭîb), and if she should happen to have been a witness of them, decorum requires that she should retire into the mountains, though only for a few hours. Some tribes require that she should remain among the mountains for the three days preceding the marriage, but among the Ṭâwara she spends them in a tent erected beside that of her father, whence she is removed to the dwelling of her future husband. It occasionally happens that the girl flees of her own accord to the mountains, and seriously resists and throws stones at an unacceptable suitor (comp. p. 497). Each tribe has a Shêkh, or chief, a title of honour which is also sometimes applied to the older and most respected members of the community. The dress of these Beduins is very simple. They wear a tarbûsh or a turban, and a grey gown fastened with a girdle round the waist. In cold weather they wear a burnous of coarse material; many of them are bare-footed, but the wealthier wear sandals of camel-leather. Their usual weapons consist of sabres and knives, the guns they use for hunting are of great length and simple construction. They neither use horses nor lances, but the men often carry staves, which are still made in the form of the Egyptian . From their girdles usually hang amulets, tinder, and tobacco pipes. Those tribes, with whom the traveller chiefly comes in contact, call themselves Ṭâwara (people of Ṭûr), and are generally honest. The principal sub-divisions of this tribe are the Ṣibjaneddêr, Mezêneh, Garârisheh, Ṣawâliha, Sa'îdiyeh, Awârimeh, 'Alêkât, Râdanîyeh, and Shahîn. The Beduins of the E. and N.E., and particularly the 'Alawîn, are wild, warlike, and insolent. The Tîyâheh, who conduct the traveller from Nakhleh to Hebron, are less objectionable. With regard to the servants of the monastery (Jebelîyeh), and the families dependent on them, who are settled in the oasis of Fîrân and in Ṭûr, see p. 503. Each tribe has its particular district, the boundaries of which are indicated by stones at doubtful points. These Beduins have long professed El-Islâm, but know little or nothing of the Prophet and his religion. They are seldom seen to pray, but they celebrate festivals to Sâlih and Mûsa (Moses), their national saints, and sacrifice victims in their honour (see pp. 500, 520).

History of the Peninsula. The history of this region is as old as that of Egypt itself, for we find that the first Pharaoh, of whose reign we possess contemporaneous monuments bearing inscriptions (Snefru), signalised himself as the conqueror of these mountain tribes, and the discoverer of the mines. The mines in the desolate Wâdi Maghâra (p. 491) and Ṣarbût el-Khâdem (p. 522) were worked by Egyptians more than 5000 years ago; and copper, malachite, and turquoises were brought thence to the treasury of Memphis. Down to the time of the invasion of Egypt by the Hyksos (p. 88), we learn that the peninsula was dependent on the Pharaohs, and was impoverished for their advantage. Whilst the latter, having been supplanted by the new masters of Egypt, maintained themselves in the S. part of the valley of the Nile, it seems that the working of the mines was suspended, and that the mountain tribes succeeded in shaking off the yoke of their oppressors. Immediately after the expulsion of the Hyksos, these tribes were subjugated anew by the powerful monarchs of the 18th Dynasty, who conquered all the states adjoining Egypt on the East. This is proved by the inscriptions of Sarbûṭ el-Khâdem, extending down to the 20th Dynasty. The names of the springs, mountains, and valleys, resemble those of the Book of Exodus; and the Biblical traditions, which the Beduins attach to them, doubtless owe their origin to the Christians who settled at an early period in this wilderness. With regard to the battle with the Amalekites, and Mount Sinai as the scene of the promulgation of the law, see p. 481 *et seq.* We may, however, remark here, that the Israelites of a later period never made pilgrimages from Palestine to the sacred mount, and that, throughout the Mosaic writings, Elijah

(p. 511) alone is mentioned as a visitor to Mount Sinai. Down to the time of the first settlement of the early Christians, we rarely have any mention of travellers in the peninsula, but they are mentioned on some Egyptian inscriptions, on the occasion of the journeys to Ophir (1 Kings ix 26, 28), and lastly in a few notices of the history of the Nabatæans, a people from the N E, who took possession of the commercial route abandoned by the Phœnicians, and, from the famous rocky city of Petra, commanded the peninsula down to about the period of the birth of Christ Numerous rocks in the districts we are about to visit bear inscriptions (p 494) which owe their origin to the heathen Nabatæans. Down to the beginning of the Christian era, the population probably led a similar life to that of the present day. Shepherds pastured their flocks here, and merchants and pilgrims traversed the wâdis on camels, or ascended to the summit of the sacred Mount Serbâl. The caravans of the merchants, however, were more richly freighted than at the present day, while the natives, instead of praying to Allah and the Prophet, worshipped the brilliant stars in the cloudless sky of this almost rainless country On the diffusion of Christianity, the deserts of the peninsula were peopled by a new race, and assumed a new appearance and a more important position. Arabia Petræa lay between the two lands which had embraced Christianity most ardently, namely Syria and Egypt, and soon became an asylum for the believers of these two countries who longed for pardon and redemption, and who hoped, by subjecting themselves to misery and privations in this world, to attain salvation in the next Their great exemplars were Moses and Elijah, both of whom had trodden the sacred soil of the peninsula, and this region therefore appeared to them a most appropriate place of retirement from the business and pleasures of a wicked world. The first seeds of Christianity, which bore fruit in Trajan's reign, were perhaps sown here by St Paul about A.D. 40 In A D 105 the peninsula was annexed to the Roman empire by Cornelius Palma, prefect of Syria After the middle of the 4th cent the peninsula was gradually peopled with Anchorites and numerous Cœnobites, who were bound by a common monastic rule. Tradition ascribes the foundation of the brotherhoods of hermits and monks to St Paul of Thebes and St. Anthony of Koma, but the most recent investigations (comp p 385) prove this conjecture to be improbable. On Mt Serbâl and in the Wâdi Fîrân, the ancient Pharan, was situated the most thickly inhabited settlement (laura) of anchorites known to have existed in any of the localities frequented by the early Christians. The penitents were not only exposed to privations of every kind, but to the attacks of the cruel and rapacious Saracens and Blemmyes About the year 305 forty of the monks of Sinai were massacred by the Saracens. In 361-63 St. Julian founded a church on Sinai (Mt Serbâl?). Terrible massacres of the monks of Sinai were again perpetrated by the Saracens in 373 and 395 or 411, of which Ammonius and Nilus, two eye-witnesses, have given accounts In the 5th cent many of the monks and anchorites embraced heretical doctrines, which exposed them to severe persecutions. In the reign of Justinian, according to the account of Procopius, a church, dedicated to the Virgin, was built halfway up Mount Sinai (on the site of the present chapel of Elijah), while a very strong fortress was constructed at the foot of the hill, and provided with a garrison, to prevent the Saracens of the peninsula from invading Palestine (see p. 500). In the 7th cent the armies of Mohammed began their victorious career. They did *not* penetrate into the interior of the peninsula, but doubtless took possession of Aila ('Akaba), which was chiefly inhabited by Jews. In the course of subsequent expeditions, the peninsula of Sinai was found to be almost exclusively occupied by a Christian population. The wandering tribes of the natives readily embraced the new religion, and the monasteries and cells of the anchorites were ere long deserted. The monks of the Monastery of the Transfiguration alone continued to maintain their position in spite of many difficulties, partly by their resolute conduct, and partly by stratagem (p. 504). In the time of the Crusades, Aila (p. 519) became one of the chief scenes of the battles between Saladin, who captured it in 1170, and the Franks, who were afterwards unable to maintain possession of it, notwithstanding the efforts made by Count Rainold. After the Crusades the history of the peninsula was merged in that of Egypt. Its sequestered valleys were traversed by hosts of Mecca pilgrims, while there was also, as at the present day, no lack of Christian pilgrims of the Greek faith, wending their way to the monastery of Sinai.

The Exodus Until recently the Bible was the only source of information regarding the emigration of the Jews from Egypt, but the monuments and papyrus-scrolls which have been handed down to us by the ancient Egyptians, and deciphered by modern ingenuity, now convey to us a distinct idea of the condition of Egypt at the time of the Exodus, which we may compare with the contemporaneous Biblical accounts On collating the Bible narrative with the monuments, we find that they agree on all material points On the other hand, however, it seems obvious, that the vicissitudes undergone by the Israelites in Egypt and during the Exodus, must have been gradually embellished by legendary and poetical additions, before they were recorded in writing. These embellishments doubtless originated in the fertile imagination of the people, and in their profound gratitude, which prompted them to paint in the most glowing and picturesque colours the great things which God had done for them, Most of the camping-places of the people seem, as we shall see, to be capable of identification, since the list of stations in the wilderness, as given by Moses (Numb xxxiii), was doubtless made from contemporaneous records †.

The Period of the Oppression. After Joseph's death the Israelites had multiplied greatly, and, together with other Semitic tribes, occupied the whole of the N E. part of the Delta, whilst the early Pharaohs of the 19th Dynasty were constantly at war with the nations whose territory adjoined the Delta on the N E. It was therefore natural that the Egyptian kings should fear that, during their absence and that of the Egyptian army, the Jews should ally themselves with the enemies of Egypt, who were of cognate race, and this apprehension is distinctly mentioned by Pharaoh in the Bible narrative *Ramses II.*, after whom one of the scenes of the compulsory labour of the Israelites was named, was the Pharaoh of the oppression, and his son *Merenptah* (the Menephthes of Manetho) was the Pharaoh of the Exodus. The monuments inform us, that these two monarchs decorated Tanis, the ancient city of the Hyksos, anew with magnificent monuments, the place having long been shunned by their

† The following theory regarding the Exodus, which was started during last century by G H Richter, and maintained more recently by Schleiden, has again been adopted by *Brugsch* (comp , however, the observation at p 470).

'According to the monuments, the Sethroitic nome was also called *Suku* or *Succoth*. This region was covered with marshes, lakes, and canals, so that it was impossible to erect towns in the *Interior* of the district, and accordingly the Egyptian texts, as well as the classic authors, mention towns on its boundaries only. The three following are those oftenest mentioned One named *Khetam* (i e. fortress) *of Succoth* lay to the N., near Pelusium, and was intended to protect the N. frontier. A second, bearing the Semitic name of *Segol*, or *Segor* (i.e. key), *of Succoth*, and situated on the S.W. frontier of the district, was intended to protect the district of Tanis-Ramses against invasion The third, known by the Semitic name of *Migdol* (i e tower), or by the Egyptian name of *Samut* (also signifying a tower), lay on the outskirts of the Arabian desert, on the E. frontier of the district of Succoth, the site being probably identical with that of the modern *Tell es-Samût* (see Map of the Suez Canal to the E. of Kantara). Brugsch identifies the Biblical *Succoth* with Segol in Succoth, and *Migdol* with the above-mentioned Migdol-Samut The Biblical *Etham*, however, which is wanting to complete the list of the stations, is also capable of identification, for it can be no other than the Egyptian *Khetam*, which signifies fortress, the same word being preserved also in the Khetam of Succoth (see above).

predecessors on account of the Semitic religious rites practised there. Tanis is the Zoan of the Bible, where Moses performed his miracles in the presence of Pharaoh This place was doubtless often visited by Ramses II., who was a powerful conqueror and founder of cities, not only when on his way to battle, and on his return as a victor, but because his presence must often have been necessary for the prevention of rebellion among the numerous foreigners resident in these E districts. The Israelitish records only mention the oppression they underwent towards the end of their sojourn in Egypt Ramses, however, was far from being a capricious tyrant, but was a wise, though severe military prince, who employed the Semitic settlers in his kingdom in the construction of useful works, in order to prevent them from endangering his empire. The Jews, perhaps, also assisted in strengthening the double series of bastions, known as the wall of Sesostris, but constructed before the time of Ramses, which closed the Isthmus of Suez and afterwards obstructed the progress of the emigrants. The 'Egyptian wall' with its forts and frontier fortresses also afforded protection against the Asiatics, and commanded the district of Goshen

The Pharaoh of the Exodus. Ramses II. was succeeded by his thirteenth son Merenptah (p 90), a man of mature age. At the beginning of his reign Merenptah came into serious collision with the Libyans, who had allied themselves with the warlike inhabitants of the Mediterranean islands, and had attacked the coast of Egypt He succeeded, however, in subduing them, and was thus enabled to march victoriously to Thebes, where he caused spacious buildings to be erected, and encouraged the scientific labours of the priests Like his father, he also occasionally resided at Tanis, as the monuments inform us, and seems to have accorded greater liberty to the Semitic inhabitants of the Delta than his predecessor. Being, however, less powerful and resolute, he was more exposed to danger from his Asiatic neighbours than Ramses, who had not only rendered them tributary, but had leagued himself with them by intermarriages and treaties of peace, of which valuable records are still preserved. Moreover, before his accession to the throne the fortification of the E. frontier of the empire had been completed. He continued, nevertheless, to employ the bondsmen in Goshen, and to keep them in check, as they might have become very formidable if they had succeeded in uniting their forces against Egypt Accordingly, when Moses requested Pharaoh to allow him to lead his people into the desert, Merenptah's policy was to refuse, his great object being to prevent the union of the Israelites with other

---

Now the monuments mention a Khetam called *Khetam in the Province of Zor* (*i e* Tanis-Ramses, p 452), to distinguish it from other fortresses of the same name. A representation of this Khetam is preserved on a monument of Seti I in Karnak, in the form of a fortress on both banks of the river (the Pelusiac arm of the Nile), the opposite parts being connected by a bridge (Kantara), while a town, named Tabenet, lies in the vicinity. [This Tabenet is probably to be identified with the 'Pelusian *Daphnae*' (the plural form being applied to the double fortress), of which Herodotus (ii 30) expressly says, that it was occupied in his time, and before it, by an Egyptian garrison for the protection of the frontier towards Arabia and Syria] This Khetam, together with the town of Tabenet, is probably to be sought for in the ruins of ***Tell Defenneh*** (see Map of the Canal of Suez, W. of Kantara, p 424) The memory of the bridge (kantara) connecting the double fortress still survives in *Kantara* (see p. 435), which lies a little to the E. of Tell Defenneh. The accuracy of this theory, according to Brugsch, is also proved by the Egyptian and classical accounts of the roads which led to the E from Ramses (i e Tanîs-Sân) Two such roads are said to have existed; one of these led to the N.E. by Pithom (p. 412) through the marshy district of Succoth, with its numerous canals, and, according to the Egyptian texts and the authority of Pliny, was unsuitable for caravans and therefore but little frequented; the second was used by the Pharaohs when they marched towards the E. with their chariots and horsemen, and led from Ramses to Segol in Succoth, Khetam, and Migdol. In the British

cognate tribes. This accounts for his obstinate resistance to the apparently simple request of Moses The story of the plagues, and the destroying angel is well known. The historical foundation of the embellished narrative is corroborated by Egyptian and Greek records, which state that Merenptah was compelled by various disastrous occurrences to allow the foreigners (or 'lepers', as they are called in Egyptian reports) to quit the country

The Exodus Moses and his people doubtless started from Ramses; but it is difficult to follow the route taken by the emigrants during the first few days. Notwithstanding the ingenious theory of Brugsch (see Note, p 481), there seems little doubt that it was the Red Sea which the Israelites crossed, when we consider that their route to the E. was obstructed by a line of fortifications Believing this, we at once succeed in identifying the stations at which they halted, and in accounting for the apparently eccentric route chosen by Moses. The following passage occurs in Numbers xxxiii. 5, *et seq.*: — 'And the children of Israel removed from *Rameses*, and pitched in *Succoth*; and they departed from Succoth and pitched in *Etham*, which is in the edge of the wilderness. And they removed from Etham, and *turned again unto Pi-Hahiroth*, which is before *Baal Zephon*; and they pitched before Migdol. And they departed from before Pi-Hahiroth, and passed through the midst of the sea into the wilderness'. — Ramses (Maskhûta), on the fresh-water canal between Tell el-Kebîr and the Lake of Timsâh, was their rallying point; the Israelites assembled here from On (Heliopolis), Belbês, Bubastis, and Pithom, from the E. and S E, and joined those coming from Tanis and the N. pastoral districts The various detachments were here united; their hearts were filled with joyous hopes of reaching the happy, promised land, and, with their swords ready to resist opposition, if necessary, the Israelites thus departed from Egypt 'armed', and with a 'high hand' On leaving Ramses they took the road to Syria, and encamped at *Succoth*, to the S. of the modern Lake Balah. On the following day they passed *Etham* (or Khetam, 'the entrenchment'), *i e.* the line of fortifications above mentioned Here their march was arrested by towers, moats, and troops of well-armed soldiers Hereupon the people, who while under the yoke of their oppressors had little opportunity of learning to use their swords, lost courage and desired to return Moses knew the character of the multitude under his care, and was aware that they were as yet unable to resist disciplined forces, and to defy death for the sake of gaining their liberty, and now 'God led them not', we are

Museum is preserved a papyrus letter upwards of 3000 years old, in which an Egyptian writer describes his departure from the royal palace at Ramses, observing that his object was to follow two fugitive servants. The writer mentions that he started from Ramses on the 9th day of the third summer month, that he arrived on the 10th at Segol in Succoth, and on the 12th at Khetam, and that he there learned, that the fugitives had taken the route in the direction of the wall (*i e* Anbu-Gerrha-Shûr, see p 426), to the N. of Migdol. If Moses and the Israelites are substituted for the two fugitive servants, and the pursuing Pharaoh for the writer, the route is precisely the same as that followed by the Hebrews on their Exodus As the writer arrived on the first day at Segol, and on the third arrived at Etham, and as the fugitives took the route thence to Migdol and Anbu-Gerrha-Shûr, so also did the Israelites. On their arrival there the Israelites were then on the bank of the *Sirbonic Lake* (see p. 426, and the Map), a long sheet of water to the E. of Port Sa'îd This lake was well known to the ancients, but has long since been filled with sand, and has therefore fallen into oblivion According to ancient accounts the lake was in the form of a long strip, separated from the Mediterranean by a narrow barrier only, and extending along the coast. Diodorus informs us that the lake was entirely overgrown with reeds and papyrus plants, and that it was very dangerous to travellers, particularly when a violent S. wind drove the sand of the desert over its surface so as entirely to conceal the water, as the surface might then easily be taken for land, and thus lure the ignorant to their de-

informed by Exodus xiii 17, 'through the way of the land of the Philistines, although that was near; for God said, lest peradventure the people repent when they see war, and they return to Egypt. But God led the people about (before Etham) through the way of the wilderness of the Red Sea' Moses, accordingly, made them leave the route to Syria, and turn towards the S in the neighbourhood of the fortifications, probably near the modern Bîr Makhdal, anciently called Migdol, which, like the Egyptian Khetam (Etham), signifies a castle and the tower of a fortress. During his long sojourn in the wilderness, after he had slain the Egyptian, their great leader had become familiar with all the routes in this region, and as soon as he observed the weakness of his people, almost the only course open to him was to avoid the forts, and turn towards the S, in order to lead them round the N. end of the modern Gulf of Suez, and through the wilderness of Arabia Petræa to Canaan. From the outset he appears to have had a twofold object in view; the first being to emancipate the people from the Egyptian yoke with the least possible loss, and the second to discipline them, and accustom them to order, obedience, and nobler pursuits in life, in a locality suited for his purpose. At *Etham* ('the bastions') the wanderers accordingly changed the direction of their route, and turned to the S. between the W. bank of the bitter lakes and the E slope of the Gebel Ahmed Taher, and, after a long and fatiguing march, encamped at *Pi-Hahiroth*, the name of which has been identified with the modern *'Agrûd* ('pi' being the Egyptian for place). They then camped for the last time in Egypt near the Red Sea, between Migdol, a frontier fort, near the ancient Kâmbysu, where a Roman military hospital afterwards stood (about 9 M. to the N. of the head of the bay and the scanty remains of the ancient Arsinoe), and the 'Atâka mountains This range was anciently called Ba'al Zephon, and on its commanding summit the Phœnician sailors used to offer sacrifices to Ba'al Zephon, or the N wind, which wafted their ships towards the South. —When Pharaoh heard that the people had not crossed the line of fortifications, and had quitted the route to Syria, on which lay the famous temple of the desert on Mount Casius, where Moses had intended sacrificing to his God, it was natural for him to say —'they are entangled in the land, the wilderness hath shut them in' (Exodus xiv. 3) His mistrust was next aroused —'And it was told the king of Egypt that the people fled: and the heart of Pharaoh and of his servants was turned against the people, and

---

struction Diodorus also mentions an expedition undertaken by Artaxerxes, King of Persia, against Egypt, during which part of the Persian army was lost in the Sirbonic lake, with the dangers of which they were entirely unacquainted The main route from Egypt to Syria traversed the narrow neck of land between the Sirbonic lake and the Mediterranean (see p 426). The Jews, after their arrival at the lake, first encamped at *Pi-Hahiroth* (*i e.* the 'mouth of the chasms covered with reeds'), and then followed the usual military route between the waters to the shrine of Ba'al Zephôn (see p 426) They then turned to the S in consequence of the divine command, traversed the desert of *Shûr* (see p. 426), and arrived in three days at Marah (*i.e* bitter), or the three bitter lakes in the isthmus (see p 433) They proceeded thence to *Elim*, which is doubtless identical with the Aa-lim or Tenthim (*i e.* town of the fishes) mentioned by the monuments, a place situated near the Gulf of Suez. The Egyptians, however, in the course of the pursuit, as they were traversing the narrow neck of land between the Sirbonic lake and the Mediterranean, were overtaken by a storm and inundation, lost their way, fell into the Sirbonic lake, and were drowned. The occurrence of such floods in this district is borne out by an observation of Strabo, that a great flood took place during his residence in this region near Mount Casius (see Note, p 426), overflowing the country to such an extent, that Mount Casius appeared like an island, and that the road to Palestine near it was navigable for vessels The sea mentioned in the Bible, through which the Israelites passed, would, according to this theory, noi be the Red Sea but the Sirbonic lake'.

they said: why have we done this, that we have let Israel go from serving us?' (Exodus xiv 5) The pursuit now began; 'he made ready his chariot, and took his people with him and he took 600 chosen chariots, and all the chariots of Egypt, and captains over every one of them. And the Lord hardened the heart of Pharaoh, king of Egypt, and he pursued after the children of Israel'. Whilst the Israelites were encamped at Pi-Hahiroth the disciplined army approached; they departed hastily, and succeeded in crossing the head of the gulf at low tide, as was frequently done by the caravans before the construction of the canal The Egyptians, in hot pursuit, reached the ford before the tide had begun to set in; but a violent gale from the S W. sprang up, the waters rose suddenly and 'covered the chariots, and the horsemen, and all the host of Pharaoh that came into the sea after them; there remained not so much as one of them

From Suez to Mount Sinai by Maghâra and Wadi Firân.

From Suez to ($2^1/_2$ hrs.) *'Ain Mûsa*, see p. 419.

Beyond 'Ain Mûsa the route traverses the *Wâdi el-'Irân*, and afterwards an undulating region. On the hill-sides specimens of isinglass-stone are frequently found. To the right stretches the sea, beyond which rise the spurs of the 'Atâḳa mountains (p. 415); on the left are the heights of the *Jebel er-Râḥa*, and, farther on, those of the *Tîh Chain* (p. 524). About 9 M. from 'Ain Mûsa begins a monotonous tract, which extends for a distance of 20 M. in the direction of the Wâdi el-'Amâra. The whole distance to the Wâdi Gharandel (p. 487), which takes two days, is destitute of variety, and is particularly fatiguing on the return-route, even in fine weather. If, moreover, the Khamsîn (p. 69) begins to blow and to raise dense clouds of dust, the patience of the traveller is severely tried, and the journey seems interminable. Near the beginning of the plain, the so-called *Derb Far'ûn* (or 'road of the Pharaohs'), skirting the coast, diverges to the right to the Jebel Ḥammâm Far'ûn (p. 488), while another route to the left leads to the Jebel er-Râha and the desert of Et-Tîh. We follow the camel track which runs between these two.

We next cross (2 hrs.) several wâdis, the most important of which is the broad *Wâdi Ṣudûr*, adjoined by the *Jebel Bishr* or *Ṣudûr* on the left, and separating the hills of Er-Râḥa and Et-Tîh. After a journey of fully 5 hrs. from the beginning of the plain we reach the **Wâdi Werdân.** The surface of the desert is sprinkled at places with sharp flints, which are perhaps fragments of nodules burst by the heat, and resemble arrow-heads, knives, and other implements (comp. p. 370).

We traverse the Wâdi Werdân in $1^1/_4$ hour. Yellow hills of sand rise on the right, and the sea and the African coast continue visible for some time. On the left the *Wuṭa Hills*, which belong to the Tîh chain, approach the route, and we obtain a fine retrospect of the Jebel Ṣudûr (see above). The sea disappears, but is afterwards again visible. The hills assume more picturesque forms. The light-coloured limestone hills, and the whitish yellow surface of the desert, present a remarkably colourless appearance, but the soil is not entirely destitute of vegetation, especially in spring. One of the commonest plants is the *Betharân* (Cantolina fragrantissima), of which the camels are very fond, and which is full of aromatic juice; it is collected by the natives in the N. part of the peninsula. Golden colocynths (*Ḥandal;* Citrullus colocynthis) are sometimes seen lying on the way-side, having fallen from their dark green stems The dried shells are sometimes used by the Beduins for holding water, or as a receptacle for butter. The inside of the fruit is sometimes used as a medicine. The *Seyâl* (Acacia tortilis) occurs frequently farther S.; the juice which it exudes (Gum Arabic) is collected by the Beduins for sale. Chewing the gum is said to be a good remedy for thirst.

The ($2^1/_2$ hrs.) **Wâdi el-'Amâra**, and beyond it the *Ḥajer er-Rekkâb* ('rider's stone'), consisting of several masses of rock, are next reached. The ground becomes more undulating. In the distance, to the S., rise the *Jebel Ḥammâm Far'ûn* (p. 488) and the long *Jebel Gharandel* (p. 487). In less than 2 hrs. we next reach the sand-hills in the **Wâdi Hawâra**, on the summit of which a bitter spring rises. Around it grow a number of stunted palm-bushes and a few thorns. This is believed to be the *Marah* of the Bible, mentioned by Moses (Exodus, xv. 23-25). † Burckhardt conjectures that the juice of the berry of the gharkad (Nitrasia tridentata Desf.), a shrub growing in the neighbouring Wâdi Gharandel, may have the property, like the juice of the pomegranate, of improving brackish water; but the Arabs know of no plant possessing the virtue of that thrown into the spring by Moses.

Stations of the Israelites in the Wilderness, and number of the Emigrants The Biblical record of these stations continues as follows (Numb. xxxiii 8). — 'And they departed from before Pi-Hahiroth, and passed through the midst of the sea into the wilderness, and went three days journey in the wilderness of Etham, and pitched in Marah. 9. And they removed from Marah, and came unto Elim. and in Elim were twelve fountains of water, and threescore and ten palm trees; and they pitched there.' The desert of Etham (which adjoined the bastions of Khetam) may now be traversed more quickly by a Sinai pilgrim with little luggage; but it could hardly have been crossed by a whole nation in less than three days. *Marah* is thus the bitter spring in the *Wâdi Hawâra*, and *Elim*, with its twelve springs and seventy palms, has long been sought for in the *Wâdi Gharandel*, although, as we shall see, the distance from Hawâra to Gharandel (2 hrs) is a very short journey, even for so large a number

Standing on the margin of the spring of Hawâra, the thoughtful traveller will naturally ask, how 600,000 men with their families, that is, at least two million persons, could possibly have drunk of its waters. ††

† 23 'And when they came to Marah, they could not drink of the waters of Marah, for they were bitter; therefore the name of it was called *Marah* (*i e.* bitter) 24. And the people murmured against Moses, saying What shall we drink? 25. And he cried unto the Lord, and the Lord shewed him a tree, which when he had cast into the waters, the waters were made sweet'.

†† Exodus xii 37 'And the children of Israel journeyed from Rameses to Succoth about 600,000 men on foot that were men, beside children'.

Even if we assume that the volume of water was more copious in the time of the Exodus, owing to the more luxuriant vegetation, many other circumstances would still combine to render it improbable that two million persons could have partaken of it The probability is that these high figures are a mythical embellishment of the historical facts. Schleiden has pointed out, that if the Israelites had numbered two million as the Bible records, they would have formed a sufficiently dense population for the whole peninsula. For such a gigantic caravan a million gallons of water a day would hardly have sufficed, without allowing for the cattle, and at the present day the Beduins begin to feel anxious, when a party of a few hundreds encamps around their springs. The number 600,000 has probably originated from the poetical accounts of the miraculous preservation of the people, who gratefully ascribed so great miracles to their protecting God, in order the more effectually to extol his power. These numbers should, doubtless, be very greatly reduced, and so also should the forty years, which the Israelites are said to have spent in the wilderness. It was obviously the purpose of their leaders to inure the people to the privations of the desert, in order to prepare them for the battles they were about to fight in Palestine, but the sacred number forty, which is so often repeated, and which was used to signify a generation, most probably indicates a term of years; we may also observe that Moses was forty years old when he fled, eighty when he led the people into the wilderness, and one hundred and twenty when he died. The fact that the Arabian literature contains a number of writings called 'Arbainât', or tales in which the number forty plays a conspicuous part, affords a confirmation of the above view

Immediately before us rises the curiously shaped *Jebel Gharandel* (Gerendel, Kharandel, Gurundel), the name of which occurs at an early period. Its slopes have been compared to 'petrified cushions'. It is possible that the wâdi which descends to the Gulf of Suez gave its name of *Charandra*, used during the Roman period, to the N. part of the Arabian gulf, where Ptolemy II. founded the town of Arsinoë. In the Itinerary of Antonine the place is called *Gurandela.*

The **Wâdi Gharandel** (reached in 2 hrs. from the spring in the Wâdi Ḥawâra), which runs for a long distance to the N.E., affords, near the sea, and particularly at the spot crossed by the Sinai route, a moderate supply of slightly brackish, but drinkable, water, especially after heavy rain, in consequence of which the desert here is clothed with pleasing, though not luxuriant, vegetation. Among the plants are several lofty and bushy palms, seyâl trees (p. 486), gharḳad shrubs, and tamarisks. Small groups of rocks on the margin of the oasis enhance the comparative picturesqueness of the valley, which was perhaps once better watered and more richly clothed with vegetation. Thus B. von Breidenbach (15th cent.), one of the first travellers who identified Gharandel with Elim, observed here a shrub bearing nuts, about the size of hazel-nuts, and known as Pharaoh nuts, but which is now extinct. If this is the *Elim* of the Bible, the 12 springs and 70 palm-trees are greatly reduced in number. The remains of two hermit-cells, hewn in the rocks, are not worth visiting. The Wâdi Gharandel, owing to its supply of water, is a favourite camping-place for the night.

The route, farther on, at first ascends slowly. In 1 hr. we reach the sepulchral mound of *Hoṣân Abû Zenneh* (horse of Abû Zenneh), on which the Beduins, in passing, throw a stone or a handful of sand, as a mark of contempt, exclaiming — 'here is food for the horse of Abû Zenneh.' The story goes, that an Arab called Abû Zenneh cruelly over-rode his mare, and, when she broke down, spurred her so violently, that she gave a final, long bound, and then dropped down dead. The hard-hearted rider marked the marvellous length of the last leap of his horse with stones, and every passer-by now adds to the heap in token of disapproval.

A little farther on we obtain a fine view: facing us rises the three-peaked *Sarbûṭ el-Jemel* (p. 524), to the S.E. tower the summits of the *Jebel Serbâl* and the *Jebel el-Benât*, to the left are the heights of *Et-Tîh*, and to the right the *Jebel Ḥammâm Far'ûn* and *Jebel Uṣêṭ*. We next cross the (3/4 hr.) *Wâdi Uṣêṭ*, which contains several pools of water and palm saplings, and which has erroneously been identified with the Elim of the Bible (see above). The only circumstance in favour of this theory is, that the Wâdi Uṣêṭ is more distant from the Wâdi Hawâra (Marah) than the Wâdi Gharandel, which, however, lies much nearer the latter than a full day's journey.

About 2 hrs. beyond the above-mentioned hillock of stones we enter the *Wâdi Ḳuwêseh*, a spacious basin enclosed and traversed by low sand-hills, and lying at the base of the Jebel Uṣêṭ and Jebel Hammâm Far'ûn.

The **Jebel Ḥammâm Far'ûn** (1567 ft. above the sea-level), or the '*Bath of Pharaoh*', is most conveniently ascended from this point, and is chiefly interesting to geologists. Half-a-day at least is required for the excursion, and the traveller should be provided with refreshments. The mountain is in the form of a blunted pyramid, with a very extensive base; the limestone on its slopes is remarkably jagged and furrowed. At several places there are warm springs, which are still used by the Arabs, particularly as a cure for rheumatism. Before using the water they are in the habit of presenting a cake or other offering, to the spirit of Pharaoh, which still haunts the spot, in order to propitiate him. One tradition is, that Pharaoh still lies here in the hot water, where he is to be eternally boiled for his sins. Another legend is to the effect, that, when Pharaoh was drowned in the Red Sea, he saw Moses standing on a rock of the Jebel Ḥammâm Far'ûn, and was so infuriated at the sight, that the water closing over him was spouted up to a great height by the violence of his panting. Ever since then his spirit has haunted this spot, and every ship that approaches the Jebel Ḥammâm Far'ûn is doomed to sink. — This legend is supplemented by another, which is also told by the Arabs, that, when the Jews would not believe that Pharaoh was really drowned, God ordered the sea to throw up his body. Since then bodies of drowned persons have been invariably cast up on the beach.

'The caverns in the Jebel Ḥammâm Far'ûn, which are frequently tubular in form and resemble long pipes, slope rapidly downwards in the direction of the strata of the rock, from W. to E. and from S.W. to N.E., communicating, doubtless, with the hot springs, as I found them completely filled with steam. In the largest of these caverns, the entrance of which is 13 ft. wide, and which lies several fathoms above the hot springs, I observed, at a distance of 6 ft. from the entrance, that the temperature was 102° Fahr., while that of the outer air was 90°. The vapour which filled the chamber had a sulphureous smell, and a slight incrustation of sulphur covered the wall at places.' *(J. Russegger.)*

The hot springs are situated on the N. side of the mountain, facing the sea; they are easily found without a guide, owing to the steam which envelopes them. There is a good bathing-place at the point where they flow into the sea from the white rock, but the bather should beware of sharks. Higher up, the springs are very hot When the temperature of the air was 90°, that of the water was found to be 153°. The water is slightly saline; according to an analysis made by J. Russegger of Vienna, it contains soda, lime, talc, chloride of hydrogen, and sulphuric acid.

The route continues to follow the Wâdi Kuwêseh for $1^1/_4$ hr., and then crosses the *Wâdi eth-Thâl*, a valley of considerable breadth, which descends to the sea towards the S.W. in the form of a narrow gorge. In about $^1/_2$ hr. more we reach the *Wâdi Shebêkeh.* In less than 1 hr. more we reach the junction of this valley with the *Wâdi el-Ḥomr*, through which (to the E) runs the route to Sinai viâ *Ṣarbûṭ el-Khâdem*, described at p. 524.

We follow the valley descending towards the sea, now called the **Wâdi Ṭayyibeh**, with numerous windings, some remarkable rock formations, several springs of bad water, and a few stunted palms. The route traverses a number of round hollows of considerable size, enclosed amphitheatrically by barren slopes of whitish grey sand and by rocks. The steep sides of these basins look from a distance as if they had been made artificially. The area in the centre is often so completely enclosed that no outlet is visible. Each quarter of an hour we obtain a different view, though the colouring is always the same. A striking exception to the last remark is afforded by the very curious appearance of the *Jebel Ṭayyibeh*, situated near the sea, and consisting of oblique strata of different colours; the lowest of these is of a golden yellow tint, the next is red, which is followed by a rusty black stratum, while the whole is surmounted by a yellow layer.

After $1^3/_4$ hr. the valley expands, and we approach the open sea, washing the banks of the sandy plain of *El-Meḳḥâr*. After a walk of $1^1/_2$ hr. along the coast we reach the **Râs Abû Zenîmeh**, which still bears the tomb of the saint, and affords a beautiful and sheltered camping-ground. At this spot (more probably than in the Wâdi Ṭayyibeh, as supposed by some authorities) was situated the encampment of the Israelites on the Red Sea (Numb. xxxiii. 10). The old harbour is still occasionally used by the fishing-boats of the Arabs. In ancient times the roads, by which ore and stone were brought from the mines of the Wâdi Maghâra and Ṣarbûṭ el-Khâdem for farther conveyance by water, converged here.

Beyond Abû Zenîmeh the route at first skirts the sea for $1^1/_2$ hour. Travellers usually walk here, and amuse themselves by picking up shells, as Sinai travellers have done from time immemorial. This custom is mentioned by Thiedmarus in the 13th cent., by Fabri, and by Breidenbach, the last of whom says, that 'various kinds of shells are to be found on the coast of the Red Sea, and also white coral, and many beautiful stones', probably meaning by the last expression the smooth fragments of quartz on the beach. On the margin of the narrow plain of the coast, to the left of the route, rise curiously formed, yellowish, limestone hills piled up in strata, one apparently resting on gigantic, shell-shaped pedestals which have been formed by the action of the water. At the S. end of these hills rises the *Jebel el-Nokhel*, a bold eminence abutting so closely on the sea that it is washed by the waves at high water, in which case the traveller must cross it by a path ascending in steps.

Beyond this hill we reach a plain, called *El-Markha*, of considerable extent, and not destitute of vegetation. It is bounded on the N.E. by the *Jebel el-Markha* (590 ft.), a black hill, contrasting strongly with its light-coloured neighbours. Proceeding to the S.E. for $2^1/_4$ hrs. more, we at length reach the more mountainous part of the peninsula, which we enter by the *Ḥanak el-Laḳam*, a valley varying in width, and flanked with barren rocks of reddish and grey tints. After $^3/_4$ hr. we reach the mouth of the *Wâdi Ba'ba'* on the N., which is commanded by the dark *Jebel Ba'ba'*, while on the S. (right) begins the *Wâdi Shelâl*. Traversing the latter for $^1/_4$ hr., we next enter the **Wâdi Budra** The winding route ascends gradually. We pass several mountain slopes resembling huge walls of blocks of stone, artificially constructed. Farther on we observe grey and red granite rocks amidst other formations. In every direction lie long heaps of black, volcanic slag, strongly resembling the refuse from foundries. Beside them lie numerous fragments of brown, grey, and red stone, including felsite porphyry, which is remarkable for the bright, brick-red colour of the orthoclase felspar. Along the slopes rise cliffs and pinnacles of various colours and grotesque forms. The route leads from one basin into another, each of which has a horizon of its own, until ($1^1/_4$ hr.) we come to a frowning barrier of rock which seems to preclude farther progress. We soon find, however, that a steep bridle-path ascends in $^1/_4$ hr. to the **Naḳb el-Budra** (or 'pass of the sword's point', 1263 ft.), by which we surmont the apparent barrier. This pass was traversed in ancient times by the beasts of burden which transported the minerals obtained in the Wâdi Maghâra to the sea; it then fell into disrepair, but was restored in 1863 by a Major Macdonald, who made an unsuccessful search for turquoises in the old mines. The summit of the pass commands a fine retrospective view of the wild Wâdi Budra, the Râs Abû Zenîmeh, the Jebel Ḥammâm Far'ûn, and the sea. Beyond the pass the valley is called the *Wâdi Naḳb el-Budra*, through which we descend in $1^1/_4$ hr. to the **Wâdi Sidr**, a winding valley enclosed by rocks of red granite.

We soon reach the *Wâdi Umm Themân* on the left, where Messrs Palmer and Wilson (in 1869) discovered mines similar to those at Maghâra. The ($^3/_4$ hr.) *Wâdi Maghâra* next diverges to the left. At the angle formed by the latter with the *Wâdi Ḳeneh*, descending from the E., are situated the famous old mines of *Ma-*

ghâra, which deserve a visit (2 hrs.; or, if a thorough inspection is made, half-a-day)

The Mines of Maghâra. The brown and brick-red slopes of the Wâdi Maghâra rise precipitously to a considerable height. They belong partly to the sandstone, and partly to the granite formation. The mines are situated on the slopes on the N.W. side, about 145 ft. above the bottom of the valley. The traveller has to scramble over heaps of rubble before reaching the broad but low openings of the mines, which seem once to have been protected by a gallery, now scarcely traceable. The shaft penetrates the rock to a considerable depth, being very wide at first, but afterwards contracting. Numerous pillars have been left for the support of the roof; old chisel marks are still observable. At many places the reddish stone contains small bluish-green, very impure turquoises, which may easily be detached with a penknife. These stones lose their colour entirely after a few years On the route to the Wâdi Fîrân (p. 494) the Beduins frequently offer for sale large, but worthless, turquoises at exorbitant prices.

Small pillars with hieroglyphic inscriptions still commemorate the period when the mines were worked for the benefit of the Pharaohs. On large smooth surfaces of the rocky walls these ancient monarchs have handed down to posterity, by means of figures and writing, the fact that they conquered the Mentu, who inhabited these regions, and provided for the wants of their miners. A gigantic Pharaoh is represented grasping the necks of a number of the vanquished with one hand, while with the other he is brandishing a weapon (khopsh). Sacrifices are also represented, and festivals, and a visit paid to the mines by inspectors of high rank. The oldest king named here is Snefru (p. 523), the first king of the 4th Dynasty. The next are Khufu (Cheops, p. 86), the builder of the Great Pyramid of Gîzeh, another monarch of the 4th dynasty; Sahura, Kaka, Raenuser, Menkauhor, Tatkara (Assa), of the 5th Dynasty; Pepi-Merira and Neferkara, of the 6th Dynasty (p. 87); Usertesen II. and Amenemha III., of the 12th Dynasty. During the domination of the Hyksos the mines were neglected; but after their expulsion, the working was resumed by Hatasu, the energetic sister and co-regent of Thothmes III., who has caused her ships, returning richly-laden from Arabia, to be represented at Dêr el-Baḥri (Thebes). There is also a pillar here dating from the time of Ramses II., but no monument now exists of the reign of his son Merenptah, the Pharaoh of the Exodus, nor of the later kings.

The mineral obtained here is called *Mafkat* in the inscriptions. It was of a decided green colour, and is elsewhere represented in bars of this  shape, and marked 'genuine' to distinguish it from the 'imitation'. The results of the careful researches of Lepsius have also been confirmed by Professor Credner's geological investigations. The genuine mafkat, which does not occur here, was probably the emerald, while the inferior quality, which was often imitated, was malachite, verdigris, green smalt, and the green colour prepared from the last. The imitation emerald, which is frequently mentioned by ancient authors was a green paste coloured with copper, which, when ground, yielded the best green paint. This raw material was used by the Egyptians for colouring glass, of which many pieces are preserved, and was probably the malachite which is called by Theophrastus 'false emerald', or copper green; and which, being much used for soldering gold, was named 'chrysocolla'. — The inscriptions always mention mafkat with khesbet, *i.e.* lapis lazuli (either genuine, inferior, or artificial), as the two minerals which are generally found together, principally in association with copper ores, malachite being carbonate of copper with a certain proportion of water, while lapis lazuli sometimes occurs interspersed with malachite, and sometimes in small nodules by itself. In the Wâdi Maghâra copper was formerly worked, and along with it was doubtless found malachite, which was either used as a precious stone, or manufactured into paint. The district

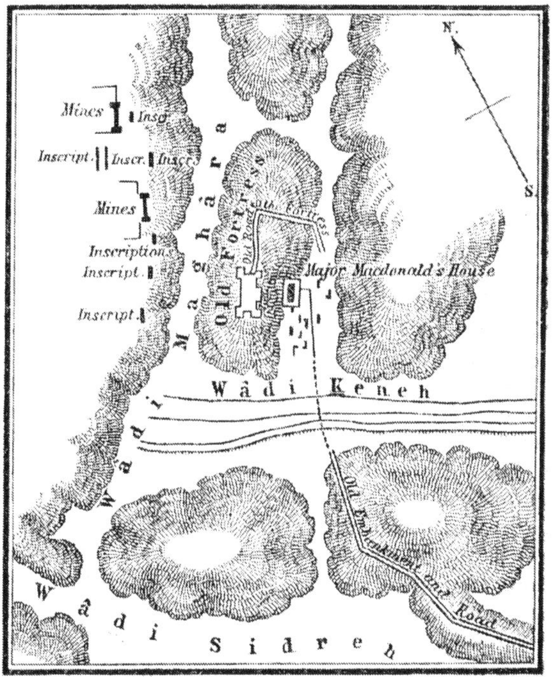

was called the Mafkat (malachite) region, after the most precious mineral obtained in it. The miners were condemned criminals, particularly political offenders and prisoners of war. The relations also of the prisoners were frequently condemned to the mines and compelled to work in fetters. As, at a later period, the Christians were compelled to work in the porphyry quarries, so in the reign of Ramses II. the refractory Israelites were employed in the mines.

Clambering up the rugged slope of the hill from the entrance to the mines, and passing several shafts, we reach a number of figures engraved on the rock, discovered by Prof. Palmer, and consisting of the hawk, the bird sacred to Horus, five human forms, and some illegible hieroglyphics. The first figure, now almost obliterated, seems to hold a chisel in its left hand, and may represent a miner;

the second wears the crown of Upper Egypt , and the third that of Lower Egypt , both representing Pharaoh as the monarch of S. and N. Egypt respectively. The rope, hammer, and chisel (implements which were still used in the time of the Ptolemies whenever a foundation-stone was laid), which they hold in their hands, show that the king was once present here to inaugurate the opening of a new mine. The shape of the chisel is curious. The fourth and fifth figures represent Pharaoh chastising the miners.

The hill, about 200 ft. in height, opposite to the entrance of the mines, is also worthy of a visit. On the further side are the ruins of Major Macdonald's house, and the summit is crowned with the remains of a fort and of the mining settlement of the period of the Pharaohs. Here also are found various tools of flint, particularly arrow-heads and sharp instruments, which were perhaps used for engraving inscriptions. The old road, once used by the miners, descending the hill and leading towards the S., with a bend towards the E., is still traceable. — There is a spring about 25 min. distant from Major Macdonald's ruined house.

Wâdi Maghâra, a station of the Israelites during the Exodus. The neighbourhood of the Râs Abû Zenîmeh is believed by most expounders of the Bible to have been the site of the camp on the Red Sea (p. 489). The sacred narrative (Numb xxxiii 11) continues as follows — 'And they removed from the Red sea, and encamped in the wilderness of Sin 12 And they took their journey out of the wilderness of Sin, and encamped in Dophkah' In the book of Exodus (xvi 1. *et seq.*) we find farther particulars of this portion of the journey We are informed there, that the whole of the people complained bitterly against Moses and Aaron for having led them out of Egypt, accusing them of having brought them 'forth into this wilderness, to kill this whole assembly with hunger.'

Many authorities identify the wilderness of Sin with the bleak coast-plain of El-Kâ'a, which extends from Râs Abû Zenîmeh to Ṭûr and beyond it, but it is more probably identical with the desolate, rocky tract which we traversed on the route from Râs Abû Zenîmeh to the Wâdi Maghâra Dophkah is the Wâdi Maghâra Enclosed by bleak and abrupt rocks, the multitude, accustomed to the extensive plain, would naturally be alarmed and depressed, and would murmur against their leaders

A little beyond the mouth of the Wâdi Maghâra, the Wâdi Sidr turns to the S., skirting the *Jebel Abû 'Alâḳa* (2623 ft.), and after fully an hour leads to a large table-land. To the E., opposite to us, is the mouth of the *Wâdi Neba'*, and to the S. lies the **Wâdi Mokatteb**, *i.e.* 'Valley of Inscriptions', which we now follow. On the W. side of this broad valley rises the *Jebel Mokatteb* (2380 ft.), at the foot of which, extending down to the floor of the valley, are strewn blocks of sandstone, several of them bearing the famous so-called 'Inscriptions of Sinai'. Most of them are on the western side of the valley. Those who do not intend to make scientific investigations need only devote a few minutes to the inscriptions in passing.

Most of the *Sinaitic Inscriptions* are in the Nabatæan character, others in Greek, and a few in Coptic and Arabic. They are roughly and superficially engraved on the rock, which has been very rarely smoothed for the purpose, and the small figures are often extremely rude and inartistic. They represent armed and unarmed men, travellers and warriors, laden and unladen camels, horses with and without riders and attendants, mountain goats, ships, crosses, and stars. A priest with raised arms, and an equestrian performer, are worthy of notice. Cosmas (Indicopleustes, or the 'Indian traveller'), who visited the Peninsula of Sinai in A D 535 and saw these inscriptions, believed them to be in the Hebrew language, and to have been executed by the Israelites during the Exodus, and marvellously preserved by providence, in order that they might serve as 'witnesses to the unbelieving'. It is now ascertained that the oldest of these inscriptions cannot have been written earlier than the 2nd century B C, while the most recent are not later than the beginning of the 4th cent. A D, and that most of them are to be ascribed to the *heathen* Nabatæans, who adhered to the Sabæan rites, and worshipped the sun, moon, and stars, especially on high mountains, such as Mounts Serbâl and Sinai. No Christian names occur, but many of the writers call themselves 'servants', 'reverers', or 'priests' of the 'sun', the 'moon', and 'Baal', and other early Arabian divinities. — The authors of these inscriptions were doubtless travellers, partly merchants, and partly pilgrims to the holy places in the Wâdi Mokatteb, among which Mount Serbâl was certainly reckoned at a very early period. The inscriptions which they rudely engraved to commemorate their visit, were first deciphered by Prof Beer (d 1864) of Leipsic, and afterwards more completely by Tuch Near the sacred places, and particularly in the Wâdi Mokatteb, festivals, with markets and shows, were held. Some of the Greek inscriptions are of later date, having evidently been engraved over the Nabatæan By the figure of a 'Diakonos Hiob', a soldier, who was hostile to the Nazarenes, has written · — 'a bad set of people these'; I, the soldier, have written this with my own hand '

The S. entrance to the Wâdi Mokatteb, a valley about 3½ M. in length, is closed by a spur of the mountain of that name, which our route crosses. Beyond the pass (1520 ft.), whence we obtain an excellent survey of the imposing mass of Mt. Serbâl, the route traverses heights and hollows strewn with small stones. The red rubble looks like fragments of bricks, and the slopes resemble dilapidated walls of loose stones.

After ¾ hr. we enter the **Wâdi Fîrân**, which is here of considerable breadth. This valley, which is probably the most important in the peninsula, begins above the Oasis of Fîrân, at the base of the Serbâl, and, after describing a wide curve, terminates near the coast. The granite slopes, flanking the valley, are not far apart at places, while in other parts the valley expands to a considerable width. The grey primitive rock, veined with reddish-brown porphyry and black diorite, rises in picturesque forms; these veins run almost invariably from N. to S. The picturesqueness of the scene is greatly enhanced by the imposing summits of the barren mountains towering above the slopes of the valley to the south. At the entrance of the valley, where at the foot of the *Jebel Nesrîn* the small wâdi of that name opens on the left, are several round heaps of stones belonging to ancient tombs. On our right next diverges the *Wâdi Nedîyeh*, on the left the *Wâdi er-Remmâneh* and the *Wâdi Mokhêres*, and to the right again the *Wâdi el-Feshêheh*, the two last being commanded by peaks of the same names. The next valleys on the right are the *Wâdis ed-Dêr*, *Nehbân*, *Eṭ-Ṭarr*, and *Abû Gerrâyât;* and opposite the latter opens the *Wâdi Ḳoṣêr*, a valley of greater extent. A little before reaching the oasis, we pass a rock called the *Ḥêsi el-Khattâtîn*, which is entirely covered with small stones. Prof. Palmer was the first traveller who was told by the Beduins that this rock was the one which yielded water when struck by Moses.

The plants of the desert now occur more frequently, and are of more vigorous growth; bushes of tamarisk, the nebḳ, the seyâl, and palm-trees, make their appearance, and the scene is enlivened by the notes of birds of grey and dark plumage. We now quit the desert, and with feelings of unmitigated delight, after a hot journey of more than 5 hrs. in the Wâdi Fîrân, we enter the **Oasis of Fîrân**, the 'Pearl of Sinai', and by far the most fertile tract in the whole peninsula. We first reach the dale of *El-Ḥesweh*, a few hundred paces only in length, watered by an inexhaustible brook which is suddenly swallowed up by the earth here, after having converted the whole of the valley above this point into a luxuriant garden in the midst of the desert. The gardens are watered by means of Shâdûfs or buckets; the dates grown here are celebrated. Every tree has its proprietor, who obtains the whole of its produce, even when he lives at a distance, his property being protected by the honest Beduins of the oasis and the inmates of the monastery. On the road-side, and on the left slope of the valley, are Beduin huts, gardens, and the ruins of stone houses, dating from the time of the ancient Fîrân. In $^1/_4$ hr. more we reach a second small group of palms, and for a few minutes we obtain a view of the W. side of Mount Serbâl. In 20 min. more we reach a wider part of the valley, in which the rocky and isolated hill of *El-Meḥarret* rises to a height of about 100 ft., bearing on its summit the traces of an early Christian monastery and church. Exactly opposite the ruin of the monastery the traveller should notice a very curious geological formation, consisting of a vein of green diorite in flesh-coloured porphyry, which is in its turn imbedded in green mica-slate. The largest fragment of the ruins, called *Ḥererât el-Kebîr*, stands on the summit of the hill which the Beduins regard as the spot where Moses prayed during the battle with the Amalekites (Exodus, xvii. 10), and at its base the relics of a large church are still traceable. Fragments of columns and ornaments, which once belonged to it, are to be found built into the walls of the houses. The Wâdis *Ejeleh* and *'Aleyât*, valleys diverging here, are watered in winter by streams from the mountains which are sometimes covered with snow. This picturesque spot is a favourite halting-place with the Beduins owing to the facilities for watering the camels. The best camping-ground is a little to the E. of the entrance to the Wâdi 'Aleyât, and in such a position as to command a view of the pinnacled summit of Mt. Serbâl (p. 497).

History The Oasis of Fîrân was probably occupied at a very early period by the Amalekites, and outside of its gates was doubtless fought the battle in which they were defeated by the Israelites. The town of the Oasis is even called by Makrîzi a city of the Amalekites, long after the Christians had been expelled from it by the Muslims. The Oasis is mentioned by Diodorus only before the Christian period, but in the 2nd cent A D Claudius Ptolemæus speaks of the town of *Pharan*, which soon became an Episcopal See and the central point of the monastic and anchorite fraternities of the peninsula Remains of old monasteries and hermits' cells are nowhere more numerous than here, and on the rocky slopes and plateaus of the Serbâl. In the 4th cent. we hear of the town being governed by a senate, and about the year 400 the spiritual affairs of the country were presided over by Bishop Nateras or Nathyr. The council of Chalcedon accorded to the oasis an archbishop of its own, who, however, was subordinate to the recently founded patriarchate of Jerusalem. In 454 Macarius is mentioned as bishop of Pharan. The solitary monasteries among the mountains suffered frequently from the attacks of the Blemmyes and Saracens, who, however, did not venture to attack the well-guarded city of the oasis, which paid tribute to their shêkhs. The Romans were nominally masters of Pharan, but in reality it was subject to the sway of the Saracen princes; and one of these, named Abokharagor, presented it to Justinian, who, as a reward, appointed him phylarch of the Saracens of Palestine. Early in the 5th cent. the monks and anchorites of Pharan began to embrace heretical principles, and we frequently hear of admonitions and threats directed by the orthodox synods and the Emperors against them as Monothelites and Monophysites — According to the trustworthy testimony of Procopius, his contemporary Justinian (527-565) was not the founder of the present monastery of Sinai, as inscriptions of the 13th cent built into its walls erroneously state, but he erected a church to the Virgin halfway up the Jebel Mûsa, probably on the site of the present chapel of Elijah, and also constructed and garrisoned a strong fortress at the foot of the mountain, on the site of the present monastery of St. Catharine, in order to prevent the Saracens of the peninsula from invading Palestine. It was doubtless the protection afforded by this castle that gradually attracted the numerous hermits of the peninsula from the Serbâl to the Jebel Mûsa, which they made the scene of a number of old Christian legends. Pharan was at an early period regarded as the site of the Rephidîm of the Bible (see below) Eusebius of Cæsarea (b 270), and his translator Jerome, state that the battle of the Amalekites took place near Pharan. Cosmas (535), who visited the Oasis in person, states that Rephidîm, where Moses struck the rock, lay near Pharan, and the account of Antoninus Martyr of his entry into Pharan shows that regularly organised pilgrimages to Rephidîm took place Among other objects the natives offered small casks of radish-oil (Rhaphanino oleo) to the pilgrims, which were probably carried off as mementoes of Rephidîm, as its name (raphanus, raphaninus) imports — After the dissemination of El-Islâm the anchorites gradually became extinct

Rephidîm and the Bible Narrative (comp p. 493). In the Book of Numbers (xxxiii. 13-14) we find the following passage: 'And they departed from Dophkah, and encamped in Alush And they removed from Alush, and encamped at *Rephidim*, where was no water for the people to drink' — Alush was probably situated between the Wâdi Maghâra and the Wâdi Fîrân, and Rephidim in the Wâdi Fîrân at the entrance of the oasis The 17th chapter of the Book of Exodus contains important additional information We are there informed that the people murmured against Moses, and reproached him with having led them out of Egypt to die of thirst, whereupon 'Moses cried unto the Lord', who commanded him to strike the rock with his staff And Moses did so, and the rock yielded a copious spring. Amalek then came and fought with the Israelites at Rephidîm, and the battle is described. The Bible narrative presents to us a picture of Moses stationed on a rock which commanded the battle-field, and praying, while Aaron and Hur 'stayed up his hands';

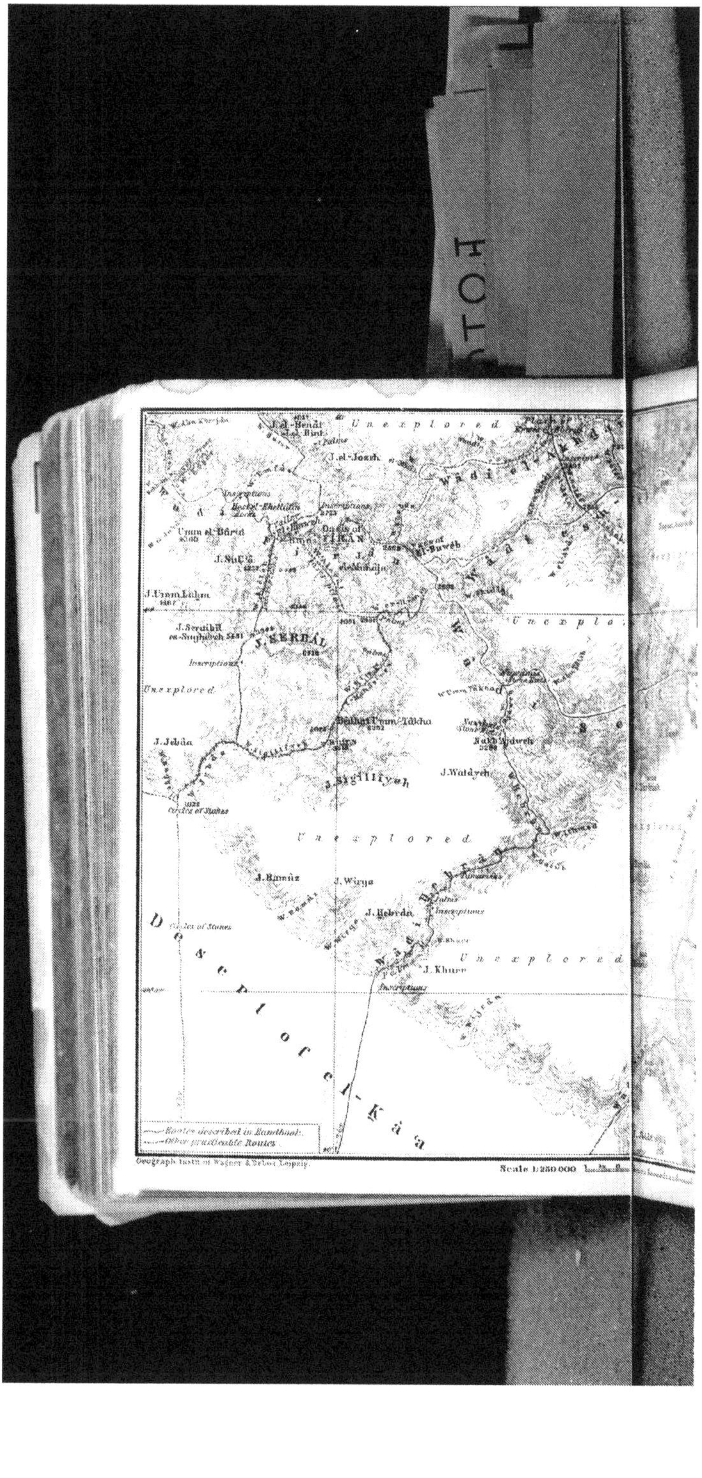
Unexplored
J. el-Jôzeh
Inscriptions
Umm el-Bûrid
Oasis of FIRÂN
J. Umm Lahm
J. SERBÂL
Unexplored
J. Jebâ
Circles of Stones
J. Sigilliyeh
J. Watiyeh
Unexplored
J. Wirya
Inscriptions
Unexplored
J. Khure
Desert of el-Kâa
Routes described in Handbook.
Other practicable Routes.
Scale 1:250 000

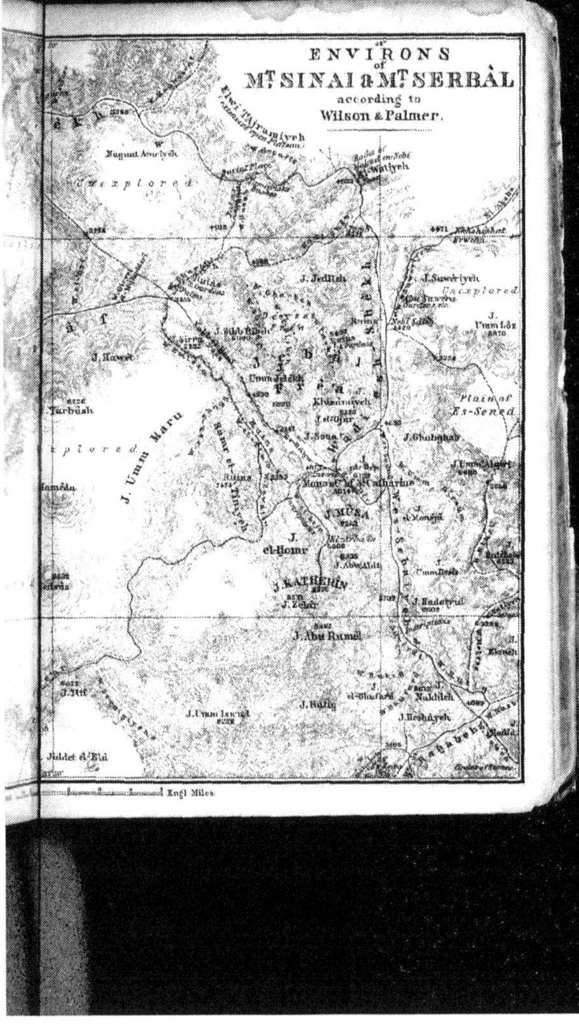

ENVIRONS
of
M^T. SINAI & M^T. SERBÂL
according to
Wilson & Palmer.
Unexplored
J. Jedîdeh
J. Suwêriyeh
J. Umm Lôz
Plain of Es-Sened
J. Howet
Tarbûsh
J. Umm Maru
J. Ghubshah
J. MÛSA
J. KATHERÎN
J. Abu Rumeil
J. Umm Iswêd
J. Rutig
Jiddet el 'Eld
Engl. Miles

INSERT FOLD-OUT OR MAP HERE!

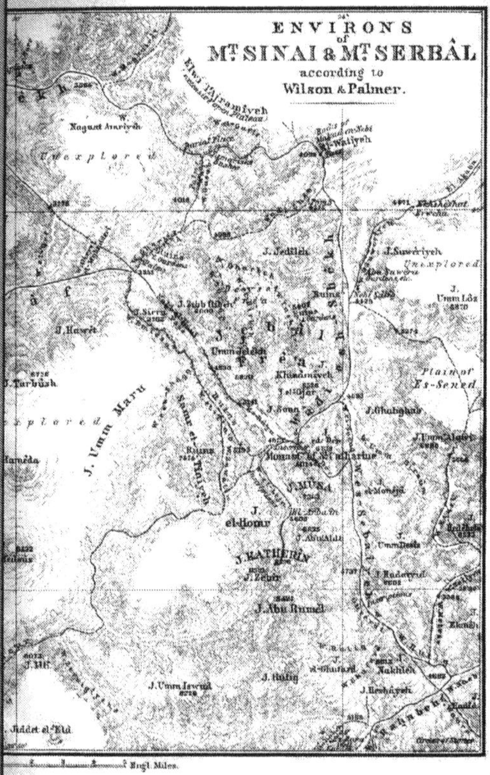
ENVIRONS of Mt. SINAI & Mt. SERBÂL
according to
Wilson & Palmer.
Unexplored
J. Jedîleh
J. Sumriyeh
Umm Lôz
Plain of Es-Sened
J. Tarbûsh
J. Umm Maru
J. Ghubghab
J. Mûsa
J. el-Homr
J. Katherin
J. Zebir
J. Abu Rumeil
J. Umm Jswud
J. Bulig
Nakhleh
J. Huwit
Engl. Miles.

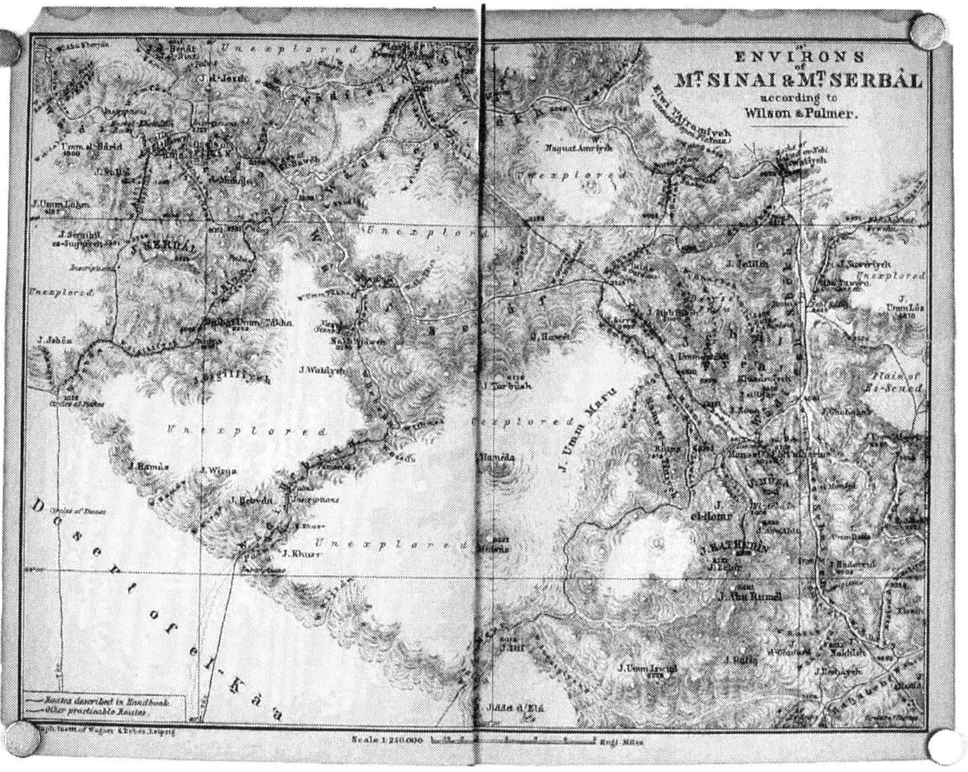

ENVIRONS
of
Mt. SINAI & Mt. SERBÂL
according to
Wilson & Palmer.
Unexplored
J. Umm Maru
J. Serbâl
J. Mûsa
J. Katherin
J. Abu Rumeil
J. Tarbûsh
J. Umm Lôz
J. Jeḥân
J. Bahâmeh
J. Hamûs
J. Wirga
J. Hawâ
J. Khuzr
J. el-Jerdi
J. Umm Lûhm
Umm el-Bârid
Umm Shomer
J. el-Homr
J. Fuṛeia
Desert of el-Kâa
Scale 1:250,000
Engl. Miles
Routes described in Handbook.
Other practicable Routes.

and we are told, tnat when he raised his hands, Israel had the mastery, and when he let them fall, Amalek had the mastery. 'And Joshua discomfited Amalek and his people with the edge of the sword'. — It is natural that a battle should have been fought on the outskirts of the oasis, as the Amalekite possessors of this fertile island in the midst of the desert would be very unlikely to yield up their valuable property without a blow. We are then informed (Exodus xviii.), that Moses, 'where he encamped at the mount of God', organised the people by the advice of Jethro, his father-in-law, who came to visit him, and chose valiant men from all Israel, whom he set over them 'to be rulers of thousands, and rulers of hundreds, rulers of fifties, and rulers of tens'. 'And (Numb. xxxiii. 15) they departed from Rephidîm, and pitched in the wilderness of Sinai', and (Exodus xix. 2) 'they were departed from Rephidîm, and were come to the desert of Sinai, and had pitched in the wilderness; and there Israel camped before the mount And Moses went up unto God'. (Comp. R. Lepsius, 'Reise nach der Halbinsel des Sinai', Berlin 1876; and also, 'Briefe aus Egypten', 1852, pp. 417-452)

The most conspicuous of the hills visible hence is the *Jebel eṭ-Ṭâḥûneh* (or Mill-Mountain), situated in a line with the monastery hill (to the N.), rising above the bed of the valley to the height of 700 ft., and crowned with the ruin of a handsome church. The steep, neglected path ascending to it is flanked with the remains of ancient chapels; and near it are many houses built of loose stones. The windows of these look towards the outside, and not into the court according to Oriental usage. The settlement is enlivened with children, poultry, and dogs, and with its babbling brook almost resembles a Tyrolese mountain village. Farther N. rises the summit of the lofty *Jebel el-Benât* (4917 ft.), or the 'Mountain of the Virgins', sometimes called the *Jebel el-Bint*, or 'Mountain of the Virgin'. It is probably so called from a chapel of the Virgin situated here, but the Beduins maintain that it derives its name from two Ṭawara maidens, who had been ordered to marry against their wishes, and who therefore fled to the mountains. They were overtaken by their pursuers on the Jebel el-Benât, but, rather than be captured, they plaited their tresses together and precipitated themselves from the rocky summit into the abyss. On the N. side of the valley are numerous tombs of hermits and monks who spent their lives on Mt. Serbâl and in the monastery of the bishopric of Pharan. These tombs are mentioned by Maḳrîzi so early as 1445. Prof. Palmer re-discovered them, and observed that the bodies had been buried in a line from E. to W., in coarse shrouds and coffins of which traces remained.

Mount Serbâl (6712 ft.; *i.e.* Serb Ba'al, or 'palm-grove of Baal') rises to the S. in the form of a broad, serrated pyramid.

The Ascent of Mount Serbâl is difficult and fatiguing, and should be attempted by experienced mountaineers only, especially as the guides afford little assistance (the best of them is *Husan el-Harbi*). The expedition takes a whole day (the ascent 5 hrs), so that the start should be made before sunrise. Strong boots are essential, the rocks being hard and sharp

The ascent is most conveniently made through the Wâdi 'Aleyât on the N. side, but it may also be made through the *Wâdi Selâf* (p. 501) and the *Wâdi er-Rimm* on the S. side If the traveller starts early enough to reach the first oasis in the Wâdi er-Rimm by 8 a m., the ascent had better be undertaken thence. In 3/4 hr. the second oasis is reached, and in 1/4 hr. more the third, each of which contains ṭarfa bushes, arundo, and three or four palms After a steep ascent of an hour we reach a ruined house; the route then passes (20 min) a small pond bordered with the jassa plant (Colutea haleppica Link , Arabic kasnûr) from which the 'staves of Moses' (p 512) are cut, and (40 min) several caverns in the flesh-coloured porphyry which were once occupied by anchorites. After a gradual ascent of one hour more, we reach the table-land of *Siḳelyîh*, with the ruins of a monastery. If Mt. Serbâl is the Sinai of the early hermits, this building must have been the scene of the atrocities committed by the Saracens which cost forty monks their lives (comp. p. 514), and which have been described by Ammonius and Nilus. The ascent of one of the peaks of Mt Serbâl begins here The nearest N. peak is too steep and dangerous to be attempted, but the second peak may be ascended by following a ridge of granite projecting from the crumbling diorite. If the ascent of Mt Serbâl has been made from the N , the traveller may return by Dêr Sikelyîh, but not unless he has satisfied himself, in the course of the ascent, that his guides are trustworthy.

Ascent of Mt. Serbâl from the N.E. side through the *Wâdi 'Aleyât*. The old Derb es-Serbâl, or Serbâl route, being now impracticable, there is no proper path. The route at first follows a narrow path, and traverses ridges of rocks, hollows, and ravines, and small plains watered with springs and richly clothed with vegetation. It passes several cells of anchorites and traces of walls, and then, for 3 hrs., ascends rapidly through the *Wâdi Abû Ḥamâd* (or valley of the wild figs). The ascent of the actual summit (3/4 hr.) is extremely laborious, and should not be attempted by persons inclined to giddiness. The veins of diorite afford the best footing. The traveller should observe the caverns in the rock which were once occupied by hermits, the ruins of their huts, the Sinaitic inscriptions, and the traces of old paths, and of a flight of steps, particularly near the summit.

The highest of the five peaks which form the summit of Mt. Serbâl, and which are separated by deep ravines and chasms, is called *El-Meḍawwa* (the 'beacon-house'). Fires used to be lighted here either in honour of Baal, or, as Prof. Palmer conjectures, to warn the anchorites of approaching danger. Many Sinaitic inscriptions still exist here. On the lower terrace of the peak is an artificial circle of stones in which the beacon-fires were probably lighted. The view from the summit is very imposing; towards three points of the compass the prospect is unimpeded, but towards the S. it is concealed by the intervening pinnacles of Mt. Serbâl and the still higher Mûsa group. Towards the E. we survey the Bay of 'Aḳaba, part of the arid territory of Arabia, and the interminable desert plateau of Tîh, stretching to the distant heights of Petra; towards the N. lies the Bay of Suez, and towards the W. rise the hills between the Nile and the Red Sea. 'Every detail of these remarkable formations is distinctly visible hence. The wâdis, including the long, crescent-shaped Wâdi esh-Shêkh, are seen turning and winding in every direction. The innumerable hills stand forth in prominent relief, with as well-defined colours as in Russegger's geological plan which we held in our hands; the dark granite, the brown sandstone, the yellow desert, the strips of vegetation flanking the Wâdi Fîrân, and the solitary green spot occupied by the large groups of palms of Rephidîm (assuming its identity to be established), are all surveyed at a glance'.

Geological Formation. According to Fraas the chief formations of Mount Serbâl are: — (1) *Gneiss* of grey colour and very fine grain, the component parts of which are uniformly distributed, the mica giving it a somewhat stratified appearance; (2) *Red granite* of great beauty, containing little or no mica; (3) *Diorite porphyry*, which frequently veins the masses of gneiss and granite. The following are the principal forms of diorite: — (1) Black diorite porphyry; (2) Dark green, and somewhat dingy diorite; (3) Diorite resembling porphyry; (4) Polyhedric porphyry of a pale-red colour, containing occasional crystals of albite, and a few grains of quartz; (5) Porphyry varying in colour from brownish to blood-red, and rough and granulated to the touch; (6) Porphyry in which pieces of oligoclase, about an inch in length, are imbedded. *Turquoises* of finer quality than those in the Wâdi Maghâra are also found here

Is Mount Serbâl the Sinai of Scripture? The traveller is reminded that during the battle of the Amalekites, Moses prayed on a rock of Horeb, that he received Jethro after the battle, when the people were encamped by the Mount of God, and that from the entrance to the oasis (Rephidîm) to the foot of Mt Sinai one day's journey only is reckoned, while a large caravan takes two days to reach the Jebel Mûsa, and lastly, that a person acquainted with the peninsula, as the leader of the Israelites undoubtedly was, would scarcely have acted wisely, if, while receiving the tables of the law, he had compelled the multitude entrusted to his care to encamp for a prolonged period far from the best watered and most fruitful spot on the whole route. As, moreover, Mt. Serbâl is by far the most imposing mountain in the peninsula, as many traditions declare it to be the scene of God's revelation to Moses, as it has long been regarded as holy, as Eusebius, followed by Cosmas and other Christian authors, identifies it with the Horeb of the Bible, and as Pharan and Sinai are always associated in the monkish chronicles and the resolutions of the Councils, it would seem more justifiable to identify Mt Serbâl with the Sinai of Scripture, than the Jebel Mûsa group. If Mt Serbâl is the Sinai of Scripture, Moses must have conducted his people from Rephidîm through the oasis, where both space and water were inadequate to their wants, and through the defile of Buwêb, into one of the neighbouring plains in the Wâdi esh-Shêkh, whence the mountain is visible in all its majesty. Whilst we are almost surrounded by an amphitheatre of hills of moderate height, the imposing rocky mass of Mt Serbâl, towering above them all, rises to the S W, being more prominently and distinctly visible here, than from any other part of the peninsula. 'Mount Serbâl', observes Prof. Palmer, 'seen from a little distance, exhibits such boldness of outline, and such huge and conspicuous forms, that it is justly entitled to be considered the grandest and most characteristic feature of the peninsula'. Although the traveller must not expect to be able to identify on Mt Serbâl every spot referred to in the Scriptural account of the promulgation of the law, there is no doubt that the general topography of the district harmonises well with that narrative. On again referring to the book of Exodus (xix. 17) we find this passage: — 'And Moses brought forth the people out of the camp to meet with God; and they stood at the nether part of the mount'. We shall see that there would have been no room for such a movement in the wâdis Er-Râha or Sebâ'iyeh, adjoining the Jebel Mûsa group, whereas it was possible, and even necessary, to lead the people who were encamped beyond the oasis, towards the foot of the mountain before us, perhaps as far as the hill of Meharret and the lower part of the Wâdi 'Aleyât. No one can look upon the conspicuous and majestic Mt. Serbâl, without being convinced that it was far more worthy of being the throne of Jehovah, than any of the less imposing peaks of the Jebel Mûsa group. If it be asked, how the glorious title of the 'Mount of the Lord' came to be transferred from one mountain to another, the question may be answered without much difficulty. When the early Christians settled in the peninsula, they foud no memorials of the Exodus, but arbitrarily assigned Old Testament names to the various hills and valleys, a practice which, as we shall afterwards see, was imitated to excess by the monks of the monastery of St. Catharine on the Jebel Mûsa. One group of anchorites identified Mt. Serbâl, and another the imposing mountain situated farther to the S, with 'Mount Horeb' As long as Pharan was a powerful place and an episcopal see, its right to claim the title was generally recognised, but after it had lapsed into heresy, this right was denied by the orthodox church, and the hermits of the Jebel Mûsa group were expressly recognised as the genuine Sinaites, for whose protection Justinian caused a castle to be built The anchorites and Cœnobites of Mt. Serbâl, who were decimated by the frequently recurring attacks of the Saracens, accordingly emigrated to the Jebel Mûsa for safety. We have already cited a remarkable passage of early date, in which it is expressly stated, that the monks of Sinai had emigrated from another mountain, and had settled on the modern Sinai by God's command See the writings of Lepsius already mentioned (p 497), where these views were expressed for the first time, and are fully discussed Many critics have since adopted the same theory

Leaving the Meharret hill (see p. 495), we proceed towards the N.E. under palm-trees. The ground becomes soft, and is carpeted with turf, moss, and reeds, interspersed with blue and red flowers. We pass rich fields of wheat, besides tobacco and other industrial crops; the bushes are enlivened by birds, and flocks of sheep and goats lie by the side of the brooks under the shade of the trees. After 1 hr. the palm-trees leave off, and are succeeded by a thicket of ṭarfa shrubs, which we traverse in $1/4$ hour. Many of these shrubs assume the form of trees, $2^1/_2$-3 ft. in circumference.

It is only in the lower part of the Wâdi esh-Shêkh (p. 520), and here in its prolongation, the Wâdi Fîrân, so far as the latter is watered by the brook, that these tarfa plants yield the well-known *Manna*. Minute holes are bored in the fine bark of the thin, brown twigs, by an insect (Coccus manniparus) which was first observed by Ehrenberg, and from the almost invisible openings issues a transparent drop of juice, which then falls off and hardens in the sand. This sweet gum, resembling honey, which is still called 'man' by the Arabians, is collected and preserved in considerable quantities; the monks in the monastery generally keep a supply, partly for their own use, and partly for sale, in tin boxes In 1845 Lepsius found the whole valley fragrant with manna as early as the end of March, but it is usually most plentiful from the end of April to the end of June, and the more so in proportion to the moisture of the preceding winter.

Adjoining the rocky slopes on the left rise numerous tent-shaped mounds of earth, upwards of 100 ft. in height, which Fraas takes to be the remains of ancient moraines. After $1/2$ hr. the *Wâdi el-Akhdar* (p. 521), leading towards the E., diverges to the left Opposite to it opens the *Wâdi Rattameh*, to the W. of which rises a hill situated to the S. (right) of the road, called the *Jebel el-Munâja*, *i.e.* 'Mountain of the conversation between God and Moses'. The Arabs still offer sacrifices here to Moses within a circle of stones on the summit of the hill, singing — 'O mountain of the conversation of Moses, we seek thy favour; preserve thy good people, and we will visit thee every year'. Farther to the E. we reach in $^1/_4$ hr. the defile of *El-Buwêb*, *i.e.* little gate, or *El-Bâb*, *i.e.* gate, where the valley contracts to a width of about 20 ft. The Wâdi Fîrân terminates here, and the **Wâdi esh-Shêkh** (p. 520) begins.

The part of the Wâdi Fîrân between the Buwêb and the Ḥererât, which now forms the most fertile oasis in the peninsula, was once a lake, as is proved by the deposits of earth, 60-100 ft. in height, in the angles of the valley throughout its whole distance, a feature observable nowhere else. In consequence of the peculiar configuration of the surrounding mountains, including the Jebel Mûsa group and the Serbâl, every fall of rain, snow, and dew in the whole neighbourhood of this extensive region, found its way through different channels into this basin; and, after the barrier at Ḥererât had been removed, the brook still remained as a relic of the ancient lake. The sudden appearance of this streamlet in the rocky valley, and its as sudden disappearance in the rock at El-Ḥesweh, must have been a constant source of wonder to the vivid imagination of the inhabitants of the desert, and it therefore seems natural that the phenomenon should have been ascribed to the miraculous rod of Moses.

Two routes lead from El-Buwêb to the Sinai monastery. The easier, through the Wâdi esh-Shêkh (11 hrs. to the monastery), is more suitable for the return-journey viâ Ṣarbûṭ el-Khâdem (p. 522); the other, rougher ($10^1/_2$ hrs. to the monastery), but more picturesque, leads through the Wâdi Selâf and across the interesting Naḳb el-Ḥâwi. We select the second of these routes.

The Wâdi esh-Shêkh, which frequently expands into picturesque basins, soon diverges to the N.E. (see p. 520), and we reach ($^1/_4$ hr.) the entrance to the **Wâdi Selâf**, a monotonous and winding valley through which our route runs for nearly 6 hours. On the right opens the *Wâdi er-Rimm* (p. 497) ascending to Mt. Serbâl, and on the same side the *Wâdi Umm Tâkha*, containing several curious stone-huts in the form of beehives, called 'nawâmîs', to which the absurd tradition attaches, that the Israelites sought refuge in them from tormenting flies. In less than 2 hrs. we reach the *Wâdi 'Ejjâwi*, through which the road from Ṭûr (p. 518) on the Red Sea joins our route from the S.W. Mt. Serbâl now at length becomes visible in all its majesty, and remains in sight behind us for $^1/_2$ hour. We next pass the *Wâdi Abû Ṭâlib* to the left, at the entrance of which the prophet Moḥammed, when he was marching against Syria (Shâm) with his uncle Ṭâlib, is said to have rested. Several other small wâdis are passed on the right and left. At the upper end of the valley at the foot of the Naḳb el-Ḥâwi Pass, there is a good camping-place, commanding a fine distant view of Mt. Serbâl. At this point begins the ascent of the **Naḳb el-Ḥâwi Defile** (4930 ft.), occupying $2^1/_2$ hrs., though an active walker might reach the top in one hour. The camels progress very slowly in this narrow, steep, rocky pass, so that the traveller will find it pleasanter to dismount, and walk up the hill. The granite rocks on each side, weathered into singularly fantastic forms, are upwards of 800 ft. in height; the gorge is strewn with stones of all sizes; the camel-path skirts the hard and uneven cliffs which bound the gorge. Lepsius has proved that the laborious task of making this path was first undertaken by the Christian monks. The torrents in this rocky gorge in winter are often so violent as to carry everything before them. In 1867 they were swelled to such a height, that they washed away a camp of the Beduins in the Wâdi Selâf, causing a loss of 40 lives and of numerous cattle, in the midst of the arid desert. The last part of the ascent is less precipitous, and we now observe a few traces of vegetation. The rocks here also bear some Sinaitic inscriptions. — At the upper end of the defile the barren cliffs of the Sinai group become visible, and a view is at length obtained of the *Râḥa* plain, surrounded by lofty mountains, and not unlike a huge amphitheatre. At the end of the valley rises the bold and conspicuous rock, known as the *Râs eṣ-Ṣafṣâf* (p. 513), which the members of the last Sinai expedition, following Dr. Robinson, believe to be the true scene of the promulgation of the law. The plain of Er-Râḥa, which we reach by at first descending a little, and afterwards ascending, the path improving as we advance, is supposed by the same travellers and explorers to have been the camping-place of the Israelites. A dark-green spot, in which antimony is probably to be found, is called *Koḥli* after that mineral. After having crossed another slight eminence, we reach the sand of the plain. A block of rock lying here (perhaps an old boundary stone), bearing peculiar marks, is the subject of an Arabian tradition, to the effect that the Gindî tribe, having been unjustly treated by the monks of the monastery of St. Catharine, who favoured the Jebelîyeh (p. 503), struck their lances into this block in token of confirmation of the oath of their Shêkh, that the monks should never pass this stone. About $1^1/_2$ hr. after leaving the summit of the Naḳb el-Ḥâwi, we pass, on the left, the mouth of the *Wâdi esh-Shêkh* (p. 520), which is commanded by the *Jebel ed-Dêr* (p. 520) on the E. The gorge, called the *Wâdi ed-Dêr*, or the *Wâdi Shu'aib* (valley of Jethro), ascending gradually, and closed by the hill of *Munâja*, opens before us. To the left of its entrance rises the hill of *Hârûn*, on the summit of which Aaron (Hârûn) is said to have set up the golden calf. In the vicinity are the remains of stone huts, built by 'Abbâs Pasha in 1853 and 1854 for the workmen and soldiers who attended him. We enter the Shu'aib valley, flanked by enormous cliffs of reddish-brown granite, towering to a dizzy height. In $^1/_2$ hr. more we reach the terraces of the green garden of the monastery which lies to the right of the path, and the caravan stops in front of the monastery.

Accommodation. Formerly, when the monks were frequently attacked by the Beduins of the peninsula, visitors were drawn up into the monastery through an opening over the gate, which was always carefully closed, by means of a rope with a wooden cross attached to the end. At the present day the traveller presents the letter of introduction which he has obtained through his Consulate at Cairo, and is admitted by a side-door. The Beduins and camels remain outside. The monastery

ENVIRONS OF THE MONASTERY OF M^T SINAI AND OF THE JEBEL MŪSA.

Engl. Mile — Scale, 1:50.000 — Paces

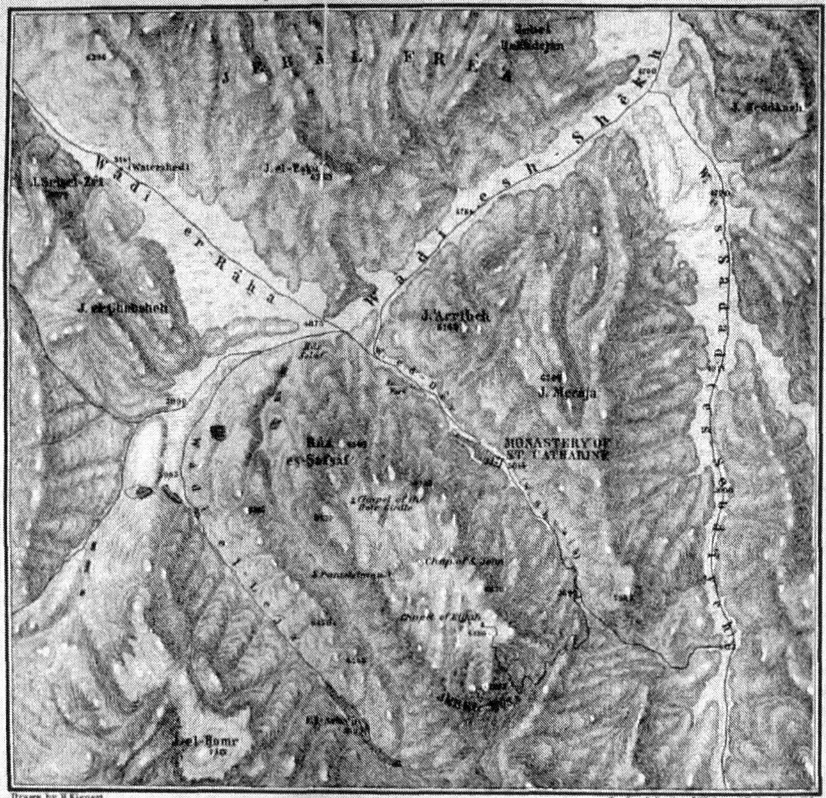

Drawn by H. Kiepert.

Geograph. Instit. of Wagner & Debes, Leipzig.

contains visitors' rooms, beds, sofas, and a kitchen. If the dragoman has undertaken to provide for the party throughout the whole journey, he must make his own bargain with the monks, to whom the traveller may afterwards present a gift on his own account. Those who have to pay their own expenses, are generally charged at least 5 fr. a day each for lodging alone. It is healthier during the cold nights in these mountains in spring, as well as more interesting, to lodge in the monastery; but the traveller will find it more independent and less expensive to camp in some suitable spot in the lower Wâdi Shu'aib, and thence to visit the monastery, the various heights of the Sinai group, and the 'Sacred Places'. The Jebelîyeh, as the servants of the monks are called, are excellent guides, and will accompany the traveller for a trifling fee. Sportsmen who wish to shoot the mountain-goat, which abounds here, may apply to the intendant of the monastery, who will provide them with a suitable guide.

•Monastery of St. Catharine on Mt. Sinai.

The only mention of Mt. Sinai in the Old Testament, after the great event of the promulgation of the law, is in connection with the flight of Elijah, who sought refuge here after having slain the priests of Baal on the brook Kishon (1 Kings, xviii. 40; xix 8) At an early part of the Christian period a number of anchorites settled here amid the springs of these rocky mountains, and pronounced the Jebel Mûsa to be the Mountain of the Lord. As early as the 4th cent they were terribly persecuted, and stories are told in connection with the Dêr el-Arba'în (monastery of the forty) in the Wâdi Leja (p. 513) of the cruel attack which cost 38 or 40 Cœnobites their lives (p. 498). While Mt Serbâl afforded a better situation for monastic settlements, Mt. Sinai attracted numerous anchorites and hermits, owing to its seclusion and greater safety, especially after Justinian, according to the statement of Procopius, his private secretary, and that of Eutychius (Sa'îd ibn el-Batrîk, 9th cent), had erected the church of the Virgin already mentioned and a castle, in A D. 530, for the protection of the monks and the neighbouring region against the attacks of the Saracens. The emperor is said to have been so dissatisfied with the site chosen by the architect, that he caused him to be beheaded. He justly objected that the fortress was commanded by the slope of the valley rising immediately above it. The desire attributed to Justinian, that the slope should have been removed, and the execution of the architect in consequence of his answer — 'if we spent the whole treasures of Rome, Egypt, and Syria, we could not level the mountain', are by no means characteristic of so sagacious an emperor The monastery might certainly have easily been destroyed by rocks rolled down from the E slope of the valley. Justinian and his wife Theodora are also said to have founded the Church of the Transfiguration (p. 506). The monastery was also greatly benefited by a gift from Justinian of a hundred Roman, and a hundred Egyptian slaves, with their wives and children. From these retainers are descended the *Jebelîyeh*, who still render service to the monks, but are despised by the Beduins and stigmatised as 'Nazarenes' and 'fellâḥîn'. Although originally Christians, and living under the supervision of their monkish masters, they could not be prevented from embracing El-Islâm, which they all now profess. In the reign of the Khalîf 'Abd el-Melik ibn Merwân there seem to have been many compulsory conversions to Mohammedanism which cost many lives; but the shrewd monks contrived to ward off their Mohammedan persecutors, by pretending that they had accorded a hospitable reception to the prophet on one of his journeys, that one of the monks of Sinai had predicted his future career, and that the prophet had given them a letter promising them the protection of his followers. The document is said to have been written by 'Ali, and to have been impressed with the blackened sign manual of the prophet, who could not himself write. Sulṭân Selîm is reported to have carried the document to Constantinople, after the conquest of Egypt, for the purpose of enriching his collection of relics, and to have sent the monks, in its stead, a copy authenticated by his own seal; this copy is also said to have been lost, but another copy of very doubtful genuineness is now preserved in the monastery of the order at Cairo The safety of the monks is now better secured by a letter of protection accorded to them by each new sultan. The mosque, which stands within the walls of the monastery, is said to have been built in order to induce Sultân Selîm (d. A.D. 1520) to abstain from his purpose of destroying the monastery, within the walls of which a young Greek priest, to whom he was attached, had died. The mosque, however, has been proved to have existed at least a century and a half earlier than the reign of Selîm, having doubt less been built out of consideration for the Muslims, whom it was absolutely necessary to conciliate. So far was this policy carried, that when King Baldwin I. of Jerusalem wished to visit Mt Sinai during the Crusades, at the beginning of the 12th cent., the monks entreated him to give up his intention, as such a visit might excite the suspicion of the Muslim rulers, and prove detrimental to the monastery. Several Beduin tribes of the peninsula were constituted the well-paid 'Ghafirs', or guardians of the monastery, one of their duties being to escort the caravans of pilgrims, a great number of whom visited the sacred places in the middle ages. The Egyptian government also, even during the Mameluke period, entered into friendly relations with the monks, partly in consequence of the pretended letter of the prophet which they possessed, partly for the sake of ensuring the safety of the Mecca pilgrims, whose route passed the territory of the monks, and partly from its desire to protect those places which were regarded as sacred by Christians and Muslims alike. Down to the reign of Mohammed 'Ali, whose patronage they enjoyed, the monks were entitled to part of the custom-house dues levied at Cairo, and that city had to supply them with the materials for their gowns; and they still enjoy the privilege of conveying their property to or from Cairo free of duty 'Abbâs Pasha visited Mt Sinai in 1853, and formed the extravagant plan of building himself a villa on a rock of Mt. Horeb (p. 510), but he was assassinated in 1854 before his design could be carried out. Although a fanatical Muslim, he did not scruple to pray in the church of the Transfiguration at the 'Place of the Burning Bush'. The safety of the monks is now perfectly insured, partly owing to the favour shown to the Christians by the Egyptian government, and partly to the protection of Russia. — Notwithstanding the ample revenues of the monastery, the number of the monks has greatly diminished. In the 14th cent it is said to have contained 3-400 inmates, together with a prelate and an archbishop, but the number is now reduced to 20-30 only, who are chiefly natives of the Greek islands, where the monastery possesses estates, particularly in Crete and Cyprus. — The most famous offshoot of the monastery of the Wâdi Shu'aib is that of the Sinaites at Cairo, but the monks also maintain constant communication with the other churches of their order, which are scattered over a great part of the East Thus we find fraternities in Roumania, Servia, Turkey (Constantinople), the Greek Archipelago, in Greece itself, and even in India, closely connected with the monastery of Mt. Sinai. The order belongs to the orthodox Greek church, which regards Sinai as no less sacred than Jerusalem

The *Monastic Rule* is very strict The monks are prohibited from partaking of meat or wine, and even oil is forbidden during the long fasts, but they are permitted to eat fish, and to drink an excellent liqueur which they prepare from dates ('Araki). They assemble for prayer twice during the day, and twice during the night. Women were formerly rigorously excluded, and even cats and hens, as belonging to the same obnoxious sex Female pilgrims, however, and enterprising lady tourists, are now lodged without difficulty in the rooms set apart for visitors. The monastery is presided over by an archbishop, who is elected by the monks here and their brethren in Cairo; the election, however, requires confirmation by the patriarch of Jerusalem, who recently exercised his right of veto in a very emphatic manner. Between 1760 and 1872 no archbishop resided on Mt. Sinai, as, in accordance with ancient treaties, large sums had to be paid and gifts presented to the Beduins upon the installation of every new prelate. After a lapse of 112 years a new archbishop *(Kallistratos)* was installed in the monastery in 1872, but his election was attended with great difficulties If the quaint old writer Schiltberger of Munich (1394-1427) could have foreseen these modern events, he would hardly have recorded the following miracle: — 'A great wonder takes place in the monastery, where there are many monks, who have as many lamps, which are always burning And when a monk is about to die his lamp begins to wane, and when it goes out, he dies. And when th, Abbot dies, the monk, who sings his praise after the mass, finds on the altar a letter on which is written the name of the man who is to be Abbot. And the lamp of the dead Abbot thereupon lights itself.' The absent archbishop is represented by a prior or wekîl, but the affairs oe the monastery are actually managed by an intendant. Most of the monksf who are quite uneducated, practise some handicraft; and they are most, successful in the distilling of brandy, and in gardening Among them are also a tailor and a shoemaker who charge exorbitantly for their primitive workmanship The bread of coarse flour is also baked on the premises. Many of the monks spend a few years only on Mt Sinai, after which they return home as 'martyrs' The monastery is also considered as a kind of penal establishment. The healthy mountain air enjoyed by the inmates of the monastery of St. Catharine has always contributed greatly to their longevity, but most of them suffer from rheumatism.

The Monastery of Sinai, an irregular pile of buildings, lies 5014 ft. above the sea-level, on the N.E. granite slopes of the Jebel Mûsa or Mount Sinai, in the Wâdi Shu'aib or valley of Jethro. Into the outer wall, facing the garden, are built two fragments of marble bearing inscriptions, one in Greek, and one in Arabic (published by Lepsius). They both date from the 12th or 13th century, and are to the same effect. The longer, in Arabic, runs as follows: — 'The monastery of Mt. (Ṭûr) Sînâi, and the church of the Mountain of the Conversation, was built by Justianus (*i. e.* Justinianus), the pious king of the Greek confession, dependent on the aid of God, and waiting for the promise of his Lord, to remind himself and his wife Theodora of the flight of time, in order that God might inherit the earth and everyone thereon, for he is the best of heirs. And his building was ended after thirty years of his reign; and he appointed over it a superintendant named Dhulas. And this happened in the year 6021 after Adam, which corresponds with the year 527 of the year of the Lord Christ'. It appears from the style of the characters, that the inscriptions date from the 12th or 13th cent., and it has already been mentioned, that the date of the foundation of the monastery has been confounded with that of the castle built by Justinian. The same wall contains another large stone, which, to judge from its ornamentation, probably bears a third inscription on one of its sides. The monastery was often destroyed and rebuilt, and consequently exhibits great incongruity of form; we therefore find cubes and round arches, pointed and flat roofs, and a church and mosque in close contact with each other. The whole building presents the appearance of a fortress externally, but the bold and menacing defences consist of the walls of houses, and massive walls of stones connecting the different buildings, which take the place of a regular rampart. The apartments occupied by the monks, pilgrims, and travellers, are situated on the first floor of the houses, which are only one room in depth, their doors being connected by a long, wooden gallery. The white-washed walls bear numerous Greek inscriptions, some of which were written by a monk of Athos, named Cyril, who was formerly librarian here. The different buildings are separated by small courts; one of these contains a well, and a small group of apricot trees enclosed by stakes. The low buildings are commanded by a lofty cypress. From the embrasures in the walls and ramparts a few small cannons still frown on the now peaceful 'Saracens'. In the midst of the buildings is situated the church (see below), with its handsome tower, adjoining which is the ill-preserved mosque. The wells yield excellent water, particularly one in a shed at the back of the church, which the monks point out as the one at which Moses watered the flocks of Jethro's daughters.

The *Church of the Transfiguration* is an early Christian basilica. The exterior is uninteresting. In the centre of the W. side, which forms a kind of façade, a large cross, with a window in the centre, takes the place of the usual rose-window; and on each side of it is a palm-tree engraved on the stone. — The church is entered by a porch, and a flight of steps descending beyond it, both of which have been restored. In the middle of each of the topmost steps is a letter of the name of St. James ('I-A-K-Ω-B-O-Σ). — We first enter a vestibule (narthex) with a Byzantine window, containing a large, modern basin for holy water with small silver eagles. The framework of the door leading into the nave is richly decorated and the panels are embellished with old pictures in enamel, of small size. The basilica, which we next enter, notwithstanding the lowness of its aisles, and the superabundant decoration peculiar to Greek churches, is not devoid of effect. Each of the lofty walls bearing the entablature of the nave rests on thick columns of granite, covered with stucco and painted green, the capitals of which are adorned with boldly executed foliage. The ceiling has been recently re-painted, and divided into bright coloured sections containing indifferent medallion figures of John the Baptist, the Virgin and Child, and the Saviour.

The *Aisles* are lighted by five Byzantine windows on each side, and are covered by a sloping roof. A coloured *Marble Pavement* in the nave now replaces one of admirable mosaic which was destroyed by Arabian treasure-seekers. Adjoining the third column on the left side of the nave is a marble *Pulpit* adorned with pleasing miniatures, which was presented to the church in 1787. Near the fourth column on the right is the *Episcopal Throne*, dating from the last century, and interesting on account of a representation of the monastery at that period, painted by an Armenian artist, and held by figures of Moses and St. Catharine. The inscription repeats the date 527 which is erroneously stated by the monks as that of the foundation of the monastery by Justinian (p. 503). Between each pair of columns are rudely-carved choir-stalls. From the ceiling are suspended three candelabra, which are lit at the evening service and made to swing from side to side; also a hundred lamps of every shape and size, some of which are adorned with ostriches' eggs, and so low, that they may be reached with the hand. The raised *Tribuna* projects into the nave far beyond the choir. A wooden *Screen* ('septum'), coloured blue, yellow, and red, and overladen with carving, with a broad gate flanked with gilded columns and rich ornamentation, separates the choir from the nave and aisles. The large crucifix, reaching to the ceiling, bears the figure of the Saviour, painted in bright colours. The candelabra, placed in front of the screen and covered with red velvet, stand on very ancient bronze lions of curious workmanship, perhaps executed before the Christian era. — The beautiful rounded **Apse* is adorned with *Mosaics* of great value, executed by European artists as early as the 7th or 8th cent. The most important of these, which, like the others, is well preserved, is the **Transfiguration of Christ*, in memory of which the church was originally consecrated. In the centre of the mosaic the youthful and somewhat commonplace figure of the Saviour soars towards heaven. Elijah, the prophet of Mt. Sinai, is pointing to the Messiah; St. John kneels at the feet of his master; Moses points to the latter as the fulfiller of his law, and St. Peter lies on the ground, while St. James is kneeling. Each figure is accompanied by the name of the person it represents. A kind of frame is formed to this picture by a series of busts of prophets, apostles, and saints in mosaic, admirably executed: —

1. John the deacon; 2. Luke; 3. Simon; 4 James; 5. Mark; 6. Bartholomew, 7. Andrew; 8. Paul; 9. Philip, 10. Thomas, 11. Matthew; 12 Thaddeus; 13. Matthias; 14 Ὁ ἅγιος ἡγούμενος, the 'Holy Superior' of the monastery; 15. Daniel; 16 Jeremiah; 17 Malachi; 18 Haggai; 19. Habakkuk; 20. Joel; 21. Amos; 22 David; 23 Hosea; 24. Micah; 25. Obadiah; 26. Nahum; 27. Zephaniah; 28. Zachariah; 29 Isaiah, 30. Ezekiel.

Above the apse, on the right, Moses kneels before the burning bush; on the left, he stands before Mt. Sinai, with the tables of the law in his hand. Between these scenes and the arch of the apse hover two angels adjoining two medallion figures (perhaps Moses and St. Catharine), which the monks point out as portraits of Justinian and Theodora, although they do not in the least resemble other portraits of the emperor and his wife. Under the scene of the Transfiguration is an inscription (Ἐν ὀνόματι Πατρὸς καὶ Υἱοῦ καὶ Ἁγίου πνεύματος γέγονεν τὸ πᾶν ἔργον τοῦτο ὑπὲρ σωτηρίας τῶν καρποφορησάντων ἐπὶ Λογγίνου τοῦ ὁσιωτάτου πρεσβυτέρου καὶ ἡγουμένου) to the effect that the mosaic was executed under *Longinus*, the Presbyter and Superior of the monastery, for the salvation of the souls of those who had contributed towards the cost of the work.

Among the sacred utensils in the choir are a finely executed Ciborium, or stand for the communion chalice, and a short marble sarcophagus said to contain the head and one hand of *St. Catharine*, who is specially revered by the Greek orthodox church. Here, too, is shown a valuable, but unpleasing reliquary, presented by Russian Christians. The head of St. Catharine is represented on a silver pillow, her face and hands being enamelled. Another similar reliquary, bearing a figure of the saint in gilded silver, was presented by the Empress Catharine of Russia.

The *Chapel of the Burning Bush*, at the back of the apse, marking the spot where God is said to have appeared to Moses, is probably the oldest part of the structure. Visitors must remove their shoes before entering. The walls are covered with slabs of porcelain. The spot where the bush is said to have stood is indicated by a plate of chased silver; over it is placed a kind of altar, within which are suspended three burning lamps. At the back of this sanctuary is a small niche adorned with figures, in a line with the apse, the semicircular wall of which encloses the whole E. end of the building. A ray of the sun is said to enter this sanctuary once only in the course of the year, gaining admission through a cleft of the rock on the E. side of the valley. From a cross erected there the hill has been named the Jebel es-Ṣalîb.

The *Chapels* surrounding the nave contain no objects of interest. Each is dedicated to an evangelist, saint, or martyr (SS. Anna, the holy martyrs of Sinai, James, Constantia and Helena, Demetrius and Sergius). Adjoining the right aisle of the basilica are the chapels of SS. Simon Stylites, Cosmas, and Damianus; adjoining the left aisle are those of SS. Anna, Marina, and Antipas. The chapel for the Latins, near the visitors' rooms, is now disused, as the Roman Catholics no longer make pilgrimages to this monastery.

The *Mosque*, a building of simple construction, is badly preserved. The stone wall of an out-building near the mosque and an arch between the mosque and the church still bear several coats of arms in the early mediæval style, perhaps those of Crusaders. Opposite is the chapel of the Panagia, which contains several portraits of bishops and archbishops of Sinai and a large model of a projected reconstruction of the monastery. It is now, however, very problematical whether this scheme of reconstruction will ever be carried out, since the property of the convent in Russia and Walachia has been secularised.

The *Library* of the monastery, which is sadly cramped for want of room, is more valuable than many better arranged and outwardly more imposing collections in Europe. Among its treasures are a great many Greek and Arabic MSS., besides others in Syrian, Æthiopian, Persian, Armenian, Slavonic, and Russian. The most valuable MSS., however, are kept stored away in cases, and the only ones exhibited to visitors are a few 'show' pieces in the treasury and a selection of comparatively uninteresting modern MSS. in a room adjoining the archbishop's house. Implicit belief should not be vouchsafed to all that the monks have to say about the MSS. in the treasury. Thus, some loose pages of a Greek Bible which they show do not belong, as they assert, to the Codex Sinaiticus. The so-called *Evangelium Theodosianum*, a collection of passages from the New Testament, is described without any ground whatever as a gift of the Emp. Theodosius (766 A.D.), and in all likelihood does not date farther back than 1000 A.D. It is written on white parchment, both sides of each sheet having two columns in golden characters. A kind of frontispiece is formed by a series of elaborate miniatures of Jesus, Mary, the four Evangelists, and St. Peter. The *Psalterianum Cassianum*, containing the whole of the Psalms written in microscopical characters on six leaves, was not executed by a nun of the 9th cent., named Cassia, but is a piece of laborious trifling dating from the period of the Renaissance. — In the 'Small Library' is a copy of the famous *Codex Sinaiticus*, discovered by Prof. Tischendorf, printed most carefully from the original, and presented by the Emperor of Russia. Several leaves of the precious MS. are preserved at the university of Leipsic, under the name of the 'Codex Friderico-Augustanus', but the greater part of it is at St. Petersburg, having been purchased from the monastery by Alexander II. for a large sum. The codex contains a complete copy of the New Testament, most of the books of the Old Testament, a part of the 'Shepherd of Hermas', and the 'Epistle of St. Barnabas'. The great value of the Codex Sinaiticus is due to its completeness, the care with which it is written, the consistency of the peculiarities of its text, and, above all, its great antiquity. It is pretty well ascertained to date from about 400 A.D., and is surpassed by the celebrated Codex Vaticanus alone in age and in importance in determining the Biblical text.

On the N. side of the monastery is the *Burial Place* of the monks, reached by several dark passages, and consisting of a strongly vaulted crypt. The remains of the bishops are preserved in coffins, and those of the priests in a separate part of the vault, while the bones and skulls of the monks are merely piled up together. The skeletons of several highly revered hermits are suspended from the wall. At the gate of the priests' vault is placed the skeleton of St. Stephanos (d. 580), wearing a skull-cap of violet velvet. Not far from this vault is a well, and beyond it is the rarely used burial-ground for pilgrims who have died here.

A flight of steps descends from this court to the **Garden*, the trees of which blossom most luxuriantly in March and April, presenting a grateful sight in the midst of this rocky wilderness. It is laid out in the form of terraces, and contains peach-trees, orange-trees, vines, etc., overshadowed by some lofty cypresses.

The Jebel Mûsa and Râs eṣ-Ṣafṣâf.

The ascent of the Jebel Mûsa occupies 3 hrs, and presents no difficulty. The start should be made about 5 a. m or earlier. Five different paths lead to the top, but the two following are almost exclusively used. The more interesting, but also more fatiguing, ascends the old pilgrimage-steps (see below), while the other begins in the Wâdi Shuʿaib, and ascends the Jebel Mûsa by a circuitous route. This last was to have been made practicable for the carriage of ʿAbbâs Pasha, who intended building himself a villa on Mt. Sinai; but he was assassinated before the completion of the work (p. 501). Those who wish to ascend the Jebel Mûsa and Râs eṣ-Ṣafṣâf separately may return by the second of these routes; in this case they may remain long enough on the Jebel Mûsa to enjoy the magnificent spectacle of a sunset By starting immediately after the disappearance of the sun, and walking rapidly, the traveller will have time and light enough to descend to the cypress plain (Chapel of Elijah), whence, with the aid of a guide, he may reach the monastery in an hour without difficulty, even in the dark, by following the road of ʿAbbâs Pasha The pilgrims' steps should on no account be descended at night. If necessary the night may be spent in the chapel of Elijah, in which case the monks provide blankets

One or two of the monks or Jebelîyeh (Arabian servants of the monastery) act as guides, carrying the necessary provisions, and rendering help in the ascent of the Râs eṣ-Ṣafṣâf.

Those who ascend by the pilgrims' steps quit the monastery by a small side-gate in its W. wall, and mount the bare granite of the W. side of the Shuʿaib valley, by a path which gradually becomes steeper, but is unattended with danger. This path, which, like many of the Oriental churches, is said to date from the time of the Empress Helena, was probably constructed for the pilgrims in the 6th or 7th cent. In 20 min. we reach a small spring which contains the same quantity of water in winter and summer, and where, according to the Arabs, Moses once tended the sheep of Jethro, whom they call Shuʿaib. The monks, on the other hand, declare that it issued from the rock in consequence of the prayers of the holy abbot Sangarius, when the wells in the monastery dried up, and that it is a cure for diseases of the eye. In 12 min. more we come to a hut, styled the *Chapel of Mary*, which is said to have been erected in memory of a vision of the Virgin. The monks, according to the story, were so terribly plagued with vermin, that they determined to leave the monastery, and ascended the mountain in procession, intending to quit the holy places. On the way, however, on the site of this hut, the Virgin appeared to them, promised to deliver them from their tormentors, and commanded them to return. They obeyed, and found that all the vermin had disappeared. The traveller, however, even at a late period of the year, will have abundant opportunity of observing that the foe has since returned. — Farther up, the route crosses a small ravine, and then passes through two rude gates. Monks are said formerly to have been stationed here for the purpose of receiving from the pilgrims, who wished to take the sacrament on the top of Mt. Sinai, a certificate that they had attended the confessional in the monastery. At the first gate they were handed a receipt, which they gave up at the second. After a few minutes more we reach a pleasant green plain, called the 'plain of the Cypress', after a gigantic cypress which rises in the middle of it. It is enclosed by bold and barren masses of rock, and reddish-brown and grey pinnacles of hard granite. Exactly to the S. of the cypress rises the peak of the Jebel Mûsa; farther distant, to the S.W., towers the lofty Jebel Katherîn (p. 515), and to the N. is the cliff of the Ṣafṣâf rising from the Râḥa plain. On a plateau to the right of the path is a nursery of saplings by the side of a fresh spring. We turn to the left of the cypress, and mount the rugged blocks over which lies the route to the summit of the Jebel Mûsa. On a small eminence, which unites the cypress plain with the Jebel Mûsa, on the left of the path, is a simple white stone building, containing two chapels dedicated to the prophets Elijah and Elisha. The rudely-whitewashed interior contains a hollow which the monks point out as the cavern in which Elijah concealed himself after he had slain the priests of Baal on the brook Kishon and had wandered 40 days and 40 nights in the wilderness. Jehovah commanded him to ascend to the top of the mountain.

'And behold', we read in 1 Kings xix 11, *et seq.*, 'the Lord passed by, and a great and strong wind rent the mountains, and brake in pieces the rocks before the Lord, but the Lord was not in the wind. and after the wind an earthquake, but the Lord was not in the earthquake: 12. And after the earthquake a fire, but the Lord was not in the fire. and after the fire a still small voice. 13 And it was so, when Elijah heard it, that he wrapped his face in his mantle, and went out, and stood in the entering in of the cave. And, behold, there came a voice unto him, and said, What doest thou here, Elijah?' — We may remind the reader how effectively Mendelssohn has set this sublime passage to music.

Beyond the Chapel of Elijah (6900 ft.) the route, or rather the flight of steps (3000 in all, according to Pococke; 500 to the spring of Sangarius, 1000 to the Chapel of Mary, 500 to the chapel of Elijah, and 1000 to the top) becomes steeper, but by daylight it is nowhere attended with danger. The granite is at first speckled red, afterwards grey, green, and yellow. After an ascent of 40 min. more, a natural hollow in the granite is pointed out by the Arabs (to the left of the path) as a foot-print of the camel which the prophet rode on his visit to Sinai, before his call. According to another legend, the camel is said to have stood with one foot in Damascus, another in Cairo, the third in Mecca, and the fourth on Mt. Sinai, where the impression is still to be seen, and thence to have been carried up into heaven with his rider by the angel Gabriel. In $^3/_4$ hr. more we reach the summit of the **Jebel Mûsa** (7363 ft.), which rises 2350 ft. above the monastery. On the small plateau at the top, to the left, partly built on ancient foundations, is situated a small and simple chapel, which those of the guides who are monks enter with candles and incense. On the right rises a small mosque in bad preservation, which the Arabs revere highly, and which, until recently, they were only permitted to enter clothed in the *iḥrâm*, or single, plain garment which they wear when pilgrims at Mecca. After the Ṣâliḥ festival (p. 520) in the Esh-Shêkh valley the Beduins sacrifice animals to Mûsa (Moses) here. At the N.E. angle of the rock which bears the chapel there is a hollow, where Moses is said to have stood when 'the Lord's glory passed by', and the monks show the impression of the prophet's head and shoulders on the stone. The tradition is to the effect that Moses remained fasting for forty days in a hollow resembling a cistern near the mosque, while writing the ten commandments.

The view is wild and imposing. Towards the S.W. rise the barren, sombre, and majestic Jebel Zebîr and Jebel Katherîn, the highest mountains in the peninsula. To the S.E. we survey the Sebâ'îyeh Valley, near the foot of the Jebel Mûsa, which some authorities take to be the camping-place of the Jews. Above it rises a multitude of mountain chains and peaks, picturesquely interspersed with intervening wâdis. Towards the E. the Jebel el-Me'allawi is particularly conspicuous. In clear weather the Red Sea, and even the greater part of the Bay of 'Aḳaba, are visible. The island of Tîrân to the S.E. of the peninsula is also sometimes descried. Towards the N.W. is the Râs eṣ-Ṣafṣâf, while below us lie the valleys of the two monasteries. Beyond these, on the right, framing the picture, rise the Jebel 'Arîbeh, El-Ferî', and Eṣ-Ṣannâ'; on the left, the Jebel er-Rabba and Eẓ-Ẓafarîyeh, with the château of 'Abbâs Pasha. Towards the N., beyond the Râs eṣ-Ṣafṣâf, we obtain a glimpse through the defile of the Naḳb el-Ḥâwi of the less mountainous region of the peninsula in that direction.

We descend in 20 min. to the cypress plain, whence the guides conduct us in 3/4 hr. through two fertile hollows by a slightly descending path to a third valley, picturesquely commanded by rocks. The first dale contains the remains of a cistern and a chapel dedicated to John the Baptist. From the valley in which this path terminates, it is usual to make the ascent of the **Râs eṣ-Ṣafṣâf** ('mountain of the willow'), which many authorities, particularly since the time of Dr. Robinson, who is also followed by Prof. Palmer, identify with the mountain where the commandments were given. We may here enjoy a cool draught from a spring near a dilapidated chapel dedicated to the 'Sacred girdle of the Virgin Mary', and inspect the venerable willow which gives its name to the mountain, and from which Moses is said to have cut his miraculous rod. The monks formerly pointed out another bush in the monastery garden from which the rod was cut. The ascent of the Ṣafṣâf (6540 ft.) is at first facilitated by steps. Farther up the path becomes steeper, and the extreme summit can only be attained by persons with steady heads by dint of scrambling. Those who are not disposed for this undertaking should take their stand by the opening of a chasm which descends precipitously into the Râḥa plain, situated about 50 paces below the summit of the mountain.

This point commands an admirable survey of the broad Wâdi, which is believed by many to have been the camping-place of the Jews, and is picturesquely enclosed by huge mountains of granite.

Opposite the cliffs of the Ṣafsâf, on the other side of the valley, rise the red porphyry masses of the Jebel Frêʿa, forming the nucleus of a labyrinth of other mountains extending towards the N. The S. side of it is called the *Jebel Sona*, to which belong the granite slopes commanding the Wâdi er-Râha at the traveller's feet and the Wâdi ed-Dêr. On the right (E.) rises the *Jebel ed-Dêr*, and on the left (W.) are seen numerous cliffs of granite, including the narrow *Ughret el-Mehd* at the entrance of the *Wâdi Leja*, and the *Jebel el-Ghabsheh*. Far below us in the valley, at the mouth of the ravine above which we stand, rises a mound of sand with some ruined buildings and a few fruit-trees.

The *Plain of Er-Râḥa*, which we here survey, is, according to the measurements of Prof. Palmer, two million sq. yds. in area. There is no doubt that this valley is sufficiently extensive to have been the camping-place of a large multitude like that of the Israelites. If the Mt. Sinai of the monks, and not Mt. Serbâl, is to be regarded as the mountain where the commandments were given, the Râs eṣ-Ṣafṣâf, and not the Jebel Mûsa, must have been the peak ascended by Moses. — If the Jebel Mûsa alone has been climbed, and the traveller wishes afterwards to visit the Râs eṣ-Ṣafṣâf, he should ascend with a guide through a cleft immediately behind the monastery, a little to the W. of the pilgrims' steps. There are steps here also, but the route is not recommended to those who are inclined to dizziness, and it is much more fatiguing than the pilgrims' route. The descent may be made by a cleft opening into the Râḥa plain, but this route is also very rough, and cannot be recommended for the ascent. Huge masses of rock have fallen into the cleft, and the path often leads below them.

Those who desire to compare the form of the group of Mt. Sinai with the account given of the 'Mount of the Lord' in the Bible narrative should keep in mind the following points suggested by Dr Robinson, which may also be considered in reference to Mt. Sinai There must be the summit of a mountain commanding the camp of the people, and a space contiguous to the mountain from which a large multitude could witness the scene on the heights The camping-place must be so situated with regard to the mountain, that the people could approach the latter, and stand upon its lower slopes; there must be the possibility of touching the mountain, and of placing an enclosure round it to prevent the people from ascending it, or touching its extremity

Those who wish to return hence to the monastery, and not to visit the Wâdi Leja and the El-Arbaʿîn monastery (p. 514) at present, may descend by the ravine called the *Sikket Shuʿaib*. The route is difficult, and reminds one of the question asked by Recha of the Knight Templar in Lessing's 'Nathan', whether 'it was really so much easier to ascend the mountain than to descend it'.

The *Wâdi el-Leja* and the *El-Arbaʿîn Monastery* may be reached even on horseback and without a guide. The whole excursion, which presents no difficulties, takes 4 hrs.; numerous sacred spots are pointed out on the route. Before entering the valley from the Râḥa plain, the place is shown where the earth is supposed to have swallowed up the company of Korah, although, according to the Bible narrative, the scene of that event must have been at a considerable distance from Mt. Sinai. A hole in the rock is also pointed out as the mould of the golden calf.

The **Leja Valley**, which flanks the W. side of the Jebel Mûsa, owes its name to an Arabian tradition that Leja was a daughter of Jethro, and a sister of Zipporah (Arabic Zafûrîya). At the entrance we first observe, on the right, the dilapidated hermitages dedicated to SS. Cosmas and Damianus, and a disused chapel of the Twelve Apostles. On the left is the ruinous monastery of *El-Bustân* with a few plantations; farther on we come to a mass of rock, called by the Arabs *Hajer Mûsa*, or 'Stone of Moses', and declared by the monks to be the *Rock of Horeb*, from which the spring issued when struck by Moses. It is probably in accordance with an ancient Jewish tradition, with which both St. Paul (1 Cor. x. 4), and the expounders of the Korân seem to have been familiar, that the monks assure us that this rock accompanied the Jews throughout their wanderings in the desert, and then returned to its old place. It is of reddish-brown granite, measures about 130 cubic yds. in content, and is about 12 ft. high. The S. side is bisected somewhat obliquely by a band of porphyry about 16 in. wide, from holes in which jets of water for each of the 12 tribes are said to have flowed. Two of the holes, however, seem to have disappeared. — Several Sinaitic inscriptions (p. 494) are to be seen here.

About 20 min. to the S. of this point is the unpretending *Dêr el-Arba'în*, or Monastery of the Forty (i.e. martyrs), with an extensive garden containing olive and other trees. In the upper and rocky part of the site rises a spring with a grotto near it, which is said once to have been occupied by St. Onofrius. The monastery was inhabited from the 16th down to the middle of the 17th century. Two or three monks reside here occasionally to look after the garden. The forty martyrs, from whom the monastery derives its name, are said to have been monks who were slain by the Saracens, but that event may as probably have taken place at the monastery of Sikelyîh on Mt. Serbâl (p. 498).

The Jebel Katherîn.

The ascent of the Jebel Katherîn is more difficult than that of the Jebel Mûsa, and is hardly suitable for ladies The start should be made very early, or the previous night should be spent at the Arba'în monastery (see above) See map, p. 496

Route as far as the (2 hrs.) *Dêr el-Arba'în*, see above. We then follow a gorge to the S.W. which soon contracts considerably, and observe several Sinaitic inscriptions. After $1^1/_4$-$1^1/_2$ hr. we reach the *Bîr esh-Shunnâr*, or 'partridges' well', which God is said to have called forth for behoof of the partridges which followed the corpse of St. Catharine (see below) when borne to Mt. Sinai by angels. The route now inclines more to the W., and is very steep and fatiguing until ($1^1/_2$ hr.) we reach the ridge of rocks leading to the top. The pilgrims have indicated the direction of the path by heaping up small pyramids of stones on larger masses of rock. After another hour of laborious climbing we reach the summit. The **Jebel Katherin** has three peaks, the *Jebel Katherîn*, the *Jebel Zebîr*, and the *Jebel Abû Rumêl*, the first of which, according to the most recent and careful English measurements, is the highest (8537 ft.), being the loftiest mountain in the peninsula. The air is often bitterly cold here, and snow lies in the rocky clefts till summer. Half of the narrow plateau on the summit is occupied by a small and rudely constructed chapel. The unevenness of the floor is declared by the monks to be due to miraculous impression of the body of St. Catharine (p. 508), which was found here 300, or according to others, 500 years after her execution, and to which attention was attracted by the rays of light emanating from it. The view is magnificent in fine weather, but towards the S.W. it is intercepted by the Jebel Umm Shomar. Towards the S.E. lies the broad Wâdi Naṣb. The greater part of the Gulf of ʿAḳaba, the Arabian mountains, and even sometimes the Râs Moḥammed (to the S.) are visible. The Gulf of Suez is surveyed as far as the African coast, on which rises the conspicuous Jebel Ghârib (p. 474). On the W. coast of the peninsula lies the sterile plain of El-Ḳâʿa, which terminates near Ṭûr. To the N. tower Mt. Serbâl and the Jebel el-Benât, and farther distant lie the light-coloured sandy plain of Er-Ramleh and the long range of the Et-Tîh hills.

The **Wâdi Sebâʿîyeh** (afternoon excursion of 3 hrs.) is interesting from its being regarded by Laborde, Strauss, Tischendorf, Graul, and others, as the camping-place of the Jews. We ascend the Wâdi Shuʿaib (p. 502), cross the moderate height of the *Jebel Munâja* ('Mountain of the Conversation'), and enter the rocky *Wâdi Sebâʿîyeh*, which is filled with heaps of rocks and small stones, whence the rocky Jebel Mûsa presents a similar appearance to that of the Râs eṣ-Ṣafṣâf from the Er-Râha plain. We may now return by the *Wâdi es-Sadad*, a valley farther to the N.E., from the Wâdi Sebâʿîyeh into the Wâdi esh-Shêkh, and thence by a longer and easier route through the Wâdi ed-Dêr. On reaching the Wâdi esh-Shêkh (p. 520) we keep to the left until the entrance of the Shuʿaib valley and the monastery comes in sight.

The **Jebel Umm Shomar** ('mother of fennel', 8448 ft.) was long considered the highest mountain in the peninsula, but it was proved by the measurements made by the English Expedition to be lower than the Jebel Katherîn. We quit Mt. Sinai by the Wâdi Sebâʿîyeh, enter the broad *Wâdi Raḥabeh*, and pass the night at the *Wâdi Zêtûn*. Next morning we first ascend the *Jebel Abû Shejer* rising 1180 ft. above the valley. The *Wâdi Zeraḳîyeh*, on the right, contains the scanty ruins of the old monastery of *Mar Antus*. The majestic granite masses of the Jebel Umm Shomar, with its huge pinnacles, somewhat resemble Mt. Serbâl.

Route to Mt. Sinai viâ Ṭûr.

From Suez to *Ṭûr*, see p. 474. **Ṭûr** is a place of some importance, inhabited by Arabs, whose property, estimated at several hundred thousand francs, is partly derived from the numerous shipwrecks which take place near the island of Shadwân. The harbour is admirably protected by coral reefs, which, however, are dangerous to those unacquainted with their situation. Ṭûr affords the only good anchorage in the Gulf of Suez, beside Suez itself, and has lately been made the chief quarantine station of the Mecca pilgrims. As the desert air here comes into contact with the fresh sea-breezes and as there is abundance of drinking-water, the choice of the government seems a very judicious one. On the return of the pilgrims, the desert to the S. of Ṭûr presents a scene of great animation. Long rows of tents, arranged in six groups, afford ample accommodation for the largest concourse of pilgrims, while the throng is swelled by traders from Suez and Cairo, who sell their inferior wares at the most exorbitant prices. On the side next Ṭûr is the camp of the soldiers who maintain the quarantine. To the N. of the town the *Jebel Ḥammâm Sidna Mûsa* ('Mountain of the baths of our Lord Moses'; 375 ft.), a spur of the low range of coast-hills, projects into the sea. At the foot of this hill lie sulphur-springs of the temperature of 92-94°, roofed over by ʿAbbâs Pasha, which irrigate plantations of palms, and are used by the natives chiefly as a cure for rheumatism. The *Ḳalʿat el-Ṭûr*, a castle erected by Sulṭân Murâd, is in a dilapidated condition. Most of the palm-plantations belong to the monks of Mt. Sinai, and are managed by their servants. Both the church and the secular building of the Greek convent at Ṭûr, which is said to have once been occupied by a bishop and 1000 monks, are modern and uninteresting. As an inscription on the exterior of the wall of the church records, they were built at the expense of the treasurer Gregorius. A few monks are always stationed here, officiating partly as chaplains to a few Christian residents, and partly as caterers for the Sinaitic monastery, which is supplied with provisions and fish from Ṭûr. The caravans between the sea and the monastery are conducted by the Beduins of the convent. Excellent fish, numerous shells, and interesting marine animals abound here.

Excursions. The palm-garden of *El-Wâdi*, about a mile to the N.W. of the town, is noted for its salubrity. In the limestone slopes of the *Jebel Hammâm Mûsa* are numerous dilapidated hermitages, with Christian crosses, and several Greek and Armenian inscriptions, dating from A D 633. To the N rises the *Jebel Mokatteb*, which boasts of several Sinaitic inscriptions. None of these places present much attraction.

The *Jebel Nâḳûs*, or 'Bell Mountain', is 4½ hrs distant from Ṭûr. It rises amphitheatrically about 1 M from the shore of the Red Sea, and is the scene of a phenomenon which was first observed by Seetzen. On ascending the sand which covers its slope we hear a peculiar sound, resembling that of distant bells, which gradually increases until it terminates in a strange kind of roar.

'The noise at first resembled the faint tones of an Æolian harp when first struck by the wind, and when the motion of the sand became more rapid and violent, it rather assumed the sound produced by rubbing the moistened finger on glass; but when the sand approached the foot of the mountain, the reverberation was as loud as thunder, causing the rock on which we sat to tremble. Our camels were so alarmed at the sound, that the attendants could scarcely hold them in.'

The phenomenon is easily explained; in ascending over the sand, when *dry* (in which case alone the sound is heard) the traveller loosens it and causes it to fall into the clefts of the sandstone rock on which it lies; a slight and gradually increasing sound is thus produced by this miniature avalanche. The Arabs believe that these curious sounds proceed from a monastery buried under the sand. It had been accidentally discovered by an Arab, who received hospitable entertainment from the monks, and swore not to betray its existence, but when he afterwards broke his oath, the monastery vanished.

From Tûr to the Monastery of St. Catharine there are two routes, one through the Wâdi Ḥebrân, the other through the Wâdi es-Slêh (Isléh). The latter is the shorter and preferable route, as the Wâdi es-Slêh is one of the most romantic ravines in the whole peninsula, while the route through the Wâdi Ḥebrân is for some distance the same as the shorter route from Suez to Sinai.

(1) Through the Wâdi es-Slêh. The start should be made at a very early hour, in order that the desert *El-Ḳâ'a* may be crossed before the heat of the day. We ride due E. for 6 hrs. through the gradually ascending desert in the direction of the huge Umm Shomar (p. 515). On reaching the base of the mountain, we descend very rapidly into a basin resembling the bed of a lake, which has been formed by the mountain torrent issuing from the Wâdi es-Slêh. At the bottom of this basin we enter the narrow, rocky defile of the **Wâdi es-Slêh.** After ascending this romantic gorge with its turbulent brook for half-an-hour, we reach a charming resting-place where there is excellent water The brook, which of course varies greatly in volume at different seasons, sometimes disappears altogether in the upper parts of the valley, but there is water enough everywhere to support the vegetation, which is very luxuriant at places. Palms and numerous tamarisks thrive in the lower part of the valley. The route is not always practicable for riding, but if the rider dismounts, the camels contrive to thread their way through the most difficult part of the ravine, while the traveller will find it a relief to walk for a quarter-of-an-hour. A little above the resting-place large masses of rock compel us again to dismount for half-an-hour's walk. About 2 hrs. from the entrance of the valley, and 280 ft. above that point, the route divides, and we turn to the left. At the next bifurcation, 10 min. farther, our route leads to the right. We enter a rocky gorge which soon contracts to a defile of 12 ft. only in width, then expands, and again contracts. We pass a few palm-trees, many tamarisks, Solaneæ, and thickets of reed. At the next bifurcation (1 hr.) we turn to the right. We pass (20 min.) the precipitous bed of a torrent on the right, and then a second descending from a curious looking hill crowned with a huge mass of rock. The stony channel of an old torrent here is deeply furrowed by that of another watercourse which now crosses it. The valley becomes wilder and more barren. We ascend the *Wâdi Ṭarfa* for 5-6 hrs. to a height of about 1875 ft. We then enter the broad *Wâdi Raḥabeh*, and traverse an open and undulating basin for 6 hrs. more, first towards

the N.E. and then towards the N.W., and at length reach the *Wâdi Sebâ'îyeh*, at the S.E. base of the Jebel Mûsa, recognisable by its church and monastery. (Towards the N. the Wâdi Sebâ'îyeh is connected with the Wâdi esh-Shêkh by the *Wâdi Sadad*; comp. p. 520). A saddle of moderate height separates the Wâdi Sebâ'îyeh from the *Wâdi ed-Dêr* ('valley of the monastery'). To the left, on the precipitous Jebel Mûsa, which is quite perpendicular at the top, we perceive the zigzags of the road constructed by 'Abbâs Pasha (p. 510). We at length descend the narrow Wâdi ed-Dêr (Shu'aib), and reach the lofty walls of the monastery of St. Catharine (see p. 503).

(2) Through the Wâdi Ḥebrân. 1st Day. For one hour we ascend a gradual slope with a saline soil to the *Umm Sa'ad*, where a spring of fresh water affords support to a few families. The waterskins should be filled here, and a supply of dates purchased, as the desert of *El-Ḳâ'a*, 6 hrs. in width, has now to be traversed. We follow the road of 'Abbâs Pasha, which, though sometimes covered with sand on the low ground, is always sufficiently marked to indicate the direction to the Wâdi Ḥebrân. For the first hour or two we pass a number of dûm-palms, but these also at length disappear. A single seyâl-tree stands about halfway, but otherwise we are surrounded by the hot desert, which is at first covered with fine sand, afterwards with rubble, and at length with enormous blocks of stone in the vicinity of the precipitous mountains. The **Wâdi Ḥebrân** is reached about sunset. At the point where it issues from the mountains it is a deep and very narrow rocky ravine. A rocky recess close to the entrance affords quarters for the first night.

2nd Day. The route through the Wâdi Ḥebrân winds considerably; the formation is granite, in which syenite predominates; it contains thick veins of hornblende, slate, geenstone, and various kinds of basalt. The volume of the brook varies according to the season; its banks are bordered with vegetation. The path, which is comparatively good, and passes a number of Sinaitic inscriptions, was to have been converted into a carriage-road by 'Abbâs Pasha, but his plan was never carried out. After $1^3/_4$ hr. the valley divides, and the road of 'Abbâs Pasha leads to the N. At a second bifurcation ($^3/_4$ hr.) the valley expands, and in $^1/_2$ hr. more we reach a clear and abundant spring, but disagreeably warm. The ṭarfa bushes and palms here form an impenetrable thicket. Water now disappears (10 min.), the vegetation becomes scantier, and we proceed to cross the precipitous *Naḳb el-'Ejjâwi* (3290 ft.). Our quarters for the second night are near the *Wâdi Selâf* (p. 501). On the third day we reach the direct route leading from Mt. Serbâl to the Naḳb el-Hâwi, etc. (see p. 501).

'Aḳaba will be visited by scientific travellers only (5-6 days' journey). The first day from the monastery of St. Catharine is generally short on account of the late start. — On the 2nd Day the watershed between the Gulf of Suez and that of 'Aḳaba is crossed, and the *Wâdi Sa'l* traversed.

Beyond the *Wâdi Marra* the route is not easily found, even by the Beduins, until after 2 hrs. we reach a sandy plain extending to the foot of the Jebel et-Tîh. After 4 hrs. we pass the *'Ain el-Khadra*, a spring with a few palms, lying to the right, probably the Biblical *Hazeroth*. After having passed through a narrow defile, we proceed to the N E. by a sandy path, enter the plain of *El-Ghôr*, traverse the spurs of the Tîh chain, and reach the *Wâdi Ghazâl*, with its steep slopes of sandstone. The night is passed in the *Wâdi er-Ruwêhibîyeh* — 3rd Day. Beyond the wâdi expands a plain of sandstone, varied with granite and diorite. In 2½ hrs. we reach the broad *Wâdi Ṣamghi*, quit it (1¾ hr.), turn towards the N.E., and traverse huge masses of rock and slopes by a gradually narrowing path The narrowest part is called *El-Buwêb*, 'the little gate'. The path, which now expands and is covered with gravel, gradually approaches the Red Sea, or rather the beautiful, bluish green Gulf of 'Akaba. In another hour we come to the good spring of *Et-Terrâbîn*, bordered with palms. The night is spent on the sea-shore — 4th Day The route skirts the shell-strewn shore. The coast mountains are formed of grey granite. Towards noon the spring of *Abû Suwêra* is reached, and we pitch our tents near the *Wâdi Huwêmirât* We observe curious crabs here which take up their abode in empty shells, and walk about with them on their backs. The hills on the opposite coast of the *Bahr 'Akaba*, or Gulf of 'Akaba, are insignificant. From our quarters for the night the Arabian village of *Haḳl* is visible — 5th Day. The route leads across promontories stretching far out into the sea, a precipitous pass, and then several more promontories, particularly near the *Wâdi Merâkh* The territory of the Ṭâwara terminates here, and that of the Huwêtât Beduins begins. Negociations for a new escort must be made with the latter, who are often unreasonable About 4 hrs from the Wâdi Ḥuwêmirât we observe a small island of granite a few hundred yards from the shore, with two hills bearing the ruins of a castle of the Saracens, probably the Fort *Aila*, which was unsuccessfully besieged by Rainald of Chatillon in 1182. The island is now called *Kureiyeh*, *Gezîret Far'ûn*, or Pharaoh's island The broad *Wâdi Ṭâba'*, farther N, contains a bitter spring and dûm-palms. Dr. Robinson found a square cistern excavated here, lined with red stone The *Râs el-Masri*, a promontory of dark-coloured stone, must be rounded, the mountains recede, and we soon reach the broad *Derb el-Hajj*, or route of the Mecca pilgrims We now skirt the extremity of the gulf, cross a saline swamp, leave the ruins of a town on the left, proceed to the S, and at length enter the fortress which lies on the E bank of the bay.

'Akaba (*Kal'at el-'Akaba*) In this neighbourhood lay the *Elath* of Scripture, which is mentioned on the occasion of the voyages to Ophir, and which was garrisoned during the Roman period by the tenth legion. It was afterwards called *Aila*, and was still inhabited by Jews as well as Christians at the time of the Crusades. In order to protect themselves against the attacks of the Saracens, the inhabitants pretended to possess a letter of protection from Mohammed. (According to another account they possess a robe which the prophet is said to have given to John, son of Rubah, the Jewish prince, as a pledge that the Jews might carry on their trade without hindrance.) Down to the 15th cent the town is spoken of as a large and prosperous commercial place During the Byzantine period it paid tribute to the emperors, but was afterwards under the protection of the governors and Mohammedan princes of Egypt, and was especially patronised by Aḥmed Ibn Ṭulûn. During the crusades it was taken by the Franks, but in A. D. 1170 Saladin caused boats to be brought by camels from the Mediterranean to the Red Sea, and recaptured Aila. The place, moreover, though on the great pilgrimage-route to Mecca, soon decayed, till at last nothing of it remained but a fort on the mainland, and one on the island of Kureiyeh. The Turkish fortress of 'Akaba is rectangular in form, each angle of its massive walls being defended by a tower. The entrance, with its iron-clad gate (bearing an old Arabic inscription), is also protected by towers.

Travellers interested in Biblical geography may visit the *Wâdi Them*, as far as the *Jebel Barghîr* (4-5 hrs.). This mountain, which is said to be known to the Arabs as the *Jebel en-Nûr* ('Mountain of Light'), has been recently supposed by Dr Beke to be the Mt. Sinai of Scripture, on he grounds that the Arabs regard it as sacred, and say that Moses once conversed here with the Lord; that sacrifices were once offered on its summit; and that stones in an upright position, and Sinaitic inscriptions, have been found here.

From 'Akaba to Petra. The 'Alawîn Arabs at 'Akaba are very exorbitant in their demands, often rude in their manners, and rarely trustworthy. At times the route through their territory to the ancient Rock City is not unattended with danger, and careful enquiry on the subject should be made at Cairo and Suez before starting. An experienced dragoman, and one who is acquainted with the Shêkhs, will be found very useful From 'Akaba to Petra, by the direct route, is a journey of 3 days, but viâ *Nakhleh* 4-5 days From Petra to Hebron, 5-6 days, if nothing untoward occurs. Attractive as Petra itself is, this route to it is not more interesting than those leading to Sinai, and the traveller can hardly be recommended to enter Palestine from this direction. A description of Petra, and of the journey to Jerusalem, will be found in *Baedeker's Palestine and Syria.*

Return Route from the Monastery of Sinai to Suez by the Wâdi esh-Shêkh, and viâ Sarbuṭ el-Khâdem (comp. p 475, and Maps pp. 496, 470).

On starting from the monastery, we first turn to the N.W. in the Wâdi ed-Dêr (p. 502), leave the plain of Er-Râḥa (p. 513) to the left, and turn to the N.E. into the *Wâdi esh-Shêkh*, which is joined by the *Wâdi es-Sadad* (p. 518) on the S., 1 hr. farther on. On the right rises the *Jebel ed-Dêr*, or 'Mountain of the Monastery' (p. 502), and on the left the *Jebel Sona* (p. 513), both of which are barren and precipitous On the left, farther on, is the *Jebel Khuzamîyeh.* The broad **Wâdi esh-Shêkh,** which is inhabited at places, extends in a large semicircle of about 15 hours' journey from the Jebel Mûsa towards the N.W. down to the Wâdi Fîrân (p. 500), presenting on the whole but little attraction After $1^1/_4$ hr. more we observe the *Tomb of the Shêkh Ṣâliḥ (Nebi Ṣâliḥ)*, which is highly revered by the Beduins, and from which the valley derives its name. Like all these weli's (p. 184), the monument is an insignificant cubical building, whitewashed, and covered with a dome, and contains an empty sarcophagus. The interior contains votive offerings, such as tassels, shawls, ostriches' eggs, camels'-halters, and bridles. The Ṭawâra Beduins regard Shêkh Ṣâliḥ as their ancestor; he was probably, however, an early Mohammedan prophet celebrated for his eloquence, who is extolled in the Ḳorân as one of the most venerable of the patriarchs. He is said to have called forth a living camel out of the rocks, and to have destroyed by an earthquake some of the proud Thamudites, to whom he had been sent, for their unbelief and for their wickedness in mutilating the knees of the sacred camel. Every May a great festival takes place here, accompanied with sacrifices, feasting, and games, at which women also are present, and a smaller festival takes place after the date harvest. At the close of the proceedings the children of the desert ascend the Jebel Mûsa, and there offer sacrifices to Moses (p. 512).

To the W. of the tomb a hill, bearing a few ruins, rises from the valley. We next pass (1/4 hr.) the entrance to the *Wâdi Ṣuwêrîyeh* on the right, which is traversed by the route to ʿAḳaba (p. 518). Opposite us, to the left, are several small towers, above which rises the pointed *Jebel Ferʿ*. The valley contracts, but after 1/2 hr. expands into a wide basin, bounded on the N. by a chain of precipitous rocky slopes. Beyond this basin (40 min.), and beyond the mouth of the *Wâdi Shiʿb*, on the left, the route traverses (10 min.) the **El-Watiyeh Pass** (4022 ft.), enclosed by imposing masses of granite. Immediately beyond it rises a stone, resembling an altar, with a white summit, which the Beduins point out as the scene of Abraham's sacrifice. A rock near it, in the form of a chair, is called the *Maḳʿad Nebi Mûsa*, or seat of the prophet Moses, which he is said to have occupied while tending the sheep of his father-in-law Jethro (p. 502).

At this point begins the lower part of the Esh-Shêkh valley. The character of the region becomes less mountainous, and the route enters an undulating district. In less than an hour we reach a luxuriant growth of ṭarfa shrubs, which extends for a distance of about 1 1/2 M. (comp. p. 500). Beyond these shrubs, on the left, opens the *Wâdi Ḳaṣab*, which leads to the S. to the Naḳb el-Ḥâwi (p. 501), and contains a number of palm-trees. Near the (1 1/4 hr.) *Wâdi Magherât*, which lies to the right, is the valley of Esh-Shêkh, which, according to Prof. Palmer's measurements, lies 3566 ft. above the sea-level. The imposing mass of Mt. Serbâl now becomes visible. Near the (1 hr.) *Wâdi eṭ-Ṭarr* (right) are a few inscriptions (p. 494). The next valley on the right is the (35 min.) *Wâdi Ṣolêf;* and opposite to it opens the broad *Wâdi Sahab*, through which the Naḳb el-Ḥâwi (p. 501) may be reached in 5 hrs. At this point (2856 ft.) our route quits the Wâdi Esh-Shêkh, which leads to the (2 3/4 hrs.) defile of El-Buwêb (p. 501) farther S. We ascend rapidly to the N.W. in the western part of the *Wâdi Ṣolêf*, which soon contracts to a gorge. Several valleys are now crossed, particularly the *Wâdi el-Akhḍar* and the *Wâdi el-ʿIshsh*, as well as the low ranges of hills which separate them; and in 1 3/4 hr. we reach the long **Wâdi Berâḥ**, lying at the base of the Jebel of the same name. We now ascend this valley, obtaining at first a fine retrospect of the Sinai group, the Jebel Mûsa, and the Katherîn, and reach the top of the pass at the base of the pyramidal hill of *Zibb el-Bahêr Abû Baḥarîyeh* (3895 ft.). We next enter the broad **Wâdi Lebweh,** through which the route, now monotonous and nearly straight, descends in less than 2 hrs. to the foot of the *Naḳb Wâdi Barak.* The Wâdi Lebweh, which makes a bend here and descends to the Wâdi Fîrân, now takes the name of *Wâdi el-ʿAḳir.* Our route ascends in 1/2 hr. to the top of the Naḳb Wâdi Barak Pass, beyond which begins the **Wâdi Barak,** a wild, stone-besprinkled valley, sometimes contracting to a gorge, and overgrown with remarkably fine old seyâl trees. Near the head of the valley are several 'Nawâmîs' (stone huts; see p. 501), Sinaitic inscriptions, and large fragments of a rude granite wall. The latter is said to have been erected by the Ṭawâra Beduins, in order to arrest the progress of troops sent by Mohammed 'Ali to punish them for pillaging a caravan; but it appears to be of earlier date. It extends along both slopes of the valley, but there is a wide opening where the route passes through it.

On the right opens the *Wâdi Mesakkar*, and on the left, lower down, the *Wâdi Ṭayyibeh*, at the base of the lofty *Dabbûs 'Ilâḳ*. In $2\frac{1}{4}$ hrs. more the Wâdi Barak reaches the *Wâdi Sîk*, which after $\frac{3}{4}$ hr. turns sharply to the left, leading to the Wâdi Sidr, while the *Wâdi el-Merayiḥ* on the right leads to the *Debbet er-Ramleh*. Our route runs to the N.W., gradually ascending, and and in $\frac{1}{2}$ hr. reaches a narrow sandy plain called the *Debêbet Shêkh Aḥmed*, from the tomb of a Beduin chief of that name to the right of the path. We then descend into the *Wâdi Khamîleh*, in which we again ascend to (2 hrs.) the *Râs Sûwik* (2475 ft.). On the left is the picturesque *Jebel Gharâbi*, a curiously eroded mass of sandstone, with several Sinaitic inscriptions. An extensive view is obtained over the Tîh hills and the plain of Ramleh.

We descend from the pass by a steep zigzag path into the *Wâdi Sûwik*, in which after $1\frac{1}{2}$ hr. we reach the mouth of the small *Wâdi Merattameh*, situated at the foot of the hills called **Ṣarbûṭ el-Khâdem.**

On the neighbouring hill, 690 ft. in height, are situated a number of interesting monuments, dating from the period of the Pharaohs, and re-discovered by Niebuhr in 1762. The ascent from the Wâdi Merattameh, which is somewhat fatiguing, and requires a steady head, occupies fully an hour. On the level plateau on the top are numerous monuments with hieroglyphic inscriptions. There are traces of an old enclosing wall, 57 yds. long, and 23 yds. broad, surrounded by sixteen ancient Egyptian upright monuments . Similar stones bearing inscriptions are lying on the ground, and there are the ruins of a small temple. The sanctuary and a pronaos of this edifice were hewn in the rocks in the reign of Amenemha III. (12th Dyn.), and furnished with handsomely painted inscriptions (which, however, are nearly obliterated), and niches for images. In the reign of Thothmes III. (18th Dyn.) the temple was extended towards the W. by the erection of a pylon and anterior court, and several rooms on the W. side were afterwards added by other kings The dimensions of the whole building are comparatively small. As in the Wâdi Maghâra (p. 491), the goddess Hathor, and particularly the Hathor of Mafkat (p. 492), was principally worshipped here. The inscriptions indicate that this spot, instead of being a burial-place with its tombstones, as one would at first have supposed, was a religious edifice with a number of chambers for various purposes.

Khâdem (Khatem) is the ancient Egyptian word for an enclosed space, a fort, or castle; and Ṣarbûṭ (pl. Ṣerâbîṭ) signifies a hill, or peak, in the language of the Beduins in the peninsula; so that Ṣerâbîṭ el-Khâdem signifies 'the heights of the fortified place'. In the neighbourhood copper and mafkat were formerly worked, and the plateau was occupied with smelting furnaces, and a temple where the miners and the overseers assembled to celebrate various festivals. The dwellings of the workmen and their overseers, and the magazines, must have been nearer the mines, several of which in the Wâdi Nasb (see below) still yield a considerable quantity of copper. Most of the monuments on the plateau were erected by the superior mining officials, who wished to hand down their names and merits to posterity, mentioning the king in whose reign they obtained their appointments, the mineral (mafkat and ore) they worked, the number of miners they employed, the zeal with which they performed their duties, and the accidents which befell them during their term of office. Victories over the native mountain tribes are sometimes also mentioned.

The large heaps of black stone in the vicinity, resembling the slag from a foundry, are partly of natural form; but artificially produced slag also occurs in the valleys between Ṣarbûṭ el-Khâdem and the Wâdi Naṣb. The old mines were re-discovered by Mr. Holland, a member of the last English Survey expedition, while others had already been discovered and described by Rüppell in the Wâdi Naṣb. It appears from the inscriptions that the mines of Ṣarbûṭ el-Khâdem, like those of the Wâdi Maghâra, were first sunk in the reign of Snefru (p. 491) at an early period of the Primæval Monarchy, and that they were worked for a still longer period than the latter, and certainly down to the 20th Dynasty. The cartouche of Ramses IV. is also said to have been found here. The mines of Ṣarbûṭ el-Khâdem must therefore have been worked after the period of the Exodus, while in those of the Wâdi Maghâra the name of Ramses II., the Pharaoh of the oppression, is the last which occurs in the inscriptions

About $^3/_4$ hr. to the S.E. of the plateau are several tombs of the 18th Dyn. discovered by Sir Gardner Wilkinson, probably those of overseers of the mines. At a distance of 2 hrs. thence the remains of miners' dwellings were found by Major Macdonald (p. 490).

A visit to these monuments takes half-a-day. Those who desire to make a thorough inspection, and to visit the Wâdi Naṣb, will require a whole day. They should then walk from Ṣarbûṭ el-Khâdem along the hills to the *Wâdi Naṣb*, at the entrance to which are a spring, shaded by palms, some ruins, the traces of old gardens, and a quantity of slag brought from the mines, $1^1/_2$ hr. to the N.W.

'We find here a number of unusually thick layers of earthy oxide of copper, inserted in wedge-like form between the horizontal strata of sandstone. At many places the metalliferous formation seems to be about 200 ft. in thickness. The ancient natives have driven shafts through these rocks in many different directions, and excavated them in the form of labyrinths, whilst (as in the Wâdi Maghâra) they left pillars here and there to prevent the roof from falling in. To judge from the extent of the mines the quantity of ore obtained must have been very considerable. To this day one of the mines contains a considerable quantity of copper ore, while another, where chambers 80 ft. in length have been excavated, seems to have been given up as exhausted'. *(Ruppell.)*

On the hill above the mines stands an ancient Egyptian obelisk with half-obliterated hieroglyphics.

Descending the Wâdi Naṣb towards the N. we reach the mouth of the Wadi Ḥobûz (see below), where the caravan should be ordered to await our arrival.

Beyond the Wâdi Merattameh the Suez route continues to follow the Wâdi Sûwik, to the N.W., passing a number of fine seyâl trees of great age. After 1 hr. the valley takes the name of *Wâdi Ḥobûz*, and in less than 1 hr. more it unites with the *Wâdi Naṣb*, which almost immediately joins the *Wâdi Ba'ba'*, a valley leading to the S.E. to the *Ḥanak el-Laḳam* (p. 490). At the junction of the Ḥobûz and Naṣb valleys our route turns to the right, and leads across the sandy table-land of *Debbet el-Ḳerai* in 3 hrs. to the beginning of the Wâdi el-Ḥomr. Ascending a little towards the middle of the lofty plain, we enjoy a fine view of the *Ṣarbûṭ el-Jemel* (2175 ft.), rising to the W. opposite to us, beyond the Wâdi Ḥomr. To the left, in the distance, are picturesquely shaped mountains with flat summits; to the right is the Tîh range; and behind us are the hills of Ṣarbûṭ el-Khâdem, the Jebel Ghârâbi, and the distant Mt. Serbâl.

We now descend to the broad route leading to *Nakhleh* (p. 520). On the right rises the long *Jebel Bêda'*. On the ground here we observe a number of curious geological formations, consisting of slabs and fragments of sandstone encrusted with nodules of iron ore, with a large admixture of silica, grouped like bunches of grapes. Some of these are perfectly spherical.

The **Wâdi el-Ḥomr** is a broad valley flanked by low limestone hills. It is commanded on the N. side by the Ṣarbûṭ el-Jemel (see above). From this valley a path, practicable for camels, traverses the *Wâdi Mesakkar* and several other valleys, and leads direct to the *Wâdi eth-Thâl* (p. 489). The regular route follows the Wâdi el-Ḥomr to its union with the *Wâdi Shebêkeh* (see p. 489). Thence to Suez, see pp. 489-485.

INDEX.

Besides the names of the places described, this Index also contains a number of names of persons and other words occurring in the Routes and in the Introduction. Ancient names are printed in *Italics* The following is a short list of Arabic words of frequent occurrence (comp vocabulary, p. 192): —

'Ain, Spring.	*Birkeh*, Pond.	*Kasr*, Castle
Bâb, Gate.	*Dêr*, Monastery.	*Kôm*, Mound of rubbish.
Bahr, Sea, river (Nile)	*Derb*, Road.	*Medîneh*, Town
Behêreh, Lake.	*Gebel*, Mountain.	*Nakb*, Pass.
Beled, Village.	*Gezîreh*, Island.	*Râs*, Promontory.
Bêt, House.	*Kafr*, Village	*Tell*, Hill.
Bilâd, Land, District.	*Kal'a*, Fortress.	*Wâdi*, Valley.
Bîr, Cistern.	*Kanṭara*, Bridge.	*Weli*, Saint's tomb.

Leipsic. Printed by Breitkopf & Härtel.

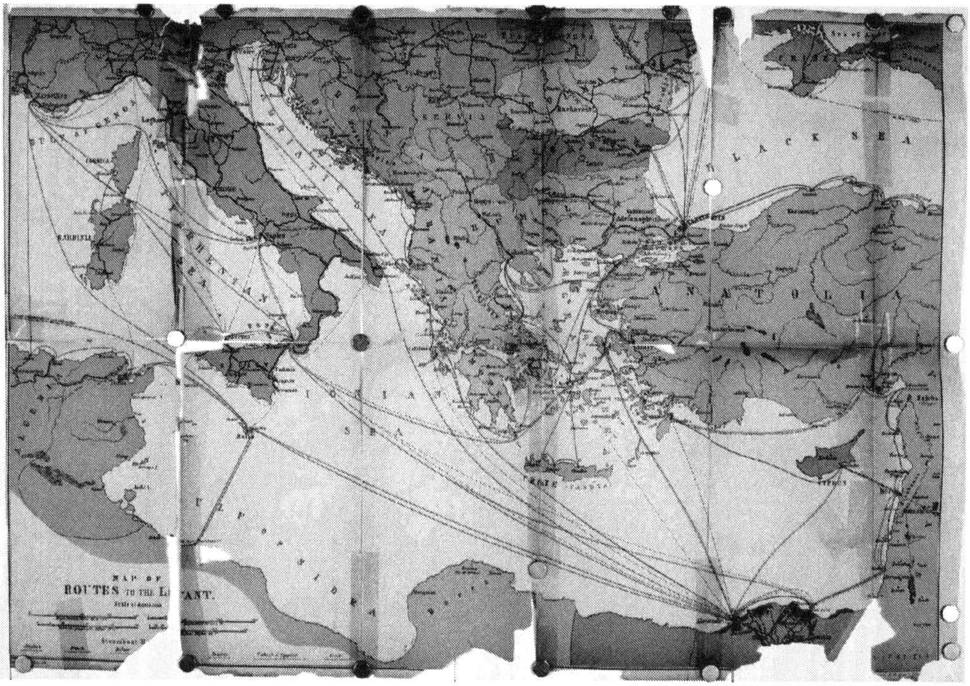
MAP OF
ROUTES TO THE L ANT.
BLACK SEA
ANATOLIA
IONIAN SEA

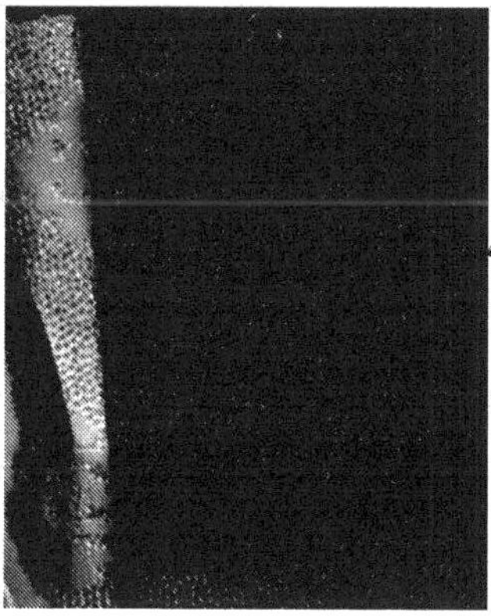

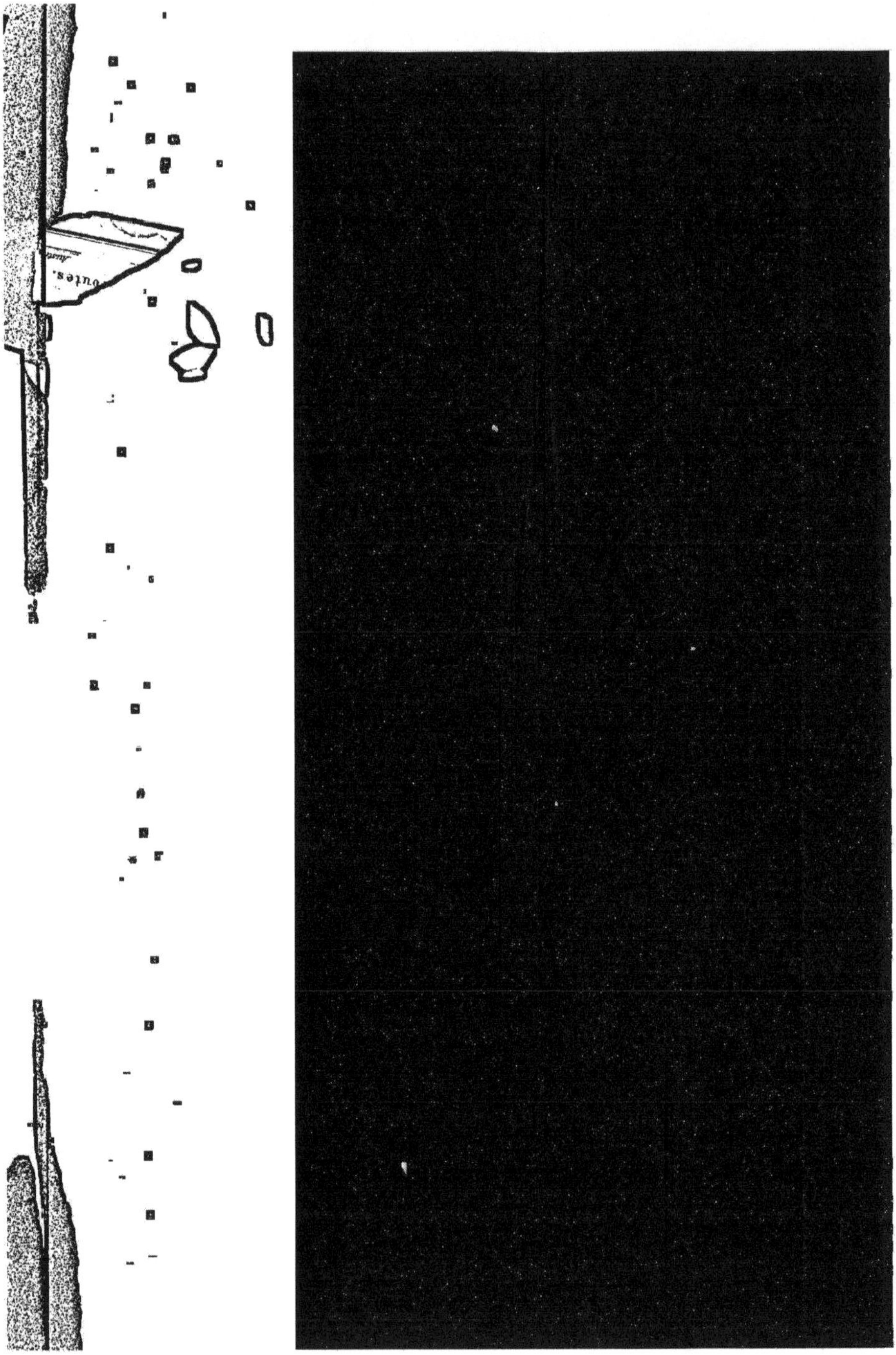

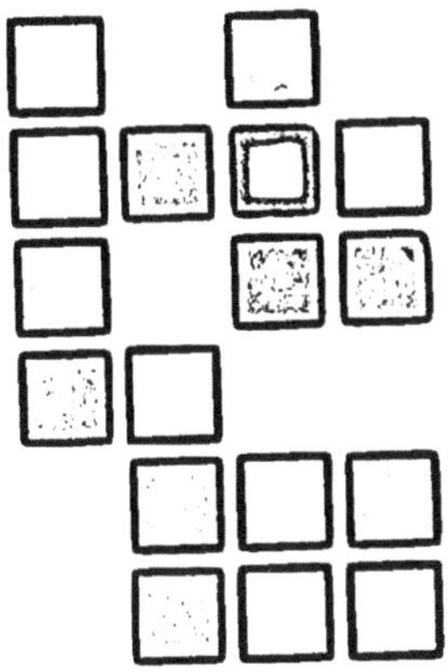

Lightning Source UK Ltd.
Milton Keynes UK
UKHW021508280921
391322UK00005B/1251

9 781361 994689